~~F(S~~

$F = S(1+p)$

IRP =

$p = \frac{(1+ih)}{(1+if)} - 1$

PPP

$ef = \frac{(1+Ih)}{(1+If)} - 1$

IFE

$ef = \frac{(1+ih)}{(1+if)} - 1$

Absolute forecast error $= \frac{\text{Forecasted Value} - \text{Realised Value}}{\text{Realised value}}$

INTERNATIONAL FINANCIAL MANAGEMENT

6th Edition

JEFF MADURA
Florida Atlantic University

Cincinnati • Albany • Boston • Detroit • Johannesburg • London • Madrid • Melbourne • Mexico City
New York • Pacific Grove • San Francisco • Scottsdale • Singapore • Tokyo • Toronto

Team Director: Jack W. Calhoun
Acquisitions Editor: Michael B. Mercier
Senior Developmental Editor: Susanna C. Smart
Marketing Manager: Lisa L. Lysne
Production Editor: Sandra Gangelhoff
Manufacturing Coordinator: Georgina Calderon
Internal and Cover Design: Joe Devine
Cover Photograph: Pete Seward/Tony Stone Images
Production House: WordCrafters Editorial Services, Inc.
Compositor: Publishers' Design and Production Services, Inc., Sagamore Beach, MA
Printer: World Color–Taunton, MA

Printed in the United States of America
2 3 4 5 6 7 8 9 10

International Thomson Publishing Europe
Berkshire House
168-173 High Holborn
London, WC1V7AA, United Kingdom

Nelson ITP, Australia
102 Dodds Street
South Melbourne
Victoria 3205 Australia

Nelson Canada
1120 Birchmount Road
Scarborough, Ontario
Canada M1K 5G4

International Thomson Publishing South Africa
Building 18, Constantia Square
138 Sixteen Road, P.O. Box 2459
Halfway House, 1685 South Africa

International Thomson Editores
Seneca, 53
Colonia Polanco
11560 México D.F. México

International Thomson Publishing Asia
60 Alberta Street #15-01
Albert Complex
Singapore 189969

International Thomson Publishing Japan
Hirakawa-cho Kyowa Building, 3F
2-2-1 Hirakawa-cho, Chiyoda-ku
Tokyo 102, Japan

Library of Congress Cataloging-in-Publication Data

Madura, Jeff.
International financial management / Jeff Madura. —6th ed.
p. cm.
Includes bibliographical references and index.
ISBN 0-324-00955-0
1. International finance. 2. Foreign exchange. Asset—liability management. 4. Banks and banking, International. 5. International business enterprises—Finance. I. Title.
HG3881.M2765 2000
658.15'99—dc21 99-26766

This book is printed on acid-free paper.

To My Parents

About the Author

Jeff Madura is presently the SunTrust Bank Professor of Finance at Florida Atlantic University. He has written several textbooks, including *Financial Markets and Institutions*. His research on international finance has been published in numerous journals, including *Journal of Financial and Quantitative Analysis, Journal of Money, Credit and Banking, Journal of Banking and Finance, Journal of International Money and Finance, Journal of Financial Research, Financial Review, Journal of Multinational Financial Management,* and *Global Finance Journal*. He has received awards for excellence in teaching and research, and has served as a consultant for international banks, securities firms, and other multinational corporations. He has served as a director for the Southern Finance Association and Eastern Finance Association, and also served as president of the Southern Finance Association.

BRIEF CONTENTS

CONTENTS

Part II Exchange Rate Behavior

Chapter 6 Government Influence on Exchange Rates 153

Chapter 7 International Arbitrage and Interest Rate Parity 189

Part IV Long-Term Asset and Liability Management

Chapter 16 Country Risk Analysis 441

Chapter 17 Multinational Cost of Capital and Capital Structure 471

PREFACE

OVERVIEW

The international financial environment has experienced major changes in recent years. Many foreign countries in Asia, Eastern Europe, and Latin America that were previously governed by socialist policies and closed to the rest of the world have undergone a transition toward free enterprise and international integration. In particular, government-owned businesses have been privatized, companies have become publicly owned, and free trade agreements have been created. While the transition has created more efficient economies, it has had some adverse side effects. In particular, free enterprise can result in failure of the less competitive companies and can make a country more susceptible to economic crises experienced by other countries.

The transmission of economic crises across countries has created a volatile global marketplace. The multinational corporations (MNCs) that compete in the global marketplace must not only be properly managed to withstand the effects of crises in foreign countries, but must also have the flexibility to capitalize on these crises. While some events (such as the Asian crisis) have adversely affected the performance of MNCs, they also present some long-term opportunities. Crises in countries tend to reduce the value of assets such as land and businesses. Those MNCs with more astute management may be positioned to increase their investment when temporary crises result in lower asset prices within a specific country.

Furthermore, numerous countries around the world that have recently allowed more capital inflows into their county are now subjected to the threat of a local currency crisis if investors withdraw the funds they invested there. Consequently, MNCs are more exposed to abrupt declines in the currencies they use to conduct international business. The higher degree of exchange rate uncertainty places more pressure on MNCs to effectively manage exchange rate risk.

The inception of a single currency (the euro) among numerous western European countries in 1999 was another major event in the global marketplace. All MNCs need to recognize how the euro will not only affect exposure to exchange rate risk, but how it will change competition within Europe, the pricing of products in Europe, and the valuations of companies in Europe. Those MNCs with more astute management should benefit from the transition to the euro, while other MNCs could be adversely affected.

In general, the recent events have made international financial management more challenging. MNCs will respond by meeting the challenge rather than retreating. Those MNCs that are most capable of responding to changes in the international financial environment will be rewarded. The same can be said for the students today who may become the future managers of MNCs.

Intended Market

This text presumes an understanding of basic corporate finance. It is suitable for both undergraduate and master's level courses in international financial management. Some master's courses may attempt to maximize student comprehension by assigning the more difficult questions, problems, and cases in each chapter.

Organization of the Text

This text is organized first to provide a background on the international environment and then to focus on the managerial aspects from a corporate perspective. Managers of MNCs must first understand the environment before they can manage within it. The first two parts of the text provide the macroeconomic framework for the text. Part I (Chapters 1 to 5) introduces the major markets that facilitate international business. Part II (Chapters 6 to 8) describes relationships between exchange rates and economic variables, and explains the forces that influence these relationships.

The remainder of the text provides a microeconomic framework, with a focus on the managerial aspects of international financial management. Part III (Chapters 9 to 12) explains the measurement and management of exchange rate risk. Part IV (Chapters 13 to 18) describes the management of long-term assets and liabilities, including motives for direct foreign investment, multinational capital budgeting, country risk analysis, and capital structure decisions. Part V (Chapters 19 to 21) concentrates on the MNC's management of short-term assets and liabilities, including trade financing, other short-term financing, and international cash management.

Each chapter is self-contained, so that professors can use classroom time to focus on the more comprehensive topics and rely on the text to cover the other concepts. Chapters can be rearranged without a loss in continuity. The chapters in this edition have been revised to place the MNC's management of long-term assets and liabilities (Part IV) ahead of the MNC's management of long-term assets and liabilities (Part V). This organization covers the strategic aspects such as motives for direct foreign investment and decisions on whether to conduct direct foreign investment before it covers the operational aspects such as short-term financing or investment. Yet, some professors prefer to cover the MNC's management of short-term assets and liabilities before the MNC's management of long-term assets and liabilities. The organization can be easily revised because the two parts are self-contained.

Furthermore, chapters within a part can be reorganized. This edition has organized Part IV to cover the management of long-term assets (with separate chapters on direct foreign investment, multinational capital budgeting, multinational restructuring, and country risk analysis) before the management of the long-term liabilities (chapters on capital structure and long-term financing). Yet, the text illustrates how management of long-term assets and long-term liabilities is integrated within the chapters.

Approach of the Text

The approach of the text is to reinforce the key concepts in the following ways.

1. PART-OPENING DIAGRAM: A diagram is provided at the beginning of each part to illustrate in general terms how the key concepts covered in that part are related. This offers some intuition about the organization of chapters in that part.

2. OBJECTIVES: The key concepts are identified within a bulleted list of objectives at the beginning of each chapter.
3. EMPHASIS: The key concepts are thoroughly described in the chapter and supported by examples and illustrations.
4. NIKE PROBLEM: Some of the key concepts are applied to Nike's international business near the end of the chapter to illustrate the reality of these concepts.
5. VALUATION OF THE MNC: Since the underlying objective of an MNC's managers is to maximize the value of the MNC, it is important to recognize how the concepts discussed in the text relate to the MNC's value. Some key concepts in the chapter are applied to the MNC valuation diagram near the end of each chapter to demonstrate how the concepts can affect the value of an MNC.
6. SUMMARY: The key concepts are summarized at the end of the chapter in a bulleted list that corresponds to the list of objectives at the beginning of the chapter.
7. SELF-TEST: A "Self-Test" at the end of the chapter challenges students on the key concepts. The answers to these questions are provided in Appendix A.
8. QUESTIONS AND APPLICATIONS: Many of the questions and other applications at the end of the chapter test the student's knowledge of the key concepts in the chapter. Near the end of this section is the "Internet Application" that identifies a specified Web site related to key concepts and requires students to access the Web site to answer questions about the concepts. There is also an application called "Running Your Own MNC" at the end of this section that allows students to apply the key concepts to a small business that they created at the beginning of the school term. This not only gives students practice in applying theory to practice, but also enhances their entrepreneurial skills.
9. CONTINUING CASE: At the end of each chapter, the continuing case allows students to use the key concepts to solve problems experienced by a firm called Blades, Inc. (a producer of roller blades). By working on cases from each chapter that relate to the same firm over a school term, students see how a firm can develop its international business over time and the rewards and challenges resulting from its growth in international business.
10. SMALL BUSINESS DILEMMA: The Small Business Dilemma at the end of each chapter places students in a position where they must use concepts introduced in the chapter to make decisions about a dilemma experienced by one particular small business called Sports Exports Company.
11. INTEGRATIVE PROBLEM: The Integrative Problem at the end of each part integrates the key concepts across chapters within that part.
12. FOCUS ON AN MNC: The "Focus on an MNC" application in Appendix D and on-line at the text's Web site enables students to apply many of the chapter concepts to a specific MNC of their choice. It also gives students experience in retrieving an annual report on-line, on reviewing an annual report, and in recognizing the link between theory provided by the text and practice.

    Students can copy the on-line assignments onto a file and infuse their responses to each chapter over the school term. By the end of the term, the file will contain a consolidated set of their response across all assigned chapters.
13. SUPPLEMENTAL CASES: Supplemental cases (called Case Problems in previous editions) allows students to apply chapter concepts to a specific situation of an MNC. All Supplemental Cases are located in Appendix B at the end of the text.

This text is designed in recognition that each professor has his or her unique style for reinforcing the key concepts within a course. Numerous methods of reinforcing the key concepts are provided in this text so that professors can select the methods that fit their style. Beyond the in-chapter applications within each chapter (such as the "Nike Problem" and "Valuation of an MNC") and the traditional end-of-chapter questions, professors have a choice of assigning international applications to: (1) various large corporations ("Supplemental Cases"), (2) small businesses ("Small Business Dilemma"), (3) the same MNC throughout the term ("Continuing Case of Blades, Inc."), (4) an MNC developed by each student ("Running Your Own MNC"), (5) a real MNC selected by each student ("Focus on an MNC"), and (6) related information on a specified Web site ("Internet Application"). While these methods vary in perspective, they all reinforce the key concepts in each chapter.

Major Changes to This Edition

Euro. This edition has been completely revised to account for the inception of the euro, the single currency adopted by numerous western European countries in 1999. Although the individual currencies will still exist for some retail transactions for a few more years, the euro is now used for most commercial transactions in the participating European countries. The examples in this text using European currencies in the previous edition have been revised to use other currencies in this edition. In addition, the impact of the euro on the international financial management by MNCs is discussed in various chapters where appropriate.

Asian Crisis. The Asian crisis has not only had a major impact on the performance of MNCs, but on the lessons to be learned in international financial management. It is discussed in managerial chapters related to exchange rate risk, direct foreign investment, multinational restructuring, and country risk. It is also related to chapters on the behavior of exchange rates (Part II). In particular, it is closely related to Chapter 6 on central bank intervention because of all the intervention efforts by the Asian countries during the Asian crisis. For this reason, a comprehensive appendix on the Asian crisis has been created and is at the end of Chapter 6.

Reorganization. The part of the text focusing on the management of long-term assets and liabilities has been moved in front of the part on management of short-term assets and liabilities. This new organization reflects the outline of many corporate finance text books in which the long-term (strategic) decisions are discussed before the short-term (operating) decisions. The long-term decisions tend to be more complex, and therefore may receive more attention. Professors who prefer to cover the management of short-term assets and liabilities before the management of long-term assets and liabilities may reverse the order without a loss in continuity, because the chapters (and the parts) are still self-contained.

A new chapter called "Multinational Restructuring" has been created (Chapter 15). It follows the chapter on capital budgeting, and applies the capital budgeting framework to suggest how an MNC can assess various types of restructuring decisions, such as acquisitions, joint ventures, and divestitures. This chapter was created in response to the large amount of restructuring by MNCs in recent years.

The chapters related to long-term management of assets and liabilities have been reorganized as follows. The Part still leads off with a chapter on the motives for direct foreign investment (Chapter 13), followed by a chapter on multinational capital budgeting. The new chapter on multinational restructuring (Chapter 15) is inserted just after the chapter on multinational capital budgeting, since it applies the capital budgeting framework. The next chapter is on country risk analysis (Chapter

16), as this chapter is closely tied to the investment decisions discussed in the previous three chapters. The chapter on multinational cost of capital and capital structure has been moved to Chapter 17, just after country risk analysis and just before the long-term financing chapter. This new arrangement reflects six chapters in this part; the first four chapters are focused on long-term investing, while the last two chapters are focused on long-term financing. The integration between long-term investing and financing is discussed in the chapters, where appropriate.

The chapter on taxation of MNCs (Chapter 21) from the previous edition has been converted to an appendix for the chapter on multinational capital budgeting (Chapter 14). This appendix describes how tax laws can vary among countries, and explains how differential tax laws among countries can affect the estimated cash flows of a proposed foreign project.

Nike Problem. The "Nike Problem" in each chapter applies one or more key concepts in the chapter to Nike and requests opinions on related issues; this is designed to stimulate class discussion on key concepts as they relate to a large U.S.-based MNC.

Valuation of an MNC. The "Valuation of an MNC" section near the end of each chapter explains how each of the key chapter concepts can affect the value of the MNC. Since the underlying theme of international financial management is to maximize the value of the MNC, this section summarizes how the concepts covered in each chapter relate to the main managerial objective of maximizing the MNC's value.

Continuing Case. A continuing case has been added to the end of every chapter. It allows students to use the key concepts to solve problems experienced by a firm called Blades, Inc. (a producer of roller blades). By working on cases from each chapter that relate to the same firm over a school term, students see how a firm can develop its international business over time, and the rewards and challenges resulting from its growth in international business.

The Supplemental Cases, which were called "Case Problems" in the previous edition, present short cases on different MNCs. The cases are now located in Appendix B.

Internet Margin Notes. Internet margin notes have been added to provide students with suggested Web sites containing materials pertinent to the topics being discussed. The text Web site at *http://madura.swcollege.com* contains links to all sites and is updated periodically to revise any changes in Internet addresses.

Study Guide. A new study guide, written by Jeff Madura and Oliver Schnusenberg, of St. Joseph's University, now accompanies the text. This study guide focuses on helping students test their knowledge of the material.

On-Line Resources

The following resources are available to students using this text:

- **Data Bank.** A data bank provides quarterly data on spot exchange rates, forward rates, interest rates, inflation rates, balance of trade data, and additional economic data for several countries since 1973.
- **References.** References to related readings are provided for every chapter.

- **Web Site Links.** Web site links related to the material in each chapter are provided.
- **Focus on an MNC.** The "Focus on an MNC" is available on-line to facilitate the consolidation of student responses to the assignments among chapters.
- **Using the World Wide Web for Finance.** Material on how to get around the Internet to find financial information provides tips to navigating the World Wide Web. This appendix, prepared by Ufuk Ince of Georgia State University, introduces students to using the World Wide Web for finance and helps students locate the information needed to solve the Internet Applications. It is available on the text Web site.

SUPPLEMENTS

The following supplements are available

For the Student

- A **Study Guide**, written by Jeff Madura and Oliver Schnusenberg, of St. Joseph's University, is a new addition to the text package. This study guide focuses on helping students test their knowledge of the material. It simulates test questions for key terms and key concepts, with numerous matching, multiple choice, and true/false questions for every chapter.
- **South-Western Finance Resource Center (http://finance.swcollege.com).** The South-Western Finance Resource Center provides unique features, customer service information, and links to book-related Web sites. Learn about valuable products and services to help with your finance studies, contact the finance editors, register for Thomson Investors Network, and more.

For the Instructor

- An **Instructor's Manual**, which contains the chapter theme, topics to stimulate class discussion, and answers to end of chapter Questions, Case Problems, Continuing Cases (Blades, Inc.), Small Business Dilemmas, Integrative Problems, and Supplemental Cases. An expanded **Test Bank** containing 880 questions in multiple choice or true/false format includes content questions as well as problems.
- **Thomson World Class Testing.** The *Thomson World Class Testing Tools*™ computerized testing program contains all of the questions in the printed test bank. *Thomson World Class Testing Tools*™ is an easy-to-use test creation software compatible with Microsoft Windows. Instructors can add or edit questions, instructions, and answers, and select questions by previewing them on the screen; selecting them randomly, or selecting them by number. Instructors can also create and administer quizzes online, whether over the Internet, a local area network (LAN), or a wide area network (WAN).
- **Transparency Masters.** A set of Transparency Masters selected from the key exhibits illustrated in the text are available to instructors.
- **PowerPoint Presentation Slides,** completely revised for this edition by Yee-Tien Fu of National Cheng-Chi University, are intended to enhance lectures and provide a guide for student note-taking. These can be downloaded from the text Web site.

- **South-Western Finance Resource Center (http://finance.swcollege.com)** The South-Western Finance Resource Center provides unique features, customer service information, and links to book-related websites. In particular, you may learn how to become an author with South-Western, request review copies, contact the finance editors, register for Thomson Investors Network, and more.
- **Thomson Investors Network** is complimentary to adopters! Instructors using *International Financial Management*, 6th Edition, may receive a complimentary password to Thomson Investors Network. This web site provides individual investors with a wealth of information and tools, including portfolio-tracking software, live stock quotes, and company and industry reports. Contact your ITP/South-Western College sales rep for more information about this offer.
- **CaseNet® Internet Resources** brings the practical lessons of real business to your classroom with our premier teaching cases, all based on data from business and industry. Cases help students make the connection between theory and practice, build analytical skills, and solve realistic problems. For more information, contact your ITP/South-Western sales representative or visit CaseNet at **http://casenet.thomson.com**

ACKNOWLEDGMENTS

Several people have contributed to the textbook. First, the motivation to write the textbook was primarily due to encouragement by professors Robert L. Conn (Miami University of Ohio), E. Joe Nosari and William Schrode (Florida State University), Anthony E. Scaperlanda (Northern Illinois University), and Richard A. Zuber (University of North Carolina at Charlotte).

Many of the revisions and expanded sections contained in this edition are due to comments and suggestions of students who used previous editions. In addition, many professors reviewed various editions of the text and had a major influence on its content and organization. All are acknowledged in alphabetical order:

Raj Aggarwal
John Carroll University

Alan Alford
Northeastern University

H. David Arnold
Auburn University

Robert Aubey
University of Wisconsin

Bruce D. Bagamery
Central Washington University

James C. Baker
Kent State University

Gurudutt Baliga
University of Delaware

Bharat B. Bhalla
Fairfield University

Rita Biswas
State University of New York at Albany

Sarah Bryant
George Washington University

Francisco Carrada-Bravo
American Graduate School of International Management

Andreas C. Christofi
Monmouth University

Alan Cook
Baylor University

W. P. Culbertson
Louisiana State University

Andrea L. DeMaskey
Villanova University

Robert Driscill
Ohio State University

Paul Fenton
Bishop's University

Stuart Fletcher
Appalachian State University

Robert D. Foster
American Graduate School of International Management

Hung-Gay Fung
University of Baltimore

Juli-Ann E. Gasper
Texas A&M University

Deborah W. Gregory
Bentley College

Nicholas Gressis
Wright State University

Indra Guertler
Babson College

Ann M. Hackert
Idaho State University

Joel Harper
Florida Atlantic University

John M. Harris, Jr.
Clemson University

Ghassem Homaifar
Middle Tennessee State University

Nathaniel Jackendoff
Temple University

Kurt R. Jesswein
Texas A&M International

Manuel L. Jose
University of Akron

Rauv Kalra
Moorhead State University

Ho-Sang Kang
University of Texas at Dallas

Frederick J. Kelly
Seton Hall University

Coleman S. Kendall
University of Illinois—Chicago

Dara Khambata
American University

Suresh Krishman
Pennsylvania State University

Boyden E. Lee
New Mexico State University

Jeong W. Lee
University of North Dakota

Carl Luft
DePaul University

K. Christopher Ma
KCM Investment Co.

Anna D. Martin
Fairfield University

Wendell McCulloch, Jr.
California State University—Long Beach

Carl McGowan
University of Michigan at Flint

Stuart Michelson
University of Central Florida

Edward Omberg
San Diego State University

Ali M. Parhizgari
Florida International University

Anne Perry
American University

Frances A. Quinn
Merrimack College

S. Ghon Rhee
University of Rhode Island

William J. Rieber
Butler University

Ashok Robin
Rochester Institute of Technology

Oliver Schnusenberg
St. Joseph's University

Jacobus T. Severiens
Kent State University

Peter Sharp
California State University—Sacramento

Dilip K. Shome
Virginia Tech University

Joseph Singer
University of Missouri—Kansas City

Naim Sipra
University of Colorado at Denver

Jacky So
Southern Illinois University at Edwardsville

Luc Soenen
California Polytechnic State University—San Luis Obisbo

Ahmad Sohrabian
California State Polytechnic University—Pomona

Caroline Spencer
Dowling College

Angelo Tarallo
Ramapo College

Amir Tavakkol
Kansas State University

Stephen G. Timme
Georgia State University

Mahmoud S. Wahab
University of Hartford

Ralph C. Walter III
Northeastern Illinois University

Elizabeth Webbink
Rutgers University

Ann Marie Whyte
University of Dayton

Marilyn Wiley
Florida Atlantic University

Glenda Wong De Paul University	Emilio Zarruk Florida Atlantic University	Stephen Zera California State University—San Marcos

This edition also benefited from the input of Jorg Bley (Florida Atlantic University), Steve Borde (University of Central Florida), Mike Dosal (Barnett Bank of Central Florida, Orlando), Victor Kalafa, and Alan Tucker (Pace University).

The people at South-Western College Publishing made many contributions to this edition. Editors Susan Smart and Mike Mercier were helpful in all stages of the writing and revising. A special thanks is due to the production editor, Sandra Gangelhoff, and the production house, WordCrafters, for their efforts to ensure a quality final product.

Finally, I wish to thank my parents, Arthur and Irene Madura, and my wife, Mary, for their moral support.

Jeff Madura
Florida Atlantic University

PART I

The International Financial Environment

Part I (Chapters 1 through 5) provides an overview of the multinational corporation (MNC) and the environment in which it operates. Chapter 1 explains the goals of the MNC, along with the motives and risks of international business. Chapter 2 describes the international flow of funds between countries. Chapter 3 describes the international financial markets and how these markets facilitate ongoing operations. Chapter 4 explains how exchange rates are determined, while Chapter 5 provides a background on the currency futures and options markets. Managers of MNCs must understand the international environment described in these chapters in order to make proper decisions.

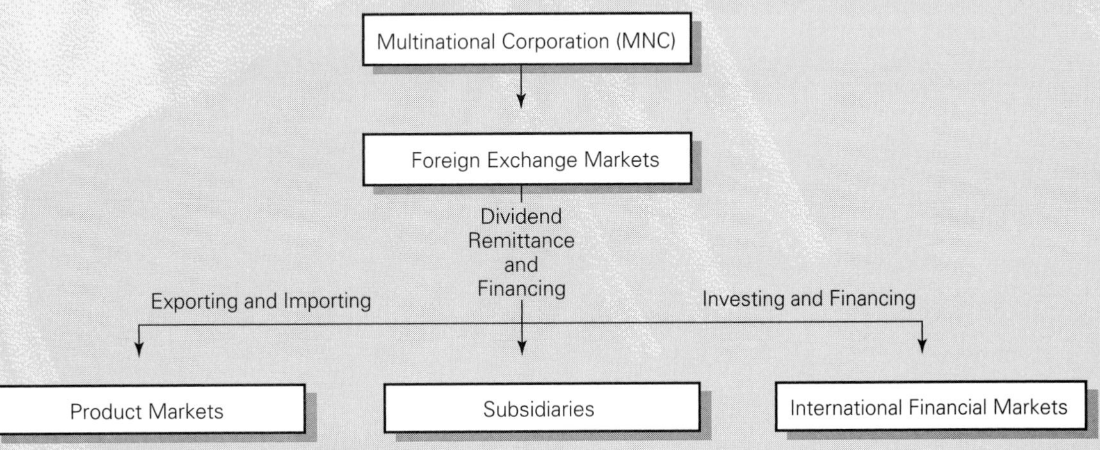

1 Multinational Financial Management: An Overview

Firms continually enact strategies to improve their cash flows and therefore enhance shareholder wealth. Some strategies involve the penetration of foreign markets. Since foreign markets can be distinctly different from local markets, they create opportunities for improving the firm's cash flows. Many barriers to entry into foreign markets have been reduced or removed recently, thereby encouraging firms to pursue international business (producing and/or selling goods in foreign countries). Consequently, many firms have evolved into multinational corporations (MNCs), which are defined as firms that engage in some form of international business.

Initially, firms may merely attempt to export products to a particular country or import supplies from a foreign manufacturer. Over time, however, many of them recognize additional foreign opportunities and eventually establish subsidiaries in foreign countries. Some businesses, such as Dow Chemical, Exxon, American Brands, and Colgate-Palmolive, commonly generate more than half their sales in foreign countries. A prime example is the Coca-Cola Company, which distributes its products in more than 160 countries and uses 40 different currencies. Over 60 percent of its total annual operating income is typically generated outside the United States.

An understanding of international financial management is crucial to not only the large MNCs with numerous foreign subsidiaries but also to the small firms that conduct international business. Many small U.S. firms generate more than 20 percent of their sales in foreign markets, including AMSCO International (Pennsylvania), Ferro (Ohio), Interlake (Illinois), Medtronic (Minnesota), Sybron (Wisconsin), and Synoptics (California). The small U.S. firms that conduct international business tend to focus on the niches that have made them successful in the United States. They tend to penetrate specialty markets where they will not have to compete with large firms that could capitalize on economies of scale. While some of the small firms have established subsidiaries, many of them use exporting to penetrate foreign markets. Seventy-five percent of U.S. firms that export have fewer than 100 employees.

International business is even important to companies that have no intention of engaging in international business, since these companies must recognize how their foreign competitors will be affected by movements in exchange rates, foreign interest rates, labor costs, and inflation. Such economic characteristics can affect the foreign competitors' cost of production and pricing policy.

Companies must also recognize how domestic competitors that obtain foreign supplies or foreign financing will be affected by economic conditions in foreign countries. If these domestic competitors are able to reduce their costs by capitalizing on opportunities in international markets, they may be able to reduce their prices without reducing their profit margins. This could allow them to increase market share at the expense of the purely domestic companies.

This chapter provides a background on the goals of an MNC and the potential risk and returns from engaging in international business.

The specific objectives of this chapter are to:

- identify the main goal of the MNC and conflicts with that goal,
- describe the key theories that justify international business, and
- explain the common methods used to conduct international business.

Goal of the MNC

The commonly accepted goal of an MNC is to maximize shareholder wealth. Developing a goal is necessary since all decisions should contribute to its accomplishment. Thus, if the objective were to maximize earnings in the near future, the firm's policies would be different than if the objective were to maximize shareholder wealth.

The focus of this text is on U.S.-based MNCs. Most of the concepts are generally transferable to MNCs that are based in other countries, but there are several exceptions that would have to be considered if the focus was not on MNCs based in the United States. For example, even a general statement about the goal of the MNC might be questioned when considering MNCs based in other countries; some MNCs based outside the United States tend to focus more on satisfying the respective goals of their respective governments, banks, or employees.

The focus of this text is also on MNCs whose parents wholly own any foreign subsidiaries, which implies that the U.S. parent is the sole owner of the subsidiaries. This is the most common form of ownership of U.S.-based MNCs, and it enables financial managers throughout the MNC to have a single goal of maximizing the value of the entire MNC instead of maximizing the value of any particular foreign subsidiary.

Conflicts Against the MNC Goal

It has often been argued that managers of a firm may make decisions that conflict with the firm's goal to maximize shareholder wealth. For example, a decision to establish a subsidiary in one location versus another may be based on the location's appeal to a particular manager rather than on its potential benefits to shareholders. Decisions to expand may be determined by the desires of managers to make their respective divisions grow in order to receive more responsibility and compensation. If a firm were composed of only one owner who was also the sole manager, a conflict of goals would not occur. However, for corporations with shareholders who differ from their managers, a conflict of goals can exist. This conflict is often referred to as the **agency problem.**

The costs of ensuring that managers maximize shareholder wealth (referred to as *agency costs*) are normally larger for MNCs than for purely domestic firms, for the following reasons. First, MNCs that have subsidiaries scattered around the world may experience larger agency problems because monitoring managers of distant subsidiaries in foreign countries is more difficult. Second, foreign subsidiary managers raised in different cultures may not follow uniform goals. Third, the sheer size of the larger MNCs can also create large agency problems. Fourth, some non-U.S. managers tend to downplay the short-term effects of decisions, which may result in decisions for foreign subsidiaries of the U.S.-based MNCs that are inconsistent with maximizing shareholder wealth.

Financial managers of an MNC with several subsidiaries may be tempted to make decisions that maximize the values of their respective subsidiaries. This objective will not necessarily coincide with maximizing the value of the overall MNC. Consider a subsidiary manager who obtained financing from the parent firm (headquarters) to develop and sell a new product. The manager estimated the costs and benefits of the project from the subsidiary's perspective and determined that the project was feasible. However, the manager neglected to realize that any earnings from this project remitted to the parent would be taxed heavily by the host government. The estimated after-tax benefits received by the parent were more than offset by the cost of financing the project. While the subsidiary's individual value was enhanced, the MNC's overall value was reduced. If financial managers are to maximize the wealth of their MNC's shareholders, they must implement policies that maximize the value of the overall MNC rather than the value of their respective subsidiaries. For many MNCs, major decisions by subsidiary managers must be approved by the parent. However, it is difficult for the parent to monitor all decisions made by subsidiary managers.

Impact of Management Control

The magnitude of agency costs can vary with the management style of the MNC. A centralized management style, as illustrated in the top section of Exhibit 1.1, can reduce agency costs because it allows managers of the parent to control foreign subsidiaries and therefore reduces the power of subsidiary managers. However, the parent's managers may make poor decisions for the subsidiary if they are not as informed as subsidiary managers about financial characteristics of the subsidiary.

The alternative style of organizing an MNC's management is a decentralized management style, as illustrated in the bottom section of Exhibit 1.1. This style is more likely to result in higher agency costs because subsidiary managers may make decisions that do not focus on maximizing the value of the entire MNC. Yet, this style gives more control to those managers who are closer to the subsidiary's operations and environment. To the extent that subsidiary managers recognize the goal of maximizing the value of the overall MNC and are compensated in accordance with that goal, the decentralized management style may be more effective.

Given the obvious tradeoff between centralized and decentralized management styles, some MNCs attempt to achieve the advantages of both styles. That is, they allow subsidiary managers to make the key decisions about their respective operations, but the decisions are monitored by the parent's management to ensure that they are in the best interests of the entire MNC.

Impact of Corporate Control

An MNC is subject to various forms of corporate control that can be used to reduce agency problems. First, an MNC may partially compensate its board members and its executives with its stock, which can encourage them to make decisions that maximize the MNC's stock price. However, this may only effectively control decisions by

Exhibit 1.1
Management Styles of MNCs

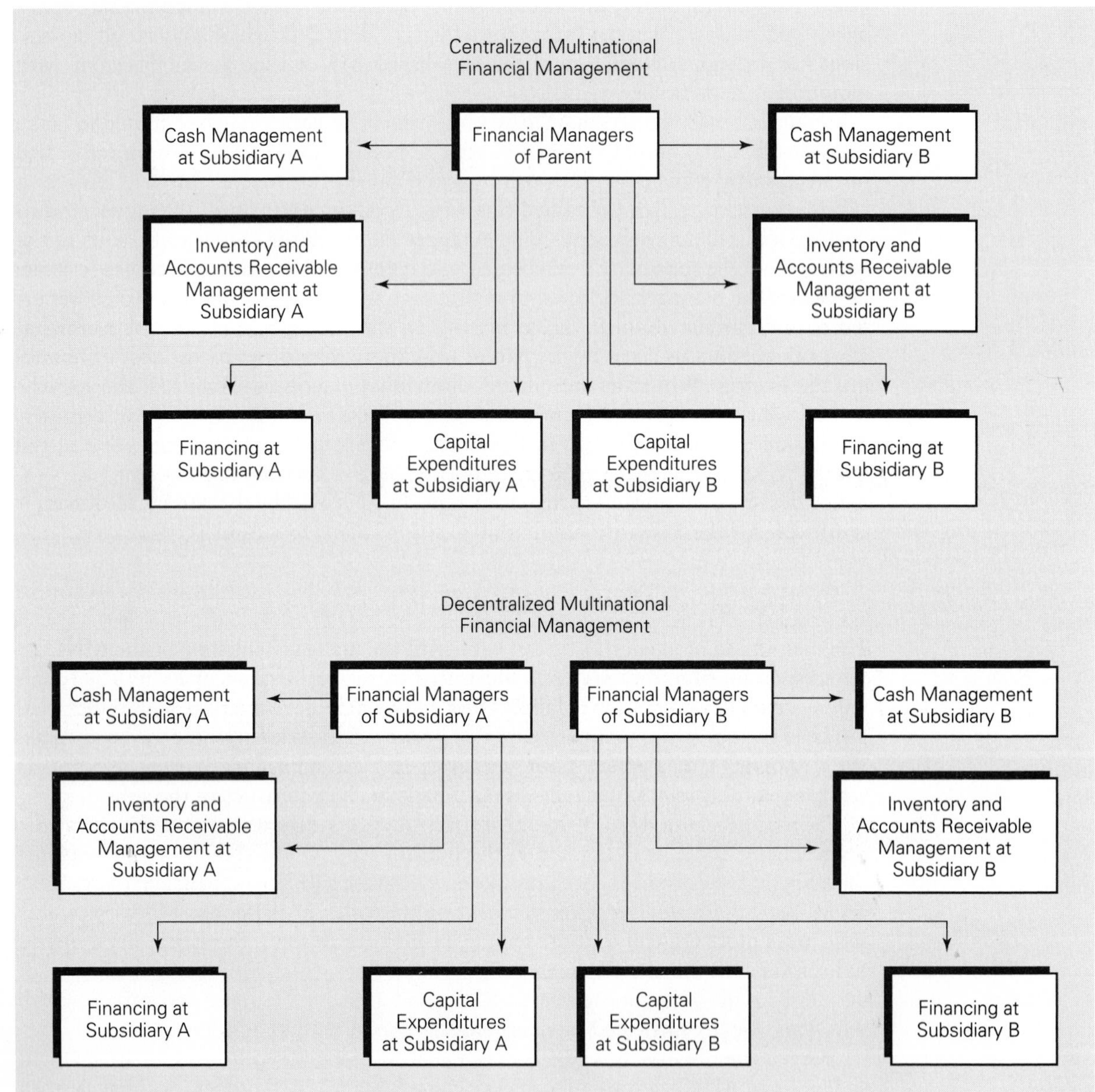

managers and board members who receive stock as compensation. In addition, some managers may still make decisions that conflict with the MNC's goal if they do not expect their decisions to have much of an impact on the stock price.

A second form of corporate control is the threat of a hostile takeover if the MNC is inefficiently managed. In theory, this threat is supposed to encourage managers to make decisions that enhance the MNC's value, since other types of decisions would cause the MNC's stock price to decline. Other firms would be more likely to acquire the MNC at such a low price and might terminate the existing managers. In the past, this threat was not very imposing for managers of subsidiaries in foreign countries because foreign governments commonly protected the employees; therefore, the potential benefits from a takeover were effectively eliminated. However, governments have recently recognized that such protectionism may promote inefficiencies and they are now more willing to accept takeovers and the subsequent layoffs that occur following takeovers.

A third form of corporate control is monitoring by large shareholders. U.S.-based MNCs are commonly monitored by mutual funds and pension funds because a large proportion of their outstanding shares are held by these institutions. Their monitoring tends to focus on broad issues to ensure that the MNC uses a compensation system that motivates managers or board members to make decisions to maximize the MNC's value; to use excess cash for repurchasing shares of stock rather than investing in questionable projects; and to ensure that the MNC does not insulate itself from the threat of a takeover (by implementing anti-takeover amendments, for example). Those MNCs that tend to make decisions that appear inconsistent with maximizing shareholder wealth are subjected to shareholder activism in which pension funds and other large institutional shareholders lobby for management changes or other changes. For example, MNCs such as Eastman Kodak, IBM, and Sears Roebuck were subjected to various forms of shareholder activism.

Like U.S. mutual funds and pension funds, foreign-owned banks also maintain large stock portfolios (unlike U.S. commercial banks, which do not use deposited funds to purchase stocks). The foreign banks are large and hold a sufficient proportion of shares of numerous firms (including some U.S.-based MNCs) to have some influence on key corporate policies. Their additional role as a lender to many of these firms enhances their ability to monitor corporate policies. However, these banks have not played a major role in corporate control. In general, they do not attempt to intervene unless a particular firm is experiencing major financial problems.

Corporate control on MNCs based in the United States has increased and is sometimes cited as the reason for the unusually strong stock price performance of U.S. firms during the 1990s, since corporate policies are now undertaken with more awareness about their impact on the stock price. Other countries are adopting U.S. corporate control practices as a means of forcing local firms to make decisions that satisfy their respective shareholders.

Constraints Interfering with the MNC's Goal

When financial managers of MNCs attempt to maximize their firm's value, they are confronted with various constraints that can be classified as environmental, regulatory, or ethical in nature.

Environmental Constraints. Each country enforces its own environmental constraints. Some countries may enforce more of these restrictions on a subsidiary whose parent is based in a different country. Building codes, disposal of production waste materials, and pollution controls are examples of the restrictions that force subsidiaries to incur additional costs. Many European countries have recently imposed tougher anti-pollution laws as a result of severe pollution problems.

Regulatory Constraints. Each country also enforces its own regulatory constraints pertaining to taxes, currency convertibility rules, earnings remittance restrictions, and other regulations that can affect cash flows of a subsidiary established there. Because these regulations can influence cash flows, they must be recognized by financial managers when assessing policies. Also, any change in these regulations may require revision of existing financial policies, so financial managers should not only recognize the regulatory restrictions that exist in a given country but also monitor them for any potential changes over time.

Ethical Constraints. There is no consensus standard of business conduct that applies to all countries. A business practice that is perceived to be unethical in one country may be totally ethical in another. For example, the U.S.-based MNCs are well aware of common business practices in some less developed countries that would be declared illegal in the United States. Bribes to governments in order to receive special tax breaks or other favors are common. A recent report presented to Congress estimated that U.S. firms lost out on at least $36 billion of international business transactions because of bribes provided by foreign competitors. The MNCs face a dilemma. If they do not participate in such practices, they may be at a competitive disadvantage. Yet, if they do participate, they receive poor reputations in countries that do not approve of such practices. Some U.S.-based MNCs have made the costly choice to refrain from business practices that are legal in certain foreign countries but not legal in the United States. That is, they follow a worldwide code of ethics. This may enhance their worldwide credibility, which can increase global demand for the products they produce.

THEORIES OF INTERNATIONAL BUSINESS

The commonly held theories as to why firms become motivated to expand their business internationally are (1) the theory of comparative advantage, (2) the imperfect markets theory, and (3) the product cycle theory. The three theories overlap to a degree and can complement each other in developing a rationale for the evolution of international business.

Theory of Comparative Advantage

Multinational business has generally increased over time. Part of this growth is due to the heightened realization that specialization by countries can increase production efficiency. Some countries, such as Japan and the United States, have a technology advantage, while countries such as Jamaica, Mexico, and South Korea have an advantage in the cost of basic labor. Since these advantages cannot be easily transported, countries tend to use their advantages to specialize in the production of goods that can be produced with relative efficiency. This explains why countries such as Japan and the United States are large producers of computer components, while countries such as Jamaica and Mexico are large producers of agricultural and handmade goods.

Specialization in some products may result in no production of other products, so that trade between countries is essential. This is the argument made by the classical theory of **comparative advantage.** Due to comparative advantages, it is easy to understand why firms are able to penetrate foreign markets. Many of the Virgin Islands rely completely on international trade for most products, while they specialize in tourism. Although the production of some goods is possible on these islands, there is more efficiency in the specialization of tourism. That is, the islands are better off using some revenues earned from tourism to import products rather than attempting to produce all the products that they need.

Imperfect Markets Theory

Countries differ with respect to resources available for the production of goods. Yet, even with such comparative advantages, the volume of international business would be limited if all resources could be easily transferred among countries. If markets were perfect, factors of production (except land) would be mobile and freely transferable. The unrestricted mobility of factors creates equality in costs and returns and removes the comparative cost advantage, the rationale for international trade and investment. However, the real world suffers from **imperfect market** conditions where factors of production are somewhat immobile. There are costs and often restrictions related to the transfer of labor and other resources used for production. There also may be restrictions on funds and other resources transferred among countries. Because markets for the various resources used in production are "imperfect," firms often capitalize on a foreign country's resources. Imperfect markets provide an incentive for firms to seek out foreign opportunities.

Product Cycle Theory

One of the more popular explanations as to why firms evolve into MNCs is introduced in the **product cycle theory.** According to this theory, firms become established in the home market as a result of some perceived advantage they would have over existing competitors, such as a need by the market for at least one more supplier of the product. Because information about markets and competition is more readily available at home, a firm is likely to establish itself first in its home country. Foreign demand for the firm's product will initially be accommodated by exporting. As time passes, the firm may feel the only way to retain its advantage over competition in foreign countries is to produce the product in foreign markets, thereby reducing its transportation costs. Over time, the competition in the foreign markets may increase as other producers become more familiar with the firm's product. Thus, the firm may develop strategies to prolong the foreign demand for its product. A common approach is to attempt to differentiate the product so that other competitors cannot offer exactly the same product. These phases of the cycle are illustrated in Exhibit 1.2. As an example, 3M Company uses one new product to penetrate foreign markets. After entering the market, it expands its product line.

There is more to the product cycle theory than is summarized here. This discussion merely suggests that, as a firm matures, it may recognize additional opportunities outside its home country. Whether the firm's foreign business diminishes or expands over time will depend on how successful it is at maintaining some advantage over its competition. The advantage could represent an edge in its production or financing approach that reduces costs. Alternatively, the advantage could reflect an edge in its marketing approach that generates and maintains a strong demand for its product.

Exhibit 1.2
International Product Life Cycle

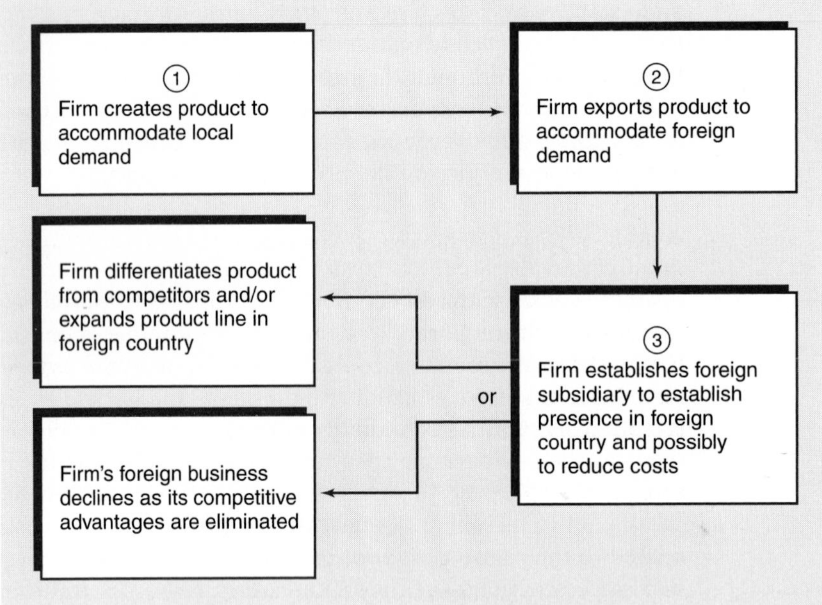

International Business Methods

There are several methods by which firms conduct international business. The most common methods are these:

- international trade
- licensing
- franchising
- joint ventures
- acquisitions of existing operations
- establishing new foreign subsidiaries

Each method is discussed in turn, with some emphasis on its risk and return characteristics.

International Trade

International trade is a relatively conservative approach that can be used by firms to penetrate markets (by exporting) or to obtain supplies at a low cost (by importing). There is minimal risk to this approach, since the firm does not place any of its capital at risk. If the firm experiences a decline in its exporting or importing, it can normally reduce or discontinue this part of its business at a low cost.

Many large U.S.-based MNCs, including Boeing, DuPont, General Electric, and IBM, generate more than $4 billion in annual sales from exporting. Yet, more than 20 percent of the value of all U.S. exports is provided by small businesses.

Licensing

Licensing obligates a firm to provide its technology (copyrights, patents, trademarks, or trade names) in exchange for fees or some other specified benefits. For example, AT&T and Nynex Corp. have licensing agreements to build and operate parts of India's telephone system. Sprint Corp. has a licensing agreement to develop telecommunications services in the United Kingdom. Eli Lilly & Co. has a licensing agreement to produce drugs for Hungary and other countries. IGA Inc., which operates more than 3,000 supermarkets in the United States, has a licensing agreement to operate supermarkets in China and Singapore. Licensing allows firms to use their technology in foreign markets without a major investment in foreign countries, and without the transportation costs that result from exporting. A major disadvantage of licensing is that it is difficult for the firm providing the technology to ensure quality control in the foreign production process.

Franchising

Franchising obligates a firm to provide a specialized sales or service strategy, support assistance, and possibly an initial investment in the franchise in exchange for periodic fees. For example, McDonald's, Pizza Hut, Subway Sandwiches, Blockbuster Video, Micro Age Computers, and Dairy Queen have franchises that are owned and managed by local residents in many foreign countries. Like licensing, franchising allows firms to penetrate foreign markets without a major investment in foreign countries. The recent relaxation of barriers in foreign countries throughout Eastern Europe and South America has resulted in numerous franchising arrangements.

Joint Ventures

A **joint venture** is a venture that is jointly owned and operated by two or more firms. Many firms penetrate foreign markets by engaging in a joint venture with firms that reside in those markets. Most joint ventures allow two firms to apply their respective comparative advantages in a given project. For example, General Mills Inc. joined in a venture with Nestlé SA, so that the cereals produced by General Mills could be sold through the overseas sales distribution network established by Nestlé.

Xerox Corp. and Fuji Co. (of Japan) engaged in a joint venture that allowed Xerox Corp. to penetrate the Japanese market and allowed Fuji to enter the photocopying business. Sara Lee Corp. and Southwestern Bell have engaged in joint ventures with Mexican firms, as such ventures have allowed entry into Mexico's markets. There are numerous joint ventures between automobile manufacturers, as each manufacturer can offer its technological advantages. General Motors has ongoing joint ventures with automobile manufacturers in several different countries, including Hungary and the former Soviet states.

Acquisitions of Existing Operations

Firms frequently acquire other firms in foreign countries as a means of penetrating foreign markets. For example, American Express recently acquired offices in London, while Procter & Gamble recently purchased a bleach company in Panama. Acquisitions allow firms to have full control over their foreign businesses and to quickly obtain a large portion of foreign market share. However, an acquisition of existing corporations is normally riskier than the other methods previously mentioned because of the large investment required. In addition, if the foreign operations perform poorly, it may be difficult to sell the operations at a reasonable price.

Some firms engage in partial international acquisitions in order to obtain a stake in foreign operations. This requires a smaller investment than full international acquisitions and therefore exposes the firm to less risk. On the other hand, the firm will not have complete control over foreign operations that are partially acquired.

Establishing New Foreign Subsidiaries

Firms can also penetrate foreign markets by establishing new operations in foreign countries to produce and sell their products. Like a foreign acquisition, this method requires a large investment. The establishment of new subsidiaries may be preferred to foreign acquisitions because the operations can be tailored exactly to the firm's needs. In addition, the investment amount may be less than that required to purchase existing operations. However, the firm will not reap any rewards from the investment until the subsidiary is built and a customer base established.

Summary of Methods

The methods of increasing international business extend from the relatively simple approach of international trade to the more complex approach of acquiring foreign firms or establishing new subsidiaries. Any method of increasing international business that requires a direct investment in foreign operations normally is referred to as a **direct foreign investment (DFI).** International trade and licensing usually are not considered to be DFI because they do not involve direct investment in foreign operations. Franchising and joint ventures tend to require some investment in foreign operations, but to a limited degree. Foreign acquisitions and the establishment of new foreign subsidiaries require substantial investment in foreign operations and represent the largest portion of DFI.

The optimal method for increasing international business may depend on the characteristics of the MNC. Exhibit 1.3 provides a sampling of U.S.-based MNCs with substantial international business. Some MNCs, such as Exxon and the Coca-Cola Company, derive most of their revenue from outside the United States. Yet, the Coca-Cola Company engages in various licensing agreements to derive some of its foreign revenue, so it does not require as much direct foreign investment to generate its foreign revenue.

International Opportunities

http://

Visit lcweb2.loc.gov/frd/cs/cshome.html, a page of the Library of Congress's Web site, for detailed studies of 85 countries.

Because of possible cost advantages from producing in foreign countries or possible revenue opportunities from demand by foreign markets, the growth potential becomes much greater for firms that consider international business. Exhibit 1.4 illustrates how a firm's growth can be affected by foreign investment and financing opportunities. The hypothetical investment opportunities for both a purely domestic firm and an MNC with similar operating characteristics are shown here. Each horizontal step represents a specific project. Each proposed project is expected to generate a marginal return to the firm.

Exhibit 1.3
Sampling of U.S.-Based MNCs with Substantial International Business

	Annual Foreign Revenue (in billions of $)	Annual Foreign Revenue as a % of Total Revenue	Foreign Assets (in billions of $)	Foreign Assets as a % of Total Assets
Exxon	$93	77%	55	57%
Ford Motor	47	32	67	30
IBM	46	58	41	50
Hewlett Packard	24	36	18	57
Procter & Gamble	17	49	11	39
Motorola	13	45	10	37
Coca-Cola Company	12	66	6	36
McDonald's	7	60	10	55
Gillette	6	63	7	62
Microsoft	4	34	4	26
Nike	4	40	3	42

Source: *Forbes,* July 27, 1998. Numbers are rounded.

Moving from left to right in Exhibit 1.4, the projects are prioritized according to marginal return. Assume that these projects are independent of each other and that their expected returns as shown have been adjusted to account for risk. With these assumptions, a firm would select the project with the highest marginal return as most

Exhibit 1.4
Cost-Benefit Evaluation for Purely Domestic Firms versus MNCs

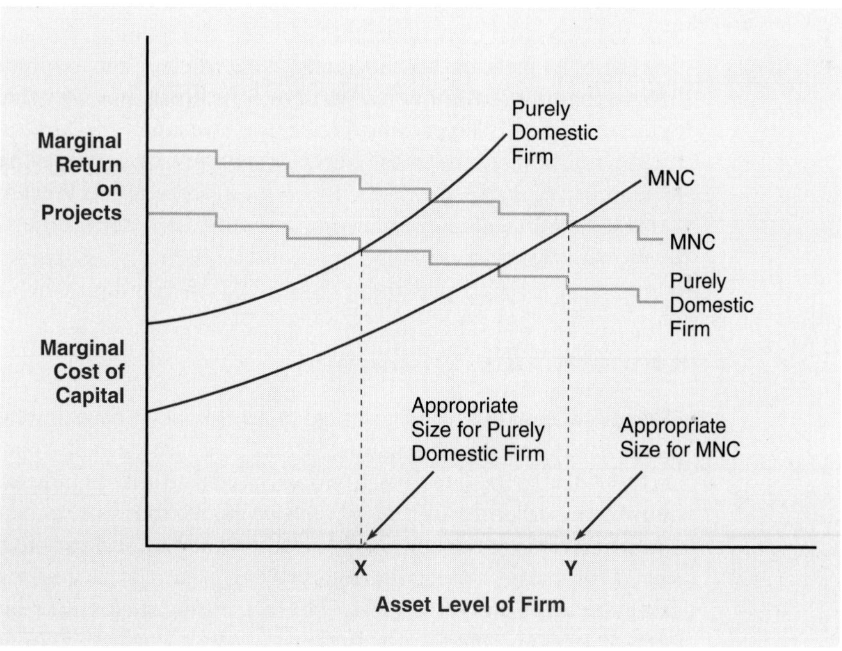

feasible and would undertake this project. Then, it would undertake the proposed project with the next highest marginal return, and so on. The marginal return on projects for the MNC is above that of the purely domestic firm because of the expanded opportunity set of possible projects from which to select.

Exhibit 1.4 also displays cost-of-capital curves for the MNC and purely domestic firm. The cost of capital is shown to increase with asset size for either type of firm. This is based on the premise that creditors or shareholders require a higher rate of return as the firm grows. Growth in asset size requires increased debt, which forces the firm to increase its periodic interest payments to creditors. Consequently, the firm has a greater probability of being unable to meet its debt obligations. To the extent that creditors and shareholders require a higher return for a more highly indebted firm, the cost of capital to the firm rises with its volume of assets. The MNC is shown to have an advantage in obtaining capital funding at a lower cost than can the purely domestic firm. This is due to its larger opportunity set of funding sources around the world.

Once the marginal cost of financing projects exceeds the marginal return on projects, the firm should not pursue such projects. As shown in Exhibit 1.4, a purely domestic firm will continue to accept projects up to point X. After that point, the marginal cost of additional projects exceeds the expected benefits.

When foreign resources, funds, and potential projects are considered, the firm's volume of feasible projects would be greater. The MNC's projects become unacceptable after point Y. This optimal level of assets exceeds that of the purely domestic firm. The difference here is due to cost advantages and opportunities in foreign countries. This comparison illustrates why firms may desire to become internationalized.

There are several limitations to the concept illustrated in Exhibit 1.4. First, there may be some cases where there are no feasible foreign opportunities for a firm. In addition, an argument could be made that foreign projects are riskier than domestic projects and therefore result in a higher cost of capital. Finally, some critics contend that the marginal cost of capital will not rise as more projects are added if the firm diversifies its projects appropriately. Nevertheless, the exhibit offers insight as to why firms expand internationally. Moreover, it illustrates why the optimal size of a given firm will typically be greater if that firm considers foreign opportunities.

In addition to capitalizing on cost advantages and opportunities, firms that enter foreign markets can also reduce their exposure to their local economy. That is, diversifying their business internationally reduces the sensitivity of their performance to the home country conditions. For example, while a U.S. recession may lower the U.S. demand for a firm's product, the non-U.S. demand may be unaffected.

Opportunities in Europe

Over time, economic and political conditions can change; this creates new opportunities in international business. A classic example is Europe in the late 1980s and early 1990s. In the late 1980s, industrialized countries in Europe agreed to make regulations more uniform and to remove many taxes on goods traded between these countries. This agreement, supported by the Single European Act of 1987, was followed by a series of negotiations among countries to begin phasing in policies that achieved uniformity by 1992. The act allows firms in a given European country greater access to supplies from firms in other European countries.

Many firms, including European subsidiaries of U.S.-based MNCs, have capitalized on the agreement by attempting to penetrate markets in border countries. Before the Single European Act, some subsidiaries conducted business only in their host countries because opportunities in border countries were discouraged by taxes and other barriers. As these barriers were reduced in the late 1980s, firms began to enter new markets. By producing more of the same product and distributing it across European countries, firms are now more able to achieve economies of scale. CPC International is one of many MNCs that was able to increase efficiency by streamlining manufacturing operations as a result of the reduction in barriers.

In 1989, another historic event occurred in Europe when the Berlin Wall separating East Germany from West Germany was removed. This was symbolic of new relations between East Germany and West Germany and was followed by efforts to reunify the two countries. In addition, it created momentum to encourage free enterprise in all Eastern European countries and privatization of businesses that were owned by the government. A key motive for pursuing opportunities in Eastern Europe was the lack of products available there. Coca-Cola Company, Reynolds Metals Company, CPC International, General Motors, and numerous other MNCs aggressively pursued expansion in Eastern Europe as a result of the momentum toward free enterprise.

While the Single European Act of 1987 and the momentum toward free enterprise in Eastern Europe offered new opportunities to MNCs, they also posed new risks. As the Single European Act removed cross-border barriers, it exposed firms to additional competition. As in other historical examples of deregulation, the more efficient firms benefit at the expense of less efficient firms.

In 1999, several European countries conformed to the euro as their currency for business transactions between these countries. This allowed firms (including European subsidiaries of U.S.-based MNCs) to engage in international transactions with the use of one currency and eliminated transactions costs resulting from exchanging currencies. It also eliminated concerns about potential effects of exchange rate fluctuations on the cash flows resulting from this type of international business. While the full effects are not yet known, the single currency system in Europe should definitely encourage more trade among European countries. In addition, the use of a single currency in most of Europe allows for a single monetary policy in Europe; MNCs that assess the economic growth in Europe can focus on one monetary policy rather than country-specific monetary policies that were prevalent before 1999.

Opportunities in Latin America

As a result of the North American Free Trade Agreement (NAFTA) of 1993, trade barriers between the United States and Mexico were eliminated. Some U.S. firms attempted to capitalize on this by exporting goods that had previously been restricted by barriers to Mexico. Other firms established subsidiaries in Mexico to produce their goods at a lower cost than was possible in the United States and then sell the goods in the United States. The removal of trade barriers essentially allowed U.S. firms to penetrate product and labor markets that previously had not been accessible.

The removal of trade barriers between the United States and Mexico allows Mexican firms to export some products to the United States that were previously restricted. Thus, U.S. firms that produce these goods are now subject to competition from Mexican exporters. Given the low cost of labor in Mexico, some U.S. firms have lost some of their market share. The effects should normally be most pronounced in the labor-intensive industries.

Within a month after the NAFTA accord, the momentum for free trade continued with a GATT (General Agreement on Tariffs and Trade) accord. This accord was the conclusion of trade negotiations from the so-called Uruguay Round that had begun seven years earlier. It called for the reduction or elimination of trade restrictions on specified imported goods over a ten-year period across 117 countries. The accord was expected to generate more international business for firms that had previously been unable to penetrate foreign markets because of trade restrictions.

Opportunities in Asia

Many U.S. firms such as PepsiCo, Coca-Cola Company, Apple Computer, and International Paper have increased their international business in Asia. In particular, China is viewed by many U.S. firms as the country with the most potential for growth. General Motors, Ford Motor Co., Procter & Gamble, and AT&T have invested billions of dollars in China to capitalize on the expected growth.

Many U.S. breweries have expanded into China to capitalize on the large increase in the demand for beer in that market. Pabst Blue Ribbon, which has lost much of its market share in the United States, has been very successful in China. Heilman Brewing has also had success with its Lone Star Beer, as the American cowboy image has been a useful marketing tool in China. Miller High Life has expanded into China through a licensing agreement, while Anheuser-Busch (producer of Budweiser) has partially acquired a Chinese beer company.

http://
These Web sites provide a background on the Asian Crisis:
www.stern.nyu.edu/~nroubini/asia/AsiaHomepage.html
www.policy.com/issuewk
www.asiehaus.org/links/crisis/htm
www.nyse.com/public/intview/4b/4bix.htm

In 1997, Asian countries such as Indonesia, Malaysia, and Thailand experienced severe economic problems. Many local companies went bankrupt, and concerns about the countries caused financial outflows of funds. These outflows left limited funds to support the economy. Interest rates increased because of the outflow of funds; this placed even more strain on firms that needed to borrow money. The so-called Asian crisis lingered in 1998 and adversely affected numerous U.S.-based MNCs that conducted business in these countries.

Yet, the crisis also created international business opportunities. The values of local firms were depressed and governments of the Asian countries reduced restrictions on acquisitions, which allowed MNCs from the United States and other countries to pursue acquisitions in the Asian countries. The crisis created opportunities for some U.S.-based MNCs to purchase local companies at a relatively low cost, improve the efficiency of the firms, and benefit from future expected economic growth. For example, during the Asian crisis in 1997–1998, South Korea's large conglomerate firms (called *chaebols*) experienced financial problems and began to sell many of their business units to obtain cash. U.S.-based MNCs such as General Electric, Procter & Gamble, and Coca-Cola Company acquired business units in Asia during this period.

Exposure to International Risk

While international business can reduce an MNC's exposure to its home country's economic conditions, it usually increases an MNC's exposure to (1) exchange rate movements, (2) foreign economic conditions, and (3) political risk. Each of these forms of exposure is briefly described here and is discussed in more detail in various sections of the text. These forms of exposure should be considered by MNCs that plan to pursue international business.

Exposure to Exchange Rate Movements

Most international business results in the exchange of one currency for another to make payment. Since exchange rates fluctuate over time, the cash outflows required to make payments change accordingly. Consequently, the number of units of a firm's home currency needed to purchase foreign supplies can change even if the suppliers have not adjusted their prices.

Exchange rate fluctuations can also affect the foreign demand for a firm's product. When the home currency strengthens, products denominated in that currency become more expensive to foreign customers, which may cause a decline in the demand and, therefore, a decline in cash inflows.

For MNCs with subsidiaries in foreign countries, exchange rate fluctuations affect the value of cash flows remitted by subsidiaries to the parent. When the parent's home currency is strong, the remitted funds will convert to a smaller amount of the home currency. A classic example of this type of exchange rate risk is the Asian crisis in 1998, when currencies of some Asian countries (such as Korea) depreciated by more than 20 percent against the dollar within a week. Thus, the U.S.-dollar value of earnings remitted by Asian subsidiaries of the U.S.-based MNCs was cut by more than 20 percent in a single week simply because of the weakening of the local currencies. Over the nine-month period ending in April 1998, the Indonesian rupiah depreciated by about 80 percent against the dollar. Thus, the U.S. dollars received by the U.S. parent from a given amount of remitted earnings by an Indonesian subsidiary were about 80 percent less in April 1998 than they had been nine months earlier.

Exposure to Foreign Economies

http://
Visit the Fed's data bank at www.stls.frb.org/fred for numerous economic and financial time series, e.g., on balance of payment statistics, interest rates, and foreign exchange rates.

When MNCs enter foreign markets to sell products, the demand for these products is dependent on the economic conditions in those markets. Thus, the cash flows of the MNC are subject to foreign economic conditions. For example, U.S. firms such as DuPont and Nike experienced lower-than-expected cash flows because of weak European economies in the 1992–93 period. U.S.-based MNCs such as Nike and 3M Co. that conducted business in Asia were adversely affected by the Asian crisis in 1998, as the weak Asian economies reduced the Asian demand for products. Mirage Resorts was adversely affected when gambling by its Asian customers declined.

Exposure to Political Risk

When MNCs establish subsidiaries in foreign countries, they become exposed to **political risk,** which represents political actions taken by the host government or the public that affect the MNC's cash flows (political risk is often viewed as a subset of **country risk,** which is explained later). For example, the host government may impose higher taxes on U.S.-based subsidiaries in retaliation for actions by the U.S. government. Alternatively, the host government may decide to buy out a subsidiary at whatever price it decides is fair. Milder forms of risk include actions by the host government that place foreign firms at a disadvantage. For example, the Mexican government was slow to respond to the request of United Parcel Service (UPS) to use its large vehicles for providing delivery services.

Nike Problem

International Business Opportunities and Risk

In every chapter, some of the key concepts discussed in the chapter are applied to Nike Inc., a firm known for its growth through penetration of foreign markets.

The evolution of Nike began in 1962, when Phil Knight, a business student in Stanford's business school, wrote a paper on how a U.S. firm could use Japanese technology to break the German dominance of the athletic shoe industry in the United States. After graduation, Knight visited the Unitsuka Tiger shoe company in Japan. He subcontracted that company to produce a shoe that he would sell in the United States under the name Blue Ribbon Sports (BRS). During the 1960s, he focused his business within the United States. In 1972, he experimented with international business by exporting his shoes to Canada. In 1974, he opened his first U.S. factory (in New Hampshire) and also expanded his operations into Australia. The firm's annual revenues were $4.8 million at that time. In 1977, the firm subcontracted factories in Taiwan and Korea to produce athletic shoes and then sold the shoes in Asian countries. In 1978, BRS became Nike Inc. and began to export shoes to Europe and South America. Nike expanded internationally as it developed a global image through its name recognition at world Olympic events and other sporting events. Its image represents a comparative advantage in many countries. As a result of its exporting and its direct foreign investment, Nike's international sales reached $1 billion by 1992.

Even with substantial international growth, Nike is not near the end of its product cycle. It has focused most of its European sales in five countries, with 70 percent of European sales attributed to the United Kingdom. Thus, there is potential for much growth in the other European countries, including Eastern Europe. In addition, while sales in Asia have declined during the Asian crisis, sales should increase over time as Asian economies rebound. Furthermore, there is still much room for growth in South American countries. Nike not only has many opportunities to expand its athletic shoe business internationally, but it could also expand its product line and sell new athletic products internationally as well.

Discussion: What factors do you think Nike considers about each country when deciding where to expand next?

Overview of an MNC's Cash Flows

Most U.S.-based MNCs have some local business within the United States, similar to other purely domestic firms. However, the types of cash flow streams of U.S.-based MNCs differ from those of purely domestic firms because of the international operations conducted by MNCs. Exhibit 1.5 shows cash flow diagrams for three common profiles of MNCs. Profile A in this exhibit reflects an MNC whose only international business is international trade. Thus, its international cash flows result from either paying for imported supplies or receiving payment in exchange for products that it exports.

Profile B reflects an MNC that engages in both international trade and some international arrangements (which can include international licensing, franchising, or joint ventures). Any of these international arrangements can require cash outflows by the MNC in foreign countries to comply with the arrangement, such as the

Exhibit 1.5
Cash Flow Diagrams for MNCs

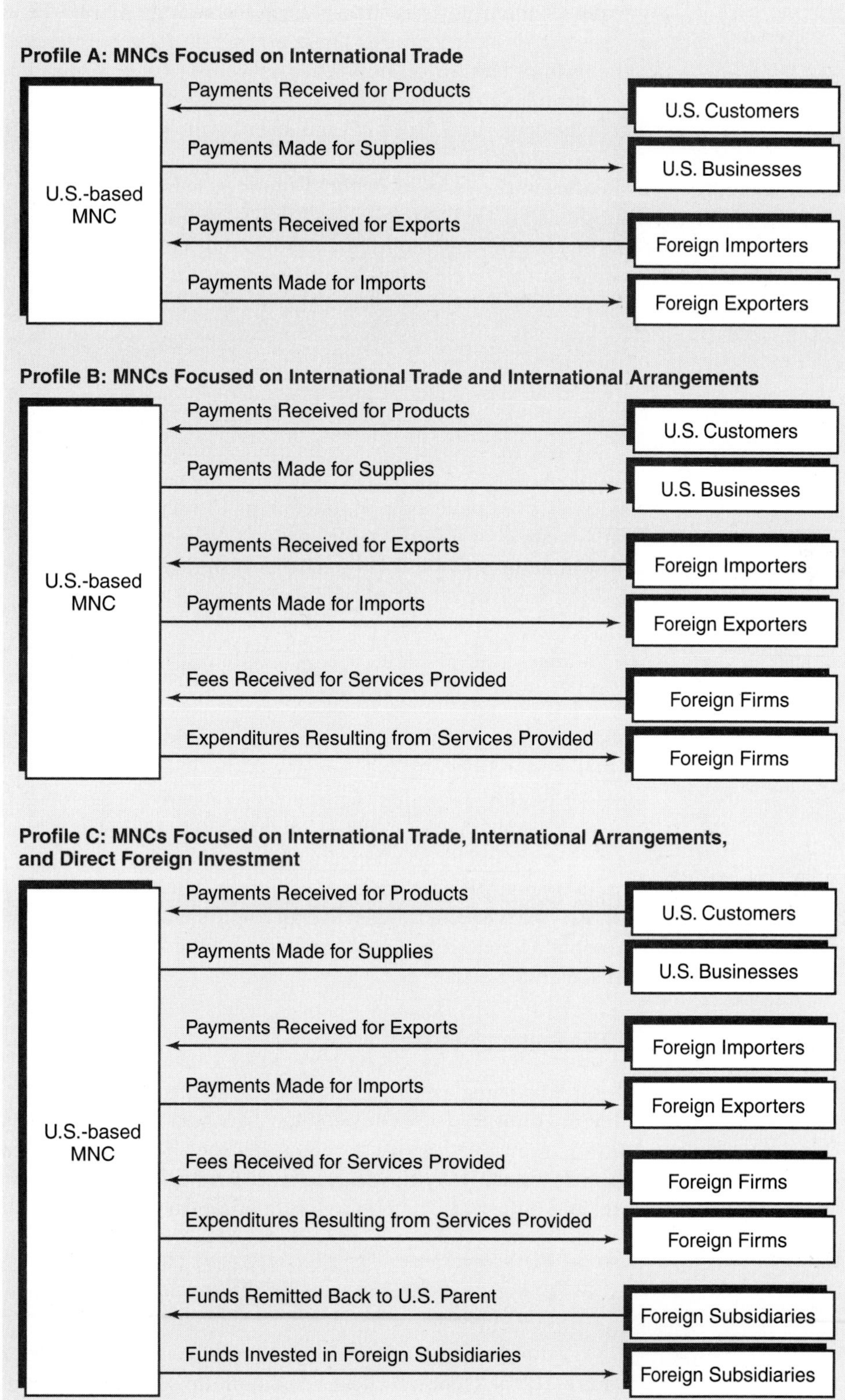

expenses incurred from transferring technology or offering partial investment in a franchise or joint venture. These arrangements generate cash flows to the MNC in the form of fees for services (such as technology or support assistance) it provides.

Profile C reflects an MNC that engages in international trade, international arrangements, and direct foreign investment. This type of MNC has one or more foreign subsidiaries. There can be cash outflows from the U.S. parent to its foreign subsidiaries in the form of invested funds to help finance the operations of the foreign subsidiaries. There are also cash flows from the foreign subsidiaries to the U.S. parent in the form of remitted earnings and fees for services provided by the parent, which can all be classified as remitted funds from the foreign subsidiaries. In general, the cash outflows associated with international business by the U.S. parent are to pay for imports, to comply with its international arrangements, or to support the creation or expansion of foreign subsidiaries. Conversely, it will receive cash flows in the form of payment for its exports, fees for the services it provides within its international arrangements, and remitted funds from the foreign subsidiaries.

Many MNCs initially conduct international business in the manner illustrated by Profile A. Some of these MNCs develop international arrangements and foreign subsidiaries over time; others are content to focus on exporting or importing as their only method of international business. While the three profiles vary, they all show how international business generates cash flows. These cash flows represent the cash inflows received by the MNC minus the cash outflows.

Valuation Model for an MNC

The value of an MNC is relevant to its shareholders and its debtholders. When managers make decisions that maximize the value of the firm, they maximize shareholder wealth (assuming that the decisions are not intended to maximize the wealth of debtholders at the expense of shareholders). Since international financial management should be conducted with the goal of increasing the value of the MNC, it is useful to review some basics of valuation. There are numerous methods of valuing an MNC, and some methods will lead to the same valuation. The one valuation method described here can be used to understand the key factors that affect an MNC's value in a general sense.

Domestic Model

Before modeling an MNC's value, consider the valuation of a purely domestic firm that does not engage in any foreign transactions. The value (V) of a purely domestic firm in the United States is commonly specified as the present value of its expected cash flows, whereby the discount rate used reflects the weighted average cost of capital and represents the required rate of return by investors:

$$V = \sum_{t=1}^{n} \left\{ \frac{[E(CF_{\$,t}]}{(1+k)^t} \right\}$$

where $E(CF_{\$,t})$ represents expected cash flows to be received at the end of period t, n represents the number of periods into the future in which cash flows are received, and k represents the required rate of return by investors. The dollar cash flows in period t represent funds received by the firm minus funds needed to pay expenses or taxes, or to reinvest in the firm (such as an investment to replace old computers or machinery). The expected cash flows are estimated from knowledge about various existing projects as well as other projects that will be implemented in the future. A firm's decisions about how it should invest funds to expand its business can affect its expected future cash flows and therefore can affect the firm's value. Holding other factors constant, an increase in expected cash flows over time should increase the value of the firm.

The required rate of return (k) in the denominator of the valuation equation represents the cost of capital (including both the cost of debt and the cost of equity) to the firm and is essentially a weighted average of the cost of capital based on all of the firm's projects. As the firm makes decisions that affect its cost of debt or its cost of equity for one or more projects, it affects the weighted average of its cost of capital and therefore affects the required rate of return. For example, if the firm's credit rating is suddenly lowered, its cost of capital will probably increase and so will its required rate of return. Holding other factors constant, an increase in the firm's required rate of return will reduce the value of the firm, because expected cash flows must be discounted at a higher interest rate. Conversely, a decrease in the firm's required rate of return will increase the value of the firm because expected cash flows are discounted at a lower required rate of return.

Valuing International Cash Flows

An MNC's value can be specified in the same manner as a purely domestic firm. However, consider that the expected cash flows generated by a U.S.-based MNC's parent in the period t may be coming from various countries and may therefore be denominated in different foreign currencies. The foreign currency cash flows will be converted into dollars. Thus, the expected dollar cash flows to be received at the end of period t are equal to the sum of the products of cash flows denominated in each currency j times the expected exchange rate at which currency j could be converted into dollars by the MNC at the end of period t.

$$E(CF_{\$,t}) = \sum_{j=1}^{m} [E(CF_{j,t}) \times E(ER_{j,t})]$$

where $CF_{j,t}$ represents the amount of cash flow denominated in a particular foreign currency j at the end of period t, and $ER_{j,t}$ represents the exchange rate at which the foreign currency (measured in dollars per unit of the foreign currency) can be converted to dollars at the end of period t.

For example, an MNC that does business in two currencies could measure its expected dollar cash flows in any period by multiplying the expected cash flow in each currency times the respective expected exchange rate at which that currency could be converted to dollars and then summing those two products. If the firm does not use various techniques (discussed later in the text) to hedge its transactions in foreign currencies, the expected exchange rate in a given period would be used in the valuation equation to estimate the corresponding expected exchange rate at which the foreign currency can be converted into dollars in that period. Conversely, if the MNC hedges these transactions, the exchange rate at which they can hedge those transactions would be used within the valuation equation.

It may help to think of an MNC as a portfolio of currency cash flows, one for each currency in which it conducts business. The expected dollar cash flows derived from each of those currencies can be combined to determine the total expected dollar cash flows in each future period. The present value of those cash flows serves as the estimate of the MNC's value. It is easier to derive an expected dollar cash flow value for each currency before combining the cash flows among currencies within a given period, because each currency's cash flow amount must be converted to a common unit (the dollar) before combining the amounts.

Example. To illustrate how the dollar cash flows of an MNC can be measured, consider a U.S. firm that had expected cash flows of $100,000 from local business and 1,000,000 Mexican pesos from business in Mexico at the end of period t. Assuming that the peso's value is expected to be $.09, the expected dollar cash flows are:

$$\begin{aligned} E(CF_{\$,t}) &= [E(CF_{j,t}) \times E(ER_{j,t})] \\ &= [\$100{,}000] + [1{,}000{,}000 \text{ pesos} \times (\$.09)] \\ &= [\$100{,}000] + \$[90{,}000] \\ &= \$190{,}000. \end{aligned}$$

The cash flows of $100,000 from U.S. business were already denominated in U.S. dollars and therefore did not have to be converted into U.S. dollars.

The MNC's dollar cash flows at the end of every period in the future can be estimated in the same manner. Then, the MNC's value can be measured by determining the present value of the expected dollar cash flows, which is the sum of the discounted dollar cash flows that are expected in all future periods. This example uses only two currencies, but if the MNC had transactions involving 40 currencies, the same process could be used. The expected dollar cash flows for each of the 40 currencies would be estimated separately for each future period. The expected dollar cash flows for each of the 40 currencies within each period could then be combined to derive the total dollar cash flows per period. Finally, the cash flows in each period would be discounted to derive the value of the MNC.

The general formula for the dollar cash flows received by the MNC in any particular period can be written as:

$$E(CF_{\$,t}) = \sum_{j=1}^{m} [E(CF_{j,t}) \times E(ER_{j,t})]$$

The value of an MNC can be more clearly differentiated from the value of a purely domestic firm by substituting this expression $[E(CF_{j,t}) \times E(ER_{j,t})]$ for $E(CF_{\$,t})$ in the valuation model, as shown here:

$$V = \sum_{t=1}^{n} \left\{ \frac{\sum_{j=1}^{m} [E(CF_{j,t}) \times E(ER_{j,t})]}{(1+k)^t} \right\}$$

where $CF_{j,t}$ represents the cash flow denominated in a particular currency (including dollars), and $ER_{j,t}$ represents the exchange rate at which the MNC can convert the foreign currency at the end of period t. Thus, the value of an MNC can be affected by a change in expectations about $CF_{j,t}$ or $ER_{j,t}$. Only those cash flows that are to be received by the MNC's parent in the period of concern should be counted. To avoid double-counting, cash flows of the MNC's subsidiaries are only considered in the valuation model when they reflect transactions with the U.S. parent. Thus, any expected cash flows received by foreign subsidiaries should not be counted in the valuation equation until they are expected to be remitted to the parent.

The denominator of the valuation model for the MNC remains unchanged from the original valuation model for the purely domestic firm. However, recognize that the weighted average cost of capital for the MNC is based on funding some projects that reflect business in different countries. Thus, any decision by the MNC's parent that affects the cost of its capital supporting projects in a specific country can affect its weighted average cost of capital (and its required rate of return) and therefore can affect its value.

In general, the valuation model shows that an MNC's value can be affected by forces that influence the amount of its cash flows in a particular currency (CF_j), the exchange rate at which that currency is converted into dollars (ER_j), or the MNC's weighted average cost of capital (k).

How Chapters Relate to Valuation

The international opportunities described in this chapter can affect the valuation of an MNC, as illustrated in Exhibit 1.6. New international opportunities can enhance the expected currency cash flows and therefore enhance the value of the firm. How-

Exhibit 1.6
Impact of New International Opportunities on an MNC's Value

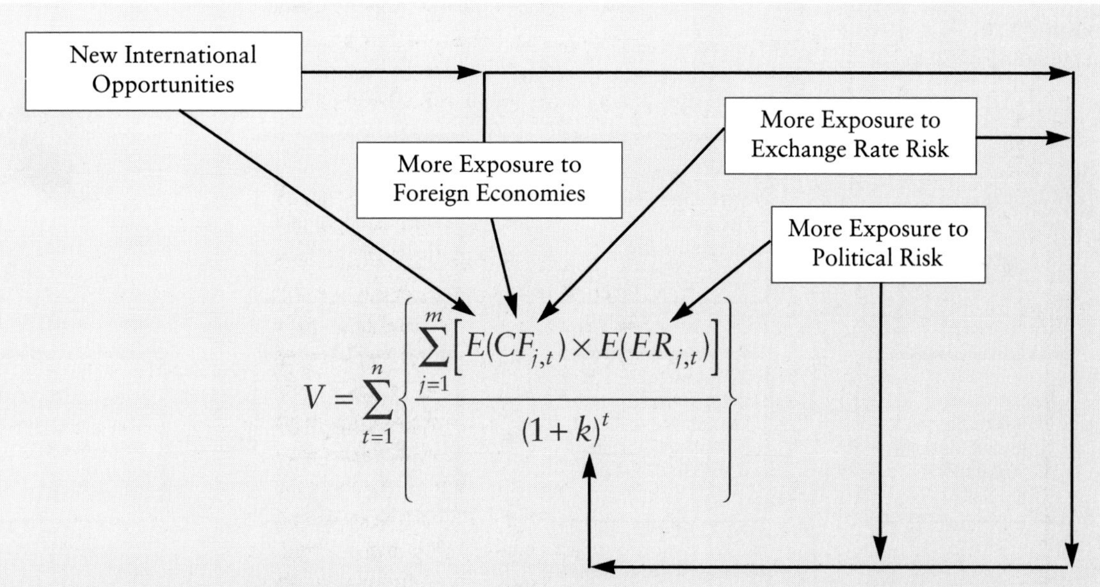

$$V = \sum_{t=1}^{n} \left\{ \frac{\sum_{j=1}^{m} \left[E(CF_{j,t}) \times E(ER_{j,t}) \right]}{(1+k)^t} \right\}$$

V = value of the U.S.-based MNC
$E(CF_{j,t})$ = expected cash flows denominated in currency j to be received by the U.S. parent in period t
$E(ER_{j,t})$ = expected exchange rate at which currency j can be converted to dollars at the end of period t
k = the weighted average cost of capital of the U.S. parent company
m = number of currencies
n = number of periods

ever, this potential advantage must be weighed against the exposure to foreign economies, exchange rate risk, and political risk, which can cause a reduction in cash flows, or to a higher weighted average cost of capital; this could reduce the value of the firm. MNCs that focus primarily on importing are exposed to exchange rate movements but are not heavily exposed to foreign economies or political risk. MNCs that are engaged in international arrangements such as licensing or joint ventures have more exposure to foreign economies and to political risk than importers but not as much exposure as MNCs with foreign subsidiaries.

Near the end of each chapter, the main concepts explained in that chapter are related to the valuation model to illustrate how those concepts are relevant to the valuation of an MNC. Thus, the potential impact of these concepts on MNCs becomes more obvious.

The organization of chapters in this text is illustrated in Exhibit 1.7. Chapters 2 through 8 of this text discuss international markets and conditions from a macroeconomic perspective and therefore focus on external forces that can affect the value of the MNC. While financial managers may not have control over these forces, they do have some control over their degree of exposure to these forces. These macroeconomic chapters provide the background necessary to make financial decisions.

Chapters 9 through 21 of this text are based on a microeconomic perspective and focus on how the financial management of an MNC can affect its value. Financial decisions by MNCs are commonly distinguished as either investing decisions or financing decisions. In general, investing decisions by an MNC tend to affect the numerator of the valuation model because such decisions affect expected cash flows. Yet, investing decisions by the MNC's parent may also affect the denominator of the

Exhibit 1.7
Organization of Chapters

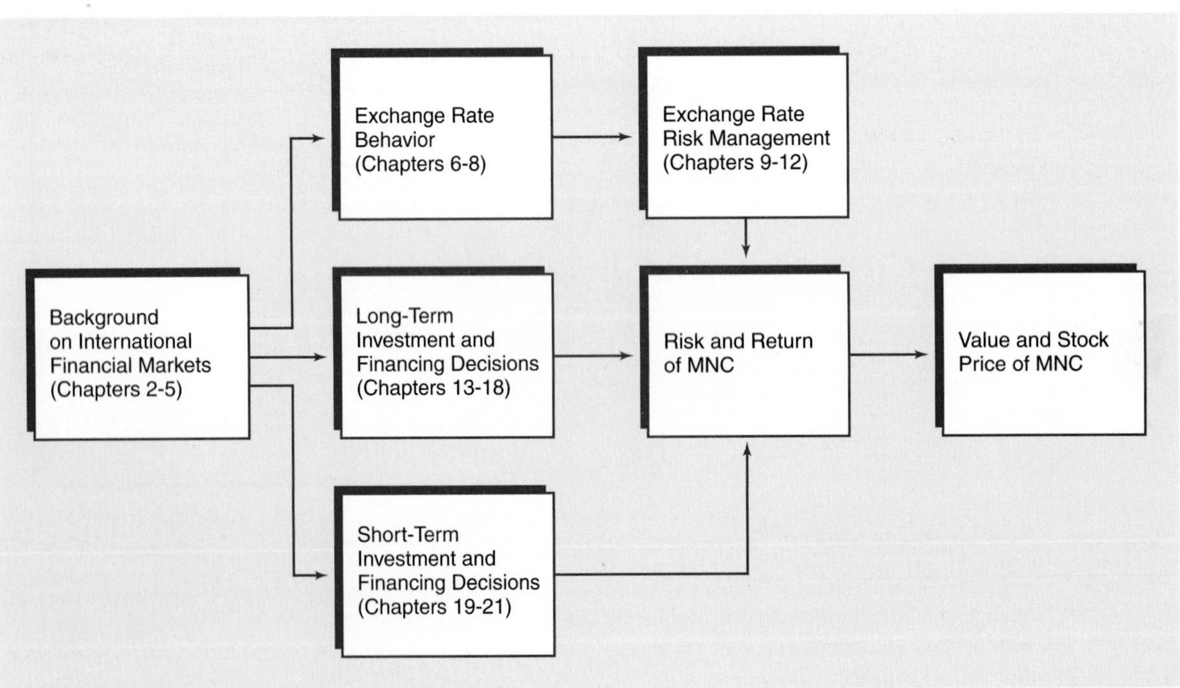

valuation model if they alter the firm's weighted average cost of capital. Long-term financing decisions by an MNC's parent tend to affect the denominator of the valuation model because they affect the MNC's cost of capital.

SUMMARY

- The main goal of the MNC is to maximize shareholder wealth. When managers are tempted to serve their own interests instead of those of shareholders, an agency problem exists. Managers also face environmental, regulatory, and ethical constraints that can conflict with the goal of maximizing shareholder wealth.
- International business is justified by three key theories. The theory of comparative advantage suggests that each country should use its comparative advantage to specialize in its production and rely on other countries to meet other needs. The imperfect markets theory suggests that because of imperfect markets, factors of production are immobile, which encourages countries to specialize based on the resources they have. The product cycle theory suggests that after firms are established in their home countries, they commonly expand their product specialization in foreign countries.
- The most common methods by which firms conduct international business are international trade, licensing, franchising, joint ventures, acquisitions of foreign firms, and formation of foreign subsidiaries. Methods such as licensing and franchising involve little or low capital investment but distribute some of the profits to other parties. Acquisition of foreign firms and formation of foreign subsidiaries involve a substantial capital investment but offer the potential for large returns.

SELF-TEST FOR CHAPTER 1

(Answers are provided in Appendix A at the back of the text.)

1. Describe typical reasons that MNCs expand internationally.
2. Describe the changes in Europe, Canada, and Mexico that have created new opportunities for U.S.-based MNCs.
3. Describe the more obvious risks faced by MNCs that expand internationally.

QUESTIONS AND APPLICATIONS

1. Explain the agency problem of MNCs. Why might agency costs be larger for the MNC as opposed to a purely domestic firm?
2. Explain how the theory of comparative advantage relates to the need for international business.
3. Explain how the existence of imperfect markets has led to the establishment of subsidiaries in foreign markets.
4. If perfect markets existed, would wages, prices, and interest rates among countries be more similar or less similar than under conditions of imperfect markets? Why?
5. Explain how the product cycle theory relates to the growth of the MNC.
6. How does access to international opportunities affect the size of corporations? Describe a scenario wherein the size of the corporation is not affected by access to international opportunities.
7. What factors cause some firms to become more internationalized than others?

8. What are some potential disadvantages of international business that are often not relevant to domestic business? Briefly state how an MNC can be adversely affected by these disadvantages.

9. Explain how the adoption of the euro as the single currency by European countries could be beneficial to MNCs based in Europe and to MNCs based in the U.S.

10. As an overall review of this chapter, identify possible reasons for growth in international business. Then, list the various disadvantages that may discourage international business.

11. Describe constraints that interfere with the MNC's objective.

12. The managers of Loyola Corporation recently had a meeting to discuss new opportunities in Europe as a result of the recent integration between European countries. They decided not to penetrate new markets because of their present focus on expanding market share in the United States. Financial managers of Loyola Corporation developed forecasts for earnings based on the 12 percent market share (defined here as its percentage of total European sales) that Loyola presently has in Europe. Is 12 percent an appropriate estimate for next year's European market share? If not, would it likely overestimate or underestimate the actual European market share next year?

13. Would the agency problem be more pronounced for Berkeley Corporation, which has its parent company make most major decisions for its foreign subsidiaries, or Oakland Corporation, which has a decentralized approach?

14. Explain why more standardized product specifications across countries can increase global competition.

15. How can German subsidiaries of U.S.-based MNCs capitalize on the removal of the Berlin Wall that separated East and West Germany?

16. Describe the Single European Act, and explain how it may affect international business by U.S. firms.

17. Review the table of contents and identify whether each of the chapters from Chapter 2 through Chapter 21 have a macro- or microperspective.

18. Explain why MNCs such as Coca-Cola and PepsiCo Inc. still have numerous opportunities for international expansion.

19. An MNC desires to penetrate a foreign market by entering a licensing agreement with a foreign firm or by acquiring a foreign firm. Explain the differences in potential risk and return between a licensing agreement with a foreign firm and the acquisition of a foreign firm.

20. Anheuser-Busch, the producer of Budweiser and other beers, has recently expanded into Japan by engaging in a joint venture with Kirin Brewery, the largest brewery in Japan. The joint venture enables Anheuser-Busch to have its beer distributed through Kirin's distribution channels in Japan. In addition, it can utilize Kirin's facilities to produce beer that will be sold locally. In return, Anheuser-Busch provides information about the American beer market to Kirin.

    a. Explain how the joint venture can enable Anheuser-Busch to achieve its objective of maximizing shareholder wealth.
    b. Explain how the joint venture can limit the risk of international business.
    c. Many international joint ventures are intended to circumvent barriers that normally prevent foreign competition. What barrier in Japan is Anheuser-Busch circumventing as a result of the joint venture? What barrier in the U.S. is Kirin circumventing as a result of the joint venture?
    d. Explain how Anheuser-Busch could lose some of its market share in countries outside of Japan as a result of this particular joint venture.

Internet Application

Assessing Direct Foreign Investment Trends

21. The Web site address of the Bureau of Economic Analysis is:

    www.bea.doc.gov

    a. Use this Web site to assess recent trends in direct foreign investment (DFI) abroad by the U.S. firms. Compare the DFI in the United Kingdom to the DFI in France. Offer a possible reason for the large difference.

b. Based on the recent trends in DFI, are U.S.-based MNCs pursuing opportunities in Asia? In Eastern Europe? In Latin America?

Running Your Own MNC

22. In each chapter of this text, you have the opportunity to apply the key concepts to your own idea about running an MNC. Many existing MNCs are small firms that focus on exporting a single product to a single country. The exported products could be sold to a single distributor based in a foreign country or could even be sold through the mail based on demand from mail-order ads. Your idea may be an extension of an idea you had for a business within the United States. It should focus on one particular foreign country and one particular foreign currency (the local currency of that country), since many of the questions within this project will allow you to learn more about that country and currency. This project can be assigned to individual students or to teams of students. For this chapter, the focus is on creating the idea for your own MNC.

    Create an idea for your own MNC to conduct international business. Your idea should be simplified to the degree that you could possibly implement it someday. However, your idea should also be sufficiently creative to be successful if done properly. Your idea should focus on one country and one foreign currency, since many MNCs are focused in this manner when they are first created. So that you can recognize the issues regarding exchange rate risk that are discussed throughout this text, you should assume that you will receive foreign currency when selling your product. Your idea should be for a small MNC instead of a large MNC because even most large MNCs began as small firms. The following questions will help you define your MNC idea:

    a. What is the product that you plan to sell?
    b. What foreign country do you plan to target?
    c. How will you sell the product in that country? (i.e., Through a distributor? By mail?)
    d. Is there some evidence that consumers in that country would buy this type of product?
    e. Do you need to purchase supplies or to hire labor?
    f. Will any expenses you incur from producing the product be in dollars or some other currency?

Blades, Inc. Case

Decision to Expand Internationally

Blades, Inc. is a U.S.-based company that has been incorporated in the United States for three years. Blades is a relatively small company, with total assets of only $200 million dollars. The company produces a single type of product, roller blades. Due to the booming roller blade market in the United States at the time of the company's establishment, the company has been quite successful. For example, in its first year of operation, it reported a net income of $3.5 million. Recently, however, the demand for Blades' "Speedos," the company's primary product in the United States, has been slowly tapering off, and Blades has not been performing well. Last year, it reported a return on assets of only 7 percent. In response to the company's annual report for its most recent year of operations, Blades' shareholders have been pressuring the company to improve its performance; their stock price has fallen from a high of $20 per share three years ago to $12 last year. Blades produces high quality roller blades and employs a unique production process, but the prices it charges are among the top 5 percent in the industry.

In light of these circumstances, Ben Holt, the company's chief financial officer, is contemplating his alternatives regarding the future of Blades, Inc. There are no other cost cutting measures Blades can implement in the U.S. that would not affect the quality of Blades' product. Also, production of alternative products would require major modifications to the existing plant setup. Furthermore, and because of these limitations, expansion within the United States at this time seems pointless.

Ben Holt is considering the following: If Blades cannot penetrate the U.S. market further or reduce costs here, why not import some parts from overseas and/or expand the company's sales to foreign countries? Similar strategies have proven successful for numerous companies that expanded into Asia in recent years to increase their profit margins. The CFO's initial focus is on Thailand. Thailand recently experienced weak economic conditions, and Blades could purchase components there at a low cost. Ben Holt is aware that many of Blades' competitors have begun importing production components from Thailand.

Not only would Blades be able to reduce costs by importing rubber and/or plastic from Thailand due to the low costs of these inputs, but it might also be able to augment weak U.S. sales by exporting to Thailand, an economy still in its infancy and just beginning to appreciate leisure products such as roller blades. Thus, while several of Blades' competitors import components from Thailand, few are exporting to the country. Long-term decisions would also eventually have to be made; maybe Blades, Inc., could establish a subsidiary in Thailand and gradually shift its focus away from the United States if its sales in the United States do not rebound again. Establishing a subsidiary in Thailand would also make sense for Blades due to its superior production process. Ben Holt is reasonably sure that Thai firms could not duplicate the high quality production process employed by Blades. Furthermore, if the company's initial approach of exporting works well, establishing a subsidiary in Thailand would preserve Blades' sales before Thai competitors are able to penetrate the Thai market.

As a financial analyst for Blades, Inc., you are assigned to analyze international opportunities and risk resulting from international business. Your initial assessment should focus on the barriers and opportunities that international trade may offer. Ben Holt has never been involved in international business in any form and is unfamiliar with any constraints that may inhibit his plan to export to and import from a foreign country. Mr. Holt has presented you with a list of initial questions you should answer.

1. What are the advantages Blades could gain from importing from and/or exporting to a foreign country such as Thailand?
2. What are some of the disadvantages Blades could face as a result of foreign trade in the short run? In the long run?
3. Which theories of international business described in this chapter apply to Blades, Inc., in the short run? The long run?
4. What long-range plans other than establishment of a subsidiary in Thailand are options for Blades and may be more suitable for the company?

Small Business Dilemma

Developing a Multinational Sporting Goods Corporation

In every chapter of this text, some of the key concepts are illustrated with an application to a small sporting goods firm that conducts international business. The "Small Business Dilemma" in each chapter allows students to recognize the dilemmas and possible decisions that firms (such as this sporting goods firm) may face in a global environment. For this chapter, the application is on the development of the sporting goods firm that would conduct international business.

Last month, Jim Logan completed his undergraduate degree in finance and decided to pursue his dream of managing his own sporting goods business. Jim had worked in a sporting goods shop while going to college, and he had noticed that many customers wanted to purchase a low-priced football. However, the sporting goods store where he worked, like many others, only sold top-of-the-line footballs. From his experience, he was aware that top-of-the-line footballs had a high markup and that a low-cost football could possibly penetrate the U.S. market. He also knew how to produce footballs. His goal was to create a firm that would produce low-priced footballs and sell them on a wholesale basis to various sporting goods stores in the United States. Unfortunately, many sporting goods stores began to sell low-priced footballs just before Jim was about to start his business. The firm that began to produce the low-cost footballs already provided many other products to sporting goods stores in the United States and therefore had already established a business relationship with these stores. Jim did not believe that he could compete with this firm in the U.S. market.

Rather than pursue a different business, Jim decided to implement his idea on a global basis. While football (as it is played in the United States) has not been a traditional sport in foreign countries, it has become more popular in some foreign countries in recent years. Furthermore, the expansion of cable networks in foreign countries would allow for much more exposure to U.S. football games in foreign countries in the future. To the extent that this would increase the popularity of football (U.S. style) as a hobby in the foreign countries, it would result in a demand for footballs in foreign countries. Jim asked many of his foreign friends from college days if they recalled seeing footballs sold in their home countries. Most of them said they rarely noticed footballs being sold in sporting goods stores but that they expected the demand for footballs to increase in their home countries. Consequently, Jim decided to start a business of producing low-priced footballs and exporting them to sporting goods distributors in foreign countries. Those distributors would then sell the footballs at the retail level. Jim planned to expand his product line over time once he identified other sports products that he might sell to foreign sporting goods stores. He decided to call his business "Sports Exports Company." To avoid any rent and labor expenses, Jim planned to produce the footballs in his garage and to perform the work himself. Thus, his main business expenses were the cost of the material used to produce footballs and expenses associated with finding distributors in foreign countries who would attempt to sell the footballs to sporting goods stores.

1. Is Sports Exports Company a multinational corporation?
2. Why are the agency costs lower for Sports Exports Company than for most MNCs?
3. Does Sports Exports Company have any comparative advantage over potential competitors in foreign countries that could produce and sell footballs there?
4. How would Jim Logan decide in which foreign markets to pursue his business idea? Should he initially attempt to focus on one or many foreign markets?
5. The Sports Exports Company has no immediate plans to conduct direct foreign investment. However, it might consider other less costly methods to establish its business in foreign markets. What methods might the Sports Exports Company use to increase its presence in foreign markets by working with one or more foreign companies?

2 International Flow of Funds

International business is facilitated by markets that allow for the flow of funds between countries. The transactions arising from international business cause money flows from one country to another. The balance of payments represents a measure of international money flows and is discussed in this chapter.

The specific objectives of this chapter are to:

- explain the key components of the balance of payments, and
- explain how the international flow of funds is influenced by economic factors and other factors.

Balance of Payments

The **balance of payments** is a measurement of all transactions between domestic and foreign residents over a specified period of time. The use of the words "all transactions" can be somewhat misleading, since some transactions may be estimated. The recording of transactions is done by **double-entry bookkeeping.** That is, each transaction is recorded as both a credit and a debit. Thus, total credits and debits will be identical for a country's balance of payments in aggregate; however, for any subset of the balance-of-payments statement, there may be a deficit or surplus position. A balance-of-payments statement can be broken down into various components. Those that receive the most attention are the current account and the capital account. The **current account** represents a summary of the flow of funds between one specified country and all other countries due to the purchases of goods or services, or the provision of income on financial assets. The **capital account** represents a summary of the flow of funds resulting from the sale of assets between one specified country and all other countries over a specified period of time. Transactions that reflect inflows of funds create a positive number (credit) to the country's balance, while transactions that reflect outflows of funds create a negative number (debit) to the country's balance.

Current Account

An example of the current account is shown in Exhibit 2.1. The current account is primarily composed of merchandise exports and imports and service exports and

Exhibit 2.1
U.S. Current Account, 1997 (in billions of $)

Merchandise Exports	$679
Merchandise Imports	–877
Balance of Trade	–198
Service Exports	253
Service Imports	–168
Transfer Payments and Other	– 42
Balance on Current Account	–155

imports. A key component of the current account is the **balance of trade,** which is simply the difference between merchandise exports and merchandise imports. A deficit in the balance of trade represents a greater value of imported goods than exported goods. Conversely, a surplus reflects a greater value of exported goods than imported goods. Merchandise exports and imports represent tangible products, such as computers and clothing, that are transported between countries. Service exports and imports represent services, such as legal, insurance, and consulting services provided for customers based in other countries. Thus, service exports by the United States result in an inflow of funds to the United States, while service imports by the United States result in an outflow of funds from the United States.

Another component is factor income, which represents income received by investors on foreign investments in financial assets (securities). Thus, factor income received by the United States reflects an inflow of funds into the United States. Factor income paid by the United States reflects an outflow of funds from the United States.

Capital Account

The key components of the capital account are shown in Exhibit 2.2. The capital account is segmented by direct foreign investment, portfolio investment, and other capital investment. Direct foreign investment represents the investment in fixed assets in foreign countries that can be used to conduct business operations. Examples of direct foreign investment include a firm's acquisition of a foreign company, its creation of a new manufacturing plant, or its expansion of an existing plant in a foreign country.

Portfolio investment represents transactions involving long-term financial assets (such as stocks and bonds) between countries that do not affect the transfer of control. Thus, a purchase of Heineken (Netherlands) stock by a U.S. investor would reflect portfolio investment because it represents a purchase of foreign financial assets, while control of Heineken's operations is unchanged. If all of Heineken's stock was purchased by a U.S. firm as the result of an acquisition, this transaction would result in a transfer of control and therefore would be classified as direct foreign investment instead of portfolio investment.

In addition to direct foreign investment and portfolio investment, other capital investment is another component of the capital account, which represents transactions involving short-term financial assets (such as money market securities) between countries. In general, direct foreign investment measures the expansion by firms in foreign

Exhibit 2.2
Key Components of U.S. Capital Account, 1997 (in billions of $)

Direct Foreign Investment in the U.S.	93
Direct Foreign Investment by the U.S.	122
Net U.S. Outflow Due to DFI	– 29
Portfolio Investment in the U.S.	598
Portfolio Investment by the U.S.	355
Net U.S. Inflow Due to Portfolio Investment	243

operations, while the portfolio investment and other capital measures the net flow of funds due to financial asset transactions between individual or institutional investors.

International Trade Flows

The volume of international trade (exports plus imports) relative to gross domestic product (GDP) is reported for some major countries in Exhibit 2.3. Note that the international trade volume as a percentage of GDP is generally much larger for Canada and European countries than it is for the United States or Japan. Yet, international trade has grown for most countries since the 1970s.

Distribution of U.S. Exports

The distribution of U.S. exports among countries during 1997 is illustrated in Exhibit 2.4. The amounts of U.S. exports are rounded to the nearest billion. For example, exports to Canada were valued at $150 billion.

Exhibit 2.3
International Trade as a Percentage of GDP for Major Countries

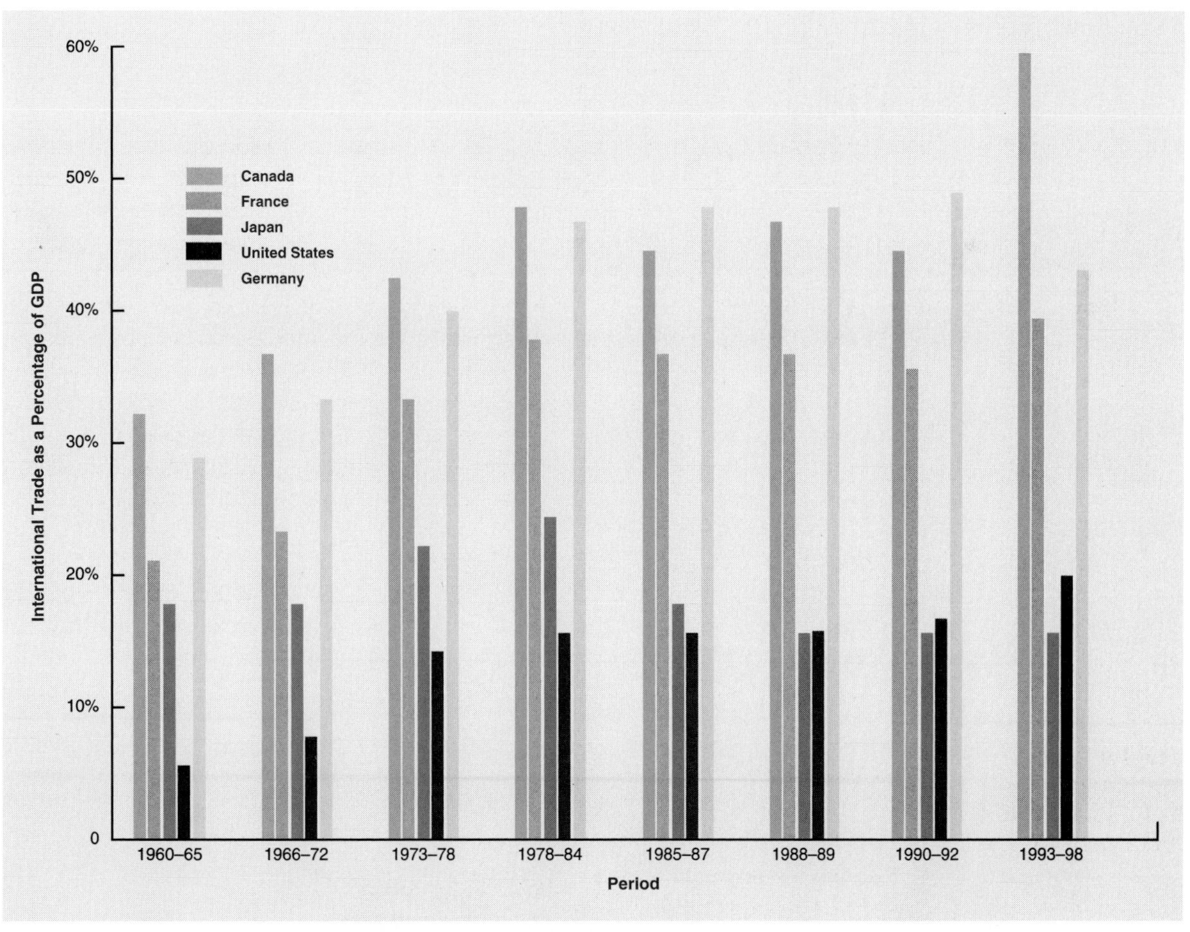

Source: *International Economic Conditions,* Federal Reserve Bank of St. Louis, June 1985, updated by author.

Exhibit 2.4
Distribution of Export Markets for U.S. Firms (in billions of $)

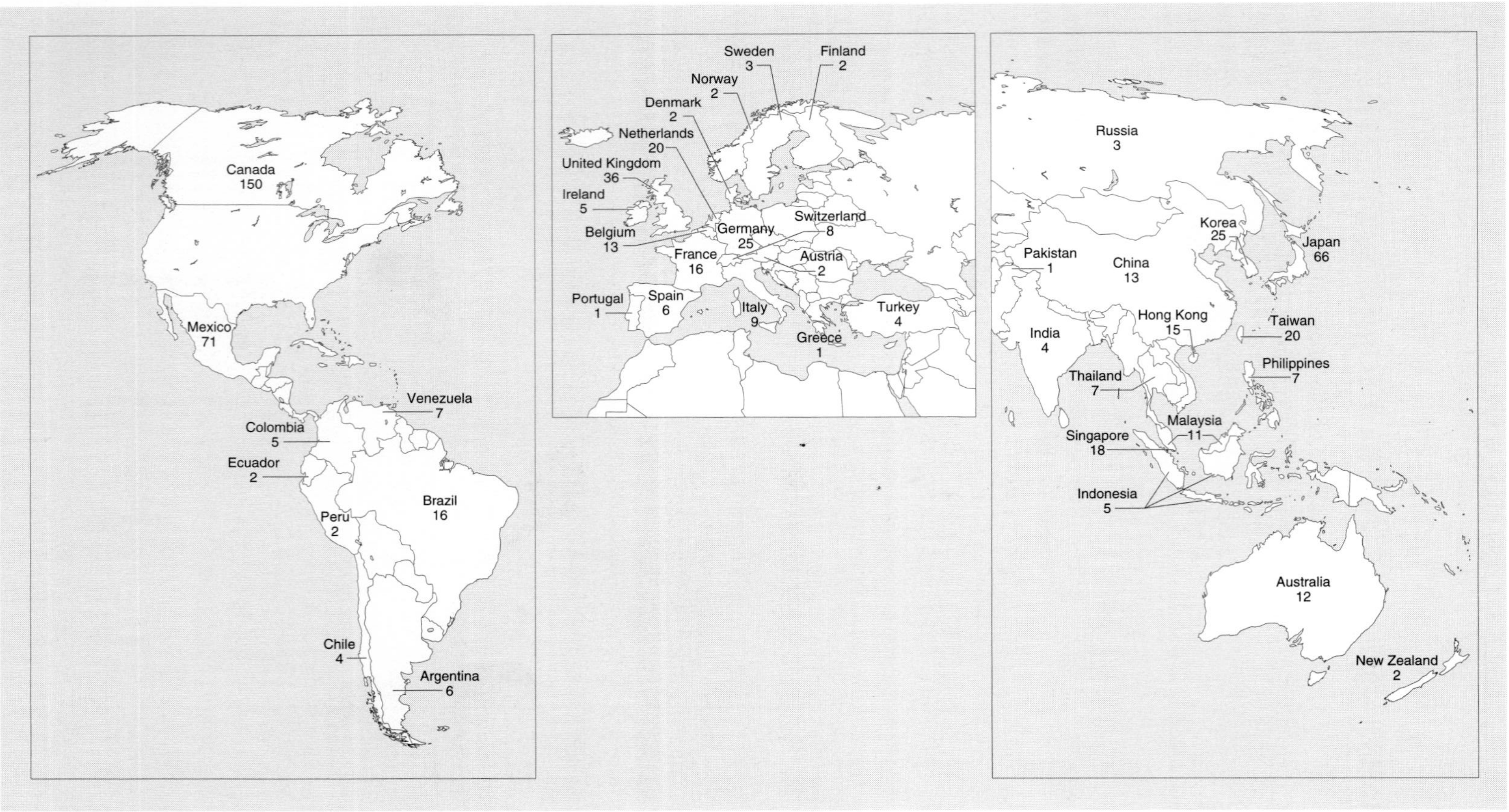

Source: U.S. Census Bureau, 1998.

Exhibit 2.5
Distribution of Annual Exports by the U.S. (in billions of $)

Source: *Survey of Current Business*, July 1998.

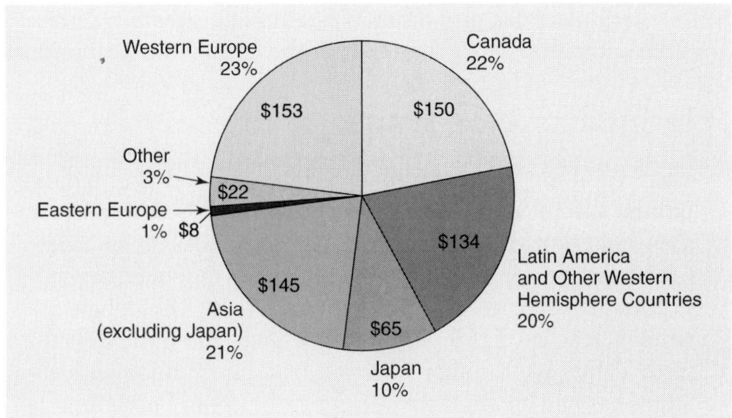

The distribution of U.S. exports by region is shown in Exhibit 2.5 to provide more insight on the relative importance of specific regions as a target for U.S. exports. Japan and the rest of Asia account for about 31 percent of all U.S. exports. Western Europe accounts for 23 percent of all U.S. exports, while Eastern Europe accounts for only one percent. Canada purchases more U.S. exports (22 percent of the total) than any other single country.

Distribution of U.S. Imports

The distribution of U.S. imports is shown in Exhibit 2.6. One-third of all U.S. imports comes from Canada and Japan. Another 20 percent comes from Western Europe, while 27 percent comes from Asian countries other than Japan. In particular, China has become a key source of U.S. imports, as the U.S. imports from China exceed that of any single European country.

Exhibit 2.6
Distribution of Annual Imports by the U.S. (in billions of $)

Source: *Survey of Current Business*, July 1998.

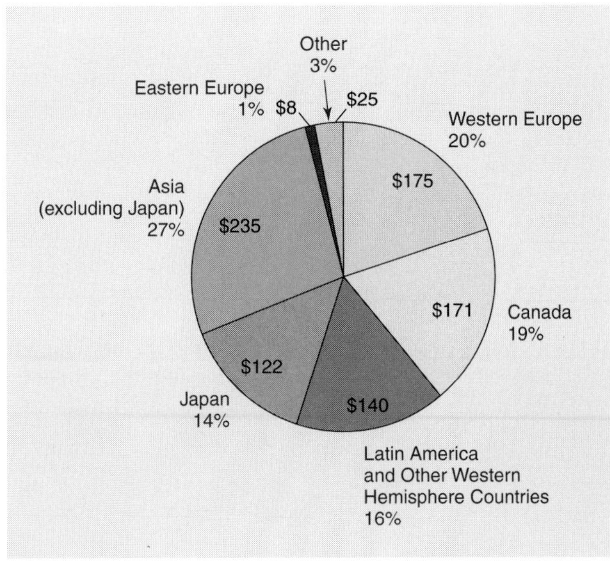

Latin America and other Western Hemisphere countries account for 16 percent of U.S. imports. More than half of the Latin American imports comes from Mexico.

U.S. Balance of Trade Trend

http://
The International Trade Administration's site at www.ita.doc.gov provides access to a variety of trade-related country and sector statistics.

The trends for U.S. exports, U.S. imports, and U.S. balance of trade are shown in Exhibit 2.7. Notice that the recent value of U.S. exports and U.S. imports is more than eight times the 1975 value. This illustrates the increase in international business over time. Since 1976, the value of U.S. imports has exceeded the value of U.S. exports, causing a balance of trade deficit. The deficit grew over time until 1986 when it reached $156 billion. Since then, the trade deficit has declined. The recent trade deficit is primarily due to a trade imbalance with two countries. The United States has had an annual trade deficit of about $60 billion with Japan and an annual trade deficit of about $34 billion with China. If the trade with these two countries

Exhibit 2.7
U.S. Balance of Trade Over Time

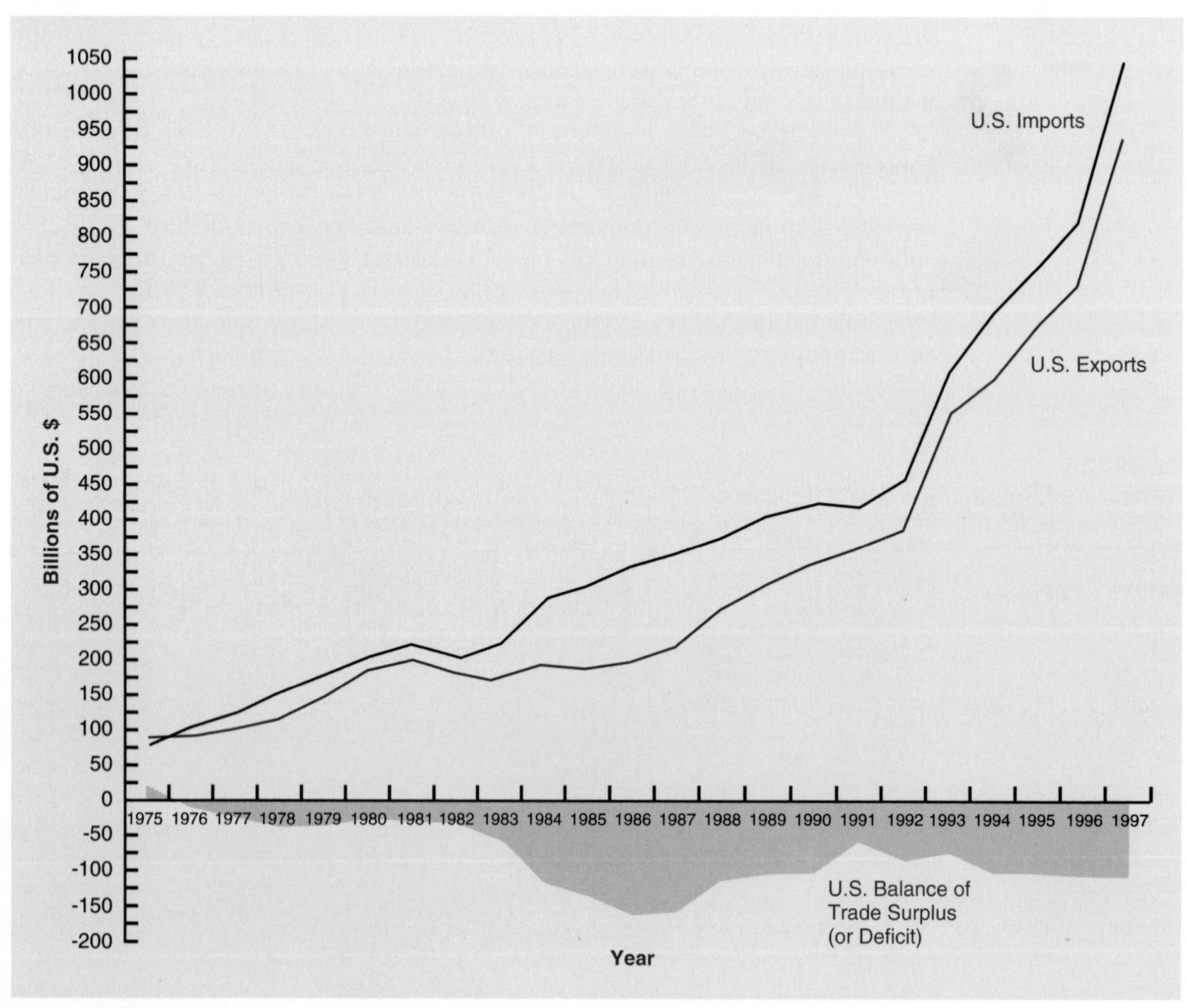

becomes more balanced over time, the overall trade deficit of the United States will likely be reduced.

Recent Changes in North American Trade

In January 1988, the United States and Canada agreed to a free trade pact, which was initiated in January 1989 and was completely phased in by 1998. As a result of this agreement, trade barriers on numerous products were reduced. The trade pact resulted in increased competition within various industries. Some firms that had focused exclusively on domestic business were encouraged to consider exporting or importing as the barriers were removed.

In 1993, the North American Free Trade Agreement (NAFTA) was passed, which removed numerous restrictions on trade between Canada, Mexico, and the United States. The agreement is an extension of the 1989 treaty that reduced trade barriers between the United States and Canada. The three countries involved in NAFTA have combined production similar to that of the European Community and a larger population (365 million versus 330 million in Europe). NAFTA also removed some restrictions on direct foreign investment in Mexico. Before the agreement, most of the direct foreign investment in Mexico was restricted to the so-called *maquiladoras* located near the U.S. border.

Opponents of NAFTA argue that the agreement will reduce the number of U.S. jobs as a result of lower labor costs in Mexico. However, proponents of NAFTA argue that there will be a redistribution of U.S. jobs, as low-skilled jobs are transferred to Mexico, some high-skilled jobs will be created as a result of increased trade to Mexico. They also suggest that a portion of the income earned in Mexico resulting from NAFTA will be spent on U.S. goods.

There is some concern that the United States will need a massive retraining program to allow for the redistribution of U.S. jobs. Any government-sponsored programs would further increase the U.S. budget deficit.

Opponents of NAFTA argue that environmental standards will not be enforced in Mexico, which would give Mexico an extra advantage beyond its labor cost advantage. However, a counterargument is that the free trade pact could enhance Mexico's economy and help finance the environmental expenses there.

Related concerns about NAFTA include differences in safety and health laws for workers and in child labor laws. These differences may give Mexico an extra cost advantage. Again, a counterargument is that Mexico may upgrade such laws if its economy is improved.

http://

Visit www.whitehouse.gov/fsbr/ for access to the economic statistics briefing room of the White House, which publishes the latest national economic and international trade statistics.

The effects of NAFTA will not be fully realized for many years. As with most guidelines that loosen trade barriers, those firms that were prevented by the barriers from pursuing international business may benefit. Conversely, those firms that were protected by the barriers may lose. The effects on many firms depend on how those firms respond to reduced trade barriers. Some firms that will face more competition must either become more efficient or consider diversifying into other industries in which they can compete more effectively.

Recent Changes in European Trade

Since the Single European Act was implemented to remove explicit and implicit barriers to trade, exports and imports between European countries have increased. Another recent event that will affect trade is the momentum for free enterprise in the former East Germany and other countries in Eastern Europe. Consumers in these countries now have more freedom to purchase imported goods, which should enhance net exports of other European countries in the near future. However, as time passes and private enterprise evolves in Eastern Europe, firms residing there may be able to develop some comparative advantages.

The single currency system in Europe also encouraged additional trade between European countries because it allowed for a single currency (the euro) to be used for trade among many European countries. This eliminated the need to convert currencies and the exchange rate risk associated with trade between the participating countries.

Trade Agreements Around the World

International trade has grown in response to trade agreements among countries. Some of the more well-known free trade areas are shown in Exhibit 2.8. Many trade agreements specify reductions in trade barriers, while others specify free trade between the countries in the group.

In December 1993, a **General Agreement on Tariffs and Trade (GATT)** accord between 117 countries called for lower tariffs around the world. The accord resulted from the so-called Uruguay Round of trade negotiations that had begun seven years earlier. The provisions of the accord reduced some tariffs by 30 percent on average and removed other tariffs over a five- to ten-year period. Existing tariffs were not reduced in some protected industries. In general, more progress was made on reducing tariffs in manufacturing industries than in service industries. Many of the large MNCs that had subsidiaries in numerous countries were affected less by the accord because they already had been producing their goods in the foreign markets they served and therefore had circumvented the tariffs. The accord was a major boost to exporting firms that had previously been subject to tariffs. Yet, because some of the tariffs will not be removed until after the year 2000, the complete effects of the accord will take time.

In fact, discussions have begun on a potential free-trade agreement between the United States and all Latin American countries, which would represent the largest free-trade zone in the world. Such an agreement is not likely to be completed for many years, but initial discussions at least show some willingness among countries to consider free trade throughout the Americas.

Friction Surrounding Trade Agreements. Trade agreements are sometimes broken when one country is harmed by another country's actions. One example is **dumping,** which reflects the exporting of products by one country to other countries at prices below cost. Some governments have been accused of creating local jobs by producing goods and dumping them. Another situation that can break a trade agreement is copyright piracy, in which a country allows local people to violate copyright protection on imported products. For example, the United States periodically criticizes the Chinese government for failing to prevent copyright piracy on U.S. movies, software, and CDs. In 1996, the United States threatened to break its trade agreements with China unless the Chinese government took actions to discourage copyright piracy by its residents. The Chinese government agreed to close factories that were illegally copying U.S. CDs and videos and to close more than 5,000 mini-theaters that showed pirated movies.

Exhibit 2.8
Trade Agreements Around the World

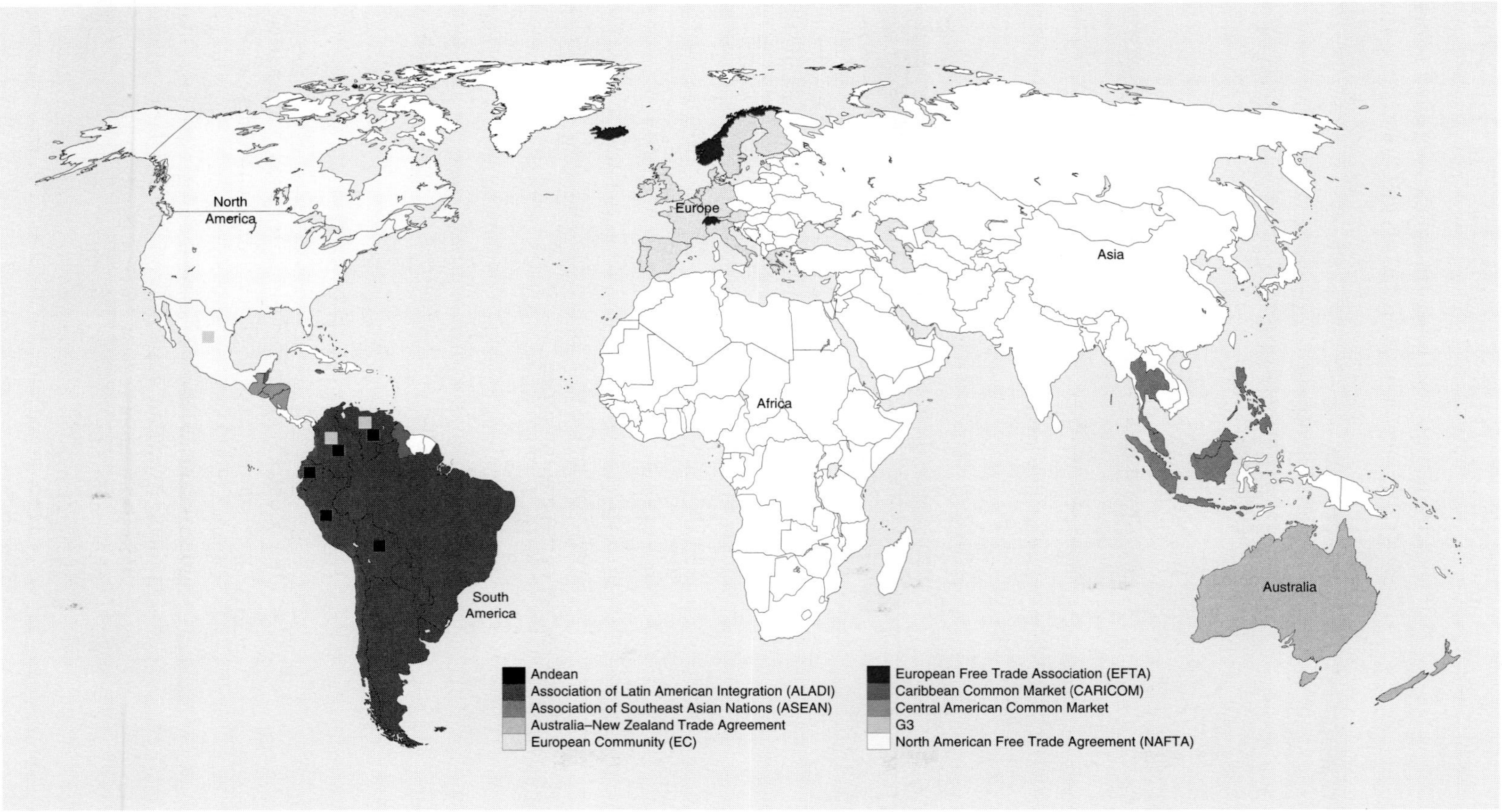

Factors Affecting International Trade Flows

Because international trade can significantly affect a country's economy, it is important to identify and monitor the factors that influence it. The most influential factors are

- inflation
- national income
- government restrictions
- exchange rates

http://

Visit www.census.gov for access to the latest economic, financial, socioeconomic, and political surveys and statistics.

Impact of Inflation

If a country's inflation rate increases relative to the countries with which it trades, its current account would be expected to decrease, other things being equal. Consumers and corporations within the country will most likely purchase more goods overseas (due to high local inflation), while the country's exports to other countries will decline.

Impact of National Income

If a country's income level (national income) increases by a higher percentage than those of other countries, its current account is expected to decrease, other things being equal. As the real income level (adjusted for inflation) rises, so does consumption of goods. A percentage of that increase in consumption will most likely reflect an increased demand for foreign goods. To illustrate the potential impact of national income on the current account balance, consider the frequent requests by the United States that other countries stimulate their respective economies, so that the foreign demand for U.S. goods increases. Yet, when countries are not willing to enact stimulative policies, the U.S. government must search for other solutions to reduce its large balance of trade deficit.

The removal of the Iron Curtain boosted Europe's economy in late 1989 and in 1990, which led to a higher demand for U.S. goods and improved the U.S. balance of trade with Europe.

During the 1997–1998 Asian crisis, the national income of Asian countries declined, causing a decline in the Asian demand for imported products manufactured by firms based in many countries. Thus, the amount of exports sold by the United States and some other countries to Asian countries was reduced as a result of the Asian crisis.

Impact of Government Restrictions

If a country's government imposes a tax on imported goods (often referred to as a tariff), the prices of foreign goods to consumers are effectively increased. Tariff rates imposed by the U.S. government are on average lower than those imposed by other governments. However, some industries are more highly protected by tariffs than others. American apparel products and farm products have historically received more protection against foreign competition as a result of high tariffs on related imports. An increase in the use of tariffs is expected to increase the U.S. current account balance, unless other governments retaliate.

There are significant differences in tariffs among countries. For example, the United States recently charged a tariff of 13.5 cents per case of foreign beer, while

Canada charged 24 cents per case, most European countries charged $2.93 per case, and China charged $14.64 per case.

In addition to tariffs, a government can reduce its country's imports by enforcing a **quota,** or a maximum limit that can be imported. Quotas have been commonly applied to a variety of goods imported by the United States and other countries.

Trade restrictions may save jobs, but only at a cost. A recent study by the Institute for International Economics estimated the cost per job saved to be $705,000 for the U.S. automobile industry and $1 million for the specialty steel industry. Furthermore, trade restrictions tend to benefit only some industries at the expense of others, as other countries retaliate by imposing their own trade restrictions. In this case, imports by both countries may be reduced so that the current account level might not be much different from where it was before the first round of trade restrictions.

http://

Dr. Ed Yardeni's Economics Network at www.yardeni.com reviews international and political economic events and their presumed global impact and presents economic and political analyses of major economies. A variety of national and international economic and financial market charts are also available.

As an example of trade restrictions, the U.S. government enforced quotas on U.S.-imported specialty steel in July 1983 at the request of the U.S. steel industry to help the industry compete against foreign producers. The quotas were imposed on steel imported from European countries. This action is not considered legal based on the General Agreement on Tariffs and Trade (GATT) provisions established in 1947. The GATT rules allow for trade restrictions only in retaliation against illegal trade actions of other countries, such as a government's subsidizing of exports. The U.S. government-enforced trade restrictions were deemed illegal because they were simply intended to give the U.S. steel industry a competitive edge in its home market. Consequently, the U.S. government was forced to accept restrictions of equal value on U.S. exports. A group of European countries announced shortly thereafter that they would retaliate by imposing tariffs and quotas on U.S. chemicals, plastics, and sporting goods exported to their countries. The U.S. government felt that such retaliatory actions were excessive and considered counter-retaliation on other goods imported by the United States from these European countries. In this example, the U.S. steel industry benefited from the U.S. government-enforced trade restrictions, but the chemicals, plastics, and sporting goods industries were adversely affected by the retaliatory actions of the European countries.

During the 1990s, U.S. steel companies continued their claim that steel exported to the United States was being subsidized by foreign governments, allowing foreign

Nike Problem

Response to Potential Trade Barriers

Given its large volume of international business, Nike closely monitors any existing or potential trade barriers. In 1997, the European Commission imposed anti-dumping taxes on some shoes imported from China and Indonesia. Nike produces some shoes in these countries that are then shipped to Europe for sale in European countries. Although the taxes were not focused on athletic shoes, Nike was prepared if its exports to Europe should be subject to such taxes. Specifically, Nike was ready to shift some production if its athletic shoes exported to Europe were subject to the anti-dumping taxes.

Discussion: Why would Nike produce shoes in Indonesia to be sold in Europe? If anti-dumping taxes are imposed, how could Nike shift its production so that it would not be subject to such taxes? Describe in general terms why it could be costly to shift production.

steel firms an unfair advantage. In 1993, the U.S. International Trade Commission, which is charged with the task of reviewing such claims, ruled that many of the claims were unfounded.

Impact of Exchange Rates

Each country's currency is valued in terms of other currencies through the use of exchange rates, so that currencies can be exchanged to facilitate international transactions. The values of most currencies can fluctuate over time because of market and government forces (as discussed in detail in Chapter 4). If a country's currency begins to rise in value against other currencies, its current account balance should decrease, other things being equal. Goods exported by the country will become more expensive to the importing countries if its currency strengthens. As a consequence, the demand for such goods will decrease. For example, a tennis racket selling in the United States for $100 would require a payment of C$125 by the Canadian importer if the Canadian dollar was valued at C$1 = $.80. Yet, it would require a payment of C$143 if C$1 = $.70, which might discourage the Canadian demand for U.S. tennis rackets. A strong local currency is expected to reduce the current account balance if the traded goods are **price-elastic** (sensitive to price changes).

Just as a strong dollar is expected to cause a lower (or more negative) U.S. balance of trade, a weak dollar is expected to cause a higher balance of trade. The dollar's weakness lowers the price paid for U.S. goods by foreign customers and can cause an increase in the demand for U.S. products. A weak dollar also tends to increase the dollar price paid for foreign goods and to reduce the U.S. demand for foreign goods.

During the 1997–1998 Asian crisis, the exchange rates of Asian currencies declined substantially, which caused the prices of Asian products to decline from the perspective of the United States and many other countries. Consequently, the demand for Asian products increased and sometimes replaced the demand for products of other countries. For example, the weakness of the Thailand baht during this period caused an increase in the global demand for types of fish from Thailand's fish products and a decline in the demand for these same types of products from the United States (Seattle).

Interaction of Factors

Since the factors that affect the balance of trade interact, their simultaneous influence on the balance of trade is complex. For example, as a high U.S. inflation rate reduces the current account, it places downward pressure on the value of the dollar (as discussed in detail in Chapter 4). Since a weaker dollar can improve the current account, it may partially offset the impact of inflation on the current account.

Correcting a Balance of Trade Deficit

By reconsidering some of the factors that affect the balance of trade, it is possible to develop some common methods for correcting a deficit. Any policy that will increase foreign demand for the country's goods and services will improve the balance of trade position. Foreign demand may increase if export prices become more attractive. This can occur when the country's inflation is low or when its currency's value is reduced, thereby making the prices cheaper from a foreign perspective.

A floating exchange rate could possibly correct any international trade imbalances in the following way. A deficit in a country's balance of trade suggests that the country is spending a greater amount of funds on foreign products than it is receiving from exports to foreign countries. Because it is selling its currency (to buy foreign goods) in greater volume than the foreign demand for its currency, the value of its currency should decrease. This decrease in value should encourage more foreign demand for its goods in the future.

While this theory seems rational, it does not always work in the manner stated. It is possible that, instead, a country's currency will remain stable or appreciate even when it has a balance of trade deficit. Other forces upon the currency's value can offset the forces created by the balance of trade deficit. For example, consider a situation where foreign investors are purchasing the currency to invest in the country's securities. This demand for the currency places upward pressure on its value, thereby offsetting the downward pressure caused by the trade imbalance. Consequently, a country cannot always rely on currency movements to correct a trade deficit.

Why a Weak Home Currency Is Not a Perfect Solution

Even if a country's home currency weakens, its balance of trade will not necessarily improve. One reason is the possibility of a revised pricing policy by foreign competition in response to exchange rate movements. When the dollar weakened in recent periods and U.S. prices became more attractive to non-U.S. customers, many non-U.S. companies lowered their prices to remain competitive with U.S. firms. Thus, the U.S. demand for foreign goods was not affected much, because foreign producers lowered prices to compensate U.S. importers for the weaker dollar.

A second reason why the dollar's general weakness does not always affect the current account is that currencies of some other countries may have also weakened, allowing their local firms the same competitive advantages of U.S. firms. For example, when the dollar weakens in Europe, the dollar's exchange rate with the currencies of Hong Kong, Singapore, South Korea, and Taiwan may remain somewhat stable. As some U.S. firms terminate their demand for supplies produced in European countries, they tend to increase their demand for goods produced in Asian countries. Consequently, the dollar's weakness in European countries causes a change in international trade behavior but does not eliminate the U.S. current account deficit.

A third reason why a weak dollar will not always reduce the U.S. trade deficit is that international trade transactions are prearranged and cannot be immediately adjusted. Thus, non-U.S. importing companies may be attracted to U.S. firms as a result of the weaker dollar but not immediately sever their relationships with suppliers from other countries. Over time, they may begin to take advantage of the weaker dollar by purchasing U.S. imports, if they believe that the weakness will continue. The lag time between the dollar's weakness and the non-U.S. firm's increased demand for U.S. products has sometimes been estimated to be 18 months or even longer.

There is also a lagged relationship between the value of the dollar and the amount of U.S. imports for the same reason. U.S. importers will not immediately switch to purchase U.S.-made goods when the dollar weakens. They may have established long-term relations with non-U.S. suppliers, or they may believe that there are no qualified substitutes for these goods in the United States. Given a stable amount of imports purchased and a weaker dollar, the dollar value of imports rises. There-

Exhibit 2.9
J-Curve Effect

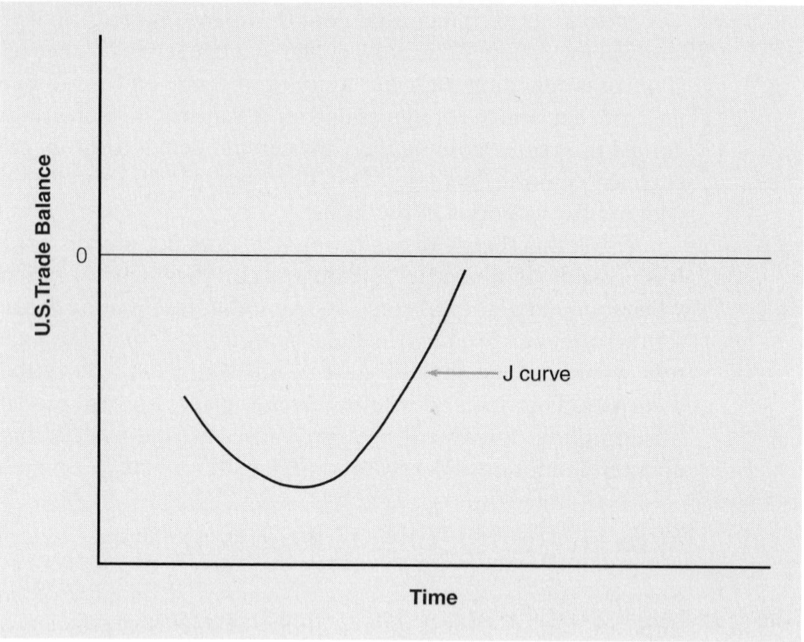

fore, the U.S. balance of trade may actually deteriorate in the short run as a result of dollar depreciation. It only improves once U.S. and non-U.S. importers respond to the change in purchasing power that is caused by the weaker dollar. This represents the so-called **J-curve effect,** as illustrated in Exhibit 2.9. The further decline in the trade balance before a reversal creates a trend that can look like the letter J.

A fourth reason why exchange rates will not always improve the U.S. balance of trade is that there are unique relationships between those importers and exporters that are under the same ownership. Many firms purchase products that are produced by their subsidiaries in what is referred to as **intracompany trade.** This type of trade makes up more than 50 percent of all international trade. The trade between the two parties will normally continue regardless of exchange rate movements because a decline in intracompany trade adversely affects the producer in the intracompany agreement. Thus, the impact of exchange rate movements on intracompany trade patterns is limited.

International Capital Flows

Capital flows usually represent direct foreign investment or portfolio investment. The direct foreign investment (DFI) positions by U.S. firms and by non-U.S. firms in the United States are illustrated in Exhibit 2.10. The DFI positions inside and outside the United States have risen substantially over time, which confirms increasing globalization. Both DFI positions leveled off during recessionary periods (such as in the early 1980s and in the early 1990s) but increased during periods of strong economic growth.

Exhibit 2.10
Comparative Direct Foreign Investment Positions

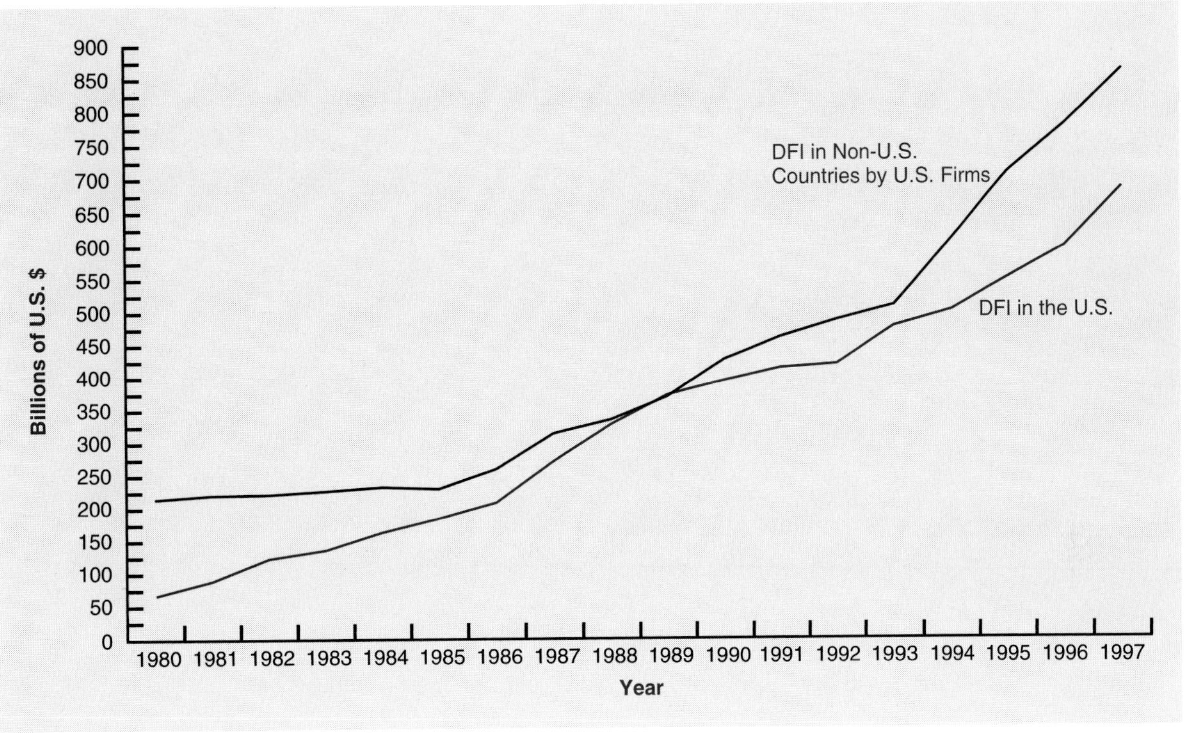

Source: *Survey of Current Business.*

Distribution of DFI by U.S. Firms

The distribution of DFI by U.S. firms is illustrated in Exhibit 2.11. The United Kingdom and Canada are the biggest targets. Latin American countries received a larger portion of DFI in aggregate than did Asian countries. The DFI by U.S. firms in Latin American and Asian countries has increased substantially as these countries have opened their markets to U.S. firms.

Distribution of DFI in the United States

Just as U.S. firms have used direct foreign investment to enter markets outside the United States, non-U.S. firms have penetrated the U.S. market. Much of the direct foreign investment in the United States comes from the United Kingdom, Japan, the Netherlands, Germany, and Canada. Seagram generates 81 percent of its business from the United States, Food Lion generates 65 percent of its revenue from the United States, and Honda generates 42 percent of its business from the United States. Many well-known firms that operate in the United States are owned by foreign companies, including Shell Oil (Netherlands), Burger King (United Kingdom), Pillsbury (United Kingdom), Citgo Petroleum (Venezuela), Canon (Japan), and Fireman's Fund (Germany). Many other firms operating in the United States are partially owned by foreign companies, including MCI Communications (United Kingdom), Universal Studios (Canada), and Northwest Airlines (Netherlands). While U.S.-based

Exhibit 2.11
Distribution of DFI by U.S. Firms (in billions of $)

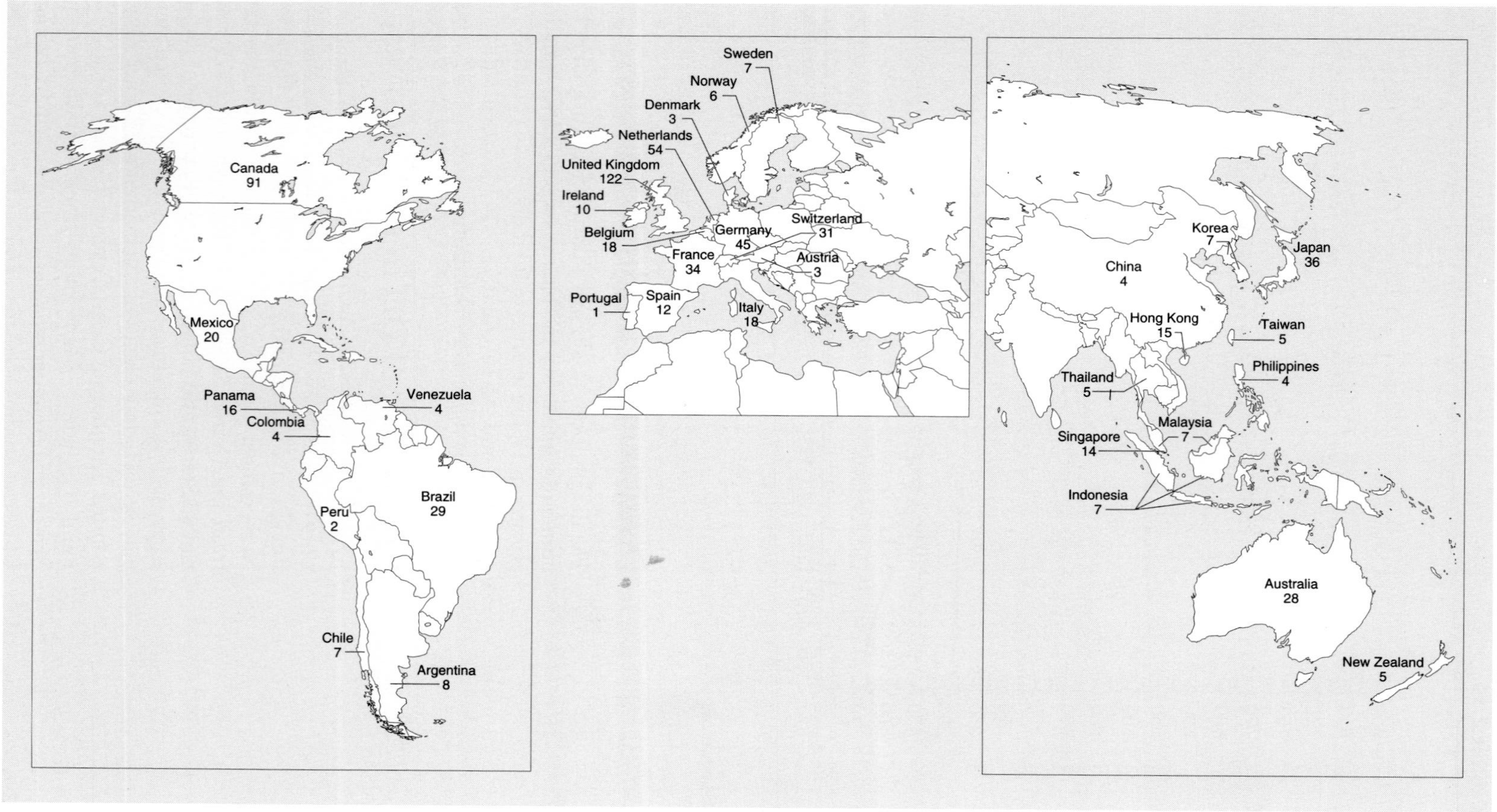

MNCs consider expanding in other countries, they must also compete with foreign firms in the United States.

Factors Affecting Direct Foreign Investment

Many U.S.-based MNCs have recently increased their direct foreign investment in foreign countries. Exhibit 2.12 identifies some U.S.-based MNCs that have substantial direct foreign investment. Notice that Exxon, IBM, and Hewlett-Packard have at least 50% of their assets in foreign countries.

Capital flows resulting from direct foreign investment change whenever conditions occur in a country that change the desire of firms to conduct business operations there. Some of the more common factors that could affect a country's appeal for direct foreign investment are identified here.

Changes in Restrictions. Restrictions have been reduced in many Eastern European countries during the mid–1990s and in Asian countries following the Asian crisis in the late 1990s. This allowed for more direct foreign investment in these countries than what would have occurred otherwise.

Globalization continues to increase in response to the reduction in tariffs and other barriers imposed by governments of countries. For example, PepsiCo Inc. (owner of KFC, Pizza Hut, and Taco Bell) has recently entered various markets in the Caribbean and Asia that were previously restricted, in pursuit of its goal to be in any country where people desire chicken, pizza, or tacos. Many U.S.-based MNCs, including Bausch & Lomb, Colgate-Palmolive, and General Electric, have been penetrating less developed countries such as Argentina, Chile, Mexico, India, China, and Hungary. New opportunities in these countries have arisen from the removal of government barriers.

Privatization. Direct foreign investment has also been stimulated by the movement toward free enterprise, whereby several national governments have sold some of their operations to corporations and other investors. This so-called **privatization** has

Exhibit 2.12
List of U.S.-Based MNCs with Substantial Direct Foreign Investment

	Foreign Revenue (measured in billions of $)	Total Revenue (in billions of $)	Foreign Revenue as % of Total Revenue	Foreign Profit as % of Total Profit	Foreign Assets as % of Total Assets
Exxon	$92	$120	76%	60%	57%
Ford Motor	47	145	32	24	30
IBM	46	79	58	61	50
General Electric	27	90	30	21	32
Hewlett-Packard	24	43	56	64	58
Procter & Gamble	17	36	49	36	39
Coca-Cola Company	12	19	66	75	36
Sara Lee	8	20	40	47	53
McDonald's	7	11	60	64	55
Gillette	6	10	60	49	61

Source: *Forbes*, July 27, 1998.

already taken place in some Latin American countries such as Brazil and Mexico, in Eastern European countries such as Poland and Hungary, and in such Caribbean territories as the Virgin Islands. Privatization allows for greater international business as foreign firms can acquire operations sold by national governments.

The reasons for promoting privatization have varied across countries. Privatization was used in Chile to prevent a few investors from controlling all the shares and in France to prevent the possible reversal to a more nationalized economy. In the United Kingdom, privatization was promoted to spread stock ownership across investors, which allowed more people to have a direct stake in the success of British industry.

http://
Visit www.heritage.org/index/execsum.html for executive summaries and charts of economic freedom rankings of countries around the world.

The primary reason that the market value of a firm may increase in response to privatization is the anticipated improvement in managerial efficiency. The goal of maximizing shareholder wealth is more focused than in management of a state-owned business, since the state must consider the economic and social ramifications of any business decision. Also, managers of a privately-owned enterprise are more motivated to ensure profitability because their careers may depend on it. For these reasons, privatized firms will search for local and global opportunities that could enhance their value. The trend toward privatization will undoubtedly create a more competitive global marketplace.

Potential Economic Growth. Countries that have more potential economic growth are more likely to attract direct foreign investment, since firms recognize that they may be able to capitalize on that growth by establishing more business there. During the Asian crisis, expected economic growth was reduced, which limited the desire of MNCs to expand there (even though they were subject to fewer restrictions when acquiring Asian companies).

Tax Rates. Countries that impose relatively low tax rates on corporate earnings are more likely to attract direct foreign investment. Firms estimate the after-tax cash flows that they would expect to earn when assessing the feasibility of direct foreign investment.

Exchange Rates. Firms would typically prefer direct foreign investment in countries where the local currency strengthens against their own. Under these conditions, they could invest funds to establish their operations in a country while that country's currency is relatively cheap (weak). Then, earnings resulting from the new operations in that country would periodically be converted back to the firm's currency at a more favorable exchange rate.

Factors Affecting International Portfolio Investment

The desire by individual or institutional investors to enact international portfolio investment in a specific country is influenced by the following factors.

Tax Rates on Interest or Dividends. Investors would normally prefer to invest in a country where the taxes on interest or dividend income from the investments are relatively low. Investors assess their potential after-tax earnings from investments in foreign securities.

Interest Rates. Portfolio investment can also be affected by interest rates. Money tends to flow to countries with high interest rates, as long as the local currencies are not expected to weaken.

Exchange Rates. If a country's home currency is expected to strengthen, foreign investors may be willing to invest in the country's securities to benefit from the currency movement. Conversely, if a country's home currency is expected to weaken, foreign investors may decide to purchase securities in other countries.

AGENCIES THAT FACILITATE INTERNATIONAL FLOWS

A variety of agencies have been established to facilitate international trade and financial transactions. These agencies often represent a collection of nations. A description of some of the more important agencies follows.

International Monetary Fund

http://
The home page of the IMF at www.imf.org makes the latest international economic news, data, and surveys available.

The United Nations Monetary and Financial Conference held in Bretton Woods, New Hampshire, in July 1944, was called to develop a structured international monetary system. As a result of this conference, the **International Monetary Fund (IMF)** was formed. The major objectives of the IMF set by the charter are to (1) promote cooperation among countries on international monetary issues, (2) promote stability in exchange rates, (3) provide temporary funds to member countries attempting to correct imbalances of international payments, (4) promote free mobility of capital funds across countries, and (5) promote free trade. It is clear from these objectives that the IMF goals encourage increased internationalization of business.

Before 1973, when exchange rates were maintained within tight boundaries, the IMF concentrated on removing currency exchange restrictions and ensuring currency convertibility, with the goal of encouraging international trade. The inception of floating exchange rates in 1973 and the onset of the 1974–75 recession caused concern by the IMF that countries would attempt to reduce their respective currency values as a means of stimulating exports and reducing imports. Thus, the IMF offered financing arrangements to countries experiencing large balance of trade deficits.

During the international debt crisis that erupted in August 1982, the IMF provided financing to many of the countries experiencing debt-repayment difficulties. It worked with each of these countries individually to develop and implement policies that would improve their balance of trade positions.

One of the key duties of the IMF is its **compensatory financing facility (CFF)**, which attempts to reduce the impact of export instability on country economies. While it is available to all IMF members, it is mainly used by developing countries. A country experiencing financial problems due to reduced export earnings must demonstrate that the reduction is temporary and beyond its control. In addition, it must be willing to work with the IMF in resolving the problem.

Each member country of the IMF is assigned a quota based on a variety of factors reflecting that country's economic status. Members are required by the IMF to pay this assigned quota. The amount of funds that each member can borrow from the IMF is dependent on its particular assigned quota.

The financing by the IMF is measured in **special drawing rights (SDRs)**. The SDR is not a currency but simply a unit of account. It is an international reserve asset created by the IMF and allocated to member countries to supplement currency reserves. The SDR's value fluctuates in accordance with the value of five major currencies: (1) U.S. dollar, (2) German mark, (3) French franc, (4) Japanese yen, and (5) British pound. This five-currency composite, designed January 1, 1981, replaced the prevailing 16-currency formula, which was more complex. Each of the five currencies represented by the revised formula was assigned weights (in accordance with their international importance) to determine the SDR value. The U.S. dollar received a 42-percent weight, the German mark received a 19-percent weight, and remaining currencies each received a 13-percent weight.

The IMF played a major role in attempting to reduce adverse effects of the Asian crisis. In 1997 and 1998, it provided funding to various Asian countries in exchange for promises made by the respective governments to take specific actions intended to improve economic conditions. Though the IMF had good intentions, the funding agreements were not always successful. For example, the IMF agreed to $43 billion funding for Indonesia. The negotiations of the agreement were tense, as the IMF demanded that President Suharto break up some of the monopolies run by Suharto's friends and family members and to close some weak banks. Yet, citizens of Indonesia interpreted the closure of weak banks as a banking crisis and began to withdraw their deposits from all banks. In January 1998, the IMF negotiated many types of economic reform, and Suharto agreed to them. However, the reforms may have been overly ambitious, and President Suharto did not accommodate the demands of the IMF to reform Indonesia's economy. The IMF agreed to renegotiate terms in March 1998 in a continuing effort to rescue Indonesia, but this effort signaled that a country did not have to meet the terms of the agreement to obtain funding. A new agreement was completed in April, and the IMF resumed its payments to support a bailout of Indonesia. In May 1998, Suharto abruptly discontinued subsidies for gasoline and food, which led to riots. Suharto blamed the riots on the IMF and on foreign investors who wanted to acquire assets in Indonesia at depressed prices.

World Bank

http://

See www.worldbank.org/, the Web site of the World Bank.

The **International Bank for Reconstruction and Development (IBRD)**, also referred to as the **World Bank,** was established in 1944. Its primary objective is to make loans to countries in order to enhance economic development. For example, the World Bank recently extended a loan to Mexico for about $4 billion over a ten-year period for environmental projects to facilitate industrial development near the U.S. border. Its main source of funds is the sale of bonds and other debt instruments to private investors and governments. The philosophy behind the World Bank's objective is profit-oriented. Therefore, loans are not subsidized but are extended at market rates to governments (and their agencies) that are likely to make repayment.

One of the World Bank's key facilities is the **Structural Adjustment Loan (SAL)** facility established in 1980. The SALs are intended to enhance a country's long-term economic growth. For example, SALs have been provided to Turkey and to some of the less developed countries (LDCs) that are attempting to improve their balance of trade.

Because the World Bank provides only a small portion of the financing needed by developing countries, it attempts to spread its funds by entering into **cofinancing agreements.** Cofinancing is performed in the following ways:

- *Official aid agencies.* Development agencies may join the World Bank in financing development projects in low-income countries.
- *Export credit agencies.* The World Bank cofinances some capital-intensive projects that are also financed through export credit agencies.
- *Commercial banks.* The World Bank has joined with commercial banks to provide financing for private sector development. In recent years, more than 350

banks from all over the world have participated in cofinancing, including BankAmerica, Bankers Trust, Chemical Bank, and Citibank.

The World Bank has recently established the **Multilateral Investment Guarantee Agency (MIGA)**, which offers various forms of political risk insurance. This is an additional means (along with its SALs) by which the World Bank can encourage the development of international trade and investment.

The World Bank is one of the largest borrowers in the world; its borrowings have amounted to the equivalent of $70 billion. Its loans are well diversified among numerous currencies and countries. It has received the highest credit rating (AAA) possible.

World Trade Organization

The **World Trade Organization** was created as a result of the Uruguay Round of trade negotiations that led to the GATT accord in 1993. This organization was established to provide a forum for multilateral trade negotiations and to settle trade disputes related to the GATT accord. It began its operations in 1995 with a membership of 81 countries, and more countries are expected to join. Member countries are given voting rights that are used to make judgments about trade disputes and other issues.

International Financial Corporation

In 1956 the **International Financial Corporation (IFC)** was established to promote private enterprise within countries. Like the IMF, it is composed of a collection of nations as members. While it aims to enhance economic development, it uses the private rather than the government sector to achieve its objectives. It not only provides loans to corporations but it also purchases stock, thereby becoming part owner in some cases rather than just a creditor. The IFC typically provides 10 to 15 percent of the necessary funds in the private enterprise projects in which it invests, and the remainder of the project must be financed through other sources. Thus, the IFC acts as a catalyst, as opposed to a sole supporter, for private enterprise development projects. It traditionally has obtained financing from the World Bank but can borrow within the international financial markets.

International Development Association

The **International Development Association (IDA)** was created in 1960 with country development objectives somewhat similar to those of the World Bank. Yet, its loan policy is more appropriate for less prosperous nations. The IDA extends loans at low interest rates to poor nations that cannot qualify for loans from the World Bank.

Bank for International Settlements

The **Bank for International Settlements (BIS)** attempts to facilitate cooperation among countries with regard to international transactions. It also provides assistance to countries experiencing a financial crisis. The BIS is sometimes referred to as the "central banks' central bank" or the "lender of last resort." It played an important role in supporting some of the less developed countries during the international debt crisis in the early and mid–1980s. It commonly provides financing for central banks in Latin American and Eastern European countries.

Regional Development Agencies

There are several other agencies with more regional (as opposed to global) objectives relating to economic development. These include, for example, the Inter-American Development Bank (focusing on the needs of Latin America), the Asian Development Bank (established to enhance social and economic development in Asia), and the African Development Fund (focusing on development in African countries).

In 1990, the European Bank for Reconstruction and Development was created to help the Eastern European countries adjust from communism to capitalism. Twelve Western European countries hold 51-percent interest, while Eastern European countries hold 13.5-percent interest. The United States is the biggest shareholder, holding 10-percent interest. There are 40 member countries in aggregate.

How International Trade Affects an MNC's Value

An MNC's value can be affected by international trade as shown in Exhibit 2.13. The cash flows (and therefore the value) of an MNC's subsidiaries that export to a specific country are typically expected to increase in response to a higher inflation rate (causing local substitutes to be more expensive) or a higher national income (which increases the level of spending) in that country. The expected cash flows of

Exhibit 2.13
Impact of International Trade on an MNC's Value

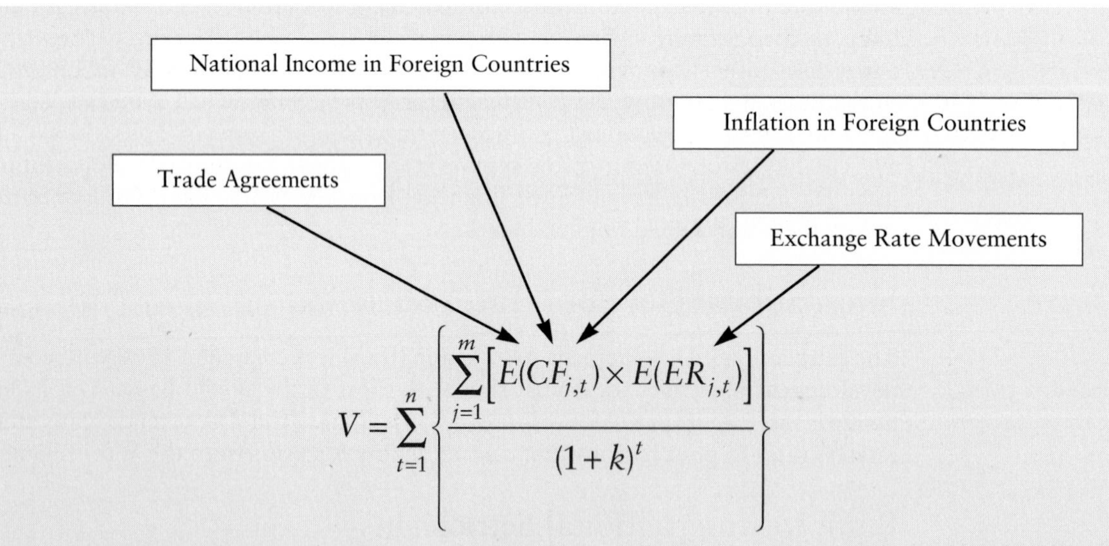

$$V = \sum_{t=1}^{n} \left\{ \frac{\sum_{j=1}^{m} \left[E(CF_{j,t}) \times E(ER_{j,t}) \right]}{(1+k)^t} \right\}$$

V = value of the U.S.-based MNC
$E(CF_{j,t})$ = expected cash flows denominated in currency j to be received by the U.S. parent in period t
$E(ER_{j,t})$ = expected exchange rate at which currency j can be converted to dollars at the end of period t
k = the weighted average cost of capital of the U.S. parent company
m = number of currencies
n = number of periods

the MNC's subsidiaries that export or import may increase as a result of country trade agreements that reduce tariffs or other trade barriers. The expected cash flows of some subsidiaries may be reduced if they now face increased competition from foreign exporters as a result of trade agreements.

Cash flows to U.S.-based MNCs that occur in the form of payments for exports manufactured in the United States are expected to increase as a result of a weaker dollar because the demand for its dollar-denominated exports should increase. However, cash flows of U.S.-based importers may be reduced by a weaker dollar because it will take more dollars (increased cash outflows) to purchase the imports. A stronger dollar will have the opposite effects on cash flows of U.S.-based MNCs involved in international trade.

SUMMARY

- The key components of the balance of payments are the current account and the capital account. The current account represents a broad measure of the country's international trade balance. The capital account is a measure of the country's long-term and short-term capital investments, including direct foreign investment and investment in securities (portfolio investment).
- A country's international trade flows are affected by inflation, national income, government restrictions, and exchange rates. High inflation, a high national income, low or no restrictions on imports, and a strong local currency tend to result in a strong demand for imports and a current account deficit. While some countries attempt to correct current account deficits by reducing the value of their currencies, this strategy is not always successful.
- A country's international capital flows are affected by any factors that influence direct foreign investment or portfolio investment. Direct foreign investment tends to occur in those countries that have no restrictions and much potential for economic growth. Portfolio investment tends to occur in those countries where there are no excessive taxes, where interest rates are high, and where the local currencies are not expected to weaken.

SELF-TEST FOR CHAPTER 2

(Answers are provided in Appendix A at the back of the text.)

1. Briefly explain how changes in various economic factors affect the U.S. current account balance.
2. Explain why U.S. tariffs will possibly change the composition of U.S. exports but will not necessarily reduce a U.S. balance of trade deficit.
3. Explain how the Asian crisis affected the trade between the U.S. and Asia.

QUESTIONS AND APPLICATIONS

1. What is the current account generally composed of?
2. What is the capital account generally composed of?
3. Discuss the trend in the U.S. balance of trade since 1980. How can you explain the trend?
4. How would a relatively high home inflation rate affect the home country's current account, other things being equal?

5. How would a weakening home currency affect the home country's current account, other things being equal?

6. How can government restrictions affect international payments among countries?

7. Is a negative current account harmful to a country? Discuss.

8. More than 500 U.S. firms have developed offices or factories in China. Many other U.S. firms have become exporters to China in recent years. However, the U.S. government has periodically threatened to restrict business between the United States and China until China improves its human rights record. The U.S. Chamber of Commerce has estimated that heavy restrictions of U.S.-China business could cause layoffs of 150,000 U.S. workers. Should the United States use trade restrictions as a means of encouraging improvements in human rights in some countries? If so, how will this affect U.S. firms that are considering business in less developed countries?

9. It is sometimes suggested that a floating exchange rate will adjust to reduce or eliminate any current account deficit. Explain why this adjustment would occur. Why does the exchange rate not always adjust to a current account deficit?

10. What are some of the major objectives of the IMF?

11. In some periods, the dollar substantially depreciated, but the U.S. demand for particular foreign imports was not significantly affected. Explain why.

12. If a U.S. importer is charged higher prices for its imported supplies, what will influence its decision to switch to a U.S. supplier?

13. In some periods, the dollar depreciated against most major currencies but not against the currencies of South Korea and Singapore. Explain why the balance of trade between the United States and these countries would shift in reaction to the dollar's depreciation against major currencies. Would the U.S. balance of trade deficit have been larger or smaller if the dollar depreciated against all currencies during this period? Explain.

14. Explain how a country may assess the historical impact of exchange rate movements on its imports. How can it use this information to forecast the expected impact of exchange rate movements on future imports?

15. When South Korea's export growth stalled, some South Korean firms suggested that South Korea's primary export problem was the weakness in the Japanese yen. How would you interpret this statement?

16. A relatively small U.S. balance of trade deficit is commonly attributed to a strong demand for U.S. exports. What do you think is the underlying reason for the strong demand for U.S. exports?

17. In recent years there has been considerable momentum to reduce or remove trade barriers in an effort to achieve "free trade." Yet, one disgruntled executive of an exporting firm stated, "Free trade is not conceivable; we are always at the mercy of the exchange rate. Any country can use this mechanism to impose implicit trade barriers." What does this statement mean?

18. The Single European Act was expected to promote more cross-border trade within Europe. Yet, there was some concern that firms exporting to Europe would lose business. Why?

19. € Explain how the existence of the euro could affect U.S. international trade.

20. Explain how German reunification has affected U.S. interest rates.

21. Describe the trends in the volume of U.S. direct foreign investment over time.

22. Describe privatization, and explain why it may allow for a greater degree of international business.

23. In recent years many U.S.-based MNCs have increased their investments in foreign securities, which are not as susceptible to negative shocks in the U.S. market. Also, when MNCs believe that the U.S. securities are overvalued, they can pursue non-U.S. securities that are driven by a different market. Moreover, in periods of low U.S. interest rates, U.S. corporations tend to seek investments in foreign securities. In general, the flow of funds into foreign countries

tends to decline when U.S. investors anticipate a strong dollar.

a. It was mentioned that expectations of a strong dollar can affect the tendency of U.S. investors to invest abroad. Explain this effect.
b. It was mentioned that low U.S. interest rates can affect the tendency of U.S.-based MNCs to invest abroad. Explain this effect.
c. In general terms, what is the attraction of the foreign investments to U.S. investors?

Internet Application

24. The Web site address of the Bureau of Economic Analysis is:

www.bea.doc.gov

a. Use this Web site to assess recent trends in exporting and importing by U.S. firms. How has the balance of trade changed over the last 12 months?
b. Offer possible reasons for this change in the balance of trade.

Running Your Own MNC

Assessing Country Factors That Will Affect the Demand for Your Product

25a. Identify the factors that can affect the balance of trade between the United States and the country that you targeted for your business. Explain how each of these factors may affect the demand for your product.

b. Which of these factors is likely to be most important in affecting the demand for your product?

Blades, Inc. Case

Exposure to International Flow of Funds

Ben Holt, chief financial officer (CFO) of Blades, Inc., has decided to counteract the decreasing demand for "Speedos" roller blades by exporting this product to Thailand. Furthermore, due to the low cost of rubber and plastic in Southeast Asia, Mr. Holt has decided to import some of the components needed to manufacture "Speedos" from Thailand. Ben Holt feels that importing rubber and plastic components from Thailand provides Blades with a cost advantage (the components imported from Thailand are about 20 percent cheaper than similar components in the United States). Currently, approximately $20 million, or 10 percent, of Blades' sales are contributed by its sales in Thailand. Conversely, only about 4 percent of Blades' cost of goods sold is attributable to rubber and plastic imported from Thailand.

The competition in Thailand from other U.S. roller blades manufacturers is sparse. Those competitors that export roller blades to Thailand invoice their exports in U.S. dollars. Currently, Blades follows a policy of invoicing in Thai baht (Thailand's currency). Ben Holt felt that this strategy would give Blades a competitive advantage, since Thai importers can plan more easily when they do not have to worry about paying differing amounts due to currency fluctuations. Furthermore, Blades' primary customer in Thailand (a retail store) has committed itself to the purchase of a certain amount of "Speedos" annually if the store were invoiced in baht for a period of three years. Blades' purchases of components from Thai exporters are currently invoiced in Thai baht.

Ben Holt is rather content with the current arrangements and sees the lack of competitors in Thailand and Blades' approach to pricing as ensuring Blades' position in the future Thai roller blade market. Specifically, Ben Holt feels that Thai importers will prefer Blades over its competitors because Blades invoices in Thai baht. Furthermore, Ben Holt thinks that the high quality of Blades' products will ensure the company's future success in the Thai market.

You, Blades' financial analyst, have your doubts as to Blades' "guaranteed" future success. Although you believe Blades' strategy regarding its Thai sales and imports is sound, you are also aware of the Asian crisis, which has weakened the Thai economy.

Specifically, you are concerned about current expectations of the future state of the Thai economy and how these developments might affect Blades. Current forecasts indicate a high level of anticipated inflation, a decreasing level of national income, and a continued depreciation of the Thai baht. In your opinion, all of these future developments could affect Blades financially given the current arrangement the company has both with its suppliers and the Thai importers. Both Thai consumers and firms might adjust their spending habits should certain developments occur.

In the past, it has seemed difficult to convince Ben Holt of potential problems that could arise in Thailand. Consequently, you have developed a list of questions for yourself, which you plan to present to the company's CFO after you have answered them. Your questions are listed here:

1. How could a higher level of inflation in Thailand affect Blades (assume U.S. inflation remains constant)?
2. How would Blades be affected relative to competition both from firms in Thailand and from U.S. firms conducting business in Thailand?
3. How could a decreasing level of national income in Thailand affect Blades?
4. How could a continued depreciation of the Thai baht affect Blades? How would it affect Blades relative to U.S. exporters invoicing their roller blades in U.S. dollars?
5. If Blades increases its business in Thailand and experiences serious financial problems, are there any international agencies that the company could approach for loans or other financial assistance?

Small Business Dilemma

Identifying Factors That Will Affect the Foreign Demand at the Sports Exports Company

Recall from Chapter 1 that Jim Logan planned to pursue his dream of establishing his own business (called the Sports Exports Company) of exporting footballs to one or more foreign markets. Jim has decided to initially pursue the market in the United Kingdom because there appears to be some interest by British citizens in football as a possible hobby, and no other firm has capitalized on this idea in the United Kingdom. (The sporting goods shops in the United Kingdom do not sell footballs but might be willing to sell them.) Jim has contacted one sporting goods distributor that has agreed to purchase footballs on a monthly basis and distribute (sell) them to sporting goods stores throughout the United Kingdom. The demand for footballs by the distributor is ultimately influenced by the demand for footballs by British citizens who shop in British sporting goods stores. The Sports Exports Company will receive British pounds when selling the product to the distributor and will then convert pounds into dollars. Jim recognizes that products (such as the footballs his firm will produce) exported from U.S. firms to foreign countries can be affected by various factors.

Identify the factors that affect the current account balance between the United States and the United Kingdom. Explain how each factor may possibly affect the British demand for the footballs that are produced by the Sports Exports Company.

3 INTERNATIONAL FINANCIAL MARKETS

Due to growth in international business over the last 30 years, various international financial markets have been developed. The specific objectives of this chapter are to describe the background and corporate use of the following international financial markets:

- foreign exchange market
- Eurocurrency market
- Eurocredit market
- Eurobond market
- international stock markets

MOTIVES FOR USING INTERNATIONAL FINANCIAL MARKETS

Several barriers prevent the markets for real or financial assets from becoming completely integrated, such as tax differentials, tariffs, quotas, labor immobility, cultural differences, financial reporting differences, and significant costs of communicating information across countries. Yet, the barriers can also create unique opportunities for specific geographic markets that will attract foreign creditors and investors. For example, barriers such as tariffs, quotas, and labor immobility can cause a given country's economic conditions to be distinctly different from others. Investors and creditors may want to do business in that country to capitalize on favorable conditions unique to that country. The existence of imperfect markets has precipitated the internationalization of financial markets.

Motives for Investing in Foreign Markets

Investors have one or more of the following motives for investing in foreign markets:

- *Economic conditions.* Firms in a particular foreign country may be expected to achieve more favorable performance than those in the investor's home country. For example, the loosening of restrictions in Eastern European countries created favorable economic conditions there. Such conditions attracted foreign investors and creditors.

- *Exchange rate expectations.* Some investors purchase financial securities denominated in a currency that is expected to appreciate against their own. From a foreign investor's perspective, the performance of such an investment is highly dependent on the currency movement over the investment horizon.
- *International diversification.* Investors may achieve benefits from internationally diversifying their asset portfolio. Empirical evidence indicates considerable risk reduction from international diversification. The risk-reduction benefits can be explained by cross-border differences in economic conditions, so that an investor's entire portfolio does not depend solely on a single country's economy. Furthermore, access to foreign markets allows investors to spread their funds across a more diverse group of industries that may not be available domestically. This is especially true for investors residing in countries whose firms are concentrated in a relatively small number of industries.

Motives for Providing Credit in Foreign Markets

Creditors (including individual investors who purchase debt securities) have one or more of the following motives for providing credit in foreign markets:

http://
Visit www.bloomberg.com for the latest information from financial markets around the world.

- *High foreign interest rates.* Some countries experience a shortage of loanable funds, which can cause market interest rates to be relatively high, even after considering default risk. Foreign creditors may attempt to capitalize on the higher rates, thereby providing capital to overseas markets. Yet, relatively high interest rates are often perceived to reflect relatively high inflationary expectations of that country. To the extent that inflation can cause depreciation of the local currency against others, high interest rates in the country may be somewhat offset by a weakening of the local currency over the time period of concern. However, the relation between a country's expected inflation and its local currency movements is not precise, since several other factors can influence currency movements as well. Thus, some creditors may believe that the interest rate advantage in a particular country will not be offset by a local currency depreciation over the period of concern.
- *Exchange rate expectations.* Creditors may consider supplying capital to countries whose currencies are expected to appreciate against their own. Whether the form of the transaction is a bond or a loan, the creditor benefits when the currency of denomination appreciates against the creditor's home currency.
- *International diversification.* Creditors can benefit from international diversification, which may reduce the probability of simultaneous bankruptcy across borrowers. The effectiveness of such a strategy depends on the correlation between the economic conditions of countries. If the countries of concern tend to experience somewhat similar business cycles, diversification across countries will be less effective.

Motives for Borrowing in Foreign Markets

Borrowers may have one or more of the following motives for borrowing in foreign markets:

- *Low interest rates.* Some countries have a large supply of funds available compared to the demand for funds, which can cause relatively low interest rates. Borrowers may attempt to borrow funds from creditors in these countries because the interest rate charged is lower. A country with relatively low interest rates is often expected to have a relatively low rate of inflation, which can place upward pressure on the foreign currency's value and offset any advantage of lower interest rates. However, since the relation between expected inflation differentials and currency movements is not precise, some borrowers will choose to borrow from a market in which nominal interest rates are low, since they do not expect an adverse currency movement to fully offset this advantage.

- *Exchange rate expectations.* Borrowers who expect a foreign currency to depreciate may consider borrowing that currency and converting it to their home currency for use. The value of the foreign currency when converted to their local currency would exceed the value when the borrowers repurchase the currency to repay the loan. This favorable currency effect can offset part or all of the interest owed on the funds borrowed.

FOREIGN EXCHANGE MARKET

The **foreign exchange market** allows currencies to be exchanged in order to facilitate international trade or financial transactions. The system for establishing exchange rates has changed over time. From 1876 to 1913, exchange rates were dictated by the **gold standard.** Each currency was convertible into gold at a specified rate. Thus, the exchange rate between two currencies was determined by their relative convertibility rates per ounce of gold. Each country used gold to back its currency.

In 1914, World War I began, and the gold standard was suspended. Some countries reverted to the gold standard in the 1920s but abandoned it as a result of a banking panic in the United States and Europe following the Great Depression. In the 1930s, some countries attempted to peg their currency to the dollar or the British pound, but there were frequent revisions. As a result of the instability in the foreign exchange market and the severe restrictions on international transactions during this period, the volume of international trade declined.

In 1944, an arrangement between countries (known as the **Bretton Woods Agreement**) called for fixed exchange rates between currencies. This arrangement lasted until 1971, as governments would intervene to prevent exchange rates from moving more than 1 percent above or below their initially established levels.

By 1971, the U.S. dollar appeared to be overvalued, since the foreign demand for U.S. dollars was substantially less than the supply of dollars for sale (to be exchanged for other currencies). Representatives from the major nations met to discuss how to deal with this dilemma. As a result of this conference, which became known as the **Smithsonian Agreement,** the U.S. dollar was devalued relative to the major currencies. The degree to which the dollar was devalued varied with each foreign currency. Not only was the dollar's value reset, but exchange rates were also allowed to fluctuate by 2 percent in either direction from the newly set rates. This was the first step in letting market forces (supply and demand) determine the appropriate price of a currency. Although boundaries still existed for exchange rates, they were widened, allowing for the currency values to move more freely toward their appropriate levels.

Even after the Smithsonian Agreement, governments were still having difficulty maintaining exchange rates within the stated boundaries. By March 1973, the more widely traded currencies were allowed to fluctuate in accordance with market forces, and the official boundaries were eliminated.

Foreign Exchange Transactions

The term "foreign exchange market" should not be thought of as a specific building or location where traders exchange currencies. Requests by companies to exchange one currency for another with commercial banks are normally made by telephone.

Spot Transactions. The most common type of foreign exchange transaction is for immediate exchange at the so-called **spot rate.** The market in which these transactions occur is known as the **spot market.** The average daily foreign exchange trading by banks around the world now exceeds $1.5 trillion. The average daily foreign exchange trading in the United States alone now exceeds $200 billion. While there are hundreds of banks in the world that can handle foreign exchange transactions, only 20 or so large banks accommodate 50 percent of the total volume of transactions. The U.S. dollar is not part of every transaction. Foreign currencies can be traded for each other. For example, a Japanese firm may need British pounds to pay for imports from the United Kingdom. Much of the foreign exchange trading is conducted by banks in London, New York, and Tokyo. Thus, these cities are perceived to represent the three largest foreign exchange trading centers.

At any given point in time, the spot exchange rate between two currencies should be similar across the various banks that provide foreign exchange services. If there is a large discrepancy, customers or other banks would purchase large amounts of a currency from whatever bank quoted a relatively low price and immediately sell it to whatever bank quoted a relatively high price. Such actions should cause adjustments in the exchange rate quotations that would eliminate any discrepancy.

If a bank begins to experience a shortage in a particular foreign currency, it can purchase that currency from other banks. This trading between banks occurs in what is often referred to as the **interbank market.** Within this market, banks can obtain quotes, or they can contact brokers who sometimes act as middlemen, matching one bank desiring to sell a given currency with another bank desiring to buy that currency. About ten foreign exchange brokerage firms handle much of the interbank transaction volume.

Although foreign exchange trading is conducted only during normal business hours in a given location, these hours vary among locations due to different time zones. Thus, at any given time on a weekday, there is a bank open and ready to accommodate foreign exchange requests.

When the foreign exchange market opens in the United States each morning, the opening exchange rate quotations will be based on the prevailing exchange rate quoted by banks in London and other locations where the foreign exchange markets have been open. For example, the quoted spot rate of the British pound could have been $1.80 at the previous close of the U.S. foreign exchange market, but by the time the market opens the following day, the opening spot rate may be $1.76. In this example, news occurring in the morning before the U.S. market opened could have caused changes in the supply and demand conditions for British pounds in the London foreign exchange market, which reduced the quoted price for the pound.

With the newest electronic devices, foreign currency trades are negotiated on computer terminals, and a push of a button confirms the trade. Traders now use electronic trading boards that allow them to instantly register transactions and check their banks' positions in various currencies. Also, several U.S. banks have developed night trading desks. The largest banks established these night trading desks to capitalize on foreign exchange movements at night and to accommodate corporate requests for currency trades. Even some medium-sized banks have begun to use night trading to accommodate corporate clients.

Many foreign transactions do not require an exchange of currencies but allow for a given currency to cross country borders. For example, the U.S. dollar is commonly accepted by merchants in many countries as a medium of exchange, especially in countries such as Bolivia, Brazil, China, Cuba, Indonesia, Russia, and Vietnam where the home currency is either weak or subject to foreign exchange restrictions. Many merchants accept U.S. dollars because they can use them to purchase goods from other countries. The U.S. dollar is the official currency of Liberia and Panama.

Forward Transactions. In addition to the spot market, there is a forward market for currencies that enables an MNC to lock in the exchange rate (called a **forward rate**) at which it will buy or sell a currency. A **forward contract** specifies the amount of a particular currency that will be purchased or sold by the MNC at a specified future point in time and at a specified exchange rate. Commercial banks accommodate the MNCs that desire forward contracts. MNCs commonly use the forward market to hedge future payments that they expect to make or receive in a foreign currency. In this way, they do not have to worry about fluctuations in the spot rate until the time of their future payments.

Attributes of Banks That Provide Foreign Exchange. The following characteristics of banks are important to customers in need of foreign exchange:

1. *Competitiveness of quote.* A savings of 1¢ per unit on the order of one million units of currency is worth $10,000.
2. *Special relationship with the bank.* The bank may offer cash management services or be willing to make a special effort to obtain even hard-to-find foreign currencies for the corporation.
3. *Speed of execution.* Banks may vary in the efficiency with which they handle a trade that has been ordered. A corporation needing the currency will prefer a bank that conducts the transaction promptly and properly handles any paperwork.
4. *Advice about current market conditions.* Some banks may provide assessments of foreign economies and relevant activities in the international financial environment that relate to corporate customers.
5. *Forecasting advice.* Some banks may provide forecasts of the future state of foreign economies, the future value of exchange rates, etc.

This list suggests that a corporation needing a foreign currency should not automatically choose a bank that will sell that currency at the lowest price. Most corporations that often need foreign currencies develop a close relationship with at least one major bank in case they ever need favors from a bank.

Bid/Ask Spread of Banks. Commercial banks provide foreign exchange transactions for a fee. At any given point in time, a bank's **bid** (buy) quote for a foreign currency will be less than its **ask** (sell) quote. The **bid/ask spread** is intended to cover the costs involved in accommodating requests to exchange currencies.

To understand how a bid/ask spread could affect you, assume you have $1,000 and plan to travel from the United States to the United Kingdom. Assume further that the bank's bid rate for the British pound is $1.52 and its ask rate is $1.60. Before leaving on your trip, you go to this bank to exchange dollars for pounds. Your $1,000 will be converted to 625 pounds (£), as follows:

$$\frac{\text{Amount in U.S. dollars to be converted}}{\text{Price charged by bank per pound}} = \frac{\$1{,}000}{\$1.60} = £625$$

Now suppose that because of an emergency you cannot take the trip, and you reconvert the £625 back to U.S. dollars, just after purchasing the pounds. If the exchange rate has not changed, you will receive

$$£625 \times (\text{Bank's bid rate of \$1.52 per pound}) = \$950.$$

Due to the bid/ask spread, you have $50 (5 percent) less than what you started with. Obviously, the dollar amount of the loss would be larger if you originally converted more than $1,000 into pounds.

The nominal bid/ask spread will look much smaller for currencies worth less than the British pound. For example, the Japanese yen is worth less than a penny. If the bank's bid price for yen is $.007, its ask price may be $.0074. In this case, the nominal bid/ask spread is $.0074 – $.007, or just four-hundredths of a penny. Yet, the bid/ask spread in percentage terms is actually slightly higher for the yen in this example than for the pound in the previous example. To prove this, consider a traveler who sells $1,000 for yen at the bank's ask price of $.0074. The traveler receives about ¥ 135,135 (computed as $1,000/$.0074). If the traveler decides to cancel the trip and converts the yen back to dollars, then, assuming no changes in the bid/ask quotations, the bank will sell these yen back at the bank's bid price of $.007 for a total of about $946 (computed by ¥ 135,135 × $.007), $54 (or 5.4 percent) less than what the traveler started with. This spread exceeds that of the British pound (5 percent in the previous example). A common way to compute the bid/ask spread in percentage terms follows:

$$\text{Bid/ask spread} = \frac{\text{Ask rate} - \text{Bid rate}}{\text{Ask rate}}$$

Using this formula, the bid/ask spreads are computed in Exhibit 3.1 for both the British pound and the Japanese yen.

Notice that these numbers coincide with those derived earlier. Such spreads are common for so-called "retail" transactions serving consumers. For larger so-called "wholesale" transactions between banks or for large corporations, the spread will be much smaller. The spread is normally greater for those currencies that are less frequently traded.

The bid/ask spread as defined here represents the discount in the bid rate as a percentage of the ask rate. An alternative bid/ask spread uses the bid rate as the denominator instead of the ask rate and measures the percentage markup of the ask rate above the bid rate. The spread would be slightly higher when using this formula because the bid rate used in the denominator is always less than the ask rate. The bid/ask spread is larger for currencies that are used less frequently. Commercial

Exhibit 3.1
Computation of the Bid/Ask Spread

Currency	Bid Rate	Ask Rate	$\frac{\text{Ask Rate} - \text{Bid Rate}}{\text{Ask Rate}}$	=	Bid/Ask Percentage Spread
British pound	\$1.52	\$1.60	$\frac{\$1.60 - \$1.52}{\$1.60}$	=	.05 *or* 5%
Japanese yen	\$ .0070	\$ .0074	$\frac{\$.0074 - \$.007}{\$.0074}$	=	.054 *or* 5.4%

banks are normally exposed to more exchange rate risk when maintaining these currencies.

In the following discussion and in examples throughout much of the text, the bid/ask spread will be ignored. That is, only one price will be shown for a given currency. This allows one to concentrate on understanding other relevant concepts. These examples depart slightly from reality because the bid and ask prices are, in a sense, assumed to be equal. While the ask price will always exceed the bid price by a small amount in reality, the implications from examples should nevertheless hold, even though the bid/ask spreads are not accounted for. In particular examples where the bid/ask spread can contribute significantly to the concept, it will be accounted for.

Interpreting Foreign Exchange Quotations

Exchange rate quotations for widely traded currencies are provided in *The Wall Street Journal* and in business sections of many newspapers on a daily basis. Each country has its own currency, although there are some exceptions. In 1999, several European countries (including Germany, France, and Italy) adopted the "euro" as their new currency for commercial transactions, replacing their own currencies. Their own currencies are available for tourists and some retail transactions, but these currencies will be phased out by the year 2002.

Quotations of Forward Rates. Some quotations of exchange rates include forward rates for the most widely traded currencies. Other forward rates are not quoted in business newspapers but are quoted by the banks that offer forward contracts in various currencies.

Direct Versus Indirect Quotations. The quotations of exchange rates for currencies normally reflect the ask prices for large transactions. Since exchange rates change throughout the day, the exchange rates quoted in a newspaper reflect only one specific point in time during the day. Quotations that represent the value of a foreign currency in dollars (number of dollars per currency) are referred to as **direct quotations.** Conversely, quotations that represent the number of units of a foreign currency per dollar are referred to as **indirect quotations.** The indirect quotation is the reciprocal of the corresponding direct quotation.

The discussion of exchange rate movements can be confusing because some comments refer to direct quotations while other comments refer to indirect quotations. For consistency, direct quotations are used throughout this text unless an example can be clarified by the use of indirect quotations. The direct quotations are easier to link with comments about any foreign currency.

IN PRACTICE

Foreign Exchange Rate Quotations

Foreign exchange quotations are provided for currencies each day in *The Wall Street Journal*, as shown here. The euro is shown at the bottom of the right-hand column. The European currencies that are being phased out are still shown in this table, as those currencies are still used for retail transactions.

CURRENCY TRADING

Thursday, March 18, 1999

EXCHANGE RATES

The New York foreign exchange mid-range rates below apply to trading among banks in amounts of $1 million and more, as quoted at 4 p.m. Eastern time by Telerate and other sources. Retail transactions provide fewer units of foreign currency per dollar. Rates for the 11 Euro currency countries are derived from the latest dollar-euro rate using the exchange ratios set 1/1/99.

	U.S. $ equiv.		Currency per U.S. $	
Country	**Thu**	**Wed**	**Thu**	**Wed**
Argentina (Peso)	1.0001	1.0005	.9999	.9995
Australia (Dollar)	.6285	.6274	1.5911	1.5939
Austria (Schilling)	.07973	.07990	12.542	12.515
Bahrain (Dinar)	2.6525	2.6525	.3770	.3770
Belgium (Franc)	.02720	.02726	36.770	36.689
Brazil (Real)	.5405	.5333	1.8500	1.8750
Britain (Pound)	1.6296	1.6300	.6136	.6135
1-month forward	1.6290	1.6293	.6139	.6138
3-months forward	1.6285	1.6285	.6141	.6141
6-months forward	1.6287	1.6284	.6140	.6141
Canada (Dollar)	.6584	.6574	1.5189	1.5212
1-month forward	.6583	.6573	1.5191	1.5214
3-months forward	.6583	.6573	1.5191	1.5214
6-months forward	.6583	.6573	1.5191	1.5214
Chile (Peso)	.002044	.002042	489.35	489.75
China (Renminbi)	.1208	.1208	8.2788	8.2787
Colombia (Peso)	.0006431	.0006403	1554.85	1561.74
Czech. Rep. (Koruna)				
Commercial rate	.02909	.02892	34.379	34.577
Denmark (Krone)	.1476	.1480	6.7735	6.7585
Ecuador (Sucre)				
Floating rate	.00009615	.0001042	10400.00	9600.00
Finland (Markka)	.1845	.1849	5.4195	5.4077
France (Franc)	.1673	.1676	5.9790	5.9660
1-month forward	.1675	.1679	5.9702	5.9566
3-months forward	.1680	.1684	5.9521	5.9367
6-months forward	.1690	.1693	5.9177	5.9055
Germany (Mark)	.5609	.5622	1.7827	1.7788
1-month forward	.5618	.5631	1.7801	1.7760
3-months forward	.5634	.5649	1.7748	1.7701
6-months forward	.5659	.5679	1.7672	1.7608
Greece (Drachma)	.003413	.003425	293.02	292.00
Hong Kong (Dollar)	.1290	.1290	7.7495	7.7490
Hungary (Forint)	.004329	.004333	230.98	230.81
India (Rupee)	.02359	.02359	42.385	42.395
Indonesia (Rupiah)	.0001108	.0001119	9025.00	8938.00
Ireland (Punt)	1.3930	1.3922	.7179	.7183
Israel (Shekel)	.2485	.2491	4.0240	4.0140
Italy (Lira)	.0005666	.0005678	1764.90	1761.05
Japan (Yen)	.008506	.008464	117.56	118.15
1-month forward	.008541	.008498	117.08	117.67
3-months forward	.008611	.008570	116.13	116.68
6-months forward	.008720	.008677	114.68	115.25
Jordan (Dinar)	1.4104	1.4104	.7090	.7090
Kuwait (Dinar)	3.2873	3.2862	.3042	.3043
Lebanon (Pound)	.0006631	.0006631	1508.00	1508.00
Malaysia (Ringgit-b)	.2632	.2632	3.8000	3.8000
Malta (Lira)	2.5530	2.5556	.3917	.3913
Mexico (Peso)				
Floating rate	.1036	.1035	9.6550	9.6610
Netherland (Guilder)	.4978	.4989	2.0087	2.0043
New Zealand (Dollar)	.5309	.5272	1.8836	1.8968
Norway (Krone)	.1296	.1291	7.7188	7.7488
Pakistan (Rupee)	.02006	.01981	49.850	50.485
Peru (new Sol)	.2988	.2973	3.3470	3.3640
Philippines (Peso)	.02573	.02571	38.865	38.890
Poland (Zloty)	.2570	.2554	3.8905	3.9150
Portugal (Escudo)	.005472	.005484	182.74	182.34
Russia (Ruble) (a)	.04228	.04272	23.650	23.410
Saudi Arabia (Riyal)	.2666	.2666	3.7504	3.7504
Singapore (Dollar)	.5795	.5805	1.7255	1.7228
Slovak Rep. (Koruna)	.02456	.02470	40.713	40.492
South Africa (Rand)	.1600	.1606	6.2490	6.2278
South Korea (Won)	.0008160	.0008147	1225.50	1227.40
Spain (Peseta)	.006594	.006608	151.66	151.33
Sweden (Krona)	.1232	.1224	8.1137	8.1713
Switzerland (Franc)	.6860	.6890	1.4577	1.4514
1-month forward	.6882	.6912	1.4531	1.4468
3-months forward	.6924	.6956	1.4443	1.4376
6-months forward	.6989	.7016	1.4308	1.4253
Taiwan (Dollar)	.03021	.03020	33.107	33.115
Thailand (Baht)	.02671	.02681	37.435	37.300
Turkey (Lira)	.00000277	.00000276	361521.50	361849.50
United Arab (Dirham)	.2723	.2723	3.6725	3.6725
Uruguay (New Peso)				
Financial	.08971	.09007	11.147	11.103
Venezuela (Bolivar)	.001724	.001726	580.20	579.50
SDR	1.3703	1.3673	.7298	.7314
Euro	1.0971	1.0995	.9115	.9095

Special Drawing Rights (SDR) are based on exchange rates for the U.S., German, British, French , and Japanese currencies. Source: International Monetary Fund.

a-Russian Central Bank rate. Trading band lowered on 8/17/98. b-Government rate.

The Wall Street Journal daily foreign exchange data from 1996 forward may be purchased through the Readers' Reference Service (413) 592-3600.

The term **SDR** is sometimes included within a table of exchange rate quotations; it represents **special drawing rights,** which are international reserve assets that were initially allocated by the International Monetary Fund to specific countries and are exchanged between governments to cover debt obligations. The SDR's value is based on a weighted index of five currencies: U.S. dollar, British pound, French franc, German mark, and Japanese yen. It has been used as a unit of account to denominate the value of international bonds, international airline fares, and other international transactions. Its use as a unit of account has caused various firms to monitor its value over time relative to their home currencies.

Cross Exchange Rates. Most exchange rate quotation tables express currencies relative to the dollar. Yet, there are some instances where one is concerned about the exchange rate between two nondollar currencies. For example, if a Canadian firm needs Mexican pesos to buy Mexican goods, it is concerned about the Mexican peso value relative to the Canadian dollar. The type of rate desired here is known as a **cross exchange rate,** since it reflects the amount of one foreign currency per unit of another foreign currency. Cross exchange rates can be easily determined with the use of foreign exchange quotations. The general formula follows.

$$\text{Value of 1 unit of Currency A in units of Currency B} = \frac{\text{Value of Currency A in \$}}{\text{Value of Currency B in \$}}$$

For example, if the peso is worth \$.07, and the Canadian dollar is worth \$.70, the value of the peso in Canadian dollars (C\$) is calculated as follows:

$$\text{Value of peso in C\$} = \frac{\text{Value of peso in \$}}{\text{Value of C\$ in \$}} = \$.07 / \$.70 = \text{C\$}.10$$

Thus, a Mexican peso is worth C\$.10. An alternative way of expressing the exchange rate is as the number of pesos equal to one Canadian dollar. This figure can be computed by taking the reciprocal: .70/.07=10.0, which suggests that a Canadian dollar is worth about 10.0 pesos according to the information provided.

Currency Futures and Options Markets

Some MNCs involved in international trade use the currency futures and options markets to hedge their positions. A **currency futures contract** specifies a standard volume of a particular currency to be exchanged on a specific settlement date. An MNC that desires to hedge payables would buy futures contracts to lock in the price paid for a foreign currency at a future point in time. Conversely, an MNC that desires to hedge receivables would sell futures contracts to lock in the price received in exchange for a foreign currency at a future point in time. Futures contracts are somewhat similar to forward contracts except that they are sold on an exchange while forward contracts are offered by commercial banks. Additional details on futures contracts, including other differences from forward contracts, are provided in Chapter 5.

Currency options contracts can be classified as calls or puts. A **currency call option** provides the right to buy a specific currency at a specific price (called the **strike price** or **exercise price**) within a specific period of time. It is used to hedge future payables. A **currency put option** provides the right to sell a specific currency

IN PRACTICE

Cross Exchange Rate Quotations

Cross exchange rate quotations are summarized for major currencies each day in *The Wall Street Journal,* as shown here. Each country is listed in the left column, with various currencies listed in the columns. For example, the top row represents quotations of exchange rates from Canada's perspective. Each number in the top row represents the number of Canadian dollars per currency listed at the top of the column. The second row represents quotations of exchange rates from France's perspective. Each number in that row represents the number of French francs per currency listed at the top of the column. The euro is shown in this table along with some of the European currencies that are being phased out.

Key Currency Cross Rates Late New York Trading Mar. 22, 1999

	Dollar	Euro	Pound	SFranc	Guilder	Peso	Yen	Lira	D-Mark	FFranc	CdnDlr
Canada	1.5030	1.6393	2.4466	1.0272	.74388	.15487	.01272	.00085	.83817	.24991	....
France	6.0141	6.5596	9.7898	4.1102	2.9765	.61969	.05090	.00339	3.3538	....	4.0014
Germany	1.7932	1.9558	2.9190	1.2255	.88750	.18477	.01518	.00101	....	.29817	1.1931
Italy	1775.3	1936.3	2889.8	1213.3	878.62	182.92	15.025	....	989.99	295.18	1181.1
Japan	118.15	128.87	192.32	80.748	58.476	12.174	....	.06655	65.888	19.645	78.609
Mexico	9.7050	10.585	15.798	6.6327	4.8033	....	.08214	.00547	5.4121	1.6137	6.4571
Netherlands	2.0205	2.2038	3.2890	1.3809	....	.20819	.01710	.00114	1.1268	.33596	1.3443
Switzerland	1.4632	1.5959	2.3818	....	.72418	.15077	.01238	.00082	.81597	.24329	.97352
U.K.	.61433	.67005	....	.41985	.30405	.06330	.00520	.00035	.34259	.10215	.40873
Euro	.91684	....	1.4924	.62660	.45377	.09447	.00776	.00052	.51129	.15245	.61001
U.S.	....	1.0907	1.6278	.68343	.49493	.10304	.00846	.00056	.55766	.16628	.66534

Source: Telerate

at a specific price within a specific period of time. It is used to hedge future receivables.

Currency call and put options can be purchased on an exchange. They offer more flexibility than the forward or futures contracts because they do not require any obligation. That is, the firm can elect not to exercise the option.

Currency options have become a popular means of hedging. The Coca-Cola Company has replaced about 30 to 40 percent of its forward contracting with currency options. FMC, a U.S. manufacturer of chemicals and machinery, now emphasizes currency options in place of forward contracts to hedge its foreign sales. A recent study by the Whitney Group found that 85 percent of U.S.-based MNCs use currency options. Additional details about currency options, including other differences from futures and forward contracts, are provided in Chapter 5.

EUROCURRENCY MARKET

Within each given country, financial markets exist in order to most efficiently transfer funds from surplus units (savers) to deficit units (borrowers). These markets are overseen by various regulators that attempt to enhance their safety and efficiency. The primary reason for the existence of financial institutions that serve these financial markets is to provide information and expertise. The surplus units do not typically know who needs to borrow funds at any particular point in time. Furthermore, they often cannot adequately evaluate the credit risk of any potential borrowers, nor establish the documentation necessary when providing loans. Financial institutions specialize in collecting funds from surplus units and then repackaging and transferring the funds to deficit units.

Development of the Eurocurrency Market

Like domestic firms, MNCs sometimes obtain funding through short-term loans from local financial institutions or through issuing short-term securities such as commercial paper. However, they can also obtain funds from the financial institutions in foreign markets. The role of international financial intermediation emerged in the 1960s and 1970s as MNCs expanded their operations. During this period, the Eurodollar market, or what is now referred to as the **Eurocurrency market,** grew to accommodate the increasing international business. The Eurodollar market was created as corporations in the United States deposited U.S. dollars in European banks. These European banks were willing to accept dollar deposits, since they could then lend dollars to corporate customers based in Europe.

Because the U.S. dollar is widely used even by foreign countries as a medium for international trade, there is a consistent need for dollars in Europe. U.S.-dollar deposits placed in banks located in Europe and other continents became known as **Eurodollars.**

The growth of the Eurodollar market was partially due to U.S. regulations in 1968, which limited foreign lending by U.S. banks. Foreign subsidiaries of U.S.-based MNCs could obtain U.S. dollars from banks in Europe. In addition, ceilings were placed on the interest rates of dollar deposits in the United States. This motivated the transfer of dollars to the Eurodollar market where such regulations were nonexistent. Furthermore, reserve requirements were nonexistent for Eurodollar deposits. Thus, banks could reduce the spread between what they paid on such deposits and charged on loans and still make a reasonable profit. This added to the popularity of the Eurodollar market, since banks could offer attractive deposit rates to corporations and governments with excess cash and attractive loan rates to corporations and governments with deficient funds.

Composition of the Eurocurrency Market

The Eurocurrency market is composed of several large banks (referred to as **Eurobanks**) that accept deposits and provide loans in various currencies. Countries within the Organization of Petroleum Exporting Countries (OPEC) also use the Eurocurrency market to deposit a portion of their petroleum revenues. The deposits usually have been denominated in U.S. dollars, since OPEC generally requires payment for oil in dollars. Those dollar deposits by OPEC countries are sometimes referred to as **petrodollars.** The Eurocurrency market has historically recycled the oil revenues from the oil-exporting countries to other countries. That is, oil revenues deposited in the Eurobanks are sometimes lent to those oil-importing countries that are short of cash. As these countries purchase more oil, funds are again transferred to oil-exporting countries, which in turn results in new deposits. This recycling process has been an important source of funds for some countries.

Eurocurrency market transactions normally represent large deposits and loans, often the equivalent of $1 million or more. Large financial transactions such as these can reduce operating expenses for a bank. This is another reason why Eurobanks can offer attractive rates on deposits and loans.

When a currency is deposited in or loaned from a Eurobank, it is often described with a "Euro" prefix attached to it. For example, a loan in Swiss francs by a Eurobank is referred to as a "Euro-Swiss franc" loan, and a deposit of Japanese yen in a Eurobank is called a "Euroyen" deposit. One should not become confused by the "Euro" prefix. The interest rate for each Eurocurrency is somewhat representative of that currency's rate in its home country. That is, the Eurodollar loan rate may be just slightly less than a similar dollar loan in the United States, and the Euro-Swiss franc loan rate may be just slightly less than the loan rate for Swiss francs in Switzerland. However, the rates charged for loans in different foreign currencies vary substantially among currencies, since funds denominated in each currency have their own supply and demand.

Syndicated Eurocurrency Loans

Although the Eurocurrency market concentrates on large-volume transactions, there are often times when no single Eurobank is willing to provide the amount needed by a particular corporation or government agency. In this case, a **syndicate** of Eurobanks may be composed. Each bank within the syndicate participates in the lending. A lead bank is responsible for negotiating terms with the borrower. Then the lead bank organizes a group of banks to underwrite the loans. The syndicate of banks is usually formed in about six weeks, or less if the borrower is well known, since the credit evaluation can then be conducted more quickly.

Borrowers who receive a syndicated loan incur various fees besides the interest on the loan. Front-end management fees are paid to represent the costs of organizing the syndicate and underwriting the loan. In addition, a commitment fee of about .25 percent or .50 percent is charged annually on the unused portion of the available credit extended by the syndicate.

Syndicated loans can be denominated in a variety of currencies. The interest rate depends on the currency denominating the loan, the maturity of the loan, and the creditworthiness of the borrower. Interest rates on syndicated loans are commonly adjustable according to movements in an interbank lending rate, and the adjustment may occur every six months or every year.

Syndicated Eurocurrency loans not only reduce the default risk of a large loan to the degree of participation for each individual bank, but they can also add an extra incentive for the borrower to repay the loan. If a government defaults on a loan to a syndicate, word will spread among banks quickly, and the government will likely have difficulty in obtaining future loans. Borrowers are therefore strongly encouraged to make prompt loan repayments on syndicated loans. From the perspective of the banks, syndicated Eurocurrency loans increase the probability of prompt repayment.

Standardizing Bank Regulations Within the Eurocurrency Market

The trend toward globalization in the banking industry is attributed to the recent standardization of regulations around the world. Two of the more significant regulatory events allowing for a more competitive global playing field are (1) the Single European Act and (2) the Basel Accord, which are described next.

Single European Act. One of the most significant events affecting international banking is the **Single European Act,** which was phased in by 1992 throughout the European Economic Community (EEC) countries. The following are some of the more relevant provisions of the Single European Act for the banking industry:

- Capital can flow freely throughout Europe.
- Banks can offer a wide variety of lending, leasing, and securities activities in the EEC.
- The regulations regarding competition, mergers, and taxes will be similar throughout the EEC.
- A bank established in any one of the EEC countries will have the right to expand into any or all of the other EEC countries.

As a result of this act, the banks have expanded across European countries. Efficiency in the European banking markets has increased because banks can more easily cross countries without concern for country-specific regulations that have prevailed in the past.

Another key provision of the act is that banks entering Europe receive the same banking powers as other banks there. Similar provisions are allowed for non-U.S. banks that enter the United States.

Basel Accord. Before 1987, capital standards imposed on banks varied across countries, which allowed some banks to have a comparative global advantage over others. As an example, consider a bank in the United States that is subject to a 6-percent capital ratio, which is twice that of a foreign bank. The foreign bank could achieve the same return on equity as the U.S. bank by generating a return on assets that is only one-half that of the U.S. bank. In essence, the foreign bank's **equity multiplier** (assets divided by equity) would be double that of the U.S. bank, which would offset the low return on assets. Given these conditions, foreign banks could accept lower profit margins while still achieving the same return on equity. This would afford them a stronger competitive position. In addition, growth would be more easily achieved, as a relatively small amount of capital is needed to support an increase in assets.

Some analysts would counter that these advantages are somewhat offset by the higher risk perception of banks having low capital ratios. Yet, if the governments in those countries are more likely to back banks that experience financial problems, banks with low capital may not necessarily be too risky. Therefore, some non-U.S. banks would have globally competitive advantages over U.S. banks, without being subject to excessive risk. In December 1987, twelve major industrialized countries attempted to resolve the disparity by proposing uniform bank standards. In July 1988, central bank governors of the twelve countries agreed on standardized guidelines, in what was referred to as the **Basel Accord.** Capital was classified as either Tier 1 ("core") capital or Tier 2 ("supplemental") capital (Tier 1 capital being at least 4 percent of risk-weighted assets). The use of risk weightings on assets implicitly created a higher required capital ratio for riskier assets. Off-balance sheet items were also accounted for, so that banks could not circumvent capital requirements by focusing on services (such as letters of credit and interest rate swaps) that are not explicitly shown on a balance sheet. Even with uniform capital requirements across countries, some analysts may still contend that U.S. banks are at a competitive disadvantage because they are subject to different accounting and tax provisions. Nevertheless, the uniform capital requirements represent significant progress toward a more level global field.

Asian Dollar Market

The Eurocurrency market can be broadly defined to include banks in Asia that accept deposits and make loans in foreign currencies (mostly dollars). Yet, this market is sometimes referred to separately as the **Asian dollar market.** Most activity takes place in Hong Kong and Singapore. The only significant difference between the Asian market and the Eurocurrency market is location. Like the Eurocurrency market, the Asian dollar market grew to accommodate needs of businesses that were using the U.S. dollar (and some other foreign currencies) as a medium of exchange for international trade. These businesses could not rely on banks in Europe because of the inconveniences of distance and different time zones.

The major sources of Asian dollar deposits are MNCs with excess cash and government agencies. Major borrowers in this market are manufacturers.

The primary function of banks in the Asian dollar market is to channel funds from depositors to borrowers. Another function is interbank lending and borrowing. Banks that have more qualified loan applicants than they can accommodate use the interbank market to obtain additional funds. Banks in the Asian market commonly borrow from or lend to banks in the Eurocurrency market.

EUROCREDIT MARKET

Multinational corporations and domestic firms sometimes obtain medium-term funds through term loans from local financial institutions or through the issuance of notes (medium-term debt obligations) in their local markets. However, MNCs also have access to medium-term funds through Eurobanks located in foreign markets. Loans of one year or longer extended by Eurobanks to MNCs or government agencies are commonly called Eurocredits or **Eurocredit loans.** These loans are provided in the so-called **Eurocredit market.** The loans can be denominated in dollars or many other currencies and commonly have a maturity of five years.

Because Eurobanks accept short-term deposits and sometimes provide longer term loans, their asset and liability maturities do not match. This can adversely affect a bank's performance during periods of rising interest rates, since the bank may have locked in a rate on its Eurocredit loans while its rate paid on short-term deposits was rising over time. To avoid this risk, Eurobanks now commonly use floating rate Eurocredit loans. The loan rate floats in accordance with the movement of some market interest rate, such as the **London Interbank Offer Rate (LIBOR),** which is the rate commonly charged for loans between Eurobanks. For example, a Eurocredit loan may have a loan rate that adjusts every six months and is set at "LIBOR plus 3 percent." The premium paid above LIBOR will depend on the credit risk of the borrower.

EUROBOND MARKET

MNCs, like domestic firms, can obtain long-term debt by issuing bonds in their local markets. MNCs can access long-term funds in foreign markets by issuing bonds in the international bond markets. International bonds are typically classified as either foreign bonds or Eurobonds. A **foreign bond** is issued by a borrower foreign to the country where the bond is placed. For example, a U.S. corporation may issue a bond denominated in Japanese yen, which is sold to investors in Japan. In some cases, a firm may issue a variety of bonds in various countries. The currency denominating each type of bond is determined by the country where it is sold. These foreign bonds are sometimes specifically referred to as **parallel bonds.**

Eurobonds are sold in countries other than the country represented by the currency denominating them. They have been very popular during the last decade as a means of attracting long-term funds. U.S.-based MNCs such as McDonald's and Walt Disney commonly use the Eurobond market. Non-U.S. firms such as Guinness, Nestlé, Volkswagen, and Volvo also use this market as a source of funds.

In recent years, governments and corporations from emerging markets have frequently utilized the Eurobond market. In 1997, Russian issuers raised almost $4 billion, while issuers from Croatia, Ukraine, Romania, and Hungary raised over $400 million per country. The new corporations that have been established in emerging markets are relying on the Eurobond market to finance their growth. Issuers from these countries commonly pay between three and six percentage points annually above the U.S. Treasury bond rate on dollar-denominated Eurobonds, but they are able to find buyers of their bonds in the Eurobond market.

Development of the Eurobond Market

The emergence of the Eurobond market is partially the result of the **Interest Equalization Tax (IET)** imposed by the U.S. government in 1963 in order to discourage U.S. investors from investing in foreign securities. Thus, non-U.S. borrowers that historically had sold securities to U.S. investors began to look elsewhere for funds.

Before 1984, investors that directly purchased U.S.-placed bonds were subject to a 30-percent withholding tax. The issuers of these bonds retained 30 percent of the interest payments to satisfy the withholding tax laws. A variety of tax treaties between the United States and other countries existed, causing this withholding tax to affect investors in some countries more than those in others. Because of the withholding tax, many U.S. bonds were issued in the Eurobond market through financing subsidiaries in the Netherlands Antilles. A tax treaty allowed interest payments from Antilles subsidiaries of U.S.-based corporations to non-U.S. investors to be exempt from the withholding tax. U.S. firms that used this method of financing were able to sell their bonds at a relatively high price because of the tax exemption. Thus, they obtained funds at a relatively low cost. Some U.S. firms did not use this financing method, since it entailed the cost of their establishing financing subsidiaries in the Netherlands Antilles and because they knew this method of circumventing the withholding tax might be prohibited by the U.S. government at some point in the future.

Indeed, in July 1984, the U.S. government abolished the withholding tax and allowed U.S. corporations to issue bearer bonds directly to non-U.S. investors. The result was a large increase in the volume of bonds sold by U.S. corporations to non-U.S. investors.

Underwriting Process

Eurobonds are underwritten by a multinational syndicate of investment banks and simultaneously placed in many countries, providing a wide spectrum of fund sources to tap. The underwriting process takes place within a stepwise sequence. The multinational managing syndicate sells the bonds to a large underwriting crew. In many cases, a special distribution to regional underwriters is allocated before the bonds finally reach the bond purchasers. One problem with the distribution method is that the second- and third-stage underwriters do not always follow up on their promise to sell the bonds. The managing syndicate is therefore forced to redistribute the unsold bonds or to sell them directly, which creates "digestion" problems in the market and adds to the distribution cost. To avoid such problems, bonds are often distributed in higher volume to the underwriters that have fulfilled their commitments in the past at the expense of those that have not. This has helped the Eurobond market maintain its desirability as a bond placement center.

Features

Eurobonds have several distinguishing features. They usually are issued in bearer form, and coupon payments are made yearly. Some Eurobonds carry a convertibility clause allowing them to be converted into a specified number of common stock shares. Eurobonds typically have few, if any, protective covenants, which is an advantage to the issuer. Also, call provisions are contained within even the short-maturity Eurobonds. Some Eurobonds, called **floating rate notes (FRNs)**, have a variable rate provision that adjusts the coupon rate over time according to prevailing market rates.

Denominations. Various currencies are commonly used to denominate Eurobonds. The U.S. dollar is used the most, denominating 70 to 75 percent of the Eurobonds, but many Eurobonds will likely be denominated in euros in the future.

The Japanese yen has been used by some firms to denominate debt recently because of its extremely low interest rates. For example, some MNCs were able to issue bonds at a yield of about 1 percent in the late 1990s.

Although firms prefer low interest rates, they tend to denominate debt in whatever currency they receive from their operations. General Electric recently issued bonds denominated in Japanese yen, Canadian dollars, British pounds, Australian dollars, New Zealand dollars, and Polish zloty to finance its foreign operations.

Interest rates for each currency and credit conditions in the Eurobond market change constantly, causing the popularity of the Eurobond market to vary among currencies. MNCs that need funds attempt to "read" market conditions so that they can properly time their bond offerings. They prefer to issue bonds in the desired currency when the respective interest rate for that currency is low and when the institutional investors who invest in the Eurobond market charge a minimal premium (above the currency's risk-free rate) for credit risk. In the late 1990s, the credit risk premium required by institutional investors in various currencies was generally low (especially for MNCs with limited exposure to Asia) which encouraged many MNCs to obtain funds through the issuance of Eurobonds.

Secondary Market. Eurobonds have a secondary market. The market makers are in many cases the same underwriters who sell the primary issues. A technological advancement called **Euro-clear** helps to inform all traders about outstanding issues for sale, thus allowing a more active secondary market. The middlemen, or intermediaries, within the secondary market are based in ten different countries, with those in the United Kingdom dominating the action. They can act not only as brokers but also as dealers that hold inventories of Eurobonds. Many of these intermediaries, such as Bank of America International, Salomon Brothers, and Citicorp International, are subsidiaries of U.S. corporations.

Ratings. While ratings are available for most Eurobond issues, there has been a tendency of the purchasers to ignore ratings in favor of a well-known name. This provides an advantage for well-known U.S. firms that have not been assigned the highest rating. About one-fourth of the debt issues in the Eurobond market are for less than $100 million, while more than one-third of the issues are for more than $300 million. For example, Gillette, which is known worldwide, raised $300 million in the Eurobond market in 1997 and paid an annual yield of just .14 percent above U.S. Treasury bonds.

Comparing Interest Rates among Currencies

Recently quoted annualized interest rates are disclosed in Exhibit 3.2. Notice the wide disparity among interest rates of different countries. At one extreme, Japan's annualized interest rate was about 1 percent, while Russia's annualized interest rate was 60 percent. In fact, Russia's annualized rate exceeded 100 percent in some periods during the late 1990s.

The interest rates in debt markets (such as in the Eurobond and Eurocurrency markets) are crucial because they affect the MNC's cost of financing. Since interest rates can vary substantially among currencies, the cost of local financing for foreign projects varies among countries. The interest rate on a debt instrument denominated in a specific currency in the Eurocurrency, Eurocredit, and Eurobond markets is determined by the demand for funds denominated in that currency and the supply of funds available in that currency.

For example, the supply and demand schedules for the U.S. dollar and for Brazil's currency (the real) are compared for a given point in time in Exhibit 3.3. The demand schedule for loanable funds is downward sloping for any currency, which simply means that the quantity of funds demanded at any point in time is inversely related to the interest rate level. That is, the total amount of loanable funds demanded (borrowed) at a given point in time is higher if the cost of borrowing is lower.

The supply schedule for loanable funds denominated in a given currency is upward sloping, which implies that the total amount of loanable funds supplied (such as savings by individuals) at a given point in time is positively related to the interest rate level. That is, the total amount of loanable funds supplied to the market is higher if the interest rate offered on savings accounts is higher.

Exhibit 3.2
Comparison of Annualized Short-Term Interest Rates Among Countries in 1999

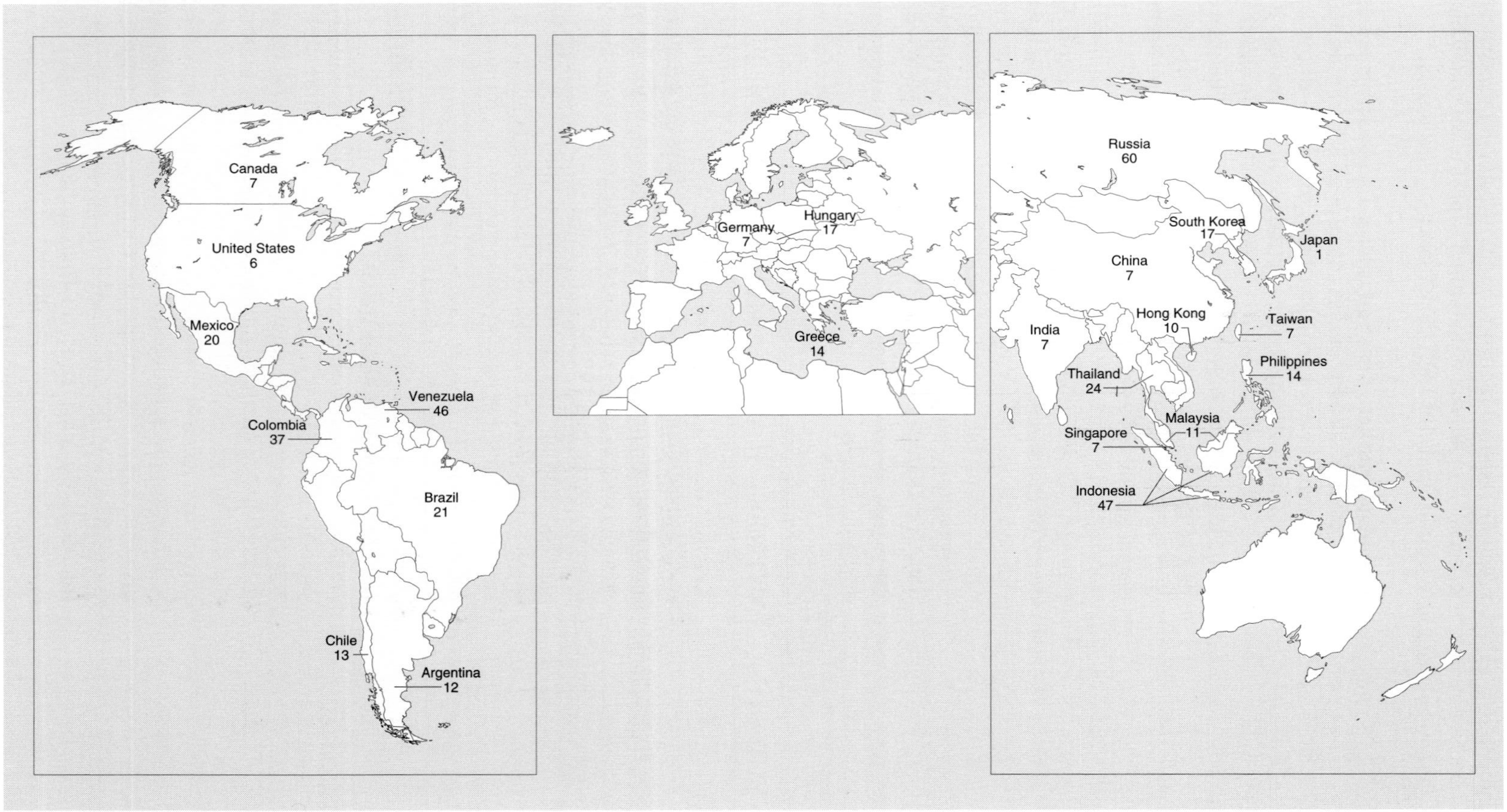

Rates are rounded to the nearest percent.

Exhibit 3.3
Why U.S. Dollar Interest Rates Differ from Brazilian Real Interest Rates

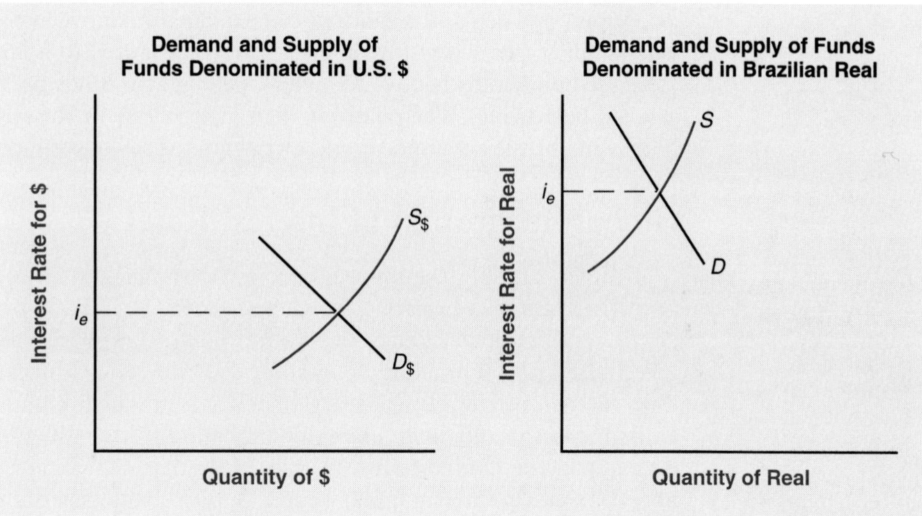

While the demand schedule for loanable funds should be downward sloping for every currency and the supply schedule of loanable funds should be upward sloping for every currency, the actual positions of these schedules vary among currencies. First, notice that the demand and supply curves are further to the right for the dollar than for the Brazilian real. The amount of dollar-denominated loanable funds supplied and demanded is much greater than the Brazilian real-denominated loanable funds, since the U.S. economy is much larger than Brazil's economy.

Also notice that the positions of the demand and supply schedules for loanable funds are much higher for the Brazilian real than for the dollar. The supply schedule for loanable funds denominated in Brazilian real shows that hardly any amount of savings would be supplied at low interest rate levels because the high inflation there encourages households to spend all of their disposable income before prices increase more. It discourages households from saving unless the interest rate is sufficiently high. In addition, the demand for loanable funds in Brazilian real shows that borrowers are willing to borrow even at very high rates of interest because they would rather borrow funds to make purchases now before prices increase. Firms would be willing to pay 70-percent interest on a loan to purchase machines whose prices will increase by 90 percent next year.

Because of the differences in the positions of the demand and supply schedules for each of the two currencies shown in Exhibit 3.3, the equilibrium interest rate for the Brazilian real is much higher than the dollar. As the demand and supply schedules change over time for a specific currency, so will the equilibrium interest rate. For example, if Brazil's government was able to substantially reduce the local inflation, the supply schedule of loanable funds denominated in Brazilian real would shift out (to the right) while the demand schedule of loanable funds denominated in real would shift in (to the left), which would result in a lower equilibrium interest rate. It may seem as though investors from other countries should invest in savings accounts in high-inflation countries such as Brazil. However, the currencies of these high-inflation countries usually weaken over time, which may more than offset the interest rate advantage as is explained later in the text. Second, savings deposits in some of these countries are not insured, which presents another risk to foreign investors. Third, there may be restrictions in some of the emerging countries that discourage investors from investing funds there.

Supply and demand conditions can explain the relative interest rate for any currency. The Japanese yen's very low interest rate is attributed to a large supply of savings by Japanese households relative to a weak demand for funds because of a weak economy (limited borrowing). The relatively high interest rate in Russia is attributed to massive borrowing by the government and a very limited savings (supply) by households.

Global Integration of Interest Rates

Many investors shift their savings around currencies of the more developed countries to take advantage of relatively high interest rates. In addition, borrowers sometimes borrow a different currency from what they need to take advantage of a relatively low interest rate. For example, assume that U.S. and Canadian interest rates are initially at the same level. Consider a situation in which high economic growth in the United States results in an increased demand for loanable funds, which causes interest rates in the United States to rise. Now that U.S. interest rates are significantly above Canadian interest rates, some U.S. borrowers may obtain funding in Canadian dollars where interest rates are relatively low. This results in an increased demand for loanable funds denominated in Canadian dollars, which can also place upward pressure on Canadian interest rates. Thus, the Canadian interest rate rises as well.

Since U.S. and Canadian interest rates have risen, some borrowers in these countries may consider borrowing European currencies if European interest rates are relatively low; this may ultimately place upward pressure on European interest rates. The impact of a change in one currency's interest rate on another can happen within the same day, week, or month. The point is that the freedom to transfer funds across countries causes the demand and supply conditions for funds to be somewhat integrated, which can cause interest rate movements to be integrated.

International Stock Markets

http://

Visit pacific.commerce.ubc.ca/xr/euro for basic information about the new single European currency (euro) and the process to achieve monetary union.

MNCs and domestic firms commonly obtain long-term funding by issuing stock locally. Yet, MNCs can also attract funds from foreign investors by issuing stock in international markets. New issues of stock are increasingly being floated by U.S.-based MNCs in the United States and non-U.S. markets simultaneously. The issuance of stock may be more easily digested when access to various markets is allowed. In addition, the issuance of stock overseas can enhance the image and name recognition of a U.S.-based MNC.

The recent conversion of many European countries to a single currency (the euro) is likely to cause more stock offerings in Europe by U.S.- and European-based MNCs. In the past, an MNC needed a different currency in every country in which it conducted business and therefore borrowed currencies from local banks in those countries. Now, it can use the euro to finance its operations across several European countries and may be able to obtain all the financing it needs with one stock offering in which the stock is denominated in euros. The MNCs can then use a portion of the revenue (in euros) to pay dividends to shareholders who have purchased the stock.

Non-U.S. corporations or governments that need large amounts of funds will sometimes issue the stock in the United States (these are called **Yankee stock offerings**) due to the liquidity of the new-issues market there. That is, a foreign corporation or government may be more likely to sell an entire issue of stock in the U.S. market, whereas in other, smaller markets, the entire issue may not necessarily sell.

The U.S. investment banks commonly serve as underwriters of the stock targeted for the U.S. market and receive underwriting fees ranging from about 3 to 6 percent of the value of stock issued. Since many financial institutions in the United States purchase non-U.S. stocks as investments, non-U.S. firms may be able to place an entire stock offering within the United States.

Firms that issue stock in the United States typically are required to satisfy more stringent disclosure rules on their financial condition. However, they are exempt from some of these disclosure rules when they qualify for a Securities and Exchange Commission guideline (called Rule 144a) through a direct placement of stock to institutional investors.

Many of the recent stock offerings in the United States by non-U.S. firms have resulted from privatization programs in Latin America and Europe, whereby businesses that were previously government-owned are being sold to U.S. shareholders. Given the large size of some of these businesses, the local stock markets are not large enough to digest stock offerings. Consequently, U.S. investors are financing many privatized businesses based in foreign countries.

When a non-U.S. firm issues stock in its own country, its shareholder base is quite limited, as a few large institutional investors may own most of the shares. By issuing stock in the United States, such a firm diversifies its shareholder base, which can reduce share price volatility caused when large investors sell shares.

Non-U.S. firms also obtain equity financing by using **American depository receipts (ADRs)**, which are certificates representing bundles of stock. The use of ADRs circumvents some disclosure requirements imposed on stock offerings in the United States, yet enables non-U.S. firms to tap the U.S. market for funds. The ADR market grew after businesses were privatized in the early 1990s, as some of these businesses issued ADRs to obtain financing.

Although the U.S. market offers an advantage for new stock issues due to size, the registration requirements can sometimes cause delays in selling the new issues. For this reason, some U.S. firms have issued new stock in foreign markets in recent years. Other U.S. firms are issuing stock in foreign markets simply to enhance their global image. The existence of various markets for new issues provides a choice for corporations in need of equity. This competition between various new-issues markets should increase the efficiency of new issues.

International stock issues tend to sell better in foreign markets when the issuing MNC has a global image. Yet, some less well-known MNCs also issue stock in foreign markets to establish a global image. In addition, the issuance of stock across several markets may avoid the downward price pressure that could occur if the entire issue were sold in a single market.

The locations of the MNC's operations can influence the decision about where to place stock, as the MNC may desire a country where it is likely to generate enough future cash flows to cover dividend payments. The stocks of some U.S.-based MNCs are widely traded on numerous stock exchanges around the world. For example, the stock of The Coca-Cola Company is traded on stock exchanges in the United States, Frankfurt, and Switzerland. The stock of TRW Inc. is traded on stock exchanges in the United States, London, and Frankfurt. CPC International, Allied-Signal, and many other U.S.-based MNCs have their stock listed on more than five different stock exchanges overseas. By listing their stock on foreign stock exchanges, MNCs can easily have their stock traded by foreign investors who have access to those stock exchanges.

A summary of the major stock markets is provided in Exhibit 3.4. Numerous other exchanges are also available. Some foreign stock markets are much smaller

Exhibit 3.4
Characteristics of Stock Exchanges

Stock Exchange	Number of Companies Listed	Market Capitalization (in billions of dollars)	Average Daily Volume (millions of shares)	Restrictions on Foreign Ownership
Australia	1,219	560	350	Only on strategic industries, such as uranium.
Belgium	263	136	NA	None
Canada (Montreal)	577	484	17	Some financial institutions are subject to a maximum limit.
Canada (Toronto)	1,323	758	88	See above.
Denmark	249	94	NA	None
Finland	126	74	NA	None
France	886	970	NA	Non-European investors are subject to a maximum limit.
Germany	3,003	824	NA	None
Hong Kong	674	278	887	None
Italy	213	490	NA	None
Japan	2,387	1,917	454	Investors may be subject to maximum limit.
Mexico	309	NA	33	Various restrictions apply.
Netherlands	350	91	NA	None
New Zealand	387	15	7	Nonresidents are subject to maximum limits.
Norway	217	66	NA	Nonresidents are subject to a maximum limit.
Singapore	326	NA	NA	Some restrictions apply.
South Korea	762	57	88	Nonresidents can invest only through mutual funds.
Switzerland	3,890	56	NA	Registered shares are restricted to residents.
Taiwan	NA	92	NA	Restrictions apply to nonresidents.
United Kingdom	2,991	2,063	NA	None
United States	3,047	8,450	540	None

http://
The site at quote.yahoo.com provides access to various domestic and international financial markets and financial market news, as well as links to national financial news servers.

than the U.S. markets because their firms have relied more on debt financing than equity financing in the past. However, firms outside the United States have recently been issuing stock more frequently, which has resulted in the growth of non-U.S. stock markets. The percentage of individual versus institutional ownership of shares varies across stock markets. Financial institutions and other firms own a large proportion of the shares outside the United States, while individual investors own a relatively small proportion of shares.

Large MNCs have begun to simultaneously float new stock issues in various countries. Investment banks underwrite stocks through one or more syndicates across countries. The global distribution of stock can reach a much larger market, so greater quantities of stock can be issued at a given price.

As a result of recent events, the stock markets have progressed toward a global around-the-clock trading system. The event known as the "Big Bang" allowed for the opening of a computerized network (called SEAQ) in London in October 1986 that is somewhat similar to the NASDAQ system in the United States. In addition, the London stock exchange now allows large investment firms in the United States and Japan to trade there. Stocks traded on London, Japanese, and U.S. exchanges allow for trading almost around the clock.

In recent years, many new stock markets have been developed. These so-called emerging markets enable foreign firms to raise large amounts of capital by issuing stock. These markets may enable U.S. firms doing business in emerging markets to raise funds by issuing stock there and listing their stock on the emerging market stock exchanges. Market characteristics such as the amount of trading relative to market capitalization and the applicable tax rates can vary substantially among emerging markets.

Comparison of International Financial Markets

Exhibit 3.5 illustrates the foreign cash flow movements of a typical MNC. These cash flows can be classified into four corporate functions, all of which generally require use of the foreign exchange markets. The spot market, forward market, currency futures market, and currency options market are all classified as foreign exchange markets.

Exhibit 3.5
Foreign Cash Flow Chart of an MNC

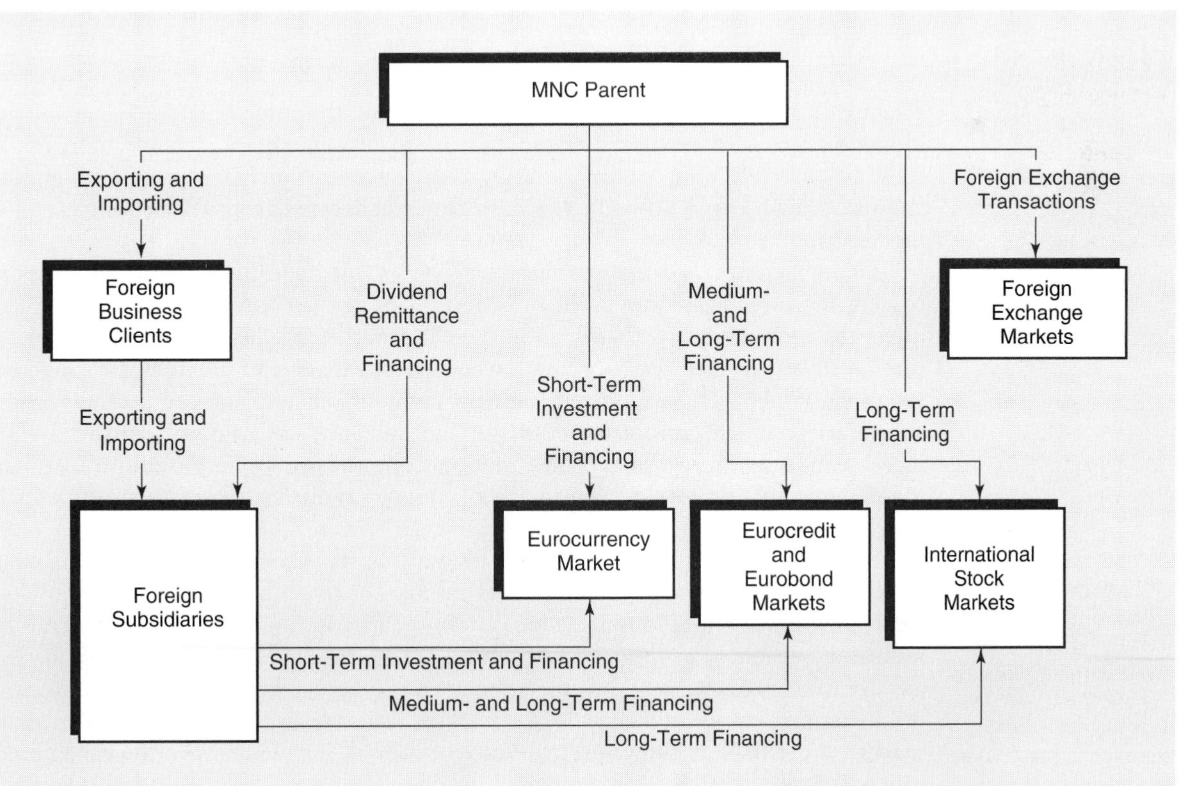

Nike Problem

Use of International Financial Markets

Like most MNCs, Nike frequently uses international financial markets to facilitate its international business operations. Since its cash flows are going to or coming from foreign subsidiaries, Nike frequently uses the foreign exchange market to facilitate its transactions. It also maintains short-term deposits at foreign banks and has access to short-term debt from foreign banks. It recently issued bonds denominated in Japanese yen to borrow the equivalent of about $100 million.

Discussion: Why do you think that Nike's foreign subsidiaries do not just rely on a large bank in the United States to provide all of its foreign exchange services and its deposit or loan services?

The first function is foreign trade with business clients. Exports generate foreign cash inflows, while imports require cash outflows. A second function is direct foreign investment, or the acquisition of foreign real assets. This function requires cash outflows but generates future inflows through remitted dividends back to the MNC parent or the sale of these foreign assets. A third function is short-term investment or financing in foreign securities. The Eurocurrency market is commonly used for this purpose. A fourth function is longer-term financing in the Eurocredit, Eurobond, or international stock markets.

How Financial Markets Affect an MNC's Value

The use of international financial markets can affect the value of an MNC, as shown in Exhibit 3.6. To the extent that issuing stock in a foreign market creates more name recognition in a foreign country, an MNC may be able to increase its presence in that country, which can lead to higher cash flows generated from that country and a higher valuation.

Financial markets can also affect an MNC's value by influencing the cost of borrowing for foreign customers of the MNC. Changes in foreign interest rates can affect the economic growth, which in turn affects the demand for products sold by foreign subsidiaries of the MNC. A lower interest rate can stimulate borrowing and spending, which results in a higher demand for products produced by the foreign subsidiaries, and therefore increases foreign currency cash flows. Conversely, an increase in local interest rates would reduce economic growth in the country, reduce the demand for the foreign subsidiary's products, reduce its foreign currency cash flows, and therefore reduce its value.

http://
The home page of Princeton's Global Market Watch at www.pei-intl.com/Quotes/WATCH.htm provides details on current financial market trends and indicators.

Since interest rates commonly vary among countries, an MNC's parent may use the Eurocurrency, Eurocredit, or Eurobond market to obtain funds at a lower cost than the cost of funds obtained locally. It reduces its cost of debt and therefore reduces its weighted average cost of capital, which results in a higher valuation.

An MNC's parent may be able to achieve a lower weighted average cost of capital by issuing equity in some foreign markets rather than issuing equity in its local market. If the MNC achieves a lower cost of capital, it can achieve a lower required rate of return and a higher valuation.

Exhibit 3.6
Impact of Global Financial Markets on an MNC's Value

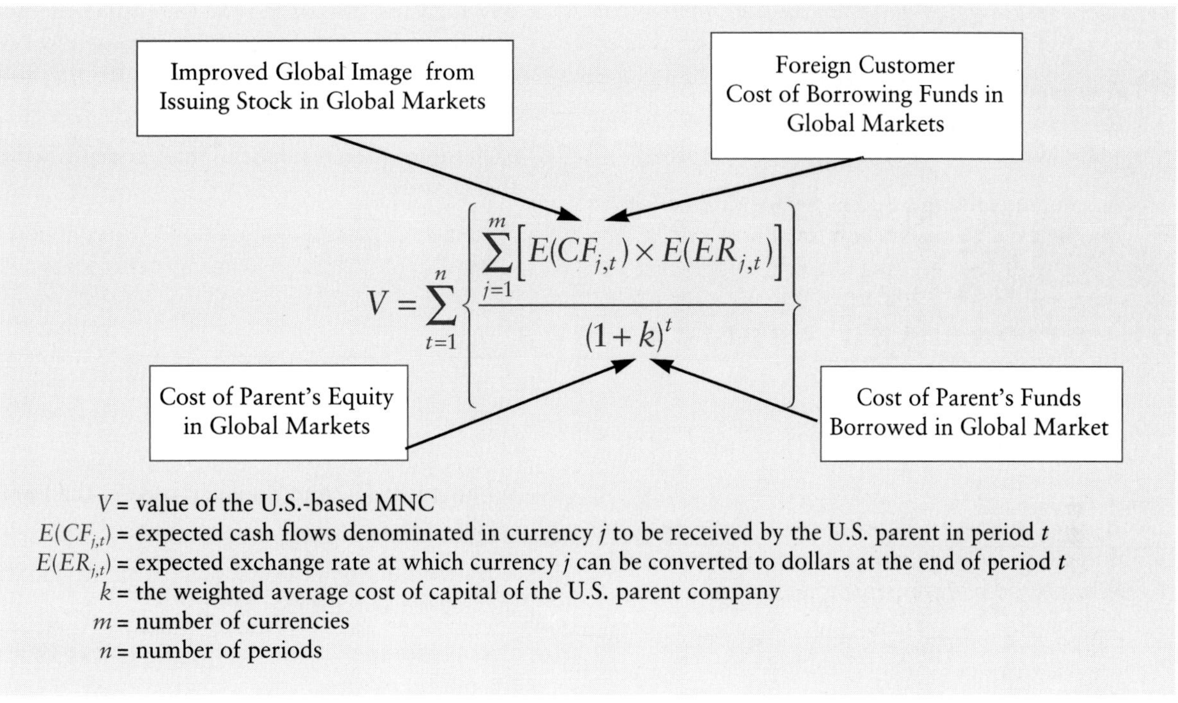

V = value of the U.S.-based MNC
$E(CF_{j,t})$ = expected cash flows denominated in currency j to be received by the U.S. parent in period t
$E(ER_{j,t})$ = expected exchange rate at which currency j can be converted to dollars at the end of period t
k = the weighted average cost of capital of the U.S. parent company
m = number of currencies
n = number of periods

SUMMARY

- The existence of market imperfections prevents markets from being completely integrated. Consequently, investors and creditors can attempt to capitalize on unique characteristics that make foreign markets more attractive than domestic markets. This motivates the international flow of funds and results in the development of international financial markets.
- The foreign exchange market allows currencies to be exchanged in order to facilitate international trade or financial transactions. Commercial banks serve as financial intermediaries in this market. They stand ready to exchange currencies on the spot or at a future point in time with the use of forward contracts.
- The Eurocurrency market is composed of several large banks that accept deposits and provide short-term loans in various currencies. This market is primarily used by governments and large corporations.
- The Eurocredit market is composed of the same commercial banks that serve the Eurocurrency market. These banks convert some of the deposits received into Eurocredit loans (for medium-term periods) to governments and large corporations.
- The Eurobond market facilitates the international transfers of long-term credit, which enables governments and large corporations to borrow funds from various countries. Eurobonds are underwritten by a multinational syndicate of investment banks and are placed in various countries.
- Just as the Eurocurrency, Eurocredit, and Eurobond markets enable firms to borrow funds in foreign countries, international stock markets enable firms to obtain equity financing in foreign countries. Thus, these markets have helped MNCs finance their international expansion.

SELF-TEST FOR CHAPTER 3

(Answers are provided in Appendix A at the back of the text.)

1. A commercial bank quotes a bid rate of $.784 for the Australian dollar and an ask rate of $.80. What is the bid/ask percentage spread?

2. A commercial bank quotes a spot rate of $.190 for the Peruvian currency (new sol) and a 90-day forward rate of $.188. Determine the forward premium (or discount) of the new sol on an annualized basis.

3. Briefly explain how MNCs can make use of each international financial market described in this chapter.

QUESTIONS AND APPLICATIONS

1. List some of the important characteristics of bank foreign exchange services that MNCs should consider.

2. Assume that a bank's bid price for Canadian dollars is $.7938, while its ask price is $.81. What is the bid/ask percentage spread?

3. Compute the forward discount or premium for the Mexican peso whose 90-day forward rate is $.102 and spot rate is $.10. State whether your answer is a discount or premium.

4. Of what use is a forward contract to an MNC?

5. How can a forward contract backfire?

6. If a dollar is worth 1.7 Singapore dollars, what is the U.S.-dollar value of a Singapore dollar?

7. Assume Poland's currency (the zloty) is worth $.17 and a Japanese yen is worth $.008. What is the cross rate of the zloty with respect to yen? That is, how many yen equal a zloty?

8. Explain how the Eurocurrency, Eurocredit, and Eurobond markets differ from one another.

9. Briefly describe the historical developments that led to floating exchange rates as of 1973.

10. What is the function of the Eurocurrency market?

11. Briefly describe the reasons for the development and the growth in the Eurocurrency market.

12. Why do interest rates vary among countries?

13. With regard to Eurocredit loans, who are the common borrowers?

14. What is LIBOR, and how is it used in the Eurocredit market?

15. Why would a bank desire to participate in syndicated Eurocredit loans?

16. Discuss some reasons for the popularity of the Eurobond market.

17. Compute the forward discount or premium for the British pound whose 180-day forward rate is $1.75 and spot rate is $1.78. State whether your answer is a discount or premium.

18. The Wolfpack Corporation is a U.S. exporter that invoices its exports to the United Kingdom in British pounds. If it expects that the pound will appreciate against the dollar in the future, should it hedge its exports with a forward contract? Explain.

19. Explain why firms may consider issuing stock in foreign markets.

20. Bullet Inc., a U.S. firm, is planning to issue new stock in the United States during this month. The only decision it has left is the specific day in which the stock should be issued. Why do you think this firm monitors results of the Tokyo stock market every morning?

21. Recently, Wal-Mart established two retail outlets in the city of Shanzen, China, which has a population of 3.7 million. These outlets are massive and contain products purchased locally

as well as imports. As Wal-Mart generates earnings beyond what it needs in Shanzen, it may remit those earnings back to the United States. Wal-Mart is likely to build additional outlets in Shanzan or in other cities in the future.

a. Explain how the Wal-Mart outlets in China would use the spot market in foreign exchange.
b. Explain how Wal-Mart's parent may utilize the Eurocurrency market when it is establishing other Wal-Mart stores in Asia.
c. Explain how Wal-Mart could use the Eurobond market to finance the establishment of new outlets in foreign markets.

22. Explain how the Asian crisis would have affected the returns to a U.S. firm investing in the Asian stock markets as a means of international diversification. [See the appendix.]

Internet Application

23. The Bloomberg Web site provides quotations of various exchange rates and stock market indexes. Its Web site address is:

www.bloomberg.com

a. Use this Web site to determine the cross exchange rate between the Japanese yen and Australian dollar. That is, determine how many yen must be converted to an Australian dollar for Japanese importers that purchase Australian products today.
b. Use this Web site to review how stock markets performed today. (This relates to the appendix of this chapter). Does it appear that returns on Asian stock markets today are related? Does it appear that the returns on the European stock markets today are related?

Running Your Own MNC

Using the Foreign Exchange Market

24. Explain how you will use the spot market for your business.

25. What bank do you plan to use to exchange the foreign currency received for dollars? What is the bid/ask spread on a recent quotation by that bank? (Call the bank to obtain quotations.)

26. Will you possibly need the forward market? Explain.

Blades, Inc. Case

Decisions to Use International Financial Markets

As a financial analyst for Blades, Inc. you are reasonably satisfied with Blades' current setup of exporting "Speedos" (roller blades) to Thailand. Due to the unique arrangement with Blades' primary customer in Thailand, forecasting the revenue to be generated there is a relatively easy task. Specifically, your customer has agreed, for a period of three years, to purchase 180,000 pairs of Speedos annually at a price of THB4,594 per pair. The current direct quotation of the dollar-baht exchange rate is $0.024.

The cost of goods sold incurred in Thailand (due to imports of the rubber and plastic components from Thailand) runs at approximately THB2,871 per pair of Speedos, but Blades currently only imports materials sufficient to manufacture about 72,000 pairs of Speedos. Blades' primary reason for using a Thai supplier is both the high quality of the components as well as the low cost, which has been facilitated by a continuing depreciation of the Thai baht against the U.S. dollar. If the dollar cost of buying components becomes more expensive in Thailand than in the United States, Blades is contemplating providing its U.S. supplier with the additional business.

Your plan is quite simple; Blades is currently using its Thai-denominated revenues to cover the cost of goods sold incurred there. During the last year, excess revenue was converted to U.S. dollars at the prevailing exchange rate. However, although your cost of goods sold is not fixed contractually as the Thai revenues are, you expect them to remain relatively constant in the near future. Consequently, the baht-denominated cash inflows are fairly predictable each year because the Thai customer has committed to the purchase of 180,000 pairs of Speedos at a fixed price. The excess dollar revenue resulting from the conversion of baht is used either to support the U.S. production of Speedos if needed or to invest in the United States. Specifically, the revenues are used to cover cost of goods sold in the U.S. manufacturing plant, located in Omaha, Nebraska.

Ben Holt, Blades' CFO, notices that Thailand's interest rates are approximately 15 percent (versus 8 percent in the United States). You interpret the high interest rates in Thailand as an indication of the uncertainty resulting from the Asian crisis. Ben Holt asks you to assess the feasibility of investing Blades' excess funds from Thailand operations in Thailand at an interest rate of 15 percent. After you communicate your opposition to his plan, Ben Holt asks you to detail the reasons in a detailed report.

1. One point of concern for you is that there is a tradeoff between the higher interest rates in Thailand and the delayed conversion of baht into dollars. Explain what this means.
2. If the net baht received from the Thailand operation are invested in Thailand, how will U.S. operations be affected? (Assume that Blades is currently paying 10 percent on dollars borrowed and needs more financing for its firm.)
3. Construct a spreadsheet to compare the cash flows resulting from two plans. Under the first plan, net baht-denominated cash flows (received today) will be invested in Thailand at 15 percent for a one-year period, after which the baht will be converted to dollars. The expected spot rate for the baht in one year is about $0.022 (Ben Holt's plan). Under the second plan, net baht-denominated cash flows are converted to dollars immediately and invested in the United States for one year at 8 percent. For this question, assume that all baht-denominated cash flows are due today. Does Ben Holt's plan seem like the superior plan in terms of dollar cash flows available after one year? Compare the choice of investing the funds versus using the funds to provide needed financing to the firm (a spreadsheet is not needed).

Small Business Dilemma

Use of the Foreign Exchange Markets by the Sports Exports Company

Each month, the Sports Exports Company (a U.S. firm) receives an order for footballs from a British sporting goods distributor. The monthly payment for the footballs is denominated in British pounds, as was requested by the British distributor. Jim Logan, owner of the Sports Exports Company, must convert the pounds received into dollars.

1. Explain how the Sports Exports Company could utilize the spot market in order to facilitate the exchange of currencies. Be specific.
2. Explain how the Sports Exports Company is exposed to exchange rate risk and how it could use the forward market to hedge this risk.

APPENDIX 3

Investing in International Financial Markets

http://

Visit www.cnnfn.com for current national and international market data and analyses.

The trading of financial assets (such as stocks or bonds) by investors in international financial markets has a major impact on MNCs. First, this type of trading can influence the level of interest rates in a specific country (and therefore the cost of debt to an MNC) because it affects the amount of funds available there. Second, it can affect the price of an MNC's stock (and therefore the cost of equity to an MNC) because it influences the demand for an MNC's stock. Third, it enables MNCs to sell securities in foreign markets. So, even though international investing in financial assets is not the most crucial activity of MNCs, international investing by individual and institutional investors can indirectly affect the actions and performance of MNCs. Consequently, an understanding of the motives and methods of international investing is necessary to anticipate how the international flow of funds may change in the future and how that change may affect MNCs.

BACKGROUND ON INTERNATIONAL STOCK EXCHANGES

The international trading of stocks has grown over time but has been limited by three barriers: transaction costs, information costs, and exchange rate risk. However, these barriers have been reduced as explained here.

Reduction in Transaction Costs

Most countries tend to have their own stock exchanges, where the stocks of local publicly-held companies are traded. In recent years, exchanges have been consolidated within a country, which has increased efficiency and reduced transaction costs. Some European stock exchanges now have extensive cross-listings, so that investors in a given European country can easily purchase stocks of companies based in other European countries.

In particular, because of its efficiency, the stock exchange of Switzerland may serve as a model that will be applied to many other stock exchanges around the world. The Swiss stock exchange is now fully computerized, so a trading floor is not needed. Orders by investors to buy or sell flow to financial institutions that are certified members of the Swiss stock exchange. These institutions may not necessarily be based in Switzerland. The details of the orders to the members, such as name of stock, number of shares to be bought or sold, and the price at which the investor is willing to buy or sell, are fed into a computer system. The system matches buyers and sellers and then sends information confirming the transaction to the financial institutions, which then informs the investor that the transaction is completed.

When there are many more buy orders than sell orders for a given stock, the computer will not be able to accommodate all orders. Yet, some buyers will then increase the price at which they are willing to pay for the stock. Thus, the price adjusts in response to the demand (buy orders) for the stock and the supply (sell orders) of the stock for sale recorded by the computer system. Similar dynamics occur when a trading floor is used, but the computerized system has documented criteria by which it prioritizes the execution of orders; traders on a trading floor may execute some trades in ways that favor themselves at the expense of the investors.

Over time, it is likely that a computerized system like that used for the Swiss stock exchange will be used at other stock exchanges. For example, the Brussels stock exchange already has conformed to the computerized system. Furthermore, the Internet now allows investors to bypass a phone call to the financial institutions and can instead place orders on their computers (through the Web site of a member of the stock exchange) that will then be executed and confirmed by the computer system through the Internet to the investor. Thus, all parts of the trading process from the placement of the order to the confirmation that the transaction has been executed will be conducted by computers. The ease with which such orders could occur, regardless of the locations of the investor and the stock exchange, is sure to increase the volume of international stock transactions in the future.

Reduction in Information Costs

The Internet allows investors access to much information about foreign stocks, so investors can make more informed decisions without having to purchase information about these stocks. Consequently, investors should be more comfortable in assessing foreign stocks. Differences in accounting rules may still limit the degree to which financial data about foreign companies can be interpreted or compared to firms in other countries, but there is some momentum toward making accounting standards uniform across some countries.

Exchange Rate Risk

When investing in a foreign stock that is denominated in a foreign currency, investors are subject to the possibility that the currency denominating the stock may depreciate against the investor's currency over time.

The potential for a major decline in the stock's value simply because of a large degree of depreciation is more likely for emerging markets, such as Indonesia or Russia, where the local currency can change by 10 percent or more on a single day.

INTERNATIONAL STOCK DIVERSIFICATION

A substantial amount of research has demonstrated that investors in stocks can benefit by diversifying internationally. The stocks of most firms are highly influenced by the countries in which those firms reside (although some firms are more vulnerable to economic conditions than others).

Since stock markets partially reflect the current and/or forecasted state of their countries' economies, they do not move in tandem. Thus, particular stocks of the various markets are not expected to be highly correlated. This contrasts with a purely domestic portfolio, in which most stocks are often moving in the same direction and by a somewhat similar magnitude.

To assess how countries' stock markets move relative to one another, correlation coefficients of monthly stock market returns (from a U.S. investor's perspective) are disclosed for some countries over the 1992–1998 period and are displayed in Exhibit 3A.1. Some pairs of indexes, such as France/Germany, exhibit relatively high correlations. Yet, most stock index correlations shown in the exhibit are less than .50. Consequently, investors should be able to reduce variability in portfolio returns by diversifying among stocks from several countries.

Limitations of International Diversification

In general, stock correlations between stock indexes in recent years are higher than they were several years ago. The general increase in correlations among stock market returns may provide implications for MNCs that attempt to diversify business internationally. To the extent that stock prices in each market reflect anticipated earnings, the increased correlations may suggest expectations of more highly correlated anticipated earnings among countries. Thus, the potential risk reduction benefits to an MNC that diversifies its business may be limited.

Exhibit 3A.2 shows how correlations between the returns of some markets (from a U.S. investor's perspective) changed recently. For example, the correlation coefficient between stock returns of the U.S. and Canadian stock markets was .47 for the 1992–1994 period but .86 during the 1995–1998 period. However, the correlations for some other pairs of stock markets declined over time. While it is difficult to generalize how stock market correlations will change in the future, it is safe to say that some correlations between stock market returns will change over time, so that the benefits of diversifying among stocks of different countries will change as well.

One reason for the increased correlations among stock market returns is increased integration of business between countries. Increased integration results in more intercountry trade flows and capital flows, which causes each country to have more influence on other countries. In particular, many European countries have become more integrated because of a movement to standardize regulations throughout Europe to facilitate trade between countries. In addition, several European countries now use the "euro" as their currency, thereby removing exchange rate risk for trade between participating countries.

The conversion to the euro also allows portfolio managers of European countries to invest in stocks of other participating European countries without concern for exchange rate risk, because these stocks are also invested in euros. This facilitates a more regional approach for European investors, who are not restricted to stocks within the investors' respective countries.

Exhibit 3A.1
Correlation Coefficients of Monthly Stock Returns January 1992–September 1998

	U.S.	Canada	France	Germany	Japan	Mexico	New Zealand
Canada	0.76						
France	0.50	0.45					
Germany	0.54	0.51	0.71				
Japan	0.21	0.27	0.28	0.21			
Mexico	0.48	0.51	0.34	0.29	0.14		
New Zealand	0.44	0.49	0.43	0.43	0.41	0.43	
Australia	0.54	0.61	0.54	0.54	0.43	0.45	0.71

Exhibit 3A.2 Comparison of Stock Market Correlations During Two Subperiods

Source: Dow Jones Country Indices.

	Subperiod	U.S.	Canada	France	Germany	Japan	Mexico
Canada	1	0.47					
	2	0.86					
France	1	0.44	0.25				
	2	0.53	0.56				
Germany	1	0.27	0.24	0.73			
	2	0.54	0.64	0.72			
Japan	1	0.12	0.26	0.26	0.20		
	2	0.36	0.31	0.37	0.27		
Mexico	1	0.45	0.43	0.16	0.00	−0.10	
	2	0.59	0.63	0.44	0.51	0.35	
New Zealand	1	0.66	0.55	0.53	0.48	0.42	0.39
	2	0.46	0.52	0.39	0.47	0.37	0.47

Subperiod 1 represents monthly market returns from January 1992 to December 1994.

Subperiod 2 represents monthly returns from January 1995 to September 1998. All market index returns are from a U.S. investor's perspective.

Since some stock market correlations may become more pronounced during a crisis, international diversification will not necessarily be as effective as it is during more favorable conditions. Two events that had an adverse effect on many markets are the 1987 crash and the Asian crisis, which are discussed next.

Market Movements During the 1987 Crash. Further evidence on the relationships between stock markets is obtained by assessing market movements during the stock market crash in October 1987. Exhibit 3A.3 shows the stock market movements for four major countries during the crash. While the magnitude of the decline was not exactly the same, all four markets were adversely affected. When institutional investors anticipated a general decline in stocks, they sold some stocks from all markets, instead of just the U.S. market.

Many stock markets experienced larger declines in prices than the United States' stock markets did. For example, during the month of October 1987, the U.S. market index declined by about 21 percent, while the German market index declined by about 23 percent and the United Kingdom index by 26 percent. The stock market indexes of Australia and Hong Kong decreased by more than 50 percent over this same month.

Some critics have suggested that the institutional forces in the United States (such as computer-assisted trading, specialists, and concurrent trading in stock index futures), along with the strong U.S. influence in the world, caused a worldwide crash. Yet, a study by Roll shows no evidence that the United States was the sole culprit.[1] Roll shows that during October 1987, countries' stock indices became more highly correlated than normal, which was likely due to some underlying factor that was capable of disrupting all markets. If computerized trading did not precipitate the

[1]Richard Roll, "The International Crash of October 1987," *Financial Analysts Journal* (October 1988), pp. 19–35.

Exhibit 3A.3
Integration Among Foreign Stock Markets During the 1987 Crash

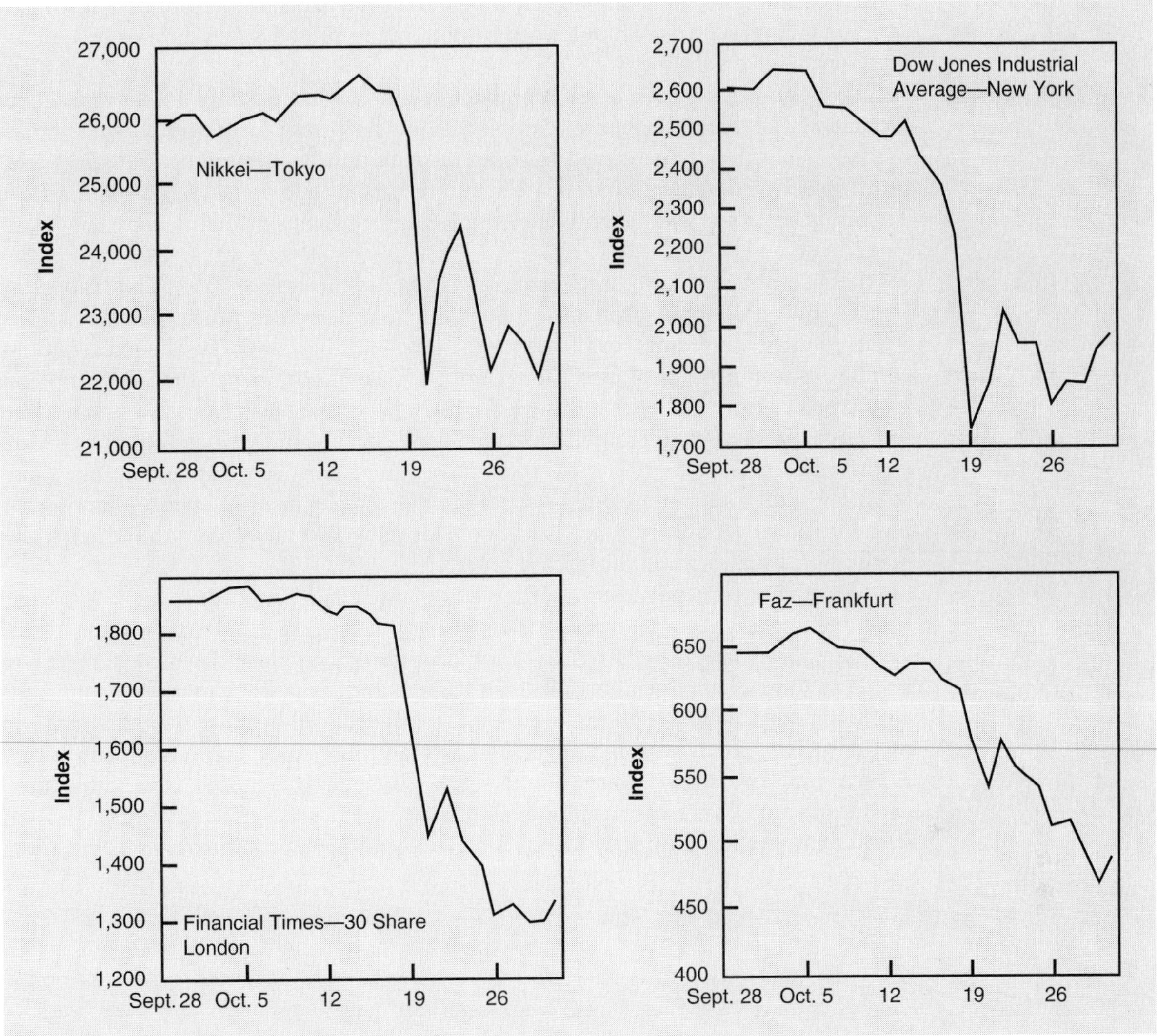

Source: *Economic Trends,* Federal Reserve Bank of Cleveland (November 1987), p. 17.

crash, however, it could have exacerbated it. Roll compared the markets in which computerized trading was prevalent during the 1987 crash (Canada, France, Japan, United Kingdom, United States) to other markets. In local currency terms, the five markets with computerized trading had an average decline of about 21 percent over October 1987, versus a 28-percent average decline for the other markets. This comparison suggests that computerized trading may even have reduced market volatility. Asian markets such as Hong Kong, Malaysia, and Singapore experienced substantial market declines on Black Monday (October 19, 1987) several hours before the U.S.

market even opened. In fact, other markets throughout Europe also experienced declines prior to the United States. It appears that the non-U.S. markets could have caused paranoia in the U.S. market, rather than the other way around. Thus, institutional factors such as computerized trading in the United States did not precipitate the worldwide crash.

Roll also assessed the possible impact of liquidity on declines across markets in October 1987. He used market capitalization as a proxy for liquidity, since larger markets are generally perceived as being more liquid. Roll found no statistical relationship between market capitalization and the magnitude of decline across markets. Therefore, liquidity did not influence market performance during the crash.

Market Movements During the Asian Crisis. In the summer of 1997, Thailand experienced severe economic problems, followed by economic downturns in several other Asian countries. Investors revalued stocks downward because of weakened economic conditions, more political uncertainty, and a lack of confidence that the problems would be resolved. The effects during the first year of the Asian crisis are summarized in Exhibit 3A.4. This crisis demonstrated how quickly stock prices could adjust to changing conditions and how adverse market conditions could spread across countries. Thus, diversification across Asia did not effectively insulate investors during the Asian crisis. Diversification across all continents would have been a more effective method of diversification during the crisis.

While there has not been another world stock market crash since 1987, there have been several mini-crashes. For example, on August 27, 1998 (referred to as "Bloody Thursday"), the Russian stock and currency values declined abruptly in response to severe financial problems in Russia, and most stock markets around the world experienced losses on that day. U.S. stocks declined by more than 4 percent on this day. The effects of some adverse events on most stock markets illustrate that even a well-diversified international stock portfolio is exposed to a substantial decline in value. In the case of Bloody Thursday, the adverse effects extended beyond stocks that would be directly affected by financial problems in Russia as paranoia

Exhibit 3A.4
How Stock Market Levels Changed During the Asian Crisis from a U.S. Perspective

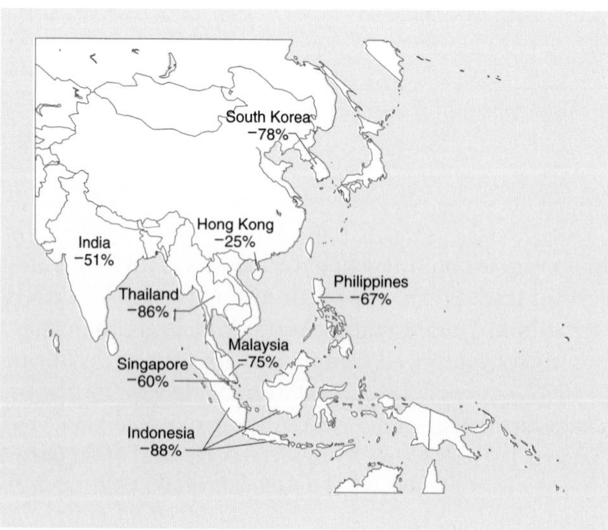

caused investors to sell stocks across all markets due to fears that all stocks might be overvalued.

Valuation of Foreign Stocks

When investors consider investing in foreign stocks, they need methods for valuing those stocks. First, they may attempt to use the dividend discount model, but with an adjustment to account for expected exchange rate movements. Foreign stocks pay dividends in the currency in which they are denominated. Thus, the cash flow per period to U.S. investors is the dividend (denominated in the foreign currency) multiplied by the value of that foreign currency in dollars. The dividend can normally be forecasted with more accuracy than the value of the foreign currency. Because of exchange rate uncertainty, the value of the foreign stock from a U.S. investor's perspective is subject to much uncertainty.

An alternative method of valuing foreign stocks is to apply price-earnings ratios. The expected earnings per share of the foreign firm are multiplied by the appropriate price-earnings ratio (based on the firm's risk and industry) to determine the appropriate price of the firm's stock. While the method is easy to use, it is subject to some limitations when applied to valuing foreign stocks. The price-earnings ratio for a given industry may change continuously in some foreign markets, especially when the industry is composed of just a few firms. Thus, it is difficult to determine the proper price-earnings ratio that should be applied to a specific foreign firm. In addition, the price-earnings ratio for any particular industry may need to be adjusted for the firm's country, since reported earnings can be influenced by the firm's accounting guidelines and tax laws. Furthermore, even if U.S. investors are comfortable with their estimate of the proper price-earnings ratio, the value derived by this method is denominated in the local foreign currency (since the estimated earnings are denominated in the local foreign currency). Therefore, U.S. investors would still need to consider exchange rate effects. Even if the stock is undervalued in the foreign country, it may not necessarily generate a reasonable return for U.S. investors if the foreign currency depreciates against the dollar.

A third method of valuing foreign stocks is to first focus on the country's macroeconomic conditions. Once the foreign country's economic conditions are assessed, any foreign firm within that country can be valued based on its sensitivity to the macroeconomic conditions. This method tends to allocate funds to stocks in those countries that are expected to experience strong economic conditions and is less focused on searching for individual stocks within a country that may be undervalued.

Some investors combine two or more methods when selecting foreign stocks. For example, they may first assess the macroeconomic conditions of all countries to screen out those countries that are expected to experience poor conditions in the future. Then, they can use other methods such as a dividend discount model or the price-earnings method to value specific firms within the countries that are appealing.

Methods Used to Invest Internationally

If investors attempt international stock diversification, there are five common approaches available:

- Direct purchases of foreign stocks
- Investment in MNC stocks

IN PRACTICE

INTERNATIONAL STOCK MARKET QUOTATIONS

International stock market prices are quoted for major stock markets each day in *The Wall Street Journal,* as shown here. For any given country, the stock index value is quoted, along with the percentage change in the index value (from the previous day) in the country's local currency (see the second and third columns).

DOW JONES GLOBAL INDEXES

5:30 p.m., Thursday, March 18, 1999

REGION/ COUNTRY	DJ GLOBAL INDEXES, LOCAL CURRENCY	PCT. CHG.	IN U.S. DOLLARS: 5:30 P.M. INDEX	CHG.	PCT. CHG.	12-MO HIGH	12-MO LOW	12-MO CHG.	PCT. CHG.	FROM 12/31	PCT. CHG.
Americas			**302.27**	**+3.94**	**+1.32**	**302.27**	**219.47**	**+45.39**	**+17.67**	**+18.49**	**+6.51**
Brazil†	1051	+2.51	216.24	+6.42	+3.06	489.24	155.25	−263.31	−54.91	−22.35	−9.37
Canada	199.34	−0.35	151.73	−0.28	−0.18	181.01	117.73	−21.94	−12.64	+5.48	+3.75
Chile	188.59	+0.41	144.49	+0.71	+0.49	183.88	96.32	−35.46	−19.71	+13.55	+10.35
Mexico	360.09	+0.23	114.67	+0.78	+0.68	136.26	60.60	−10.38	−8.30	+25.65	+28.81
U.S.	1246.50	+1.37	1246.50	+16.85	+1.37	1246.50	900.71	+213.61	+20.68	+77.16	+6.60
Venezuela	294.91	−0.93	31.37	−0.31	−0.98	78.54	23.01	−42.34	−57.44	−8.56	−21.44
Latin America			**137.73**	**+2.00**	**+1.47**	**221.07**	**90.39**	**−77.20**	**−35.92**	**+9.41**	**+7.33**
Europe/Africa			**232.52**	**−1.41**	**−0.60**	**251.61**	**185.07**	**+11.61**	**+5.26**	**−2.47**	**−1.05**
Austria	123.89	−0.48	105.54	−0.82	−0.77	141.18	93.22	−14.45	−12.04	+0.21	+0.20
Belgium	306.82	−0.80	261.60	−2.88	−1.09	307.75	212.28	+49.32	+23.23	−27.81	−9.61
Denmark	186.17	+0.98	162.85	+1.65	+1.02	210.95	156.84	−37.10	−18.55	−27.28	−14.35
Finland	871.45	−0.89	666.17	−7.94	−1.18	697.57	365.19	+253.41	+61.39	+61.65	+10.20
France	253.00	−0.33	219.21	−1.37	−0.62	238.23	173.04	+29.81	+15.74	−1.80	−0.82
Germany	280.22	−0.73	238.14	−2.45	−1.02	280.68	195.52	+16.59	+7.49	−9.87	−3.98
Greece	575.17	+0.73	344.93	+0.91	+0.26	344.93	169.27	+175.66	+103.78	+62.93	+22.32
Ireland	409.80	+0.14	341.05	−0.53	−0.16	369.89	247.45	+28.44	+9.10	+5.41	+1.61
Italy	330.37	+0.91	230.92	+1.43	+0.62	252.46	169.16	+35.43	+18.12	−3.51	−1.50
Netherlands	383.21	−0.06	325.70	−1.15	−0.35	366.66	258.60	+20.47	+6.71	−20.34	−5.88
Norway	163.06	+0.75	126.60	+1.83	+1.47	190.12	96.85	−47.67	−27.36	+10.48	+9.02
Portugal	345.67	−2.12	255.65	−6.28	−2.40	361.91	221.49	−52.89	−17.14	−42.25	−14.18
South Africa	183.54	−0.83	80.60	−1.13	−1.38	136.11	57.78	−36.35	−31.09	+9.89	+13.99
Spain	402.08	−0.77	258.64	−2.77	−1.06	293.48	194.86	+24.32	+10.38	−11.98	−4.43
Sweden	375.68	−1.74	257.20	−3.27	−1.26	317.82	190.08	−23.62	−8.41	+3.75	+1.48
Switzerland	407.33	−0.38	378.88	−3.37	−0.88	421.91	295.28	+12.83	+3.51	−17.05	−4.31
United Kingdom	232.86	−0.47	203.03	−0.98	−0.48	211.29	162.40	−0.04	−0.02	+4.45	+2.24
Europe/Africa (ex. South Africa)			**241.20**	**−1.42**	**−0.59**	**260.76**	**191.94**	**+14.39**	**+6.34**	**−3.19**	**−1.31**
Europe/Africa (ex. U.K. & S. Africa)			**265.14**	**−1.69**	**−0.63**	**292.44**	**210.59**	**+22.42**	**+9.24**	**−7.75**	**−2.84**
Asia/Pacific			**87.74**	**−1.42**	**−1.59**	**89.16**	**62.38**	**+4.28**	**+5.13**	**+6.71**	**+8.28**
Australia	185.65	−0.60	153.70	−0.19	−0.12	157.89	112.56	+11.14	+7.81	+12.68	+8.99
Hong Kong	211.26	−2.46	212.03	−5.33	−2.45	241.43	134.48	−22.75	−9.69	+7.97	+3.90
Indonesia	157.64	0.00	34.99	−0.02	−0.06	53.67	15.47	−4.94	−12.37	−5.46	−13.50
Japan	76.68	−2.41	81.45	−1.47	−1.77	82.92	57.38	+7.76	+10.54	+7.25	+9.77
New Zealand	139.82	−1.60	138.12	−0.13	−0.09	168.59	99.94	−27.91	−16.81	+8.72	+6.74
Philippines	191.46	+2.37	128.05	+3.00	+2.40	153.00	60.68	−18.13	−12.40	+0.77	+0.60
Singapore	111.02	−0.91	104.38	−0.81	−0.77	125.42	59.89	−21.04	−16.78	−5.02	−4.59
South Korea	98.32	−3.54	60.86	−2.10	−3.34	72.10	25.38	+15.99	+35.63	−0.37	−0.61
Taiwan	168.10	+2.06	130.83	+2.62	+2.04	168.59	106.17	−32.43	−19.87	+7.54	+6.11
Thailand	62.37	+1.23	39.31	+0.36	+0.92	52.94	20.88	−11.71	−22.96	−0.45	−1.13
Asia/Pacific (ex. Japan)			**136.72**	**−1.52**	**−1.10**	**150.29**	**91.45**	**−9.73**	**−6.64**	**+6.02**	**+4.61**
World (ex. U.S.)			**149.82**	**−1.28**	**−0.85**	**153.61**	**115.37**	**+4.13**	**+2.84**	**+2.81**	**+1.91**
DJ WORLD STOCK INDEX			**210.95**	**+0.69**	**+0.33**	**211.77**	**160.36**	**+21.70**	**+11.46**	**+8.16**	**+4.02**

Indexes based on 6/30/82=100 for U.S., 12/31/91=100 for World.
†Local currency index shown in 000s.

Source: Reprinted by permission of *The Wall Street Journal,* © 1999, Dow Jones & Company, Inc. All Rights Reserved Worldwide.

- American depository receipts (ADRs)
- World Equity Benchmark Shares (WEBS)
- International mutual funds (IMFs)

Each approach is discussed in turn.

Direct Purchases of Foreign Stocks. Foreign stocks could be purchased on foreign stock exchanges. This requires the services of brokerage firms that can contact floor brokers who work on the foreign stock exchange of concern. However, this approach is inefficient because of market imperfections such as insufficient information, transaction costs, and tax differentials among countries.

An alternative method of investing directly in foreign stocks is to purchase stocks of foreign companies that are sold on the local stock exchange. In the United States, for example, Royal Dutch Shell (of the Netherlands), Sony (of Japan), and many other foreign stocks are sold on U.S. stock exchanges. Because the number of foreign stocks listed on any local stock exchange is typically quite limited, this method by itself may not be adequate to achieve full benefits of international diversification.

Investment in MNC Stocks. The operations of an MNC represent international diversification. Like an investor with a well-managed stock portfolio, an MNC can reduce risk (variability in net cash flows) by diversifying sales not only among industries but also among countries. In this sense, the MNC as a single firm can achieve stability similar to that of an internationally diversified stock portfolio.

If MNC stocks behave like an international stock portfolio, then they should be sensitive to the stock markets of the various countries in which they operate. The sensitivity of returns of MNCs based in a particular country to specific international stock markets could be measured as:

$$\mathrm{R}_{MNC} = a_o + a_1\mathrm{R}_L + b_1\mathrm{R}_{I,1} + b_2\mathrm{R}_{I,2} + \ldots + b_n\mathrm{R}_{I,n} + u,$$

where R_{MNC} is the average return on a portfolio of MNCs from the same country, a_o is the intercept, R_L is the return on the local stock market, $\mathrm{R}_{I,1}$ through $\mathrm{R}_{I,n}$ are returns on foreign stock indices I_1 through I_n, and u is an error term. The regression coefficient a_1 measures the sensitivity of MNC returns to their local stock market, while coefficients b_1 through b_n measure the sensitivity of MNC returns to the various foreign stock markets. Studies have applied the time series regression model specified here, and found that MNCs based in a particular country were typically affected only by their respective local stock markets and were not affected by other stock market movements. This method does not achieve diversification benefits.

American Depository Receipts. Another approach is to purchase American depository receipts (ADRs), which are certificates representing ownership of foreign stocks. There are more than 1,000 ADRs available in the United States, primarily traded on the over-the-counter (OTC) stock market. Because most of these ADRs are not actively traded, their prices typically are not reported on a consistent basis. This may change over time, however, as they are becoming increasingly popular.

An investment in ADRs may be an adequate substitute for direct investment in foreign stocks. However, the limited number of ADRs available and the relatively high transaction costs may encourage some investors to use an alternative approach.

World Equity Benchmark Shares. While investors have closely monitored international stock indexes for years, they were typically unable to invest directly in these indexes. The index was simply a measure of performance for a set of stocks but was not traded. World equity benchmark shares (WEBS) represent indexes that reflect composites of stocks for particular countries; they have been created to allow investors to invest directly in a stock index representing any one of several countries. For example, investors could purchase WEBS if they wanted to invest in an index representing Mexico's stock market.

International Mutual Funds. A final approach to consider is purchasing shares of **international mutual funds (IMFs)**, which are portfolios of stocks from various countries. Several investment firms, such as Fidelity, Vanguard, and Merrill Lynch, have constructed IMFs for their customers. Like domestic mutual funds, IMFs are popular due to (1) the low minimum investment necessary to participate in the funds, (2) the presumed expertise of the portfolio managers, and (3) the high degree of diversification achieved by the portfolios' inclusion of several stocks. Yet, an IMF is often thought to be more capable of reducing risk than a purely domestic mutual fund, since it includes foreign securities. An IMF represents a prepackaged portfolio, so investors who use it do not need to construct their own portfolios. While some investors prefer to construct their own portfolios, the existence of numerous IMFs on the market today allows investors to select the one that most closely resembles the type of portfolio they would have constructed on their own. Moreover, there are some investors who feel more comfortable with a professional manager composing the international portfolio.

Exchange Rate Risk of Foreign Stocks

As the foreign currency denominating a foreign stock appreciates, the return to the investor is enhanced. However, if the foreign currency depreciates, the return is reduced. The volatility of exchange rates causes returns on foreign stocks to be volatile as well.

Reducing Exchange Rate Risk of Foreign Stocks. The exchange rate risk resulting from foreign stock holdings can be reduced by diversification among stocks of different countries. For example, a U.S. investor can reduce exchange rate risk by spreading whatever funds are to be used for foreign investments across various non-U.S. countries. If correlations between foreign currency movements (against the U.S. dollar) are low or negative, exchange rate risk can be effectively reduced through diversification.

Many foreign currencies move in tandem against the dollar, especially the European currencies (including the euro). Thus, if one of these currencies depreciates substantially against the dollar, the others will as well, and all foreign stocks denominated in these currencies will be adversely affected to a similar degree. Investors would achieve more effective diversification of currencies by spreading the foreign investment across continents.

Another method of reducing exchange rate risk is to take short positions in the foreign currencies denominating the foreign stocks. For example, a U.S. investor holding Mexican stocks who expects the stocks to be worth 10 million Mexican pesos one year from now could sell forward contracts (or futures contracts) representing 10 million pesos. The stocks could be liquidated at that time and the pesos could be exchanged for dollars at a locked-in price.

While hedging the exchange rate risk of an international stock portfolio can be effective, it has three limitations. First, the number of foreign currency units to be converted to dollars at the end of the investment horizon is unknown. If the units received from liquidating the foreign stocks are more (less) than the amount hedged, the investor has a net long (short) position in that foreign currency, and the return will be unfavorably affected by its depreciation (appreciation). Nevertheless, while investors may not perform a perfect hedge for this reason, they normally should be able to hedge most of their exchange rate risk.

A second limitation of hedging exchange rate risk is that the investors may decide to retain the foreign stocks beyond the initially planned investment horizon. Of course, they can create another short position after the initial short position is terminated. If they ever decide to liquidate the foreign stocks prior to the forward delivery date, the hedge will be less effective. They could use the proceeds to invest in foreign money market securities denominated in that foreign currency in order to postpone conversion to dollars until the forward delivery date. But this prevents them from using the funds for other opportunities until that delivery date.

A third limitation of hedging is that forward rates for some currencies may not exist or may exhibit a large discount. This limitation generally does not apply to the widely traded currencies.

4 EXCHANGE RATE DETERMINATION

Firms that conduct international business must continuously monitor exchange rates because their cash flows are highly dependent on them. This chapter provides a foundation for understanding how exchange rates are determined.

The specific objectives of this chapter are to

- explain how exchange rate movements are measured,
- explain how the equilibrium exchange rate is determined, and
- examine factors that affect the equilibrium exchange rate.

MEASURING EXCHANGE RATE MOVEMENTS

An exchange rate measures the value of one currency in units of another currency. As economic conditions change, exchange rates can change substantially. To illustrate, Exhibit 4.1 shows the value of the British pound over time. The percentage changes from year to year are displayed in the second graph. A decline in a currency's value is often referred to as **depreciation.** When the British pound depreciates against the U.S. dollar, this means that the U.S. dollar is strengthening relative to the pound. This increase in a currency value is often referred to as **appreciation.**

When the spot rates of two specific points in time are compared, the spot rate as of the more recent date is denoted as S and the spot rate as of the earlier date is denoted as S_{t-1}. The percentage change in the value of a foreign currency is computed as

$$\text{Percent } \Delta \text{ in foreign currency value} = \frac{S - S_{t-1}}{S_{t-1}}$$

A positive percentage change represents appreciation of the foreign currency, while a negative percentage change represents depreciation. Such large percentage changes in a currency as those annual percentage changes disclosed in Exhibit 4.1 would not normally exist on a daily or weekly basis. Yet, rates of change of as much as 5 percent have occurred over a 24-hour period for some currencies.

Exhibit 4.1
Fluctuation of the British Pound Value Over Time

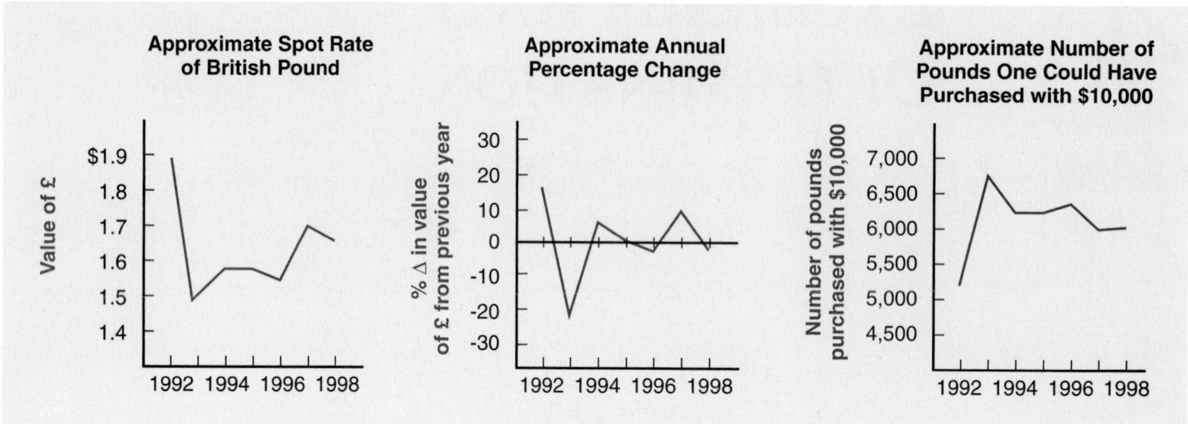

On some days, most foreign currencies appreciate against the dollar, although by different degrees. On other days, most currencies depreciate against the dollar, but by different degrees. There are also some days on which some currencies appreciate while others depreciate against the dollar; the media reports on this scenario by stating that "the dollar was *mixed* in trading."

Exchange Rate Equilibrium

While it is easy to measure the percentage change in the value of a currency, it is more difficult to explain why the value changed or to forecast how it may change in the future. To achieve either of these objectives, the concept of an **equilibrium exchange rate** must be understood, as well as the factors that affect the equilibrium rate.

Before considering why an exchange rate changes, realize that an exchange rate at a given point in time represents a *price* of a currency. Like any other products sold in markets, the price of a currency is determined by the demand for that currency relative to supply. Thus, for each possible price of a British pound, there would be a corresponding demand for pounds and a corresponding supply of pounds for sale. At any point in time, a currency should exhibit the price at which the demand for that currency is equal to supply, and this represents the equilibrium exchange rate. Of course, conditions can change over time, causing the supply or demand for a given currency to adjust, which would force movement in the currency's price. This topic is more thoroughly discussed in this section.

Demand for a Currency

The British pound is used here to explain exchange rate equilibrium. Since the United Kingdom has not adopted the euro as its currency, it continues to use the pound as its currency. Exhibit 4.2 shows a hypothetical number of pounds that would be demanded under various possibilities for the exchange rate. At any one point in time there is only one exchange rate. The exhibit shows the quantity of pounds that would be demanded for various exchange rates. The reason for the downward-sloping

Exhibit 4.2
Demand Schedule for British Pounds

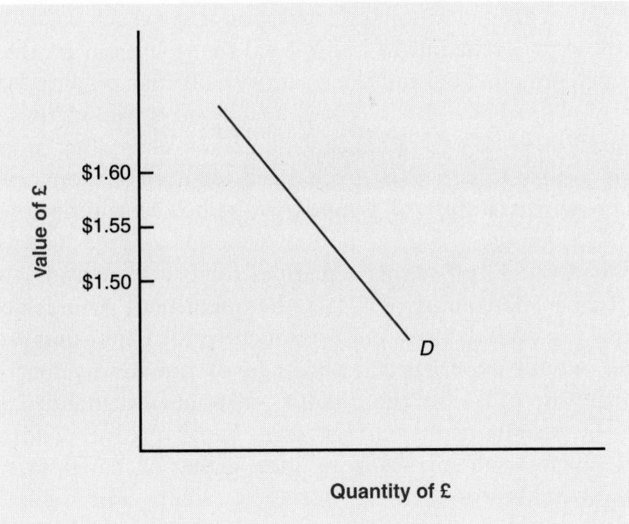

demand schedule is that U.S. corporations would be encouraged to purchase more British goods when the pound was worth less, since it would take fewer dollars to obtain the desired amount of pounds.

Supply of a Currency for Sale

Up to this point, only the U.S. demand for pounds has been considered, but the British demand for U.S. dollars must also be considered. This can be referred to as a British *supply of pounds for sale,* since pounds are supplied in the foreign exchange market in exchange for U.S. dollars.

A supply schedule of pounds for sale in the foreign exchange market can be developed in a manner similar to the method for the demand schedule for pounds. Exhibit 4.3 shows the quantity of pounds for sale (supplied to the foreign exchange

Exhibit 4.3
Supply Schedule of British Pounds for Sale

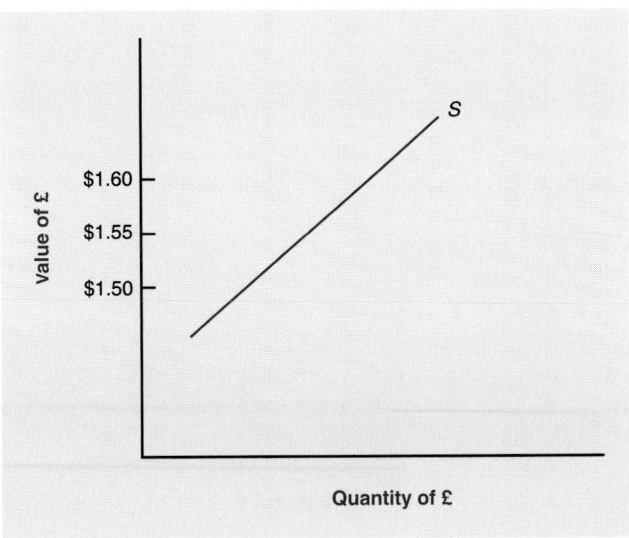

market in exchange for dollars) corresponding to each possible exchange rate. Notice from the supply schedule in Exhibit 4.3 that there is a positive relationship between the British pound value and the quantity of British pounds for sale (supplied), which can be explained as follows. When the pound is valued high, British consumers and firms are more likely to purchase U.S. goods. Thus, they supply a greater number of pounds to the market, to be exchanged for dollars. Conversely, when the pound is valued low, the supply of pounds for sale is less, reflecting less British desire to obtain U.S. goods.

The demand and supply schedules for British pounds are combined in Exhibit 4.4. At an exchange rate of $1.50, the quantity of pounds demanded would exceed the supply of pounds for sale. Consequently, the banks that provide foreign exchange services would experience a shortage of pounds at that exchange rate. At an exchange rate of $1.60, the quantity of pounds demanded would be less than the supply of pounds for sale. Therefore, banks providing foreign exchange services would experience a surplus of pounds at that exchange rate. According to Exhibit 4.4, the equilibrium exchange rate is presently $1.55, since this rate equates the quantity of pounds demanded to the supply of pounds for sale.

FACTORS THAT INFLUENCE EXCHANGE RATES

The equilibrium exchange rate will change over time as supply and demand schedules change. The factors that cause currency supply and demand schedules to change are discussed here by relating each factor's influence to the demand and supply schedules graphically displayed in Exhibit 4.4.

Relative Inflation Rates

Changes in relative inflation rates can affect international trade activity, which influences the demand and supply of currencies, and therefore influences exchange rates.

Exhibit 4.4
Equilibrium Exchange Rate Determination

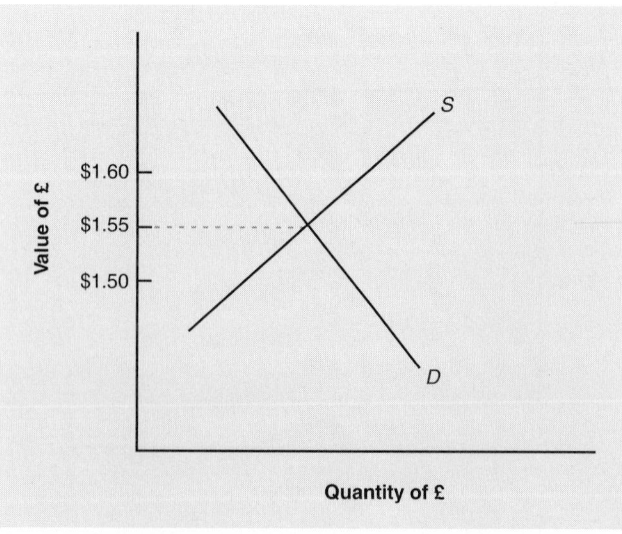

What would happen to the demand and supply schedules displayed in Exhibit 4.4 if U.S. inflation suddenly increased substantially while British inflation remained the same? (Assume that both British and U.S. firms sell goods that can serve as substitutes for each other.) The sudden jump in U.S. inflation should cause an increase in the U.S. demand for British goods and therefore also cause an increase in the U.S. demand for British pounds. In addition, the jump in U.S. inflation should reduce the British desire for U.S. goods and therefore reduce the supply of pounds for sale. These market reactions are illustrated in Exhibit 4.5. At the previous equilibrium exchange rate of $1.55, there would be a shortage of pounds in the foreign exchange market. The increased U.S. demand for pounds and the reduced supply of pounds for sale places upward pressure on the value of the pound. According to Exhibit 4.5, the new equilibrium value is $1.57.

In reality, the actual demand and supply schedules, and therefore the true equilibrium exchange rate, will reflect several factors simultaneously. The point of the preceding example is to logically work through the mechanics of the way higher inflation in a country can affect an exchange rate. Each factor is assessed one at a time to determine its separate influence on exchange rates, holding all other factors constant. Then, all factors can be tied together to fully explain why an exchange rate moves the way it does.

As another example, assume there is a sudden and substantial increase in British inflation while U.S. inflation is low. Based on this information, answer the following questions: (1) How is the demand schedule for pounds affected? (2) How is the supply schedule of pounds for sale affected? (3) Will the new equilibrium value of the pound increase, decrease, or remain unchanged? The answers based on the information given are (1) the demand schedule for pounds should shift inward, (2) the supply schedule of pounds for sale should shift outward, and (3) the new equilibrium value of the pound will decrease. Of course, the actual amount by which the pound value will decrease depends on the magnitude of the shifts. There is not enough information to determine the exact magnitude of shifts.

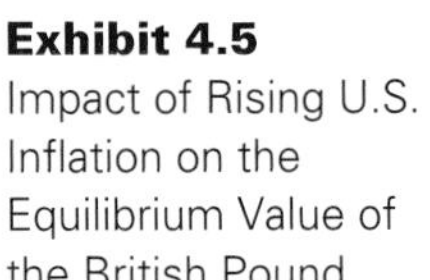

Exhibit 4.5
Impact of Rising U.S. Inflation on the Equilibrium Value of the British Pound

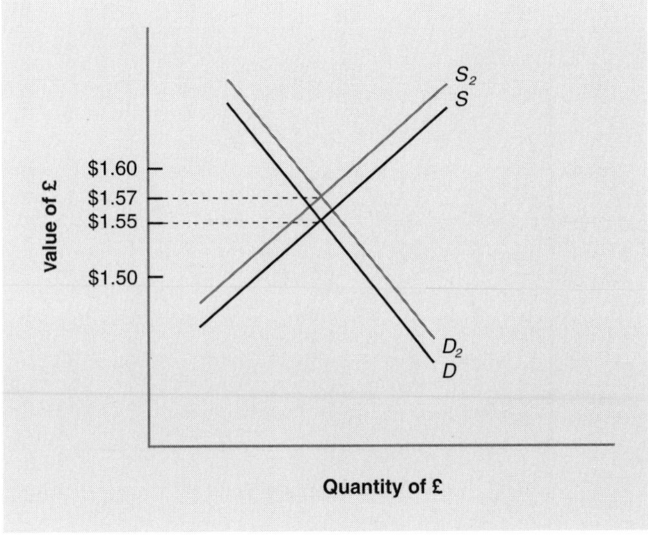

Relative Interest Rates

Changes in relative interest rates affect investment in foreign securities, which influences the demand and supply of currencies and therefore influences exchange rates. Assume that U.S. interest rates rise while British interest rates remain constant. In this case, U.S. corporations will likely reduce their demand for pounds, since the U.S. rates are now more attractive relative to British rates, and there is less desire for British bank deposits. Since U.S. rates will now look more attractive to British corporations with excess cash, the supply of pounds for sale by British corporations should increase as they establish more bank deposits in the United States. Due to an inward shift in demand for pounds and an outward shift in supply of pounds for sale, the equilibrium exchange rate should decrease. This is graphically represented in Exhibit 4.6. If U.S. interest rates decreased relative to British interest rates, we would expect the opposite shifts of those just stated.

In some cases, an exchange rate between two countries' currencies can be affected by changes in a third country's interest rate. For example, when the Canadian interest rate increases, it can become more attractive to British investors than the U.S. rate. This encourages British investors to purchase fewer dollar-denominated securities. That is, the supply of pounds to be exchanged for dollars would be smaller than it would have been without the increase in Canadian interest rates, which placed upward pressure on the value of pounds against the U.S. dollar.

http://
Visit www.bloomberg.com for the latest information from financial markets around the world.

Real Interest Rates. While a relatively high interest rate may attract foreign inflows (to invest in securities offering high yields), the relatively high interest rate may reflect expectations of relatively high inflation. Since high inflation can place downward pressure on the local currency, this may discourage some foreign investors from investing in securities denominated in that currency. For this reason, it is helpful to consider the **real interest rate,** which adjusts the nominal interest rate for inflation:

Real interest rate = Nominal interest rate – Inflation rate.

This relationship is sometimes called the Fisher effect.

Exhibit 4.6
Impact of Rising U.S. Interest Rates on the Equilibrium Value of the British Pound

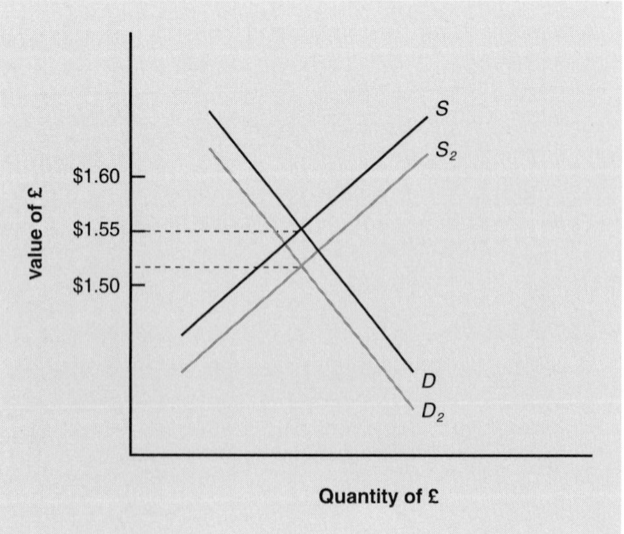

The real interest rate is commonly compared among countries to assess exchange rate movements because it combines nominal interest rates and inflation, both of which influence exchange rates. Other things held constant, there should be a high correlation between the real interest rate differential and the dollar's value.

To illustrate the potential impact of interest rates on exchange rates, in 1997 and 1998, long-term interest rates were less than 2 percent in Japan on an annualized basis versus between 6 and 7 percent in the United States. During this period, the Japanese yen depreciated substantially against the dollar, reaching a seven-year low as funds flowed from Japan to the United States to capitalize on the relatively high U.S. interest rates. The flow of funds caused a large supply of yen to be exchanged for dollars in the foreign exchange market over this period.

Relative Income Levels

A third factor affecting exchange rates is relative income levels. Assume that the U.S. income level substantially rises while the British income level remains unchanged. Consider the impact of this scenario on (1) the demand schedule for pounds, (2) the supply schedule of pounds for sale, and (3) the equilibrium exchange rate. First, the demand schedule for pounds will shift outward, reflecting an increase in U.S. income and therefore increased demand for British goods. Second, the supply schedule of pounds for sale is not expected to change. Therefore, the equilibrium exchange rate of the pound is expected to rise, as shown in Exhibit 4.7. When the indirect effect of changing income levels on exchange rates through effects on interest rates is considered, the impact may differ from the theory presented here, as will be explained shortly.

Government Controls

A fourth factor affecting exchange rates is government controls. The governments of foreign countries can influence the equilibrium exchange rate in many ways, including

Exhibit 4.7
Impact of Rising U.S. Income Levels on the Equilibrium Value of the British Pound

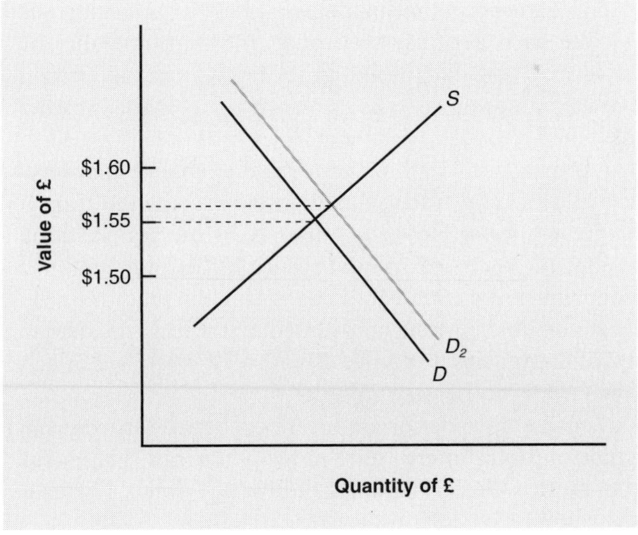

(1) the imposition of foreign exchange barriers, (2) the imposition of foreign trade barriers, (3) intervening (buying and selling currencies) in the foreign exchange markets, and (4) affecting macro variables such as inflation, interest rates, and income levels. Chapter 6 covers these methods in detail. At this point, one example will be given to illustrate potential governmental influence. Recall the example in which U.S. interest rates rose relative to British interest rates. The expected reaction was an increase in British supply of pounds for sale to obtain more U.S. dollars (in order to capitalize on high U.S. money market yields). Yet, if the British government placed a heavy tax on interest income earned by its people from foreign investments, this could discourage the exchange of pounds for dollars.

Expectations

A fifth factor affecting exchange rates is market expectations of future exchange rates. Like other financial markets, foreign exchange markets react to any news that may have a future effect. For example, news of a potential surge in U.S. inflation may cause currency traders to sell dollars, anticipating a future decline in the dollar's value. This response places immediate downward pressure on the dollar.

Many institutional investors (such as commercial banks and insurance companies) take currency positions based on anticipated interest rate movements in various countries. For example, they may temporarily invest funds in Canada if they expect Canadian interest rates to increase; such a rise may cause further capital flows into Canada, which could place upward pressure on the Canadian dollar's value. By taking a position based on expectations, they can fully benefit from the change in the Canadian dollar's value because they will have purchased Canadian dollars before the change occurred. While there is an obvious risk here that their expectations may be wrong, the point is that expectations can influence exchange rates because they commonly motivate institutional investors to take foreign currency positions.

During the Asian crisis in 1997 and 1998, many commercial banks around the world sold off Asian currencies in exchange for other currencies because they anticipated that the Asian currencies were overvalued. These actions placed downward pressure on the Asian currencies, and the commercial banks were criticized by some people for perpetuating the weakness of these currencies. However, when the banks take such actions, they push the market value of a currency toward its proper level. Thus, they make the foreign exchange market more efficient in that the market values of currencies adjust to relevant information that affects expectations.

The transactions within the foreign exchange markets facilitate either trade or financial flows. The trade-related foreign exchange transactions are generally less responsive to news. However, financial flow transactions are very responsive to news, since the decisions to hold securities denominated in a particular currency are often dependent on anticipated changes in currency values. To the extent that news affects anticipated currency movements, it affects the demand for currencies and the supply of currencies for sale. Because of such speculative transactions, foreign exchange rates can be very volatile.

Day-to-day speculation on future exchange rate movements is commonly driven by signals of future interest rate movements, but this speculation can also be driven by other factors. Some examples of how the dollar's value responded to speculation and the cause of speculation are described here.

Date	Status of Dollar	Explanation
October 24, 1991	Weakened	Economic indicators for U.S. were poor (causing an expected decline in future U.S. interest rates).
October 29, 1991	Weakened	U.S. consumer confidence indicators declined (causing an expected decline in future U.S. interest rates).
January 16, 1992	Weakened	Correction following a week-long rally (speculators believed there was an overreaction).
January 30, 1992	Strengthened	Federal Reserve Chairman Alan Greenspan suggests that the Fed is unlikely to cut U.S. interest rates.
July 15, 1992	Weakened	Expectations of a tight German monetary policy (could cause higher German interest rates).
April 19, 1993	Weakened	Foreign exchange market participants interpreted President Clinton's comments as a desire to weaken the dollar's value against the Japanese yen (to reduce the trade deficit with Japan).
June 15, 1993	Strengthened	Comments from the German central bank signaled a possible decline in German interest rates.
November 7, 1996	Strengthened	Comments from Japanese officials that the dollar should continue to strengthen against the Japanese yen.
August 26, 1998	Strengthened	Financial problems in Russia caused foreign exchange market participants to sell the Russian currency (the ruble) and other currencies of emerging markets in exchange for dollars.

http://
VIBES provides over 1,300 links to Internet sources of international business and economic information at www.uncc.edu/lis/library/reference/intbus/vibehome.htm.

Since signals of the future economic conditions that affect exchange rates can change quickly, the speculative positions in currencies may adjust quickly, causing unclear patterns in exchange rates. It is not unusual for the dollar to strengthen substantially on a given day, only to weaken substantially on the next day. This can occur when speculators overreact to news on one day (causing the dollar to be overvalued), which results in a correction during the next day. Overreactions occur because speculators are commonly taking positions based on signals of future actions (rather than the confirmation of actions), and these signals may be misleading.

Speculators can be especially influential on the exchange rate movements of emerging markets because those markets have a smaller amount of foreign exchange trading for other purposes (such as international trade) and therefore are less liquid than the larger markets. For example, the abrupt decline in the Russian ruble on some days during 1998 was partially attributed to speculative trading (although the decline may have occurred anyway over time). The decline in the ruble created a lack of confidence in other emerging markets as well and caused speculators to sell off other emerging market currencies, such as those of Poland and Venezuela.

Interaction of Factors

Trade-related factors and financial factors sometimes interact. For example, an increase in income levels sometimes causes expectations of higher interest rates. So even though a stronger income level can result in more imports, it may also indirectly attract more financial inflows (assuming interest rates increase). When considering the interaction, an increase in income levels is frequently expected to strengthen the local currency, because the favorable financial flows may overwhelm the unfavorable trade flows. Exhibit 4.8 separates payment flows between countries into trade-related and finance-related flows, and summarizes the factors that affect these flows.

Over a particular period, some factors may place upward pressure on the value of a foreign currency while other factors place downward pressure on the currency's value. For example, assume the simultaneous existence of (1) a sudden increase in U.S. inflation and (2) a sudden increase in U.S. interest rates. If the British economy were relatively unchanged, the increase in U.S. inflation would place upward pressure on the pound's value while the increase in U.S. interest rates would place downward pressure on the pound's value. The sensitivity of an exchange rate to these factors is dependent on the volume of international transactions between the two countries. If the two countries engage in a large volume of international trade but very small international capital flows, the relative inflation rates would likely be more influential. However, if the two countries engage in a large volume of capital flows, interest rate fluctuations may be most influential.

Example. Assume that Morgan Company, a U.S.-based multinational corporation (MNC), desires to forecast the direction of the Venezuela bolivar and Japanese yen, since it commonly purchases supplies from Venezuela and Japan. The following one-year projections have been developed for economic conditions by financial analysts of Morgan:

Exhibit 4.8
Summary of How Factors Can Affect Exchange Rates

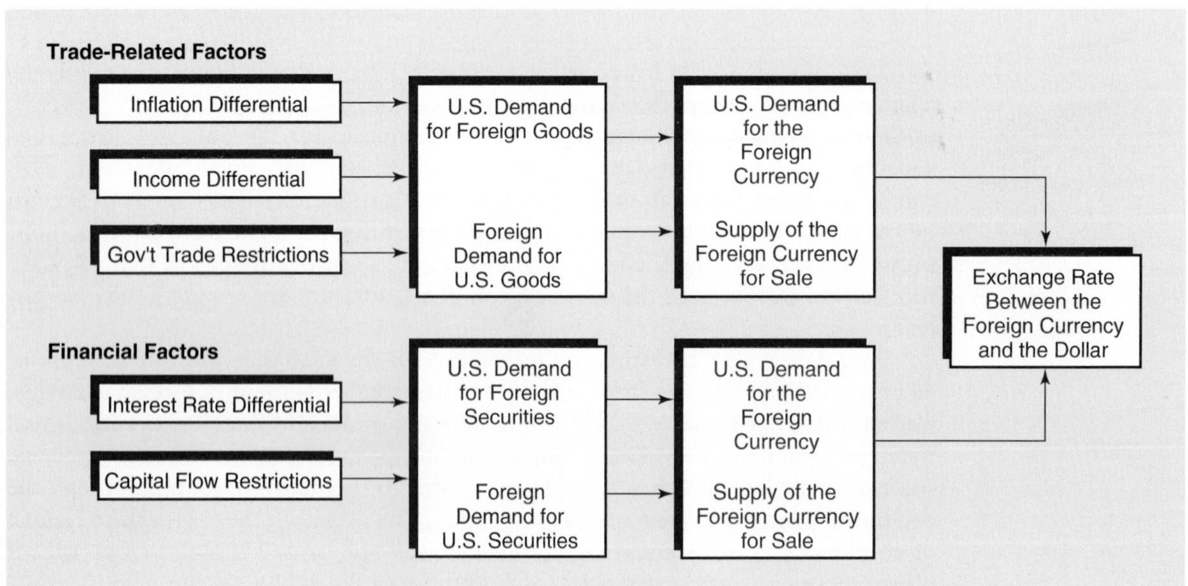

Factor	United States	Venezuela	Japan
Change in interest rates	–1%	–2%	–4%
Change in inflation	+2%	–3%	–6%

Assume that the United States and Venezuela conduct a large volume of international trade but engage in minimal capital flow transactions. Also assume that the United States and Japan conduct very little international trade but frequently engage in capital flow transactions. What should Morgan expect regarding the future value of the Venezuela bolivar and Japanese yen?

The bolivar should be influenced most by trade-related factors because of Venezuela's assumed heavy trade with the United States. The expected inflationary changes should place upward pressure on the value of the bolivar. Interest rates are not expected to have much of a direct impact on the bolivar because of the assumed infrequent capital flow transactions between the United States and Venezuela.

The Japanese yen should be most influenced by interest rates because of Japan's assumed heavy capital flow transactions with the United States. The expected interest rate changes should place downward pressure on the yen. The inflationary changes are not expected to have much of a direct impact on the yen because of the assumed infrequent trade between the two countries.

An understanding of exchange rate equilibrium does not guarantee accurate forecasts of future exchange rates since that will depend in part on how the factors that affect exchange rates will change in the future. Even if analysts fully realize how factors influence exchange rates, this does not mean they can predict how those factors will change.

How Factors Have Influenced Exchange Rates

http://
Visit the Fed's data bank at www.stls.frb.org/fred for numerous economic and financial time series, e.g., on balance of payment statistics, interest rates.

The dollar's value changes by different magnitudes relative to each foreign currency of concern. In many cases, analysts measure the dollar's general strength or weakness with an index. That is, several currencies are consolidated into a single composite. The weight assigned to each currency is determined by its relative importance in international trade and/or finance. For simplicity, most indexes are based on only the industrialized countries. However, an index representing currencies of the industrialized countries would not be useful for assessing how the dollar's changing value has affected trade with less developed countries (LDCs).

The value of a foreign currency index is illustrated over time in Exhibit 4.9. This exhibit shows that the major foreign currencies increased in value against the dollar in the late 1970s and decreased in value during the early 1980s. After the index reached its low point in 1985, it increased during the late 1980s and during the 1990s. By 1995, its value was almost twice that of 1985.

In the late 1970s, the dollar weakened against most currencies, primarily because of a relatively high U.S. inflation rate. In 1980, U.S. interest rates hit an all-time high that was at least partially due to the high U.S. inflation and growth in the late 1970s. The high interest rates caused a slowdown in the economy. While inflation was lowered, so was total spending. The combination of high U.S. interest rates, a somewhat depressed U.S. economy, and low inflation caused the dollar to strengthen against most currencies. It continued to strengthen throughout the early 1980s and often set all-time high records in 1984 and early 1985.

Exhibit 4.9
Value of Foreign Currency Index (with Respect to the Dollar) Over Time

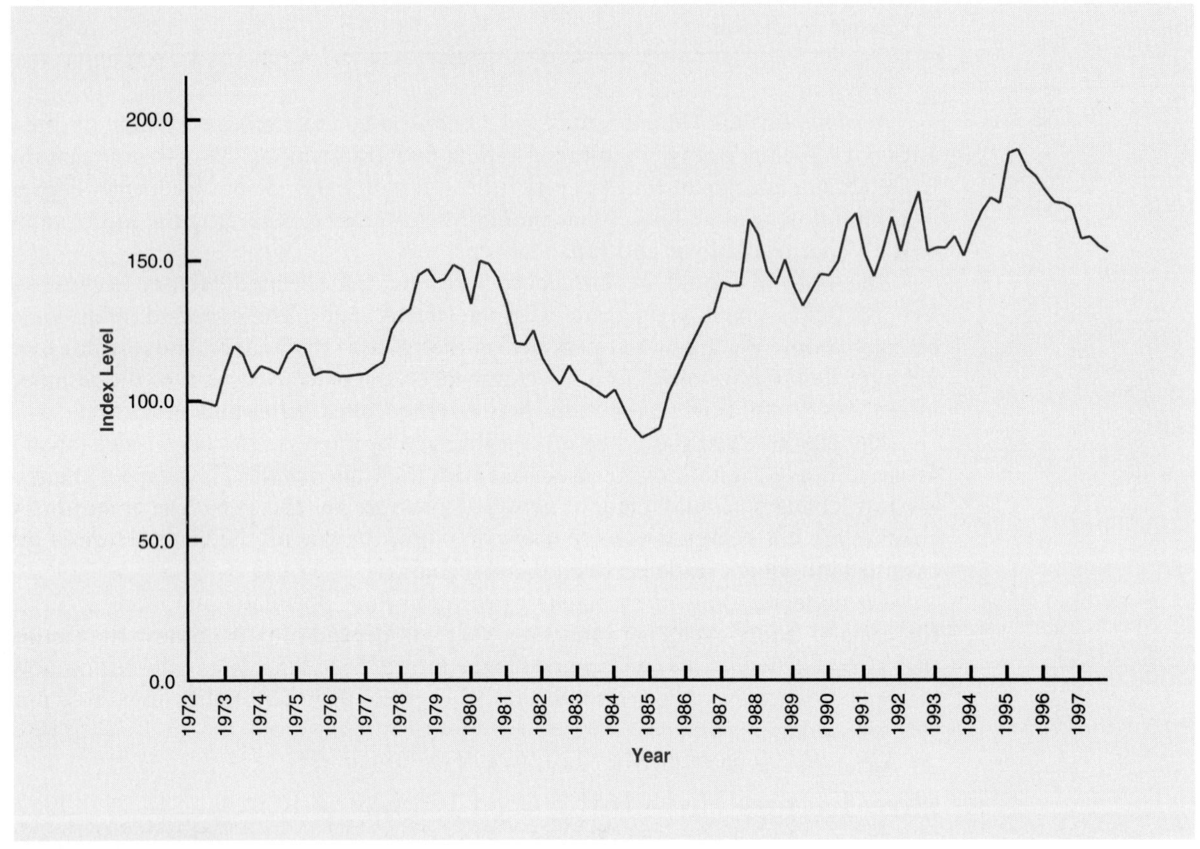

Note: The index reflects movements in the British pound, French franc, German mark, Japanese yen, and Swiss franc; the index is based on equal weights applied to these currencies.

http://
Visit www.ny.frb.org/pihome/mktrates for current and historic exchange rates.

The dollar's value declined consistently from 1985 to 1988, mainly because of the large balance of trade deficit during that period. In 1989, the dollar strengthened as relatively high U.S. interest rates had attracted capital inflows from foreign countries. In addition, the U.S. balance of trade deficit had declined.

In 1990, the dollar weakened during the Persian Gulf War. The weakness was partially attributed to expectations of higher oil prices and therefore higher U.S. inflation. It strengthened as the war ended but resumed its decline in late 1991 and 1992 as U.S. interest rates declined. However, by 1998, the dollar had regained much of the strength that it lost in the early 1990s.

Speculating on Anticipated Exchange Rates

Many commercial banks attempt to capitalize on their speculation of anticipated exchange rate movements. To illustrate how a bank may attempt to capitalize on the expected change in a currency's value, assume the following:

- Chicago Bank expects the exchange rate of the New Zealand dollar (NZ$) to appreciate from its present level of $.50 to $.52 in 30 days.
- Chicago Bank is able to borrow $20 million on a short-term basis from other banks.
- Present short-term interest rates (annualized) in the interbank market are as follows:

Currency	Lending Rate	Borrowing Rate
U.S. Dollars	6.72%	7.20%
New Zealand dollars (NZ$)	6.48%	6.96%

Because brokers sometimes serve as intermediaries between banks, the lending rate differs from the borrowing rate. Given the information, Chicago Bank could

1. Borrow $20 million.
2. Convert the $20 million to NZ$40 million (computed as $20,000,000/$.50).
3. Lend the New Zealand dollars at 6.48 percent annualized, which represents a .54 percent return over the 30-day period [computed as 6.48% × (30/360)]. After 30 days, the bank would receive NZ$40,216,000 [computed as NZ$40,000,000 × (1 + .0054)].
4. Use the proceeds of the New Zealand dollar loan repayment (on Day 30) to repay the dollars borrowed. The annual interest on the U.S. dollars borrowed is 7.2 percent, or .6 percent over the 30-day period [computed as 7.2% × (30/360)]. The total U.S. dollar amount necessary to repay the loan is therefore $20,120,000 [computed as $20,000,000 × (1 + .006)].

Assuming that the exchange rate on Day 30 is $.52 per New Zealand dollar as anticipated, the number of New Zealand dollars necessary to repay the dollar loan is NZ$38,692,308 (computed as $20,120,000/$.52 per New Zealand dollar). Given that the bank accumulated NZ$40,216,000 from its New Zealand dollar loan, it would earn a speculative profit of NZ$1,523,692, which is the equivalent of $792,320 (given a spot rate of $.52 per New Zealand dollar on Day 30). This speculative profit would be earned by the bank without using any funds from deposit accounts, since the funds would have been borrowed through the interbank market.

If Chicago Bank expected that the New Zealand dollar would depreciate, it could attempt to make a speculative profit by taking positions opposite to those described in the previous example. To illustrate, assume that the bank expects an exchange rate of $.48 for the New Zealand dollar on Day 30. It could borrow New Zealand dollars, convert them to U.S. dollars, and lend the U.S. dollars out. On Day 30, it could close out these positions. Using the rates quoted in the previous example, and assuming the bank can borrow NZ$40 million, the following steps could be taken:

1. Borrow NZ$40 million.
2. Convert the NZ$40 million to $20 million (computed as NZ$40,000,000 × $.50).
3. Lend the U.S. dollars at 6.72 percent, which represents a .56 percent return over the 30-day period. After 30 days, the bank would receive $20,112,000 [computed as $20,000,000 × (1 + .0056)].

Nike Problem

Factors That May Be Considered When Assessing Exchange Rates

Since Nike has international business in numerous countries, it closely monitors exchange rate movements. In particular, Nike has major business in Japan and in the United Kingdom. It has even begun to sell its shoes in Eastern European countries. Nike recognizes that it must monitor movements in currencies that were not allowed to fluctuate in the past. It has also recently expanded its business in Latin America, where currencies can be quite volatile.

Discussion: What specific factors do you think Nike considers when determining how the value of the Japanese yen may change in the near future? Would it consider the same factors when determining how the value of the Czech Republic's currency (the koruna)?

4. Use the proceeds of the U.S. dollar loan repayment (on Day 30) to repay the New Zealand dollars borrowed. The annual interest on the New Zealand dollars borrowed is 6.96 percent, or .58% over the 30-day period [computed as 6.96 × (30/360)]. The total New Zealand dollars necessary to repay the loan is therefore NZ$40,232,000 [computed as NZ$40,000,000 × (1 + .0058)].

Assuming that the exchange rate on Day 30 is $.48 per New Zealand dollar as anticipated, the number of U.S. dollars necessary to repay the NZ$ loan is $19,311,360 (computed as NZ$40,232,000 × $.48 per New Zealand dollar). Given that the bank accumulated $20,112,000 from its U.S. dollar loan, it would earn a speculative profit of $800,640 without using any of its own money (computed as $20,112,000 – $19,311,360).

Most money center banks continue to take some speculative positions in foreign currencies. In fact, some banks' currency trading profits have averaged over $100 million per quarter in the 1990s.

Banks may attempt to speculate in the foreign exchange market. The potential return from foreign currency speculation is high for banks that have large borrowing capacity. Yet, foreign exchange rates are very volatile, and a poor forecast could result in a large loss. One of the best known bank failures, Franklin National Bank in 1974, was primarily attributed to massive speculative losses from foreign currency positions.

How Exchange Rates Affect an MNC's Value

The manner by which exchange rate determination affects unhedged cash flows of an MNC is shown in Exhibit 4.10. A higher foreign inflation rate tends to place downward pressure on a foreign currency's value, which reduces the expected dollar cash flows received by a U.S.-based parent. A higher foreign interest rate tends to place upward pressure on the foreign currency and can therefore have a favorable effect on expected dollar cash flows.

These statements do not consider the effects that those factors can have on the economic growth of the foreign country and therefore the demand for the MNC's products and the expected cash flows in that foreign currency (CF_f). Nevertheless, the

Exhibit 4.10
Impact of Factors That Influence Exchange Rates on an MNC's Value

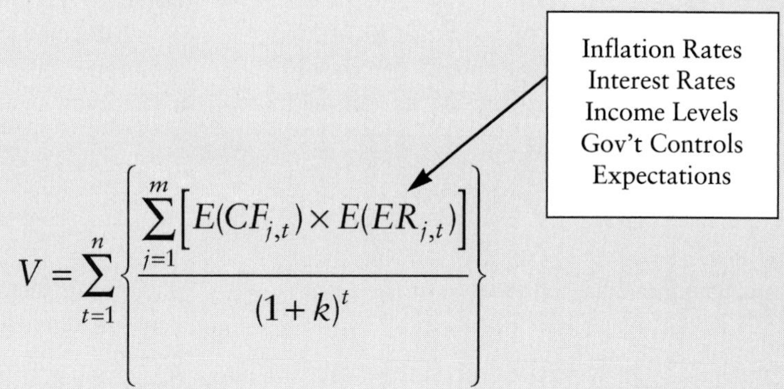

V = value of the U.S.-based MNC
$E(CF_{j,t})$ = expected cash flows denominated in currency j to be received by the U.S. parent in period t
$E(ER_{j,t})$ = expected exchange rate at which currency j can be converted to dollars at the end of period t
k = the weighted average cost of capital of the U.S. parent company
m = number of currencies
n = number of periods

concepts in this chapter can be assessed by an MNC to determine how a spot rate of a foreign currency remitted to the parent will change because of expectations about economic conditions in that country versus the United States. This information is useful as partial input when assessing how these conditions will affect the value of the MNC.

SUMMARY

- Exchange rate movements are commonly measured by the percentage change in their values over a specified period, such as a month or a year. MNCs closely monitor exchange rate movements over the period in which they have cash flows denominated in the foreign currencies of concern.
- The equilibrium exchange rate between two currencies at any point in time is based on the demand and supply conditions. Changes in the demand for a currency or the supply of a currency for sale will affect the equilibrium exchange rate.
- The key economic factors that can influence exchange rate movements through their effects on demand and supply conditions are relative inflation rates, interest rates, and income levels, as well as government controls. As these factors cause a change in international trade or financial flows, they affect the demand for a currency or the supply of currency for sale and therefore affect the equilibrium exchange rate.
- The two factors that are most closely monitored by foreign exchange market participants are relative inflation and interest rates. If a foreign country experiences high inflation (relative to the United States), its exports to the United States should decrease (U.S. demand for its currency decreases), its imports should increase (supply of its currency to be exchanged for dol-

lars increases), and there is downward pressure on its currency's equilibrium value.

If a foreign country experiences an increase in interest rates (relative to U.S. interest rates), the inflow of U.S. funds to purchase its securities should increase (U.S. demand for its currency increases), the outflow of its funds to purchase U.S. securities should decrease (supply of its currency to be exchanged for U.S. dollars decreases), and there is upward pressure on its currency's equilibrium value.

All relevant factors must be considered simultaneously to assess the likely movement in a currency's value.

SELF-TEST FOR CHAPTER 4

(Answers are provided in Appendix A at the back of the text.)

1. Briefly describe how various economic factors can affect the equilibrium exchange rate of the Japanese yen's value with respect to that of the dollar.
2. A recent shift in the interest rate differential between the United States and Country A had a large effect on the value of Currency A. However, the same shift in the interest rate differential between the United States and Country B had no effect on the value of Currency B. Explain why the effects may vary.
3. Smart Banking Corp. can borrow $5 million at 6% annualized. It can use the proceeds to invest in Canadian dollars at 9% annualized over a six-day period. The Canadian dollar is worth $.95 and is expected to be worth $.94 in six days. Based on this information, should Smart Banking Corp. borrow U.S. dollars and invest in Canadian dollars? What would be the gain or loss in U.S. dollars?

QUESTIONS AND APPLICATIONS

1. Assume the spot rate of the British pound is $1.73. The expected spot rate one year from now is assumed to be $1.66. What percentage depreciation does this reflect?
2. Assume the U.S. inflation rate becomes high relative to Canadian inflation. Other things being equal, how should this affect the (a) U.S. demand for Canadian dollars, (b) supply of Canadian dollars for sale, and (c) equilibrium value of the Canadian dollar?
3. Assume the U.S. interest rates fall relative to British interest rates. Other things being equal, how should this affect the (a) U.S. demand for British pounds, (b) supply of pounds for sale, and (c) equilibrium value of the pound?
4. Assume the U.S. income level rises at a much higher degree than does the Canadian income level. Other things being equal, how should this affect the (a) U.S. demand for Canadian dollars, (b) supply of Canadian dollars for sale, and (c) equilibrium value of the Canadian dollar?
5. Assume the Japanese government relaxes its controls on imports by Japanese companies. Other things being equal, how should this affect the (a) U.S. demand for Japanese yen, (b) supply of yen for sale, and (c) equilibrium value of the yen?
6. What is the expected relationship between the relative real interest rates of two countries and the exchange rate of their currencies?
7. Explain the recent trend in the dollar's value.
8. Explain why a public forecast by a respected economist about future interest rates could affect the value of the dollar today. Why do some forecasts by well-respected economists have no impact on today's value of the dollar?
9. Assume that substantial capital flows occur between the United States, Country A, and Coun-

try B, in all directions. If interest rates in Country A declined, how could this affect the value of Currency A against the dollar? How might this decline in Country A's interest rates possibly affect the value of Currency B against the dollar?

10. Tarheel Company plans to determine how changes in U.S. and Mexican real interest rates will affect the value of the U.S. dollar. (See Appendix C.)

    a. Describe a regression model that could be used to achieve this objective. Also explain the expected sign of the regression coefficient.
    b. If Tarheel Company thought that the existence of a quota in particular historical periods may have affected exchange rates, how might this be accounted for in the regression model?

11. What factors affect the future movements in the € value of the euro against the dollar?

12. Blue Demon Bank expects that the Chinese currency (the yuan) will depreciate against the dollar from its spot rate of $.15 to $.14 in 10 days. The following interbank lending and borrowing rates exist:

	Lending Rate	Borrowing Rate
U.S. dollar	8.0%	8.3%
Chinese yuan	8.5%	8.7%

    Assume that Blue Demon Bank has a borrowing capacity of either $10 million or 70 million yuan in the interbank market, depending on which currency it wants to borrow.

    a. How could Blue Demon Bank attempt to capitalize on its expectations without using deposited funds? Estimate the profits that could be generated from this strategy.
    b. Assume all the preceding information, with this exception: Blue Demon Bank expects the yuan to appreciate from its present spot rate of $.15 to $.17 in 30 days. How could it attempt to capitalize on its expectations without using deposited funds? Estimate the profits that could be generated from this strategy.

13. Assume that the United States heavily invests in government and corporate securities of Country K. In addition, residents of Country K heavily invest in the United States. Approximately $10 billion worth of investment transactions occur between these two countries each year. The total dollar value of trade transactions per year is about $8 million. This information is expected to also hold in the future.

    Because your firm exports goods to Country K, your job as international cash manager requires you to forecast the value of Country K's currency (the "krank") with respect to the dollar. Explain how each of the following conditions will affect the value of the krank, holding other things equal. Then, aggregate all of these impacts to develop an overall forecast of the krank's movement against the dollar.

    a. U.S. inflation has suddenly increased substantially, while Country K's inflation remains low.
    b. U.S. interest rates have increased substantially, while Country K's interest rates remain low. Investors of both countries are attracted to high interest rates.
    c. The U.S. income level has increased substantially, while Country K's income level has remained unchanged.
    d. The United States is expected to place a small tariff on goods imported from Country K.
    e. Combine all expected impacts to develop an overall forecast.

14. Every month, the U.S. trade deficit figures are announced. The foreign exchange traders often react to this announcement and even attempt to forecast the figures before they are announced.

    a. Why do you think the trade deficit announcement sometimes has such an impact on foreign exchange trading?
    b. In some periods, foreign exchange traders do not respond to a trade deficit announcement, even when the announced deficit is

very large. Offer an explanation for such a lack of response.

15. Explain why the value of the British pound against the dollar will not always move in tandem with the value of the euro against the dollar.

16. The currencies of some Latin American countries depreciate against the U.S. dollar on a daily basis. What do you think is the major factor that places such severe downward pressure on the value of these currencies? What obvious change in Latin American economic policy is needed to prevent further depreciation of Latin American currencies?

17. In the early 1990s, Russia was attempting to import more goods but had little to offer other countries in terms of potential exports. In addition, Russia's inflation rate was high. Explain the type of pressure that these factors placed on the Russian currency.

18. Analysts commonly attribute the appreciation of a currency to expectations that economic conditions will strengthen. Yet, this chapter suggests that when other factors are held constant, increased national income could increase imports and cause the local currency to weaken. In reality, other factors are not constant. What other factor is likely to be affected by increased economic growth, which could place upward pressure on the value of the local currency?

19. Mexico tends to have much higher inflation than the United States and also much higher interest rates than the United States. The inflation and interest rates are much more volatile in Mexico than in industrialized countries. The value of the Mexican peso is typically more volatile than the currencies of industrialized countries from a U.S. perspective; it has typically depreciated from one year to the next, but the degree of depreciation has varied substantially. The bid/ask spread tends to be wider for the peso than currencies in industrialized countries.

    a. Identify the most obvious economic reason for the persistent depreciation in the value of the peso.
    b. High interest rates are commonly expected to strengthen a country's currency because they can encourage foreign investment in securities in that country, which results in the exchange of other currencies for that currency. Yet, the peso's value has declined against the dollar over most years even though the Mexican interest rates are typically much higher than the U.S. interest rates. Thus, it appears that the high Mexican interest rates do not attract substantial U.S. investment in Mexico's securities. Why do you think U.S. investors do not try to capitalize on the high interest rates in Mexico?
    c. Why do you think the bid/ask spread is higher for pesos than for currencies of industrialized countries? How does this affect a U.S. firm that does substantial business in Mexico?

20. If the Asian countries experience a decline in economic growth (and therefore experience a decline in inflation and interest rates as a result), how will their currency values (relative to the U.S. dollar) be affected?

21. Why do you think most crises in countries (such as the Asian crisis) cause their local currency to weaken abruptly? Is it because of trade flows or capital flows?

Internet Application

22. The Web site of the Federal Reserve Bank of St. Louis provides exchange rate trends of various currencies. Its address is:

    www.stls.frb.org

    a. Use this Web page to determine how exchange rates of various currencies have changed in recent months. Note that most of these currencies (except the British pound) are quoted in units per dollar. In general, have most currencies strengthened or weakened against the dollar over the last three months? Offer one or more reasons to explain the general movements in currency values against the dollar recently.
    b. Does it appear that the Asian currencies move in the same direction relative to the dollar? Does it appear that the Latin American currencies move in the same direction against the dollar? Explain.

Running Your Own MNC

Monitoring Movements in the Foreign Currency's Value

23. What key factors likely affect the value of the foreign currency of concern over time? For each factor that is expected to affect the foreign currency's value, describe the manner by which this factor affects the value.

Blades, Inc. Case

Assessment of Future Exchange Rate Movements

As the chief financial officer of Blades, Inc., Ben Holt is pleased that his current system of exporting "Speedos" to Thailand seems to be working well. Blades' primary customer in Thailand, a retailer called Entertainment Products, has committed itself to purchasing a fixed number of Speedos annually for the next three years at a fixed price denominated in baht, Thailand's currency. Furthermore, Blades is using a Thai supplier for some of the components needed to manufacture Speedos. Mr. Holt is, however, concerned with the recent developments in Asia. Foreign investors from various countries had invested heavily in Thailand to take advantage of the high interest rates there. As a result of the Asian crisis, however, many foreign investors have lost their confidence in Thailand and have withdrawn their funds.

Ben Holt has two major concerns regarding these developments. First, he is wondering how these changes in Thailand's economy could affect the value of the Thai baht and, consequently, Blades. More specifically, he is wondering whether the effects on the Thai baht may affect Blades even though its primary Thai customer is committed to Blades over the next three years.

Second, Ben Holt believes that Blades may be able to speculate on the anticipated movement of the baht. Yet, he is uncertain about the procedure needed to accomplish this. To facilitate Mr. Holt's understanding of exchange rate speculation, he has asked you, Blades' financial analyst, to provide him with detailed illustrations of two scenarios. In the first, the baht would move from a current level of $0.022 to $0.020 within the next 30 days. Under the second scenario, the baht would move from its current level to $0.025 within the next 30 days.

Based on Mr. Holt's needs, he has provided you with the following list of questions to be answered:

1. How are percentage changes in a currency's value measured? Illustrate your answer numerically by assuming a change in the Thai baht's value from a value of $0.022 to $0.026.
2. What are the basic factors that determine the value of a currency? In equilibrium, what is the relationship between these factors?
3. If the baht had not been linked to the U.S. dollar in the early 1990s, how would the relatively high levels of inflation and interest rates have affected its value? (Assume a constant level of U.S. inflation and interest rates.)
4. How do you think the loss of confidence in the Thai baht, evidenced by the withdrawal of funds from Thailand, affected the baht's value? Would Blades be affected by the change in value, given the primary Thai customer's commitment?
5. Assume that Thailand's central bank wishes to prevent a withdrawal of funds from its country in order to prevent further changes in the currency's value. How could it accomplish this objective using interest rates?
6. Construct a spreadsheet illustrating the steps Blades' treasurer would need to follow in order to speculate on expected movements in the baht's value over the next 30 days. Also show the speculative profit (in dollars) resulting from each scenario. Use both of Ben Holt's examples to illustrate possible speculation. Assume that

Blades can borrow either $10 million or the baht equivalent of this amount. Furthermore, assume that the following short-term interest rates (annualized) are available to Blades:

Currency	Lending Rate	Borrowing Rate
Dollars	8.10%	8.20%
Thai baht	14.80%	15.40%

Small Business Dilemma

Assessment by the Sports Exports Company of Factors That Affect the British Pound's Value

Since the Sports Exports Company (a U.S. firm) receives payments in British pounds every month and converts those pounds into dollars, it needs to closely monitor the value of the British pound in the future. Jim Logan, owner of the Sports Exports Company, expects that inflation will rise substantially in the United Kingdom, while inflation in the United States will remain low. He also expects that the interest rates in both countries will rise by about the same amount.

1. Given Jim's expectations, forecast whether the pound will appreciate or depreciate against the dollar over time.

2. Given Jim's expectations, will the Sports Exports Company be favorably or unfavorably affected by the future changes in the value of the pound?

5 CURRENCY DERIVATIVES

This chapter is devoted entirely to currency derivatives, often used by speculators interested in trading currencies simply to achieve profits but also used by firms to cover their foreign currency positions. Since firms commonly use currency derivatives, it is important to understand the background of these derivatives and how they can help achieve corporate goals.

The specific objectives of this chapter are to

- explain how forward contracts are used to hedge based on anticipated exchange rate movements,
- explain how currency futures contracts are used to speculate or hedge based on anticipated exchange rate movements, and
- explain how currency options contracts are used to speculate or hedge based on anticipated exchange rate movements.

FORWARD MARKET

The forward market facilitates the trading of forward contracts on currencies. A **forward contract** is an agreement between a corporation and a commercial bank to exchange a specified amount of a currency at a specified exchange rate (called the **forward rate**) on a specified date in the future. When multinational corporations (MNCs) anticipate future need or future receipt of a foreign currency, they can set up forward contracts to lock in the rate at which they can purchase or sell a particular foreign currency. Virtually all MNCs use forward contracts. Some MNCs, such as CPC International and TRW, have forward contracts outstanding worth more than $100 million to hedge various positions.

Because forward contracts accommodate large corporations, the forward transaction will often be valued at $1 million or more. Forward contracts are not normally used by consumers or small firms. In some cases, a bank may request an initial deposit by the corporation to assure that it will fulfill its obligation. In other cases, the bank may fully trust the corporation and will not require an initial deposit.

How MNCs Use Forward Contracts

Consider a firm that will need 1,000,000 Singapore dollars in 90 days to purchase Singapore imports. Assume that it can buy Singapore dollars for immediate delivery at the spot rate of $.50 per Singapore dollar (S$). At this spot rate, the firm would need $500,000 (computed as S$1,000,000 × $.50 per Singapore dollar). However, it may not have the funds right now to exchange for Singapore dollars. It could wait 90 days and then exchange dollars for Singapore dollars at the spot rate existing at that time. Yet, the firm does not know what the spot rate will be at that time. If the rate rises to $.60 by then, the firm will need $600,000 (computed as S$1,000,000 × $.60 per Singapore dollar). This represents an additional outlay of $100,000 due simply to the firm's waiting 90 days to make payment. Clearly, if the firm had known that the Singapore dollar value was going to rise to $.60, it would have purchased the Singapore dollars 90 days earlier just to avoid the additional expense. Even if the firm did not have the money at the time, it would have been better off borrowing U.S. dollars and using those dollars to buy the Singapore dollars.

A preferable situation would be for a firm to be able to lock in the rate it will pay for Singapore dollars 90 days from now without having to exchange dollars for Singapore dollars immediately. This is exactly what the forward contract can do. Specifically, the firm would have contacted a bank to purchase S$1,000,000 ninety days forward. The most common forward contracts are for 30, 60, 90, 180, and 360 days, although other periods (including longer periods) are available. The forward rate of a given currency will typically vary with the length (number of days) of the forward period.

Corporations also use the forward market to lock in the rate at which they can sell foreign currencies. This strategy is used to hedge against the possibility of those currencies depreciating over time.

As with the case of spot rates, there is a bid/ask spread on forward rates. For example, a given bank may have set up a contract with one firm where it will sell the firm Singapore dollars 90 days from now at $.510 per Singapore dollar. This represents the ask rate. At the same time, it may have agreed to purchase (bid) Singapore dollars 90 days from now from some other firm at $.505 per Singapore dollar.

Forward contracts are even available at some banks on currencies of developing countries, such as Chile, Mexico, South Korea, Taiwan, and Thailand. Since these markets have relatively few orders for forward contracts, banks are less able to match up willing buyers and sellers. This lack of liquidity causes banks to widen the bid/ask spread when quoting forward contracts. The contracts in these countries are generally available only for short-term horizons.

Premium or Discount on the Forward Rate. If the forward rate exceeds the existing spot rate, it contains a **premium.** If it is less than the existing spot rate, it contains a **discount.** This premium or discount is normally computed on an annual basis as shown in Exhibit 5.1. For example, assume the forward exchange rates shown in Column 2 of Exhibit 5.1 were quoted for the British pound. Based on those forward rates, the forward discount has been computed for each maturity. The forward discounts can first be computed in decimal form, which is easily converted into percentage form.

Forward rates typically differ from the spot rate for any given currency. If the forward rate were the same as the spot rate, and interest rates of the two countries differed, it would be possible for some investors (under certain assumptions) to use

Exhibit 5.1
Computation of Forward Rate Premiums or Discounts

Type of Exchange Rate for £	Value	Maturity	Forward Rate Premium or Discount for £
Spot rate	$1.681		
30-day forward rate	$1.680	30 days	$\frac{\$1.680 - \$1.681}{\$1.681} \times \frac{360}{30} = -.71\%$
90-day forward rate	$1.677	90 days	$\frac{\$1.677 - \$1.681}{\$1.681} \times \frac{360}{90} = -.95\%$
180-day forward rate	$1.672	180 days	$\frac{\$1.672 - \$1.681}{\$1.681} \times \frac{360}{180} = -1.07\%$

arbitrage so as to earn higher returns than would be possible domestically without incurring additional risk. Consequently, the forward rate will usually contain a premium (or discount) that reflects the difference between the home interest rate and the foreign interest rate.

Non-Deliverable Forward Contracts

A new type of forward contract called **non-deliverable forward contracts (NDFs)** is frequently used for currencies in emerging markets. Like a regular forward contract, an NDF represents an agreement regarding a position in a specified amount of a specified currency, a specified exchange rate, and a specified future settlement date. However, an NDF does not result in an actual exchange of the currencies at the future date. That is, there is no delivery. Instead, a payment is made by one party in the agreement to the other party based on the exchange rate at the future date.

To illustrate, assume that Jackson Inc., a U.S.-based MNC, determines as of April 1 that it will need 100 million Chilean pesos to purchase supplies on July 1. It can negotiate an NDF with a local bank as follows. The NDF specified the currency (Chilean peso), the settlement date (90 days from now), and a so-called reference rate, which identified the type of exchange rate that will be marked to market at the settlement. In our example, the NDF may contain the following information:

Buy 100 million Chilean pesos

Settlement date: July 1

Reference index: Chilean peso's closing exchange rate (in dollars) quoted by Chile's central bank in 90 days.

Assume that the Chilean peso (which is the reference index) is presently valued at $.0020, so that the dollar amount of the position is $200,000 at the time of the agreement. At the time of the settlement date (July 1), the value of the reference index is determined, and a payment is made between the two parties to settle the NDF agreement. For example, if the peso value increased to $.0023 by July 1, the value of the position specified in the NDF contract would be $230,000 ($.0023 × 100 million pesos). Since the value of Jackson's NDF position is $30,000 higher than when the agreement was created, Jackson will receive a payment of $30,000 from the bank involved in the NDF agreement.

Recall that Jackson needs 100 million pesos to buy imports. Since the peso's spot rate rose from April 1 to July 1, Jackson will need to pay $30,000 more for the imports than if it paid for them when it ordered the supplies from Chile. Yet, it would have received a payment of $30,000 due to its NDF agreement. Thus, the NDF agreement hedged the exchange rate risk.

If the Chilean peso had depreciated to $.0018 in the previous example, Jackson's position in its NDF would have been valued at $180,000 (100 million pesos × $.0018) at the settlement date, which is $20,000 less than what the value was when the agreement was created. Therefore, Jackson would have owed the bank $20,000 at that time. However, the decline in the spot rate of the peso means that Jackson would pay $20,000 less for the imports than if it had paid for them when it ordered the supplies from Chile. Thus, an offsetting effect would also occur in this example.

These examples show that while the NDF does not involve delivery, it can effectively hedge future foreign currency payments that are anticipated by the MNC.

Since an NDF can specify that any payments between the two parties be in dollars or some other available currency, firms can even use NDFs to hedge existing positions of foreign currencies that are not convertible. For example, an MNC may expect to receive payment in a foreign currency that cannot be converted into dollars. While it may use the currency to make purchases in the local country of concern, it still may desire to hedge against a decline in the value of the currency over the period before it receives payment. It could take a sell position in NDF and use the closing exchange rate of that currency as of the settlement date as the reference index. If the currency depreciated against the dollar over time, the firm would receive the difference between the dollar value of position when the NDF contract was created and the dollar value of the position as of the settlement date. Thus, it would receive a payment in dollars from the NDF contract to offset any depreciation in the currency over the period of concern.

Currency Futures Market

http://

The *Futures* magazine Web site at www.futuresmag.com/library/contents.html covers various aspects of derivatives trading such as new products, strategies, and market analyses.

Currency futures contracts are contracts specifying a standard volume of a particular currency to be exchanged on a specific settlement date. They are commonly traded on the trading floor of the Chicago Mercantile Exchange (CME). Firms (or individuals) can execute orders by calling brokerage firms that serve as intermediaries. The order to buy or sell a currency futures contract for a specific currency and a specific settlement date is communicated to the brokerage firm, which in turn communicates the order to the CME. A floor broker at the CME who specializes in that type of currency futures contract stands at a specific spot at the trading pit where that type of contract is traded and attempts to find a counter-party to fulfill the order. For example, if an MNC requested the purchase of a Mexican peso futures contract with a December settlement date, the floor broker assigned to execute this order would look for another floor broker who has an order to sell a Mexican peso futures contract with a December settlement date.

Trading on the floor (in the trading pits) of the CME is possible from 7:20 a.m. to 2:00 p.m. (Chicago time) Monday through Friday. Yet, currency futures contracts

http://
Visit the Chicago Mercantile Exchange site at www.cme.com for a time series on financial futures and option prices. The site also allows for the generation of historic price charts.

can still be traded after the CME's floor is closed on the CME's automated order-entry and matching system called GLOBEX from 2:30 p.m. until 7:05 a.m. the following morning. The GLOBEX system matches buy and sell orders for each type of currency futures contract.

Typical settlement dates are the third Wednesdays in March, June, September, and December. There is also an over-the-counter currency futures market, in which various financial intermediaries facilitate trading of currency futures contracts with specific settlement dates. Contracts have to be standardized, or floor trading would be slowed down considerably as brokers would have to assess contract specifications.

The trading volume of currency futures has consistently increased over time and, as growth in international transactions continues, the market should grow as well. Futures contracts are available for several widely traded currencies at the Chicago Mercantile Exchange (see Exhibit 5.2), and the contract for each currency specifies a standardized number of units. The trading of the French franc and German mark futures are being phased out over time as a result of the replacement of those currencies with the euro in 1999. The trading of euro futures will increase over time as euros are increasingly used to make payments.

Comparison of Currency Futures and Forward Contracts

Currency futures contracts are similar to forward contracts in that they allow a customer to lock in the exchange rate at which a specific currency is purchased or sold for a specific date in the future. Yet, there are some differences between currency futures contracts and forward contracts, which are summarized in Exhibit 5.3. Currency futures contracts are sold on an exchange, while each forward contract is negotiated between a firm and a commercial bank over the telephone. Thus, forward contracts can be tailored to the needs of the firm, while the currency futures contracts are standardized.

Corporations that have established relationships with large banks tend to use forward contracts rather than futures contracts because forward contracts are tailored to the precise amount of currency to be purchased or sold in the future and the precise forward date that they prefer. Conversely, small firms and individuals who do not have established relationships with large banks or prefer to trade in smaller amounts tend to use currency futures contracts.

Exhibit 5.2
Currency Futures Contracts Traded on the Chicago Mercantile Exchange

Currency	Units per Contract
Australian dollar	100,000
Brazilian real	100,000
British pound	62,500
Canadian dollar	100,000
Euro	125,000
Japanese yen	12,500,000
Mexican peso	500,000
New Zealand dollar	100,000
Russian ruble	500,000
South African rand	500,000
Swiss franc	125,000

Exhibit 5.3
Comparison of the Forward and Futures Markets

	Forward	Futures
Size of contract	Tailored to individual needs.	Standardized.
Delivery date	Tailored to individual needs.	Standardized.
Participants	Banks, brokers, and multinational companies. Public speculation not encouraged.	Banks, brokers, and multinational companies. Qualified public speculation encouraged.
Security deposit	None as such, but compensating bank balances or lines of credit required.	Small security deposit required.
Clearing operation	Handling contingent on individual banks and brokers. No separate clearinghouse function.	Handled by exchange clearinghouse. Daily settlements to the market price.
Marketplace	Over the telephone worldwide.	Central exchange floor with worldwide communications.
Regulation	Self-regulating.	Commodity Futures Trading Commission; National Futures Association.
Liquidation	Most settled by actual delivery. Some by offset, at a cost.	Most by offset, very few by delivery.
Transaction costs	Set by "spread" between bank's buy and sell prices.	Negotiated brokerage fees.

Source: Reprinted with the permission of the Chicago Mercantile Exchange.

Pricing Currency Futures

The price of currency futures normally will be similar to the forward rate for a given currency and settlement date. To understand why, assume that the currency futures price on the pound is $1.50 and that forward contracts for a similar period are available for $1.48. Firms may attempt to purchase forward contracts and simultaneously sell currency futures contracts. If they could exactly match the settlement dates of the two contracts, they could generate guaranteed profits of $.02 per unit. These actions would place downward pressure on the currency futures price. The futures contract and forward contracts of a given currency and settlement date should have the same price, or else guaranteed profits are possible (assuming no transaction costs).

The currency futures price differs from the spot rate for the same reasons that a forward rate differs from the spot rate. If a currency's spot and futures prices were the same and the currency's interest rate were higher than the U.S. rate, U.S. speculators could lock in a higher return than they would receive on U.S. investments. They could purchase the foreign currency at the spot rate, invest the funds at the attractive interest rate, and simultaneously sell currency futures to lock in the exchange rate, at which they could reconvert the currency back to dollars. If the spot and futures rates were the same, there would be neither a gain nor a loss on the currency conversion. Thus, the higher foreign interest rate would provide a higher yield on this type of investment. The actions of investors to capitalize on this opportunity would place upward pressure on the spot rate and downward pressure on the currency futures price, causing the futures price to fall below the spot rate.

Closing Out a Futures Position

If a firm holding a currency futures contract decides before settlement date that it no longer wants to maintain such a position, it can close out its position by selling an identical futures contract. The gain or loss to the firm from its previous futures position is dependent on the price of purchasing futures versus selling futures.

The price of a futures contract changes over time in accordance with movements in the spot rate and also by changing expectations about the spot rate's value as of the settlement date. For example, if the spot rate of a currency increased substantially over a one-month period, the futures price would likely increase by about the same amount. In this case, the purchase and subsequent sale of a futures contract would be profitable. Conversely, a decline in the spot rate over time would correspond with a decline in the currency futures price, meaning that the purchase and subsequent sale of a futures contract would result in a loss. While the purchasers of the futures contract could decide not to close out their position under such conditions, the losses from that position could increase over time.

Sellers of futures contracts could close out their positions by purchasing currency futures contracts with similar settlement dates. Most currency futures contracts are closed out before the settlement date.

Credit Risk of Currency Futures Contracts

Each currency futures contract represents an agreement between a client and the exchange clearinghouse, even though the exchange has not taken a position. To illustrate, assume you call a broker to request the purchase of a British pound futures contract with a March settlement date. Meanwhile, another person unrelated to you calls a broker to request the sale of a similar futures contract. Neither party needs to worry about the credit risk of the counterparty. The exchange clearinghouse assures that you will receive whatever is owed to you as a result of your currency futures position.

To minimize its risk in such a guarantee, the CME imposes **margin requirements** to cover fluctuations in the value of a contract, meaning that the participants must place a deposit with their respective brokerage firms when they take a position. The initial margin requirement is typically between $1,000 and $2,000 per currency futures contract. However, if the value of the futures contract declines over time, the buyer may be asked to add to the initial margin. Margin requirements are not always required for forward contracts, due to the more personal nature of the agreement; the bank knows the firm it is dealing with and may trust it to fulfill its obligation.

Corporate Use of Currency Futures

Corporations that have open positions in foreign currencies can consider the purchase or sale of futures contracts to offset such positions. The ownership of futures contracts locks in the price at which a firm can purchase a currency. For example, assume a U.S. firm orders Canadian goods and upon delivery will need to send C$500,000 to the Canadian exporter. Thus, the U.S. firm could purchase Canadian dollar futures contracts today, which would lock in the price to be paid for Canadian dollars at a future settlement date. By holding futures contracts, the firm does not have to worry about changes in the spot rate of the Canadian dollar over time.

Alternatively, a firm may consider selling a futures contract when it plans to receive a currency it will not need (perhaps from exporting products invoiced in the foreign currency preferred by the importer). By selling a futures contract, the firm is locking in the price at which it will be able to sell this currency as of the settlement date. Such an action can be appropriate if the firm expects this currency to depreciate against its home currency. The manner in which a firm can use futures contracts to cover, or **hedge,** its currency positions is described more thoroughly in Chapter 11.

Speculation with Currency Futures

Currency futures contracts are sometimes purchased by speculators who are simply attempting to capitalize on their expectation of a currency's future movement. If, for example, they expect the British pound to appreciate in the future, they might purchase a futures contract that will lock in the price at which they can buy pounds at a specified settlement date. On the settlement date, they can purchase their pounds at the rate specified by the futures contract and then sell these pounds at the spot

IN PRACTICE

CURRENCY FUTURES QUOTATIONS

Currency futures quotations are summarized each day in *The Wall Street Journal,* as shown here. Each currency is listed in bold, with the specified number of units per contract to the right. Each row under a given currency represents a particular settlement month as specified in the left margin. For any particular currency and settlement month, the opening, high, low, and settle (closing) futures prices are disclosed. Changes in the futures price from the previous trading day are also disclosed. The popularity of any currency futures contract is indicated by the "open interest" in the far right column, which represents the number of existing contracts that have not been offset.

CURRENCY

	Open	High	Low	Settle	Change	Lifetime High	Lifetime Low	Open Interest
JAPAN YEN (CME)-12.5 million yen; $ per yen (.00)								
June	.8641	.8647	.8536	.8563	– .0064	.9430	.7086	70,392
Sept	.8688	.8688	.8640	.8671	– .0064	.9500	.7680	1,635
Dec	....	....	....	.8779	– .0064	.9600	.8410	402
Est vol 17,982; vol Fri 11,356; open int 72,432, –292.								
DEUTSCHEMARK (CME)-125,000 marks; $ per mark								
June	.5605	.5608	.5570	.5605	+ .0012	.6285	.5530	31,670
Sept	....	....	....	.5635	+ .0012	.6300	.5580	1,195
Dec	....	....	....	.5667	+ .0012	.6120	.5610	96
Est vol 5,386; vol Fri 5,519; open int 32,961, –17.								
CANADIAN DOLLAR (CME)-100,000 dlrs.; $ per Can $								
June	.6597	.6655	.6597	.6649	+ .0052	.7172	.6300	48,723
Sept	.6615	.6655	.6615	.6650	+ .0052	.7080	.6310	2,194
Dec	.6634	.6660	.6630	.6653	+ .0052	.6785	.6320	1,621
Mr00	....	....	....	.6656	+ .0052	.6750	.6425	253
June	....	....	....	.6659	+ .0052	.6760	.6547	91
Est vol 8,496; vol Fri 4,902; open int 52,882, +612.								
BRITISH POUND (CME)-62,500 pds.; $ per pound								
June	1.6280	1.6288	1.6240	1.6272	+ .0002	1.7060	1.5880	54,599
Sept	1.6260	1.6290	1.6250	1.6276	+ .0002	1.6980	1.5940	1,251
Est vol 2,583; vol Fri 5,561; open int 55,880, +1,144.								
SWISS FRANC (CME)-125,000 francs; $ per franc								
June	.6885	.6900	.6856	.6897	+ .0025	.7930	.6695	58,191
Sept	....	....	....	.6960	+ .0025	.7831	.6915	311
Est vol 6,963; vol Fri 8,168; open int 58,508, –41.								
AUSTRALIAN DOLLAR (CME)-100,000 dlrs.; $ per A.$								
June	.6320	.6365	.6305	.6359	+ .0058	.6545	.5818	16,419
Est vol 768; vol Fri 932; open int 16,421, +60.								
MEXICAN PESO (CME)-500,000 new Mex. peso, $ per MP								
June	.09858	.09870	.09830	.09858	– 00150	.10230	.06900	16,098
Sept	....	....	....	.09420	– 00150	.09510	.06350	1,915
Dec	....	....	....	.09015	– 00150	.84345	.06700	773
Mr00	....	....	....	.08625	– 00150	.08705	.08135	352
Est vol 912; vol Fri 2,963; open int 19,138, –947.								
BRAZILIAN REAL (CME)-100,000 Braz. reais; $ per reais								
Apr	.53300	.54000	.53300	.53980	+ 00380	.79760	.44410	4,453
May	....	....	....	.53150	+ 00550	.78400	.44300	398
June	.52000	.52000	.52000	.52300	+ 00600	.77050	.43000	1,945
Est vol 513; vol Fri 375; open int 6,808, +70.								
EURO FX (CME)-Euro 125,000; $ per Euro								
June	1.1050	1.1050	1.0903	1.0964	+ .0026	1.2339	1.0848	32,693
Est vol 6,908; vol Fri 7,723; open int 32,815, +3,054.								

rate. If the spot rate has appreciated by this time in accordance with their expectations, they will profit from this strategy.

Currency futures are often sold by speculators who expect that the spot rate of a currency will be less than the rate for which they would be obligated to sell it. For example, assume a Mexican peso futures contract specifies a price of $.10 per unit. Also assume speculators expect the spot rate of the peso to be $.08 on the settlement date. They could profit from selling a futures contract as follows. If their expectations are correct, they will be able to purchase 500,000 pesos for $40,000 in the spot market as of the settlement date. Then, by selling their pesos at $.10 per peso as specified by the futures contract, they will receive $50,000, and their gain will be $10,000 ($50,000 – $40,000). Of course, expectations are often incorrect. It is because of different expectations that some speculators prefer to purchase futures contracts while other speculators prefer to sell the same contracts at a given point in time.

Transaction Costs of Currency Futures

Brokers that fulfill orders to buy or sell futures contracts charge a transaction or brokerage fee in the form of a bid/ask spread. That is, they buy a futures contract for one price (their "bid" price) and simultaneously sell the contract to someone else for a slightly higher price (their "ask" price). The difference between a bid and an ask price on a futures contract may be as little as $7.50. Yet, even this amount is larger in percentage terms than the transaction fees for forward contracts.

CURRENCY OPTIONS MARKET

In late 1982, exchanges in Amsterdam, Montreal, and Philadelphia allowed for trading in standardized foreign currency options. Since that time, options have been offered on the Chicago Mercantile Exchange and the Chicago Board Options Exchange. A currency option is an alternative type of contract that can be purchased or sold by speculators and firms. Currency options are presently available for many currencies, including the British pound, Canadian dollar, Japanese yen, euro, Swiss franc, and Australian dollar.

The options exchanges in the United States are regulated by the Securities and Exchange Commission. Options can be purchased or sold through brokers for a commission. The commission per transaction is commonly $30 to $60 for a single option currency option, but it can be much lower per contract when the transaction involves multiple contracts. Brokers require that a margin be maintained during the life of the contract. The margin is increased for clients whose option positions have deteriorated. This protects against possible losses if the clients do not fulfill their obligations.

In addition to the exchanges on which currency options are available, there is an over-the-counter market in which currency options are offered by commercial banks and brokerage firms. Unlike the currency options traded on an exchange, currency options are tailored to the specific needs of the firm. Since these options are not standardized, all the terms must be specified in the contracts. The number of units, desired strike price, and expiration date can be tailored to the specific need of the client. The minimum size of currency options offered by financial institutions is normally about $5 million. Since these transactions are conducted with a specific financial institution rather than an exchange, there are no credit guarantees. Thus, the agreement made is only as safe as the parties involved. For this reason, financial institutions may require some collateral from any individuals or firms desiring to purchase or sell currency options. Currency options are classified as either **calls** or **puts.** Each is discussed here.

Currency Call Options

The **currency call option** grants the right to buy a specific currency at a designated price within a specific period of time. The price at which the owner is allowed to buy that currency is known as the **exercise price** or **strike price,** and there are monthly expiration dates for each option.

Call options are desirable when one wishes to lock in a maximum price to be paid for a currency in the future. If the spot rate of the currency rises above the strike price, owners of call options can "exercise" their options by purchasing the currency at the strike price, which will be cheaper than the prevailing spot rate. This strategy is somewhat similar to that used by purchasers of futures contracts, but the futures contracts require an obligation, which the currency option does not. The owner can choose to let the option expire on the expiration date without ever exercising it. Owners of expired call options will have lost the premium they initially paid, but that is the most they can lose.

Currency options quotations are summarized each day in *The Wall Street Journal* and other business newspapers. While currency options have typically expired

IN PRACTICE

Currency Options Quotations

Currency options quotations are provided each day by *The Wall Street Journal*, as shown here. Some of these options are American style, while others are European style, as noted. Some currency options use an end-of-the-month (EOM) expiration date for the month of concern.

OPTIONS

PHILADELPHIA EXCHANGE

		Calls		Puts	
		Vol.	Last	Vol.	Last
CDollr					**65.67**
50,000 Canadian Dollar EOM-European style					
65½	Mar	4	0.31	4	0.32
65½	Apr	20	0.65	...	...
66	Apr	40	0.46	...	0.01
Australian Dollar					**62.91**
50,000 Australian Dollars-European style.					
62½	May	...	0.01	50	0.68
50,000 Australian Dollars-cents per unit.					
65½	May	1	0.38	...	0.01
British Pound					**162.32**
31,250 Brit. Pounds-European Style.					
158	Jun	1	5.05	...	0.01
162	Apr	...	...	16	1.33
31,250 Brit. Pounds-cents per unit.					
163	May	50	1.74	...	0.01
164	Apr	1	0.95	...	...
Canadian Dollar					**65.67**
50,000 Canadian Dollars-cents per unit.					
66½	Apr	7	0.20	6	1.30
67½	Jun	...	...	24	2.30
Euro					**109.15**
62,500 Euro-European style					
108	Apr	...	0.01	800	0.75
112	Apr	800	0.59	...	0.01
German Mark					**55.92**
62,500 German Marks-European Style.					
57	Apr	70	0.26	...	...
Japanese Yen					**83.92**
6,250,000 J.Yen EOM-European style.					
84	Mar	80	1.80	...	0.01
86	Apr	80	2.02	...	0.01
6,250,000J.Yen-100ths of a cent per unit.					
72	Jun	...	0.01	1	0.25
81	Jun	...	0.01	3	1.40
82	May	...	0.01	5	1.40
82	Jun	...	0.01	3	1.60
83	May	...	0.01	86	1.56
85	Jun	...	0.01	7	2.71
86	Apr	...	...	3	2.34
92	Jun	12	1.11	...	0.01
6,250,000J.Yen-European Style.					
88	Apr	8	1.00	...	0.01
6,250,000J.Yen-EuropeanStyle.					
85	Jun	...	...	20	2.62
Swiss Franc					**68.25**
62,500 Swiss Francs-European Style.					
69	Apr	...	...	12	1.08
69	May	12	1.08	...	0.01
71	Apr	4	0.19	...	...
62,500 Swiss Francs-cents per unit.					
68½	Apr	35	0.83	...	0.01
Call Vol 5,657			**Open Int ... 37,667**		
Put Vol 1,139			**Open Int ... 46,187**		

near the middle of the specified month, some of them expire at the end of the specific month and are designated as EOM. Some options are listed as "European Style," which means that those options can be exercised only upon expiration.

A currency call option is classified as *in the money* when the present exchange rate exceeds the strike price, *at the money* when the present exchange rate equals the strike price, and *out of the money* when the present exchange rate is less than the strike price. For a given currency and expiration date, an in-the-money call option will require a higher premium than options that are at the money or out of the money.

Factors Affecting Currency Call Option Premiums

Premiums of call options vary due to three main factors:

http://
Visit www.ino.com for the latest information and prices of options and financial futures as well as the corresponding historic price charts.

1. *Level of existing spot price relative to strike price.* The higher the spot rate relative to the strike price, the higher will be the option price. This is due to the higher probability of buying the currency at a substantially lower rate than what you could sell it for. This relationship can be verified by comparing premiums of options for a specified currency and expiration date that have different strike prices.
2. *Length of time before the expiration date.* It is generally expected that the spot rate has a greater chance of rising high above the strike price if it has a longer period of time to do so. A settlement date in June allows two additional months beyond April for the spot rate to move above the strike price. This explains why December option prices exceed November option prices given a specific strike price. This relationship can be verified by comparing premiums of options for a specified currency and strike price that have different expiration dates.
3. *Potential variability of currency.* The greater the variability of the currency, the higher the probability that the spot rate will be above the strike price. Thus, more volatile currencies will have higher call option prices. For example, the Canadian dollar is a more stable currency than most other currencies. If all other factors are similar, Canadian call options should be less expensive than call options on other foreign currencies.

The potential currency variability can also vary over time for one particular currency. For example, at the beginning of the Asian crisis in 1997, the Asian countries experienced financial problems, and their currency values were subject to much more uncertainty. Consequently, the premium on over-the-counter options of Asian currencies such as the Thailand baht, Indonesian rupiah, and Korean won increased. The higher premium was necessary to compensate one who might be willing to sell options in these currencies, as the risk to that seller had increased since the currencies had become more volatile.

Hedging with Currency Call Options

Corporations with open positions in foreign currencies can sometimes use currency call options to cover these positions. If, for example, a U.S. firm orders Australian goods, it may need to send Australian dollars to the Australian exporter upon delivery. An Australian dollar call option locks in a maximum rate at which a U.S. firm can exchange dollars for Australian dollars. This exchange of currencies at the specified strike price on the call option contract can be executed at any time before the expiration date. In essence, the call option contract has specified the maximum price the U.S. firm must pay to obtain these Australian dollars. Yet, if the Australian dollar's value remains below the strike price, the U.S. firm can purchase Australian dollars at the prevailing spot rate when it needs to pay for its imports and can simply let its call option expire.

Sometimes a firm anticipates a possible need for a foreign currency but is not yet certain of that need. Consider a firm that bids on a project required by the Canadian government. If the bid is accepted, the firm will need approximately C$500,000 to purchase Canadian materials and services. However, the firm will not know whether the bid is accepted until three months from now. In this case, it could purchase call options with a three-month expiration date. Ten call option contracts would cover the entire amount of potential exposure. If the bid is accepted, the firm can use the options to purchase the Canadian dollars needed. If the Canadian dollar has depreciated over time, the firm will likely let the options expire.

Assume that the exercise price on Canadian dollars is $.70 and the call option premium is $.02 per unit. The firm will pay $1,000 per option (since there are 50,000 units per Canadian dollar option), or $10,000 for the ten option contracts. With the options, the maximum amount necessary to purchase the C$500,000 is $350,000 (computed as $.70 per Canadian dollar × C$500,000). The amount of U.S. dollars needed could be less if the Canadian dollar's spot rate were below the exercise price at the time the Canadian dollars were purchased.

Even if the project's bid is rejected, the currency call option will be exercised if the Canadian dollar's spot rate exceeds the exercise price before the option expires. Any gain from exercising may partially or even fully offset the premium paid for the options.

As another example, a U.S. firm involved in a foreign acquisition bid may purchase call options on the currency that would be needed to purchase the foreign company's shares. The call options hedge the U.S. firm against the potential appreciation of the currency that may be needed if the acquisition occurs. If the acquisition does not occur and the spot rate remains below the strike price, the firm can let the call options expire. If the acquisition does not occur and the spot rate exceeds the strike price, the firm can exercise the option and sell the foreign currency in the spot market. Alternatively, the firm could sell the call options it was holding. Either of these actions may offset part or all of the premium paid for the option.

These examples suggest that options may be more appropriate than futures or forward contracts for some situations. Chrysler Corporation uses options for about 50 percent of its hedging transactions and forward contracts for the remaining 50 percent. Intel Corporation uses options to hedge its order backlog in semiconductors. If an order is cancelled, it has the flexibility to let the options contract expire. With a forward contract, it would be obligated to fulfill its obligation even though the order was cancelled. When Air Products and Chemicals was hired to perform some projects, it needed capital equipment from Germany. The purchase of equipment was contingent on whether the firm was hired for the projects. The company used options to hedge this possible future purchase.

Speculating with Currency Call Options

Because this text focuses on multinational financial management, the corporate use of currency options is more important than the speculative use. The use of options for hedging is discussed in detail in Chapter 11. Speculative trading is discussed here in order to provide more of a background on the currency options market.

Individuals may speculate in the currency options market based on their expectation of the future movements in a particular currency. For example, speculators who expect that the Japanese yen will appreciate can purchase Japanese yen call options. Once the spot rate of Japanese yen appreciates, the speculators can exercise their option by purchasing yen at the strike price and then sell the yen at the prevailing spot rate.

Just as is the case with currency futures, for every buyer of a currency call option there must be a seller. A seller (sometimes called a **writer**) of a call option is obligated to sell a specified currency at a specified price (the strike price) up to a specified expiration date. Speculators may sometimes want to sell a currency call option on a currency that is expected to depreciate in the future. The only way a currency call option will be exercised is if the spot rate is higher than the strike price. Thus, a seller of the currency call option will receive the premium when the option is purchased and can keep the entire amount if the option is not exercised. When it appears that an option will be exercised, there will still be sellers of options. However, such options will sell for high premiums due to the high risk that the option will be exercised at some point.

Numerical Examples. Suppose that Jim is a speculator who buys a British pound call option with a strike price of $1.40 and a December settlement date. The current spot price as of that date is about $1.39. Jim pays a premium of $.012 per unit for the call option. Assume there are no brokerage fees. Just before the expiration date, the spot rate of the British pound reaches $1.41. At this time, Jim exercises the call option and then immediately sells the pounds at the spot rate to a bank. To determine Jim's profit or loss, first compute his revenues from selling the currency. Then, subtract from this amount the purchase price of pounds when exercising the option, and also subtract the purchase price of the option. The computations follow. Assume one option contract specifies 31,250 units.

	Per Unit	Per Contract
Selling price of £	$1.41	$44,063 ($1.41 × 31,250 units)
– Purchase price of £	–1.40	–43,750 ($1.40 × 31,250 units)
– Premium paid for option	–.012	–375 ($.012 × 31,250 units)
= Net profit	– $.002	–$62 (– $.002 × 31,250 units)

Assume that Linda was the seller of the call option purchased by Jim. Also assume that Linda would only purchase British pounds if and when the option was exercised, at which time she must provide the pounds at the exercise price of $1.40. Using the information in this example, Linda's net profit from selling the call option is derived here:

	Per Unit	Per Contract
Selling price of £	$1.40	$43,750 ($1.40 × 31,250 units)
– Purchase price of £	–1.41	–44,063 ($1.41 × 31,250 units)
+ Premium received	+.012	+375 ($.012 × 31,250 units)
= Net profit	$.002	$62 ($.002 × 31,250 units)

As a second example, assume the following information:

- Call option premium on Canadian dollars (C$) = $.01 per unit
- Strike price = $.70
- 1 option contract represents C$50,000

A speculator who had purchased this call option decided to exercise the option shortly before the expiration date, when the spot rate reached $.74. The Canadian dollars were immediately sold in the spot market by the speculator. Given this information, the net profit to the speculator was

	Per Unit	Per Contract
Selling price of C$	$.74	$37,000 ($.74 × 50,000 units)
– Purchase price of C$	–.70	–35,000 ($.70 × 50,000 units)
– Premium paid for option	–.01	–500 ($.01 × 50,000 units)
= Net profit	$.03	$1,500 ($.03 × 50,000 units)

If the seller of the call option did not obtain Canadian dollars until the option was about to be exercised, the net profit to the seller of the call option was

	Per Unit	Per Contract
Selling price of C$	$.70	$35,000 ($.70 × 50,000 units)
– Purchase price of C$	– .74	–37,000 ($.74 × 50,000 units)
+ Premium received	+ .01	+500 ($.01 × 50,000 units)
= Net profit	– $.03	–$1,500 (–$.04 × 50,000 units)

When brokerage fees are ignored, the currency call purchaser's gain will be the seller's loss. The currency call purchaser's expenses represent the seller's revenues, and the purchaser's revenues represent the seller's expenses. Yet, because it is possible for purchasers and sellers of options to close out their positions, the relationship described here will not hold unless both parties begin and close out their positions at the same time.

An owner of a currency option may simply sell the option to someone else before the expiration date rather than exercising it. The owner can still earn profits, since the option premium changes over time, reflecting the probability that the option can be exercised and the potential profit from exercising it.

Break-Even Point from Speculation. The purchaser of a call option will break even if the revenue from selling the currency equals the payments for (1) the currency (at the strike price) and (2) the option premium. In other words, regardless of the number of units in a contract, a purchaser will break even if the spot rate at which the currency is sold is equal to the strike price plus the option premium. In the previous example, the strike price is $.70 and the option premium is $.01. Thus, in order for the purchaser to break even, the spot rate existing at the time the call is exercised must be $.71 ($.70 + $.01). Of course, speculators would not have purchased the call option if they thought the spot rate would only reach this break-even point without going higher before the expiration date. The computation of the break-even point is useful for a speculator deciding whether to purchase a currency call option.

Currency Put Options

The owner of a **currency put option** is granted the right to sell a currency at a specified price (the strike price) within a specified period of time. As with currency call options, the owner of a put option is not obligated to exercise the option. Therefore, the maximum potential loss to the owner of the put option is the price (or premium) paid for the option contract.

A currency put option is classified as *in the money* when the present exchange rate is less than the strike price, *at the money* when the present exchange rate equals the strike price, and *out of the money* when the present exchange rate exceeds the strike price. For a given currency and expiration date, an in-the-money put option will require a higher premium than options that are at the money or out of the money.

Factors Affecting Currency Put Option Premiums

The three main factors influencing call option premiums also influence put option premiums. First, the spot rate of a currency relative to the strike price is important. The lower the spot rate is relative to the strike price, the more valuable will be the put option, since there is a higher probability that the put option will be exercised. Recall that just the opposite relationship held for the call option. A second factor influencing the put option premium is the length of time until the expiration date. As with currency call options, the longer the time is to expiration, the greater will be the put option premium. A longer period creates a higher probability for the currency to move within a range where it would be feasible to exercise the option (whether it is a put or a call). These relationships can be verified by assessing quotations of put option premiums for a specified currency. A third factor that influences the put option premium is the variability of a currency. As with currency call options, the greater the variability, the greater will be the put option premium, again reflecting a higher probability that the option may be exercised.

Hedging with Currency Put Options

Corporations with open positions in foreign currencies can use currency put options in some cases to cover these positions. For example, assume a U.S. firm has exported products to Canada and invoiced the products in Canadian dollars (at the request of the Canadian importers). This firm may be concerned that the Canadian dollars it is receiving will depreciate over time. To insulate itself against possible depreciation, it could purchase Canadian dollar put options, which would entitle the firm to sell Canadian dollars at the specified strike price. In essence, the firm would lock in the minimum rate at which it could exchange Canadian dollars for U.S. dollars over a specified period of time. Yet, if the Canadian dollar appreciated over this time period, the firm could let the put options expire and sell the Canadian dollars received at the prevailing spot rate.

Speculating with Currency Put Options

Individuals may speculate with currency put options based on their expectations of the future movements in a particular currency. For example, speculators who expect that the British pound will depreciate could purchase British pound put options, which would entitle them to sell British pounds at a specified strike price. If the pound's spot rate did depreciate as expected, the speculators could then purchase pounds at the spot rate and exercise their put options by selling these pounds at the strike price.

Speculators could also attempt to profit from selling currency put options. The seller of such options is obligated to purchase the specified currency at the strike price from the owner who exercises the put option. Speculators who believe the currency will appreciate (or at least will not depreciate) may consider selling a currency put option. If the currency appreciated over the entire period, the option would not be exercised. This is an ideal situation for put option sellers, since they keep the premiums received when selling the options and bear no cost.

Numerical Example. To illustrate how to determine the net profit from speculating with put options, assume the following information:

- Put option premium on British pound (£) = $.04 per unit
- Strike price = $1.40
- 1 option contract represents £31,250

A speculator who had purchased this put option decided to exercise the option shortly before the expiration date, when the spot rate of the pound was $1.30. The pounds were purchased in the spot market at that time by the speculator. Given this information, the net profit to the purchaser of the put option was

	Per Unit	Per Contract
Selling price of £	$1.40	$43,750 ($1.40 × 31,250 units)
– Purchase price of £	–1.30	–40,625 ($1.30 × 31,250 units)
– Premium paid for option	–.04	–1,250 ($.04 × 31,250 units)
= Net profit	$.06	$ 1,875 ($.06 × 31,250 units)

Assuming that the seller of the put option sold the pounds received immediately after the option was exercised, the net profit to the seller of the put option was

	Per Unit	Per Contract
Selling price of £	$1.30	$40,625 ($1.30 × 31,250 units)
– Purchase price of £	–1.40	–43,750 ($1.40 × 31,250 units)
+ Premium received	+.04	+1,250 ($.04 × 31,250 units)
= Net profit	–$.06	– $1,875 (–$.06 × 31,250 units)

The seller of the put options could simply refrain from selling the pounds (after being forced to buy them at $1.40 per pound) until the spot rate of the pound rose. However, there is no guarantee that the pound will reverse its direction and begin to appreciate. The seller's net loss could potentially be greater if the pound's spot rate continued to fall, unless the pounds were sold immediately.

Whatever an owner of a put option gains, the seller loses, and vice versa. This relationship would hold if brokerage costs did not exist and if the buyer and seller of options entered and closed their positions at the same time. Brokerage fees for currency options exist, however, and are very similar in magnitude to those of currency futures contracts.

Speculating with Combined Put and Call Options. For volatile currencies, one possible speculative strategy is to purchase a **straddle,** which represents both a put option and a call option at the same exercise price. This may seem unusual, since owning a put option is appropriate for expectations that the currency will depreciate while owning a call option is appropriate for expectations that the currency will appreciate. However, it is possible that the currency will depreciate (at which time the put is exercised) and then reverse direction and appreciate (allowing for profits when exercising the call). Also, one might anticipate that the currency will be substantially affected by current economic events yet be uncertain of the exact way in which it will be affected. By purchasing a put option and a call option, the speculator will gain if the currency moves substantially in either direction. Although two options are purchased and only one is exercised, the gains could more than offset the costs.

Contingency Graphs for Currency Options

Assume that a British pound call option is available, with a strike price of $1.50 and a call premium of $.02. The speculative profits to be earned are dependent on the future spot rate of the pound. Assume that the speculator plans to exercise the option on the expiration date (if appropriate at that time) and to then immediately sell the pounds received in the spot market. Under these conditions, a **contingency graph** can be created to measure the profit or loss per unit (see the upper-left graph in Exhibit 5.4). Notice that if the future spot rate is $1.50 or less, the net gain per unit is –$.02 (ignoring transaction costs). This represents the loss of the premium per unit paid for the option, as the option would not be exercised. At $1.51, $.01 per unit would be earned by exercising the option, but considering the $.02 premium paid, the net gain would be –$.01. At $1.52, $.02 per unit would be earned by exercising the option, which would offset the $.02 premium per unit. This is the break-even point. At any rate above this point, the premium paid would be more than offset by the gain from exercising the option, resulting in a positive net gain. The maximum loss to the speculator in this example is the premium paid for the option.

A contingency graph could also be developed for the seller of this call option. The lower-left graph shown in Exhibit 5.4 assumes that this seller would purchase the pounds in the spot market just as the option was exercised (ignoring transaction costs). At future spot rates of less than $1.50, the net gain to the seller would be the premium of $.02 per unit, as the option would not have been exercised. If the future spot rate were $1.51, the seller would have lost $.01 per unit on the option transaction (paying $1.51 for pounds in the spot market and selling pounds for $1.50 to fulfill the exercise request). Yet, this loss would be more than offset by the premium of $.02 per unit, resulting in a net gain of –$.01 per unit. The break-even point is at $1.52, and the net gain to the seller of a call option becomes negative at all future spot rates higher than that point. Notice that the contingency graphs for the buyer and seller of this call option are mirror images of one another in our example.

A contingency graph for a buyer of a put option can also be developed. The upper-right graph in Exhibit 5.4 shows the net gains to a buyer of a British pound put option with an exercise price of $1.50 and a premium of $.03 per unit. If the future spot rate were above $1.50, the option would not be exercised. At a future spot rate of $1.48, the put option would be exercised. However, considering the premium of $.03 per unit, there would be a net loss of $.01 per unit. The break-even

Exhibit 5.4
Contingency Graphs for Currency Options

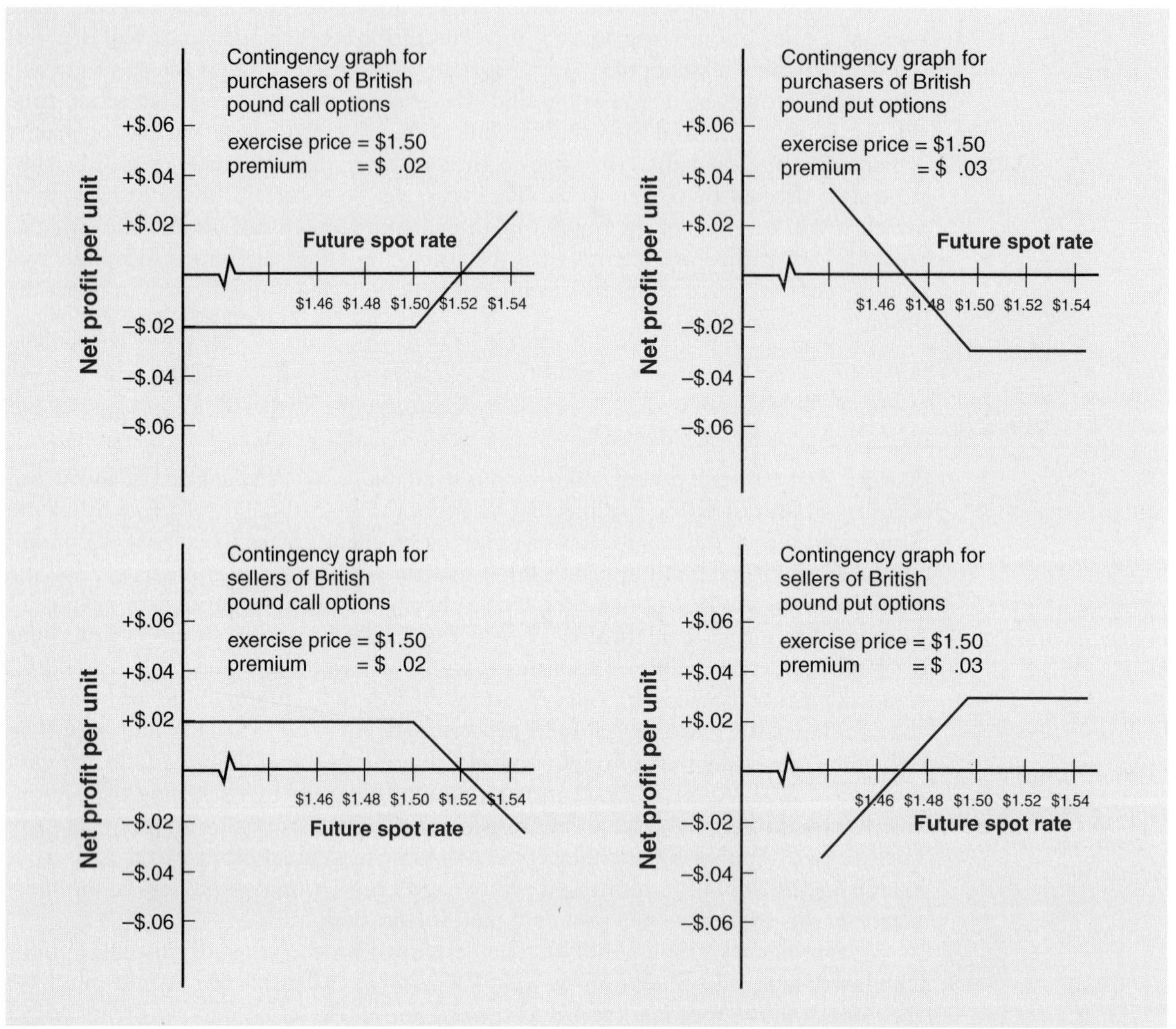

point in this example is $1.47, since this is the future spot rate that would generate $.03 per unit from exercising the option to offset the $.03 premium. At any future spot rates of less than $1.47, the buyer of the put option would earn a positive net gain.

A contingency graph for the seller of this put option is shown in the lower-right graph in Exhibit 5.4. It is the mirror image of the contingency graph for the buyer of a put option.

There are various reasons why an option buyer's net gain will not always represent an option seller's net loss. The buyer may be using call options to hedge a foreign currency, rather than to speculate. In this case, the buyer does not evaluate the options position taken by measuring a net gain or loss; the option is used simply for protection. In addition, sellers of call options on a currency in which they currently maintain a position would not need to purchase the currency at the time an option is exercised. They could simply liquidate their position in order to provide the currency to the person exercising the option.

CONDITIONAL CURRENCY OPTIONS

Some currency options are structured with a conditional premium, meaning that the premium is conditioned on the actual movement in the currency's value over the period of concern. For example, assume that Jensen Co., a U.S.-based MNC, needs to sell British pounds that it will receive in 60 days. Assume it can negotiate a traditional currency put option on pounds in which the exercise price is \$1.70 and the premium is \$.02 per unit.

Alternatively, it could negotiate a conditional currency option with a commercial bank, which has an exercise price of \$1.70, and a so-called trigger of \$1.74. If the pound's value falls below the exercise price by the expiration date, Jensen will exercise the option, thereby receiving \$1.70 per pound, and it does not need to pay a premium for the option.

If the pound's value is between the exercise price (\$1.70) and the trigger (\$1.74), the option will not be exercised, and Jensen will not need to pay a premium. If the pound's value exceeds the trigger of \$1.74, Jensen will pay a premium of \$.04 per unit. Notice that this premium may be higher than the premium that it would have paid if it had purchased a basic put option. However, Jensen may not mind this outcome because it will be receiving a high dollar amount from converting its pound receivables in the spot market.

Jensen must determine whether the potential advantage of the conditional option (avoiding the payment of a premium under some conditions) outweighs the potential disadvantage (paying a higher premium than the premium for a traditional put option on British pounds).

The potential advantage and disadvantage are illustrated in Exhibit 5.5. At exchange rates less than or equal to the trigger level (\$1.74), the conditional option

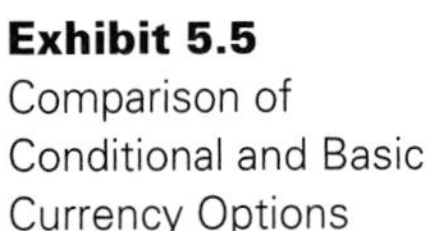

Exhibit 5.5
Comparison of Conditional and Basic Currency Options

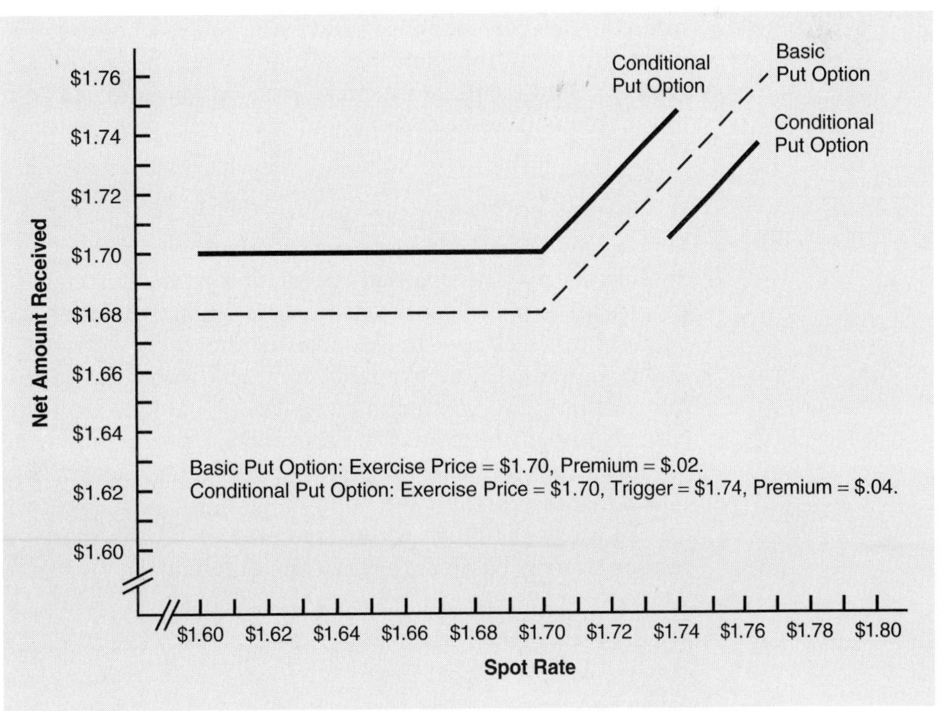

results in a larger payment to Jensen by the amount of the premium that would have been paid for the basic option. Conversely, at exchange rates above the trigger level, the conditional option results in a lower payment to Jensen, as its premium of $.04 exceeds the premium of $.02 per unit paid on a basic option.

The choice of a basic option versus a conditional option is dependent on expectations of the currency's exchange rate over the period of concern. A firm that was very confident that the pound's value would not exceed $1.74 in the previous example would prefer the conditional currency option.

Conditional currency options are also available for U.S. firms that need to purchase a foreign currency in the near future. For example, a conditional call option on pounds may specify an exercise price of $1.70, and a trigger of $1.67. If the pound's value remains above the trigger of the call option, a premium will not have to be paid for the call option. However, if the pound's value falls below the trigger, a large premium (such as $.04 per unit) would be required. Some conditional options require a premium if the trigger is reached anytime up until the expiration date; others only require a premium if the exchange rate is beyond the trigger as of the expiration date.

There are also numerous combinations of currency options used by firms. For example, a firm may purchase a currency call option to hedge payables and finance the purchase of the call option by selling a put option on the same currency.

European Currency Options

The discussion of currency options up to this point has been solely related to American-style options. European-style currency options are also available for speculating and hedging in the foreign exchange market. They are similar to American-style options except that they must be exercised on the expiration date if they are to be exercised at all. Consequently, they do not offer as much flexibility; however, this is not relevant to some situations. For example, firms that purchase options to hedge future foreign currency cash flows will probably not desire to exercise their options before the expiration date anyway. If European-style options are available for the same expiration date as American-style options and can be purchased for a slightly lower premium, some corporations may prefer them for hedging.

Efficiency of Currency Futures and Options

Speculators may believe that speculation in the currency futures and/or currency options markets can consistently generate abnormally large profits. This would not be possible if such foreign exchange markets were "efficient." In an efficient foreign exchange market, any available contracts would be priced to reflect all relevant information; thus, speculators would not be able to exploit existing information to earn abnormally large profits. Any valuable information would already have caused an adjustment in "sell" or "buy" requests, thereby forcing the contract price to reflect that information.

To assess the efficiency of the currency futures market, Thomas[1] developed a trading strategy based on interest rate differentials. This strategy generated a return

[1]Lee R. Thomas III, "A Winning Strategy for Currency-Futures Speculation," *Journal of Portfolio Management* (Fall 1985), pp. 65–69.

Nike Problem

Use of Currency Derivative Contracts

Like many MNCs, Nike uses currency derivative contracts to hedge some future transactions that are denominated in foreign currencies. Nike's policy is to use currency derivatives for hedging and not for speculating in the foreign exchange market. In general, Nike uses forward contracts to hedge payables or receivables but purchases currency options to hedge some anticipated foreign transactions that are not confirmed commitments. Its hedged transactions are typically denominated in European currencies, the Japanese yen, or the Canadian dollar. Nike mentions in a recent annual report that the estimated fair market values of its currency derivative positions will fluctuate over time, and that these values should not be assessed by themselves but in relation to the market values of the transactions that are to be hedged. For example, consider a purchase of yen future contracts by Nike that is intended to hedge future yen payments. The market value of a purchased futures position in yen could lose market value due to a decline in the yen's value. Yet, the dollar market value of the hedged position would decline by a similar amount. Thus, a reduction in the value of any currency derivative positions does not necessarily create more risk because there may be an offsetting effect when the currency derivatives are used to hedge future transactions.

Discussion: Explain why Nike may use forward contracts to hedge committed transactions, while it uses currency options to hedge contracts that are anticipated but not committed. That is, why would forward contracts possibly be an advantage for committed transactions, and why would currency options possibly be an advantage for anticipated transactions?

of about 10.3 percent above the three-month Treasury bill rate on average, suggesting that currency futures are not priced efficiently (if the excess return is assumed to more than compensate for the risk involved).

The efficiency of the currency options market has also been tested. Research by Bodurtha and Courtadon[2] and by Tucker[3] found that when accounting for transaction costs, the currency options market is efficient. This suggests that currency option prices generally reflect all available information.

A speculative strategy requires the speculator to incur risk, since the actual results from investing funds in a speculative instrument are uncertain. While a high return (profit as a percent of the amount invested) can sometimes be achieved by speculating in foreign exchange markets, there is considerable risk involved. "Abnormal" profits from a speculative strategy would reflect above-average returns *after* accounting for the risk involved. Individuals who speculate in futures and options markets must believe that they know something the market doesn't. Yet, corpora-

---

[2]James Bodurtha and Georges Courtadon, "Tests of an American Option Pricing Model on the Foreign Currency Options Market," *Journal of Financial Quantitative Analysis* (June 1987), pp. 153–168.

[3]Alan L. Tucker, "Empirical Tests of the Efficiency of the Currency Option Market," *Journal of Financial Research* (Winter 1985), pp. 275–285.

Exhibit 5.6
Impact of Currency Derivatives on an MNC's Value

Currency Futures
Currency Options

$$V = \sum_{t=1}^{n} \left\{ \frac{\sum_{j=1}^{m} \left[E(CF_{j,t}) \times E(ER_{j,t}) \right]}{(1+k)^t} \right\}$$

V = value of the U.S.-based MNC
$E(CF_{j,t})$ = expected cash flows denominated in currency j to be received by the U.S. parent in period t
$E(ER_{j,t})$ = expected exchange rate at which currency j can be converted to dollars at the end of period t
k = the weighted average cost of capital of the U.S. parent company
m = number of currencies
n = number of periods

tions may use these markets even if they believe in market efficiency. Their positions in currency futures and currency options are usually intended to reduce exposure to fluctuating exchange rates rather than to earn a speculative profit.

How the Use of Currency Futures and Options Affects an MNC's Value

The use of currency futures and options can affect an MNC's value, as shown in Exhibit 5.6. Currency futures can prevent the possibility that the value of foreign currency receipts will decline because of depreciation of that currency against the dollar. In this way, the use of currency futures can increase the expected dollar cash flows to be received from converting foreign currency cash flows to dollars. Yet, by using currency futures, the MNC forgoes the possibility of a favorable effect resulting from the appreciation of foreign currencies that will be converted into dollars.

Currency options can offer the same type of protection against depreciation of currencies that will be received but allow more flexibility to capitalize on the potential appreciation of the foreign currency before conversion into dollars. However, premiums are paid for the options, which reduce cash flows of the MNC.

SUMMARY

- A currency futures contract specifies a standard volume of a particular currency to be exchanged on a particular date. Such a contract can be purchased by speculators who expect that currency to appreciate. If the currency appreciates, the value of the futures contract rises, allowing the speculators to benefit when they close out their positions.

- A currency futures contract can be sold by speculators who expect that currency to depreciate. If the currency depreciates, the value of the futures contract declines, allowing the speculators to benefit when they close out their positions.
- Futures contracts on a particular currency can be purchased by corporations that have payables in that currency and wish to hedge against the possible appreciation of that currency. Conversely, these contracts can be sold by corporations that have receivables in that currency and wish to hedge against the possible depreciation of that currency.
- Currency options are classified as call options or put options. Call options allow the right to purchase a specified currency at a specified exchange rate by a specified expiration date. Put options allow the right to sell a specified currency at a specified exchange rate by a specified expiration date.
- Call options on a specific currency can be purchased by speculators who expect that currency to appreciate. Put options on a specific currency can be purchased by speculators who expect that currency to depreciate.
- Currency call options are commonly purchased by corporations that have payables in a currency that is expected to appreciate. Currency put options are commonly purchased by corporations that have receivables in a currency that is expected to depreciate.

SELF-TEST FOR CHAPTER 5

(Answers are provided in Appendix A at the back of the text.)

1. A call option on Canadian dollars is available with a strike price of $.60 and is purchased by a speculator for the premium of $.06 per unit. Assume there are 50,000 units in this option contract. If the Canadian dollar's spot rate is $.65 at the time the option is exercised, what is the net profit per unit to the speculator? What is the net profit for one contract? What would the spot rate need to be at the time the option is exercised for the speculator to break even? What is the net profit per unit to the seller of this option?
2. A put option on Australian dollars is available with a strike price of $.80 and is purchased by a speculator for the premium of $.02. If the Australian dollar's spot rate is $.74 on the expiration date, should the speculator exercise the option on this date or let the option expire? What is the net profit per unit to the speculator? What is the net profit per unit to the seller of this put option?
3. Longer-term currency options are becoming more popular for hedging exchange rate risk. Why do you think some firms decide to hedge by using other techniques instead of purchasing long-term currency options?

QUESTIONS AND APPLICATIONS

1. Compare and contrast the forward and futures contracts.
2. How can currency futures be used by corporations?
3. How can currency futures be used by speculators?
4. What is a currency call option?
5. What is a currency put option?
6. When would a U.S. firm consider purchasing a call option in euros for hedging?
7. When would a U.S. firm consider purchasing a put option in euros for hedging?
8. When should a speculator purchase a call option on Australian dollars?
9. When should a speculator purchase a put option on Australian dollars?

10. List the factors that affect currency call option premiums, and briefly explain the relationship that exists for each. Do you think an at-the-money call option in euros has a higher or lower premium than an at-the-money call option in British pounds (assuming the expiration date and the total dollar value represented by each option are the same for both options)?

11. List the factors that affect currency put option premiums, and briefly explain the relationship that exists for each.

12. Assume a speculator purchased a call option on British pounds for $.02 per unit. The strike price was $1.45, and the spot rate at the time the pound option was exercised was $1.46. Assume there are 31,250 units in a British pound option. What was the net profit on this option to the speculator?

13. Assume a U.S. speculator purchased a put option on British pounds for $.04 per unit. The strike price was $1.80, and the spot rate at the time the pound was exercised was $1.59. Assume there are 31,250 units in a British pound option. What was the net profit on the option?

14. Assume a U.S. speculator sold a call option on Canadian dollars for $.01 per unit. The strike price was $.76, and the spot rate at the time the option was exercised was $.82. Assume the speculator did not obtain Canadian dollars until the option was exercised. Also assume there are 50,000 units in a Canadian dollar option. What was the net profit to the seller of the call option?

15. Assume a U.S. speculator sold a put option on Canadian dollars for $.03 per unit. The strike price was $.75, and the spot rate at the time the Canadian dollar was exercised was $.72. Assume the speculator immediately sold off the Canadian dollars received when the option was exercised. Also assume there are 50,000 units in a Canadian dollar option. What was the net profit to the seller of the put option?

16. What are the advantages and disadvantages to a U.S. corporation that uses currency options on euros rather than a forward contract on euros to hedge against its exposure in euros?

17. Assume that the euro's spot rate has moved in cycles over time. How might you try to use futures contracts on pounds to capitalize on this tendency? How could you determine whether such a strategy would have been profitable in previous periods?

18. Assume that the transactions listed in Column 1 of the following table are anticipated by U.S. firms that have no other foreign transactions. Place an "X" in the table wherever you see possible ways to hedge each of the transactions.

	Forward Contract		Futures Contract		Options Contract	
	Forward Purchase	Forward Sale	Buy Futures	Sell Futures	Purchase a Call	Purchase a Put
a. Georgetown Company plans to purchase Japanese goods denominated in yen.						
b. Harvard Inc. will sell goods to Japan, denominated in yen.						
c. Yale Corporation has a subsidiary in Australia that will be remitting funds to the U.S. parent.						
d. Brown Inc. needs to pay off existing loans soon that were denominated in Canadian dollars.						
e. Princeton Company may purchase a company in Japan in the near future (but the deal may not go through).						

19. Assume that on November 1 the spot rate of the British pound was $1.58 and the price on a December futures contract was $1.59. Assume that the pound depreciated over November, so that by November 30 it was worth $1.51.

a. What do you think happened to the futures price over the month of November? Why?
b. If you had known that this would occur, would you have purchased or sold a December futures contract in pounds on November 1? Explain.

20. Assume that a March futures contract on Mexican pesos was available in January for $.09 per unit. Also assume that forward contracts were available for the same settlement date at a price of $.092 per peso. How could speculators capitalize on this situation, assuming zero transaction costs? How would such speculative activity affect the difference between the forward contract price and the futures price?

21. LSU Corporation purchased Canadian dollar call options for speculative purposes. If these options are exercised, LSU will immediately sell the Canadian dollars in the spot market. Each option was purchased for a premium of $.03 per unit, with an exercise price of $.75. LSU plans to wait until the expiration date before considering whether to exercise the options. Of course, it will exercise the options at that time only if it is feasible to do so. In the following table, fill in the net profit (or loss) per unit to LSU Corporation based on the listed possible spot rates of the Canadian dollar that may exist on the expiration date.

Possible Spot Rate of Canadian Dollar on Expiration Date	Net Profit (Loss) per Unit to LSU Corporation If Spot Rate Occurs
$.76	
.78	
.80	
.82	
.85	
.87	

22. Auburn Company has purchased Canadian dollar put options for speculative purposes. Each option was purchased for a premium of $.02 per unit, with an exercise price of $.76 per unit. Auburn Company will purchase the Canadian dollars just before it exercises the options (if it is feasible to exercise the options). It plans to wait until the expiration date before considering whether to exercise the options. In the following table, fill in the net profit (or loss) per unit to Auburn Company based on the listed possible spot rates of the Canadian dollar that may exist on the expiration date.

Possible Spot Rate of Canadian Dollar on Expiration Date	Net Profit (Loss) per Unit to Auburn Company If Spot Rate Occurs
$.76	
.79	
.84	
.87	
.89	
.91	

23. Bama Corporation has sold British pound call options for speculative purposes. The option premium was $.06 per unit and the exercise price was $1.58. Bama will purchase the pounds on the day the options are exercised (if the options are exercised) in order to fulfill its obligation. In the following table, fill in the net profit (or loss) to Bama Corporation if the listed spot rate exists at the time the purchaser of the call options considers exercising them.

Possible Spot Rate at the Time Purchaser of Call Options Considers Exercising Them	Net Profit (Loss) per Unit to Bama Corporation If Spot Rate Occurs
$1.53	
1.55	
1.57	
1.60	
1.62	
1.64	
1.68	

24. Bulldog Inc. has sold Australian dollar put options at a premium of $.01 per unit and with an exercise price of $.76 per unit. It has fore-

casted the Australian dollar's lowest level over the period of concern as shown in the following table. If that level occurs and the put options are exercised at that time, determine the net profit (or loss) per unit to Bulldog Inc.

Possible Value of Australian Dollar	Net Profit (Loss) to Bulldog Inc. If Value Occurs
$.72	
.73	
.74	
.75	
.76	

25. A U.S. professional football team plans to play an exhibition game in the United Kingdom next year. Assume all expenses will be paid by the British government, and a check of 1 million pounds will be provided to the team. The team anticipates that the pound will depreciate substantially by the scheduled date of the game. In addition, the National Football League must approve the deal, and approval (or disapproval) will not occur for three months. How could the team hedge its position? What is there to lose by waiting three months to see if the exhibition game is approved before hedging?

26. Because changes in economic conditions are uncertain, there can be large changes in currency values in a single day due to a sudden shift in expectations. As funds shift toward different currencies, the demand and supply conditions in the foreign exchange market change, and so do currency values. Currency futures markets are commonly used as a means of capitalizing on shifts in currency values because the value of a futures contract tends to move in line with the change in the corresponding currency value. Thus, the currency futures pits of the Chicago Mercantile Exchange are most exciting on days when there is major news that signals a potential shift in economic conditions. Furthermore, unanticipated actions by the Federal Reserve to adjust a currency's value tends to cause panic as participants maneuver in response to the Fed's actions.

To illustrate how the environment can be affected, consider a recent situation in which many currencies appreciated against the dollar. Most speculators anticipated that these currencies would continue to strengthen and took large buy positions in currency futures. However, the Fed intervened in the foreign exchange market by selling foreign currencies in exchange for dollars, causing an abrupt decline in the values of foreign currencies (as the dollar strengthened). Participants that had purchased currency futures contracts incurred large losses. One floor broker responded to the effects of the Fed's intervention by selling at once 300 futures contracts on British pounds (with a value of about $30 million). These types of actions caused even more panic on the futures market.

a. Explain the logic of how central bank intervention caused sheer panic for currency futures traders with buy positions.
b. Explain the concern caused when a floor broker was willing to sell 300 pound futures contracts at the going market rate. What might this action signal to the brokers?
c. Explain why speculators with short (sell) positions could benefit as a result of the central bank intervention.
d. Some traders with buy positions may have responded immediately to the central bank intervention by selling futures contracts. Why would some speculators with buy positions leave their positions unchanged or even increase their positions by purchasing more futures contracts in response to the central bank intervention?

Internet Application

26. The Web site of the Chicago Mercantile Exchange provides information about currency futures and options. Its address is:

www.cme.com

a. Use this Web site to review the prevailing prices of currency futures contracts. Do today's futures prices (for contracts with the closest settlement date) generally reflect an increase or decrease from the day before? Is there any news today that might explain the change in the futures prices?

b. Does it appear that changes in futures prices among currencies (for the closest settlement date) are in the same direction? Explain.
c. If you purchased a British pound futures contract with the closest settlement date, what is the futures price? Given that a contract is based on 62,500 pounds, what is the dollar amount you will need at settlement date to fulfill the contract?

Running Your Own MNC

Using Currency Futures and Options

27a. How can you use currency futures to hedge the exchange rate risk of your MNC?

b. How can you use currency options to hedge the exchange rate risk of your MNC?

Blades, Inc. Case

Use of Currency Derivative Instruments

Blades, Inc. needs to order supplies two months ahead of the delivery date. It is considering an order from a Japanese supplier that requires a payment of 12.5 million yen payable as of the delivery date. Its choices are to either

- Purchase two call options contracts (since each option contract represents 6,250,000 yen) or
- Purchase one futures contract (which represents 12.5 million yen).

The futures price on yen has historically exhibited a slight discount from the existing spot rate. However, the firm would like to use currency options to hedge payables in Japanese yen for transactions two months in advance. Blades would prefer hedging its yen payable position because it is uncomfortable leaving the position open given the historical volatility of the yen. Nevertheless, the firm would be willing to remain unhedged if the yen becomes more stable someday.

Ben Holt, Blades' chief financial officer (CFO), prefers the flexibility that options offer over forward contracts or futures contracts because he can let the options expire if the yen depreciates. He would like to use an exercise price that is about 5 percent above the existing spot rate to ensure that Blades will have to pay no more than 5 percent above the existing spot rate for a transaction two months beyond its order date, as long as the option premium is no more than 1.6 percent of the price it would have to pay per unit when exercising the option.

In general, the options on the yen have required a premium that is about 1.5 percent of the total transaction amount that would be paid if the option is exercised. For example, recently the yen spot rate was $0.0072, and the firm purchased a call option with an exercise price of $0.00756, which is 5 percent above the existing spot rate. The premium for this option was $0.0001134, which is 1.5 percent of the price to be paid per yen if the option is exercised.

A recent event caused more uncertainty about the yen's future value, although it did not affect the spot rate or the forward or futures rate of the yen. Specifically, the yen's spot rate was still $0.0072, but the option premium for a call option with an exercise price of $0.00756 was now $0.0001512. There is an alternative call option available with an expiration date of two months from now that has a premium of $0.0001134 (which is the size of the premium that would have existed for the option desired before the event), but it is for a call option with an exercise price of $.00792.

The table below summarizes the option and futures information available to the firm:

	Before Event	After Event	
Spot Rate	$.0072	$.0072	$.0072
Option Information:			
Exercise Price ($)	$.00756	$.00756	$.00792
Exercise Price (% Above Spot)	5%	5%	10%
Option Premium Per Yen ($)	$.0001134	$.0001512	$.0001134

	Before Event	After Event	
Option Premium (% of Exercise Price)	1.5%	2.0%	1.5%
Total Premium ($)	$1,417.50	$1,890.00	$1,417.50
Amount Paid for Yen if Option Is Exercised (Not Including Premium)	$94,500.00	$94,500.00	$99,000.00
Futures Contract Information:			
Futures Price	$.006912	$.006912	

As an analyst for Blades, you have been asked to offer insight on how to hedge. Use a spreadsheet to support your analysis of questions 4 and 6.

1. If Blades uses call options to hedge its yen payables, should it use the call option with the exercise price of $0.00756 or the call option with the exercise price of $0.00792? Describe the tradeoff.
2. Should Blades allow its yen position to be unhedged? Describe the tradeoff.
3. Assume there are speculators who attempt to capitalize on their expectation of the yen's movement over the two months between order and delivery dates by either buying or selling yen futures now and buying or selling yen at the future spot rate. Given this information, what is the expectation on the order date of the yen spot rate by the delivery date? (Your answer should consist of one number.)
4. Assume that the firm shares the market consensus of the future yen spot rate. Given this expectation and given that the firm makes a decision (i.e., option, futures contract, remain unhedged) purely on a cost basis, what would be its optimal choice?
5. Will the choice you made as to the optimal hedging strategy in question 4 definitely turn out to be the lowest cost alternative in terms of actual costs incurred? Why or why not?
6. Now assume that you have determined that the historical standard deviation of the yen is about $0.0005. Based on your assessment, you believe it to be highly unlikely that the future spot rate will be more than two standard deviations above the expected spot rate by the delivery date. Also assume that the futures price remains at its current level of $0.006912. Based on this expectation of the future spot rate, what is the optimal hedge for the firm?

Small Business Dilemma

Use of Currency Futures and Options by the Sports Exports Company

The Sports Exports Company receives pounds each month as payment for the footballs that it exports. It anticipates that the pound will depreciate over time against the dollar.

1. How can the Sports Exports Company use currency futures contracts to hedge against exchange rate risk? Are there any limitations of using currency futures contracts that would prevent the Sports Exports Company from locking in a specific exchange rate at which it can sell all the pounds it expects to receive in each of the upcoming months?
2. How can the Sports Exports Company use currency options to hedge against exchange rate risk? Are there any limitations of using currency options contracts that would prevent the Sports Exports Company from locking in a specific exchange rate at which it can sell all the pounds it expects to receive in each of the upcoming months?
3. Jim Logan, owner of the Sports Exports Company, is concerned that the pound may depreciate substantially over the next month, but he also believes that the pound could appreciate substantially if specific situations occur. Should Jim use currency futures or currency options to hedge the exchange rate risk? Is there any disadvantage of selecting this method for hedging?

Appendix 5
Currency Option Pricing

It is useful to understand what drives the premiums paid for currency options in order to recognize the various factors that must be monitored when anticipating future movements in currency option premiums. Since participants in the currency options market typically take positions based on their expectations of how the premiums will change over time, they can benefit from understanding how options are priced.

Boundary Conditions

The first step in pricing currency options is to recognize boundary conditions that force the option premium to be within lower and upper bounds.

Lower Bounds

The call option premium (C) has a lower bound of at least zero or the spread between the underlying spot exchange rate (S) and the exercise price (X), whichever is greater, as shown below:

$$C \geq \text{MAX}(0, S - X).$$

This floor is enforced by arbitrage restrictions. For example, assume that the premium on a British pound call option is \$.01, while the spot rate of the pound is \$1.62 and the exercise price is \$1.60. In this example, the spread ($S - X$) exceeds the call premium, which would allow for arbitrage. One could purchase the call option for \$.01 per unit, immediately exercise the option at \$1.60 per pound, and then sell the pounds in the spot market for \$1.62 per unit. This would generate an immediate profit of \$.01 per unit. Arbitrage would continue until the market forces realigned the spread ($S - X$) to be less than or equal to the call premium.

The put option premium (P) has a lower bound of zero or the spread between the exercise price (X) and the underlying spot exchange rate (S), whichever is greater, as shown below:

$$P \geq \text{MAX}(0, X - S)$$

This floor is also enforced by arbitrage restrictions. For example, assume that the premium on a British pound put option is \$.02, while the spot rate of the pound is \$1.60 and the exercise price is \$1.63. One could purchase the pound put option for \$.02 per unit, purchase pounds in the spot market at \$1.60, and immediately exercise the option by selling the pounds at \$1.63 per unit. This would generate an immediate profit of \$.01 per unit. Arbitrage would continue until the market forces realigned the spread ($X - S$) to be less than or equal to the put premium.

Upper Bounds

The upper bound for a call option premium is equal to the spot exchange rate (S), as shown below:

$$C \leq S$$

If the call option premium ever exceeds the spot exchange rate, one could engage in arbitrage by selling call options for a higher price per unit than the cost of purchasing the underlying currency. Even if those call options are exercised, one could provide the currency that was purchased earlier (the call option was covered). The arbitrage profit in this example is the difference between the amount received when selling the premium and the cost of purchasing the currency in the spot market. Arbitrage would occur until the call option's premium was less than or equal to the spot rate.

The upper bound for a put option is equal to the option's exercise price (X), as shown below:

$$P \leq X$$

If the put option premium ever exceeds the exercise price, one could engage in arbitrage by selling put options. Even if the put options are exercised, the proceeds received from selling the put options exceed the price paid (which is the exercise price) at the time of exercise.

Given these boundaries that are enforced by arbitrage, option premiums lie within these boundaries.

APPLICATION OF PRICING MODELS

While boundary conditions can be used to determine the possible range for a currency option's premium, they do not precisely indicate the appropriate premium for the option. However, pricing models have been developed to price currency options. Based on information about an option (such as the exercise price and time to maturity) and about the currency (such as its spot rate, standard deviation, and interest rate), pricing models can derive the premium on a currency option. The currency option pricing model of Biger and Hull[4] is

$$C = e^{-r^*T} S \cdot N(d_1) - e^{-rT} X \cdot N(d_1 - \sigma\sqrt{T})$$

where

$d_1 = \{[\ln(S/X) + (r - r^* + (\sigma^2/2))T]/\sigma\sqrt{T}\}$
C = the price of the currency call option
S = the underlying spot exchange rate
X = the exercise price
r = the U.S. riskless rate of interest
r^* = the foreign riskless rate of interest
σ = the instantaneous standard deviation of the return on a holding of foreign currency

[4]Nahum Biger and John Hull, "The Valuation of Currency Options," *Financial Management* (Spring 1983), pp. 24–28.

T = the option's time maturity expressed as a fraction of a year
$N(\cdot)$ = the standard normal cumulative distribution function.

This equation is based on the stock option pricing model (OPM) when allowing for continuous dividends. Since the interest gained on holding a foreign security (r^*) is equivalent to a continuously paid dividend on a stock share, this version of the OPM holds completely. The key transformation in adapting the stock OPM to value currency options is the substitution of exchange rates for stock prices. Thus, the percentage change of exchange rates is assumed to follow a diffusion process with constant mean and variance.

Bodurtha and Courtadon[5] have tested the predictive ability of the currency option of the pricing model. They computed pricing errors from the model using 3,326 call options. The model's average percentage pricing error for call options was –6.90 percent, which is smaller than the corresponding error reported for the dividend-adjusted Black-Scholes stock OPM. Hence, the currency option pricing model has been more accurate than the counterpart stock OPM.

The model developed by Biger and Hull is sometimes referred to as the European model because it does not account for early exercise. European currency options do not allow for early exercise (before the expiration date), while American currency options do allow for early exercise. The extra flexibility of American currency options may justify a higher premium on American currency options than on European currency options with similar characteristics. However, there is not a closed-form model for pricing American currency options. While there are various techniques used to price American currency options, the European model is commonly applied to price American currency options because the European model can be just as accurate.

Bodurtha and Courtadon found that the application of an American currency options pricing model does not improve predictive accuracy. Their average percentage pricing error was –7.07 percent for all sample call options when using the American model.

Given all other parameters, the currency option pricing model can be used to impute the standard deviation σ. This implied parameter represents the option's market assessment of currency volatility over the life of the option.

Pricing Currency Put Options According to Put-Call Parity

Given the premium of a European call option (called C), the premium for a European put option (called P) on the same currency and same exercise price (X) can be derived from put-call parity, which is shown below:

$$P = C + Xe^{-rT} - Se^{-r^*T}$$

where

r = the U.S. riskless rate of interest
r^* = the foreign riskless rate of interest
T = the option's time to maturity expressed as a fraction of the year

[5]James Bodurtha and Georges Courtadon, "Tests of an American Option Pricing Model on the Foreign Currency Options Market," *Journal of Financial Quantitative Analysis* (June 1987), pp. 153–168.

If the actual put option premium is less than what is suggested by the put-call parity equation above, arbitrage can be conducted. Specifically, one could (1) buy the put option, (2) sell the call option, and (3) buy the underlying currency. The purchases are financed with the proceeds from selling the call option and from borrowing at the rate r. Meanwhile, the foreign currency that was purchased can be deposited to earn the foreign rate r^*. Regardless of the scenario for the path of the currency's exchange rate movement over the life of the option, the arbitrage will result in a profit. First, if the exchange rate is equal to the exercise price such that each option expires worthless, the foreign currency can be converted in the spot market to dollars, and this amount will exceed the amount required to repay the loan. Second, if the foreign currency appreciates and therefore exceeds the exercise price, there will be a loss from the call option being exercised. While the put option would expire, the foreign currency would be converted in the spot market to dollars, and this amount will exceed the amount required to repay the loan and the amount of the loss on the call option. Third, if the foreign currency depreciates and therefore is below the exercise price, the amount received from exercising the put option plus the amount received from converting the foreign currency to dollars will exceed the amount required to repay the loan. Since the arbitrage generates a profit under any exchange rate scenario, it will force an adjustment in the option premiums so that put-call parity is no longer violated.

If the actual put option premium is more than what is suggested by put-call parity, arbitrage would again be possible. The arbitrage strategy would be the reverse of that used when the actual put option premium was less than what is suggested by put-call parity (as was just described). The arbitrage would force an adjustment in option premiums so that put-call parity is no longer violated. The arbitrage that can be applied when there is a violation of put-call parity on American currency options differs slightly from the arbitrage applicable to European currency options. Nevertheless, the concept still holds that the premium of a currency put option can be determined according to the premium of a call option on the same currency and the same exercise price.

Part I Integrative Problem

The International Financial Environment

Mesa Co. specializes in the production of small fancy picture frames, which are exported from the United States to the United Kingdom. Mesa invoices the exports in pounds and converts the pounds to dollars when they are received. The British demand for these frames is positively related to economic conditions in the United Kingdom. Assume that British inflation and interest rates are similar to the rates in the United States. Mesa believes the U.S. balance of trade deficit from trade between the United States and the United Kingdom is expected to adjust to changing prices between the two countries, while capital flows will adjust to interest rate differentials. Mesa believes that the value of the pound is very sensitive to changing international flows and is moderately sensitive to changing international trade flows. The following information was considered by Mesa:

- The U.K. inflation rate is expected to decline, while the U.S. inflation rate is expected to rise.
- British interest rates are expected to decline, while U.S. interest rates are expected to increase.

Questions

1. Explain how the international trade flows should initially adjust in response to the changes in inflation (holding exchange rates constant). Explain how the international capital flows should adjust in response to the changes in interest rates (holding exchange rates constant).
2. Using the information provided, will Mesa expect the pound to appreciate or depreciate in the future? Explain.
3. Mesa believes international capital flows shift in response to changing interest rate differentials. Is there any reason why the changing interest rate differentials in this example will not necessarily cause international capital flows to change significantly? Explain.
4. Based on your answer to Question 2, how would Mesa's cash flows be affected by the expected exchange rate movements? Explain.
5. Based on your answer to Question 4, should Mesa consider hedging its exchange rate risk? If so, explain how it could hedge using forward contracts, futures contracts, and currency options.

Part II

Exchange Rate Behavior

Part II (Chapters 6 through 8) focuses on critical relationships pertaining to exchange rates. Chapter 6 explains how governments can influence exchange rate movements and how such movements can affect economic conditions. Chapter 7 explores the relationships among foreign currencies. It also explains how the forward exchange rate is influenced by the differential between interest rates of any two countries. Chapter 8 discusses prominent theories regarding the impact of inflation on exchange rates and the impact of interest rate movements on exchange rates.

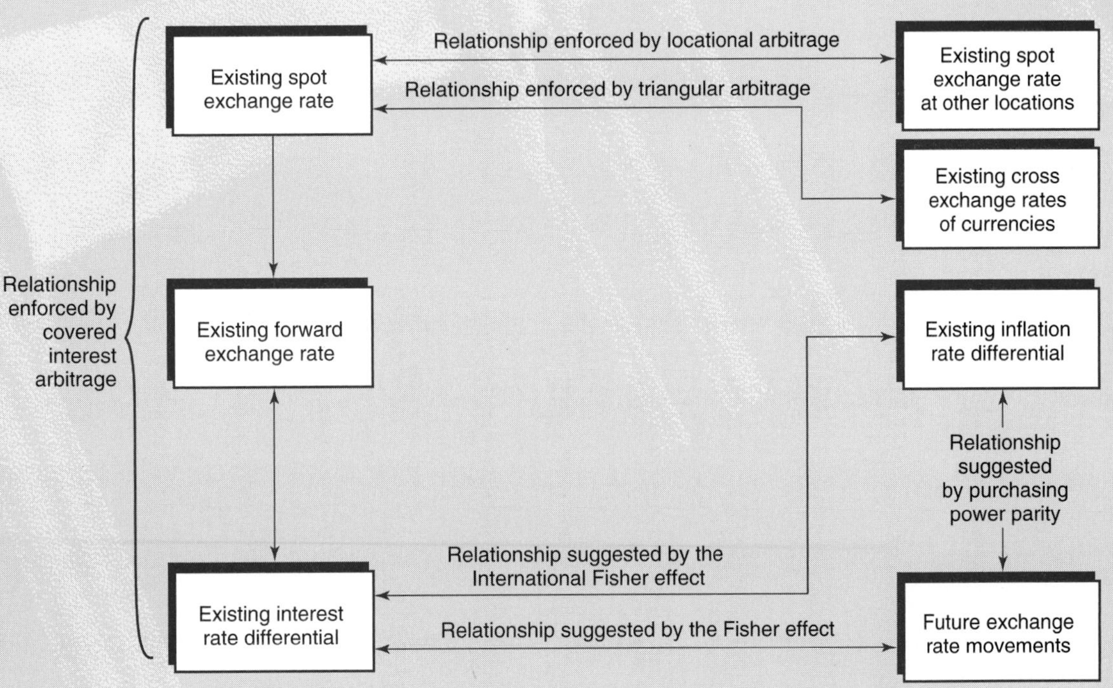

6 GOVERNMENT INFLUENCE ON EXCHANGE RATES

Government policies affect exchange rates, which can influence a country's economy and financial markets. Because the performance of a multinational corporation (MNC) is affected by both the economy and exchange rates, it is important to understand how the government affects exchange rates.

The specific objectives of this chapter are to

- describe the exchange rate systems used by various governments,
- explain how the governments can use direct intervention to influence exchange rates,
- explain how the governments can use indirect intervention to influence exchange rates, and
- explain how government intervention in the foreign exchange market can affect economic conditions.

EXCHANGE RATE SYSTEMS

Exchange rate systems can be classified according to the degree by which exchange rates are controlled by the government. Exchange rate systems normally fall into one of the following categories:

- Fixed
- Freely floating
- Managed float
- Pegged

Each of these exchange rate systems is discussed in turn.

Fixed Exchange Rate System

In a **fixed exchange rate system,** exchange rates are either held constant or allowed to fluctuate only within very narrow boundaries. If an exchange rate begins to move too much, governments can intervene to maintain it within the boundaries. The methods used by governments to control exchange rates are mentioned later in this chapter.

From 1944 to 1971, exchange rates were typically fixed according to a system planned at the Bretton Woods conference (in Bretton Woods, New Hampshire, 1944) by representatives from various countries. Because this arrangement, known as the **Bretton Woods Agreement,** lasted from 1944 to 1971, that period is sometimes referred to as the Bretton Woods era. Each currency was valued in terms of gold; for example, the U.S. dollar was valued as 1/35 ounce of gold. Since all currencies were valued in terms of gold, their values with respect to each other were fixed. Governments intervened in the foreign exchange markets to ensure that exchange rates drifted no more than 1 percent above or below the initially set rates.

During the Bretton Woods era, the United States often experienced balance of trade deficits, which may imply that the dollar's value was too strong, since the use of dollars for foreign purchases exceeded the demand by foreign countries for dollar-denominated goods. By 1971, it appeared that some currency values would need to be adjusted in order to restore a more balanced flow of payments between countries. As of December 1971, a conference among representatives of various countries concluded with the **Smithsonian Agreement,** which called for a devaluation of the U.S. dollar by about 8 percent against other currencies. In addition, boundaries for the currency values were expanded to within 2.25 percent above or below the rates initially set by the agreement. However, international payments imbalances continued, and as of February 1973, the dollar was again devalued. By March 1973, most governments of the major countries were no longer attempting to maintain their home currency values within the boundaries established by the Smithsonian Agreement.

Under a fixed exchange rate environment, the managerial duties of an MNC are less difficult. However, there is still the risk that the government will alter the value of a specific currency. Currency devaluation can boost a country's exports, and therefore productivity (and jobs), since it encourages foreign consumers and firms to purchase goods denominated in that devalued currency. Revaluation (increasing the value) of a currency can increase competition that local firms receive from foreign firms, since foreign currencies can be purchased cheaply. Revaluation is a useful strategy by governments to restrain inflation, since it may prevent local firms from substantially raising the prices of their products. Of course, not all currencies can be revalued or devalued simultaneously. If the U.S. dollar, for example, is devalued against other currencies, this implies that the other currencies have been revalued against the U.S. dollar.

Freely Floating Exchange Rate System

In a **freely floating exchange rate system,** exchange rate values would be determined by market forces without intervention by various governments. Under such a system, MNCs would need to devote substantial resources to measuring and managing exposure to exchange rate fluctuations.

Advantages of a Freely Floating Exchange Rate System. From a macro viewpoint, where the stability of the entire world is concerned, a freely floating system could be preferable to a fixed exchange rate system. To illustrate, assume that there are only two countries in the world: the United States and the United Kingdom. These countries trade frequently with each other. Now assume a fixed exchange rate system. If the United States experiences a much higher inflation rate than the United Kingdom, we might expect U.S. consumers to buy more goods in the United Kingdom and British consumers to reduce their imports of U.S. goods (due to the high U.S. prices). This reaction would force U.S. production down and unemployment up. It could also cause higher inflation in the United Kingdom due to the excessive demand for British goods relative to the supply of British goods produced. Thus, the high inflation in the United States could cause high inflation in the United Kingdom. In the mid- and late 1960s, the United States experienced relatively high inflation and was accused of "exporting" this inflation to some European countries.

The results would not necessarily be the same in a freely floating exchange rate environment. As a consequence of high U.S. inflation, the increased U.S. demand for British goods would place upward pressure on the value of the British pound. As a second consequence of high U.S. inflation, the reduced British demand for U.S. goods would imply a reduced supply of pounds for sale (exchanged into dollars), which would also place upward pressure on the British pound value. The pound would appreciate due to these market forces (it would not be allowed to appreciate under the fixed rate system). This appreciation would make British goods more expensive to the U.S. consumers, even though British producers did not raise their prices. The higher prices would simply be due to the pound's appreciation, requiring a greater number of U.S. dollars to buy the same number of pounds as before. In the United Kingdom, the actual price of the goods as measured in British pounds might possibly be unchanged. Even though U.S. prices increased, British consumers would continue to purchase U.S. goods because their pounds could be exchanged for more U.S. dollars (due to the British pound's appreciation against the U.S. dollar).

This discussion indicates that U.S. inflation would have a greater impact on inflation in other countries within a fixed exchange rate system than it would in a floating exchange rate system. Problems experienced in one country would not necessarily be as contagious to other countries in a freely floating exchange rate environment. In our example, the United Kingdom is somewhat insulated from the U.S. inflation due to movement in the exchange rate.

Consider a second common economic problem: unemployment. Under a fixed rate system, high U.S. unemployment will cause a reduction in U.S. income and a decline in U.S. purchases of British goods. Consequently, productivity in the United Kingdom might decrease and unemployment may rise. Under a floating rate system, the decline in U.S. purchases of British goods would reflect a reduced U.S. demand for British pounds. Such a shift in demand could cause the pound to depreciate against the dollar (under the fixed rate system, the pound would not be allowed to depreciate). The depreciation of the pound would make British goods look cheap to U.S. consumers, offsetting the possible reduction in demand for these goods that could result from a lower level of U.S. income. As was true with inflation, a sudden change in unemployment appears to be less influential on a foreign country under a floating rate system than under a fixed rate system.

An additional advantage of freely floating rates is that a central bank is not required to constantly maintain exchange rates within specified boundaries. Therefore, it is not forced to implement an intervention policy that may have an unfavorable effect on the economy just to control exchange rates. Furthermore, governments can implement policies without concern as to whether the policies will maintain the exchange rates within specified boundaries. Finally, if exchange rates were not allowed to float, investors would invest funds in whatever country had the highest interest rate. This would likely cause governments in countries with low interest rates to restrict investors' funds from leaving the country. Thus, there would be more capital flow restrictions, and financial market efficiency would be reduced.

Disadvantages of a Freely Floating System. In the previous examples, the United Kingdom is somewhat insulated from the problems experienced in the United States due to the freely floating exchange rate system. While this is an advantage in protecting one country (the United Kingdom), it can be a disadvantage to the country that initially experienced the economic problems. For instance, if the United States experiences high inflation, the dollar may weaken, thereby insulating the United Kingdom from the inflation, as discussed earlier. However, from the U.S. perspective, a weaker U.S. dollar causes import prices to be higher. This can increase the price of U.S. materials and supplies, which will in turn increase U.S. prices of finished goods. In addition, higher foreign prices (from the U.S. perspective) can force U.S. consumers to purchase domestic products. As U.S. producers recognize that their foreign competition has been reduced due to the weak dollar, they can more easily raise their prices without losing their customers to foreign competition.

As a second example, consider a situation in which the U.S. unemployment rate is increasing. This tends to force the value of the dollar up because the demand for imports decreases. A stronger dollar will then reignite the desire for foreign goods, since they can be purchased cheaply. Yet, such a reaction can actually be detrimental to the United States during periods of high unemployment.

The preceding examples illustrate that a country's problems can sometimes be compounded by freely floating exchange rates. On the other hand, our earlier examples show that in a fixed exchange rate environment a country's problems are more contagious to other countries. The designation of one system as more desirable may depend on a country's political environment, economic conditions, goals, and policies.

Managed Float Exchange Rate System

The exchange rate system that exists today for some currencies lies somewhere between fixed and freely floating. It resembles the freely floating system in that exchange rates are allowed to fluctuate on a daily basis and official boundaries do not exist. Yet, it is similar to the fixed system in that governments can and sometimes do intervene to prevent their currencies from moving too much in a certain direction. This type of system is known as a **managed float** or "dirty" float (as opposed to a "clean" float where rates float freely without government intervention). The various forms of intervention used by governments to manage exchange rate movements are discussed later in this chapter.

Some governments impose bands around their currency to limit the degree of movement. South Korea used this strategy to stabilize its currency (the won) in 1997, but discontinued it when it could not contain the value of the won within bands. Russia implemented a band of 15 percent above and below the prevailing exchange rate of its currency (the ruble) relative to the dollar in November 1997, but could not maintain the ruble's value within these bands. Brazil managed the depreciation of its currency (the real) to be about 7 percent per year, but recently allowed the real to float. Venezuela uses a floating peg system in which its currency is guided to depreciate by 1.5 percent per month against the dollar, but it is allowed flexibility to deviate above or below this level by 7.5 percent.

http://
The Investorlinks site at www.investorlinks.com/global-central-banks.html provides links to central banks around the world.

Criticism of a Managed Float System. Some critics suggest that a managed float system allows a government to manipulate exchange rates in a manner that could benefit its own country at the expense of others. For example, a government may attempt to weaken its currency to stimulate a stagnant economy. The increased aggregate demand for products that results from such a policy may reflect a decreased aggregate demand for products in other countries, as the weakened currency attracts foreign demand. While this criticism is valid, it could apply as well to the fixed exchange rate system, where governments have the power to devalue their currencies.

Pegged Exchange Rate System

Some countries use a **pegged exchange rate** arrangement, in which their home currency's value is pegged to a foreign currency or to some unit of account. While the home currency's value is fixed in terms of the foreign currency (or unit of account) to which it is pegged, it moves in line with that currency against other currencies.

Some Asian countries such as Malaysia and Thailand had pegged their currency's value to the dollar. During the Asian crisis, though, they were unable to maintain the peg and allowed their currencies to float against the dollar.

Europe's Exchange Rate Mechanism (ERM).

One of the best-known pegged exchange rate arrangements was established by the European Economic Community (EEC) in April 1972, when EEC members determined that their currencies were to be maintained within established limits of each other. This arrangement became known as the **snake.** Market pressure caused some currencies to move outside their established limits. Consequently, some members withdrew from the snake arrangement; it was difficult to maintain, and some currencies were realigned.

Due to continued problems with the snake arrangement, the European Monetary System (EMS) was pushed into operation as of March 1979. The EMS concept is similar to the snake arrangement, but the specific characteristics differ. Under the EMS arrangement, exchange rates of member countries were held together within specified limits and were also tied to the European Currency Unit (ECU), which was a unit of account. Its value was a weighted average of exchange rates of the member countries, each weight determined by a member's relative gross national product and activity in intra-European trade. The currencies of these member countries were allowed to fluctuate by no more than 2.25 percent (6 percent for some currencies) from the initially established par values. In 1993, these boundaries were widened substantially, allowing more fluctuation in exchange rates between European currencies.

The method of linking European currency values with the ECU was known as the **exchange rate mechanism (ERM).** The participating governments intervened in the foreign exchange markets to maintain the exchange rates within boundaries established by the ERM.

The exchange rate mechanism experienced severe problems in the fall of 1992, as economic conditions and goals varied among European countries. The German government focused on controlling inflation and implemented a tight monetary policy, which increased German interest rates. Money flowed out of other European countries into Germany to capitalize on the relatively high German interest rates. Since exchange rates between European currencies were tied (within boundaries), European investors could capitalize on the high German interest rates without much concern about exchange rate risk. The flow of funds out of other European countries reduced the supply of funds in these countries. Consequently, interest rates increased in these countries as well, at a time when their respective governments were attempting to lower interest rates in order to stimulate their economies. The end result was less aggregate spending in countries because of the increase in interest rates. Such a result was especially undesirable during 1992 because some European countries were in the midst of a recession.

http://
Visit the European Union site at europa.eu.int/index-en.htm for access to the server of the European Union's parliament, Council, Commission, Court of Justice, and other bodies. It includes basic information on all related political and economic issues.

In the fall of 1992, the central banks of European countries attempted to maintain exchange rates through direct intervention in the foreign exchange markets. They also attempted to increase interest rates, which would discourage investors from investing in marks to capitalize on high German interest rates. However, this form of intervention conflicted with the goals of stimulating European economies. In an attempt to stabilize the ERM, the central banks of some European countries were prevented from using more stimulative monetary policies.

In the fall of 1992, Germany had experienced a large budget deficit in financing the reunification of East and West Germany. The German government was more concerned about inflation and less concerned about unemployment because its economy was relatively strong. However, other European governments were more concerned about stimulating their economies to reduce their high unemployment levels.

In October 1992, the British and Italian governments suspended their participation in the ERM because their own goals for a stronger economy could not be satisfied if their interest rates were to be so highly influenced by the German interest rates. This suspension of participation in the ERM meant that their currencies were no longer tied to the German mark and other European currencies. Therefore, even if interest rates were higher in some European countries, funds in the United Kingdom and in Italy would not necessarily flow to those countries because of exchange rate risk. In this way, the British and Italian interest rates would be more dependent on local conditions than on the conditions of other European countries.

Ireland's unemployment rate was 17 percent at the time, and high interest rates were preventing any possible stimulus in Ireland's economy. Since the United Kingdom suspended its ties with the ERM, the British pound depreciated substantially against European currencies, including the Irish punt (mainly because of the relatively high interest rates in these countries). About one-third of Ireland's exports are to the United Kingdom. The Irish punt appreciated by about 15 percent against the British pound, causing a reduced British demand for Irish goods. Ireland responded to the crisis by devaluing its currency against other European currencies in an attempt to enhance exports and stimulate its economy.

Meanwhile, Denmark attempted to maintain its currency position in the ERM, while Finland, Norway, and Sweden allowed their currencies to decline against ERM currencies in an attempt to stimulate their economies. Since 20 percent of Denmark's trade is with these three countries, its exports were severely reduced because Denmark's exports were now priced relatively high as compared to these other countries.

€

The demise of Europe's exchange rate mechanism provided momentum for the single European currency (the euro), which began in 1999, and is discussed later in this chapter.

The Mexican Peso Crisis. In 1994, Mexico's central bank used a special form of a pegged exchange rate system. It linked the peso to the U.S. dollar, but allowed a band within which the peso's value could fluctuate against the dollar. It enforced the link through frequent intervention. In fact, it partially supported its intervention by issuing short-term debt securities denominated in dollars, and using the dollars to purchase pesos in the foreign exchange market. Limiting the degree of depreciation in the peso was intended to reduce inflationary pressure that can be caused when a home currency is very weak because it reduces competition from foreign firms. However, Mexico experienced a large balance of trade deficit in 1994, perhaps because the peso was stronger than it should have been and encouraged Mexican firms and consumers to buy an excessive amount of imports.

By December 1994, there was substantial downward pressure on the peso. On December 20, 1994, Mexico's central bank devalued the peso by about 13 percent. Mexico's stock prices plummeted, as many foreign investors sold their shares and withdrew their funds from Mexico in anticipation of further devaluation of the peso. On December 22, the central bank allowed the peso to float freely, and it declined by 15 percent. This was the beginning of the so-called Mexican peso crisis. The central bank increased interest rates in an attempt to discourage foreign investors from withdrawing their investments in Mexico's debt securities. Yet, the higher interest rates increased the cost of borrowing for Mexican firms and consumers, thereby slowing economic growth.

As the central bank of Mexico's short-term debt obligations denominated in dollars matured, it used its weak pesos to obtain dollars and repay the debt. Since the peso weakened, the effective cost of financing with dollars was very expensive for the central bank of Mexico. The financial problems in Mexico caused a lack of confidence by investors in peso-denominated securities, which encouraged them to liquidate their peso-denominated securities and transfer their funds to other countries. These actions placed additional downward pressure on the peso. In the four-month period beginning December 20, 1994, the value of the peso had declined by more than 50 percent. Over time, Mexico's economy improved and the paranoia leading to the withdrawal of funds by foreign investors subsided. The Mexican crisis may not have occurred if the peso was allowed to float throughout 1994, because the peso would have gravitated toward its natural level. The crisis illustrates why central bank intervention will not necessarily be able to overwhelm market forces, and may serve as an argument for letting a currency float freely.

Currency Boards. A **currency board** is a system for maintaining the value of the local currency with respect to some other specified currency. For example, Hong Kong has tied the value of its currency (the Hong Kong dollar) to the U.S. dollar (HK$7.8=$1) since 1983; Argentina has tied the value of its peso to the U.S. dollar (one peso equals one U.S. dollar) since 1991.

For the currency board to be successful at maintaining the value of the local currency with respect to some other specified currency, it must have credibility in its promise to maintain the exchange rate. If some economic conditions place downward pressure on the local currency's value, the currency board must use intervention to defend the currency's value. If speculators believe that the currency board will not support the specified exchange rate, they may take positions that would generate profits if the currency board discontinues its support of the local currency. For example, if speculators were concerned about the potential weakness of the Hong Kong dollar against the U.S. dollar, they would exchange Hong Kong dollars for U.S. dollars. They would maintain the U.S. dollars until the Hong Kong dollar weakened and then exchange the U.S. dollars back into Hong Kong dollars at a more favorable exchange rate. The actions of speculators to move money out of the currency that might weaken places even more pressure on that currency and makes it more difficult for the currency board to defend its position. There have been some speculative actions taken in anticipation of a weakening of the Hong Kong dollar, but the Hong Kong government successfully maintained the Hong Kong dollar's value. In 1995, Argentina experienced financial problems, and some speculators withdrew their bank deposits and transferred funds overseas, anticipating a possible decline in the peso's value. The government successfully maintained the peso's value, but there was a cost, as it may have been more able to increase demand for its exports if it allowed the peso to weaken. Yet, the effort to maintain the value of the peso gave the currency board credibility and reduced the chances of future speculative actions.

When Indonesia was experiencing financial problems during the 1997–1998 Asian crisis, businesses and investors sold the local currency (rupiah) because of expectations that it would weaken further. Such actions perpetuated the weakness, as the exchange of rupiah for other currencies placed more downward pressure on the value of the rupiah. Indonesia considered implementing a currency board to stabilize its currency and therefore discourage the flow of funds out of the country. Yet, businesses and investors had no confidence in Indonesia's government to maintain a fixed exchange rate, as economic pressures on the rupiah would ultimately lead to a decline in the rupiah's value. Thus, Indonesia's government did not implement a currency board.

A country that uses a currency board does not have complete control over its local interest rates, as its interest rates must be aligned with the interest rates of the currency to which it is tied. For example, if Hong Kong lowered its interest rates to stimulate its economy, its interest rate would then be lower than U.S. interest rates. Investors based in Hong Kong would be enticed to exchange Hong Kong dollars for U.S. dollars and invest in the United States where interest rates are higher. Since the Hong Kong dollar is tied to the U.S. dollar, the investors could exchange the proceeds of their investment at the end of the investment period back to Hong Kong dollars without concern about exchange rate risk because the exchange rate is fixed.

Conversely, if U.S. interest rates were lower than interest rates in Hong Kong (on securities with similar risk), U.S. investors could capitalize on the higher Hong Kong interest rates by investing in Hong Kong. In some cases, the interest rate on a specific type of security will not be exactly the same in each country because of risk. For example, while Argentina's peso is tied to the dollar, the interest rates in Argentina are commonly about 4 percentage points higher than in the United States, but this reflects the perception of higher credit risk (risk that the borrower will not repay the creditor). Nevertheless, an adjustment in the interest rates in the United States will normally cause somewhat similar adjustments in the interest rates of other currencies that are tied to the dollar.

Impact of Exchange Rates on Countries with Pegged Currencies. To illustrate how a currency that is pegged to the U.S. dollar can be affected by other exchange rate movements, consider a world of three countries: (1) the United States, (2) a country called FLOAT, whose currency fluctuates against the dollar, and (3) a country called PEG, whose currency is pegged to the dollar. Assume that FLOAT's currency is currently valued at $.50 while PEG's currency is valued at $1.20. This implies that the cross exchange rate between FLOAT's and PEG's currencies is 2.4 units of FLOAT's currency for each unit of PEG's currency (computed as $1.2/$.50 = 2.4). Assume that each country trades with the other two countries and that some of the products traded are also produced in the other countries. Now assume that over the next six months, FLOAT's currency depreciates against the dollar and is worth only $.40 by the end of this six-month period. The most obvious result is an increase in the U.S. demand for FLOAT's products, because FLOAT's products can be purchased with fewer dollars. In addition, there is a decrease in FLOAT's demand for U.S. products, because these products cost more to FLOAT's firms and consumers. Yet, PEG's trade positions are also affected, as follows.

When FLOAT's currency depreciates against the dollar, it also depreciates against PEG's currency, since PEG's currency is pegged to the dollar. In this example, the cross rate has changed to three units of FLOAT's currency for each unit of PEG's currency (computed as \$1.2/\$.40 = 3). This causes FLOAT's consumers and firms to reduce their demand for PEG's products and PEG's consumers and firms to increase their demand for FLOAT's products.

Even though the value of PEG's currency with respect to the U.S. dollar is unchanged, the trade between the United States and PEG will be affected. Because U.S. consumers and firms can purchase FLOAT's products with fewer dollars, they will substitute FLOAT's exports for PEG's exports. In addition, PEG's consumers and firms will substitute FLOAT's exports for U.S. exports, because the price they pay for FLOAT's exports has been reduced.

Overall, the depreciation of FLOAT's currency against the dollar (and therefore against PEG's currency) causes an increase in FLOAT's exports to the other two countries and a decrease in FLOAT's demand for imports from those countries. In addition, the volume of trade between the United States and PEG decreases. FLOAT's economy is stimulated by these actions.

If our example is revised to assume appreciation of FLOAT's currency against the U.S. dollar, the opposite effects will likely occur. The United States and PEG will increase their demand for each other's products and reduce their demand for FLOAT's products. FLOAT will increase demand for U.S. and PEG's products. In general, the economies of the United States and PEG will be stimulated by this event.

The validity of this theory can be reinforced with a realistic example. The Hong Kong dollar is pegged to the U.S. dollar, while the Japanese yen floats against the dollar. Significant adjustments in international trade can occur when the yen appreciates against the U.S. dollar, as Japanese products become more expensive to U.S. importers (except when the Japanese firms reduced the price to fully compensate for the weak dollar). Therefore, some U.S. importers switch their purchases to products produced by Hong Kong manufacturers. Conversely, some U.S. importers switch back to Japan when the yen weakens, since the relative purchasing power of U.S. importers that purchase Japanese imports increases.

Classification of Exchange Rate Arrangements

Exhibit 6.1 categorizes exchange rate arrangements used by various countries. Many countries allow the value of their currency to float against others but intervene periodically to influence its value. Several small countries peg their currencies to the U.S. dollar, while others peg their currencies to a currency composite. Although a country can attempt to peg its value against any particular currency, it cannot peg its value to all currencies. For example, when Argentina pegs the value of its peso to the dollar, the peso's value is fixed relative to the U.S. dollar, but its value moves in tandem with the dollar against other currencies, including other Latin American currencies. Thus, if the Mexican peso depreciates against the U.S. dollar, it will also depreciate against the Argentina peso during a period when the Argentina peso is pegged to the dollar.

The Mexican peso has a controlled exchange rate that applies to international trade and a floating market rate that applies to tourism. The floating market rate is influenced by central bank intervention. In recent years, Mexico has reduced its inflation rate and has been able to stabilize the value of the peso. Argentina intervenes frequently to stabilize its currency's value. Chile intervenes to maintain its cur-

Exhibit 6.1
Exchange Rate Arrangements

Floating Rate System

This list includes some currencies that are pegged to another currency, but the value is allowed to float within a range.

Country	Currency
Afghanistan	afghani
Australia	dollar
Bolivia	boliviano
Brazil	real
Canada	dollar
Chile	peso
Greece	drachma
India	rupee
Indonesia	rupiah
Israel	new shekel
Jamaica	dollar
Japan	yen
Mexico	peso
Norway	krone
Paraguay	guarani
Peru	new sol
Poland	zloty
Romania	leu
Russia	ruble
Singapore	dollar
South Africa	rand
South Korea	won
Sweden	krona
Switzerland	franc
Taiwan	new dollar
Thailand	baht
U.K.	pound
Venezuela	bolivar

European Monetary System

Country	Currency
Austria	schilling*
Belgium	franc*
Denmark	krone
Finland	markka*
France	franc*
Germany	mark*
Ireland	pound*
Italy	lire*
Luxembourg	franc*
Netherlands	guilder*
Portugal	escudo*
Spain	peseta*

*Designates a currency that was replaced by the euro for commercial transactions as of 1999 and will be phased out even for retail transactions by the year 2002.

Pegged Rate System		
The following currencies are pegged to a currency or a composite of currencies.		
Country	**Currency**	**Currency Is Pegged to**
Argentina	peso	U.S. dollar
Bahamas	dollar	U.S. dollar
Barbados	dollar	U.S. dollar
Bermuda	dollar	U.S. dollar
China	yuan	U.S. dollar
Hong Kong	dollar	U.S. dollar
Hungary	forint	Composite of European currencies
Saudi Arabia	riyal	U.S. dollar

rency within 10 percent of a specified exchange rate with respect to major currencies. Venezuela intervenes to limit exchange rate fluctuations within wide bands.

Some Eastern European countries that recently opened their markets have tied their currencies to a single widely traded currency. The arrangement was sometimes temporary, as these countries were searching for the proper exchange rate that would stabilize or enhance their economic conditions. For example, the government of Slovakia devalued its currency (the koruna) in an attempt to increase the foreign demand for its goods and reduce unemployment.

Many governments attempt to impose exchange controls in order to prevent their exchange rates from fluctuating. However, when these governments remove the controls, the exchange rates abruptly adjust to a new market-determined level. For example, in October 1994, the Russian authorities allowed the Russian ruble to fluctuate, and the ruble depreciated by 27 percent against the dollar on that day. In April 1996, Venezuela's government removed controls on the bolivar (its currency), and the bolivar depreciated by 42 percent on that day.

A Single European Currency

In 1991, the Maastricht treaty called for the goal of a single European currency. As of January 1, 1999, the euro replaced national currencies of 11 European countries for the purpose of commercial transactions executed through electronic transfers and other forms of payment. By June 1, 2002, the national currencies are to be withdrawn from the financial system and replaced with the euro. Of the 15 member countries that are part of the European Union, 11 countries have initially agreed to participate in the euro: Austria, Belgium, Finland, France, Germany, Ireland, Italy, Luxembourg, Netherlands, Portugal, and Spain. Three other members (United Kingdom, Denmark, and Sweden) have decided not to participate initially but may join later. The participating countries comprise almost 20 percent of the world's total gross domestic product, which is similar to the level of production in the United States. Greece does not qualify because its federal deficit level is too high, but it may participate once it reduces its debt level. Other emerging countries in Europe, such as the Czech Republic or Hungary, may also join the European Union later if they satisfy the limitations imposed on government deficits.

The euro enables participating countries to engage in cross-border trade flows and capital flows without converting to a different currency. This avoids transaction costs and exposure to exchange rate movements. However, the euro's value will fluctuate against currencies of other countries, based on supply and demand conditions. For example, its value with respect to the dollar will be influenced by the trade flows and capital flows between the set of participating European countries and the United States, since these flows affect the supply and demand conditions. Its value with respect to the Japanese yen will be influenced by the trade flows and capital flows between the set of participating European currencies and Japan. Since the euro's value is essentially derived from a portfolio of European currencies, it should be less volatile than the currencies it replaced, such as the German mark or the French franc.

Impact on European Monetary Policy

The euro allows for a single money supply throughout much of Europe, rather than a separate money supply for each participating currency. Thus, European monetary policy is consolidated, because any effects on the supply of money impact all European countries using that one currency as their form of money. The implementation of a common monetary policy may create more political unification among European countries with similar national defense and foreign policies. The new European Central Bank (ECB) will be based in Frankfurt and will be responsible for setting monetary policy for all participating European countries. Its objective will be to control inflation in the participating countries and to stabilize (within reasonable boundaries) the value of the euro with respect to other major currencies. Thus, the ECB's monetary goals of price stability and currency stability are somewhat similar to those of individual countries around the world, but these goals are distinguished in that they are focused on a group of countries instead of a single country.

Although a single European monetary policy may allow for more consistent economic conditions across countries, it prevents any individual European country from solving local economic problems with its own unique monetary policy. European governments may disagree on the ideal monetary policy to enhance their local economies, but they must agree on a single European monetary policy. Any given policy used in a particular period may enhance some countries and adversely affect others. Yet, each participating country will still be able to apply its own fiscal policy (tax and government expenditure decisions). The use of a common currency may someday create more political harmony among European countries.

Impact on Business within Europe

The elimination of currency movements among European countries encourages more long-term business arrangements between firms of different countries, as there would not be a concern about adverse effects due to currency movements. Thus, there should be an increase in all types of business arrangements including licensing, joint ventures, and acquisitions between firms in different European countries.

Prices of products will become more comparable among European countries, as the exchange rate between the countries will be fixed. Thus, buyers will be more able to determine where they can obtain products at the lowest cost.

There should be more trade flows between the participating European countries, as exporters and importers can conduct trade without concern about exchange rate movements. To the extent that there are more trade flows between these countries, economic conditions in each of these countries should have a larger impact on the other European countries, and economies of these countries may become more integrated.

Impact on the Valuation of Businesses in Europe

When firms consider acquiring targets in Europe, they will be more able to compare the prices (market values) of targets among countries because their values will be denominated in the same currency (the euro). In addition, the future currency movements of the target's currency against any non-European currency will be the same. Therefore U.S. firms could more easily conduct valuations of firms across the participating European countries because there are no longer any differences in exchange rate effects when funds are remitted to the U.S. parent. The level of appreciation or depreciation when funds are remitted to the United States from any of the participating countries will be the same for a particular period.

Because firms can be more easily compared among the participating European countries, these firms will be pressured to perform well when measured against all other firms in the same industry throughout these countries, not just within its own country. Therefore, these firms will become more focused on meeting various performance goals.

Impact on Financial Flows

Stock prices are now more comparable among the European countries because they are denominated in the same currency. Investors in the participating European countries are now able to invest in stocks throughout these countries without concern about exchange rate risk. Thus, there will be more cross-border investing than there was in the past. Since stock market prices are influenced by expectations of economic conditions, the stock prices among the European countries may become more highly correlated if economies among these countries become more highly correlated. Investors from other countries who invest in European countries may not achieve as much diversification as in the past because of the integration and because the exchange rate effects will be the same for all markets whose stocks are denominated in euros. Stock markets in these European countries are also likely to consolidate over time now that they use the same currency for denomination.

http://
Visit pacific.commerce.ubc.ca/xr/euro for basic information about the new single European currency (euro) and the process to achieve monetary union.

Bond investors based in these European countries will be able to invest in bonds issued by governments and corporations in these countries without concern about exchange rate risk, as long as the bonds are denominated in euros. Some European governments have already issued bonds that will be redenominated in euros, because some bonds placed in Europe with other currency denominations will not have an active secondary market once euro-denominated bonds become popular. The bond yields in these European countries will not necessarily be similar even though they will now be denominated in the same currency; the credit risk may generally be higher for issuers in a particular country.

Impact on Exchange Rate Risk

One major advantage of a single European currency is the complete elimination of exchange rate risk between the participating European countries, which could encourage more trade and capital flows across European borders. In addition, foreign exchange transactions costs associated with transactions between European countries would be eliminated. The single European currency is consistent with the goal of the Single European Act to remove trade barriers between European borders, since exchange rate risk is an implicit trade barrier.

European countries that participate in the single European currency may still be affected by movements in the euro's value with respect to other existing currencies such as the dollar. Furthermore, many U.S. firms will still be affected by movements in the euro's value with respect to the dollar.

A single European currency forces the interest rate offered on government securities to be similar across the participating European countries. Any discrepancy in rates would encourage investors within these European countries to invest in the currency with the highest rate, which would realign the interest rates among these countries.

Government Intervention

Each country has a government agency that may intervene in the foreign exchange markets to control its currency's value. In the United States, for example, the central bank is the Federal Reserve System (the Fed). Central banks have more duties than intervention in the foreign exchange market. They attempt to control the growth of money supply in their respective countries in a way that will favorably affect economic conditions.

Reasons for Government Intervention

The degree to which the home currency is controlled, or "managed," varies among central banks. Three common reasons for central banks to manage exchange rates are

- To smooth exchange rate movements.
- To establish implicit exchange rate boundaries.
- To respond to temporary disturbances.

Smooth Exchange Rate Movements. If a central bank is concerned that its economy will be affected by abrupt movements in its home currency's value, it may attempt to smooth the currency movements over time. Its actions may keep business cycles less volatile. It may also increase international trade by reducing exchange rate uncertainty. Furthermore, smoothing currency movements may reduce fears in the financial markets and speculative activity that could cause a major decline in a currency's value.

Establish Implicit Exchange Rate Boundaries. Some central banks attempt to maintain their home currency rates within some unofficial, or implicit, boundaries. Analysts are commonly quoted as forecasting that a currency will not fall below or rise above a particular benchmark value because the central bank would intervene to prevent that.

The Federal Reserve periodically intervened between 1983 and 1985 in an attempt to reverse the U.S. dollar's upward momentum and from 1986 through the beginning of 1988 to reverse the dollar's downward momentum. This implies that the Fed may have established implicit boundaries for the dollar. Yet, even if boundaries did exist, they would likely be modified over time. A very weak or strong dollar would be more tolerable in some periods than in others.

Respond to Temporary Disturbances. In some cases, a central bank may intervene to insulate a currency's value from a temporary disturbance. In fact, the stated objective of the Fed's intervention policy is to counter disorderly market conditions. For example, the news that oil prices might rise could cause expectations of a future decline in the Japanese yen value, since Japan exchanges yen for dollars to purchase oil from oil-exporting countries. Foreign exchange market speculators may exchange yen for dollars in anticipation of this decline. Central banks may therefore intervene to offset the immediate downward pressure on the yen caused by such market transactions.

Several studies have found that government intervention does not have a permanent impact on exchange rate movements. In many cases, intervention is overwhelmed by market forces. Central banks operate, however, on the theory that currency movements would be even more volatile in the absence of intervention.

Direct Intervention

The Fed's direct method of intervention to force dollar depreciation is to exchange dollars that it holds as reserves for other foreign currencies in the foreign exchange market. This so-called "flooding the market with dollars" places downward pressure on the dollar. If the Fed desires to strengthen the dollar, it can exchange foreign currencies for dollars in the foreign exchange market, thereby placing upward pressure on the dollar.

The effects of direct intervention on the value of the British pound is illustrated in Exhibit 6.2. To strengthen the pound's value (or to weaken the dollar), the Fed exchanges dollars for pounds, which reflects an outward shift in the demand for pounds in the foreign exchange market (as shown in the graph on the left). Conversely, to weaken the pound's value (or to strengthen the dollar), the Fed exchanges pounds for dollars, which reflects an outward shift in the supply of pounds for sale in the foreign exchange market (as shown in the graph on the right).

Direct intervention is usually most effective when there is a coordinated effort among central banks. If all central banks simultaneously attempt to strengthen or weaken the dollar in the manner just described, they can exert greater pressure on the dollar's value.

Examples of Direct Intervention. In September 1985, the central banks of the United States, Germany, the United Kingdom, France, and Japan implemented a coordinated program to weaken the dollar. These actions were the result of an agreement among country representatives in the Plaza Hotel in New York, an agreement now referred to as the **Plaza Accord.** The foreign exchange markets were flooded with billions of dollars as these central banks exchanged dollars for foreign currencies. This action added momentum to the dollar's fall. However, while direct intervention was frequently used in 1986 and 1987 to strengthen the dollar, the dollar still continued to weaken.

Exhibit 6.2
Effects of Direct Central Bank Intervention in the Foreign Exchange Market

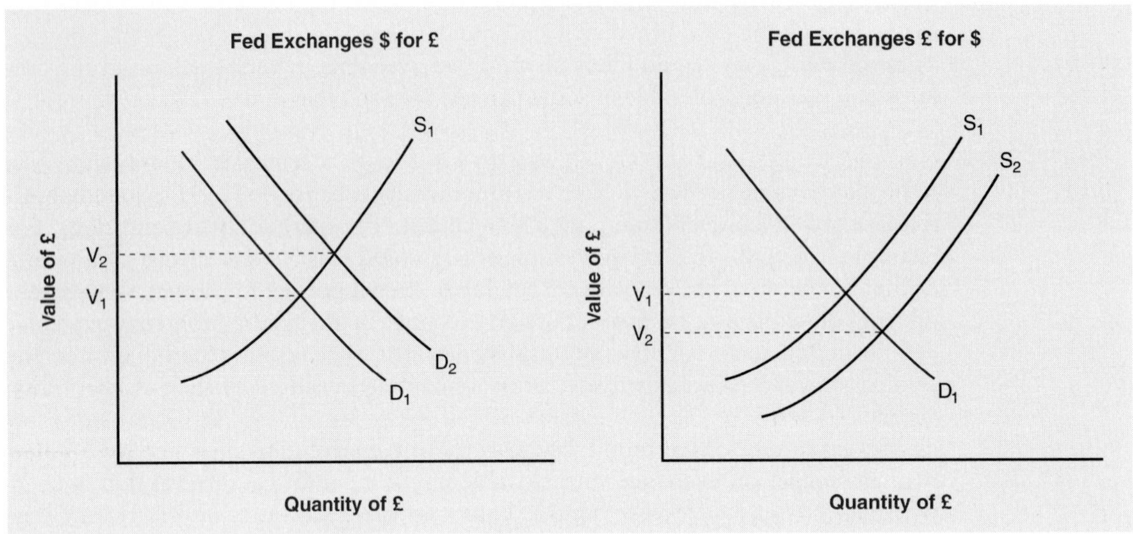

The dollar began to strengthen in 1988. As it continued to strengthen in the summer of 1989, there was some concern by the industrialized countries that a stronger dollar could adversely affect the world economy. Five central banks intervened on September 14, 1989, precipitating an abrupt decline in the dollar's value. However, additional central bank intervention in the following month was overwhelmed by market transactions. With the growth in foreign exchange activity, central bank intervention is less effective. The volume of foreign exchange transactions on a single day exceeds the combined values of reserves at all central banks.

In 1989, the Fed intervened on 97 different days. Since then, the Fed has not intervened on more than 20 days in any year.

In 1992, the dollar was weak, causing the Federal Reserve to intervene by purchasing dollars with European currencies. In 1993, the concern was focused on the Japanese yen, which appreciated against the dollar by 13 percent over the first five months of 1993 and reached a post-World War II high. The Federal Reserve intervened seven times on May 27, 1993, to prevent further momentum. Specifically, the Fed repeatedly purchased dollars with yen in the foreign exchange market on this day. Though the efforts may have temporarily slowed the yen's momentum, the yen was not weakened.

On August 8, 1994, the Fed and 15 other central banks intervened to prevent further weakening of the dollar. They exchanged foreign currencies for about $1.5 billion in the foreign exchange market. The intervention effort was not successful, as the value of the dollar continued to decline.

On August 15, 1995, central banks intervened in the foreign exchange market by purchasing dollars. This intervention caused the yen to decline by more than 3 percent against the dollar on that day.

On June 17, 1998, the Federal Reserve and Japan's central bank directly intervened in the foreign exchange market by using more than $3 billion to purchase Japanese yen. The Fed was concerned that the continued depreciation of the yen would place more downward pressure on other Asian currencies. The yen's value increased by 5 percent on the day of the intervention, but some of that gain was lost over the following days. Then, on January 12, 1999, Japan's central bank used yen to purchase dollars and caused the yen to decline by 4 percent at one point during the day.

Nonsterilized Versus Sterilized Intervention. When the Fed intervenes in the foreign exchange market without adjusting for the change in money supply, it is engaging in **nonsterilized intervention.** For example, if the Fed exchanges dollars for foreign currencies in the foreign exchange markets in an attempt to strengthen foreign currencies (weaken the dollar), the dollar money supply increases.

If the Fed desires to intervene in the foreign exchange market while retaining the dollar money supply, it uses **sterilized intervention,** achieved by simultaneous transactions in the foreign exchange markets and Treasury securities markets. For example, if the Fed desires to strengthen foreign currencies (weaken the dollar) without affecting the dollar money supply, it (1) exchanges dollars for foreign currencies and (2) sells some of its holdings of Treasury securities for dollars. The net effect is an increase in investors' holdings of Treasury securities and a decrease in bank foreign currency balances.

The difference between nonsterilized and sterilized intervention is illustrated in Exhibit 6.3. In one scenario, the Federal Reserve attempts to strengthen the Canadian dollar (top section of exhibit), and in a second scenario, the Federal Reserve attempts to weaken the Canadian dollar (bottom section of exhibit). For each scenario, this exhibit shows how the sterilized intervention (graph on the right) involves an exchange of Treasury securities for U.S. dollars that offsets the U.S. dollar flows resulting from the exchange of currencies. That is, the sterilized intervention achieves the same exchange of currencies in the foreign exchange market as nonsterilized intervention, but it involves an additional transaction to prevent adjustments in the U.S. dollar money supply.

Exhibit 6.3
Forms of Central Bank Intervention in the Foreign Exchange Market

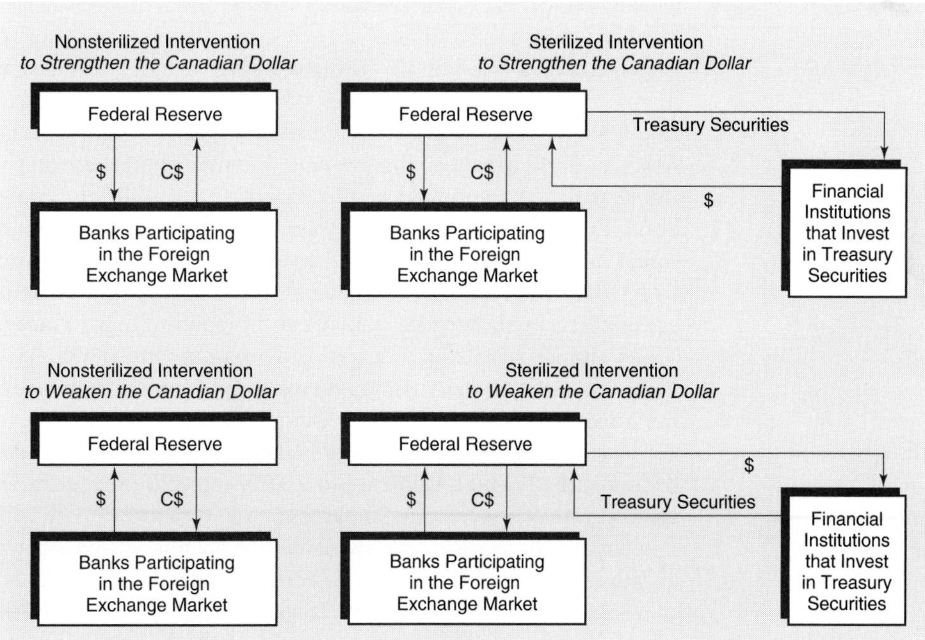

Speculating on Direct Intervention. Some traders in the foreign exchange market attempt to determine when Federal Reserve intervention is occurring, and the extent of the intervention, in order to capitalize on the anticipated results of the intervention effort. Normally, the Federal Reserve attempts to intervene without being noticed. However, dealers at the major banks that trade with the Fed often pass the information to other market participants. Also, when the Fed deals directly with numerous commercial banks, markets are well aware that the Fed is intervening. To hide its strategy, the Fed may pretend to be interested in selling dollars when it is actually buying dollars, or vice versa. It calls commercial banks and obtains both bid and ask quotes on currencies, so the banks are not sure whether the Fed is considering purchases or sales of these currencies.

Intervention strategies vary among central banks. Some arrange for one large order when they intervene; others arrange several smaller orders, of the equivalent of $5 million to $10 million. Even if traders determine the extent of central bank intervention, they still cannot know with certainty the impact of that intervention on exchange rates.

Indirect Intervention

The Fed can affect the dollar's value indirectly by influencing the factors that determine it. For example, the Fed could attempt to lower interest rates by increasing the U.S. money supply (assuming that inflationary expectations are not affected). Lower U.S. interest rates tend to discourage foreign investors from investing in U.S. securities, thereby placing downward pressure on the value of the dollar. Or, to boost the dollar's value, the Fed could attempt to increase interest rates by reducing the U.S. money supply. It has commonly used this strategy along with direct intervention in the foreign exchange market.

When countries experience substantial net outflows of funds (which places severe downward pressure on their currency), they commonly use indirect intervention by raising interest rates to discourage excessive outflows of funds and therefore limit any downward pressure on the value of their currency. However, this adversely affects local borrowers (government agencies, corporations, and consumers) and may weaken the economy. For example, in October 1997, there was concern that the Asian crisis might adversely affect Brazil and other Latin American countries. Speculators pulled funds out of Brazil and reinvested them in other countries, causing major capital outflows, and therefore placing extreme downward pressure on the currency. The Central Bank of Brazil responded at the end of October by doubling its interest rates from about 20 percent to about 40 percent. This action discouraged investors from pulling funds out of Brazil because they could now earn twice the interest from investing in some securities there. While the action was successful in defending the real, it reduced economic growth because the cost of borrowing funds was too high for many firms.

A similar situation occurred in Russia in May 1998. The Russian currency (the ruble) had consistently declined over the previous four months, and the stock market prices had declined by more than 50 percent over the previous four months. Since the lack of confidence in Russia's currency and stocks could cause massive outflows of funds, the Russian Central Bank attempted to prevent further outflows by tripling interest rates (from about 50 percent to 150 percent). The ruble was temporarily stabilized, but the stock prices continued to decline as investors were concerned that the high interest rates would reduce economic growth.

Some governments attempt to use foreign exchange controls (such as restrictions on the exchange of the currency) as a form of indirect intervention to maintain the exchange rate of their currency. Yet, when there is severe pressure, they tend to let the currency float temporarily toward its market-determined level and set new bands around that level. During the mid–1990s, Venezuela imposed foreign exchange controls on its currency (the bolivar). In April 1996, Venezuela removed its controls on foreign exchange, and the bolivar declined by 42 percent the next day. This result suggests the market-determined exchange rate of the bolivar was substantially lower than the exchange rate at which the bolivar was artificially set by the government.

During the Asian crisis in 1997 and 1998, central banks of some Asian countries increased their interest rates in order to prevent their currencies from weakening. The higher interest rates were expected to make the local securities more attractive and therefore encourage them to maintain their holdings of securities, which would reduce an exchange of the local currency for other currencies. This effort was not successful for most Asian countries but was successful for China and Hong Kong.

EXCHANGE RATE TARGET ZONES

In recent years, many economists have criticized the present exchange rate system because of the wide swings in exchange rates of major currencies. Some have suggested that **target zones** be used for these currencies. An initial exchange rate would be established, with specific boundaries surrounding that rate. Such a target zone is similar to the bands used in the fixed exchange rate system, but a target zone system would likely allow wider boundaries. Proponents of the target zone system suggest that it would stabilize international trade patterns by reducing exchange rate volatility.

There are some complications involved in implementing a target zone system. First, what initial exchange rate should be established for each country? Second, how wide should the target zone be? The ideal target zone allows exchange rates to adjust to economic factors without causing wide swings in international trade and fear in financial markets.

If target zones were implemented, governments would be responsible for intervening to maintain their currencies within the zones. If the zones were sufficiently wide, government intervention would rarely be necessary; however, such wide zones would basically resemble the exchange rate system as it exists today. Governments tend to intervene when a currency's value moves outside some implicitly acceptable zone.

Unless governments could maintain a currency's value within the target zone, this system could not provide stability in international markets. A country experiencing a large balance of trade deficit might intentionally allow its currency to float below the lower boundary in order to stimulate foreign demand for its exports. Wide swings in international trade patterns could result. Furthermore, financial market prices would be more volatile because financial market participants would expect some currencies to move outside of their zones. The result would be a system no different from what exists today.

In February 1987, representatives of the United States, Japan, West Germany, France, Canada, Italy, and the United Kingdom (also known as the Group of Seven or G-7 countries) signed the **Louvre Accord** to establish acceptable ranges (not disclosed to the public) for the dollar's value relative to other currencies. The Federal Reserve intervened heavily in the foreign exchange market for two years after the Louvre Accord, but it has generally intervened only in small doses in recent years. Thus, recent central bank intervention policy has been similar to the policy that existed before the Louvre Accord.

Intervention as a Policy Tool

The federal government of any country can implement its own fiscal and monetary policies to control its economy. In addition, it may attempt to influence the value of its home currency in order to improve its economy, weakening its currency under some conditions and strengthening it under others. In essence, the exchange rate becomes a tool, like tax laws and money supply, with which the government can work to achieve its desired economic objectives.

Influence of a Weak Home Currency on the Economy

A weak home currency can stimulate foreign demand for products. A weak dollar, for example, can substantially boost U.S. exports and U.S. jobs. In addition, it may also reduce U.S. imports.

While a weak currency can reduce unemployment at home, it can lead to higher inflation. For example, in the late 1970s the U.S. dollar was weak, causing U.S. imports from foreign countries to be highly priced. The dollar was also weak in the early 1990s; this situation priced firms such as Bayer, Volkswagen, and Volvo out of the U.S. market. Under these conditions, U.S. companies were therefore able to raise their local prices, since it was difficult for foreign producers to compete. In addition, U.S. firms that are heavy exporters, such as Goodyear Tire & Rubber Co., Litton Industries, Merck, and Maytag Corp., also benefit from a weaker dollar.

Influence of a Strong Home Currency on the Economy

A strong home currency can encourage consumers and corporations of that home country to buy goods from other countries. This situation intensifies foreign competition and forces domestic producers to refrain from increasing prices. Therefore, we expect the country's overall inflation rate to be lower if its currency is strengthened, other things being equal.

http://

Visit www.clev.frb.org/research for the Fed's latest research on monetary, economic, and banking topics.

While a strong currency is a possible cure for high inflation, it may cause higher unemployment due to the attractive foreign prices that result from a strong home currency. The ideal value of the currency depends on the perspective of the country and the officials who are involved with these decisions. The strength or weakness of a currency is just one of many factors that influence a country's economic conditions.

We can combine the above discussion of how exchange rates affect inflation with the discussion in Chapter 4 on how inflation can affect exchange rates, for a more complete picture of the dynamics of the exchange rate–inflation relationship. A weak dollar places upward pressure on U.S. inflation, which in turn places further downward pressure on the value of the dollar. A strong dollar places downward pressure on inflation and on U.S. economic growth, which in turn places further upward pressure on the dollar's value.

The interaction between exchange rates, government policies, and economic factors is illustrated in Exhibit 6.4. As already mentioned, factors other than the home currency's strength affect unemployment and/or inflation. Likewise, factors other than the unemployment or inflation level influence a currency's strength. The cycles that have been described here will often be interrupted by these other factors and therefore will not continue indefinitely.

Exhibit 6.4
Impact of Government Actions on Exchange Rates

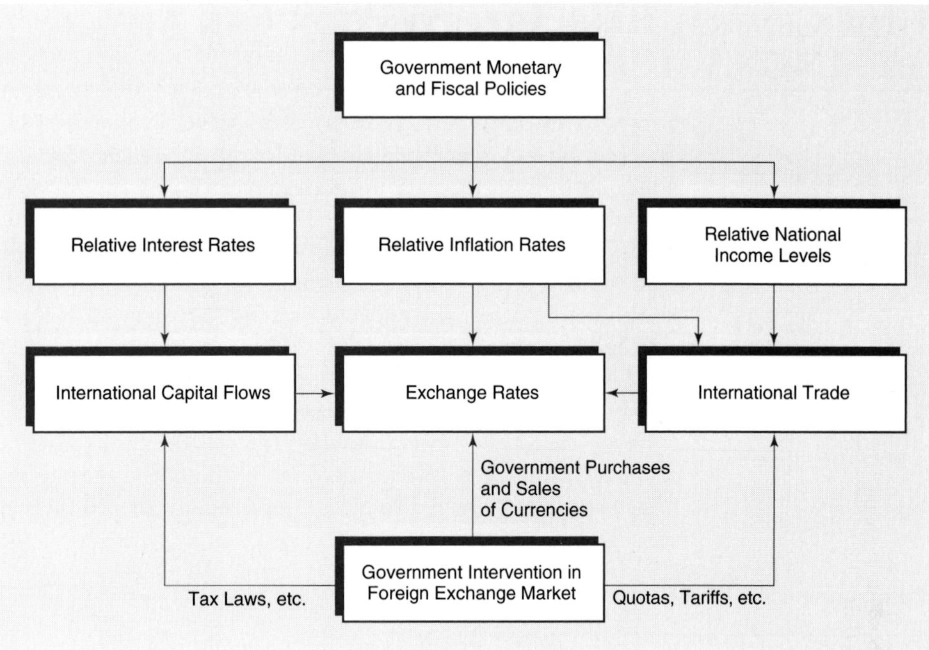

Nike Problem

How Business Can Be Affected by Foreign Government Intervention

Like many MNCs, Nike is subject to the change in exchange rate regimes by governments of the foreign countries. Nike has some cash flows between Western European countries, some of which have agreed to participate in the single European currency (the euro). The cash flows between Nike's subsidiaries in these countries are no longer subject to exchange rate movements since each country is using the same currency. Nike should also benefit because it can avoid transactions costs associated with exchanging one currency for another. However, there is still exchange rate risk whenever these subsidiaries conduct business outside those countries that participate in Europe. In addition, there is still exchange rate risk when these subsidiaries remit funds to the U.S. parent.

During the Asian crisis, the government of Indonesia searched for ways to create a fixed or pegged exchange rate system to encourage investors to keep their investments in these countries. Yet, there was not much confidence that Indonesia would be able to enforce a pegged exchange rate between its currency (the rupiah) and the dollar. The governments also intervened in the foreign exchange market to limit the potential degree of depreciation. The high degree of volatility of the rupiah's value not only affected the cash flows of committed transactions but also affected the future orders of Nike's products in these countries. Some potential purchasers of athletic shoes reduced their orders because of the uncertainty about the price they would pay.

Discussion: If the value of the Indonesian rupiah was temporarily pegged to the U.S. dollar, how would this affect the cash flows of Nike? Would any future remittances of earnings from Nike's Indonesian subsidiary to the U.S. parent be free from exchange rate risk? Explain.

HOW CENTRAL BANK INTERVENTION CAN AFFECT AN MNC'S VALUE

Central bank intervention can affect an MNC's value as shown in Exhibit 6.5. Direct intervention can affect the values of foreign currencies, which determine the expected dollar cash flows that are ultimately received by the MNC's parent as earnings are remitted by foreign subsidiaries. To the extent that direct intervention coincidentally affects foreign economic conditions as a result of influencing the value of foreign currency values, it may affect the demand for products produced by foreign subsidiaries, and therefore affect the expected foreign currency cash flows generated by the foreign subsidiaries.

Like direct intervention, indirect intervention can affect the values of foreign currencies. In addition, indirect intervention can have an impact on the expected foreign currency cash flows, because when the central banks affect economic conditions in order to influence a foreign currency's value, the change in these economic conditions is usually expected to affect the demand for products produced by the foreign subsidiaries.

Exhibit 6.5
Impact of Central Bank Intervention on an MNC's Value

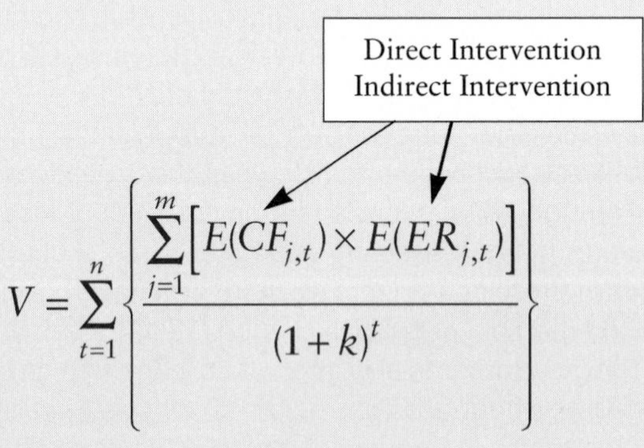

$$V = \sum_{t=1}^{n} \left\{ \frac{\sum_{j=1}^{m} \left[E(CF_{j,t}) \times E(ER_{j,t}) \right]}{(1+k)^t} \right\}$$

V = value of the U.S.-based MNC
$E(CF_{j,t})$ = expected cash flows denominated in currency j to be received by the U.S. parent in period t
$E(ER_{j,t})$ = expected exchange rate at which currency j can be converted to dollars at the end of period t
k = the weighted average cost of capital of the U.S. parent company
m = number of currencies
n = number of periods

SUMMARY

- Exchange rate systems can be classified as fixed rate, freely floating, managed float, and pegged. In a fixed exchange rate system, exchange rates are either held constant or allowed to fluctuate only within very narrow boundaries. In a freely floating exchange rate system, exchange rate values are determined by market forces without intervention. In a managed float system, exchange rates are not restricted by boundaries but are subject to government intervention. In a pegged exchange rate system, a currency's value is pegged to a foreign currency or a unit of account and moves in line with that currency (or unit of account) against other currencies.
- Governments can use direct intervention by purchasing or selling currencies in the foreign exchange market, thereby affecting demand and supply conditions, and in turn affecting the equilibrium values of the currencies. When a government purchases a currency in the foreign exchange market, it places upward pressure on its equilibrium value. When a government sells a currency in the foreign exchange market, it places downward pressure on its equilibrium value.
- Governments can use indirect intervention by influencing the economic factors that affect equilibrium exchange rates.
- When government intervention is used to weaken the U.S. dollar, it stimulates the U.S. economy by reducing the U.S. demand for imports and increasing the foreign demand for U.S. exports. Thus, the weak dollar tends to reduce U.S. unemployment, but it can increase U.S. inflation.

  When government intervention is used to strengthen the U.S. dollar, it can increase the U.S. demand for imports, which intensifies foreign competition. It can reduce U.S. inflation but may cause a higher level of U.S. unemployment.

SELF-TEST FOR CHAPTER 6

(Answers are provided in Appendix A at the back of the text.)

1. Explain why it would be virtually impossible to set an exchange rate between the Japanese yen and the dollar and to maintain a fixed exchange rate.
2. Assume the Federal Reserve believes that the dollar should be weakened against the Mexican peso. Explain how it could use direct and indirect intervention to weaken the dollar's value with respect to the peso. Assume that future inflation in the United States is expected to be low, regardless of the Fed's actions.
3. Briefly explain why the Federal Reserve may attempt to weaken the dollar.

QUESTIONS AND APPLICATIONS

1. Compare and contrast the fixed, freely floating, and managed float exchange rate systems.
2. What are some advantages and disadvantages of a freely floating exchange rate system versus a fixed exchange rate system?
3. € Assume that Belgium, one of the European countries that uses the euro as its currency, would prefer that its currency depreciate against the dollar. Can it apply central bank intervention in order to achieve this objective? Explain.
4. How can a central bank use direct intervention to change the value of a currency?
5. How can a central bank use *indirect* intervention to change the value of a currency?
6. The media frequently report that "the dollar's value strengthened against many currencies in

response to the Federal Reserve's plan to increase interest rates." Explain why the dollar's value may change even before the Federal Reserve affects interest rates.

7. Assume there is concern that the United States may experience a recession. Provide recommendations to the Federal Reserve regarding how it should attempt to directly influence the dollar to prevent a recession. How might U.S. exporters react to this policy (favorably or unfavorably)? What about U.S. importing firms?

8. What is the impact of a weak home currency on the home economy, other things being equal?

9. What is the impact of a *strong* home currency on the home economy, other things being equal?

10. Explain the potential feedback effects of a currency's changing value on inflation.

11. € Explain why the European Central Bank may desire to smooth exchange rate movements in the euro.

12. Why do foreign market participants attempt to monitor the Fed's direct intervention efforts? How does the Fed attempt to hide its intervention actions?

13. In the fall of 1992, France was experiencing a relatively high unemployment rate. During this period, the United Kingdom and Italy suspended their participation in the exchange rate mechanism (ERM), but France continued to participate. Some analysts stated that France "paid a high price" for its continued participation in the ERM during this period. Interpret this statement.

14. Why would the Fed's indirect intervention have a stronger impact on some currencies than others?

15. Why might a central bank's indirect intervention have a stronger impact than its direct intervention?

16. The Hong Kong dollar's value is tied to the U.S. dollar. Explain how the following trade patterns would be affected by appreciation in the Japanese yen against the U.S. dollar: (a) Hong Kong exports to Japan and (b) Hong Kong exports to the United States.

17. Assuming that U.S. bond prices are normally inversely related to U.S. inflation, offer your opinion on why expectations of a weak dollar can reduce bond prices, other things being equal.

18. The Argentine peso is tied to the U.S. dollar. Why would Argentina's economy be affected if the Fed uses central bank intervention to increase the U.S. dollar's value against several currencies.

19. € If most countries in Europe experience a recession, how might the European Central Bank (ECB) use direct intervention to stimulate economic growth?

20. Explain the difference between sterilized and nonsterilized intervention.

21. Consider a recent action taken by the government of Chile to reduce one of its key interest rates. The values of several Latin American currencies were expected to change against the Chilean peso substantially in response to the news.

    a. Explain why the Latin American currencies could be affected by a cut in Chile's interest rates.
    b. Explain how the central banks of other Latin American countries likely would adjust interest rates in these countries and how their currencies would respond to the central bank intervention.
    c. How would a U.S. firm that exports products to Latin American countries be affected by the central bank intervention? (Assume the exports are denominated in the corresponding Latin American currency for each country).

22. Should the governments of Asian countries allow their currencies to float freely? What would be the advantages of letting their currencies float freely? What would be the disadvantages?

23. During the Asian crisis, some Asian central banks raised their interest rates to prevent their currencies from weakening. Yet, the currencies weakened anyway. Offer your opinion as to why the central bank's indirect intervention did not work.

Internet Application

24. The Web site for Japan's central bank, the Bank of Japan, provides information about its mission and its policy actions. Its address is

    www.boj.or.jp/en/index.htm

    a. Use this Web site to summarize the mission of the Bank of Japan. How does this mission relate to intervening in the foreign exchange market?
    b. Review the minutes of recent meetings by Bank of Japan officials. Summarize at least one recent meeting that was associated with possible or actual intervention to affect the yen's value.
    c. Why might the foreign exchange intervention strategies of the Bank of Japan be relevant to the U.S. government and to U.S.-based MNCs?

Running Your Own MNC

Monitoring Central Bank Intervention

25a. How can your business be affected if the Fed attempts to strengthen the dollar in the foreign exchange market?

b. If the Fed decides to weaken the dollar, how will your business be affected?

c. How can indirect central bank intervention affect your business even if there is no impact on exchange rates?

Blades, Inc. Case

Assessment of Government Influence on Exchange Rates

Recall that Blades, the U.S. manufacturer of roller blades, generates most of its revenue and incurs most of its expenses in the United States. However, the company has recently begun exporting roller blades to Thailand. The company has an agreement with Entertainment Products, Inc., a Thai importer, for a three-year period. According to the terms of the agreement, Entertainment Products will purchase 180,000 pairs of "Speedos," Blades' primary product, annually at a fixed price of 4,594 Thai baht per pair. Due to quality and cost considerations, Blades is also importing certain rubber and plastic components from a Thai exporter. The cost of these components runs at approximately 2,871 Thai baht per pair of Speedos. No contractual agreement exists between Blades, Inc. and the Thai exporter. Consequently, the cost of the rubber and plastic components imported from Thailand is subject not only to exchange rate considerations but to economic conditions (such as inflation) in Thailand as well.

Shortly after Blades, Inc. began exporting to and importing from Thailand, the Southeast Asian region experienced weak economic conditions. Consequently, foreign investors in Thailand quickly realized the baht's weakness and withdrew their investments, resulting in an excess supply of Thai baht for sale. Because of the resulting downward pressure on the baht's value, the Thai government attempted to stabilize the baht's exchange rate. In order to maintain the baht's value, the Thai government intervened in the foreign exchange market. Specifically, it swapped its baht reserves for dollar reserves at other central banks and then used its dollar reserves to purchase the baht in the foreign exchange market. However, this agreement required Thailand to reverse this transaction by exchanging dollars for baht at a future date. Unfortunately, the Thai government's intervention was unsuccessful, as it was overwhelmed by market forces. Consequently, the Thai government ceased its intervention efforts, and the value of the Thai baht declined by more than 20 percent against the dollar over a five-week period.

When the Thai government stopped intervening in the foreign exchange market, Ben Holt, Blades' CFO, was concerned that the value of the Thai baht would continue to decline indefinitely. Since Blades generated net inflow in Thai baht, this would seriously affect the company's profit margin.

Furthermore, one of the reasons Blades expanded into Thailand was to appease the company's shareholder demands for senior management action with respect to the firm's low profit margins at last year's annual shareholder meeting. Expanding into Thailand had been Ben Holt's suggestion, and he was now afraid that his career might be at stake. Because of these deliberations, Ben Holt felt that the Asian crisis and its impact on Blades demanded his serious attention. One of the factors Ben Holt felt he should consider was the issue of government intervention and how it could affect Blades in particular. Specifically, he wondered whether the decision to enter into a fixed agreement with Entertainment Products had been a good idea under the circumstances. Another issue was how the future completion of the swap agreement initiated by the Thai government would affect Blades. To address these issues and to gain a little more understanding of the process of government intervention, Ben Holt has prepared the following list of questions for you, Blades' financial analyst, since he knows that you understand international financial management.

1. Did the intervention effort by the Thai government constitute direct or indirect intervention? Explain.
2. Did the intervention by the Thai government constitute sterilized or nonsterilized intervention? What is the difference between the two types? Which of the two types do you think would be more effective in increasing the value of the baht? Why? (Hint: Think about the effect of nonsterilized intervention on U.S. interest rates).
3. If the Thai baht was virtually fixed with respect to the dollar, how could this have affected U.S. levels of inflation? Do you think these effects on the U.S. economy will be more pronounced for companies such as Blades that operate under trade arrangements involving commitments or for firms that do not? How are companies such as Blades affected by a fixed exchange rate?
4. What are some of the potential disadvantages for Thai levels of inflation associated with the floating exchange system that is now used in Thailand? Do you think Blades contributes to these disadvantages to a great extent? How are companies such as Blades affected by a freely floating exchange rate?
5. What do you think will happen to the Thai baht's value when the swap arrangement is completed? How will this affect Blades?

Small Business Dilemma

Assessment of Central Bank Intervention by the Sports Exports Company

Jim Logan, owner of the Sports Exports Company, is concerned about the value of the British pound over time because his firm receives pounds as payment for footballs exported to the United Kingdom. He recently read that the Bank of England (the central bank of the United Kingdom) is likely to use direct intervention in the foreign exchange market by flooding the market with British pounds.

1. Forecast whether the British pound will weaken or strengthen based on the information provided.
2. How would the performance of the Sports Exports Company be affected by the Bank of England's policy of flooding the foreign exchange market with British pounds (assuming that it does not hedge its exchange rate risk)?

Appendix 6

Government Intervention During the Asian Crisis

From 1990 to 1997, Asian countries achieved higher economic growth than any other countries. They were viewed as models for advancement in technology and economic improvement. However, in the summer and fall of 1997, they experienced financial problems, leading to what is commonly referred to as the "Asian Crisis," and resulting in bailouts of countries by the International Monetary Fund (IMF).

Much of the crisis is attributed to the substantial depreciation of Asian currencies, which caused severe financial problems for firms and governments throughout Asia, as well as some other regions. This crisis demonstrated how exchange rate movements can affect country conditions and therefore affect the firms that operate in those countries.

The specific objectives of this appendix are to describe the conditions in the foreign exchange market that contributed to the Asian crisis, explain how governments intervened in an attempt to control their exchange rates, and describe the consequences of their intervention efforts.

Crisis in Thailand

Up until July 1997, Thailand was one of the fastest growing economies. In fact, Thailand was the fastest growing country over the 1985–1994 period. Thai consumers spent freely, which resulted in lower savings compared to other Southeast Asian countries. The high level of spending and low level of saving placed upward pressure on prices of real estate and products, and on its local interest rate. Normally, countries with high inflation tend to have weak currencies because of forces from purchasing power parity. However, Thailand's currency was linked to the dollar prior to July 1997, which made Thailand an attractive site for foreign investors; they could earn a high interest rate on funds invested while being protected (until the crisis) from a large depreciation in the baht.

Bank Lending Situation

The large inflow of funds is normally desired by countries because it can help support the country's growth. However, it provided Thailand's banks with an abundance of funds beyond what the banks could use for making loans. Consequently, the banks provided many loans that were very risky in their attempt to make use of all of their funds. Commercial developers borrowed heavily without having to prove that the expansion was feasible. Lenders were willing to lend large sums of money based on the previous success of the developers. The loans may have been viewed as feasible when using assumptions of a continual high-growth economy, but such high growth could not last forever. The corporate structure of Thailand also led to excessive lending. Many of the corporations are tied in with banks, such that some of the bank lending is not an "arms-length" business transaction, but a loan to a friend who needs funds.

Flow of Funds Situation

In addition to the lending situation, the large inflow of funds made Thailand more susceptible to a massive outflow of funds if the foreign investors ever lost their confidence in Thailand. Given the large amount of risky loans and the potential for a massive outflow of funds, Thailand was sometimes referred to as a house of cards, waiting to collapse.

While the large inflow of funds placed downward pressure on interest rates, the supply was offset by a strong demand for funds as developers and corporations sought to capitalize on the growth economy by expanding. Also, Thailand's government was borrowing heavily to improve the country's infrastructure. Thus, the massive borrowing was occurring at relatively high interest rates, making the debt expensive to the borrowers.

Export Competition

During the first half of 1997, the dollar strengthened against the Japanese yen and European currencies, which reduced the prices of Japanese and European imports. Although the dollar was linked to the baht over this period, Thailand's products were not priced as competitively to U.S. importers.

Pressure on the Thai Baht

The baht experienced downward pressure in July 1997 as some foreign investors recognized potential weakness in the baht. The outflow of funds expedited the weakening of the baht, as foreign investors exchanged their baht for their home currencies. The baht's value relative to the dollar was pressured by the large sale of baht in exchange for dollars. On July 2, 1997, the baht's link to the dollar was detached. Thailand's central bank attempted to maintain the baht's value by intervention. Specifically, it swapped its baht reserves for dollar reserves at other central banks and then used its dollar reserves to purchase the baht in the foreign exchange market (this swap agreement required Thailand to reverse this exchange by exchanging dollars for baht at a future date). The intervention was intended to offset the sales of baht by foreign investors in the foreign exchange market. However, its intervention efforts were overwhelmed by market forces. The supply of baht for sale exceeded the demand for baht in the foreign exchange market, which caused the government to surrender in its effort to defend the baht's value. In July 1997, the value of Thailand's currency plummeted. Over a five-week period, the baht declined by more than 20 percent against the dollar.

Damage to Thailand

The central bank used more than $20 billion to purchase baht in the foreign exchange market as part of its direct intervention efforts. Due to the decline in the value of the baht, Thailand needed more baht to be exchanged for the dollars that it needed to repay the other central banks.

The amount of defaulted loans by Thailand's banks was estimated at over $30 billion. Meanwhile some corporations in Thailand had borrowed funds in other currencies (including the dollar) because the interest rates in Thailand were relatively high. This strategy backfired because the weakening of the baht forced these corporations to exchange larger amounts of baht for the currencies needed in order to pay off the loans. Consequently, the effective financing rate (which accounts for the exchange rate effect to determine the true cost of borrowing) incurred by these corporations was much higher than what they would have paid if they had borrowed funds locally in Thailand. The higher borrowing cost was an additional strain on corporations.

Rescue Package for Thailand

On August 5, 1997, the IMF and several countries agreed to provide Thailand with a $16 billion dollar rescue package. Japan provided $4 billion, while the IMF provided $4 billion. This was the second largest bailout plan for a single country (Mexico received a $50 million bailout in 1994). In return for the monetary support it received, Thailand agreed to reduce its budget deficit, prevent inflation from rising above the 9 percent level, raise the value-added tax from 7 percent to 10 percent, and to clean up the financial statements of the local banks, which had many bad loans not disclosed.

The rescue package took time to finalize because Thailand's government was unwilling to shut down all the banks that were experiencing financial problems as a result of their overly generous lending policies. The success of the rescue package has been questioned by many critics since there was much business corruption that caused some of the funding to be misallocated.

Spread of the Crisis throughout Southeast Asia

The crisis in Thailand was contagious to other countries in Southeast Asia. The Southeast Asian economies are somewhat integrated because of the trade between countries. The Thailand crisis was expected to weaken Thailand's economy, which would result in a reduction in the demand for products produced in the other countries of Southeast Asia. As the demand for products declines in those countries, so does their national income, and their demand for products in the other Southeast Asian countries. Thus, the effects could perpetuate. These countries also had very high growth in recent years, which led to overly optimistic assessments of future economic conditions, and therefore resulted in excessive loans being extended for projects that had a high risk of default.

The other Southeast Asian countries also were similar to Thailand in that they had relatively high interest rates, and their governments tended to stabilize their currency. Consequently, these countries had attracted a large amount of foreign investment as well. Thailand's crisis made foreign investors realize that such a crisis could also hit the other countries in Southeast Asia. Consequently, they began to withdraw funds from these countries.

Effects on Other Asian Currencies

In July and August of 1997, the values of the Malaysian ringgit, Singapore dollar, Philippine peso, Taiwan dollar, and Indonesian rupiah also declined. The Philippine peso was devalued in July. Malaysia initially attempted to maintain the ringgit's value within a narrow band but then surrendered and let the ringgit float to its market-determined level.

In August 1997, Bank Indonesia (the central bank) used more than $500 million in direct intervention to purchase rupiah in the foreign exchange market in an attempt to boost the value of the rupiah. However, by mid–August, it gave up on its effort to maintain the rupiah's value within a band and let the rupiah float to its natural level. This decision by Bank Indonesia to let the rupiah float may have been influenced by the failed outcome of Thailand's costly efforts to maintain the baht. The market forces were too strong and could not be offset by direct intervention. On October 30, 1997, a rescue package for Indonesia was announced, but the IMF and Indonesia's government did not agree on the terms of the package until the spring of 1998. One of the main points of contention was that President Suharto wanted to peg its exchange rate, but the IMF believed there would be renewed speculative attacks on the currency because Indonesia's central bank would not be able to maintain the rupiah's exchange rate at a fixed level. The package represented about $43 billion in aid from the IMF.

While Southeast Asian countries gave up on their fight to maintain their currencies within bands, they imposed restrictions on their forward and futures markets to prevent excessive speculation. For example, Indonesia and Malaysia imposed a limit on the size of forward contracts created by banks for foreign residents. These actions limit the degree to which speculators may sell these forward based on expectations that the currencies will weaken over time. In general, efforts to protect the currencies failed because investors and firms had no confidence that the fundamental factors causing weakness in the currencies were being corrected. Therefore, the flow of funds continued out of the Asian countries, which led to even more sales of Asian currencies in exchange for other currencies, which placed additional downward pressure on the values of these currencies.

Effects on Financing Expenses

As the values of the Southeast Asian currencies declined, speculators responded by withdrawing more of their funds from these countries, which led to further weakness in the currencies. As in Thailand, many corporations in these countries borrowed in other countries (such as the United States) where interest rates were relatively low. The decline in the values for their local currencies caused their effective rate of financing to be excessive, which strained their cash flow situation.

Due to the integration of Southeast Asian economies, the excessive lending by the local banks across the countries, and the susceptibility of all these countries to massive fund outflows, the crisis was not really focused on one country. What was initially referred to as the Thailand crisis became the Asian crisis.

Impact of the Asian Crisis on Hong Kong

On October 23, 1997, the Hong Kong stock market prices declined by 10.2 percent on average, and when considering the three trading days before that, the cumulative four-day effect was a decline of 23.3 percent. The decline was primarily attributed to speculation that Hong Kong's currency might be devalued and that it could experience financial problems similar to the Southeast Asian countries. The fact that the market value of Hong Kong companies could decline by almost one-fourth over a four-day period demonstrated the perceived exposure of Hong Kong to the crisis.

Hong Kong maintained its pegged exchange rate system during this period, as its Hong Kong dollar was tied to the U.S. dollar. However, it had to increase interest rates to discourage investors from transferring their funds out of the country.

Impact of the Asian Crisis on Russia

Just as investors lost confidence in the values of Southeast Asian currencies and transferred funds out of those countries, they began to transfer funds out of Russia during the crisis. In response to the downward pressure placed on the Russian ruble by the actions of investors, the central bank of Russia used direct intervention by using dollars to purchase rubles in the foreign exchange market. It also used indirect intervention by raising interest rates to make them more attractive to investors, thereby discouraging additional outflows.

In July 1998, the IMF organized a loan package (with some help from Japan and the World Bank) worth $22.6 billion to Russia. The package requires that Russia boost its tax revenue, reduce it budget deficit, and create a more capitalist environment for its businesses.

During August 1998, Russia's central bank commonly intervened to prevent the ruble from declining substantially. However, on August 26, it gave up its fight to defend the ruble's value, and market forces caused the ruble to decline by more than 50 percent against most currencies on that day. This led to fears of a new crisis, and the next day (called "Bloody Thursday"), paranoia swept stock markets around the world. Some stock markets (including the U.S. stock market) experienced declines of more than 4 percent.

Impact of the Asian Crisis on South Korea

By November 1997, seven of South Korea's conglomerates (called *chaebols*) had collapsed. The banks that financed the operations of the chaebols were stuck with the equivalent of $52 billion in bad debt as a result. Like the Southeast Asian countries, South Korea's banks were too willing to provide loans to corporations (especially the chaebols) without conducting a thorough credit analysis. This was partially attributed to the assumption that economic growth would continue at a rapid pace, which exaggerated the future cash flows that borrowers would have available to pay off their loans. It was also attributed to the tradition of banks extending loans to any conglomerates without assessing whether the loans could be repaid. In November, South Korea's currency (the won) declined substantially, and the central bank attempted to use its reserves to prevent a free fall in the won, with little success. Meanwhile, the credit ratings of several banks in Asian countries were downgraded because of recognition of their bad loans.

On December 3, 1997, the International Monetary Fund agreed to enact a $55 million dollar rescue package for South Korea. The World Bank and Asian Development Bank joined with the IMF to provide a standby credit line of $35 billion. If that credit amount was not sufficient, other countries (including Japan and the United States) had agreed to provide a credit line of $20 billion. The total available credit (assuming it is all used) exceeds the credit provided in the Mexican bailout of 1994 and would make this the largest bailout ever. In exchange for the funding,

South Korea agreed to reduce its economic growth and to restrict the conglomerates from excessive borrowing. This resulted in some bankruptcies and unemployment, as the banks could not automatically provide loans to all conglomerates needing funds unless the funding was economically justified.

There was skepticism about whether the bailout will work. The people in South Korea have witnessed a strong growth period for two decades that has improved the economy, and they had some difficulty adjusting to a more market-oriented approach in which firms have to justify their desire to grow in order to obtain funding. To the extent that conglomerates will only be given loans to grow when there is an economic rationale, the loans will be paid back and the default rate on loans should be reduced. Meanwhile, the credit ratings of several banks in Asian countries have been downgraded because of recognition of their bad loans.

Impact of the Asian Crisis on Japan

Japan was also affected by the Asian crisis because it exports products to these countries, and many of its corporations have subsidiaries in these countries whose business performance is affected by the local economic conditions. Japan also had been experiencing its own problems. Its financial industry had been struggling, primarily because of defaulted loans. In November 1997, one of Japan's 20 largest banks failed. A week later, Yamaichi Securities Co. (a brokerage firm) announced that it would shut down its business. Yamaichi was the largest firm in Japan to fail since World War II. The news was shocking because the Japanese government had historically bailed out large firms such as Yamaichi because of the possible adverse effects on other firms. This made market participants question the potential failure of other large financial institutions that were previously perceived to be protected ("too big to fail"). The Japanese yen continued to weaken against the dollar during the spring of 1998, which placed more pressure on other Asian currencies; Asian countries wanted to gain a competitive advantage in exporting to the United States as a result of their weak currencies. In April 1998, the Bank of Japan used more than $20 billion to purchase yen in the foreign exchange market. This effort to boost the yen's value was unsuccessful. In July 1998, Prime Minister Hashimoto resigned, causing more uncertainty about the outlook for Japan.

Impact of the Asian Crisis on China

It is ironic that China did not experience the adverse economic effects of the crisis, because China's growth in the years prior to the crisis was not as strong as those countries in Southeast Asia. The government of China had more control over economic conditions because it still owned most real estate and still controlled most of the banks that provided credit to support growth. Thus, there were fewer bankruptcies resulting from the crisis in China. In addition, China's government was able to maintain the value of the yuan against the dollar, which limited speculative flows of funds out of China. While interest rates increased during the crisis, they remained relatively low. This allowed firms to obtain funding at a reasonable cost, which enabled Chinese firms to continue to meet their interest payments.

However, concerns about China mounted because it relies heavily on exports to stimulate its economy; China was now at a competitive disadvantage relative to the other Southeast Asian countries whose currencies had depreciated. Thus, importers from the United States and Europe shifted some of their purchases to those countries where the currencies weakened substantially. In addition, the decline in the other Asian currencies against the Chinese yuan encouraged Chinese consumers to purchase imports instead of locally manufactured products.

Impact of the Asian Crisis on Latin American Countries

The Asian crisis also affected Latin American countries. Countries such as Chile, Mexico, and Venezuela were adversely affected because they export products to Asia, and the weak Asian economies resulted in a lower demand for the Latin American exports. In addition, the Latin American countries lost some business to other countries that switched to Asian products because of the substantial depreciation of Asian currencies, which made their products cheaper than those of Latin America.

The adverse effects on Latin American countries placed pressure on Latin American currency values, as there was a concern of speculative outflows of funds that would have weakened these currencies in the same way that Asian currencies weakened. In particular, there was pressure on Brazil's currency (called the *real*) in late October 1997. Some speculators believed that since most Asian countries could not maintain their currencies within bands under the existing conditions, Brazil would be unable to achieve its goal of stabilizing the value of its currency.

The central bank of Brazil used about $7 billion of reserves as a form of direct intervention to purchase real in the foreign exchange market and protect the real from depreciation. It also used indirect intervention by raising short-term interest rates in Brazil. This encouraged foreign investment in Brazil's short-term securities to capitalize on high interest rates and also encouraged local investors to invest locally rather than in foreign markets. The adjustment of interest rates to maintain the value of the real signaled that the central bank of Brazil was serious about maintaining the stability of the real. Yet, this type of intervention was costly because it increased the cost of borrowing for households, corporations, and government agencies in Brazil, which could reduce economic growth as a result. If Brazil's currency had weakened, the speculative forces might have spread to the other Latin American currencies, as well.

The Asian crisis also caused bond ratings of many large corporations and government agencies in Latin America to be downgraded. For example, in November 1997, the top-grade government-backed bonds in South Korea were reduced to junk-level status in the international credit markets. Rumors that banks were dumping Asian bonds caused fears that all emerging-market debt would be dumped in the bond markets. Furthermore, there was a concern that many banks experiencing financial problems (because their loans were not being paid back) would sell bond holdings in the secondary market in order to raise funds. Consequently, prices of bonds issued in emerging markets declined, including those of Latin American countries.

Impact of the Asian Crisis on Europe

During the Asian crisis, European countries were experiencing strong economic growth. However, many European firms were adversely affected by the Asian crisis. Like firms in Latin America, some firms in Europe experienced a reduced demand for their exports to Asia during the crisis. In addition, they lost some exporting business to Asian exporters as a result of the weakened Asian currencies that reduced the Asian prices from an importer's perspective.

European banks were especially affected by the Asian crisis, since they provided large loans to numerous Asian firms which had defaulted.

Impact of the Asian Crisis on the United States

The effects of the Asian crisis were even felt in the United States. Stock values of U.S. firms, such as 3M Co., Motorola, Hewlett-Packard, and Nike, that conducted much business in Asia were adversely affected. Many U.S. engineering and construction firms were adversely affected as Asian countries reduced their plans to improve infrastructure. Stock values of U.S. exporters to those countries were adversely affected because of the decline in spending by consumers and corporations in Asian countries and because of the weakening of the Asian currencies, which made U.S. products more expensive. Some large U.S. commercial banks experienced significant stock price declines because of their exposure (primarily loans and bond holdings) to Asian countries. For example, Citibank had loans and investments in South Korea amounting to more than $2 billion during the crisis, and Chase Manhattan had close to $2 billion in loans and investments there.

Lessons about Exchange Rates and Intervention

The Asian crisis demonstrated to central banks the degree to which the currencies of countries could depreciate in response to a lack of confidence by investors and firms in the central bank's ability to stabilize its local currency. If investors and firms had expected the central banks to prevent the free fall in currency values, they would not have transferred their funds to other countries. This would have reduced the downward pressure on the currency values.

Exhibit 6A.1 shows how exchange rates of some Asian currencies changed against the U.S. dollar within one year of the crisis (from June 1997 to June 1998). In particular, currencies of Indonesia, Malaysia, South Korea, and Thailand declined substantially.

The Asian crisis also demonstrated how interest rates could be affected in response to the flow of funds out of countries. Exhibit 6A.2 illustrates how interest

Exhibit 6A.1
How Exchange Rates Changed During the Asian Crisis (June 1997–June 1998)

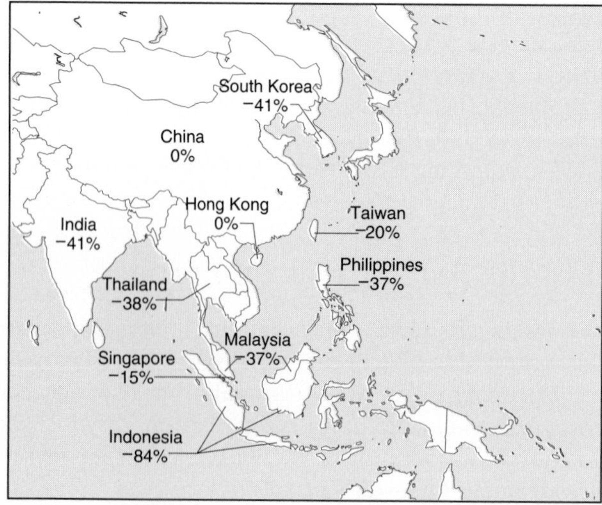

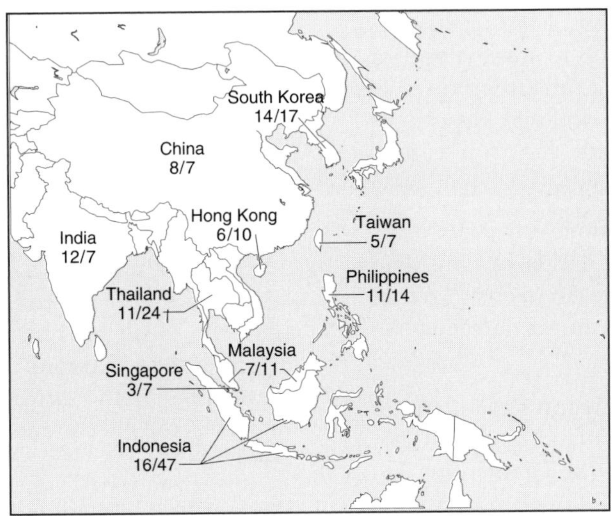

Exhibit 6A.2 How Interest Rates Changed During the Asian Crisis (Number before slash represents annualized interest rate as of June 1997; number after slash represents annualized interest rate as of June 1998)

rates changed from June 1997 (just before the crisis) to June 1998 for various Asian countries. The increase in interest rates could be attributed to the indirect intervention intended to prevent the local currencies from depreciating further, or to the massive outflow of funds from the country, or to both of these conditions. In particular, interest rates of Indonesia, Malaysia, and Thailand increased substantially from their pre-crisis levels. Those countries whose local currencies experienced more depreciation had higher upward adjustments. Since the substantial increase in interest rates (which tends to reduce economic growth) may have been caused by the outflow of funds, it may be indirectly due to the lack of confidence by investors and firms in the ability of each Asian central bank to stabilize its local currency.

Finally, the Asian crisis demonstrated how integrated country economies are, especially during a crisis. Just as the U.S. and European economies can affect emerging markets, they are susceptible to conditions in emerging markets. Even if a central bank can withstand the pressure on its currency caused by conditions in other countries, it cannot necessarily insulate its economy from other countries that are experiencing financial problems.

DISCUSSION QUESTIONS

The following discussion questions related to the Asian crisis illustrate how the foreign exchange market conditions are integrated with the other financial markets around the world. Thus, participants in any of these markets must understand the dynamics of the foreign exchange market. These discussion questions can be used in several ways. They may serve as an assignment on a day that the professor is unable to attend class. They are especially useful for group exercises. The class could be segmented into small groups; each group is asked to assess all of the issues and determine a solution. Each group should have spokesperson. For each issue, one of the groups will be randomly selected and asked to present their solution, and then other students not in that group may be allowed a chance to suggest alternative answers if they feel that the answer can be improved. Some of the issues have no perfect solution, which allows for different points of view to be presented by students.

1. Was the depreciation of the Asian currencies during the Asian crisis due to trade flows or capital flows? Why do you think the degree of movement over a short period may depend on whether the reason is trade flows or capital flows.

2. Why do you think the Indonesian rupiah was more exposed to an abrupt decline in value than the Japanese yen during the Asian crisis (even if their economies experienced the same degree of weakness)?

3. During the Asian crisis, direct intervention did not prevent depreciation of currencies. Offer your explanation for why the intervention did not work.

4. During the Asian crisis, some local firms in Asia borrowed dollars rather than local currency to support local operations. Why would they borrow dollars when they really need their local currency to support operations? Why did this strategy backfire?

5. The Asian crisis showed that a currency crisis could affect interest rates. Why did the Asian crisis place upward pressure on Asian interest rates in Asian countries? Why did it place downward pressure on U.S. interest rates?

6. According to the international Fisher effect (IFE), how would expectations of the Asian exchange rate change after the interest rates in Asia increased? Why? Is the underlying reason logical?

7. During the Asian crisis, why did the discount of the forward rate of Asian currencies change? Do you think it increased or decreased? Why?

8. During the Hong Kong crisis, the Hong Kong stock market declined substantially over a three-day period due to concerns in the foreign exchange market. Why would stock prices decline due to concerns in the foreign exchange market? Why would some countries be more susceptible to this type of situation than others?

9. On August 26, 1998 Russia decided to let the ruble float freely, the ruble declined by about 50 percent on that day. On the following day, called "Bloody Thursday" stock markets around the world (including the U.S.) declined by more than 4 percent. Why do you think the decline in the ruble had such a global impact on stock prices? Is the market's reaction rational? Would the effect have been different if the ruble's plunge occurred in an earlier time period, such as four years earlier? Why?

10. Normally, a weak local currency is expected to stimulate the local economy. Yet, it appeared that the weak currencies of Asia adversely affected their economies. Why do think the weakening of the currencies did not initially improve their economies during the Asian crisis?

11. During the Asian crisis, Hong Kong and China successfully intervened (by raising their interest rates) to protect their local currencies from depreciating. Yet, these countries were also adversely affected by the Asian crisis. Why do you think the actions to protect the values of their currencies would have affected their economies? Why do you think the weakness of other Asian currencies against the dollar and the stability of their currencies against the dollar would have adversely affected their economies?

12. During the Asian crisis, why do you think the values of bonds issued by Asian governments declined? Why do you think the values of Latin American bonds declined in response to the Asian crisis?

13. Why do you think the depreciation of the Asian currencies adversely affected U.S. firms? (There are at least three reasons, each related to a different type of exposure of some U.S. firms to exchange rate risk).

14. During the Asian crisis, the currencies of many Asian countries declined even though their respective governments attempted to intervene with direct intervention or by raising interest rates. Given that the abrupt depreciation of currencies was attributed to an abrupt outflow of funds in the financial markets, what alternative Asian government action may have been more successful in preventing a substantial decline in their currency's value? Are there any possible adverse effects of your proposed solution?

7 INTERNATIONAL ARBITRAGE AND INTEREST RATE PARITY

If there are discrepancies within the foreign exchange market, in which quoted prices of currencies vary from what the market prices should be, certain market forces will realign the rates. The mechanics of this realignment take place as a result of international arbitrage.

The specific objectives of this chapter are to

- explain the conditions that will result in various forms of international arbitrage, along with realignments that will occur in response to various forms of international arbitrage, and
- explain the concept of interest rate parity, and how it prevents arbitrage opportunities.

INTERNATIONAL ARBITRAGE

Arbitrage can be loosely defined as capitalizing on a discrepancy in quoted prices. In many cases, there is no investment of funds tied up for any length of time and no risk involved in the strategy. To illustrate, suppose two coin shops buy and sell coins. If Shop A is willing to sell a particular coin for \$120, while Shop B is willing to buy that same coin for \$130, a person can execute arbitrage by purchasing the coin at Shop A for \$120 and selling it to Shop B for \$130. The prices at coin shops can vary, since demand conditions may vary among shop locations. If two coin shops are not aware of each other's prices, the opportunity for arbitrage may occur.

The act of arbitrage will cause prices to realign. In our example, arbitrage would cause Shop A to raise its price (due to high demand for the coin). At the same time, Shop B would reduce its bid price after receiving a surplus of coins as arbitrage occurs. The type of arbitrage discussed in this chapter is primarily international in scope; it is applied to foreign exchange and international money markets and takes three common forms:

- Locational arbitrage
- Triangular arbitrage
- Covered interest arbitrage

Each form will be discussed in turn.

Locational Arbitrage

Commercial banks providing foreign exchange services will normally quote about the same rates on currencies, so shopping around may not necessarily lead to a more favorable rate. If the demand and supply conditions for a particular currency vary among banks, that currency may be priced at different rates among banks, and market forces will force realignment in the following manner.

Consider two banks that buy and sell currencies. Assume that there is no bid/ask spread, and that the single rate quoted at Bank A for a British pound is $1.60, while the single rate quoted at Bank B is $1.61. If you had funds available, you could use them to buy pounds at Bank A for $1.60 per pound and then sell pounds at Bank B for $1.61 per pound. Under the condition that there is no bid/ask spread and there are no other costs to conducting this arbitrage strategy, your gain would be $.01 per pound. The gain is risk-free in that you knew as you purchased pounds how much you could sell them for. Also, in this example you did not have to tie your funds up for any length of time. The term **locational arbitrage** implies capitalizing on the differential exchange rates between locations.

Since banks have a bid/ask spread on currencies, the next example accounts for this spread. The information on British pounds at both banks is revised to include the bid/ask spread in Exhibit 7.1. The information in this exhibit shows that you can no longer profit from locational arbitrage. If you buy pounds from Bank A at $1.61 (the bank's ask price) and then sell the pounds at Bank B at its bid price of $1.61, you just break even. The point of this example is to demonstrate that even when the bid prices between two banks or the ask prices between two banks are different, this does not guarantee that locational arbitrage will be possible. For you to achieve profits from locational arbitrage, the bid price of one bank must be higher than the ask price of another bank.

Realignment Due to Locational Arbitrage. An example in which locational arbitrage is possible can be helpful in demonstrating how market forces will cause a realignment in the exchange rates of the banks. Examine the quotations for the New Zealand dollar (NZ$) at two banks as shown in Exhibit 7.2. Information contained in Exhibit 7.2 shows that you can obtain New Zealand dollars from Bank C at the ask price of $.640 and then sell New Zealand dollars to Bank D at the bid price of $.645. This represents one "round-trip" transaction in locational arbitrage. If you started with $10,000 and conducted one round-trip transaction, how many U.S. dollars would you end up with? The $10,000 is initially exchanged for NZ$15,625 ($10,000/$.640 per New Zealand dollar) at Bank C. Then the NZ$15,625 are sold for $.645 each, for a total of $10,078. Thus, your gain from locational arbitrage is $78. This does not sound like much relative to your investment of $10,000. However, consider that you did not have to tie up your funds. Your round-trip transaction could take place over a telecommunications network within a matter of seconds. Also, if you could use a larger sum of money for the transaction, your gains would

Exhibit 7.1
Currency Quotes for Locational Arbitrage Example

	Bank A			Bank B	
	Bid	Ask		Bid	Ask
British pound quote	$1.60	$1.61	British pound quote	$1.61	$1.62

Exhibit 7.2 Currency Quotes for Second Locational Arbitrage Example

	Bank C			Bank D	
	Bid	Ask		Bid	Ask
New Zealand dollar quote	$.635	$.640	New Zealand dollar quote	$.645	$.650

be larger. Finally, you could continue to repeat your round-trip transactions until Bank C's ask price is no longer less than Bank D's bid price.

Quoted prices will react to the locational arbitrage strategy used by investors. Due to the high demand for New Zealand dollars at Bank C (resulting from arbitrage activity), a shortage of New Zealand dollars may soon develop there. As a result of this shortage, Bank C will raise its ask price for New Zealand dollars. The excess supply of New Zealand dollars at Bank D (resulting from sales of New Zealand dollars to Bank D in exchange for U.S. dollars) will force Bank D to lower its bid price. As the currency prices are adjusted, gains from locational arbitrage will be reduced. Once the ask price of Bank C is not any lower than the bid price of Bank D, locational arbitrage will no longer occur. The time from which locational arbitrage occurs to the time at which prices adjust may be just a matter of minutes.

This discussion is not intended to make you believe you could pay for your education through part-time locational arbitrage. Foreign exchange dealers can compare quotes from banks on computer terminals, which will immediately signal to the dealer any opportunity to employ locational arbitrage. Thus, they will most likely beat you to the profits. The concept of locational arbitrage is relevant in that it explains why exchange rate quotations among banks at different locations will not normally differ by a significant amount. This applies not only to banks on the same street or within the same city but to all banks across the world.

Triangular Arbitrage

Foreign exchange quotations are typically expressed in U.S. dollars, regardless of the country in which the quote is provided. Yet, there are many instances where the U.S. dollar is not part of the foreign exchange transaction. **Cross exchange rates** are used to determine the relationship between two nondollar currencies.

Given two nondollar currencies called X and Y, the value of X with respect to Y is determined as follows:

http://

The site at quote.yahoo.com/m3?u provides a currency converter for over 100 currencies with frequent daily foreign exchange rate updates.

$$\text{Value of Currency X in units of Currency Y} = \frac{\text{Value of X in \$}}{\text{Value of Y in \$}}$$

For example, if the British pound (£) is worth $1.60, while the Canadian dollar (C$) is worth $.80, the value of the British pound with respect to the Canadian dollar is calculated

$$\text{Value of £ in units of C\$} = \$1.60/\$.80 = 2.0$$

The value of the C$ in units of £ can also be determined from the cross exchange rate formula:

$$\text{Value of C\$ in units of £} = \$.80/\$1.60 = .50$$

http://
The site at pacific.commerce.ubc.ca/xr/data.html provides foreign exchange time series for over 60 countries, which can be customized with respect to period and base currency.

Notice that the value of a Canadian dollar in units of pounds is simply the reciprocal of the value of a pound in units of Canadian dollars. Assume that a quoted cross exchange rate differs from the appropriate cross exchange rate (as determined by the preceding formula). Under these conditions, **triangular arbitrage** can be used, whereby currency transactions are conducted in the spot market to capitalize on a discrepancy in the cross exchange rate between two currencies.

If the cross exchange rate is not set properly, arbitrage may be used to capitalize on the discrepancy. For example, assume that a bank has quoted the British pound (£) at $1.60, the Malaysian ringgit (MYR) at $.20, and the cross exchange rate at £1 = MYR8.10. Your first task is to use the pound value in U.S. dollars and Malaysian ringgit value in U.S. dollars to develop the cross exchange rate that should exist between the pound and the Malaysian ringgit. The cross rate formula discussed earlier reveals that the pound should be worth MYR8.0. When quoting a cross exchange rate of £1 = MYR8.1, the bank is exchanging too many ringgit for a pound, and is asking for too many ringgit in exchange for a pound. Based on this information, you could engage in triangular arbitrage by purchasing pounds with dollars, converting the pounds to ringgit, and then exchanging the ringgit for dollars. If you have $10,000, how many dollars will you end up with if you implement this triangular arbitrage strategy? To answer the question, consider the following steps.

- First, determine the number of pounds received for your dollars: $10,000 = £6,250, based on the bank's quote of $1.60 per pound.
- Second, determine how many ringgit you will receive in exchange for pounds: £6,250 = MYR50,625, based on the bank's quote of 8.1 ringgit per pound.
- Finally, determine how many U.S. dollars you will receive in exchange for the ringgit: MYR50,625 = $10,125 based on the bank's quote of $.20 per ringgit (5 ringgit to the dollar). The triangular-arbitrage strategy generates $10,125, which is $125 more than you started with.

Like locational arbitrage, triangular arbitrage does not tie up funds. Also, the strategy is risk-free, since there is no uncertainty about the prices at which you will buy and sell the currencies. To make the scenario more realistic, however, consider the information in Exhibit 7.3, which discloses bid and ask rates quoted by a bank. Using Exhibit 7.3, you can determine whether triangular arbitrage is possible by starting with some fictitious amount (say $10,000) of U.S. dollars and estimating the number of dollars you would generate after implementing the strategy. The only difference between what is shown in Exhibit 7.3 and the previous example is that bid/ask spreads are now considered.

In the example, the triangular arbitrage strategy suggested exchanging dollars for pounds, pounds for ringgit, and then ringgit for dollars. Apply this strategy to the bid and ask exchange rate quotations disclosed in Exhibit 7.3. If you start out with $10,000, that will be converted into £6,211 (based on the bank's ask price of $1.61

Exhibit 7.3
Currency Quotes for a Triangular Arbitrage Example

	Quoted Bid Price	Quoted Ask Price
Value of a British pound in U.S. dollars	$1.60	$1.61
Value of a Malaysian ringgit (MYR) in U.S. dollars	$.200	$.201
Value of a British pound in Malaysian ringgit (MYR)	MYR8.10	MYR8.20

Exhibit 7.4
Impact of Triangular Arbitrage

Activity	Impact
1. Participants use dollars to purchase pounds.	Bank increases its ask price of pounds with respect to the dollar.
2. Participants use pounds to purchase Malaysian ringgit.	Bank reduces its bid price of the British pound with respect to the ringgit; that is, it reduces the number of ringgit to be exchanged per pound received.
3. Participants use Malaysian ringgit to purchase U.S. dollars.	Bank reduces its bid price of ringgit with respect to the dollar.

per pound). Then the £6,211 are converted into MYR50,309 (based on the bank's bid price for pounds of MYR8.1 per pound, £6,211 × 8.1 = MYR50,309). Next, the MYR50,309 are converted to $10,062 (based on the bank's bid price of $.200). The profit is $10,062 – $10,000 = $62. The profit is lower here than in the previous example because bid and ask quotations are used. Any possible profit opportunities from triangular arbitrage should be only temporary, since realignment in exchange rates occurs, as explained next.

Realignment Due to Triangular Arbitrage. The realignment that results from the triangular arbitrage activity is summarized in the second column of Exhibit 7.4. The realignment will likely occur quickly to prevent continued benefits from triangular arbitrage. The discrepancies assumed here are unlikely to occur within a single bank. A more likely case of triangular arbitrage would be three transactions at three separate banks.

Given three currencies, the exchange rate between each pair is displayed in Exhibit 7.5. If any two of these three exchange rates are known, the exchange rate of the third pair can be determined. When the actual cross exchange rate differs from the appropriate cross exchange rate, the exchange rates of the currencies are not in equilibrium. Triangular arbitrage would force the exchange rates back into equilibrium.

As with locational arbitrage, triangular arbitrage is not normally a strategy that most of us can take advantage of. This is especially true in light of the computer technology available to foreign exchange dealers, which can easily detect misalignment in cross exchange rates. The point of this discussion is that because of triangular arbitrage, cross exchange rates are usually aligned correctly. If they are not, triangular arbitrage will take place until the rates are aligned correctly.

Exhibit 7.5
Relationship between Three Currencies

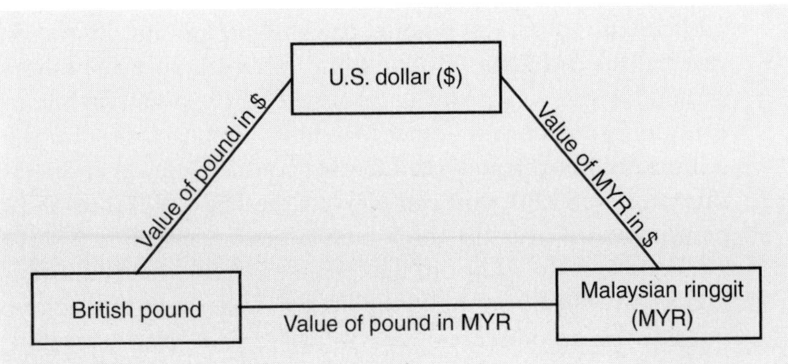

Covered Interest Arbitrage

Up to this point, two types of arbitrage have been considered. Locational arbitrage forces any particular exchange rate to be similar among banks. Triangular arbitrage forces a quoted cross exchange rate to be appropriately priced. Another arbitrage concept, called **covered interest arbitrage,** tends to force a relationship between the interest rates of two countries and their forward exchange rate premium or discount. Covered interest arbitrage involves investing in a foreign country and covering against exchange rate risk. Some of the literature in international finance specifies that the funds to be invested be borrowed locally. In this case, the investors would not be tying up any of their own funds. Other research, however, does not make this specification. That is, the investors would use their own funds. In this case, the term "arbitrage" is loosely defined, since there is a positive dollar amount invested over a period of time. The following discussion is based on this latter meaning of covered interest arbitrage; yet, arbitrage under either interpretation should have a similar impact on currency values and interest rates.

To illustrate how covered interest arbitrage works, assume that you desire to capitalize on relatively high rates of interest in the United Kingdom, and have funds available for 90 days. The interest rate is fixed; only the future exchange rate at which you will exchange pounds back to U.S. dollars is uncertain. A forward sale of pounds can be used to guarantee the rate at which you could exchange pounds for dollars at a future point in time. This actual strategy is as follows:

1. On Day 1, convert your U.S. dollars to pounds and set up a 90-day deposit account in a British bank.
2. On Day 1, engage in a forward contract to sell pounds 90 days forward.
3. In 90 days when the deposit matures, convert the pounds to U.S. dollars at the rate that was agreed upon in the forward contract.

The next example uses numbers to illustrate how this would work:

- You have $800,000 to invest.
- The current spot rate of the pound is $1.60.
- The 90-day forward rate of the pound is $1.60.
- The 90-day interest rate in the United States is 2 percent.
- The 90-day interest rate in the United Kingdom is 4 percent.

Based on this information, you could first convert the $800,000 to £500,000, deposit the £500,000 in a British bank, and then simultaneously set up a forward contract with a bank to sell the pounds at $1.60 per pound. By the time the deposit matures, you will have £520,000 (including interest), so this is the amount of pounds that should be sold forward. The spot rate of the pound at the time the deposit matures is no longer important, since you have already locked in the rate at which you can sell the pounds through the forward contract. Based on the assumed 90-day forward rate of £1 = $1.60, you can convert the £520,000 into $832,000. This reflects a 4-percent return over the three-month period, which is 2 percent above the return on a U.S. deposit. In addition, the return on this foreign deposit has been locked in, since you know when you make the deposit exactly how much you will get back for the pounds you accumulate.

Recall that locational and triangular arbitrage do not tie up funds; thus, any profits are achieved instantaneously. In the case of covered interest arbitrage, the funds are tied up for a period of time (90 days in our example). This would not be a valuable strategy if it earned 2 percent or less, since you could earn 2 percent on a domestic deposit. The term "arbitrage" here suggests that you can guarantee a return on your funds that exceeds the returns you could achieve domestically.

Realignment Due to Covered Interest Arbitrage. As with the other forms of arbitrage, market forces resulting from covered interest arbitrage will cause a market realignment. Once the realignment takes place, excess profits from arbitrage are no longer possible.

In the previous discussion, four variables (pound spot rate, British interest rate, U.S. interest rate, and pound forward rate) could be affected by covered interest arbitrage. It is difficult to forecast the exact magnitude of each change. Yet, it should be clear that each change reduces the excess return initially achieved from covered interest arbitrage.

The impact of covered interest arbitrage on exchange rates and interest rates is summarized in Exhibit 7.6. If we assume no adjustment in interest rates, covered interest arbitrage would be feasible until the forward rate of the pound was sufficiently below the spot rate to offset the interest rate advantage. Given that the British interest rate is 2 percent above the U.S. interest rate, U.S. investors could benefit from covered interest arbitrage until the forward rate was about 2 percent less than the spot rate.

If interest rates change in response to the flow of funds into the United Kingdom, the interest rate differential would be reduced. Consequently, it would take a smaller differential between the spot and forward rate of the pound to offset the interest rate differential. However, most or all of the adjustments would most likely be focused on the exchange rates.

Assume that the exchange rates change in response to covered interest arbitrage as shown in Exhibit 7.7. With these new rates, further efforts to conduct covered interest arbitrage no longer provide a return to U.S. investors that is higher than the prevailing U.S. interest rate. This can be shown by computing the return earned from covered interest arbitrage, as follows (assume an initial investment of $800,000):

1. Convert $800,000 to pounds:

   $$\$800{,}000/\$1.62 = £493{,}827.$$

2. Calculate accumulated pounds over 90 days at 4 percent:

   $$£493{,}827 \times 1.04 = £513{,}580.$$

Exhibit 7.6
Impact of Covered Interest Arbitrage

Activity	Impact
1. Use dollars to purchase pounds in the spot market.	Upward pressure on the spot rate of the pound.
2. Engage in a forward contract to sell pounds forward.	Downward pressure on the forward rate of the pound.
3. Invest funds from the U.S. in the United Kingdom.	Possible upward pressure on U.S. interest rates and downward pressure on British interest rates.

Exhibit 7.7
Adjustments in Exchange Rates Due to Covered Interest Arbitrage

	Original Value	Value after Being Affected by Covered Interest Arbitrage
British pound spot rate in U.S. dollars	$1.60	$1.6200
British pound 90-day forward rate in U.S. dollars	1.60	1.5888

3. Reconvert pounds to dollars (at the forward rate of $1.5888) after 90 days:

$$£513{,}580 \times \$1.5888 = \$815{,}976.$$

4. Determine yield earned from covered interest arbitrage:

$$(\$815{,}976 - \$800{,}000)/\$800{,}000 = .02, \text{ or } 2\%.$$

This example shows that those individuals who initially conduct covered interest arbitrage cause exchange rates and possibly interest rates to move in such a way that future attempts at covered interest arbitrage provide a return that is no better than what is possible domestically. Due to the market forces from covered interest arbitrage, a relationship between the forward rate premium and interest rate differentials should exist. This relationship is discussed shortly.

Comparison of Arbitrage Effects

A comparison of the three types of arbitrage is provided in Exhibit 7.8. The threat of locational arbitrage ensures that quoted exchange rates are similar across banks in different locations. The threat of triangular arbitrage ensures that cross exchange rates are properly set. The threat of covered interest arbitrage ensures that forward exchange rates are properly set. Any discrepancy will trigger arbitrage, which should eliminate the discrepancy. Thus, arbitrage tends to allow for a more orderly foreign exchange market.

Interest Rate Parity (IRP)

Once market forces cause the interest rates and exchange rates to be such that covered interest arbitrage is no longer feasible, there is an equilibrium state referred to as **interest rate parity (IRP)**. In equilibrium, the forward rate differs from the spot rate by a sufficient amount to offset the interest rate differential between two currencies. In the previous example, the U.S. investor receives a higher interest rate from the foreign investment, but there is an offsetting effect due to the investor's paying more per unit of foreign currency (at the spot rate) than what is received per unit when the currency is sold forward (at the forward rate). Recall that when the forward rate is less than the spot rate, this implies the forward rate exhibits a discount.

Exhibit 7.8
Comparing Arbitrage Strategies

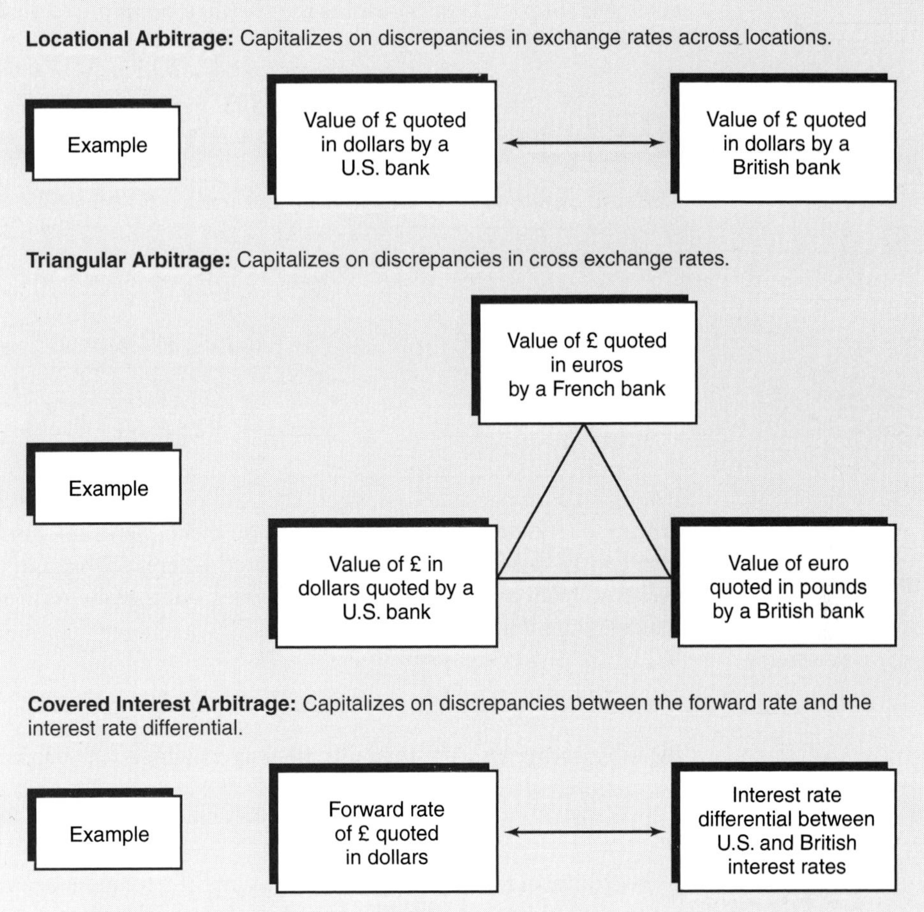

Derivation of Interest Rate Parity

The relationship between a forward premium (or discount) of a foreign currency and the interest rates representing these currencies according to IRP can be determined as follows. Consider a U.S. investor who attempts covered interest arbitrage. The return to a U.S. investor from using covered interest arbitrage can be determined given

- The amount of the home currency (U.S. dollars in our example) that is initially invested (A_h).
- The spot rate (S) in dollars when the foreign currency is purchased.
- The interest rate on the foreign deposit (i_f).
- The forward rate (F) in dollars at which the foreign currency will be converted back to U.S. dollars.

The amount of the home currency received at the end of the deposit period due to such a strategy (called A_n) is

$$A_n = (A_h/S)(1 + i_f)F$$

Since F is simply S times one plus the forward premium (called p), we can rewrite this equation as

$$\begin{aligned} A_n &= (A_h/S)(1 + i_f)[S(1 + p)] \\ &= A_h(1 + i_f)(1 + p) \end{aligned}$$

The rate of return from this investment (called R) is as follows:

$$\begin{aligned} R &= \frac{A_n - A_h}{A_h} \\ &= \frac{[A_h(1+i_f)(1+p)] - A_h}{A_h} \\ &= (1+i_f)(1+p) - 1 \end{aligned}$$

If interest rate parity exists, then the rate of return achieved from covered interest arbitrage (R) should be equal to the rate available in the home country. Set the rate that can be achieved from using covered interest arbitrage to the rate that can be achieved from an investment in the home country (the return on a home investment is simply the home interest rate called i_h):

$$R = i_h$$

By substituting into the formula the way in which R is determined, we obtain

$$(1 + i_f)(1 + p) - 1 = i_h$$

By rearranging terms, we can find out what the forward premium of the foreign currency should be under conditions of interest rate parity:

$$\begin{aligned} (1+i_f)(1+p) - 1 &= i_h \\ (1+i_f)(1+p) &= (1+i_h) \\ (1+p) &= \frac{(1+i_h)}{(1+i_f)} \\ p &= \frac{(1+i_h)}{(1+i_f)} - 1 \end{aligned}$$

Numerical Example of Interest Rate Parity

As an example, assume that the Mexican peso exhibits a six-month interest rate of 6 percent, while the U.S. dollar exhibits a six-month interest rate of 5 percent. From a U.S. investor's perspective, the U.S. dollar is the home currency. According to IRP, the forward rate premium of the peso with respect to the U.S. dollar should be

$$\begin{aligned} p &= \frac{(1+.05)}{(1+.06)} - 1 \\ &= -.0094, \text{ or } -.94\% \text{ (not annualized)} \end{aligned}$$

Thus, the peso should exhibit a forward discount of about .94 percent. This implies that U.S. investors would receive .94 percent less when selling pesos six months from now (based on a forward sale) than the price they pay for pesos today at the spot rate. Such a discount would offset the interest rate advantage of the peso. If the peso's spot rate is \$.10, a forward discount of .94 percent means that the six-month forward rate is as follows:

$$\begin{aligned} F &= S(1 + p) \\ &= \$.10(1 - .0094) \\ &= \$.09906 \end{aligned}$$

The following numerical example confirms that if interest rate parity exists, covered interest arbitrage will not be feasible. Use the information on the spot rate and six-month forward rate of the peso, as well as Mexico's interest rate, to determine a U.S. investor's return from using covered interest arbitrage. Assume the investor begins with \$1,000,000 to invest.

Step 1. On the first day, the U.S. investor converts \$1,000,000 into pesos (MXP) at \$.10 per peso:

$$\$1{,}000{,}000/\$.10 \text{ per peso} = \text{MXP}10{,}000{,}000$$

Step 2. On the first day, the U.S. investor also sells pesos six months forward. The number of pesos to be sold forward is the anticipated accumulation of pesos over the six-month period, which is estimated as

$$\text{MXP}10{,}000{,}000 \times (1 + 6\%) = \text{MXP}10{,}600{,}000$$

Step 3. After six months, the U.S. investor withdraws the initial deposit of pesos along with the accumulated interest, amounting to a total of 10,600,000 pesos. The investor converts the pesos into dollars in accordance with the forward contract agreed upon six months earlier. The forward rate was \$.09906, so the number of U.S. dollars received from the conversion is

$$\text{MXP}10{,}600{,}000 \times (\$.09906 \text{ per peso}) = \$1{,}050{,}036$$

Results. The act of covered interest arbitrage achieves a return of about 5 percent here. Rounding the forward discount at .94 percent causes the slight deviation from the 5 percent return.

The results suggest that, in this instance, using covered interest arbitrage generates a return that is about what the U.S. investors would have received anyway if they had simply invested their funds domestically. This confirms that covered interest arbitrage is not worthwhile if interest rate parity exists.

The relationship between the forward premium (or discount) and the interest rate differential according to interest rate parity is simplified in an approximated form as follows:

$$p = \frac{F - S}{S} \cong i_h - i_f$$

where

p = forward premium (or discount)
F = forward rate in dollars
S = spot rate in dollars
i_h = home interest rate
i_f = foreign interest rate

This approximated form provides a reasonable estimate when the interest rate differential is small. The variables in this equation are not annualized. In our previous example, the U.S. (home) interest rate is less than the foreign interest rate, so the forward rate contains a discount (the forward rate is less than the spot rate). The larger the degree by which the foreign interest rate exceeds the home interest rate, the larger will be the forward discount of the foreign currency specified by the IRP formula.

If the foreign interest rate is less than the home interest rate, the interest rate parity relationship suggests that the forward rate should exhibit a premium. There may be reason for investors to attempt covered interest arbitrage even if the home interest rate is higher than the foreign interest rate. Consider a situation in which the foreign interest rate is just slightly less than the home rate. In this case, interest rate parity would exist if the forward rate were just slightly larger than the spot rate (exhibiting a slight premium). Then, the amount U.S. investors gained from the forward rate premium would be offset by the slightly lower interest rate. However, if the forward rate exhibited a large premium, the U.S. investors could achieve a higher return through covered interest arbitrage than by investing domestically.

Graphic Analysis of Interest Rate Parity

The interest rate differential can be compared to the forward premium (or discount) with the aid of a graph like that in Exhibit 7.9. All the possible points that represent interest rate parity can be plotted by using the approximation expressed earlier and plugging in numbers. For example, if the foreign interest rate (i_f) exceeds the home interest rate (i_h) by 1 percent ($i_h - i_f = -1\%$), then the forward rate should exhibit a discount of 1 percent. This is represented by point A on the graph. If the foreign interest rate exceeds the home rate by 2 percent, then the forward rate should exhibit a discount of 2 percent, as represented by point B on the graph, and so on. For cases in which the foreign interest rate is less than the home interest rate, the forward rate should exhibit a premium approximately equal to that differential. For example, if the home interest rate exceeds the foreign rate by 1 percent ($i_h - i_f = 1\%$), then the forward premium should be 1 percent, as represented by point C. If the home interest rate exceeds the foreign rate by 2 percent ($i_h - i_f = 2\%$), then the forward premium should be 2 percent, as represented by point D, and so on. Any points lying on the diagonal line cutting the intersection of axes represent interest rate parity. For this reason, that diagonal line is referred to as the **interest rate parity (IRP) line.**

http://
Visit www.bloomberg.com for the latest information from financial markets around the world.

An individual or corporation could at any time examine all currencies to compare forward rate premiums (or discounts) to interest rate differentials. From a U.S. perspective, interest rates in Japan are usually lower than the home interest rates. Consequently, the forward rate of the Japanese yen will usually exhibit a premium and may be represented by points such as C or D or even points above D along the diagonal line in Exhibit 7.9. Conversely, the United Kingdom often has higher interest rates than the United States, and their forward rates often exhibit a discount, represented by point A or B.

Exhibit 7.9
Illustration of Interest Rate Parity

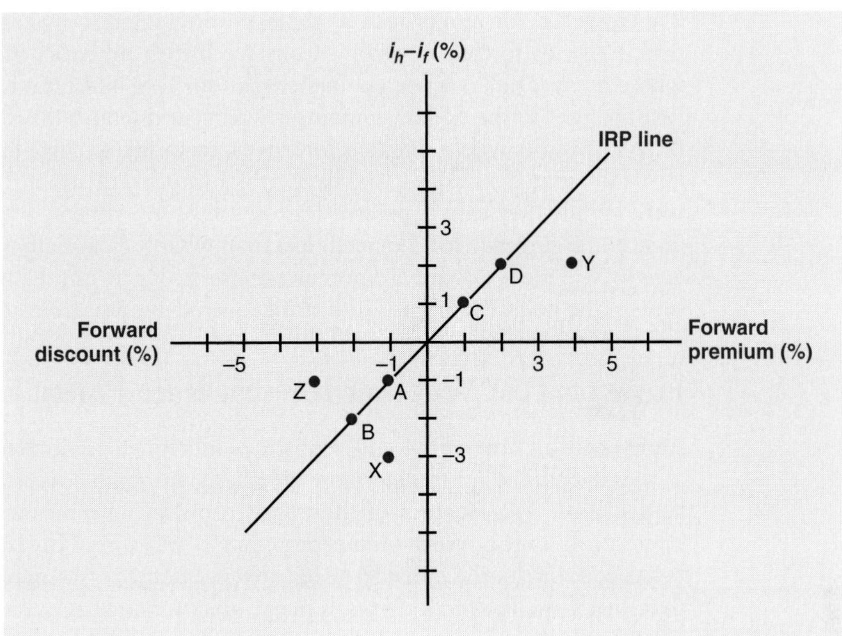

Exhibit 7.9 can be used whether or not you annualize the rates, as long as you are consistent. That is, if you annualize the interest rates to determine the interest rate differential, you should also annualize the forward premium or discount.

What if a three-month deposit represented by a foreign currency offers an annualized interest rate of 10 percent, versus an annualized interest rate of 7 percent in the home country? Such a scenario is represented on the graph by $i_h - i_f = -3\%$. Also assume that the foreign currency exhibits an annualized forward discount of 1 percent. The combined interest rate differential and forward discount information can be represented by point X on the graph. Since point X is not on the IRP line, we should expect that covered interest arbitrage is beneficial for some investors. The investor attains an additional 3 percentage points for the foreign deposit, and this advantage is only partially offset by the 1-percent forward discount.

Assume that the annualized interest rate for the foreign currency is 5 percent, as compared to 7 percent for the home country. The interest rate differential expressed on the graph is $i_h - i_f = 2\%$. However, assume that the forward premium of the foreign currency is 4 percent (point Y in Exhibit 7.9). Thus, what the investor loses on the lower interest rate from the foreign investment is more than made up by the high forward premium.

Shift to the left side of the IRP line. Take point Z, for example. This represents a foreign interest rate that exceeds the home interest rate by 1 percent, while the forward rate exhibits a 3-percent discount. This point, like all points to the left of the interest rate parity line, represents a situation in which U.S. investors would achieve a lower return on a foreign investment than they would on a domestic one. The reason for this lower return is normally either (1) the advantage of the foreign interest rate relative to the U.S. interest rate is more than offset by the forward rate discount (which reflects point Z), or (2) the degree by which the home interest rate exceeds the foreign rate more than offsets the forward rate premium.

However, for points such as these, covered interest arbitrage is feasible from the perspective of foreign investors. Consider British investors in the United Kingdom, whose interest rate is 1 percent higher than the U.S. interest rate, and the forward rate (with respect to the dollar) contains a 3-percent discount (as represented by point Z). British investors would sell their foreign currency in exchange for dollars, invest in dollar-denominated securities, and engage in a forward contract to purchase pounds forward. While they earn 1 percent less on a U.S. investment, they are able to purchase their home currency for 3 percent less than what they initially sold it for. This type of activity will place downward pressure on the spot rate of the pound and upward pressure on the pound's forward rate, until covered interest arbitrage is no longer feasible.

How to Test Whether Interest Rate Parity Exists

An investor or firm can plot all realistic points for various currencies on a graph such as that in Exhibit 7.9 to determine whether gains from covered interest arbitrage can be achieved. The location of the points provides an indication of whether covered interest arbitrage is worthwhile. For points to the right of the IRP line, investors in the home country should consider using covered interest arbitrage, since a return higher than the home interest rate (i_h) is achievable. Of course, as investors and firms take advantage of such opportunities, there will be a tendency for the point to move toward the IRP line. Covered interest arbitrage should continue until the IRP relationship holds.

The points to the left of the IRP line are not suitable for covered interest arbitrage by home-country investors, but are suitable for foreign investors. In our example, foreign investors would conduct covered interest arbitrage by purchasing and depositing the home currency (dollars), while simultaneously purchasing their currency forward for the date at which the U.S. deposit matures.

Interpretation of Interest Rate Parity

Interest rate parity is sometimes mistakenly summarized as follows: "If IRP exists, then foreign investors will earn the same returns as U.S. investors." To prove that this statement is incorrect, consider two countries: the United States, with a 10-percent interest rate, and the United Kingdom, with a 14-percent interest rate. U.S. investors could achieve 10 percent domestically or attempt to use covered interest arbitrage. If they attempt covered interest arbitrage while IRP exists, then the result will be a 10-percent return, the same as that possible for them in the United States. If British investors attempt covered interest arbitrage while IRP exists, then the result will be a 14-percent return, the same as that possible for them in the United Kingdom. Thus, U.S. investors and British investors do *not* achieve the same nominal return here, even though IRP exists. An appropriate summary explanation of interest rate parity is that if interest rate parity exists, investors cannot use covered interest arbitrage to achieve higher returns than those achievable in their respective home countries.

Does Interest Rate Parity Hold?

To correctly determine whether IRP holds, it is necessary to compare the forward rate (or discount) and interest rate quotations that occur at the same time. If the forward rate and interest rate quotations do not reflect the same time of day, then results could be somewhat distorted. Due to limitations in access to data, it is difficult to get quotations that reflect the same point in time. Consequently, the testing of IRP is subject to some error. Yet, that should not discourage attempts to determine whether IRP exists. Empirical examination of IRP has been conducted by numerous academic studies over the last several years. The actual relationship between the forward rate premium and interest rate differentials generally supports IRP. While there are deviations, they are often not large enough to make covered interest arbitrage worthwhile, as we will now discuss in more detail.

Considerations When Assessing Interest Rate Parity

If IRP does not hold, there is still the possibility that covered interest arbitrage is not worthwhile. This is due to potential costs that arise from foreign investments but not from domestic investments. Such costs could include transaction costs, currency restrictions, and differential tax laws.

If an investor wishes to account for transaction costs, the actual point reflecting the interest rate differential and forward rate premium must be farther from the IRP line to make covered interest arbitrage worthwhile. Exhibit 7.10 identifies the areas that reflect potential for covered interest arbitrage *after* accounting for transaction costs. Notice the band surrounding the IRP line. For points not on the IRP line but within this band, covered interest arbitrage is not worthwhile (because the excess return is offset by costs). For points to the right (or below) the band, investors residing in the home country could gain through covered interest arbitrage. For points to

Exhibit 7.10
Potential for Covered Interest Arbitrage When Considering Transaction Costs

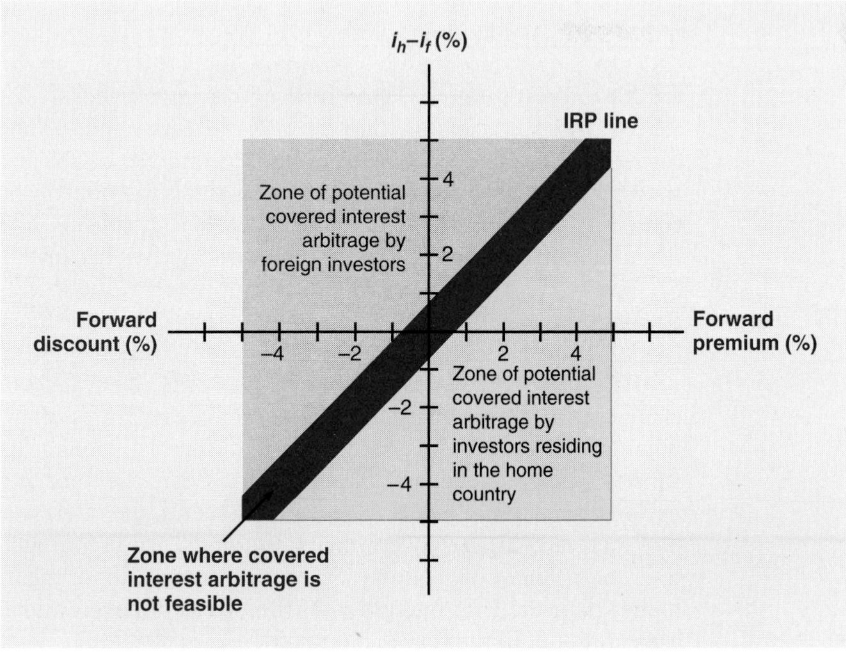

the left (or above) the band, foreign investors could gain through covered interest arbitrage.

Even if covered interest arbitrage appears feasible after accounting for transaction costs, the act of investing funds overseas is subject to political risk. While the forward contract locks in the rate at which the foreign funds should be reconverted, there is no guarantee that funds will be allowed to be reconverted. A crisis in the foreign country could cause its government to restrict any exchange of the local currency for other currencies. In this case, the investor would be unable to use these funds until the foreign government eliminated the restriction. Investors may also perceive a slight default risk on foreign investments such as foreign Treasury bills, since they might not be assured that the foreign government will guarantee full repayment of interest and principal upon default.

Firms and investors recognize the impact that taxes may have on income. Because tax laws vary among countries, investors and firms that set up deposits in other countries must be aware of the existing tax laws. It is possible that covered interest arbitrage could be feasible when considering before-tax returns but not necessarily when considering after-tax returns. Such a scenario would be due to differential tax rates.

If IRP does not hold, the possibility of covered interest arbitrage deserves consideration. However, the existence of all these factors could eliminate the possibility of abnormal returns from covered interest arbitrage. Covered interest arbitrage should be attempted only if abnormal returns remain after considering transaction costs, potential currency restrictions, and taxes.

Correlation between Spot and Forward Rates

Because of interest rate parity, a foreign currency's forward rate will normally move in tandem with the spot rate. This correlation of movement depends on interest rate movements, as shown in Exhibit 7.11. Currency A's spot rate (S_A) and forward rate (F_A) are shown, along with a comparison of the U.S. interest rate ($i_{U.S.}$) and Country A's interest rate (i_A). From time t_0 to t_1, i_A exceeds $i_{U.S.}$, and F_A is therefore less than S_A by approximately that interest rate differential. The size of the interest rate differential declines over this period, causing the discount on F_A to decline along with it. At time t_1, the interest rates of the two countries are equal, so that F_A is equal to S_A. From time t_1 to t_2, i_A is below $i_{U.S.}$, causing F_A to be above S_A. At the beginning of this period, the premium on F_A rises because the differential between $i_{U.S.}$ and i_A becomes larger. As time t_2 approaches, the interest rate differential narrows until $i_A = i_{U.S.}$ at time t_2, causing F_A to equal S_A. After time t_2, i_A exceeds $i_{U.S.}$, forcing F_A to fall below S_A.

The 1997–1998 Asian crisis offers a useful illustration of why the forward rate changes over time. During this crisis, the forward rates offered to U.S. firms on currencies such as the Malaysian ringgit, Indonesian rupiah, and Thailand baht were substantially reduced, for two reasons. First, the spot rates of these currencies declined substantially during the crisis. Second, the interest rates of these currencies had increased as the governments attempted to discourage investors from pulling their funds out of the country. Since the interest rates of these currencies had become higher than the U.S. interest rate, the threat of covered interest arbitrage forced a large discount in the forward rate of these currencies.

Exhibit 7.11
Relationship between Interest Rate Differentials and Forward Rate Premiums over Time

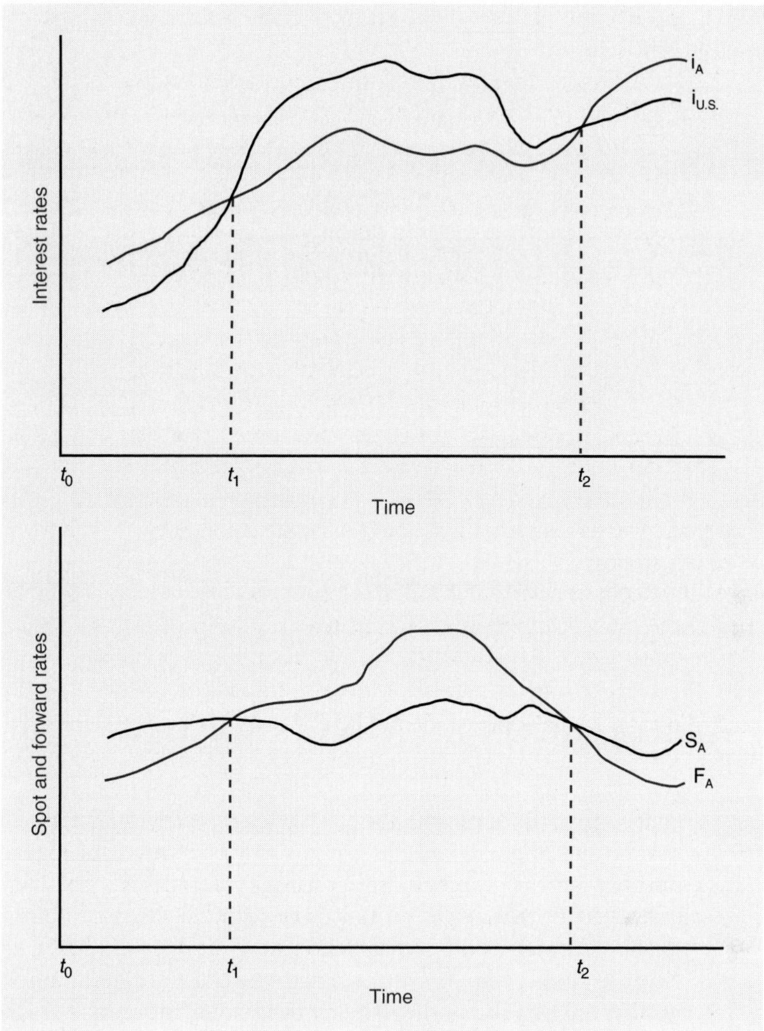

Nike Problem

How the Asian Crisis Affected the Hedging Decision

Since the Asian crisis, interest rates in some of the Asian countries increased substantially as the respective governments attempted to prevent an outflow of funds by offering attractive interest rates on local investments. Such economic conditions resulted in challenging dilemmas for MNCs such as Nike that conduct business in these countries. For example, consider a situation in which Nike had planned to remit funds from Indonesia to the U.S. parent in six months. It could sell the Indonesian currency (the rupiah) six months forward, but the forward rate on the rupiah would exhibit a much larger discount, as the very high interest rate relative to the U.S. interest rate forces a large forward rate discount through interest rate parity.

Discussion: Given the large forward discount, should Nike no longer consider hedging its future remittances from Indonesia to the U.S. parent?

Exhibit 7.12
Impact of Arbitrage on an MNC's Value

Forces of Arbitrage

$$V = \sum_{t=1}^{n} \left\{ \frac{\sum_{j=1}^{m} \left[E(CF_{j,t}) \times E(ER_{j,t}) \right]}{(1+k)^t} \right\}$$

V = value of the U.S.-based MNC
$E(CF_{j,t})$ = expected cash flows denominated in currency j to be received by the U.S. parent in period t
$E(ER_{j,t})$ = expected exchange rate at which currency j can be converted to dollars at the end of period t
k = the weighted average cost of capital of the U.S. parent company
m = number of currencies
n = number of periods

Impact of Arbitrage on an MNC's Value

Arbitrage can affect an MNC's value, as shown in Exhibit 7.12. Arbitrage tends to ensure that the spot and forward rates of foreign currency in the foreign exchange market are aligned, such that firms can be assured of exchanging one currency for another at the appropriate exchange rate. Thus, the cash flows of MNCs are enhanced because they do not have to incur costs of continuously monitoring the exchange rates at all commercial banks at a given point in time. The value of an MNC is higher than if arbitrage activities had not maintained exchange rates at their appropriate levels, as the MNC would incur more monitoring costs prior to executing each foreign exchange transaction.

SUMMARY

- Locational arbitrage may occur if foreign exchange quotations differ among banks. The act of locational arbitrage should force the foreign exchange quotations of banks to become realigned, and locational arbitrage will no longer be possible.
- Triangular arbitrage is related to cross exchange rates. A cross exchange rate between two currencies is determined by the values of these two currencies with respect to a third currency. If the actual cross exchange rate of these two currencies differs from the rate that should exist, triangular arbitrage is possible. The act of triangular arbitrage should force cross exchange rates to become realigned, at which time triangular arbitrage will no longer be possible.
- Covered interest arbitrage is based on the relationship between the forward rate premium and the interest rate differential. The size of the premium or discount exhibited by the forward rate of a currency should be about the same as the differential between the interest rates of the two countries of concern. In general terms, the for-

ward rate of the foreign currency will contain a discount (premium) if its interest rate is higher (lower) than the U.S. interest rate. If the forward premium deviates substantially from the interest rate differential, covered interest arbitrage is possible. This type of arbitrage represents a foreign short-term investment in a foreign currency covered by a forward sale of that foreign currency in the future. In this manner, the investor is not exposed to fluctuation in the foreign currency's value.

- Interest rate parity (IRP) is a theory which states that the size of the forward premium (or discount) should be equal to the interest rate differential between the two countries of concern. When IRP exists, covered interest arbitrage is not feasible, because any interest rate advantage in the foreign country will be offset by the discount on the forward rate. Thus, the act of covered interest arbitrage would generate a return that is no higher than what would be generated by a domestic investment.

SELF-TEST FOR CHAPTER 7

(Answers are provided in Appendix A at the back of the text.)

1. Assume that the following spot exchange rates exist today:

   £1 = $1.50
   C$ = $.75
   £1 = C$2

   Assume no transaction costs. Based on these exchange rates, can triangular arbitrage be used to earn a profit? Explain.

2. Assume the following information:

   Spot rate of £ = $1.60
   180-day forward rate of £ = $1.56
   180-day British interest rate = 4%
   180-day U.S. interest rate = 3%

   Based on this information, is covered interest arbitrage by U.S. investors feasible? Explain.

3. Using the information in the previous question, does interest rate parity exist? Explain.

4. Explain in general terms how various forms of arbitrage can remove any discrepancies in the pricing of currencies.

5. Assume that the British pound's one-year forward rate exhibits a discount. Assume that interest rate parity continually exists. Explain how the discount on the British pound's one-year forward discount would change if British one-year interest rates rose by 3 percentage points while U.S. one-year interest rates rose by 2 percentage points.

QUESTIONS AND APPLICATIONS

1. Explain the concept of locational arbitrage and the scenario necessary for it to be plausible.

2. Assume the following information:

	Bank X	Bank Y
Bid price of New Zealand dollars	$.401	$.398
Ask price of New Zealand dollars	$.404	$.400

   Given this information, is locational arbitrage possible? If so, explain the steps that would reflect locational arbitrage, and compute the profit from this arbitrage if you had $1,000,000 to use.

3. Based on the information in the previous question, what market forces would occur to eliminate any further possibilities of locational arbitrage?

4. Explain the concept of triangular arbitrage and the scenario necessary for it to be plausible.

5. Assume the following information for a particular bank:

	Quoted Price
Value of Canadian dollar in U.S. dollars	$.90
Value of New Zealand dollar in U.S. dollars	$.30
Value of Canadian dollar in New Zealand dollars	NZ$3.02

Given this information, is triangular arbitrage possible? If so, explain the steps that would reflect triangular arbitrage, and compute the profit from this strategy if you had $1,000,000 to use.

6. Based on the information in the previous question, what market forces would occur to eliminate any further possibilities of triangular arbitrage?

7. Explain the concept of covered interest arbitrage and the scenario necessary for it to be plausible.

8. Assume the following information:

Spot rate of Canadian dollar	= $.80
90-day forward rate of Canadian dollar	= $.79
90-day Canadian interest rate	= 4%
90-day U.S. interest rate	= 2.5%

Given this information, what would be the yield (percentage return) to a U.S. investor who used covered interest arbitrage? (Assume the investor invests $1,000,000.)

9. Based on the information in the previous question, what market forces would occur to eliminate any further possibilities of covered interest arbitrage?

10. Assume the following information:

Spot rate of Mexican peso	= $.100
180-day forward rate of Mexican peso	= $.098
180-day Mexican interest rate	= 6%
180-day U.S. interest rate	= 5%

Given this information, is covered interest arbitrage worthwhile for Mexican investors? Explain your answer.

11. Explain the concept of interest rate parity. Provide the rationale for its possible existence.

12. Describe a method for testing whether interest rate parity exists.

13. Why are transaction costs, currency restrictions, and differential tax laws important when evaluating whether covered interest arbitrage can be beneficial?

14. Assume that the existing U.S. one-year interest rate is 10 percent and the Canadian one-year interest rate is 11 percent. Also assume that interest rate parity exists. Should the forward rate of the Canadian dollar exhibit a discount or a premium? If U.S. investors attempted covered interest arbitrage, what would be their return? If Canadian investors attempted covered interest arbitrage, what would be their return?

15. € Why would U.S. investors consider covered interest arbitrage in France when the interest rate on euros in France is lower than the U.S. interest rate?

16. Consider investors that invest in either U.S. or British one-year Treasury bills. Assume zero transaction costs and no taxes.

    a. If interest rate parity exists, then the return for U.S. investors who use covered interest arbitrage would be the same as the return for U.S. investors who invest in U.S. Treasury bills. Is this statement true or false? If false, correct the statement.
    b. If interest rate parity exists, then the return for British investors who use covered interest arbitrage would be the same as the return for British investors who invest in British Treasury bills. Is this statement true or false? If false, correct the statement.

17. Assume that the Japanese yen's rate currently exhibits a premium of 6 percent, and that interest rate parity exists. How will this premium change if U.S. interest rates decrease, in order for interest rate parity to be maintained? Why might we expect the premium to change?

18. € Assume that the forward rate premium of the euro was higher last month than the premium today. What does this imply about interest rate

differentials between the United States and Europe today compared to those last month?

19. If the relationship that is specified by interest rate parity does not exist at any period but does exist on average, then covered interest arbitrage should not be considered by U.S. firms. Do you agree or disagree with this statement? Explain.

20. The one-year interest rate in New Zealand is 6 percent. The one-year U.S. interest rate is 10 percent. The spot rate of the New Zealand dollar (NZ$)is $.50. The forward rate of the New Zealand dollar is $.54. Is covered interest arbitrage feasible for U.S. investors? Is it feasible for New Zealand investors? Explain why each of these opportunities for covered interest arbitrage is or is not feasible.

21. Assume that the one-year U.S. interest rate is 11 percent, while the one-year interest rate in a specific less developed country (LDC) is 40 percent. Assume that a U.S. bank is willing to purchase the currency of that country from you one year from now at a discount of 13 percent. Would covered interest arbitrage be worth considering? Is there any reason why you should not attempt covered interest arbitrage in this situation? (Ignore tax effects.)

22. Why do you think currencies of countries with high inflation rates tend to have forward discounts?

23. Assume that Mexico's economy expanded significantly, causing a high demand for loanable funds there by local firms. How might these conditions affect the forward discount of the Mexican peso?

24. € Assume that the 30-day forward premium of the euro is –1 percent, while the 90-day forward premium of the euro is 2 percent. Explain the likely interest rate conditions that would cause these conditions. Does this ensure that covered interest arbitrage is worthwhile?

25. € Assume that the annual U.S. interest rate is currently 8 percent and Germany's annual interest rate is currently 9 percent. The euro's one-year forward rate currently exhibits a discount of 2 percent.
    a. Does interest rate parity exist?
    b. Can a U.S. firm benefit from investing funds in Germany using covered interest arbitrage?
    c. Can a German subsidiary of a U.S. firm benefit by investing funds in the U.S. through covered interest arbitrage?

26. Before the Asian crisis began, Asian central banks were maintaining a somewhat stable value for their respective currencies. Yet, the forward rate of Southeast Asian currencies exhibited a discount. Explain.

Internet Application

27. The Web site of Bloomberg provides quotations in foreign exchange markets. Its address is:

    www.bloomberg.com

    Use this Web page to determine the cross exchange rate between the Canadian dollar and the Japanese yen. Notice that the value of the pound (in dollars) and the value of the yen (in dollars) are also disclosed. Based on these values, is the cross rate between the Canadian dollar and the yen what you expected it to be? Explain.

Running Your Own MNC

Assessing Spot and Forward Rates

28 a. Obtain a quotation for the spot rate of the foreign currency (that you will receive from your business) from the bank where you intend to conduct your foreign exchange transactions. Then, obtain a quotation for the spot rate of the foreign currency from another bank. Does it appear that the spot rates are aligned across locations at a given point in time?

   b. Obtain a quotation for the one-year forward rate of the foreign currency from the bank where you intend to conduct your foreign exchange transactions. Then, use a business periodical to determine the prevailing one-year interest rates in the United States and the foreign country of concern. Does it appear that interest rate parity exists?

c. Review the data on forward rates from *The Wall Street Journal* or another source to determine whether the foreign currency of concern typically exhibits a discount or a premium. Then review data on interest rates to compare the foreign country of concern and the U.S. interest rates. Does it appear that the forward rate of the foreign currency exhibits a premium (discount) when its interest rate is lower (higher) than the U.S. interest rate, as suggested by interest rate parity?

Blades, Inc. Case

Assessment of Potential Arbitrage Opportunities

Recall that Blades, a U.S. manufacturer of roller blades, has chosen Thailand as its primary export target for "Speedos," Blades' primary product. Moreover, Blades' primary customer in Thailand, Entertainment Products, has committed itself to the purchase of 180,000 Speedos annually for the next three years at a fixed price denominated in baht, Thailand's currency. Because of quality and cost considerations, Blades also imports some of the rubber and plastic components needed to manufacture Speedos.

Lately, Thailand has experienced weak economic growth and political uncertainty. As investors lost confidence in the Thai baht as a result of political uncertainty, they withdrew their funds from the country. This resulted in an excess supply of baht for sale over the demand for baht in the foreign exchange market, which put downward pressure on the baht's value. As foreign investors continued to withdraw their funds from Thailand, the baht's value continued to deteriorate. Since Blades has net cash flows in baht resulting from its exports to the country, a deterioration in the baht's value would affect the company negatively.

Ben Holt, Blades' CFO, would like to ensure that the spot and forward rates Blades is quoted by its bank are reasonable. If the exchange rate quotes are reasonable, then arbitrage would not be possible. However, if the quotations are not appropriate, arbitrage may be possible. Under these conditions, Ben Holt would like Blades, Inc. to use some form of arbitrage to take advantage of possible mispricing in the foreign exchange market. Although Blades is not an arbitrageur, Ben Holt believes that arbitrage opportunities could offset the negative impact resulting from the baht's depreciation, which would otherwise seriously affect Blades' profit margins.

Ben Holt has identified three arbitrage opportunities as profitable and would like to know which one of these is the most profitable. Thus, Ben Holt has asked you, Blades' financial analyst, to prepare an analysis of the arbitrage opportunities he has identified. This would allow the CFO to assess the profitability of arbitrage opportunities very quickly.

1. The first arbitrage opportunity identified by Ben Holt relates to locational arbitrage. He has received spot rate quotations from two banks in Thailand: Minzu Bank and Sobat Bank, both located in Bangkok. The bid and ask prices of Thai baht for each bank are displayed in the table below:

	Minzu Bank	Sobat Bank
Bid	\$0.0224	\$0.0228
Ask	\$0.0227	\$0.0229

Determine whether the foreign exchange quotations are appropriate. If they are not appropriate, determine the profit you could generate by withdrawing \$100,000 from Blades' checking account and engaging in arbitrage before the rates are adjusted.

2. Besides the bid and ask quotes for the Thai baht provided in the previous question, Minzu Bank has provided the following quotations for the U.S. dollar and the Japanese yen:

	Quoted Bid Price	Quoted Ask Price
Value of a Japanese yen in U.S. dollars	\$0.0085	\$0.0086
Value of a Thai baht in Japanese yen	JY2.69	JY2.70

Determine whether the cross exchange rate between the Thai baht and Japanese yen is appropriate. If it is not appropriate, determine the profit you could generate for Blades, Inc. by withdrawing $100,000 from Blades' checking account and engaging in triangular arbitrage before the rates are adjusted.

3. Ben Holt has obtained several forward contract quotations for the Thai baht to determine whether covered interest arbitrage may be possible. He was quoted a forward rate of $0.0225 per Thai baht for a 90-day forward contract. The current spot rate is $0.0227. Ninety-day interest rates available to Blades in the United States are 2 percent, while 90-day interest rates in Thailand are 3.75 percent (these rates are not annualized). Ben Holt is aware that covered interest arbitrage, unlike locational and triangular arbitrage, requires an investment of funds. Thus, he would like to be able to estimate the dollar profit resulting from arbitrage over and above the dollar amount available on a 90-day U.S. deposit.

   Determine whether the forward rate is priced appropriately. If it is not priced appropriately, determine the profit you could generate for Blades by withdrawing $100,000 from Blades' checking account and engaging in covered interest arbitrage. Measure the profit as the excess amount above what you could generate by investing in the U.S. money market.

4. Why are arbitrage opportunities likely to disappear soon after they have been discovered? To illustrate your answer, assume that covered interest arbitrage involving the immediate purchase and forward sale of baht is possible. Discuss how the baht's spot and forward rates would adjust until covered interest arbitrage is no longer possible. What is the resulting equilibrium state called?

Small Business Dilemma

Assessment of Prevailing Spot and Forward Rates by the Sports Exports Company

As the Sports Exports Company exports footballs to the United Kingdom, it receives British pounds. The check (denominated in pounds) for last month's exports just arrived. Jim Logan (owner of the Sports Exports Company) normally deposits the check with his local bank and requests that the bank convert the check to pounds at the prevailing spot rate (assuming that he did not use a forward contract to hedge this payment). Jim's local bank provides foreign exchange services for many of its business customers who need to buy or sell widely traded currencies. However, Jim decided to check the quotations of the spot rate among other banks before converting the payment into dollars.

1. Do you think Jim will be able to find a bank that provides him with a more favorable spot rate than his local bank? Explain.

2. Do you think that Jim's bank is likely to provide more reasonable quotations for the spot rate of the British pound if it is the only bank in town that provides foreign exchange services? Explain.

3. Jim is considering the use of a forward contract to hedge the anticipated receivables in pounds next month. His local bank quoted him a spot rate of $1.65 and a one-month forward rate of $1.6435. Before Jim decides to sell pounds one month forward, he wants to be sure that the forward rate is reasonable, given the prevailing spot rate. A one-month Treasury security in the United States currently offers a yield (not annualized) of 1 percent, while a one-month Treasury security in the United Kingdom offers a yield of 1.4 percent. Do you believe that the one-month forward rate is reasonable given the spot rate of $1.65?

8 RELATIONSHIPS BETWEEN INFLATION, INTEREST RATES, AND EXCHANGE RATES

Inflation rates and interest rates can have a strong impact on exchange rates, as explained in Chapter 4. Given their potential importance, they deserve to be studied more closely.

The specific objectives of this chapter are to

- explain the purchasing power parity (PPP) theory and its implications for exchange rate changes,
- explain the international Fisher effect (IFE) theory and its implications for exchange rate changes, and
- compare the PPP theory, IFE theory, and theory of interest rate parity (IRP), which was introduced in the previous chapter.

PURCHASING POWER PARITY (PPP)

In Chapter 4, the expected impact of relative inflation rates on exchange rates was discussed. Recall from this discussion that when one country's inflation rate rises relative to that of another, the demand for its currency declines as its exports decline (due to its higher prices). In addition, consumers and firms in the country with higher inflation tend to increase their importing. Both of these forces place downward pressure on the currency of the high-inflation country. Inflation rates often vary among countries, causing international trade patterns and exchange rates to adjust accordingly.

One of the most popular and controversial theories in international finance is the **purchasing power parity (PPP) theory,** which focuses on the inflation–exchange rate relationship. There are various forms of PPP theory. The **absolute form,** also called the "law of one price," suggests that prices of similar products of two different countries should be equal when measured in a common currency. If a discrepancy in prices as measured by a common currency exists, the demand should shift so that these prices should converge. For example, if the same product is produced by the United States and the United Kingdom, and the price in the United Kingdom is lower when measured in a common currency, the demand for that product should increase in the United Kingdom while it declines in the United States. Consequently, the actual price charged in each country may be affected and/or the exchange rate may adjust. Both forces would cause the prices of the products to be similar when measured in a common currency. Realistically, the existence of transportation costs, tariffs, and quotas may prevent the absolute form of PPP. If transportation costs were high in this example, the demand for the products might not shift in the manner suggested. Thus, the discrepancy in prices would continue.

The **relative form** of PPP is an alternative version that accounts for the possibility of market imperfections such as transportation costs, tariffs, and quotas. This version acknowledges that because of these market imperfections, prices of similar products of different countries will not necessarily be the same when measured in a common currency. However, it states that the rate of change in the prices of products should be somewhat similar when measured in a common currency, as long as the transportation costs and trade barriers are unchanged. To illustrate the relative form of PPP, assume that two countries initially have zero inflation. Also assume that the current exchange rate between the two countries' currencies is in equilibrium. As time passes, both countries may experience inflation; for PPP to hold, the exchange rate should adjust to offset the differential in the inflation rates of the two countries. If this occurs, the prices of goods in either country should appear similar to consumers. That is, consumers should note little difference in their purchasing power in the two countries.

Derivation of Purchasing Power Parity

Assume that the price indexes of the home country (h) and a foreign country (f) are equal. Now assume that over time, the home country experiences an inflation rate of I_h, while the foreign country experiences an inflation rate of I_f. Due to inflation, the price index of goods in the consumer's home country (P_h) becomes

$$P_h(1 + I_h)$$

The price index of the foreign country (P_f) will also change due to inflation in that country:

$$P_f(1 + I_f)$$

If $I_h > I_f$, and the exchange rate between the currencies of the two countries does not change, then your purchasing power is greater on foreign goods than on home goods. In this case, PPP does not exist. If $I_h < I_f$, and the exchange rate between the currencies of the two countries does not change, then your purchasing power is greater on home goods than on foreign goods. In this case also, PPP does not exist.

The theory of PPP suggests that the exchange rate will not remain constant but will adjust to maintain the parity in purchasing power. If inflation occurs and the exchange rate of the foreign currency changes, the foreign price index from the home consumer's perspective becomes

$$P_f(1 + I_f)(1 + e_f)$$

where e_f represents the percentage change in the value of the foreign currency. According to PPP theory, the percentage change in the foreign currency (e_f) should change to maintain parity in the new price indexes of the two countries. We can solve for e_f under conditions of PPP by setting the formula for the new price index of the foreign country equal to the formula for the new price index of the home country, as follows:

$$P_f(1 + I_f)(1 + e_f) = P_h(1 + I_h)$$

Solving for e_f, we obtain

$$(1+e_f) = \frac{P_h(1+I_h)}{P_f(1+I_f)}$$

$$e_f = \frac{P_h(1+I_h)}{P_f(1+I_f)} - 1$$

Since P_h equals P_f (because price indexes were initially assumed equal in both countries), they cancel, leaving

$$e_f = \frac{(1+I_h)}{(1+I_f)} - 1$$

This formula reflects the relationship between relative inflation rates and the exchange rate according to PPP. Notice that if $I_h > I_f$, e_f should be positive. This implies that the foreign currency will appreciate when the home country's inflation exceeds the foreign country's inflation. Conversely, if $I_h < I_f$, then e_f should be negative. This implies that the foreign currency will depreciate when the foreign country's inflation exceeds the home country's inflation.

Numerical Examples of Purchasing Power Parity

As a numerical example, assume that the exchange rate is in equilibrium initially. Then the home currency experiences a 5-percent inflation rate, while the foreign country experiences a 3-percent inflation rate. According to PPP, the foreign currency will adjust as shown:

$$\begin{aligned} e_f &= \frac{1+I_h}{1+I_f} - 1 \\ &= \frac{1+.05}{1+.03} - 1 \\ &= .0194, \textit{ or } 1.94\% \end{aligned}$$

The implications are that the foreign currency should appreciate by 1.94 percent in response to the higher inflation of the home country relative to the foreign country. If this exchange rate change does occur, the price index of the foreign country will be as high as that in the home country from the perspective of consumers in the home country. Even though inflation is lower in the foreign country, appreciation of the foreign currency pushes the foreign country's price index up from the perspective of consumers in the home country. When considering the exchange rate effect, price indexes of both countries rise by 5 percent from the home country perspective. Thus, the purchasing power on foreign goods is equal to that on the home goods.

In a second example, again assume that the exchange rate is in equilibrium initially. Then the home country experiences a 4-percent inflation rate, while the foreign country experiences a 7-percent inflation rate. According to PPP, the foreign currency will adjust as shown:

$$\begin{aligned} e_f &= \frac{(1+I_h)}{1+I_f)} - 1 \\ &= \frac{1+.04}{1+.07} - 1 \\ &= -.028, \text{ or } -2.8\% \end{aligned}$$

The implications are that the foreign currency should depreciate by 2.8 percent in response to the higher inflation of the foreign country relative to the home country. Even though the inflation is lower in the home country, the depreciation of the foreign currency places downward pressure on the foreign country's prices from the perspective of the consumers in the home country. When considering the exchange rate impact, prices of both countries rise by 4 percent. Thus, PPP would still exist, due to the adjustment in the exchange rate.

A more simplified but less precise relationship based on PPP is

$$e_f \cong I_h - I_f$$

That is, the exchange rate percentage change should be approximately equal to the differential in inflation rates between two countries. This simplified formula is appropriate only when the inflation differential is small. To illustrate the use of this simplified formula, consider two countries, the United States and the United Kingdom, which trade extensively with each other. Assume an equilibrium state in which the exchange rate of the British pound is initially worth $2.00. Now assume that the United States experiences a 9-percent inflation rate, while the United Kingdom experiences a 5-percent inflation rate. Under these conditions, PPP theory would suggest that the British pound should appreciate by approximately 4 percent, the differential in inflation rates.

Rationale behind Purchasing Power Parity Theory

If two countries produce products that are substitutes for each other, the demand for products should adjust as inflation rates differ. In our previous example, prices increase in the United States by 9 percent versus 5 percent in the United Kingdom. This should initially cause U.S. consumers to increase imports from the United Kingdom and British consumers to lower their demand for the U.S. goods (since prices of British goods have increased by a lower rate). Such forces place upward pressure on the British pound value. The shifting in consumption from the United States to the United Kingdom will continue until the British pound value has appreciated to the extent that (1) the prices paid for British goods by U.S. consumers are no lower than the prices for the comparable products made in the United States and (2) the prices paid for U.S. goods by British consumers are no higher than the prices for the comparable products made in the United Kingdom. The level of appreciation in the pound needed to achieve this new equilibrium situation is approximately 4 percent, as will be verified here.

Given British inflation of 5 percent and the pound's appreciation of 4 percent, U.S. consumers would be paying about 9 percent more for the British goods than they paid in the initial equilibrium state. This is equal to the 9-percent increase in prices of U.S. goods from the U.S. inflation. Consider a situation in which the pound appreciated by only 1 percent. In this case, the increased price of British goods to U.S. consumers would be approximately 6 percent (5-percent inflation and 1-percent appreciation in the British pound), which is less than the 9-percent increase in the price of U.S. goods to U.S. consumers. Thus, we would expect U.S. consumers to continue to shift their consumption to British goods. Purchasing power parity suggests that the increasing U.S. consumption of British goods by U.S. consumers would persist until the pound appreciated by about 4 percent. Any level of appreciation lower than this would represent more attractive British prices relative to U.S. prices from the U.S. consumer's viewpoint.

From the British consumer's point of view, the price of U.S. goods would have initially increased by 4 percent more than British goods. Thus, British consumers would continue to reduce imports from the United States until the pound appreciated enough to make U.S. goods no more expensive than British goods. Once the pound appreciated by 4 percent, this would partially offset the increase in U.S. prices of 9 percent from the British consumer's perspective. To be more precise, the net effect is that the prices of U.S. goods would increase by approximately 5 percent to British consumers (9-percent inflation minus the 4-percent savings to British consumers due to the pound's 4-percent appreciation).

Graphic Analysis of Purchasing Power Parity

Using PPP theory, we should be able to assess the potential impact of inflation on exchange rates. Exhibit 8.1 is a graphic representation of PPP theory. The points on the exhibit suggest that, given the inflation differential between the home and the for-

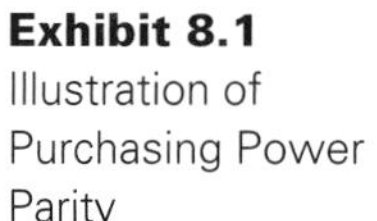
Exhibit 8.1
Illustration of Purchasing Power Parity

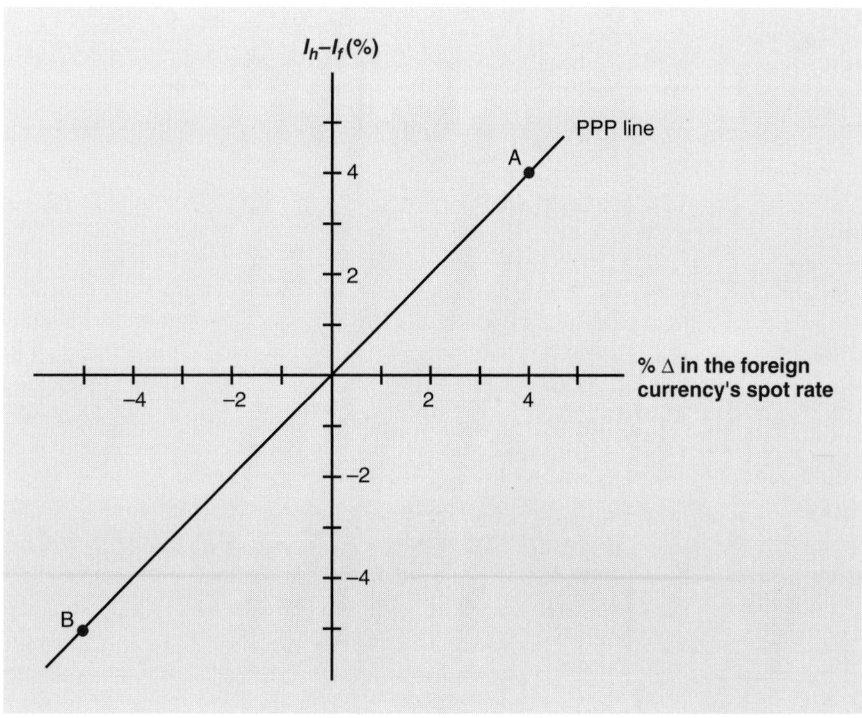

eign country of X percent, the foreign currency should adjust by X percent due to that inflation differential. The diagonal line connecting all these points together is known as the **PPP line.** Point A represents our example in which the U.S. (to be considered as the home country here) and British inflation rates were assumed to be 9 percent and 5 percent, respectively, so that $I_h - I_f = 4\%$. Recall that this led to the anticipated appreciation in the British pound of 4 percent, as illustrated by point A. Point B reflects an example in which the U.S. and foreign inflation rates were assumed to be 1 percent and 6 percent respectively, so that $I_h - I_f = -5\%$. This would lead to anticipated depreciation of the foreign currency by 5 percent, as illustrated by point B. If the exchange rate does respond to inflation differentials according to PPP theory, the actual points should lie on or close to the PPP line.

Exhibit 8.2 identifies areas of purchasing power disparity. Assume an initial equilibrium situation, then a change in the inflation rates of the two countries. If the exchange rate does not move as PPP theory would suggest, there is a disparity in the purchasing power of the two countries.

Point C in Exhibit 8.2 represents home inflation (I_h) in excess of foreign inflation (I_f) by 4 percent. Yet, the foreign currency appreciated by only 1 percent in response to this inflation differential. Consequently, purchasing power disparity exists. The home consumer's purchasing power on foreign goods has become more favorable relative to the purchasing power on the home country's goods. The PPP theory would suggest that such a disparity in purchasing power should exist only in the short run. Over time, as the home country consumers take advantage of the disparity by purchasing more foreign goods, upward pressure on the foreign currency's value will cause point C to move toward the PPP line. All points to the left of (or above) the PPP line represent more favorable purchasing power on foreign goods than on home goods.

Exhibit 8.2
Identifying Disparity in Purchasing Power

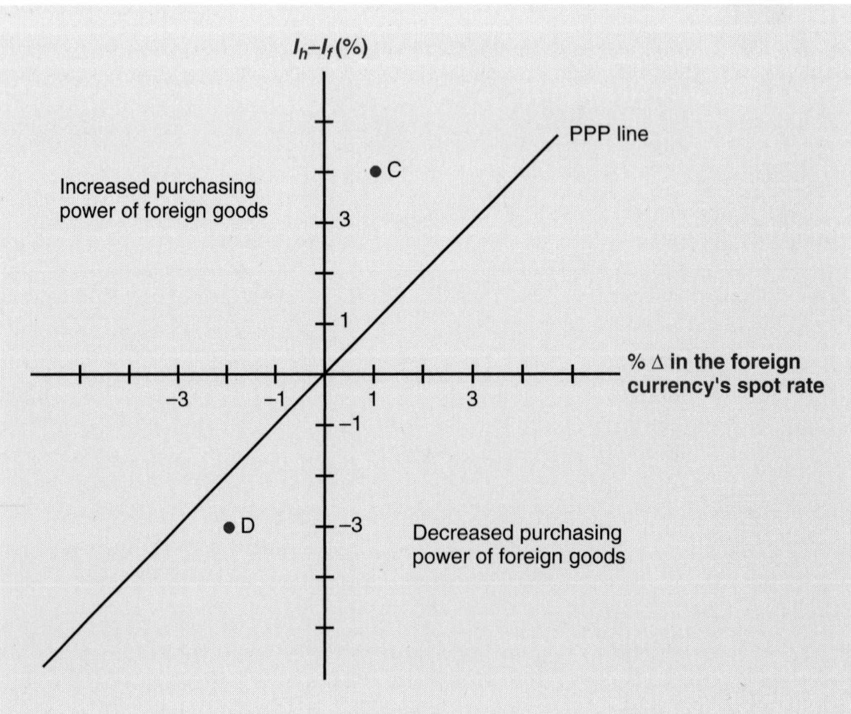

Point D in Exhibit 8.2 represents home inflation below foreign inflation by 3 percent. Yet, the foreign currency has depreciated by only 2 percent. Again, purchasing power disparity exists. The purchasing power on foreign goods has become less favorable relative to the purchasing power on the home country's goods. The PPP theory would suggest that the foreign currency in this example should have depreciated by 3 percent to fully offset the 3-percent inflation differential. Since the foreign currency did not weaken to this extent, the home country consumers may discontinue their purchasing of goods in the foreign country, causing the foreign currency to weaken to the extent anticipated by PPP theory. If so, point D would move toward the PPP line. All points to the right of (or below) the PPP line represent more favorable purchasing power on home country goods than on foreign goods.

Testing the Purchasing Power Parity Theory

The PPP theory not only provides an explanation of how relative inflation rates between two countries can influence an exchange rate, but it also provides information that could be used to forecast exchange rates. Substantial research has been conducted to examine whether PPP exists. The results of these tests will be discussed shortly. But first, how would you go about testing whether PPP exists? One simple method would be to choose two countries (say, the United States and a foreign country) and compare their differential in inflation rates to the percentage change in the foreign currency's value during several time periods. We could plot on a graph similar to Exhibit 8.2 each point representing the inflation differential and exchange rate percentage change for each specific time period, and then determine whether these points closely resemble the PPP line as drawn in Exhibit 8.2. If the points deviate significantly from the PPP line, then the percentage change in the foreign currency is not being influenced by the inflation differential in the manner PPP theory suggests.

As an alternative test of PPP, several foreign countries could be compared with the home country over a given time period. Each foreign country would exhibit an inflation differential relative to the home country, which could be compared to the exchange rate change during the period of concern. Thus, a point could be plotted on a graph such as Exhibit 8.2 for each foreign country analyzed. If the points deviated significantly from the PPP line, then the exchange rates would not be responding to the inflation differentials in accordance with PPP theory. PPP theory can be tested for any countries on which inflation information is available.

Statistical Test of PPP. A somewhat simplified statistical test of purchasing power parity could be developed by applying regression analysis to historical exchange rates and inflation differentials (see Appendix C for more information on regression analysis). To illustrate, let's focus on one particular exchange rate. The quarterly percentage changes in the foreign currency value (e_f) can be regressed against the inflation differential that existed at the beginning of the quarter, as shown here:

$$e_f = a_0 + a_1\left(\frac{(1+I_{U.S.})}{(1+I_f)} - 1\right) + \mu$$

where a_0 is a constant, a_1 is the slope coefficient, and μ is an error term. Regression analysis would be applied to quarterly data to determine the regression coefficients. The hypothesized values of a_0 and a_1 are 0 and 1.0, respectively. These coefficients imply that for a given inflation differential, there is an equal offsetting percentage change in the exchange rate, on average. The appropriate t-test for each regression coefficient requires a comparison to the hypothesized value, and division by the standard error (s.e.) of the coefficient, as follows:

$$\text{Test for } a_0 = 0: \quad t = \frac{a_0 - 0}{\text{s.e. of } a_0} \qquad \text{Test for } a_1 = 1 \quad t = \frac{a_1 - 1}{\text{s.e. of } a_1}$$

The t-table would then be used to find the critical t-value. If either t-test finds that the coefficients differ significantly from what is expected, the relationship between the inflation differential and the exchange rate differs from that stated by PPP theory. It should be mentioned that the appropriate lag time between the inflation differential and exchange rate is subject to controversy.

http://
The World Bank's Web site at www.worldbank.org offers socio-economic development and performance indicators as well as links to statistical and project-oriented publications and analyses.

Results of Tests of PPP. Much research has been conducted to test whether PPP exists. Recent studies by Mishkin, Adler, and Dumas, and Abuaf and Jorion[1] found evidence of significant deviations from PPP, persisting for lengthy periods. A related study by Adler and Lehman[2] provided evidence against PPP even over the long term.

However, recent research by Hakkio[3] found that when an exchange rate deviated far from the value that would have been expected according to PPP, it moved toward that value. While the relationship between inflation differentials and exchange rates is not perfect even in the long run, it supports the use of inflation differentials to forecast long-run movements in exchange rates.

To further examine whether PPP is valid, Exhibit 8.3 illustrates the relationship between relative inflation rates and exchange rate movements over time. The inflation differential shown in each of the four graphs (each graph represents one foreign currency) is measured as the U.S. inflation rate minus the foreign inflation rate. The annual differential in inflation between the United States and each foreign country is represented on the vertical axis of Exhibit 8.3. In addition, the annual exchange rate percentage change of each foreign currency (relative to the U.S. dollar) is represented on the horizontal axis. If PPP existed during the period examined, the points plotted on the graph should be near an imaginary 45-degree line, which would split the axes (like the PPP line shown in Exhibit 8.2). The annual inflation differentials and exchange rate percentage changes from 1982 to 1998 are plotted.

http://
The site at www.singstat.gov.sg compares the actual values of foreign currencies with the value that should exist under conditions of purchasing power parity.

While the results for each graph are different, some general comments apply to all graphs. The percentage changes in exchange rates are typically much more volatile than the inflation differentials. Thus, the exchange rates are changing to a greater degree than would be anticipated by PPP theory. In some years, even the

[1]Frederic S. Mishkin, "Are Real Interest Rates Equal Across Countries? An Empirical Investigation of International Parity Conditions," *Journal of Finance* (December 1984), pp. 1345–1357; Michael Adler and Bernard Dumas, "International Portfolio Choice and Corporate Finance: A Synthesis," *Journal of Finance* (June 1983), pp. 925–984; Niso Abuaf and Philippe Jorion, "Purchasing Power in the Long Run," *Journal of Finance* (March 1990), pp. 157–174.

[2]Michael Adler and Bruce Lehman, "Deviations from Purchasing Power Parity in the Long Run," *Journal of Finance* (December 1983) pp. 1471–1487.

[3]Craig S. Hakkio, "Interest Rates and Exchange Rates—What Is the Relationship?" *Economic Review*, Federal Reserve Bank of Kansas City (November 1986), pp. 33–43.

Exhibit 8.3
Comparison of Annual Inflation Differentials and Exchange Rate Movements for Four Major Countries

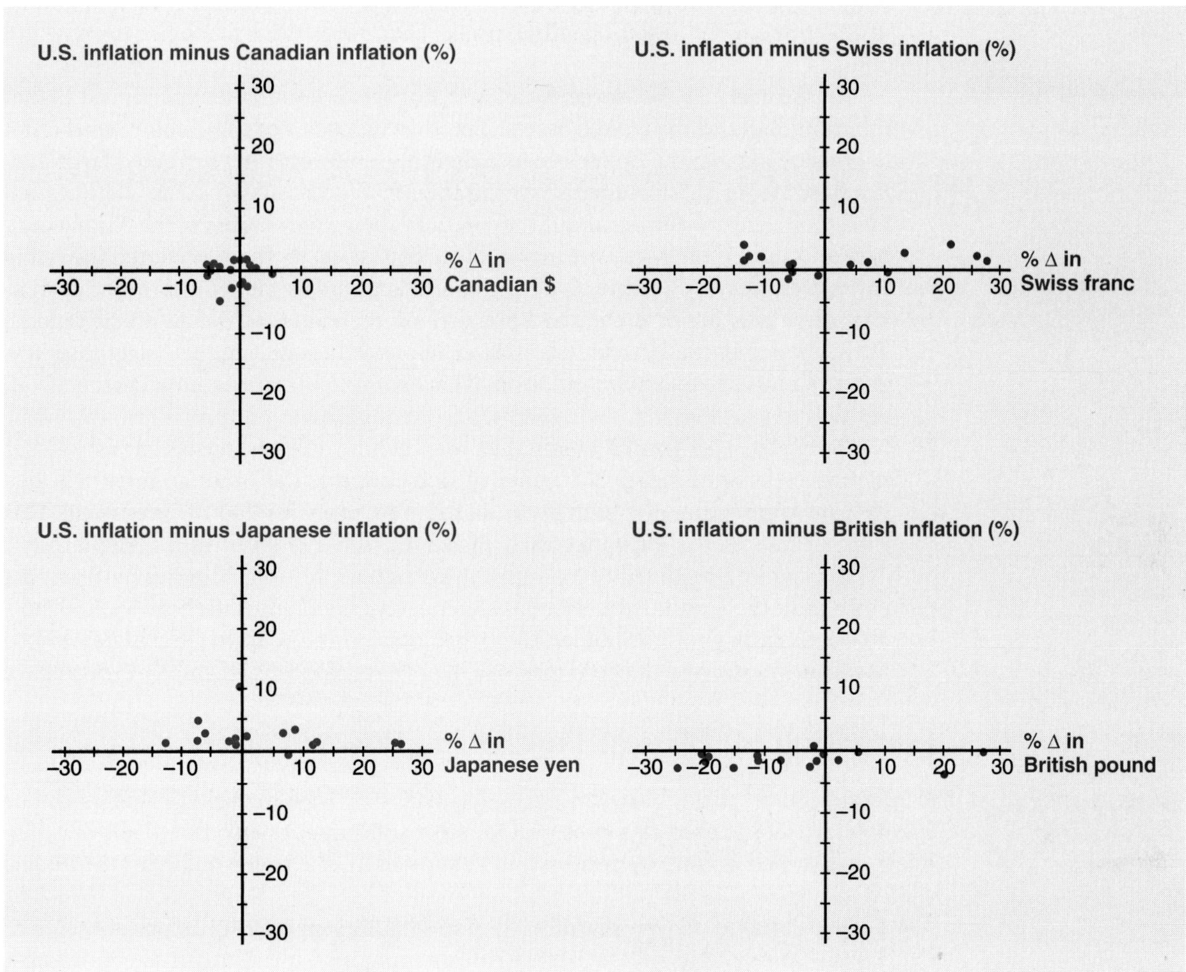

direction of a currency could not have been anticipated by PPP theory. The results in Exhibit 8.3 suggest that the relationship between inflation differentials and exchange rate movements often becomes distorted.

Why Purchasing Power Parity Does Not Occur

Two of the most commonly proposed reasons that PPP does not consistently occur are discussed next:

1. *Other influential factors.* Exchange rates are affected by other factors in addition to the inflation differential. Recall that differentials in interest rates and income levels as well as government controls are important. To illustrate, assume Mexico's inflation rate is 5 percent above the U.S. inflation rate. From this informa-

tion, PPP theory would suggest the Mexican peso should depreciate by 5 percent against the U.S. dollar. Yet, if the government of Mexico imposed trade barriers on U.S. exports, Mexican consumers and firms could not adjust their spending in reaction to the inflation differential. Therefore, the exchange rate will not adjust.

In the early 1990s, some Asian and European countries experienced higher inflation than did the United States. Yet, the currencies of these countries did not depreciate against the dollar because their high interest rates attracted large capital flows from U.S. investors. During the 1997–1998 Asian crisis, institutional investors were concerned about the safety of their investments in the Asian countries and shifted their investments to other countries. As they converted the Asian currencies received from liquidating their Asian investments into other currencies, there was major downward pressure on the values of the Asian currencies. Thus, the substantial decline of Asian currency values during the Asian crisis was not attributed to excessive inflation. This example illustrates how currency values will not necessarily be driven by purchasing power parity.

2. *No substitutes for traded goods.* The idea behind PPP theory is that as soon as the prices become relatively higher in one country, the other country will discontinue importing and shift to domestic purchases instead of importing. This shift influences the exchange rate. However, what if substitute goods are not available domestically? For example, if Mexico's inflation increases by 5 percent more than the U.S. inflation rate, U.S. consumers may not necessarily find suitable substitute goods at home. Thus, they may continue to buy the highly priced Mexican goods, and the peso may *not* depreciate as it was originally expected to.

Limitation in Tests of Purchasing Power Parity

A limitation in testing PPP is that the results will vary with the base period used. For example, if 1978 is used as a base period, most subsequent periods will show a relatively overvalued dollar; by contrast, if 1984 is used, the dollar may appear undervalued in subsequent periods.

The base period chosen should reflect an equilibrium position, since subsequent periods are evaluated in comparison to it. Unfortunately, it is difficult to choose such a base period. In fact, one of the main reasons for abolishing fixed exchange rates was the difficulty in identifying an appropriate equilibrium exchange rate.

http://
Dr. Ed Yardeni's Economics Network at www.yardeni.com reviews international and political economic events and their presumed global impact and presents economic and political analyses of major economies. A variety of national and international economic and financial market charts are also available.

Purchasing Power Parity in the Long Run

Purchasing power parity (PPP) can be tested by assessing a "real" exchange rate between two currencies over time. The real exchange rate is the actual exchange rate adjusted for inflationary effects in the two countries of concern. In this way, the exchange rate serves as a measure of purchasing power. If a currency weakens by 10 percent but its home inflation is 10 percent more than inflation in the foreign country, the real exchange rate has not changed. The degree of weakness in the currency is offset by the lower inflationary effects on foreign goods.

If the real exchange rate reverts to some mean level over time, this would suggest that it is constant in the long run, and any deviations from the mean are temporary. Conversely, if the real exchange rate follows a random walk, this implies that it moves randomly without any predictable pattern. That is, it does not tend to revert to some mean level and therefore cannot be viewed as constant in the long run.

Under these conditions, the notion of purchasing power parity is rejected because the movements in the real exchange rate appear to be more than temporary deviations from some equilibrium value.

A recent study by Abuaf and Jorion[4] tested PPP by assessing the long-run pattern of the real exchange rate. They state that the typical findings rejecting PPP in previous studies are questionable because of limitations in the methods used to test PPP. The authors find that the notion of a constant real exchange rate in the long run cannot be rejected, offering some support for PPP in the long run. They suggest that deviations from PPP are substantial in the short run but are reduced by about half in three years. Thus, even though exchange rates deviate from the levels predicted by PPP in the short run, their deviations are reduced over the long run.

International Fisher Effect (IFE)

Along with PPP theory, another major theory in international finance is the **international Fisher effect (IFE)** theory. It uses interest rate rather than inflation rate differentials to explain why exchange rates change over time, but it is closely related to the PPP theory because interest rates are often highly correlated with inflation rates. According to the so-called **Fisher effect,** nominal risk-free interest rates contain a real rate of return and anticipated inflation. If investors of all countries require the same real return, interest rate differentials between countries may be the result of differentials in expected inflation.

Recall that PPP theory suggests that exchange rate movements are caused by inflation rate differentials. If real rates of interest are the same across countries, any difference in nominal interest rates could be attributed to the difference in expected inflation. The IFE theory suggests that foreign currencies with relatively high interest rates will depreciate because the high nominal interest rates reflect expected inflation. The nominal interest rate would also incorporate the *default risk* of an investment. The following examples focus on investments that are risk-free, so that default risk will not have to be accounted for.

Assume that investors in the United States expect a 6-percent rate of inflation over one year and require a real return of 2 percent over one year; the nominal interest rate on one-year Treasury securities would be 8 percent. If investors in all countries required the same real rate of return for one year, then the differential in nominal interest rates among any two countries would represent their respective inflation differentials. For example, assume that the nominal interest rate is 8 percent in the United States and 5 percent in Japan. If investors in both countries require a real return of 2 percent, then the differential in expected inflation is 3 percent (6 percent in the United States versus 3 percent in Japan). According to PPP theory, the Japanese yen would be expected to appreciate by the expected inflation differential of 3 percent. If the exchange rate changes as expected, Japanese investors that attempt to capitalize on the higher U.S. interest rate would earn a return similar to what they could have earned in their own country. While the U.S. interest rate is 3 percent higher, the Japanese investors would have repurchased their yen for 3 percent more than the price at which they sold yen.

[4]Niso Abuaf and Philippe Jorion, "Purchasing Power in the Long Run," *Journal of Finance* (March 1990), 157–174.

To reinforce the concept, assume that the nominal interest rate in Canada is 13 percent. Given that investors in Canada also require a real return of 2 percent, the expected inflation rate in Canada must be 11 percent. According to PPP theory, the Canadian dollar is expected to depreciate by approximately 5 percent against the U.S. dollar (since the Canadian inflation rate is 5 percent higher). Therefore, U.S. investors would not benefit from investing in Canada because the 5-percent interest rate differential would be offset by investing in a currency that would be worth 5 percent less by the end of the period. U.S. investors would earn 8 percent on the Canadian investment, which is the same they could earn in the United States.

Given this information, the expected inflation differential between Canada and Japan is 8 percent. According to PPP theory, this inflation differential suggests that the Canadian dollar should depreciate by 8 percent against the yen. Therefore, even though Japanese investors would earn an additional 8-percent interest on a Canadian investment, the Canadian dollar would be valued at 8 percent less by the end of the period. Under these conditions, the Japanese investors would earn a return of 5 percent, which is the same as what they would earn on an investment in Japan. These possible investment opportunities, along with some others, are summarized in Exhibit 8.4. Note that wherever investors of a given country invest their funds, the expected nominal return is the same.

Derivation of the International Fisher Effect

The precise relationship between the interest rate differential of two countries and the expected exchange rate change according to IFE can be derived as follows. First, the actual return to investors who invest in money market securities (such as short-term bank deposits) in their home country is simply the interest rate offered on those securities. However, the actual return to investors who invest in a foreign money market security depends on not only the foreign interest rate (i_f) but also the percent change in the value of the foreign currency (e_f) denominating the security. The formula for the actual or so-called "effective" (exchange rate adjusted) return on a foreign bank deposit (or any money market security) is

$$r = (1 + i_f)(1 + e_f) - 1$$

According to the IFE, the effective return on a foreign investment should on average be equal to the effective return on a domestic investment. Therefore, the IFE suggests that the expected return on a foreign money market investment is equal to the interest rate on a local money market investment:

$$E(r) = i_h$$

where r is the effective return on the foreign deposit and i_h is the interest rate on the home deposit. We can determine the degree by which the foreign currency must change in order to make investments in both countries generate similar returns. Take the previous formula for what determines r, and set it equal to i_h as follows:

$$r = i_h$$
$$(1 + i_f)(1 + e_f) - 1 = i_h$$

Exhibit 8.4

Illustration of the International Fisher Effect (IFE) from Various Investor Perspectives

Investors Residing in	Attempt to Invest in	Expected Inflation Differential (Home Inflation Minus Foreign Inflation)	Expected Percentage Change in Currency Needed by Investors	Nominal Interest Rate to Be Earned	Return to Investors After Considering Exchange Rate Adjustment	Inflation Anticipated in Home Country	Real Return Earned by Investors
Japan	Japan		—	5%	5%	3%	2%
	U.S.	3% – 6% = –3%	–3%	8	5	3	2
	Canada	3% – 11% = –8%	–8	13	5	3	2
U.S.	Japan	6% – 3% = 3%	3	5	8	6	2
	U.S.		—	8	8	6	2
	Canada	6% – 11% = –5%	–5	13	8	6	2
Canada	Japan	11% – 3% = 8%	8	5	13	11	2
	U.S.	11% – 6% = 5%	5	8	13	11	2
	Canada		—	13	13	11	2

Now solve for e_f:

$$(1+i_f)(1+e_f) = (1+i_h)$$

$$(1+e_f) = \frac{(1+i_h)}{(1+i_f)}$$

$$e_f = \frac{(1+i_h)}{(1+i_f)} - 1$$

As verified here, the IFE theory contends that when $i_h > i_f$, e_f will be positive, because the relatively low foreign interest rate reflects relatively low inflationary expectations in the foreign country. That is, the foreign currency will appreciate when the foreign interest rate is lower than the home interest rate. This appreciation will improve the foreign return to investors from the home country, making returns on foreign securities similar to returns on home securities. Conversely, when $i_f > i_h$, e_f will be negative. That is, the foreign currency will depreciate when the foreign interest rate exceeds the home interest rate. This depreciation will reduce the return on foreign securities from the perspective of investors in the home country, making returns on foreign securities no higher than returns on home securities.

As a numerical example, assume that the interest rate on a one-year insured home bank deposit is 11 percent, and the interest rate on a one-year insured foreign bank deposit is 12 percent. For the actual returns of these two investments to be similar from the perspective of investors in the home country, the foreign currency would have to change over the investment horizon by the following percentage:

$$\begin{aligned} e_f &= \frac{(1+i_h)}{(1+i_f)} - 1 \\ &= \frac{(1+.11)}{(1+.12)} - 1 \\ &= -.0089, \textit{ or } -.89\% \end{aligned}$$

The implications are that the foreign currency denominating the foreign deposit would need to depreciate by .89 percent in order to make the actual return on the foreign deposit equal to 11 percent from the perspective of investors in the home country. This would then make the return on the foreign investment equal to the return on a domestic investment. A more simplified but less precise rule of the IFE is

$$e_f \cong i_h - i_f$$

That is, the exchange rate percentage change over the investment horizon will equal the interest rate differential between two countries. This approximation provides reasonable estimates only when the interest rate differential is small. For example, if the British rate on six-month deposits were 2 percent above the U.S. interest rate, the British pound would depreciate by approximately 2 percent over six months, according to IFE. If this occurred, U.S. investors would earn about the same return on British deposits as they would on U.S. deposits. Thus, there would be no advantage to the foreign investments, even though they exhibited a higher interest rate than domestic investments.

Graphic Analysis of the International Fisher Effect

Exhibit 8.5 displays the set of points that conform to the argument behind IFE theory. For example, point E reflects a situation in which the foreign interest rate exceeded the home interest rate by three percentage points. Yet, the foreign currency has depreciated by 3 percent to offset its interest rate advantage. Thus, an investor setting up a deposit in the foreign country would achieve a return similar to what is possible domestically. Point F represents a home interest rate 2 percent above the foreign interest rate. If investors from the home country establish a foreign deposit, they are at a disadvantage regarding the foreign interest rate. However, IFE theory suggests that the currency should appreciate by 2 percent to offset the interest rate disadvantage.

Point F in Exhibit 8.5 can also illustrate the IFE from a foreign investor's perspective. The home interest rate would appear attractive to the foreign investor. However, IFE theory suggests that the foreign currency will appreciate by 2 percent, which, from the foreign investor's perspective, implies the home country's currency denominating the investment instruments would depreciate to offset the interest rate advantage.

All the points along the so-called **IFE line** in Exhibit 8.5 reflect exchange rate adjustment to offset the differential in interest rates. This means an investor will end up achieving the same yield (adjusted for exchange rate fluctuations) whether investing at home or in a foreign country.

To be precise, IFE theory does not suggest this relationship will exist over each time period. The point of IFE theory is that if a corporation periodically makes foreign investments to take advantage of higher foreign interest rates, it will achieve a

Exhibit 8.5
Illustration of IFE Line (When Exchange Rate Changes Perfectly Offset Interest Rate Differentials)

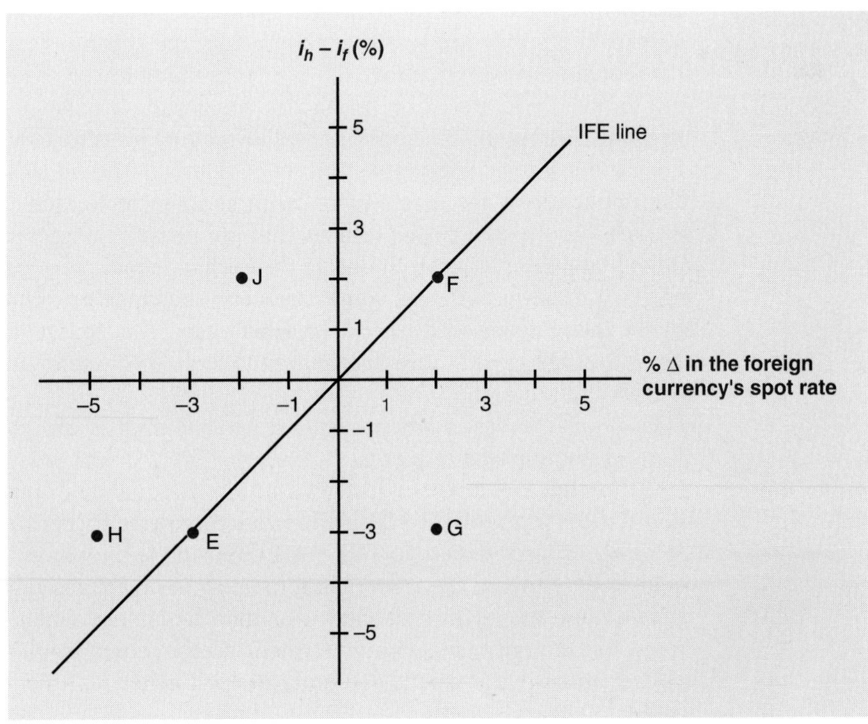

yield that is sometimes above and sometimes below the domestic yield. Periodic investments by a U.S. corporation in an attempt to capitalize on the higher interest rates would, on the average, achieve a yield similar to that by a corporation simply making domestic deposits periodically.

Points below the IFE line generally reflect the higher returns from investing in foreign deposits. For example, point G in Exhibit 8.5 suggests that the foreign interest rate exceeds the home interest rate by 3 percent. In addition, the foreign currency has appreciated by 2 percent. The combination of the higher foreign interest rate plus the appreciation of the foreign currency will cause the foreign yield to be higher than what is possible domestically. If actual data were compiled and plotted, and the vast majority of points were below the IFE line, this would suggest that investors of the home country could consistently increase their investment returns by establishing foreign bank deposits. Such results would refute the IFE theory.

Points above the IFE line generally reflect returns from foreign deposits that are lower than the returns possible domestically. For example, point H reflects a foreign interest rate that is 3 percent above the home interest rate. Yet, point H suggests that the exchange rate of the foreign currency has depreciated by 5 percent to more than offset its interest rate advantage.

As another example, point J represents a situation in which an investor of the home country is hampered in two ways by investing in a foreign deposit. First, the foreign interest rate is lower than the home interest rate. Second, the foreign currency has depreciated during the time the foreign deposit has been held. If actual data were compiled and plotted, and the vast majority of points were above the IFE line, this would suggest that investors of the home country would receive consistently lower returns from foreign investments as opposed to investments in the home country. Such results would refute the IFE theory.

http://
Visit the Fed's data bank at www.stls.frb.org/fred for numerous economic and financial time series, e.g., on balance of payment statistics, interest rates.

If the actual points (one for each period) of interest rates and exchange rate changes were plotted over time on a graph such as Exhibit 8.5, we could determine whether the points are systematically below the IFE line (suggesting higher returns from foreign investing), above the line (suggesting lower returns from foreign investing), or evenly scattered on both sides (suggesting a balance of higher returns from foreign investing in some periods and lower foreign returns in other periods).

Exhibit 8.6 is an example of a set of points that tend to support the IFE theory. The implications are that returns from short-term foreign investments are on the average about equal to the returns that are possible domestically. Notice that each individual point reflects a change in the exchange rate that does not exactly offset the interest rate differential. In some cases, the exchange rate change does not fully offset the interest rate differential. In other cases, the exchange rate change has more than offset the interest rate differential. Overall, the results balance out such that the interest rate differentials are *on the average* offset by changes in the exchange rates. Thus, foreign investments have generated yields that are on the average equal to those of domestic investments.

If foreign yields are expected to be about equal to domestic yields, a U.S. firm would most probably prefer the domestic investments because the yield on domestic short-term securities (such as bank deposits) is known in advance. However, the yield to be attained from foreign short-term securities is uncertain, due to the uncertainty of the spot exchange rate that will exist when the security matures. Investors generally prefer an investment whose return is known over an investment whose return is uncertain, assuming that all other features of the investments are similar.

Exhibit 8.6
Illustration of IFE Concept (When Exchange Rate Changes Offset Interest Rate Differentials on Average)

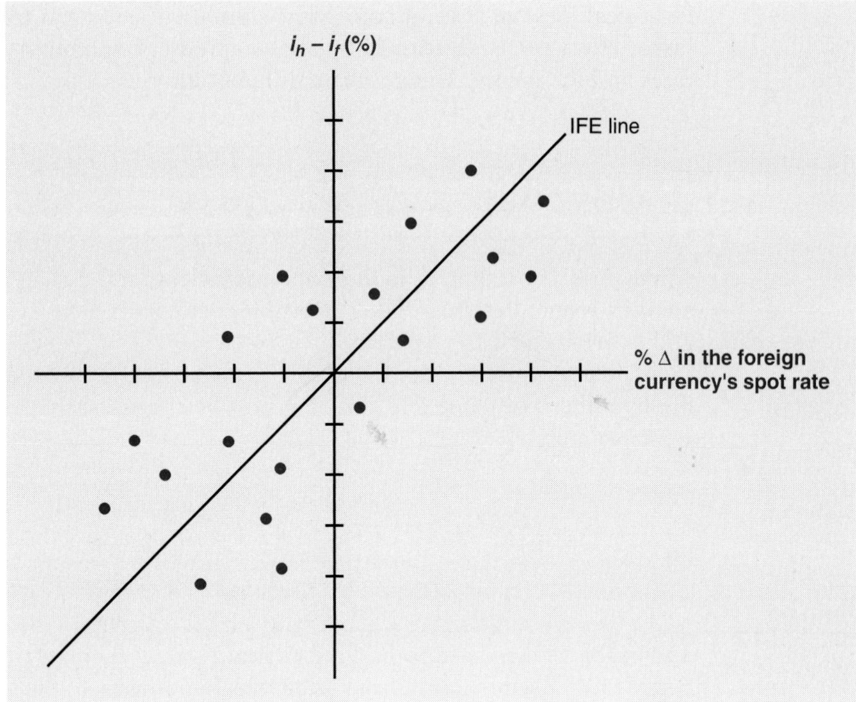

Tests of the International Fisher Effect

Whether the IFE holds in reality depends on the particular time period examined. In 1978–1979, the U.S. interest rates were generally higher than foreign interest rates, and the foreign currency values strengthened during this period (again supporting IFE theory to an extent). However, during the 1980–1984 period, the foreign currencies consistently weakened far beyond what would have been anticipated according to IFE theory. Furthermore, during the 1985–1987 period, foreign currencies strengthened to a much greater degree than suggested by the interest differential. While the IFE theory may hold during some time frames, there is evidence that it does not consistently hold.

A study by Thomas[5] tested the IFE theory by examining the results of (1) purchasing currency futures contracts of currencies with high interest rates that contained discounts (relative to the spot rates) and (2) selling futures on currencies with low interest rates that contained premiums. If the high-interest-rate currencies depreciated and the low-interest-rate currencies appreciated to the extent suggested by the IFE theory, the strategy described here would not generate significant profits. However, 123 (57 percent) of the 216 transactions created by this strategy were profitable. In addition, the average gain was much higher than the average loss. The rate of return averaged 77 percent on an annual basis. This study indicates that the IFE does not hold, which is not to say that all MNCs should immediately place all excess cash in high-interest-rate currencies. There is significant risk in such a strategy, as verified by the existence of losses generated in some periods of the study.

[5]Lee R. Thomas, "A Winning Strategy for Currency-Futures Speculation," *Journal of Portfolio Management* (Fall 1985), pp. 65–69.

Statistical Test of IFE. A somewhat simplified statistical test of the international Fisher effect can be developed by applying regression analysis to historical exchange rates and the nominal interest rate differential.

$$e_f = a_0 + a_1\left[\frac{1+i_{U.S.}}{1+i_f} - 1\right] + \mu$$

where a_0 is a constant, a_1 is the slope coefficient, and μ is an error term. Regression analysis would determine the regression coefficients. The hypothesized values of a_0 and a_1 are 0 and 1.0, respectively.

The appropriate *t*-test for each regression coefficient requires a comparison to the hypothesized value and then division by the standard error (s.e.) of the coefficients, as follows:

Test for $a_0 = 0$	Test for $a_1 = 1$
$t = \dfrac{a_0 - 0}{\text{s.e. of } a_0}$	$t = \dfrac{a_1 - 1}{\text{s.e. of } a_1}$

The *t*-table is then used to find the critical *t*-value. If either *t*-test finds that the coefficients differ significantly from what was hypothesized, the IFE is refuted.

Why the International Fisher Effect Does Not Occur

As mentioned earlier in this chapter, purchasing power parity (PPP) has not held over certain periods. Since the international Fisher effect is based on purchasing power parity, it does not consistently hold either. Because there are factors other than inflation that affect exchange rates, the exchange rates do not adjust in accordance with the inflation differential. Assume a nominal interest rate in a foreign country that is 3 percent above the U.S. rate because expected inflation in that country is 3 percent above expected U.S. inflation. Even if these nominal rates properly reflect inflationary expectations, the exchange rate of the foreign currency will react to other factors in addition to the inflation differential. If these other factors place upward pressure on the foreign currency's value, they will offset the downward pressure placed by the inflation differential. Consequently, foreign investments will achieve higher returns for the U.S. investors than domestic investments will.

Application of the International Fisher Effect to the Asian Crisis

The international Fisher effect (IFE) would suggest that when the Southeast Asian countries had high interest rates before the Asian crisis, they could not attract foreign investment because of exchange rate expectations. Specifically, the high nominal interest rate should reflect a high level of expected inflation. When combining the inflation and interest rate relationship with purchasing power parity, the high interest rate should result in a weaker currency because of the implied market expectations of high inflation. Foreign investors using this theory would not expect to benefit from the high Southeast Asian interest rates because the currency that they would invest in to attain the high interest would be expected to depreciate, thereby offsetting the interest rate advantage.

Yet, foreign investors did attempt to capitalize on the high foreign interest rates in Southeast Asia (at least before the Asian crisis). This suggests that they did not expect the IFE to hold. Since central banks of some southeast countries were maintaining their currencies within narrow bands, they were effectively preventing the exchange rate from depreciating in a manner that would offset the interest rate differential. Therefore, the IFE could not hold, and there was motivation for foreign investors to attempt capitalizing on the high interest rates in Southeast Asia. However, the strategy backfired for any investors who attempted to capitalize on the high interest rates during the Asian crisis, because the central bank efforts to maintain a stable currency were overwhelmed by market forces. Consequently, the effective yield (which accounts for exchange rate movements) earned by foreign investors who attempted to capitalize on the high interest rates in Southeast Asia was commonly negative. In essence, the depreciation in the currency that these investors invested wiped out the high level of interest earned on the investment, so that the investors received less at the end of their investment horizon than they initially invested.

Comparison of IRP, PPP, and IFE Theories

At this point, it may be helpful to compare three related theories of international finance: (1) interest rate parity (IRP), discussed in Chapter 7, (2) purchasing power parity (PPP), and (3) the international Fisher effect (IFE). Exhibit 8.7 summarizes the main theme of each theory. Note that all three theories relate to the determination of exchange rates. Yet, they differ in their implications. The theory of IRP focuses on why the forward rate differs from the spot rate and on the degree of difference that should exist. This relates to a specific point in time. Conversely, PPP theory and IFE theory focus on how a currency's spot rate will change over time. While PPP theory

Nike Problem

Impact of Inflation, Interest Rates, and Exchange Rate Relationships on Nike's Latin American Business

As Nike considers expanding in Latin American markets, the relationships between nominal interest rates, inflation rates, and exchange rates are very important. Some Latin American countries have very high interest rates, which reflect the expectation of high inflation rates (Fisher effect), and the high inflation rates could cause currencies of Latin American countries to weaken. The higher inflation may increase the amount of Nike's profits when measured in local currency (assuming that revenues and costs increase by a similar percentage, the nominal amount of profits should increase). Yet, it would also cause downward pressure (due to purchasing power parity) on the exchange rates of the Latin American currencies against the dollar, so that the funds will convert to fewer dollars over time. In fact, the exchange rate effects could more than offset any favorable effect on profits earned by a Latin American subsidiary.

Discussion: If Nike expands its business throughout Latin American countries, some of which have very high inflation rates, do you think Nike should hedge future remittances of funds from Latin American countries to the United States? Explain.

Exhibit 8.7
Comparison of IRP, PPP, and IFE Theories

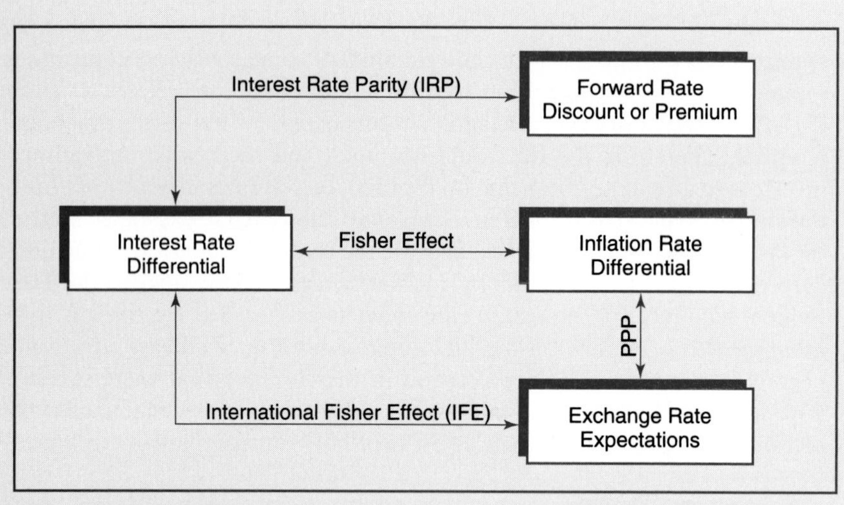

Theory	Key Variables of Theory		Summary of Theory
Interest rate parity (IRP)	Forward rate premium (or discount)	Interest rate differential	The forward rate of one currency with respect to another will contain a premium (or discount) that is determined by the differential in interest rates between the two countries. As a result, covered interest arbitrage will provide a return that is no higher than a domestic return.
Purchasing power parity (PPP)	Percentage change in spot exchange rate	Inflation rate differential	The spot rate of one currency with respect to another will change in reaction to the differential in inflation rates between the two countries. Consequently, the purchasing power for consumers when purchasing goods in their own country will be similar to their purchasing power when importing goods from the foreign country.
International Fisher effect (IFE)	Percentage change in spot exchange rate	Interest rate differential	The spot rate of one currency with respect to another will change in accordance with the differential in interest rates between the two countries. Consequently, the return on uncovered foreign money market securities will on average be no higher than the return on domestic money market securities from the perspective of investors in the home country.

suggests that the spot rate will change in accordance with inflation differentials, IFE theory suggests that it will change in accordance with interest rate differentials. PPP is nevertheless related to IFE because inflation differentials influence the nominal interest rate differentials between two countries.

IMPACT OF FOREIGN INFLATION ON THE VALUE OF THE MNC

The IFE and PPP can affect an MNC's value, as shown in Exhibit 8.8. High interest rates in a country can reflect the expectation of high inflation (the Fisher effect), which may be expected to place downward pressure on the local currency against the dollar. High inflation can increase the expected foreign currency cash flows of an MNC's foreign subsidiaries, assuming that it increases the revenue and the expenses by the same percentage (as earnings will be increased by that percentage as well). However, since high inflation can result in a weaker currency (as suggested by PPP), the foreign currency cash flows that are to be remitted and are not hedged will be expected to convert into fewer dollar cash flows. The impact of high inflation in a foreign country on the MNC's value is dependent on whether the expected favorable impact on foreign currency cash flows is greater than the expected unfavorable effect on the exchange rate at which the foreign currency will ultimately be converted into dollars.

Exhibit 8.8
Impact of Foreign Inflation on an MNC's Value

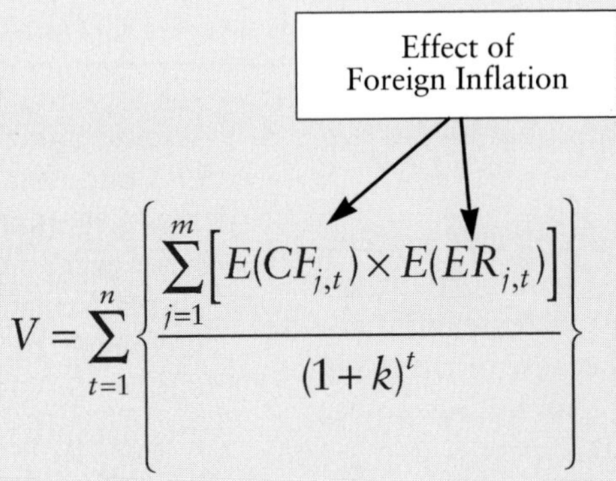

$$V = \sum_{t=1}^{n} \left\{ \frac{\sum_{j=1}^{m} \left[E(CF_{j,t}) \times E(ER_{j,t}) \right]}{(1+k)^t} \right\}$$

V = value of the U.S.-based MNC
$E(CF_{j,t})$ = expected cash flows denominated in currency j to be received by the U.S. parent in period t
$E(ER_{j,t})$ = expected exchange rate at which currency j can be converted to dollars at the end of period t
k = the weighted average cost of capital of the U.S. parent company
m = number of currencies
n = number of periods

SUMMARY

- Purchasing power parity (PPP) theory specifies a precise relationship between relative inflation rates of two countries and their exchange rate. In inexact terms, PPP theory suggests that the equilibrium exchange rate will adjust by the same magnitude as the differential in inflation rates between two countries. While PPP continues to be a valuable concept, there is evidence of sizable deviations from the theory in the real world.
- The international Fisher effect (IFE) specifies a precise relationship between relative interest rates of two countries and their exchange rates. It suggests that an investor who periodically invests in foreign interest-bearing securities will on average achieve a return similar to what is possible domestically. This implies that the exchange rate of the country with high interest rates will depreciate to offset the interest rate advantage achieved by foreign investments. However, there is evidence that during some periods the IFE does not hold. Thus, investment in foreign short-term securities may achieve a higher return than what is possible domestically. If a firm attempts to achieve this higher return, however, it does incur the risk that the currency denominating the foreign security might depreciate against the investor's home currency during the investment period. In this case, the foreign security could generate a lower return than a domestic security, even if it exhibits a higher interest rate.
- The PPP theory focuses on the relationship between the inflation rate differential and future exchange rate movements. The IFE focuses on the interest rate differential and future exchange rate movements. The theory of interest rate parity (IRP) focuses on the relationship between the interest rate differential and the forward rate premium (or discount) at a given point in time.
- If IRP exists, it is not possible to benefit from covered interest arbitrage. Investors can still attempt to benefit from high foreign interest rates if they remain uncovered (do not sell the currency forward). But IFE suggests that this strategy will not generate higher returns than what are possible domestically because the exchange rate is expected to decline on average by the amount of the interest rate differential.

SELF-TEST FOR CHAPTER 8

(Answers are provided in Appendix A at the back of the text.)

1. A U.S. importer of Japanese computer supplies pays for the supplies in yen. The importer is not concerned about the possible increase in Japanese prices (charged in yen) because of the likely offsetting effect caused by purchasing power parity (PPP). Explain what this means.
2. Use what you know about tests of PPP to answer this question. Using the information in the first question, explain why the U.S. importer of Japanese supplies would be concerned about its future payments.
3. Use purchasing power parity to explain how the values of the currencies of Eastern European countries might change if those countries experience high inflation, while the United States experiences low inflation.
4. Assume that the Canadian dollar's spot rate is $.85 and that the Canadian and U.S. inflation rates are similar. Then assume that Canada experiences 4-percent inflation, while the United States experiences 3-percent inflation. According to purchasing power parity, what will be the new value of the Canadian dollar after it adjusts to the inflationary changes? (You may use the approximate formula to answer this question.)
5. Assume that the Australian dollar's spot rate is $.90 and that the Australian and U.S. one-year interest rates were initially 6 percent. Then assume that the Australian one-year interest rate increases by 5 percentage points, while the U.S. one-year interest rate remains unchanged. Using this information and the international Fisher effect (IFE) theory, forecast the spot rate for one year ahead.

6. In the previous question, the Australian interest rates increased from 6 percent to 11 percent. According to the international Fisher effect (IFE), what is the underlying factor that would cause such a change? Give an explanation based on IFE of the forces that would cause a change in the Australian dollar. If U.S. investors believed in the IFE, would they attempt to capitalize on the higher Australian interest rates? Explain.

QUESTIONS AND APPLICATIONS

1. Explain the theory of purchasing power parity (PPP). Based on this theory, what is the general forecast of the values of currencies in highly inflated countries?

2. Explain the rationale behind purchasing power parity theory.

3. Explain how you could determine whether purchasing power parity exists.

4. Inflation differentials between the United States and industrialized countries have typically been a few percentage points in any given year. Yet, there have been many years in which annual exchange rates between the corresponding currencies have changed by 10 percent or more. What does this information suggest about purchasing power parity (PPP)?

5. Explain why purchasing power parity does not hold.

6. Describe a limitation in testing whether purchasing power parity holds.

7. Explain the international Fisher effect (IFE). What are the implications of IFE to firms with excess cash that consistently invest in foreign Treasury bills?

8. What is the rationale for the existence of the international Fisher effect?

9. Assume U.S. interest rates are generally above foreign interest rates. What does this suggest about the future strength or weakness of the dollar based on the international Fisher effect? Explain.

10. Compare and contrast interest rate parity (discussed in the previous chapter), purchasing power parity (PPP), and the international Fisher effect (IFE).

11. One assumption made in developing the international Fisher effect is that all investors in all countries require the same real return. What does this mean?

12. How could you use regression analysis to determine whether the relationship specified by purchasing power parity (PPP) exists on average? Specify the model, and describe how you would assess the regression results to determine if there is a *significant* difference from the relationship suggested by PPP.

13. Describe a statistical test for the international Fisher effect.

14. If investors in the United States and Canada required the same real return, and the nominal rate of interest were 2 percent higher in Canada, what would this imply about expectations of U.S. inflation and Canadian inflation? What do these inflationary expectations suggest about future exchange rates?

15. € Assume several European countries that use the euro as their currency experienced higher inflation than the U.S., while two European countries that use the euro as their currency experienced lower inflation than the U.S. According to purchasing power parity, how would the euro's value against the dollar be affected?

16. Currencies of some Latin American countries, such as Brazil and Venezuela, frequently weaken against most other currencies. What concept in this chapter would explain this occurrence?

17. Japan has typically had lower inflation than the United States. How would one expect this to affect the Japanese yen's value? Why does this expected relationship not always occur?

18. Assume that the nominal interest rate in Mexico is 48 percent and the interest rate in the United States is 8 percent for one-year securities that are

free from default risk. What would the international Fisher effect suggest about the differential in expected inflation in these two countries? Using this information and the purchasing power parity theory, describe the expected nominal return to U.S. investors who invest in Mexico.

19. Shouldn't the international Fisher effect discourage investors from attempting to capitalize on higher foreign interest rates? Why do some investors continue to invest overseas, even when they have no other transactions overseas?

20. Assume that the inflation rate in Brazil is expected to increase substantially. How would this affect Brazil's nominal interest rates and the value of its currency (called the real)? If the international Fisher effect holds, how would the nominal return to U.S. investors who invest in Brazil be affected by the higher inflation in Brazil? Explain.

21. How is it possible for purchasing power parity to hold if the international Fisher effect does not?

22. Explain why the international Fisher effect may not hold.

23. Assume that the spot exchange rate of the British pound is $1.73. How would this spot rate adjust according to purchasing power parity if the United Kingdom experiences an inflation rate of 7 percent while the United States experiences an inflation rate of 2 percent?

24. Assume the spot exchange rate of the Singapore dollar is $.70. The one-year interest rate is 11 percent in the United States and 7 percent in Singapore. What would be the spot rate in one year according to the international Fisher effect? (You may use the approximate formula to answer this question.)

25. As of today, assume the following information is available:

	U.S.	Mexico
Real rate of interest required by investors	2%	2%
Nominal interest rate	11%	15%
Spot rate	—	$.20
One-year forward rate	—	$.19

a. Use the forward rate to forecast the percentage change in the Mexican peso over the next year.
b. Use the differential in expected inflation to forecast the percentage change in the Mexican peso over the next year.
c. Use the spot rate to forecast the percentage change in the Mexican peso over the next year.

26. Would PPP be more likely to hold between the United States and Hungary if trade barriers were completely removed and if Hungary's currency were allowed to float without any government intervention? Explain.

27. Would IFE be more likely to hold between the United States and Hungary if trade barriers were completely removed and if Hungary's currency were allowed to float without any government intervention? Explain.

28. The opening of Russia's market has resulted in a highly volatile Russian currency (the ruble). Russia's inflation has commonly exceeded 20 percent per month. Russian interest rates commonly exceed 150 percent, but this is sometimes less than the annual inflation rate in Russia.

a. Explain why the high Russian inflation was placing severe pressure on the value of the Russian ruble.
b. Does the effect of Russian inflation on the decline of the ruble's value support the theory of purchasing power parity (PPP)? How might the relationship be distorted by political conditions in Russia?
c. Does it appear that the prices of Russian goods will be equal to the prices of U.S. goods from the perspective of Russian consumers (after considering exchange rates)? Explain.
d. Given high Russian inflation and the decline in the ruble, will the effects offset each other for U.S. importers? That is, how will U.S. importers of Russian goods be affected by the conditions?

29. Why does the international Fisher effect (IFE) suggest that the Asian countries would not attract foreign investment before the Asian crisis despite the high interest rates prevailing in those countries?

30. Before the Asian crisis, many investors attempted to capitalize on the high interest rates prevailing in the Asian countries, although the level of interest rates primarily reflected an increase in expected inflation. Explain why investors behaved in this manner.

31. € Given the recent conversion of several European currencies into the euro, what would cause the euro's value to change against the dollar according to purchasing power parity (PPP) theory?

32. € Assume that the inflation rates of the countries represented by the euro are very low, while other European countries that have their own currencies experience high inflation. Explain how and why the euro's value could be expected to change against these currencies according to the purchasing power parity (PPP) theory.

33. € Given the recent conversion of several European currencies into the euro, explain what would cause the euro's value to change against the dollar according to the international Fisher effect (IFE).

Internet Application

34. The "Market" section of the Bloomberg Web site provides interest rate quotations for numerous currencies. Its Web site address is:

    www.bloomberg.com

    a. Go to the "Markets" section and then to "International Yield Curves." Determine the prevailing one-year interest rate of the Australian dollar, the Japanese yen, and the U.K. pound. Assuming a 2-percent real rate of interest for savers in any country, determine the expected rate of inflation over the next year in each of these countries that is implied by the nominal interest rate (according to the Fisher effect).
    b. What is the approximate expected percentage change in the value of each of these currencies against the dollar over the next year, when applying purchasing power parity to the inflation level of each of these currencies versus the dollar?

Running Your Own MNC

Determining Whether IFE Holds

35. Use *The Wall Street Journal* or another data source to record the interest rate differential between the interest rate of the foreign country in which you plan to do business and the U.S. rate over the last five or so quarters. Then, review the exchange rate percentage change in the foreign currency of concern over each of those corresponding quarters to determine whether the international Fisher effect (IFE) appears to hold over those quarters for that currency.

Blades, Inc. Case

Assessment of Purchasing Power Parity

Blades, the U.S.-based roller blades manufacturer, is currently both exporting to and importing from Thailand. The company has chosen Thailand as an export target for its primary product, "Speedos," because of Thailand's growth prospects and the lack of competition from both Thai and U.S. roller blade manufacturers in Thailand. Under an existing arrangement, Blades sells 180,000 pairs of Speedos annually to Entertainment Products, Inc., a Thai retailer. The arrangement involves a fixed, baht-denominated price and will last for three years. Blades generates approximately 10 percent of its revenue in Thailand.

Blades has also decided to import certain rubber and plastic components needed to manufacture Speedos because of cost and quality considerations. Specifically, the weak economic conditions in Thailand resulting from recent events have allowed Blades to import components from the country at a relatively low cost. However, Blades did not enter into a long-term arrangement to import these components and pays market prices (in baht) prevailing in Thailand at the time of purchase. Currently, Blades incurs about 4 percent of its cost of goods sold in Thailand.

Although Blades has no immediate plans for expansion in Thailand, it may establish a subsidiary there in the future. Moreover, even if Blades does not establish a subsidiary in Thailand, it will continue exporting to and importing from the country for several years. Due to these considerations, Blades' management is very concerned with the recent events taking place in Thailand and its neighboring countries, as they may affect both Blades' current performance and the company's future plans.

Ben Holt, Blades' CFO, is particularly concerned with the level of inflation in Thailand. The nature of Blades' export arrangement with Entertainment Products, while allowing for a minimum level of revenue to be generated in Thailand in a given year, prevents Blades from adjusting prices according to the level of inflation in Thailand. In retrospect, Ben Holt is wondering whether Blades should have entered into the export arrangement at all. Since Thailand's economy was growing very fast when Blades agreed to the arrangement, the high level of consumer spending there resulted in a high level of inflation and interest rates in Thailand. Naturally, Blades would have preferred an agreement whereby the price per pair of Speedos would be adjusted for the Thai level of inflation. However, to take advantage of the growth opportunities in Thailand, Blades accepted the arrangement when Entertainment Products insisted on a fixed price level. Currently, however, the baht is freely floating, and Ben Holt is wondering how a relatively high level of Thai inflation may affect the baht-dollar exchange rate and, consequently, Blades' revenue generated in Thailand.

Ben Holt is also concerned with Blades' cost of goods sold incurred in Thailand. Since no fixed-price arrangement exists and the components are invoiced in Thai baht, Blades has been subject to increases in the prices of rubber and plastic. Mr. Holt is wondering how a potentially high level of inflation will impact the baht-dollar exchange rate and the cost of goods sold incurred in Thailand now that the baht is freely floating.

When Mr. Holt started thinking about the future economic conditions in Thailand and the resulting impact on Blades, he found that he needed your help. In particular, Ben Holt is vaguely familiar with the concept of purchasing power parity (PPP) and is wondering about this theory's implications for Blades, Inc., if there are any. Furthermore, Mr. Holt also remembers that relatively high interest rates in Thailand will attract capital flows and place upward pressure on the baht.

Because of these concerns, and to gain some insight into the impact of inflation on Blades, Inc., Ben Holt has asked you to provide him with answers to the following questions:

1. What is the relationship between the exchange rates and relative inflation levels of the two countries? How would this relationship affect Blades' Thai revenue and costs given that the baht is freely floating? What is the net effect of this relationship on Blades?
2. What are some of the factors that prevent purchasing power parity (PPP) from occurring in the short run? Would you expect PPP to hold better because of trade arrangements under which countries commit themselves to the purchase or sale of a fixed number of goods over a specified time period? Why or why not?
3. How do you reconcile the high level of interest rates in Thailand with the expected change of the baht-dollar exchange rate according to purchasing power parity?
4. Given Blades' future plans in Thailand, should the company be concerned with PPP? Why or why not?
5. PPP may hold better for some countries than for others. Given that the Thai baht has only been freely floating for a short period of time, how do you think Blades could gain insight into whether PPP will hold for Thailand?

Small Business Dilemma

Assessment of the IFE by the Sports Exports Company

Every month, the Sports Exports Company receives a payment denominated in British pounds for the footballs it exports to the United Kingdom. Jim Logan, owner of the Sports Exports Company, decides each month whether to hedge the payment with a forward contract for the following month. However, he has questioned whether this decision is worth the trouble. He suggests that if the international Fisher effect (IFE) holds, the pound's value should change (on average) by an amount that reflects the differential between the interest rates of the two countries of concern. Since the forward premium reflects that same interest rate differential, the results from hedging should equal the results from not hedging on average.

1. Is Jim's interpretation of the international Fisher effect (IFE) theory correct?
2. If you were in Jim's position, would you spend time trying to decide whether to hedge the receivables each month, or do you believe that the results would be the same (on average) whether you hedged or didn't hedge?

PART II
INTEGRATIVE PROBLEM

Exchange Rate Behavior

Questions

1. As an employee of the foreign exchange department for a large company, you have been given the following information.

Beginning of Year
Spot rate of £ = $1.596
Spot rate of Australian dollar (A$) = $.70
Cross exchange rate: £1 = A$2.28
One-year forward rate of A$ = $.71
One-year forward rate of £ = $1.58004
One-year U.S. interest rate = 8.00%
One-year British interest rate = 9.09%
One-year Australian interest rate = 7.00%

   Determine whether triangular arbitrage is feasible and, if so, how it would be conducted to make a profit.
2. Using the information in Question 1, determine whether covered interest arbitrage is feasible and, if so, how it would be conducted to make a profit.
3. Based on the information in Question 1 for the beginning of the year, use the international Fisher effect (IFE) theory to forecast the annual percentage change in the British pound's value over the year.
4. Assume that at the beginning of the year, the pound's value is in equilibrium. Assume that over the year the British inflation rate is 6 percent, while the U.S. inflation rate is 4 percent. Assume that any change in the pound's value due to the inflation differential has occurred by the end of the year. Using this information and the information provided in Question 1, determine how the pound's value changed over the year.
5. Assume that the pound's depreciation over the year has been attributed directly to central bank intervention. Explain the type of direct intervention that would place downward pressure on the value of the pound.

PART III

Exchange Rate Risk Management

Part III (Chapters 9 through 12) explains the various functions involved in managing exposure to exchange rate risk. Chapter 9 describes various methods used to forecast exchange rates and explains how to assess forecasting performance. Chapter 10 demonstrates how to measure exposure to exchange rate movements. Given a firm's exposure and forecasts of future exchange rates, Chapters 11 and 12 explain how to hedge that exposure.

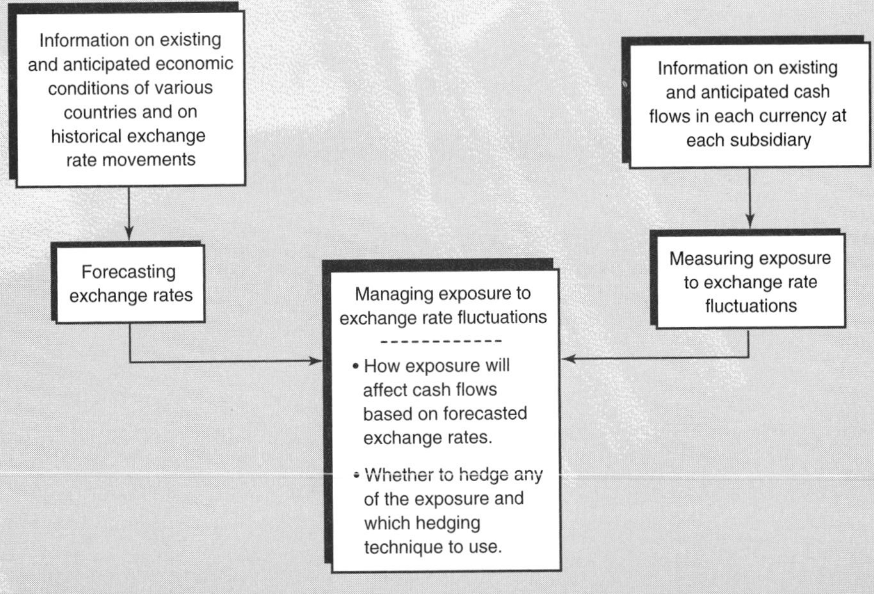

9 Forecasting Exchange Rates

The decisions of a multinational corporation (MNC) are influenced by exchange rate projections.

The specific objectives of this chapter are to

- explain how firms can benefit from forecasting exchange rates,
- describe the common techniques used for forecasting, and
- explain how forecasting performance can be evaluated.

Why Firms Forecast Exchange Rates

Virtually every operation of an MNC can be influenced by changes in exchange rates. Several corporate functions for which exchange rate forecasts are necessary follow:

1. *Hedging decision.* MNCs are constantly confronted with the decision of whether to hedge future payables and receivables in foreign currencies. Whether a firm hedges may be determined by its forecasts of foreign currency values. As a simple example, consider a firm in the United States that plans to pay for clothing imported from Mexico in 90 days. If the forecasted value of the peso in 90 days is sufficiently below the 90-day forward rate, the MNC may decide not to hedge.
2. *Short-term financing decision.* When large corporations borrow, they have access to several different currencies. The currency they borrow will ideally (1) exhibit a low interest rate and (2) weaken in value over the financing period. If, for example, a U.S. firm borrowed Japanese yen, and the yen depreciated against the U.S. dollar over the financing period, the firm could pay back the loan with fewer dollars (when converting those dollars in exchange for the amount owed in yen). This financing decision should therefore be influenced by exchange rate forecasts of any currencies available for financing.
3. *Short-term investment decision.* Corporations sometimes have a substantial amount of excess cash available for a short time period. Large deposits can be established in several currencies. The ideal currency for deposits would (1) exhibit a high interest rate and (2) strengthen in value over the investment

period. Consider, for example, a U.S. corporation that has excess cash deposited into a British bank account, and assume the British pound has appreciated against the dollar by the end of the deposit period. As the British pounds are withdrawn and exchanged for U.S. dollars, more dollars will be received, due to the pound's appreciation against the dollar. Exchange rate forecasts of the currencies denominating available deposit accounts should therefore be considered when determining where to invest the short-term cash.

4. *Capital budgeting decision.* When an MNC attempts to determine whether to establish a subsidiary in a given country, a capital budgeting analysis is conducted. Forecasts of the future cash flows used within the capital budgeting process will be dependent on future currency values. This dependency can be due to (1) future inflows or outflows denominated in foreign currencies that will require conversion to the home currency, and/or (2) the influence of future exchange rates on demand for the corporation's products. There are several additional ways by which exchange rates can affect the estimated cash flows, but the main point here is that accurate forecasts of currency values will improve the estimates of the cash flows and therefore enhance the MNC's decision-making abilities.
5. *Long-term financing decision.* Corporations that issue bonds to secure long-term funds may consider denominating the bonds in foreign currencies. As with short-term financing, corporations would prefer the currency borrowed (denominating the debt) to depreciate over time against the currency they are receiving from sales. To estimate the cost of issuing bonds denominated in a foreign currency, forecasts of exchange rates are required.
6. *Earnings assessment.* When earnings of an MNC are reported, subsidiary earnings are consolidated and translated into the currency representing the parent firm's home country. For example, consider an MNC with its home office in the United States and subsidiaries in Canada and the United Kingdom. The Canadian subsidiary's earnings in Canadian dollars must be measured by translation to U.S. dollars. The British subsidiary's earnings in pounds must also be measured by translation to U.S. dollars. "Translation" does not suggest that the earnings are physically converted to U.S. dollars. It is simply a recording process to periodically report consolidated earnings in a single currency. Using the scenario just described, appreciation of the Canadian dollar will boost the Canadian subsidiary's earnings when reported in (translated to) U.S. dollars. Forecasts of exchange rates thus play an important role in the overall forecast of an MNC's consolidated earnings.

The need for accurate exchange rate projections should now be clear. The following section describes forecasting methods available.

Forecasting Techniques

The numerous methods available for forecasting exchange rates can be categorized into four general groups: (1) technical, (2) fundamental, (3) market-based, and (4) mixed.

Technical Forecasting

Technical forecasting involves use of historical exchange rate data to predict future values. For example, the fact that a given currency has increased in value over four consecutive days may provide an indication of how the currency will move tomor-

http://
See pacific.commerce.ubc.ca/xr/data.html for a foreign exchange time series for over 60 countries which can be customized with respect to period and base currency.

row. In some cases, a more complex statistical analysis is applied in technical forecasting. For example, a computer program can be developed to detect particular historical trends.

There are also several **time series models** that examine moving averages and thus allow a forecaster to develop some rule, such as, "The currency tends to decline in value after a rise in moving average over three consecutive periods." Normally, consultants who use such a method will not disclose their particular rules for forecasting. If they did, their potential clients might apply the rules themselves instead of paying for the consultant's advice.

Technical forecasting of exchange rates is similar to technical forecasting of stock prices. If the pattern of currency values over time appears random, then technical forecasting is not appropriate. Unless historical trends in exchange rate movements can be identified, examination of past movements will not be useful for indicating future movements.

Technical factors have sometimes been cited as the main reason for changing speculative positions that cause an adjustment in the dollar's value. For example, it is not unusual to see headlines about the dollar's value changing because of the following possible explanations:

- Technical factors overwhelmed economic news
- Technical factors triggered sales of dollars
- Technical factors indicated that dollars had been recently oversold, triggering purchases of dollars

These examples suggest that technical forecasting appears to be widely used by speculators who frequently attempt to capitalize on day-to-day exchange rate movements.

Technical forecasting models have helped some speculators in the foreign exchange market at various times. However, a model that has worked well in one particular period will not necessarily work well in another. With the abundance of technical models existing today, some are bound to generate speculative profits in any given period.

Many foreign exchange participants argue that even if a particular technical forecasting model is shown to lead consistently to speculative profits, it will no longer be useful once other participants begin to use it. The trading based on its recommendation would push the currency value to a new position immediately. Speculators using technical exchange rate forecasting often incur large transaction costs due to frequent trading. In addition, it can be time-consuming to monitor currency movements in the search for any systematic pattern. Furthermore, speculators need sufficient capital to absorb losses that may occur.

From the corporate point of view, use of technical forecasting may be limited in that it typically focuses on the near future, which is not that helpful for developing corporate policies. Also, it rarely provides point estimates or a range of possible future values, as pointed out by Goodman.[1] Because technical analysis will not typically estimate future exchange rates in precise terms, it is not, by itself, an adequate forecasting tool for financial managers of MNCs.

---

[1]Stephen H. Goodman, "Foreign Exchange Rate Forecasting Techniques: Implications for Business and Policy," *Journal of Finance* (May 1979), pp. 415–427.

Fundamental Forecasting

Fundamental forecasting is based on fundamental relationships between economic variables and exchange rates. Given current values of these variables along with their historical impact on a currency's value, corporations can develop exchange rate projections. For example, high inflation in a given country can lead to depreciation in the currency representing that country. Of course, all other factors that may influence exchange rates also should be considered.

A forecast may arise simply from a subjective assessment of the degree to which general movements in economic variables in one country are expected to affect exchange rates. From a statistical perspective, a forecast would be based on quantitatively measured impacts of factors on exchange rates. While some of the full-blown fundamental models are beyond the scope of this text, a simplified discussion follows.

Example of Fundamental Forecasting. The focus here is on only two of the many factors that affect currency values. Before identifying them, consider that the corporate objective is to forecast the percentage change (rate of appreciation or depreciation) in the British pound with respect to the U.S. dollar during the next quarter. For simplicity, assume the firm's forecast for the British pound is dependent on only two factors that affect the pound's value:

1. Inflation in the United States relative to inflation in the United Kingdom.
2. Income growth in the United States relative to income growth in the United Kingdom (measured as a percentage change).

http://

See www.yardeni.com for reviews of international political and economic events and their presumed global impact. The site also presents economic and political analyses of major economies.

The first step is to determine how these variables have affected the percentage change in the pound value based on historical data. This is commonly achieved with regression analysis. First, quarterly data can be compiled for the inflation and income growth levels of both the United Kingdom and the United States. The dependent variable is the quarterly percentage change in the British pound value (called *BP*). The independent (influential) variables may be set up as follows:

1. Previous quarterly percentage change in the inflation differential (U.S. inflation rate minus British inflation rate), referred to as INF_{t-1}.
2. Previous quarterly percentage change in the income growth differential (U.S. income growth minus British income growth), referred to as INC_{t-1}.

The regression equation can be defined as

$$BP_t = b_0 + b_1 INF_{t-1} + b_2 INC_{t-1} + \mu_t$$

where b_0 is a constant, b_1 measures the sensitivity of BP_t to changes in INF_{t-1}, b_2 measures the sensitivity of BP_t to changes in INC_{t-1}, and μ_t represents an error term. A set of historical data would be needed to obtain previous values of *BP, INF,* and *INC*. Using this data set, regression analysis will generate the values of the regression coefficients (b_0, b_1, and b_2). That is, regression analysis determines the direction and degree to which *BP* is affected by each independent variable. The coefficient b_1 will exhibit a positive sign if, when INF_{t-1} changes, BP_t changes in the same direction (other things held constant). A negative sign indicates that BP_t and INF_{t-1} move in opposite directions. In the equation given, b_1 is expected to exhibit a positive sign, because when inflation in the United States relative to the United Kingdom increases, upward pressure is exerted on the pound's value.

The regression coefficient b_2 (which measures the impact of INC_{t-1} on BP_t) is expected to be positive, since when U.S. income growth exceeds British income growth, there is upward pressure on the pound's value. These relationships have already been thoroughly discussed in Chapter 4.

Once regression analysis is employed to generate values of the coefficients, these coefficients can be used to forecast. To illustrate, assume the following values: b_0 = .002, b_1 = .8, and b_2 = 1.0. The coefficients can be interpreted as follows. For a one-unit percentage change in the inflation differential, the pound is expected to change by .8 percent in the same direction, other things held constant. For a one-unit percentage change in the income differential, the British pound is expected to change by 1.0 percent in the same direction, other things held constant. To develop forecasts, assume that the most recent quarterly percentage change in INF_{t-1} (the inflation differential) is 4 percent, and that INC_{t-1} (the income growth differential) is 2 percent. Using this information along with our estimated regression coefficients, the forecast for BP_t is

$$\begin{aligned} BP_t &= b_0 + b_1\, INF_{t-1} + b_2\, INC_{t-1} \\ &= .002 + .8(4\%) + 1(2\%) \\ &= .2\% + 3.2\% + 2\% \\ &= 5.4\% \end{aligned}$$

Thus, given the current figures for inflation rates and income growth, the pound should appreciate by 5.4 percent during the next quarter.

This example is simplified to illustrate how fundamental analysis can be implemented for forecasting. A full-blown model may include many more than two factors. Yet, the application would still be somewhat similar. A large time series database would be necessary to warrant any confidence in the relationships detected by such a model.

Use of Sensitivity Analysis for Fundamental Forecasting. When a regression model is used for forecasting, and the values of the influential factors have a lagged impact on exchange rates, the actual value of those factors can be used as input for the forecast. For example, if the inflation differential has a lagged impact on exchange rates, the inflation differential in the previous period may be used to forecast the percentage change in the exchange rate over the future period. However, some factors may have an instantaneous influence on exchange rates. Since these factors are not known, forecasts must be used. Firms recognize that poor forecasts of these factors can cause poor forecasts of the exchange rate movements, so they may attempt to account for the uncertainty by using **sensitivity analysis,** in which more than one possible outcome is considered for the factors exhibiting uncertainty.

To illustrate how sensitivity analysis can be applied to the forecasting of exchange rate movements, assume that Phoenix Corporation develops a regression model to forecast the percentage change in the Mexican peso's value. We will simplify our example by assuming that the real interest rate differential and the inflation differential are the only factors that affect exchange rate movements, as shown in this regression model:

$$e_t = a_0 + a_1\, INT_t + a_2\, INF_{t-1} + \mu_t$$

where

e_t = percentage change in the peso's exchange rate over period t
INT_t = real interest rate differential over period t
INF_{t-1} = inflation differential in the previous period
a_0, a_1, a_2 = regression coefficients
μ_t = error term

Historical data are used to determine values for e_t along with values for INT_t and INF_{t-1} for several periods (preferably, 30 or more periods are used to build the database). The length of each historical period (quarter, month, etc.) should match the length of the period for which the forecast is needed. The historical data needed per period for the Mexican peso model are (1) percentage change in peso value, (2) U.S. real interest rate minus Mexican real interest rate, and (3) U.S. inflation rate in the previous period minus Mexican inflation rate in the previous period. Assume that regression analysis has provided the following estimates for the regression coefficients:

Regression Coefficient	Estimate
a_0	.001
a_1	–.7
a_2	.6

The negative sign of a_1 suggests a negative relationship between INT_t and the peso's movements, while the positive sign of a_2 suggests a positive relationship between INF_{t-1} and the peso's movements.

To forecast the peso's percentage change over the upcoming period, INT_t and INF_{t-1} must be estimated. Assume that INF_{t-1} was 1 percent. However, INT_t is not known at the beginning of the period and must therefore be forecasted. Assume that Phoenix Corporation has developed the following probability distribution for INT_t:

Probability	Possible Outcome
20%	–3%
50%	–4%
30%	–5%
100%	

A separate forecast of e_t can be developed from each possible outcome of INT_t, as follows:

Forecast of INT	Forecast of e_t	Probability
–3%	.1% + (–.7)(–3%) + .6(1%) = 2.8%	20%
–4%	.1% + (–.7)(–4%) + .6(1%) = 3.5%	50%
–5%	.1% + (–.7)(–5%) + .6(1%) = 4.2%	30%

If other currencies were to be forecasted, the probability distributions of their movements over the upcoming period could also be developed in a similar manner. For example, the percentage change in the Japanese yen could be forecasted by regressing historical percentage changes in the yen's value against (1) the differential between U.S. real interest rates and Japanese real interest rates, and (2) the differential between U.S. inflation in the previous period and Japanese inflation in the previous period. The regression coefficients estimated by regression analysis for the yen model will differ from those for the peso model. The estimated coefficients could then be used along with estimates for the interest rate differential and inflation rate differential to develop a forecast of the percentage change in the yen. Sensitivity analysis could be used to reforecast the yen's percentage change based on alternative estimates of the interest rate differential.

Use of PPP for Fundamental Forecasting. Recall that the theory of purchasing power parity (PPP) specifies the fundamental relationship between the inflation differential and the exchange rate. In simple terms, PPP states that the currency of the relatively inflated country will depreciate by an amount that reflects that country's inflation differential. Recall that according to PPP, the percentage change in the foreign currency's value (e) over a period should reflect the differential between the home inflation rate (I) and the foreign inflation rate (I_f) over that period. For example, assume that the United States inflation rate was expected to be 1 percent over the next year, while the Australian inflation rate was expected to be 6 percent over the next year. According to PPP, the Australian dollar's exchange rate should change as follows:

$$
\begin{aligned}
e &= \frac{(1+I_{U.S.})}{(1+I_f)} - 1 \\
&= \frac{1.01}{1.06} - 1 \\
&\cong -4.7\%
\end{aligned}
$$

This forecast of the percentage change in the rand can be applied to the existing spot rate of the rand to forecast the future spot rate at the end of one year. For example, if the spot rate (S_t) of the rand was \$.20, the expected spot rate of the Australian dollar at the end of one year, $E(S_{t+1})$, would be about \$.1906, as shown:

$$
\begin{aligned}
E(S_{t+1}) &= S_t(1+e) \\
&= \$.20\,[1+(-.047)] \\
&= \$.1906
\end{aligned}
$$

In reality, the inflation rates of the two countries over an upcoming period are uncertain and therefore would have to be forecasted when using PPP to forecast the future exchange rate at the end of the period. This complicates the use of PPP to forecast future exchange rates. Even if the inflation rates in the upcoming period were known with certainty, PPP might not be able to forecast exchange rates accurately.

If the PPP theory were accurate in reality, there would be no need to even consider alternative forecasting techniques. However, using the inflation differential of two countries to forecast their exchange rate is not always accurate. Problems arise because (1) the timing of the impact of inflation fluctuations on changing trade patterns, and therefore on exchange rates, is not known with certainty, (2) data used to measure relative prices of two countries may be somewhat inaccurate, (3) barriers to trade can disrupt the trade patterns that should emerge in accordance with PPP theory, and (4) other factors, such as the interest rate differential between countries, can also affect exchange rates. For these reasons, the inflation differential by itself is not sufficient to accurately forecast exchange rate movements. Yet, it should be included in any fundamental forecasting model.

Limitations of Fundamental Forecasting. While fundamental forecasting accounts for the expected fundamental relationships between factors and currency values, the following limitations exist:

- Uncertain timing of impact
- Forecasts needed for factors with instantaneous impact
- Omission of other relevant factors from model
- Change in sensitivity of currency movements to each factor over time

First, the precise timing of the impact of some factors on a currency's value is not known. It is possible that the impact of inflation on exchange rates will not completely occur until two, three, or four quarters later. The regression model would need to be adjusted accordingly.

A second limitation (as mentioned earlier) is related to those factors that exhibit an immediate impact on exchange rates. Their inclusion in a fundamental forecasting model would be useful only if forecasts could be obtained for them. Forecasts of these factors should be developed for a period that corresponds to the period in which a forecast for exchange rates is necessary. In this case, the accuracy of the exchange rate forecasts will be somewhat dependent on the forecasting accuracy of these factors. Even if firms knew exactly how movements in these factors affected exchange rates, their exchange rate projections could be inaccurate if they could not predict the values of the factors.

A third limitation is that there may be factors that deserve consideration in the fundamental forecasting process that cannot be easily quantified. For example, what if large Australian exporting firms experienced an unanticipated labor strike, causing shortages? This would reduce the availability of Australian goods for U.S. consumers and therefore reduce U.S. demand for Australian dollars. Such an event, which would place downward pressure on the Australian dollar value, is not normally incorporated into the forecasting model.

A fourth limitation of the fundamental model is that coefficients derived from the regression analysis will not necessarily remain constant over time. In the previous example, the coefficient for INF_{t-1} was .6, suggesting that for a one-unit change in INF_{t-1}, the Mexican peso would appreciate by .6 percent. Yet, if the Mexican or U.S. governments imposed new trade barriers, or eliminated existing barriers, the impact of the inflation differential on trade (and therefore on the Mexican peso's exchange rate) could be affected.

These limitations of fundamental forecasting are discussed to emphasize that even the most sophisticated forecasting techniques (fundamental or otherwise) are not going to provide consistently accurate forecasts. MNCs that use forecasting techniques must allow for some margin of error and recognize the possibility of error when implementing corporate policies.

http://

See www.cme.com for quotes on currency futures which can be used to create market-based forecasts.

Market-Based Forecasting

The process of developing forecasts from market indicators, known as **market-based forecasting,** is usually based on either (1) the spot rate or (2) the forward rate.

Use of the Spot Rate. To clarify why the spot rate can serve as a market-based forecast, assume the British pound is expected to appreciate against the dollar in the very near future. This will encourage speculators to buy the pound with U.S. dollars today in anticipation of its appreciation, and these purchases could force the pound's value up immediately. Conversely, if the pound is expected to depreciate against the dollar, speculators will sell off pounds now, hoping to purchase them back at a lower price after they decline in value. Such action could force the pound to depreciate immediately. Thus, the current value of the pound should reflect the expectation of the pound's value in the very near future. Corporations can use the spot rate to forecast, since it represents the market's expectation of the spot rate in the near future.

Use of the Forward Rate. To understand why the forward rate can serve as a forecast of the future spot rate, consider the following example. Assume the 30-day forward rate of the British pound is $1.40, and the general expectation of speculators is that the future spot rate of the pound will be $1.45 in 30 days. If speculators expect the future spot rate to be $1.45, and the prevailing forward rate is $1.40, they might buy pounds 30 days forward at $1.40 and then sell them when received (in 30 days) at the spot rate existing then. If their forecast is correct, they will earn $.05 ($1.45 – $1.40) per pound. If a large number of speculators implement this strategy, the substantial forward purchases of pounds will cause the forward rate to increase until this speculative demand stops. Perhaps this speculative demand will terminate when the forward rate reaches $1.45, since at this rate, no profits will be expected by implementing the strategy described. This example shows that the forward rate should move toward the market's general expectation of the future spot rate. In this sense, the forward rate serves as a market-based forecast, since it reflects the market's expectation of the spot rate at the end of the forward horizon (30 days from now in the previous example).

While the focus of this chapter is on corporate forecasting rather than speculation, it is speculation that helps to push the forward rate to the level that reflects the general expectation of the future spot rate. If corporations are convinced that the forward rate is a reliable indicator of the future spot rate, they can simply monitor this publicly quoted rate to develop exchange rate projections.

Long-Term Forecasting with Forward Rates. While forward rates are sometimes available for two to five years, such rates are rarely quoted. However, the quoted interest rates on risk-free instruments of various countries can be used to determine what the forward rates would be under conditions of interest rate parity. For example, assume that the U.S. five-year interest rate is 10 percent, annualized, while the British five-year interest rate is 13 percent. The five-year compounded return on investments in each of these countries is computed as follows:

Country	Five-Year Compounded Return
United States	$(1.10)^5 - 1 = 61\%$
United Kingdom	$(1.13)^5 - 1 = 84\%$

Thus, the appropriate five-year forward rate premium (or discount) of the British pound would be

$$\begin{aligned} p &= \frac{(1+i_{\text{U.S.}})}{(1+i_{\text{U.K.}})} - 1 \\ &= \frac{1.61}{1.84} - 1 \\ &= -.125, \text{ or } -12.5\% \end{aligned}$$

The results of our computation suggest that the five-year forward rate of the pound should contain a 12.5-percent discount. That is, the spot rate of the pound is expected to depreciate by 12.5 percent over the five-year period for which the forward rate is used to forecast.

Skepticism about the Forward Rate Forecast. One reason firms might not accept the forward rate as a predictor is because of a second market force. Recall that according to interest rate parity, the forward premium (or discount) is determined by the interest rate differential. If, for example, the 30-day interest rate of the British pound is above the 30-day U.S. interest rate, we expect the forward rate on the pound to exhibit a discount. The size of the discount will be such that U.S. investors cannot achieve abnormal returns by using covered interest arbitrage (converting dollars to pounds, investing pounds in a British 30-day account, and simultaneously selling pounds 30 days forward in exchange for dollars). Based on this information, consider that the forward rates of some currencies such as the British pound are usually below their current spot rates. That is, they almost always exhibit a forward discount (since their interest rates are typically above the U.S. rates). The discount within the forward rate suggests that the pound should depreciate, even when all other factors suggest that these currencies will appreciate.

Mixed Forecasting

Because no single forecasting technique has been found to be consistently superior to the others, some MNCs may prefer to use a combination of forecasting techniques. This method is referred to as **mixed forecasting.** Various forecasts for a particular currency value could be developed using several forecasting techniques. Each of the techniques used could be assigned weights in such a way that the weights totaled 100 percent, with the techniques thought to be more reliable being assigned higher weights. The actual forecast of the currency by the MNC would be a weighted average of the various forecasts developed. To illustrate the use of mixed forecasting, consider the following example.

Assume that a U.S. firm desires to assess the value of the Mexican peso because it is considering the expansion of more business in Mexico. The conclusions drawn from each forecast technique are shown in Exhibit 9.1. Notice that, in this example, the forecasted direction of the peso's value is dependent on the technique used. The peso is expected to appreciate when using the fundamental forecast, but depreciate when using the technical forecast or the market-based forecast. In fact, the fundamental and market-based forecasts were both driven by the same factor (interest rates), and yet results were distinctly different. The ultimate forecast about the peso is dependent on one's view of the technique that is most accurate. It is possible that

Exhibit 9.1
Forecasts of the Mexican Peso Drawn from Each Forecast Technique

	Factors Considered	Situation	Forecast
Technical Forecast	Recent Movement in Peso	The peso's value declined in the last few weeks below a specific threshold level.	The peso's value will continue to fall now that it is beyond the threshold level.
Fundamental Forecast	Economic Growth, Inflation, Interest Rates	Mexico's interest rates are high, and inflation should remain low.	The peso's value will rise as U.S. investors capitalize on the high interest rates by investing in Mexican securities.
Market-Based Forecast	Spot Rate, Forward Rate	The peso's forward rate exhibits a significant discount, which is attributed to Mexico's relatively high interest rates.	Based on the forward rate of a forecast, the peso's value will decline.

the firm may assign one technique a lower weight when forecasting in one period, but a higher weight when forecasting in a later period; some conditions can become more influential over time. Some firms may even weight a given technique more for some currencies than for others at a given point in time. For example, an MNC may think the pound is predicted best by the market-based forecast, while the New Zealand dollar's value is mainly driven by fundamental factors, and the Mexican peso's value may seem to follow technical factors.

While each forecasting method has its merits, some changes in exchange rates are not easily predicted. For example, during the Asian crisis, the Indonesian rupiah depreciated by more than 80 percent within a nine-month period against the dollar. Before the decline of the rupiah, technical factors did not indicate any potential weakness, fundamental factors did not indicate potential weakness, and the forward rate did not indicate potential weakness. The depreciation of the rupiah was primarily attributed to concerns by institutional investors about the safety of their investments in Indonesia, which encouraged them to liquidate the investments and convert the rupiah into other currencies, placing downward pressure on the rupiah. This type of influence is more likely to be captured by a subjective assessment of conditions in a country and not by quantitative methods described here. Thus, MNCs may benefit from using the methods described in this chapter along with their own sense of the conditions in a particular country.

Forecasting Services

The corporate need to forecast currency values has prompted the emergence of several consulting firms, including Business International, Conti Currency, Predex, and Wharton Econometric Forecasting Associates. In addition, some large investment banks such as Goldman Sachs and commercial banks such as Citibank offer forecasting services. Many consulting services use at least two different types of analysis to generate separate forecasts and then determine the weighted average of the forecasts.

Some forecasting services, such as Capital Techniques, FX Concepts, and Preview Economics, focus on technical forecasting, while other services, such as Corporate Treasury Consultants Ltd. and WEFA, focus on fundamental forecasting. Many services, such as Chemical Bank and Forexia Ltd., use both technical and fundamental forecasting. In some cases, the technical forecasting techniques are emphasized by the forecasting firms for short-term forecasts, while fundamental techniques are emphasized for long-run forecasts.

Forecasts are even provided for currencies that are not widely traded. Firms provide forecasts on any currency for time horizons of interest to their clients, ranging from one day to ten years from now. In addition, some firms will offer advice on international cash management, assessment of exposure to exchange rate risk, and hedging. Many of the firms provide their clients with forecasts and recommendations monthly, or even weekly, for an annual fee.

Given the recent volatility in foreign exchange markets, it is quite difficult to forecast currency values. One way for a corporation to determine whether a forecasting service is valuable is to compare the accuracy of its forecasts to that of alternative publicly available and free forecasts. The forward rate serves as a benchmark for comparison here, since it is quoted in many newspapers and magazines. A study by Richard Levich[2] compared the forecasts of several currency forecasting services regarding nine different currencies to the forward rate. Only 5 percent of the forecasts (when considering all forecasting firms and all currencies forecasted) for one month ahead were more accurate than the forward rate, while only 14 percent of forecasts for three months ahead were more accurate. These results are frustrating to the corporations that have paid substantial amounts per year or more for expert opinions. Perhaps some corporate clients of these consulting firms believe the fee is worth it even when the forecasting performance is poor, if other services (such as cash management) are included in the package. It is also possible that a corporate treasurer, in recognition of the potential for error in forecasting exchange rates, may prefer to pay a consulting firm for its forecasts. Then the treasurer is not (in a sense) directly responsible for corporate problems that result from inaccurate currency forecasts. Not all MNCs hire consulting firms to do their forecasting. For example, Kodak, Inc., once used a service but became dissatisfied with it, and it has now developed its own forecasting system.

EVALUATION OF FORECAST PERFORMANCE

An MNC that forecasts exchange rates must monitor its performance over time to determine whether the forecasting procedure is satisfactory. For this purpose, a measurement of the forecast error is required. There are various ways to compute forecast errors. Only one possible measurement will be discussed here and is defined as follows:

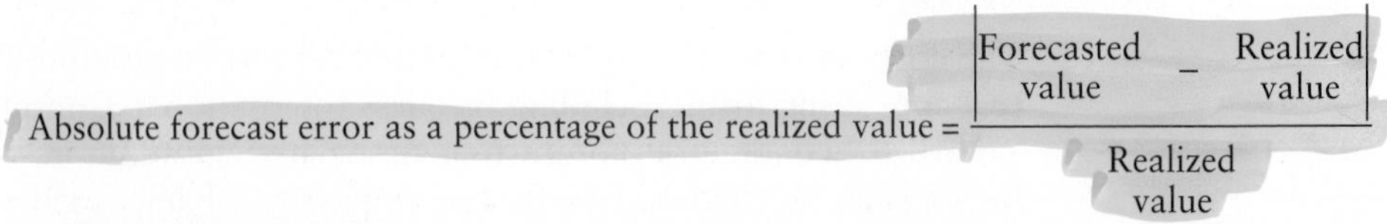

$$\text{Absolute forecast error as a percentage of the realized value} = \frac{\left|\text{Forecasted value} - \text{Realized value}\right|}{\text{Realized value}}$$

[2]Richard M. Levich, "Are Forward Exchange Rates Unbiased Predictors of Future Spot Rates?" *Columbia Journal of World Business* (Winter 1979), pp. 49–61.

The error is computed using an absolute value, since this avoids a possible offsetting effect when determining the mean forecast error. For example, consider a simplified example, in which the forecast error is .05 in the first period and –.05 in the second period (if the absolute value is not taken). The mean error here over the two periods is zero. Yet, that is misleading because the forecast was not perfectly accurate in either period. The absolute value avoids such a distortion.

When measuring forecast performance of different currencies, it is often useful to adjust for their relative sizes, so forecasting ability can be compared among currencies. As an example, consider the following forecasted and realized values by a U.S. firm during one period:

	Forecasted Value	Realized Value
British pound	\$1.35	\$1.50
Mexican peso	\$ .12	\$ .10

In this case, the difference between the forecasted value and the realized value is \$.15 for the pound, compared to \$.02 for the peso. This does not necessarily imply that the forecast of the peso is more accurate. When considering the size of what is forecasted (dividing the difference by the realized value), one can see that the British pound has been predicted with more accuracy on a percentage basis. With the data given, the forecasting error (as defined earlier) of the British pound is

$$\frac{|\$1.35-\$1.50|}{\$1.50}=\frac{\$.15}{\$1.50}=.10,\text{ or }10\%$$

In comparison, the forecast error of the Mexican peso is

$$\frac{|.12-.10|}{.10}=\frac{.02}{.10}=.20,\text{ or }20\%$$

Thus, the peso has been predicted with less accuracy.

Forecast Accuracy Over Time

MNCs are likely to have more confidence in their measurement of the forecast error when they measure it over each of several periods. The absolute forecast error as a percentage of the realized value can be estimated for each period in order to derive the mean error over all of these periods. For example, if an MNC was most interested in forecasting the value of a currency 90 days (one quarter) from now, it would assess errors from the application of various forecast procedures over the last several quarters.

Has there been any improvement in forecasting in recent years? The answer depends on the method used to develop forecasts. With regard to the forward rate as a predictor, the magnitude of the absolute errors is shown for the British pound over time in Exhibit 9.2. The size of the errors changes over time. However, there does not appear to be a consistent movement toward larger or smaller errors.

Exhibit 9.2
Absolute Forecast Errors Over Time for the British Pound (Using the Forward Rate to Forecast)

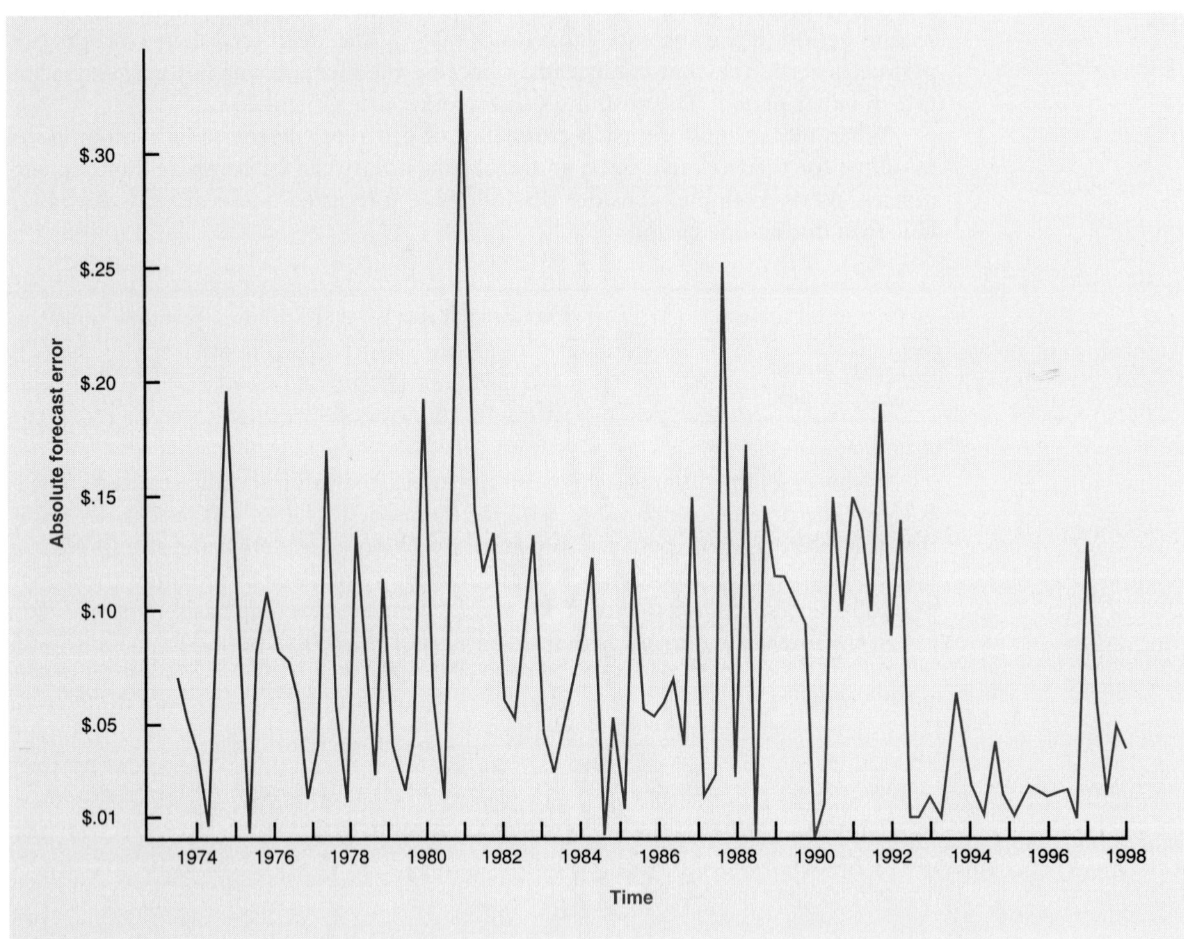

The year 1981 stands out as a period in which forecasts were worse than ever. U.S. interest rates were extremely high at the time, which attracted foreign (including British) demand for U.S. dollars to buy U.S. securities. Consequently, the British pound depreciated to such a degree that the 90-day forecasts based on the forward rate were off by as much as $.32 per pound.

Forecast Accuracy among Currencies

The ability to forecast currency values may vary with the currency of concern. For example, Exhibit 9.3 discloses the mean forecast errors of major currencies over the 1974–1998 period. These errors are derived when the 90-day forward rate is being used to forecast. The Canadian dollar stands out as the currency most accurately predicted. Its mean error is less than one-third of the mean absolute forecast errors of the Japanese yen and Swiss franc over the 1974–1998 period. This is important information, since a financial manager of a U.S. firm can feel more confident about the number of dollars to be received (or needed) on Canadian transactions. Conversely, it

Exhibit 9.3
Comparison of Forecast Errors among Currencies (1974–1998 Period)

Currency	Mean Absolute Forecast Error as a Percent of the Realized Value		
	1974–1998	1974–1984	1985–1998
British pound	4.61%	5.06%	4.21%
Canadian dollar	1.73	1.70	1.75
Japanese yen	5.60	5.22	5.93
Swiss franc	5.69	5.81	5.58

appears much more difficult to forecast the future value of the Japanese yen. The higher degree of accuracy when forecasting the Canadian dollar versus the other currencies is attributed to less volatility in the Canadian dollar's exchange rate over time.

The absolute forecast errors of the currencies can change over time, as illustrated in Exhibit 9.3. For example, the absolute forecast error of the British pound was 5.06 percent over the period from 1974 to 1984 but declined to 4.21 percent over the period from 1985 to 1998. The Canadian dollar exhibited a much lower absolute forecast error than the other currencies in all periods assessed.

Search for Forecast Bias

The difference between the forecasted and realized exchange rates for a given point in time represents a nominal forecast error. A time series of nominal forecast errors for the British pound is illustrated in Exhibit 9.4. Negative errors over time represent underestimating, while positive errors represent overestimating. If the errors are consistently positive or negative over time, then a bias in the forecasting procedure does exist. In this example, it appears that a bias did exist in distinct periods. During the strong-pound periods, the forecasts underestimated, while in weak-pound periods, the forecasts overestimated.

Statistical Test of Forecast Bias

If the forward rate is a biased predictor of the future spot rate, this implies that there is a systematic forecast error, which could be corrected to improve forecast accuracy. If the forward rate is unbiased, it fully reflects all available information about the future spot rate. Any forecast errors would be the result of events that could not have been anticipated from existing information at the time of the forecast. A conventional method of testing for a forecast bias is to apply the following regression model to historical data:

$$S_t = a_0 + a_1 F_{t-1} + \mu_t$$

where

S_t = spot rate at time t
F_{t-1} = forward rate at time $t-1$
μ_t = error term
a_0 = intercept
a_1 = regression coefficient

Exhibit 9.4
Comparison of Forecasted and Realized Spot Rates Over Time for the British Pound (Using the FR to Forecast)

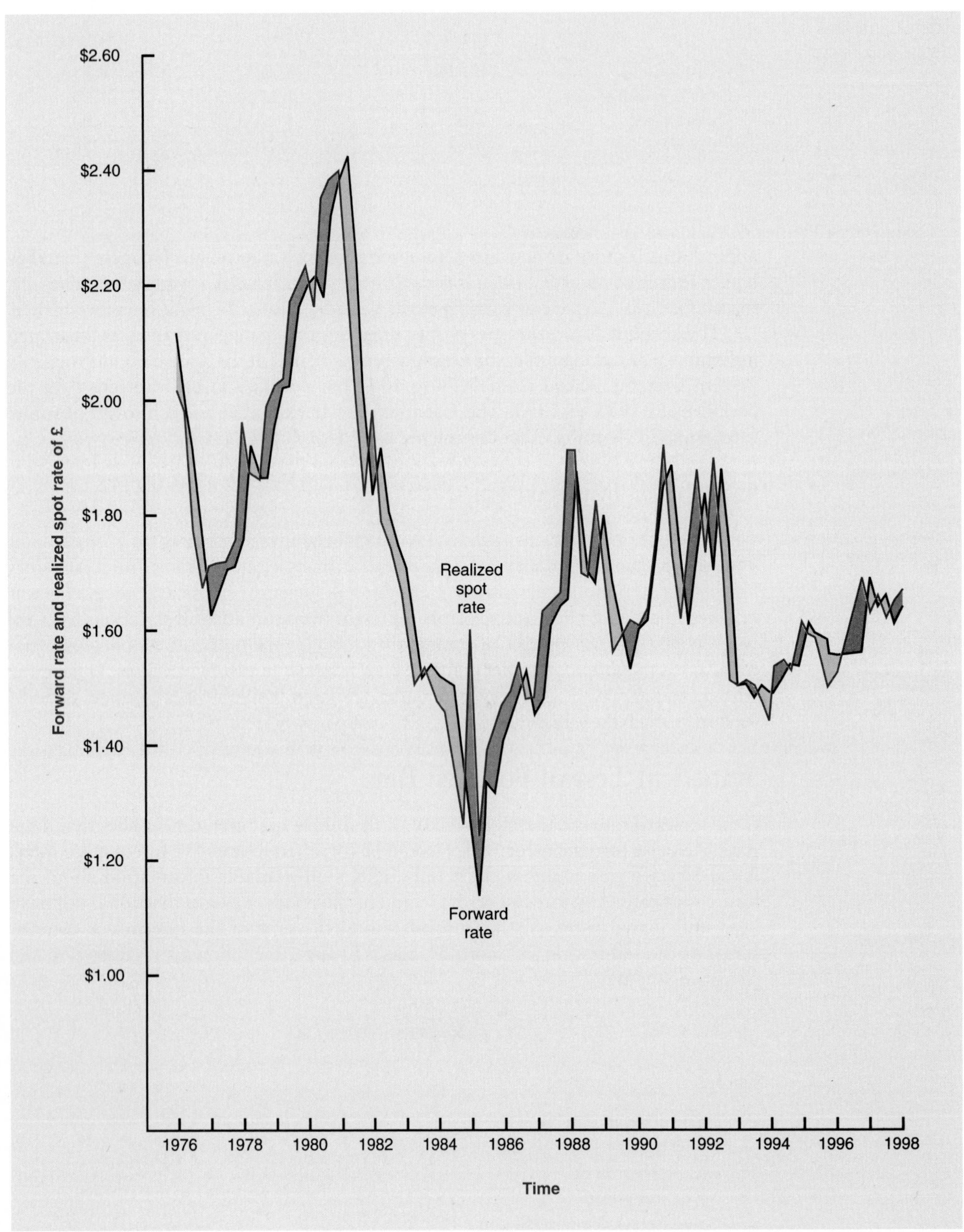

If the forward rate is unbiased, the intercept should equal zero, and the regression coefficient a_1 should equal 1.0. The t-test for a_1 is

$$t = \frac{a_1 - 1}{\text{standard error of } a_1}$$

If $a_0 = 0$ and a_1 is significantly less than 1.0, this implies that the forward rate is systematically overestimating the spot rate. For example, if $a_0 = 0$ and $a_1 = .90$, the future spot rate is estimated to be 90 percent of the forecast generated by the forward rate. Conversely, if $a_0 = 0$ and a_1 is significantly greater than 1.0, this implies that the forward rate is systematically underestimating the spot rate. For example, if $a = 0$ and $a_1 = 1.1$, the future spot rate is estimated to be 1.1 times the forecast generated by the forward rate. When a bias is detected and anticipated to persist in the future, future forecasts may incorporate the bias detected. Using the example in which $a_1 =$ 1.1, future forecasts of the spot rate may incorporate this information by multiplying the forward rate by 1.1 to create a forecast of the future spot rate.

By detecting a bias, an MNC may be able to revise its forecast to adjust for the bias so it can improve its forecasting accuracy. For example, if the errors are consistently positive, an MNC could adjust today's forward rate downward to reflect the bias detected. Over time, a forecasting bias can change (from underestimating to overestimating, or vice versa). Any adjustment to the forward rate used as a forecast would need to reflect the anticipated bias for the period of concern.

Graphic Evaluation of Forecast Performance

Performance from forecasting can be examined with the use of a graph that compares forecasted values with the realized values for various time periods. As a hypothetical example, consider the corporate exchange rate projections for Currency Q with respect to the U.S. dollar that appear in Exhibit 9.5. The predicted and realized exchange rate values in Exhibit 9.5 can be compared graphically, as shown in Exhibit 9.6. For example, in period 1, the predicted value of Currency Q was \$.20 and the realized value was \$.16. This point is illustrated in Exhibit 9.6 and designated with a "1."

The 45-degree line in Exhibit 9.6 represents perfect forecasts. To clarify, consider a case in which the realized value turned out to be exactly what was predicted

Exhibit 9.5 Hypothetical Evaluation of Forecast Performance

Period	Predicted Value of Currency Q for End of Period	Realized Value of Currency Q as of End of Period
1	\$.20	\$.16
2	.18	.14
3	.24	.16
4	.26	.22
5	.30	.28
6	.22	.26
7	.16	.14
8	.14	.10

Exhibit 9.6
Comparison of Forecasted and Realized Spot Rates

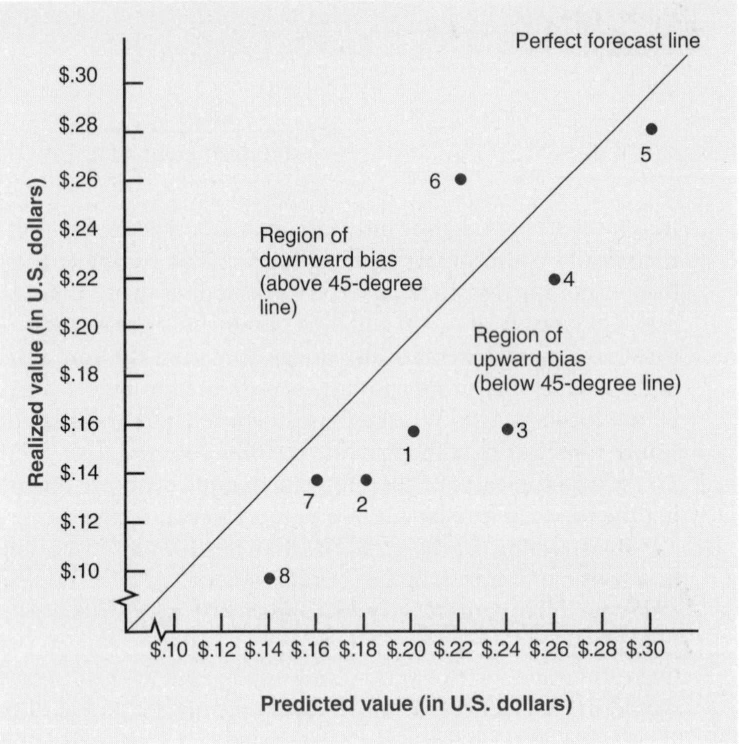

over several periods. All points would be located on that 45-degree line in Exhibit 9.6. For this reason, the line is referred to as the **perfect forecast line.** While in our example the forecasts are not perfectly accurate, the perfect forecast line still can be useful for assessing forecasting performance. The closer the points reflecting the eight periods are vertically to the 45-degree line, the better the forecast. The vertical distance between each point and the 45-degree line is the forecast error. For example, the 45-degree line is $.04 above the point representing period 1. This implies that the forecast for period 1 was $.04 above the realized value. All points below the 45-degree line reflect overestimation by the forecasts. In Exhibit 9.6, seven of the eight points are in this range. Thus, it appears that the forecasts tend to be *upward biased* (typically above the realized value).

All points above the 45-degree line reflect underestimation by the forecasts. In Exhibit 9.6, only one of the eight points is in this range. None of the eight points is on the 45-degree line. This means that Currency Q was not predicted with perfect accuracy in any of the eight periods.

If points appear to be scattered evenly on both sides of the 45-degree line, then the forecasts are said to be *unbiased,* since they are not consistently above or below the realized values. Whether evaluating the size of forecast errors or attempting to search for a bias, more reliable results are obtained when examining a large number of periods. Only eight periods have been evaluated here, in order to provide a simplified example.

The forecast evaluation procedure described here is applied to the British pound and shown in Exhibit 9.7. Separating the entire period into subperiods (as shown in Exhibit 9.8) reveals a forecast bias in various time periods.

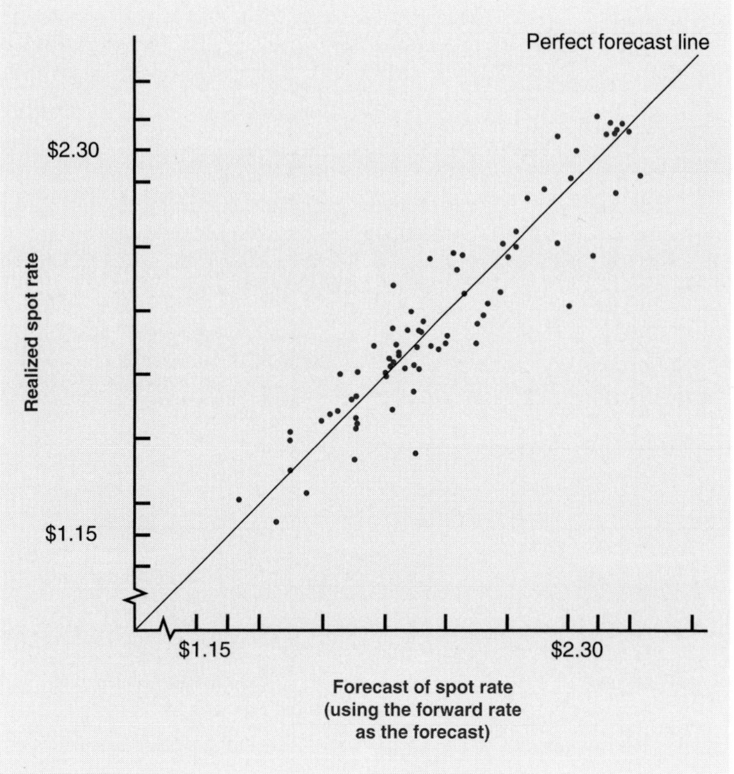

Exhibit 9.7
Graphic Comparison of Forecasted and Realized Spot Rates for the British Pound (Using the Forward Rate as the Forecast)

Comparison of Forecasting Techniques

When an MNC evaluates its forecasting performance, it must realize that errors will commonly occur. To at least minimize the errors, it may desire to compare forecasting errors of various available methods. This can be done by plotting the points relating to both methods on a graph similar to Exhibit 9.7, which is based on forecasts of the British pound over time. The points pertaining to each method could be distinguished by a particular mark or color. The performance of the two methods could be evaluated by comparing distances of points from the 45-degree line. In some cases, neither forecasting method may stand out as superior when compared graphically. If so, a more precise comparison could be conducted by computing the forecast errors for all periods for each method and then comparing these errors.

As an example, the data from Exhibit 9.5 will be used as one set of forecasts assumed to be developed by a U.S. firm for Currency Q's value. Assume that the firm also has a second forecast for each period based on an alternative forecasting model. The assumed forecasts of Currency Q, using what shall be called Model 1 and Model 2, are shown in Columns 2 and 3, respectively, of Exhibit 9.9, along with the realized value of Currency Q in Column 4.

The absolute forecast errors of forecasting with Model 1 and Model 2 are shown in Columns 5 and 6, respectively. Notice that Model 1 has outperformed Model 2 in six of the eight periods. The mean absolute forecast error when using Model 1 is $.04, meaning that forecasts with Model 1 are off by $.04 on the average. While Model 1 is not perfectly accurate, it does a better job than Model 2, whose mean

Exhibit 9.8
Graphic Comparison of Forecasted and Realized Spot Rates in Different Subperiods for the British Pound (Using the Forward Rate as the Forecast)

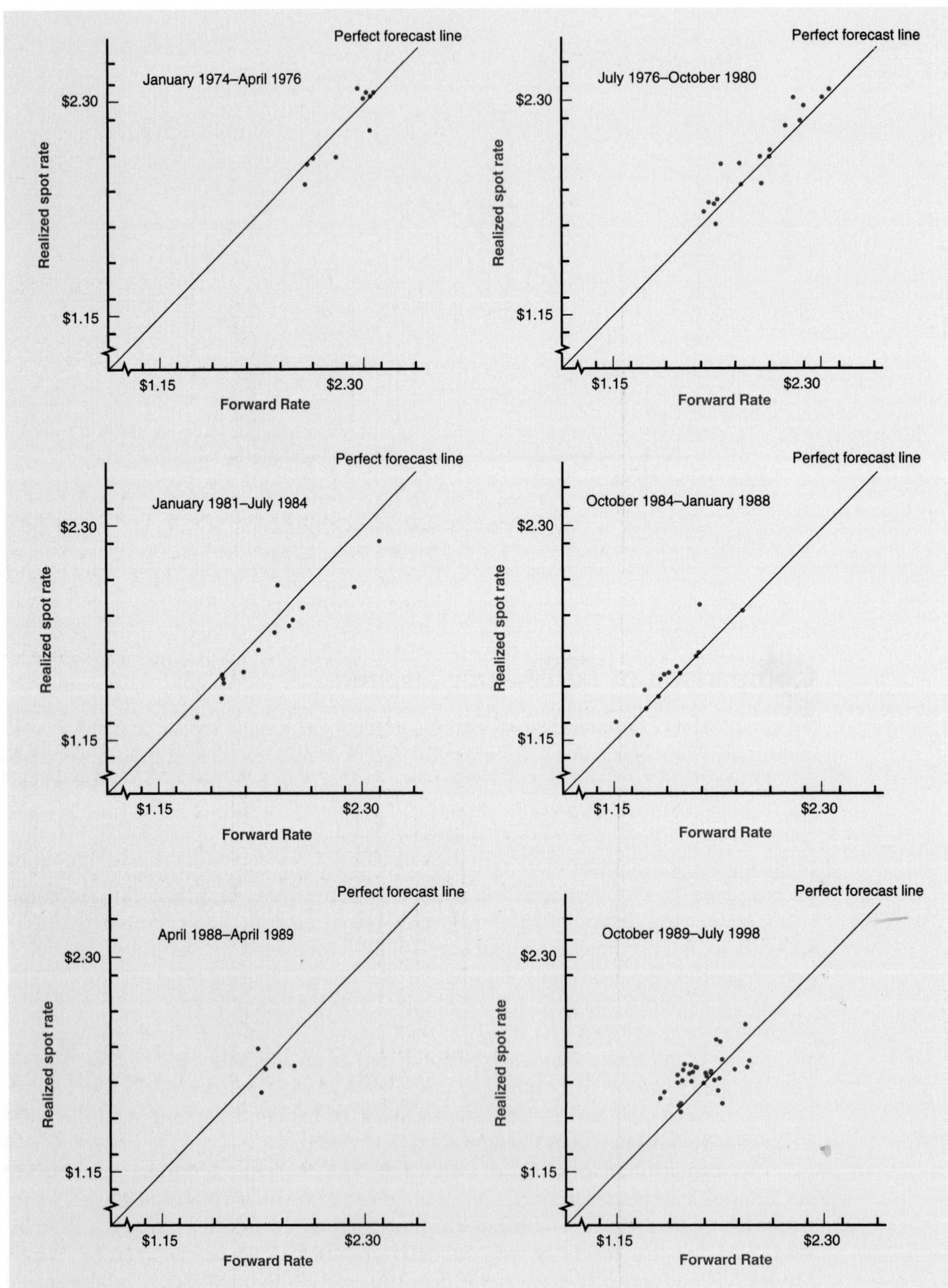

Exhibit 9.9
Comparison of Forecast Techniques

(1)	(2)	(3)	(4)	(5)	(6)	(7) = (5) – (6)
Period	Predicted Value of Currency Q by Model 1	Predicted Value of Currency Q by Model 2	Realized Value of Currency Q	Absolute Forecast Error Using Model 1	Absolute Forecast Error Using Model 2	Difference in Absolute Forecast Errors (Model 1 – Model 2)
1	$.20	$.24	$.16	$.04	$.08	$–.04
2	.18	.20	.14	.04	.06	–.02
3	.24	.20	.16	.08	.04	.04
4	.26	.20	.22	.04	.02	.02
5	.30	.18	.28	.02	.10	–.08
6	.22	.32	.26	.04	.06	–.02
7	.16	.20	.14	.02	.06	–.04
8	.14	.24	.10	.04	.14	–.10
				Sum = .32 Mean = .04	Sum = .56 Mean = .07	Sum = –.24 Mean = –.03

absolute forecast error is $.07. Overall, predictions with Model 1 are on the average $.03 closer to the realized value.

For an MNC to do a complete comparison of performance among forecasting techniques, it should evaluate as many periods as possible. Only eight periods are used in our example, since that is enough to illustrate how to compare forecasting performance. If the MNC has a large number of periods to evaluate, it could statistically test for significant differences in forecasting errors using a *t*-test or a nonparametric test. Results from such a test would determine whether there is a significant difference in the accuracy of the forecasting techniques.

Forecasting Under Market Efficiency

If the foreign exchange rate market is **weak-form efficient,** then historical and current exchange rate information is not useful for forecasting exchange rate movements, since today's exchange rates reflect all of this information. That is, technical analysis would not be capable of improving forecasts. If the foreign exchange market is **semistrong-form efficient,** then *all* relevant public information is already reflected in today's exchange rates. If today's exchange rates fully reflected any historical trends in exchange rate movements, but not other public information on expected interest rate movements, the foreign exchange market would be weak-form efficient, but not semistrong-form efficient. Much research has tested the efficient market hypothesis for foreign exchange markets. Research by Cornell and Dietrich[3] and others suggests that foreign exchange markets appear to be weak-form efficient and semistrong-form efficient.

[3]Bradford Cornell and J. Kimball Dietrich, "The Efficiency of the Market for Foreign Exchange Under Floating Exchange Rates," *Review of Economics and Statistics* (February 1978), pp. 111–120.

Nike Problem

How Nike Can Benefit from Exchange Rate Forecasts

Since Nike has cash flows in several different currencies, it can benefit from accurate forecasts of exchange rate movements. For example, if it was confident that the Asian currencies would depreciate against European currencies, Nike could allow European customers purchasing products in Asia to pay in their own currencies. Thus, the Asian subsidiaries would have European currencies that they could convert in the spot market. Second, Nike would be more capable of determining what the demand for its athletic shoes produced in various countries would be; some consumers adjust their demand to the price they pay, which is affected by the exchange rate. Third, Nike could improve decision-making on where to establish future subsidiaries if it knew how future exchange rates would move. Fourth, Nike could more accurately predict how much dollar cash flows would be received by the U.S. parent by the end of each year if it could properly forecast exchange rates.

Discussion: Assume that the forward rate is an unbiased but not necessarily accurate forecast of the future exchange rate of the yen over the next several years. Based on this information, do you think Nike should hedge its remittance of expected Japanese yen profits to the U.S. parent by selling yen forward contracts? Why would this strategy be an advantage? Under what conditions would this strategy be a disadvantage?

If foreign exchange markets are **strong-form efficient,** then all relevant public *and* private information is already reflected in today's exchange rates. This form of efficiency cannot be tested, since private information is not available.

Even though foreign exchange markets are generally found to be at least semi-strong-form efficient, forecasts of exchange rates by MNCs may still be worthwhile. Their goal is not necessarily to earn speculative profits but to use reasonable exchange rate forecasts to implement policies. When MNCs assess proposed policies, they usually prefer to develop their own forecasts of exchange rates over time rather than simply use market-based rates as a forecast of future rates. MNCs are often interested in more than a point estimate of an exchange rate one year, three years, or five years from now. They prefer to determine a variety of scenarios and assess how exchange rates may change for each scenario. Even if today's forward exchange rate properly reflects all available information, it does not indicate to the MNC the possible deviation of the realized future exchange rate from what is expected. MNCs need to determine the range of various possible exchange rate movements in order to assess the degree to which their operating performance could be affected.

Forecasting Exchange Rate Volatility

MNCs not only forecast future exchange rates but they also forecast exchange rate volatility in future periods. One reason for forecasting exchange rate volatility is that MNCs recognize how difficult it is to accurately forecast the exchange rates. If they can forecast the volatility, they can determine the potential range surrounding their forecast. This enables them to develop best-case and worst-case scenarios along with their point estimate forecast for a particular currency.

The first step in forecasting exchange rate volatility is to determine the relevant period of concern. For example, if an MNC is forecasting the value of the Canadian dollar each day over the next quarter, it may attempt also to forecast the standard deviation of daily exchange rate movements over this quarter. This information could be used along with the point estimate forecast of the Canadian dollar for each day to derive confidence intervals around each forecast.

There are numerous methods that could be used to forecast the volatility of exchange rate movements for a future period. First, the volatility of historical exchange rate movements could be used as a forecast of the future. In our example, the standard deviation of daily exchange rate movements in the Canadian dollar during the previous month could be used as an estimate of the standard deviation of daily exchange rate movements in the Canadian dollar during the upcoming month.

A second method for forecasting exchange rate volatility is to use a time series of volatility patterns in previous periods. In our example, the standard deviation of daily exchange rate movements in the Canadian dollar could be determined for each of the last several months. Then, a time series trend of these standard deviation levels could be used to form an estimate for the standard deviation of daily exchange rate movements in the Canadian dollar over the next month. This method differs from the first method in that it uses information beyond that contained in the previous month. For example, the forecast may be based on a weighting scheme such as 50 percent times the standard deviation in the last month, plus 25 percent times the standard deviation in the month before that, plus 15 percent times the standard deviation in the month before that, plus 10 percent times the standard deviation in the month before that. This scheme places more weight on the most recent data to derive the forecast but allows data from the last four months to influence the forecast. Normally, the weights that achieved the most accuracy (lowest forecast error) over previous periods and the number of previous periods (lags) would be used when applying this method. However, since various economic and political factors can cause exchange rate volatility to change abruptly, even sophisticated time series models do not necessarily generate accurate forecasts of exchange rate volatility.

A third method for forecasting exchange rate volatility is to derive the exchange rate's implied standard deviation (ISD) from the currency option pricing model. Recall that the premium on a call option for a currency is dependent on factors such as the relationship between the spot exchange rate and the exercise (strike) price of the option, the number of days until the expiration date of the option, and the anticipated volatility of the currency's exchange rate movements. There is a formula for estimating the call option premium based on various factors. The actual values of each of these factors are known, except for the anticipated volatility. However, by plugging in the option premium paid by investors for that specific currency option, it is possible to derive the anticipated volatility level. In our example, the MNC would consider a call option on Canadian dollars that has 30 days to expiration (since it wishes to forecast volatility over a 30-day period). This measurement represents the anticipated volatility of the Canadian dollar over a 30-day period by investors who are trading currency options. An MNC may use this measurement as its own forecast of the Canadian dollar's volatility.

Application of Exchange Rate Forecasting to the Asian Crisis

Just before the Asian crisis, the spot rate (in dollars) would have served as a reasonable predictor of the future spot rate because the central banks were maintaining a somewhat stable value for their respective currencies. The forward rate (in dollars) of these Southeast Asian currencies would not have been as accurate because it would have exhibited a discount to reflect the differential between the Southeast Asian country's interest rate and the U.S. interest rate (based on interest rate parity). However, the currency value was prevented from gravitating towards its appropriate level because it was restricted by the central banks to maintain currency stability.

The use of fundamental factors may not have achieved an accurate forecast just before the crisis; some of the conditions (such as high local inflation) would be expected to place downward pressure on the currencies, yet the values were prevented from declining.

Once the crisis began, the use of the spot rate would have generated a poor forecast because it would have predicted stability, while the currency value declined substantially. The forward rate would have been more accurate than the spot rate during the Asian crisis because it contained a discount which suggests an expected depreciation of the currencies. However, the currencies depreciated by much more than what would have been predicted according to the forward rate.

Many fundamental forecasts may have correctly predicted the direction of the currency's movement. However, it is unlikely that the fundamental forecast models would have predicted the degree of the decline in Asian currency values, regardless of how the model would have been structured. Two key factors that led to the substantial decline in currency values were (1) the large amount of foreign investment prior to the crisis (which allowed for the possibility of a massive outflow of funds) and (2) fear of a massive selloff of the currencies, which perpetuated the problem. These two factors cannot easily be incorporated in a fundamental forecasting model in a manner that will precisely identify the timing and magnitude of a major decline in a currency's value.

How Exchange Rate Forecasting Affects an MNC's Value

Exchange rate forecasting affects the value of the MNC as shown in Exhibit 9.10. The forecasts lead to decisions about whether the firm should remain exposed to exchange rate fluctuations or hedge their foreign currency positions. The forecasts can affect the expected foreign currency cash flows if those cash flows are partially generated by foreign subsidiaries from transactions with other countries.

The forecasts have a direct effect on the expected values of the exchange rates at which the foreign currency cash flows will be converted into dollars when those cash flows are remitted to the U.S. parent. Since the forecasts lead to decisions about whether to hedge, they influence the actual exchange rate at which the future foreign currency cash flows will be converted to dollars when remitted to the U.S. parent. Thus, they determine the expected dollar cash flows to be received by the U.S. parent.

Exhibit 9.10
Impact of Forecasted Exchange Rates on an MNC's Value

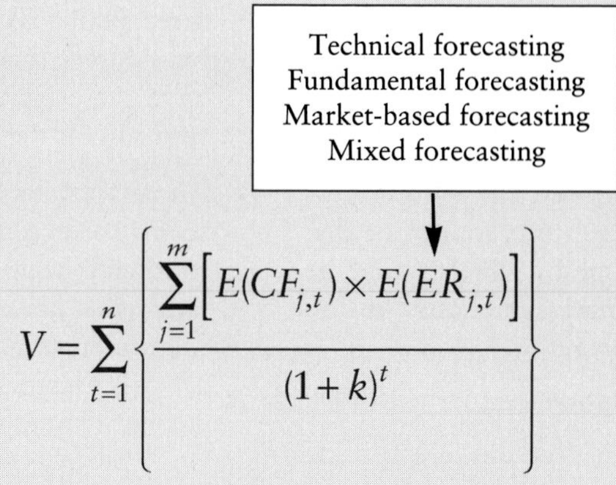

$$V = \sum_{t=1}^{n} \left\{ \frac{\sum_{j=1}^{m} \left[E(CF_{j,t}) \times E(ER_{j,t}) \right]}{(1+k)^t} \right\}$$

V = value of the U.S.-based MNC
$E(CF_{j,t})$ = expected cash flows denominated in currency j to be received by the U.S. parent in period t
$E(ER_{j,t})$ = expected exchange rate at which currency j can be converted to dollars at the end of period t
k = the weighted average cost of capital of the U.S. parent company
m = number of currencies
n = number of periods

SUMMARY

- Multinational corporations need exchange rate forecasts to make decisions on hedging payables and receivables, short-term financing and investment, capital budgeting, and long-term financing.
- The most common forecasting techniques can be classified as (1) technical, (2) fundamental, (3) market-based, and (4) mixed. Unfortunately, these techniques have generally performed rather poorly in recent years. Yet, due to the high variability in exchange rates, it should not be surprising that forecasts will not always be accurate. Also, floating rates have been in existence only since the early 1970s; this has not allowed much time to improve forecasting ability by experience.
- Forecast methods can be evaluated by comparing the actual values of currencies to the values predicted according to the forecast method. This comparison should be conducted over several periods in order to draw meaningful implications. Two criteria used to evaluate performance of a forecast method are bias and accuracy. When comparing the forecast accuracy between two currencies, the absolute forecast error should be divided by the realized value of the currency to control for differences in the relative values of currencies.

SELF-TEST FOR CHAPTER 9

(Answers are provided in Appendix A at the back of the text.)

1. Assume that the annual U.S. return is expected to be 7 percent for each of the next four years, while the annual interest rate in Mexico is expected to be 20 percent. Determine the appropriate four-year forward rate premium or discount on the Mexican peso, which could be used to forecast the percentage change in the peso over the next four years.

2. Consider the following information:

Currency	90-Day Forward Rate	Spot Rate That Occurred 90 Days Later
Canadian dollar	$.80	$.82
Japanese yen	$.012	$.011

Assuming the forward rate was used as the forecast of the future spot rate, determine whether the Canadian dollar or the Japanese yen was forecasted with more accuracy, based on the absolute forecast error as a percentage of the realized value.

3. Assume that the forward rate and spot rate of the Mexican peso are normally similar at a given point in time. Assume that the peso has depreciated consistently and substantially over the last three years. Would the forward rate have been biased over this period? If so, would it typically have overestimated or underestimated the future spot rate of the peso (in dollars)? Explain.

4. An analyst has stated that the British pound seems to increase in value over the two weeks following announcements by the Bank of England (the British central bank) that it would raise interest rates. If this statement is true, what are the inferences regarding weak-form or semi-strong-form efficiency?

5. Assume that the Mexican interest rates are much higher than U.S. interest rates. Also assume that interest rate parity (discussed in Chapter 7) exists. If you use the forward rate of the Mexican peso to forecast the Mexican peso's future spot rate, would you expect the peso to appreciate or depreciate? Explain.

6. Warden Co. is considering a project in Venezuela, which will be very profitable if the local currency (bolivar) appreciates against the dollar. If the bolivar depreciates, the project will result in losses. Warden Co. forecasts that the bolivar will appreciate. The bolivar's value historically has been very volatile. As a manager of Warden Co., would you be comfortable with this project? Explain.

QUESTIONS AND APPLICATIONS

1. Explain corporate motives for forecasting exchange rates.
2. Explain the technical technique for forecasting exchange rates.
3. Explain the fundamental technique for forecasting exchange rates.
4. Explain the market-based technique for forecasting exchange rates.
5. Explain the mixed technique for forecasting exchange rates.
6. What are some limitations of using technical forecasting to predict exchange rates?
7. What are some limitations of using a fundamental technique to forecast exchange rates?
8. What is the rationale for using market-based forecasts?
9. Explain how to assess performance in forecasting exchange rates.
10. Explain how to detect a bias in forecasting exchange rates.
11. You are hired as a consultant to assess a firm's ability to forecast. The firm has developed a point forecast for two different currencies. It wants to determine which currency was forecast with greater accuracy. The information is provided.

Period	Yen Forecast	Actual Yen Value	Pound Forecast	Actual Pound Value
1	$.0050	$.0051	$1.50	$1.51
2	.0048	.0052	1.53	1.50
3	.0053	.0052	1.55	1.58
4	.0055	.0056	1.49	1.52

12. You are hired as a consultant to determine whether there is a bias from forecasting the percentage change in the Canadian dollar (C$). A set of 200 data points was used to develop the following regression equation.

    Actual % Δ in C$ over period t =
    $a_0 + a_1$ (Forecasted % Δ in C$ over period t)

    The regression results are as follows:

Coefficient	Standard error
$a_0 = .006$	.011
$a_1 = .800$	.05

    Based on these results, is there a bias in the forecast? Verify your conclusion. If there is a bias, explain whether it is an overestimate or an underestimate.

13. Syracuse Corporation believes that future real interest rate movements will affect exchange rates, and it has applied regression analysis to historical data in order to assess the relationship. It will use the regression coefficient derived from this analysis along with forecasted real interest rate movements in order to predict exchange rates in the future. Explain at least three limitations of this method.

14. Lexington Company is a U.S.-based MNC with subsidiaries in most major countries. Each subsidiary is responsible for forecasting the future exchange rate of its local currency, relative to the U.S. dollar. Comment on this policy. How might Lexington Company ensure consistent forecasts among the different subsidiaries?

15. Assume that the following regression model was applied to historical quarterly data:

$$e_t = a_0 + a_1 INT_t + a_2 INF_{t-1} + \mu_t$$

    where

    e_t = percentage change in exchange rate of the Japanese yen in period t
    INT_t = average real interest rate differential (U.S. interest rate minus Japanese interest rate) over period t
    INF_{t-1} = inflation differential (U.S. inflation rate minus Japanese inflation rate) in the previous period
    a_0, a_1, a_2 = regression coefficients
    μ_t = error term

    Assume that the regression coefficients were estimated as follows:

$$a_0 = 0.0$$
$$a_1 = .9$$
$$a_2 = .8$$

    Also assume that the inflation differential in the most recent period was 3 percent. The real interest rate differential in the upcoming period is forecasted as follows:

Interest Rate Differential	Probability
0%	30%
1	60
2	10

    If Stillwater Inc. uses this information to forecast the Japanese yen's exchange rate, what will be the probability distribution of the yen's percentage change over the upcoming period?

16. Assume that the four-year annualized interest rate in the United States is 9 percent and the four-year interest rate in Singapore is 6 percent. Assume interest rate parity holds for a four-year horizon. Assume that the spot rate of the Singapore dollar is $.60. If the forward rate is used to forecast exchange rates, what will be the forecast for the Singapore dollar's spot rate in four years? What percentage appreciation or depreciation does this forecast imply over the four-year period?

17. € Assume that foreign exchange markets were found to be weak-form efficient. What does this suggest about utilizing technical analysis to speculate in euros?

18. If MNCs believed that foreign exchange markets are strong-form efficient, why would they develop their own forecasts of future exchange rates? Why wouldn't they simply use today's quoted rates as indicators about future rates? After all, today's quoted rates should reflect all relevant information.

19. € If the euro appreciates substantially against the dollar during a specific period, would market-based forecasts have overestimated or underestimated the realized values over this period? Explain.

20. The director of currency forecasting at Champaign-Urbana Corporation made the statement, "The most critical task of forecasting exchange rates is not to derive a point estimate of a future exchange rate but to assess how wrong our estimate might be." What does this statement mean?

21. When some countries in Eastern Europe initially allow their currencies to fluctuate against the dollar, would the fundamental technique based on historical relationships be useful for forecasting future exchange rates of these currencies? Explain.

22. Royce Company is a U.S. firm with future receivables one year from now in Canadian dollars and British pounds. Its pound receivables are known with certainty, while its estimated Canadian dollar receivables are subject to a 2-percent error in either direction. The dollar values of both types of receivables are similar. There is no chance of default by the customers involved. The treasurer of Royce stated that the estimate of dollar cash flows to be generated from the British pound receivables is subject to greater uncertainty than that of the Canadian dollar receivables. Explain the rationale for such a statement.

23. € Cooper Inc., a U.S.-based MNC, periodically obtains euros to purchase German products. It assesses U.S. and German trade patterns and inflation rates to develop a fundamental forecast for the euro. How could Cooper possibly improve its method of fundamental forecasting as applied to the euro?

24. Assume that you obtain a quote for a one-year forward rate on the Mexican peso. Assume that Mexico's one-year interest rate is 40 percent, while the U.S. one-year interest rate is 7 percent. Over the next year, the peso depreciates by 12 percent. Do you think the forward rate overestimated the spot rate one year ahead in this example? Explain.

25. € The treasurer of Glencoe Inc. detected a forecast bias when using the 30-day forward rate of the euro to forecast future spot rates of the euro over various periods. He believed he could use such information to determine whether imports ordered every week should be hedged (payment is made 30 days after each order). The president of Glencoe stated that in the long run the forward rate is unbiased and suggested that the treasurer should not waste time trying to "beat the forward rate" but should just hedge all orders. Who is correct?

26. The value of each Latin American currency relative to the dollar is dictated by supply and demand conditions between that currency and the dollar. The values of Latin American currencies have generally declined substantially against the dollar over time. Most of these countries have high inflation rates and high interest rates. The data on inflation rates, economic growth, and other economic indicators are subject to error, as limited resources are used to compile economic data.
    a. If the forward rate was used as a market-based forecast, would this rate result in a forecast of appreciation, depreciation, or no change in any particular Latin American currency? Explain.
    b. If technical forecasting was used, would this result in a forecast of appreciation, depreciation, or no change in the value of a specific Latin American currency? Explain.
    c. Do you think that U.S. firms can accurately forecast the future values of Latin American currencies? Explain.

27. Explain why the current spot rate was probably a better forecast of the future spot rate than the forward rate for the Southeast Asian countries before the Asian crisis.

28. Explain why the use of the spot rate for forecasting purposes would have generated a poor forecast for the Southeast Asian countries' currencies once the Asian crisis began.

Internet Application

29. The Web site of the Chicago Mercantile Exchange (CME) provides information about the exchange and the futures contracts offered on the exchange. Its address is

    http://www.cme.com

    a. Go to the section on "Prices" and then to the "Daily and Weekly Charts." Describe the trend of a peso futures contract over the last few months. What does this trend suggest about changes in forecasts of the peso over the period assessed (assuming that the futures rate was used as a forecast method)? What do you think caused the futures prices to change over the last few months?
    b. Select a peso futures contract that has at least one month until its settlement date. Determine whether that futures contract would have underestimated or overestimated the spot rate as of settlement date if it was used to forecast the future spot rate. Was the forecast accurate?
    c. The following Web site provides data on daily exchange rates for numerous currencies during recent months:

       http://pacific.commerce.ubc.ca/xr/data.html

       Use this Web site to determine whether there appears to be a trend in the Australian dollar exchange rate for the last 20 days, using the U.S. dollar as a base currency. Repeat the assessment for the Thai baht and the Mexican peso. Forecast the direction of each of these currencies based on the trend you see.

Running Your Own MNC

Monitoring Exchange Rate Trends

30. Use a business periodical or the Internet to determine how the value of the foreign currency of concern has changed in each of the last five weeks. Does it appear that there is a trend over the last five weeks? What is the mean percentage change over these weeks? If you believed that the currency's value would continue following the recent trend, would it appreciate or depreciate in the near future?

Blades, Inc. Case

Forecasting Exchange Rates

Recall that Blades, Inc., the U.S.-based manufacturer of roller blades, is currently both exporting to and importing from Thailand. Ben Holt and you, a financial analyst of Blades, Inc., are reasonably happy with Blades' current performance in Thailand. Entertainment Products, Inc., a Thai retailer for sporting goods, has committed itself to the purchase of a minimum number of Blades' "Speedos" annually. The agreement will terminate after three years. Blades also imports certain components needed to manufacture its products from Thailand. Both Blades' imports and exports are denominated in Thai baht. Because of these practices, Blades generates approximately 10 percent of its revenue and 4 percent of its cost of goods sold in Thailand.

Currently, Blades' only business in Thailand consists of export and import trade. However, Ben Holt, Blades' chief financial officer (CFO), is thinking about using Thailand to augment Blades' U.S. business in other ways as well in the future. For example, Mr. Holt is contemplating the establishment of a subsidiary in Thailand in order to increase the percentage of its sales to Thailand. Furthermore, if Blades establishes a subsidiary in Thailand, it may access the money and capital markets in Thailand. For instance, Blades may instruct its Thai subsidiary to invest excess funds in the Thai money market or to satisfy its short-term needs for funds in the Thai money market. Furthermore, part of the subsidiary financing may be obtained by utilizing investment banks in Thailand.

Due to current practices and future plans, Mr. Holt is concerned with the recent developments in Thailand and with their potential impact on the future of Blades, Inc. in Thailand. Economic conditions in Thailand have been unfavorable recently. In addition to the unfavorable economic conditions, the Thai government has recently abandoned the Thai baht's peg to the dollar, and the baht is now a freely floating currency. Since this action, movements in the value of the baht have been highly volatile, and foreign investors in Thailand have lost their confidence in the baht, causing massive capital outflows from Thailand. Consequently, the baht has been depreciating.

When Thailand was experiencing a high economic growth rate, few analysts anticipated an economic downturn. Consequently, Ben Holt never found it necessary to forecast economic conditions in Thailand even though Blades was doing business there. Now, however, Mr. Holt's attitude has changed. A continuation of the unfavorable economic conditions prevailing in Thailand could affect the demand for Blades' products in the country. Thus, Entertainment Products may not renew its commitment for another three years.

Since the baht is now a freely floating currency, and since Blades generates net cash inflows denominated in baht, a continued depreciation of the baht could adversely affect Blades, as these net inflows would be converted into fewer dollars. Thus, Blades is also considering the hedging of its baht-denominated inflows.

Because of these deliberations, Ben Holt has decided to reassess the importance of forecasting the baht-dollar exchange rate. His primary objective is to forecast the baht-dollar exchange rate for the next quarter. A secondary objective is to determine which forecasting technique is the most accurate and should be used in future periods. In order to accomplish this, he has asked you, a financial analyst of Blades, for help in forecasting the baht-dollar exchange rate for the next quarter.

Mr. Holt is aware of the forecasting techniques available. He has collected some economic data and conducted a preliminary analysis to use in your analysis. For example, he has conducted a time series analysis for the exchange rates over the last fifty quarters for a country very similar to Thailand in terms of economic conditions and trade relationships with the United States. He then used this analysis to forecast the baht's value next quarter. The technical forecast indicates a depreciation of the baht by 6 percent over the next quarter from the baht's current level of $.023 to $.02162. He has also conducted a fundamental forecast of the baht-dollar exchange rate using historical inflation and interest rate data from the country similar to Thailand. The fundamental forecast that was conducted, however, depends on what happens to Thai interest rates during the next quarter, and therefore reflects a probability distribution. There is a 30-percent chance that Thai interest rates will be such that the baht will depreciate by 2 percent, a 15-percent chance that the baht will depreciate by 5 percent, and a 55-percent chance that the baht will depreciate by 10 percent.

Ben Holt has provided you with the following questions he would like you to answer:

1. Considering both Blades' current practices and future plans, how can it benefit from forecasting the baht-dollar exchange rate?
2. Given that the baht has been freely floating for only a very short period of time, which forecasting technique (i.e., technical, fundamental, or market-based) would be easiest to use in forecasting the future value of the baht? Why?
3. Blades is considering the use of either current spot rates or available forward rates to forecast the future value of the baht. Available forward rates currently exhibit a large discount. Do you think the spot or the forward rate will yield a better market-based forecast? Why?
4. The current 90-day forward rate for the baht is $.021. By what percentage is the baht expected to change over the next quarter according to a market-based forecast using the forward rate? What is the forecasted value of the baht in 90 days using this forecast?
5. Assume that the technical forecast has been more accurate than the market-based forecast in recent weeks. What does this indicate about market efficiency for the baht-dollar exchange rate? Do you think this means that technical analysis will always be superior to other forecasting techniques in the future? Why of why not?
6. What is the expected percentage change in the value of the baht during the next quarter based on the fundamental forecast? What is the forecasted value of the baht using this forecast? If the value of the baht 90 days from now turns out to be $.022, which forecasting technique is

the most accurate? (Use the absolute forecast error as a percentage of the realized value to answer the last part of this question.)

7. Do you think the technique you have identified in question 6 will always be the most accurate? Why or why not?

Small Business Dilemma

Exchange Rate Forecasting by the Sports Exports Company

The Sports Exports Company converts British pounds into dollars every month. The prevailing spot rate is about $1.65, but there is much uncertainty about the future value of the pound. Jim Logan, owner of the Sports Exports Company, expects that British inflation will rise substantially in the future. In previous years when British inflation was high, the pound depreciated. The prevailing British interest rate is slightly higher than the prevailing U.S. interest rate. The pound has risen slightly over each of the last several months. Jim wants to forecast the value of the pound for each of the next 20 months.

1. Explain how Jim could use technical forecasting to forecast the future value of the pound. Based on the information provided, do you think that a technical forecast of the pound would reflect future appreciation or depreciation in the pound?
2. Explain how Jim could use fundamental forecasting to forecast the future value of the pound. Based on the information provided, do you think that a fundamental forecast of the pound would reflect appreciation or depreciation in the pound?
3. Explain how Jim could use a market-based forecast to forecast the future value of the pound. Do you think the market-based forecast would reflect appreciation, depreciation, or no change in the value of the pound?
4. Does it appear that all of the forecast techniques will lead to the same forecast of the pound's future value? Which forecast technique would you prefer to use in this situation?

10 MEASURING EXPOSURE TO EXCHANGE RATE FLUCTUATIONS

Exchange rate risk can be broadly defined as the risk that a company's performance will be affected by exchange rate movements. Multinational corporations (MNCs) closely monitor their operations to determine how they are exposed to various forms of exchange rate risk.

The specific objectives of this chapter are to

- discuss the relevance of an MNC's exposure to exchange rate risk,
- explain how transaction exposure can be measured,
- explain how economic exposure can be measured, and
- explain how translation exposure can be measured.

IS EXCHANGE RATE RISK RELEVANT?

Arguments have been made to suggest that exchange rate risk is irrelevant, which have resulted in counterarguments, as summarized here.

Purchasing Power Parity Argument

Some critics may suggest that a firm's exposure to exchange rate risk is not relevant and that firms therefore need not measure or manage their exposure. One argument for exchange rate irrelevance is that, according to purchasing power parity (PPP) theory, exchange rate movements should be matched by price movements. For example, consider the case of Office Import Company, a U.S. importer of office supplies that distributes these supplies throughout the country. Assume that Office Import Company currently competes against several U.S. companies that produce their own office supplies. If the dollar depreciates, Office Import Company will need more dollars to cover its import payments. Yet, according to PPP, a decline in the dollar would be associated with relatively high inflation in the United States. Thus, while the local competitors would not be affected by the dollar's decline, their cost of producing supplies would increase as a result of inflation. And although Office Import Company would be adversely affected by the dollar's decline, it would avoid the higher production costs in the United States. It may therefore be argued that this offsetting effect makes exchange rate risk irrelevant.

Since PPP does not necessarily hold, the exchange rate will not change in accordance with the inflation differential between the two countries. Since a perfect offsetting effect is unlikely, the firm's competitive capabilities may indeed be influenced by exchange rate movements. Even if PPP did hold over a very long period of time, this would not comfort managers of MNCs that are focusing on the next year or even over the next five years.

The Investor Hedge Argument

A second argument for exchange rate irrelevance is that investors in MNCs could hedge this risk on their own. For example, if investors in Office Import Company are aware that performance may be affected by exchange rate fluctuations, they may choose to take positions (in futures contracts or options contracts) to offset any adverse impact of dollar depreciation on Office Import Company. The reasoning is that exchange rate risk is not relevant to corporations because shareholders can deal with this risk individually.

The investor hedge argument assumes that investors have complete information on corporate exposure to exchange rate fluctuations as well as the capabilities to correctly insulate their individual exposure. To the extent that investors prefer that corporations perform the hedging for them, exchange rate exposure is relevant to corporations.

Currency Diversification Argument

It may be argued that if a U.S.-based MNC is well diversified across numerous countries, its value will not be affected by exchange rate movements because of offsetting effects. However, it is naive to presume that exchange rate effects will offset each other just because an MNC may have transactions in many different currencies.

Stakeholder Diversification Argument

It may be argued that if stakeholders (such as creditors or stockholders) are well diversified, they will be somewhat insulated against losses experienced by an MNC due to exchange rate risk. However, several MNCs in which they have a stake could be affected in the same way because of exchange rate risk. For example, in 1998, numerous U.S.-based MNCs were adversely affected by the depreciation of Asian currencies against the dollar.

Since creditors could experience large loan losses if the MNCs that were granted loans experienced financial problems, they may prefer that the MNCs maintain low exposure to exchange rate risk. Consequently, MNCs that hedge exposure to risk may be able to borrow funds at a lower cost.

To the extent that the MNCs can stabilize their earnings over time by hedging their exchange rate risk, they may also reduce their general operating expenses over time (by avoiding costs of downsizing and restructuring). Many MNCs, including Colgate, Eastman Kodak, and Merck, have attempted to stabilize their earnings with hedging strategies, which confirms their view that exchange rate risk is relevant.

TYPES OF EXPOSURE

As mentioned in the previous chapter, exchange rates cannot be forecasted with perfect accuracy, but the firm can at least measure its exposure to exchange rate fluctuations. If the firm is highly exposed to exchange rate fluctuations, it can consider techniques to reduce its exposure. Such techniques are identified in the following chapter. Before choosing among them, the firm should first measure its degree of exposure.

Exposure to exchange rate fluctuations comes in three forms:

- Transaction exposure
- Economic exposure
- Translation exposure

Each type of exposure will be discussed in turn.

TRANSACTION EXPOSURE

The value of a firm's cash inflows received in various currencies will be affected by respective exchange rates of these currencies when converted into the currency desired. Similarly, the value of a firm's cash outflows in various currencies will be dependent on the respective exchange rates of these currencies. The degree to which the value of future cash transactions can be affected by exchange rate fluctuations is referred to as **transaction exposure.**

To illustrate the potential impact of transaction exposure, consider those U.S. exporters that sold products to Asian countries during the 1997–1998 Asian crisis, when some Asian currencies depreciated by 80 percent. If the exporters had invoiced their products in Asian currencies, their cash flows may have been 80-percent less than what they anticipated. If they invoiced the products in dollars, they would have not been subject to the transaction exposure, but the Asian importing companies would have been subjected to transaction exposure. The impact of large swings in currency values can be devastating to a firm that relies heavily on international trade for its business.

Two steps are involved in measuring transaction exposure: (1) determine the projected net amount of inflows or outflows in each foreign currency and (2) determine the overall risk of exposure to those currencies. Each of these steps is discussed in turn.

Transaction Exposure to "Net" Cash Flows

MNCs tend to focus on transaction exposure over an upcoming short-term period (such as at the next month or the next quarter) in which they can anticipate foreign currency cash flows with reasonable accuracy. Measurement of transaction exposure requires projections of the consolidated net amount in currency inflows or outflows for all subsidiaries, categorized by currency. One foreign subsidiary may have inflows of a foreign currency while another may have outflows of that same currency. Thus, the net cash flows of that currency for the MNC overall may be negligible. Yet, the net cash flows in some other currency could be substantial if most subsidiaries had future inflows in that currency. Estimating the consolidated net cash flows per currency is a useful first step when assessing an MNC's exposure, since it helps to determine the MNC's overall position in each currency.

Example. Consider a U.S.-based MNC called Miami Company that conducts its international business in four currencies. Its objective is to first measure the exposure in each currency in the next quarter and then estimate its consolidated cash flows for one quarter ahead, as shown in Exhibit 10.1. For example, it expects Canadian dollar inflows of C$12,000,000 and outflows of C$2,000,000 over the next month. Thus, it expects net inflows of C$10,000,000. Given an expected exchange rate of $.80, it can convert the expected net inflow of Canadian dollars into an expected net inflow of $8,000,000 (estimated as C$10,000,000 × $.80).

The same process described for the Canadian dollar is used to determine the net cash flows of each of the other three currencies. Notice from the last column of Exhibit 10.1 that the expected net cash flows in three of the currencies are positive, while the net cash flows in Swedish kronar are negative (reflecting cash outflows).

The information in Exhibit 10.1 needs to be converted into dollars so that Miami Company can assess the exposure of each currency by using a standardized measure. For each currency, the net cash flows is converted into dollars to determine the dollar amount of exposure. Notice that Miami Company has a smaller dollar amount of exposure in Mexican pesos than in any of the other currencies. However, this does not necessarily mean that it will be affected less by its peso exposure, as will be illustrated shortly.

Recognize that the net inflows or outflows in each foreign currency and the exchange rates at the end of the period are uncertain. Thus, the MNC might develop a range of possible exchange rates for each currency instead of a point estimate, as shown in Exhibit 10.2. Under these conditions, there is a range of net cash flows in dollars rather than a point estimate. Notice that the range of dollar cash flows resulting from Miami's peso transactions is wide; this reflects the high degree of uncertainty surrounding the peso's value over the next quarter. Conversely, the range of dollar cash flows resulting from the Canadian dollar transactions is narrow, because the Canadian dollar is expected to be relatively stable over the next quarter.

In the example, the net cash flow situation is assessed for only one quarter. Miami Company could also derive the expected net cash flows for other periods, such as a week or a month. Some MNCs desire to assess their transaction exposure

Exhibit 10.1
Consolidated Net Cash Flow Assessment of Miami Company

Currency	Total Inflow	Total Outflow	Net Inflow or Outflow	Expected Exchange Rate	Net Inflow or Outflow as Measured in U.S. Dollars
British pound	£17,000,000	£7,000,000	+£10,000,000	$1.50	+$15,000,000
Canadian dollar	C$12,000,000	C$2,000,000	+C$10,000,000	$ .80	+$ 8,000,000
Swedish krona	SK20,000,000	SK120,000,000	–SK100,000,000	$ .15	–$15,000,000
Mexican peso	p90,000,000	p10,000,000	+p80,000,000	$ .10	+$ 8,000,000

Exhibit 10.2
Estimating the Range of Net Inflows or Outflows for Miami Company

Currency	Net Inflow or Outflow	Range of Possible Exchange Rates at End of Period	Range of Possible Net Inflows or Outflows in U.S. Dollars (Based on Range of Possible Exchange Rates)
British pound	+£10,000,000	$1.40 to $1.60	+$14,000,000 to +$16,000,000
Canadian dollar	+C$10,000,000	$.79 to $.81	+$ 7,900,000 to +$ 8,100,000
Swedish krona	–SK100,000,000	$.14 to $.16	–$14,000,000 to –$16,000,000
Mexican peso	+p80,000,000	$.06 to $.11	+$ 4,800,000 to +$ 8,800,000

during several periods. To do this, the same methods that were described could be applied to each period. The further into the future the MNC attempts to measure transaction exposure, the less accurate will be the measurement. This is due to greater uncertainty about inflows or outflows in each foreign currency, as well as future exchange rates, over periods further into the future. An MNC's overall exposure can only be assessed after considering each currency's variability and correlations among currencies. The overall exposure of Miami Company will be assessed after the following discussion of currency variability and correlations.

Transaction Exposure Based on Currency Variability

In the previous example, the expected exchange rates for the end of the period are given without any explanation as to how they were derived. Each MNC may have its own method for developing exchange rate projections. Some methods have been described in the previous chapter. While it is difficult to predict future currency values with much accuracy, an MNC can evaluate historical data in order to at least assess the potential degree of movement for each currency.

http://
See www.ny.frb.org/pihome/mktrates for current and historic exchange rates and implied currency option volatilities.

Measurement of Currency Variability. The standard deviation statistic serves as one possible way to measure the degree of movement for each particular currency. To demonstrate the use of such information, consider a U.S.-based MNC trying to assess currency movements. It could evaluate the historical variability in each foreign currency based on the standard deviation statistics. Exhibit 10.3 displays the standard deviation of foreign currencies (based on monthly data) over two separate periods. When comparing currencies within either period, it is clear that some currencies fluctuate much more than others. For example, the standard deviation of the monthly movements in the Japanese yen and the Swiss franc are more than twice that of the Canadian dollar. Based on this information, the potential for these other currencies to deviate far from their projected future values is greater than the same potential for the Canadian dollar (from the U.S. firm's perspective). Some currencies in emerging markets are much more volatile than those shown here. For example, the standard deviation of the Mexican peso was more than twice that of any currency shown in Exhibit 10.3 over the 1994–1998 period.

Exhibit 10.3
Standard Deviations of Exchange Rate Movements (Based on Monthly Data)

Currency	Time Period	
	1981–1993	1994–1998
British pound	0.0309	0.0148
Canadian dollar	0.0100	0.0110
Indian rupee	0.0219	0.0168
Japanese yen	0.0279	0.0298
New Zealand dollar	0.0289	0.0190
Swedish krona	0.0287	0.0195
Swiss franc	0.0330	0.0246
Singapore dollar	0.0111	0.0174

Currency Variability Over Time. The variability of a currency will not necessarily remain consistent from one time period to another. Exhibit 10.3 illustrates how standard deviations can change over time. For example, the British pound's value has become less volatile.

Since currency variability levels change over time, the MNC's assessment of a currency's future variability will not be perfect when a previous time period is used as the indicator. However, the MNC can benefit from information such as that in Exhibit 10.3 if it is used wisely. Although the MNC may not be able to predict a currency's future variability with perfect accuracy, it can identify currencies whose values are *most likely* to be stable or highly variable in the future. For example, the Canadian dollar consistently exhibits lower variability than the other currencies. This explains the findings in the previous chapter that the forecast errors when forecasting the value of the Canadian dollar are consistently smaller than when forecasting values of other currencies.

Transaction Exposure Based on Currency Correlations

To illustrate how MNCs would assess exposure based on currency movements, consider the historical exchange rate fluctuations as shown in Exhibit 10.4 for Currencies X, Y, and Z. Assume you are treasurer of a U.S.-based MNC when examining the following two scenarios.

Scenario 1. Assume that you expect as of one year from now to need $10 million for the purchase of Currency X and another $20 million to purchase Currency Y. You also expect to receive about $30 million when converting inflows of Currency Z one year from now. There is much transaction exposure in this scenario, as explained next.

Exhibit 10.4 suggests that Currencies X and Y are highly correlated with each other but negatively correlated with Currency Z. If Currencies X and Y appreciate against the U.S. dollar, more dollars will be needed to purchase them. And if they appreciate against the dollar, Currency Z will likely depreciate against the dollar, based on its historical co-movements with Currencies X and Y. Since Currency Z is to be received by the MNC in the future, this cash inflow will convert to fewer U.S. dollars if it does depreciate. Thus, the MNC could possibly end up receiving fewer dollars and paying out more dollars than it currently expects to.

Exhibit 10.4
Illustration of Currency Movements for Scenarios

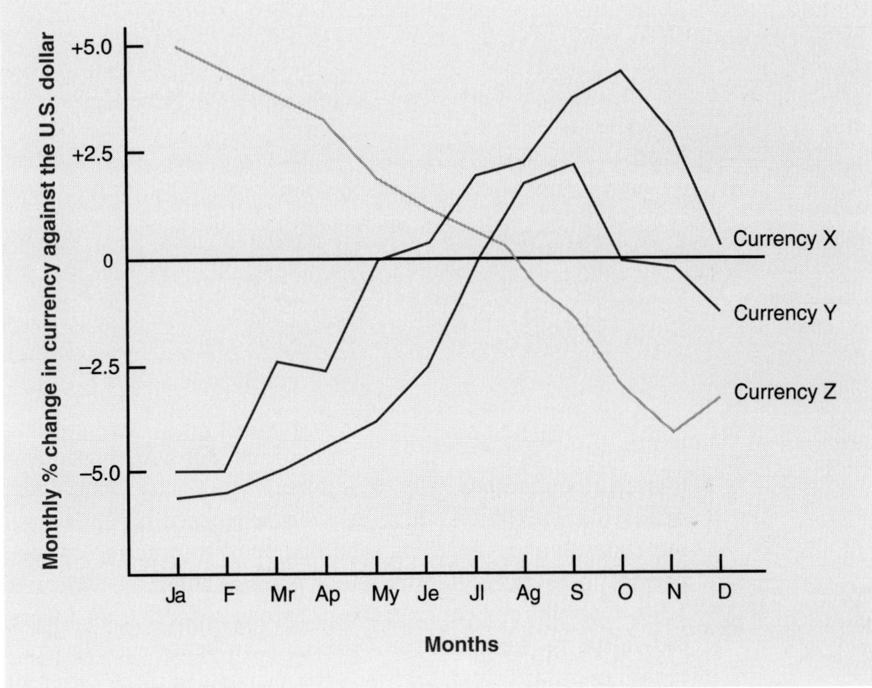

Scenario 2. Assume that you expect as of one year from now to need $10 million for the purchase of Currency X and another $20 million to purchase Currency Y (as in Scenario 1). Also assume that you expect to need another $30 million to purchase Currency Z one year from now. Finally, assume that you have no projected inflows in foreign currencies. There is not much transaction risk in this scenario, when you consider all currencies simultaneously. Based on the correlations that appear to exist as shown in Exhibit 10.4, the changes in values of Currencies X and Y will be somewhat offset by opposite movements in Currency Z. For example, if Currencies X and Y appreciate by 20 percent, the MNC will need $36 million instead of $30 million to buy these currencies. Yet, Currency Z will likely depreciate under this situation. A perfect offset would occur if Currency Z depreciated by 20 percent so that it would take only $24 million to purchase the necessary amount of Currency Z. Then, the additional $6 million needed to purchase Currencies X and Y would be offset by the $6 million saved due to depreciation of Currency Z. A perfect offset is not likely to occur, but the point here is to be able to detect positions that could somewhat offset each other.

In summary, the first step when assessing transaction exposure is to determine the size of the position in each currency. The second step is to determine how that individual currency position could affect the firm. This is accomplished by assessing the standard deviations and correlations of the currencies. Even if a particular currency is perceived as risky, its impact on the firm's overall exposure will not be severe if the firm has taken just a minor position in that currency. For this reason, both of these steps must be considered simultaneously when developing an overall assessment of the firm's transaction risk.

Exhibit 10.5
Correlations Among Exchange Rate Movements

	British pound	Canadian dollar	Japanese yen	New Zealand dollar	Swedish krona	Swiss franc
British pound	1.00					
Canadian dollar	.18	1.00				
Japanese yen	.45	.06	1.00			
New Zealand dollar	.39	.20	.33	1.00		
Swedish krona	.62	.16	.46	.33	1.00	
Swiss franc	.63	.12	.61	.37	.70	1.00

Measurement of Currency Correlations. The correlations among currency movements can be measured by their *correlation coefficients,* which indicate the degree to which two currencies move in relation to each other. Thus, MNCs could use such information when deciding their degree of transaction exposure. The extreme case is perfect positive correlation, which is represented by a correlation coefficient equal to 1.00. Correlations can also be negative, reflecting an inverse relationship between individual movements, the extreme case being –1.00. The correlation coefficients (based on quarterly data) for currency pairs in three different periods are illustrated in Exhibit 10.5. It is clear that some currency pairs exhibit a much higher correlation than others. At the other extreme, the Canadian dollar has a very low correlation with other currencies. Currency correlations are generally positive; this implies that currencies tend to move in the same direction against the U.S. dollar (though by different degrees). The positive correlation may not always occur on a day-to-day basis, but it appears to hold over longer periods of time for most currencies.

Currency Correlations Over Time. Currency correlations are not constant over time. Therefore, the MNC cannot use previous correlations to predict future correlations with perfect accuracy. However, there are some general relationships that tend to hold over time. Movements in currencies of western European currencies tend to be highly correlated, from a U.S. perspective. In addition, the Canadian dollar consistently moves almost independently of the other currencies, based on its continued low correlations with them.

Exhibit 10.6 provides a trend of exchange rate movements of various currencies against the dollar. It confirms that correlations and variability levels of currencies vary among currencies and vary over time.

Transaction Exposure Based on Value-at-Risk

http://
See pacific.commerce.ubc.ca/xr/data.html for a foreign exchange time series for over 60 countries which can be customized with respect to period and base currency.

A related method for assessing exposure is the value-at-risk (VAR) method, which incorporates volatility and currency correlations to determine the potential maximum one-day loss on the value of positions of the MNC that are exposed to exchange rate movements. For example, an MNC that typically has receivables in Japanese yen could first determine the maximum one-day loss that would be likely. By using a recent historical period such as 90 days to determine the potential one-day decline in yen, the MNC then applies that potential decline to its receivables to determine the potential loss in the dollar value of its receivables if that one-day decline in

Exhibit 10.6
Movements of Major Currencies Against the Dollar

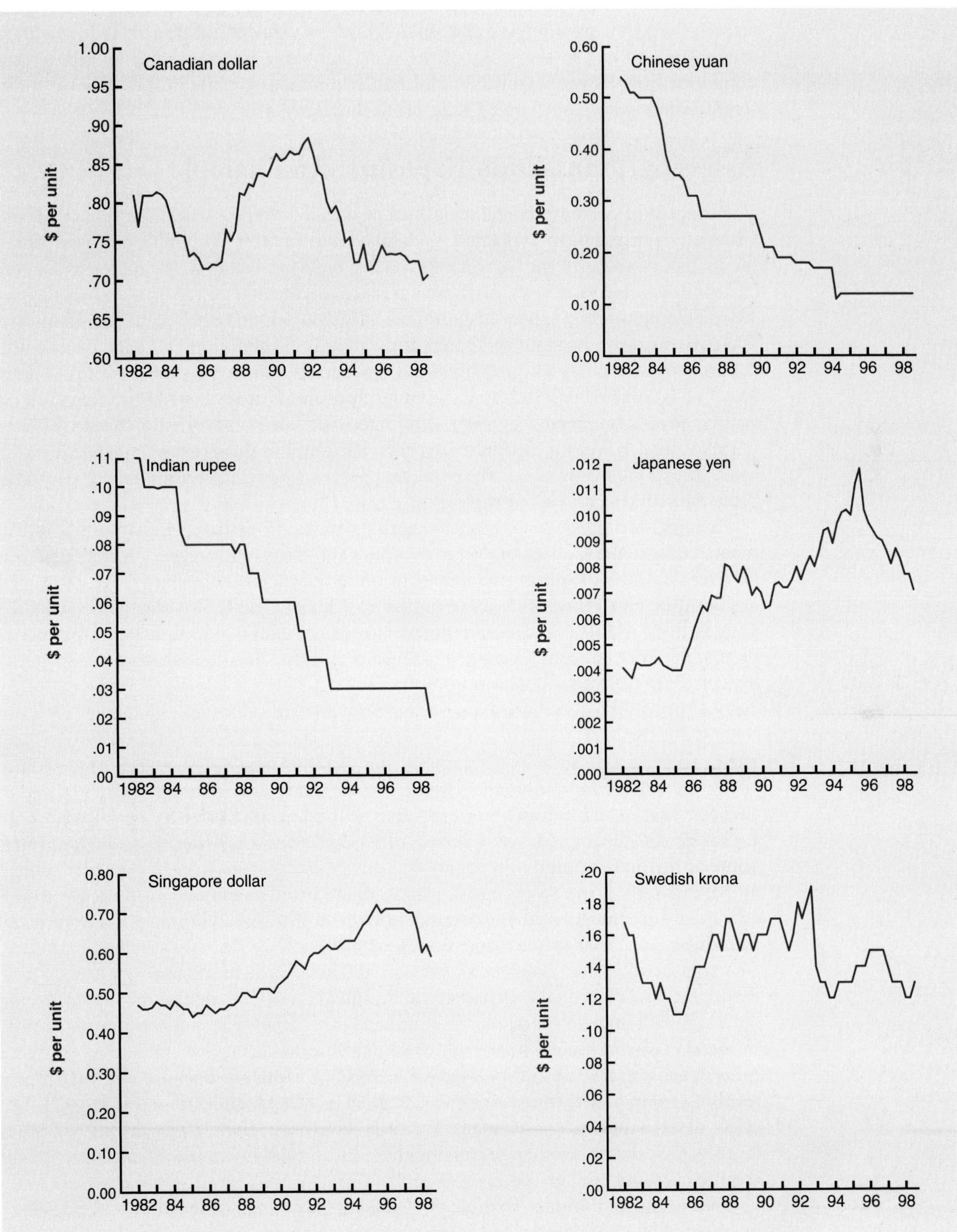

the yen does occur. If the MNC has other positions in yen (such as a Japanese subsidiary), it would also determine the potential reduction in value on those positions due to a maximum one-day decline in the yen's value. When aggregating these effects, the MNC would have determined how its value could be affected by a maximum one-day loss in the value of the yen. This same process could be repeated to determine how its value could be affected by a maximum loss in the yen over a different time horizon, such as a 7-day or 30-day horizon.

Assessing Transaction Exposure: An Example

The concept of currency correlations can be applied to the earlier example of Miami Company's transaction exposure, as displayed in Exhibit 10.2. Since movements in the British pound and the Swedish krona are highly correlated, the exposures to the cash inflows and outflows in these currencies will offset each other to a degree. Miami Company anticipates cash inflows in British pounds equivalent to $15 million and cash outflows in Swedish kronar equivalent to $15 million. Thus, if a weak-dollar cycle occurs, Miami Company will be adversely affected by its exposure to kronar, but favorably affected by its pound exposure. During a strong-dollar cycle, it will be adversely affected by the pound exposure but favorably affected by its kronar exposure. If Miami Company expects that these two currencies will move in the same direction and by about the same degree over the next period, the exposures to these two currencies are partially offset.

Miami may not be too concerned with its exposure to the Canadian dollar movements because the Canadian dollar is somewhat stable with respect to the U.S. dollar over time; risk of substantial depreciation of the Canadian dollar is low. However, it should be concerned with its exposure to Mexican peso movements because the peso is quite volatile and could depreciate substantially within a short period of time. Therefore, Miami Company should seriously consider whether to hedge its expected net cash flow position in pesos.

Economic Exposure

The degree to which a firm's present value of future cash flows can be influenced by exchange rate fluctuations is referred to as **economic exposure** to exchange rates. Some of the more common international business transactions that typically subject an MNC's cash flows to economic exposure are listed in the first column of Exhibit 10.7. They are categorized as affecting inflows or outflows. Those transactions listed in Exhibit 10.7 that require conversion of currencies reflect transaction exposure. The transactions that require conversion are exports denominated in foreign currency, interest received from foreign investments, imports denominated in foreign currency, and interest owed on foreign loans. The other transactions do not require conversion of currencies and therefore do not reflect transaction exposure. Yet, these other transactions are also a form of economic exposure because the cash flows resulting from these transactions can be influenced by exchange rate movements. The effect of exchange rate movements on cash flows from these transactions can be as large as the effect of exchange rate movements on cash flows from transactions that require currency conversion.

The second column of Exhibit 10.7 suggests how each of these transactions may be affected by appreciation of the firm's local currency, while the third column sug-

Exhibit 10.7
Economic Exposure to Exchange Rate Fluctuations

Transactions That Influence the Firm's Local Currency Inflows	Impact of Local Currency Appreciation on Transactions	Impact of Local Currency Depreciation on Transactions
Local sales (relative to foreign competition in local markets)	Decrease	Increase
Firm's exports denominated in local currency	Decrease	Increase
Firm's exports denominated in foreign currency	Decrease	Increase
Interest received from foreign investments	Decrease	Increase
Transactions That Influence the Firm's Local Currency Outflows		
Firm's imported supplies denominated in local currency	No Change	No Change
Firm's imported supplies denominated in foreign currency	Decrease	Increase
Interest owed on foreign funds borrowed	Decrease	Increase

gests how each transaction is affected by depreciation of the firm's local currency. A discussion of the impact of local currency appreciation on each transaction follows.

Economic Exposure to Local Currency Appreciation

The following discussion of economic exposure to local currency appreciation is related to Column 2 in Exhibit 10.7. With regard to the firm's cash inflows, its local sales (within the firm's country) are expected to decrease as a result of appreciation in the local currency. This is due to the increased foreign competition, as local customers could obtain foreign substitute products cheaply with their strengthened currency. The extent of reduced local sales would depend on the degree of foreign competition within the local market.

Cash inflows from exports denominated in the local currency would likely be reduced as a result of appreciation in the local currency. The reason is that foreign importers would need more of their own currency to pay for these products. Exports denominated in the foreign currency also would likely cause reduced cash inflows, but for a different reason. Demand for the firm's product by foreign importers would not change, since they could use their own currency and would not need to obtain the firm's local currency. However, when the firm received the foreign currency inflows, it would convert them to its local currency. If the local currency had appreciated, these inflows would convert to a reduced amount. Finally, any interest or dividends received from foreign investments would convert to a reduced amount in local currency inflows if the local currency had strengthened.

With regard to the firm's cash outflows, the cost of imported supplies denominated in the local currency would not be directly affected by any changes in exchange rates. However, the cost of imported supplies denominated in the foreign currency would be reduced if the local currency appreciated. In addition, any interest to be paid on financing in foreign currencies would be reduced (in terms of the local currency) if the local currency appreciated. This would be due to exchange of the strengthened local currency for the foreign currency in order to make interest payments.

Overall, appreciation in the firm's local currency causes a reduction in both cash inflows and outflows. Thus, it is difficult to generalize whether net cash flows will increase or decrease due to the local currency's appreciation. The impact of local currency appreciation on a firm's net cash flows depends on whether the inflow transactions are affected more or less than the outflow transactions. If, for example, the firm is in the exporting business but obtains its supplies and borrowed funds locally, its inflow transactions will be reduced by a greater degree than its outflow transactions. In this case, net cash flows will be reduced. Conversely, cash inflows of a firm concentrating its sales locally with little foreign competition will not be severely reduced by appreciation of the local currency. If such a firm obtains supplies and borrowed funds overseas, its outflows will be reduced. Overall, this firm's net cash flows will be enhanced by the appreciation of its local currency.

A prominent example of an MNC's economic exposure is Caterpillar Inc., which has relied heavily on exports for a large portion of its sales. The strengthening of the dollar increases the price paid by importers for Caterpillar's products. Caterpillar is especially vulnerable to the value of the dollar because its key competitor is Komatsu of Japan, whose exports are denominated in Japanese yen. When the value of the yen was relatively weak, many firms switched from Caterpillar to Komatsu. Caterpillar's performance improved substantially in periods when the yen and other foreign currencies strengthened against the dollar.

Economic Exposure to Local Currency Depreciation

If the firm's local currency depreciates (see Column 3 of Exhibit 10.7), the transactions will be affected in a manner opposite to the way they are influenced by appreciation. Local sales should increase due to reduced foreign competition (since prices denominated in strong foreign currencies would seem high to the local customers). The firm's exports denominated in the local currency would appear cheap to importers, thereby increasing foreign demand for them. Even exports denominated in the foreign currency could increase cash flows, since a given amount in foreign currency inflows to the firm would convert to a larger amount of the local currency. In addition, interest or dividends from foreign investments would now convert to more of the local currency.

With regard to cash outflows, imported supplies denominated in the local currency would not be directly affected by any change in exchange rates. However, the cost of imported supplies denominated in the foreign currency would rise, since it would take more of the weakened local currency to obtain the foreign currency needed. Any interest payments paid on financing in foreign currencies would increase.

In general, depreciation of the firm's local currency causes an increase in both cash inflows and outflows. Because a partial offsetting effect is likely, it is difficult to generalize as to whether net cash flows will increase or decrease due to the local currency's depreciation. The end result depends on whether inflow variables are affected more than outflow variables. A firm that concentrates on exporting and obtains supplies and borrowed funds locally would likely benefit from a depreciated local currency. This is the case for Caterpillar, Chrysler, Ford, and General Motors in periods when the dollar weakens substantially against most major currencies. Conversely, a firm that concentrates on local sales, has very little foreign competition, and obtains foreign supplies (denominated in foreign currencies) would likely be hurt by a depreciated local currency.

Economic Exposure of Domestic Firms

Although our focus is on the financial management of MNCs, even purely domestic firms are affected by economic exposure. For example, consider a local steel producer that purchases all of its supplies locally and sells all of its steel locally. Because the firm's transactions are solely in the local currency, it is not subject to transaction exposure. However, if there is foreign competition within the local markets this firm sells to, then it is subject to economic exposure. If the exchange rate of the foreign competitor's invoice currency depreciates against the local currency, then customers interested in steel products may shift their purchases toward the foreign steel producer. Consequently, demand for the local firm's steel will likely decrease, and so will net cash inflows. This example illustrates how a firm can be subject to economic exposure without being subject to transaction exposure.

Economic Exposure of MNCs

The degree of economic exposure to exchange rate fluctuations likely will be much greater for a firm involved in international business than for a purely domestic firm. As an example of an MNC's economic exposure, General Corporation arranged to sell software to Mexican customers in the early 1980s. However, the Mexican peso was devalued by 40 percent against the dollar, substantially increasing the Mexican customer's purchase price. Consequently, sales by General Corporation to Mexico declined. DuPont Company, a large U.S.-based MNC, is adversely affected by the weakness of foreign currencies against the dollar. The adverse effects are due to weak foreign currency cash flows being converted to U.S. dollars and a decline in the demand for DuPont's exports.

The impact of the U.S. dollar's movements varies across U.S.-based MNCs because of their differences in operating characteristics. Even those U.S.-based MNCs that can be classified as heavy exporters may be affected differently, depending on how their competitors react to exchange rate movements. A U.S. exporter whose foreign competitors are willing to reduce their profit margin during a weak-dollar period may not necessarily benefit from the exchange rate movements.

The effects of exchange rate movements on MNCs can also vary with the currency of concern, since exchange rates can change by varying degrees. For example, while the Japanese yen appreciated against the dollar in the first half of 1993, some European currencies depreciated. Thus, U.S.-based MNCs with exports concentrated in Europe were adversely affected by their exposure, while those with exports concentrated in Japan were favorably affected. However, in 1997, the opposite trends occurred, such that U.S.-based MNCs with exports concentrated in Europe were favorably affected, while others with exports concentrated in Japan were adversely affected.

In 1997 and 1998, many U.S.-based MNCs were adversely affected by exchange rates because of their economic exposure to Asian currencies (such as the Indonesian rupiah, Thailand baht, and Korean won). First, the weakening of Asian currencies raised the prices of the exports that were sold by U.S.-based MNCs to Asia, from the perspective of Asian importers (since the exports were usually denominated in dollars). Thus, even though these exporters were not affected by transaction exposure in this case, they were affected by economic exposure. Second, many U.S. exporters also experienced a decline in the demand from importers based in other countries, as some importers switched their demand to Asian exporters because the weak Asian currencies caused the prices of the products to be lower than prices charged by U.S. exporters from their perspective.

Many European firms that exported to Asia and other countries were also adversely affected for the same reason. Even exporters in China and Hong Kong suffered from economic exposure; they attempted to maintain stable exchange rates of their currencies, so their prices were no longer as competitive as those of exporters based in Indonesia, Thailand, or Korea where currency values declined by more than 50 percent during the 1997–1998 period.

The numerous examples provided here illustrate that (1) exchange rate movements can affect an MNC's performance, (2) the impact is sometimes favorable, and (3) the impact is dependent on the MNC's degree of exposure to the specific currency of concern.

Measuring Economic Exposure

While economic exposure can force either a favorable or an unfavorable impact on a company, it is critical for the company to assess the potential degree of exposure that exists and then determine whether it should attempt to insulate itself against this exposure. Assessing the economic exposure of an MNC with subsidiaries scattered across countries is difficult, due to the interaction of cash flows denominated in various currencies into, out of, and within the MNC. The overall impact of a given currency's fluctuation on all of the subsidiaries is extremely complex.

Sensitivity of Earnings to Exchange Rates. One method of measuring an MNC's economic exposure is to classify the cash flows into different income statement items and subjectively predict each income statement item based on a forecast of exchange rates. Then an alternative exchange rate scenario can be considered and the forecasts for the income statement items revised. By reviewing how the earnings forecast in the income statement changes in response to alternative exchange rate scenarios, the firm can assess the influence of currency movements on earnings and cash flows. This procedure is especially useful for firms that have more expenses than revenue in a particular foreign currency as is illustrated next.

To illustrate this procedure, consider Madison Inc., which is a U.S.-based company that conducts a portion of its business in Canada. Its U.S. sales are denominated in U.S. dollars, while its Canadian sales are denominated in Canadian dollars. Its pro forma income statement for next year is shown in Exhibit 10.8. The income statement items are segmented into those for the United States and for Canada. Assume that Madison Inc. desires to assess how its income statement items would be affected by three possible exchange rate scenarios for the Canadian dollar over the period of concern: (1) \$.75, (2) \$.80, and (3) \$.85. These scenarios are separately analyzed in the second, third, and fourth columns of Exhibit 10.9.

If the U.S. sales are unaffected by the possible exchange rates, the impact of exchange rates on all income statement items can be assessed from the information contained in Exhibit 10.8. However, to make the example more realistic, assume that Madison's sales in the United States are higher when the Canadian dollar (C\$) is stronger, since Canadian competitors will be priced out of the U.S. market. To be specific, assume the following forecasts for U.S. sales corresponding to each possible exchange rate scenario:

Exhibit 10.8
Revenue and Cost Estimates: Madison Inc. (in Millions of U.S. Dollars and Canadian Dollars)

	U.S. Business	Canadian Business
Sales	$304.00	C$ 4
Cost of goods sold	50.00	200
Gross profit	$254.00	C$–196
Operating expenses:		
Fixed	$ 30.00	—
Variable	30.72	—
Total	$ 60.72	—
Earnings before interest and taxes	$193.28	C$–196
Interest expense	3.00	10
Earnings before taxes (EBT)	$190.28	C$–206

Possible Exchange Rate of C$	Forecasted U.S. Sales (in Millions)
$.75	$300
.80	304
.85	307

The impact of an exchange rate on local sales for any firm would depend on the foreign competition of concern. Historical data could be used to assess how local sales had been affected by exchange rates in the past. For our example, the impact of the exchange rate on local sales is given, so there is no need to assess historical data.

Given this information, Madison Inc. can determine how its pro forma statement would be affected by each exchange rate scenario, as shown in Exhibit 10.9. The assumed impact of exchange rates on U.S. sales is shown in row 1. Row 2 shows the amount in U.S. dollars to be received as a result of Canadian sales (after converting the forecasted C$4 million of Canadian sales into U.S. dollars). Row 3 represents the estimated U.S. dollars to be received from total sales, which is determined by combining rows 1 and 2. Row 4 shows the cost of goods sold in the United States. Row 5 converts the estimated C$200 million cost of goods sold into U.S. dollars for each exchange rate scenario. Row 6 measures the estimated U.S. dollars needed to cover the total cost of goods sold, which is determined by combining rows 4 and 5. Row 7 estimates the gross profit in U.S. dollars, as determined by subtracting row 6 from row 3. Rows 8 through 10 show estimated operating expenses, and row 11 subtracts total operating expenses from gross profit to determine earnings before interest and taxes (EBIT). Row 12 estimates the interest expenses paid in the United States, while row 13 estimates the U.S. dollars needed to make interest payments in Canada. Row 14 combines rows 12 and 13 to estimate total U.S. dollars needed to make all interest payments. Row 15 shows earnings before taxes (EBT), estimated by subtracting row 14 from row 11.

The effect of exchange rates on Madison's revenues and costs can now be reviewed. Exhibit 10.9 illustrates how both U.S. sales and the dollar value of Canadian

Exhibit 10.9
Impact of Possible Exchange Rate Movements on Earnings of Madison Inc. (in Millions)

	Exchange Rate Scenario					
	C$ = $.75		C$ = $.80		C$ = $.85	
Sales:						
(1) U.S.		$300.0		$304.00		$307.00
(2) Canadian	C$4 =	3.0	C$4 =	3.20	C$4 =	3.40
(3) Total		$303.0		$307.20		$310.40
Cost of goods sold:						
(4) U.S.		$ 50.0		$ 50.00		$ 50.00
(5) Canadian	C$200 =	150.0	C$200 =	160.00	C$200 =	170.00
(6) Total		$200.0		$210.00		$220.00
(7) Gross Profit		$103.0		$ 97.20		$ 90.40
Operating expenses:						
(8) U.S.: Fixed		$ 30.0		$ 30.00		$ 30.00
(9) U.S.: Variable (10% of total sales)		30.3		30.72		31.04
(10) Total		$ 60.3		$ 60.72		$ 61.04
(11) EBIT		$ 42.7		$ 36.48		$ 29.36
Interest expense:						
(12) U.S.		$ 3.0		$ 3.00		$ 3.00
(13) Canadian	C$10 =	7.5	C$10 =	8.00	C$10 =	8.50
(14) Total		$ 10.5		$ 11.00		$ 11.50
(15) EBT		$ 32.2		$ 25.48		$ 17.86

sales would increase as a result of a stronger Canadian dollar. Because Madison's Canadian cost of goods sold exposure (C$200 million) is much greater than its Canadian sales exposure (C$4 million), there is a negative overall impact of a strong Canadian dollar on gross profit. The total amount in U.S. dollars needed to make interest payments is also higher when the Canadian dollar is stronger. In general, Madison Inc. would be adversely affected by a stronger Canadian dollar. It would be favorably affected by a weaker Canadian dollar, since the reduced value of total revenue would be more than offset by the reduced cost of goods sold and interest expenses.

A general conclusion from our example is that firms with more (less) in foreign costs than in foreign revenue will be unfavorably (favorably) affected by a stronger foreign currency. Yet, the precise anticipated impact can be determined only by utilizing the procedure described here, or some alternative procedure. Our example is based on a one-period time horizon. If firms have developed forecasts of sales, expenses, and exchange rates for several periods ahead, they can assess their economic exposure over time. Their economic exposure will be affected by any change in operating characteristics over time.

Sensitivity of Cash Flows to Exchange Rates. Another possible method of assessing the firm's economic exposure to currency movements is to apply regression analysis to historical cash flow and exchange rate data as follows:

$$PCF_t = a_0 + a_1 e_t + \mu_t$$

where

PCF_t = percentage change in inflation-adjusted cash flows measured in the firm's home currency over period t
e_t = percentage change in the exchange rate of the currency over period t
μ_t = random error term
a_0 = intercept
a_1 = slope coefficient

The regression coefficient a_1, estimated by regression analysis, would indicate the sensitivity of PCF_t to e_t. If the firm anticipated no major adjustments in its operating structure, it would expect the sensitivity detected from regression analysis to be somewhat similar in the future.

This regression model may be revised to handle more complex situations. For example, if additional currencies were to be assessed, they could be included in the model as additional independent variables. Each currency's impact would be measured by the estimate of its respective regression coefficient. If an MNC were influenced by numerous currencies, it could measure the sensitivity of PCF_t to an index (or composite) of currencies.

The analysis just described for a single currency could also be assessed over separate subperiods, as the sensitivity of a firm's cash flows to a currency's movements may change over time. This would be indicated by a shift in the regression coefficient, which may occur if the firm's exposure to exchange rate movements changed.

Some MNCs may prefer to use their stock price as a proxy for the firm's value and then assess how their stock price changes in response to currency movements. Regression analysis could also be applied to this situation, by replacing PCF_t with the percentage change in stock price in the models specified here.

Some researchers, including Adler and Dumas,[1] suggest the use of regression analysis for this purpose. By assigning stock returns as the dependent variable, regression analysis can indicate how firm value is sensitive to exchange rate fluctuations.

Some companies may assess the impact of exchange rates on particular corporate characteristics, such as earnings, exports, or sales. For example, Toyota Motor Corporation has measured the sensitivity of exports to the yen exchange rate (relative to the U.S. dollar). Consequently, the firm can forecast the expected impact of a forecasted yen value on future exports.

TRANSLATION EXPOSURE

The exposure of the MNC's consolidated financial statements to exchange rate fluctuations is known as **translation exposure.** For example, if the assets or liabilities of the MNC's subsidiaries are translated at something other than historical exchange rates, the balance sheet will be affected by fluctuations in currency values over time. In addition, subsidiary earnings translated into the reporting currency on the consolidated income statement are subject to changing exchange rates.

[1]Michael Adler and Bernard Dumas, "Exposure to Currency Risk: Definition and Measurement," *Financial Management,* 13, no. 2 (Summer 1984), pp. 41–50.

Does Translation Exposure Matter?

Translation of financial statements for consolidated reporting purposes does not affect an MNC's cash flows. For this reason, some analysts suggest that translation exposure is not relevant. MNCs could argue that the subsidiary earnings do not actually have to be converted into the parent's currency. Therefore, if the subsidiary's local currency is currently weak, the earnings could be retained rather than converted and sent to the parent. The earnings could be reinvested in the subsidiary's country if feasible opportunities exist. Because the subsidiary's earnings do not necessarily have to be exchanged for the parent's currency, the translation of a weakened subsidiary currency might distort the true performance of the subsidiary. If financial analysts recognize this distortion, they will not automatically assign a poor evaluation to MNCs whose consolidated earnings are reduced due to weakened subsidiary currencies.

However, the consolidated earnings of MNCs with foreign subsidiaries are affected as a result of translation exposure. Since earnings can affect stock prices, many MNCs are concerned about translation exposure. To illustrate how translation exposure can indirectly affect the stock price of a firm through its impact on consolidated earnings, consider the case of IBM. In 1996, the chief financial officer of IBM announced that the second quarter's earnings would be reduced by $.25 per share simply because of the impact of exchange rates on the foreign earnings as they are translated in dollars to consolidate all of IBM's earnings. If this decline in earnings is not important to investors because it only affects reported earnings and does not affect cash flow, then investors should not have reacted to the announcement. Yet, investors did react by selling their shares of IBM stock.

There are numerous cases in which news that an MNC's earnings were adversely affected by translation exposure resulted in an immediate decline in their respective stock prices. Many investors tend to use earnings when valuing firms, either by deriving estimates of expected cash flows from previous earnings or by applying a price-earnings (P/E) ratio to expected annual earnings to derive a value per share of stock. Since an MNC's translation exposure affects its consolidated earnings, which affect the MNC's value, it is understandable that MNCs are concerned about translation exposure.

If the translation effect on consolidated earnings was distorting the true value of an MNC, investors could attempt to remove the translation effect on consolidated earnings every quarter before deriving a value. However, there is some logic to considering the translation effect when deriving the value of an MNC. Consider an example in which the local currency of an MNC's foreign subsidiary declined by 30 percent against the dollar over the last year. If we assume that the foreign subsidiary earnings are not remitted to the U.S. parent, there is no immediate effect of exchange rate movements on the dollar cash flows received by the U.S. parent. Thus, the total dollar cash flows of the U.S. parent are not immediately affected by the weakening of the subsidiary's currency. However, investors may use the most recent exchange rate as a forecast of the future exchange rate when foreign currency cash flows are actually remitted to the U.S. parent and converted into dollars. In this example, there is no immediate effect on the cash flows received by the parent, but there is an adverse effect on the expected future cash flows that will be received by the parent from the subsidiary in the future. Thus, the translation of earnings this year may be a useful base to derive the expected future dollar cash flows that will be received by the U.S. parent as earnings are remitted by the foreign subsidiary in the future, which suggests that the translation effects in any year should not be removed when determining the MNC's value.

Because many firms believe that translation exposure is relevant, it is important to understand what influences a firm's degree of exposure to translation gains and losses. This topic is discussed in the following section.

Determinants of Translation Exposure

Translation exposure is dependent on

- The degree of foreign involvement by foreign subsidiaries.
- The locations of foreign subsidiaries.
- The accounting methods used.

Degree of Foreign Involvement. The greater the percentage of an MNC's business conducted by its foreign subsidiaries, the larger will be the percentage of a given financial statement item that is susceptible to translation exposure. For example, the foreign involvement of some MNCs may be mostly in the form of exporting. These MNCs don't have much of their business conducted by foreign subsidiaries. Thus, the consolidated financial statements will not be substantially affected by exchange rate fluctuations (although such firms may exhibit a high degree of transaction and economic exposure).

Locations of Foreign Subsidiaries. The locations of the subsidiaries can also influence the degree of translation exposure, since the financial statement items of each subsidiary are typically measured by that country's home currency. For example, consider the reporting situation of a U.S. MNC with a Mexican subsidiary. The Mexican subsidiary's assets, liabilities, earnings, etc., are measured in Mexican pesos. The MNC must develop consolidated quarterly financial statements that require translation of the Mexican subsidiary figures into U.S.-dollar terms. If the subsidiaries are located in countries such as Canada, where the currency is somewhat stable against the U.S. dollar, then translation risk will be lower.

Accounting Methods. Finally, the MNC's degree of accounting exposure can be greatly affected by the accounting procedures it uses to translate when consolidating financial statement data. Under the Financial Accounting Standards Board No. 52 (FASB-52), adopted in December 1981, the consolidated accounting rules for U.S.-based MNCs changed dramatically. Listed are some of the more important points of FASB-52:

1. The functional currency of an entity is the currency of the economic environment in which the entity operates.
2. The current exchange rate as of the reporting date is used to translate the assets and liabilities of a foreign entity from its functional currency into the reporting currency.
3. The weighted average exchange rate is used to translate revenue, expenses, and gains and losses of a foreign entity from its functional currency into the reporting currency.
4. Translated income gains or losses due to changes in foreign currency values are not recognized in current net income but are reported as a second component of stockholder's equity; an exception to this rule is a foreign entity located in a country with high inflation.

5. Realized income gains or losses due to foreign currency transactions are recorded in current net income, although there are some exceptions.

Under FASB-52, consolidated earnings are sensitive to the functional currency's weighted average exchange rate. Consider a British subsidiary of a U.S.-based MNC that earned £10,000,000 in Year 1 and £10,000,000 in Year 2. When these earnings are consolidated along with other subsidiary earnings, they are translated at the weighted average exchange rate in that year. Assume the weighted average exchange rate is $1.90 in Year 1 and $1.50 in Year 2. The translated earnings for each reporting period in U.S. dollars are determined as follows:

Reporting Period	Assumed Local Earnings of British Subsidiary	Weighted Average Exchange Rate of Pound Over the Reporting Period	Translated U.S. Dollar Earnings of British Subsidiary
Year 1	£10,000,000	$1.90	$19,000,000
Year 2	£10,000,000	$1.50	$15,000,000

Notice that even though local earnings in pounds were the same in each year, consolidated MNC dollar earnings translated from the British subsidiary were reduced by $4 million in Year 2. The discrepancy here is due to the change in the weighted average of the British pound exchange rate. It is possible that financial analysts may give the MNC a poor evaluation due to its British subsidiary's reduced earnings (when measured in dollars) in Year 2. Yet, the drop in earnings is not the fault of the British subsidiary, but rather of a weakened British pound that makes its Year 2 earnings look small (when measured in U.S. dollars). The pound's exchange rate has varied by the amount shown in the example during the 1990s, which partially explains the variability in earnings of MNCs over time.

Examples of Translation Exposure

Consolidated earnings of Black & Decker, The Coca-Cola Company, and other MNCs are very sensitive to exchange rates because more than a third of their assets and sales are overseas. Their earnings in foreign countries are reduced when foreign currencies depreciate against the dollar.

The earnings of numerous U.S.-based MNCs were favorably affected by the weakened dollar over the 1985–1988 period. The boost in earnings was primarily attributed to the foreign subsidiary earnings that were translated into dollars at a higher exchange rate.

In the early 1990s, many currencies experienced volatile cycles, causing wide swings in the translation effects on the consolidated earnings of U.S.-based MNCs. During the 1997–1998 Asian crisis, currencies of some Asian countries depreciated by more than 50 percent against the dollar. Thus, a given amount of earnings by an Asian subsidiary of a U.S.-based MNC translated into less than half the dollar value of earnings than the translated value that would have occurred prior to the Asian crisis. While much of the attention to the Asian crisis is focused on how foreign subsidiaries based there experienced lower earnings, the translation effect caused additional adverse effects because it forced Asian earnings (which were lower than normal for most subsidiaries during the crisis) to be translated at very low exchange rates, which had a negative effect on the consolidated earnings of the U.S.-based MNCs.

The impact of the Asian crisis on translation exposure is not restricted to MNCs that had subsidiaries in countries such as Thailand, Malaysia, and Indonesia, although those countries were affected the most. The substantial depreciation of these currencies also encouraged Japan to weaken its currency (the yen) so that its export prices would still be competitive. Thus, the earnings of Japanese subsidiaries of U.S.-based MNCs translated into relatively small amounts of dollar earnings because of the weakness of the yen over the period that the earnings occurred.

According to World Research Advisory estimates, translated earnings of U.S.-based MNCs in aggregate were reduced by $20 billion in the third quarter of 1998 alone simply because of the depreciation of Asian currencies against the dollar.

When foreign subsidiaries of an MNC have many growth opportunities locally, they tend to reinvest most or all of their earnings in that local country. In this case, there is less concern about translation exposure because the earnings will not have to be converted into a different currency. However, when subsidiaries do not have local growth opportunities, they are more likely to remit those earnings to the parent. Under these conditions, translation exposure is more critical and may even signal increased economic exposure in the near future (when the earnings are remitted). In general, translation exposure is more closely monitored when the foreign earnings of the subsidiaries are more likely to be remitted to the parent because it signals a business operation that is subject to economic exposure.

Integrative Example of Exposure. As a final example that integrates translation exposure with transaction and economic exposure, Minnesota Mining & Manufacturing (3M) Co. experienced significantly lower earnings in 1998 during the Asian crisis because of its exposure to exchange rate movements of Asian currencies against the dollar. 3M normally relies on Asia for about 17 percent of its total worldwide revenue. First, 3M has receivables in some Asian currencies that are converted to dollars

Nike Problem

Nike's Translation Exposure

Nike has foreign subsidiaries that facilitate its international business. Its consolidated earnings are partially attributed to earnings generated by its foreign subsidiaries. Since the foreign earnings must be translated to U.S.-dollar earnings, the consolidated statements are subject to translation exposure; that is, the exchange rates at which the earnings are translated into dollars to derive the consolidated earnings are dependent on exchange rates over the time period of concern. In those years (such as 1997) when the local currencies of the foreign subsidiaries depreciate against the dollar, the earnings of those subsidiaries are reduced because of translation exposure. Nike states in a recent annual report that any little earnings blip can cause a significant impact on the stock price. Thus, it appears that the decline in Nike's stock price during 1997 was at least partially attributed to its translation exposure. Even though translation exposure does not directly affect cash flows, it can affect Nike's value through its effect on consolidated earnings.

Discussion: Should Nike be concerned with its translation exposure, or will the effects even out over time?

(transaction exposure), and the substantial depreciation of the Asian currencies caused 3M's receivables to be converted to a smaller amount of dollars. Second, 3M was subject to economic exposure beyond its transaction exposure because the Asian demand for 3M's products that are denominated in dollars declined as the Asian currencies weakened. Third, 3M suffered from its translation exposure because its Asian subsidiary earnings were translated into the reported consolidated earnings at weak exchange rates, which reduced the level of reported earnings. In June 1998, 3M announced that its earnings were significantly below the level that was expected, which caused its stock price to decline by more than 6 percent in a single day.

Impact of Exchange Rate Exposure on an MNC's Value

An MNC's exposure to exchange rate movements can affect its value, as shown in Exhibit 10.10. The foreign currency cash flows generated by the foreign subsidiaries are subject to transaction exposure if those subsidiaries had transactions with foreign countries that involved the exchange of the local currency for other currencies. Transaction exposure definitely affects the dollar cash flows that are ultimately received when exchanging foreign currency cash flows because the future exchange

Exhibit 10.10
Impact of Exposure on an MNC's Value

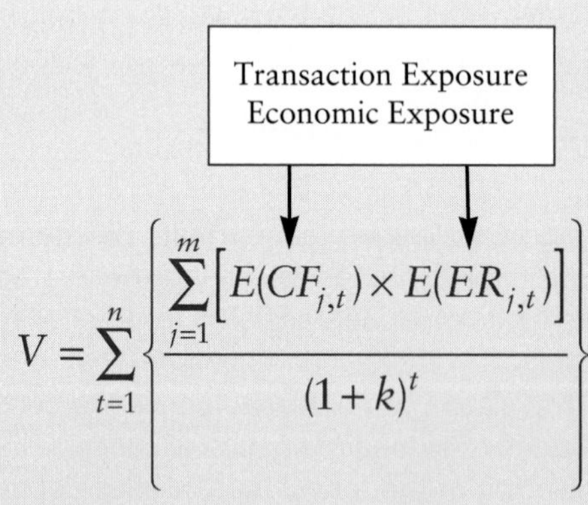

$$V = \sum_{t=1}^{n} \left\{ \frac{\sum_{j=1}^{m} \left[E(CF_{j,t}) \times E(ER_{j,t}) \right]}{(1+k)^t} \right\}$$

V = value of the U.S.-based MNC
$E(CF_{j,t})$ = expected cash flows denominated in currency j to be received by the U.S. parent in period t
$E(ER_{j,t})$ = expected exchange rate at which currency j can be converted to dollars at the end of period t
k = the weighted average cost of capital of the U.S. parent company
m = number of currencies
n = number of periods

rates at which the foreign currency cash flows will be converted to dollars will change over time.

The foreign currency cash flows generated by the foreign subsidiaries may be subject to economic exposure even before those cash flows are converted into dollars. For example, the subsidiaries may compete with firms in other countries, and the demand for their products (and therefore foreign currency cash flows received) are dependent on the exchange rates of the currencies denominating the competitor's products.

While the diagram does not show any effect of exposure on the parent's cost of capital, an effect is possible in some cases. If the foreign subsidiaries are subject to a very high degree of economic exposure, their cost of capital (and therefore the required return on their investment) may be affected, which also influences the MNC's value.

SUMMARY

- MNCs with less risk can obtain funds at lower financing costs. Since they may experience more volatile cash flows because of exchange rate movements, exchange rate risk can affect their financing costs. Thus, MNCs may benefit from hedging exchange rate risk.
- Transaction exposure represents the exposure of an MNC's future cash transactions to exchange rate movements. MNCs can measure their transaction exposure by determining their future payables and receivables positions in various currencies, along with the variability levels and correlations of these currencies. From this information, they can assess how their revenue and costs may change in response to various exchange rate scenarios.
- Economic exposure represents any exposure of an MNC's cash flows (direct or indirect) to exchange rate movements. MNCs can attempt to measure their economic exposure by determining the extent to which their cash flows will be affected by their exposure to each foreign currency.
- Translation exposure represents the exposure of an MNC's consolidated financial statements to exchange rate movements. To measure translation exposure, MNCs can forecast their earnings in each foreign currency and then determine the potential exchange rate movements of each currency relative to their home currency.

SELF-TEST FOR CHAPTER 10

(Answers are provided in Appendix A at the back of the text.)

1. Given that shareholders can diversify away an individual firm's exchange rate risk by investing in a variety of firms, why are firms concerned about exchange rate risk?
2. A U.S. firm considers importing its supplies from either Canada (denominated in C$) or Mexico (denominated in pesos) on a monthly basis. The quality is the same for both sources. Once the firm completes the agreement with a supplier, it will be obligated to continue using that supplier for at least three years. Based on existing exchange rates, the dollar amount to be paid (including transportation costs) would be the same. The firm has no other exposure to exchange rate movements. Given that the firm prefers to have less exchange rate risk, which alternative is preferable? Explain.
3. Assume your U.S. firm currently exports to Mexico on a monthly basis. The goods are

priced in pesos. Once material is received from a source, it is quickly used to produce the product in the United States and then the product is exported. Currently, there is no other exposure to exchange rate risk. You have a choice of purchasing the material from Canada (denominated in C$), from Mexico (denominated in pesos), or from within the United States (denominated in U.S. dollars). The quality and your expected cost are similar across the three sources. Which source would be preferable, given that you prefer minimal exchange rate risk?

4. Using the information in the previous question, consider the proposal to price the exports to Mexico in dollars and to use the U.S. source for material. Would this proposal eliminate the exchange rate risk?

5. Assume that the dollar is expected to strengthen over the next several years against the euro. Explain how this will affect the consolidated earnings of U.S.-based MNCs with subsidiaries in Europe.

QUESTIONS AND APPLICATIONS

1. Why would an MNC consider examining only its "net" cash flows in each currency when assessing its transaction exposure?

2. Your employer, a large MNC, has asked you to assess its transaction exposure. Its projected cash flows are as follows for the next year:

Currency	Total Inflow	Total Outflow	Current Exchange Rate in U.S. Dollars
Danish krone	(DK) DK50,000,000	DK40,000,000	$ .15
British pound	(£) £2,000,000	£1,000,000	$1.50

Assume that the movements in the Danish krona and the pound are highly correlated. Provide your assessment as to your firm's degree of transaction exposure (as to whether the exposure is high or low). Substantiate your answer.

3. What factors affect a firm's degree of transaction exposure in a particular currency? For each factor, explain the desirable characteristics that would reduce transaction exposure.

4. Are currency correlations perfectly stable over time? What does your answer imply about using past data on correlations as an indicator for the future?

5. If a firm has net receivables in several currencies that are highly correlated with each other, what does this imply about the firm's overall degree of transaction exposure?

6. Compare and contrast transaction exposure and economic exposure.

7. How should appreciation of a firm's home currency generally affect its cash inflows? Why?

8. How should depreciation of a firm's home currency generally affect its cash outflows? Why?

9. Fischer, Inc. exports products from Florida to Europe. It obtains its supplies and borrows funds locally. How would appreciation of the euro likely affect its net cash flows? Why?

10. Why are even the cash flows of a purely domestic firm exposed to exchange rate fluctuations?

11. Assume an MNC hires you as a consultant to assess its degree of economic exposure to exchange rate fluctuations. How would you handle this task? Be specific.

12. a. In using regression analysis to assess the sensitivity of cash flows to exchange rate movements, what is the use of breaking the database into subperiods?
    b. Assume the regression coefficient based on assessing economic exposure was much higher in this second subperiod than in the first subperiod. What does this tell you about the firm's degree of economic exposure over time? Why might such results occur?

13. a. Present an argument for why translation exposure is relevant to an MNC.
b. Present an argument for why translation exposure is not relevant to an MNC.

14. What factors affect the firm's degree of translation exposure? Explain how each factor influences translation exposure.

15. How can a U.S. company use regression analysis to assess its economic exposure to fluctuations in the British pound?

16. Consider a period in which the U.S. dollar weakens against the euro. How will this affect the reported earnings of a U.S.-based MNC with European subsidiaries?

17. Consider a period in which the U.S. dollar strengthens against most foreign currencies. How will this affect the reported earnings of a U.S.-based MNC with subsidiaries all over the world?

18. Walt Disney World built an amusement park in France that opened in 1992. How do you think this project has affected Disney's overall economic exposure to exchange rate movements? Explain.

19. Using the cost and revenue information shown for DeKalb Inc., determine how the costs, revenue and earnings items would be affected by three possible exchange rate scenarios for the New Zealand dollar (NZ$): (1) NZ$ = $.50, (2) NZ$ = $.55, and (3) NZ$ = $.60. (Assume U.S. sales will be unaffected by the exchange rate.) Assume that NZ$ earnings will be remitted to the U.S. at the end of the period.

Revenue and Cost Estimates: DeKalb Inc.
(in millions of U.S. dollars and New Zealand dollars)

	U.S. Business	New Zealand Business
Sales	$ 800	NZ$ 800
Cost of goods sold	500	100
Gross profit	$ 300	NZ$ 700
Operating expenses	300	0
Earnings before interest and taxes	$0	NZ$ 700
Interest expenses	100	0
Earnings before taxes	$–100	NZ$ 700

20. Aggie Company produces chemicals. It is a major exporter to Europe, where its main competition is from other U.S. exporters. All of these companies invoice the products in U.S. dollars. Is Aggie's transaction exposure likely to be significantly affected if the euro strengthens or weakens? Explain. If the euro weakens for several years, can you think of any change that might occur within the global chemicals market?

21. Longhorn Company produces hospital equipment. Most of its revenues are in the United States. About half of its expenses require outflows in Philippine pesos (to pay for Philippine materials). Most of Longhorn's competition is from U.S. firms that have no international business at all. How will Longhorn Company be affected if the peso strengthens?

22. Lubbock Inc. produces furniture and has no international business. Its major competitors import most of their furniture from Brazil and then sell it out of retail stores in the United States. How will Lubbock Inc. be affected if Brazil's currency (the real) strengthens over time?

23. Sooner Company is a U.S. wholesale company that imports expensive high-quality luggage and sells it to retail stores around the United States. Its main competitors also import high-quality luggage and sell it to retail stores. None of these competitors hedge their exposure to exchange rate movements. The treasurer of Sooner Company told the board of directors that the firm's performance would be more volatile over time if it hedged its exchange rate exposure. How could a firm's cash flows be more stable as a result of such high exposure to exchange rate fluctuations?

24. Boulder Inc. exports chairs to Europe (invoiced in U.S. dollars) and competes against local European companies. If purchasing power parity exists, why would Boulder not benefit from a stronger euro?

25. Toyota Motor Corporation measures the sensitivity of exports to the yen exchange rate (relative to the U.S. dollar). Explain how regression analysis could be used for such a task. Identify the expected sign of the regression coefficient if Toyota primarily exported to the United States.

If Toyota established plants in the United States, how might the regression coefficient on the exchange rate variable change?

26. Cornhusker Company is an exporter of products to Singapore. It wants to know how its stock price is affected by changes in the Singapore dollar's exchange rate. It believes that the impact may occur with a lag of one to three quarters. How could regression analysis be used to assess the impact?

27. Vegas Corporation is a U.S. firm that exports most of its products to Canada. It historically invoiced its products in Canadian dollars to accommodate the importers. However, it was adversely affected when the Canadian dollar weakened against the U.S. dollar. Since Vegas did not hedge, its Canadian dollar receivables were converted into a relatively small amount of U.S. dollars. After a few more years of continual concern about possible exchange rate movements, Vegas called its customers and requested that they pay for future orders with U.S. dollars instead of Canadian dollars. At this time, the Canadian dollar was valued at $.81. The customers decided to oblige, since the number of Canadian dollars to be converted to U.S. dollars when importing the goods from Vegas was still slightly smaller than the number of Canadian dollars that would be needed to buy the product from a Canadian manufacturer. Based on this situation, has transaction exposure changed for Vegas Corporation? Has economic exposure changed? Explain.

28. Cieplak Inc. is a U.S.-based MNC that has recently expanded into Asia. Its U.S. parent exports to some Asian countries, with its exports denominated in the Asian currencies. It also has a large subsidiary in Malaysia that serves that market. Offer at least two reasons related to exposure to exchange rates why Cieplak's earnings were reduced during the Asian crisis.

29. During the Asian crisis in 1998, there were rumors that China would weaken its currency (the yuan) against many currencies in the United States and in Europe. This caused investors to reduce the valuation of stocks in Asian countries such as Japan, Taiwan, and Singapore. Offer an intuitive explanation for such an effect. What types of Asian firms would be affected the most?

Internet Application

30. The following Web site provides daily exchange rate data for several currencies over the last few months.

    http://pacific.commerce.ubc.ca/xr/data.html

    a. Use this Web site to assess the volatility of recent daily exchange rates of the Canadian dollar and Australian dollar over the last two months. Which currency appears to be more volatile? What are the implications for U.S. firms that recently had cash flows denominated in Australian dollars versus Canadian dollars?
    b. The following Web site contains annual reports of many MNCs:

       http://www.reportgallery.com

       Review the annual report of your choice. Look for any comments in the report that describe the MNC's transaction exposure, economic exposure, or translation exposure. Summarize the MNC's exposure based on the comments in the annual report.

Running Your Own MNC

Recognizing Exposure to Exchange Rate Risk

31. Recall that when you created your business idea, it was assumed that your receivables would be denominated in the foreign currency of concern upon the sale of your products.

    a. Describe your exposure to exchange rate risk. That is, describe the exchange rate conditions affecting the performance of your business.
    b. Is your business subject to transaction exposure? economic exposure? translation exposure? Explain why your business is or is not subject to each of these types of exposure.

Blades, Inc. Case

Assessment of Exchange Rate Exposure

Blades, Inc. is currently exporting roller blades to Thailand and importing certain components needed to manufacture roller blades from Thailand. Under a fixed contractual agreement, Blades' primary customer in Thailand has committed itself to the purchase of 180,000 pairs of roller blades annually at a fixed price of 4,594 Thai baht (THB) per pair. Blades is importing rubber and plastic components from various suppliers in Thailand at a cost of approximately THB2,871 per pair, although the exact price (in baht) depends on current market prices. Blades imports materials sufficient to manufacture 72,000 pairs of roller blades from Thailand each year. The decision to import materials from Thailand was reached because rubber and plastic components needed to manufacture Blades' products are inexpensive, yet high quality, in Thailand.

Blades has also conducted business with a Japanese supplier in the past. Although Blades' analysis indicates that the Japanese components are of a lower quality than the Thai components, Blades has occasionally imported components from Japan if the prices of these components were low enough. Currently, Ben Holt, Blades' chief financial officer (CFO), is considering the possibility of importing components from Japan more frequently. Specifically, he would like to reduce Blades' baht exposure by taking advantage of the recently high correlation between the baht and the yen. Since Blades has net inflows denominated in baht and would have outflows denominated in yen, its net transaction exposure would be reduced if these two currencies were highly correlated. If Blades decides to import components from Japan, it would probably import materials sufficient to manufacture 1,700 pairs of roller blades annually at a price of ¥7,440 per pair.

Ben Holt is also contemplating a further expansion into foreign countries. Although he would eventually like to establish a subsidiary or acquire an existing business overseas, his immediate focus is on increasing Blades' foreign sales. Mr. Holt's primary reason for this decision is that the profit margin resulting from Blades' imports and exports exceeds 25 percent, while the profit margin resulting from Blades' domestic production is below 15 percent. Consequently, he sees a further foreign expansion of Blades as beneficial to the company's future.

While Blades' current exporting and importing practices have been profitable, Ben Holt is contemplating the extension of Blades' trade relationships to countries in different regions of the world. One reason for this decision is that various Thai roller blade manufacturers have recently established subsidiaries in the United States. Furthermore, various Thai roller blade manufacturers have recently targeted the U.S. market by advertising their products over the Internet. As a result of this increased competition from Thailand, Blades is uncertain whether its primary customer in Thailand will renew the current commitment to purchase a fixed number of roller blades annually. The current agreement will terminate in two years. Another reason for engaging in transactions with other, non-Asian, countries is that the Thai baht has depreciated substantially recently, which has somewhat reduced Blades' profit margins. The sale of roller blades to other countries with more stable currencies may increase Blades' profit margins.

While Blades will continue exporting to Thailand under the current agreement for the next two years, it may also export roller blades to Jogs Ltd., a British retailer. Preliminary negotiations indicate that Jogs would be willing to commit itself to the purchase of 200,000 pairs of "Speedos," Blades' primary product, for a fixed price of £80 per pair.

Mr. Holt is aware that a further expansion of Blades would increase its exposure to exchange rate fluctuations, but he believes that Blades can further supplement its profit margins through this expansion. He is vaguely familiar with the different types of exchange rate exposure but has asked you, a financial analyst of Blades, Inc., to help him assess how the contemplated changes would affect Blades' financial position. Among other concerns, Ben Holt is aware that recent economic problems in Thailand have had an effect on Thailand and other Asian countries. Whereas the correlation between Asian currencies such as the Japanese yen and the Thai baht is generally not very high and very unstable, these recent problems have increased the correlation among most Asian currencies. Conversely, the correlation between the British pound and the Asian currencies is quite low.

To aid you in your analysis, Ben Holt has provided you with the following data:

Currency	Expected Exchange Rate	Range of Possible Exchange Rates
British pound	$1.50	$1.47 to $1.53
Japanese yen	$0.0083	$0.0079 to $0.0087
Thai baht	$0.024	$0.020 to $0.028

Ben Holt has provided with the following list of questions he would like you to answer:

1. What type(s) of exposure (i.e., transaction, economic, or translation exposure) is Blades subject to? Why?
2. Using a spreadsheet, conduct a consolidated net cash flow assessment of Blades, Inc., and estimate the range of net inflows and outflows for Blades, Inc., for the coming year. Assume that Blades enters into the agreement with Jogs Ltd.
3. If Blades does not enter into the agreement with the British firm and continues to export to Thailand and import from Thailand and Japan, do you think the increased correlations between the Japanese yen and the Thai baht would increase or reduce Blades' level of transaction exposure?
4. Do you think Blades should import components from Japan to reduce its net transaction exposure in the long run? Why or why not?
5. Assuming Blades enters into the agreement with Jogs Ltd., how will its overall transaction exposure be affected?
6. Given that Thai roller blade manufacturers located in Thailand have begun targeting the U.S. roller blade market, how do you think Blades' U.S. sales were affected by the depreciation of the Thai baht? How do you think its exports to Thailand and its imports from Thailand and Japan were affected by the depreciation?

Small Business Dilemma

Assessment of Exchange Rate Exposure by the Sports Exports Company

At the current time, the Sports Exports Company is willing to receive payments in pounds for the monthly exports it sends to the United Kingdom. While all of its receivables are denominated in British pounds, it has no payables in British pounds or in any other foreign currency. Jim Logan, owner of the Sports Exports Company, wants to assess his firm's exposure to exchange rate risk.

1. Would you describe the exposure of the Sports Exports Company to exchange rate risk as transaction exposure? economic exposure? translation exposure?
2. Jim Logan considers a change in the pricing policy in which the importer must pay in dollars, so that Jim does not have to worry about converting pounds to dollars every month. If this policy was implemented, would this eliminate the transaction exposure of the Sports Exports Company? Would it eliminate the economic exposure of the Sports Exports Company? Explain.
3. If Jim decided to implement the policy described in the previous question, how would the Sports Exports Company be affected (if at all) by appreciation of the pound? by depreciation of the pound? Would these effects on the Sports Exports Company differ if Jim retained his original policy of pricing the exports in British pounds?

APPENDIX 10

Estimating the Variability of a Currency Portfolio

To illustrate how the variability of foreign currency cash flows is affected by correlations, consider a simplified example in which an MNC has only two foreign currencies. Fifty percent of the MNC's funds are expected to come from Currency A, and the remaining funds from Currency B. Assume that over an annual period, the standard deviation of exchange rate movements is 4 percent for Currency A and 4 percent for Currency B. Also assume that these two currencies are perfectly positively correlated, so that their correlation coefficient is 1.00. The standard deviation of this two-currency portfolio (σ_p) can be determined from the following equation:

$$\sigma_p = \sqrt{W_A^2\sigma_A^2 + W_B^2\sigma_B^2 + 2W_A W_B \sigma_A \sigma_B CORR_{AB}}$$

where

W_A = percentage of funds to be received from receivables in Currency A
W_B = percentage of funds to be received from receivables in Currency B
σ_A = standard deviation of exchange rate movements for Currency A
σ_B = standard deviation of exchange rate movements for Currency B
$CORR_{AB}$ = correlation coefficient of exchange rate movements between Currencies A and B

Using the information provided, the variability of the combined (portfolio) cash flows of Currencies A and B can be estimated as

$$\begin{aligned}\sigma_p &= \sqrt{.5^2(.04)^2 + .5^2(.04)^2 + 2(.5)(.5)(.04)(.04)(1.0)} \\ &= \sqrt{.0004 + .0004 + .0008} \\ &= \sqrt{.0016} \\ &= .04, \text{ or } 4\%\end{aligned}$$

Notice that the standard deviation in the portfolio is as high as the standard deviation of either individual currency. The diversification between these two currencies does not reduce variability because the currency movements are perfectly positively correlated. Diversification between currencies with a low correlation could substantially reduce the variability of the portfolio of inflow currencies. For example, if the two currencies had a correlation coefficient of .2, the portfolio variability (assuming 50-percent weight to each currency) would be

$$\begin{aligned}\sigma_p &= \sqrt{.5^2(.04)^2 + .5^2(.04)^2 + 2(.5)(.5)(.04)(.04)(0.2)} \\ &= \sqrt{.0004 + .0004 + .0016} \\ &= \sqrt{.0096} \\ &= \text{about } .031, \text{ or } 3.1\%\end{aligned}$$

A negative correlation coefficient between Currencies A and B would reduce the portfolio variability to even a greater degree. For example, consider an extreme example in which Currencies A and B are perfectly negatively correlated, as represented by a correlation coefficient of –1.00. The portfolio variability (assuming 50 percent weight to each currency) would be

$$\begin{aligned}\sigma_p &= \sqrt{.5^2(.04)^2 + .5^2(.04)^2 + 2(.5)(.5)(.04)(.04)(-1.0)} \\ &= \sqrt{.0004 + .0004 + (-.0008)} \\ &= \sqrt{.0} \\ &= 0\end{aligned}$$

The portfolio's exchange rate movements against the dollar would be stable because of the offsetting effects between Currencies A and B, if they are perfectly negatively correlated. Such a situation would normally be favorably perceived by an MNC, since the home currency value of the portfolio of foreign currencies could be virtually insulated from movements in these currencies.

It is unlikely that the MNC will be able to structure its foreign cash flows so that it is totally insulated against exchange rate movements. However, the examples given here demonstrate that a set of foreign currency cash inflows is less volatile if the correlations are low. The cash flows would also be less volatile if the standard deviations of the individual currencies were lower. This can be verified by assuming a standard deviation of less than 4 percent for each currency in the preceding examples and recomputing the portfolio's standard deviation.

11 Managing Transaction Exposure

Recall from the previous chapter that there are three forms by which a multinational corporation (MNC) is exposed to exchange rate fluctuations: (1) transaction exposure, (2) economic exposure, and (3) translation exposure. This chapter focuses on the management of transaction exposure, while the following chapter focuses on the management of economic and translation exposure.

The specific objectives of this chapter are to

- identify the commonly used techniques for hedging transaction exposure,
- explain how each technique can be used to hedge future payables and receivables,
- compare the advantages and disadvantages among hedging techniques, and
- suggest other methods of reducing exchange rate risk when hedging techniques are not available.

Transaction Exposure

Transaction exposure exists when the future cash transactions of a firm are affected by exchange rate fluctuations. For example, a U.S. firm that purchases Mexican goods may need pesos to buy the goods. While the firm may know exactly how many pesos it will need, it doesn't know how many dollars will be needed to be exchanged for those pesos. This uncertainty occurs because the exchange rate between pesos and dollars fluctuates over time. Also consider a U.S.-based MNC that will be receiving a foreign currency. Its future receivables are exposed, since it is uncertain of the dollars it will obtain when exchanging the foreign currency received.

Selective Hedging of Transaction Exposure

Before MNCs take the time to manage transaction exposure, they may question whether hedging is worthwhile. Consider the firm that is deciding whether to hedge its periodic future payables denominated in a foreign currency. The forward contract is a common hedging device against this foreign currency position. If the spot rate in the future exceeds today's forward rate, then the MNC will save money by hedging its net payables (as opposed to no hedge). If the spot rate in the future is less than today's forward rate, then the MNC will lose money by hedging its net payables. A forward rate that serves as an unbiased forecast of the future spot rate will underestimate and overestimate the future spot rate with equal frequency. In this case, periodic hedging with the forward rate will be more costly in some periods and less costly in other periods. On the average, it will not reduce the MNC's costs. Thus, it could be argued that hedging is not worthwhile.

http://

See www.ibm.com as an example of an MNC's Web site. The Web sites of various MNCs make financial statements such as annual reports available that disclose the use of financial derivatives for the purpose of hedging interest rate risk and foreign exchange rate risk.

Many MNCs, such as Black & Decker, Eastman Kodak Co., Merck & Co., and Zenith Electronics Corp., choose to hedge only in those situations in which they expect the currency to move in a direction that will make hedging feasible. That is, they may hedge future payables if they foresee appreciation in the currency denominating the payables. In addition, they may hedge future receivables if they foresee depreciation in the currency denominating the receivables. For example, Zenith hedges its imports of Japanese components only when it expects the yen to appreciate.

The strategy of selective hedging is illustrated by the following quotations from annual reports:

> The purpose of the Company's foreign currency hedging activities is to reduce the risk that the eventual dollar net cash inflows resulting from sales outside the U.S. will be adversely affected by exchange rates. [The Coca-Cola Company]

> Decisions regarding whether or not to hedge a given commitment are made on a case-by-case basis by taking into consideration the amount and duration of the exposure, market volatility, and economic trends. [DuPont Corporation]

> We selectively hedge the potential effect of the foreign currency fluctuations related to operating activities . . . [General Mills Co.]

Some MNCs, such as Seagram Company, tend to hedge most or all of their net positions in foreign currency. Westinghouse tends to hedge most of its foreign transactions, including any foreign transactions in excess of $250,000. Its policy is intended to ensure that changes in exchange rates will not have a significant impact on its performance.

MNCs that hedge most of their exposure do not necessarily expect that hedging will always be beneficial. In fact, such MNCs may even believe that hedging will, on the average, result in the same cash inflows or outflows as not hedging. Yet, they may prefer knowing what their future cash inflows or outflows in terms of their home currency will be in each period, since this could enhance corporate planning. A hedge allows the firm to know the future cash flows (in terms of the home currency) that will result from any foreign transactions that have already been negotiated.

In general, decisions on whether to hedge, how much to hedge, and how to hedge will vary with the MNC management's degree of risk aversion and its forecasts of exchange rates. MNCs that are more conservative tend to hedge more of their exposure.

Most MNCs do not perceive their foreign exchange management as a profit center. Thus, it is normally inappropriate for the foreign exchange management group to set a profit goal, as it may even use some hedges that will likely result in slightly worse outcomes than no hedges at all, just to avoid the possibility of a major adverse movement in exchange rates.

If transaction exposure does exist, the firm faces three major tasks. First, it must identify the degree of transaction exposure. Second, it must decide whether to hedge this exposure. Finally, if it decides to hedge part or all of the exposure, it must choose among the various hedging techniques available. Each of these tasks is discussed in turn.

Identifying Net Transaction Exposure

Before the MNC makes any decisions related to hedging, it should identify the individual **net transaction exposure** on a currency-by-currency basis. The term "net" here refers to the consolidation of all expected inflows and outflows for a particular time and currency. The management at each subsidiary plays a vital role in the process of reporting its expected inflows and outflows. Then a centralized group consolidates subsidiary reports in order to identify, for the MNC as a whole, the expected net positions in each foreign currency during several upcoming periods. The MNC can identify its exposure by reviewing this consolidation of subsidiary positions. For example, one subsidiary may have net receivables in Mexican pesos three months from now, while a different subsidiary may have net payables in pesos. If the peso appreciates, this will be favorable to the first subsidiary and unfavorable to the second subsidiary. However, the impact on the MNC as a whole is at least partially offset. Each subsidiary may desire to hedge its net currency position in order to avoid the possible adverse impacts on its performance due to fluctuation in the currency's value. However, the overall performance of the MNC could already be insulated by the offsetting positions between subsidiaries. Therefore, hedging the position of each individual subsidiary may not be necessary.

Examples. As an example of centralization used to measure net transaction exposure, consider Eastman Kodak Company's centralized currency management approach. Kodak bills subsidiaries in their local currencies. The rationale for a change in strategies was to shift the foreign exchange exposure from subsidiaries to the parent company. Because the parent was reorganized to concentrate its resources and expert personnel, it centralized the currency exposure management. The parent now receives foreign currencies from its subsidiaries overseas and converts them to U.S. dollars. It can maintain the currencies as foreign deposits if it believes such currencies will strengthen against the U.S. dollar in the near future.

Another example is Borg-Warner Corporation, which has set up a central clearinghouse system that also reflects a centralized management approach. Thus, its assessment and management of currency exposure is conducted on the entire portfolio of all subsidiaries, rather than on each subsidiary individually.

Fiat, the Italian auto manufacturer, implemented such a system to monitor 421 subsidiaries dispersed among 55 countries. A key to its success is a comprehensive reporting system that keeps track of its aggregate cash flows in each currency. The net inflow or outflow position for each currency can then be assessed as to whether and how the position should be balanced out.

At the beginning of 1998, DuPont Corporation used a centralized approach to determine that it had the equivalent of about $2 billion in anticipated British pound inflows and the equivalent of about $1 billion in anticipated British pound outflows, resulting in a net position of $1 billion in pound inflows. Consequently, it used hedging techniques to hedge almost all of its net exposure in pounds.

These examples support the centralized approach to hedging, in which net transaction exposure in each currency must be identified. Then, the MNC must decide whether to hedge these positions.

Adjusting the Invoice Policy to Manage Exposure

In some circumstances, the U.S. firm may be able to modify its pricing policy to hedge against transaction exposure. That is, the firm may be able to invoice (price) its exports in the same currency that will be needed to pay for imports. For example, assume the firm has continual payables in Mexican pesos, perhaps because a Mexican exporter sends goods to the U.S. firm under the condition that the goods be invoiced in Mexican pesos. Consequently, the U.S. firm is now exposed to fluctuations in the value of the peso. Assume the U.S. firm exports products (invoiced in U.S. dollars) to other corporations in Mexico. It could modify its invoicing policy from U.S. dollars to pesos in order to match its future payables in pesos. In this way, the peso receivables from these exports can be used to pay off the U.S. firm's future payables in pesos.

It would be difficult, if not impossible, to (1) invoice the precise amount for exports in pesos in order to exactly match the peso payables and (2) perfectly match the timing of inflows and outflows. Because the matching of inflows and outflows in foreign currencies does have its limitations, it will not completely hedge all of the firm's exposed positions in foreign currencies. Therefore, hedging techniques deserve consideration.

Techniques to Eliminate Transaction Exposure

If the MNC decides to hedge part or all of its transaction exposure, it may select from the following hedging techniques:

- Futures hedge
- Forward hedge
- Money market hedge
- Currency option hedge

MNCs will normally compare the cash flow that would be expected from each hedging technique before determining which technique to apply. The selection of the proper hedging technique can vary over time, as the relative advantages of each technique may change over time. Each of these hedging techniques is discussed in turn, with examples provided. After all techniques have been discussed, a comprehensive example illustrates how all the techniques can be compared to determine the appropriate technique to hedge a particular position.

Futures Hedge

Currency futures can be used by firms that desire to hedge transaction exposure. A futures contract hedge is very similar to that of a forward contract (to be discussed shortly), except that forward contracts are common for large transactions, whereas futures contracts may be more appropriate for firms that prefer to hedge in smaller amounts. Also, futures contracts represent a standardized number of units for each currency.

A firm that buys a currency futures contract is entitled to receive a specified amount in a specified currency for a stated price on a specified date. To hedge payment on future payables in a foreign currency, the firm may desire to purchase a currency futures contract representing the currency it will need in the near future. By holding this contract, it locks in the amount of its home currency needed to make payment on the payables.

Although currency futures can reduce the firm's transaction exposure, they sometimes backfire on the firm. If the firm is hedging payables, the locked-in futures price for the currency could end up being higher than the future spot rate of the currency (if the currency depreciates over time). If the firm expected the currency's value to depreciate by the time it would need to make payment, it would not purchase a currency futures contract.

A firm that sells a currency futures contract is entitled to sell a specified amount in a specified currency for a stated price on a specified date. To hedge the home currency value of future receivables in a foreign currency, the firm may desire to sell a currency futures contract representing the currency it will be receiving. Therefore, the firm knows how much of its home currency it will receive after converting the foreign currency receivables into its home currency. By locking in the exchange rate at which it will be able to exchange the foreign currency for its home currency, the firm insulates the value of its future receivables from the fluctuations in the foreign currency's spot rate over time.

As with the purchase of currency futures, a sale of currency futures can backfire. In our example in which the firm is hedging future receivables, the locked-in currency futures price at which the firm will sell the foreign currency may end up being lower than the spot rate of the currency (if the foreign currency appreciates over time). Nonetheless, due to the uncertainty of future currency values, the firm may be more comfortable hedging than remaining exposed to exchange rate fluctuations.

Forward Hedge

Forward contracts are commonly used by large corporations that desire to hedge. To recognize the uses of forward contracts, consider the following quotes by U.S.-based MNCs:

> Outstanding foreign currency forward contracts used as a means of offsetting earnings fluctuations from anticipated foreign currency cash flows totaled $182 million. . . . [Union Carbide]

> The Company enters into forward currency exchange contracts to hedge its equity investments in certain foreign subsidiaries and to manage its exposure against fluctuations in foreign currency rates . . . The Company has entered into forward currency exchange contracts to reduce its exposure to currency fluctuations on the proceeds of its sale of its investment in Asahi Fiber Glass Company, Ltd. . . The Company entered into forward currency exchange contracts to reduce its exposure to currency fluctuations on earnings of certain European subsidiaries. [Owens Corning Co.]

> USX uses forward currency contracts to reduce exposure to currency price fluctuations when transactions require settlement in a foreign currency. . . . [USX Corporation]

To use the forward contract hedge, the MNC purchases that currency denominating the payables forward. For example, if a U.S.-based MNC must pay a Singapore supplier 1,000,000 Singapore dollars (S$) in 30 days, it can request from a bank a forward contract to accommodate this future payment. The bank agrees to provide the Singapore dollars to the MNC in 30 days in exchange for U.S. dollars. The forward contract specifies the exchange rate at which the currencies will be exchanged. This exchange rate reflects the so-called 30-day forward rate. The MNC hedges its position by locking in the rate it will pay for S$ in 30 days. Thus, it now knows the number of dollars it will need to exchange for S$.

If the U.S.-based MNC expects receivables in Singapore dollars in 30 days, it would like to lock in the rate at which it can sell these dollars for U.S. dollars. In this case, a request for a forward sale of Singapore dollars is appropriate. Many MNCs commonly implement the forward hedging technique. For example, DuPont Company often has the equivalent of $300 million to $500 million in forward contracts at any one time, to cover open currency positions.

Forward and futures contracts are available to hedge positions in Mexican pesos. This is important to U.S. firms that have receivables in pesos from their businesses in Mexico, since the peso frequently depreciates against the U.S. dollar. However, the forward rate (and the futures rate) would contain a substantial discount, because Mexico's interest rate is normally much higher than the U.S. interest rate. For interest rate parity to exist (which prevents any arbitrage opportunities), the forward rate on pesos must contain a large discount whenever Mexico's interest rate is much higher than the U.S. interest rate.

Forward Hedge Versus No Hedge on Payables. The decision as to whether to hedge a position with a forward contract or to keep it unhedged can be made by comparing the known result of hedging to the possible results of remaining unhedged. To illustrate, assume that a U.S. firm will need £100,000 in 90 days to pay for British imports. Assume that today's 90-day forward rate of the British pound is $1.40. To assess the future value of the British pound, the firm may develop a probability distribution, as shown in Exhibit 11.1. This is graphically illustrated in Exhibit 11.2, which breaks down the probability distribution. Both exhibits can be used to determine the probability that a forward hedge will be more costly than no hedge. This is achieved by estimating the **real cost of hedging** payables (RCH_p). The real cost of hedging measures the additional expenses beyond those incurred without hedging. The term "real" here does not mean "inflation-adjusted." The real cost of hedging payables is measured as

$$RCH_p = NCH_p - NC_p$$

where

NCH_p = nominal cost of hedging payables
NC_p = nominal cost of payables without hedging

When the real cost of hedging is negative, this implies that hedging is more favorable than not hedging. The RCH_p is estimated for each scenario in Column 5 of Exhibit 11.1. While NCH_p is certain, NC_p is uncertain, causing RCH_p to be uncertain.

While the firm doesn't know RCH_p in advance, it can at least use the information in Exhibits 11.1 and 11.2 to decide whether a hedge is feasible. First, it could estimate the expected value of the RCH_p. This expected value is determined by

$$\text{Expected value of } RCH_p = \Sigma\, P_i RCH_i$$

Exhibit 11.1
Feasibility Analysis for Hedging

Possible Spot Rate of £ in 90 Days	Probability	Nominal Cost of Hedging £100,000	Amount in $ Needed to Buy £100,000 If Firm Remains Unhedged	Real Cost of Hedging £100,000
$1.30	5%	$140,000	$1.30 × 100,000 = $130,000	$10,000
$1.32	10	$140,000	$1.32 × 100,000 = $132,000	$ 8,000
$1.34	15	$140,000	$1.34 × 100,000 = $134,000	$ 6,000
$1.36	20	$140,000	$1.36 × 100,000 = $136,000	$ 4,000
$1.38	20	$140,000	$1.38 × 100,000 = $138,000	$ 2,000
$1.40	15	$140,000	$1.40 × 100,000 = $140,000	$ 0
$1.42	10	$140,000	$1.42 × 100,000 = $142,000	–$ 2,000
$1.45	5	$140,000	$1.45 × 100,000 = $145,000	–$ 5,000

where P_i represents the probability that the ith outcome will occur. In our example, the expected value of the RCH_p can be computed as

$$\begin{aligned} E(RCH_p) &= \Sigma P_i RCH_i \\ &= 5\%(10{,}000) + 10\%(8{,}000) + 15\%(6{,}000) \\ &\quad + 20\%(4{,}000) + 20\%(2{,}000) + 15\%(0) \\ &\quad + 10\%(-2{,}000) + 5\%(-5{,}000) \\ &= \$500 + \$800 + \$900 \\ &\quad + \$800 + \$400 + 0 \\ &\quad - \$200 - \$250 \\ &= \$2{,}950 \end{aligned}$$

While this expected value is useful in assessing RCH_p, it does not clearly indicate the overall probability that hedging will be more costly. Such additional information

Exhibit 11.2
Comparison of Costs of Hedging versus No Hedge

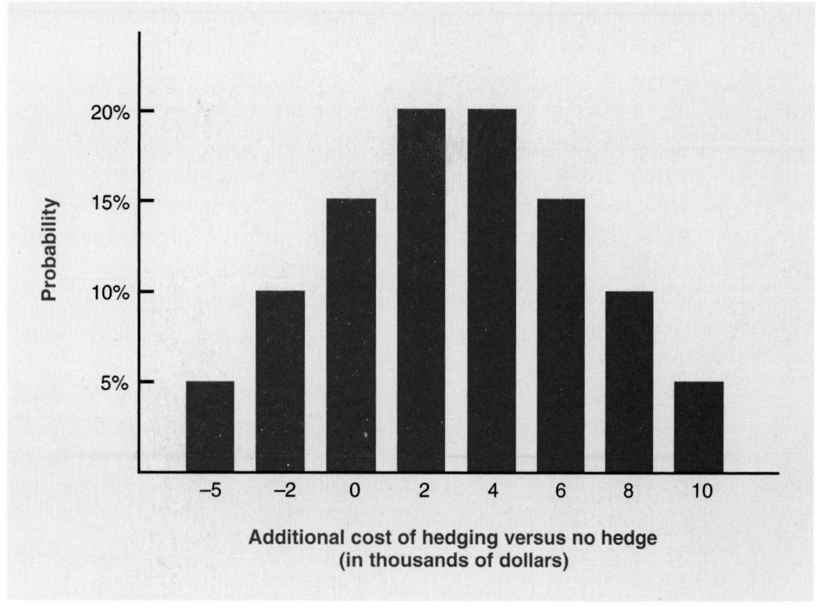

could be determined by reviewing Exhibit 11.1 or 11.2. The data indicate there is a 15-percent chance that the RCH_p will be negative (that the nominal cost of hedging will be lower than remaining unhedged). Some firms may be more comfortable hedging, since this way they will know the exact amount of U.S. dollars needed for future purchases. Other firms may be willing to remain unhedged if the projected unhedged cost will most likely be less than the nominal cost of hedging. In our example, the probability of incurring a lower cost when remaining unhedged is 85 percent. The hedge-versus-no-hedge decision will be based on the firm's degree of risk aversion. Firms with a greater desire to avoid risk would be expected to hedge their open positions in foreign currencies more often than firms that are less concerned with risk.

If the forward rate is an accurate predictor of the future spot rate, the RCH_p will be zero. Because the forward rate often underestimates or overestimates the future spot rate, RCH_p differs from zero. If, however, the forward rate is an unbiased predictor of the future spot rate, RCH_p will be zero on average, as the differences between the forward rate and future spot rate will offset each other over time. If a firm believes that the forward rate is an unbiased predictor of the future spot rate, it will consider hedging its payables, since the forecasted RCH_p is zero, and the transaction exposure can be eliminated.

Forward Hedge Versus No Hedge on Receivables. For firms with exposure in receivables, the real cost of hedging receivables (RCH_r) can be estimated as

$$RCH_r = NR_r - NRH_r$$

where

NR_r = nominal home currency revenues received without hedging
NRH_r = nominal home currency revenues received from hedging

This equation is structured so that the real cost of hedging receivables is positive when hedging results in lower revenue than not hedging. This allows for consistency between RCH_p and RCH_r, since a negative (positive) value of either implies that hedging has had a more (less) favorable result than not hedging.

As with payable positions, firms can determine whether to hedge receivable positions by first developing a probability distribution for the future spot rate and then using it to develop a probability distribution of RCH_r. If the RCH_r was likely to be negative, hedging would be preferred. If the RCH_r was likely to be positive, the firm would need to evaluate whether the potential benefits from remaining unhedged were worth the risk. If the forward rate was believed to be an unbiased predictor of the future spot rate, firms would consider hedging their receivables positions at an expected real cost of zero (ignoring transaction costs).

The *RCH* has been defined here in terms of the MNC's home currency (U.S. dollars, in our example). It can also be expressed as a percentage of the nominal hedged amount. This may be a useful measurement when comparing the *RCH* for various currencies. For example, if a U.S. firm was hedging various currencies in different amounts, a comparison of the dollar amount of *RCH* among currencies would be distorted by the dollar amount of payables or receivables hedged. For this reason, *RCH*s for each currency should be measured as a percentage of their respective hedged amounts if they are to be compared.

The *RCH* cannot be determined until the payables or receivables period is over. Firms should be pleased when they hedge if the *RCH* turns out to be very low, and especially pleased if it is negative. Conservative firms, however, may feel hedging is worthwhile even if the *RCH* turns out to be high.

The real cost of hedging British pounds over time (from a U.S. firm's perspective) is displayed in Exhibit 11.3. The top graph shows the real cost of hedging payables, while the lower graph shows the real cost of hedging receivables. Ninety-day periods were used to measure the real costs of hedging. The costs were measured on a per-unit basis. The real cost of hedging pound payables (shown in the top graph of Exhibit 11.3) was high in the early 1980s, since the pound was weakening over this period. Thus, the existing spot rate at the time payables were due was typically below the forward rate available at the beginning of each corresponding 90-day period. The real cost of hedging pound payables was commonly negative in the late 1970s, late 1980s, and early 1990s, since the pound was strengthening over these periods. In the mid- and late 1990s, the real cost of hedging was closer to zero, as the pound's value was not as volatile over that period.

The real cost of hedging receivables is shown in the bottom graph of Exhibit 11.3. Since transaction costs were ignored when measuring the real costs of hedging in Exhibit 11.3, the real cost of hedging receivables is the exact opposite of the real cost of hedging payables.

Money Market Hedge

A **money market hedge** involves taking a money market position to cover a future payables or receivables position. The money market hedge on payables will be discussed separately from the hedge on receivables.

Money Market Hedge on Payables. First, a simplified money market hedge, in which the firm has excess cash, will be illustrated. Then, a second example will show how a firm can use a money market hedge to hedge payables, even if it does not have excess cash.

If a firm has excess cash, it can create a short-term deposit in the foreign currency that it will need in the future. For example, if a U.S. firm needs NZ$1,000,000 in 30 days and it can earn 6 percent annualized (.5 percent for 30 days) on a New Zealand security over this period, the amount needed to purchase a New Zealand one-month security is

$$\text{Deposit amount to hedge NZ\$ payables} = \frac{\text{NZ\$1,000,000}}{1+.005}$$
$$= \text{NZ\$995,025}$$

Assuming that the New Zealand dollar's spot rate is $.65, then $646,766 is needed to purchase the New Zealand securities (computed as NZ$995,025 × $.65). In 30 days, the security will mature and provide NZ$1,000,000 to the U.S. firm, which can then use this money to cover its payables. Regardless of how the New Zealand dollar exchange rate changes over this period, the U.S. firm's New Zealand investment will be able to cover the payables position.

In many cases, firms would prefer to hedge payables without using their cash balances. A money market hedge can still be used in this situation, but it requires two money market positions: (1) borrowed funds in the home currency and (2) a short-term investment in the foreign currency. To illustrate, reconsider the previous exam-

Exhibit 11.3
Real Cost of Hedging British Pounds Over Time

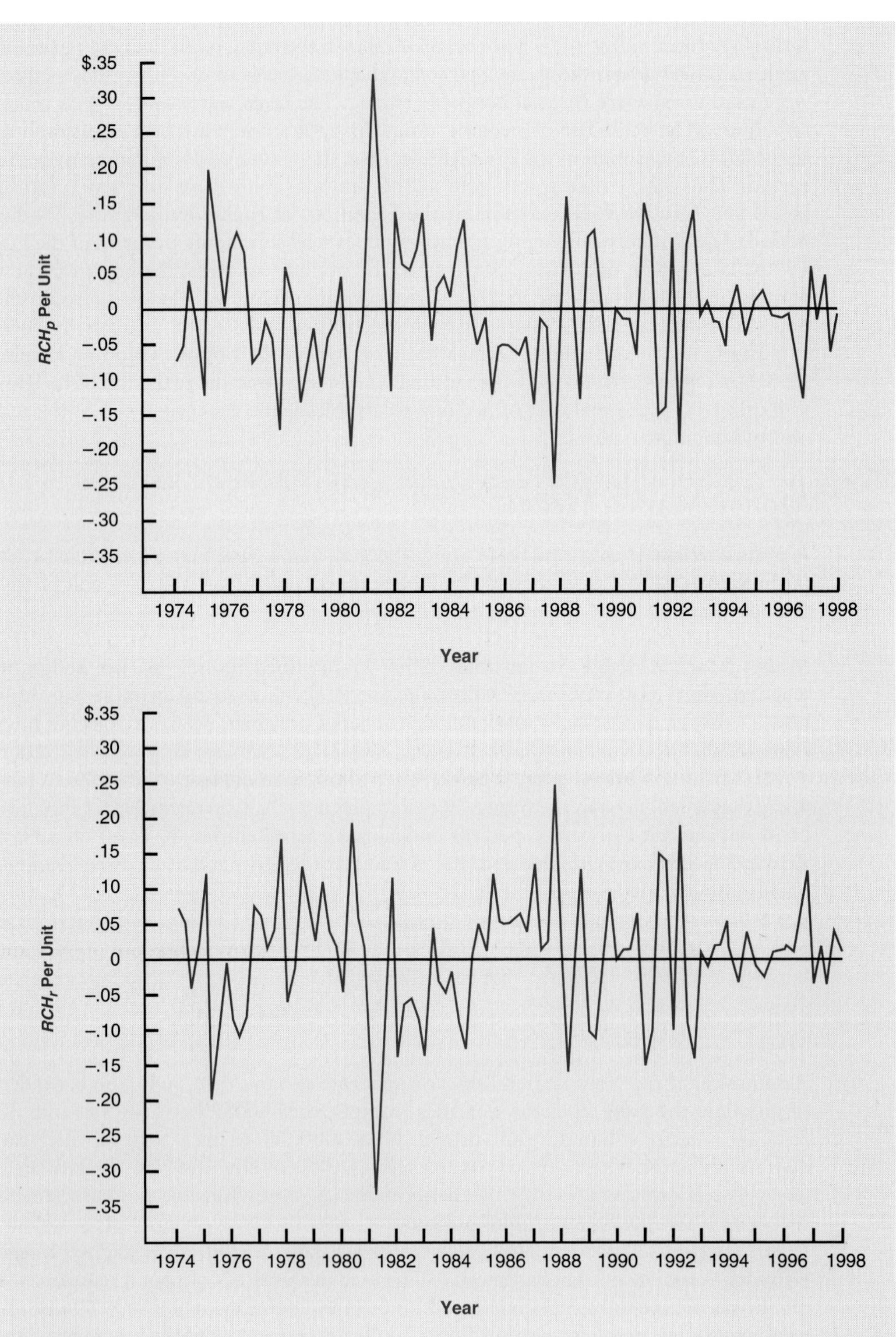

ple, in which NZ$1,000,000 is needed in 30 days. Recall that $646,766 is needed to obtain the investment of NZ$995,025, which in turn will accumulate to the NZ$1,000,000 needed in 30 days. If the U.S. firm has no excess cash, it can borrow $646,766 from a U.S. bank and exchange those dollars for New Zealand dollars in order to purchase the New Zealand security.

Because the New Zealand investment will cover the future payables position, the U.S. firm needs to be concerned only about the dollars owed back on the loan in 30 days. The firm's money market hedge used to hedge payables can be summarized as follows:

Step 1. Borrow $646,766 from a U.S. bank; assume a .7-percent interest rate over the 30-day loan period.

Step 2. Convert the $646,766 to NZ$995,025, given the exchange rate of $.65 per NZ$.

Step 3. Use the NZ$ to purchase a New Zealand security that offers .5 percent over one month.

Step 4. Repay the U.S. loan in 30 days, plus interest; the amount owed is $651,293 (computed as $646,766 × 1.007).

Consider a U.S. firm that plans to implement either a forward contract hedge or a money market hedge to cover its future payables. Which of these two hedging techniques would be most appropriate for the MNC? The answer can be determined by comparing the payment dictated by the forward contract to the loan repayment made on borrowed funds when using the money market hedge. The forward hedge and the money market hedge are directly comparable as long as the firm's cash balances are not used in the money market hedge. Thus, a firm can determine which hedge is preferable before implementing a hedge. Of course, it cannot determine whether either hedge will outperform an unhedged strategy until the period of concern has elapsed.

Money Market Hedge on Receivables. Consider a U.S. firm that transported goods to Singapore and expects to receive S$400,000 in 90 days. A simplified money market hedge could be implemented if the firm needed to borrow U.S. funds for 90 days anyway. Instead of borrowing U.S. dollars, it could borrow Singapore dollars and convert them into U.S. dollars for use. Assuming an annualized interest rate of 8 percent, or 2 percent over the 90-day period, the amount of Singapore dollars to be borrowed to hedge the future receivables would be

$$\text{Borrowed amount to hedge S\\$ receivables} = \frac{\text{S\\$400,000}}{1+.02} = \text{S\\$392,157}$$

If the firm borrows S$392,157 and converts those Singapore dollars to U.S. dollars, then the receivables can be used to pay off the Singapore-dollar loan in 90 days. Meanwhile, the proceeds of the loan can be used for whatever purpose the firm desires.

In some cases, the firm may not need to borrow funds for a 90-day period. In these situations, a money market hedge can still be used to hedge receivables if the firm takes two positions in the money markets: (1) borrow the foreign currency representing future receivables and (2) invest in the home currency. To illustrate, reconsider the previous example of S$400,000 in receivables. Even if the U.S. firm does not have a use for the S$392,157 borrowed, it can invest them in a 90-day U.S. security. Assuming that a Singapore dollar is worth $.55, the Singapore dollars borrowed can be converted to $215,686. Assuming an annualized U.S. interest rate of 7.2 percent (1.8 percent over 90 days) on 90-day securities, the U.S. investment will be worth $219,568 (computed as $215,686 × 1.018) in 90 days. Since the receivables can cover the existing loan, the firm will have $219,568 as a result of enacting the money market hedge.

The results of the money market hedge in this example can be compared to the results of a forward hedge in order to determine which type of hedge is preferable. Since the results of either hedge are known beforehand, the firm can implement the one that is more feasible. As with hedging payables, the firm will not know whether the chosen hedge on receivables will outperform an unhedged strategy until the period of concern has elapsed.

Implications of IRP for the Money Market Hedge. If interest rate parity (IRP) exists, and transaction costs do not exist, the money market hedge will yield the same results as the forward hedge. This is so because the forward premium on the forward rate reflects the interest rate differential between the two currencies. The hedging of future payables with a forward purchase will be similar to borrowing at the home interest rate and investing at the foreign interest rate. The hedging of future receivables with a forward sale will be similar to borrowing at the foreign interest rate and investing at the home interest rate. Even if the forward premium generally reflects the interest rate differential between countries, the existence of transaction costs may cause the results from a forward hedge to differ from those from the money market hedge.

Currency Option Hedge

Firms recognize that hedging techniques such as the forward hedge and money market hedge can backfire when a payables currency depreciates or a receivables currency appreciates over the hedged period. In these situations, an unhedged strategy would likely outperform the forward hedge or money market hedge. The ideal type of hedge would insulate the firm from adverse exchange rate movements but allow the firm to benefit from favorable exchange rate movements. Currency options exhibit these attributes. However, a firm must assess whether the advantages of a currency option hedge are worth the price (premium) paid for it. Details on currency options are provided in Chapter 5. The following discussion illustrates how they can be used in hedging.

http://

See www.futures.com/library/contents.html, the Web site of *Futures* magazine, for coverage of various aspects of derivatives trading such as new products, strategies, and market analyses.

Hedging Payables with Currency Call Options. A currency call option provides the right to buy a specified amount of a particular currency at a specified price (the exercise price) within a given period of time. Yet, unlike a futures or forward contract, the currency call option *does not obligate* its owner to buy the currency at that price. To illustrate, consider a firm that has payables in British pounds. If the spot rate of the pound remains lower than the exercise price throughout the life of the option, the firm that needs pounds could let the option expire and simply purchase them at the existing spot rate. On the other hand, if the spot rate of the pound appreciates over time, the call option allows the firm to purchase pounds at the exercise price. That is, the firm owning a call option has locked in a maximum price (the exercise price) to pay for the currency. It also has the flexibility, though, to let the option expire and obtain the currency at the existing spot rate when the currency is to be sent for payment.

Consider Clemson Corporation, which has payables of £100,000, 90 days from now. Assume there is a call option available with an exercise price of $1.60. Assume that the option premium is $.04 per unit. For options that cover the 100,000 units, the total premium is $4,000 (100,000 × $.04). Clemson doesn't have to exercise its call option if it can obtain pounds at a lower spot rate.

Assume that Clemson expects the spot rate of the pound to be either $1.58, $1.62, or $1.66 when the payables are due. The effect of each of these scenarios on Clemson's cost of payables is shown in Exhibit 11.4. The first two columns simply identify the scenario to be analyzed. The third column shows the premium per unit paid on the option, which is the same regardless of the spot rate that occurs when payables are due. The fourth column shows the amount that Clemson would pay per pound for the payables under each scenario, assuming that it owned call options. If Scenario 1 occurs, Clemson will let the options expire and purchase pounds in the spot market for $1.58 each. If Scenarios 2 or 3 occur, Clemson will exercise the options and therefore purchase pounds for $1.60 per unit, and it will use the pounds to make its payment. The fifth column is the sum of the third and fourth columns, as it determines the amount paid per unit when including the premium paid on the call option. The sixth column converts the fifth column into a total dollar cost, based on the £100,000 hedged.

Hedging Receivables with Currency Put Options. Like the currency call option, the currency put option can also be a valuable hedging device. The currency put option provides the right to sell a specified amount in a particular currency at a specified price (the exercise price) within a given period of time. It could be used by firms to hedge future receivables in foreign currencies, since it guarantees a certain price (the exercise price) at which the future receivables can be sold. The currency put option *does not obligate* its owner to sell the currency at a specified price. If the existing spot rate of the foreign currency is above the exercise price when the firm receives the foreign currency, the firm can sell the currency received at the spot rate and let the put option expire. The application of put options for hedging will now be discussed.

Assume that Knoxville Inc. transported goods to New Zealand and expects to receive NZ$600,000 in about 90 days. If Knoxville is concerned about the possibility

Exhibit 11.4

Use of Currency Call Options for Hedging British Pound Payables (Exercise Price = $1.60; Premium = $.04)

(1)	(2)	(3)	(4)	(5) = (4) + (3)	(6)
Scenario	Spot Rate When Payables Are Due	Premium per Unit Paid on Call Options	Amount Paid per Unit When Owning Call Options	Total Amount Paid per Unit (Including the Premium) When Owning Call Options	$ Amount Paid for £100,000 When Owning Call Options
1	$1.58	$.04	$1.58	$1.62	$162,000
2	1.62	.04	1.60	1.64	164,000
3	1.66	.04	1.60	1.64	164,000

of the New Zealand dollar's depreciation against the U.S. dollar, it could purchase put options to cover its receivables. Assume that the NZ$ put options considered here have an exercise price of $.50 and a premium of $.03 per unit. Also assume that Knoxville anticipates the spot rate in 90 days to be either $.44, $.46, or $.51. The amount to be received as a result of owning currency put options is shown in Exhibit 11.5. Columns 2 through 5 are on a per-unit basis. Column 6 is determined by multiplying the per-unit amount received in Column 5 by 600,000 units.

Comparison of Hedging Techniques

Each of the hedging techniques is briefly summarized in Exhibit 11.6. When using a futures hedge, forward hedge, or money market hedge, the firm can estimate the funds (denominated in its home currency) that it will need for future payables, or the funds it will receive after converting foreign currency receivables. Thus, it can compare the costs or revenue and determine which of these hedging techniques is appropriate. However, the cash flow associated with the currency option hedge cannot be determined with certainty because the costs of purchasing payables and the revenue generated from receivables are not known ahead of time.

Payables Example. To reinforce an understanding of the hedging techniques, a comprehensive example is provided here. Assume that Fresno Corporation will need £200,000 in 180 days. It considers using (1) a forward hedge, (2) a money market hedge, (3) an option hedge, or (4) no hedge. Its analysts develop the following information, which can be used to assess the alternative solutions:

- Spot rate of pound as of today = $1.50
- 180-day forward rate of pound as of today = $1.47

Interest rates are as follows:

	U.K.	U.S.
180-day deposit rate	4.5%	4.5%
180-day borrowing rate	5.0%	5.0%

Exhibit 11.5

Use of Currency Put Options for Hedging New Zealand Dollar Receivables (Exercise Price = $.50; Premium = $.03)

(1)	(2)	(3)	(4)	(5) = (4) − (3)	(6)
Scenario	Spot Rate When Payment on Receivables Is Received	Premium per Unit on Put Options	Amount Received per Unit When Owning Put Options	Net Amount Received per Unit (After Accounting for Premium Paid)	Dollar Amount Received from Hedging NZ$600,000 Receivables With Put Options
1	$.44	$.03	$.50	$.47	$282,000
2	.46	.03	.50	.47	282,000
3	.51	.03	.51	.48	288,000

Exhibit 11.6
Review of Techniques for Hedging Transaction Exposure

Hedging Technique	To Hedge Payables	To Hedge Receivables
1. Futures hedge	Purchase a currency futures contract (or contracts) representing the currency and amount related to the payables.	Sell a currency futures contract (or contracts) representing the currency and amount related to the receivables.
2. Forward hedge	Negotiate a forward contract to purchase the amount of foreign currency needed to cover the payables.	Negotiate a forward contract to sell the amount of foreign currency that will be received as a result of the receivables.
3. Money market hedge	Borrow local currency and convert to currency denominating payables. Invest these funds until they are needed to cover the payables.	Borrow the currency denominating the receivables, convert it to the local currency, and invest it. Then pay off the loan with cash inflows from the receivables.
4. Currency option hedge	Purchase a currency call option (or options) representing the currency and amount related to the payables.	Purchase a currency put option (or options) representing the currency and amount related to the receivables.

- A call option on pounds that expires in 180 days has an exercise price of \$1.48 and a premium of \$.03.
- A put option on pounds that expires in 180 days has an exercise price of \$1.49 and a premium of \$.02.
- Fresno Corporation forecasted the future spot rate in 180 days as follows:

Possible Outcome	Probability
\$1.43	20%
1.46	70
1.52	10

Each alternative solution to the existing problem is assessed in Exhibit 11.7. Now these solutions will be compared to determine the best one.

Each of the alternative solutions has been analyzed to estimate the nominal dollar cost of paying for the payables denominated in pounds. The cost is known with certainty for the forward rate hedge and money market hedge. However, the cost when either using the call option or remaining unhedged is dependent on the spot rate 180 days from now. The costs of the four alternatives are also compared with the use of probability distributions, as shown in Exhibit 11.8. A review of this exhibit shows that the forward hedge is superior to the money market hedge, since the dollar cost is definitely less. A comparison of the forward hedge to the call option hedge shows that there is an 80-percent chance that the call option hedge will be more expensive. Thus, the forward hedge appears to be the optimal hedge.

The probability distribution of outcomes for the no-hedge strategy appears to be more favorable than that for the forward hedge. Fresno Corporation is likely to perform best if it remains unhedged, but it should choose the forward hedge if it prefers to hedge. If Fresno does not hedge, it should periodically reassess the hedging deci-

Exhibit 11.7
Comparison of Hedging Alternatives for Fresno Corporation

Forward Hedge
Purchase pounds 180 days forward.

$$\text{Dollars needed in 180 days} = \text{Payables in £} \times \text{Forward rate of £}$$
$$= £200{,}000 \times \$1.47$$
$$= \$294{,}000$$

Money Market Hedge
Borrow \$, Convert to £, Invest £, Repay \$ loan in 180 days.

$$\text{Amount in £ to be invested} = \frac{£200{,}000}{(1 + .045)}$$
$$= £191{,}388$$

$$\{\text{Amount in \$ needed to convert into £ for deposit}\} = £191{,}388 \times \$1.50$$
$$= \$287{,}082$$

$$\{\text{Interest and principal owed on \$ loan after 180 days}\} = \$287{,}082 \times (1 + .05)$$
$$= \$301{,}436$$

Call Option
Purchase call option (the following computations assume that the option is to be exercised on the day pounds are needed, or not at all. Exercise price = \$1.48, premium = \$.03.)

Possible Spot Rate in 180 days	Premium per Unit Paid for Option	Exercise Option?	Total Price (Including Option Premium) Paid per Unit	Total Price Paid for £200,000	Probability
\$1.43	\$.03	No	\$1.46	\$292,000	20%
1.46	.03	No	1.49	298,000	70
1.52	.03	Yes	1.51	302,000	10

Remain Unhedged
Purchase £200,000 in the spot market 180 days from now.

Future Spot Rate Expected in 180 Days	Dollars Needed to Purchase £200,000	Probability
\$1.43	\$286,000	20%
1.46	292,000	70
1.52	304,000	10

sion. For example, after 60 days it should repeat the analysis shown here, based on the applicable spot rate, forward rate, interest rates, call option information, and forecasts of the spot rate 120 days into the future (when the payables are due).

Receivables Example. A similar analysis of transaction exposure could be conducted if a firm desired to hedge receivables. For example, assume that Gator Corporation

Exhibit 11.8
Nominal Dollar Cost of Pound-Denominated Payables

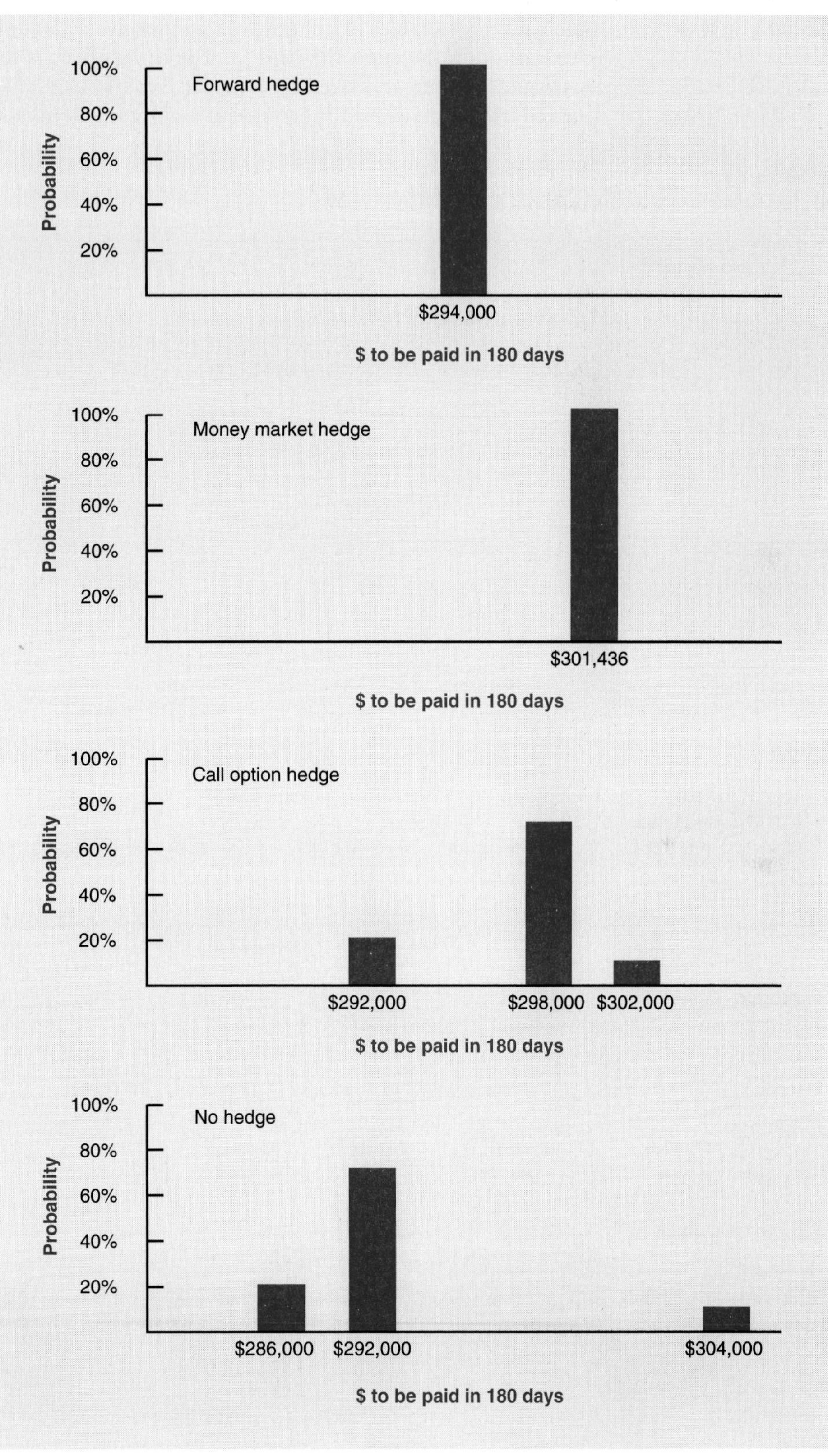

anticipates no payables in pounds, but will receive £300,000 in 180 days. The same information on the spot, forward, and options prices is used to compare hedging techniques and an unhedged strategy in Exhibit 11.9. The dollar amounts to be received from each of the four alternatives are compared in Exhibit 11.10. It appears

Exhibit 11.9
Comparison of Hedging Alternatives for Gator Corporation

Forward Hedge
Sell pounds 180 days forward.

Dollars to be received in 180 days = Receivables in £ × Forward rate of £
= £300,000 × $1.47
= $441,000

Money Market Hedge
Borrow £, convert to $, invest $, use receivables to pay off loan in 180 days.

$$\text{Amount in £ Borrowed} = \frac{£300{,}000}{(1 + .05)}$$
$$= £285{,}714$$

$ received from converting £ = £285,714 × $1.50 per £
= $428,571

$ accumulated after 180 days = $428,571 × (1 + .045)
= $447,857

Put Option Hedge
Purchase put option (assume the options are to be exercised on the day pounds are to be received, or not at all. Exercise price = $1.49; premium = $.02.)

Possible Spot Rate in 180 days	Premium per Unit Paid for Option	Exercise Option?	Total Dollars Received per Unit (After Accounting for the Premium)	Total Dollars Received From Converting £300,000	Probability
$1.43	$.02	Yes	$1.47	$441,000	20%
1.46	.02	Yes	1.47	441,000	70
1.52	.02	No	1.50	450,000	10

Remain Unhedged

Possible Spot Rate in 180 Days	Total Dollars Received From Converting £300,000	Probability
$1.43	$429,000	20%
1.46	438,000	70
1.52	456,000	10

Exhibit 11.10
Dollars Received from Pound-Denominated Receivables

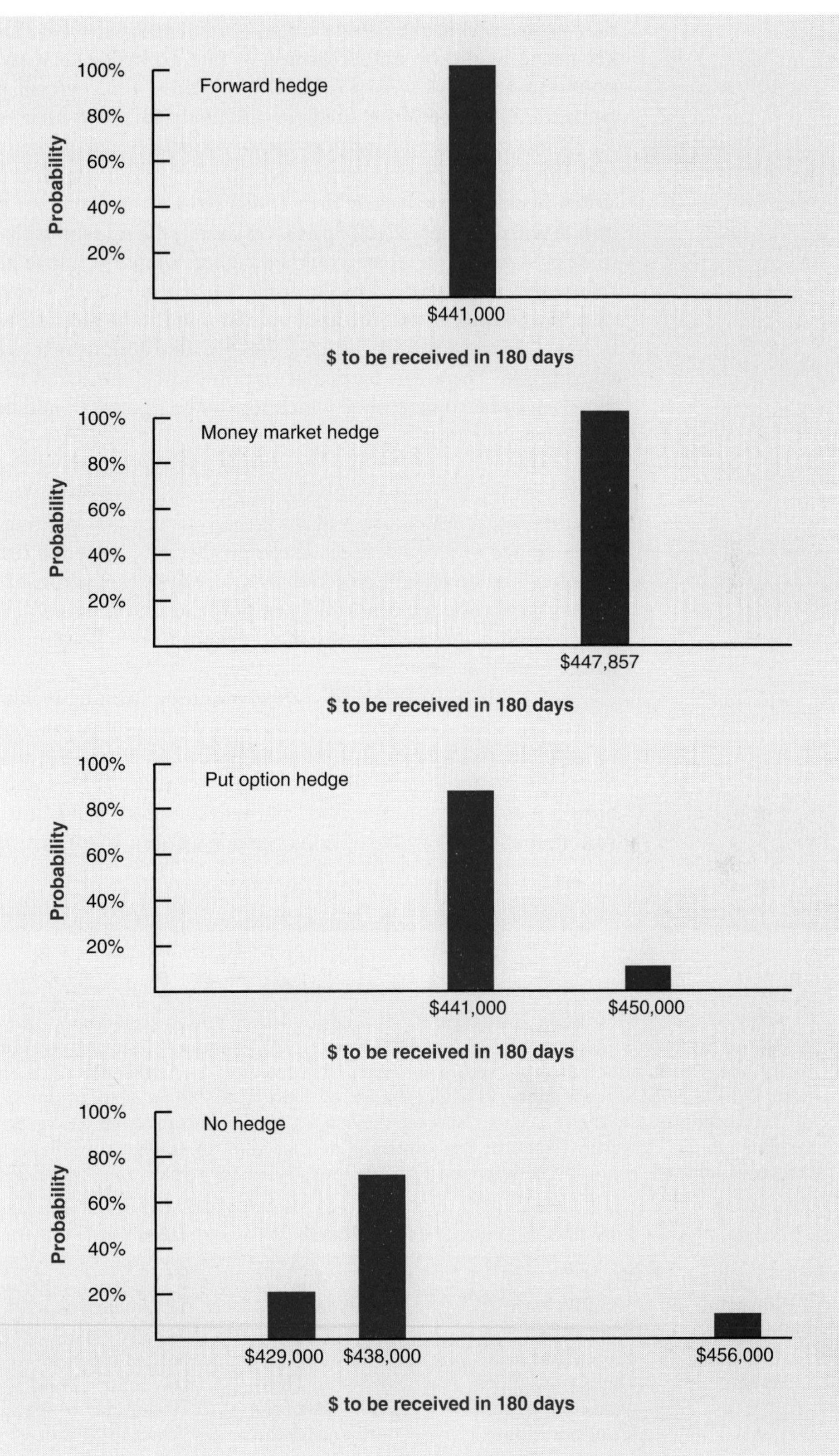

that the money market hedge is the optimal hedge for this example. The money market hedge would be outperformed by the no-hedge strategy if the spot rate of the pound in 180 days were $1.52. There is only a 10-percent probability of that outcome, though. Therefore, the firm will likely decide to hedge its receivables position.

While this example includes the assessment of one particular currency option, several alternative currency options are normally available with different exercise prices. When hedging payables, a firm could reduce the premium paid by choosing a call option with a higher exercise price. Of course, the tradeoff is that the maximum amount to be paid for the payables would be higher. Similarly, a firm hedging receivables could reduce the premium paid by choosing a put option with a lower exercise price. In this case, the tradeoff is that the minimum amount to be received for the receivables would be lower. Firms generally compare the available options first to determine which is most appropriate. Then, this particular option can be compared to the other hedging techniques in order to determine which technique (if any) should be used.

Determining the Optimal Hedge. Most MNCs (including DuPont, W.R. Grace, and IBM) do not use one type of hedging technique exclusively but determine which technique is optimal on a case-by-case basis. The optimal hedging technique is dependent on exchange rate projections. If the projections cause the firm to believe that it will definitely be adversely affected by its transaction exposure, a forward hedge or money market hedge is normally appropriate. Conversely, if the firm believes that it may benefit from its exposure, the currency option hedge is more appropriate (if any hedge is used at all).

As a realistic example of choosing among hedging techniques, consider the case of Merck, with worldwide sales of over $6 billion. It has recently used put options to hedge its receivables denominated in foreign currencies because it did not want to forgo the potential benefits if the dollar weakened. Under this type of scenario, the option would not be exercised, as the receivables would be worth more at the prevailing spot rate. Yet, the options provide insurance just in case the dollar strengthens.

IN PRACTICE

FUTURES CONTRACTS ON EUROS

The Chicago Mercantile Exchange (CME) has developed futures contracts on euros so that MNCs can easily hedge their positions in euros, as summarized here. U.S.-based MNCs commonly consider the use of the futures contract on the euro with respect to the dollar (column 2). However, there are also futures contracts available on cross-rates between the euro and the British pound (column 3), the euro and the Japanese yen (column 4), and (3) the euro and the Swiss franc (column 5). Settlement dates on all of these contracts are available on March, June, September, and December. The futures contracts on cross-rates allow for easy hedging by foreign subsidiaries that wish to exchange euros for widely used currencies other than the dollar.

	Euro/U.S. $	Euro/Pound	Euro/Yen	Euro/Swiss franc
Ticker Symbol	EC	RP	RY	RF
Trading Unit	125,000 euros	125,000 euros	125,000 euros	125,000 euros
Quotation	$ per euro	Pounds per euro	Yen per euro	SF per euro
Last Day of Trading	Second Business Day Before Third Wednesday of the Contract Month	Second Business Day Before Third Wednesday of the Contract Month	Second Business Day Before Third Wednesday of the Contract Month	Second Business Day Before Third Wednesday of the Contract Month

Also, recognize that there may be other currency options available with the same expiration date, but different exercise prices. There may also be other types of currency options, such as conditional currency options whose premiums may be conditional on the movement of the spot rate by the time of expiration. Additional hedging techniques such as these could be compared by including them in the analysis that was just illustrated.

LIMITATIONS OF HEDGING

While hedging transaction exposure can be effective, there are some limitations that deserve to be mentioned here.

Limitation of Hedging an Uncertain Amount

Some international transactions involve an uncertain amount of goods ordered and therefore involve an uncertain transaction amount in a foreign currency. In the receivables example, it is assumed that the £300,000 will be received in 180 days. If the receivables amount could actually be as low as £200,000, should the firm still hedge the expected inflow of £300,000? If the firm overhedges, it will have to make up the difference to fulfill the hedging strategy. For example, if it uses the money market hedge to hedge £300,000, and receivables amount to only £200,000, it will have to purchase £100,000 in the spot market to achieve the £300,000 needed to pay off the loan. If the pound appreciates over the 180-day period, the firm will need a large amount in dollars to obtain the £100,000. This example shows how **overhedging** (hedging a larger amount in a currency than the actual transaction amount) can adversely affect a firm.

A solution to avoid overhedging is to hedge only the minimum known amount in the future transaction. In our example, if the future receivables may be as low as £200,000, the firm could hedge this amount. However, under these conditions the firm may not have completely hedged its position. If the actual transaction amount

Nike Problem

Nike's Management of Transaction Exposure

Since Nike conducts business across many countries, it can be exposed to exchange rate movements. It commonly hedges its transaction exposure. In a recent annual report, Nike states that its foreign currency hedging activities are intended to protect itself from the risk that the eventual dollar cash flows resulting from the sale and purchase of products in foreign currencies will be adversely affected by changes in exchange rates. The annual report also states that Nike nets its foreign exchange exposures to capitalize on natural offsets that occur through intracompany transactions and other business transactions. In those cases where there is not a natural offset, it commonly hedges by negotiating forward contracts and currency options contracts with high-quality financial institutions.

Discussion: Since Nike conducts much business in Japan, it is likely to have cash flows in yen that will periodically be remitted by its Japanese subsidiary to the U.S. parent. What are the limitations of hedging these remittances one year in advance over each of the next 20 years? What are the limitations of creating a hedge today that will hedge these remittances over each of the next 20 years?

turns out to be £300,000 as expected, the firm will be only partially hedged and will need to sell the extra £100,000 in the spot market.

This dilemma is very common for firms, since the precise amount in a foreign currency to be received at the end of a period can be uncertain, especially for firms heavily involved in exporting. Based on this example, it should be clear that most MNCs cannot completely hedge all of their transactions. Nevertheless, by hedging a portion of those transactions that affect them, they can reduce the sensitivity of their cash flows to exchange rate movements.

Limitation of Repeated Short-Term Hedging

The continual hedging of repeated transactions that are expected to occur in the near future has limited effectiveness over the long run. To illustrate, consider a U.S. importer that specializes in importing particular Japanese stereos in one large shipment per year and then selling them to retail stores throughout the year. Assume that today's exchange rate of the Japanese yen is \$.005 and that the stereos are worth ¥60,000, or \$300. Further assume that the forward rate of the yen generally exhibits a premium of 2 percent. Exhibit 11.11 shows the dollar/yen exchange rate to be paid by the importer over time. As the spot rate changes, the forward rate will often change by a similar amount. Thus, if the spot rate increases by 10 percent over the year, the forward rate may increase by about the same amount, and the importer will pay 10 percent more for next year's shipment of stereos (assuming no change in the yen price quoted by the Japanese exporter). The use of a one-year forward contract during a strong-yen cycle is preferable to no hedge in this case but will still result in subsequent increases in prices paid by the importer each year. This illustrates that the use of short-term hedging techniques does not completely insulate a firm from exchange rate exposure, even if they are repeatedly used over time.

If the hedging techniques could be applied to longer-term periods, they could more effectively insulate the firm from exchange rate risk over the long run. To illus-

Exhibit 11.11
Illustration of Repeated Hedging of Foreign Payables When the Foreign Currency Is Appreciating

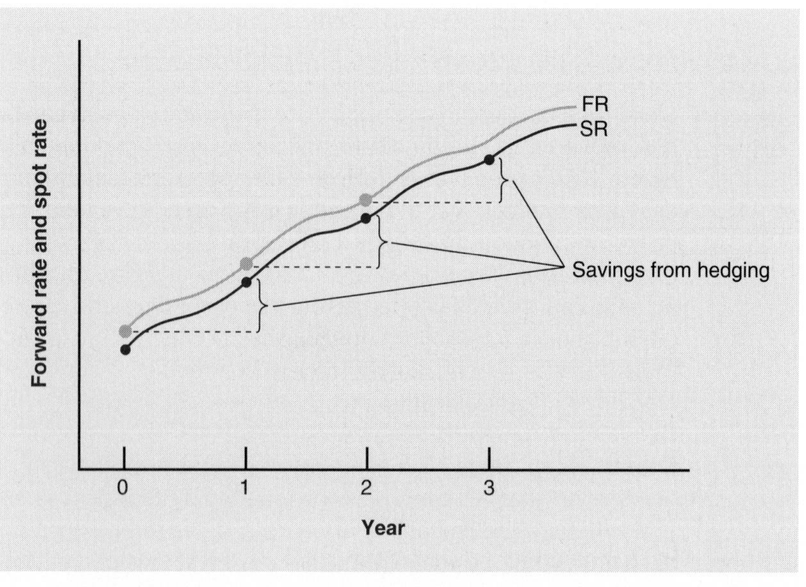

Exhibit 11.12
Long-Term Hedging of Payables When the Foreign Currency Is Appreciating

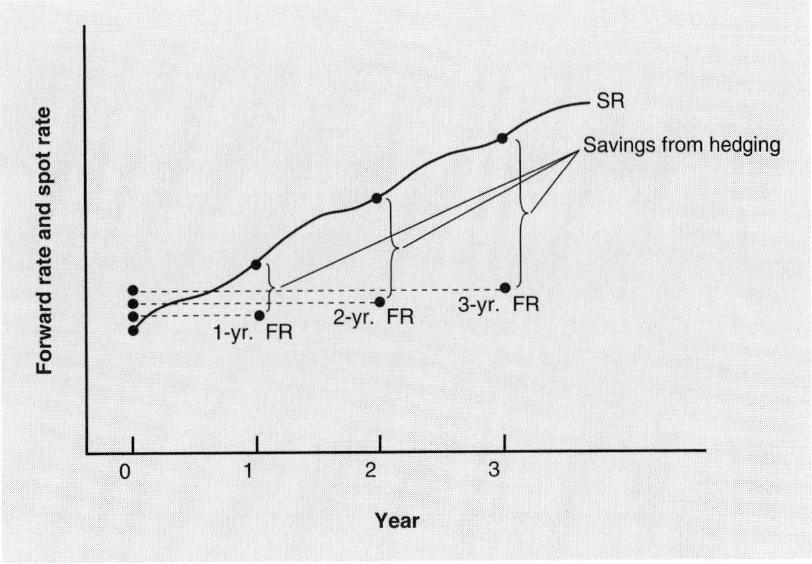

trate, the stereo importer could, as of Time 0, create a hedge for shipments to arrive at the end of each of the next several years. The forward rate for each hedge would be based on the spot rate as of today, as shown in Exhibit 11.12. During a strong-yen cycle, such a strategy would save a substantial amount of money. However, the limitation of this strategy is that the amount in yen to be hedged further into the future is more uncertain, since the shipment size will be dependent on economic conditions or other factors at that time. If a recession occurs, the importer may reduce the number of stereos ordered, but the amount in yen to be received by the importer is dictated by the forward contract that was created. If the stereo manufacturer goes bankrupt, or simply experiences stockouts, the importer is still obligated to purchase the yen, even if a shipment is not forthcoming.

Hedging Long-Term Transaction Exposure

Some MNCs are certain of having cash flows denominated in foreign currencies for several years and attempt to use long-term hedging. For example, Walt Disney Company has hedged its Japanese yen cash flows that would be remitted to the United States (from the Japanese theme park) 20 years ahead. Eastman Kodak Co. and General Electric Co. incorporate foreign exchange management into their long-term corporate planning. Thus, techniques for hedging long-term exchange rate exposure are needed.

For firms that can accurately estimate foreign currency payables or receivables that will occur several years from now, there are three commonly used techniques to hedge such long-term transaction exposure:

- Long-term forward contract
- Currency swap
- Parallel loan

Each technique is discussed in turn.

Long-Term Forward Contract

Until recently, **long-term forward contracts,** or long forwards, were seldom used. Today the long forward is quite popular. Most large international banks will routinely quote forward rates for terms of up to five years for British pounds, Canadian dollars, Japanese yen, and Swiss francs. Long forwards are especially attractive to firms that have set up fixed-price exporting or importing contracts over a long period of time and want to protect their cash flow from exchange rate fluctuations.

Like a short-term forward contract, the long forward can be tailored to accommodate the specific needs of the firm. Maturities of up to 10 years or more can sometimes be set up for the major currencies. Because a bank is trusting that a firm will fulfill its long-term obligation specified in the forward contract, it will consider only very creditworthy customers.

Currency Swap

A **currency swap** is a second technique for hedging long-term transaction exposure to exchange rate fluctuations. It can take many forms. One type of currency swap accommodates two firms that have different long-term needs. Consider a U.S. firm, hired to build an oil pipeline within the U.K., that expects to receive payment in British pounds in five years when the job is completed. At the same time, a British firm is hired by a U.S. bank for a long-term consulting project. Assume that payment to this British firm will be in U.S. dollars and that much of the payment will occur in five years. The U.S. firm will be receiving British pounds in five years and the British firm will be receiving U.S. dollars in five years. These two firms could arrange a currency swap that allows for an exchange of pounds for dollars in five years at some negotiated exchange rate. In this way, the U.S. firm could lock in the number of U.S. dollars the British pound payment will convert to in five years. Likewise, the British firm could lock in the number of British pounds the U.S. dollar payment will convert to in five years.

To create a currency swap, firms rely on financial intermediaries who can accommodate their needs. There are brokers employed by large banks and investment firms that act as intermediaries for swaps. They are notified by those corporations that want to eliminate transaction exposure to specific currencies at certain future dates. Using this information, they can match up firms when one firm needs the currency the other firm wants to dispose of (and vice versa). The brokers receive a fee for their service.

Over time, the currency swap obligation may become undesirable to one of the parties involved. Using our example, if the British pound appreciates substantially over time, the U.S. company that agreed to swap pounds for dollars will be worse off than if it had been able to obtain its dollars in the spot market. Of course, it did not know this when it engaged in a swap agreement. The swap agreement may require periodic payments from one party to the other to account for exchange rate movements, so as to reduce the possibility that one party will not fulfill its obligation by the time the exchange of currencies is supposed to occur.

Parallel Loan

A **parallel loan** (or "back-to-back loan") involves an exchange of currencies between two parties, with a promise to reexchange currencies at a specified exchange rate and future date. It represents two swaps of currencies, one swap at the inception of the loan contract and another swap at the specified future date. A parallel loan is interpreted by accountants as a loan and is therefore recorded on financial statements.

Alternative Hedging Techniques

Sometimes a firm is not able to completely eliminate its transaction exposure. For example, a firm cannot always accurately forecast the sales (representing inflow payments) on products and/or the purchases (representing outflow payments) on supplies denominated in foreign currencies. Thus, it does not know the precise amount to hedge in each foreign currency. In addition, projected costs of the hedging techniques may seem too high to be worthwhile. Finally, there is also the possibility that the currencies a firm is exposed to cannot be hedged, perhaps due to the nonexistence of a forward market or currency options market for such currencies. Even the money market hedge may not be possible if there are barriers to foreign investing or borrowing in the home country of a particular currency. Also, the swap arrangement may be difficult to set up if the currency is not widely traded, since there would not be an active market for swaps in that currency.

When a perfect hedge is not available (or is too expensive) to eliminate transaction exposure, the firm should consider methods to at least reduce exposure. Such methods include

- Leading and lagging
- Cross-hedging
- Currency diversification

Each method is discussed in turn.

Leading and Lagging

The act of leading and lagging represents an adjustment in the timing of payment request or disbursement to reflect expectations about future currency movements. For example, consider a multinational corporation based in the United States that has subsidiaries dispersed around the world. The focus here will be on a subsidiary within the U.K. that purchases some of its supplies from a subsidiary in Hungary. Assume these supplies are denominated in Hungary's currency (the forint). If the British subsidiary expects that the pound will soon depreciate against the forint, it may attempt to accelerate the timing of its payment before the pound depreciates. This strategy is referred to as **leading.**

As a second possibility, consider a scenario in which the British subsidiary expects the pound to appreciate against the forint soon. In this case, the British subsidiary may attempt to stall its payment until after the pound appreciates. In this way it could use fewer pounds to obtain the forint needed for payment. This strategy is referred to as **lagging.** General Electric and other well-known MNCs commonly use leading and lagging strategies in countries that allow them.

Some countries' governments limit the length of time involved on leading and lagging strategies, so that the flow of funds into or out of a country is not disrupted. Consequently, a multinational corporation must be aware of government restrictions of any countries in which it conducts business before using these strategies.

Cross-Hedging

Cross-hedging is a common method of reducing transaction exposure when the currency cannot be hedged. Assume a U.S. firm has payables in Currency X 90 days from now. Because it is worried that Currency X may appreciate against the U.S. dollar, it may desire to hedge this position. If forward contracts and the other hedging techniques are not possible for this currency, the firm may consider cross-hedging, in which case it needs to first identify a currency that can be hedged and is highly correlated with Currency X. It could then set up a 90-day forward contract on this currency. If two currencies are highly correlated relative to the U.S. dollar (that is, they move in a similar direction against the U.S. dollar), then the exchange rate between these two currencies should be somewhat stable over time. When purchasing the one currency 90 days forward, the U.S. firm can then exchange that currency for Currency X. The effectiveness of this strategy depends on the degree to which these two currencies are positively correlated. The stronger the positive correlation, the more effective will be the cross-hedging strategy.

To illustrate a second use of cross-hedging, consider a U.S. firm that has net inflows denominated in Danish kroner and net outflows denominated in Swiss francs. Because these two currencies often move in tandem against the U.S. dollar, a cross-hedge exists. If by chance the krone depreciates, the U.S. firm will obtain fewer dollars when exchanging those kroner received. Of course, the Swiss franc will probably also have depreciated (though not necessarily by the same degree) against the dollar. Thus, fewer dollars will be needed to obtain francs when sending outflow payments. Regardless of whether these currencies depreciate or appreciate against the U.S. dollar, the U.S. firm in this example will be somewhat insulated from the exchange rate fluctuations if the two currencies are highly positively correlated.

Currency Diversification

A third method for reducing transaction exposure is **currency diversification.** Consider a multinational firm based in the United States that is heavily involved in exporting and importing and has more inflows than outflows in each foreign currency. In this case, the MNC will be hurt by a strong dollar, since the foreign currencies received will not be worth as many dollars. If all the inflows are denominated in one or a few foreign currencies, substantial depreciation of one of these currencies would severely affect the *dollar value* of the firm's inflows. However, substantial depreciation in one foreign currency would not be as damaging if that currency were only one of several to which the firm was exposed. This is so because the single currency would represent only a small portion of total inflows and would therefore not severely affect the dollar value of the total inflows. Some MNCs, such as The Coca-Cola Company, PepsiCo, and Philip Morris, claim that their exposure to exchange rate movements is significantly reduced because they diversify their business among numerous countries.

The dollar value of future inflows in foreign currencies will be more stable if the foreign currencies received are *not* highly positively correlated. The reason is that lower positive correlations or negative correlations can reduce the variability of the dollar value of all foreign currency inflows. If the foreign currencies were highly correlated with each other, diversifying among them would not be a very effective way to reduce risk. If one of the currencies substantially depreciated, the others would do so as well, given that all these currencies move in tandem.

Exhibit 11.13
Impact of Hedging Transaction Exposure on an MNC's Value

Hedging Decisions on Transaction Exposure

$$V = \sum_{t=1}^{n} \left\{ \frac{\sum_{j=1}^{m} \left[E(CF_{j,t}) \times E(ER_{j,t}) \right]}{(1+k)^t} \right\}$$

V = value of the U.S.-based MNC
$E(CF_{j,t})$ = expected cash flows denominated in currency j to be received by the U.S. parent in period t
$E(ER_{j,t})$ = expected exchange rate at which currency j can be converted to dollars at the end of period t
k = the weighted average cost of capital of the U.S. parent
m = number of currencies
n = number of periods

How Transaction Exposure Management Affects an MNC's Value

An MNC's management of transaction exposure can affect its value, as shown in Exhibit 11.13. If the MNC's foreign subsidiaries exchange their local currencies when conducting normal business, their expected foreign currency cash flows are dependent on whether they hedge those transactions or remain unhedged. Whether hedging each transaction results in higher or lower cash flows to those subsidiaries is not known until the transaction occurs.

Regardless of whether the business transactions of the foreign subsidiaries are hedged, the expected dollar value of the foreign currency cash flows remitted by the foreign subsidiaries is dependent on whether those remitted cash flows are hedged. Hedging decisions on remitted funds affect the expected value of the exchange rate at which the funds are converted to dollars and therefore affect the dollar cash flows that are ultimately received by the U.S. parent.

SUMMARY

- MNCs use the following techniques to hedge transaction exposure: (1) futures hedge, (2) forward hedge, (3) money market hedge, and (4) currency options hedge.

- To hedge payables, a futures or forward contract on the foreign currency can be purchased. Alternatively, a money market hedge strategy can be used, in which the MNC borrows its home currency and converts the proceeds into the foreign currency that will be needed in the future. Finally, call options on the foreign currency can be purchased.

  To hedge receivables, a futures or forward contract on the foreign currency can be sold. Alternatively, a money market hedge strategy can be used, in which the MNC borrows the foreign currency to be received and converts the funds into its home currency; the loan is to be repaid by the receivables. Finally, put options on the foreign currency can be purchased.

- Futures contracts and forward contracts normally yield similar results. Forward contracts are more flexible because they are not standardized. The money market hedge yields results similar to those of the forward hedge if interest rate parity exists. The currency options hedge has an advantage over the other hedging techniques in that it does not have to be exercised if the MNC would be better off unhedged. Yet, a premium must be paid to purchase the currency options, as there is a cost for the flexibility they provide.
- When hedging techniques are not available, there are still some methods of reducing transaction exposure, such as leading and lagging, cross-hedging, and currency diversification.

SELF-TEST FOR CHAPTER 11

(Answers are provided in Appendix A at the back of the text.)

1. Montclair Co., a U.S. firm, plans to use a money market hedge to hedge its payment of A$3,000,000 for Australian goods in one year. The U.S. interest rate is 7 percent, while the Australian interest rate is 12 percent. The spot rate of the Australian dollar is $.85, while the one-year forward rate is $.81. Determine the amount of U.S. dollars needed in one year if a money market hedge is used.
2. Using the information in the previous question, would Montclair Co. be better off hedging the payables with a money market hedge or with a forward hedge?
3. Using the information about Montclair from the first question, explain the possible advantage of a currency option hedge over a money market hedge for Montclair Co. What is a possible disadvantage of the currency option hedge?
4. Sanibel Co. purchases British goods (denominated in £) every month. It negotiates a one-month forward contract at the beginning of every month to hedge its payables. Assume the British pound appreciates consistently over the next five years. Will Sanibel be affected? Explain.
5. Using the information from question 4, suggest how Sanibel Co. could more effectively insulate itself from the possible long-term appreciation of the British pound.
6. Hopkins Co. transported goods to Switzerland and will receive SF2,000,000 in three months. It believes the 3-month forward rate will be an accurate forecast of the future spot rate. The 3-month forward rate of the Swiss franc is $.68. A put option is available with an exercise price of $.69 and a premium of $.03. Would Hopkins prefer a put option hedge to no hedge? Explain.

QUESTIONS AND APPLICATIONS

1. Quincy Corporation estimates the following cash flows in 90 days at its subsidiaries as follows:

	Net Position in Each Currency Measured in the Parent's Currency		
Subsidiary	Currency 1	Currency 2	Currency 3
A	+200	−300	−100
B	+100	− 40	− 10
C	−180	+200	− 40

Determine the consolidated net exposure of the MNC to each currency.

2. Assume that Stevens Point Company has net receivables of 100,000 Singapore dollars in 90 days. The spot rate of the S$ is $.50, and the Singapore interest rate is 2 percent over 90 days. Suggest how the U.S. firm could implement a money market hedge. Be precise.
3. Assume that Vermont Company has net payables of 200,000 Mexican pesos in 180 days.

The Mexican interest rate is 7 percent over 180 days, and the spot rate of the peso is $.10. Suggest how the U.S. firm could implement a money market hedge. Be precise.

4. Assume that Citadel Company purchases some goods in Chile that are denominated in Chilean pesos. It also sells goods denominated in U.S. dollars to some firms in Chile. At the end of each month, it has a large net payables position in Chilean pesos. How can this U.S. firm use an invoicing strategy to reduce this transaction exposure? List any limitations on the effectiveness of this strategy.

5. € Explain how a U.S. corporation could hedge net receivables in euros with futures contracts.

6. Explain how a U.S. corporation could hedge net payables in Japanese yen with futures contracts.

7. Explain how a U.S. corporation could hedge net receivables in Malaysian ringgit with a forward contract.

8. Explain how a U.S. corporation could hedge payables in Canadian dollars with a forward contract.

9. Assume that Loras Corporation imported goods from New Zealand and needs 100,000 New Zealand dollars 180 days from now. It is trying to determine whether or not to hedge this position. It has developed the following probability distribution for the New Zealand dollar:

Possible Value of New Zealand Dollar in 180 days	Probability
$.40	5%
.45	10
.48	30
.50	30
.53	20
.55	5

The 180-day forward rate of the New Zealand dollar is $.52. The spot rate of the New Zealand dollar is $.49. Develop a table showing a feasibility analysis for hedging. That is, determine the possible differences between the costs of hedging and those of not hedging. What is the probability that hedging will be more costly to the firm than not hedging?

10. Using the information from question 9, determine the expected value of the additional cost of hedging.

11. If hedging is expected to be more costly than not hedging, why would a firm even consider hedging?

12. Assume that Suffolk Company negotiated a forward contract to purchase 200,000 British pounds in 90 days. The 90-day forward rate was $1.40 per British pound. The pounds to be purchased were to be used to purchase British supplies. On the day the pounds were delivered in accordance with the forward contract, the spot rate of the British pound was $1.44. What was the real cost of hedging the payables for this U.S. firm?

13. Repeat question 12, except assume that the spot rate of the British pound was $1.34 on the day the pounds were delivered in accordance with the forward contract. What was the real cost of hedging the payables in this example?

14. Assume that Bentley Company negotiated a forward contract to sell 100,000 Canadian dollars in one year. The one-year forward rate on the Canadian dollar was $.80. This strategy was designed to hedge receivables in Canadian dollars. On the day the Canadian dollars were to be sold off in accordance with the forward contract, the spot rate of the Canadian dollar was $.83. What was the real cost of hedging receivables for this U.S. firm?

15. Repeat question 14, except assume that the spot rate of the Canadian dollar was $.75 on the day the Canadian dollars were to be sold off in accordance with the forward contract. What was the real cost of hedging receivables in this example?

16. Assume the following information:

90-day U.S. interest rate	4%
90-day Malaysian interest rate	3%
90-day forward rate of Malaysian ringgit	$.400
Spot rate of Malaysian ringgit	$.404

Assume that Santa Barbara Company in the United States will need 300,000 ringgit in 90 days. It wishes to hedge this payables position.

Would it be better off using a forward hedge or a money market hedge? Substantiate your answer with estimated costs for each type of hedge.

17. Assume the following information:

180-day U.S. interest rate	8%
180-day British interest rate	9%
180-day forward rate of British pound	$1.50
Spot rate of British pound	$1.48

Assume that Riverside Corporation from the United States will receive 400,000 pounds in 180 days. Would it be better off using a forward hedge or a money market hedge? Substantiate your answer with estimated revenue for each type of hedge.

18. Why would a firm consider hedging net payables or net receivables with currency options rather than forward contracts? What are the disadvantages of hedging with currency options as opposed to forward contracts?

19. Relate the use of currency options to hedging net payables and receivables. That is, when should currency puts be purchased, and when should currency calls be purchased?

20. € Can an MNC determine whether currency options will be more or less expensive than a forward hedge when considering both hedging techniques to cover net payables in euros? Why or why not?

21. How can a firm hedge long-term currency positions? Elaborate on each method.

22. Under what conditions would an MNC's subsidiary consider use of a "leading" strategy to reduce transaction exposure?

23. Under what conditions would an MNC's subsidiary consider use of a "lagging" strategy to reduce transaction exposure?

24. Explain how cross-hedging can be used by a firm to reduce transaction exposure.

25. Explain how currency diversification can be used by a firm to reduce transaction exposure.

26. a. Assume that Carbondale Company expects to receive S$500,000 in one year. The existing spot rate of the Singapore dollar is $.60. The one-year forward rate of the Singapore dollar is $.62. Carbondale created a probability distribution for the future spot rate in one year as follows:

Future Spot Rate	Probability
$.61	20%
.63	50
.67	30

Assume that one-year put options on S$ are available, with an exercise price of $.63 and a premium of $.04 per unit. One-year call options on S$ are available with an exercise price of $.60 and a premium of $.03 per unit. Assume the following money market rates:

	U.S.	Singapore
Deposit rate	8%	5%
Borrowing rate	9	6

Given this information, determine whether a forward hedge, money market hedge, or currency options hedge would be most appropriate. Then, compare the most appropriate hedge to an unhedged strategy, and decide whether Carbondale should hedge its receivables position.

b. Assume that Baton Rouge Inc. expects to need S$1 million in one year. Using any relevant information in Part A of this question, determine whether a forward hedge, money market hedge, or a currency options hedge would be most appropriate. Then, compare the most appropriate hedge to an unhedged strategy, and decide whether Baton Rouge should hedge its payables position.

27. SMU Corporation has future receivables on NZ$4,000,000 in one year. It must decide whether to use options or a money market hedge to hedge this position. Use any of the following information to make the decision. Verify your answer by determining the estimate (or probability distribution) of dollar revenue to be received in one year for each type of hedge.

Spot rate of NZ$	$.54	
One-year call option	exercise price = $.50; premium = $.07	
One-year put option	exercise price = $.52; premium = $.03	

	U.S.	New Zealand
One-year deposit rate	9%	6%
One-year borrowing rate	11	8

	Rate	Probability
Forecasted spot rate of NZ$	$.50	20%
	.51	50
	.53	30

28. As treasurer of Tucson Corporation (a U.S. exporter to New Zealand), you must decide how to hedge (if at all) future receivables of 250,000 New Zealand dollars 90 days from now. Put options are available for a premium of $.03 per unit and an exercise price of $.49 per NZ$. The forecasted spot rate of the NZ$ in 90 days follows:

Future Spot Rate	Probability
$.44	30%
.40	50
.38	20

Given that you hedge your position with options, create a probability distribution for dollars to be received in 90 days.

29. As treasurer of Tempe Corporation, you are confronted with the following problem. Assume the one-year forward rate of the British pound is $1.59. You plan to receive 1 million pounds in one year. There is a one-year put option available. It has an exercise price of $1.61. The spot rate as of today is $1.62, and the option premium is $.04 per unit. Your forecast of the percentage change in the spot rate was determined from the following regression model:

$$e_t = a_0 + a_1\, DINF_{t-1} + a_2\, DINT_t + \mu$$

where

e_t = percentage change in British pound value over period t

$DINF_{t-1}$ = differential in inflation between the United States and the United Kingdom in period $t-1$

$DINT_t$ = average differential between United States interest rate and British interest rate over period t

a_0, a_1, and a_2 = regression coefficients

μ = error term

The regression model was applied to historical annual data, and the regression coefficients were estimated as follows:

$$a_0 = 0$$
$$a_1 = 1.1$$
$$a_2 = .6$$

Assume last year's inflation rates were 3 percent for the United States and 8 percent for the United Kingdom. Also assume that the interest rate differential ($DINT_t$) is forecasted as follows for this year:

Forecast of $DINT_t$	Probability
1%	40%
2	50
3	10

Using any of the available information, decide whether the treasurer should choose the forward hedge or a put option hedge. Show your work.

30. Would a U.S. firm's real cost of hedging Australian dollar payables every 90 days have been positive, negative, or about zero on average over a period in which the dollar weakened consistently? What does this imply about the forward rate as an unbiased predictor of the future spot rate? Explain.

31. € If interest rate parity exists, would a forward hedge be more favorable, equally favorable, or less favorable than a money market hedge on euro payables? Explain.

32. Would a U.S. firm's real cost of hedging Japanese yen receivables have been positive, negative, or about zero on average over a period in which the dollar weakened consistently? Explain.

33. If you are a U.S. importer of Mexican goods and you believe that today's forward rate of the peso is a very accurate estimate of the future spot rate, do you think Mexican peso call options would be a more appropriate hedge than the forward hedge? Explain.

34. You are an exporter of goods to the United Kingdom, and you believe that today's forward rate of the British pound substantially underestimates the future spot rate. Company policy requires you to hedge your British pound receivables in some way. Would a forward hedge or a put option hedge be more appropriate? Explain.

35. Explain how a Malaysian firm can use the forward market to hedge periodic purchases of U.S. goods denominated in U.S. dollars.

36. Explain how a French firm can use foward contracts to hedge periodic sales of goods sold to the U.S. that are invoiced in dollars.

37. Explain how a British firm can use the forward market to hedge periodic purchases of Japanese goods denominated in yen.

38. Cornell Company purchases computer chips denominated in euros on a monthly basis from a Dutch supplier. To hedge its exchange rate risk, this U.S. firm negotiates a three-month forward contract three months before the next order will arrive. In other words, Cornell is always covered for the next three monthly shipments. Because Cornell consistently hedges in this manner, it is not concerned with exchange rate movements. Is Cornell insulated from exchange rate movements? Explain.

39. Malibu Inc. is a U.S. company that imports British goods. It plans to use call options to hedge payables of £100,000 in 90 days. Three call options are available which have an expiration date 90 days from now. Fill in the number of dollars needed to pay for the payables (including the option premium paid) for each option available under each possible scenario.

Scenario	Spot Rate of Pound 90 Days From Now	Exercise Price = \$1.74; Premium = \$.06	Exercise Price = \$1.76; Premium = \$.05	Exercise Price = \$1.79; Premium = \$.03
1	\$1.65			
2	1.70			
3	1.75			
4	1.80			
5	1.85			

If each of the five scenarios had an equal probability of occurrence, which option would you choose? Explain.

40. Wedco Technology of New Jersey exports plastics products to Europe. Wedco decided to price its exports in dollars. Telematics International, Inc. (of Florida), exports computer network systems to the United Kingdom (denominated in British pounds) and other countries. Telematics decided to use hedging techniques such as forward contracts to hedge its exposure.

    a. Does Wedco's strategy of pricing its materials for European customers in dollars avoid economic exposure? Explain.
    b. Explain why the earnings of Telematics International, Inc., were affected by changes in the value of the pound. Why might Telematics leave its exposure unhedged sometimes?

41. If a U.S. firm exports products (denominated in U.S. dollars) to Asian countries, describe how the Asian crisis could reduce the cash flows of exporters.

42. If a U.S. firm exported products (denominated in U.S. dollars) to Asia, and anticipated the Asian crisis before it began, how could it have insulated itself from any currency effects while still exporting to Asia?

Internet Application

43. The following Web site contains annual reports of many MNCs:

    http://www.reportgallery.com

a. Review the annual report of your choice. Look for any comments in the report that describe the MNC's hedging of transaction exposure. Summarize the MNC's hedging of transaction exposure based on the comments in the annual report.

b. The following Web site provides exchange rate movements against the dollar over recent months:

http://pacific.commerce.ubc.ca/xr/data.html

Based on the exposure of the MNC you assessed in exercise (a), determine whether the exchange rate movements of whatever currency (or currencies) it is exposed to moved in a favorable or unfavorable direction over the last few months.

Running Your Own MNC

Hedging with Forward Contracts

44a. Given your exposure to exchange rate risk, explain how you could use forward contracts to hedge.

b. Explain how you could use currency options to hedge your exposure.

c. Review the currency options quotations for the foreign currency of concern in *The Wall Street Journal,* or from an Internet source, and determine the premium that would be paid to be able to sell the currency at today's spot rate. (If the currency option data are not available for the currency of concern, skip this question.)

Blades, Inc. Case

Management of Transaction Exposure

Blades, Inc. has recently decided to expand its international trade relationship by exporting to the United Kingdom. Jogs Ltd., a British retailer, has committed itself to the annual purchase of 200,000 pairs of "Speedos," Blades' primary product, for a price of £80 per pair. The agreement is to last for two years, at which time it may be renewed by Blades and Jogs.

In addition to this new international trade relationship, Blades continues to export to Thailand. Its primary customer there, a retailer called Entertainment Products, is committed to the purchase of 180,000 pairs of Speedos annually for another two years at a fixed price of 4,594 Thai baht per pair. When the agreement terminates, it may be renewed by Blades and Entertainment Products.

Blades also incurs costs of goods sold denominated in Thai baht. It imports materials sufficient to manufacture 72,000 pairs of Speedos annually from Thailand. These imports are denominated in baht, and the price depends on current market prices for the rubber and plastic components imported.

Under the two export arrangements, Blades sells quarterly amounts of 50,000 and 45,000 pairs of Speedos to Jogs and Entertainment Products, respectively. Payment for these sales is made on the first of January, April, July and October. The annual amounts are spread over quarters in order to avoid excessive inventories for the British and Thai retailers. Similarly, in order to avoid excessive inventories, Blades usually imports materials sufficient to manufacture 18,000 pairs of Speedos quarterly from Thailand. Although payment terms call for payment within sixty days of delivery, Blades generally pays for its Thai imports upon delivery on the first day of each quarter in order to maintain its trade relationships with the Thai suppliers. Blades feels that early payment is beneficial, as other customers of the Thai supplier only pay for their purchases when it is required.

Since Blades is relatively new to international trade, Ben Holt, Blades' chief financial officer (CFO), is concerned with the potential impact of exchange rate fluctuations on Blades' financial performance. Mr. Holt is vaguely familiar with various techniques available to hedge transaction exposure, but he is not certain whether one technique is superior to the others. Mr. Holt would like to know more about the forward, money market, and option hedges and has asked you, a financial analyst of

Blades, to help him identify the hedging technique most appropriate for Blades. Unfortunately, no options are available for Thailand, but British call and put options are available for 31,250 pounds per option.

Ben Holt has gathered and provided you with the following information for Thailand and the United Kingdom:

	Thailand	United Kingdom
Current Spot Rate	$0.0230	$1.50
90-Day Forward Rate	$0.0215	$1.49
Put Option Premium	Not available	$0.020 per unit
Put Option Exercise Price	Not available	$1.47
Call Option Premium	Not available	$0.015 per unit
Call Option Exercise Price	Not available	$1.48
90-Day Borrowing Rate (nonannualized)	4%	2%
90-Day Lending Rate (nonannualized)	3.5%	1.8%

In addition to this information, Ben Holt has informed you that the 90-day borrowing and lending rates in the U.S. are 2.3 percent and 2.1 percent, respectively on a nonannualized basis. He has also identified the following probability distributions for the exchange rates of the British pound and the Thai baht in 90 days:

Probability	Spot Rate for the British Pound in 90 Days	Spot Rate for the Thai Baht in 90 Days
5%	$1.45	$0.0200
20%	$1.47	$0.0213
30%	$1.48	$0.0217
25%	$1.49	$0.0220
15%	$1.50	$0.0230
5%	$1.52	$0.0235

Blades' next sales to and purchases from Thailand will occur one quarter from now. If Blades decides to hedge, Ben Holt will want to hedge the entire amount subject to exchange rate fluctuations, even if it requires overhedging (i.e., hedging more than the needed amount). Currently, Ben Holt expects the imported components from Thailand to cost approximately 3,000 baht per pair of Speedos. Ben Holt has asked you to answer the following questions for him:

1. Using a spreadsheet, compare the hedging alternatives for the Thai baht with a scenario under which Blades remains unhedged. Do you think Blades should hedge or remain unhedged? If Blades should hedge, which hedge is most appropriate for Blades?
2. Using a spreadsheet, compare the hedging alternatives for the British pound receivables with a scenario under which Blades remains unhedged. Do you think Blades should hedge or remain unhedged? Which hedge is the most appropriate for Blades?
3. In general, do you think it is easier for Blades to hedge its inflows or its outflows denominated in foreign currencies? Why?
4. Would any of the hedges you compared in question 2 for the British pounds to be received in 90 days require Blades to overhedge? Given Blades' exporting arrangements, do you think it is subject to overhedging with a money market hedge?
5. Could Blades modify the timing of the Thai imports in order to reduce its transaction exposure? What is the tradeoff of such a modification?
6. Could Blades modify its payment practices for the Thai imports in order to reduce its transaction exposure? What is the tradeoff of such a modification?
7. Given Blades' exporting agreements, are there any long-term hedging techniques Blades could benefit from? For this question only, assume that Blades incurs all of its costs in the United States.

Small Business Dilemma

Hedging Decisions by the Sports Exports Company

Jim Logan, owner of the Sports Exports Company, will be receiving about 10,000 British pounds about one month from now as payment for exports produced and sent by his firm. Jim is concerned about his exposure because he expects that there are two possible scenarios: (1) the pound will depreciate by 3 percent over the next month or (2) the pound will appreciate by 2 percent over the next month. There is a 70-percent chance that Scenario 1 will occur. There is a 30-percent chance that Scenario 2 will occur.

Jim notices that the prevailing spot rate of the pound is $1.65, and the one-month forward rate is about $1.645. Jim can purchase a put option over the counter from a securities firm that has an exercise (strike) price of $1.645, a premium of $.025, and an expiration date of one month from now.

1. Determine the amount of dollars received by the Sports Exports Company if the receivables to be received in one month are not hedged, under each of the two exchange rate scenarios.
2. Determine the amount of dollars received by the Sports Exports Company if a put option is used to hedge receivables in one month under each of the two exchange rate scenarios.
3. Determine the amount of dollars received by the Sports Exports Company if a forward hedge is used to hedge receivables in one month under each of the two exchange rate scenarios.

12 Managing Economic Exposure and Translation Exposure

The means by which multinational corporations (MNCs) can manage the exposure of their international transactions to exchange rate movements (referred to as transaction exposure) are described in the previous chapter. However, cash flows of MNCs may still be sensitive to exchange rate movements (economic exposure) even if anticipated international transactions are hedged. Furthermore, the consolidated financial statements of MNCs may still be exposed to exchange rate movements (translation exposure).

The specific objectives of this chapter are to

- explain how an MNC's economic exposure can be hedged, and
- explain how an MNC's translation exposure can be hedged.

In general, it is more difficult to effectively hedge economic or translation exposure than to hedge transaction exposure, for reasons explained in this chapter.

Economic Exposure

From a U.S. firm's perspective, transaction exposure represents only the exchange rate risk when converting net foreign cash inflows to U.S. dollars or when purchasing foreign currencies to send payments. Economic exposure represents any impact of exchange rate fluctuations on a firm's future cash flows. Corporate cash flows can be affected by exchange rate movements in ways not directly associated with foreign transactions. Thus, firms cannot just focus on hedging their foreign currency payables or receivables but must also attempt to determine how all their cash flows will be affected by possible exchange rate movements.

Furthermore, the management of transaction exposure tends to focus only on foreign currency cash flows in an upcoming short-term period (such as the next year). Conversely, the management of economic exposure tends to serve as a long-term solution rather than just a short-term solution, as will be illustrated shortly.

Importance of Managing Economic Exposure

To illustrate the importance of managing economic exposure, consider the case of Laker Airways, a British Airline. Laker generated much of its revenue in British pounds. However, a large proportion of its expenses (such as fuel, oil, and debt payments) were denominated in dollars. As the dollar strengthened in 1981, Laker needed larger amounts in pounds to cover the dollar-denominated expenses.

In January 1981, Laker borrowed $131 million from a group of U.S. and European banks. The debt was denominated in U.S. dollars and therefore required debt repayments in U.S. dollars. By borrowing U.S. dollars in 1981, Laker further increased its degree of economic exposure. As the dollar continued to strengthen, the firm's revenues could not adequately cover its dollar-denominated expenses. Consequently, Laker Airways went bankrupt. It might have avoided bankruptcy if it had reduced its economic exposure, either by reducing its dollar-denominated expenses or by increasing its dollar-denominated revenue.

The importance of managing economic exposure can also be illustrated from the 1997–1998 Asian crisis. Those MNCs from the United States and other countries that exported to Asia and invoiced the products in their own currencies were not subject to transaction exposure from this business. However, when the Asian currencies declined by as much as 80 percent over this period, Asian importers simply could not afford to purchase products denominated in other currencies. Thus, they discontinued orders for foreign imports unless the exporters were willing to accept the Asian currencies as payment. If those MNCs had some of their expenses denominated in the Asian currencies, they could have reduced their economic exposure.

http://

See www.ibm.com as an example of an MNC's Web site. The Web sites of various MNCs make financial statements such as annual reports available that disclose the use of financial derivatives for the purpose of hedging interest rate risk and foreign exchange rate risk.

MNCs typically recognize the importance of managing economic exposure. For example, the section of a recent annual report of IBM identified "the continued adverse effects of a strong dollar on our non-U.S. results" as one of its primary challenges. In addition, a recent annual report by PepsiCo states that:

> The economic impact of currency exchange rates on us is complex because such changes are often linked to variability in real growth, inflation, interest rates, governmental actions, and other factors. These changes, if material, can cause us to adjust our financing and operating strategies.

Assessing Economic Exposure

To illustrate how economic exposure can be managed, reconsider the case of Madison Inc. discussed in Chapter 10. Madison's economic exposure to exchange rate movements can be assessed by determining the sensitivity of expenses and revenue to various possible exchange rate scenarios. The original revenue and expense information from Exhibit 10.9 of Chapter 10 is restated in Exhibit 12.1. The U.S. revenues are assumed to be sensitive to different exchange rate scenarios because of the foreign competition. Canadian sales are expected to be C$4 million, regardless of the exchange rate scenario. Yet, the dollar amount received from these sales will depend on the scenario. The cost of goods sold attributable to U.S. orders is assumed to be $50 million and insensitive to exchange rate movements. The cost of goods sold attributable to Canadian orders is assumed to be C$200 million. The U.S. dollar amount of this cost varies with the exchange rate scenario. The gross profit shown in Exhibit 12.1 is determined by subtracting the total dollar value of cost of goods sold from the total dollar value of sales.

Exhibit 12.1
Original Impact of Exchange Rate Movements on Earnings: Madison Inc. (in Millions)

		C$ = $.75		C$ = $.80		C$ = $.85
Sales:						
(1) U.S.		$300.0		$304.00		$307.00
(2) Canadian	C$4 =	3.0	C$4 =	3.20	C$4 =	3.40
(3) Total		$303.0		$307.20		$310.40
Cost of goods sold:						
(4) U.S.		$ 50.0		$ 50.00		$ 50.00
(5) Canadian	C$200 =	150.0	C$200 =	160.00	C$200 =	170.00
(6) Total		$200.0		$210.00		$220.00
(7) Gross profit		$103.0		$ 97.20		$ 90.40
Operating expenses:						
(8) U.S.: Fixed		$ 30.0		$ 30.00		$ 30.00
(9) U.S.: Variable (10% of total sales)		30.3		30.72		31.04
(10) Total		$ 60.3		$ 60.72		$ 61.04
(11) Earnings before interest and taxes		$ 42.7		$ 36.48		$ 29.36
Interest expense:						
(12) U.S.		$ 3.0		$ 3.00		$ 3.00
(13) Canadian	C$10 =	7.5	C$10 =	8.00	C$10 =	8.50
(14) Total		$ 10.5		$ 11.00		$ 11.50
(15) Earnings before taxes		$ 32.2		$ 25.48		$ 17.86

Operating expenses are separated into fixed and variable categories. The fixed expenses are $30 million per year, while the projected variable expenses are dictated by projected sales. The earnings before interest and taxes are determined by the total U.S.-dollar amount of gross profit minus the total U.S.-dollar amount of operating expenses. The interest owed to U.S. banks is insensitive to the exchange rate scenario. However, the projected amount of dollars needed to pay interest on existing Canadian loans varies with the exchange rate scenario. Earnings before taxes are estimated by subtracting total interest expense from earnings before interest and taxes.

Exhibit 12.1 enables Madison to assess how its income statement items would be affected by different exchange rate movements. A stronger Canadian dollar results in an increase in Madison's U.S. sales and in the dollar revenue earned from Canadian sales. However, it also increases Madison's cost of materials purchased from Canada and its amount in dollars needed to pay interest on loans from Canadian banks. The higher expenses more than offset the higher revenue in the strong Canadian dollar scenario. Thus, the amount of Madison's earnings before taxes is inversely related to the strength of the Canadian dollar.

If the Canadian dollar strengthens consistently over the long run, Madison's cost of goods sold and interest expense likely will rise at a higher rate than U.S.-dollar revenue. Consequently, it may wish to enact some policies to create a more balanced impact of Canadian dollar movements on its revenue and expenses. At the current time, its high exposure to exchange rate movements is due to its expenses being more susceptible than its revenue to the changing value of the Canadian dollar. A policy to either increase Canadian sales or reduce orders of Canadian materials would provide more balance.

How Restructuring Can Reduce Economic Exposure

Madison could create more balance by increasing Canadian sales. It believes that it can achieve Canadian sales of C$20 million if it spends $2 million more on advertising (which is part of its fixed operating expenses). The increased sales will also require an additional expenditure of $10 million on materials from U.S. suppliers. In addition, it plans to reduce its reliance on Canadian suppliers and increase its reliance on U.S. suppliers. This strategy is expected to reduce the cost of goods sold attributable to Canadian suppliers by C$100 million and increase the cost of goods sold attributable to U.S. suppliers by $80 million (not including the $10 million increase resulting from increased sales to the Canadian market). Furthermore, it plans to borrow additional funds in the United States and retire some existing loans from Canadian banks. The result will be an additional interest expense of $4 million to U.S. banks and a reduction of C$5 million owed to Canadian banks. The anticipated impact of these strategies on the projected income statement is shown in Exhibit 12.2. For each of the three exchange rate scenarios, the initial projections are in the left column, while the revised projections (as a result of the proposed strategy) are in the right column.

Each of the revised estimates of the income statement items will be explained. First, the projected total sales increase, in response to intentions of penetrating the Canadian market. Second, the U.S. cost of goods sold is now $90 million higher than before, resulting from a $10 million increase to accommodate increased Canadian sales and an $80 million increase due to the shift from Canadian suppliers to U.S. suppliers. The Canadian cost of goods sold decreases from C$200 million to C$100 million as a result of this shift. The revised fixed operating expenses of $32 million include the increase in advertising expenses necessary to penetrate the Canadian market. The variable operating expenses are revised because of revised estimates for total sales. The interest expenses are revised because of the increased loans from the U.S. banks and reduced loans from Canadian banks.

If Madison increases its Canadian dollar inflows and reduces its Canadian dollar outflows as proposed, its revenue and expenses will be affected by Canadian dollar movements in a somewhat similar manner. Thus, its performance will be less susceptible to movements in the Canadian dollar. Exhibit 12.3 illustrates the sensitivity of Madison's earnings before taxes to the three exchange rate scenarios (derived from Exhibit 12.2). The reduced sensitivity of Madison's proposed restructured operations to exchange rate movements is obvious.

The way a firm restructures its operations to reduce economic exposure to exchange rate risk depends on the form of exposure. For Madison Inc., future expenses are more sensitive than future revenue to the possible values of a foreign currency. Therefore, economic exposure could be reduced by increasing the sensitivity of revenue and reducing the sensitivity of expenses to exchange rate movements. Firms that have a greater level of exchange-rate-sensitive revenue than expenses, however, would reduce economic exposure by decreasing the level of exchange-rate-sensitive revenue or by increasing the level of exchange-rate-sensitive expenses.

Exhibit 12.2

Impact of Possible Exchange Rate Movements on Earnings Under Two Alternative Operational Structures (in Millions)

	Exchange Rate Scenario C$ = $.75				Exchange Rate Scenario C$ = $.80				Exchange Rate Scenario C$ = $.85			
		Original Operational Structure		*Proposed Operational Structure*		Original Operational Structure		*Proposed Operational Structure*		Original Operational Structure		*Proposed Operational Structure*
Sales:												
U.S.		$300.0		$300.00		$304.00		$304		$307.00		$307.00
Canadian	C$4 =	3.0	C$20 =	15.00	C$4 =	3.20	C$20 =	16	C$4 =	3.40	C$20 =	17.00
Total		$303.0		$315.00		$307.20		$320		$310.40		$324.00
Cost of goods sold:												
U.S.		$ 50.0		$140.00		$ 50.00		$140		$ 50.00		$140.00
Canadian	C$200 =	150.0	C$100 =	75.00	C$200 =	160.00	C$100 =	80	C$200 =	170.00	C$100 =	85.00
Total		$200.0		$215.00		$210.00		$220		$220.00		$225.00
Gross profit		$103.0		$100.00		$ 97.20		$100		$ 90.40		$ 99.00
Operating expenses:												
U.S.: Fixed		$ 30.0		$ 32.00		$ 30.00		$ 32		$ 30.00		$ 32.00
U.S.: Variable (10% of total sales)		30.3		31.50		30.72		32		31.04		32.40
Total		$ 60.3		$ 63.50		$ 60.72		$ 64		$ 61.04		$ 64.40
Earnings before interest and taxes		$ 42.7		$ 36.50		$ 36.48		$ 36		$ 29.36		$ 34.60
Interest expense:												
U.S.		$ 3.0		$ 7.00		$ 3.00		$ 7		$ 3.00		$ 7.00
Canadian	C$10 =	7.5	C$5 =	3.75	C$10 =	8.00	C$5 =	4	C$10 =	8.50	C$5 =	4.25
Total		$ 10.5		$ 10.75		$ 11.00		$ 11		$ 11.50		$ 11.25
Earnings before taxes		$ 32.2		$ 25.75		$ 25.48		$ 25		$ 17.86		$ 23.35

Exhibit 12.3
Economic Exposure Based on the Original and Proposed Operating Structures

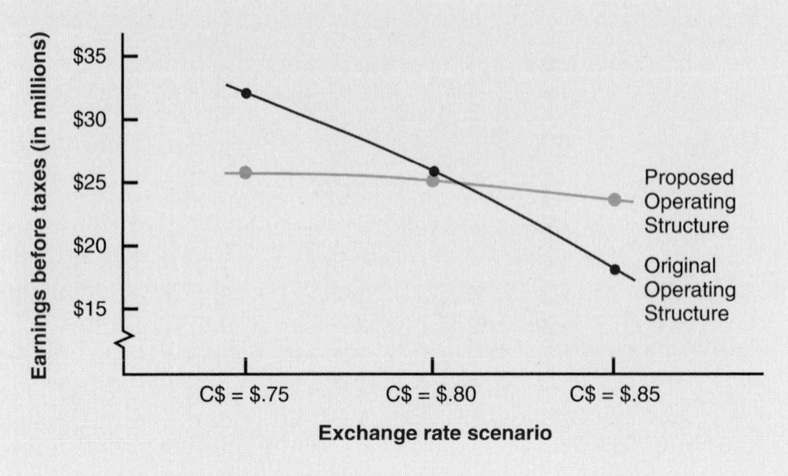

It should be mentioned that some revenue or expenses may be more exchange-rate-sensitive than others. Therefore, simply matching the level of exchange-rate-sensitive revenue to the level of exchange-rate-sensitive expenses may not completely insulate a firm from exchange rate risk. The firm can best evaluate a proposed restructuring of operations by forecasting various income statement items for various possible exchange rate scenarios (as shown in Exhibit 12.2) and then assessing the sensitivity of earnings to these different scenarios.

Expediting the Analysis with Computer Spreadsheets. Determining the sensitivity of earnings before taxes to alternative exchange rate scenarios could also be expedited by computer. A spreadsheet similar to Exhibit 12.2 could be created. Forecasts could be input by the analyst for items such as sales, cost of goods sold, and fixed operating expenses. The remaining items could be defined by formula, so that they could be estimated by computer after forecasts of the other items were input. For example, the exchange rate forecast influences projections of (1) dollars received from Canadian sales, (2) cost of goods sold attributable to purchases of Canadian materials, and (3) amount in dollars needed to cover the Canadian interest payments. The firm could revise the input in accordance with proposed restructured operations, in order to determine how economic exposure would be affected. A computerized spreadsheet would allow the analyst to assess several possible operational structures.

Recall that Madison Inc. assessed one alternative operational structure in which it increased foreign Canadian sales by C$16 million, reduced its purchases of Canadian materials by C$100 million, and reduced its interest owed to Canadian banks by C$5 million. If it had computerized the spreadsheet, it could easily have assessed the impact of alternative strategies, such as increasing Canadian sales by other amounts and/or reducing the Canadian expenses by other amounts. This would have offered Madison more information about its economic exposure under various operational structures and would therefore have enabled it to devise the operational structure that would reduce economic exposure to the degree desired.

Issues Involved in the Restructuring Decision

The restructuring of operations to reduce economic exposure is a more complex task than hedging any single foreign currency transaction, which is why the management of economic exposure is normally perceived to be more difficult than the management of transaction exposure. However, the management of economic exposure serves as a long-term solution, because once the restructuring is complete, it should reduce economic exposure over the long run. This differs from the hedging of transaction exposure, which deals with each upcoming foreign currency transaction separately. Yet, any restructuring that is used to reduce economic exposure may only be reversed or eliminated at a high cost. Therefore, MNCs must be very confident about the potential benefits before they decide to restructure their operations.

When deciding how to restructure operations to reduce economic exposure, one must address the following questions:

- Should the firm attempt to increase or reduce sales in new or existing foreign markets?
- Should the firm increase or reduce its dependency on foreign suppliers?
- Should the firm establish or eliminate production facilities in foreign markets?
- Should the firm increase or reduce its level of debt denominated in foreign currencies?

Each of these four questions reflects a different part of the firm's income statement. The first relates to foreign cash inflows and the remaining ones to foreign cash outflows. Some of the more common solutions to balancing a foreign currency's inflows and outflows are summarized in Exhibit 12.4. Any restructuring of operations that can reduce the periodic difference between a foreign currency's inflows and outflows can reduce the firm's economic exposure to that currency's movements.

MNCs that have production and marketing facilities in various countries may be able to shift their allocation of operations in order to reduce any adverse impact of economic exposure. For example, consider a U.S.-based MNC that produces products in the United States, Japan, and Mexico and sells these products (denominated in the currency where they are produced) to several countries. If the Japanese yen strengthens against many currencies, the MNC may boost production in Mexico, expecting a decline in demand for the Japanese subsidiary's products. The MNC parent may even request that some machinery be transported from Japan to Mexico and

Exhibit 12.4
How to Restructure Operations to Balance the Impact of Currency Movements on Cash Inflows and Outflows

Type of Operation	Recommended Action When a Foreign Currency Has a Greater Impact on Cash Inflows	Recommended Action When a Foreign Currency Has a Greater Impact on Cash Outflows
Sales in foreign currency units	Reduce foreign sales	Increase foreign sales
Reliance on foreign supplies	Increase foreign supply orders	Reduce foreign supply orders
Proportion of debt structure representing foreign debt	Restructure debt to increase debt payments in foreign currency	Restructure debt to reduce debt payments in foreign currency

allocate more marketing funds to the Mexican subsidiary at the expense of the Japanese subsidiary. This type of strategy may force the firm to forgo economies of scale that could be achieved if production were concentrated at one particular subsidiary while other subsidiaries focused on warehousing and distribution.

Examples of Restructuring That Reduced Exposure

To illustrate how the shifting of production can reduce economic exposure, consider the actual case of Honda, the Japanese automobile producer. By developing plants in the United States to produce automobiles for sale there, Honda not only circumvents possible trade restrictions but also reduces its economic exposure to exchange rate risk. When the automobiles were exported to the United States, the U.S. demand for Hondas would decline in response to appreciation of the yen, because the dollar cost of the purchase increased. Thus, Honda's cash flows were adversely affected as the strong yen caused less demand for its exports. By producing automobiles in the United States and invoicing them in dollars, Honda is trying to ensure that the U.S. demand for these automobiles will not be so sensitive to the value of the Japanese yen. However, Honda is not completely insulated from exchange rate risk for two reasons. First, the Honda plants in the United States purchase various components from Japan (invoiced in yen), causing the dollar costs of these components to rise when the yen appreciates. Second, earnings remitted from Honda's plants in the United States to its parent in Japan will convert to a smaller number of yen when the yen appreciates. Nevertheless, the transfer of production to the location where the product is sold has reduced the economic exposure.

U.S.-based automobile manufacturers are subject to economic exposure because they compete with manufacturers in different countries, and a weakening of the yen or other currencies can result in lower prices paid by U.S. automobile dealers for imported cars, which may decrease the U.S. demand for U.S. cars. It can also reduce the non-U.S. demand for U.S. cars because the price of the imported U.S. cars from a foreign perspective increases as foreign currencies weaken against the dollar. However, the U.S. automobile manufacturers have revised their operations to create some offsetting effects when foreign currencies weaken. As an example, Chrysler purchases engines and other components from Japan. When the yen weakens, the adverse effects on the demand for Chrysler's cars is partially offset by the favorable effects of obtaining engines and components from Japan at a lower price. During the Asian crisis in 1997 and 1998, the yen weakened substantially against the dollar, but Chrysler's performance remained stable because it had offsetting types of exposure to the yen's exchange rate movements.

Managing Translation Exposure

Translation exposure occurs when an MNC translates each subsidiary's financial data to its home currency for consolidated financial statements. Because cash flow is not affected, some people would argue that it is not necessary to hedge or even reduce accounting exposure. Still, some firms are concerned with translation exposure because of its potential impact on reported consolidated earnings. Based on a recent survey of firms by *Institutional Investor* magazine, more than one-third of firms believe that the hedging of translation exposure is a major concern.

Nike Problem

Management of Economic Exposure

Nike's economic exposure comes in various forms. First, it is subject to transaction exposure because of its numerous purchase and sale transactions in foreign currencies, and this transaction exposure is a subset of economic exposure. Second, any remitted earnings from foreign subsidiaries to the U.S. parent also reflect transaction exposure and therefore reflect economic exposure. Third, a change in exchange rates that affects the demand for shoes at other athletic shoe companies (such as Adidas) can indirectly affect the demand for Nike's athletic shoes. Nike attempts to hedge some of its transaction exposure, but it cannot eliminate transaction exposure because it cannot predict all future transactions ahead of time. Moreover, even if it could eliminate its transaction exposure, it cannot perfectly hedge its remaining economic exposure; it is difficult to determine exactly how a specific exchange rate movement will affect the demand for a competitor's athletic shoes, and therefore how it will indirectly affect the demand for Nike's shoes.

Discussion: Given that Nike conducts much business in Japan, what are the expected results from a regression analysis of percentage changes in Nike's stock price against percentage changes in the value of the yen over several months (after controlling for U.S. stock market movements)? That is, should Nike's stock return be positively or inversely related to movements in the yen's value (measured in dollars)? Explain.

Some MNCs attempt to avoid translation exposure by matching foreign liabilities with foreign assets. For example, Philip Morris uses foreign financing to match its level of foreign assets.

Use of Forward Contracts to Hedge Translation Exposure

http://

See www.futures.com/library/contents/html, the Web site of *Futures* magazine, for coverage of various aspects of derivatives trading such as new products, strategies, and market analyses.

MNCs can use forward contracts or futures contracts to hedge translation exposure, as described in the following example. Consider a U.S.-based MNC that has just one subsidiary located within the U.K. Assume the British subsidiary as of the beginning of its fiscal year forecasts earnings at £20,000,000. Assume this subsidiary plans to reinvest the entire amount in earnings within the U.K. and does not plan to remit any earnings back to the parent in the United States. While there is no foreseeable transaction exposure from the future earnings (since the pounds will remain in the U.K.), translation exposure does exist for the MNC.

The British earnings would be translated at the weighted average value of the pound over the course of the year. If the British pound is currently worth $1.50 and if its value was constant during the year, the forecasted translation of British earnings into U.S. dollars would be $30 million (computed as £20,000,000 × $1.50 per pound).

The MNC may be concerned that the translated value of British earnings will be reduced if the pound's average value decreases during the year. To hedge this translation exposure, it could implement a forward hedge on the expected earnings by selling £20,000,000 one year forward. Assume the forward rate at that time is $1.50, the same as the spot rate. At the end of the year, the MNC could buy £20,000,000 at the spot rate and fulfill its forward contract obligation to sell £20,000,000. If the pound depreciates during the fiscal year, then the MNC will be able to purchase pounds at the end of the fiscal year at a cheaper rate than it could sell them for ($1.50 per pound) to fulfill the forward contract. Thus, it will have generated income that could offset the translation loss.

The precise level of income generated by the forward contract will depend on the spot rate of the pound at the end of the fiscal year. Under conditions in which the pound depreciates, the translation loss will be somewhat offset by the gain generated from the forward contract position.

Limitations of Hedging Translation Exposure

There are four limitations in hedging translation exposure:

- inaccurate earnings forecasts
- inadequate forward contracts for some currencies
- accounting distortions
- increased transaction exposure

Inaccurate Earnings Forecasts. A subsidiary's forecasted earnings for the end of the year are not guaranteed. In our example, British earnings were projected to be 20 million pounds. If the actual earnings turned out to be much higher, the translation loss in the previous example likely would exceed the gain generated from the forward contract strategy.

Inadequate Forward Contracts for Some Currencies. A second limitation is that forward contracts are not available for all currencies. Thus, an MNC with subsidiaries in some smaller countries may not be able to obtain forward contracts for the currencies of concern.

Accounting Distortions. A third limitation is that the forward-rate gain or loss reflects the difference between the forward rate and future spot rate, whereas the translation gain or loss reflects the difference between the average exchange rate over the period of concern and the future spot rate. In addition, the translation losses are not tax deductible, whereas gains on forward contracts used to hedge translation exposure are taxed.

Increased Transaction Exposure. The fourth and most critical limitation with a hedging strategy (forward or money market hedge) on translation exposure is that the MNC may be increasing its transaction exposure. For example, consider a situation in which the subsidiary's currency appreciates during the fiscal year, resulting in a translation gain. If the MNC enacts a hedge strategy at the start of the fiscal year, this strategy will generate a transaction loss that will somewhat offset the translation gain. Some MNCs may not be comfortable with this offsetting effect. The translation gain is simply a paper gain; that is, the reported dollar value of earnings is higher due to the subsidiary currency's appreciation. Yet, the parent does not receive any more income due to this appreciation if the subsidiary reinvests the earnings. The MNC parent's net cash flow is not affected. Conversely, the loss resulting from a hedge strategy is a *real* loss. That is, the net cash flow to the parent will be reduced due to this loss. In this example, the MNC reduces its translation exposure at the expense of increasing its transaction exposure.

Alternative Solution to Hedging Translation Exposure

Perhaps the best way for MNCs to deal with translation exposure is to clarify how their consolidated earnings have been affected by exchange rate movements. In this way, shareholders and potential investors will be more aware of the translation effect. An unusually low level of consolidated earnings may not discourage shareholders and potential investors if it is attributed to translation of subsidiary earnings at low exchange rates.

Some MNCs do not consider hedging translation exposure because they do not perceive this exposure to be relevant. For example, Phillips Petroleum has stated in its annual report that translation exposure is not hedged because translation effects do not influence cash flows. Many other MNCs follow similar policies. PepsiCo's view on the hedging of translation exposure is consistent with these comments and is summarized in a recent annual report:

> We do not generally hedge translation risks because cash flows from international operations are generally reinvested locally. We do not enter into hedges to minimize volatility of reported earnings because we do not believe it is justified by the exposure or the cost.

How Managing Economic Exposure Affects an MNC's Value

An MNC's management of economic exposure can affect its value, as shown in Exhibit 12.5. First, since transaction exposure is a subset of economic exposure, foreign subsidiaries that exchange their local currencies for others as part of their nor-

Exhibit 12.5
Impact of an MNC's Value

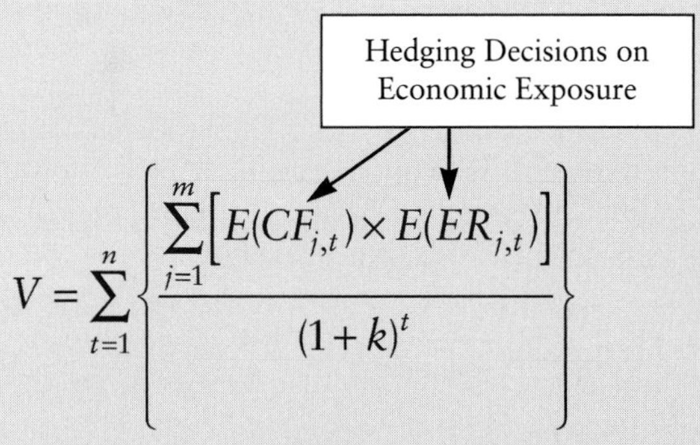

$$V = \sum_{t=1}^{n} \left\{ \frac{\sum_{j=1}^{m} \left[E(CF_{j,t}) \times E(ER_{j,t}) \right]}{(1+k)^t} \right\}$$

V = value of the U.S.-based MNC
$E(CF_{j,t})$ = expected cash flows denominated in currency j to be received by the U.S. parent in period t
$E(ER_{j,t})$ = expected exchange rate at which currency j can be converted to dollars at the end of period t
k = the weighted average cost of capital of the U.S. parent
m = number of currencies
n = number of periods

mal business must manage their transaction exposure, which affects their expected foreign currency cash flows. Second, the dollar cash flows that the U.S. parent expects to receive from the foreign subsidiaries are dependent on the expected exchange rates at which foreign currency cash flows are remitted from the foreign subsidiaries to the U.S. parent, which are determined by management of transaction exposure (whether to hedge those transactions).

An MNC's value is also affected by management of other forms of economic exposure that are unrelated to transaction exposure. For example, foreign subsidiaries may attempt to restructure their operations such that their levels of foreign currency cash flows generated each period are less sensitive to exchange rate movements, and therefore are more predictable. They may attempt to sell most of their products locally so that the demand for their products denominated in their local currency is less sensitive to exchange rate movements. However, managing economic exposure in this way may result in the loss of some additional business for the foreign subsidiaries, which will affect the expected foreign currency cash flows of the MNC.

SUMMARY

- Economic exposure can be managed by balancing the sensitivity of revenue and expenses to exchange rate fluctuations. To accomplish this, however, the firm must first recognize how its revenue and expenses are affected by exchange rate fluctuations. For some firms, revenue are more susceptible. These firms are most concerned that their home currency will appreciate against foreign currencies, since the unfavorable effects on revenue will more than offset the favorable effects on expenses. Conversely, firms whose expenses are more exchange-rate-sensitive than their revenue are most concerned that their home currency will depreciate against foreign currencies. When firms reduce their economic exposure, they reduce not only these unfavorable effects but also the favorable effects if the home currency value moves in the opposite direction.

- Translation exposure can be reduced by creating a forward sale in the foreign currency used to measure a subsidiary's income. If the foreign currency depreciates against the home currency, the adverse impact on the consolidated income statement can be offset by the gain on the forward sale in that currency. If the foreign currency appreciates over the time period of concern, there will be a loss on the forward sale that is offset by a favorable effect on the reported consolidated earnings. However, many MNCs would not be satisfied with a "paper gain" that offsets a "cash loss."

SELF-TEST FOR CHAPTER 12

(Answers are provided in Appendix A at the back of the text.)

1. Salem Exporting Co. purchases chemicals from U.S. sources and uses them to make pharmaceutical products that are exported to Canadian hospitals. Salem prices its products in C$ and is concerned about the possibility of the long-term depreciation of C$ against the dollar. It periodically hedges its exposure with short-term forward contracts, but this does not insulate against the possible trend of continuing C$ depreciation. How could Salem offset some of its exposure resulting from its export business?

2. Using the information in question 1, give a possible disadvantage of offsetting exchange rate exposure from the export business.

3. Coastal Corp. is a U.S. firm with a subsidiary in the United Kingdom. It expects that the pound will depreciate this year. Explain Coastal's translation exposure. How could Coastal hedge its translation exposure?

4. Arlington Co. has substantial translation exposure in European subsidiaries. The treasurer of Arlington Co. suggests that the translation effects are not relevant because the earnings generated by the European subsidiaries are not being remitted to the U.S. parent, but are simply being reinvested in Europe. Yet, the vice president of finance of Arlington Co. is concerned about translation exposure because the stock price is highly dependent on the consolidated earnings, which are dependent on the exchange rates at which the earnings are translated. Who is correct?

5. Lincolnshire Co. exports 80 percent of its total production of goods in New Mexico to Latin American countries. Kalafa Co. sells all the goods it produces in the United States, but it has a subsidiary in Spain that usually generates about 20 percent of its total earnings. Compare the translation exposure of these two U.S. firms.

QUESTIONS AND APPLICATIONS

1. St. Paul Company does business in the United States and New Zealand. In attempting to assess its economic exposure, it compiled the following information.

   a. Its U.S. sales are somewhat affected by the New Zealand dollar's value because it faces competition from New Zealand exporters. It forecasts the U.S. sales based on the following three exchange rate scenarios.

Exchange Rate of NZ$	Revenue from U.S. Business (in millions)
NZ$ = $.48	$100
NZ$ = .50	105
NZ$ = .54	110

   b. Its New Zealand dollar revenue on sales to New Zealand invoiced in NZ$ are expected to be NZ$600 million.
   c. Its anticipated cost of goods sold is estimated at $200 million from the purchase of U.S. materials and NZ$100 million from the purchase of New Zealand materials.
   d. Fixed operating expenses are estimated at $30 million.
   e. Variable operating expenses are estimated at 20 percent of total sales (after including New Zealand sales, translated to a U.S. dollar amount).
   f. Interest expense is estimated at $20 million on existing U.S. loans, and the company has no existing New Zealand loans.

   Create a forecasted income statement for St. Paul Company under each of the three exchange rate scenarios. Explain how St. Paul's projected earnings before taxes are affected by possible exchange rate movements. Explain how it can restructure its operations to reduce the sensitivity of its earnings to exchange rate movements, without reducing its volume of business in New Zealand.

2. Baltimore Inc. is a U.S.-based MNC that obtains 10 percent of its supplies from European manufacturers. Sixty percent of its revenues are due to exports to Europe, where its product is exported and invoiced in euros. Explain how Baltimore Inc. could attempt to reduce its economic exposure to exchange rate fluctuations in the euro.

3. UVA Company is a U.S.-based MNC that obtains 40 percent of its foreign supplies from Thailand. It also borrows Thailand's currency (the baht) from Thai banks and converts the baht to dollars to support U.S. operations. It currently receives about 10 percent of its revenue from Thai customers. Its sales to Thai customers are denominated in baht. Explain how UVA Company can reduce its economic exposure to exchange rate fluctuations.

4. Albany Corporation is a U.S.-based MNC that has a large government contract with Australia. The contract will continue for several years and generate more than half of Albany's total sales volume. The Australian government pays Albany in Australian dollars. About 10 percent of Albany's operating expenses are in Australian dollars; all other expenses are in U.S. dollars. Explain how Albany Company can reduce its economic exposure to exchange rate fluctuations.

5. When an MNC restructures its operations to reduce its economic exposure, it may sometimes forgo economies of scale. Explain.

6. Explain how a U.S.-based MNC's consolidated earnings are affected during a period such as the Asian crisis.

7. Explain how a firm can hedge its translation exposure.

8. Theis Inc. is a U.S.-based MNC that has European subsidiaries and wants to hedge its translation exposure to fluctuations in the euro's value. Explain some limitations for Theis when it hedges translation exposure.

9. Would a more established MNC or a less established MNC be more capable of effectively hedging its given level of translation exposure? Why?

10. If a U.S.-based MNC is concerned with how shareholders react to changes in consolidated earnings but prefers not to hedge its translation exposure, how can it attempt to reduce shareholder reaction to a decline in consolidated earnings that results from a strengthened dollar?

11. Carlton Company and Palmer Inc. are U.S.-based MNCs with subsidiaries in Mexico that distribute medical supplies (produced in the United States) to customers throughout Latin America. Both subsidiaries purchase the products at cost and sell the products at 90-percent markup. The other operating costs of the subsidiaries are very low. Carlton Company has a research and development center in the United States which focuses on improving its medical technology. Palmer Inc. has a similar center that is based in Mexico. The parent of each firm subsidizes its respective research and development center on an annual basis. Which firm is subject to a higher degree of economic exposure? Explain.

12. Nelson Company is a U.S. firm with annual export sales to Singapore worth about S$800 million. Its main competitor is Mez Company, also based in the United States, with a subsidiary in Singapore that generates about S$800 million in annual sales. Any earnings generated by the subsidiary are reinvested to support its operations. Based on the information provided, which firm is subject to a higher degree of translation exposure? Explain.

Internet Application

13. The following Web site provides annual reports of numerous MNCs:

    http://reportgallery.com

    a. Review an annual report of an MNC of your choice. Look for any comments that relate to the MNC's economic or translation exposure. Does it appear that the MNC hedges its economic exposure or translation exposure? If so, what are the methods it uses to hedge its exposure?
    b. The following web site provides exchange rate movements against the dollar over recent months:

    http://dominostat-usa.gov/econtest.nsf

    Based on the translation exposure of the MNC you assessed in exercise (a), determine whether the exchange rate movements of whatever currency (or currencies) it is exposed to moved in a favorable or unfavorable direction over the last few months.

Running Your Own MNC

14. Recall that it was assumed that your receivables would be denominated in the foreign currency of concern. For this question only, assume that you could switch your pricing policy so that the receivables would be denominated in dollars instead of the foreign currency. How would this switch affect the transaction exposure and the economic exposure of your business? Explain the conditions that could still cause the performance of your business to be affected by exchange rate movements.

Blades, Inc. Case

Assessment of Economic Exposure

Blades, Inc. has been exporting to Thailand since its decision to supplement its declining U.S. sales by exporting there. Furthermore, Blades has recently begun exporting to a retailer in the United Kingdom. The suppliers of the components needed by Blades for roller blade production (such as rubber and plastic) are located in the United States and Thailand. The decision to use Thai suppliers for rubber and plastic components needed to manufacture roller blades was reached because of cost and quality considerations. All of Blades' exports and imports are denominated in the respective foreign currency; for example, Blades pays for the Thai imports in baht.

The decision to export to Thailand was supported by the fact that Thailand was among the world's fastest growing economies in recent years. Furthermore, Blades found an importer in Thailand that was willing to commit itself to the annual purchase of 180,000 pairs of Blades' "Speedos," which are among the highest quality roller blades in the world. The commitment began last year and will last another two years, at which time it may be renewed by the two parties. Due to this commitment, Blades is selling its roller blades for THB4,594 per pair (approximately $100 at current exchange rates) instead of the usual $120 per pair. Although this price represents a substantial discount from the regular price for a pair of Speedo blades, it still constitutes a considerable markup above cost. Because importers in other Asian countries were not willing to make this type of commitment, this was a decisive factor in the choice of Thailand for exporting purposes. Although Ben Holt, Blades' chief financial officer (CFO), believes Asia to be a region of the world with very high future growth potential in the sports product market, Blades has recently begun exporting to Jogs Ltd., a British retailer. Jogs has committed itself to the purchase of 200,000 pair of Speedos annually for a fixed price of £80 per pair.

For the coming year, Blades expects to import rubber and plastic components from Thailand sufficient to manufacture 80,000 pairs of Speedos, at a cost of approximately 3,000 Thai baht per pair of Speedos.

You, as Blades' financial analyst, have pointed out to Ben Holt that recent events in Asia have fundamentally affected the economic condition of Asian countries, including Thailand. For example, you have pointed out to Mr. Holt that the high level of consumer spending on leisure products such as roller blades has declined considerably. Thus, the Thai retailer may not renew its commitment with Blades in two years. Furthermore, you are worried that the current economic conditions in Thailand may lead to a substantial depreciation of the Thai baht, which would affect Blades negatively.

Despite recent developments, however, Ben Holt remains optimistic, as he strongly believes that the growth opportunities in Southeast Asia are among the most promising when the impact of recent events in Asia subsides. Consequently, Mr. Holt has no doubts that the Thai customer will renew its commitment for another three years when the current agreement terminates. In your opinion, Ben Holt is not considering all of the factors that might directly or indirectly affect Blades. Moreover, you are worried that Mr. Holt is ignoring Blades' future in Thailand even if the Thai importer will renew its commitment for another three years. In fact, you believe that a renewal of the existing agreement with the Thai customer may affect Blades negatively due to the high level of inflation in Thailand.

Since Ben Holt is interested in your opinion, and since he would like to assess Blades' economic exposure in Thailand, he has asked you to conduct an analysis of the impact of the value of the baht on next year's earnings to assess Blades' economic exposure. You have gathered the following information:

- Blades has forecasted sales in the United States of 520,000 pairs of Speedos at regular prices; exports to Thailand of 180,000 pairs of Speedos for THB4,594 a pair; and exports to the United Kingdom of 200,000 pairs of Speedos for £80 per pair.
- Cost of goods sold for 80,000 pairs of Speedos are incurred in Thailand; the remainder is

incurred in the United States, where the cost of goods sold per pair of Speedos runs at approximately $70.

- Fixed costs are $2,000,000, and variable operating expenses other than costs of goods sold represent approximately 11 percent of U.S. sales. All fixed and variable operating expenses other than cost of goods sold are incurred in the United States.
- The recent events in Asia have increased the uncertainty regarding certain Asian currencies considerably, making it extremely difficult to forecast the value of the baht at which the Thai revenues will be converted. The current spot rate of the baht is $.022 and the current spot rate of the pound is $1.50. You have created three scenarios and derived an expected value on average for the upcoming year based on each scenario:

Scenario	Effect on the Average Value of Baht	Average Value of Baht	Average Value of Pound
1	No Change	$.0220	$1.530
2	Depreciate by 5 Percent	$.0209	$1.485
3	Depreciate by 10 Percent	$.0198	$1.500

- Blades currently has no debt in its capital structure. However, it may borrow funds in Thailand if it establishes a subsidiary in the country.

Ben Holt has asked you to answer the following questions:

1. How would Blades be negatively affected by the high level of inflation in Thailand if the Thai customer renews its commitment for another three years?
2. Ben Holt believes that the Thai importer will renew its commitment in two years. Do you think he is correct in this assessment? Why or why not? Also, assume that the Thai economy returns to the high growth level that existed prior to the recent unfavorable economic events. Under this assumption, how likely is it that the Thai importer will renew its commitment in two years?
3. For each of the three possible values of the Thai baht and the British pound, use a spreadsheet to construct a pro forma income statement for the next year. Briefly comment on the level of Blades' economic exposure.
4. Now repeat your analysis in question 3 but assume that the British pound and the Thai baht are perfectly correlated. For example, if the baht depreciates by 5 percent, the pound will also depreciate by 5 percent. Under this assumption, is Blades subject to a greater degree of economic exposure? Why or why not?
5. Based on your answers to the previous three questions, what actions could Blades take to reduce its level of economic exposure to Thailand?

Small Business Dilemma

Hedging the Sports Exports Company's Economic Exposure to Exchange Rate Risk

Jim Logan, owner of the Sports Exports Company, remains concerned about his exposure to exchange rate risk. Even if Jim hedges his transactions from one month to another, he recognizes that a long-term trend of depreciation in the British pound could have a severe impact on his firm. He believes that he must continue to focus on the British market for selling his footballs. However, he plans to consider various ways in which he can reduce his economic exposure. At the current time, he obtains material from a local manufacturer and uses a machine to produce the footballs, which are then exported. He still uses his garage as a place of production and would like to continue using his garage to maintain low operating expenses.

1. How could Jim adjust his operations in order to reduce his economic exposure? What is a possible disadvantage of such an adjustment?
2. Offer another solution to hedging the economic exposure in the long run, as Jim's business grows. What are the disadvantages of applying this solution?

PART III
INTEGRATIVE
PROBLEM

Exchange Rate Risk Management

Vogl Co. is a U.S. firm conducting a financial plan for the next year. It has no foreign subsidiaries, but more than half of its sales are from exports. Its foreign cash inflows to be received from exporting and cash outflows to be paid for imported supplies over the next year are disclosed below.

Currency	Total Inflow	Total Outflow
Canadian dollar (C$)	C$32,000,000	C$2,000,000
New Zealand dollar (NZ$)	NZ$5,000,000	NZ$1,000,000
Mexican peso (MXP)	MXP11,000,000	MXP10,000,000
Singapore dollar (S$)	S$4,000,000	S$8,000,000

The spot rates and one-year forward rates as of today are

Currency	Spot Rate	One-Year Forward Rate
C$	$.90	$.93
NZ$	.60	.59
MXP	.18	.15
S$	.65	.64

Questions

1. Based on the information provided, determine the net exposure of each foreign currency in dollars.
2. Assume that today's spot rate is used as a forecast of the future spot rate one year from now. The New Zealand dollar, Mexican peso, and Singapore dollar are expected to move in tandem against the U.S. dollar over the next year. The Canadian dollar movements are expected to be unrelated to movements of the other currencies. Since exchange rates are difficult to predict, the forecasted net dollar cash flows per currency may be inaccurate. Do you anticipate any offsetting exchange rate effects from whatever exchange movements do occur? Explain.
3. Given the forecast of the Canadian dollar along with the forward rate of the Canadian dollar, what is the expected increase or decrease in dollar cash flows that would result from hedging the net cash flows in Canadian dollars? Would you hedge the Canadian dollar position?
4. Assume that the Canadian dollar net inflows may range from C$20,000,000 to C$40,000,000 over the next year. Explain the risk of hedging C$30,000,000 in net inflows. How can Vogl Co. avoid such a risk? Is there any tradeoff resulting from your strategy to avoid that risk?
5. Vogl Company recognizes that its year-to-year hedging strategy hedges the risk only over a given year but does not insulate it from long-term trends in the C$ value. It has considered establishing a subsidiary in Canada. The goods would be

sent from the United States to the Canadian subsidiary and distributed by the subsidiary. The proceeds received would be reinvested by the Canadian subsidiary in Canada. In this way, Vogl Company would not have to convert C$ to dollars each year. Has Vogl eliminated its exposure to exchange rate risk by using this strategy? Explain.

PART IV

Long-Term Asset and Liability Management

Part IV (Chapters 13 through 18) focuses on the multinational corporation's (MNC's) management of long-term assets and liabilities. Chapter 13 explains how MNCs can benefit from international business. Chapter 14 describes the information MNCs must have when considering multinational projects and demonstrates how the capital budgeting analysis is conducted. Chapter 15 identifies the common forms of multinational restructuring and illustrates how to assess the feasibility of proposed forms of restructuring. Chapter 16 explains how MNCs assess country risk associated with their prevailing projects as well as with their proposed projects. Chapter 17 explains the capital structure decision for MNCs, which affects the cost of financing new projects. Chapter 18 describes the MNC's long-term financing decision.

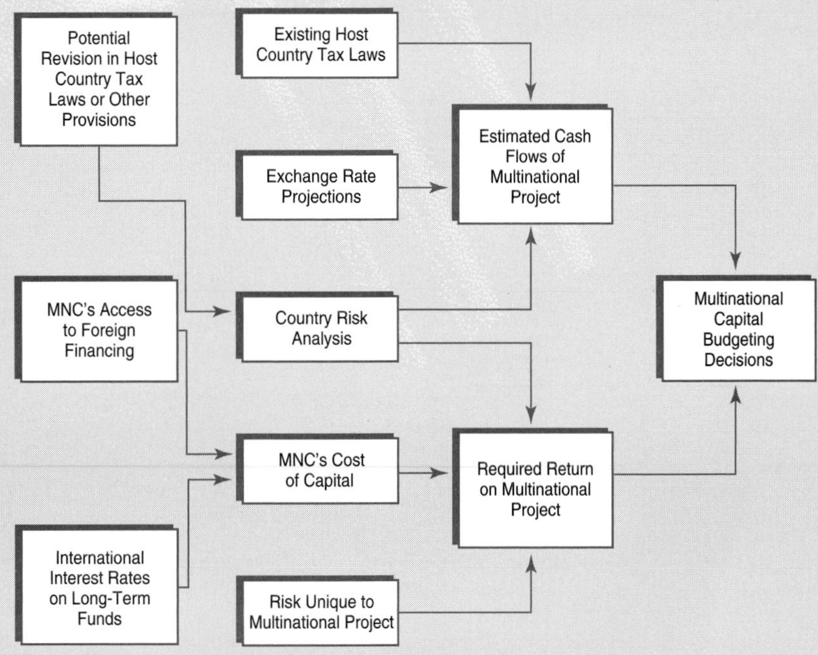

13 Direct Foreign Investment

The global expansion of multinational corporations (MNCs) has become more widespread following the actions of many governments to remove various barriers. MNCs commonly capitalize on foreign business opportunities by engaging in **direct foreign investment (DFI),** which represents investment in real assets (such as land, buildings, or even existing plants) in foreign countries.

MNCs conduct DFI through joint ventures with foreign firms, acquisitions of foreign firms, and formations of new foreign subsidiaries. Any of these types of DFI can generate high returns when managed properly. However, DFI requires a substantial investment and can therefore place much capital at risk. Moreover, when the investment does not perform as well as expected, the MNC may be unable to easily sell the foreign project it created. Given these return and risk characteristics of DFI, MNCs tend to analyze carefully the potential benefits and costs before implementing any type of DFI.

The specific objectives of this chapter are to

- describe common motives for initiating direct foreign investment, and
- illustrate the benefits of international diversification.

Motives for Direct Foreign Investment

Direct foreign investment is commonly considered by MNCs because it can improve profitability and enhance shareholder wealth. There are several ways in which DFI can boost revenues or reduce costs.

1. *Attract new sources of demand.* A corporation often reaches a stage at which growth is limited in its home country. This may be due to intense competition for the product it sells. Even if there is little competition, its market share in its home country may already be near its potential peak. Thus, a possible solution is to consider foreign markets where there is potential demand. Many of the developing countries, such as Argentina, Chile, Mexico, Hungary, and China, have been perceived as the most attractive sources of new demand. Many MNCs have penetrated these countries since barriers have been removed. Because the con-

sumers in these countries have historically been restricted from purchasing goods produced by firms outside their countries, the markets for some goods are not well established and offer much potential for penetration by MNCs. For example, Blockbuster Entertainment Corp. has recently established video stores in Australia, Chile, Japan, and several European countries where the video-rental concept is relatively new. With over two thousand stores in the United States, Blockbuster's growth potential in the United States was limited.

Motorola has recently invested more than $1 billion in joint ventures in China; The Coca-Cola Company has invested about $500 million in bottling facilities in China; and PepsiCo has invested about $200 million in bottling facilities, KFC franchises, and Pizza Hut franchises. Other MNCs, such as Ford Motor Company, United Technologies, General Electric, Hewlett-Packard, and IBM, have also invested more than $100 million in China to attract demand by consumers in China.

2. *Enter markets in which superior profits are possible.* If other corporations within the industry have proven that excessive earnings can be realized in other markets, an MNC may also decide to sell in those markets. It may plan to undercut the prevailing, excessively high prices. A common problem with this strategy is that previously established sellers in a new market may prevent a new competitor from taking away their business by lowering their prices just when the new competitor attempts to break into this market.
3. *Fully benefit from economies of scale.* The corporation that attempts to sell its primary product in new markets may increase its earnings and shareholder wealth due to **economies of scale** (lower average cost per unit resulting from increased production). Such a motive is more likely for firms that utilize much machinery.

   As the Single European Act removed trade barriers, it allowed MNCs to achieve greater economies of scale. For example, some U.S.-based MNCs have consolidated their European plants, as the removal of tariffs between European countries allows economies of scale at one European plant without excessive exporting costs. The act also enhances economies of scale by making regulations on television ads, automobile standards, and other products and services uniform across European countries. As a result, Colgate-Palmolive Company, Prime Computer, and other MNCs are manufacturing more homogeneous products that can be sold in all European countries. The adoption of the euro also allowed for consolidation, as exchange rate risk within these countries was eliminated.

4. *Use foreign factors of production.* Labor and land costs can vary dramatically among countries. MNCs often attempt to set up production in locations where land and labor are cheap. Due to market imperfections (as discussed in Chapter 1) such as imperfect information, relocation transaction costs, and barriers to industry entry, specific labor costs do not necessarily become equal among markets. Thus, it is worthwhile for MNCs to survey markets to determine whether they can benefit from cheaper costs by producing in those markets.

   The minimum daily wage rate is less than $6 in Mexico, versus over $30 in the U.S. Many U.S.-based MNCs have subsidiaries in Mexico to achieve lower labor costs, including Black & Decker Corp., Eastman Kodak Co., Ford Motor Co., General Electric Co., RCA Corp., Smith Corona, and Zenith Corp.

   Baxter Travenol has established manufacturing plants in Mexico and Malaysia to capitalize on lower costs of production (primarily wage rates). Honeywell has some of its joint ventures in countries such as Korea and India where production costs are low. It also has established subsidiaries in countries where production costs are low, such as Mexico, Malaysia, Hong Kong, and Taiwan.

In fact, Mexico has attracted almost $8 billion in direct foreign investment from firms in the automobile industry, primarily because of the low-cost labor. Sedans and trucks are produced by General Motors subsidiaries, and wages for the workers there are about $13 per day, which is less than the average hourly rate for similar workers in the United States. Trucks are also produced by Ford subsidiaries based there.

Non-U.S. automobile manufacturers also capitalize on the low-cost labor in Mexico. Volkswagen of Germany has its Beetle produced in Mexico. Daimler-Benz of Germany has its 12-wheeler trucks produced in Mexico. Nissan Motor Co. of Japan has some of its wagons produced in Mexico.

Other Japanese companies are also increasingly using Mexico and other low-wage countries for production. For example, Sony Corporation recently established a plant in Tijuana. Matsushita Electrical Industrial Company has a large plant in Tijuana.

5. *Use foreign raw materials.* Due to transportation costs, a corporation attempts to avoid importing raw materials from a given country, especially when it plans to then sell the finished product back to consumers in that foreign country. Under such circumstances, a more feasible solution may be to develop the product in the country where the raw materials are located.
6. *Use foreign technology.* Corporations are increasingly establishing overseas plants or acquiring existing overseas plants to learn about the technology of foreign countries. This technology is then used to improve their own production processes at all subsidiary plants around the world.
7. *Exploit monopolistic advantages.* Industrial organization theory states that firms may become internationalized if they possess resources or skills not available to competing firms. If a particular firm possesses advanced technology and has exploited this advantage successfully in local markets, it may attempt to exploit it internationally as well. Technology is not restricted to developing a new product. It can even represent a more efficient production, marketing, or financing process. To the extent to which the firm has an advantage over competitors, it should be able to benefit from becoming internationalized.
8. *React to exchange rate movements.* When a foreign currency is perceived by a firm to be undervalued, the firm may consider direct foreign investment in that country, as the initial outlay should be relatively low. For example, assume that a U.S. firm could build a manufacturing plant in the United Kingdom for £40 million. The dollar cost of this project would have been $77.2 million at the beginning of 1991, when the British pound was valued at $1.93. However, just six months later, the dollar cost of this project would have been $65.2 million (or $12 million less) since the pound's value had declined to $1.63 by that time. The exchange rate declined even further during the 1990s, before reverting back to about $1.63 by 1999. Since the decision regarding whether to engage in direct foreign investment is partially dependent on the cost, exchange rate movements may influence this decision.

   A related reason for such DFI is to offset the changing demand for a company's exports due to exchange rate fluctuations. For example, when Japanese automobile manufacturers build plants in the United States, they can reduce exposure to exchange rate fluctuations by incurring dollar costs that offset dollar revenues. Although MNCs do not simply engage in large projects as an indirect means of speculating on currencies, the feasibility of proposed projects may be dependent on existing and expected exchange rate movements.

The conversion of European currencies to the euro in 1999 reduces the influence of exchange rates on the selection of a European country for direct foreign investment because the future exchange rate effects will be similar across all countries that use the euro as their currency. For example, the decision by a U.S.-based MNC to build a manufacturing plant in Germany versus Italy or Spain will not be determined by the exchange rate effects because those countries have adopted the euro as their currency. However, exchange rates will still be considered if the MNC is considering European countries that have not adopted the euro along with those that have.

9. *React to trade restrictions.* In some cases, an MNC uses direct foreign investment as a defensive rather than an aggressive strategy. For example, Japanese automobile manufacturers established plants in the United States in anticipation that their exports to the United States would be subject to more stringent trade restrictions. Japanese companies recognized the potential trade barriers that could either limit or prohibit their exports. Since 1980, there have been numerous trade restrictions enforced on automobile imports by the United States.
10. *Diversify internationally.* Since economies of countries do not move perfectly in tandem over time, net cash flow from sales of products across countries should be more stable than comparable sales if the products were sold in a single country. By diversifying sales (and possibly even production) internationally, a firm can make its net cash flows less volatile. Thus, the possibility of a liquidity deficiency is less likely. In addition, the firm may enjoy a lower cost of capital as shareholders and creditors perceive the MNC's risk to be lower as a result of more stable cash flows. Potential benefits to MNCs that diversify internationally are examined more thoroughly later in the chapter.

Summary of Benefits of Direct Foreign Investment

The optimal method for a firm to penetrate a foreign market is partially dependent on the characteristics of the market. For example, direct foreign investment by U.S. firms is common in Europe but not so common in Asia, where the people are accustomed to purchasing products from Asians. Thus, licensing arrangements or joint ventures may be more appropriate when firms are expanding into Asia.

Exhibit 13.1 summarizes the possible benefits of DFI and explains the means by which MNCs could use DFI to achieve those benefits. Most MNCs pursue DFI based on their expectations of capitalizing on one or more of the potential benefits summarized in Exhibit 13.1. While most attempts to increase international business are motivated by one or more of the benefits listed here, there are some corresponding disadvantages as well. For example, the potential cost savings associated with establishing a subsidiary in a less developed country are obvious. However, the expense of establishing the subsidiary, the uncertainty of inflation and exchange rate movements, and the political risk should not be ignored. Decisions to invest in a foreign country must weigh the potential benefits against such costs or additional risks.

http://
Visit Morgan Stanley's Economic Forum at www.ms.com/GEF for analyses, discussions, statistics, and forecasts related to non-U.S. economies.

As conditions change over time, so do possible benefits from pursuing direct foreign investment in various countries. Thus, some countries may become more attractive targets while other countries become less attractive. The choice of target countries for DFI has changed over time, as illustrated in Exhibit 13.2. Canada now

Exhibit 13.1
Summary of Motives for Direct Foreign Investment

Possible Benefit	Means of Using DFI to Achieve This Benefit
1. Attract new sources of demand.	Establish a subsidiary or acquire a competitor in a new market.
2. Enter markets in which superior profits are possible.	Acquire a competitor that has controlled its local market.
3. Fully benefit from economies of scale.	Establish a subsidiary in a new market that can sell products produced elsewhere; this allows for increased production and possibly greater production efficiency.
4. Use foreign factors of production.	Establish a subsidiary in a market that has relatively low costs of labor or land; sell the finished product to countries where the cost of production is higher.
5. Use foreign raw materials.	Establish a subsidiary in a market in which raw materials are cheap and accessible; sell the finished product to countries in which the raw materials are more expensive.
6. Use foreign technology.	Participate in a joint venture in order to learn about a production process or other operations.
7. Exploit monopolistic advantages.	Establish a subsidiary in a market in which competitors are unable to produce the identical product; sell products in that country.
8. React to exchange rate movements.	Establish a subsidiary in a new market in which the local currency is weak but expected to strengthen over time.
9. React to trade restrictions.	Establish a subsidiary in a market in which tougher trade restrictions will adversely affect the firm's export volume.
10. Diversify internationally.	Establish subsidiaries in markets whose business cycles differ from those where existing subsidiaries are based.

Exhibit 13.2
Change in Distribution of Direct Foreign Investment (DFI) by U.S. Firms Over Time

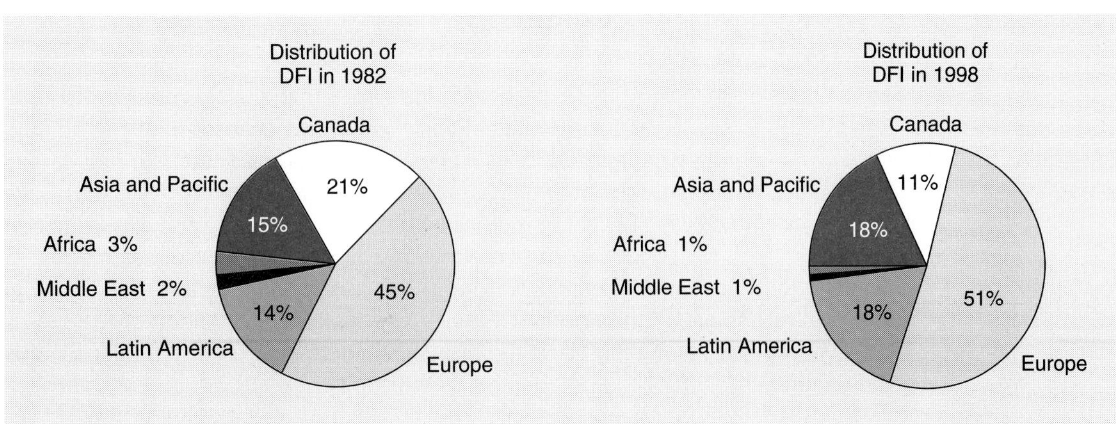

Source: *Survey of Current Business.*

receives a smaller proportion of total DFI than it received in the past, while Europe, Latin America, and Asia receive a larger proportion of DFI than they received in the past. More than one-half of all DFI by U.S. firms is in European countries. The increased focus of DFI in Europe is partially attributed to the opening of the Eastern European countries. The increased focus on Latin America is partially attributed to its high economic growth, which has encouraged MNCs to capitalize on new sources of demand for their products. In addition, MNCs have targeted Latin America and Asia to use factors of production that are less expensive in foreign countries than in the United States.

Application of Direct Foreign Investment to the Asian Crisis

To illustrate how an MNC may use the factors just described to determine whether DFI is worthwhile, consider an MNC that contemplated DFI in Thailand in 1997 but delayed its assessment until 1999 because of the Asian crisis. A new subsidiary in Thailand might not attract new sources of demand after the crisis due to Thailand's weak economy. In addition, the MNC may be unable to earn excessive profits there because the crisis caused existing firms to keep their prices very low in order to survive. However, other factors may favor DFI in Thailand. For example, the MNC could probably achieve low production costs in Thailand because empty factories and office buildings could be purchased at a discount after the crisis. In addition, the Thai baht depreciated substantially against the dollar during the crisis, which would allow the MNC to invest in Thailand at a time when the dollar could be exchanged at a favorable exchange rate. The ultimate decision to engage in direct foreign investment would depend on the specific characteristics of the business that the MNC was planning in Thailand. The favorable aspects of DFI in Thailand would have to be compared to the unfavorable aspects by using multinational capital budgeting, which is explained in the following chapter.

Nike Problem

Motives for Direct Foreign Investment

Nike is a classic example of a firm that has pursued international business in Asia and Europe because of some of the motives described in this chapter. It attracted new sources of demand by consumers in foreign countries, as many consumers viewed Nike athletic shoes as unique (global name, image). In some cases, Nike may have increased its economies of scale by increasing production capacity and exporting part of the production. Nike benefits from relatively low labor costs by producing some of its athletic footwear in Indonesia, China, and Vietnam. It has also diversified so that it does not rely solely on the demand within any one country or region of the world. Therefore, Nike's overall cash flows are less sensitive to economic conditions in any given region.

Discussion: Nike has plans for expansion of its athletic footwear in Latin America. What motives do you think have encouraged Nike to expand in Latin America?

BENEFITS OF INTERNATIONAL DIVERSIFICATION

A numerical example is presented next to illustrate how an international project can reduce the firm's risk to a greater degree than a local project can. Then the potential diversification benefits from multiple projects are discussed.

Numerical Example of Diversification Benefits

Consider a U.S. firm that plans to invest in a new project that will be located either in the United States or in the United Kingdom. Once the project is completed, it will constitute 30 percent of the firm's total funds invested in itself. Assume the firm's current investment in its business (the remaining 70 percent) is exclusively in the United States. Characteristics of the proposed project are forecasted for a five-year period for both a U.S. and a British location, as shown in Exhibit 13.3.

Assume that the firm plans to assess the feasibility of each proposed project based on expected risk and return, using a five-year time horizon. Also assume that the firm's expected annual after-tax return on investment on its prevailing business is 20 percent, and its variability of returns (as measured by standard deviation) is expected to be .10. The firm can assess its expected overall performance based on developing the project in the United States. Then it can repeat the analysis based on developing the business in the United Kingdom. It is essentially comparing two portfolios. The first portfolio is 70 percent of its total funds invested in its prevailing U.S. business, plus the remaining 30 percent of funds is invested in a new project located in the United States. The second portfolio again represents 70 percent of the firm's total funds invested in its prevailing business, but the remaining 30 percent of funds is invested in a new project located in the United Kingdom. Therefore, 70 percent of each portfolio's investment is identical. The difference is reflected in the remaining 30 percent of funds invested.

If the new project is located in the United States, the overall firm's expected after-tax return (r_p) is

r_p =	[(70%)	×	(20%)]	+	[(30%)	×	(25%)]	=	21.5%
	% of funds invested in prevailing business		Expected return on prevailing business		% of funds invested in new U.S. project		Expected return on new U.S. project		Firm's overall expected return

This computation is based on weighting the returns according to the percentage of total funds invested in each investment.

If the firm calculates its overall expected return when locating the new project in the U.K. instead of the United States, the results would remain unchanged. This is because the new project's expected return is the same regardless of the country of location. Therefore, in terms of return, neither new project has an advantage.

With regard to risk, the new project is expected to exhibit slightly less variability in returns during the five-year period if located in the United States (see Exhibit 13.3). Since firms typically prefer more stable returns on their investments, this is an advantage. However, estimating the risk of the individual project without consideration of the overall firm would be a mistake. The expected correlation of the new

Exhibit 13.3
Evaluation of Proposed Projects in Alternative Locations

	Characteristics of Proposed Project If Located in the United States	Characteristics of Proposed Project If Located in the U.K.
Mean expected annual return on investment (after taxes)	25%	25%
Standard deviation of expected annual after-tax returns on investment	.09	.11
Correlation of expected annual after-tax returns on investment with after-tax returns of prevailing U.S. business	.80	.02

project's returns with those of the prevailing business must also be considered. Recall that portfolio variance is determined by the individual variability of each component as well as their pairwise correlations. The variance of a portfolio (σ_p^2) composed of only two investments (A and B) is computed as

$$\sigma_p^2 = w_A^2\sigma_A^2 + w_B^2\sigma_B^2 + 2w_A w_B \sigma_A \sigma_B (CORR_{AB})$$

where w_A and w_B represent the percentage of total funds allocated to Investments A and B, respectively; σ_A and σ_B are the standard deviations of returns on Investments A and B, respectively, and $CORR_{AB}$ is the correlation coefficient of returns between Investments A and B. This equation for portfolio variance can be applied to the problem at hand. The portfolio reflects the overall firm. First, compute the overall firm's variance in returns assuming it locates the new project in the United States (based on the information provided in Exhibit 13.3). This variance (σ_p^2) is

$$\begin{aligned}\sigma_p^2 &= (.70)^2\,(.10)^2 + (.30)^2\,(.09)^2 + 2\,(.70)(.30)(.10)(.09)(.80)\\ &= (.49)(.01) + (.09)(.0081) + .003024\\ &= .0049 + .000729 + .003024\\ &= .008653\end{aligned}$$

If the firm decides to locate the new project in the U.K. instead of the United States, its overall variability in returns will be different, because that project differs from the new U.S. project in terms of individual variability in returns and correlation with the prevailing business. The overall variability of the firm's returns based on locating the new project in the U.K. is estimated by variance in the portfolio returns (σ_p^2):

$$\begin{aligned}\sigma_p^2 &= (.70)^2\,(.10)^2 + (.30)^2\,(.11)^2 + 2(.70)\,(.30)\,(.10)\,(.11)\,(.02)\\ &= (.49)\,(.01) + (.09)\,(.0121) + .0000924\\ &= .0049 + .001089 + .0000924\\ &= .0060814\end{aligned}$$

Thus, the firm will generate more stable returns if the new project is located in the U.K. The firm's overall variability in returns is almost 29.7 percent less if the new project is located in the U.K. rather than in the United States.

The reason for the reduced variability when locating in the foreign country is based on the correlation of the new project's expected returns with the expected returns of the prevailing business. If the new project is located in the firm's home country (the United States), its returns are expected to be more highly correlated with those of the prevailing business than they would be if the project was located in the U.K. When economic conditions of two countries (such as the United States and the U.K.) are not highly correlated, then a firm may reduce its risk by diversifying its business in both countries instead of concentrating in just one.

Diversification Benefits of Multiple Projects

By extending the previous example to multiple projects, one can gain further insight on the benefits from international diversification. Consider a set of 40 possible U.S. projects, each of which has expected returns to a firm over the next five years. Assume that the variance of each project's expected returns has been estimated and that the average variance of these 40 projects also has been determined. Now consider all possible sets of two projects combined (and equally weighted). If the returns on these projects are not all perfectly positively correlated, the average variance of a typical two-project portfolio will be less than the average variance of individual projects. Similarly, the variance of all possible three-project portfolios (equally weighted) should be even lower. As more projects are added, the portfolio variance should decrease on average. Initially, the average reduction in variance of returns (a measure of risk) associated with the addition of one more project is substantial. However, after some point, the average reduction in variance becomes negligible, meaning that the remaining risk cannot be diversified away by adding more U.S. projects. This is illustrated as the U.S. curve in Exhibit 13.4.

Now consider another set of 40 projects, of which some are in the United States and the rest are in various foreign countries. If the procedure just described is applied to this set, the outcome will be similar to the global curve in Exhibit 13.4. Notice that

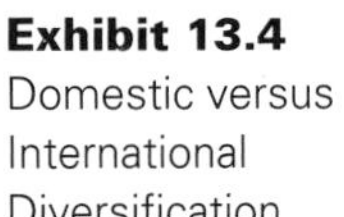

Exhibit 13.4
Domestic versus International Diversification

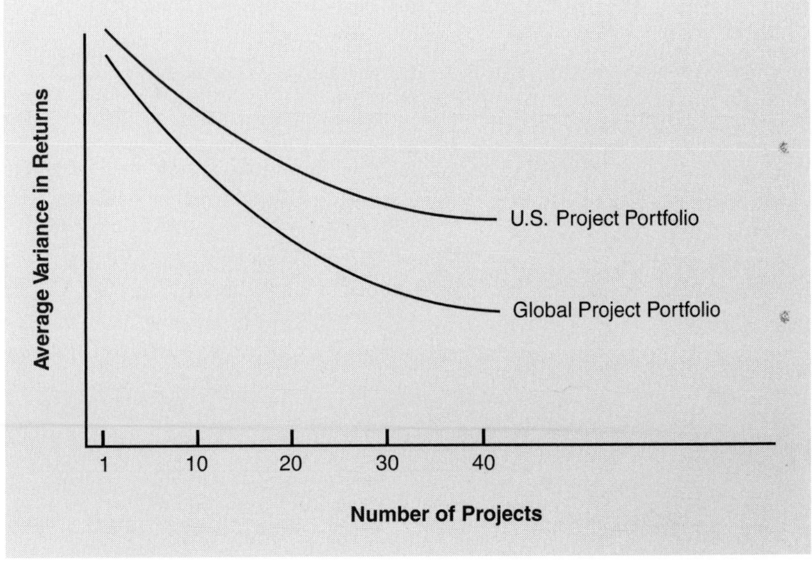

the degree of risk reduction resulting from adding an additional project is greater for the global set than for the U.S. set. For any given number of projects, the global portfolio has less risk. The advantage to the global set is attributed to the lower correlations between returns of projects implemented in different economies.

Risk-Return Analysis of International Projects

Like any investor, an MNC with projects positioned around the world is concerned with the risk and return characteristics of the projects. The portfolio of all projects reflects the MNC in aggregate. From a conceptual perspective, the MNC's global strategy of developing projects can be examined using Exhibit 13.5. Each point on the graph reflects a specific project that either has been implemented or is being considered. The return axis may be measured by potential return on assets or return on equity. The risk may be measured by potential fluctuation in the returns generated by each project.

Exhibit 13.5 shows that Project A has the highest expected return of all the projects. While the MNC could devote most of its resources toward this project to attempt to achieve such a high return, its risk is possibly too high by itself. In addition, such a project may not be able to absorb all available capital anyway if its potential market for customers is limited. Thus, the MNC develops a portfolio of projects. By combining Project A with several other projects, the MNC may decrease its expected return. On the other hand, risk could also be reduced substantially. If the MNC appropriately combines projects, its project portfolio may be able to achieve a risk-return trade-off exhibited by any of the points on the curve in Exhibit 13.5. This curve represents a frontier of efficient project portfolios that exhibit desirable risk-return characteristics, in that no single project could outperform any of these portfolios. The term "efficient" refers to a minimum risk for a given expected return. Project portfolios outperform the individual projects because of the diversification attributes discussed earlier. The lower, or more negative, the correlation in project returns over time, the lower will be the project portfolio risk.

http://
The CIA's homepage at www.odci.gov/cia/ciahome.html provides access to various national and international surveys, analyses, maps, and publications such as the World Factbook.

Exhibit 13.5
Risk-Return Analysis of International Projects

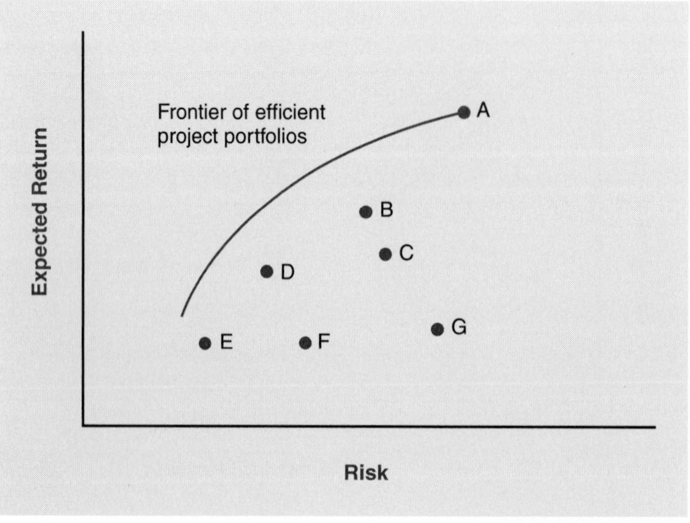

As new projects are proposed, the frontier of efficient project portfolios may shift. An MNC is better off if the efficient frontier is further to the left since this reflects less risk.

Along the frontier of efficient project portfolios, no portfolio can be singled out as "optimal" for all MNCs. This is because MNCs vary in their willingness to accept risk. If the MNC is very conservative and has the choice of any portfolios represented by the frontier in Exhibit 13.5, it will probably prefer one that exhibits low risk (near the bottom of the frontier). Conversely, a more aggressive strategy would be to implement a portfolio of projects that exhibit risk-return characteristics such as those near the top of the frontier.

The actual location of the frontier of efficient project portfolios depends on the business in which the firm is involved. Consider an MNC that sells steel solely to European nations and is considering other related projects. Its frontier of efficient project portfolios would exhibit considerable risk (because it sells just one product to countries whose economies move in tandem). Yet, another MNC that sells a wide range of products to countries all over the world could reduce its project portfolio risk to a greater degree. Therefore, its frontier of efficient project portfolios would be closer to the vertical axis. This comparison is illustrated in Exhibit 13.6. Of course, this comparison assumes the multiproduct MNC is knowledgeable about all of its products and the markets to which it sells.

Our discussion suggests that MNCs can achieve more desirable risk-return characteristics from their project portfolios if they sufficiently diversify among products *and* geographical markets. This also relates to the advantage an MNC has over a purely domestic firm with only a local market. The MNC may be able to develop a more efficient portfolio of projects than its domestic counterpart.

The international diversification of sales is shown for three U.S.-based MNCs in Exhibit 13.7. Notice that each of these MNCs has diversified its sales across several regions. By diversifying their business across foreign regions, these firms have reduced their exposure to economic conditions in the United States. However, they have become more exposed to conditions in foreign countries.

Exhibit 13.6
Risk-Return Advantage of a Diversified MNC

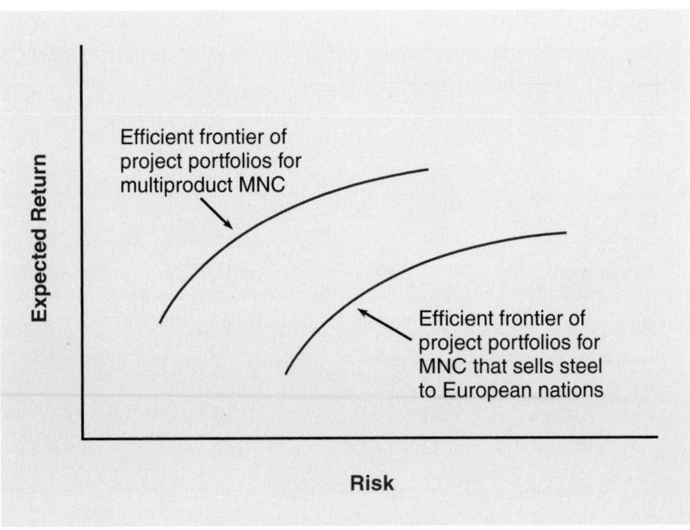

Exhibit 13.7
International Diversification of Sales (1998)

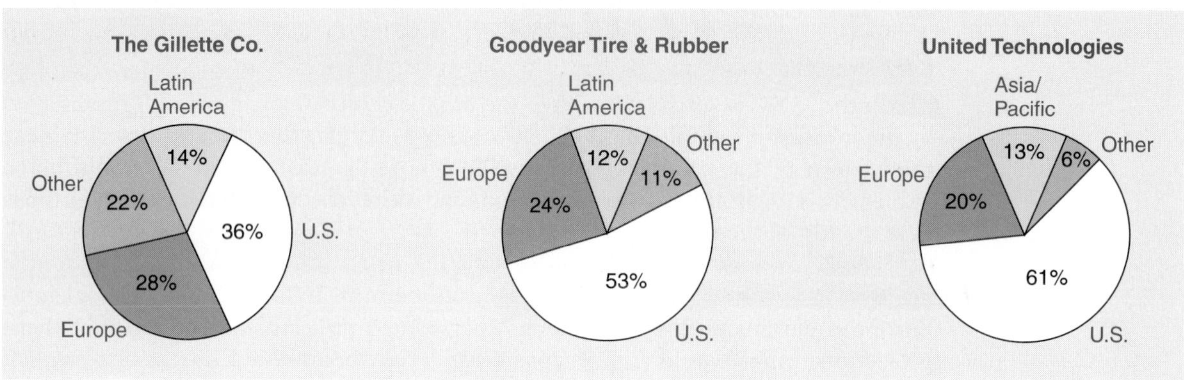

DECISIONS SUBSEQUENT TO DFI

Once DFI takes place, periodic decisions are necessary to determine whether further expansion should take place in a given location. In addition, as the project generates earnings, the MNC must decide whether to have the funds remitted to the parent or used by the subsidiary. If the subsidiary has a use for the funds that would be of more value than the parent's use, the subsidiary should retain the funds. Of course, a certain percentage of the funds will be needed to maintain operations, but the remaining funds could be sent to the parent, sent to another subsidiary, or reinvested for expansion purposes.

Facts relevant to the decision regarding whether the subsidiary should reinvest the earnings should be analyzed on a case-by-case basis. That is, there is no simple guideline to follow. The appropriate decision depends on the economic conditions in the subsidiary's country and the parent's country, as well as restrictions imposed by the host country government. Exhibit 13.8 provides a breakdown of reported earnings from U.S. DFI in regions as of 1998. The total earnings for each region are divided into "distributed" (sent to parent or elsewhere) and "reinvested" earnings. Notice how the reinvestment ratio (computed as reinvested earnings divided by total earnings) varies among regions.

Exhibit 13.8
Earnings from Direct Foreign Investment Abroad by U.S.-Based MNCs Reported in 1998 (in Millions of Dollars)

	Earnings			
Location	Total	Distributed	Reinvested	Reinvestment Ratio
All areas	95,067	37,182	57,885	0.61
Canada	8,642	1,767	6,875	0.80
Europe	46,183	2,713	43,470	0.94
Latin America	17,404	3,105	14,299	0.82
Asia and Pacific	18,937	4,185	14,752	0.78

Source: *Survey of Current Business,* U.S. Department of Commerce.

HOST GOVERNMENT VIEW OF DFI

DFI may be perceived as a cause of or the remedy for national problems. For example, DFI may provide needed employment or technology. However, locally owned companies may lose business due to the new competition. These effects could lead to proposals for increased protectionism.

The ability of a host government to attract DFI is dependent on the country's markets and resources, as well as government regulations and incentives. Countries such as Singapore and Hong Kong have attracted substantial DFI because they enforce few restrictions. Conversely, Japan has attracted a very limited amount of DFI because of major barriers to entry.

Some governments offer incentives by reducing production restrictions. For example, Mexico recently reduced its restrictions on automobiles produced there. It had required that Mexican parts make up 65 percent of an automobile produced for the domestic market and 30 percent of one produced for export. This policy was changed to encourage automobile manufacturers from other countries to establish plants in Mexico. Mexico also recently announced that it would allow foreign companies to own 100 percent of their subsidiaries established in Mexico.

http://

The Price Waterhouse Coopers site at www.pwcglobal.com provides access to country-specific information such as general business rules and regulations, tax environments, and some other useful statistics and surveys.

Each government must weigh the advantages and disadvantages of DFI in its country. Some types of DFI will be more attractive to some governments than others. The ideal DFI solves problems such as unemployment and lack of technology without taking business away from local firms. An example would be a production plant that uses local labor and produces goods that are not direct substitutes of other locally produced goods. In this case, the plant will not cause a reduction in sales by local firms. A second ideal situation would be a plant that uses local labor and then exports the products (assuming no other local firm exports such products to the same areas).

In most cases, there may be both advantages and disadvantages to a country's allowing a given type of DFI into the country. If the advantages appear to outweigh the disadvantages, the government may attempt to provide additional incentives in order to encourage the DFI to take place. Such incentives could include tax breaks on the income earned there, rent-free land and buildings, low-interest loans, subsidized energy, and reduced environmental (pollution, etc.) restrictions. The degree to which a government would offer such incentives depends on the extent to which the MNC's DFI would benefit that country.

As an example of a government incentive, consider the recent decision by Allied Research Associates Inc. to build a production facility and office in Belgium. The Belgian government subsidized a large portion of the expenses, offering tax concessions and favorable interest rates on loans to Allied. Finland and Ireland attracted MNCs in the late 1990s by imposing a very low corporate tax rate on specific businesses.

IMPACT OF THE DFI DECISION ON AN MNC'S VALUE

An MNC's direct foreign investment decision affects its value, as shown in Exhibit 13.9. Decisions on which countries to target for expansion affect the revenue generated by the foreign subsidiaries and the operating expenses of the foreign subsidiaries. Thus, the direct foreign investment decisions determine the expected foreign currency cash flows that will be earned by each foreign subsidiary and will therefore affect the expected dollar cash flows ultimately received by the U.S. parent.

Exhibit 13.9
Impact of Direct Foreign Investment Decisions on an MNC's Value

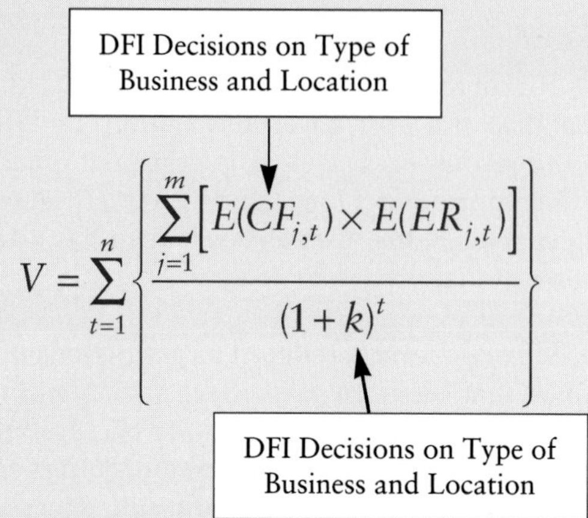

$$V = \sum_{t=1}^{n} \left\{ \frac{\sum_{j=1}^{m} \left[E(CF_{j,t}) \times E(ER_{j,t}) \right]}{(1+k)^t} \right\}$$

V = value of the U.S.-based MNC
$E(CF_{j,t})$ = expected cash flows denominated in currency j to be received by the U.S. parent in period t
$E(ER_{j,t})$ = expected exchange rate at which currency j can be converted to dollars at the end of period t
k = the weighted average cost of capital of the U.S. parent
m = number of currencies
n = number of periods

Since the direct foreign investment decisions by the U.S. parent determine the types of new operations and the locations of foreign operations, they can affect the perceived risk of these operations that are supported by the parent's direct foreign investment. Therefore direct foreign investment decisions can affect the MNC's cost of capital, which also affects the MNC's value.

SUMMARY

- MNCs may be motivated to initiate direct foreign investment because they can attract new sources of demand or enter markets where superior profits are possible. These two motives are normally based on opportunities to generate more revenue in foreign markets. There are many other motives for using direct foreign investment that are typically related to cost efficiency, such as using foreign factors of production, raw materials, or technology.

  There are other motives for direct foreign investment that MNCs consider to protect their foreign market share, such as reacting to exchange rate movements or trade restrictions.

- International diversification is a common motive for direct foreign investment. It allows an MNC to reduce its exposure to domestic economic conditions. In this way, the MNC may be able to stabilize its cash flows and reduce its risk. Such a goal is desirable because it may reduce the firm's cost of financing.

  International projects can possibly allow MNCs to achieve lower risk than what is possible from only domestic projects, without reducing their expected returns. International diversification tends to be more capable of risk reduction when the direct foreign investment is targeted for countries whose economies are somewhat unrelated to an MNC's home country economy.

SELF-TEST FOR CHAPTER 13

(Answers are provided in Appendix A at the back of the text.)

1. Offer some reasons for U.S. firms' preference for direct foreign investment in Canada over DFI in Mexico.
2. Offer some reasons for U.S. firms' preference for direct foreign investment in Mexico over DFI in Canada.
3. € One U.S. executive stated that Europe was not considered as a location for direct foreign investment because of the euro's value. Interpret this statement.
4. Why do you think joint ventures are a common strategy used by U.S. firms to enter China?
5. Why would the United States offer large incentives to a foreign automobile manufacturer for establishment of a production subsidiary in the United States? Isn't this strategy indirectly subsidizing the foreign competitors of U.S. firms?

QUESTIONS AND APPLICATIONS

1. Describe some potential benefits to the MNC as a result of direct foreign investment (DFI). Elaborate on each type of benefit.
2. Packer Inc., a U.S. producer of computer diskettes, plans to establish a subsidiary in Mexico in order to penetrate the Mexican market. Executives of Packer believe that the Mexican peso's value is relatively strong and will weaken against the dollar over time. If their expectations about the peso value are correct, how will this affect the feasibility of the project? Explain.
3. Bear Company and Viking Inc. are automobile manufacturers that desire to benefit from economies of scale. Bear Company has decided to establish distributorship subsidiaries in various countries, while Viking Inc. has decided to establish manufacturing subsidiaries in various countries. Which firm is more likely to benefit from economies of scale?
4. Raider Chemical Company and Ram Inc. had similar intentions to reduce the volatility of their cash flows. Raider implemented a long-range plan to establish 40 percent of its business in Canada. Ram Inc. implemented a long-range plan to establish 30 percent of its business in Europe and Asia, scattered among 12 different countries. Which company would more effectively reduce cash flow volatility once the plans are achieved?
5. If the United States placed long-term restrictions on imports, would the amount of direct foreign investment by non-U.S. MNCs in the United States increase, decrease, or be unchanged? Explain.
6. In 1972, Tandy Corporation established a manufacturing facility in South Korea to produce computer components. One of the attractions was the relatively low cost of labor. In 1989, Tandy closed the facility as the cost advantage dissipated. Why do you think the relative cost advantage has dissipated in South Korea and other Asian countries such as Hong Kong, Singapore, and Taiwan? (Ignore possible exchange rate effects.)
7. Offer your opinion on why economies of some less developed countries with strict restrictions on international trade and direct foreign investment are somewhat independent from economies of other countries. Why would MNCs desire to enter such countries? If these countries relaxed their restrictions, would their economies continue to be independent of other economies? Explain.
8. € Dolphin Inc., a U.S.-based MNC with a European subsidiary, expects that the euro will appreciate for several years. How might Dolphin Inc. adjust its policy on remitted earnings from the European subsidiary?

9. Bronco Corporation has decided to establish a subsidiary in Taiwan that would produce stereos and sell them in Taiwan. It expects that its cost of producing these stereos will be one-third the cost of producing them in the United States. Assuming that its production cost estimates are accurate, is Bronco's strategy sensible? Explain.

10. What does this chapter reveal about the relationship between the degree of international business and risk of MNCs? What does this imply about the feasibility of increasing international business?

11. Starter Corp. of New Haven, Connecticut, produces sportswear that is licensed by professional sports teams. It recently decided to expand in Europe. What are the potential benefits for this firm to use direct foreign investment?

12. What potential benefits do you think were most important in the decision of Walt Disney Company to build a theme park in France?

13. Once an MNC establishes a subsidiary, DFI remains an ongoing decision. What does this statement mean?

14. Why would foreign governments provide MNCs with incentives to undertake DFI there?

15. This chapter concentrates on possible benefits to a firm that increases its international business. What are some risks of international business that may not exist for local business?

16. J.C. Penney recognized numerous opportunities to expand in foreign countries and has assessed many foreign markets, including Brazil, Greece, Mexico, Portugal, Singapore, and Thailand. It opened new stores in Europe, Asia, and Latin America. However, it did not have a sufficient understanding of the culture of each country that it had targeted. Thus, J.C. Penney engaged in joint ventures with local partners of each foreign country who knew the opinions of the local customers.

    a. What comparative advantage does J.C. Penney have when establishing a store in a foreign country, relative to an independent variety store?
    b. Why might the overall risk of J.C. Penney decrease or increase as a result of its recent global expansion?
    c. J.C. Penney has been more cautious about entering China. Explain the potential obstacles associated with entering China.

17. Consider the typical motives for a U.S. firm to engage in direct foreign investment. Which of these motives might be used to encourage a U.S. firm to invest in Asia since the Asian crisis began? (Assume the firm currently has no business in Asia.)

18. From the perspective of a U.S. firm that has direct foreign investment throughout Asia, did the Asian crisis increase or decrease the international diversification benefits achievable in the Asian countries?

Internet Application

19. Information related to direct foreign investment can be retrieved from the following Web site of the Michigan State University Center for International Business Education and Research:

    http://ciber.bus.msu.edu

    a. Use this Web page to identify emerging markets that appear to have favorable characteristics for DFI.
    b. The following Web site provides information about conditions that could affect the decision for an MNC to invest in a specific country:

       http://lcweb2.loc.gov/gov/frd/cs/cshome.html

    Use this Web site to review the related information about a country of your choice. Describe the current economic environment and political environment of that country.

Running Your Own MNC

20. a. Assuming that your international business is successful, identify reasons why it may be feasible to establish a small subsidiary in the foreign country rather than continue exporting.
    b. Identify the disadvantages associated with establishing a small subsidiary in the foreign country of concern.

Blades, Inc. Case

Consideration of Direct Foreign Investment

For the last year, Blades, Inc. has been exporting to Thailand in order to supplement its declining U.S. sales. Under the existing arrangement, Blades sells 180,000 pairs of roller blades annually to Entertainment Products, a Thai retailer, for a fixed price denominated in Thai baht. The agreement will last for another two years. Furthermore, in order to diversify internationally and to take advantage of an attractive offer by Jogs Ltd., a British retailer, Blades has recently begun exporting to the United Kingdom. Under the resulting agreement, Jogs will purchase 200,000 pairs of "Speedos," Blades' primary product, annually at a fixed price of £80 per pair.

Blades' suppliers of the needed components for its roller blade production are located primarily in the United States, where Blades incurs the majority of its cost of goods sold. Although prices for inputs needed to manufacture roller blades vary, recent costs have run at approximately $70 per pair. Blades also imports components from Thailand because of the relatively low price of rubber and plastic components and because of their high quality. These imports are denominated in Thai baht, and the exact price (in baht) depends on prevailing market prices for these components in Thailand. Currently, inputs sufficient to manufacture a pair of roller blades cost approximately 3,000 Thai baht per pair of roller blades.

Although Thailand had been among the world's fastest growing economies, recent events in Thailand have increased the level of economic uncertainty. Specifically, the Thai baht, which had been pegged to the dollar, is now a freely floating currency and has depreciated substantially in recent months. Furthermore, recent levels of inflation in Thailand have been very high. Future economic conditions in Thailand are currently highly uncertain.

Ben Holt, Blades' chief financial officer (CFO), is seriously considering direct foreign investment in Thailand. He believes that the time to either establish a subsidiary or to acquire an existing business in Thailand is perfect, since uncertain economic conditions and the depreciation of the baht have substantially lowered the initial costs required for direct foreign investment. Ben Holt believes the growth potential in Asia will be extremely high once the Thai economy stabilizes.

Although Mr. Holt has also considered direct foreign investment in the United Kingdom, he would prefer that Blades invest in Thailand as opposed to the United Kingdom. Forecasts indicate that the demand for roller blades in the United Kingdom is similar to that of the United States; since Blades' U.S. sales have recently declined because of the high prices its charges, direct foreign investment in the United Kingdom is expected to yield similar results, especially since the components required to manufacture roller blades are more expensive in the United Kingdom than they are in the United States. Furthermore, both domestic and foreign roller blade manufacturers are relatively well established in the United Kingdom, and the growth potential there is limited. Conversely, there is more growth potential for the Thai roller blade market.

Blades can sell its products at a lower price but generate higher profit margins in Thailand than it can in the United States. This is because the Thai customer has committed itself to purchase a fixed number of Blades' products annually only if it can purchase Speedos at a substantial discount from the U.S. price. Nevertheless, since the cost of goods sold incurred in Thailand is substantially below that incurred in the United States, Blades has managed to generate higher profit margins from its Thai exports and imports than in the United States.

As a financial analyst for Blades, Inc., you generally agree with Ben Holt's assessment of the situation. However, you are concerned that Thai consumers have not been affected yet by the unfavorable economic conditions. You believe that they may reduce their spending on leisure products within the next year. Therefore, you think it would be beneficial to wait until next year, when the unfavorable economic conditions in Thailand may subside, to make a decision regarding direct foreign investment in Thailand. However, if economic conditions in Thailand improve over the next year, direct foreign investment may become more expensive both because existing firms will be more expensive and because the baht may appreciate.

You are also aware that several of Blades' U.S. competitors are considering expansion into Thailand within the next year.

If Blades acquires an existing business in Thailand or establishes a subsidiary there by the end of next year, it would fulfill its agreement with Entertainment Products for the subsequent year. The Thai retailer has expressed an interest in renewing the contractual agreement with Blades at that time if Blades establishes operations in Thailand. However, Ben Holt believes that Blades could charge a higher price for its products if it establishes its own distribution channels.

Ben Holt has asked you to answer the following questions:

1. Identify and discuss some of the benefits of direct foreign investment that apply to Blades, Inc.
2. Do you think Blades should wait until next year to undertake direct foreign investment in Thailand? What is the tradeoff if Blades undertakes the direct foreign investment now?
3. Do you think Blades should renew its agreement with the Thai supplier for another three years? What is the tradeoff if Blades renews the agreement?
4. Assume a high level of unemployment in Thailand and a unique production process employed by Blades, Inc. How do you think the Thai government would view the establishment of a subsidiary in Thailand by firms such as Blades? Do you think the Thai government would be more or less supportive of an acquisition by firms such as Blades of existing businesses in Thailand? Why?

Small Business Dilemma

Direct Foreign Investment Decision by the Sports Exports Company

Jim Logan's business, the Sports Exports Company, continues to grow. His primary product is the footballs he produces and exports to a distributor in the United Kingdom. However, his recent joint venture with a British firm has also been successful. The venture arranges for a British firm to produce other sporting goods for Jim's firm; these goods are then delivered to that distributor. Jim intentionally started his international business by exporting because it was easier and cheaper to export than to establish a place of business in the United Kingdom. However, he is considering the establishment of a firm in the United Kingdom that would produce the footballs there instead of in his garage (in the United States). Also, this firm would produce the other sporting goods that he now sells, so he would no longer have to rely on another British firm (through the joint venture) to produce those goods.

1. Given the information provided here, what are Jim's advantages in establishing the firm in the United Kingdom?
2. Given the information provided here, what are Jim's disadvantages in establishing the firm in the United Kingdom?

14 Multinational Capital Budgeting

Multinational corporations (MNCs) evaluate international projects by using multinational capital budgeting, which compares the benefits and costs of these projects. Given that many MNCs spend more than $100 million per year on international projects, multinational capital budgeting is a critical function. Many international projects are irreversible and cannot be easily sold to other corporations at a reasonable price. Proper use of multinational capital budgeting can separate the international projects worthy of implementation from those that are not.

The most popular form of capital budgeting is to determine the project's net present value by estimating the present value of the project's future cash flows and subtracting the initial outlay required for the project. Multinational capital budgeting typically involves a similar process. However, special circumstances of international projects that affect the future cash flows or the discount rate used to discount cash flows make multinational capital budgeting more complex.

The specific objectives of this chapter are to

- compare the capital budgeting analysis of an MNC's subsidiary versus its parent,
- demonstrate how multinational capital budgeting can be applied to determine whether an international project should be implemented, and
- explain how the risk of international projects can be assessed.

Subsidiary versus Parent Perspective

Should capital budgeting for a multinational project be conducted from the viewpoint of the subsidiary that will administer the project or the parent that will most likely finance much of the project? Some would say the subsidiary's perspective should be used since it will be responsible for administering the project. In addition, since the subsidiary is a subset of the MNC, what is good for the subsidiary would appear to be good for the MNC. This reasoning, however, is not necessarily correct. One could argue that if the parent is financing the project, then it should be evaluating the results from its point of view. The feasibility of the capital budgeting analysis can vary with the perspective because the net after-tax cash inflows to the subsidiary can differ substantially from those to the parent. Such a difference is due to several factors, some of which are discussed here.

Tax Differentials

http://
See www.tax.kmpg.net/library for detailed information on the tax regimes, rates, and regulations of over 75 countries.

Assume that the parent considers expanding a subsidiary's marketing department. Also assume that the host country government imposes a very low tax rate on earnings generated by the subsidiary. If the earnings due to the project will someday be remitted to the parent, the MNC needs to consider how the parent's government taxes these earnings. If the parent's government imposes a high tax rate on the remitted funds, the project may be feasible from the subsidiary's point of view, but not from the parent's point of view. Under such a scenario, the parent should not consider implementing such a project, even though it appears feasible from the subsidiary's perspective.

Restricted Remittances

Consider a potential project to be implemented in a country where government restrictions require that a percentage of the subsidiary earnings remain in the country. Since the parent may never have access to such funds, the project is not attractive to the parent. Yet, the project may be attractive to the subsidiary. One possible solution to such a problem is to let the subsidiary obtain partial financing for the project within the host country. In this case, the portion of funds not allowed to be sent to the parent can be used to cover the financing costs over time.

Excessive Remittances

Consider a parent that charges its subsidiary very high administrative fees, since management is centralized at the headquarters. To the subsidiary, the fees represent an expense. To the parent, the fees represent revenue that may substantially exceed the actual cost of managing the subsidiary. In this case, the project's earnings may appear low from the subsidiary's perspective and high from the parent's perspective. The feasibility of the project again depends on perspective. In most cases, neglecting the parent's perspective will distort the true value of a foreign project.

Exchange Rate Movements

When earnings are remitted to the parent, they are normally converted from the subsidiary's local currency to the parent's currency. The amount received by the parent is therefore influenced by the existing exchange rate. If the subsidiary project is assessed from the subsidiary's perspective, the cash flows forecasted for the subsidiary do not have to be converted to the parent's currency.

Summary of Factors

Exhibit 14.1 illustrates the process from the time earnings are generated by the subsidiary until remitted funds are received by the parent. The exhibit shows that the earnings are reduced initially by corporate taxes paid to the host government. Then, some of the earnings are retained by the subsidiary (either by choice of the subsidiary or according to host government rules), with the residual targeted as funds to be

Exhibit 14.1
Process of Remitting Subsidiary Earnings to the Parent

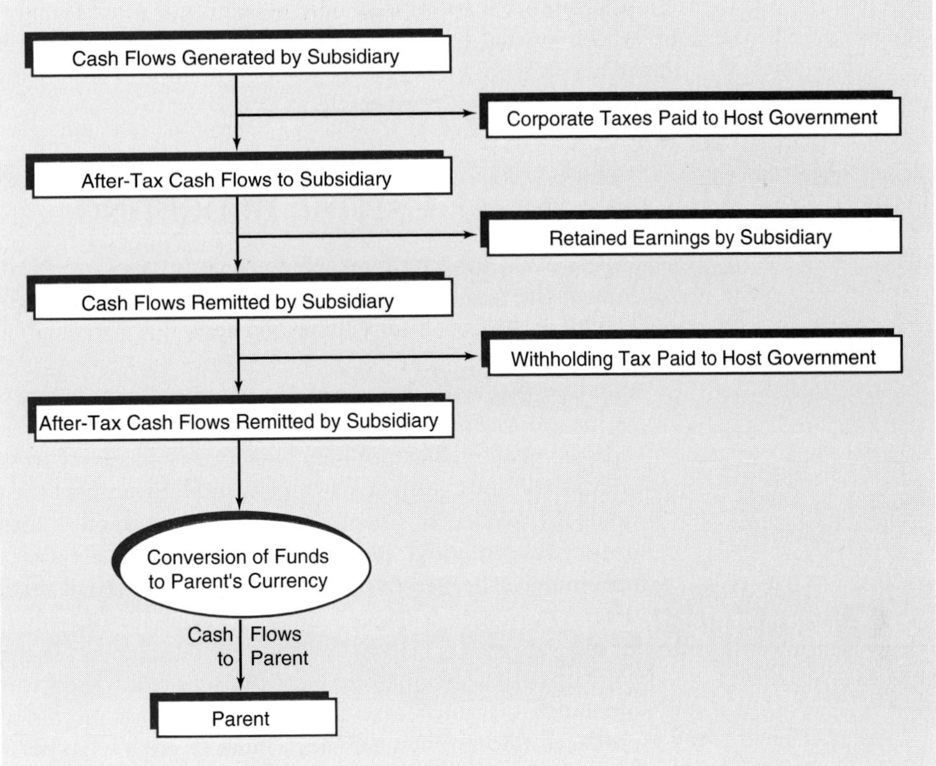

remitted. Those funds that are remitted may be subject to a withholding tax by the host government. The remaining funds are converted to the parent's currency (at the prevailing exchange rate) and remitted to the parent. Given the various factors shown here that can drain subsidiary earnings, the cash flows actually remitted by the subsidiary may represent only a small portion of the earnings generated by the subsidiary. The feasibility of the project from the parent's perspective is dependent not on the subsidiary cash flows but on the cash flows that it ultimately receives.

A parent's perspective is appropriate in attempting to determine whether a project will enhance the firm's value. Given that the parent's shareholders are its owners, it should make decisions that satisfy its shareholders. Each project, whether foreign or domestic, should ultimately generate sufficient cash flows to the parent in order to enhance shareholder wealth. Any project that can create a positive net present value for the parent should enhance shareholder wealth.

One exception to the rule of using a parent's perspective occurs when the foreign subsidiary is not wholly owned by the parent and when the foreign project is partially financed with retained earnings of the parent and of the subsidiary. In this case, the foreign subsidiary has a group of shareholders that it must satisfy. Any arrangement made between the parent and the subsidiary should be acceptable to the two entities only if the arrangement enhances the values of both entities. The decisions are not intended to transfer wealth from one entity to another but are in the interest of both groups of shareholders.

While this exception has been recognized, most foreign subsidiaries of MNCs are wholly owned by the parents. Examples in this text implicitly assume that the subsidiary is wholly owned by the parent (unless noted otherwise) and therefore focus on the parent's perspective.

INPUT FOR MULTINATIONAL CAPITAL BUDGETING

Regardless of the long-term project to be considered, an MNC will normally require forecasts of the economic and financial characteristics related to the project. Each of these characteristics is briefly described here:

1. *Initial investment.* The parent's initial investment in a project may constitute the major source of funds to support a particular project. Funds initially invested in a project may include not only whatever is necessary to start the project but also additional funds, such as working capital, to support the project over time. Such funds are needed to finance inventory, wages, etc., until the revenue from the project are generated. Because cash inflows will not always be sufficient to cover upcoming cash outflows, working capital is needed throughout a project's lifetime.
2. *Consumer demand.* An accurately forecasted consumer demand for a product is quite valuable when projecting a cash flow schedule. However, future demand is often difficult to forecast. For example, if the project is a plant in Germany that produces automobiles, the MNC must forecast what percentage of the auto market in Germany it can pull from prevailing auto producers. Once a market share percentage is forecasted, projected demand can be computed with ease. Yet, the forecast of market share is subject to error. Demand forecasts can sometimes be aided by historical data on what market share other MNCs in the industry pulled when they entered this market. However, historical data are not always an accurate indicator of the future. In addition, many projects reflect a first attempt, so there are no predecessors to review as an indicator of the future.
3. *Price.* The price at which the product could be sold can be forecasted using competitive products in the markets as a comparison. However, a long-term capital budgeting analysis requires projections for not only the upcoming period but the expected lifetime of the project as well. The future prices will most likely be responsive to the future inflation rate in the host country (where the project is to take place). Yet, the future inflation rate is not known. Thus, future inflation rates must be forecasted in order to develop projections of the product price over time.
4. *Variable cost.* Like the price estimate, variable-cost forecasts can be developed from assessing prevailing comparative costs of the components (such as hourly labor costs, etc.) that make it up. Such costs should normally move in tandem with the future inflation rate of the host country. Even if the variable cost per unit can be accurately predicted, the projected total variable cost (variable cost per unit times quantity produced) may be wrong if the demand is inaccurately forecasted.
5. *Fixed cost.* On a periodic basis, the fixed cost may be easier to predict than the variable cost since it is not normally sensitive to changes in demand. It is, however, sensitive to any change in the host country's inflation rate from the point at which the forecast is made until the point at which the fixed costs are incurred.

6. *Project lifetime.* While it is difficult to assess the life of some projects, other projects are designated specific lifetimes, at the end of which they will be liquidated. This makes the capital budgeting analysis easier to apply. It should be recognized that the MNC does not always have complete control over the lifetime decision. In some cases, political events may force a liquidation of the project earlier than planned. The probability that such events will occur varies among countries.
7. *Salvage (liquidation) value.* The after-tax salvage value of most projects is difficult to forecast. It will depend on several factors, including the success of the project and the attitude of the host government toward the project. As an extreme possibility, the host government could take over the project without adequately compensating the MNC.
8. *Fund-transfer restrictions.* In some cases, a host government will prevent a subsidiary's earnings from being sent to the parent. This restriction may reflect an attempt to encourage additional local spending or to avoid excessive sales of the local currency in exchange for some other currency. Since the fund-transfer restrictions prevent cash from coming back to the parent, projected net cash flows from the parent's perspective will be affected by the restrictions. If the parent is aware of these restrictions, it can incorporate them when projecting net cash flows. However, the host government may adjust its fund-transfer restrictions over time, in which case the MNC can only forecast the future fund-transfer restrictions and incorporate these forecasts into the analysis.
9. *Tax laws.* The tax laws on earnings generated by a foreign subsidiary or remitted to the MNC's parent vary among countries. Under some circumstances, they allow tax deductions or credits for the MNC due to tax payments by subsidiaries to their respective host countries (see the chapter appendix for more details). Because after-tax cash flows are necessary for an adequate capital budgeting analysis, international tax effects must be determined on any proposed foreign projects.
10. *Exchange rates.* Any international project will be affected by exchange rate fluctuations during the life of the project, but these movements are often very difficult to forecast. There are methods of hedging against them, though most hedging techniques are used to cover short-term positions. While it is possible to hedge over longer periods (with long-term forward contracts or currency swap arrangements), the MNC has no way of knowing the amount of funds that it should hedge. This is because it is only guessing at its future costs and revenue due to the project. Thus, the MNC may decide not to hedge the projected foreign currency net cash flows.
11. *Required rate of return.* Once the relevant cash flows of a proposed project are estimated, they can be discounted at the project's required rate of return, which may differ from the MNC's cost of capital because of that particular project's risk.

http://
The Virtual International Business and Economic Sources (VIBES) at www.uncc.edu/lis/library/reference/intbus/vibehome.htm provides 1,300 links to Internet sources of international business and economic information.

Additional considerations will be discussed after a simplified multinational capital budgeting example is provided. In the real world, magic numbers aren't provided to MNCs for insertion into their computers. The challenge revolves around accurately forecasting the variables relevant to the project evaluation. If garbage (inaccurate forecasts) is input into the computer, the analysis output generated by the computer will also be garbage. Consequently, an MNC may take on a project by mistake. Since such a mistake may be worth millions of dollars, it is understandable that MNCs need to assess the degree of uncertainty for any input that is used in the project evaluation. This is discussed more thoroughly later in this chapter.

MULTINATIONAL CAPITAL BUDGETING EXAMPLE

Capital budgeting for the MNC is necessary for all long-term projects that deserve consideration. The projects may range from a small expansion of a subsidiary division to the creation of a new subsidiary. The example that follows reflects the possible development of a new subsidiary. It begins with assumptions that simplify the capital budgeting analysis. Then, additional considerations are discussed in order to emphasize the potential complexity of such an analysis.

The forthcoming example illustrates one of many possible methods available that would achieve the same result. Also, keep in mind that a real-world problem would involve more extenuating circumstances than those shown here.

Example: Background

Spartan Inc. is considering the development of a subsidiary in Singapore that could manufacture and sell tennis rackets locally. Various departments of Spartan Inc. were asked to supply relevant information for a capital budgeting analysis. In addition, some executives of Spartan Inc. met with government officials of Singapore regarding the proposed subsidiary. All relevant information follows.

1. *Initial investment.* An estimated 20 million Singapore dollars (S$), which includes funds to support working capital, would be needed for the project. Given the existing spot rate of $.50 per Singapore dollar, the U.S.-dollar amount of the parent's initial investment is $10 million.
2. *Project life.* The project is expected to end in four years. The host government of Singapore has promised to make a payment to the parent in order to purchase the plant after four years.
3. *Price and demand.* The estimated price and demand schedules during each of the next four years are shown here:

Year	Price per Racket	Demand in Singapore
1	S$350	60,000 units
2	S$350	60,000 units
3	S$360	100,000 units
4	S$380	100,000 units

4. *Costs.* The variable costs (for materials, labor, etc.) per unit were estimated and consolidated as shown here:

Year	Variable Costs (VC) per Racket
1	S$200
2	S$200
3	S$250
4	S$260

The expense of leasing extra office space is S$1 million per year. Other annual overhead expenses are expected to be S$1 million per year.

5. *Exchange rates.* The spot exchange rate of the Singapore dollar is \$.50. The spot rate is used by Spartan Inc. as its best forecast of the exchange rate that will exist in the future periods. Thus, the forecasted exchange rate for all future periods is \$.50.
6. *Host country taxes on income earned by subsidiary.* The Singapore government will allow Spartan Inc. to establish the subsidiary and will impose a 20-percent tax rate on income. In addition, it will impose a 10-percent withholding tax on any funds remitted by the subsidiary to the parent.
7. *U.S. government taxes on income earned by Spartan subsidiary.* The U.S. government will allow a tax credit on taxes paid in Singapore, so that earnings remitted by the parent will not be taxed by the U.S. government.
8. *Cash flows from Spartan subsidiary to parent.* The Spartan subsidiary plans to send all net cash flows received back to the parent firm at the end of each year. The Singapore government promises no restrictions on the cash flows to be sent back to the parent firm but does impose a 10-percent withholding tax on any funds sent to the parent, as mentioned earlier.
9. *Depreciation.* The Singapore government will allow the subsidiary of Spartan Inc. to depreciate the cost of the plant and equipment at a maximum rate of S\$2 million per year, which is the rate to be used by the subsidiary.
10. *Salvage value.* The Singapore government will send a payment of S\$12 million to the parent to assume ownership of the subsidiary at the end of four years. Assume that there is no capital gains tax on the sale of the subsidiary.
11. *Required rate of return.* Spartan Inc. requires a 15-percent return on this project.

Example: Analysis

The capital budgeting analysis will be conducted from the parent's perspective, based on the assumption that the subsidiary is intended to generate cash flows that will ultimately be passed on to the parent. Thus, the net present value from the parent's perspective is based on a comparison of the present value of the cash flows received by the parent to the initial outlay by the parent. As illustrated earlier in this chapter, an international project's *NPV* is dependent on whether a parent or subsidiary perspective is used. Since the U.S. parent's perspective is used, the cash flows of concern are the dollars ultimately received by the parent as a result of the project. The initial outlay of concern is the investment by the parent. The required rate of return is based on the cost of capital used by the parent to make its investment, with an adjustment for the risk of the project. If the establishment of the subsidiary is beneficial to Spartan's parent, the present value of future cash flows (including the salvage value) ultimately received by the parent should exceed the parent's initial outlay.

The capital budgeting analysis to determine whether Spartan Inc. should establish the subsidiary is provided in Exhibit 14.2 (review this exhibit as you read on). The first step is to incorporate demand and price estimates in order to forecast total revenue (see lines 1 through 3). Then, the expenses are summed up to forecast total expenses (see lines 4 through 9). Next, before-tax earnings are computed (in line 10) by subtracting total expenses from total revenues. Host government taxes (line 11) are then deducted from before-tax earnings to determine after-tax earnings for the subsidiary (line 12).

The depreciation expense is added to the after-tax subsidiary earnings to compute the net cash flow to the subsidiary (line 13). All of these funds are to be remitted by the subsidiary, so line 14 is the same as line 13. The subsidiary can afford to

Exhibit 14.2
Capital Budgeting Analysis: Spartan Inc.

	Year 0	Year 1	Year 2	Year 3	Year 4
1. Demand		60,000	60,000	100,000	100,000
2. Price per unit		S$350	S$350	S$360	S$380
3. Total revenue = (1) × (2)		**S$21,000,000**	**S$21,000,000**	**S$36,000,000**	**S$38,000,000**
4. Variable cost per unit		S$200	S$200	S$250	S$260
5. Total variable cost = (1) × (4)		S$12,000,000	S$12,000,000	S$25,000,000	S$26,000,000
6. Annual lease expense		S$1,000,000	S$1,000,000	S$1,000,000	S$1,000,000
7. Other fixed annual expenses		S$1,000,000	S$1,000,000	S$1,000,000	S$1,000,000
8. Noncash expense (depreciation)		S$2,000,000	S$2,000,000	S$2,000,000	S$2,000,000
9. Total expenses = (5) + (6) + (7) + (8)		**S$16,000,000**	**S$16,000,000**	**S$29,000,000**	**S$30,000,000**
10. Before-tax earnings of subsidiary = (3) – (9)		S$5,000,000	S$5,000,000	S$7,000,000	S$8,000,000
11. Host government tax (20%)		S$1,000,000	S$1,000,000	S$1,400,000	S$1,600,000
12. After-tax earnings of subsidiary		S$4,000,000	S$4,000,000	S$5,600,000	S$6,400,000
13. Net cash flow to subsidiary = (12) + (8)		**S$6,000,000**	**S$6,000,000**	**S$7,600,000**	**S$8,400,000**
14. S$ remitted by subsidiary (100% of net cash flow)		S$6,000,000	S$6,000,000	S$7,600,000	S$8,400,000
15. Withholding tax on remitted funds (10%)		S$600,000	S$600,000	S$760,000	S$840,000
16. S$ remitted after withholding taxes		**S$5,400,000**	**S$5,400,000**	**S$6,840,000**	**S$7,560,000**
17. Salvage value					S$12,000,000
18. Exchange rate of S$		$.50	$.50	$.50	$.50
19. Cash flows to parent		$2,700,000	$2,700,000	$3,420,000	$9,780,000
20. *PV* of parent cash flows (15% discount rate)		**$2,347,826**	**$2,041,588**	**$2,248,706**	**$5,591,747**
21. Initial investment by parent	$10,000,000				
22. Cumulative *NPV*		–$7,652,174	–$5,610,586	–$3,361,880	$2,229,867

send all net cash flow to the parent since the initial investment provided by the parent includes working capital. The funds remitted to the parent are subject to a 10-percent withholding tax (line 15), so the actual amount of funds to be sent after these taxes is shown in line 16. The salvage value of the project is shown in line 17. The funds to be remitted must first be converted into dollars at the exchange rate (line 18) existing at that time. The parent's cash flow from the subsidiary is shown in line 19. The periodic funds received from the subsidiary are not subject to U.S. corporate taxes since it was assumed that the taxes paid in Singapore would represent a credit offsetting taxes owed to the U.S. government.

Although several capital budgeting techniques are available, a commonly used technique is to estimate the cash flows and salvage value to be received by the parent and compute the net present value (NPV) of the project, as shown here:

$$NPV = -IO + \sum_{t=1}^{n} \frac{CF_t}{(1+k)^t} + \frac{SV_n}{(1+k)^n}$$

where

IO = initial outlay (investment)
CF_t = cash flow in period t
SV_n = salvage value
k = required rate of return on the project
n = lifetime of the project (number of periods)

The *present value (PV)* of each period's net cash flow is computed using a 15-percent discount rate (line 20). The discount rate should reflect the parent's cost of capital with an adjustment for the project's risk. Finally, the cumulative *NPV* (line 22) is determined by consolidating the discounted cash flows for each period and subtracting the initial outlay (in line 21). For example, as of the end of Year 2, the cumulative *NPV* was –$5,610,586. This was determined by consolidating the $2,347,826 in Year 1, the $2,041,588 in Year 2, and subtracting the initial investment of $10,000,000. The critical value in line 22 is in the last period, since this reflects the *NPV* of the project.

In our example, the cumulative *NPV* as of the end of the last period is $2,229,867. Because the *NPV* is positive, the MNC may accept this project if the discount rate of 15 percent has fully accounted for the project's risk. However, if the analysis has not yet accounted for risk, the decision may be to reject the project. The manner by which the MNC can account for risk in capital budgeting is discussed shortly.

Factors to Consider in Multinational Capital Budgeting

The example of Spartan Inc. ignores a variety of factors that may affect the capital budgeting analysis, namely

1. exchange rate fluctuations
2. inflation
3. financing arrangement
4. blocked funds
5. uncertain salvage value
6. impact of project on prevailing cash flows
7. host government incentives

Each of these factors is discussed in turn.

Exchange Rate Fluctuations

Recall that Spartan Inc. uses the Singapore dollar's current spot rate ($.50) as a forecast for all future periods of concern. While the company realizes that the exchange rate will typically change over time, it does not know whether the Singapore dollar will strengthen or weaken in the future. While the difficulty in accurately forecasting exchange rates is well known, a multinational capital budgeting analysis could at least incorporate other scenarios for exchange rate movements, such as a pessimistic scenario and an optimistic scenario. From the parent's point of view, appreciation of the Singapore dollar would be favorable since the Singapore dollar inflows would someday be converted to more U.S. dollars. Conversely, depreciation would be unfavorable since the weakened Singapore dollars would convert to fewer U.S. dollars over time.

Weak-S$ and strong-S$ scenarios are illustrated in Exhibit 14.3. At the top of the table, the anticipated after-tax Singapore-dollar cash flows (including salvage value) are shown for the subsidiary from lines 16 and 17 in Exhibit 14.2. The amount in U.S. dollars that these Singapore dollars convert to depends on the exchange rates existing in the various periods in which they are converted. The number of Singapore dollars multiplied by the forecasted exchange rate will determine the estimated number of U.S. dollars received by the parent.

Notice from Exhibit 14.3 the differences in cash flow received by the parent in the strong-S$ scenario from those received in the weak-S$ scenario. A strong Singapore dollar is clearly beneficial, as verified by the increased U.S.-dollar value of cash flows received. The large differences in cash flow received by the parent in the different scenarios illustrate the impact of exchange rate expectations on the feasibility of an international project.

Exhibit 14.3
Analysis Using Different Exchange Rate Scenarios: Spartan Inc.

	Year 0	Year 1	Year 2	Year 3	Year 4
S$ remitted after withholding taxes (including salvage value)		S$5,400,000	S$5,400,000	S$6,840,000	SF19,560,000
Strong-S$ Scenario					
Exchange rate of S$		$.54	$.57	$.61	$.65
Cash flows to parent		$2,916,000	$3,078,000	$4,172,400	$12,714,000
PV of cash flows (15% discount rate)		$2,535,652	$2,327,410	$2,743,421	$7,269,271
Initial investment by parent	$10,000,000				
Cumulative *NPV*		–$7,464,348	–$5,136,938	–$2,393,517	$4,875,754
Weak-S$ Scenario					
Exchange rate of S$		$.47	$.45	$.40	$.37
Cash flows to parent		$2,538,000	$2,430,000	$2,736,000	$7,237,200
PV of cash flows (15% discount rate)		$2,206,957	$1,837,429	$1,798,964	$4,137,893
Initial investment by parent	$10,000,000				
Cumulative *NPV*		–$7,793,043	–$5,955,614	–$4,156,650	–$18,757

The *NPV* forecasts based on projections for exchange rates are illustrated in Exhibit 14.4. The estimated *NPV* is highest if the Singapore dollar is expected to strengthen and lowest if it is expected to weaken. The estimated *NPV* is negative for the weak-S$ scenario but positive for the stable-S$ and strong-S$ scenarios. This project's true feasibility would depend on the probability distribution of these three scenarios for the Singapore dollar during the project's lifetime. If there is a high probability that the weak-S$ scenario will occur, this project should not be accepted.

Inflation

Our example implicitly considers inflation, since variable cost per unit and product prices generally have been rising over time. However, inflation can be quite volatile

Exhibit 14.4
Sensitivity of the Project's *NPV* to Different Exchange Rate Scenarios: Spartan Inc.

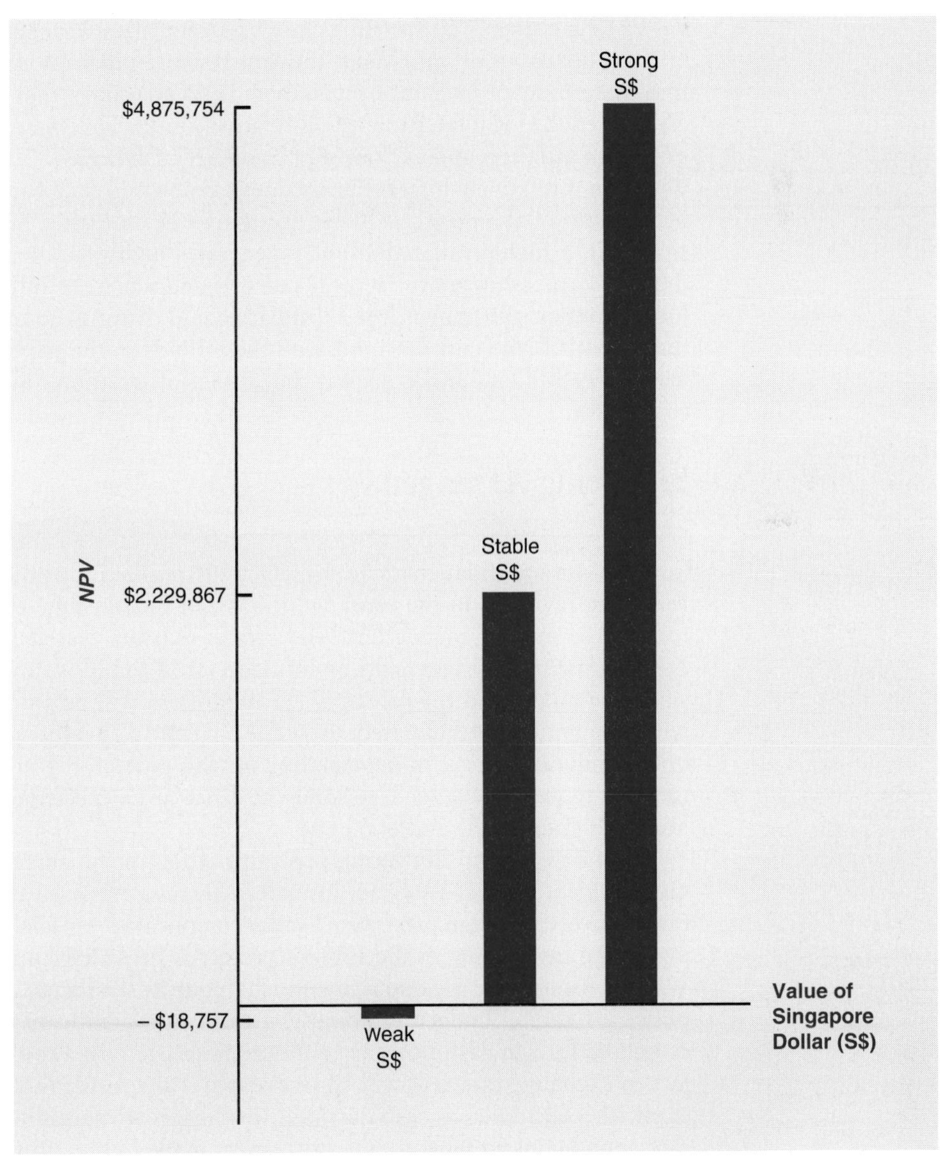

from year to year in some countries and can therefore strongly influence a project's net cash flows. Inaccurate inflation forecasts could lead to inaccurate net cash flow forecasts. The inflation rate in many less developed countries may be 200 percent or more in any given year. It would be virtually impossible for any subsidiary in these countries to accurately forecast inflation each year.

While both costs and revenues should be affected in the same direction by inflation fluctuations, their magnitudes may be very different from each other. This is especially true when the project involves importing partially manufactured components and selling the finished product locally. The local economy's inflation will most likely have a stronger impact on revenues than on costs in such cases.

The joint impact of inflation and exchange rate fluctuations on a subsidiary's net cash flows may produce a partial offsetting effect, from the viewpoint of the parent. The exchange rates of highly inflated countries tend to weaken over time. Thus, even if subsidiary earnings are inflated, they will be deflated when converted into the parent's home currency (if the subsidiary's currency has weakened). Such an offsetting effect is not exact or consistent, though. Because inflation is only one of many factors that influence exchange rates, there is no guarantee that a currency will depreciate when the local inflation rate is relatively high. Therefore, one cannot ignore the impact of inflation and exchange rates on net cash flows.

Even if relatively high inflation does cause a currency to weaken, the impact on net cash flows of a project will not necessarily be offsetting. Suppose an MNC's subsidiary in a highly inflated country generates highly inflated earnings and invests them in local securities for several years. If and when the inflation subsides and the local currency strengthens, the subsidiary could convert the accumulated earnings to the parent's home currency and send these funds to the parent. This example illustrates why MNCs cannot neglect the impact of inflation and/or exchange rates on cash flows.

Financing Arrangement

Many foreign projects are partially financed by foreign subsidiaries. To illustrate how this foreign financing can influence the feasibility of the project, consider the following revisions in the example of Spartan Inc. Assume that the subsidiary borrows S$10 million to purchase the offices that are leased in the initial example. Assume that interest payments on this loan (of S$1 million) are to be paid by the subsidiary annually and the principal (S$10 million) will be paid at the end of Year 4, when the project is terminated. Since the Singapore government permits a maximum of S$2 million per year in depreciation for this project, the subsidiary's depreciation rate will remain unchanged. Assume the offices are expected to be sold for S$10 million after taxes at the end of Year 4.

Domestic capital budgeting problems would not include debt payments in the measurement of cash flows because all financing costs are captured by the discount rate. However, foreign projects are more complicated, especially when partial financing of the investment in the foreign project is provided by the foreign subsidiary. While consolidating the initial investment made by the parent and the subsidiary simplifies the capital budgeting process, it can cause significant estimation errors. The estimated foreign cash flows that are ultimately remitted to the parent and are subject to exchange rate risk will be overstated if the foreign interest expenses are not explicitly considered as cash outflows for the foreign subsidiary. Thus, a more accurate approach is to separate the investment made by the subsidiary from the investment made by the parent. The capital budgeting analysis can focus on the parent's perspective by comparing the present value of the cash flows received by the parent to the initial investment by the parent.

Given the revised assumptions, the following revisions must be made to the capital budgeting analysis:

1. Since the subsidiary is borrowing funds to purchase the offices, the lease payments of S$1 million per year will not be necessary. However, the subsidiary will pay interest payments of S$1 million per year as a result of the loan. Thus, the annual cash outflows for the subsidiary are still the same.
2. The subsidiary must pay the S$10 million in loan principal at the end of four years. However, since the subsidiary expects to receive S$10 million (in 4 years) from the sale of the offices it purchases with the funds provided by the loan, it can use the proceeds of the sale to pay the loan principal.

Since the subsidiary's maximum depreciation expense allowed by the Singapore government already has been taken even before the subsidiary owned the offices, it cannot increase its annual depreciation expenses. In this example, the cash flows ultimately received by the parent when the subsidiary obtains financing to purchase offices are similar to the cash flows determined in the original example (when the offices are to be leased). If the numbers were not offsetting, the capital budgeting analysis would be conducted in the revised example to determine whether the *NPV* from the parent's perspective is higher than that in the initial example.

Recall that in the original example, the offices are leased by the subsidiary, while in the revised example the offices are purchased with borrowed funds by the subsidiary. Consider one more alternative arrangement, in which the parent uses its own funds to purchase the offices. That is, its initial investment is $15 million, composed of the original $10 million investment as explained earlier, plus an additional $5 million to obtain an extra S$10 million to purchase the offices. This example is provided because it illustrates how the capital budgeting analysis changes when the parent takes a bigger stake in the investment. Given the revised assumption that the parent rather than the subsidiary will purchase the offices, the following revisions must be made to the capital budgeting analysis:

1. The subsidiary will not have any loan payments (since it will not need to borrow funds), as the offices are to be purchased by the parent. Since the offices are to be purchased, there will be no lease payments either.
2. The initial investment by the parent is $15 million instead of $10 million.
3. The salvage value to be received by the parent is S$22 million instead of S$12 million because the offices are assumed to be sold for S$10 million after taxes at the end of Year 4. The S$10 million to be received from selling the offices can be added to the S$12 million to be received from selling the rest of the subsidiary.

The capital budgeting analysis for Spartan Inc. under this revised financing strategy in which the parent finances the entire $15 million investment is shown in Exhibit 14.5. This analysis uses our original exchange rate projections of $.50 per Singapore dollar for each period. The numbers that are directly affected by the revised financing arrangement are bracketed. Other numbers are also affected indirectly as a result. For example, the subsidiary's after-tax earnings increase as a result of avoiding interest or

Exhibit 14.5
Analysis with an Alternative Financing Arrangement: Spartan Inc.

	Year 0	Year 1	Year 2	Year 3	Year 4
1. Demand		60,000	60,000	100,000	100,000
2. Price per unit		S$350	S$350	S$360	S$380
3. Total revenue = (1) × (2)		**S$21,000,000**	**S$21,000,000**	**S$36,000,000**	**S$38,000,000**
4. Variable cost per unit		S$200	S$200	S$250	S$260
5. Total variable cost = (1) × (4)		S$12,000,000	S$12,000,000	S$25,000,000	S$26,000,000
6. Annual lease expense		[S$ 0]	[S$ 0]	[S$ 0]	[S$ 0]
7. Other fixed annual expenses		S$1,000,000	S$1,000,000	S$1,000,000	S$1,000,000
8. Noncash expense (depreciation)		S$2,000,000	S$2,000,000	S$2,000,000	S$2,000,000
9. Total expenses = (5) + (6) + (7) + (8)		**S$15,000,000**	**S$15,000,000**	**S$28,000,000**	**S$29,000,000**
10. Before-tax earnings of subsidiary = (3) − (9)		S$6,000,000	S$6,000,000	S$8,000,000	S$9,000,000
11. Host government tax (20%)		S$1,200,000	S$1,200,000	S$1,600,000	S$1,800,000
12. After-tax earnings of subsidiary		S$4,800,000	S$4,800,000	S$6,400,000	S$7,200,000
13. Net cash flow to subsidiary = (12) + (8)		**S$6,800,000**	**S$6,800,000**	**S$8,400,000**	**S$9,200,000**
14. S$ remitted by subsidiary (100% of S$)		S$6,800,000	S$6,800,000	S$8,400,000	S$9,200,000
15. Withholding tax on remitted funds (10%)		S$680,000	S$680,000	S$840,000	S$920,000
16. S$ remitted after withholding taxes		**S$6,120,000**	**S$6,120,000**	**S$7,560,000**	**S$8,280,000**
17. Salvage value					[S$22,000,000]
18. Exchange rate of S$		$.50	$.50	$.50	$.50
19. Cash flows to parent		$3,060,000	$3,060,000	$3,780,000	$15,140,000
20. *PV* of parent cash flows (15% discount rate)		**$2,660,870**	**$2,313,800**	**$2,485,411**	**$8,656,344**
21. Initial investment by parent	[$15,000,000]				
22. Cumulative *NPV*		−$12,339,130	−$10,025,330	−$7,539,919	$1,116,425

lease payments on its offices. The *NPV* of the project under this alternative financing arrangement is positive but less than in the original arrangement. Given the higher initial outlay of the parent and the lower *NPV*, this arrangement in which the parent finances the $15 million investment is not as feasible as the arrangement in which the offices are either leased or purchased with funds borrowed by the subsidiary.

One reason that the subsidiary financing is more feasible than complete parent financing is that the financing rate on the loan is lower than the parent's required rate of return on funds provided to the subsidiary. Yet, if local loans had a relatively high interest rate, the use of local financing would not likely be as attractive.

In general, this revised example shows that the increased investment by the parent causes more exchange rate exposure to the parent for the following reasons. First, since the parent provides the entire investment, there is no foreign financing required. Consequently, there are no interest payments paid by the subsidiary, and the cash flows to be remitted to the parent are larger. Second, the salvage value to be remitted to the parent is larger. Given the larger payments to the parent, the cash flows ultimately received by the parent are more susceptible to exchange rate movements.

The exposure is not as large when the offices are purchased by the subsidiary because the subsidiary financing forces some of the financing expenses to be incurred by the subsidiary. The subsidiary financing essentially shifts some of the expenses to the same currency as that received by the subsidiary and therefore reduces the amount that will ultimately be converted into dollars for remittance to the parent.

Some foreign projects are completely financed with retained earnings of existing foreign subsidiaries. These projects are difficult to assess from the parent's perspective because their direct effects are normally focused on the subsidiaries. One approach is to view a subsidiary's investment in a project as an opportunity cost, since the funds could be remitted to the parent rather than invested in the foreign project. Thus, the initial outlay from the parent's perspective is the amount in funds that it would have received from the subsidiary if the funds were remitted rather than invested in this project. The cash flows from the parent's perspective reflect those cash flows ultimately received by the parent as a result of the foreign project.

Even if the project generates earnings for the subsidiary that are reinvested by the subsidiary, the key cash flows from the parent's perspective are those that it ultimately receives from the project. In this way, any international factors that will affect the cash flows (such as withholding taxes and exchange rate movements) are incorporated into the capital budgeting process.

Blocked Funds

In some cases, the host country may block funds that the subsidiary attempts to send to the parent. For example, some countries may require that earnings generated by the subsidiary be reinvested locally for at least three years before they can be remitted. This can possibly affect the accept/reject decision on a project. Reconsider the example of Spartan Inc., assuming that all funds are blocked until the subsidiary is sold. This forces the subsidiary to reinvest those funds until that time. Blocked funds penalize a project if the return on such reinvestment is less than the required rate of return on the project.

Assume that these funds are used to purchase marketable securities that are expected to yield 5 percent annually, after taxes. A reevaluation of Spartan's cash flows (from Exhibit 14.2) to incorporate the blocked-funds restriction is shown in Exhibit 14.6. The withholding tax is not applied until the funds are remitted to the parent, which is in Year 4. The original exchange rate projections are used here. All parent cash flows depend on the exchange rate four years from now. The *NPV* of the project with blocked funds is still positive, but it is substantially less than the *NPV* in the original example.

If the foreign subsidiary has a loan outstanding, it may be able to better utilize blocked funds by repaying the local loan. For example, the S$6 million at the end of Year 1 could be used to reduce the outstanding loan balance instead of being invested in marketable securities, assuming that the lending bank allows early repayment.

Exhibit 14.6
Capital Budgeting with Blocked Funds: Spartan Inc.

	Year 0	Year 1	Year 2	Year 3	Year 4
S$ to be remitted by subsidiary		S$6,000,000	S$6,000,000	S$7,600,000	S$8,400,000
				→	S$7,980,000
S$ accumulated by reinvesting funds to be remitted			→		S$6,615,000
		→			S$6,945,750
					S$29,940,750
Withholding tax (10%)					S$2,994,075
S$ remitted after withholding tax					S$26,946,675
Salvage value					S$12,000,000
Exchange rate					$.50
Cash flows to parent					$19,473,338
PV of parent cash flows (15% discount rate)					$11,133,944
Initial investment by parent	$10,000,000				
Cumulative *NPV*		–$10,000,000	–$10,000,000	–$10,000,000	$1,133,944

Uncertain Salvage Value

The salvage value of an MNC's project typically has a significant impact on the project's *NPV*. When the salvage value is uncertain, the MNC may desire to incorporate various possible outcomes for the salvage value and reestimate the *NPV* based on each possible outcome. It may even desire to estimate the break-even salvage value (also called break-even terminal value), which is the salvage value necessary to achieve a zero *NPV* for the project. If the actual salvage value is expected to equal or exceed the break-even salvage value, the project is feasible. The break-even salvage value (called SV_n) can be determined by setting *NPV* equal to zero and rearranging the capital budgeting equation, as follows:

$$NPV = -IO + \sum_{t=1}^{n} \frac{CF_t}{(1+k)^t} + \frac{SV_n}{(1+k)^n}$$

$$O = -IO + \sum_{t=1}^{n} \frac{CF_t}{(1+k)^t} + \frac{SV_n}{(1+k)^n}$$

$$\left[IO - \sum_{t=1}^{n} \frac{CF_t}{(1+k)^t}\right] = \frac{SV_n}{(1+k)^n}$$

$$\left[IO - \sum_{t=1}^{n} \frac{CF_t}{(1+k)^t}\right](1+k)^n = SV_n$$

To illustrate the use of break-even salvage value, reconsider the Spartan Inc. example and assume that Spartan is not guaranteed a price for the project. The break-even salvage value for that project can be determined by (1) estimating the present value of future cash flows (excluding the salvage value), (2) subtracting the discounted cash flows from the initial outlay, and (3) multiplying the difference times $(1 + k)^n$. Using the original cash flow information from Exhibit 14.2, the present value of cash flows can be determined:

$$\begin{aligned}\text{PV of parent cash flows} &= \frac{\$2,700,000}{(1.15)^1} + \frac{\$2,700,000}{(1.15)^2} + \frac{\$3,420,000}{(1.15)^3} + \frac{\$3,780,000}{(1.15)^4} \\ &= \$2,347,826 + \$2,041,588 + \$2,248,706 + \$2,161,227 \\ &= \$8,799,347\end{aligned}$$

Given the present value of cash flows and the estimated initial outlay, the break-even salvage value is determined this way:

$$\begin{aligned}SV_n &= \left[IO - \sum \frac{CF_t}{(1+k)^t}\right](1+k)^n \\ &= [\$10,000,000 - \$8,799,347](1.15)^4 \\ &= \$2,099,950\end{aligned}$$

Given the original information in Exhibit 14.2, Spartan Inc. would accept the project only if the salvage value were estimated to be at least \$2,099,950 (assuming that the project's required rate of return is 15 percent).

Assuming the forecasted exchange rate of \$.50 per Singapore dollar (2 Singapore dollars per U.S. dollar), the project must sell for more than S\$4,199,900 (computed as \$2,099,950 divided by \$.50) to exhibit a positive *NPV* (assuming no taxes are paid on this amount). If Spartan did not have a guarantee from the Singapore government, it could assess the probability that the subsidiary would sell for more than the break-even salvage value and then incorporate this assessment in its decision to accept or reject the project.

Impact of Project on Prevailing Cash Flows

In our example, there is no presumed impact of the new project on prevailing cash flows. In reality, however, there may often be an impact. Reconsider the Spartan Inc. example, assuming this time that (1) there is no concern about the Singapore government's imposing trade restrictions on imported tennis rackets; (2) Spartan Inc. still considers establishing a subsidiary in Singapore because its production costs in Singapore are expected to be lower than they would be in the United States; and (3) without a subsidiary, Spartan's export business to Singapore is expected to generate net cash flows of \$1 million over the next four years. With a subsidiary, these cash flows would be forgone. The effects of these assumptions are shown in Exhibit 14.7. The previously estimated cash flows to the parent from the subsidiary (drawn from Exhibit 14.2) are restated in Exhibit 14.7. These estimates do not account for forgone cash flows since the possible export business was not considered. However, if the export business was established, the forgone cash flows attributable to this business would have to be considered, as shown in Exhibit 14.7. The adjusted cash flows to the parent account for the project's impact on prevailing cash flows.

The present value of adjusted cash flows and cumulative *NPV* are also shown in Exhibit 14.7. The project's *NPV* is now negative as a result of the adverse effect on

Exhibit 14.7
Capital Budgeting When Prevailing Cash Flows Are Affected: Spartan Inc.

	Year 0	Year 1	Year 2	Year 3	Year 4
Cash flows to parent, ignoring impact on prevailing cash flows		$2,700,000	$2,700,000	$3,420,000	$9,780,000
Impact of project on prevailing cash flows		–$1,000,000	–$1,000,000	–$1,000,000	–$1,000,000
Cash flows to parent, incorporating impact on prevailing cash flows		$1,700,000	$1,700,000	$2,420,000	$8,780,000
PV of cash flows to parent (15% discount rate)		$1,478,261	$1,285,444	$1,591,189	$5,019,994
Initial investment	$10,000,000				
Cumulative *NPV*		–$8,521,739	–$7,236,295	–$5,645,106	–$625,112

prevailing cash flows. Thus, the project would not be feasible if the exporting business to Singapore was established.

It should be mentioned that some foreign projects may have a favorable impact on prevailing cash flows. For example, if a manufacturer of computer components established a foreign subsidiary to manufacture computers, the subsidiary might order the components from the parent. In this case, the sales volume of the parent would increase.

Host Government Incentives

Some foreign projects proposed by MNCs would have a favorable impact on economic conditions in a host country and would therefore be encouraged by the host government. Any incentives offered by the host government must be incorporated within the capital budgeting analysis. For example, a low-rate host government loan or a reduced tax rate offered to the subsidiary would enhance periodic cash flows. If the government subsidized the initial establishment of the subsidiary, the MNC's initial investment would be reduced.

Adjusting Project Assessment for Risk

If an MNC is unsure of the estimated cash flows of a proposed project, it needs to incorporate an adjustment for this risk. Three common methods used for adjusting the evaluation for risk are

- risk-adjusted discount rate
- sensitivity analysis
- simulation

Each method is described in turn.

Nike Problem

Assessing International Projects

Given Nike's international expansion, it has clearly conducted many multinational capital budgeting analyses. The underlying reasons for the feasibility of its international expansion may vary among countries. Its expansion in Asia requires a large initial outlay in some countries (such as Hong Kong) but a low initial outlay in others (such as when it subcontracts to have shoes made in Vietnam). If Nike subcontracts production to existing shoe companies, a multinational capital budgeting analysis could still measure the discounted value of net cash flows. The difference between this type of project versus having its own facility produce shoes is that it would not need the large initial outlay for its own facility. Yet, it also would not have a salvage value if it terminates this project because it does not own the shoe factory.

Discussion: Assume that Nike decides to build a shoe factory in Brazil, of which half the initial outlay is funded by the parent's equity and half is funded by borrowing funds in Brazil. Assume that Nike wants to assess the project from its own perspective to determine whether the future cash flows of the project in Brazil will provide a sufficient return to the parent to warrant the initial investment by the parent. Why will the estimated cash flows be different from the estimated cash flows of its shoe factory in New Hampshire? Why will the initial outlay be different? Explain how Nike can conduct multinational capital budgeting in a manner that will achieve its objective.

Risk-Adjusted Discount Rate

The greater the uncertainty about a project's forecasted cash flows, the larger should be the discount rate applied to cash flows, other things being equal. This risk-adjusted discount rate tends to reduce the worth of a project by a degree that reflects the risk the project exhibits. This approach is easy to use, but it is criticized for being somewhat arbitrary. In addition, an equal adjustment to the discount rate over all periods does not reflect differences in the degree of uncertainty from one period to another. If the projected cash flows among periods have different degrees of uncertainty, the risk adjustment of the cash flows should vary also.

Consider a country whose political situation is slowly destabilizing. The probability of blocked funds, expropriation, etc., will increase over time. Thus, cash flows sent to the parent are less certain in the distant future than they are in the near future. A different discount rate should therefore be applied to each period in accordance with its corresponding risk. Even so, it will be a subjective adjustment that may not accurately reflect the risk.

Despite its subjectivity, the risk-adjusted discount rate is a commonly used technique, perhaps because of the ease with which one can arbitrarily adjust it. In addition, there is no alternative technique that will perfectly adjust for risk, although there are some (discussed next) that in certain cases may better reflect a project's risk.

Sensitivity Analysis

Once the MNC has estimated the *NPV* of a proposed project, it may want to consider alternative estimates for its input variables. For example, demand for the Spartan subsidiary's tennis rackets (in our earlier example) is estimated to be 60,000 in the first two years and 100,000 in the next two years. If demand were 60,000 in all four years, how would that change the *NPV* results? Alternatively, what if demand were 100,000 in all four years? Use of such *what-if* scenarios is referred to as **sensitivity analysis.** The objective is to determine how sensitive the *NPV* is to alternative values of the input variables. The estimates of any input variables can be revised to create new estimates for *NPV*. If the *NPV* is consistently positive during these revisions, then the MNC should become more comfortable with the project. If in many cases it is negative, the accept/reject decision for the project becomes more difficult.

The two exchange rate scenarios developed earlier represent a form of sensitivity analysis. The advantage of sensitivity analysis over the use of simple point estimates is that it reassesses the project based on various circumstances that may occur. Many computer software packages are available to perform sensitivity analysis.

Simulation

Simulation can be used for a variety of tasks, including the generation of a probability distribution for *NPV* based on a range of possible values for one or more input variables. Simulation is typically performed with the aid of a computer package. To illustrate how it can be applied to multinational capital budgeting, reconsider Spartan Inc. and assume that it expects the exchange rate to depreciate by 3 to 7 percent per year (with an equal probability of all values in this range occurring). Unlike a single point estimate, simulation can consider the entire distribution of possibilities for the Singapore dollar's exchange rate at the end of each year. It considers all point estimates for the other variables and randomly picks one of the possible values of the Singapore dollar's depreciation level for each of the four years. Based on this random selection process, the *NPV* is determined.

The procedure just described represents one iteration. Then the process is repeated: the Singapore dollar's depreciation for each year is again randomly selected (within the range of possibilities assumed earlier). Again, the *NPV* of the project, if these exchange rate fluctuations actually occurred, is computed. The simulation program may be run for, say, 100 iterations. This means that 100 different possible scenarios are created for the possible exchange rates of the Singapore dollar during the four-year project period. Each iteration reflects a different scenario. The *NPV* of the project based on each scenario is then computed. Thus, simulation generates a distribution of *NPV*s for the project. The major advantage of simulation is that the MNC can examine the range of possible *NPV*s that may occur. From the information, it can determine the probability that the *NPV* will be positive, or greater than a particular level. The greater the uncertainty of the exchange rate, the greater will be the uncertainty of the *NPV*. The risk of a project will be greater if it involves the transaction of more volatile currencies, other things being equal.

In reality, many or all of the input variables necessary for multinational capital budgeting may be uncertain in the future. Probability distributions could be developed for all variables with uncertain future values. The final result is a distribution of possible *NPV*s that might occur for the project. The simulation technique does not put all of its emphasis on any one particular *NPV* forecast but instead provides a distribution of the possible outcomes that may occur.

The project's cost of capital can be used as a discount rate when simulation is performed. The probability that the project will be successful can be estimated by measuring the area within the probability distribution in which the $NPV > 0$. This area represents the probability that the present value of future cash flows will exceed the initial outlay. MNCs can also use the probability distribution to estimate the probability that the project will backfire by measuring the area in which $NPV < 0$.

Simulation is difficult to do manually because of the iterations necessary to develop a distribution of NPVs. Yet, computer programs can run 100 iterations and generate results within a matter of seconds. The user of a simulation program must provide the probability distributions for the input variables that will affect the project's NPV. Like any model, the accuracy of results generated by simulation will be determined by the accuracy of the input.

Impact of Multinational Capital Budgeting on an MNC's Value

An MNC's multinational capital budgeting affects its value, as shown in Exhibit 14.8. Multinational capital budgeting decisions are not only used to support decisions to enter a new country, but they are also used to expand within a particular country. Thus, multinational capital budgeting dictates the types of operations and the locations of operations run by the MNC, and it therefore affects the expected foreign currency cash flows generated by the MNC's foreign subsidiaries. Since the expected foreign currency cash flows influence the amount of expected dollar cash flows received by the U.S. parent, multinational capital budgeting decisions affect the value of the MNC.

Because multinational capital budgeting decisions determine the types of operations of the MNC, they also affect the level of the MNC's risk. When the MNC's parent financially supports the foreign projects, its cost of capital is affected, which influences its required rate of return on its businesses and its value.

Exhibit 14.8
Impact of Multinational Capital Budgeting on an MNC's Value

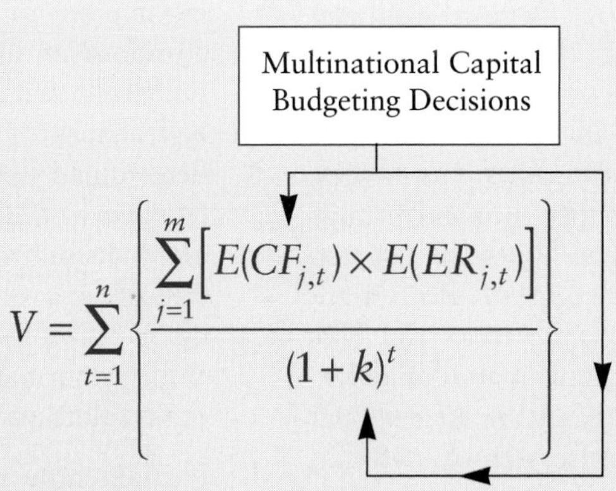

$$V = \sum_{t=1}^{n} \left\{ \frac{\sum_{j=1}^{m} \left[E(CF_{j,t}) \times E(ER_{j,t}) \right]}{(1+k)^t} \right\}$$

V = value of the U.S.-based MNC

$E(CF_{j,t})$ = expected cash flows denominated in currency j to be received by the U.S. parent in period t

$E(ER_{j,t})$ = expected exchange rate at which currency j can be converted to dollars at the end of period t

k = the weighted average cost of capital of the U.S. parent

m = number of currencies

n = number of periods

SUMMARY

- Capital budgeting conducted from an MNC's subsidiary perspective may generate different results and a different conclusion than from those obtained if it is conducted from an MNC's parent perspective. The subsidiary perspective does not consider possible exchange rate and tax effects on cash flows transferred by the subsidiary to the parent. When a parent is deciding whether to implement an international project, it should determine whether the project is feasible from its own perspective.
- Multinational capital budgeting requires any input that will help estimate the initial outlay, periodic cash flows, salvage value, and required rate of return on the project. Once these factors are estimated, the international project's *NPV* can be estimated, just as if it were a domestic project. However, it is normally more difficult to estimate these factors for an international project. Exchange rates create an additional source of uncertainty because they affect the cash flows ultimately received by the parent as a result of the project. Other international conditions that can influence the cash flows ultimately received by the parent include the financing arrangement (parent versus subsidiary financing of the project), blocked funds by the host government, and host government incentives.
- The risk of international projects can be accounted for by adjusting the discount rate used to estimate the project's net present value. However, the adjustment to the discount rate is subjective. An alternative method is to estimate the net present value based on various possible scenarios for exchange rates or any other uncertain factors. This method is facilitated by the use of sensitivity analysis or simulation.

SELF-TEST FOR CHAPTER 14

(Answers are provided in Appendix A at the back of the text.)

1. Two managers of a U.S. firm assessed a project proposed in Jamaica. Each manager used exactly the same estimates of the earnings to be generated by the project in Jamaica, as these estimates were provided by other employees. The managers agree on the proportion of funds to be remitted each year, the life of the project, and the discount rate to be applied. Both managers also assessed the project from the U.S. parent's perspective. Yet, one manager determined that this project had a large net present value, while the other manager determined that the project had a negative net present value. Explain the possible reasons for such a difference.

2. Pinpoint the parts of a multinational capital budgeting analysis that are sensitive for a proposed sales distribution center in Ireland when the forecast of a stable economy in Ireland is revised to predict a recession.

3. New Orleans Exporting Co. focuses on producing small computer components which are then sold to Mexico. It plans to expand by establishing a plant in Mexico which will produce the components and sell them locally. This plant will cut down on the amount of goods that will be transported from New Orleans. The firm has determined that the cash flows to be earned in Mexico would yield a positive net present value after accounting for tax and exchange rate effects, converting cash flows to dollars, and discounting them at the proper discount rate. What other major factor must be considered in the estimation of the project's *NPV*?

4. Explain how the present value of the salvage value of an Indonesian subsidiary will be affected (from the U.S. parent's perspective) by (a) an increase in the risk of the foreign subsidiary and (b) an expectation that Indonesia's currency (rupiah) will depreciate against the dollar over time.

5. Wilmette Co. and Niles Co. (both from the United States) are assessing the acquisition of

the same firm in Thailand and have obtained the future cash flow estimates (in Thailand's currency, baht) from the firm. Wilmette would use its retained earnings from U.S. operations to acquire the subsidiary. Niles Co. would finance the acquisition mostly with a term loan (in baht) from Thai banks. Neither firm has any other business in Thailand. Which firm's dollar cash flows would be affected more by future changes in the value of the baht (assuming that the Thai firm is acquired)?

6. Review the capital budgeting example of Spartan Inc. discussed in this chapter. Identify the specific variables assessed within the process of estimating a foreign project's net present value (from a U.S. perspective) that would cause the most uncertainty about the *NPV*.

QUESTIONS AND APPLICATIONS

1. Why should capital budgeting for subsidiary projects be assessed from the parent's perspective?
2. What additional factors deserve consideration in multinational capital budgeting that are not normally relevant for a purely domestic project?
3. What is the limitation of using point estimates of exchange rates within the capital budgeting analysis?
4. Explain how simulation can be used in multinational capital budgeting. What can it do that other risk adjustment techniques cannot?
5. Using the capital budgeting framework discussed in this chapter, explain the sources of uncertainty surrounding a proposed project in Hungary by a U.S. firm. In what ways is the estimated *NPV* of this project more uncertain than that of a similar project in a more developed European country?
6. List the various techniques for adjusting risk in multinational capital budgeting. Describe any advantages or disadvantages of each technique.
7. Project X has an *NPV* estimated by your employees to be $1.2 million. Your employees state in their report that they have not accounted for risk but, that with such a large *NPV*, the project should be accepted since even a risk-adjusted *NPV* would likely be positive. You have the final decision as to whether to accept or reject the project. What is your decision?
8. € Describe in general terms how future appreciation of the euro will likely affect the value (from the parent's perspective) of a project established in Germany today by a U.S.-based MNC. Will the sensitivity of the project value be affected by the percentage of earnings remitted to the parent each year?
9. € Repeat question 8, assuming future depreciation of the euro.
10. Explain how the financing decision can influence the sensitivity of *NPV* to exchange rate forecasts.
11. Wolverine Corporation currently has no existing business in New Zealand but is considering the establishment of a subsidiary there. The following information has been gathered to assess this project:
    - The initial investment required is NZ$50 million. Given the existing spot rate of $.50 per New Zealand dollar, the initial investment in U.S. dollars is $25 million. In addition to the NZ$50 million initial investment on plant and equipment, NZ$20 million is needed for working capital and will be borrowed by the subsidiary from a New Zealand bank. The New Zealand subsidiary of Wolverine will pay interest only on the loan each year at an interest rate of 14 percent. The loan principal is to be paid in 10 years.
    - The project will be terminated at the end of Year 3 when the subsidiary will be sold.
    - The price, demand, and variable cost of the product in New Zealand are as follows:

Year	Price	Demand	Variable Cost
1	NZ$500	40,000 units	NZ$30
2	NZ$511	50,000 units	NZ$35
3	NZ$530	60,000 units	NZ$40

- The fixed costs, such as overhead expenses, are estimated to be NZ$6 million per year.
- The exchange rate of the New Zealand dollar is expected to be $.52 at the end of Year 1, $.54 at the end of Year 2, and $.56 at the end of Year 3.
- The New Zealand government will impose an income tax of 30 percent on income. In addition, it will impose a withholding tax of 10 percent on earnings remitted by the subsidiary. The U.S. government will allow a tax credit on remitted earnings and will not impose any additional taxes.
- All cash flows received by the subsidiary are to be sent to the parent at the end of each year. The subsidiary will use its working capital to support ongoing operations.
- The plant and equipment are depreciated over 10 years using the straight-line depreciation method. Since the plant and equipment are initially valued at NZ$50 million, the annual depreciation expense is NZ$5 million.
- In three years, the subsidiary is to be sold. Wolverine plans to let the acquiring firm assume the existing New Zealand loan. The working capital will not be liquidated but will be used by the acquiring firm. Wolverine expects to receive NZ$52 million after subtracting capital gains taxes when it sells the subsidiary. Assume that this amount is not subject to a withholding tax.
- Wolverine requires a 20-percent rate of return on this project.

a. Determine the net present value of this project. Should Wolverine accept this project?
b. Assume that Wolverine is also considering an alternate financing arrangement, in which the parent invests an additional $10 million to cover the working capital requirements, so that the subsidiary avoids the New Zealand bank loan. If this arrangement is used, the selling price of the subsidiary (after subtracting any capital gains taxes) is expected to be NZ$18 million higher. Is this alternative financing arrangement more feasible for the parent than the originally proposed arrangement? Explain.
c. Would the *NPV* of this project from the parent's perspective be more sensitive to exchange rate movements if the subsidiary used New Zealand financing to cover the working capital or if the parent invested more of its own funds to cover the working capital? Explain.
d. Assume that Wolverine uses the original proposed financing arrangement and that funds are blocked until the subsidiary is sold. The funds to be remitted are reinvested at a rate of 6 percent (after taxes) until the end of Year 3. How is the project's *NPV* affected?
e. What is the break-even salvage value of this project if Wolverine Corporation uses the original proposed financing arrangement and funds are not blocked?
f. Assume that Wolverine decides to implement the project, using the original proposed financing arrangement. Also assume that after one year, a New Zealand firm offers Wolverine a price of $27 million after taxes for the subsidiary and that Wolverine's original forecasts for Years 2 and 3 have not changed. Should Wolverine divest the subsidiary? Explain.

12. Huskie Industries, a U.S.-based MNC, considers purchasing a small manufacturing company in France that sells products only within France. Huskie has no other existing business in France and no cash flows in euros. Would the proposed acquisition likely be more feasible if the euro is expected to appreciate or to depreciate over the long run? Explain.

13. When Walt Disney World considered establishing a theme park in France, were the forecasted revenues and costs associated with the French park sufficient to assess the feasibility of this project? Were there any other "relevant cash flows" that deserved to be considered?

14. Athens Inc. established a subsidiary in the United Kingdom that was independent of its operations in the United States. The subsidiary's performance was well above what was expected. Consequently, when a British firm approached Athens Inc. about the possibility of acquiring it, Athens' chief financial officer replied that the

subsidiary was performing so well that it was not for sale. Comment on this strategy.

15. Lehigh Company established a subsidiary in Switzerland that was performing below the cash flow projections developed before the subsidiary was established. Lehigh anticipated that future cash flows would also be lower than the original cash flow projections. Consequently, Lehigh decided to inform several potential acquiring firms of its plan to sell the subsidiary. Lehigh then received a few bids. Even the highest bid was very low, but Lehigh accepted the offer. It justified its decision by stating that any existing project whose cash flows were not sufficient to recover the initial investment should be divested. Comment on this statement.

16. Flagstaff Corporation is a U.S.-based firm with a subsidiary in Mexico. It plans to reinvest its earnings in Mexican government securities for the next ten years because the interest rate earned on these securities is so high. Then, after ten years, it will remit all accumulated earnings to the United States. What is a drawback of using this approach? (Assume the securities have no default or interest rate risk.)

17. Colorado Springs Company (based in the United States) plans to divest either its Singapore or its Canadian subsidiary. Assume that if exchange rates stayed constant, the dollar cash flows each of these subsidiaries provided to the parent over time would be somewhat similar. However, the firm expects the Singapore dollar to depreciate against the U.S. dollar and the Canadian dollar to appreciate against the U.S. dollar. The firm can sell either subsidiary for about the same price today. Which one should it sell?

18. San Gabriel Corporation recently considered divesting its Italian subsidiary and determined that the divestiture was not feasible. The required rate of return on this subsidiary was 17 percent. In the last week, its required return on that subsidiary increased to 21 percent. If the sales price of the subsidiary has not changed, explain why the divestiture may now be feasible.

19. Ventura Corporation is a U.S.-based MNC which plans to establish a subsidiary in Japan. It is very confident that the Japanese yen will appreciate against the dollar over time. The subsidiary will retain only enough revenue to cover expenses and will remit the rest to the parent each year. Would Ventura benefit more from exchange rate effects if its parent provided equity financing for the subsidiary or if the subsidiary were financed by local banks in Japan? Explain.

20. Santa Monica Company is a U.S.-based MNC that was considering establishing a consumer products division in Germany, which would be financed by German banks. It completed its capital budgeting analysis in August 1989. Then, in November 1989, there was evidence of possible reunification between East and West Germany. In response, Santa Monica Company increased its expected cash flows by 20 percent and did not adjust the discount rate applied to the project. Should the discount rate be affected by reunification?

21. Assume that a less developed country called LDC removes its barriers to encourage direct foreign investment (DFI) in order to reduce its unemployment rate, currently at 15 percent. Also assume that several MNCs are likely to consider DFI in LDC. The inflation rate in recent years has averaged 4 percent. The hourly wage in LDC for manufacturing is the equivalent of about $5 per hour. As Piedmont Company developed cash flow forecasts to perform a capital budgeting analysis for a project in LDC, it assumed a wage rate of $5 in Year 1 and applied a 4-percent increase to each of the next ten years. The components produced are to be exported to its headquarters in the United States, where they will be used in the production of computers. Do you think Piedmont will overestimate or underestimate the net present value of this project? Why? (Assume that LDC's currency is tied to the dollar and will remain that way.)

22. PepsiCo recently decided to invest more than $300 million for expansion in Brazil. There is much potential in Brazil because it has 150 million people and the demand for soft drinks by Brazil's consumers is increasing over time. However, soft drink consumption is still only about one-fifth of the soft drink consumption in the United States. PepsiCo's initial outlay was used to purchase three production plants and a

distribution network of almost 1,000 trucks to distribute PepsiCo's products to retail stores in Brazil. The expansion in Brazil was expected to make PepsiCo's products more accessible to consumers in Brazil.

a. Given that the investment by PepsiCo Inc. in Brazil was entirely in dollars, describe the exposure to exchange rate risk resulting from the project. Explain how the size of the parent's initial investment and the exchange rate risk would have been affected if PepsiCo Inc. had financed much of the investment with loans from banks in Brazil.
b. Describe the factors that were likely to be considered by PepsiCo Inc. when estimating the future cash flows of the project in Brazil.
c. What factors were likely to be considered by PepsiCo Inc. in deriving its required rate of return on the project in Brazil?
d. Describe the uncertainty that surrounds the estimate of future cash flows from the perspective of the U.S. parent.
e. PepsiCo's parent was responsible for assessing the expansion in Brazil. Yet, PepsiCo already had some existing operations in Brazil. When capital budgeting analysis is used to determine whether this project is feasible, should the project be assessed from the perspective of Brazil or the United States? Explain.

23. Assume that a U.S. firm was evaluating a project in Thailand (to be financed with U.S. dollars). All cash flows generated from the project are to be reinvested in Thailand for several years. Explain how the Asian crisis would have affected the expected cash flows of this project and the required rate of return on this project. If the cash flows were to be remitted to the U.S. parent, explain how the Asian crisis would have affected the expected cash flows of this project.

24. When considering the implementation of a project in one of several possible countries, what types of tax characteristics should be assessed among the countries? (See Appendix 14).

Internet Application

25. The following Web site offers regional and country-specific information:

    http://ciber.bus.msu.edu/busres.htm

    Go to the section on country-specific information on Europe, and then link to Portugal. Explain how the most recent conditions described about Portugal would possibly cause an MNC to revise its expected cash flows from a project it considered six months ago. That is, identify any factors in the environment that affect estimates of an MNC's future cash flows on proposed projects in Portugal. State whether the recent environmental changes would cause an increase or decrease in expected cash flows estimated as of today, as compared to estimates created six months ago.

Running Your Own MNC

Deriving a Required Rate of Return for an International Project

26. Consider a possible project that would result in expansion of your international business. Describe how you would derive a required rate of return for this project.

Blades, Inc. Case

Decision by Blades, Inc. to Invest in Thailand

Since Ben Holt, Blades' chief financial officer (CFO), believes the growth potential for the roller blade market in Thailand to be very high, he, together with Blades' board of directors, has decided to invest in Thailand. The purpose of the investment is to establish a manufacturing plant to produce "Speedos," Blades' high quality roller blades. The proposed investment is to take the form of establishing a subsidiary in Bangkok. Ben Holt believes that economic conditions in Thailand will be relatively strong in ten years, at which time he expects to sell the subsidiary.

Blades will continue exporting to the United Kingdom under an existing agreement with Jogs Ltd., a British retailer. Furthermore, it will continue its sales in the United States. However, under an existing agreement with Entertainment Products, Inc., a Thai retailer, Blades is committed to selling 180,000 pairs of Speedos to the retailer at a fixed price of 4,594 Thai baht per pair. Once operations in Thailand commence, the agreement will last another year, at which time the agreement may be renewed. Thus, Blades will sell 180,000 pairs of roller blades to Entertainment Products during Blades' first year of operations in Thailand whether it has operations in the country or not. However, since only materials sufficient to manufacture 72,000 pairs were imported from Thailand, Blades will save the equivalent of 300 baht per pair in variable costs on the 108,000 pairs not previously sourced from Thailand and sold in the last year of the existing agreement.

Entertainment Products has already declared its willingness to renew the agreement for another three years under identical terms. However, because of recent delivery delays, it is willing to renew the agreement only if Blades has operations in Thailand. Moreover, if Blades has a subsidiary in Thailand, Entertainment Products will keep renewing the existing agreement as long as Blades operates in Thailand. If the agreement is renewed, Blades expects to sell a total of 300,000 pairs of Speedos annually during its first two years of operation in Thailand to various retailers, including Entertainment Products. After this time, it expects to sell 400,000 pairs annually. If the agreement is not renewed, Blades will be able to sell 5,000 of the 180,000 pairs to Entertainment Products annually, but not at a fixed price. Thus, if the agreement is not renewed, Blades expects to sell a total of 125,000 pairs of Speedos annually during its first two years of operation in Thailand and 225,000 pairs annually thereafter. Pairs not sold under the contractual agreement with Entertainment Products will be sold for 5,000 Thai baht per pair, since Entertainment Products had required a lower price to compensate it for the risk of being unable to sell the pairs it purchased from Blades.

Ben Holt wishes to analyze the financial feasibility of establishing a subsidiary in Thailand. You are a financial analyst of Blades and have been given the task of analyzing the proposed project. Since future economic conditions in Thailand are highly uncertain, Ben Holt has also asked you to conduct some sensitivity analyses. Fortunately, most of the information needed to conduct a capital budgeting analysis has been provided to you by Ben Holt. This information is detailed here:

- The building and equipment needed will cost 550 million Thai baht. This amount includes additional funds to support working capital.
- The plant and equipment will be depreciated using straight-line depreciation. Thus, 30 million baht will be depreciated annually for 10 years.
- The variable costs needed to manufacture Speedos are estimated to be 3,500 baht per pair next year.
- Blades' fixed operating expenses, such as administrative salaries, will be 25 million baht next year.
- The current spot exchange rate of the Thai baht is $0.023. Blades expects the baht to depreciate by an average of 2 percent per year for the next ten years.
- The Thai government will impose a 25-percent tax rate on income and a 10-percent withholding tax on any funds remitted by the subsidiary to Blades. Any earnings remitted to the United States will not be taxed again.
- After ten years, Blades expects to sell its Thai subsidiary. It expects to sell the subsidiary for about 650 million baht, after considering any capital gains taxes.
- The average annual inflation in Thailand is expected to be 12 percent. Unless prices are contractually fixed, revenue, variable costs, and fixed costs are subject to inflation and are expected to change by the same annual rate as the inflation rate.

Blades could continue to export to and import from Thailand, which has generated a return of about 20 percent. Blades requires a return of 25 percent on this project in order to justify its investment in Thailand. All excess funds generated by the Thai subsidiary will be remitted to Blades and will be used to support U.S. operations.

Ben Holt has asked you to answer the following questions:

1. Should the sales and the associated costs of 180,000 pairs of roller blades to be sold in Thailand under the existing agreement be included in the capital budgeting analysis to decide whether Blades should establish a subsidiary in Thailand? Should the sales resulting from a renewed agreement be included? Why or why not?
2. Using a spreadsheet, conduct a capital budgeting analysis for the proposed project, assuming that Blades renews the agreement with Entertainment Products. Should Blades establish a subsidiary in Thailand under these conditions?
3. Using a spreadsheet, conduct a capital budgeting analysis for the proposed project assuming that Blades does not renew the agreement with Entertainment Products. Should Blades establish a subsidiary in Thailand under these conditions? Should Blades renew the agreement with Entertainment Products or not?
4. Since future economic conditions in Thailand are uncertain, Mr. Holt would like to know how critical the salvage value is in the project you think is most feasible.
5. The future value of the baht is highly uncertain. Under a worst case scenario, the baht may depreciate by as much as 5 percent annually. Revise your spreadsheet to illustrate how this would affect Blades' decision to establish a subsidiary in Thailand. (Use the capital budgeting analysis you have identified as the most favorable from questions 2 and 3 to answer this question.)

Small Business Dilemma

Multinational Capital Budgeting by the Sports Exports Company

Jim Logan, owner of the Sports Exports Company, has been pleased with his success in the United Kingdom. He began his business by producing footballs and exporting them to the United Kingdom. While American-style football is still not nearly as popular in the United Kingdom as it is in the United States, his firm controls the market in the United Kingdom. Jim is considering an application of the same business in Mexico. He would produce the footballs in the United States and export them to a distributor of sporting goods in Mexico, who would sell the footballs to retail stores. The distributor likely would want to make payment for the product each month in Mexican pesos. Jim would need to hire one full-time employee in the United States to perform the production. He would also need to lease one more warehouse.

1. Describe the capital budgeting steps that would be necessary to determine whether this proposed project is feasible, as related to this specific situation.
2. Explain why there is uncertainty surrounding the cash flows of this project.

APPENDIX 14

Incorporating International Tax Laws in Multinational Capital Budgeting

Tax laws can vary among countries in many ways, but any type of tax causes an MNC's before-tax cash flows to vary from its after-tax cash flows. To estimate the future cash flows that are to be generated by a proposed foreign project (such as the establishment of a new subsidiary or the acquisition of a foreign firm), MNCs must first estimate the taxes that they will incur due to the foreign project. This appendix provides a general background on some of the more important international tax characteristics that must be considered by an MNC when assessing foreign projects. Financial managers do not necessarily have to be international tax experts because they may be able to rely on the MNC's international tax department or on independent tax consultants for guidance. However, they should at least be aware of international tax characteristics that can affect the cash flows of a foreign project and recognize how those characteristics can vary among the countries where foreign projects are considered.

VARIATION IN TAX LAWS AMONG COUNTRIES

Each country varies in the way it generates tax revenue. The United States relies on corporate and individual income taxes for federal revenue. Other countries may depend more on the *value-added tax (VAT)* or excise taxes. Since each country has its own philosophy on whom to tax and how much, it is not surprising that corporations may be treated unequally among countries in terms of taxes. Because systems and tax rates are unique to each country, MNCs need to recognize the various tax provisions of each country where they consider investing in a foreign project. The more important tax characteristics of a country to be considered within an MNC's international tax assessment are (1) corporate income taxes, (2) withholding taxes, (3) personal and excise tax rates, (4) provision for carrybacks and carryforwards, (5) tax treaties, (6) tax credits, and (7) taxes on income from intercompany transactions. A discussion of each characteristic follows.

Corporate Income Taxes

In general, countries impose taxes on corporate income generated within their borders, even if the parents of those corporations are based in other countries. Each country has its unique corporate income tax laws. The United States, for example, taxes the worldwide income of U.S. "persons," a term that includes corporations.

http://
The Price Waterhouse Coopers site at www.pwcglobal.com provides access to country-specific information such as general business rules and regulations and tax environments.

However, as a general rule, foreign income of a foreign subsidiary of a U.S. company is not taxed until it is transferred to the U.S. parent by payment of dividends or a liquidation distribution. This is the concept of deferral.

An MNC planning direct foreign investment in foreign countries must determine how the anticipated earnings from a foreign project will be affected. Tax rates imposed on income earned by businesses (including foreign subsidiaries of MNCs) or income remitted to a parent are shown in Exhibit 14A.1 for several countries. The second column of this exhibit shows the extent to which corporate income tax rates can vary among host countries and illustrates why MNCs closely assess the tax

Exhibit 14A.1
Comparison of Tax Characteristics Among Countries

Country	Corp. Income Tax	Withholding Tax on: Dividends	Interest	Patent Royalties, etc.	Carryforward Losses for __ Years
Argentina	33%	0%	13%	20–30%	5
Australia	36	0	30	10	Unlimited
Austria	34	25	25	20	Unlimited
Belgium	40	25	15	15	Unlimited
Brazil	15	0	15	15	Unlimited
Canada	29	25	25	25	7
Chile	15	20	35	30	Unlimited
China	30	20	20	20	5
Czech Rep.	35	25	0–25	25	7
France	33	25	33	15	5
Germany	45	25	0	25	Unlimited
Hong Kong	17	0	0	2–17	Unlimited
Hungary	18	0–35	18	18	5
India	35	0	20	20	8
Indonesia	30	15–20	15–20	15–20	5–10
Ireland	32	0	26	26	Unlimited
Israel	36	25	25	25	Unlimited
Italy	37	32	0–27	22	5
Jamaica	33	33	33	33	Unlimited
Japan	37	20	15–20	20	5
Korea	28	0	20	0	5
Malaysia	28	0	15	10	Unlimited
Mexico	34	0	15–35	15–35	10
Netherlands	35	25	0	0	Unlimited
New Zealand	33	30	15	15	Unlimited
Singapore	26	0	15	15	Unlimited
Spain	35	25	25	25	7
Switzerland	10–27	35	35	0	7
Taiwan	25	15	25	35	5
U.K.	31	0	20	23	Unlimited
U.S.	35	30	30	30	20
Venezuela	34	0	0–5	0–34	3

Source: 1998 WorldwideCorporate Tax Guide, Ernst & Young. The numbers provided above are for illustrative purposes only, as the actual tax rate may depend on specific characteristics of the MNC.

guidelines in any foreign country in which they consider conducting direct foreign investment. Given differences in tax deductions, depreciation, business subsidies, and other factors, corporate tax differentials cannot be measured simply by comparing quoted tax rates across countries.

Corporate tax rates can also differ within a country, depending on whether the entity is a domestic corporation. Also, if it is considered to have a permanent establishment in a country, an unregistered foreign corporation may be subject to that country's tax laws on income earned within its borders. Generally, a permanent establishment includes an office or fixed place of business or a specified kind of agency (*independent* agents are normally excluded) through which active and continuous business is conducted. In some cases, the tax depends on the industry or on the form of business used (corporation, branch, partnership, etc.).

Withholding Taxes

The following types of payments by an MNC's subsidiary are commonly subject to a withholding tax by the host government. First, a subsidiary may remit a portion of its earnings, referred to as *dividends,* to its parent since the parent is the shareholder of the subsidiary. Second, the subsidiary may pay interest to the parent or to other nonresident debtholders from which it received loans. Third, the subsidiary may make payments to the parent or to other nonresident firms in return for the use of patents (such as technology) or other rights. The payment of dividends reduces the amount of reinvestment by the subsidiary in the host country. The payments by the subsidiary to nonresident firms to cover interest or patents reflect expenses by the subsidiary, which will normally reduce its taxable income, and therefore will reduce the corporate income taxes paid to the host government. Thus, withholding taxes may be a way for host governments to tax MNCs that make interest or patent payments to nonresident firms.

Since withholding taxes imposed on the subsidiary can reduce the funds remitted by the subsidiary to the parent, the withholding taxes must be accounted for within a capital budgeting analysis conducted by the parent. As with corporate tax rates, the withholding tax rate can vary substantially among countries, as shown in Exhibit 14A.1. Even within a country, the withholding tax can vary according to the purpose of the fund transfer, as shown across each row in Exhibit 14A.1.

Reducing Exposure to Withholding Taxes. Withholding taxes can be reduced by income tax treaties (discussed shortly). Because of tax treaties between some countries, the withholding taxes shown in the exhibit may be less when the MNC's parent is based in countries participating in the treaties.

If the host country government of a particular subsidiary places a high withholding tax on subsidiary earnings remitted to the parent, the parent of the MNC may instruct the subsidiary to temporarily refrain from remitting earnings and to reinvest them in that host country instead. As an alternative approach, the MNC may instruct the subsidiary to set up a research and development division that will enhance subsidiaries elsewhere. The main purpose behind this strategy is to search for a way to efficiently use the funds abroad if the funds cannot be sent to the parent without excessive taxation. Since the international tax laws can influence the timing of the transfer of funds back to the parent, they affect the timing of cash flows on proposed foreign projects. Therefore, the international tax implications must be understood before the cash flows of a foreign project can be estimated.

Personal and Excise Tax Rates

An MNC is more likely to be concerned with corporate tax rates and withholding tax rates than individual tax rates because its cash flows are directly affected by the taxes incurred. However, a country's individual tax rates can indirectly affect an MNC's cash flows because the MNC may have to pay higher wages to employees in countries (such as in Europe) where the personal income levels of employees are taxed at a relatively high rate. In addition, a country's value-added tax or excise tax may affect cash flows to be generated from a foreign project because it may make the products less competitive on a global basis (reducing the expected quantity of products to be sold).

Provision for Carrybacks and Carryforwards

Negative earnings from operations can often be carried back or forward to offset earnings in other years. The laws pertaining to these so-called **net operating loss carrybacks** and **carryforwards** can vary among countries. An MNC generally does not plan to generate negative earnings in foreign countries. Yet, if negative earnings occur, it is desirable to be able to use them to offset other years of positive earnings. Most foreign countries do not allow negative earnings to be carried back but allow some flexibility in carrying losses forward (see the last column of Exhibit 14A.1). Since many foreign projects are expected to result in negative earnings in the early years, the tax laws for the country of concern will affect the future tax deductions resulting from these losses and will therefore affect the future cash flows of the foreign project.

Tax Treaties

Countries often establish income tax treaties, whereby one partner will reduce its taxes by granting a credit for taxes imposed on corporations operating within the other treaty partner's tax jurisdiction. Income tax treaties help avoid corporate exposure to double taxation. Some treaties apply to taxes paid on income earned by MNCs in foreign income. Other treaties apply to withholding taxes imposed by the host country on foreign earnings that are remitted to the parent.

Without such treaties, subsidiary earnings could be taxed by the host country and then again by the parent's country when received by the parent. To the extent that the parent uses some of these earnings to provide cash dividends for shareholders, triple taxation could result (since the dividend income is also taxed at the shareholder level). Because income tax treaties reduce taxes on earnings generated by MNCs, they help stimulate direct foreign investment. Many foreign projects that are perceived as feasible would not be feasible without income tax treaties because the expected cash flows would be reduced by excessive taxation.

Tax Credits

Even without income tax treaties, an MNC may be allowed to credit income and withholding taxes paid in one country against taxes owed by the parent if it meets certain requirements. Like income tax treaties, tax credits help to avoid double taxation and stimulate direct foreign investment.

The tax credit policies can vary among countries, but they generally work like this. Consider a U.S.-based MNC subject to a U.S.-tax rate of 35 percent. Assume that a foreign subsidiary of this corporation has generated earnings taxed at less than 35 percent by the host country's government. The earnings remitted to the parent from the subsidiary will be subject to an additional amount of U.S. tax to bring the total tax up to 35 percent. From the parent's point of view, the tax on its subsidiary's remitted earnings are 35 percent overall, so it does not matter whether the host country of the subsidiary or the United States receives most of the taxes. From the perspective of the governments of these two countries, however, the allocation of taxes is very important. If subsidiaries of U.S. corporations are established in foreign countries, and if these countries tax income at a rate close to 35 percent, they can generate large tax revenues from income earned by the subsidiaries. The tax revenues received by them are at the expense of the parent's country (the United States, in this case).

If the corporate income tax rate in a foreign country is greater than 35 percent, the United States generally does not impose any additional taxes on earnings remitted to a U.S. parent by foreign subsidiaries in that country. In fact, under current law, the United States allows the excess foreign tax to be credited against other taxes owed by the parent, due on the same type of income generated by subsidiaries in other lower-tax countries. In a sense, this suggests that some host countries could charge abnormally high corporate income tax rates to foreign subsidiaries and still attract direct foreign investment. If the MNC in our example has subsidiaries located in some countries with low corporate income taxes, the U.S. tax on earnings remitted to the U.S. parent will normally bring up the total tax to 35 percent. Yet, credits against excessive income taxes by high-tax countries on foreign subsidiaries could offset these taxes that would otherwise be paid to the U.S. government. Due to tax credits, therefore, an MNC might be more willing to invest in a project in a country with excessive tax rates.

The current tax information of countries may not be sufficient to determine the tax effects of a particular foreign project, since tax incentives may be offered in particular circumstances, and tax rates can change over time. Consider an MNC that plans to establish a manufacturing plant in Country Y rather than Country X. Assume that while many economic characteristics favor Country X, the current tax rates within Country Y are lower. However, whereas tax rates in Country X have been historically stable and are expected to continue that way, they have been changing every few years in Country Y. In this case, the MNC must assess the future uncertainty of the tax rates. It cannot treat the current tax rate of Country Y as a constant when conducting a capital budgeting analysis. Instead, it must consider possible changes in the tax rates over time and, based on these possibilities, determine whether Country Y's projected tax advantages *over time* sufficiently outweigh the advantages of the Country X location. One approach to account for possible changes in the tax rates is to use sensitivity analysis, which measures the sensitivity of the net present value (*NPV*) of after-tax cash flows to various possible tax changes over time. For each tax scenario, a different *NPV* is projected. By accounting for each possible tax scenario, the MNC can develop a distribution of possible *NPV*s that may occur and can then compare these for each country.

There are two critical, broadly defined functions necessary to determine how international tax laws affect the cash flows of a foreign project. The first is to be aware of all the current (and possible future) tax laws that exist for each country where the MNC does (or plans to do) business. The second function is to take the information generated from the first function and apply it to forecasted earnings and remittances to determine the taxes, so that the proposed project's cash flows can be estimated.

Taxes on Income from Intercompany Transactions

Many proposed foreign projects by an MNC involve intercompany transactions. For example, a U.S-based MNC may consider acquiring a foreign firm that will produce and deliver supplies to its U.S. subsidiaries. Under these conditions, the MNC must use transfer pricing, which involves pricing the transactions between the two entities (such as subsidiaries) of the same corporation. When MNCs consider new foreign projects, they must incorporate their transfer pricing to properly estimate cash flows that will be generated from these projects. Therefore, transfer pricing decisions must be made on any anticipated intercompany transactions that would result from the new foreign project before the feasibility of the foreign project can be determined. MNCs are subject to some guidelines on transfer pricing, but they usually have some flexibility and tend to use a transfer pricing policy that will minimize taxes while satisfying the guidelines.

To illustrate the concept of transfer pricing, suppose that Oakland Corporation has established two subsidiaries to capitalize on low production costs. One of these subsidiaries (called Hitax Sub) is located in a country whose government charges a 50-percent tax rate on before-tax earnings. Hitax Sub produces partially finished products and sends them to the other subsidiary (called Lotax Sub) where the final assembly takes place. The host government of Lotax Sub charges a 20-percent tax on before-tax earnings. To simplify the example, assume that no dividends are to be remitted to the parent in the near future. Given this information, pro forma income statements would be as shown in the top part of Exhibit 14A.2 for Hitax Sub (Column 2), Lotax Sub (Column 3), and the combined subsidiaries (Column 4). The income statement items are reported in U.S. dollars to more easily illustrate how a revised transfer pricing policy can affect earnings and cash flows.

The sales level shown for Hitax Sub matches the cost of goods sold for Lotax Sub, implying that all Hitax Sub sales are to Lotax Sub. The additional expenses incurred by Lotax Sub to complete the product are classified as operating expenses.

Notice from Exhibit 14A.2 that both subsidiaries have the same earnings before taxes. Yet, because of the differences in tax rates, Hitax Sub will earn an after-tax income of $7.5 million less than Lotax Sub. If Oakland Corporation could revise its transfer pricing, its combined earnings after taxes would be increased. To illustrate, suppose that the price of products sent from Hitax Sub to Lotax Sub is reduced, causing the sales of Hitax Sub to decline from $100 million to $80 million. This would also reduce the cost of goods sold of Lotax Sub by $20 million. The revised pro forma income statement resulting from the change in the transfer pricing policy is shown in the bottom part of Exhibit 14A.2. The difference in forecasted earnings before taxes between the two subsidiaries is now $40 million, although the combined amount has not changed. Because earnings have been shifted from Hitax Sub to Lotax Sub, the total tax payments are reduced to $11.5 million from the original estimate of $17.5 million. Thus, the corporate taxes imposed on earnings are now forecasted to be $6 million less than originally expected.

It should be mentioned that there are some limitations to such an adjustment in the transfer pricing policy since host governments may enforce laws that restrict such practices when the intent is to avoid taxes. Transactions between subsidiaries of

Exhibit 14A.2
Impact of Transfer Pricing Adjustment on Pro Forma Earnings and Taxes: Oakland Corporation (in Thousands)

	Original Estimates		
	Hitax Sub	Lotax Sub	Combined[1]
Sales	$100,000	$150,000	$250,000
Less: Cost of goods sold	50,000	100,000	150,000
Gross profit	50,000	50,000	100,000
Less: Operating expenses	20,000	20,000	40,000
Earnings before interest and taxes	30,000	30,000	60,000
Interest expense	5,000	5,000	10,000
Earnings before taxes	25,000	25,000	50,000
Taxes (50% for Hitax and 20% for Lotax)	12,500	5,000	17,500
Earnings after taxes	12,500	20,000	32,500
	Revised Estimates Based on Adjusting Transfer Pricing Policy		
	Hitax Sub	Lotax Sub	Combined[1]
Sales	$80,000	$150,000	$230,000
Less: Cost of goods sold	50,000	80,000	130,000
Gross profit	30,000	70,000	100,000
Less: Operating expenses	20,000	20,000	40,000
Earnings before interest and taxes	10,000	50,000	60,000
Interest expense	5,000	5,000	10,000
Earnings before taxes	5,000	45,000	50,000
Taxes (50% for Hitax and 20% for Lotax)	2,500	9,000	11,500
Earnings after taxes	2,500	36,000	38,500

[1]The combined numbers are shown here for illustrative purposes only and do not reflect the firm's official consolidated financial statements. When consolidating sales for financial statements, intercompany transactions (between subsidiaries) would be eliminated. This example is simply intended to illustrate how total taxes paid by subsidiaries are lower when transfer pricing is structured to shift some gross profit from a high-tax subsidiary to a low-tax subsidiary.

a firm are supposed to be priced using the principle of "arm's-length" transactions. That is, the price should be set as if the buyer is unrelated to the seller and should not be adjusted simply to shift tax burdens. However, since there is some flexibility on transfer pricing policies, MNCs from all countries attempt to establish transfer pricing policies that are within legal limits, but also reduce tax burdens. Even if the transfer price reflects the "fair" price that would normally be charged in the market, one subsidiary can still charge another for technology transfers, research and development expenses, or other forms of overhead expenses incurred.

The actual mechanics of international transfer pricing go far beyond the example provided here. The U.S. laws in this area are particularly strict. Nevertheless, there are various ways MNCs can justify increasing prices at one subsidiary and reducing them at another.

There is substantial evidence that MNCs based in numerous countries use transfer pricing strategies to reduce their taxes. Moreover, several alternative methods circumvent transfer pricing restrictions. Various fees can be implemented for services, research and development, royalties, and administrative duties. While the fees may be imposed to shift earnings and minimize tax effects, the actual performance of each subsidiary is distorted. Yet, a centralized MNC approach could account for the transfer pricing strategy implemented when assessing the true performance of each subsidiary.

15 Multinational Restructuring

MNCs commonly engage in **multinational restructuring**, which represents the restructuring of the composition of their multinational assets or liabilities. Thus, multinational restructuring decisions not only determine the types of assets, but also the countries where those assets are located.

The specific objectives of this chapter are to

- provide a background on how MNCs use international acquisitions as a form of multinational restructuring,
- explain how MNCs conduct valuations of foreign target firms,
- explain why valuations of a target firm vary among MNCs that plan to restructure by acquiring a target, and
- identify other types of multinational restructuring, besides international acquisitions.

Background on Multinational Restructuring

Decisions by an MNC to build a new subsidiary in the Netherlands, to acquire a company in Italy, to sell its Singapore subsidiary, to downsize its operations in New Zealand, or to shift some production from its British subsidiary to its Mexican subsidiary all represent forms of multinational restructuring. Even the most successful MNCs continuously assess possible forms of multinational restructuring so that they can capitalize on changing economic, political, or industry conditions across countries.

MNCs reevaluate their existing businesses and other proposed projects when determining the ideal composition of assets to employ and the locations where the assets are employed. Even if an existing business adds value to the MNC, it may be worthwhile to assess whether the business would generate more value to the MNC if it was restructured.

INTERNATIONAL ACQUISITIONS

An international acquisition of a firm is similar to other international projects in that it requires an initial outlay and is expected to generate cash flows whose present value will exceed the initial outlay. Many U.S.-based MNCs including Rockwell International, Ford Motor Co., Scott Paper Co., Borden Inc., and Dow Chemical Co. have recently engaged in international acquisitions. Many more international acquisitions are motivated by the desire to increase global market share, and to capitalize on economies of scale through global consolidation.

MNCs may view international acquisitions as a better form of direct foreign investment than establishing a new subsidiary. However, there are distinct differences between these two forms of direct foreign investment. Through an international acquisition, the firm can immediately expand its international business since the target is already in place. Conversely, establishing a new subsidiary requires time. Second, an international acquisition can benefit from the customer relationships that have already been established. These advantages of an international acquisition over the establishment of a foreign subsidiary must be weighed against the higher costs of the acquisition. When viewed as a project, the international acquisition usually generates quicker and larger cash flows than the establishment of a new subsidiary but requires a larger initial outlay. International acquisitions also necessitate the integration of parent management style with that of the foreign target.

Trends in International Acquisitions

Exhibits 15.1 and 15.2 compare the volume and value of international acquisitions involving U.S. firms. The volume of foreign acquisitions of U.S. firms has increased consistently since 1993. The volume of U.S. acquisitions of foreign firms has increased consistently since 1988. In 1997, there were more than 1,000 U.S. acquisitions of foreign firms.

In particular, European firms have been attractive targets for U.S. firms attempting to establish presence in Europe due to the more uniform regulations across European countries and the momentum for free enterprise in Eastern Europe. U.S. acquisitions of European firms continued in 1998 in anticipation that the single European currency would enhance efficiency in European operations. U.S. firms acquire more targets in the United Kingdom than in any other country; British and Canadian firms are the most common non-U.S. acquirers of U.S. targets.

Exhibit 15.2 compares the values of U.S. acquisitions of foreign firms to those of foreign acquisitions of U.S. firms. The value of foreign acquisitions of U.S. firms consistently increased since 1992. The annual increases have been especially pronounced since 1994. U.S. acquisitions of foreign firms have consistently increased since 1992. By 1997, the value of U.S. acquisitions of foreign firms was more than twice the value in any year up to 1995.

http://
Visit the homepage of the CIA at www.odci.gov/cia/ciahome.html for access to various national and international surveys, analyses, maps, and publications such as the World Factbook.

Barriers to International Acquisitions

When MNCs consider acquiring a foreign company, they need to be aware of the barriers that are imposed by host government agencies. All countries have one or more agencies that monitor mergers and acquisitions. The acquisition activity in any given country is somewhat influenced by the regulations enforced by these agencies. For example, in France the Treasury can reject any deal if the acquirer is based out-

Exhibit 15.1
Trends in International Acquisitions

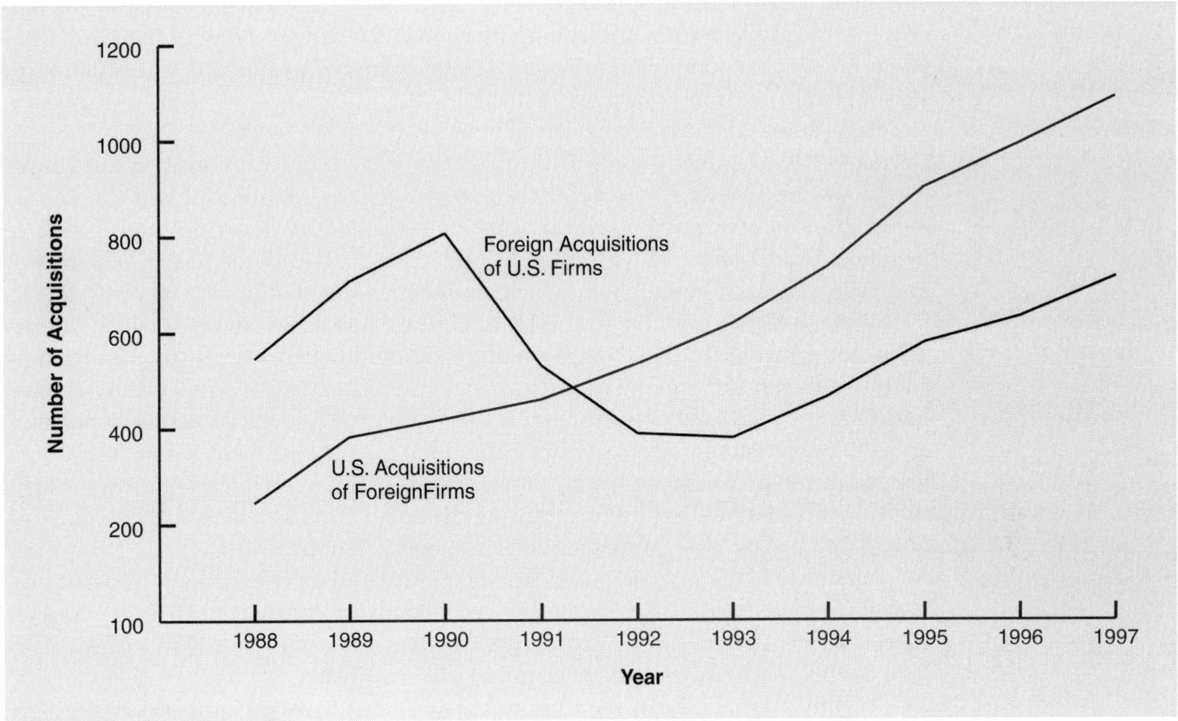

Source: *Mergers & Acquisitions.*

Exhibit 15.2
Value of International Acquisitions

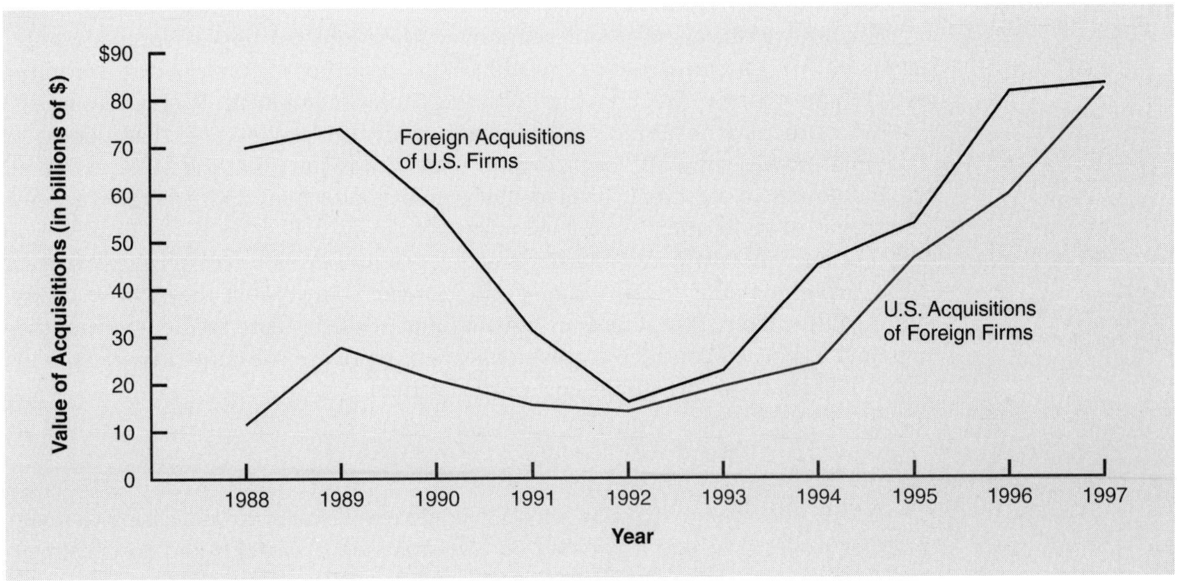

Source: *Mergers & Acquisitions.*

side the European Economic Community. The French government may also reject a deal if the target is in some closely monitored industry, such as defense or health care. The Monopolies Commission of France also reviews acquisitions to prevent any combined firms from controlling more than 25 percent of an industry or from severely reducing competition. Recently, The Coca-Cola Company's application to expand its business in France was denied.

Acquisitions in Japan are reviewed by the Fair Trade Commission, acquisitions in Germany are examined by the Antitrust Authority, and acquisitions in the United Kingdom are reviewed by several regulatory agencies. Acquisitions in the United States are also reviewed by several agencies, including the Securities and Exchange Commission, which regulates the conduct of acquisitions, and the Justice Department and Federal Trade Commission, which analyze the potential impact on competition.

Most countries prohibit or at least discourage **hostile takeovers** in which the target is not agreeable to the acquisition. Explicit and implicit barriers to even friendly acquisitions can vary among countries. For example, many governments in Asia and Latin America have restricted foreign majority ownership, which essentially prevents an MNC from another country from purchasing target firms there. These restrictions have been reduced in recent years. Governments of Asian countries removed restrictions on international acquisitions during the Asian crisis as a means of encouraging MNCs to develop new business in their respective countries.

Japan has historically imposed barriers to discourage international acquisitions, However, these barriers have been reduced recently (as long as the Japanese target is agreeable), as U.S.-based MNCs such as Corning Glass Works, Data General, Eastman Kodak, and Motorola have acquired Japanese firms.

An implicit barrier to international acquisitions in some countries is the "red tape" involved, such as procedure and documentation requirements. An acquiring firm is subject to a different set of requirements in each country. Therefore, it has been difficult for a firm to become proficient at the process unless it concentrates on international acquisitions within a single foreign country. The current efforts to make regulations uniform across Europe have simplified the paperwork involved in acquisitions of European firms.

Some governments allow international acquisitions but impose special requirements on MNCs that desire to acquire a local firm. For example, the government may require that the MNC create pollution control equipment. It may require the MNC to structure the business to export the products it produces, so that it does not take market share of other local firms. It may even require that the MNC retain all the employees of the target firm so that the unemployment and general economic conditions of the country are not adversely affected.

The existing barriers to international acquisitions do not necessarily prevent an MNC from pursuing a target in a specific foreign country, but they can be costly. Since MNCs can pursue targets in other countries where there are no barriers, they are only willing to consider acquisitions where there are substantial barriers if the potential benefits outweigh the cost of the barriers.

Model for Valuing a Foreign Target

The MNC's decision to invest in a foreign company is similar to its decision to invest in other projects, in that it is based on a comparison of benefits and costs as measured by net present value. From an MNC parent's perspective, the foreign target's value can be estimated as the present value of cash flows that it receives from the foreign target, as the foreign target would become a foreign subsidiary owned by the MNC's parent.

The MNC's parent would only consider investing in the target if the estimated present value of these cash flows it would ultimately receive from the target over time exceeds the initial outlay necessary to purchase the target. Thus, capital budgeting analysis can be used to determine whether a firm should be acquired. The net present value of a company from the acquiring firm's perspective (NPV_a) is

$$NPV_a = -IO_a + \sum_{t=1}^{n} \frac{CF_{a,t}}{(1+k)^t} + \frac{SV_a}{(1+k)^n}$$

where

IO_a = initial outlay needed by the acquiring firm to acquire the company
$CF_{a,t}$ = cash flow to be generated by the company for the acquiring firm
k = required rate of return on the acquisition of the company
SV_a = salvage value of the company (expected selling price of the company at a point in the future)
n = time at which the company will be sold by the acquiring firm

The capital budgeting analysis of a foreign target must account for the exchange rate of concern. For example, consider a U.S.-based MNC that assesses the acquisition of a foreign company. The dollar initial outlay ($IO_{U.S.}$) needed by the U.S. firm is determined by the acquisition price in foreign currency units (IO_f) and the spot rate of the foreign currency (S):

$$IO_{U.S.} = IO_f(S)$$

The dollar amount of cash flows to the U.S. firm is determined by the foreign currency cash flows ($CF_{f,t}$) per period remitted to the United States and the spot rate at that time (S_t):

$$CF_{a,t} = (CF_{f,t})S_t$$

This ignores any withholding taxes or blocked-funds restrictions imposed by the host government and any income taxes imposed by the U.S. government. The dollar amount of salvage value to the U.S. firm is determined by the salvage value in foreign-currency units (SV_f) and the spot rate at that time (period n) when it is converted to dollars (S_n):

$$SV_a = (SV_f)S_n$$

The net present value of a foreign target can be derived by substituting the equalities just described in the capital budgeting equation:

$$\begin{aligned} NPV_a &= -IO_a + \sum_{t=1}^{n} \frac{CF_{a,t}}{(1+k)^t} + \frac{SV_a}{(1+k)^n} \\ &= -(IO_f)S + \sum_{t=1}^{n} \frac{(CF_{f,t})S_t}{(1+k)^t} + \frac{(SV_f)S_n}{(1+k)^n} \end{aligned}$$

Assessing Potential Acquisitions in Asia

Some U.S. and European firms capitalized on the weak Asian currencies to invest in Asia during the Asian crisis. For example, Procter & Gamble agreed to acquire Sanyong Paper (a large conglomerate in South Korea) during the crisis. Citicorp invested in a large stake of First City Bank in Thailand. Within the first six months of 1998, U.S. firms invested more than $8 billion in Asia, which is more than double the entire amount that they invested there in all of 1997.

http://
Visit the World Bank's Web site at www.worldbank.org for socioeconomic development and performance indicators as well as links to statistical and project-oriented publications and analyses.

The initial outlay for acquiring a firm in Asia is lower as a result of the Asian crisis. First, property values have declined in Asia. Second, the parent's currency (for parents in the United States or Europe) now has more purchasing power due to the weakening of the Asian currencies. Third, many firms in Asia are near bankruptcy and may not be able to obtain necessary funding. Fourth, the governments in these countries may be more willing to allow foreign acquisitions of the local firms (especially those that are failing) as a means of resolving the crisis.

However, the obvious adverse effects of the Asian crisis must also be considered within the capital budgeting analysis. The lower economic growth will generate lower cash flows for most Asian projects, and the weak currency reduces the amount of cash flows (in the parent's currency) that is ultimately received as a return on the parent's investment.

To the extent that the firms believe that the Asian currency values have hit bottom and will rebound, any new foreign acquisitions of Asian firms would benefit from future exchange rate movements. Firms could invest their home currency in exchange for the weak Asian currency to initiate their investment in Asia. Then, if the Asian currency appreciates over time, the earnings generated over there will be worth more (in terms of the parent's currency) when remitted to the parent.

Assessing Potential Acquisitions in Europe

€

Before the adoption of the euro, a U.S.-based MNC would have to separately consider the exchange rate effects from acquiring firms in different European countries. For example, Italy's currency (the lira) was considered more likely to weaken against the dollar than some of the other European currencies, and this could affect the decision of whether to acquire an Italian firm versus a firm in Germany or France. The adoption of the euro as the local currency by several European countries simplifies the analysis for an MNC that is comparing possible target firms in those participating countries. The U.S.-based MNC can be affected by future movements in the euro's value against the dollar, but those effects should occur regardless of whether the MNC purchased a firm in Italy or in any other participating country. Thus, the MNC can make its decision on which firm to acquire within these participating countries without concern about differential exchange rate effects. However, if an MNC is also assessing some firms in European countries that have not adopted the euro as their currency, it will still have to compare the potential exchange rate effects that could result from the acquisition.

Factors That Affect the Expected Cash Flows of the Foreign Target

When an MNC estimates the future cash flows that it would ultimately receive from the foreign target after acquiring that target, it considers several factors that reflect either conditions in the country of concern or conditions of the target itself. The following factors are typically considered when estimating the cash flows that will be provided by the foreign target to the parent.

Target-Specific Factors

Target's Previous Cash Flows. Since the foreign target has been conducting business, it has a history of cash flows that it generated. The recent cash flows per period may serve as an initial base from which future cash flows per period can be estimated after accounting for other factors. Since the target firm has already been conducting business, it may be easier to estimate the cash flows to be generated by a target than to estimate the cash flows to be generated from a new foreign subsidiary.

Yet, previous cash flows of a company are not necessarily an accurate indicator of future cash flows, especially when the target's future cash flows would have to be converted into the acquirer's home currency as they are remitted to the parent. Therefore, the MNC needs to carefully consider all the factors that could influence the cash flows that will be generated from a foreign target.

Managerial Talent of the Target. An acquiring firm must assess the existing managerial talent of the target so that it can determine how the target firm would be managed after the acquisition. The manner by which the acquirer plans to deal with the managerial talent will affect the estimated cash flows to be generated by the target.

If the MNC acquires the target, it may allow the target firm to be managed as it was before the acquisition. However, under these conditions, the acquiring firm may have less potential for enhancing the target's cash flows.

A second alternative for the MNC is to downsize the target firm after acquiring it. For example, if the acquiring firm infuses new technology into the target firm that reduces the need for some of the target's employees, it can attempt to downsize the target. Downsizing reduces expenses but may also reduce productivity and revenue, so that the effect on cash flows can vary with the situation. However, there are significant barriers to increasing efficiency by downsizing in several countries. Governments of some countries are likely to intervene and prevent the acquisition if downsizing is anticipated.

A third alternative for the MNC is to maintain the existing employees of the target but restructure the operations in a manner that achieves more efficient use of labor. For example, the MNC may infuse its own technology into the target firm and then restructure operations so that many of the employees are given new job assignments. This strategy may cause the acquirer to incur some additional expenses, but there is potential for improved cash flows over time.

http://
Visit the Web page of the International Institute for Management (IMD) at www.imd.ch/wcy/wcy_online.html for the results of a comprehensive World Competitiveness Analysis that ranks about 50 countries by factors such as infrastructure, financial environment, science and technological capabilities, international business environment, and political freedom.

Country-Specific Factors

Target's Local Economic Conditions. Potential targets in countries where economic conditions are strong are more likely to experience strong demand for their products in the future and may generate higher cash flows. However, some firms are more sensitive to economic conditions than others. Also, some acquisitions of firms are intended to focus on exporting from the target's home country, so the target country's economic conditions may not be as important. Economic conditions are difficult to predict over a long-term period, especially for emerging countries.

Target's Local Political Conditions. Potential targets in countries where political conditions are favorable are less likely to experience adverse shocks to their cash flow. The sensitivity of cash flows to political conditions is dependent on the firm's type of business. Political conditions are difficult to predict over a long-term period, especially for emerging countries.

Target's Industry Conditions. Industry conditions within a country can cause some targets to be more desirable than others. Some industries in a particular country may be extremely competitive while others are not. In addition, some industries exhibit much stronger potential for growth in a particular country, while others exhibit very little potential for growth. When an MNC assesses targets among countries, it would prefer a country in which the growth potential for its respective industry is high and the competition within the industry is not excessive.

http://
Visit Fred, the Federal Reserve's data bank, at www.stls.frb.org/fred for numerous economic and financial time series, e.g., on balance of payment statistics, interest rates, and foreign exchange rates.

Target's Currency Conditions. If a U.S.-based MNC plans to acquire a foreign target, it must consider how future exchange rate movements may affect the target's local currency cash flows. It must also consider how exchange rates will affect the conversion of the target's remitted earnings to the U.S. parent. The ideal conditions would typically be a weak foreign currency at the time of the acquisition (so that the MNC's initial outlay is low) and a strengthening of the foreign currency over time as funds are periodically remitted to the U.S. parent. There can be exceptions to this general statement, but the point is that the MNC forecasts future exchange rates and then applies those forecasts to determine the impact on cash flows.

Target's Local Stock Market Conditions. Potential target firms that are publicly held are continuously valued in the market, so their stock prices can change rapidly. As the target firm's stock price changes, the acceptable bid price necessary to buy that firm would likely change as well. Thus, there are substantial swings in the purchase price that would be acceptable to a target. This is especially true for those publicly-traded firms in emerging markets in Asia, Eastern Europe, and Latin America whose stock prices commonly change by 5 percent or more within a week. Therefore, an MNC that plans to acquire a target would prefer to time its bid for the target when the local stock market prices are generally low.

Taxes Applicable to the Target. When an MNC assesses a foreign target, it must estimate the expected after-tax cash flows that it will ultimately receive in the form of remitted funds to the parent. Thus, the tax laws applicable to the foreign target are used to derive the after-tax cash flows. First, the estimated future earnings of the target must be derived, and corporate tax rates are applied to determine the after-tax earnings. Second, any withholding tax rates are applied to the funds that are expected to be remitted to the parent in each period, so that the after-tax proceeds can be determined. Third, there could be an additional tax or a tax credit applied to remitted earnings by the acquiring firm's government.

EXAMPLE OF THE VALUATION PROCESS

Consider a U.S.-based MNC that desires to expand in Latin America or Canada. The methods used by the MNC to initially screen targets in various countries and then to estimate a target's value are discussed next.

International Screening Process

The MNC may consider the factors just identified when it conducts an initial screening of prospective targets. Based on Exhibit 15.3, there are prospective targets in Mexico, Brazil, Columbia, and Canada. The target in Mexico has no plans to sell its business and is unwilling to even consider an offer from the MNC. Therefore, this firm is no longer considered. The MNC anticipates potential political problems that could create barriers to an acquisition in Columbia, even though the Columbian target is willing to be acquired. The stock market conditions are not favorable in Brazil, as the stock prices of most Brazilian companies rose substantially just prior to the MNC's assessment of the targets. The MNC does not want to pay as much as the Brazilian target is now worth based on its prevailing market value.

Based on this screening process, the only foreign target that deserves a closer assessment is Canada. The currency conditions of Canada are expected to be slightly unfavorable according to the MNC's assessment, but this is not a reason to eliminate the target from further consideration. Thus, the next step would be for the MNC to obtain as much information as possible so that it can assess the firm and conditions in Canada. Then it can use this information to derive the target's expected cash flows and to determine whether the value of the target in Canada exceeds the initial outlay that would be required to purchase the target, as explained next.

Estimating the Target's Value

Once the MNC has completed its initial screening of targets, it needs to conduct a valuation of all targets that passed the screening process. Continuing with our simplified example, the MNC 's screening process resulted in only one eligible target, a Canadian firm. Assume the Canadian firm has conducted all of its business locally. Assume that the MNC expects that it can obtain materials at a lower cost than the target can because of its relationships with some Canadian suppliers and that it also expects to implement a more efficient production process. The MNC also plans to use its existing managerial talent to manage the target and therefore reduce the administrative and marketing expenses incurred by the target. It also expects that the revenue of the target will increase when the products produced by the target are sold under the MNC's own name. It expects to maintain prices of the products as they are.

Exhibit 15.3
Example of Process Used to Screen Foreign Targets

Target Based in:	Is the Target Receptive to an Acquisition?	Local Economic and Industry Conditions	Local Political Conditions	Local Currency Conditions	Prevailing Stock Market Prices	Tax Laws
Mexico	No	Favorable	OK	OK	OK	May Change
Brazil	Maybe	OK	Volatile	OK	Too High	May Change
Colombia	Yes	Favorable	Volatile	Favorable	OK	Reasonable
Canada	Yes	OK	Favorable	Slightly Unfavorable	OK	Reasonable

The expected cash flows of the target can be measured by first determining the revenue and expense levels in recent years and then adjusting those levels to reflect the changes that would occur after the acquisition. The range of annual revenue has been between C$80 million and C$90 million over the last four years. The MNC uses C$100 million as its best guess for revenue next year because it believes that it can improve the marketing of the products and because it expects a strong Canadian economy. Furthermore, it assumes a 10-percent growth rate in revenue over each of the following two years. The cost of goods sold has been about 50 percent of the revenue in the past but is expected to become 40 percent of revenue because the MNC expects improvement in efficiency. The estimates are shown in Exhibit 15.4.

Selling and administrative expenses have been about C$20 million annually, but the MNC believes that it could restructure the target's administrative positions such that it could reduce the selling and administrative expenses to C$15 million in each of the next three years. The depreciation expenses have been about C$10 million in the past and are expected to remain at that level for the next three years. The Canadian tax rate on the target's earnings is expected to be 30 percent.

Given the information assumed here, the after-tax earnings that the target would generate under the ownership of the MNC are estimated in Exhibit 15.4. The cash flows generated by the target are determined by adding the depreciation expense back to the after-tax earnings. Assume that the target will need C$5 million in cash each year to support existing operations (including the repair of existing machinery) and that the remaining cash flow can be remitted to the U.S. parent. Assume that the target firm is financially supported only by its equity. It currently has 10 million shares of stock outstanding that are priced at C$17 per share.

Since the MNC's parent wishes to assess the target from its own perspective, it focuses on the dollar cash flows that it expects to receive. Assuming that there are no additional taxes, the expected cash flows generated in Canada that are to be remitted to the MNC's parent are converted into U.S. dollars at the expected exchange rate at the end of each year. The MNC uses the prevailing exchange rate of the Cana-

Exhibit 15.4 Valuation of Canadian Target Based on the Assumptions Provided (numbers are in millions)

	Last Year	Year 1	Year 2	Year 3
Revenue	C$90	C$100	C$110	C$121
Cost of Goods Sold	C$45	C$40	C$44	C$48.4
Gross Profit	C$45	C$60	C$56	C$72.6
Selling & Admin. Exp.	C$20	C$15	C$15	C$15
Depreciation	C$10	C$10	C$10	C$10
Earnings Before Taxes	C$15	C$35	C$31	C$47.6
Tax (30%)	C$4.5	C$10.5	C$9.3	C$14.28
Earnings After Taxes	C$10.5	C$24.5	C$21.7	C$33.32
+Depreciation		C$10	C$10	C$10
–Funds To Reinvest		C$5	C$5	C$5
Sale of Firm		—	—	C$230
Cash Flows in C$		C$29.5	C$26.7	C$268.32
Exchange Rate of C$		$.80	$.80	$.80
Cash Flows in $		$23.6	$21.36	$214.66
PV (20% disc. rate)		$19.67	$14.83	$124.22
Cumulative *PV*		$19.67	$34.50	$158.72

dian dollar (which is $.80) as the expected exchange rate for the Canadian dollar in future years.

Estimating the Target's Future Sales Price. If the MNC purchases the target, assume that it would sell the target in three years, after improving the target's performance. Assume that it expects to receive C$230 million (after removing the capital gains taxes) when selling this target in three years. The price at which the target can actually be sold will depend on the expected future cash flows of the target from that point forward, but those expected cash flows are partially dependent on the performance of the target prior to that time. Thus, the MNC can enhance its sales price by improving the target's performance over the three years in which it plans to own the target.

Valuing the Target Based on Estimated Cash Flows. The expected U.S.-dollar cash flows to the U.S.-based MNC over the next three years are shown in Exhibit 15.4. The high cash flow in Year 3 is due to the MNC's plans to sell the target at that time. Assuming a required rate of return by the MNC of 20 percent on this project, the cash flows are discounted at that rate to derive the net present value of acquiring this target. From the U.S.-based MNC's perspective, the net present value of the target is about $158.72 million.

Given that the target's shares are presently valued at C$17 per share, the 10 million shares are worth C$170 million. At the prevailing exchange rate of $.80 per dollar, the target is presently valued at $136 million by the market (computed as C$170 million × $.80). The MNC's valuation of the target of about $159 million is about 17 percent above the market valuation. However, it will have to pay a premium on the shares to entice the target's board of directors to approve the acquisition. Premiums commonly range from 10 percent to 40 percent of the market price. If the MNC allows for a premium of 10 percent above the prevailing stock price of C$17 per share, it would pay C$18.7 per share for the target. At this price per share, the price paid for the Canadian firm would be C$187 million, which is equal to $149.6 million at the existing exchange rate. This price is less than the perceived net present value of the target, so the MNC may be willing to pay this amount.

The MNC recognizes that it may be asked to pay a higher premium if the target rejects its offer of a 10-percent premium, but it would not exceed paying a premium beyond what is reflected by its estimate of the target's *NPV*. Since it values the target at about $159 million, it would not pay more than about C$199 million at the prevailing exchange rate (computed as $159 million divided by $.80 per Canadian dollar). This amount reflects a share price of C$19.90 (computed as C$199 million divided by 10 million shares), so it should not pay any more than C$19.90 per share to acquire the target.

Sources of Uncertainty. This example shows how the acquisition of a publicly traded foreign firm differs from the creation of a new foreign subsidiary. While the valuation of a publicly traded foreign firm can utilize information about an existing business, there are still several reasons why the cash flows resulting from the acquisition are subject to uncertainty. These reasons can be identified by reviewing the assumptions made in the valuation process. First, the growth rate of revenue was assumed to be 10 percent. If this rate is overestimated (perhaps because the Canadian economic growth is overestimated), the earnings generated in Canada will be lower, and cash flows remitted to the U.S. parent will be lower as well.

Second, the cost of goods sold could exceed the assumed level of 40 percent of revenue, which would reduce cash flows remitted to the parent. Third, the selling and administrative expenses could exceed the assumed amount of C$15 million, especially when considering that the annual expenses were $20 million prior to the acquisition. Fourth, the corporate tax rate imposed by the Canadian government could increase, which would reduce the cash flows remitted to the parent. Fifth, the exchange rate of the Canadian dollar may be weaker than what was assumed, which would reduce the cash flows received by the parent. Sixth, any of the five reasons just provided could cause the estimated selling price of the target three years from now to be poorly estimated, and this estimate is very influential on the valuation of the target today.

Since one or more of these conditions could occur, the estimated net present value of the target could be overestimated. Consequently, it is possible for the MNC to acquire the target at a purchase price exceeding the actual value of the target. In particular, the future cash flows are very sensitive to exchange rate movements. This can be illustrated by using sensitivity analysis and reestimating the value of the target based on different scenarios for the exchange rate over time.

Changes in Valuation Over Time. If the MNC decides not to bid for the target at this time, it will need to redo its analysis whenever it reconsiders acquiring the target. As the factors that affect the expected cash flows or the required rate of return from investing in the target change, so will the value of the target. For example, changes in the expected economic conditions in Canada will affect the cash flows generated by the target. Changes in exchange rates will affect the purchase price by the MNC's parent and the expected cash flows to be received by the parent. Changes in the MNC parent's cost of financing or political risk in Canada could cause a change in the required rate of return on the Canadian target.

While the MNC's valuation of the target changes over time, so does the market value of the target. The target's stock price may change in response to conditions that affect its expected cash flows. It may increase if investors anticipate that it will be acquired, since they are aware that stock prices of targets rise abruptly after a bid by the acquiring firm. Thus, it is important that the MNC considering the acquisition of the target keep its intentions confidential. Second, the target's stock price could change simply because of general stock market conditions in Canada.

Why Valuations of a Target May Vary among MNCs

Most MNCs that consider acquiring a specific target would use a somewhat similar process for valuing the target. However, the valuations will vary among MNCs because of differences in the manner in which they estimate the key determinants of a given target's valuation: (1) cash flows to be generated by the target, (2) exchange rate effects on funds remitted to the MNC's parent, and (3) required rate of return when investing in the target.

Estimated Cash Flows of the Foreign Target

The target's expected future cash flows will vary among MNCs because the cash flows will be dependent on the MNC's management or oversight of the target's operations. If an MNC can apply its efficient production methods to improve the production efficiency of the target without reducing the target's production volume, it can improve the target's cash flows.

Each MNC may have a different plan as to how the target would fit within its structure and how future operations would be conducted by the target. The target's expected cash flows would be influenced by the manner in which the target is to be utilized. An MNC with production plants in Asia that purchases another Asian production plant may simply be attempting to increase its market share and production capacity. This MNC's cash flows change because of a higher production and sales level. Conversely, an MNC with all of its production plants in the United States may purchase an Asian production plant to shift its production where production costs are lower. This MNC's cash flows change because of lower expenses.

Tax laws can create competitive advantages for acquirers based in some countries. Acquirers based in low-tax countries may be able to generate higher cash flows from acquiring a foreign target than acquirers in high-tax countries simply because they may be subject to less taxes on the future earnings remitted by the target (after it is acquired) to the acquirer.

Exchange Rate Effects on the Funds Remitted

The valuation of a target among MNCs can vary simply because of differences in the exchange rate effects on funds remitted by the foreign target to the MNC's parent. If the target remits funds frequently in the near future, its value would be partially dependent on the expected exchange rate of the target's local currency in the near future. However, if the target does not remit funds in the near future, its value is more dependent on its local growth strategy and on exchange rates in the distant future.

Required Return of Acquirer

The valuation of the target could also vary among MNCs because of differences in their required rate of return from investing funds to acquire the target. If an MNC targets a successful foreign company with plans to continue the target's local business in a more efficient manner, the risk of the business would be relatively low, and therefore the MNC's required return from acquiring the target would be relatively low. Conversely, if an MNC targets the company because it plans to turn the company into a major exporter, the risk of this target is much higher. It has not established itself in these foreign markets, and the cash flows that would result from the exporting business are very uncertain. Thus, the required return of the target company if it is to serve as a major exporter will be relatively high as well.

If potential acquirers are based in different countries, their required rates of return when considering a specific target will vary even if the desired use of the target is similar. Recall that the required rate of return of any project of an MNC is dependent on its local risk-free interest rate (since that influences the cost of funds for that MNC). Therefore, the required rate of return for MNCs based in countries with relatively high interest rates such as Brazil and Venezuela may differ from MNCs based in low interest rate countries such as the United States or Japan. A higher required rate of return by MNCs in Latin American countries will not necessarily lead to a lower valuation. The target's currency might be expected to appreciate substantially against Latin American currencies (since some Latin American currencies have consistently weakened over time), which enhances the amount of cash flows received as a result of remitted funds and could possibly offset the effects of the higher required rate of return.

Other Types of Multinational Restructuring

Besides acquiring foreign firms, MNCs can engage in multinational restructuring through international partial acquisitions, acquisitions of privatized businesses, international alliances, and international divestitures. Each type is described in turn.

International Partial Acquisitions

In many cases, an MNC considers a partial international acquisition of a firm, in which it purchases part of the existing stock of a foreign firm. A partial international acquisition requires less funds because only a portion of the foreign target's shares are purchased. This type of investment normally allows the foreign target to continue operating and may not necessarily cause the employee turnover that commonly occurs after a target's ownership changes. However, by acquiring a substantial fraction of the shares, the MNC may have some influence on the target's management and be in a position to complete the acquisition in the future. Some MNCs buy substantial stakes in foreign companies to have some control over their operations. For example, Coca-Cola has purchased stakes in many foreign bottle companies that serve as the bottlers of its syrup. In this way, it can ensure that the bottle operations meet its standards.

Valuation of a Foreign Firm That May Be Partially Acquired. When an MNC considers a partial acquisition of a firm, its valuation of that firm can be conducted in a similar manner as when it purchases the entire firm, especially when it plans to purchase a substantial amount of shares so that it could control the firm. However, the valuation would be different if the MNC buys only a small proportion of the firm's shares. Under these conditions, the MNC cannot restructure the firm's operations to make it more efficient, and its estimates of the firm's cash flows must be made from its perspective of a passive investor rather than as a decision-maker for the firm.

International Acquisitions of Privatized Businesses

In recent years, government-owned businesses of many developing countries in Eastern Europe and South America have been sold to individuals or corporations. Many MNCs have capitalized on this wave of so-called privatization by acquiring the businesses being sold by governments. These businesses may be attractive because of the potential for MNCs to increase their efficiency.

Valuation of a Privatized Business. The valuation of a foreign business that was owned by the government in developing countries can be conducted by using capital budgeting analysis, as illustrated earlier. However, the valuation of these businesses is difficult for the following reasons.

First, the future cash flows are very uncertain because the businesses previously have been operating in environments of little or no competition. Thus, previous sales volume figures may not be useful indicators of future sales.

Second, there are very limited data concerning what businesses are worth in some of these countries because there are not many publicly traded firms in their markets, and there is limited disclosure of prices paid for targets in other acquisitions. Consequently, there may not be any benchmarks to use when valuing a business.

Third, economic conditions in these countries are very uncertain during the transition to a market-oriented economy. Fourth, political conditions tend to be volatile during the transition, as government policies for businesses are sometimes unclear or subject to abrupt changes.

Fifth, if earnings of the foreign subsidiary are converted to the MNC parent's home currency, the exchange rate estimates are very uncertain. The exchange rates of the currencies in these countries were not determined by market forces, since the currencies were rarely traded in the foreign exchange markets in the past. Thus, the exchange rates may change substantially over time as international trade and investment become more common.

Sixth, the discount rate used to measure the present value of the business is subject to error because the cost of financing projects in these countries is so uncertain. Interest rates in the countries engaged in privatization have not been determined by market forces, since capital flows into and out of these countries were restricted. As barriers to international capital flows are removed, there is much uncertainty as to how interest rates will adjust. Since the cost of financing businesses in these countries is very uncertain, the discount rate is uncertain as well.

Even with the difficulties of measuring the value of privatized businesses, MNCs such as Gerber Products, PepsiCo, and Westinghouse have acquired these businesses as a means of entering new markets. Hungary serves as a model country for privatizations. There are more than 25,000 MNCs that have a foreign stake in Hungary's businesses. Hungary's government has been quick and efficient at selling off its assets to MNCs.

International Alliances

MNCs commonly engage in international alliances such as joint venture agreements and licensing agreements with foreign firms. The characteristics of international alliances are quite different from international acquisitions. The initial outlay is typically smaller, since the MNC is not acquiring a foreign firm. Yet, the cash flows to be received will typically be smaller as well.

Valuation of a Proposed International Alliance. To illustrate how a proposed international alliance can be valued, consider a U.S.-based MNC that plans to provide a Mexican firm with technology in return for royalty payments that are 10 percent of that firm's future sales of products resulting from use of this technology over the next five years. The MNC's initial outlay for this international alliance is the initial expense incurred as a result of providing a foreign firm with some technology. The cash flows to be received by the MNC from the Mexican firm can be estimated by first forecasting the Mexican firm's annual sales (in pesos) of products that relied on this technology. The MNC will receive 10 percent of this amount based on the proposed alliance. Then, it must forecast the value of the peso over each of the next five years so that it can determine the dollar cash flows resulting from these royalties. It must also consider any tax effects.

International Divestitures

An MNC should periodically reassess its direct foreign investments to determine whether to retain those investments or sell (divest) them. Some foreign projects that have been implemented may no longer be feasible as a result of the MNC's increased cost of capital, increased host government taxes, increased political risk in the host country, or revised projections of exchange rates. Many divestitures occur as a result of a revised assessment of industry or economic conditions. For example, Warner-Lambert Company, Johnson & Johnson, and several other U.S.-based MNCs recently divested some of their Latin American subsidiaries when economic conditions deteriorated there.

Assessing Whether to Divest Existing Operations in Asia. During the Asian crisis in the 1997–1998 period, some MNCs with direct foreign investment in Asia reassessed the feasibility of their existing operations. The expected cash flows that these operations would generate for the parent had declined in many cases for two obvious reasons. First, the economic growth in Asia declined, which led to a decline in expected local sales by the foreign subsidiaries and therefore a decline in the expected level of foreign currency cash flow. Second, the weak currencies of Asian countries led to a decline in the expected amount of the parent's currency to be received when foreign subsidiaries from Asian countries remit funds.

Valuation of an International Project That May Be Divested. The valuation of a proposed international divestiture can be determined by comparing the present value of the cash flows if the project is continued to the proceeds that would be received (after taxes) if the project is divested. To illustrate how an MNC might reevaluate a project after it has been implemented, reconsider the example from the previous chapter in which Spartan Inc. proposed a Singapore subsidiary. Assume that the Singapore subsidiary is created and, after two years, the spot rate of the Singapore dollar is $.46. In addition, forecasts have been revised for the remaining two years of the project, indicating that the Singapore dollar should be worth $.44 in Year 3 and $.40 in the project's final year. Because these forecasted exchange rates have an adverse effect on the project, Spartan Inc. considers divesting the subsidiary. For simplicity, assume that the original forecasts of the other variables remain unchanged and that a potential acquirer has offered S$13,000,000 (after adjusting for any capital gains taxes) for the subsidiary if the acquirer can retain the existing working capital.

Spartan can conduct a divestiture analysis by comparing the after-tax proceeds from the possible sale of the project (in U.S. dollars) to the present value of expected U.S.-dollar inflows that the project will generate if it is not sold. This comparison will determine the net present value of the divestiture (NPV_d), as illustrated in Exhibit 15.5. Since the present value of the subsidiary's cash flows from Spartan's perspective exceeds the price at which it could sell the subsidiary, the divestiture is not feasible. Thus, the MNC should not divest the subsidiary at the prevailing price offered for the subsidiary. Yet, it may still search for another firm that is willing to acquire the subsidiary for a price that exceeds its present value.

Restructuring Decisions as Real Options

Some restructuring issues faced by MNCs involve **real options**, or implicit options on real assets (such as buildings, machinery, and other assets used by MNCs to facilitate their production). A real option can be classified as a call option on real assets or a put option on real assets, as explained next.

Call Option on Real Assets

A **call option on real assets** represents a proposed project that contains an option of pursuing an additional venture. For example, Coral Inc., an Internet firm in the U.S., is considering the acquisition of an Internet business in Mexico. The expected dollar cash flows that would result from acquiring this business are estimated and discounted and compared to the initial outlay. At this time, the present value of the future cash flows that are directly attributable to the Mexican business is slightly lower than the initial outlay that would be required to purchase that business, so that the business appears to be an unfeasible investment.

A Brazilian Internet firm is also for sale, but its owners will only sell the business to a firm that they know and trust, and Coral Inc. has no relationship with this business. A possible advantage of the Mexican firm that is not measured by the traditional multinational capital budgeting analysis is that it commonly does business with the Brazilian Internet firm, and could use its relationship to help Coral acquire the Brazilian firm. Thus, if Coral purchased the Mexican Internet business, it would have an option to also acquire the Internet firm in Brazil. In essence, Coral would have a call option on real assets (of the Brazilian firm), because it would have the option (not an obligation) to purchase the Brazilian firm. The expected purchase price of the Brazilian firm over the next few months serves as the exercise price within the call option on real assets. If Coral acquires the Brazilian firm, it now has a second initial outlay, and will generate a second stream of cash flows.

When considering the call option on real assets, the acquisition of the Mexican Internet firm may now be feasible, even though it was not feasible when considering only the cash flows directly attributable to that firm. The project can be analyzed by segmenting it into two scenarios. The first scenario is that Coral Inc. acquires the Mexican firm, but after taking a closer look at the Brazilian firm, decides not to exercise its call option (decides not to purchase the Brazilian firm). The net present value in this scenario is simply a measure of the present value of expected dollar cash flows directly attributable to the Mexican firm minus the initial outlay necessary to purchase the Mexican firm. The second scenario is that Coral Inc. acquire the Mexican firm and then exercise its option by also purchasing the Brazilian firm. In this case, the present value of combined (Mexican firm plus Brazilian firm) cash flow streams (in dollars) would be compared to the combined initial outlays.

If the outlay necessary to acquire the Brazilian firm was made after the initial outlay of the Mexican firm, the outlay for the Brazilian firm should be discounted. If Coral Inc. knows the probability of these two scenarios, it could determine the probability of each scenario, and then determine the expected value of the net present value of the proposed project by summing the products of the probability of each scenario times the respective *NPV* for that scenario.

Put Option on Real Assets

A **put option on real assets** represents a proposed project that contains an option of divesting part or all of the project. For example, Jade Inc., an office supply firm in the United States, is considering the acquisition of a similar business in Italy. Jade Inc. believes that if future economic conditions in Italy are favorable, the net present value of this project is positive. However, given that weak economic conditions in Italy are more likely, the proposed project appears to be unfeasible.

Exhibit 15.5
Divestiture Analysis: Spartan Inc.

	End of Year 2 (Today)	End of Year 3 (One Year From Today)	End of Year 4 (Two Years From Today)
S$ remitted after withholding taxes		S$6,840,000	S$19,560,000
Selling price	S$13,000,000		
Exchange rate	\$.46	\$.44	\$.40
Cash flow received from divestiture	\$5,980,000		
Cash flows forgone due to divestiture		\$3,009,600	\$7,824,000
PV of forgone cash flows (15% discount rate)		\$2,617,044	\$5,916,068
NPV_d = \$5,980,000 – (\$2,617,044 + \$5,916,068) = \$5,980,000 – \$8,533,112 = –\$2,553,112			

Yet, reconsider the project if Jade Inc. knew that it could sell the Italian firm at a specified price to another firm over the next four years. In this case, Jade has an implied put option attached to the project.

The feasibility of this project can be assessed by determining the *NPV* under the scenario of strong economic conditions, and then determining the *NPV* under the scenario of weak economic conditions. The expected value of the *NPV* of this project can be estimated as the sum of the products of the probability of each scenario times its respective *NPV*. If economic conditions are favorable, the net present value is positive. If economic conditions are weak, Jade Inc. may sell the Italian firm at the

Nike Problem

Multinational Restructuring at Nike

An obvious starting point for Nike when considering whether to restructure its international operations is to determine its current status regarding where it generates most of its revenue and income. In recent years, Nike has generated more than 15 percent of its total revenue and its income from Europe, more than 15 percent of its total revenue and income from Asia, and about 7 percent of its total revenue and income from Canada and Latin America. However, the Asian crisis has disrupted the growth in Asia, which discouraged any plans for growth in Asia, but the Latin America and Canada rates of growth have been very high in recent years. Nike plans to pursue expansion in Latin America, which is supported by its recent revenue and income growth in Latin America.

Discussion: In 1995, Nike purchased Bauer Inc., which is the world's largest hockey equipment manufacturer. How would this form of restructuring be beneficial to Nike? Should Nike sell hockey equipment wherever it sells its athletic footwear?

locked in sales price (which resembles an exercise price of a put option), and therefore may still achieve a positive net present value over the short time that it owned the Italian firm. Thus, the put option on real assets may turn an unfeasible project into a feasible project.

Impact of Multinational Restructuring on an MNC's Value

An MNC's multinational restructuring can affect its value, as shown in Exhibit 15.6. A strategy of foreign expansion creates additional expected cash flows to be generated by the MNC's foreign subsidiaries and therefore increases the expected cash flows that will ultimately be received by the parent. The expansion also typically requires a large initial outlay by the parent. Conversely, a MNC's strategy of divesting creates an initial inflow of funds to the parent as a foreign business is sold, at the expense of a reduction in the future expected cash flows because the business will no longer be part of the MNC.

Exhibit 15.6
Impact of Multinational Restructuring on an MNC's Value

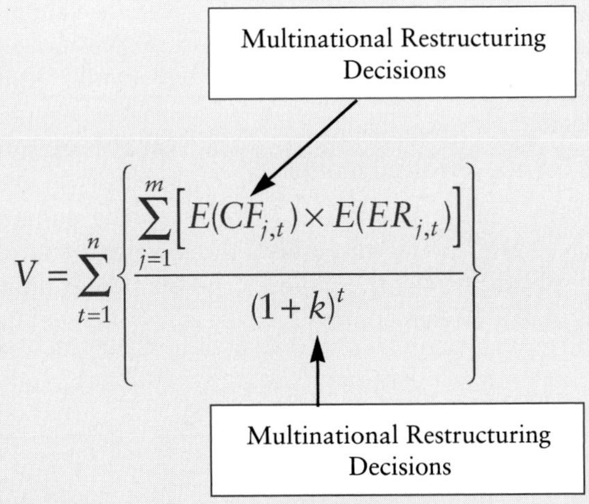

$$V = \sum_{t=1}^{n} \left\{ \frac{\sum_{j=1}^{m} \left[E(CF_{j,t}) \times E(ER_{j,t}) \right]}{(1+k)^t} \right\}$$

V = value of the U.S.-based MNC
$E(CF_{j,t})$ = expected cash flows denominated in currency j to be received by the U.S. parent in period t
$E(ER_{j,t})$ = expected exchange rate at which currency j can be converted to dollars at the end of period t
k = the weighted average cost of capital of the U.S. parent
m = number of currencies
n = number of periods

SUMMARY

- One of the most common types of multinational restructuring is international acquisitions. MNCs can use capital budgeting to determine whether a foreign target is worth acquiring. The expected cash flows of a foreign target are affected by target-specific factors (such as the target's previous cash flows and its managerial talent) and country-specific factors (such as economic conditions, political conditions, currency conditions, and stock market conditions).
- An MNC's typical valuation process is to initially screen prospective targets based on willingness to be acquired and country barriers. Then, the prospective targets are valued by estimating the target's cash flows based on target-specific characteristics, the target's respective country characteristics, and discounting their expected cash flows. The perceived value can be compared to the target's market value to determine whether the target could be purchased at a price that is below the perceived value from the MNC's perspective.
- Valuations of a foreign target may vary among potential acquirers because of differences in estimates of the target's cash flows or exchange rate movements or differences in the required rate of return among acquirers. These differences may be especially pronounced when the acquirers are from different countries.
- Besides international acquisitions of firms, the more common types of multinational restructuring include international partial acquisitions, international acquisitions of privatized businesses, international alliances (such as international licensing or joint ventures), and international divestitures. Each of these types of multinational restructuring can be assessed by applying multinational capital budgeting.

SELF-TEST FOR CHAPTER 15

(Answers are provided in Appendix A at the back of the text.)

1. Explain why more acquisitions have taken place in Europe in recent years. €
2. What are some of the barriers involved in international acquisitions?
3. Why may a U.S.-based MNC prefer the establishment of a foreign subsidiary over the acquisition of an existing firm in a foreign country?
4. Assume that a U.S. firm has been considering the divestiture of a Swedish subsidiary that produces ski equipment and sells it locally. A Swedish firm has already offered to acquire this Swedish subsidiary. Assume that the U.S. parent has just revised its projections of the Swedish krona's value downward. Will the proposed divestiture now seem more feasible or less feasible than it did before? Explain.

QUESTIONS AND APPLICATIONS

1. Why do you think MNCs continuously assess possible forms of multinational restructuring, such as foreign acquisitions or downsizing of a foreign subsidiary?
2. Maude, Inc., a U.S.-based MNC, has recently acquired a firm in Singapore. To eliminate inefficiencies, Maude downsized the target substantially, eliminating two-thirds of the workforce. Why might this action affect the regulations imposed on the subsidiary's business by the Singapore government?
3. Poki, Inc., a U.S.-based MNC, considers expanding into Thailand because of decreasing profit margins in the United States. The demand for Poki's product in Thailand is very strong. However, forecasts indicate that the baht is

expected to depreciate substantially over the next three years. Should Poki expand into Thailand? What factors may affect its decision?

4. Rastell, Inc., a U.S.-based MNC, is considering the acquisition of a Russian target to produce personal computers (PCs) and market them throughout Russia, where demand for PCs has increased substantially in recent years. Assume that stock market conditions are not favorable in Russia, as the stock prices of most Russian companies rose substantially just prior to Rastell's assessment of the target. What are some alternatives available to Rastell?

5. MNC X, a manufacturer of clothing, wants to increase market share by acquiring a target producing a popular clothing line in Europe. This clothing line is well established. Forecasts indicate a relatively stable euro over the life of the project. MNC Y wants to increase its market share in the personal computer market by acquiring a target in Thailand that currently produces radios and converting the operations. Forecasts indicate a depreciation of the baht over the life of the project. Funds resulting from both projects will be remitted to the respective U.S. parent on a regular basis. Which target do you think will result in a higher *NPV*? Why?

6. Why are valuations of privatized businesses previously owned by the governments of developing countries more difficult than valuations of existing firms in developed countries?

7. Blore, Inc., a U.S.-based MNC, has screened several targets. Based on economic and political considerations, only one eligible target remains in Malaysia. Blore would like you to value this target and has provided you with the following information:

   - Blore expects to keep the target for three years, at which time it expects to sell the firm for 300 million Malaysian ringgit (MYR) after deducting the amount for any taxes paid.
   - Blore expects a strong Malaysian economy. Consequently, the estimates for revenues for the next year are MYR200 million. Revenues are expected to increase by 8 percent over the following two years.
   - Cost of goods sold are expected to be 50 percent of revenues.
   - Selling and administrative expenses are expected to be MYR30 million in each of the next three years.
   - The Malaysian tax rate on the target's earnings is expected to be 35 percent.
   - Depreciation expenses are expected to be MYR20 million per year for each of the next three years.
   - The target will need MYR7 million in cash each year to support existing operations.
   - The target's stock price is currently MYR30 per share. The target has 9 million shares outstanding.
   - Any remaining cash flows are remitted by the target to Blore, Inc. Blore uses the prevailing exchange rate of the Malaysian ringgit as the expected exchange rate for the next three years. This exchange rate is currently $.25.
   - Blore's required rate of return on similar projects is 20 percent.

   a. Prepare a worksheet to estimate the value of the Malaysian target based on the information provided.
   b. Will Blore, Inc., be able to acquire the Malaysian target for a price lower than its valuation of the target?

8. Refer to question 7. What are some of the key sources of uncertainty in Blore's valuation of the target? Identify two reasons for the expected cash flows from an Asian subsidiary of a U.S.-based MNC to be lower as a result of the Asian crisis.

9. The reduction in expected cash flow of Asian subsidiaries as a result of the Asian crisis will likely lead to a reduced valuation of these subsidiaries from the parent's perspective. Explain why a U.S.-based MNC may not sell its Asian subsidiaries.

10. Identify two reasons why the expected cash flows from the Asian subsidiary of a U.S.-based MNC may have been lower during the Asian crisis than in the 1997–1998 period.

Internet Application

11. The following Web site provides information about recent economic events around the world:

    http://biz.yahoo.com/reports/world.html

    Use this Web site to review the international events over the last week. Select three economic events that could affect economic or political conditions in foreign countries and explain how an MNC might restructure its business in response to these events. That is, would the MNC increase or reduce its business in that country due to that event?

Running Your Own MNC

Estimating Cash Flows of an International Project

12. a. If you seriously considered whether to implement your international business idea, you would have to measure the costs and benefits of this idea. Describe how you would estimate the dollar revenue to be received from your business.
    b. Describe how you would estimate the expenses associated with your business.
    c. Describe how you would estimate the net cash flows (in dollars) of your business.
    d. Explain why your estimate of the net cash flows (in dollars) could be overestimated.

Blades, Inc. Case

Assessment of an Acquisition in Thailand

Recall that Ben Holt, Blades' chief financial officer (CFO), has suggested to the board of directors that Blades proceed with the establishment of a subsidiary in Thailand. Due to the high growth potential of the roller blade market in Thailand, his analysis suggests that the venture will be profitable. Specifically, his view is that Blades should establish a subsidiary in Thailand to manufacture roller blades, whether an existing agreement with Entertainment Products (a Thai retailer) is renewed or not. Under this agreement, Entertainment Products is committed to the purchase of 180,000 pairs of "Speedos," Blades' primary product, annually. The agreement was initially for three years, and will expire two years from now. At this time, the agreement may be renewed. Due to delivery delays, Entertainment Products has indicated that it will only renew the agreement if Blades establishes a subsidiary in Thailand. In this case, the price per pair of roller blades would be fixed at 4,594 Thai baht per pair. If Blades decides not to renew the agreement, Entertainment Products, Inc. has indicated that it would only purchase 5,000 pairs of "Speedos" annually at prevailing market prices.

According to Ben Holt's analysis, renewing the agreement with Entertainment Products and establishing a subsidiary in Thailand will result in a net present value (*NPV*) of $2,638,735. Conversely, if the agreement is not renewed and a subsidiary is established, the resulting *NPV* is $8,746,688. Consequently, Ben Holt has suggested to the board of directors that Blades establish a subsidiary without renewing the existing agreement with Entertainment Products.

Recently, a Thai roller blade manufacturer called Skates'n'Stuff has contacted Ben Holt regarding the potential sale of the company to Blades, Inc. Skates'n'Stuff entered the Thai roller blade market a decade ago and has generated a profit in every year of operation. Furthermore, Skates'n'Stuff has established distribution channels in Thailand. Consequently, if Blades would acquire the company, it could begin sales immediately and would not require an additional year to build the plant in Thailand. Initial forecasts indicate that Blades would be able to sell 280,000 pairs of roller blades annually. These sales are incremental to the acquisition of Skates'n'Stuff. Furthermore, all sales resulting from the acquisition would be made to retailers in Thailand. Moreover, Blades fixed expenses would be 20 million baht annually. Although Ben Holt has not previously considered the acquisition of an existing business, he is now wondering whether the acquisition of Skates'n'Stuff may be a better course of action than building a subsidiary in Thailand.

However, Ben Holt is also aware of some disadvantages associated with such an acquisition. Skates'n'Stuff's CFO has indicated that he would be willing to accept a price of 1 billion baht in payment for the company, which is clearly more expensive than the 550 million baht outlay that would be required to establish a subsidiary in Thailand. However, Skates'n'Stuff's CFO has indicated that it is willing to negotiate. Furthermore, Blades' employs a high quality production process, which enables it to charge relatively high prices for roller blades produced in one of its plants. If Blades were to acquire Skates'n'Stuff, which uses an inferior production process (resulting in lower quality roller blades), it would have to charge a lower price for the roller blades it produces there. Initial forecasts indicate that Blades will be able to charge a price of 4,500 Thai baht per pair of roller blades without affecting demand. However, because Skates'n'Stuff uses a production process that results in lower quality roller blades than Blades' "Speedos," operating costs incurred would be similar to the amount incurred if Blades establishes a subsidiary in Thailand. Thus, Blades estimates that it would incur operating costs of about 3,500 baht per pair of roller blades.

Ben Holt has asked you, a financial analyst for Blades, Inc., to determine whether the acquisition of Skates'n'Stuff is a better course of action for Blades, Inc. than the establishment of a subsidiary in Thailand. The acquisition of Skates'n'Stuff would be more favorable than the establishment of a subsidiary if the present value of the cash flows generated by the company exceeds the purchase price by more than $8,746,688, the *NPV* of establishing a new subsidiary. Thus, Ben Holt has asked you to construct a spreadsheet that determined the net present value of the acquisition.

To aid you in your analysis, Ben Holt has provided you with the following additional information, which he gathered from various sources, including unaudited financial statements of Skates'n'Stuff for the last three years.

- Blades, Inc. requires a return on the Thai acquisition of 25 percent, the same rate of return it would require if it established a subsidiary in Thailand.
- If Skates'n'Stuff is acquired, Blades, Inc. will operate the company for ten years, at which time Skates'n'Stuff will be sold for an estimated amount of 1.1 million baht.
- 600 million baht of the 1 billion baht purchase price constitutes the cost of the plant and equipment. These items are depreciated using straight-line depreciation. Thus, 60 million baht will be depreciated annually for ten years.
- Sales of 280,000 pairs of roller blades annually will begin immediately at a price of 4,500 baht per pair.
- Variable costs per pair of roller blades will be 3,500 per pair.
- Fixed operating costs, including salaries and administrative expenses, will be 20 million baht annually.
- The current spot rate of the Thai baht is $0.023. Blades expects the baht to depreciate by an average of 2 percent per year for the next ten years.
- The Thai government will impose a 25 percent tax rate on income and a 10 percent withholding tax on any funds remitted by Skates'n'Stuff to Blades, Inc. Any earnings remitted to the U.S. will not be taxed again in the U.S. All earnings generated by Skates'n'Stuff will be remitted to Blades, Inc.
- The average inflation rate in Thailand is expected to be 12 percent annually. Revenues, variable costs, and fixed costs are subject to inflation, and are expected to change by the same annual rate as the inflation rate.

In addition to the information outlined above, Ben Holt has informed you that Blades, Inc. will need to manufacture all of the 180,000 pairs to be delivered to Entertainment Products this year and next year in Thailand. Since Blades only used components from Thailand (which are of a lower quality but cheaper than U.S. components) sufficient to manufacture 72,000 pairs annually previously, it will incur cost savings of 32.4 million baht this year and next year. However, since Blades, Inc. would sell 180,000 pairs of Speedos annually to Entertainment Products this year and next year whether it acquires Skates'n'Stuff or not, Ben Holt has urged you not to include these sales in your analysis. The agreement with Entertainment Product will not be renewed at the end of next year.

Ben Holt would like you to answer the following questions:

1. Using a spreadsheet, determine the net present value (*NPV*) of the acquisition of Skates'n' Stuff? Based on your numerical analysis, should Blades, Inc. establish a subsidiary in Thailand or should it acquire Skates'n'Stuff?
2. If Blades, Inc. were to negotiate with Skates'n' Stuff, what is the maximum amount (in Thai baht) Blades should be willing to pay?
3. Are there any other factors Blades, Inc. should consider in making its decision? In your answer, you should consider the price Skates'n'Stuff is asking relative to your analysis in question (1), other potential businesses for sale in Thailand, the source of the information your analysis is based on, the production process that will be employed by the target in the future, and the future management of Skates'n'Stuff.

Small Business Dilemma

Multinational Restructuring by the Sports Exports Company

The Sports Exports Company has been successful in producing footballs in the United States and exporting them to the United Kingdom. Recently, Jim Logan (owner of the Sports Exports Company) has considered restructuring his company by expanding throughout Europe. He planned to export footballs and other sporting goods that were not already popular in Europe to one large sporting goods distributor in Germany; the goods would then be distributed to any retail sporting goods stores throughout Europe that were willing to purchase these goods. This distributor would make payments in euros to the Sports Exports Company.

1. Are there any reasons why the business that has been so successful in the United Kingdom will not necessarily be successful in other European countries?
2. If the business is diversified throughout Europe, will this substantially reduce the exposure of the Sports Exports Company to exchange rate risk?
3. Now that several countries in Europe participate a single currency system, will this affect the performance of new expansion throughout Europe?

16 COUNTRY RISK ANALYSIS

Country risk analysis is conducted when the firm is assessing whether to continue conducting business within a particular country. It can also be used when determining whether to implement new projects in foreign countries. Country risk can be partitioned into the country's political risk and its financial risk.

The specific objectives of this chapter are to

- identify the common factors used by MNCs to measure a country's political risk,
- identify the common factors used by MNCs to measure a country's financial risk,
- explain the techniques used to measure country risk, and
- explain how the assessment of country risk is used by MNCs when making financial decisions.

WHY COUNTRY RISK ANALYSIS IS IMPORTANT

Country risk represents the potentially adverse impact of a country's environment on the multinational corporation's (MNC's) cash flows. Country risk analysis is important to MNCs for the following reasons. First, it can be used to monitor countries where the MNC is currently doing business. If the country risk level of a particular country begins to increase, the MNC may consider divesting its subsidiaries located there. Country risk analysis can also be used by MNCs as a screening device to avoid conducting business in countries with excessive risk. Events that heighten country risk tend to discourage U.S. direct foreign investment in that particular country. Country risk analysis is not restricted to predicting major crises. It can be used to improve the analysis used to make long-term investment or financing decisions.

POLITICAL RISK FACTORS

An MNC must assess country risk not only in countries where it currently does business but also in those in which it expects to market exports or establish subsidiaries. Several risk characteristics of a country may significantly affect performance, and the MNC should be concerned about the degree of impact likely for each.

As one might expect, there are many country characteristics related to the political environment that influence an MNC. The extreme form of political risk is the possibility that the host country will take over a subsidiary. In some cases of expropriation, some compensation (the amount decided by the host country government) is awarded. In other cases, the assets are confiscated and no compensation is provided. Such events can take place peacefully or by force. Some of the more common forms of political risk include

- Attitude of consumers in the host country
- Attitude of host government
- Blockage of fund transfers
- Currency inconvertibility
- War
- Bureaucracy
- Corruption

Each of these characteristics will be examined.

Attitude of Consumers in the Host Country

A mild form of political risk (to an exporter) is a tendency of residents to purchase only homemade goods. Even if the exporter decided to set up a subsidiary in the foreign country, this philosophy could prevent its success. All countries tend to exert some pressure on consumers to purchase from locally owned manufacturers. (In the United States, consumers are encouraged to look for the "made in the U.S.A." label.) MNCs that consider entering a foreign market (or have already entered that market) must monitor the general loyalty of consumers toward homemade products. If consumers are very loyal to local products, a joint venture with a local company may be more feasible than an exporting strategy.

Attitude of Host Government

Various actions of a host government can affect the cash flow of an MNC. For example, a host government might impose pollution control standards (which affect costs) and additional corporate taxes (which affect after-tax earnings) as well as withholding taxes and fund transfer restrictions (which affect after-tax cash flows sent to the parent).

Some analysts use turnover in government members or philosophy as a proxy for a country's political risk. While this can significantly influence the MNC's future cash flows, it alone does not serve as a suitable representation of political risk. A subsidiary will not necessarily be affected by changing governments. Furthermore, a subsidiary can be affected by adjusted policies of the host government or by a changing attitude toward the subsidiary's home country (and therefore the subsidiary), even when the host government has no risk of being overthrown.

There are various ways in which the host government can make the MNC's operations coincide with its own goals. It may, for example, require the use of local employees for managerial positions at a subsidiary. In addition, it may require social facilities (such as an exercise room, nonsmoking areas, etc.) or special environmental controls (air pollution control equipment, etc.). Furthermore, it is not uncommon for a host government to require special permits, impose extra taxes, or subsidize competitors. All of these examples represent political risk, in that they reflect a country's political characteristics and could influence an MNC's cash flows.

One of the most troubling issues for MNCs is a lack of enforcement by host governments on local firms that illegally copy the MNC's product. For example, local firms in Asia commonly copy software produced by MNCs and sell it to customers at a lower price. Software producers lose an estimated $3 billion in sales annually in Asia for this reason.

Blockage of Fund Transfers

Subsidiaries of MNCs often send funds back to the headquarters for loan repayments, purchases of supplies, administrative fees, remitted earnings, or several other possible purposes. In some cases, a host government may block fund transfers, which could force subsidiaries to undertake projects that are not optimal (just to make use of the funds). Alternatively, the MNC could invest the funds in local securities that would provide some return while funds were blocked. But, this return might be inferior to what could have been earned on funds remitted to the parent.

Currency Inconvertibility

Some governments do not allow the home currency to be exchanged into other currencies. Thus, the earnings generated by a subsidiary in these countries cannot be remitted to the parent through currency conversion. When the currency is inconvertible, an MNC parent may need to exchange it for goods to extract benefits from projects in that country.

War

Some countries tend to engage in constant battles with neighboring countries or experience internal battles. This can affect the safety of employees hired by an MNC's subsidiary or by salespeople who attempt to establish export markets for the MNC. In addition, countries occasionally plagued with the threat of war typically have volatile business cycles, which make the MNC's cash flow generated from such countries more uncertain.

Bureaucracy

Another country risk factor is government bureaucracy, which can complicate the MNC's business. Although this factor may seem irrelevant, it was a major deterrent for MNCs that had considered projects in Eastern Europe in the early 1990s. Many of the Eastern European governments were not experienced at facilitating the entrance of MNCs into their markets.

Corruption

Corruption can adversely affect an MNC's international business because it can increase the cost of conducting business or reduce revenue. There are various forms of corruption between firms or between a firm and the government. For example, an MNC may lose revenue because a government contract is awarded to a local firm that paid off a government official. A sampling of corruption perception index rat-

Exhibit 16.1
Corruption Ratings Among Countries

Country	Corruption Perception Index
Denmark	9.94
New Zealand	9.23
Canada	9.10
Australia	8.85
Germany	8.23
Hong Kong	7.28
Japan	6.57
Chile	6.05
Hungary	5.18
Taiwan	5.02
Malaysia	5.01
South Korea	4.29
Brazil	3.56
Thailand	3.06
China	2.88
Argentina	2.81
Indonesia	2.72
Mexico	2.66
Russia	2.72

Source: *Euromoney,* September 1997, p. 25, and Transparency International.

ings (drawn from *Euromoney* magazine) is provided in Exhibit 16.1. The highest possible rating is 10.0. Many of the countries in Western Europe were assigned ratings of 8.0 or above, while countries in Asia and South America were assigned lower ratings.

Financial Risk Factors

Along with political factors, financial factors should also be considered when assessing country risk. One of the most obvious financial factors is the current and potential state of the country's economy. An MNC that exports to a country or develops a subsidiary in a country is highly concerned with that country's demand for its products. This demand is, of course, strongly influenced by the country's economy. A recession in the country could severely reduce demand for the MNC's exports or products sold by the MNC's local subsidiary. For example, in the early 1990s, the European business performance of Ford Motor Co., Nike, Walt Disney Co., and many other U.S.-based MNCs was severely affected by the European recession.

In some cases, financial distress in a country can encourage a government to implement policies that could limit the MNC's market penetration there. For example, Ford Motor Co. was allowed by the Spanish government to set up production facilities in Spain only if it would abide by certain provisions. These included a limit of Ford's local sales volume to 10 percent of the previous year's local automobile sales. In addition, of the total volume of automobiles produced by Ford in Spain, two-thirds had to be exported. The motivation behind these provisions was creation of jobs for workers in Spain without seriously affecting local competitors. Allowing a subsidiary that primarily exports its product achieved this objective for Spain.

In this example, the MNC (Ford) was aware of the host government's restrictions before establishing a subsidiary. In some cases the rules change after the game has begun. That is, additional host government restrictions may be enforced after an MNC establishes a foreign subsidiary. For example, during the international debt crisis, many of the less developed countries were experiencing economic problems, so governments restricted local firms from importing goods from MNCs in an attempt to boost local sales.

http://
The Department of Statistics, Singapore, site at www.singstat.gov.sg/BES provides access to the department's current business expectation surveys and country analyses.

Because the state of a country's economy is dependent on several financial factors, an MNC should consider all of these factors. Some of the more obvious ones include interest rates, exchange rates, and inflation. Higher interest rates tend to slow the growth of an economy and reduce demand for the MNC's products. Lower interest rates often stimulate the economy and increase demand for the MNC's products. Exchange rates can strongly influence the demand for the country's exports, which in turn affects the country's production and income level. Inflation can affect the purchasing power of consumers and therefore the consumer demand for an MNC's goods.

Interest rates, exchange rates, and inflation can also have an impact on each other, which makes the overall assessment of their impact on the economy more complex. Even if we know exactly how these factors influence a country's economy, we are unsure of their future values, so some uncertainty still remains. As an example, assume that for every percentage point decrease in interest rates in Country X, there will be a 2-percent increase in total production. However, it is not known with certainty how interest rates will change in the future. A firm may forecast a 3-percent

Nike Problem

Potential Exposure to Country Risk

Since Nike conducts a large amount of international business, it must monitor country risk in many countries. Nike could be affected by country risk in several ways. First, a conflict between the United States and a specific foreign country could cause either the foreign country's government or its people to vent their anger toward a Nike subsidiary in that country. That is, Nike could be a target simply because it is viewed as a U.S. company, even if all the employees at that subsidiary are locals. Second, a change in foreign government officials could result in new tax laws and other restrictions imposed on subsidiaries of U.S. firms or firms from any other country that are based in this country. Third, other local shoe manufacturers could possibly use government ties to impose more restrictions against Nike so that they could have a competitive advantage in the country of concern. Fourth, Nike's subsidiary could be adversely affected by other political problems in the country that cause a deterioration in economic conditions there. Any of these conditions can cause an increase in the subsidiary's expenses, or a decline in its revenue.

Discussion: When Nike decides to conduct a multinational capital budgeting analysis to assess the establishment of a new shoe factory in Latin America, how can it capture the potential effects of country risk in its analysis?

decrease in interest rates, which would lead to a 6-percent increase in total production. Yet, if interest rates actually increase, production may actually decrease.

Financial factors that indicate the government's purchasing power are also important in a case in which the government serves as a customer of the MNC. For example, a growing budget deficit may force the government to reduce its purchases of goods produced by the MNC and its subsidiaries.

As another example of how financial factors can affect an MNC's cash flows, consider the wage-price freeze imposed by Brazil in 1990 and 1991 in order to reduce the inflationary spiral. This action slowed down the economy and affected sales of several subsidiaries of U.S.-based MNCs, including Armco, Inc., Black & Decker Corporation, and Quaker Oats Company.

The discussion up to this point emphasizes that country risk analysis goes far beyond an MNC's estimation of the probability that its subsidiary will be taken over by the local government. It includes an assessment of all factors (political and financial) related to the foreign country that influence the MNC's cash flow. Also, after assessing country risk, an MNC must decide how to manage its exposure.

Types of Country Risk Assessment

Although there is no consensus as to how country risk can best be assessed, some guidelines have been developed. The first step is to recognize the difference between (1) an overall risk assessment of a country without consideration of the MNC's business and (2) the risk assessment of a country as related to the MNC's type of business. The first type can be referred to as **macroassessment** of country risk and the latter type as a **microassessment.** Each type is discussed in turn.

Macroassessment of Country Risk

http://

Visit lcweb2.loc.gov/frd/cs/cshome.html for detailed studies of 85 countries provided by the Library of Congress.

A macroassessment involves consideration of all variables that affect country risk except for those unique to a particular firm or industry. This type of risk is convenient in that it remains the same for a given country, regardless of the firm or industry of concern; however, it excludes relevant information that could improve the accuracy of the assessment. While a macroassessment of country risk is not ideal for any individual MNC, it serves as a foundation that can then be modified to reflect the particular business in which the MNC is involved.

Any macroassessment model should consider both political and financial characteristics of the country being assessed. Political factors include the relationship of the host government with the MNC's home country government, the attitude of the people in the host country toward the MNC's government, the historical stability of the host government, the vulnerability of the host government to political takeovers within the government, and the probability of war between the host country and neighboring countries. Consideration of such political factors will indicate the probability of political events that may affect an MNC and the magnitude of the impact.

The financial factors of a macroassessment model should include GDP growth, inflation trends, government budget levels (and the government deficit), interest rates, unemployment, the country's reliance on export income, the balance of trade, and foreign exchange controls. The list of financial factors could easily be extended several pages. The factors listed here represent just a subset of the financial factors considered when evaluating the financial strength of a country.

http://
The U.S. Department of Commerce Web page at www.stat-usa.gov provides access to a variety of micro-economic and macro-economic data on emerging markets.

Country Characteristics That Affect Profits. A recent survey by Petry and Sprow[1] was conducted to determine what country characteristics could have the greatest potential impact on the profitability of large MNCs. Each characteristic was assigned a weight from 1 to 5, with 5 reflecting the most negative impact. An average weight across all MNCs was then computed; those characteristics with a higher average weight are perceived to have a larger negative impact on the MNC's profitability. The average weights for the seven most critical characteristics are disclosed here.

The authors also found that the weights assigned by MNCs in the consumer/retail sector were lower than those assigned by MNCs in the industrial sector. MNCs with a relatively large proportion of international business assigned higher weights, or greater importance, to restrictive practices and unstable currencies.

Country Characteristic	Average Weight
Restrictive Practices	3.44
Tariffs or Regulations	3.16
Unstable Currencies	3.07
Foreign Government Subsidies	3.07
Shaky Governments in Less Developed Countries	2.84
Third World Debt Problems	2.67
Varying Standards Between Countries	2.58

There is clearly some degree of subjectivity in identifying each of the relevant political and financial factors for a macroassessment of country risk. There is also some subjectivity in determining the degree of importance of each factor in contributing to the overall macroassessment for a particular country. For instance, one assessor may assign a much higher weight (degree of importance) to real GDP growth than another assessor. Finally, there is some subjectivity in predicting these financial factors. Because of the types of subjectivity mentioned here, it is not surprising that risk assessors often differ in opinion after completing a macroassessment of country risk.

Microassessment of Country Risk

While a macroassessment of country risk provides an indication of the country's overall status, it does not assess country risk from the perspective of the particular business of concern. Consider Country Z, which has been assigned a relatively low macroassessment by most experts due to its poor financial condition. Also consider two MNCs that are deciding whether to set up subsidiaries in Country Z. One MNC is considering the development of a subsidiary that would produce automobiles, while the other MNC plans to build a subsidiary that would produce military supplies. Country Z's government may be committed to purchasing a given amount of military supplies, regardless of how weak the economy is. Thus, the military supply subsidiary may be feasible, while the automobile subsidiary may not.

[1]Glenn H. Petry and James Sprow, "International Trends and Events in Corporate Finance and Management: A Survey," *Financial Practice and Education,* Spring/Summer 1993, pp. 21–28.

There is always the possibility that Country Z's government will search for a locally owned firm to produce military supplies, since it may desire more confidentiality about the supplies it is ordering. This possibility is an element of country risk, since it is a country characteristic (or attitude) that can affect the feasibility of a project. Yet, this specific characteristic is relevant only to the military supply subsidiary and not to the automobile subsidiary. This example illustrates how an appropriate country risk assessment varies with the firm, industry, and project of concern and therefore why the macroassessment of country risk has its limitations. A microassessment is also necessary when evaluating the country risk as related to a particular project proposed by a particular firm.

In addition to political variables, financial variables are also necessary for microassessment of country risk. Microfactors would include the sensitivity of the firm's business to real GDP growth, inflation trends, interest rates, etc. Due to differences in business characteristics, some firms are more susceptible to the host country's economy than others.

In summary, the overall assessment of country risk consists of four parts:

1. Macropolitical risk
2. Macrofinancial risk
3. Micropolitical risk
4. Microfinancial risk

While these parts can be consolidated to generate a single country risk rating, it may be useful to keep them separate, so an MNC can realize the various ways by which its direct foreign investment or exporting operations are exposed to country risk.

Techniques to Assess Country Risk

Once a firm identifies all the macro- and microfactors that deserve consideration in the country risk assessment, it may wish to implement a system for evaluating these factors and determining a country risk rating. There are various techniques available to achieve this objective. Some of the more popular techniques are

- Checklist approach
- Delphi technique
- Quantitative analysis
- Inspection visits
- Combination of techniques

Each technique is briefly discussed in turn.

Checklist Approach

A checklist approach involves judgment on all the political and financial factors (both macro and micro) that contribute to a firm's assessment of country risk. Some factors (such as real GDP growth) can be measured from available data, while others (such as probability of entering into a war) must be subjectively measured. The factors should be converted if necessary to some numerical form in which they can be assessed for a particular country. Those factors thought to have a greater influence on country risk should be assigned greater weights. Both the measurement of some factors and the weighting scheme implemented are subjective.

Delphi Technique

The **Delphi technique** involves the collection of independent opinions on country risk without group discussion by the assessors who provide these opinions. The assessors here may be employees of the firm conducting the assessment or outside consultants. The MNC can average these country risk scores in some manner and even assess the degree of disagreement by measuring dispersion of opinions.

Quantitative Analysis

Once the financial and political variables have been measured for a period of time, models for quantitative analysis can attempt to identify the characteristics that influence the level of country risk. Discriminant analysis is a statistical tool commonly used for this purpose. To illustrate, assume there are some countries that historically can be classified as exhibiting tolerable risk, while other countries exhibit intolerable risk. Discriminant analysis can examine the financial and political factors of all of these countries and attempt to identify which factors help to distinguish (or discriminate) between a tolerable-risk country and an intolerable-risk country. For example, discriminant analysis may find that real growth in GDP is a crucial variable in explaining why a country is a good or bad risk. This information, along with the information determined for all other factors, can then be used in reassessing countries over time. If real GDP growth and other key variables begin to deteriorate for a particular country, this provides a signal that the country risk is increasing.

Regression analysis may also be used to assess risk, since it can measure the sensitivity of one variable to other variables. For example, a firm could regress a measure of its business activity (such as its percentage increase in sales) against country characteristics (such as real growth in GDP). Results from such an analysis will indicate the susceptibility of a particular business to a country's economy. This is valuable information to incorporate into the overall evaluation of country risk.

While statistical models can quantify the impact of variables on each other, they do have their limitations. For example, discriminant analysis applied to historical data may have found that strong real GDP growth can reduce a country's degree of country risk. But, if the firm cannot predict the real growth in GDP for a country, it may be difficult to predict how a country's risk will change over time. Because the country risk rating is to be used in assessing possible projects for the future, the ideal rating system would provide an early warning about countries that may cause problems for the firm in the future. Thus, the ideal quantitative techniques would identify characteristics that signaled problems well before they actually occurred (preferably before the firm's decision to take on a project in that country). At this point in time, such a quantitative model does not exist.

Inspection Visits

Inspection visits involve traveling to a country and meeting with government officials, firm executives, and/or consumers. Such meetings help clarify any uncertain opinions the firm has about a country. Indeed, some variables, such as intercountry relationships, may be difficult to assess without a trip to the host country.

Combination of Techniques

In some cases, it may be most appropriate to implement two or more of the techniques described here. This is common practice, since each technique has its own strengths and weaknesses. For example, an inspection visit may provide useful information, but the visit does not by itself represent a complete country risk analysis. Individual evaluations of country risk could be generated by each technique for a particular country, and if significant differences showed up, further analysis could be conducted.

Comparing Risk Ratings Among Countries

An MNC may evaluate country risk for several countries, perhaps to determine where to establish a subsidiary. One approach to comparing political and financial ratings among countries, advocated by some foreign risk managers, is a **foreign investment risk matrix (FIRM)**, which displays the financial (or economic) risk by intervals ranging across the matrix from "acceptable" to "unacceptable." It also displays political risk by intervals ranging from "stable" to "unstable." An example of this matrix is shown in Exhibit 16.2. Each country can be positioned in its appropriate location on the matrix based on its political rating and financial rating.

Exhibit 16.2
Example of Foreign Investment Risk Matrix

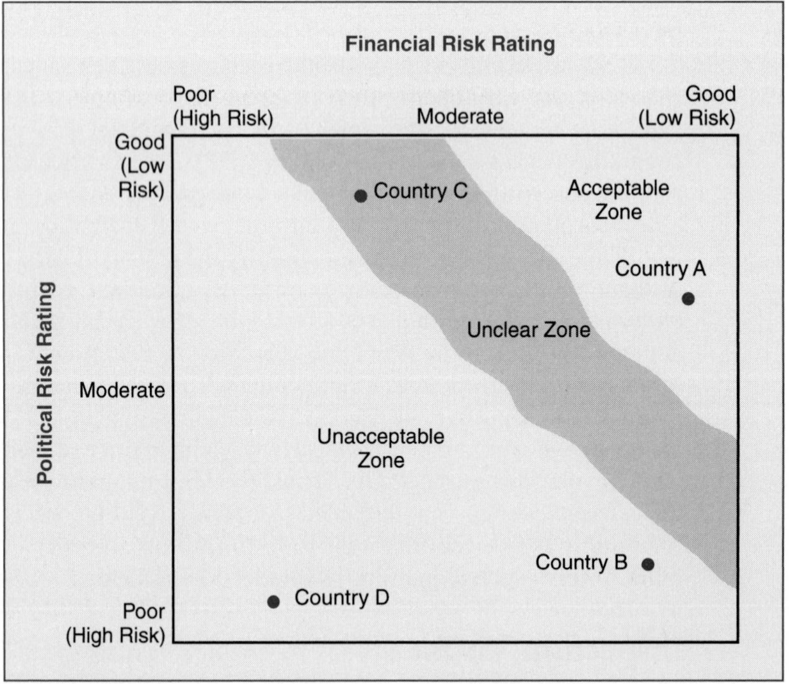

NOTE: This matrix was adapted from a matrix suggested by Bhalla; see *Euromoney*, June 1983, p. 70.

Some countries, such as Country A in the exhibit, will be acceptable because they have a low degree of political and financial risk. Other countries, such as Country B, have low financial risk but high political risk. For Country C in the exhibit, the converse is true. Still others have a high degree of financial and political risk, such as Country D. A firm that uses this matrix must determine the acceptable and unacceptable zones. Based on the zones shown in Exhibit 16.2, Country A is acceptable for implementing projects, but Country B and Country D are unacceptable. Country C is in a so-called "unclear zone," suggesting further evaluation is necessary.

As already mentioned, the importance of political risk versus financial risk varies with the intent of the MNC. Those considering direct foreign investment to attract demand in that country must be highly concerned about financial risk. Those establishing a foreign manufacturing plant and planning to export the goods from there should be more concerned with political risk.

While the FIRM approach can be useful for an MNC, it does not quantify an overall country risk rating for any individual country, since its financial and political ratings have not been weighted. An appropriate procedure for quantifying a country's overall risk is described next.

Quantifying Country Risk: An Example

To develop an overall country risk rating, it is necessary to first construct separate ratings for political and financial risk. As discussed earlier in this chapter, both political risk and financial risk depend on a variety of factors. First, the political factors can be assigned values within some arbitrarily chosen range (such as values from 1 to 5, where 5 is the best value/lowest risk). Next, these political factors are assigned weights (representing degree of importance), which should add up to 100 percent. The assigned values of the factors times their respective weights can then be summed up to derive a political risk rating.

The process described for deriving the political risk rating can then be repeated to derive the financial risk rating. That is, values can be assigned (from 1 to 5, where 5 is the best value/lowest risk) to all financial factors. The assigned values of the factors times their respective weights can be summed up to derive a financial risk rating.

Once the political and financial ratings have been derived, a country's overall country risk rating as related to a specific project can be determined by assigning weights to the political and financial ratings according to their perceived importance. For example, if the political risk were thought to be much more influential on a particular project than the financial risk, it would receive a higher weight than the financial risk rating (both weights added must total 100 percent). The political and financial ratings multiplied by their respective weights would determine the overall country risk rating for a country as related to a particular project.

As a simplified example, Exhibit 16.3 illustrates Cougar Company's country risk assessment of the hypothetical country Sunland. The company is assessing the establishment of a steel manufacturing plant there. From Exhibit 16.3, there are three political factors and five financial factors that contribute to the overall country risk rating in this example. In a realistic setting, many more factors might be included. Political risk factor A might reflect the degree of political tension within the country, while political risk factor B may reflect the degree of political tension of the country with its neighboring countries, and so on. Financial risk factor A might reflect potential internal economic growth, and so on.

Exhibit 16.3
Determining the Overall Country Risk Rating

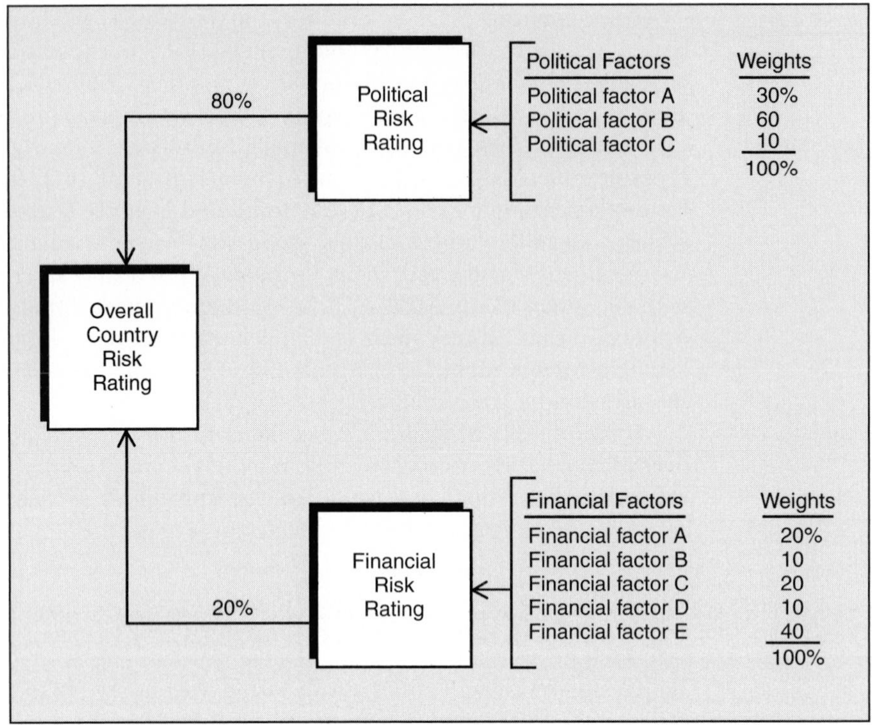

The number of relevant factors comprising both the political risk and the financial risk categories will vary with the country being assessed and the type of corporate operations planned for that country. The assignment of values to the factors, along with the degrees of importance (weights) assigned to the factors, will also vary with the country being assessed and type of corporate operations planned for that country.

To complete the example of deriving Sunland's overall country risk as related to Cougar Company's future plans, assume the company has assigned the values and weights to the factors as shown in Exhibit 16.4. In this example, the company generally assigns the financial factors higher ratings than the political factors. The financial condition of the country has therefore been assessed more favorably than the political condition. Political factor B is thought to be most important, based on a weighting of 60 percent, whereas political factors A and C receive the remaining 40-percent weighting. Financial factor E is thought to be very important, based on its 40-percent weighting, compared to 20-percent weights for factors A and C and 10-percent weights for factors B and D.

The political risk rating is determined by adding the products of assigned ratings (Column 2) and weights (Column 3) of the political risk factors. It equals 2.7, which may appear low based on the individual assigned values. Yet, political factor B carries a 60-percent weight and was assigned a low value, which explains the relatively low political risk rating.

The financial risk is computed to be 3.9, which again verifies that the financial condition of the country is better than its political condition. Once the political and financial ratings are determined, the overall country risk rating can be derived (as shown at the bottom of Exhibit 16.4), given the weights assigned to political and financial risk. Column 3 in the lower portion of Exhibit 16.4 suggests that the company perceives political risk (receiving an 80-percent weight) to be much more important than financial risk (receiving a 20-percent weight) in this country as related to the proposed project. The overall country risk rating of 2.94 may appear low given the individual category ratings. This is due to the heavy weighting to political risk, which in this example is critical, from the firm's perspective. Should Cougar Company establish a steel manufacturing plant in a country that has an overall country risk rating of 2.94 (based on a scale of 1 to 5)? The answer depends on the risk tolerance of the firm.

If the country risk is too high, then the firm does not need to analyze the feasibility of the proposed project any further. Some firms may contend that no risk is

Exhibit 16.4

Derivation of the Overall Country Risk Rating Based on Assumed Information

(1)	(2)	(3)	(4) = (2) × (3)
Political Risk Factors	Rating Assigned by Company to Factor (Within a Range of 1–5)	Weight Assigned by Company to Factor According to Importance	Weighted Value of Factor
Political factor A	4	30%	1.2
Political factor B	2	60	1.2
Political factor C	3	10	.3
		100%	2.7 = Political risk rating
Financial Risk Factors			
Financial factor A	5	20%	1.0
Financial factor B	4	10	.4
Financial factor C	4	20	.8
Financial factor D	5	10	.5
Financial factor E	3	40	1.2
		100%	3.9 = Financial risk rating

(1)	(2)	(3)	(4) = (2) × (3)
Category	Rating as Determined Above	Weight Assigned by Company to Each Risk Category	Weighted Rating
Political risk	2.7	80%	2.16
Financial risk	3.9	20%	.78
		100%	2.94 = Overall country risk rating

Exhibit 16.5
Country Risk Ratings Among Countries (Maximum Rating is 100)

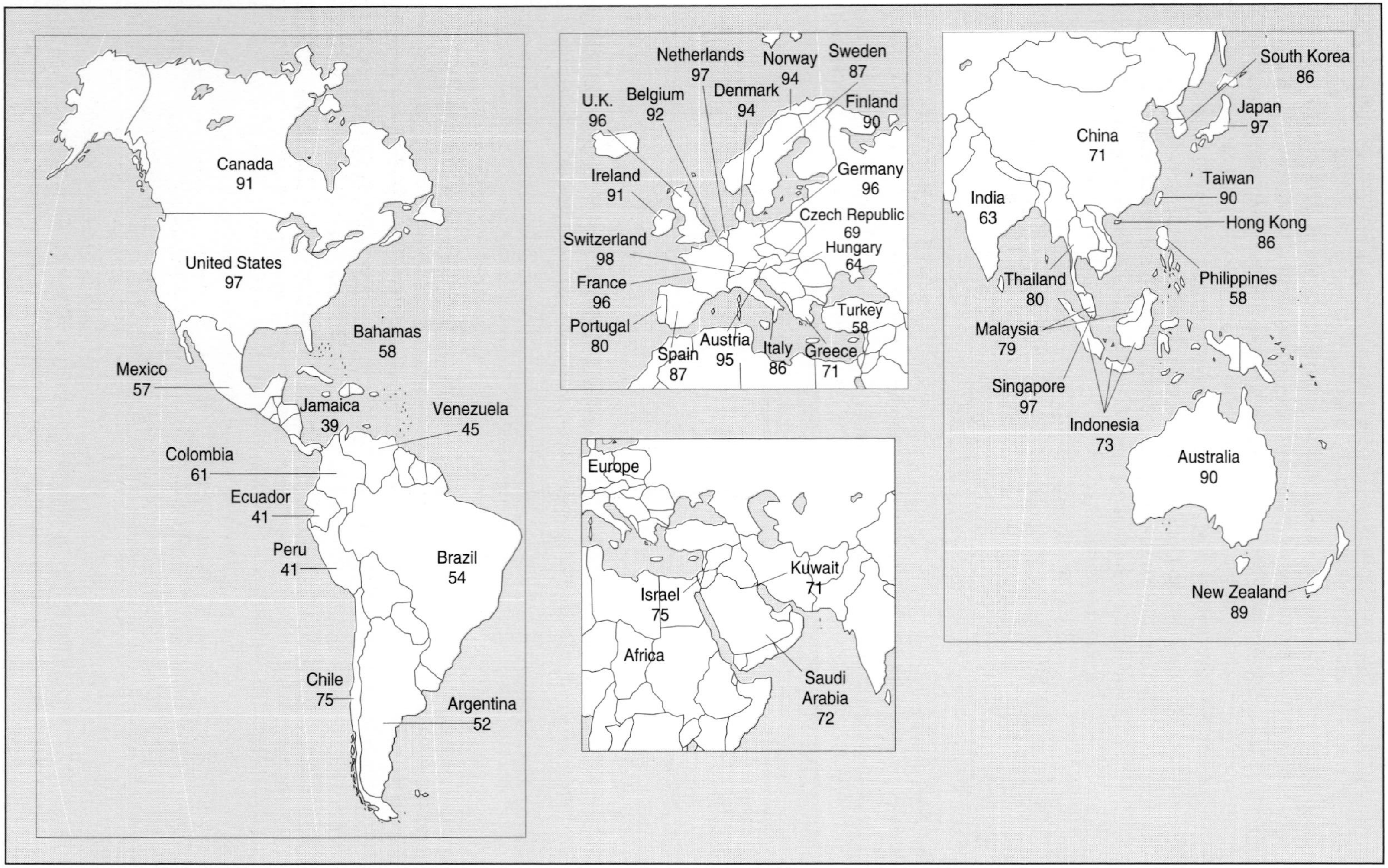

(NOTE: The ratings were based on a 1995 survey by *Euromoney* magazine (see *Euromoney*, September 1995, p. 307–311).

too high when considering a project. Their reasoning is that if the potential return is high enough, the project is worth undertaking. However, there are cases in which the degree of country risk could be too high regardless of the project's expected return. Consider a proposed development of a subsidiary that appears very profitable in Country Z. If Country Z is often engaged in war, this places a threat on the life of any employee who would be transferred to that subsidiary. In this case, Country Z should be off limits, and the proposed project should not receive further consideration.

Before moving on, it should be emphasized that country risk assessors have their own individual procedures for quantifying country risk. The procedure described here is just one of many. Most procedures are similar, though, in that they somehow assign ratings and weights to all individual characteristics relevant to country risk assessment.

ACTUAL COUNTRY RISK RATINGS ACROSS COUNTRIES

Recently, *Euromoney* magazine surveyed experts about their views of country risk in many countries. The mean overall country risk rating assigned by those experts who were surveyed is shown in Exhibit 16.5. This exhibit illustrates how the country risk rating can vary substantially among countries. Many of the industrialized countries such as Germany and Switzerland were rated highly. Some emerging markets such as Taiwan and South Korea were rated high, while other emerging markets such as China and Hungary were assigned moderate ratings. Many Latin American countries such as Ecuador, Peru, and Venezuela were assigned low country risk ratings. Country risk ratings change over time in response to the factors that influence a country's rating. The risk ratings of some Asian countries (such as Indonesia and Thailand) declined after this survey as a result of the Asian crisis.

Since the overall country risk rating is composed of various components, some countries may be rated highly according to some factors, but lower according to others. Exhibit 16.6 shows the economic performance (which is a subset of the financial risk rating) and political risk for various countries. These two factors were assigned a maximum of 50 points (25 points each), out of a total of 100 points. Other financial factors to be discussed shortly made up the other 50 points. Notice from Exhibit 16.6 that industrialized countries such as Germany and Japan are assigned a higher political risk rating than economic performance rating. Conversely, emerging markets such as China and Hungary receive a higher economic performance rating than political risk rating.

Along with political risk and economic performance, there are some other factors related to financial risk that were assessed in the *Euromoney* magazine survey. Exhibit 16.7 identifies these factors and shows the ratings assigned to one particular country, China. The exhibit also states the maximum score that was possible for each factor, which indicates the weight given to each factor. The economic performance and political risk factors have the most influence on the total score because they could each receive up to 25 points, out of a total 100 points. Yet, several financial factors reflect the ability of a subsidiary to access funds in the country of concern. China was rated relatively strong on economic performance and on "debt in default," but it was not rated as high on political risk and on the factors reflecting access to funds.

http://

Visit www.duke.edu/~charvey/Country_risk for the results of Campbell R. Harvey's political, economic, and financial country risk analysis.

Exhibit 16.6
Comparison of Economic Performance and Political Risk Across Countries

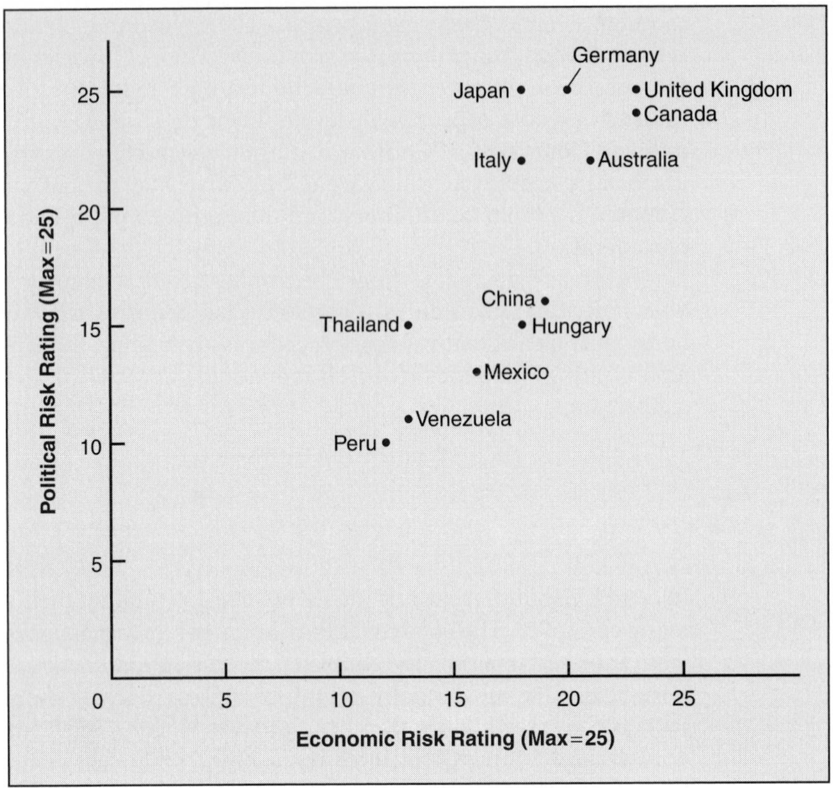

Incorporating Country Risk in Capital Budgeting

If the risk rating of a country is in the tolerable range, any project related to that country deserves further consideration. Country risk can be incorporated in the capital budgeting analysis of a proposed project by adjustment of the discount rate or by adjustment of the estimated cash flows. Each method is discussed here.

Adjustment of the Discount Rate

The discount rate of a proposed project is supposed to reflect the required rate of return on that project. Thus, the discount rate could be adjusted to account for the country risk. The lower the country risk rating, the higher is the perceived risk and the higher is the discount rate applied to the project's cash flows. This approach is convenient in that one adjustment to the capital budgeting analysis can capture country risk. However, there is no precise formula for adjusting the discount rate to incorporate country risk. The adjustment is somewhat arbitrary and may therefore cause feasible projects to be rejected or unfeasible projects to be accepted.

Exhibit 16.7
Example of How Overall Country Risk Rating was Determined for China by a *Euromoney* Magazine Survey

	Maximum Score Possible	Score for China
Political Risk	25	16.25
Economic Performance	25	19.35
Debt Indicators	10	9.54
Debt in Default	10	10.00
Credit Ratings	10	4.62
Access to Bank Finance	5	0.07
Access to Short-term Finance	5	3.00
Access to Capital Markets	5	4.00
Forfaiting Factors	5	4.24
Total		71.07

Adjustment of the Estimated Cash Flows

Perhaps the most appropriate method for incorporating forms of country risk in a capital budgeting analysis is to estimate how the cash flows would be affected by each form of risk. For example, if there is a 20-percent probability that the host government will temporarily block funds from the subsidiary to the parent, the MNC should estimate the project's net present value (*NPV*) under these circumstances, realizing that there is a 20-percent chance that this *NPV* will occur.

If there is a chance that the host government takeover will occur, the foreign project's *NPV* under these conditions should be estimated. Each possible form of risk has an estimated impact on the foreign project's cash flows and therefore on the project's *NPV*. By analyzing each possible impact, the MNC can determine the probability distribution of *NPV*s for the project. Its accept/reject decision on the project will be based on its assessment of the probability that the project will generate a positive *NPV*, as well as the size of possible *NPV* outcomes. While this procedure may seem somewhat tedious, it directly incorporates forms of country risk into the cash flow estimates and explicitly illustrates the possible results from implementing the project. The more convenient method of adjusting the discount rate in accordance with the country risk rating does not indicate the probability distribution of possible outcomes.

To illustrate how country risk can be incorporated in capital budgeting, reconsider the example for Spartan Inc. that is discussed in Chapter 14. Assume for the moment that all the initial assumptions regarding Spartan's initial investment, project life, pricing policy, exchange rate projections, etc., apply here. However, two country risk characteristics will be incorporated here that are not included in the initial analysis. First, assume that there is a 30-percent chance that the withholding tax imposed by the Singapore government will be at a 20-percent rate rather than a 10-percent rate. Second, assume that there is a 40-percent chance that the Singapore government will provide Spartan a payment (salvage value) of S$7 million rather than S$12 million. These two possibilities represent a form of country risk. Assume that these two possible situations are unrelated. To determine how the *NPV* is affected by each of these scenarios, a capital budgeting analysis similar to that shown in Exhibit 14.2 from Chapter 14 could be used. If this analysis were already on a spreadsheet, the *NPV* could be easily estimated by adjustment of line items no. 15 (withholding tax imposed on remitted funds) and no. 17 (salvage value). The capital budgeting analysis measures the effect of a 20-percent withholding tax rate in Exhibit 16.8. Since none of the items before line no. 14 are affected, these items are not shown here. If the 20-percent withholding tax rate is imposed, the *NPV* of the four-year project is $1,252,160.

Now consider the possibility of the lower salvage value, while using the initial assumption of a 10-percent withholding tax rate. The capital budgeting analysis accounts for the lower salvage value in Exhibit 16.9. The estimated *NPV* is $800,484, based on this scenario.

Finally, consider the possibility that the higher withholding tax and the lower salvage value occur. The capital budgeting analysis in Exhibit 16.10 accounts for both of these situations. The *NPV* is estimated to be –$177,223.

Once estimates for the *NPV* are derived for each scenario, the firm can attempt to determine whether the project is feasible. In our example, there are two country risk variables that are uncertain, and there are four possible *NPV* outcomes, as illustrated in Exhibit 16.11. Given the probability of each possible situation and the assumption that the withholding tax outcome is independent from the salvage value outcome, joint probabilities can be determined for each pair of outcomes by multiplying the probabilities of the two outcomes of concern. Since the probability of a 20-percent withholding tax is 30 percent, the probability of a 10-percent withholding tax is 70 percent. Given that the probability of a lower salvage value is 40 percent, the probability of the initial estimate for the salvage value is 60 percent. Thus, scenario no. 1 (10-percent withholding tax and S$12 million salvage value) created in Chapter 14 has a joint probability (probability that both outcomes will occur) of (70%) × (60%) = 42%.

Exhibit 16.8

Analysis of Project Based on a 20-Percent Withholding Tax: Spartan Inc.

	Year 0	Year 1	Year 2	Year 3	Year 4
14. S$ remitted by subsidiary		S$6,000,000	S$6,000,000	S$7,600,000	S$ 8,400,000
15. Withholding tax imposed on remitted funds (20%)		S$1,200,000	S$1,200,000	S$1,520,000	S$ 1,680,000
16. S$ remitted after withholding taxes		S$4,800,000	S$4,800,000	S$6,080,000	S$ 6,720,000
17. Salvage value					S$12,000,000
18. Exchange rate of S$		$.50	$.50	$.50	$.50
19. Cash flows to parent		$2,400,000	$2,400,000	$3,040,000	$ 9,360,000
20. *PV* of parent cash flows (15% discount rate)		$2,086,956	$1,814,745	$1,998,849	$ 5,351,610
21. Initial investment by parent	$10,000,000				
22. Cumulative *NPV*		–$7,913,044	–$6,098,299	–$4,099,450	$ 1,252,160

Exhibit 16.9
Analysis of Project Based on a Reduced Salvage Value: Spartan Inc.

	Year 0	Year 1	Year 2	Year 3	Year 4
14. S$ remitted by subsidiary		S$6,000,000	S$6,000,000	S$7,600,000	S$8,400,000
15. Withholding tax imposed on remitted funds (10%)		S$ 600,000	S$ 600,000	S$ 760,000	S$ 840,000
16. S$ remitted after withholding taxes		S$5,400,000	S$5,400,000	S$6,840,000	S$7,560,000
17. Salvage value					S$7,000,000
18. Exchange rate of S$		$.50	$.50	$.50	$.50
19. Cash flows to parent		$2,700,000	$2,700,000	$3,420,000	$7,280,000
20. *PV* of parent cash flows (15% discount rate)		$2,347,826	$2,041,588	$2,248,706	$4,162,364
21. Initial investment by parent	$10,000,000				
22. Cumulative *NPV*		–$7,652,174	–$5,610,586	–$3,361,880	$ 800,484

From Exhibit 16.11, scenario no. 4 is the only scenario in which there is a negative *NPV*. Since this scenario has a 12-percent chance of occurring, there is a 12-percent chance that the project proposed will adversely affect the value of the firm. Put another way, there is an 88-percent chance that the project will enhance the firm's value. The expected value of the project's *NPV* could be measured as the sum of each scenario's estimated *NPV* multiplied by its respective probability across all

Exhibit 16.10
Analysis of Project Based on a 20-Percent Withholding Tax and a Reduced Salvage Value: Spartan Inc.

	Year 0	Year 1	Year 2	Year 3	Year 4
14. S$ remitted by subsidiary		S$6,000,000	S$6,000,000	S$7,600,000	S$8,400,000
15. Withholding tax imposed on remitted funds (20%)		S$1,200,000	S$1,200,000	S$1,520,000	S$1,680,000
16. S$ remitted after withholding taxes		S$4,800,000	S$4,800,000	S$6,080,000	S$6,720,000
17. Salvage value					S$7,000,000
18. Exchange rate of S$		$.50	$.50	$.50	$.50
19. Cash flows to parent		$2,400,000	$2,400,000	$3,040,000	$6,860,000
20. *PV* of parent cash flows (15% discount rate)		$2,086,956	$1,814,745	$1,998,849	$3,922,227
21. Initial investment by parent	$10,000,000				
22. Cumulative *NPV*		–$7,913,044	–$6,098,299	–$4,099,450	–$ 177,223

Exhibit 16.11
Summary of Estimated *NPV*s Across the Possible Scenarios: Spartan Inc.

Scenario	Withholding Tax Imposed by Singapore Government	Salvage Value of Project	*NPV*	Probability
1	10%	S$12,000,000	$2,229,867	(70%)(60%) = 42%
2	20%	S$12,000,000	$1,252,160	(30%)(60%) = 18%
3	10%	S$ 7,000,000	$ 800,484	(70%)(40%) = 28%
4	20%	S$ 7,000,000	–$ 177,223	(30%)(40%) = 12%

$$
\begin{aligned}
E(NPV) &= \$2{,}229{,}867\ (42\%) \\
&+ \$1{,}252{,}160\ (18\%) \\
&+ \$800{,}484\ (28\%) \\
&- \$177{,}223\ (12\%) \\
&= \$1{,}364{,}801
\end{aligned}
$$

four scenarios, as shown in the bottom of Exhibit 16.11. Most MNCs would accept the proposed project, given the likelihood that the project will have a positive *NPV* and the limited loss that would occur even under the worst case scenario.

In this example, the initial assumptions for most input variables were used as if these assumptions were known with certainty. However, it is possible to account for the uncertainty of country risk characteristics (as is done in our current example) while also allowing for uncertainty in the other variables as well. This process can be facilitated if the analysis is on a computer spreadsheet. For example, if the firm wished to allow for three possible exchange rate trends, it could adjust the exchange rate projections for each of the four scenarios assessed in the current example. Each scenario would reflect a specific withholding tax outcome, a specific salvage value outcome, and a specific exchange rate trend. There would be a total of 12 scenarios, with each scenario having an estimated *NPV* and a probability of occurrence. Based on the estimated *NPV* and the probability of each scenario, the firm could then measure the expected value of the *NPV* and the probability that the *NPV* would be positive.

Even after a project is accepted and implemented, country risk must continue to be monitored. With a labor-intensive MNC, the host country may feel it is benefiting from a subsidiary's existence (due to the subsidiary's employment of local people), and the chance of expropriation may be low. Yet, there are several other forms of country risk that need to be considered. Decisions regarding subsidiary expansion, fund transfers to the parent, and sources of financing can all be affected by any changes in country risk. Since country risk can change dramatically over time, periodic reassessment is required, especially for less stable countries.

Applications of Country Risk Analysis

There are some cases in which country risk assessment has enabled MNCs to avoid further involvement and even reduce current involvement in politically tense countries. For example, four months before the fall of the Shah of Iran, a country risk assessor for Gulf Oil detected severe political pressure building within Iran. Consequently, Gulf Oil began planning to deal with the subsequent loss of Iranian oil, which at the time amounted to 10 percent of its crude supplies. While dedicating resources to country risk assessment can be well worth the cost, the art of forecasting country crises is far from being perfected.

Whether MNCs hire outside consultants or use in-house staff to perform country risk analysis, they have often been unable to predict major trouble in various countries. For example, the Iranian crisis, Poland's financial crisis, and the economic deterioration of several Latin American countries were generally not detected well in advance. It is understandable that country risk systems are prone to errors. Consider the procedure discussed earlier in this chapter in which individual country characteristics were assigned values which rate each characteristic. The values assigned are somewhat arbitrary. In addition, the assigning of weights to reflect the importance of each characteristic is also somewhat arbitrary. Thus, while an overall risk rating of a country can be useful, it cannot always detect upcoming crises.

The general inability of MNCs to predict country crises may also be due to too much reliance on statistics. Quantitative models, while valuable, cannot evaluate subjective data that cannot be quantified. In addition, historical trends of various country characteristics are not always useful for anticipating an upcoming crisis. Furthermore, warnings by country risk assessors are sometimes ignored by executives higher up in the company's organization.

Due to the exposure to error when assessing country risk, no system has been singled out as optimal. A survey of 193 corporations heavily involved in foreign business found that about half of the corporations have no formal means for making country risk assessments. This does not mean they neglect to assess country risk, but rather that there is no proven method to use. Some of the assessors' opinions of country risk are based simply on their conversations with other people whom they believe to be reliable. While such an approach is quite simplistic, there is no clear-cut evidence that even the most sophisticated technique will more properly assess country risk.

Country Risk Analysis of Eastern Bloc Countries. To illustrate the characteristics that are given much attention when assessing country risk, consider the assessment of Eastern Bloc countries in recent years. Hungary has generally received relatively high ratings because of its capable labor force, the recent ease in remitting profits from the country, and its government's efforts to promote direct foreign investment. Poland, Romania, and the countries that formerly made up Czechoslovakia and Yugoslavia have received low ratings because of internal political battles, large budget deficits, poor economic conditions, large government bureaucracies, and a lack of effort in welcoming direct foreign investment.

While these ratings may change over time, this assessment summary suggests the more relevant characteristics that influence the ratings of Eastern Bloc countries. Some other important characteristics assessed when measuring country risk in these countries are availability of hotels, office space, phone lines, and public transportation.

Country Risk Resulting from the Persian Gulf Crisis. As a result of the Persian Gulf crisis, many MNCs attempted to reassess country risk. Terrorism became a major concern. Various methods were used by MNCs to protect against terrorism. Cross-country travel by executives was reduced, as MNCs used teleconference calls instead.

Some MNCs with subsidiaries in Saudi Arabia temporarily closed some of their operations, allowing employees from other countries to return home. Some projects that were being considered for countries that could be subject to terrorist attacks were postponed. Even projects that appeared to be feasible from a financial perspective were postponed because of the potential danger to employees.

In addition to the threat of terrorism, there were many other ways in which the Persian Gulf crisis influenced cash flows of MNCs. The effects varied with the characteristics of each MNC. The more obvious effects of the crisis were reduced travel and higher oil prices. The reduction in travel adversely affected airlines, hotels, restaurants, luggage manufacturers, tourist attractions, rental car agencies, and cruise lines.

The Persian Gulf crisis is a clear example of how country risk can change over time. It would have been difficult to forecast that Iraq was going to invade Kuwait or to forecast the events following the invasion. MNCs recognize that some unpredictable events will unfold that will affect their exposure to country risk. Yet, they can at least be prepared to revise their operations in order to reduce their exposure.

Country Risk Resulting from the Asian Crisis. As a result of the 1997–1998 Asian crisis, MNCs realized that they had underestimated the potential financial problems that could occur in the high-growth Asian countries. The high degree of economic growth was overemphasized and comforted country risk analysts, even though the Asian countries had high debt levels, and commercial banks had massive loan problems. The loan problems were not obvious because commercial banks were typically not required to disclose much information about their loans. Once the problems became publicized, some of the banks were closed, some depositors shifted their money to other countries, and there was not sufficient liquidity for the firms in these countries. It appears that country risk analysts ignored some of the potential problems in these countries, and many MNCs with subsidiaries in these countries were not prepared for the Asian crisis once it occurred. A more thorough country risk analysis may have enabled some MNCs to respond more quickly to the crisis than other MNCs that ignored signs of trouble. Now the issue for country risk analysts is to reassess conditions given that somewhat depressed prices of real estate in these countries may offer some new types of investment opportunities.

Reducing Exposure to Host Government Takeovers

While there are several possible benefits to direct foreign investment, country risk can offset such benefits. The most severe country risk is a host government takeover. This type of takeover may result in major losses, especially when the MNC does not have any power to negotiate with the host government.

The most common strategies used to reduce exposure to a host government takeover are

- Use a short-term horizon
- Rely on unique supplies or technology
- Hire local labor
- Borrow local funds
- Purchase insurance

Use a Short-Term Horizon

This technique concentrates on recovering cash flow quickly, so that in the event of expropriation, losses are minimized. An MNC would also exert only a minimum effort to replace worn-out equipment and machinery at the subsidiary. It may even phase out its overseas investment by selling off its assets to local investors or the government in stages over time.

Rely on Unique Supplies or Technology

If the subsidiary can bring in supplies from its headquarters (or a sister subsidiary) that cannot be duplicated locally, the host government will not be able to take over and operate the subsidiary without such supplies. Also, the supplies could be cut off by the MNC if the subsidiary were treated unfairly.

If the subsidiary can hide the technology in its production process, a government takeover will be less likely. The only way that a takeover would work here would be if the MNC were willing to provide the necessary technology, and the MNC would provide such information only under conditions of a friendly takeover, in which it received adequate compensation.

Hire Local Labor

If local employees of the subsidiary were affected by the host government's takeover, they could pressure their government to avoid such action. However, the government could still let those employees retain their positions after taking over the subsidiary. Thus, this strategy has only limited effectiveness in avoiding or reducing a government takeover.

Borrow Local Funds

If the subsidiary borrows funds locally, local banks will be concerned about its future performance. If for any reason a government takeover would reduce the probability that the banks would receive their loan repayments promptly, they might attempt to prevent a takeover by the host government. However, the host government may guarantee repayment to the banks, so this strategy has only limited effectiveness. Nevertheless, it could still be preferable to a situation in which the MNC not only lost the subsidiary but also still owed home country creditors.

Purchase Insurance

Insurance can be purchased to cover the risk of expropriation. For example, the U.S. government provides insurance through the Overseas Private Investment Corporation (OPIC). The insurance premiums paid by a firm depend on the degree of insurance coverage and the risk associated with the firm. Yet, any insurance policy will typically cover only a portion of the company's total exposure to country risk.

Many home countries of MNCs have investment guarantee programs that insure to some extent the risks of expropriation, wars, or currency blockage. Some guarantee programs have a one-year waiting period or longer before compensation is paid on losses due to expropriation. Also, some insurance policies do not cover all forms of expropriation. Furthermore, to be eligible for such insurance, the subsidiary might be required by the country to concentrate on exporting rather than on local sales. Even if a subsidiary qualifies for insurance, there is a cost. Any insurance will typically cover only a portion of the assets and may specify a maximum duration of coverage, such as 15 or 20 years. A subsidiary must weigh the benefits of this insurance against the cost of the policy's premiums and potential losses in excess of coverage. The insurance can be helpful, but it does not by itself prevent losses due to expropriation.

In 1993, Russia established an insurance fund to protect MNCs against various forms of country risk. This action was taken to encourage more direct foreign investment in Russia.

The World Bank established an affiliate called the Multilateral Investment Guarantee Agency (MIGA) to provide political insurance for MNCs with direct foreign investment in less developed countries. MIGA offers insurance against expropriation, breach of contract, currency inconvertibility, war, and civil disturbances.

Impact of an MNC's Country Risk Analysis on Its Value

An MNC's country risk analysis can affect its value, as shown in Exhibit 16.12. The country risk analysis determines the expected cash flows derived from each foreign subsidiary in the future. For example, an MNC with an Austrian subsidiary that expects Austria to revise its environmental laws must apply that expectation to estimate the cost of complying with these laws and derive the expected cash flows to be generated by its Austrian subsidiary in the future. A country risk analysis may also

Exhibit 16.12
Impact of Country Risk on an MNC's Value

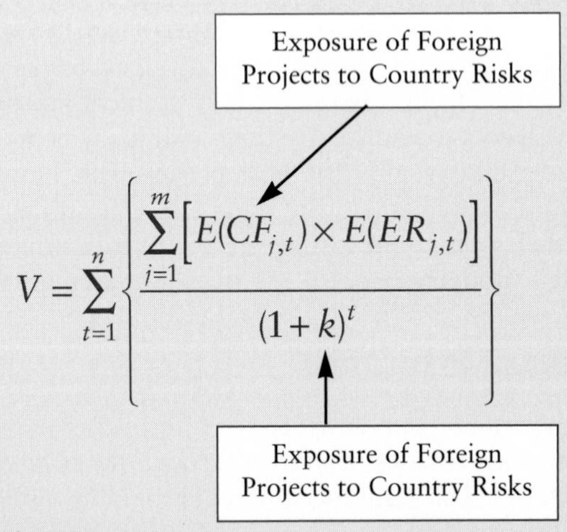

V = value of the U.S.-based MNC
$E(CF_{j,t})$ = expected cash flows denominated in currency j to be received by the U.S. parent in period t
$E(ER_{j,t})$ = expected exchange rate at which currency j can be converted to dollars at the end of period t
k = the weighted average cost of capital of the U.S. parent company
m = number of currencies
n = number of periods

lead to a decision to divest a subsidiary, which means that the expected foreign currency cash flows generated by that subsidiary will terminate after that point. Thus, the expected foreign currency cash flows that will ultimately be remitted to the U.S. parent are influenced by the country risk analysis.

The parent's required rate of return on the funds it provides to support operations in foreign countries is also affected by its country risk analysis. During the Asian crisis, many MNCs revised their country risk assessment upward for Asian countries. Thus, the required rate of return for investment in Asian operations would have been revised upward even if no other factors changed, which reduces the value of the MNC.

SUMMARY

- The factors used by MNCs to measure a country's political risk include attitude of consumers toward purchasing homemade goods, the host government's attitude toward the MNC, the blockage of fund transfers, currency inconvertibility, war, bureaucracy, and corruption. These factors can increase the costs of international business.
- The factors used by MNCs to measure a country's financial risk are the country's interest rates, exchange rates, and inflation rates.
- The techniques typically used by MNCs to measure the country risk are the checklist approach, the Delphi technique, quantitative analysis, and inspection visits. Since no one technique covers all aspects of country risk, a combination of these techniques is commonly used.

  The measurement of country risk is essentially a weighted average of the political or financial factors that are perceived to comprise country risk. Each MNC has its own view as to the weights that should be assigned to each factor. Thus, the overall rating for a country may vary among MNCs.
- Once country risk is measured, it can be incorporated into a capital budgeting analysis by adjustment of the discount rate. However, the adjustment is somewhat arbitrary and may cause improper decision making.

  An alternative method of incorporating country risk analysis into capital budgeting is to explicitly account for each factor that affects country risk. For each possible form of risk, the MNC can recalculate the foreign project's net present value under the condition that the event (such as blocked funds, increased taxes, etc.) occurs.

SELF-TEST FOR CHAPTER 16

(Answers are provided in Appendix A at the back of the text.)

1. Key West Co. exports highly advanced phone system components to its subsidiary shops on islands in the Caribbean Sea. The components are purchased by consumers to improve their phone systems. These components are not produced in other countries. Explain how political risk factors could adversely affect the profitability of Key West Co.
2. Using the information in question 1, explain how financial risk factors could adversely affect the profitability of Key West Co.
3. Given the information in question 1, do you expect that Key West Co. is more concerned about the adverse effects of political risk or those of financial risk?
4. In 1992, a bomb exploded in the World Trade Center. Explain what types of firms would be most concerned about an increase in country risk as a result of this event.

5. Rockford Co. plans to expand its successful business by establishing a subsidiary in Canada. However, it is concerned that after two years the Canadian government will either impose a special tax on any income sent back to the U.S. parent or order the subsidiary to be sold at that time. The executives have estimated that either of these scenarios has a 15-percent chance of occurring. They have decided to add four percentage points onto the project's required rate of return to incorporate the country risk that they were concerned about in the capital budgeting analysis. Is there a better way to more precisely incorporate the country risk of concern here?

QUESTIONS AND APPLICATIONS

1. List some forms of country risk other than a takeover of a subsidiary by the host government.

2. Identify common political factors for an MNC to consider when assessing country risk. Briefly elaborate on how each factor can affect the risk to the MNC.

3. Identify common *financial* factors for an MNC to consider when assessing country risk. Briefly elaborate on how each factor can affect the risk to the MNC.

4. Discuss the use of the foreign investment risk matrix (FIRM) to compare country risk among countries. Why do firms have different acceptable zones when using this matrix?

5. Describe the steps involved in assessing country risk once all relevant information has been gathered.

6. Describe the possible errors involved in assessing country risk. In other words, explain why country risk analysis is not always accurate.

7. Explain an MNC's strategy of diversifying projects internationally in order to maintain a low level of overall country risk.

8. Once a project is accepted, country risk analysis for the foreign country involved is no longer necessary, assuming that no other proposed projects are being evaluated for that country. Do you agree with this statement? Why or why not?

9. If the potential return is high enough, any degree of country risk can be tolerated. Do you agree with this statement? Why or why not?

10. An MNC has decided to call a well-known country risk consultant to conduct a country risk analysis on a small country in which the MNC plans to develop a large subsidiary. The MNC prefers to hire the consultant, since it plans to use its employees for other important corporate functions. The consultant uses a computer program that has assigned weights of importance linked to the various factors. The consultant will evaluate the factors for this small country and insert a rating for each factor into the computer. While the assigned weights to the factors are not adjusted by the computer, the factor ratings are adjusted for each particular country the consultant assesses. Do you think the MNC should use this consultant? Why or why not?

11. Explain the microassessment of country risk.

12. How could a country risk assessment be used to adjust a project's required rate of return? How could such an assessment be used instead to adjust a project's estimated cash flows?

13. Explain some methods of reducing exposure to existing country risk while maintaining the same amount of business within a particular country.

14. Why do some subsidiaries maintain a low profile as to where their parents are located?

15. Do you think that a proper country risk analysis can replace a capital budgeting analysis of a project considered for a foreign country? Explain.

16. NYU Corporation considered establishing a subsidiary in Zenland; it performed a country risk analysis to help make the decision. It first retrieved a country risk analysis performed

about one year earlier, when it had planned to begin a major exporting business to Zenland firms. Then it updated the analysis by incorporating all current information on the key variables that were used in that analysis, such as Zenland's willingness to accept exports, its existing quotas, and existing tariff laws. Is this country risk analysis adequate? Explain.

17. In the early 1990s, MNCs such as Alcoa DuPont, Heinz, and IBM donated products and technology to foreign countries where they have subsidiaries. How could these actions reduce some forms of country risk?

18. A U.S. firm plans a project in the United Kingdom, in which it would lease space for one year in a shopping mall to sell expensive clothes manufactured in the United States. The project would end in one year, when all earnings would be remitted to the U.S. firm. Assume that no additional corporate taxes would be incurred beyond those imposed by the British government. Since the firm would rent space, it would not have any long-term assets in the United Kingdom, and it expects that the salvage (terminal) value of the project will be about zero.

    Assume that the project's required rate of return is 18 percent. Also assume that the initial outlay required by the parent to fill the store with clothes is $200,000. The pretax earnings are expected to be £300,000 at the end of one year. The British pound is expected to be worth $1.60 at the end of one year, when the after-tax earnings will be converted to dollars and remitted to the U.S. The following forms of country risk must be considered:

    The British economy may weaken (probability = 30%), which would cause the expected pretax earnings to be £200,000.

    The British corporate tax rate on income earned by U.S. firms may increase from 40 percent to 50 percent (probability = 20 percent).

    These two forms of country risk are independent. Calculate the expected value of the project's net present value (*NPV*) and determine the probability that the project will have a negative *NPV*.

19. Explain how capital budgeting analysis would need to be adjusted for question 18 if there were three possible outcomes for the British pound, in addition to the possible outcomes for the British economic growth and the corporate tax rate.

20. Recently, J.C. Penney decided to consider expansion into various foreign countries; it applied a comprehensive country risk analysis before making its expansion decisions. Initial screenings of 30 foreign countries were based on political and economic factors that contribute to country risk. For the remaining 20 countries where country risk was considered to be tolerable, specific country risk characteristics of each country were considered. One of J.C. Penney's biggest targets is Mexico, where it planned to build and operate seven large stores.

    a. Identify the political factors that you think may possibly affect the performance of the J.C. Penney stores in Mexico.
    b. Explain why the J.C. Penney stores in Mexico and in other foreign markets are subject to financial risk (a subset of country risk).
    c. Assume that J.C. Penney anticipated that there was a 10-percent chance that the Mexican government would temporarily prevent conversion of peso profits into dollars because of political conditions. This event would prevent J.C. Penney from remitting earnings generated in Mexico and could adversely affect the performance of these stores (from the U.S. perspective). Offer a way in which this type of political risk could be explicitly incorporated in a capital budgeting analysis when assessing the feasibility of these projects.
    d. Assume that J.C. Penney decides to use dollars to finance the expansion of stores in Mexico. Second, assume that J.C. Penney decides to use one set of dollar cash flow estimates for any project that it assesses. Third, assume that the stores in Mexico are not subject to political risk. Do you think that the required rate of return on these projects would differ from the required rate of return on stores built in the United States at the same time? Explain.

e. Based on your answer to the previous question, does this mean that proposals for any new stores in the United States have a higher probability of being accepted than proposals for any new stores in Mexico?

Internet Application

21. The following Web site offers information on countries that are more transparent than others, which implies that one can recognize that they are having political or economic problems:

asiarisk.com/library2/html

Use this Web site to identify the Asian countries that have recently been rated very transparent. What Asian countries are not perceived to be transparent?

Running Your Own MNC

Assessing Exposure to Country Risk

22. a. Describe the financial factors that expose your business to country risk.

b. Describe the political factors that expose your business to country risk.

Blades, Inc. Case

Country Risk Assessment

Recently, Ben Holt, Blades' chief financial officer (CFO), has assessed whether it would be more beneficial for Blades to establish a subsidiary in Thailand to manufacture roller blades or to acquire an existing manufacturer, Skates'n'Stuff, which has offered to sell the business to Blades for 1 billion Thai baht. In Ben Holt's view, establishing a subsidiary in Thailand yields a higher net present value (*NPV*) than the acquisition of the existing business. Furthermore, the Thai manufacturer has rejected an offer by Blades, Inc. for 900 million baht. A purchase price of 900 million baht for Skates'n'Stuff would make the acquisition as attractive as the establishment of a subsidiary in Thailand in terms of net present value. Skates'n'Stuff has indicated that it is not willing to accept an amount below 950 million baht in payment.

Although Ben Holt is confident that the *NPV* analysis was conducted correctly, he is troubled by the fact that the same discount rate, 25 percent, was used in each analysis. In his view, establishing a subsidiary in Thailand may be associated with a higher level of country risk than acquiring Skates'n'Stuff. Although either approach would result in approximately the same level of financial risk, the political risk associated with establishing a subsidiary in Thailand may be higher then the political risk of operating Skates'n'Stuff. If the establishment of a subsidiary in Thailand is associated with a higher level of country risk overall, then a higher discount rate should have been used in this analysis. Based on these considerations, Ben Holt's objective is to measure the country risk associated with Thailand on both a macro and micro level and then to reexamine the feasibility of both approaches.

First, Ben Holt has gathered some more detailed political information for Thailand. For example, he believes that consumers in Asian countries prefer to purchase goods produced by Asians, which may prevent the success of establishing a subsidiary in Thailand. Conversely, this cultural characteristic may not affect the success of operating Skates'n'Stuff, especially if Blades retains the company's management and employees. Furthermore, the subsidiary would have to apply for various licenses and permits to be allowed to operate in Thailand, while Skates'n'Stuff has applied and received these licenses and permits long ago. However, the number of licenses required for Blades' industry is relatively low compared to other industries. Moreover, there is a high possibility that the Thai government will implement capital controls in the near future, which would prevent funds from leaving Thailand. Since Blades, Inc. has planned to remit all earnings generated by its subsidiary or by Skates'n'Stuff back to the U.S., regardless of which approach to direct foreign investment it takes, capital controls may force Blades to reinvest funds in Thailand.

Ben Holt has also gathered some information regarding the financial risk of operating in Thailand. Thailand's economy has been weak lately and recent forecasts indicate that a recovery may be slow. A weak economy may affect the demand for Blades' products, roller blades. The state of the economy is of particular concern to Blades since it produces a leisure product. In the case of an economic turndown, consumers will first eliminate these types of purchases. Ben Holt is also worried about the high level of interest rates in Thailand, which may further slow economic growth if Thai citizens begin saving more. Furthermore, Mr. Holt is also aware that inflation levels in Thailand are expected to remain high. These high inflation levels can affect the purchasing power of Thai consumers, who may adjust their spending habits to purchase more essential products than roller blades. However, high levels of inflation also indicate that consumers in Thailand are still spending a relatively high proportion of their earnings.

Another financial factor that may affect Blades' operations in Thailand is the baht-dollar exchange rate. Current forecasts indicate that the Thai baht may depreciate in the future. However, recall that Blades will sell all roller blades produced in Thailand to Thai consumers. Therefore, Blades is not subject to a lower level of U.S. demand resulting from a weak baht. However, Blades will remit the earnings generated in Thailand back to the U.S., and a weak baht would reduce the dollar amount of these translated earnings.

Based on these initial considerations, Ben Holt feels that the level of political risk of operating in Thailand may be higher if Blades decides to establish a subsidiary in Thailand to manufacture roller blades (as opposed to acquiring Skates'n'Stuff). Conversely, the financial risk of operating in Thailand will be roughly the same whether Blades establishes a subsidiary in Thailand or acquires Skates'n'Stuff. However, Ben Holt is not satisfied with this initial assessment and would like to have numbers at hand when he meets with the board of directors next week. Thus, he would like to conduct a quantitative analysis of the country risk associated with operating in Thailand. Thus, he has asked you, a financial analyst of Blades, Inc. to develop a country risk analysis for Thailand and to adjust the discount rate for the riskier venture (i.e., establishing a subsidiary or acquiring Skates'n'Stuff). Ben Holt has provided you with the following information for your analysis:

- Since Blades produces leisure products, it is more susceptible to financial than political risk factors. You should use weights of 60 percent for financial risk factors and 40 percent for political risk factors in your analysis.
- You should use the attitude of Thai consumers, capital controls, and bureaucracy as political risk factors in your analysis. Ben Holt perceives capital controls as the more important political risk factor. In his view, the consumer attitude and bureaucracy factors are of equal importance.
- You should use interest rates, inflation levels, and exchange rates as the financial risk factors in your analysis. In Ben Holt's view, exchange rates and interest rates in Thailand are of equal importance, while inflation levels are of slightly lower importance.
- Each factor used in your analysis should be assigned a rating within a range of 1 to 5, where 5 indicates the most unfavorable rating.

Ben Holt has asked you to answer the following questions for him, which he will use in his meeting with the board of directors:

1. Based on the information provided in the case, do you think the political risk associated with Thailand is higher or lower for a manufacturer of leisure products such as Blades as opposed to, say, a food producer? That is, conduct a microassessment of political risk for Blades, Inc.
2. Do you think the financial risk associated with Thailand is higher or lower for a manufacturer of leisure products such as Blades as opposed to, say, a food producer? That is, conduct a microassessment of financial risk for Blades, Inc. Do you think a leisure product manufacturer such as Blades will be more affected by political or financial risk factors?
3. Without using a numerical analysis, do you think establishing a subsidiary in Thailand or acquiring Skates'n'Stuff will result in a higher assessment of political risk? Of financial risk? Substantiate your answer.
4. Using a spreadsheet, conduct a quantitative country risk analysis for Blades, Inc. using the information Ben Holt has provided you with.

Use your judgment to assign weights and ratings to each political and financial risk factor and determine an overall country risk rating for Thailand. Conduct two separate analyses for (1) the establishment of a subsidiary in Thailand, and (2) the acquisition of Skates'n'Stuff.

5. Which method of direct foreign investment should utilize a higher discount rate in the capital budgeting analysis? Would this strengthen or weaken the tentative decision of establishing a subsidiary in Thailand?

Small Business Dilemma

Country Risk Analysis at the Sports Exports Company

The Sports Exports Company produces footballs in the United States and exports them to the United Kingdom. It also has an ongoing joint venture with a British firm that produces some sporting goods for a fee. The Sports Exports Company is considering the establishment of a small subsidiary in the United Kingdom.

1. Under the current conditions, is the Sports Exports Company subject to country risk?
2. If the firm does decide to develop a small subsidiary in the United Kingdom, will the exposure to country risk change? If so, how?

17 Multinational Cost of Capital and Capital Structure

An MNC finances its operations by using a capital structure (proportion of debt versus equity financing) that can minimize its cost of capital. By minimizing the cost of capital used to finance a given level of operations, the MNC minimizes the required rate of return necessary to make the foreign operations feasible and therefore maximizes the value of those operations.

The specific objectives of this chapter are to

- explain how corporate and country characteristics influence an MNC's cost of capital,
- explain why there are differences in the costs of capital among countries, and
- explain how corporate and country characteristics are considered by an MNC when it establishes its capital structure.

Background on Cost of Capital

A firm's capital consists of equity (retained earnings and funds obtained by issuing stock) and debt (borrowed funds). The firm's cost of retained earnings reflects an opportunity cost: what the existing shareholders could have earned if they had received the earnings as dividends and invested the funds themselves. The firm's cost of new common equity (issuing new stock) reflects an opportunity cost: what the new shareholders could have earned if they had invested their funds elsewhere instead of in the stock. This cost exceeds that of retained earnings because it also includes the expenses associated with selling the new stock (flotation costs). The firm's cost of debt is easier to measure because interest expenses are incurred by the firm as a result of borrowing funds. Firms attempt to use a specific capital structure, or mix of capital components, that will minimize their cost of capital. The lower a firm's cost of capital, the lower is its required rate of return on a given proposed project. Firms estimate their cost of capital before they conduct capital budgeting, because the net present value of any project is partially dependent on the cost of capital.

The firm's weighted average cost of capital (referred to as k_c) can be measured as

$$k_c = \left(\frac{D}{D+E}\right)k_d(1-t) + \left(\frac{E}{D+E}\right)k_e$$

where D is the amount of the firm's debt, k_d is the before-tax cost of its debt, t is the corporate tax rate, E is the equity of the firm, and k_e is the cost of financing with equity. These ratios reflect the percentage of capital represented by debt and equity respectively.

There is an advantage to using debt rather than equity as capital because the interest payments on debt are tax deductible. However, the greater the use of debt, the greater the interest expense is and the higher the probability that the firm will be unable to meet its expenses. Consequently, the rate of return required by potential new shareholders or creditors will increase to reflect the higher probability of bankruptcy.

The tradeoff between debt's advantage (tax deductibility of interest payments) and its disadvantage (increased bankruptcy probability) is illustrated in Exhibit 17.1. The firm's cost of capital is shown to initially decrease as the ratio of debt to total capital increases. However, after some point (labeled X in Exhibit 17.1), the cost of capital rises as the ratio of debt to total capital increases. This implies that it is favorable to increase the use of debt financing until the point at which the bankruptcy probability becomes large enough to offset the tax advantage of using debt. To go beyond that point would increase the firm's overall cost of capital.

COST OF CAPITAL FOR MNCS

The cost of capital for MNCs may differ from that for domestic firms because of the following characteristics that differentiate MNCs from domestic firms.

Exhibit 17.1
Searching for the Appropriate Capital Structure

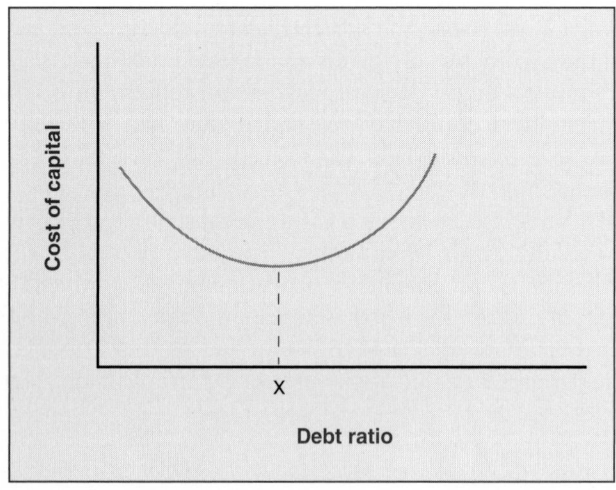

1. *Size of firm.* MNCs that often borrow substantial amounts may be given preferential treatment by creditors, thereby reducing their cost of capital. Furthermore, their relatively large issues of stocks or bonds allow for reduced flotation costs (as a percentage of the amount of financing). Yet, this is due to their size and not to their internationalized business. That is, a domestic corporation may be given the same treatment if it is large enough. However, a firm's growth is more restricted if it is not willing to operate internationally. Because MNCs may more easily achieve growth, they may be more able than purely domestic firms to reach the necessary size to receive preferential treatment from creditors.
2. *Access to international capital markets.* MNCs are normally able to obtain funds through the international capital markets. Since the cost of funds can vary among markets, the MNC's access to the international capital markets may allow it to attract funds at a lower cost than that paid by domestic firms. In addition, subsidiaries may be able to obtain funds locally at a lower cost than that available to the parent if the prevailing interest rates in the host country are relatively low. To illustrate, The Coca-Cola Company's recent annual report stated "Our global presence and strong capital position afford us easy access to key financial markets around the world, enabling us to raise funds with a low effective cost. This posture, coupled with the aggressive management of our mix of short-term and long-term debt, results in a lower overall cost of borrowing."

   The use of foreign funds will not necessarily increase the MNC's exposure to exchange rate risk since the revenues generated by the subsidiary will most likely be denominated in the same currency. In this case, the subsidiary is not relying on the parent for financing, although some centralized managerial support from the parent will most likely still exist.
3. *International diversification.* A firm's cost of capital is affected by the probability that it will go bankrupt. If a firm's cash inflows come from sources all over the world, there might be more stability in cash inflows. This reasoning is based on the premise that total sales will not be highly influenced by a single economy. To the extent that individual economies are independent of each other, net cash flows from a portfolio of subsidiaries should exhibit less variability, which may reduce the probability of bankruptcy and therefore reduce the cost of capital.
4. *Exposure to exchange rate risk.* An MNC's cash flow could be more volatile than that of a domestic firm in the same industry if it is highly exposed to exchange rate risk. If foreign earnings are remitted to the U.S. parent of an MNC, they will not be worth as much when the U.S. dollar is strong against major currencies. Thus, the capability of making interest payments on outstanding debt is reduced, and the probability of bankruptcy is higher. This could force creditors and shareholders to require a higher return, which increases the MNC's cost of capital.

   Overall, a firm more exposed to exchange rate fluctuations will usually have a wider (more dispersed) distribution of possible cash flows in future periods. Since the cost of capital should reflect that possibility, and since the possibility of bankruptcy would be higher if the cash flow expectations were more uncertain, exposure to exchange rate fluctuations could lead to a higher cost of capital.
5. *Exposure to country risk.* An MNC that establishes foreign subsidiaries is subject to the possibility that the host country government may seize the MNC's subsidiary assets. The probability of such an occurrence is influenced by many factors, including the attitude of the host country government and the industry of concern. If assets are seized and fair compensation is not provided, the prob-

ability of the MNC's going bankrupt increases. The higher the percentage of an MNC's assets invested in foreign countries and the higher the overall country risk of operating in these countries, the higher will be the MNC's probability of bankruptcy (and therefore cost of capital), other things being equal.

http://
The Price Waterhouse Coopers Web site at www.pwcglobal.com provides access to country-specific information such as general business rules and regulations, tax environments, and some other useful statistics and surveys.

There are other forms of country risk not as critical as a host government takeover that could affect an MNC subsidiary's cash flows. These less critical types of risk (such as revised tax laws by host country governments, etc.) are not necessarily incorporated within the cash flow projections since there is no reason to believe that they will arise. Yet, because there is a possibility that these events will occur, the capital budgeting process should incorporate such risk. For example, Exxon has much experience in assessing the feasibility of potential projects in foreign countries. If it detects a radical change in government or tax policy, it adds a premium to the required return of related projects. The size of the premium is determined by financial planners and political analysts.

Five factors that may distinguish between the cost of capital for an MNC and that cost for a domestic firm in a particular industry have been assessed and are summarized in Exhibit 17.2. In general, the first three factors listed (size, access to international capital markets, and international diversification) are favorable to an MNC's cost of capital, while exchange rate risk and country risk are unfavorable. It is impossible to generalize on whether MNCs have a cost of capital advantage over domestic firms. Each MNC should be assessed separately to determine whether the net effects of its international operations on the cost of capital are favorable.

Exhibit 17.2
Summary of Factors That Cause the Cost of Capital of MNCs to Differ from That of Domestic Firms

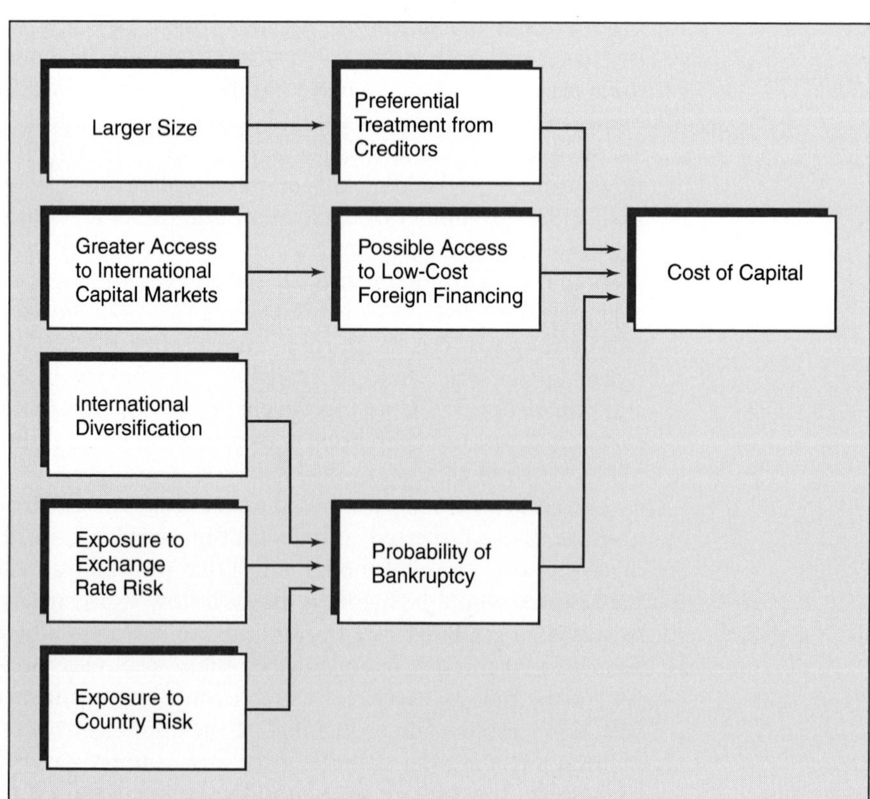

Cost of Capital Comparison Using the CAPM

To assess how required rates of return of MNCs differ from those of purely domestic firms, the capital asset pricing model (CAPM) can be applied. It defines the required return (k_e) on a stock as

$$k_e = R_f + B(R_m - R_f)$$

where

R_f = risk-free rate of return
R_m = market return
B = beta of stock

The CAPM suggests that the required return on a firm's stock is a positive function of (1) the risk-free rate of interest, (2) the market rate of return, and (3) the stock's beta. The beta represents the sensitivity of the stock's returns to market returns (a stock index is normally used as a proxy for the market). An MNC has no control over the risk-free rate of interest or over the market returns, but it may be able to influence its beta. An MNC that increases its amount in foreign sales may be able to reduce its stock's beta and therefore reduce the return required by investors. In this way, it would reduce its cost of capital.

Advocates of the CAPM may suggest that a project's beta could be used to determine the required rate of return for that project. A project's beta represents the sensitivity of the project's cash flow to the market conditions. A project whose cash flow is insulated from market conditions will exhibit a low beta.

For a well-diversified MNC with cash flows generated by several projects, each project contains two types of risk: (1) unsystematic variability in cash flows unique to the firm and (2) systematic risk. Capital asset pricing theory suggests that the unsystematic risk of projects can be ignored since it will be diversified away. However, systematic risk is not diversified away since all projects are similarly affected. The lower a project's beta, the lower is the project's systematic risk and the lower the required rate of return for such a project. If projects of MNCs exhibit lower betas than projects of purely domestic firms, then the required rates of return on MNC projects should be lower. This translates into a lower overall cost of capital.

Capital asset pricing theory would most likely suggest that the MNC cost of capital is generally lower than that of domestic firms, due to the reasoning just presented. It should be emphasized, though, that unsystematic project risk is considered to be relevant by some MNCs. And if it is also considered within the assessment of a project's risk, the required rate of return will not necessarily be lower for MNC projects than projects of domestic firms. In fact, a large project in a less developed country with very volatile economic conditions and a high degree of country risk would be perceived as being very risky by many MNCs, even if the expected cash flows of this project were uncorrelated with the U.S. market. This implies that MNCs may consider unsystematic risk as an important factor when determining a foreign project's required rate of return.

When assuming that financial markets are segmented, it is acceptable to use the U.S. market when measuring a U.S.-based MNC's project beta. If U.S. investors invest mostly in the United States, their investments are systematically affected by the U.S. market. MNCs that adopt projects with low betas may be able to reduce their own betas (the sensitivity of their stock returns to market returns). Such firms are desirable to U.S. investors because they offer more diversification benefits as a result of having low betas.

Since markets are becoming more integrated over time, one could argue that a world market is more appropriate than a U.S. market for determining the beta of U.S.-based MNCs. That is, if investors purchased stocks across many countries, their stocks would be substantially affected by world market conditions, not just U.S. market conditions. Consequently, they would prefer to invest in firms that had low sensitivity to world market conditions to achieve more diversification benefits. MNCs that could adopt projects that were somewhat isolated from world market conditions might be able to reduce their overall sensitivity to these conditions and could be viewed as desirable investments by investors.

While markets are becoming more integrated, U.S. investors still tend to focus on U.S. stocks and to capitalize on lower transaction and information costs. Thus, their investments are systematically affected by U.S. market conditions; this causes them to be most concerned about the sensitivity of investments to the U.S. market.

In summary, we cannot say with certainty whether an MNC will have a lower cost of capital than a purely domestic firm in the same industry. However, we can use this discussion to understand how an MNC may attempt to take full advantage of the favorable aspects that reduce its cost of capital, while minimizing exposure to the unfavorable aspects that increase its cost of capital.

Costs of Capital Across Countries

An understanding of why the cost of capital can vary among countries is relevant for three reasons. First, it can explain why MNCs based in some countries may have a competitive advantage over others. Just as there are differences in technology or resources across countries, there are differences in the cost of capital, which can allow some MNCs to more easily increase their world market share. Second, MNCs may be able to adjust their international operations and sources of funds to capitalize on differences in the cost of capital among countries. Third, an understanding of differences in the costs of each capital component (debt and equity) can help explain why MNCs based in some countries tend to use a more debt-intensive capital structure than MNCs based elsewhere. Country differences in the cost of debt are described first, followed by country differences in the cost of equity.

Country Differences in the Cost of Debt

The cost of debt to a firm is primarily determined by the prevailing risk-free interest rate in the currency borrowed and the risk premium required by creditors. The cost of debt for firms is higher in some countries than in others because the corresponding risk-free rate is higher at a specific point in time, or because the risk premium is higher. Explanations for country differences in the risk-free rate and in the risk premium follow.

Differences in the Risk-Free Rate. The risk-free rate is determined by the interaction of the supply and demand for funds. Any factors that influence the supply and/or demand will affect the risk-free rate. Some of the factors that have such an influence and vary among countries are tax laws, demographics, monetary policies, and economic conditions.

http://
Visit www.bloomberg.com for the latest information from financial markets around the world.

Tax laws in some countries offer more incentives to save than those in others, which can influence the supply of savings, and therefore, interest rates. A country's corporate tax laws related to depreciation and investment tax credits can also affect interest rates through their influence on the corporate demand for funds.

The demographics of a country influence the supply of savings available and the amount of loanable funds demanded. Since demographics differ among countries, so will supply and demand conditions and, therefore, nominal interest rates. Countries with younger populations are likely to experience higher interest rates since younger households tend to save less and borrow more.

The monetary policy implemented by each country's central bank influences the supply of loanable funds and therefore influences interest rates. Countries that use a loose money policy (high money supply growth) may achieve lower nominal interest rates if they can maintain a low rate of inflation. Some theories suggest that a loose money policy will cause higher interest rates by raising inflationary expectations and the demand for loanable funds. The point here is that regardless of how a monetary policy affects interest rates, each central bank implements its own monetary policy, and this can cause differences in interest rates among countries.

Since economic conditions influence interest rates, they can cause interest rates to vary across countries. However, several European countries that have adopted the euro as their currency now have the same risk-free interest rate. The cost of debt in many less developed countries is much higher than that cost in industrialized countries, primarily because of economic conditions. The high expected rate of inflation causes creditors to require a high risk-free interest rate.

Differences in the Risk Premium. The risk premium on debt must be large enough to compensate creditors for the risk that the borrower may be unable to meet its payment obligations. This risk can vary among countries because of differences in economic conditions, relationships between corporations and creditors, government intervention, and degree of financial leverage.

http://
Morgan Stanley's Economic Forum at www.ms.com/GEF provides analysis, discussions, statistics, and forecasts related to non-U.S. economies.

If economic conditions in a particular country tend to be more stable, the risk of a recession is relatively low. Thus, the probability that a firm might not meet its obligations is lower, allowing for a lower risk premium.

Relationships between corporations and creditors are closer in some countries than in others. In Japan, creditors stand ready to extend credit in the event of a corporation's financial distress, which reduces the risk of illiquidity. The cost of a Japanese firm's financial problems may be shared in various ways by the firm's management, business customers, and consumers. Since the financial problems are not borne entirely by creditors, there is more motivation for all parties involved to see that the problems are resolved. Thus, there is less likelihood (for a given level of debt) that Japanese firms will go bankrupt, which implies a lower risk premium on the debt of Japanese firms.

Governments in some countries are more willing to intervene and rescue failing firms. For example, in the United Kingdom many firms are partially owned by the government. It may be in the best interest of the government to rescue firms that it partially owns. Even if the government is not a partial owner, it may provide direct subsidies or extend loans to failing firms. In the United States, government rescues are not as well received, since taxpayers prefer not to bear the cost of corporate mismanagement. While there has been some government intervention in the United States to protect particular industries, the probability that a failing firm might be rescued by the government is lower there than in other countries. Therefore, the risk premium on a given level of debt would be higher for U.S. firms than for firms of other countries.

Firms in some countries have greater borrowing capacity because their creditors are willing to tolerate a higher degree of financial leverage. For example, firms in Japan and Germany have a higher degree of financial leverage than firms in the United States. If all other factors were equal, these high-leverage firms would have to pay a higher risk premium. However, all other factors are not equal. In fact, these firms are allowed to use a higher degree of financial leverage because of their unique relationships with the creditors and governments.

Comparative Costs of Debt Across Countries. The before-tax cost of debt (as measured by corporate bond yields) for various countries is displayed in Exhibit 17.3.

Exhibit 17.3
Costs of Debt Across Countries

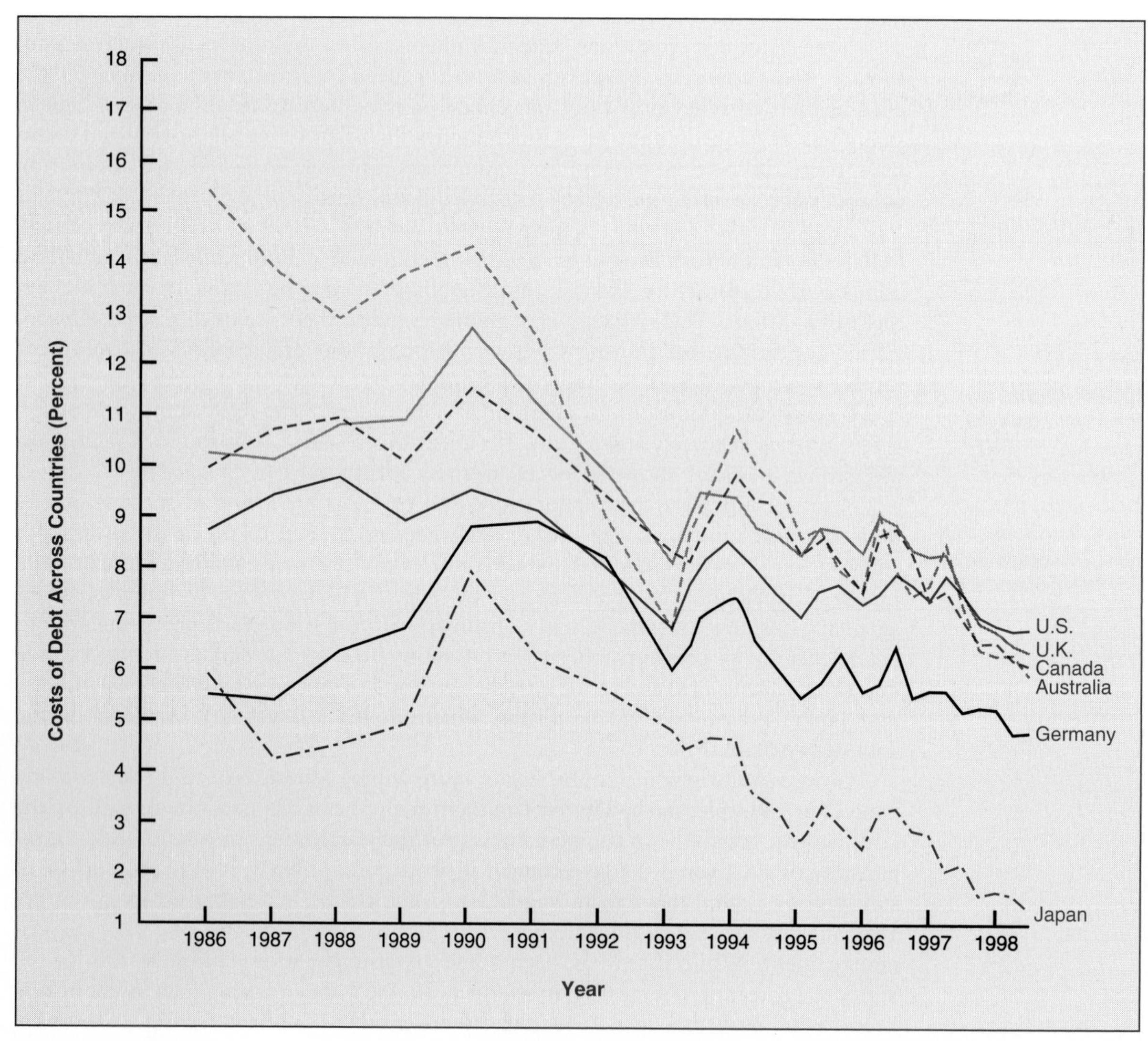

There is some positive correlation between country cost-of-debt levels over time. The nominal cost of debt for firms in many countries declined in the early 1990s during a global recession and then increased in the mid-1990s, before declining again in the late 1990s. The disparity in the cost of debt among the countries is due primarily to the disparity in their risk-free interest rates.

MNCs operating in countries with a high cost of capital will be forced to decline projects that might be feasible for MNCs operating in countries with a low cost of capital. In addition, MNCs in countries with a high cost of debt may be more likely to divest existing projects because of the high cost associated with funding them. As an example, Lloyds Bank of the United Kingdom decided to sell its U.S. commercial bank operations because the returns were not adequate, and it could do just as well by investing the funds in British money markets. If its cost of capital had been lower, Lloyds Bank might have retained this project.

Country Differences in the Cost of Equity

A country's cost of equity represents an opportunity cost: what shareholders could earn on investments with similar risk if the equity funds were distributed to them. This return on equity can be measured as a risk-free interest rate that could have been earned by shareholders, plus a premium to reflect the risk of the firm. Since risk-free interest rates vary among countries, the costs of equity can vary distinctly among countries.

The cost of equity is also based on investment opportunities in the country of concern. In a country with many investment opportunities, potential returns may be relatively high, resulting in a high opportunity cost of funds and, therefore, a high cost of capital. According to McCauley and Zimmer, a country's cost of equity can be estimated by first applying the price/earnings multiple to a given stream of earnings.[1]

The price/earnings multiple is related to the cost of capital because it reflects the share price of the firm in proportion to the firm's performance (as measured by earnings). A high price/earnings multiple implies that the firm receives a high price when selling new stock for a given level of earnings, which means that the cost of equity financing is low. However, adjustments to the price/earnings multiples must be made for the effects of a country's inflation, earnings growth, and other factors.

Combining the Costs of Debt and Equity

The costs of debt and equity can be combined to derive an overall cost of capital. The relative proportions of debt and equity used by firms in each country must be applied as weights to reasonably estimate this cost of capital. Given the differences in the costs of debt across countries and the differences in the costs of equity across countries, it is understandable that the cost of capital may be lower for firms based in specific countries. Japan has commonly been cited as having a relatively low cost of capital. It usually has a relatively low risk-free interest rate, which not only affects the cost of debt but also indirectly affects the cost of equity. In addition, the price/earnings multiples of Japanese firms are usually high, which allows Japanese firms to

[1]Robert N. McCauley and Steven A. Zimmer, "Explaining International Differences in the Cost of Capital," *FRBNY Quarterly Review* (Summer 1989), pp. 7–28.

Nike Problem

Effect of International Operations on the Cost of Capital

Nike has substantial operations in Japan, and it uses yen-denominated bonds to support these operations. It recently issued yen-denominated bonds that have a value equivalent to about $100 million. The use of yen-denominated bonds is desirable because the interest rate on yen-denominated debt instruments is very low. In addition, the yen-denominated bonds create an interest expense each year that can be offset by a portion of the revenue. This reduces the amount of yen that will ultimately have to be converted into dollars as funds are remitted to the parent, and therefore reduces Nike's exposure to exchange rate risk.

Discussion: If Nike decides to expand further in South America, why might its capital structure be affected? Why will its overall cost of capital be affected?

obtain equity funding at a relatively low cost. MNCs can attempt to access capital from countries where capital costs are low, but when the capital is used to support operations in other countries, the MNCs are usually exposed to exchange rate risk. Thus, the cost of capital may ultimately turn out to be higher than expected.

Using the Cost of Capital for Assessing Foreign Projects

When an MNC's parent proposes an investment in a foreign project that has the same risk as the MNC itself, it can use its weighted average cost of capital as the required rate of return for the project. However, many foreign projects may exhibit different risk levels than those of the MNCs. There are various ways for an MNC to account for the risk differential in its capital budgeting process. First, it can account for the risk within its cash flow estimates. Many possible values for each input variable (such as demand, price, labor cost, etc.) can be incorporated to estimate net present values (*NPV*s) under alternative scenarios and then derive a probability distribution of net present values (*NPV*s). When the weighted average cost of capital is used as the required rate of return, the probability distribution of *NPV*s can be assessed to determine the probability that the foreign project will generate a return that is at least equal to the firm's weighted average cost of capital. If the project exhibits much risk, an area of the probability distribution will reflect negative *NPV*s, which suggests that the project could backfire. This is a useful method to use in accounting for risk because it explicitly incorporates the various possible scenarios in the *NPV* estimation and therefore can measure the probability that a project may backfire. Computer software programs that perform sensitivity analysis and simulation can be used to facilitate the process.

An alternative method of accounting for a foreign project's risk is to adjust the firm's weighted average cost of capital for the risk differential. For example, if the foreign project was thought to exhibit more risk than the MNC exhibits, a premium could be added to the weighted average cost of capital to derive the required rate of return on the project. Then, the capital budgeting process would incorporate this required rate of return as the discount rate. If the foreign project exhibited lower risk, the MNC would use a required rate of return on the project that was less than its weighted average cost of capital.

This method is easy to use, but there is no perfect formula to adjust for the project's unique risk. Yet, some logic could be used to derive a reasonable risk adjustment. Recall that the weighted average cost of capital is simply the weighted average cost of equity plus the weighted average after-tax cost of debt. The MNC's parent could estimate its cost of equity and the after-tax cost of debt on the funds to be obtained to finance the foreign project. The after-tax cost of debt can be estimated with reasonable accuracy since there is public information on the present costs of debt (bond yields) incurred by other firms whose risk level is similar to the foreign project. Recall that the cost of equity is an opportunity cost: what investors could earn on alternative equity investments with similar risk. The MNC could attempt to measure the expected return on a set of stocks that exhibited the same risk as its foreign project. This expected return could serve as the cost of equity. The required rate of return on the project would be the project's weighted cost of capital, based on the estimates explained here.

The MNC's Capital Structure Decision

An MNC's capital structure decision involves the choice of debt versus equity financing within all of its subsidiaries. Thus, its overall capital structure is essentially a combination of all of its subsidiary capital structures. MNCs recognize the trade-off between using debt and using equity for financing their operations. The advantages of using debt as opposed to equity vary with corporate characteristics specific to the MNCs themselves and specific to the countries where the MNCs have established subsidiaries. Some of the more relevant corporate characteristics specific to the MNC that can affect the MNC's capital structure are identified first, followed by country characteristics.

http://
Visit www.worldbank.org for country profiles, analyses, and sectoral surveys.

Influence of Corporate Characteristics

Characteristics unique to each MNC can influence its capital structure. Some of the more common firm-specific characteristics that affect the MNC's capital structure are identified here.

Stability of MNC's Cash Flows. MNCs with more stable cash flows can handle more debt because there is a constant stream of cash inflows to cover periodic interest payments. Conversely, MNCs with erratic cash flows may prefer less debt because they are not assured of generating enough cash in each period to make larger interest payments on debt. MNCs that are diversified across several countries may have more stable cash flows since the conditions in any single country should not have a major impact on their cash flows. Consequently, these MNCs may be able to handle a more debt-intensive capital structure.

MNC's Credit Risk. MNCs that have lower credit risk (risk of default on loans provided by creditors) have more access to credit. Any factors that influence credit risk can affect an MNC's choice of using debt versus equity. For example, if an MNC's management is thought to be strong and competent, its credit risk may be low, which allows for easier access to debt. MNCs with assets that serve as acceptable collateral (such as buildings, trucks, and adaptable machinery) are more able to obtain loans and may prefer to emphasize debt financing. Conversely, MNCs with assets that are not marketable have less acceptable collateral and may need to use a higher proportion of equity financing.

MNC's Access to Retained Earnings. MNCs that are more profitable may be able to finance most of their investment with retained earnings and therefore use an equity-intensive capital structure. Conversely, MNCs that have small levels of retained earnings may rely on debt financing. Growth-oriented MNCs are less able to finance their expansion with retained earnings and tend to rely on debt financing. Yet, MNCs with less growth need less new financing and may rely on retained earnings (equity) rather than debt.

MNC's Guarantees on Debt. If the parent backs the debt of the subsidiary, the subsidiary's borrowing capacity might be increased. Therefore, the subsidiary might need less equity financing. Yet the borrowing capacity of the parent might be reduced, as creditors are not willing to provide as many funds to the parent if those funds may possibly be needed to rescue a parent's subsidiary.

MNC's Agency Problems. If the subsidiary in a host country cannot easily be monitored by investors from the parent's country, agency costs are higher. The subsidiary in a host country may be induced by the parent to issue stock rather than debt in the local market, so that the managers there are monitored to ensure maximization of the firm's stock price. In this case, the foreign subsidiary is referred to as "partially owned" rather than "wholly owned" by the MNC's parent. This strategy can affect the MNC's capital structure. It may be feasible when the MNC's parent can enhance the subsidiary's image and presence in the host country or can motivate the subsidiary's managers by allowing them partial ownership.

One concern about a partially owned foreign subsidiary is a potential conflict of interest, especially when its managers are minority shareholders. These managers may make decisions that can benefit the subsidiary at the expense of the MNC overall. For example, they may use funds for projects that are feasible from their perspective but not from the parent's perspective.

Influence of Country Characteristics

In addition to characteristics unique to each MNC, the characteristics unique to each host country can influence the MNC's choice of debt versus equity financing and therefore influence the MNC's capital structure. Specific country characteristics that can influence an MNC's choice of equity versus debt financing are described here.

Stock Restrictions in Host Countries. Investors in some countries are restricted by their governments to invest in local stocks. Even when investors are allowed to invest in other countries, they may not have complete information about stocks of companies outside their home countries. This represents an implicit barrier to cross-border investing. Furthermore, potential adverse exchange rate effects and tax effects could discourage investors from investing outside their home countries. The impediments to worldwide investing can cause some investors to have fewer stock investment opportunities than others. Consequently, an MNC operating in countries where investors have fewer investment opportunities may be able to raise equity in those countries at a relatively low cost. This could entice the MNC to use more equity by issuing stock in these countries to finance its operations.

Interest Rates in Host Countries. Because of government-imposed barriers on capital flows along with potential adverse exchange rate, tax, and country risk effects, loanable funds do not always flow to where they are needed most. Thus, the price of loanable funds (the interest rate) can vary across countries. MNCs may be able to obtain loanable funds (debt) at a relatively low cost in specific countries, while the cost of debt in other countries may be very high. Consequently, an MNC's preference for debt may depend on the costs of debt in the countries where it operates. If markets were somewhat segmented and the cost of funds in the subsidiary's country appeared excessive, the parent might use its own equity to support projects implemented by the subsidiary.

Strength of Host Country Currencies. If an MNC is concerned about the potential weakness of currencies used in foreign countries, it may attempt to finance a large proportion of its foreign operations by borrowing those currencies instead of relying on parent funds. In this way, the amount in earnings to be remitted periodically by the subsidiaries would be smaller because of interest payments on local debt. This strategy reduces the MNC's exposure to exchange rate risk.

If the parent believed that the subsidiary's local currency would appreciate against the parent's currency, it might prefer that the subsidiary retain and reinvest more of its earnings. The parent might provide an immediate cash infusion to finance growth in the subsidiary. As a result, there would be a transfer of internal funds from the parent to the subsidiary, which would possibly cause more external financing by the parent and less debt financing by the subsidiary.

Country Risk in Host Countries. A relatively mild form of country risk is the possibility that the host government will temporarily block funds to be remitted by the subsidiary to the parent. Subsidiaries that are prevented from remitting earnings over a period may prefer to use local debt financing. This strategy would reduce the amount in funds to be blocked because interest would need to be paid on local debt.

If an MNC's subsidiary is exposed to risk that a host government might confiscate the assets, it may use much debt financing in that host country. The local creditors that have lent funds to the MNC have a genuine interest in ensuring that the MNC be treated fairly by the host government. In addition, if the MNC's operations in a foreign country are terminated by the host government, it will not lose as much if its operations are financed by local creditors. Under these circumstances, the local creditors will have to negotiate with the host government to obtain all or part of the funds they have lent after the host government liquidates the assets it confiscates from the MNC.

A less likely alternative to reducing exposure to a high degree of country risk is for the subsidiary to issue stock within the host country. Minority shareholders benefit directly from a profitable subsidiary. Therefore, they could pressure their government to refrain from imposing excessive taxes, environmental constraints, or any other provisions that would reduce the profits of the subsidiary. A minority interest in a subsidiary by local investors may offer some protection against threats of any adverse actions by the host government. Another advantage of a partially owned subsidiary is that it may open up additional opportunities within the host country. The subsidiary's name may spread as a result of shares placed with minority shareholders in that country.

Tax Laws in Host Countries. Foreign subsidiaries of an MNC may be subject to a withholding tax when they remit earnings. By using local debt financing instead of relying on parent financing, they may be able to reduce the amount that is to be remitted periodically, as they would make interest payments on the local debt. Thus, they may reduce the withholding taxes by using more local debt financing. Foreign subsidiaries may also consider the use of local debt if high corporate tax rates are imposed by the host governments on foreign earnings in order to benefit from the tax advantage of using debt where taxes are high (unless the higher amount of taxes paid would be fully offset by tax credits received by the parent).

In recent years, MNCs have restructured their capital structures to reduce their withholding taxes on remitted earnings by subsidiaries. To illustrate, consider the following example, which is a typical situation for many MNCs. Clayton Inc. is a U.S.-based MNC whose parent plans to raise $50 million of capital in the United States by issuing stock in the United States. The parent plans to convert the $50 million into 70 million Australian dollars and use the funds to build a subsidiary in Australia. Since the parent may need some return on this capital to pay its shareholders' dividends, it would require that its Australian subsidiary remit A$2 million per year. Assume that the Australian government would impose a withholding tax of 10 percent on the remitted earnings, which is A$200,000 per year. There are several different ways in which Clayton Inc. can revise its capital structure to reduce or avoid these taxes. Most solutions involve reducing the reliance of the subsidiary on the parent's capital.

First, Clayton's Australian subsidiary could borrow funds in Australia as its main source of capital instead of relying on the U.S. parent. Thus, it would use some of its earnings to pay its local creditors interest instead of remitting a large amount of earnings to the U.S parent. This financing strategy minimizes the amount of funds that would be remitted and can therefore minimize the withholding taxes that would be paid to the Australian government . In addition, the subsidiary would not need as much equity investment from the parent. One limitation of this strategy is that Clayton's subsidiary may have increased its debt to an excessive level.

If Clayton Inc. preferred not to increase its debt, its subsidiary could have raised funds by issuing stock in the host country. In this case, the subsidiary would use a portion of its funds to pay dividends to local shareholders rather than remit those funds to the parent. Once again, withholding taxes are minimized because the subsidiary would not remit much money to the parent. The issuance of the stock by the subsidiary allows a minority ownership of the subsidiary in Australia and could cause a reduction in the parent's control over the subsidiary. However, the parent would still retain control over the subsidiary if it instructed the subsidiary to issue nonvoting stock.

Each of these strategies by Clayton Inc. minimizes the withholding tax, but the first strategy reflects a more debt-intensive capital structure while the second strategy reflects a more equity-intensive capital structure. The two strategies are illustrated in Exhibit 17.4. These strategies could have also been used to reduce the exposure of the MNC to exchange rate risk because they minimize the amount of Australian dollars that will be converted into U.S. dollars.

Exhibit 17.4
Adjusting the Multinational Capital Structure to Reduce Withholding Taxes

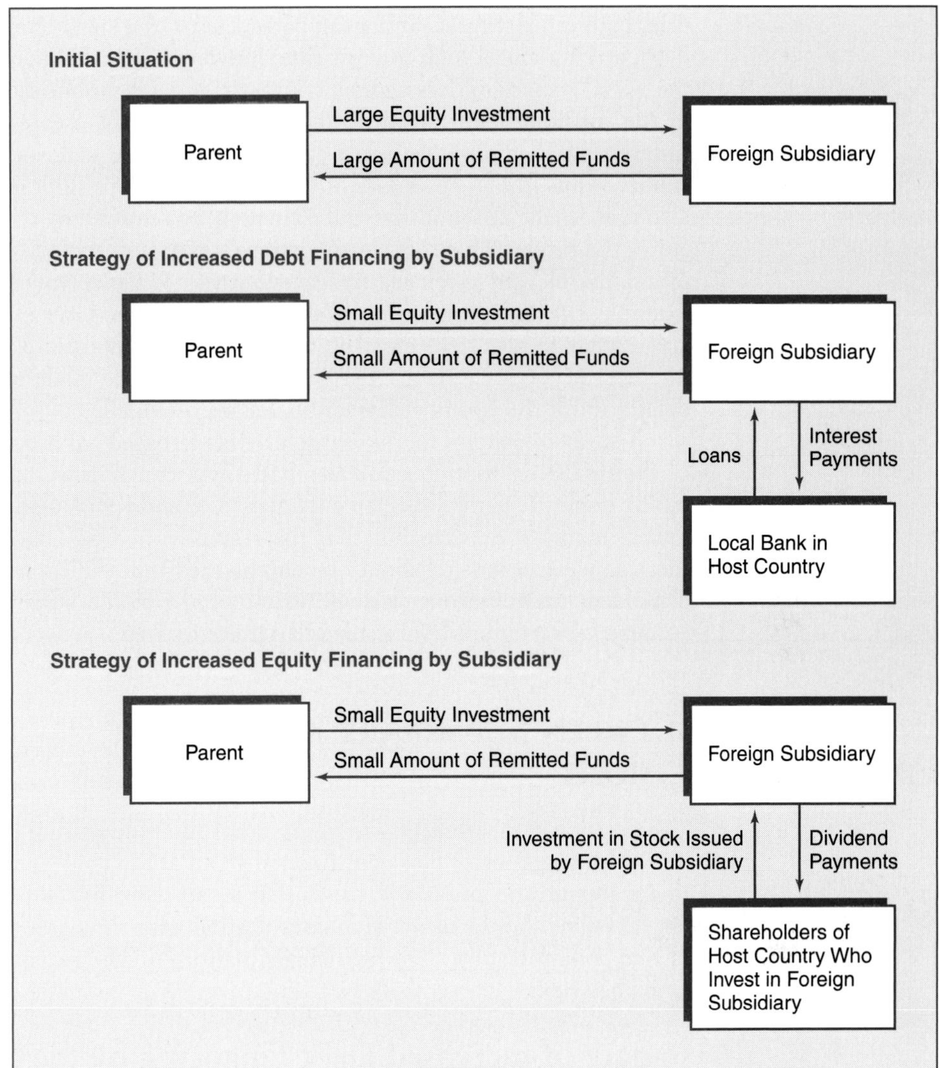

Summary of Characteristics That Affect an MNC's Capital Structure

Overall, MNCs may prefer to use a more debt-intensive capital structure when they exhibit characteristics such as stable cash flows, low credit risk, and limited access to retained earnings. Furthermore, MNCs prefer that their subsidiaries use a more debt-intensive capital structure when their subsidiaries are subject to (1) low local interest rates, (2) potentially weak local currencies, (3) a high degree of country risk, and (4) high taxes. Since the characteristics vary among host countries, some of an MNC's subsidiaries may benefit from a high degree of financial leverage, while others may not.

In some cases, the subsidiary may be located in a host country that creates some advantages for debt financing along with some advantages for internal equity financing by the subsidiary. Consider a U.S.-based MNC that has a large subsidiary in a Latin American country. Historically, Latin American countries have had high inflation, high interest rates, and weak currencies. If the subsidiary is financed with local debt, it will incur a high interest rate. However, debt financing would help insulate the MNC's shareholders against country risk, as it minimizes the equity investment in the subsidiary. In addition, the use of local debt creates future cash outflows (interest payments) in the same currency as its cash inflows generated by the subsidiary. Thus, the use of debt not only minimizes the equity investment required but also reduces the amount that will ultimately be remitted by the subsidiary to the parent in the future. This reduces the parent's exposure to exchange rate risk, which is especially relevant given the typical weakness of Latin American currencies. In this example, the advantages of local debt financing (it reduces exposure to country risk and exchange rate risk) must be weighed against the disadvantage (there is a high interest rate on local debt). The final decision can be made only after more specific details about the country characteristics are provided.

A study by Fatemi found that selected U.S.-based MNCs with at least 25 percent of their sales in foreign countries had significantly lower financial leverage than purely domestic firms.[2] A related study by Lee and Kwok also found that MNCs had lower financial leverage but that the results varied among industries.[3] Even with these generalizations, it should be emphasized that the capital structure decision is dependent on numerous characteristics specific to the individual MNC and to the countries where the MNC's subsidiaries are located.

Interaction between Subsidiary and Parent Financing Decisions

The decision by a subsidiary to use internal equity financing (retaining and reinvesting its earnings) or obtain debt financing can affect its degree of reliance on parent financing and the amount of funds that it can remit to the parent. Thus, its financing decisions should be made in consultation with the parent. The potential impact of two common subsidiary financing situations on the parent's capital structure are explained next.

Impact of Increased Debt Financing by the Subsidiary

When global conditions increase the debt financing of the subsidiary, the amount of internal equity financing needed by the subsidiary is reduced. As these extra internal funds are remitted to the parent, the parent will have a larger amount of internal funds for financing before it resorts to external financing. Assuming that the parent's operations absorb all internal funds and require some debt financing, there are offsetting effects on the capital structures of the subsidiary and the parent. The increased use of debt financing by the subsidiary is offset by the reduced debt financing of the parent. Yet, the cost of capital for the MNC overall could have changed for two reasons. First, the revised composition of debt financing (more by the subsidiary, less by the parent) could affect the interest charged on the debt. Second, it

[2]Ali M. Fatemi, "The Effect of International Diversification on Corporate Financing Policy," *Journal of Business Research* (January 1988), pp. 17–30.

[3]Kwang Chul Lee and Chuck C. Y. Kwok, "Multinational Corporations vs. Domestic Corporations: International Environmental Factors and Determinants of Capital Structure," *Journal of International Business Studies* (Summer 1988), pp. 195–217.

could affect the MNC's overall exposure to exchange rate risk and therefore influence the risk premium on capital.

There are situations in which the increased use of debt financing of the subsidiary will not be offset by reduced debt financing of the parent. For example, if there are any restrictions or excessive taxes on remitted funds, the parent may not be able to rely on the subsidiary and may need some debt financing as well. In this case, international conditions that encourage increased use of debt financing by the subsidiary will result in a more debt-intensive capital structure for the MNC. Again, the cost of capital to the MNC could be affected by the subsidiary's increased debt financing, for reasons already mentioned. Yet, an additional reason here is the use of a higher proportion of debt financing for the MNC overall.

Impact of Reduced Debt Financing by the Subsidiary

When global conditions encourage the subsidiary to use less debt financing, the subsidiary will need to use more internal financing. Consequently, it will remit fewer funds to the parent, reducing the amount of internal funds available to the parent. If the parent's operations absorb all internal funds and require some debt financing, there are offsetting effects on the capital structures of the subsidiary and parent. The reduction in debt financing of the subsidiary is offset by the increased use of debt financing of the parent. The cost of capital may change even if the MNC's overall capital structure does not, for reasons expressed earlier.

If the parent's operations can be fully financed with internal funds, the parent will not use debt financing. Thus, the reduction in debt financing of the subsidiary is not offset by increased debt financing of the parent, and the MNC's overall capital structure becomes more equity-intensive.

Summary of Interaction between Subsidiary and Parent Financing Decisions

Exhibit 17.5 provides a summary of some of the more relevant characteristics of the host country that can affect a subsidiary's preference for debt or equity financing. The decision by a subsidiary to finance with local debt affects the amount of funds

Exhibit 17.5
Effect of Global Conditions on Financing

Host Country Conditions	Amount of Local Debt Financing by Subsidiary	Amount of Internal Funds Available to Parent	Amount of Debt Financing Provided by Parent
Higher Country Risk in Host Country	Higher	Higher	Lower
Higher Interest Rates in Host Country	Lower	Lower	Higher
Lower Interest Rates in Host Country	Higher	Higher	Lower
Expected Weakness of Host Country Currency	Higher	Higher	Lower
Expected Strength of Host Country Currency	Lower	Lower	Higher
Blocked Funds Imposed by Host Government	Higher	Higher	Lower
High Withholding Taxes Imposed by Host Government	Higher	Higher	Lower
Higher Corporate Taxes Imposed by Host Government	Higher	Higher	Lower

remitted to the parent and therefore affects the amount of internal financing available to the parent. Since the subsidiary's local debt financing decisions are influenced by country-specific characteristics like those shown in Exhibit 17.5, the MNC's overall capital structure is partially influenced by the locations of the foreign subsidiaries.

Using a Target Capital Structure on a Local versus Global Basis

An MNC may deviate from its "local" target capital structure in each country where financing is obtained, yet still achieve its "global" target capital structure (based on consolidating the capital structures of all its subsidiaries). The following examples of particular foreign country conditions illustrate the motive behind deviating from a local target capital structure while still satisfying a global target capital structure.

Offsetting a Subsidiary's High Degree of Financial Leverage

First, consider that Country A does not allow MNCs with headquarters elsewhere to list their stocks on its local stock exchange. Under these conditions, an MNC's subsidiary that desired to expand its operations would likely decide to borrow funds through bond issuance or bank loans rather than by issuing stock in this country. By being forced to use debt financing here, the MNC might deviate from its target capital structure, which could raise its overall cost of capital. The parent might offset this concentration in debt by using more equity financing for its own operations.

As a second example, consider an MNC that desires financing in Country B, which is experiencing political turmoil. The use of local bank loans would be most appropriate since local banks may be able to prevent the subsidiary's operations in that country from being affected by any political conditions. If the local banks serve as creditors to the MNC's subsidiary, it is in their interest to ensure that the subsidiary's operations are sufficiently profitable to repay its loans. Since the subsidiary may have more financial leverage than what is desired for the MNC overall, the parent may use less financial leverage to finance its own operations in order to achieve the overall ("global") target capital structure.

Offsetting a Subsidiary's Low Degree of Financial Leverage

Consider an example in which Country C allows the MNC's subsidiary to issue stock there and list its stock on its local exchange. Also assume that the project to be implemented in that country will not generate net cash flows for five years, thereby limiting the ability of the subsidiary to generate internal financing. In this case, equity financing by the subsidiary may be more appropriate. The MNC's subsidiary could issue stock and, by paying low or zero dividends, it could avoid any major cash outflows for the next five years. The parent might offset the subsidiary's concentration in equity by instructing one of its other foreign subsidiaries in some other host country to use mostly debt financing. Alternatively, the parent could use more debt financing to support its own operations.

Limitations in Offsetting a Subsidiary's Abnormal Degree of Financial Leverage

The examples provided up to this point suggest that the parent can adjust the way in which it finances its own operations in order to offset the imbalance that could be created by a foreign subsidiary. However, the revision of the parent's capital structure may result in a higher cost of capital for the parent. Given that the subsidiary's financing decision could possibly affect the parent's capital structure and therefore affect the parent's cost of capital, the subsidiary must be aware of the impact of its decision on the parent. The decision by the subsidiary to use an unusually high or low degree of financial leverage should only be made if the benefits outweigh any costs for the MNC overall.

The strategy of ignoring a "local" target capital structure in favor of a "global" target capital structure is rational as long as it is acceptable by foreign creditors and investors. However, if foreign creditors and investors monitor each subsidiary's local capital structure, they may require a higher rate of return on funds provided to the MNC. For example, the "local" target capital structures for the subsidiaries based in Country A (from the earlier example) and in Country B are debt-intensive. Creditors in these two countries may penalize the subsidiary for its highly leveraged local capital structure, even though the MNC's global capital structure is more balanced, because they believe that the subsidiary may be unable to meet its high debt repayment levels. However, it the parent plans to back the subsidiaries, it could guarantee debt repayment to the creditors in the foreign countries, which might reduce the risk perception and lower the cost of the debt. Many MNC parents stand ready to financially back their subsidiaries since, if they did not, their subsidiaries would be unable to obtain adequate financing.

Capital Structures across Countries

Firms in Japan and Germany have used a much higher degree of financial leverage (on average) than have firms in the United States or the United Kingdom. However, the probability of bankruptcy may generally be lower for MNCs in other countries, since their respective governments may rescue them. Furthermore, banks in Japan and Germany commonly serve as creditors and large shareholders of firms and have a vested interest in rescuing these firms.

Impact of an MNC's Capital Structure Decisions on Its Value

An MNC's capital structure decisions affect its value, as shown in Exhibit 17.6. In general, the capital structure decisions of an MNC involve the mix of debt and equity to use for financing its businesses. Its choice of equity instead of debt reduces the perceived risk of the MNC, but it also dilutes the ownership of the MNC.

When an MNC's parent uses equity to provide most of the financing for foreign subsidiaries, this is initiated with a large cash outflow from the parent to the foreign subsidiaries. Equity financing by the parent typically increases the expected amount

Exhibit 17.6
Impact of Multinational Capital Structure Decisions on an MNC's Value

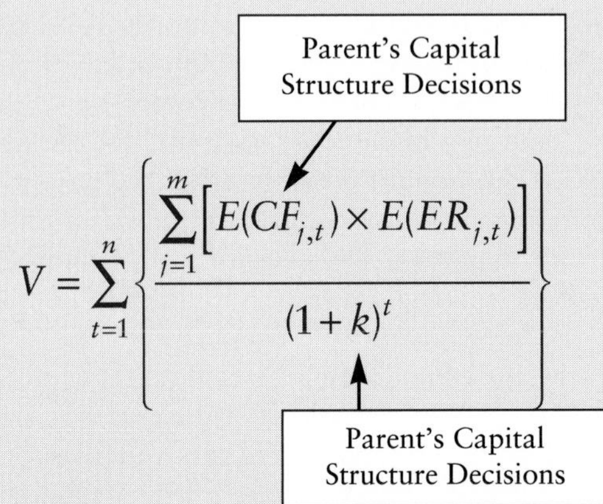

V = value of the U.S.-based MNC
$E(CF_{j,t})$ = expected cash flows denominated in currency j to be received by the U.S. parent in period t
$E(ER_{j,t})$ = expected exchange rate at which currency j can be converted to dollars at the end of period t
k = the weighted average cost of capital of the U.S. parent company
m = number of currencies
n = number of periods

of foreign currency cash flows that can be remitted by foreign subsidiaries to the parent because it reduces the need for the foreign subsidiaries to borrow funds.

Alternatively, when a foreign subsidiary uses local debt to finance most of its operations, there will be less cash flow remitted on a periodic basis to the parent because the interest payments on debt are made by the subsidiary before remitting cash flows to the parent. While this reduces the amount of foreign cash flows received by the parent, it also reduces the amount of foreign cash flows that have to be converted to dollars and therefore reduces the exposure to exchange rate risk. In addition, the local financing by subsidiaries requires less financial support from the parent. The parent must consider the tradeoff described here when determining whether its provision of equity financing for its foreign subsidiaries would enhance the MNC's overall value.

SUMMARY

- The cost of capital may be lower for an MNC than for a domestic firm because of characteristics peculiar to the MNC, including its size, access to international capital markets, and its degree of international diversification. Yet, there are some characteristics peculiar to an MNC that can increase the MNC's cost of capital, such as exposure to exchange rate risk and to country risk.
- Costs of capital vary across countries because of country differences in the components that comprise the cost of capital. Specifically, there are differences in the risk-free rate, the risk premium on debt, and the cost of equity among countries. Countries with a higher risk-free rate tend to exhibit a higher cost of capital.
- The MNC's capital structure decision is influenced by corporate characteristics such as the

stability of the MNC's cash flows, the MNC's credit risk, and the MNC's access to earnings. It also is influenced by characteristics of the countries where it conducts business, such as stock restrictions, interest rates, strength of local currencies, country risk, and tax laws. Some characteristics favor an equity-intensive capital structure because they discourage the use of debt. Other characteristics favor a debt-intensive structure because of the desire to protect against risks by creating foreign debt. Given that the relative costs of capital components vary among countries, the MNC's capital structure may be dependent on the specific mix of countries in which it conducts its operations.

SELF-TEST FOR CHAPTER 17

(Answers are provided in Appendix A at the back of the text.)

1. When Goshen Inc. focused only on domestic business in the United States, it had a low debt level. As it expanded into other countries, it increased its degree of financial leverage (on a consolidated basis). What factors would have caused Goshen to increase its financial leverage (assuming that country risk was not a concern)?
2. Lynde Co. is a U.S.-based MNC with a large subsidiary in the Philippines financed with equity from the parent. In response to news about possible turnover in the Philippine government, the subsidiary revised its capital structure by borrowing from local banks and transferring the equity investment back to the U.S. parent. Explain the likely motive behind these actions.
3. Duever Co. (a U.S. firm) noticed that its financial leverage was substantially lower than most successful firms in Germany and Japan within the same industry. Is Duever's capital structure less than optimal?
4. Consider a U.S.-based MNC with a large subsidiary in Venezuela, where interest rates are very high and the currency is expected to weaken. Assume that the country risk is perceived by the MNC to be high. Explain the tradeoff involved in financing the subsidiary with local debt versus doing so with an equity investment from the parent.
5. A U.S.-based MNC is considering a project to establish a plant for producing and selling consumer goods in an undeveloped country. Assume that the host country's economy is very dependent on oil prices, the local currency of the country is very volatile, and the country risk is very high. Also assume that the country's economic conditions are unrelated to U.S. conditions. Should the required rate of return (and therefore the risk premium) on the project be higher or lower than that of other alternative projects in the United States?

QUESTIONS AND APPLICATIONS

1. Create an argument in support of an MNC's favoring a debt-intensive capital structure.
2. Create an argument in support of an MNC's favoring an equity-intensive capital structure.
3. Do U.S.-based MNCs in general have a higher or lower degree of financial leverage than U.S. domestic firms (based on recent research)?
4. Describe general differences between the capital structures of firms based in the United States and those of firms based in Japan. Offer an explanation for this difference.
5. Why might a firm use a "local" capital structure at a particular subsidiary that differs substantially from its "global" capital structure?

6. Explain how characteristics of MNCs can affect the cost of capital.

7. Explain why managers of a wholly owned subsidiary may be more likely to satisfy the shareholders of the MNC.

8. LaSalle Corporation is a U.S.-based MNC with subsidiaries in various less developed countries where stock markets are not well established. How can LaSalle still attempt to achieve its "global" target capital structure of 50-percent debt and 50-percent equity, even if it plans to use only debt financing for the subsidiaries in these countries?

9. Drexel Company is a U.S.-based company that is establishing a project in a politically unstable country. It is considering two possible sources of financing. Either the parent could provide most of the financing, or the subsidiary could be supported by local loans from banks in that country. Which financing alternative is most appropriate to protect the subsidiary?

10. Charleston Corporation has considered establishing a subsidiary in either Germany or the United Kingdom. The subsidiary would be mostly financed with loans from the local banks in the host country chosen. It determined that the revenue generated from the British subsidiary would be slightly more favorable than the revenue generated by the German subsidiary, even after considering tax and exchange rate effects. The initial outlay is the same, and both countries appear to be politically stable. Charleston recently chose to establish the subsidiary in the United Kingdom because of the revenue advantage. Do you agree with its decision? Explain.

11. Fairfield Corporation, a U.S. firm, just established a subsidiary in a less developed country that consistently experiences an annual inflation rate of 80 percent or more. The country does not have an established stock market, but loans by local banks are available with a 90-percent interest rate. Fairfield has decided to use a strategy in which the subsidiary is financed entirely with funds from the parent. It believes that in this way it can avoid the excessive interest rate in the host country. What is a key disadvantage of using this strategy that may cause Fairfield to be no better off than if it paid the 90-percent interest rate?

12. Veer Company is a U.S.-based MNC that has most of its operations in Japan. Noticing that the Japanese companies with which it competes use more financial leverage, it has decided to adjust its financial leverage to be in line with theirs. In this way, it should reap more tax advantages with the heavy emphasis on debt. It believes that the market's perception of its risk will remain unchanged since its financial leverage is still no higher than that of Japanese competitors. Comment on this.

13. Pullman Inc., a U.S. firm, has had much profitability but prefers not to pay out higher dividends because its shareholders desire that the funds be reinvested. It plans for large growth in several less developed countries. Pullman Inc. would like to finance the growth with local debt in the host countries of concern to reduce exposure to country risk. Explain the dilemma faced by Pullman and offer possible solutions.

14. € Forest Co. produces goods in the United States, Germany, and Australia and sells the goods in the areas where they are produced. Foreign earnings are periodically remitted to the U.S. parent. As the euro's interest rates have declined to a very low level, Forest Co. has decided to finance its German operations with borrowed funds in place of the parent's equity investment. Forest will transfer the U.S. parent's equity investment in the German subsidiary over to its Australian subsidiary. These funds will be used to pay off a floating rate loan, as Australian interest rates have been high and are rising. Explain the expected effects of these actions on the consolidated capital structure and cost of capital of Forest Co.

15. € Using the information in question 14, explain how the exposure of Forest Co. to exchange rate risk may have changed.

16. Explain why the cost of capital for a U.S.-based MNC with a large subsidiary in Brazil is higher than for a U.S.-based MNC in the same industry with a large subsidiary in Japan. Assume that the subsidiary operations for each MNC are financed with local debt in the host country.

17. In recent years, several U.S. firms have penetrated Mexico's market. One of the biggest challenges is the cost of capital to finance businesses in Mexico. Mexican interest rates tend to be much higher than U.S. interest rates. In some periods, the Mexican government does not attempt to lower the interest rates because higher rates may attract foreign investment in Mexican securities.

    a. How might U.S.-based MNCs expand in Mexico without incurring the high Mexican interest expenses when financing the expansion? Are there any disadvantages associated with this strategy?
    b. Are there any additional alternatives for a Mexican subsidiary to finance its business itself after it has been well established? How might this strategy affect the subsidiary's capital structure?

Internet Application

18. The Web site of Bloomberg provides interest rate data for many countries and various maturities. Its address is

    www.bloomberg.com

    Go to the "Markets" section and then to "International Yield Curves." Assume that an MNC would pay one percent more on borrowed funds than the risk-free (government) rates shown at the Bloomberg Web site. Determine the cost of debt (use a ten-year maturity) for the U.S. parent that borrows dollars. Then determine the cost of funds for a foreign subsidiary in Japan that borrows funds locally. Then determine the cost of debt for a subsidiary in Thailand that borrows funds locally. Offer some explanations as to why the cost of debt may vary among the three countries.

Running Your Own MNC

Capital Structure Decisions

19a. Describe the capital structure that you would use to run your business.

b. Why might the proportion of equity to be used in your business be limited when the business is first created?

Blades, Inc. Case

Assessment of Cost of Capital

Recall that Blades has tentatively decided to establish a subsidiary in Thailand in order to manufacture roller blades. The new plant will be utilized to produce "Speedos," Blades' primary product. Once the subsidiary has been established in Thailand, it will be operated for ten years, at which time it is expected to be sold. Ben Holt, Blades' chief financial officer (CFO) believes the growth potential in Thailand to be extremely high over the next few years. However, his optimism is not shared by most economic forecasters, which predict a slow recovery of the Thai economy, which has been very negatively affected by recent events in the country. Furthermore, forecasts for the future value of the baht indicate that the currency may continue to depreciate over the next few years.

Despite the pessimistic forecasts, Ben Holt believes Thailand to be a good international target for Blades' products because of the high growth potential and lack of competitors in Thailand. At a recent meeting of the board of directors, Ben Holt presented his capital budgeting analysis and pointed out that the establishment of a subsidiary in Thailand had a net present value (*NPV*) of over $8 million even when a 25 percent required rate of return is used to discount the cash flows resulting from the project. Blades' board of directors, while favorable to the idea of international expansion, remained skeptical. Specifically, the directors wondered where Ben Holt obtained the 25 percent discount rate to conduct his capital budgeting analysis and whether this discount rate was high enough. Consequently, the decision to establish a subsidiary in Thailand has been delayed until the board of directors meeting next month.

The directors also asked Ben Holt to determine how operating a subsidiary in Thailand would affect Blades' required rate of return and its cost of capital. The directors would like to know how Blades' characteristics would affect its cost of capital relative to roller blade manufacturers operating solely in the United States. Furthermore, the capital asset pricing model (CAPM) was mentioned by two directors, who would like to know how Blades' systematic risk would be affected by expanding into Thailand. Another issue that was raised is how the cost of debt and equity in Thailand differ from the corresponding costs in the United States, and whether these differences would affect Blades' cost of capital. The last issue that was raised during the board of directors' meeting concerned Blades' capital structure decision and whether it would be affected by expanding into Thailand. The board of directors has asked Ben Holt to conduct a thorough analysis of these issues and report back to them at their next meeting.

Ben Holt's knowledge of cost of capital and capital structure decisions is somewhat limited and he requires your help. You are a financial analyst for Blades, Inc. Ben Holt has gathered some information regarding Blades' characteristics that distinguish it from roller blade manufacturers operating solely in the United States, its systematic risk, and the costs of debt and equity in Thailand, and he seeks to determine whether and how this information will affect Blades' cost of capital and its capital structure decision.

Regarding Blades' characteristics, Ben Holt has gathered information regarding Blades' size, its access to the Thai capital markets, the diversification benefits from a Thai expansion, its exposure to exchange rate risk, and its exposure to country risk. Although Blades expansion into Thailand classifies the company as an MNC, Blades is still relatively small compared to U.S. roller blade manufacturers. Also, Blades expansion into Thailand will give it access to the capital and money markets there. However, negotiations with various commercial banks in Thailand indicate that Blades will be able to borrow at interest rates of approximately 15 percent, versus 8 percent in the United States.

Expanding into Thailand will diversify Blades' operations. As a result of this expansion, Blades would be subject to economic conditions in Thailand as well as the United States. Ben Holt sees this as a major advantage since Blades' cash flows will now not be solely dependent on the U.S. economy. Consequently, Ben Holt believes that Blades' probability of bankruptcy is reduced. Nevertheless, if Blades establishes a subsidiary in Thailand, all of the subsidiary's earnings will be remitted back to the U.S. parent, which indicates a high level of exchange rate risk. This is of particular concern because current economic forecasts for Thailand indicate that the baht will depreciate further over the next few years. Furthermore, Ben Holt has already conducted a country risk analysis for Thailand, which resulted in an unfavorable country risk rating.

Regarding Blades' level of systematic risk, Ben Holt has determined how Blades' beta, which measures systematic risk, would be affected by Blades' establishment of a subsidiary in Thailand. Ben Holt believes that Blades' beta would drop from its current level of 2.0 to 1.8. This is because Blades' exposure to U.S. market conditions would be reduced by an expansion into Thailand. Moreover, Ben Holt estimates the risk-free interest rate to be 5 percent and the required return on the market to be 12 percent.

Ben Holt has also determined that the costs of both debt and equity are higher in Thailand than they are in the United States. Interest rates required by lenders such as commercial banks in Thailand are higher than they are in the United States. This is partially attributed to a higher risk premium, which reflects the larger degree of economic uncertainty in Thailand. Thailand's cost of equity is also higher than it is in the United States. Thailand is not as developed as the United States in many ways and various investment opportunities are available to Thai investors, which increases their opportunity cost. However, Ben Holt is not sure whether this higher cost of equity in Thailand would affect Blades, as Blades' shareholders are all located in the United States.

Ben Holt has asked you to analyze this information and to determine how it may affect Blades' cost of capital and its capital structure. To help you in your analysis, Mr. Holt would like you to provide answers to the following questions:

1. If Blades, Inc. expands into Thailand, do you think its cost of capital is higher or lower than the cost of capital of roller blade manufacturers

operating solely in the U.S.? Substantiate your answer by outlining how Blades' characteristics distinguish it from domestic roller blade manufacturers.

2. According to the CAPM, how would Blades' required rate of return be affected by an expansion into Thailand? How do you reconcile this result with your answer to question (1)? Do you think Blades should use the required rate of return resulting from the CAPM to discount the cash flows of the Thai subsidiary to determine its *NPV*?

3. If Blades borrows funds in Thailand necessary to support its Thai subsidiary, how would this affect its cost of capital? Why?

4. Given the high level of interest rates in Thailand, the high level of exchange rate risk, and the high (perceived) level of country risk, do you think Blades will be more or less likely to use debt in its capital structure as a result of its expansion into Thailand? Why?

Small Business Dilemma

Multinational Capital Structure Decision at the Sports Exports Company

The Sports Exports Company has considered a variety of projects, but it still continues to focus all of its business in the United Kingdom. Since most of its business still comes from the exporting of footballs (denominated in pounds), it remains exposed to exchange rate risk. On the favorable side, the British demand for its footballs has risen consistently every month. Jim Logan, the owner of the Sports Exports Company, has retained more than $100,000 (after the pounds were converted into dollars) in earnings since he began his business. At this point in time, his capital structure is mostly his own equity, with very little debt. Jim has periodically considered establishing a very small subsidiary in the United Kingdom that would produce the footballs there (so that he would not have to export them from the United States). If he does decide to establish a small subsidiary in the United Kingdom, he has several options for the capital structure that would be used to support this subsidiary: (1) use all of his equity to invest in the firm, (2) use pound-denominated long-term debt, or (3) use dollar-denominated long-term debt. The interest rate on British long-term debt is slightly higher than the interest rate on U.S. long-term debt.

1. What is an advantage of using equity to support the subsidiary? What is a disadvantage?
2. If Jim decided to use long-term debt as the primary form of capital to support this subsidiary, should he use dollar-denominated debt or pound-denominated debt?
3. How can the equity proportion of the capital structure increase over time after a business has been established?

18 LONG-TERM FINANCING

Multinational corporations (MNCs) typically use long-term sources of funds to finance long-term projects. They have access to domestic and foreign sources of funds. It is worthwhile for MNCs to consider all possible forms of financing before making their final decisions.

The specific objectives of this chapter are to

- explain why MNCs consider long-term financing in foreign currencies,
- explain how to assess the feasibility of long-term financing in foreign currencies, and
- explain how the assessment of long-term financing in foreign currencies is adjusted for bonds with floating interest rates.

LONG-TERM FINANCING DECISION

The long-term financing decision of the MNC is commonly influenced by the different interest rates that exist among currencies. The actual cost of long-term financing considers both the quoted interest rate and the percentage change in the exchange rate of the currency borrowed over the loan life. Just as currencies exhibit different interest rates on short-term bank loans, bond yields can vary as well among currencies. Exhibit 18.1 illustrates the long-term bond yields for several different countries as of a given point in time. The wide differentials in bond yields are evident, which reflect a difference in the cost of debt financing among firms in different countries.

Because bonds denominated in foreign currencies sometimes have lower yields, U.S. corporations often consider issuing bonds in those countries denominated in these currencies. For example, Hewlett-Packard, IBM, PepsiCo, and Walt Disney recently issued bonds denominated in Japanese yen to capitalize on low Japanese interest rates. Since the actual financing cost to a U.S. corporation issuing a foreign currency-denominated bond is affected by that currency's value relative to the U.S. dollar during the financing period, there is no guarantee that the bond will be less costly than a U.S. dollar-denominated bond. The borrowing firm must make coupon payments in the currency denominating the bond. If this currency appreciates against the firm's home

Exhibit 18.1
Annualized Bond Yields among Countries (ten-year maturity, as of June 26, 1998)

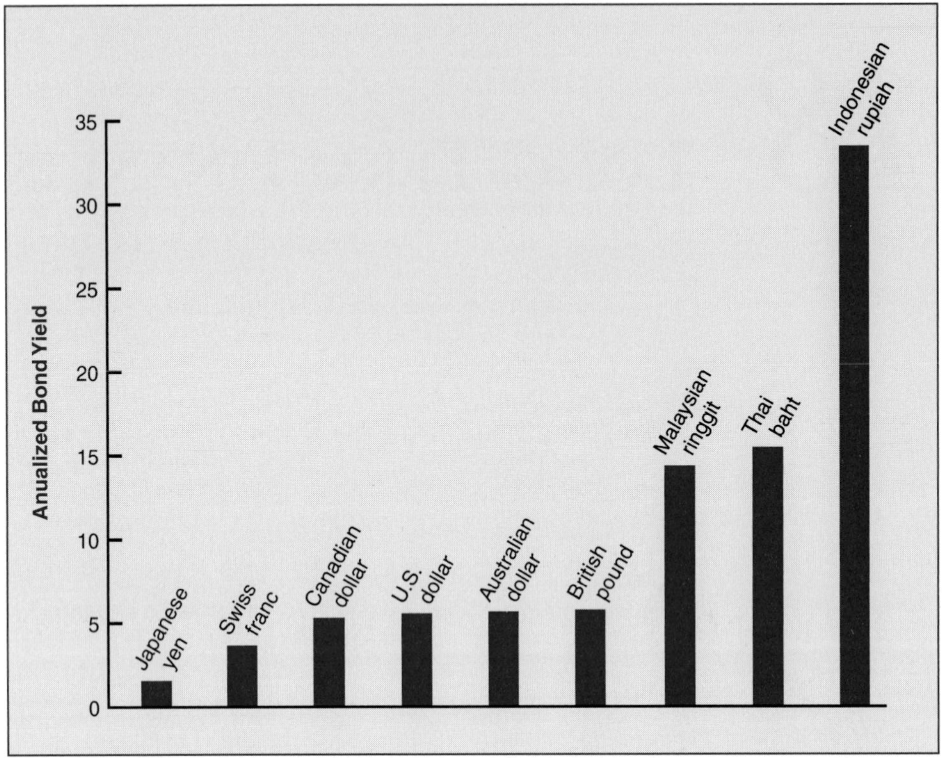

currency, the funds needed to make coupon payments will increase. For this reason, a firm will not always denominate debt in a currency that exhibits a low interest rate.

To make the long-term financing decision, the MNC must (1) determine the amount of funds needed, (2) forecast the price at which it can issue the bond, and (3) forecast periodic exchange rate values for the currency denominating the bond. This information can be used to determine the bond's financing costs, which can be compared with the financing costs the firm would incur using its home currency. Finally, the uncertainty of the actual financing costs to be incurred from foreign financing must be accounted for as well. To illustrate the borrower's analysis of financing with Eurobonds, an example is provided here.

Financing with a Stable Currency

Consider a U.S.-based MNC that needs to borrow $1,000,000 over a three-year period. This reflects a relatively small amount of funds and a short time period for bond financing but will allow for a more simplified example. Assume that the firm believes it can sell dollar-denominated bonds at par value if it provides a coupon rate of 14 percent. It also has the alternative of denominating the bonds in Singapore dollars to sell in the Eurobond market, in which case it would convert its borrowed Singapore dollars to U.S. dollars to use as needed. Then, it would need to obtain Singapore dollars annually to make the coupon payments. Assume that the current exchange rate of the Singapore dollar is $.50. The firm needs S$2,000,000 (computed as $1,000,000/$.50 per Singapore dollar) to obtain the $1 million it initially needs. The firm believes it can sell the S$-denominated bonds at par value if it provides a coupon rate of 10 percent.

The costs of both financing alternatives are illustrated in Exhibit 18.2. The outflow payment schedule of each financing method is provided here. The outflow payments if the firm finances with U.S. dollar-denominated bonds are known. In addition, the number of Singapore dollars needed at the end of each period is known if the firm finances with a S$-denominated bond. Yet, because the future exchange rate of the Singapore dollar is uncertain, the number of dollars needed to obtain the Singapore dollars each year is uncertain. If exchange rates do not change, the annual cost of financing with Singapore dollars is 10 percent, which is less than the 14-percent annual cost of financing with U.S. dollars.

A comparison between the costs of financing with the two different currencies can be conducted by determining the annual cost of financing with each bond, from the U.S. firm's perspective. The comparison is shown in the last column of Exhibit 18.2. The annual cost of financing represents the discount rate at which the future outflow payments must be discounted so that their present value equals the amount borrowed. This is similar to the so-called yield to maturity but is assessed here from the borrower's perspective rather from than the investor's perspective. When the price at which the bonds are initially issued equals the par value and there is no exchange rate adjustment, the annual cost of financing is simply equal to the coupon rate. Thus, the annual cost of financing for the U.S. dollar-denominated bond would be 14 percent. If the Singapore dollar's value were expected to change over time, the annual cost of financing could be easily determined with some calculators.

In our example, the Singapore dollar-denominated debt appears to be less costly. However, it is unrealistic to assume that the Singapore dollar will remain stable over time. Consequently, some MNCs may choose to issue U.S. dollar-denominated debt, even though it appears more costly. The potential savings from issuing bonds denominated in a foreign currency must be weighed against the potential risk of such a method. In this example, risk reflects the possibility that the Singapore dollar will appreciate to a degree that causes Singapore dollar-denominated bonds to be more costly than U.S. dollar-denominated bonds.

Financing with a Strong Currency

To illustrate the risk involved in financing with a bond denominated in Singapore dollars, assume that the Singapore dollar has appreciated from $.50 to $.55 at the end of Year 1, to $.60 at the end of Year 2, and to $.65 by the end of Year 3. In this case, the payments made by the U.S. firm are displayed in Exhibit 18.3. From a comparison of the dollar outflows in this scenario with the outflows that would have occurred from a U.S. dollar-denominated bond, the risk to a firm from denominating a bond in a foreign currency is evident. The period of the last payment is partic-

Exhibit 18.2
Financing with Bonds Denominated in Dollars versus Singapore Dollars

Financing Alternative	End of Year: 1	2	3	Annual Cost of Financing
1) U.S. dollar-denominated bonds (coupon rate = 14%)	$140,000	$140,000	$1,140,000	14%
2) Singapore dollar-denominated bonds (coupon rate = 10%)	S$200,000	S$200,000	S$2,200,000	—
Forecasted exchange rate of S$	$.50	$.50	$.50	—
Payments in dollars	$100,000	$100,000	$1,100,000	10%

Exhibit 18.3
Financing with Singapore Dollars During a Strong-S$ Period

	End of Year: 1	2	3	Annual Cost of Financing
Payments in Singapore dollars	S$200,000	S$200,000	S$2,200,000	—
Forecasted exchange rate of S$	$.55	$.60	$.65	—
Payments in dollars	$110,000	$120,000	$1,430,000	20.11%

IN PRACTICE

GLOBAL BOND MARKET QUOTATIONS

The prices and yields of government bonds in various countries are disclosed in *The Wall Street Journal,* as shown here. A bond index has been created for each country, which is monitored to measure returns in the local currency. The returns are measured as the percentage change from the previous day, from the previous month, and from the beginning of the year. The index is also measured from a U.S. perspective to indicate the performance for U.S. investors. Notice how the year-to-date return for bonds measured in local currency can vary substantially from the return for those same bonds measured from a U.S. perspective. The difference reflects the exchange rate effects on the returns to U.S. investors.

Total Rates of Return on International Bonds
In percent, based on J.P. Morgan Government Bond Index, Dec. 31, 1987=100

	LOCAL CURRENCY TERMS INDEX VALUE	1 DAY	1 MO	3 MOS	SINCE 12/31	U.S. DOLLAR TERMS INDEX VALUE	1 DAY	1 MO	3 MOS	SINCE 12/31
Japan	198.36	+ 0.53	+ 0.22	+ 1.57	+ 3.73	198.24	+ 0.47	+ 1.17	− 6.80	− 3.39
Britain	343.48	+ 0.08	+ 1.45	− 0.05	+ 0.31	290.57	+ 0.44	+ 0.56	− 3.33	− 3.81
Germany	229.42	+ 0.15	+ 1.14	+ 0.66	+ 1.25	198.66	+ 0.47	+ 0.64	− 6.89	− 6.92
France	306.42	+ 0.13	+ 1.19	+ 0.52	+ 1.04	268.16	+ 0.45	+ 0.68	− 7.01	− 7.10
Canada	314.23	− 0.20	+ 2.16	+ 1.16	+ 0.90	272.25	+ 0.09	+ 3.20	+ 1.98	+ 3.32
Netherlands	244.35	+ 0.16	+ 1.20	+ 0.64	+ 1.27	211.27	+ 0.48	+ 0.69	− 6.91	− 6.89
ECU-a	262.07	+ 0.03	+ 0.41	+ 1.50	+ 1.66	237.95	+ 0.34	− 0.10	− 6.11	− 6.53
Global-b	267.28	+ 0.15	+ 1.11	+ 0.41	+ 0.87	241.21	+ 0.29	+ 1.03	− 4.26	− 3.76
EMBI+-c	148.17	+ 0.38	+ 8.70	+ 5.91	+ 6.91	148.17	+ 0.38	+ 8.70	+ 5.91	+ 6.91

a-Dec. 31, 1989=100 b-18 int'l gov. markets c-external-currency emerging mkt. debt, Dec. 31, 1993=100.

ularly crucial for bond financing in foreign currencies. It includes not only the final coupon payment but the principal as well. Normally, exchange rates are more difficult to predict over longer time horizons. Thus, the time at which the principal is to be repaid is so far away that it may be virtually impossible to have a reliable estimate of the exchange rate at that time. For this reason, some firms may be uncomfortable issuing bonds denominated in foreign currencies.

Financing with a Weak Currency

Just as an appreciating currency increases the periodic outflow payments of the bond issuer, a depreciating currency will reduce outflow payments. To illustrate, consider the same information provided earlier on a three-year bond denominated in Singapore dollars. Also assume that the Singapore dollar depreciates from $.50 to $.48 at the end of Year 1, to $.46 at the end of Year 2, and to $.40 by the end of Year 3. In this case, the payments made by the U.S. firm are shown in Exhibit 18.4. When one compares the dollar outflows in this scenario with the outflows that would have occurred from a U.S. dollar-denominated bond, the potential savings from foreign financing are evident.

Up to this point, three scenarios have been evaluated: (1) no change in the Singapore dollar's exchange rate, (2) an appreciating Singapore dollar, and (3) a depreciating Singapore dollar. Exhibit 18.5 summarizes the results of the three scenarios, illustrating how exchange rates can influence the outflow payments from financing with bonds denominated in foreign currencies.

ACTUAL BOND FINANCING COSTS

Consider a U.S. firm that in January 1976 sold bonds denominated in British pounds with a par value of £10 million and a 10-percent coupon rate, thereby requiring coupon payments of £1 million at the end of each year. Assume that this firm had no existing business in the United Kingdom and therefore needed to exchange dollars for

Exhibit 18.4 Financing with Singapore Dollars During a Weak-S$ Period

	End of Year:			Annual Cost of Financing
	1	2	3	
Payments in Singapore dollars	S$200,000	S$200,000	S$2,200,000	—
Forecasted exchange rate of S$	$.48	$.46	$.40	—
Payments in dollars	$ 96,000	$ 92,000	$880,000	2.44%

Exhibit 18.5 Exchange Rate Effects on Outflow Payments for S$-Denominated Bonds

	Payment in U.S. Dollars at End of Year:			Annual Cost of Financing
Exchange Rate Scenario	1	2	3	
Scenario 1: No change in S$ value	$100,000	$100,000	$1,100,000	10.00%
Scenario 2: Strong S$	$110,000	$120,000	$1,430,000	20.11%
Scenario 3: Weak S$	$ 96,000	$ 92,000	$ 880,000	2.44%

pounds to make the coupon payments each year. Exhibit 18.6 shows how the dollar payments would fluctuate each year according to the actual exchange rate at that time. In 1980, when the pound was worth $2.3950, the coupon payment was $2,395,000. Just four years later, the pound was worth $1.1592, causing the coupon payment to be $1,159,200. Thus, the firm's dollar coupon payment in 1984 was less that half of that paid in 1980, even though the number of pounds needed (£1 million) was the same each year. In general, the dollar coupon payments increased during the late 1980s (as the pound appreciated) and then declined during the early 1990s (as the pound depreciated). The pound was somewhat stable in the middle 1990s, so that its effect on the coupon payment was not so pronounced. The strong influence of exchange rate movements on the cost of financing with bonds denominated in a foreign currency is very obvious in this exhibit. The actual effects would vary with the currency of denomination, since exchange rates do not move in perfect tandem against the dollar.

Exhibit 18.6
Actual Costs of Annual Financing with Pound-Denominated Bonds from a U.S. Perspective

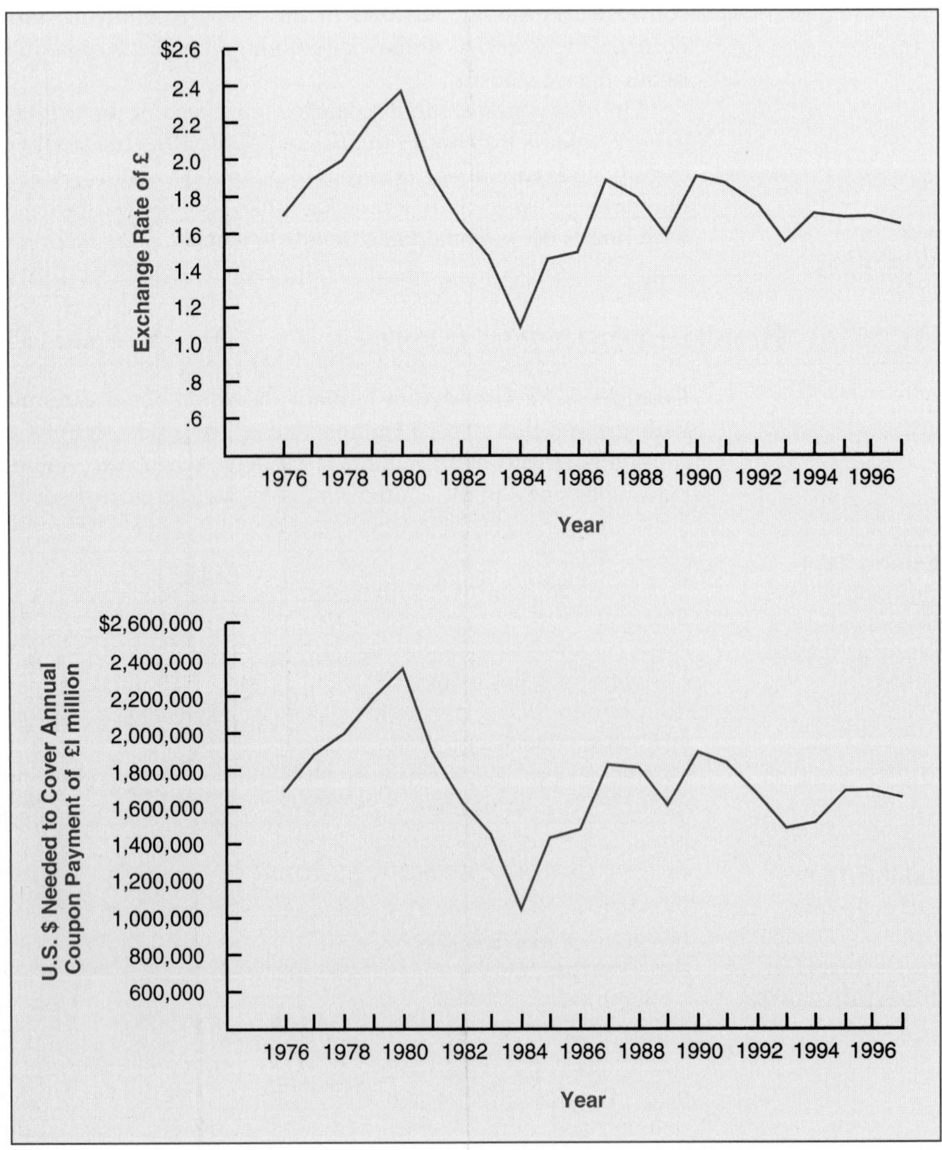

COMPARING BOND DENOMINATION ALTERNATIVES

http://
Dr. Ed Yardeni's Economics Network at www.yardeni.com reviews international political and economic events and their presumed global impact and presents economic and political analyses of major economies. A variety of national and international economic and financial markets charts are available as well.

A firm in need of long-term funds must decide which currency to use in denominating the bond. When considering a foreign currency for which it does not have future cash inflows, it must assess the potential strength or weakness of that currency. One approach to assessing the feasibility of each currency is to forecast its exchange rate for each period for which an outflow payment would be provided to bondholders and to determine the amount of the home currency needed to cover the payments according to those forecasted exchange rates. Because it is difficult to develop accurate point estimates of exchange rates, this approach can easily lead to poor decisions. Therefore, it is necessary to consider alternative techniques for projecting future exchange rates.

Use of Exchange Rate Probabilities

An alternative approach to projecting point estimates of future exchange rates is to develop a probability distribution for an exchange rate for each period for which payments are made to bondholders. In this case, the *expected value* of the exchange rate can be computed for each period by multiplying each possible exchange rate by its associated probability and totaling the products. Then, the exchange rate's expected value can be used to forecast the cash outflows necessary to pay bondholders over each period. The exchange rate's expected value may vary from one period to another. After developing probability distributions and computing the expected values, one can estimate the expected cost of financing and compare that with the cost of financing with a bond denominated in the home currency.

Using this approach, a single outflow estimate is derived for each payment period, and a single estimate is derived for the annual cost of financing over the life of the bond. Since this approach does not indicate the range of possible results that may occur, it is difficult to assess the probability that a bond denominated in a foreign currency will be more costly than a bond denominated in the home currency. It is possible to measure such risk through use of simulation, as explained next.

Use of Simulation

When a firm considers issuing bonds in a foreign currency, it can develop a probability distribution of the currency's exchange rate at the end of each year (or whenever coupons are to be paid). The U.S. firm can feed its probability distributions of exchange rates into a simulation computer program. Then, the program will randomly draw one of the possible values from the exchange rate distribution for the end of each year and determine the outflow payments necessary based on those exchange rates. Consequently, the cost of financing is determined. The procedure described up to this point represents one iteration. Next, the program will repeat the procedure by again randomly drawing one of the possible values from the exchange rate distribution at the end of each year. This will provide a new schedule of outflow payments reflecting those randomly selected exchange rates. The cost of financing for this second iteration is also determined. The simulation program continually repeats this procedure, perhaps 100 times or so (as many times as desired).

For every iteration, a possible scenario of future exchange rates is proposed, which is then used to determine the annual cost of financing if that scenario does occur. Thus, the simulation generates a probability distribution of annual financing costs that can then be compared with the known cost of financing if the bond is denominated in U.S. dollars (the home currency). Such a comparison will determine the probability that issuing bonds denominated in a foreign currency will be cheaper than dollar-denominated bonds.

Financing with Floating Rate Eurobonds

Eurobonds are often issued with a floating, rather than fixed, coupon rate. This means the coupon rate will fluctuate over time in accordance with interest rates. For example, the coupon rate is frequently tied to the **London Interbank Offer Rate (LIBOR)**, which is a rate at which Eurobanks lend funds to each other. As LIBOR increases, so does the coupon rate of a floating rate bond. A floating coupon rate can be an advantage to the bond issuer during periods of decreasing interest rates, when otherwise the firm would be locked in at a higher coupon rate over the life of the bond. It can also be a disadvantage during periods of rising interest rates.

When coupon rates are fixed, the only uncertain variable to be assessed for denominating a bond in a foreign currency is the exchange rate. If the coupon rate is floating, then projections are required not only for exchange rates but for interest rates as well. Recall that simulation can be used to examine the possible outcomes of bond financing based on several possible exchange rate scenarios. It can be used simultaneously to incorporate possible outcomes for the coupon rate over the life of the loan and can develop a probability distribution of annual costs of financing.

Exchange Rate Risk of Foreign Bonds

When financing in bonds, one must assess not only the potential savings from denominating a bond in a foreign currency but the risk resulting from exchange rate fluctuations as well. Not all foreign currencies exhibit the same risk. From a U.S. borrower's perspective, a bond denominated in Canadian dollars is less risky than a bond denominated in most other foreign currencies (assuming it has no offsetting position in these currencies). This is because the Canadian dollar exhibits less variability against the U.S. dollar over time and therefore is less likely to deviate far from its projected future exchange rate. If all other characteristics of two bonds denominated in different currencies are similar, a U.S. borrower should prefer the bond denominated in the currency that is more stable.

Hedging Exchange Rate Risk

The exchange rate risk from financing with bonds in foreign currencies can be hedged with offsetting cash inflows in that currency, or with forward contracts, as explained here.

Offsetting Cash Inflows. Some firms may have inflow payments in particular currencies, which could offset outflow payments related to bond financing. Thus, it may be possible to finance with bonds denominated in a foreign currency that exhibits a lower coupon rate without becoming exposed to exchange rate risk. Yet, it is unlikely that a firm would be able to perfectly match the timing and amount of the outflows in the foreign currency denominating the bond to the inflows in that currency. Therefore, some exposure to exchange rate fluctuations will exist. The exposure can be substantially reduced, though, if the firm receives inflows in the particular currency denominating the bond. This can help to stabilize the firm's cash flow. Many MNCs, including Allied-Signal Inc. and The Coca-Cola Company, issue bonds in some of the foreign currencies that they receive from operations. PepsiCo issues bonds in several foreign currencies and uses proceeds in those same currencies resulting from foreign operations to pay interest and principal payments. TRW Inc. typically borrows the equivalent of more than $100 million in foreign currencies, with foreign currency revenue used to cover the debt payments.

The decision of several European countries to adopt the euro as their currency has important implications for MNCs that require long-term financing and wish to offset some of their cash inflows with debt payments. MNCs that have cash inflows in many of the participating European countries could now issue bonds denominated in euros and then use their cash inflows from operations in these countries to make the debt payments. Prior to the adoption of the euro, an MNC might have preferred to finance in the currency of each European country where it was conducting business so that it could cover its financing payments with cash inflows in the same currency. This preference would have reduced the ability to use bonds because the amount of financing in every country may not have been sufficiently large enough to justify bond offerings in each of several currencies. Thus, the MNC may have used local bank financing in each of those countries instead of bond financing; local bank financing may be more expensive than bond financing. However, the MNC may require a sufficiently large amount of financing to issue bonds denominated in euros when it can distribute the proceeds for use in several European countries and then aggregate cash inflows from these countries to cover the financing payments. In this way, the adoption of the euro may increase the use of bond financing and reduce the cost of financing for MNCs conducting business in Europe.

In addition, the adoption of the euro by countries such as Italy and Spain forces their interest rates to be similar to those of the other participating countries. Thus, MNCs should be able to finance projects in these countries and use cash inflows to cover their debt payments while achieving lower financing costs than when those countries had their own currency.

The Eurobond has historically been dominated by government bond offerings. Yet, as corporations increase their issuance of bonds denominated in euros in the Eurobond market in order to offset their cash inflows in euros, the composition of the Eurobond market will change. These corporate bond offerings will not necessarily have the same yield across all issuers, since some issuers will have a lower degree of credit risk and therefore need to pay a higher yield. However, the adoption of the euro will encourage many MNCs based in the United States and Europe who conduct business in Europe to issue Eurobonds denominated in euros, so that the difference in yields paid (and therefore cost of financing) on these bonds will be primarily determined by the credit risk of the issuer rather than the currency, regardless of the participating European country where the proceeds of the bond offering are spent.

Forward Contracts. When a bond denominated in a foreign currency has a lower coupon rate than the firm's home currency, the firm may consider issuing bonds denominated in that currency and simultaneously hedging its exchange rate risk through the forward market. Because the forward market can sometimes accommodate requests of five years or longer, such an approach may be possible. The firm could arrange to purchase the foreign currency forward for each time at which payments are required. However, the forward rate for each horizon will most likely be above the spot rate. Consequently, hedging these future outflow payments may not be less costly than the outflow payments needed if a dollar-denominated bond were issued. The relationship implied here reflects the concept of interest rate parity, which was discussed in earlier chapters, except that the point of view in this chapter is long-term rather than short-term.

Nike Problem

International Long-Term Financing

Since Nike finances a substantial amount of fixed assets in foreign countries, it commonly makes long-term financing decisions about its international operations. It has issued long-term debt denominated in Japanese yen to support Japanese operations. Specific long-term financing decisions may vary from one subsidiary to another because of differences in nominal interest rates, country risk levels, and exchange rate risk levels among countries. There is no one perfect solution for long-term financing. The decision normally is based on financing with a currency that has a relatively low interest rate and does not increase exposure to exchange rate risk.

However, it is impossible to solve both objectives in some cases, such as when borrowing in Latin America. If Nike borrows in the local currency, there may be a natural offsetting effect to reduce exchange rate risk, since cash inflows can be used to cover the repayment of debt. However, interest rates in many Latin American countries are very high. The only way to avoid a high interest rate is to borrow in another currency (such as dollars) and convert that currency into the Latin American currency needed to support the project. However, this creates more exchange rate risk because Nike will have to convert cash flows generated by the Latin American currency to cover the debt repayments. Since Latin American currencies have historically depreciated against the dollar and other currencies over time, this strategy could possibly result in a higher cost of financing than borrowing the local currency in the Latin American country of concern.

Discussion: Nike could consider a strategy of borrowing dollars and converting the dollars to the currency needed and simultaneously selling forward contracts on the foreign currency to hedge the conversion when converting back to dollars to repay the loan. Do you think this strategy would achieve a lower financing cost than borrowing the local currency? Explain.

Long-Term Financing in Multiple Currencies

Up to this point, discussion has focused on choosing the most feasible currency for a bond. In some cases, the appropriate selection for a borrower may be not a single currency or bond but a portfolio of currencies. Since the lifetime of bonds is too long to single out any particular currency as being safe, a portfolio of diversified currencies could reduce the risk incurred by the bond issuer. For example, a U.S. firm may denominate bonds in several foreign currencies, rather than a single foreign currency, so that substantial appreciation of any one particular currency will not drastically increase the number of dollars necessary to cover the financing payments. To illustrate the potential advantage of bond diversification, consider the example of an MNC based in the United States that plans to issue bonds and has considered four alternatives:

1. Issue bonds denominated in U.S. dollars.
2. Issue bonds denominated in Japanese yen.
3. Issue bonds denominated in Canadian dollars.
4. Issue some bonds denominated in Japanese yen and some bonds denominated in Canadian dollars.

Assume that the MNC has no net exposure in either Japanese yen or Canadian dollars (C$). Also assume that the coupon rate for a U.S. dollar-denominated bond is 14 percent, while for a yen- or Canadian dollar-denominated bond the coupon rate is 8 percent. It is expected that any of these bonds could be sold at par value.

There is a substantial difference here between the coupon rates of the dollar-denominated bonds and those of bonds denominated in foreign currencies. If the Canadian dollar appreciates against the U.S. dollar, the actual financing cost from issuing C$-denominated bonds may be higher than that of the U.S. dollar-denominated bonds. If the Japanese yen appreciates substantially against the U.S. dollar, the actual financing cost from issuing yen-denominated bonds may be higher than that of the dollar-denominated bonds. If the exchange rates of the Canadian dollar and Japanese yen move in opposite directions against the U.S. dollar, then both types of bonds could not simultaneously be more costly than U.S. dollar-denominated bonds, so financing with both types of bonds would almost ensure that the overall financing cost to the U.S. firm would be less than the cost from issuing a U.S. dollar-denominated bond.

In reality, there is no guarantee that the exchange rates of the Canadian dollar and Japanese yen will move in opposite directions. However, if the currency movements are not highly correlated, it is unlikely that both currencies will simultaneously appreciate to an extent that will offset their lower coupon rate advantages. Therefore, financing in bonds denominated in more than one foreign currency can increase the probability that the overall cost of foreign financing will be less than that of financing with the domestic currency (U.S. dollars, in our example). This example involves only two foreign currencies. In reality, a firm may consider several currencies that exhibit lower interest rates and issue a portion of its bonds in each of these currencies. Such a strategy can increase the other costs (advertising, printing, etc.) of issuing bonds, but those costs may be offset by a reduction in cash outflows to bondholders.

Currency Cocktail Bonds

There is a method by which a firm can finance in several currencies without issuing various types of bonds (thus avoiding higher transaction costs). It can develop a **currency cocktail bond,** denominated in not one, but a mixture (or "cocktail") of currencies. Within the Eurobond market, a cocktail bond may be preferred over the single-currency bond, since it can reduce exchange rate risk.

A currency cocktail simply reflects a multicurrency unit of account. Several currency cocktails have been developed to denominate international bonds, and some have already been used in this manner. One of the more popular currency cocktails is the **Special Drawing Right (SDR)**, which was originally devised as an alternative foreign reserve asset but is now used to denominate bonds and bank deposits and to price various services. Given the creation of the euro as a single European currency, the use of a currency cocktail bond in Europe is limited because one currency is now used by numerous European countries.

Using Swaps to Hedge Financing Costs

When MNCs issue bonds that expose them to interest rate or exchange rate risk, they may use *swaps* to hedge the risk. **Interest rate swaps** can be used to hedge interest rate risk, while **currency swaps** can be used to hedge exchange rate risk.

Interest Rate Swaps

As the popularity of the Eurobond market has increased, so have interest rate swaps, which enable a firm to exchange fixed rate payments for variable rate payments. The

http://
Visit home.earthlink.net ~green for access to detailed information on interest rate swaps such as theoretical foundation and trading strategies.

interest rate swaps are used by bond issuers because they may reconfigure the future bond payments to a more preferable structure. For example, consider two firms that desire to issue bonds:

- Quality Company is a highly rated firm that prefers to borrow at a variable interest rate.
- Risky Company is a low-rated firm that prefers to borrow at a fixed interest rate.

Assume that the rates these companies would pay for issuing either variable rate or fixed rate Eurobonds are as follows:

	Fixed Rate Bond	Variable Rate Bond
Quality Company	9%	LIBOR + .5%
Risky Company	10.5%	LIBOR + 1%

LIBOR, the London interbank offer rate, changes over time. Based on the information given, Quality Company has a comparative advantage when issuing either fixed rate or variable rate bonds, but more of one with fixed rate bonds. Quality Company could issue fixed rate bonds while Risky Company issues variable rate bonds; then, Quality could provide variable rate payments to Risky in exchange for fixed rate payments.

Assume that Quality Company negotiates with Risky Company to provide variable rate payments at LIBOR + ½ percent in exchange for fixed rate payments of 9½ percent. The interest rate swap arrangement is shown in Exhibit 18.7. Quality Company benefits, since its fixed rate payments received on the swap exceed the payments owed to bondholders by ½ percent. Its variable rate payments to Risky Company are the same as what it would have paid if it issued variable rate bonds. Risky Company is receiving LIBOR + ½ percent on the swap, which is ½ percent less than what it must pay on its variable rate bonds. Yet, it is making fixed rate payments of 9½ percent, which is 1 percent less than what it would have paid if it issued fixed rate bonds. Overall, it saves ½ percent per year of financing costs.

Exhibit 18.7
Illustration of an Interest Rate Swap

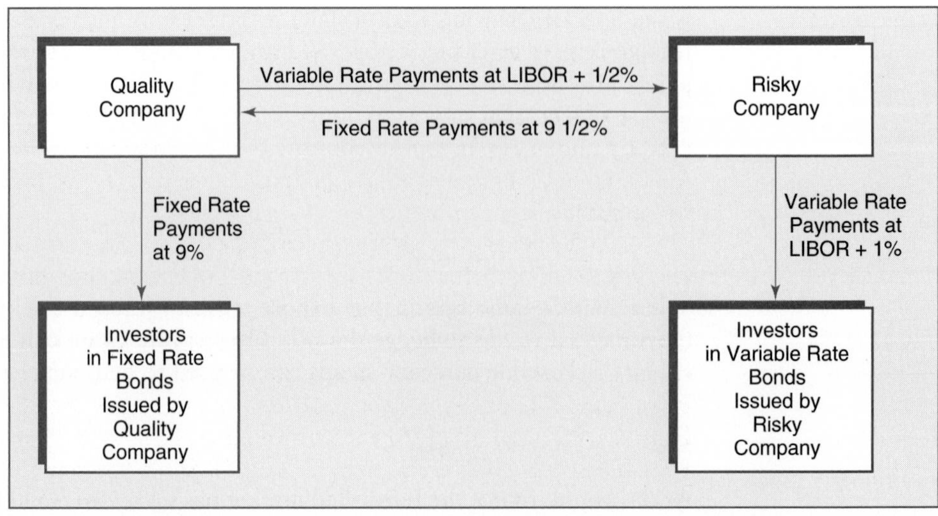

Two limitations of the swap just described are worth mentioning. First, there is a cost of time and resources associated with searching for a suitable swap candidate and negotiating the swap terms. Second, there is a risk to each swap participant that the counterparticipant could default on payments. For this reason, financial intermediaries are usually involved in swap agreements. They match up participants and also assume the default risk involved. For their role, they charge a fee, which would reduce the estimated benefits in this example, but their involvement is critical to effectively match up swap participants and reduce concern about default risk.

Ashland Oil, Campbell Soup Company, GTE, Intel Corporation, Johnson Controls, Union Carbide, and many other MNCs commonly use interest rate swaps. For example, Ashland Oil commonly issues fixed rate debt and uses interest rate swaps to achieve lower borrowing costs on variable rate debt. Campbell Soup Company uses interest rate swaps to minimize its worldwide financing costs and to achieve a targeted proportion of fixed rate versus variable rate debt. GTE recently used interest rate swaps to convert more than $500 million of variable rate debt into fixed rate debt.

Currency Swaps

Another swap used to complement bond issues, the currency swap, enables firms to exchange currencies at periodic intervals. Ford Motor Co., Johnson & Johnson, General Motors Corporation, and many other MNCs use currency swaps. Consider a U.S. firm, called Miller Company, that desires to issue a bond that is denominated in euros since it could make payments with euro inflows to be generated from existing operations. However, this firm is not well known to investors that would consider purchasing euro-denominated bonds. Also consider a firm, called Beck Company, that desires to issue dollar-denominated bonds because its inflow payments are mostly in dollars. However, it is not well known to the investors that would purchase these bonds. If Miller is known within the dollar-denominated market while Beck is known within the euro-denominated market, the following transactions would be appropriate. Miller could issue dollar-denominated bonds, while Beck issued euro-denominated bonds. Miller could provide euro payments to Beck in exchange for dollar payments. This swap of currencies would allow the companies to make payments to their respective bondholders without concern about exchange rate risk. This type of currency swap is illustrated in Exhibit 18.8.

Many MNCs simultaneously swap interest payments and currencies. For example, the Gillette Co. engaged in swap agreements that converted $500 million in fixed rate dollar-denominated debt into multiple currency variable rate debt. PepsiCo enters into interest rate swaps and currency swaps to reduce borrowing costs.

The large commercial banks that serve as financial intermediaries for currency swaps sometimes take positions. That is, they may agree to swap fixed rate payments for variable rate payments or swap currencies with firms, rather than simply search for suitable swap candidates.

An alternative method by which firms could obtain financing in a foreign currency is the parallel (or back-to-back) loan, which represents simultaneous loans provided by two parties with an agreement to repay at a specified point in the future. For example, assume that the parent of a U.S.-based MNC desires to expand its British subsidiary, while the parent of a British-based MNC desires to expand its American subsidiary. The British parent provides pounds to the British subsidiary of the U.S.-based MNC, while the U.S. parent provides dollars to the American subsidiary of the British-based MNC (as shown in Exhibit 18.9). At the time specified by the loan contract, the loans are repaid. The British subsidiary of the U.S.-based MNC uses

Exhibit 18.8
Illustration of a Currency Swap

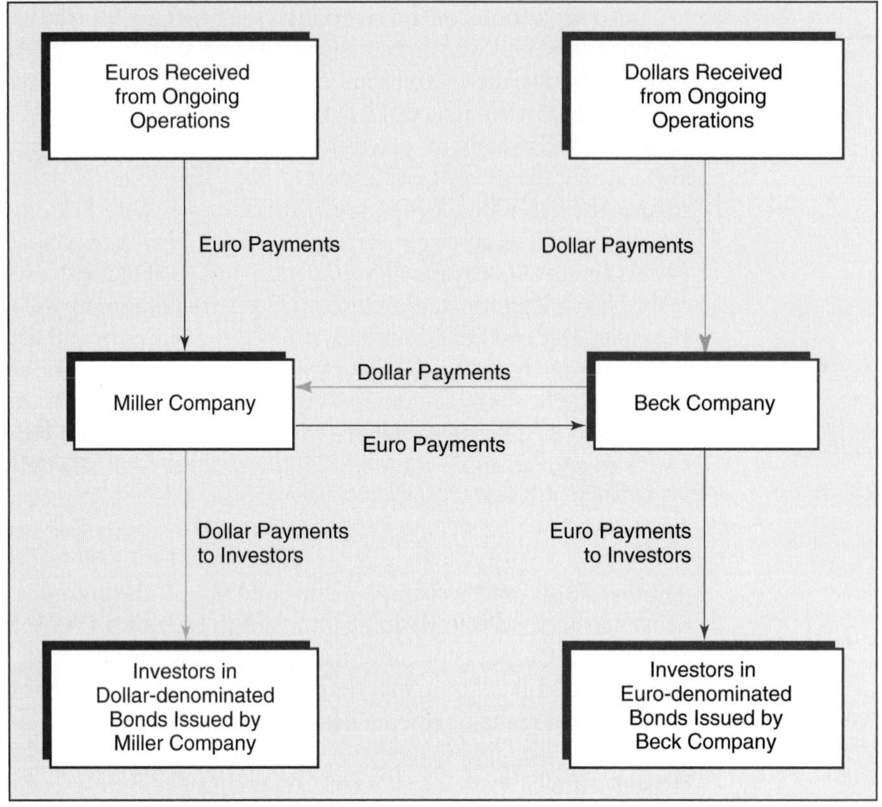

Exhibit 18.9
Illustration of a Parallel Loan

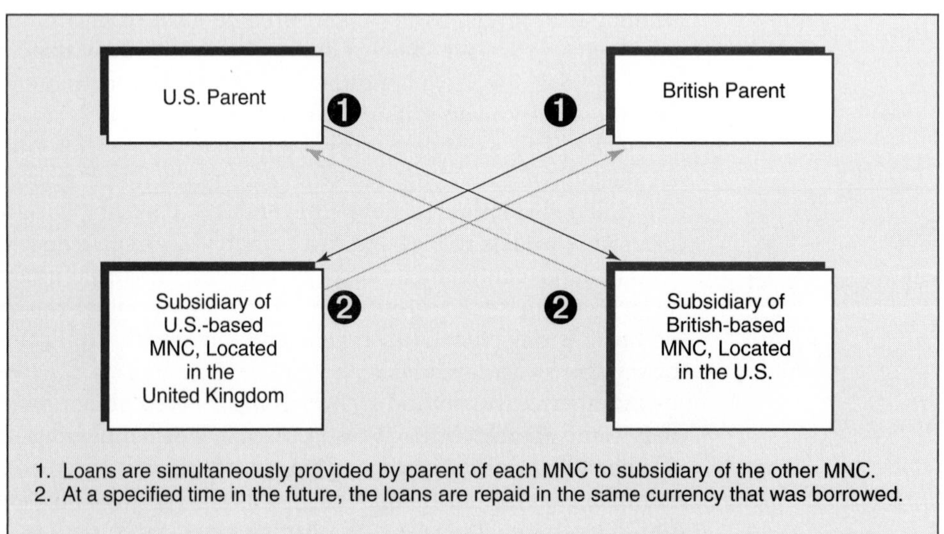

pound-denominated revenues to repay the British company that provided the loan. At the same time, the American subsidiary of the British-based MNC uses dollar-denominated revenues to repay the U.S. company that provided the loan.

Foreign Debt Maturity Decisions

Even when an MNC decides to use the local currency of the foreign country to finance business in that country, it must decide on the maturity for that debt. For this reason, it may want to assess the yield curve in that country. The yield curve illustrates the annualized yield on Treasury bonds for each of several different maturities at a specific point in time. Firms commonly assess a yield curve when deciding whether to use short-term, medium-term, or long-term debt to finance their business. While firms cannot borrow at the risk-free rates illustrated on a yield curve, the yield curve still allows a comparison across countries, because the firms' borrowing rate would exceed each risk-free rate shown on the Treasury yield curve by a premium that reflects their default risk. Some firms prefer to use long-term fixed rate debt when the yield curve has a flat slope, so that they incur a similar (or lower) interest rate as the prevailing short-term rate. When the yield curve has a steep upward slope, firms can obtain cheaper short-term debt but must accept the uncertainty about their future borrowing rate when the short-term debt matures.

http://
Visit www.bloomberg.com for the latest information from financial markets around the world.

Exhibit 18.10 shows the yield curves for various countries at a specific point in time. Since the slopes of yield curves can vary among countries, the choice of financing with long-term debt versus short-term or medium-term debt may vary among countries. Thus, an MNC may decide to use short-term or medium-term financing in one country while using long-term financing in other countries. While the United States typically has an upward-sloping yield curve, the yield curves in other countries are commonly inverted, implying a lower annualized yield on long-term debt. Thus, the cost of debt not only varies among countries but varies among maturity dates within a given country. In some countries, such as those in South America, there is not much of a market for long-term fixed rate debt, so MNCs in those countries are typically forced to finance projects with floating rate debt.

Impact of an MNC's Long-Term Financing Decision on Its Value

An MNC's long-term financing decisions affect its value, as shown in Exhibit 18.11. The parent's long-term financing decision determines how its long-term operations are to be financed with debt. In particular, this decision will dictate the maturity and other provisions on long-term debt securities issued. It will also dictate the currency used to denominate the debt. When a parent uses debt financing, its cost of debt will be affected by its choice of the currency borrowed. While it may be convenient to conduct long-term financing in the currency that matches the currency

Exhibit 18.10
Yield Curves Among Foreign Countries (as of June 26, 1998)

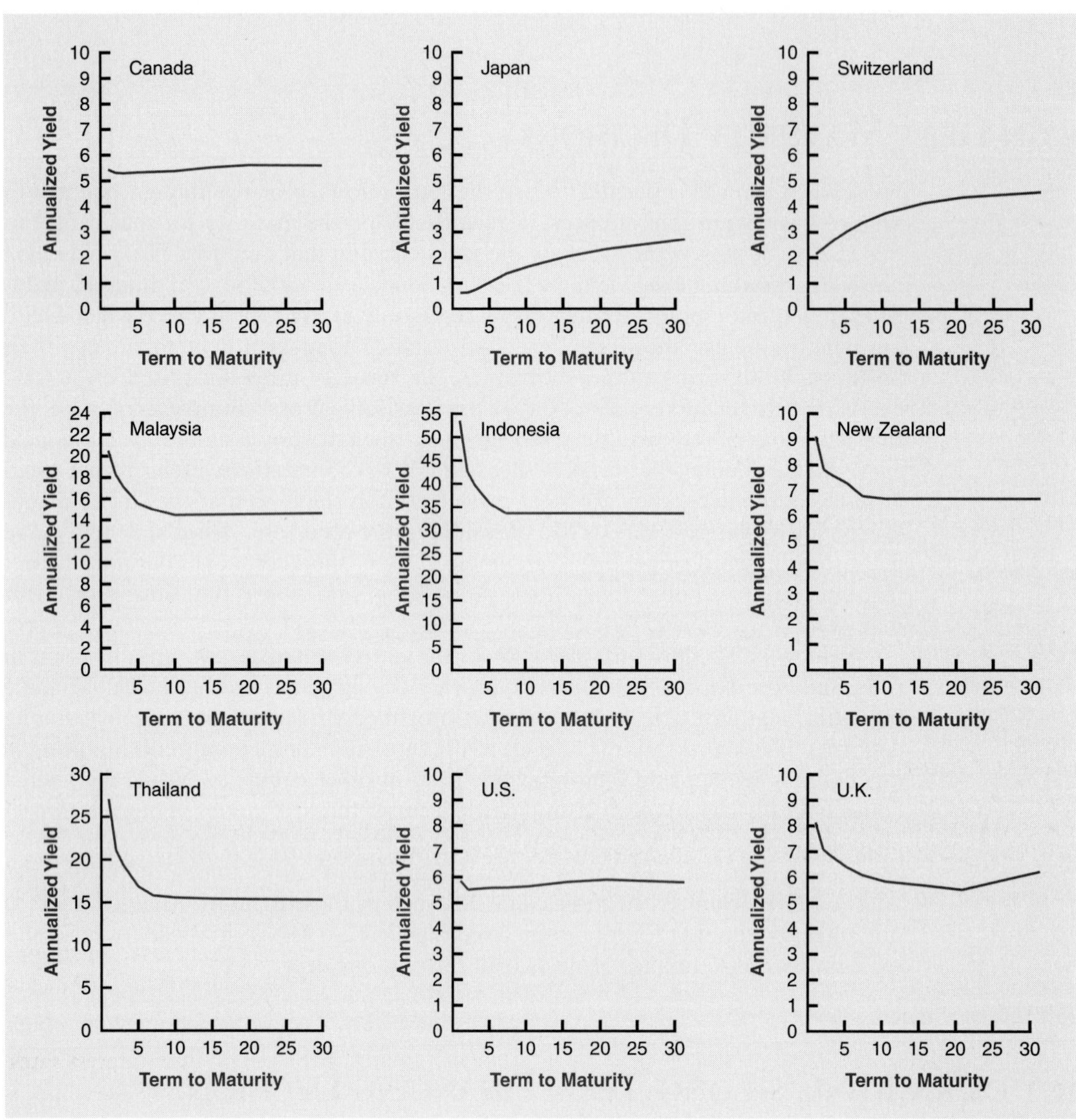

generated from operations, the disparity among interest rates of long-term debt denominated in different currencies can motivate an MNC to consider financing with long-term debt in a different currency. Since the parent's choice of the currency used to denominate debt affects the cost of debt, it also affects its cost of capital and therefore affects its required rate of return on its investments and its value.

Exhibit 18.11
Impact of Long-Term Financing Decisions on an MNC's Value

$$V = \sum_{t=1}^{n} \left\{ \frac{\sum_{j=1}^{m} \left[E(CF_{j,t}) \times E(ER_{j,t}) \right]}{(1+k)^t} \right\}$$

Parent's Decisions on Currency Used to Denominate Debt

V = value of the U.S.-based MNC
$E(CF_{j,t})$ = expected cash flows denominated in currency j to be received by the U.S. parent in period t
$E(ER_{j,t})$ = expected exchange rate at which currency j can be converted to dollars at the end of period t
k = the weighted average cost of capital of the U.S. parent company
m = number of currencies
n = number of periods

SUMMARY

- Some MNCs may consider long-term financing in foreign currencies to offset future cash inflows in those currencies and therefore reduce exposure to exchange rate risk. Other MNCs may consider long-term financing in foreign currencies to reduce financing costs. If a foreign interest rate is relatively low or the foreign currency borrowed depreciates over the financing period, long-term financing in that currency can result in low financing costs.

- An MNC can assess the feasibility of financing in foreign currencies by applying exchange rate forecasts to the periodic coupon payments and the principal payment. In this way, it determines the amount of its home currency that is necessary per period to cover the payments. The annual cost of financing can be estimated by determination of the discount rate that equates the periodic payments on the foreign financing to the initial amount borrowed (as measured in the domestic currency). The discount rate derived from this exercise represents the annual cost of financing in the foreign currency, which can be compared to the cost of domestic financing. The cost of long-term financing in a foreign currency is dependent on the currency's exchange rate over the financing period and therefore is uncertain. Thus, the MNC will not automatically finance with a foreign currency that has a lower interest rate, since its exchange rate forecasts are subject to error. For this reason, the MNC may estimate the costs of foreign financing under various exchange rate scenarios over time.

- For Eurobonds that have floating interest rates, the coupon payment to be paid to investors is uncertain. This creates another uncertain variable (along with exchange rates) in estimating the amount in the firm's domestic currency which is required per period to make the payments. This uncertainty can be accounted for through estimation of the coupon payment amount necessary under various interest rate scenarios over time. Then, with the use of these estimates, the amount of the firm's domestic currency required to make the payments can be estimated, based on various exchange rate scenarios over time.

SELF-TEST FOR CHAPTER 18

(Answers are provided in Appendix A at the back of the text.)

1. Explain why a firm may issue a bond denominated in a currency different from its home currency to finance local operations. Explain the risk involved.

2. A U.S.-based MNC is considering the issuance of a 20-year Swiss franc-denominated bond. The proceeds are to be converted to British pounds to support the firm's British operations. The MNC has no Swiss operations but prefers to issue the bond in francs rather than pounds because the coupon rate is 2 percentage points lower. Explain the risk involved in this strategy. Do you think the risk here is greater or less than it would be if the bond proceeds were used to finance U.S. operations? Why?

3. Some large companies based in Latin American countries could borrow funds (through issuing bonds or borrowing from U.S. banks) at an interest rate that would be substantially less than the interest rates in their own countries. Assuming that they are perceived to be creditworthy in the United States, why might they still prefer to borrow in their local countries when financing local projects (even if they incur interest rates of 80 percent or more)?

4. A respected economist just announced a prediction that even though Japanese inflation would not rise, Japanese interest rates would rise consistently over the next five years. Paxson Co., a U.S. firm with no foreign operations, has recently issued a Japanese yen-denominated bond to finance U.S. operations. It chose the yen denomination because the coupon rate was low. Its vice president stated, "I'm not concerned about the prediction because we issued fixed rate bonds and are therefore insulated from risk." Do you agree? Explain.

5. Long-term interest rates in some Latin American countries commonly exceed 100 percent annually. Offer your opinion as to why these interest rates are so much higher than those of industrialized countries and why some projects in these countries are feasible for local firms, even though the cost of funding the projects is so high.

QUESTIONS AND APPLICATIONS

1. What factors should be considered by a U.S. firm that plans to issue a floating rate Eurobond?

2. What is the advantage of using simulation to assess the bond financing position?

3. Explain the difference in the cost of financing with foreign currencies during a strong dollar period versus a weak dollar period for a U.S. firm.

4. € Explain how a U.S.-based MNC issuing bonds denominated in euros may be able to offset a portion of its exchange rate risk.

5. Is the risk of issuing a floating rate Eurobond higher or lower than the risk of issuing a fixed-rate Eurobond? Explain.

6. € Columbia Corporation is a U.S. company with no foreign currency cash flows. It plans to issue either (1) a bond denominated in euros with a fixed interest rate or (2) a bond denominated in U.S. dollars with a floating interest rate. It estimates its periodic dollar cash flows for each bond. Which bond do you think would have greater uncertainty surrounding these future dollar cash flows? Explain.

7. Why would a U.S. firm consider issuing bonds denominated in multiple currencies?

8. Kerr Inc., a major U.S. exporter of products to Japan, denominates its exports in dollars and has no other international business. It can borrow dollars at 9 percent to finance its operations or borrow yen at 3 percent. Yet, if it

borrowed yen, it would be exposed to exchange rate risk. How could it borrow yen and possibly reduce its economic exposure to exchange rate risk?

9. Katina Inc. is a U.S. firm that plans to finance with Eurobonds denominated in euros to obtain a lower interest rate than dollar-denominated bonds. Its cash flows are in dollars. What is the most critical point in time at which the exchange rate will have the greatest impact?

10. How would an investing firm differ from a borrowing firm in the features (i.e., interest rate and currency's future exchange rates) it would prefer a floating rate Eurobond to exhibit?

11. Assume that Seminole Inc. considers issuing a Singapore dollar-denominated bond at its present coupon rate of 7 percent, even though it has no incoming Singapore dollar cash flows to cover the bond payments. It is attracted to the low financing rate, since U.S.-dollar bonds issued in the United States would have a coupon rate of 12 percent. Assume that either type of bond would have a four-year maturity and could be issued at par value. Seminole needs to borrow $10 million. Therefore, it will issue either U.S.-dollar bonds with a par value of $10 million or bonds denominated in Singapore dollars with a par value of S$20 million. The spot rate of the Singapore dollar is $.50. Seminole has forecasted the Singapore dollar's value at the end of each of the next four years, when coupon payments are to be paid:

End of Year	Exchange Rate of S$
1	$.52
2	.56
3	.58
4	.53

Determine the expected annual cost of financing with Singapore dollars. Should Seminole Inc. issue bonds denominated in U.S. dollars or in Singapore dollars? Explain.

12. Assume that Hurricane Inc. is a U.S. company that exports products to the United Kingdom, invoiced in dollars. It also exports products to Denmark, invoiced in dollars. It currently has no cash outflows in foreign currencies, and it plans to issue bonds in the near future. It could likely issue bonds at par value in (1) dollars, with a coupon rate of 12 percent, (2) Danish kroner, with a coupon rate of 9 percent, or (3) pounds, with a coupon rate of 15 percent. It expects the Danish krone and the pound to strengthen over time. How could Hurricane revise its invoicing policy and make its bond denomination decision to achieve low financing costs without excessive exposure to exchange rate fluctuations?

13. Janutis Co. has just issued fixed rate debt at 10 percent. Yet, it prefers to convert its financing to incur a floating rate on its debt. It engages in an interest rate swap in which it swaps variable rate payments of LIBOR plus 1 percent in exchange for fixed rate payments of 10 percent. The interest rates are applied to an amount that represents the principal from its recent debt issue in order to determine the interest payments due at the end of each year for the next three years. Janutis Co. expects that the LIBOR rate will be 9 percent at the end of the first year, 8.5 percent at the end of the second year, and 7 percent at the end of the third year. Determine the financing rate that Janutis Co. expects to pay on its debt after considering the effect of the interest rate swap.

14. Grant Inc. is a well-known U.S. firm that needs to borrow 10 million British pounds to support a new business in the United Kingdom. However, it cannot obtain financing from British banks because it is not yet established within the United Kingdom. It decides to issue dollar-denominated debt (at par value) in the United States, for which it will pay an annual coupon rate of 10 percent. It then will convert the dollar proceeds from the debt issue into British pounds at the prevailing spot rate (the prevailing spot rate is one pound = $1.70). Over each of the next three years, it plans to use the revenue in pounds from the new business in the United Kingdom to make its annual debt payment. Grant Inc. engages in a currency swap in which it will convert pounds to dollars at an exchange rate of $1.70 per pound at the end of

each of the next three years. How many dollars must be borrowed initially to support the new business in the United Kingdom? How many pounds should Grant Inc. specify in the swap agreement that it will swap over each of the next three years in exchange for dollars so that it can pay its annual coupon payments to the U.S. creditors?

15. Ivax Corp. (based in Miami) is a U.S. drug company that has attempted to capitalize on new opportunities to expand in Eastern Europe. The production costs in most Eastern European countries are very low, often less than one-fourth of the cost of those in Germany or Switzerland. Furthermore, there is a strong demand for drugs in Eastern Europe. Ivax penetrated Eastern Europe by purchasing a 60-percent stake in Galena AS, a Czech firm that produces drugs.
    a. Should Ivax finance its investment in the Czech firm by borrowing dollars from a U.S. bank and converting the dollars into koruna (the Czech currency) or by borrowing koruna from a local Czech bank? What information do you need to know to answer this question?
    b. How can borrowing koruna locally from a Czech bank reduce the exposure of Ivax to exchange rate risk?
    c. How can borrowing koruna locally from a Czech bank reduce the exposure of Ivax to political risk caused by government regulations?

Internet Application

16. The Web site of Bloomberg provides interest rate data for many countries and various maturities. Its address is

    www.bloomberg.com

    Go to the "Markets" section of the Web site and then to "International Yield Curves." Consider a subsidiary of a U.S.-based MNC that is located in Australia. Assume that when it borrows in Australian dollars, it would pay 1 percent more than the risk-free (government) rates shown on the Web site. What rate would the subsidiary pay for one-year debt? for 5-year debt? for 10-year debt? Assuming that it needs funds for 10 years, do you think it should use one-year debt, 5-year debt, or 10-year debt? Explain your answer.

Running Your Own MNC

Long-Term Debt-Denomination Decision

17a. If you planned to borrow long-term funds, you could borrow dollars or you could borrow the foreign currency of concern. Using the Internet or other sources of data, compare the U.S. interest rate to the foreign interest rate over the last 8 quarters. Which interest rate is typically higher?

b. Explain why you might be able to reduce your exposure to exchange rate risk by borrowing long-term funds denominated in the foreign currency of concern.

Blades, Inc. Case

Use of Long-Term Foreign Financing

Recall that Blades, Inc. is considering the establishment of a subsidiary in Thailand to manufacture "Speedos," Blades' primary roller blade product. Alternatively, Blades could acquire an existing manufacturer of roller blades in Thailand, Skates'n' Stuff. At the most recent meeting of the board of directors of Blades, Inc., the directors voted to establish a subsidiary in Thailand. The directors voted for the establishment of a subsidiary because of the relatively high level of control it affords Blades.

The Thai subsidiary is expected to begin production by early next year, and the construction of the plant in Thailand and the purchase of necessary equipment to manufacture Speedos is to commence immediately. Initial estimates of the plant and equipment required by Blades, Inc. in order to establish the subsidiary in Bangkok indicate costs of approximately 550 million Thai baht. Since the current exchange rate of the baht is $0.023, this translates to a dollar cost of $12.65 million. Blades, Inc. currently has $2.65 million available in cash to cover a portion of the costs. The remaining $10 million (434,782,609 baht), however, will have to be obtained from other sources.

The board of directors has asked Ben Holt, Blades' chief financial officer (CFO), to line up the necessary financing to cover the remaining construction costs and purchase of equipment. Ben Holt realizes that Blades is a relatively small company whose stock is not widely held. Furthermore, Ben Holt believes that Blades' stock is currently undervalued because Blades' expansion into Thailand has not been widely publicized at this point. Because of these considerations, Ben Holt would prefer debt to equity financing in order to raise the funds necessary to complete construction of the Thai plant.

Ben Holt has identified two choices of debt financing: issue the equivalent of $10 million yen-denominated notes or issue the equivalent of approximately $10 million baht-denominated notes. Both types of notes would have a maturity of five years. In the fifth year, the face value of the notes will be repaid together with the last annual interest payment. Yen-denominated notes are available in increments of ¥125,000, while baht-denominated notes are issued in increments of 50,000 baht. Since the baht-denominated notes are issued in increments of 50,000 baht, Blades needs to issue THB434,782,609/50,000 = 8,696 baht-denominated notes. Furthermore, since the current exchange rate of the yen in baht is THB0.347826/¥, Blades needs to obtain THB434,782,609/THB0.347826 = ¥1,250,000,313. Since yen-denominated notes would be issued in increments of 125,000 yen, Blades would have to issue ¥1,250,000,313/¥125,000 = 10,000 yen-denominated notes.

Due to recent unfavorable economic events in Thailand, expansion into Thailand is viewed as relatively risky; Ben Holt's research indicates that Blades would have to offer a coupon rate of approximately 10 percent on the yen-denominated notes to induce investors to purchase these notes. Conversely, Blades could issue baht-denominated notes at a coupon rate of 15 percent. Whether Blades decides to issue baht- or yen-denominated notes, it would use the cash flows generated by the Thai subsidiary to pay the interest on the notes and to repay the principal in five years. For example, if Blades decides to issue yen-denominated notes, it would convert baht into yen to pay the interest on these notes and to repay the principal in five years.

Although Blades can finance with a lower coupon rate by issuing yen-denominated notes, Ben Holt suspects that the effective financing rate for the yen-denominated notes may actually be higher than for the baht-denominated notes. This is because forecasts for the future value of the yen indicate an appreciation of the yen (versus the baht) in the future. Although the precise future value of the yen is uncertain, Ben Holt has compiled the following probability distribution for the annual percentage change of the yen versus the baht:

Annual % Change in Yen (versus the baht)	Probability
0%	20%
2	50
3	30

Ben Holt suspects that the effective financing cost of the yen-denominated notes may actually be higher than for the baht-denominated notes once the expected appreciation of the yen (versus the baht) is taken into consideration.

Ben Holt has asked you, a financial analyst of Blades, Inc., to answer the following questions for him:

1. Given that Blades expects to use the cash flows generated by the Thai subsidiary in order to pay the interest and principal of the notes, would the effective financing cost of the baht-denominated notes be affected by exchange rate movements? Would the effective financing cost of the yen-denominated notes be affected by exchange rate movements? How?

2. Construct a spreadsheet to determine the annual effective financing percentage cost of the yen-denominated note issued in each of the three scenarios for the future value of the yen. What is the probability that the financing cost of issuing yen-denominated notes is higher than the cost of issuing baht-denominated notes?

3. Using a spreadsheet, determine the expected annual effective financing percentage cost of

issuing yen-denominated notes. How does this expected financing cost compare with the expected financing cost of the baht-denominated notes?

4. Based on your answers to the previous questions, do you think Blades should issue yen- or baht-denominated notes? What is the tradeoff involved?

Small Business Dilemma

Long-Term Financing Decision by the Sports Exports Company

The Sports Exports Company continues to focus on producing footballs in the United States and exporting them to the United Kingdom. The exports are denominated in pounds, which has continually exposed the firm to exchange rate risk. It is now considering a new form of expansion where it would sell specialty sporting goods in the United States. If it pursues this U.S. project, it would need to borrow long-term funds. The dollar-denominated debt has an interest rate that is slightly lower than the pound-denominated debt.

1. Jim Logan, owner of the Sports Exports Company, needs to determine whether dollar-denominated debt or pound-denominated debt would be most appropriate for financing this expansion, if he does expand. He was leaning toward financing the U.S. project with dollar-denominated debt, since his goal was to avoid exchange rate risk. Is there any reason why he should consider using pound-denominated debt in order to reduce exchange rate risk?
2. Assume that Jim decides to finance his proposed U.S. business with dollar-denominated debt, if he does implement the U.S. business idea. How could he use a currency swap along with the debt to reduce the firm's exposure to exchange rate risk?

PART IV
INTEGRATIVE PROBLEM

Long-Term Assets and Liability Management

Gandor Co. is a U.S. firm that is considering a joint venture with a Chinese firm to produce and sell videocassettes. Gandor will invest $12 million in this project, which will help to finance the Chinese firm's production. For each of the first three years, 50 percent of the total profits will be distributed to the Chinese firm, while the remaining 50 percent will be converted to dollars to be sent to the United States. The Chinese government intends to impose a 20-percent income tax on the profits earned by Gandor. The Chinese government has guaranteed that the after-tax profits (denominated in yuan, the Chinese currency) can be converted to U.S. dollars at an exchange rate of $.20 per yuan and sent to Gandor Co. each year. At the current time, there is no withholding tax imposed on profits to be sent to the United States as a result of joint ventures in China. Assume that even after considering the taxes paid in China, there is an additional 10-percent tax imposed by the U.S. government on profits received by Gandor Co. After the first three years, all profits earned are allocated to the Chinese firm.

The expected total profits resulting from the joint venture per year are as follows:

Year	Total Profits From Joint Venture (in yuan)
1	60 million
2	80 million
3	100 million

Gandor's average cost of debt is 13.8 percent before taxes. Its average cost of equity is 18 percent. Assume that the corporate income tax rate imposed on Gandor is normally 30 percent. Gandor uses a capital structure composed of 60-percent debt and 40-percent equity. Gandor automatically adds 4 percentage points to its cost of capital when deriving its required rate of return on international joint ventures. While this project has particular forms of country risk that are unique, Gandor plans to account for these forms of risk within its estimation of cash flows.

There are two forms of country risk that concern Gandor. First, there is the risk that the Chinese government will increase the corporate income tax rate from 20 percent to 40 percent (20-percent probability). If this occurs, additional tax credits will be allowed, resulting in no U.S. taxes on the profits from this joint venture. Second, there is the risk that the Chinese government will impose a withholding tax of 10 percent on the profits that were to be sent to the United States (20-percent probability). In this case, additional tax credits will not be allowed, and Gandor will still be subject to a 10-percent U.S. tax on profits received from China. Assume that the two types of country risk are mutually exclusive. That is, the Chinese government will only adjust one of its tax guidelines (the income tax or the withholding tax), if any.

Questions

1. Determine Gandor's cost of capital. Also, determine Gandor's required rate of return for the joint venture in China.
2. Determine the probability distribution of Gandor's net present values for the joint venture. Capital budgeting analyses should be conducted for the three scenarios:

   Scenario 1. Based on original assumptions.

   Scenario 2. Based on an increase in the corporate income tax by the Chinese government.

   Scenario 3. Based on the imposition of a withholding tax by the Chinese government.

3. Would you recommend that Gandor participate in the joint venture? Explain.
4. What do you think would be the key underlying factor that would have the most influence on the profits earned in China as a result of the joint venture?
5. Is there any reason for Gandor to revise the composition of its capital (debt and equity) obtained from the United States when financing joint ventures like this?
6. When Gandor was assessing this proposed joint venture, some of the managers of Gandor Co. recommended that it borrow the Chinese currency rather than dollars to partially obtain the necessary capital for its initial investment. They suggested that such a strategy could reduce Gandor's exchange rate risk. Do you agree? Explain.

PART V

Short-Term Asset and Liability Management

Part V (Chapters 19 through 21) focuses on the MNC's management of short-term assets and liabilities. Chapter 19 describes methods by which MNCs can finance their international trade. Chapter 20 identifies sources of short-term funds and explains the criteria used by MNCs to make their short-term financing decisions. Chapter 21 describes how MNCs optimize their cash flows and explains the criteria used to make their short-term investment decisions.

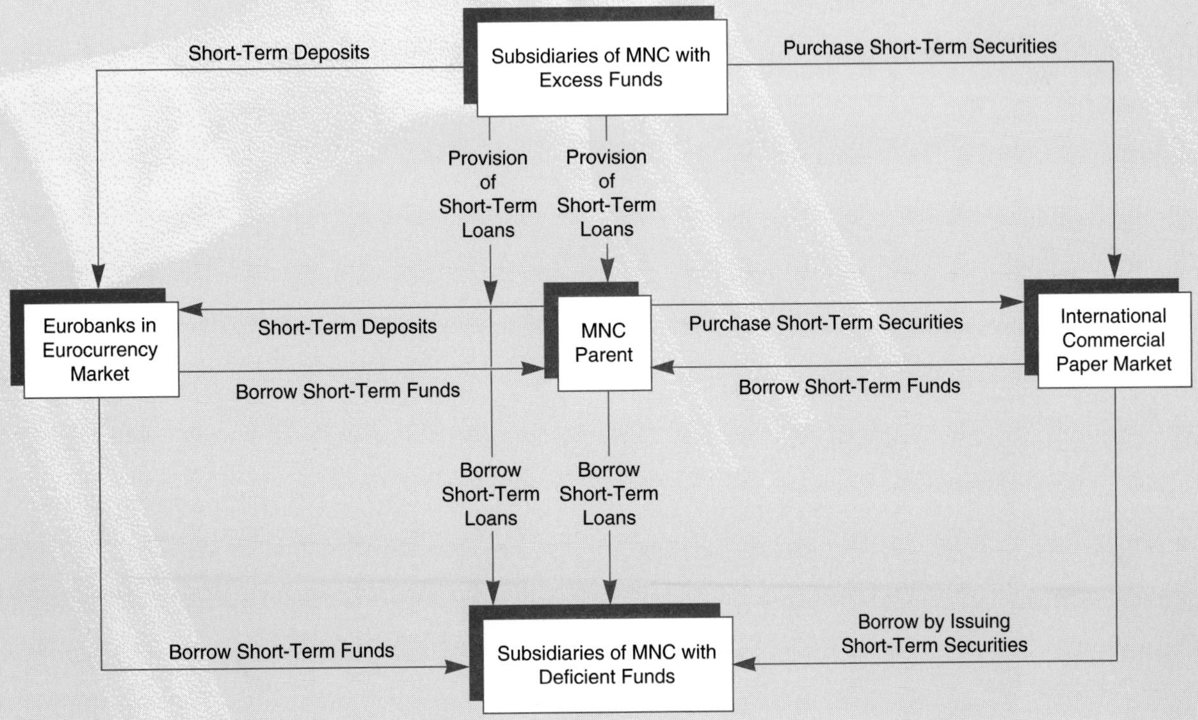

19 Financing International Trade

The international trade activities of multinational corporations (MNCs) have grown in importance over time. This trend is attributable to the increased globalization of the world economies and the availability of trade finance from the international banking community. While banks also finance domestic trade, their role in financing international trade is more critical due to the additional complications involved. First, the exporter might question the importer's ability to make payment. Second, even if the importer is creditworthy, the government might impose exchange controls that prevent payment to the exporter. Third, the importer might not trust that the exporter will ship the goods ordered. Fourth, even if the exporter does ship the goods, trade barriers or time lags in international transportation might delay arrival time.

The specific objectives of this chapter are to

- describe methods of payment for international trade,
- explain common trade finance methods, and
- describe the major agencies that facilitate international trade with export insurance and/or loan programs.

Payment Methods for International Trade

In any international trade transaction, credit is provided by either the supplier (exporter), the buyer (importer), one or more financial institutions, or any combination of these. The supplier may have sufficient cash flow to finance the entire trade cycle, beginning with the production of the product until payment is eventually made by the buyer. This form of credit is known as **supplier credit.** In some cases, the exporter may require bank financing to augment its cash flow. On the other hand, the supplier may not desire to provide financing, in which case the buyer will have to finance the transaction itself, either internally or externally, through its bank. Banks on both sides of the transaction can thus play an integral part in trade financing.

In general, five basic methods of payment are used to settle international transactions, each with a different degree of risk to the exporter and importer (Exhibit 19.1):

Exhibit 19.1
Comparison of Payment Methods

Method	Usual Time of Payment	Goods Available to Buyers	Risk to Exporter	Risk to Importer
Prepayment	Before shipment	After payment	None	Relies completely on exporter to ship goods as ordered
Letter of credit	When shipment is made	After payment	Very little or none, depending on credit terms	Assured shipment made, but relies on exporter to ship goods described in documents
Sight draft; documents against payment	On presentation of draft to buyer	After payment	If draft unpaid, must dispose of goods	Same as above unless importer can inspect goods before payment
Time draft; documents against acceptance	On maturity of drafts	Before payment	Relies on buyer to pay drafts	Same as above
Consignment	At time of sale by buyer	Before payment	Allows importer to sell inventory before paying exporter	None; improves cash flow of buyer
Open account	As agreed	Before payment	Relies completely on buyer to pay account as agreed	None

- prepayment
- letters of credit
- drafts (sight/time)
- consignment
- open account

Prepayment

Under the **prepayment** method, the exporter will not ship the goods until the buyer has remitted payment to the exporter. Payment is usually made in the form of an international wire transfer to the exporter's bank account or foreign bank draft. As technology progresses, electronic commerce will allow firms engaged in international trade to make electronic credits and debits through an intermediary bank. This method affords the supplier the greatest degree of protection, and it is normally requested of first-time buyers whose creditworthiness is unknown or whose countries are in financial difficulty. Most buyers, however, are not willing to bear all the risk by prepaying an order.

http://
Visit www.businessfinance.com/index.html for a search engine on corporate funding resources.

Letters of Credit (L/C)

A **letter of credit (L/C)** is an instrument issued by a bank on behalf of the importer (buyer) promising to pay the exporter (beneficiary) upon presentation of shipping documents in compliance with the terms stipulated therein. In effect, the bank is substituting its credit for that of the buyer. This method is a compromise between seller and buyer because it affords certain advantages to both parties. The exporter is assured of receiving payment from the issuing bank as long as it presents documents in accordance with the L/C. It is important to point out that the issuing bank is obligated to honor drawings under the L/C regardless of the buyer's ability or willingness to pay. On the other hand, the importer does not have to pay for the goods until shipment has been made and documents are presented in good order. However, the importer must still rely upon the exporter to ship the goods as described in the documents, since the L/C does not guarantee that the goods purchased will be those invoiced and shipped. Letters of credit will be described in greater detail later in this chapter.

Drafts

A **draft** (or **bill of exchange**) is an unconditional promise drawn by one party, usually the exporter, instructing the buyer to pay the face amount of the draft upon presentation. The draft represents the exporter's formal demand for payment from the buyer. A draft affords the exporter less protection than an L/C, since the banks are not obligated to honor payments on the buyer's behalf.

Most trade transactions handled on a draft basis are processed through banking channels. In banking terminology, they are known as **documentary collections.** In a documentary collection transaction, banks on both ends act as intermediaries in the processing of shipping documents and the collection of payment. If shipment is made under a sight draft, the exporter is paid once shipment has been made and the draft is presented to the buyer for payment. The buyer's bank will not release the shipping documents to the buyer until the buyer has paid the draft. This is known as **documents against payment.** It is a practice that provides the exporter with some protection, since the banks will release the shipping documents only according to the exporter's instructions. The buyer needs the shipping documents to pick up merchandise. The buyer does not have to pay for the merchandise until the draft has been presented.

If a shipment is made under a time draft, the exporter provides instructions to the buyer's bank to release shipping documents against acceptance (signing) of the draft. This method of payment is sometimes referred to as **documents against acceptance.** By accepting the draft, the buyer is promising to pay the exporter at the specified future date. This accepted draft is also known as a **trade acceptance,** which is different from a banker's acceptance. In this type of transaction, the buyer is able to obtain the merchandise prior to paying for it. It is the buyer's responsibility to honor that draft at maturity. In this case, the exporter is providing the financing and is dependent upon the buyer's financial integrity to pay the draft at maturity. Shipping on a time draft basis provides some added comfort in that banks at both ends are used as collection agents. In addition, a draft serves as a binding financial obligation in case the exporter wishes to pursue litigation on uncollected receivables. The added risk is that if the buyer fails to pay the draft at maturity, the bank is not obligated to honor payment. The exporter is assuming all the risk and must analyze the buyer accordingly.

Consignment

Under a **consignment** arrangement, the exporter ships the goods to the importer while still retaining actual title to the merchandise. The importer has access to the inventory but does not have to pay for the goods until they have been sold to a third party. The exporter is trusting the importer to remit payment for the goods sold at that time. If the importer fails to pay, the exporter has limited recourse since there is no draft involved and the goods have already been sold. As a result of the high risk, the consignment method is seldom used except by affiliated and subsidiary companies trading with the parent company. Some equipment suppliers allow importers to hold some equipment on the sales floor as demonstrator models. Once the models are sold or after a specified period, payment is sent to the supplier.

Open Account

The opposite of prepayment is the **open account transaction** in which the exporter ships the merchandise and expects the buyer to remit payment according to the agreed-upon terms. The exporter is relying fully upon the financial creditworthiness, integrity, and reputation of the buyer. As might be expected, this method is used when seller and buyer have mutual trust and a great deal of experience with each other. Despite the risks involved, open account transactions are widely utilized, particularly among the industrialized countries in North America and Europe.

Trade Finance Methods

As mentioned in the previous section, banks on both sides of the transaction play a critical role in financing international trade. Some of the more popular methods of financing international trade include

- accounts receivable financing
- factoring
- letters of credit (L/C)
- banker's acceptances
- working capital financing
- medium-term capital goods financing (forfaiting)
- countertrade

Each of these methods is described in turn.

Accounts Receivable Financing

In some cases, the exporter of goods may be willing to ship goods to the importer without an assurance of payment from a bank. This could take the form of an open account shipment or a time draft. Prior to shipment, the exporter should have conducted its own credit check on the importer to determine creditworthiness. If the exporter is willing to wait for payment, it will extend credit to the buyer.

If the exporter needs funds immediately, it may require financing from a bank. In what is referred to as **accounts receivable financing,** the bank will provide a loan to the exporter secured by an assignment of the account receivable. The bank's loan is made to the exporter based on its creditworthiness. In the event the buyer fails to pay the exporter for whatever reason, the exporter is still responsible to repay the bank.

Accounts receivable financing involves additional risks, such as government restrictions and exchange controls, that may prevent the buyer from paying the exporter. As a result, the loan rate is often higher than domestic accounts receivable financing. The length of a financing term is usually one to six months. To mitigate the additional risk of a foreign receivable, exporters and banks often require export credit insurance before financing foreign receivables.

Factoring

When an exporter ships goods before receiving payment, the accounts receivable balance increases. Unless the exporter has received a loan from a bank, it is initially financing the transaction and must monitor the collections of receivables. Since there is a danger that the buyer will never pay at all, the exporting firm may consider selling the accounts receivable to a third party, known as a **factor.** In this type of financing, the exporter sells the accounts receivable without recourse. The factor then assumes all administrative responsibilities involved in collecting from the buyer and the associated credit exposure. As one would expect, the factor performs its own credit approval process on the foreign buyer before purchasing the receivable. For providing this service, the factor usually purchases the receivable at a discount and also receives a flat processing fee.

Factoring provides several benefits to the exporter. First, by selling the accounts receivable, the exporter does not have to worry about the administrative duties involved in maintaining and monitoring an accounts receivable accounting ledger. Second, the factor assumes the credit exposure to the buyer so the exporter does not have to maintain personnel to assess the creditworthiness of foreign buyers. Finally, the sale of the receivable to the factor provides immediate payment and improves the exporter's cash flow.

Since it is the importer who must be creditworthy from a factor's point of view, **cross-border factoring** is often used. This involves a network of factors in various countries who assess credit risk. The exporter's factor contacts a correspondent factor in the buyer's country to assess the importer's creditworthiness and handle the collections of the receivable. Factoring services are usually provided by the factoring subsidiaries of commercial banks, commercial finance companies, and other specialized finance houses. Factors often utilize export credit insurance to mitigate the additional risk of a foreign receivable.

Letters of Credit (L/C)

Introduced earlier, the letter of credit (L/C) is one of the oldest forms of trade finance still in existence. Because of the protection and benefits it accords to both exporter and importer, it is a critical component of many international trade transactions. The L/C is an undertaking by a bank to make payments on behalf of a specified party to a beneficiary under specified conditions. The beneficiary (exporter) is paid upon presentation of the required documents in compliance with the terms of the L/C. The L/C process normally involves two banks, the exporter's bank and the importer's bank. The issuing bank is substituting its credit for that of the importer. It has essentially guaranteed payment to the exporter, provided the exporter complies with the terms and conditions of the L/C.

Sometimes the exporter is uncomfortable with the issuing bank's promise to pay, since the bank is located in a foreign country. Even if the issuing bank is well known worldwide, the exporter may be concerned that the foreign government might impose exchange controls or other restrictions that would prevent payment by the issuing bank. For this reason, the exporter may request that a local bank confirm the L/C and thus assure that all the responsibilities of the issuing bank will be met. The confirming bank is obligated to honor drawings made by the beneficiary in compliance with the L/C regardless of the issuing bank's ability to make that payment. Consequently, the confirming bank is trusting that the foreign bank issuing the L/C is sound. The exporter, however, need worry only about the credibility of the confirming bank.

Trade-related letters of credit are known as **commercial letters of credit** or **import/export letters of credit.** There are basically two types: revocable and irrevocable. A **revocable letter of credit** can be canceled or revoked at any time without prior notification to the beneficiary, and it is seldom used. An **irrevocable letter of credit** (see Exhibit 19.2) cannot be canceled or amended without the beneficiary's consent. The bank issuing the letter of credit is known as the **"issuing" bank.** The correspondent bank in the beneficiary's country to which the issuing bank sends the L/C is commonly referred to as the **"advising" bank.** An irrevocable L/C obligates the issuing bank to honor all drawings presented in conformity with the terms of the L/C. Letters of credit are normally issued in accordance with the provisions contained in "Uniform Customs and Practice for Documentary Credits," published by the International Chamber of Commerce.

Exhibit 19.2
Example of an Irrevocable Letter of Credit

Name of issuing bank

Address of issuing bank

Name of exporter

Address of exporter

We establish our irrevocable letter of credit:
for the account of (*importer name*),
in the amount of (*value of exports*),
expiring (*date*),
available by your draft at (*time period*) days sight and accompanied by: (any invoices, packing lists, bills of lading, etc., that need to be presented with the letter of credit)
Insurance provided by (*exporter or importer*)
covering shipment of (*merchandise description*)
From: (*port of shipment*)
To: (*port of arrival*)

(Authorized Signature)

____

The bank issuing the L/C makes payments once the required documentation has been presented in accordance with the payment terms. The importer must pay the issuing bank the amount of the L/C plus accrued fees associated with obtaining the L/C. The importer will usually have an account established at the issuing bank to be drawn upon for payment, so that the issuing bank does not tie up its own funds. However, if the importer does not have sufficient funds in its account, the issuing bank is still obligated to honor all valid drawings against the L/C. This is why the bank's decision to issue an L/C on behalf of an importer involves an analysis of the importer's creditworthiness and is analogous to the decision to make a loan. The documentary credit procedure is described in the flowchart in Exhibit 19.3. In what is commonly referred to as a *refinancing of a sight L/C,* the bank arranges to fund a loan to pay out the L/C instead of charging the importer's account immediately. The importer is responsible for repaying the bank both principal and interest at maturity. This is just another method of providing extended payment terms to a buyer when the exporter insists upon payment at sight.

The bank issuing the L/C makes payment to the beneficiary (exporter) upon presentation of documents that meet the conditions stipulated in the L/C. Letters of credit are payable either at sight (upon presentation of documents) or at a specified future date. The typical documentation required under an L/C includes a draft (sight or time), a commercial invoice, and a bill of lading. Depending upon the agreement, product, or country, other documents (such as a certificate of origin, inspection certificate, packing list, or insurance certificate) might be required. The three most common L/C documents are as follows.

Draft. Also known as a **bill of exchange,** a draft (introduced earlier) is an unconditional promise drawn by one party, usually the exporter, requesting the importer to pay the face amount of the draft at sight or at a specified future date. If the draft is

Exhibit 19.3
Documentary Credit Procedure

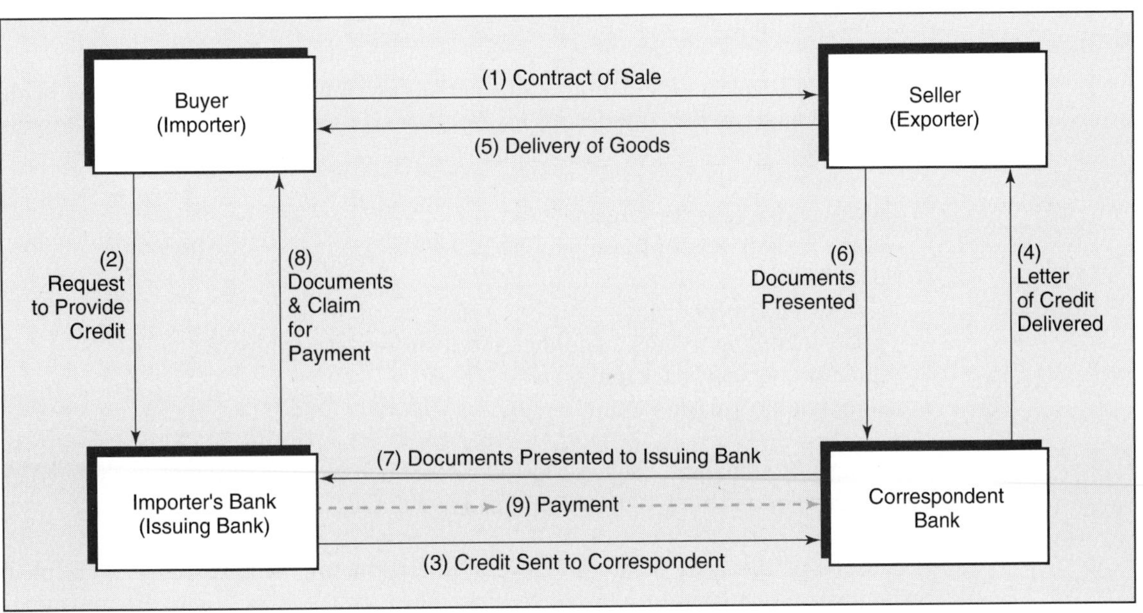

drawn at sight, it is payable upon presentation of documents. If it is payable at a specified future date (a time draft) and is accepted by the importer, it is known as a trade acceptance. A **banker's acceptance** is a time draft drawn on and accepted by a bank. When presented under a letter of credit, the draft represents the exporter's formal demand for payment. The time period, or **tenor,** of most time drafts is usually anywhere from 30 to 180 days.

Bill of Lading. The key document in an international shipment under an L/C is the **bill of lading (B/L).** It serves as a receipt for shipment and a summary of freight charges; most importantly, it conveys title to the merchandise. If the merchandise is to be shipped by boat, the carrier will issue what is known as an **ocean bill of lading.** When the merchandise is shipped by air, the carrier will issue an **airway bill.** The carrier presents the bill to the exporter (shipper), who in turn presents it to the bank along with the other required documents.

A significant feature of a B/L is its negotiability. A straight B/L is consigned directly to the importer. Since it does not represent title to the merchandise, the importer does not need it to pick up the merchandise. However, when a B/L is made out to order, it is said to be in negotiable form. The exporter normally endorses the B/L to the bank once payment is received from the bank.

The bank would not endorse the B/L over to the importer until payment had been made. The importer needs the original B/L to pick up the merchandise. With a **negotiable B/L,** title passes to the holder of the endorsed B/L. Because a negotiable B/L grants title to the holder, banks can take the merchandise as collateral. Some of the usual provisions contained within a B/L include

- a description of the merchandise
- identification marks on the merchandise
- evidence of loading (receiving) ports
- name of the exporter (shipper)
- name of the importer
- status of freight charges (prepaid or collect)
- date of shipment

Commercial Invoice. The exporter's (seller's) description of the merchandise being sold to the buyer is the **commercial invoice,** which normally contains the following information:

- name and address of seller
- name and address of buyer
- date
- terms of payment
- price, including freight, handling, and insurance if applicable
- quantity, weight, packaging, etc.
- shipping information

Under an L/C shipment, the description of the merchandise outlined in the invoice must correspond exactly to that contained in the L/C.

Variations of the L/C. There are several variations of the L/C that are useful in financing trade. A **standby letter of credit** can be used to guarantee invoice payments to a supplier. It promises to pay the beneficiary if the buyer fails to pay as agreed. Internationally, standby L/Cs often are used with government-related contracts and serve as bid bonds, performance bonds, or advance payment guarantees. In an international or domestic trade transaction, the seller would agree to ship to the buyer on standard open account terms as long as the buyer provided a standby L/C for a specified amount and term. As long as the buyer pays the seller as agreed, the standby L/C is never funded. However, if the buyer fails to pay, the exporter may present documents under the L/C and request payment from the bank. The buyer's bank is essentially guaranteeing that the buyer will make payment to the seller.

A **transferable letter of credit** is a variation of the standard commercial L/C that allows the first beneficiary to transfer all or a part of the original L/C to a third party. The new beneficiary has the same rights and protection as the original beneficiary. This type of L/C is used extensively by brokers, who are not the actual suppliers. For example, the broker asks the foreign buyer to issue an L/C for $100,000 in his favor. The L/C must contain a clause stating that the L/C is transferable. The broker has located a supplier who will provide the product for $80,000. However, the end supplier has requested payment in advance from the broker. With a transferable L/C, the broker can transfer $80,000 of the original L/C to the end supplier under the same terms and conditions, except for the amount, the latest shipment date, the invoice, and the period of validity. When the end supplier ships the product, it presents its documents to the bank. When the bank pays the L/C, $80,000 is paid to the end supplier and $20,000 goes to the broker. In effect, the broker has utilized the credit of the buyer to finance the entire transaction.

An **assignment of proceeds** under an L/C is another method of financing a transaction involving a broker. The original beneficiary of the L/C may pledge (or assign) the proceeds under an L/C to the end supplier. The end supplier has the assurance from the bank that if and when documents are presented in compliance with the

Nike Problem

Use of Letters of Credit

Nike can attribute part of its international business growth in the 1970s to the use of letters of credit. In 1971, Nike (which was then called BSR) was not well known to businesses in Japan or anywhere else. However, it was still able to subcontract the production of athletic shoes in Japan, by using letters of credit. This assured the shoe producer in Japan that it would receive payment for the shoes that would be sent to the United States, and facilitated the flow of trade without concern about credit risk. Banks served as the guarantors in the event that the Japanese shoe company was not paid in full after transporting shoes to the United States. Thus, because of the backing of the banks, the letters of credit allowed the Japanese shoe company to do international business without concern that the counterparty in its agreement would fulfill its obligation. Without such agreements, Nike (and many other firms) would not have been able to order the shipments of goods.

Discussion: When retail stores based outside the countries where Nike has its production facilities order shipments of Nike's shoes, Nike may not have sufficient information to determine the credit quality of these retail stores. How do letters of credit facilitate such international transactions?

terms of the L/C, the bank will pay the end supplier according to the assignment instructions. This assignment is valid only if the beneficiary presents documents that comply with the L/C. The end supplier must recognize that the issuing bank is under no obligation to pay the end supplier if the original beneficiary never ships the goods or fails to comply with the terms of the L/C.

Banker's Acceptances

Introduced earlier, a banker's acceptance (shown in Exhibit 19.4) is a bill of exchange, or time draft, drawn on and accepted by a bank. It is the accepting bank's obligation to pay the holder of the draft at maturity.

The first step in the creation of a banker's acceptance is for the importer to order goods from the exporter. The importer then requests its local bank to issue an L/C on its behalf. The L/C will allow the exporter to draw a time draft on the bank in payment for the exported goods. The exporter presents the time draft along with shipping documents to its local bank, and the exporter's bank sends the time draft along with shipping documents to the importer's bank. The importer's bank accepts the draft, thereby creating the banker's acceptance. If the exporter does not want to wait until the specified date to receive payment, it can request that the banker's acceptance be sold in the money market. In this case, the funds received from the sale of a banker's acceptance are less than they would be if the exporter waited to receive payment. Such a discount reflects the time value of money.

A money market investor may be willing to buy the banker's acceptance at a discount and hold it until payment is due. This investor will then receive full payment because the banker's acceptance represents a future claim on funds of the bank represented by the acceptance. The bank will make full payment at the date specified, since it expects to receive this amount plus an additional fee from the importer.

If the exporter holds the acceptance until maturity, it provides the financing for the importer as it does with accounts receivable financing. In this case, the key difference between use of a banker's acceptance and accounts receivable financing is that a banker's acceptance guarantees payment to the exporter by a bank. However, if the exporter sells the banker's acceptance in the secondary market, it is no longer providing the financing for the importer. The holder of the banker's acceptance is financing instead.

Exhibit 19.4
Banker's Acceptance

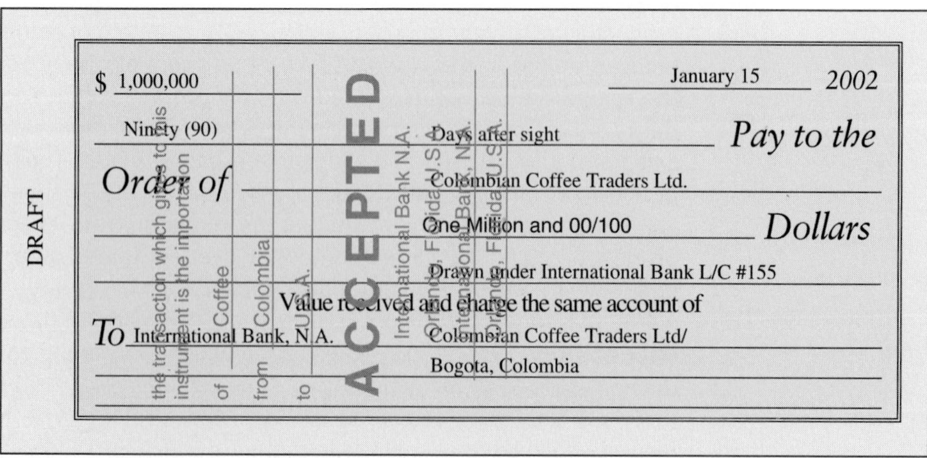

DRAFT

$ 1,000,000 January 15 2002

Ninety (90) Days after sight *Pay to the*

Order of Colombian Coffee Traders Ltd.

One Million and 00/100 *Dollars*

Drawn under International Bank L/C #155

Value received and charge the same account of

To International Bank, N.A. Colombian Coffee Traders Ltd/

Bogota, Colombia

ACCEPTED

International Bank N.A.

Orlando, Florida U.S.A.

the transaction which gives rise to this instrument is the importation of Coffee from Colombia to U.S.A.

A banker's acceptance can be beneficial to the exporter, importer, and issuing bank. The exporter does not need to worry about the credit risk of the importer and can therefore penetrate new foreign markets without concern about the credit risk of potential customers. In addition, there is little exposure to political risk or to exchange controls imposed by a government. Banks normally are allowed to meet their payment commitments even under the existence of controls. Yet, an importer may have greater difficulty in making payment to the exporter if controls are imposed. Without a banker's acceptance, an exporter might not receive payment even if the importer is willing to pay, due to exchange controls. Finally, the exporter can sell the banker's acceptance at a discount before payment is due and thus obtain funds up front from the issuing bank.

The importer benefits from a banker's acceptance in that it has greater access to foreign markets when purchasing supplies and other products. Without banker's acceptances, exporters may be unwilling to accept the credit risk of importers. Due to the documents presented along with the acceptance, the importer is assured that goods have been shipped. Even though the importer has not paid in advance, this assurance is valuable since the importer may need to know if and when supplies and other products will arrive. Finally, because the banker's acceptance allows the importer to pay at a later date, the importer's payment is financed until the maturity date of the banker's acceptance. Without an acceptance, the importer would likely be forced to pay in advance, thereby tying up funds.

The bank accepting the drafts benefits in that it earns a commission for creating an acceptance. The commission that the bank charges the customer reflects the perceived creditworthiness of the customer. The interest rate charged the customer, which is commonly referred to as the **all-in-rate,** consists of the discount rate plus the acceptance commission. In general, the all-in-rate for acceptance financing is lower than prime-based borrowings, as shown in the following comparison:

	Loan	Acceptance
Amount:	$1,000,000	$1,000,000
Term:	180 Days	180 Days
Rate:	Prime + 1.5%	BA Rate + 1.5%
	10.0% + 1.5% = 11.5%	7.60% + 1.5% = 9.10%
Interest Cost:	$57,500	$45,500

In this example, the interest savings for a six-month period is $12,000. Since the banker's acceptance is a marketable instrument with an active secondary market, the rates on acceptances usually fall between those of short-term Treasury bills and those of commercial paper. Investors are usually willing to purchase acceptances as an investment because of their yield, safety, and liquidity. When a bank creates, accepts, and sells the acceptance, it is actually using the investor's money to finance the bank's customer. As a result, the bank has created an asset at one price, sold it at another, and retained a commission (spread) as its fee.

Banker's acceptance financing can also be arranged through the refinancing of a sight letter of credit. In this case, the exporter (beneficiary) of the letter of credit may insist upon payment at sight. So that the importer can obtain terms, the bank arranges to finance the payment of the sight letter of credit under a separate acceptance-financing agreement. The importer (borrower) simply draws drafts upon the bank, which in turn accepts and discounts the drafts. Proceeds are used to pay the exporter. At maturity, the importer is responsible for repayment to the bank.

Acceptance financing can also be arranged without the use of a letter of credit under a separate acceptance agreement. Similar to a regular loan agreement, it stipulates the terms and conditions under which the bank is prepared to finance the borrower using acceptances instead of promissory notes. As long as the acceptances meet one of the underlying transaction requirements, the bank and borrower can utilize banker's acceptances as an alternative financing mechanism. The life cycle of a banker's acceptance is illustrated in Exhibit 19.5.

Exhibit 19.5

Life Cycle of a Typical Banker's Acceptance (B/A)

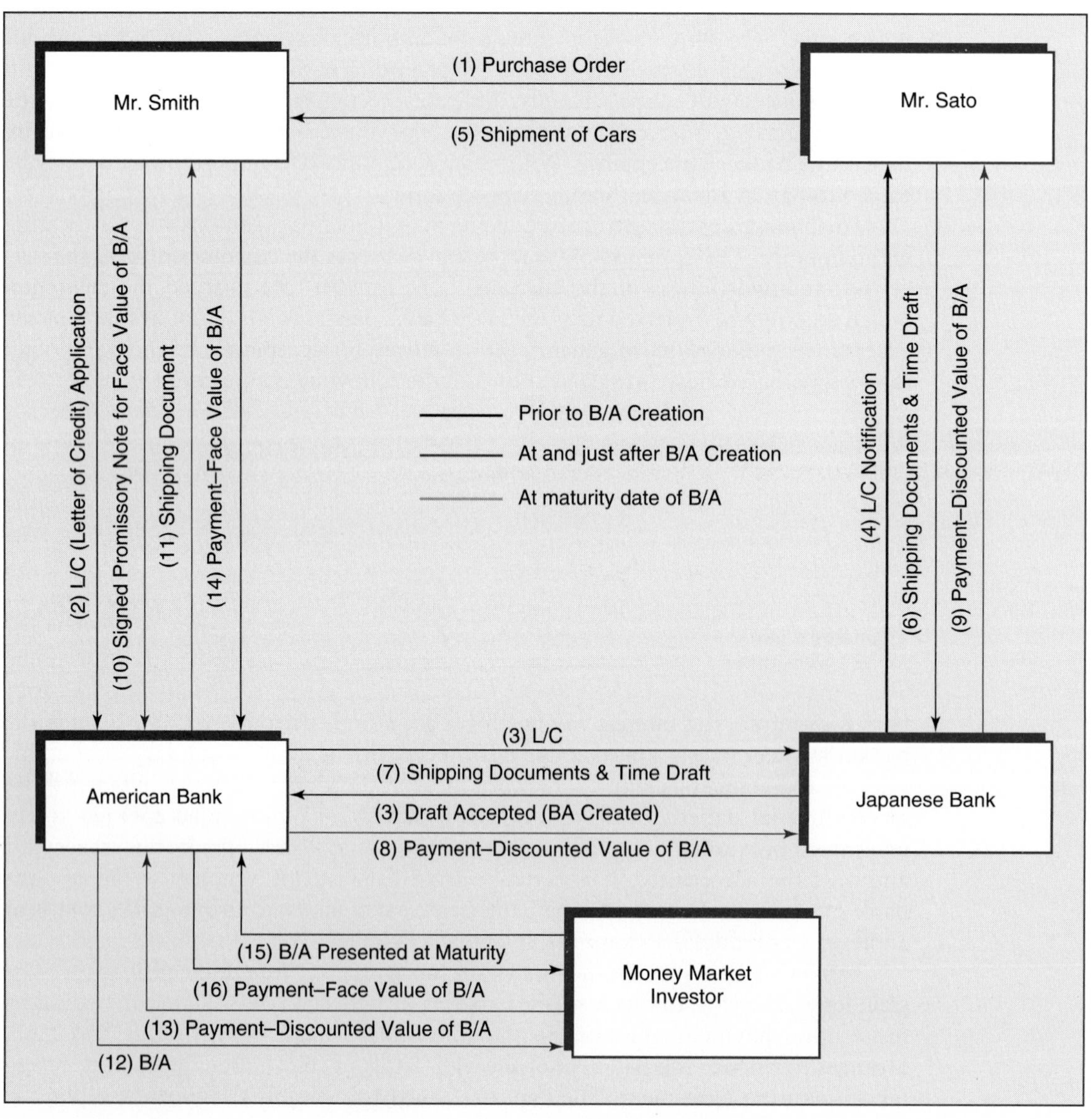

Working Capital Financing

As just explained, a banker's acceptance can allow an exporter to receive funds immediately, yet allow an importer to delay its payment until a future date. The bank may even provide short-term loans beyond the banker's acceptance period. In the case of an importer, the purchase from overseas usually represents the acquisition of inventory. The loan finances the working capital cycle that begins with the purchase of inventory and continues with the sale of the goods, creation of an account receivable, and conversion to cash. With an exporter, the short-term loan might finance the manufacture of the merchandise destined for export (pre-export financing) or the time period from when the sale is made until payment is received from the buyer. For example, the firm may have imported foreign beer, which it plans to distribute to grocery and liquor stores. The bank not only can provide a letter of credit for trade finance but it can also finance the importer's cost from the time of distribution and collection of payment.

Medium-Term Capital Goods Financing (Forfaiting)

Because capital goods are often quite expensive, an importer may not be able to make payment on the goods within a short time period. Thus, longer-term financing may be required here. The exporter might be able to provide financing for the importer but may not desire to do so, since the financing may extend over several years. In this case, a type of trade finance known as **forfaiting** could be used. Forfaiting refers to the purchase of financial obligations, such as bills of exchange or promissory notes, without recourse to the original holder, usually the exporter. In a forfait transaction, the importer would issue a promissory note in favor of the exporter to pay for the imported capital goods. The term generally ranges from three to seven years. The exporter would then sell the notes, without recourse, to the forfaiting bank. In some respects, this is similar to factoring, in that the forfaiter (or factor) assumes responsibility for the collection of payment from the buyer, the underlying credit risk, and risk pertaining to countries. Since the forfaiting bank assumes the risk of nonpayment, it should assess the creditworthiness of the importer as if it were extending a medium-term loan. Forfait transactions normally are collateralized by a bank guarantee or letter of credit issued by the importer's bank for the term of the transaction. Since financial information is usually difficult to obtain on the importer, the forfaiting bank places a great deal of reliance on the bank guarantee as the collateral in the event the buyer fails to pay as agreed. It is this guarantee backing up the transaction that has fostered the growth of the forfait market, particularly in Europe, as a practical means of trade finance.

Forfaiting transactions are usually in excess of $500,000 and can be denominated in most currencies. For some larger transactions, more than one bank may be involved. In this case, a syndicate is formed wherein each participant assumes a proportionate share of the underlying risk and profit. A forfaiting firm may decide to sell the promissory notes of the importer to other financial institutions willing to purchase them. However, the forfaiting firm is still responsible for payment on the notes in the event the importer is unable to pay.

Countertrade

The term **countertrade** denotes all types of foreign trade transactions in which the sale of goods to one country is linked to the purchase or exchange of goods from that same country. Some types of countertrade, such as barter, have been in existence for thousands of years. However, only recently has countertrade gained popularity and importance. The growth in various types of countertrade has been fueled by large balance of payment disequilibriums, foreign currency shortages, and LDC debt problems, and stagnant worldwide demand. As a result, many MNCs have been confronted with countertrade opportunities, particularly in Asia, Latin America, and Eastern Europe. The most common types of countertrade include barter, compensation, and counterpurchase.

Barter represents the exchange of goods between two parties without the use of any currency as a medium of exchange. Most barter arrangements are one-time transactions governed by one contract. An example would be the exchange of 100 tons of wheat from Canada for 20 tons of shrimp from Ecuador.

In a **compensation** or clearing-account arrangement, the delivery of goods to one party is compensated for by the seller's buying back a certain amount of the product from that same party. The transaction is governed by one contract, and the value of the goods is expressed in monetary terms. The buy-back arrangement could be for a fraction of the original sale (**partial compensation**) or more than 100 percent of the original sale (**full compensation**). An example of compensation would be the sale of phosphate from Morocco to France in exchange for purchasing a certain percentage of fertilizer. In some countries, this is also referred to as an industrial cooperation arrangement. Such arrangements often involve the construction of large projects, such as power plants, in exchange for the purchase of the project's output over an extended period of time. For example, a hydroelectric plant was sold by Brazil to Argentina in exchange for Brazil's purchase of a percentage of the plant's output over a long-term contract.

The term **counterpurchase** denotes the exchange of goods between two parties under two distinct contracts expressed in monetary terms. Delivery and payment of both goods are technically separate transactions.

The countertrade market is still developing. The primary participants are governments and multinationals, with assistance provided by specialists in the field, such as attorneys, financial institutions, and trading companies. The transactions are usually very complex and large. Many variations of countertrade exist, and the terminology used by the various market participants is still forming. Nonetheless, despite the economic inefficiencies of countertrade, it has grown in significance and is used by the experienced traders and governments.

Agencies That Motivate International Trade

Due to the inherent risks of international trade, government institutions and the private sector offer various forms of export credit, export finance, and guarantee programs to reduce risk and stimulate foreign trade.

The prominent agencies providing this service in the United States are

- Export-Import Bank of the U.S. (Ex-Imbank)
- Private Export Funding Corporation (PEFCO)
- Overseas Private Investment Corporation (OPIC)

Each of these agencies is described in turn.

http://
Visit www.exim.gov, the site of the Export-Import Bank of the United States, for interest rates charged by an export credit agency.

Export-Import Bank of the United States

Ex-Imbank was established in 1934 with the original intention to facilitate Soviet-American trade. Its mission today is to finance and facilitate the export of American goods and services and maintain the competitiveness of American companies in overseas markets. It operates as an independent agency of the U.S. government and, as such, carries the full faith and credit of the United States. In over 60 years, Ex-Imbank has supported over $300 billion in U.S. exports. In fact, since 1988, Ex-Imbank has financed, guaranteed, or insured over $14 billion in U.S. exports.

The programs of Ex-Imbank are typically designed to encourage the private sector to finance export trade by assume some of the underlying credit risk, and provide direct financing to foreign importers when private lenders are unwilling to do so. To satisfy these objectives, the Ex-Imbank offers programs that are classified as: (1) guarantees, (2) loans, (3) bank insurance, and (4) export credit insurance.

Guarantee Programs. The two most widely used guarantee programs are the **Working Capital Guarantee Program** and the **Medium-Term Guarantee Program.** The Working Capital Guarantee Program encourages commercial banks to extend short-term export financing to eligible exporters by providing a comprehensive guarantee that covers 90 to 100 percent of the loan's principal and interest. Ex-Imbank's guarantee protects the lender against the risk of default by the exporter. It does not protect the exporter against the risk of nonpayment by the foreign buyer. The loans are fully collateralized by export receivables and export inventory and require the payment of guarantee fees to Ex-Imbank. The export receivables are usually supported with export credit insurance or a letter of credit.

The Guarantee Program encourages commercial lenders to finance the sale of U.S. capital equipment and services to approved foreign buyers. The Ex-Imbank guarantees 100 percent of the loan's principal and interest. The financed amount cannot exceed 85 percent of the contract price. This program is designed to finance products sold on a medium-term basis, with repayment terms of generally between one and five years. The guarantee fees paid to Ex-Imbank are determined by the repayment terms and buyer's risk. Ex-Imbank now offers a leasing program to finance capital equipment and related services.

Loan Programs. Two of the most popular loan programs are the **Direct Loan Program** and the **Project Finance Loan Program.** Under the Direct Loan Program, Ex-Imbank offers fixed-rate loans directly to the foreign buyer to purchase U.S. capital equipment and services on a medium-term or long-term basis. The total financed amount cannot exceed 85 percent of the contract price. Repayment terms depend upon the amount but are typically one to five years for medium-term transactions and seven to ten years for long-term transactions. Ex-Imbank's lending rates are generally below market rates.

The Project Finance Loan Program allows banks, Ex-Imbank, or a combination of both to extend long-term financing for capital equipment and related services for major projects. These are typically large infrastructure projects, such as power generation, whose repayment depends on project cash flows. Major U.S. corporations are often involved in these types of projects. The program typically requires a 15 percent cash payment by the foreign buyer and allows for guarantees of up to 85 percent of the contract amount. The fees and interest rates will vary depending on project risk.

Bank Insurance Programs. Ex-Imbank offers several insurance policies to banks. The most widely used is the **Bank Letter of Credit Policy.** This policy enables banks to confirm letters of credit issued by foreign banks supporting a purchase of U.S. exports. Without this insurance, some banks would not be willing to assume the underlying commercial and political risk associated with confirming a letter of credit. The banks are insured up to 100 percent for sovereign (government) banks and 95 percent for all other banks. The premium is based on the type of buyer, repayment term, and country. The **Financial Institution Buyer Credit Policy** is issued in the name of the bank. This policy provides insurance coverage for loans by banks to foreign buyers on a short-term basis. A variety of short-term and medium-term insurance policies are available to exporters, banks, and other eligible applicants. Basically, all the policies provide insurance protection against the risk of nonpayment by foreign buyers. If the foreign buyer fails to pay the exporter because of commercial reasons such as cash flow problems or insolvency, Ex-Imbank will reimburse the exporter between 90 and 100 percent of the insured amount, depending upon the type of policy and buyer. If the loss is due to political factors, such as foreign exchange controls or war, Ex-Imbank will reimburse the exporter for 100 percent of the insured amount. The insurance policies can be used by exporters as a marketing tool by enabling them to offer more competitive terms while protecting them against the risk of nonpayment. The exporter can also use the insurance policy as a financing tool by assigning the proceeds of the policy to a bank as collateral. Certain restrictions may apply to particular countries, depending upon Ex-Imbank's experience, as well as existing economic and political conditions.

http://
The SBA's Office of International Trade, www.sbaonline.sba.gov/oit/finance/programs.html, gives information about all available trade finance programs.

The **Small Business Policy** provides enhanced coverage to new exporters and small businesses. Firms with very few export credit sales are eligible for this policy. The policy will insure short-term credit sales (under 180 days) to approved foreign buyers. In addition to providing 95 percent coverage against commercial risk defaults and 100 percent against political risk, the policy offers lower premiums and no annual commercial risk loss deductible. The exporter can assign the policy to a bank as collateral.

The **Umbrella Policy** operates in a slightly different manner. The policy itself is issued to an "administrator," such as a bank, trading company, insurance broker, or government agency. The policyholder administers the policy for multiple exporters and relieves the exporters of the administrative responsibilities associated with the policy. The short-term insurance protection is similar to the Small Business Policy and does not have a commercial risk deductible. The proceeds of the policy may be assigned to a bank for financing purposes.

The **Multi-Buyer Policy** is used primarily by the experienced exporter. It provides insurance coverage on short-term export sales to many different buyers. Premiums are based on an exporter's sales profile, credit history, terms of repayment, country, and other factors. Based upon the exporter's experience and the buyer's creditworthiness, Ex-Imbank may grant the exporter authority to preapprove specific buyers up to a certain limit.

The **Single-Buyer Policy** allows an exporter to selectively insure certain short-term transactions to preapproved buyers. Premiums are based on repayment term and transaction risk. There is also a Medium-Term Policy to cover sales to a single buyer for terms of between one and five years.

Ex-Imbank has also entered into partnership arrangements with more than 30 states to disseminate government trade promotion services to a broader audience.

For example, in Florida, the Florida Export Finance Corp provides export credit insurance consulting, trade finance, and guarantees to exporters based in Florida.

There are several private insurance carriers, such as AIG, that provide various types of insurance policies that may be used to mitigate risk. They are frequently employed when Ex-Imbank insurance is not available or desirable.

Private Export Funding Corporation (PEFCO)

PEFCO, a private corporation, is owned by a consortium of commercial banks and industrial companies. In cooperation with Ex-Imbank, PEFCO provides medium- and long-term fixed-rate financing to foreign buyers. Ex-Imbank guarantees all export loans made by PEFCO. Most PEFCO loans are to finance large projects, such as aircraft and power generation equipment, and as a result have very long terms (5 to 25 years). Since commercial banks usually do not extend such long terms, PEFCO fills a void in the market. PEFCO raises its funds in the capital markets through the issuance of long-term bonds. These bonds are readily marketable since they are in effect secured by Ex-Imbank-guaranteed loans.

Overseas Private Investment Corporation (OPIC)

OPIC, formed in 1971, is a self-sustaining federal agency responsible for insuring direct U.S. investments in foreign countries against the risks of currency inconvertibility, expropriation, and other political risks. Through the direct loan or guaranty program, OPIC will provide medium- to long-term financing to U.S. investors undertaking an overseas venture. In addition to the general insurance and finance programs, OPIC offers specific types of coverage for exporters bidding on or performing foreign contracts. American contractors can insure themselves against contractual disputes and even the wrongful calling of standby letters of credit.

Other Considerations

Beyond the insurance and financing, there are U.S. tax provisions that encourage international trade. Beginning in 1985, the Foreign Sales Corporation (FSC) replaced the Domestic International Sales Corporation (DISC) as the primary tax vehicle to promote U.S. exports. DISC provided a U.S. exporter with a tax deferral on a percentage of its income generated through export sales. The new FSC rules allow for the exporter to receive up to a 15 percent tax exemption on income earned through the FSC. However, the FSC must be incorporated offshore and meet certain procedural and administrative requirements.

Impact of International Trade Financing on an MNC's Value

International trade financing by an MNC can affect its value, as shown in Exhibit 19.6. International trade financing methods enable an MNC to do business with foreign customers that it may not be able to do otherwise. Thus, subsidiaries of an MNC can conduct more business as a result of international trade financing, which

Exhibit 19.6
Impact of Trade Financing Decisions on an MNC's Value

Trade Financing Decisions

$$V = \sum_{t=1}^{n} \left\{ \frac{\sum_{j=1}^{m} \left[E(CF_{j,t}) \times E(ER_{j,t}) \right]}{(1+k)^t} \right\}$$

V = value of the U.S.-based MNC
$E(CF_{j,t})$ = expected cash flows denominated in currency j to be received by the U.S. parent in period t
$E(ER_{j,t})$ = expected exchange rate at which currency j can be converted to dollars at the end of period t
k = the weighted average cost of capital of the U.S. parent company
m = number of currencies
n = number of periods

increases the expected foreign currency cash flows. These subsidiaries may also be able to obtain supplies at a lower cost through importing and the use of international trade financing, which increases the expected foreign currency cash flows. Thus, the expected dollar cash flows that will ultimately be received by the U.S. parent can be enhanced by the use of international trade financing.

SUMMARY

- The common methods of payment for international trade are (1) prepayment (before goods are sent), (2) letters of credit, (3) drafts, (4) consignment, and (5) open account.
- The most popular methods of financing international trade are (1) accounts receivable financing, (2) factoring, (3) letters of credit, (4) banker's acceptances, (5) working capital financing, (6) medium-term capital goods financing (forfaiting), and (7) countertrade.
- The major agencies that facilitate international trade with export insurance and/or loan programs are (1) Export-Import Bank, (2)Private Export Funding Corporation, and (3) Overseas Private Investment Corporation.

SELF-TEST FOR CHAPTER 19

(Answers are provided in Appendix A at the back of the text.)

1. Explain why so many international transactions require international trade credit facilitated by commercial banks.
2. Explain the difference in the risk to the exporter between accounts receivable financing and factoring.
3. Explain how the Export-Import Bank can encourage U.S. firms to export to less developed countries where there is political risk.

QUESTIONS AND APPLICATIONS

1. How can a banker's acceptance be beneficial to (1) an exporter? (2) an importer? (3) a bank?
2. Why would an exporter provide financing for an importer? Is there much risk in this activity? Explain.
3. What is the role of a factor within international trade transactions? How can a factor aid an exporter?
4. What is the role today of the Export-Import Bank of the United States?
5. What are bills of lading, and how do they facilitate international trade transactions?
6. What is forfaiting? Specify the type of traded goods for which forfaiting is applied.
7. Briefly describe the role of PEFCO.
8. In this chapter, many forms of government insurance and guarantee programs are described. What motivates a government to establish so many programs?
9. Describe how the desirability for foreign trade would be affected if banks did not provide trade-related services.
10. What is countertrade?
11. Briefly describe the Working Capital Guarantee Program administered by the Export-Import Bank.
12. Describe the Direct Loan Program that is administered by the Export-Import Bank.
13. Describe the Small Business Policy.
14. Describe the role of the Overseas Private Investment Corporation (OPIC).
15. Ocean Traders of North America is a firm based in Mobile, Alabama, that specializes in seafood exports and commonly uses letters of credit to ensure payment. It recently experienced a problem, however. The U.S. exporter had an irrevocable letter of credit issued by a Russian bank to ensure that it would receive payment upon shipment of 16,000 tons of fish to a Russian firm. However, this bank backed out of its obligation, stating that is it not authorized to guarantee commercial transactions.
    a. Explain how the irrevocable letters of credit would normally facilitate the business transaction between the Russian importer and Ocean Traders of North America (the U.S. exporter).
    b. Explain how the cancellation of the letter of credit could create a trade crisis between the U.S. and Russian firms.
    c. Why do you think situations like this (the cancellation of the letter of credit) are rare in industrialized countries?
    d. Can you think of any alternative strategy that the U.S. exporter could have used to protect itself better when dealing with a Russian importer?

Internet Application

16. The Web site of the Export-Import Bank of the United States offers information about trade financing. Its address is:

    http://www.exim.gov

Review the section on Small Business Programs and summarize what the Ex-Imbank does to facilitate trade by small businesses.

Running Your Own MNC

Ensuring Payment for Exports

17. Explain how your business could ensure payment for the products that you are exporting to a foreign country.

Blades, Inc. Case

Assessment of International Trade Financing in Thailand

Blades, Inc., has recently decided to establish a subsidiary in Thailand in order to produce "Speedos," Blades' primary roller blade product. The establishment of a subsidiary in Thailand was motivated by the high growth potential of the Thai roller blade market. Furthermore, Blades has decided to establish a subsidiary, as opposed to acquiring an existing Thai roller blade manufacturer for sale, in order to maintain its flexibility and control over the operations in Thailand. Moreover, Blades, Inc. has decided to issue yen-denominated notes to partially finance the cost of establishing a subsidiary in Thailand. Blades has decided to issue yen instead of baht-denominated notes to avoid the high effective interest rates associated with the baht-denominated notes.

Currently, Blades plans to sell all roller blades manufactured in Thailand to retailers in Thailand. Furthermore, Blades plans to purchase all components for roller blades manufactured in Thailand from Thai suppliers. Similarly, all of Blades' roller blades manufactured in the United States will be sold to retailers in the United States and all components needed for Blades' U.S. production will be purchased from suppliers in the United States. Consequently, Blades will have no exports and imports once the plant in Thailand is operational, which is expected to occur early next year.

Construction of the plant in Thailand has already begun, and Blades is currently in the process of purchasing the machinery necessary to produce "Speedos." Besides these activities, Ben Holt, Blades' chief financial officer (CFO), has been actively engaged in lining up suppliers of the needed rubber and plastic components in Thailand and in the identification of its Thai customers, which will consist of various sports product retailers in Thailand.

Although Ben Holt has been successful in locating both interested suppliers and interested customers, he is discovering that he has neglected certain precautions of operating a subsidiary in Thailand. First, although Blades is relatively well known in the United States, it is not recognized internationally. Consequently, the suppliers Blades would like to use in Thailand are not familiar with Blades and have no information on the firm's reputation. Moreover, Blades' previous activities in Thailand were restricted to the export of a fixed number of "Speedos" annually to one customer, a Thai retailer called Entertainment Products. However, Ben Holt has little information about Blades' potential Thai customers that would buy the roller blades produced by the newly constructed plant. Nevertheless, although letters of credit (L/Cs) and drafts are usually employed for exporting purposes, these instruments are also used for trade within a country between relatively unknown parties.

Even though Blades has identified various potential customers in Thailand, four retailers of sports products appear particularly interested. Due to the fact that Blades is not familiar with these firms and their reputation, it would like to receive payment from these firms as soon as possible. Ideally, Blades would like its customers to prepay for their purchases, as this would involve the least risk for Blades. Unfortunately, none of the four potential customers have agreed to a prepayment arrangement. In fact, one of these potential customers, Cool Runnings, Inc., insists on an open account transaction. Payment terms in Thailand for purchases of this type are typically "net 60," indicating that payment for the roller blades would be due approximately two months after a purchase has been made. Two of the remaining three retailers, Sports Equipment, Inc., and Major Leagues, Inc., have indicated that they would prefer an open account transaction; however, both of these retailers have indicated that their banks would act as intermediaries for a time draft. The fourth retailer, Sports Gear, Inc., is indifferent as to the specific payment method but has indicated to Blades that it finds a prepayment arrangement unacceptable.

Blades also needs a suitable arrangement with its various potential suppliers of rubber and plastic components in Thailand. Because Blades' financing of the Thai subsidiary involved a U.S. bank, it has virtually no contacts in the Thai banking system. Because Blades is relatively unknown in Thailand, Thai suppliers have indicated that they would prefer prepayment or at least a guarantee from a Thai bank that Blades will be able to make payment within 30 days of purchase. Blades does not currently have accounts receivable in Thailand. It does, however, have accounts receivable in the United States resulting from its U.S. sales.

Ben Holt would like to please Blades' Thai customers and suppliers in order to establish strong business relationships in Thailand. However, he is worried that Blades may be at a disadvantage if it concedes to the Thai firms' demands entirely. Consequently, he has asked you, a financial analyst of Blades, Inc., to provide him with some guidance regarding international trade financing. Specifically, Mr. Holt has asked you to answer the following questions for him:

1. Assuming that banks in Thailand issue a time draft on behalf of Sports Equipment, Inc., and Major Leagues, Inc., would Blades, Inc., receive payment for its roller blades before it delivers them? Do the banks issuing the time drafts guarantee payment on behalf of the Thai retailers if the latter default on the payment?
2. What payment method should Blades suggest to Sports Gear, Inc.? Substantiate your answer.
3. What organization could Blades contact in order to insure its sales to the Thai retailers? What type of insurance do these organizations provide?
4. How could Blades use accounts receivable financing or factoring considering that it does not currently have accounts receivable in Thailand? If Blades uses a Thai bank to obtain this financing, how do you think the fact that Blades does not have receivables in Thailand would affect the terms of financing?
5. Assuming that Blades is unable to locate a Thai bank that is willing to issue a letter of credit on Blades' behalf, can you think of a way Blades could utilize its bank in the United States to effectively obtain a letter of credit from a Thai bank?
6. What organizations could Blades contact to obtain working capital financing? If Blades is unable to obtain working capital financing from these organizations, what are its other options to finance its working capital needs in Thailand?

Small Business Dilemma

Ensuring Payment for Products Exported by the Sports Exports Company

The Sports Exports Company produces footballs and exports them to a distributor in the United Kingdom. It typically sends footballs in bulk and then receives payment after the distributor receives the shipment. The business relationship with the distributor is based on trust. Although the relationship has worked thus far, Jim Logan (owner of the Sports Exports Company) is concerned about the possibility that the distributor will not make its payment.

1. How could a letter of credit be used by Jim to ensure that he will be paid for the products he exports?
2. Jim has discussed the possibility of expanding his export business through a second sporting goods distributor in the United Kingdom; this second distributor would cover a different territory than the first distributor. The second distributor is only willing to engage in a consignment arrangement when selling footballs to retail stores. Explain the risk to Jim beyond the typical types of risk Jim incurs when dealing with the first distributor. Should Jim pursue this type of business?

20 SHORT-TERM FINANCING

All firms make short-term financing decisions periodically. Beyond the trade financing discussed in the previous chapter, multinational corporations (MNCs) obtain short-term financing to support other operations as well. Because MNCs have access to additional sources of funds, their short-term financing decisions are more complex than those of other companies.

The specific objectives of this chapter are to

- explain why MNCs consider foreign financing,
- explain how MNCs determine whether to use foreign financing, and
- illustrate the possible benefits of financing with a portfolio of currencies.

SOURCES OF SHORT-TERM FINANCING

MNC parents and their subsidiaries typically use various methods of obtaining short-term funds to satisfy their liquidity needs. One method increasingly used in recent years is the issuing of **Euronotes,** or unsecured debt securities. The interest rates on these notes are based on LIBOR (the interest rate Eurobanks charge on interbank loans). They typically have maturities of one, three, or six months. Some MNCs continually roll them over as a form of intermediate-term financing. Commercial banks underwrite the notes for MNCs, and some commercial banks purchase them for their own investment portfolios.

In addition to Euronotes, MNCs also issue **Euro-commercial paper** to obtain short-term financing. Dealers issue this paper for MNCs without the backing of an underwriting syndicate, so a selling price is not guaranteed to the issuers. Maturities can be tailored to the issuer's preferences. Dealers make a secondary market by offering to repurchase Euro-commercial paper before maturity.

Another popular source of short-term funds by MNCs is direct loans from Eurobanks, typically utilized to maintain a relationship with Eurobanks. If other sources of short-term funds become unavailable, MNCs will rely more heavily on direct loans from Eurobanks. Most MNCs maintain credit arrangements with various banks around the world. For example, Westinghouse has credit arrangements with more than 100 foreign and domestic banks.

INTERNAL FINANCING BY MNCS

Before an MNC's parent or subsidiary in need of funds searches for outside funding, it should determine whether there are any available internal funds. That is, it should check other subsidiaries' cash flow positions. If, for example, earnings have been high at particular subsidiaries and a portion of funds generated is simply invested locally in money market securities, the parent may request these funds from the subsidiaries. This is especially feasible during periods when the cost of obtaining funds in the parent's home country is relatively high.

Parents of MNCs can also attempt to be financed by subsidiaries through increasing their markups on supplies they send to the subsidiaries. In this case, the funds given to the parent by the subsidiary will never be returned. This method of supporting the parent can sometimes be more feasible than the previously discussed methods if it avoids restrictions or taxes enforced by national governments. Yet, this method itself may be restricted or limited by host governments where subsidiaries are located.

WHY MNCS CONSIDER FOREIGN FINANCING

Regardless of whether an MNC parent or subsidiary decides to obtain financing from subsidiaries or from some other source, it also must decide which currency to borrow. Even if it needs its home currency, it may prefer to borrow a foreign currency. Reasons for this preference follow.

Foreign Financing to Offset Foreign Receivables

A large firm may finance in a foreign currency to offset a net receivables position in that foreign currency. For example, consider a U.S. firm that has net receivables denominated in euros. If it needs short-term funds, it can borrow euros and convert them to U.S. dollars for the purpose for which it needs funds. Then, the net receivables in euros will be used to pay off the loan. In this example, financing in a foreign currency reduces the firm's exposure to fluctuating exchange rates. This strategy is especially appealing if the interest rate of the foreign currency is low.

How Avon Used Foreign Financing during the Asian Crisis

During the Asian crisis in 1997 and 1998, many MNCs with Asian subsidiaries were adversely affected by the weakening of Asian currencies against the dollar. Avon Products Inc. used various methods to reduce its economic exposure to the weak Asian currencies. Given that Avon had more cash inflows than cash outflows in Asian currencies, it used strategies that would reduce the excess of cash inflows denominated in Asian currencies. First, it purchased more materials locally. Second, it borrowed funds locally to finance its operations so that it could use some of its cash inflows in Asian currencies to repay the debt. Third, it hired more local salespeople (rather than rely on marketing from the United States) to help sell its products locally. Fourth, it began to remit its earnings more frequently so that excess cash flow denominated in Asian currencies would not accumulate.

http://
Morgan Stanley's Economic Forum, www.ms.com/GEF, provides analysis, discussions, statistics, and forecasts related to non-U.S. economies.

Foreign Financing to Reduce Costs

Even when an MNC parent or subsidiary is not attempting to cover foreign net receivables, it may still consider borrowing foreign currencies if the interest rates on such currencies are attractive. Financing in foreign currencies is common as a result of the development of the Eurocurrency market. The cost of financing can vary with the currency borrowed in the Eurocurrency market. A Eurocurrency loan may offer a slightly lower rate than a loan in the same currency through the home country. Therefore, a U.S.-based MNC, for example, may be able to obtain a lower rate when borrowing U.S. dollars in the Eurocurrency market than it could from a local bank. Yet, the U.S. MNC may also consider financing in a foreign currency through the Eurocurrency market, even if it needs U.S. dollars. Assume the Eurodollar financing rate is 9 percent, while the Euro-Japanese yen financing rate is 4 percent. The U.S. MNC can borrow Japanese yen and immediately convert those yen to dollars for use. Once the loan repayment is due, the U.S. firm will need to obtain Japanese yen in order to pay off the loan. If the Japanese yen value in terms of U.S. dollars has not changed from the time the loan was given until the loan is repaid, the U.S. firm will pay 4 percent on that loan.

http://
Visit www.bloomberg.com for the latest information from financial markets around the world.

Exhibit 20.1 illustrates how interest rates differ among currencies. The Japanese interest rate is lowest recently, while British and Canadian interest rates are often much higher. In some periods, there is a 7-percent differential between the highest and lowest interest rates.

Determining the Effective Financing Rate

In reality, the value of the currency borrowed will most likely change with respect to the borrower's local currency over time. The actual cost of financing by the debtor firm will depend on (1) the interest rate charged by the bank that provided the loan and (2) the movement in the borrowed currency's value over the life of the loan. Thus, the actual or "effective" financing rate may differ from the quoted interest rate. This point is illustrated in the following example.

A U.S. firm is given a one-year loan of NZ\$1,000,000 at the quoted interest rate of 8 percent. When the U.S. firm receives the loan, it converts the New Zealand dollars to U.S. dollars to pay a supplier for materials. The exchange rate at that time is \$.50 per NZ\$, so the NZ\$1,000,000 is converted to \$500,000 (computed as NZ\$1,000,000 × \$.50 per NZ\$ = \$500,000). One year later, the U.S. firm pays back the loan of NZ\$1,000,000 plus interest of NZ\$80,000 (interest computed as 8% × NZ\$1,000,000). Thus, the total amount in New Zealand dollars needed by the U.S. firm is NZ\$1,000,000 + NZ\$80,000 = NZ\$1,080,000. Assume the New Zealand dollar appreciates from \$.50 to \$.60 by the time the loan is to be repaid. The firm will need to convert \$648,000 (computed as NZ\$1,080,000 × \$.60 per NZ\$) to the necessary number of New Zealand dollars for loan repayment.

To compute the effective financing rate, first determine the amount in U.S. dollars beyond the amount borrowed that was paid back. Then divide by the number of U.S. dollars borrowed (after converting the New Zealand dollars to U.S. dollars). Given that the firm borrowed the equivalent of \$500,000 and paid back \$648,000 for the loan, the effective financing rate in this case is \$148,000/\$500,000 = 29.6%. If the exchange rate remained constant throughout the life of the loan, the total

Exhibit 20.1
Short-Term Interest Rates for Various Countries

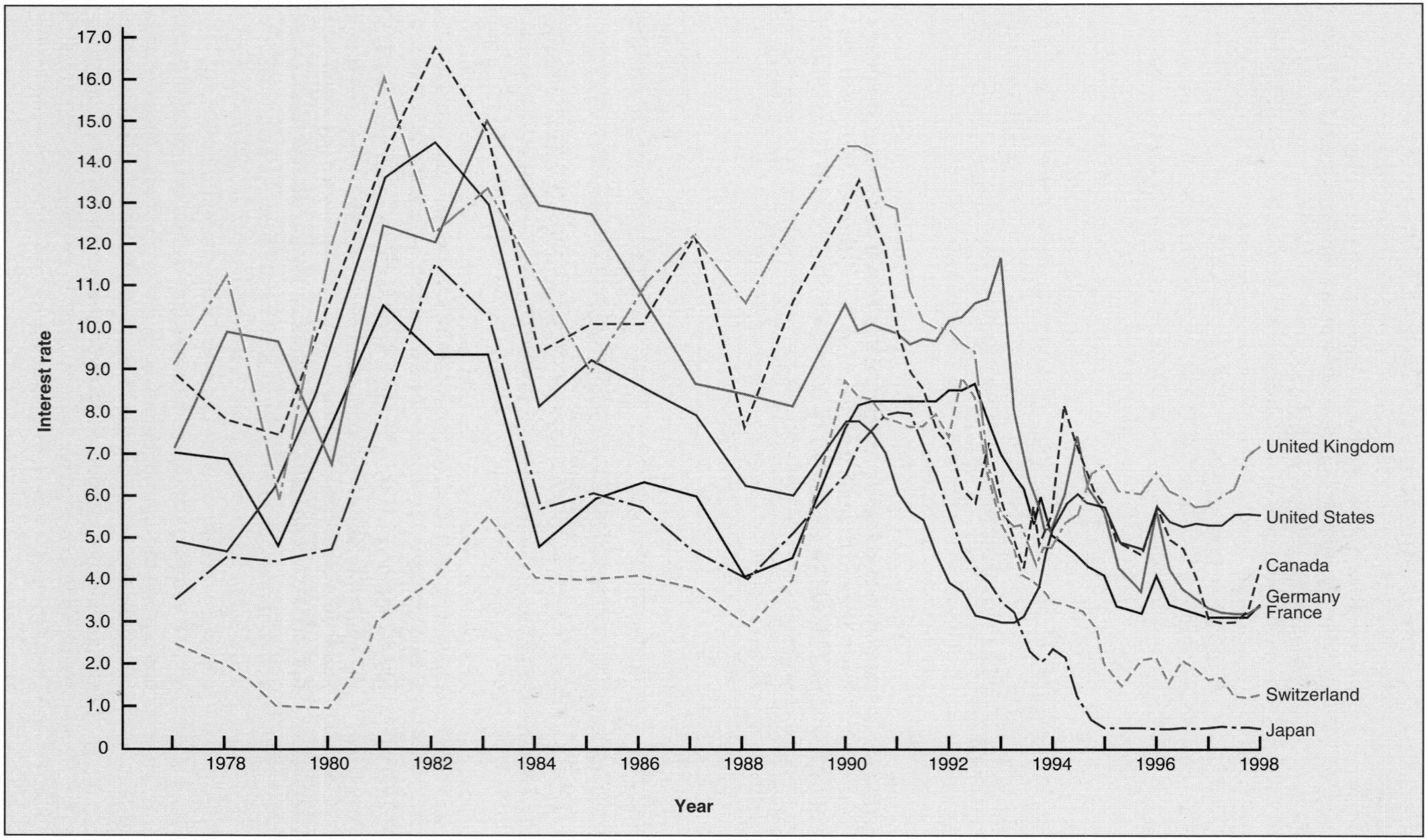

loan repayment would have been \$540,000, representing an effective rate of \$40,000/\$500,000 = 8%. Since the New Zealand dollar appreciated substantially in our example, the effective financing rate was very high. If the U.S. firm had anticipated the New Zealand dollar's substantial appreciation, it would not have borrowed the New Zealand dollars.

The effective financing rate (called r_f) is derived as follows:

$$r_f = (1 + i_f)\left[1 + \left(\frac{S_{t+1} - S}{S}\right)\right] - 1$$

where i_f represents the interest rate of the foreign currency, and S and S_{t+1} represent the spot rate of the foreign currency at the beginning and end of the financing period, respectively. Since the terms in parentheses reflect the percentage change in the foreign currency's spot rate (denoted as e_f), the preceding equation can be rewritten as

$$r_f = (1 + i_f)\,(1 + e_f) - 1$$

In the example, e_f reflects the percentage change in the New Zealand dollar (against the U.S. dollar) from the day the New Zealand dollars were borrowed until the day they were paid back by the U.S. firm. The New Zealand dollar appreciated from \$.50 to \$.60, or by 20 percent over the life of the loan. With this information and the quoted interest rate of 8 percent, the effective financing rate on New Zealand dollars by the U.S. firm can be computed as

$$\begin{aligned} r_f &= (1 + i_f)\,(1 + e_f) - 1 \\ &= (1 + .08)\,(1 + .20) - 1 \\ &= .296, \text{ or } 29.6\% \end{aligned}$$

which is the same rate determined from the alternative computational approach.

To test your understanding of financing in a foreign currency, consider a second example for the U.S. firm. Based on a quoted interest rate of 8 percent for the New Zealand dollar and depreciation in the New Zealand dollar from \$.50 (on the day funds were borrowed) to \$.45 (on the day of loan repayment), what is the effective financing rate of a one-year loan from the viewpoint of a U.S. firm? The answer can be determined by first computing the percentage change in the New Zealand dollar's value: (\$.45 – \$.50)/\$.50 = –10%. Next, the quoted interest rate (i_f) of 8% and the percentage change in the New Zealand dollar (e_f) of –10% can be inserted into the formula for the effective financing rate (r_f):

$$\begin{aligned} r_f &= (1 + .08)\,[1 + (-.10)] - 1 \\ &= [(1.08)\,(.9)] - 1 \\ &= -.028, \text{ or } -2.8\% \end{aligned}$$

A *negative* effective financing rate implies the U.S. firm actually paid fewer dollars in total loan repayment than the number of dollars borrowed. Such a result can occur if the New Zealand dollar depreciates substantially over the life of the loan. This does not imply that a loan will be basically "free" anytime the currency borrowed depreciates over the life of the loan. Yet, depreciation of any amount will cause the effective financing rate to be less than the quoted interest rate, as can be substantiated by reviewing the formula for the effective financing rate.

The examples provided so far suggest that a firm should not consider only the quoted interest rates of foreign currencies when choosing which currency to borrow. The expected rate of appreciation or depreciation should also be considered.

Criteria Considered for Foreign Financing

There are various criteria an MNC must consider in its international financing decision, including

- interest rate parity
- the forward rate as a forecast
- exchange rate forecasts

These criteria can influence the MNC's decision regarding which currency or currencies to borrow. Each is discussed in turn.

Interest Rate Parity

Recall that covered interest arbitrage was described as a foreign short-term investment with a simultaneous forward sale of the foreign currency denominating the foreign investment. From a financing perspective, covered interest arbitrage can be conducted as follows. First, borrow a foreign currency and convert that currency to the home currency for use. Also, simultaneously purchase the foreign currency forward to lock in the exchange rate of the currency needed to pay off the loan. If the foreign currency's interest rate is low, this may appear to be a feasible strategy. However, such a currency normally will exhibit a forward premium that offsets the differential between its interest rate and the home interest rate.

This can be shown by recognizing that the financing firm no longer will be affected by the percentage change in exchange rates but instead by the percentage difference between the spot rate at which the foreign currency was converted to the local currency and the forward rate at which the foreign currency was repurchased. The difference reflects the forward premium (unannualized). The unannualized forward premium (p) can substitute for e_f in the equation introduced earlier to determine the effective financing rate when covering in the forward market under conditions of interest rate parity:

$$r_f = (1 + i_f)(1 + p) - 1$$

If interest rate parity exists, the forward premium is:

$$p = \frac{(1+i_h)}{(1+i_f)} - 1$$

where i_h represents the home currency's interest rate. When this equation is used to reflect financing rates, we can substitute the formula for p to determine the effective financing rate of a foreign currency under conditions of interest rate parity:

$$
\begin{aligned}
r_f &= (1+i_f)(1+p)-1 \\
&= (1+i_f)\left[1+\frac{(1+i_h)}{(1+i_f)}-1\right]-1 \\
&= i_h
\end{aligned}
$$

Thus, if interest rate parity exists, the attempt of covered interest arbitrage to finance with a low interest rate currency will result in an effective financing rate similar to the domestic interest rate.

Exhibit 20.2 summarizes the implications of a variety of scenarios relating to interest rate parity. Even if interest rate parity exists, financing with a foreign currency may still be feasible, but it would have to be conducted on an uncovered basis (without use of a forward hedge). That is, foreign financing may result in a lower financing cost than domestic financing, but it cannot be guaranteed (unless the firm has receivables in that same currency).

The Forward Rate as a Forecast

Assume the forward rate (F) of the foreign currency borrowed is used by firms as a predictor of the spot rate that will exist at the end of the financing period. The expected effective financing rate from borrowing a foreign currency would be forecasted by substituting F for S_{t+1} in the following equation:

Exhibit 20.2 Implications of Interest Rate Parity for Financing

Scenario	Implications
1. Interest rate parity holds.	Foreign financing and a simultaneous hedge of that position in the forward market will result in financing costs similar to those in domestic financing.
2. Interest rate parity holds, and the forward rate is an accurate forecast of the future spot rate.	Uncovered foreign financing will result in financing costs similar to those in domestic financing.
3. Interest rate parity holds, and the forward rate is expected to overestimate the future spot rate.	Uncovered foreign financing is expected to result in lower financing costs than those in domestic financing.
4. Interest rate parity holds, and the forward rate is expected to underestimate the future spot rate.	Uncovered foreign financing is expected to result in higher financing costs than those in domestic financing.
5. Interest rate parity does not hold; the forward premium (discount) exceeds (is less than) the interest rate differential.	Foreign financing with a simultaneous hedge of that position in the forward market results in higher financing costs than those of domestic financing.
6. Interest rate parity does not hold; the forward premium (discount) is less than (exceeds) the interest rate differential.	Foreign financing with a simultaneous hedge of that position in the forward market results in lower financing costs than those of domestic financing.

$$r_f = (1+i_f)\left[1+\frac{S_{t+1}-S}{S}\right]-1$$

$$r_f = (1+i_f)\left[1+\frac{F-S}{S}\right]-1$$

As already shown, the right side of this equation is equal to the home currency financing rate if interest rate parity exists. If the forward rate is an accurate estimator of the future spot rate S_{t+1}, the foreign financing rate will be similar to the home financing rate.

When interest rate parity exists here, the forward rate can be used as a break-even point to assess the financing decision. When a firm is financing with the foreign currency (and not covering the foreign currency position), the effective financing rate will be less than the domestic rate if the future spot rate of the foreign currency (spot rate at the time of loan repayment) is less than the forward rate (at the time the loan is granted). Conversely, the effective financing rate in a foreign loan will be greater than the domestic rate if the future spot rate of the foreign currency turns out to be greater than the forward rate.

If the forward rate is an unbiased predictor of the future spot rate, then the effective financing rate of a foreign currency will on average be equal to the domestic financing rate. In this case, firms that consistently borrow foreign currencies will not achieve lower financing costs. While the effective financing rate in some periods may turn out to be lower than the domestic rate, it will be higher in other periods, causing an offsetting effect. Firms that believe the forward rate is an unbiased predictor of the future spot rate will prefer borrowing their home currency, where the financing rate is known with certainty and is not expected to be any higher on average than foreign financing.

Exchange Rate Forecasts

While the forecasting capabilities of firms are somewhat limited, some firms may make decisions based on cycles in currency movements. Firms may use the recent movements as a forecast of future movements to determine whether they should borrow a foreign currency. This strategy would have been successful on average if utilized in the past. It will be successful in the future if currency movements continue to move in one direction for long periods of time.

Once the firm develops a forecast for the exchange rate's percentage change over the financing period (e_f), it can use this forecast along with the foreign interest rate to forecast the effective financing rate of a foreign currency. The forecasted rate can then be compared to the domestic financing rate. For example, assume a U.S. firm needs funds for one year and is aware that the one-year interest rate in U.S. dollars is 12 percent while the interest rate from borrowing Swiss francs is 8 percent. Assume the U.S. firm forecasts that the Swiss franc will appreciate from its current rate of \$.45 to \$.459, or by 2 percent over the next year. The expected value for e_f [written as $E(e_f)$] will therefore be 2 percent. Thus, the expected effective financing rate [$E(r_f)$] will be

$$\begin{aligned} E(r_f) &= (1 + i_f)\,[1 + E(e_f)] - 1 \\ &= (1 + .08)\,(1 + .02) - 1 \\ &= .1016, \text{ or } 10.16\% \end{aligned}$$

In this example, financing in Swiss francs is expected to be less expensive than financing in U.S. dollars. However, the value for e_f is forecasted and therefore is not known with certainty. Thus, there is no guarantee that foreign financing will truly be less costly.

Deriving a Value for e_f That Equates Domestic and Foreign Rates. The U.S. firm may attempt at least to determine what value of e_f would make the effective rate from foreign financing the same as domestic financing. To determine this value, begin with the effective financing rate formula and solve e_f as shown:

$$r_f = (1+i_f)(1+e_f)-1$$

$$(1+r_f) = (1+i_f)(1+e_f)$$

$$\frac{(1+r_f)}{(1+i_f)} = (1+e_f)$$

$$\frac{(1+r_f)}{(1+i_f)} - 1 = e_f$$

Since the U.S. financing rate is 12 percent in our previous example, that rate is plugged in for r_f. We can also plug in 8 percent for i_f, so that the break-even value of e_f is

$$\begin{aligned} e_f &= \frac{(1+r_f)}{(1+i_f)} - 1 \\ &= \frac{(1+.12)}{(1+.08)} - 1 \\ &= .037037, \textit{ or } 3.7037\% \end{aligned}$$

This suggests that the Swiss franc must appreciate by about 3.7 percent over the loan period to make the Swiss franc loan as costly as a loan in U.S. dollars. Any smaller degree of appreciation would make the Swiss franc loan less costly. The U.S. firm can use this information when determining whether to borrow U.S. dollars or Swiss francs. If it expects the Swiss franc to appreciate by more than 3.7 percent over the loan life, it should prefer borrowing in U.S. dollars. If it expects the Swiss franc to appreciate by less than 3.7 percent or to depreciate, its decision is more complex. If the potential savings from financing with the foreign currency outweigh the risk involved, then the firm should choose that route. The final decision here will be influenced by the firm's degree of risk aversion.

Use of Probability Distributions. To gain more insight in the financing decision, the firm may wish to develop a probability distribution for the percentage change in value for a particular foreign currency over the financing horizon. Since forecasts are not always accurate, it is sometimes useful to develop a probability distribution instead of relying on a single point estimate. Using the probability distribution of possible percentage changes in the currency's value, along with the currency's interest rate, the firm can determine the probability distribution of the possible effective financing rates for the currency. Then, it can compare this distribution to the known financing rate of the home currency in order to make its financing decision. An example follows.

Assume a U.S. firm is deciding whether to borrow Swiss francs for one year. It finds that the quoted interest rate for the Swiss franc is 8 percent and the quoted rate for the U.S. dollar is 15 percent. The firm then develops a probability distribution for the Swiss franc's possible percentage change in value over the life of the loan. The probability distribution is displayed in Exhibit 20.3. The first row in Exhibit 20.3 shows that there is a 5-percent probability of a 6-percent depreciation in the Swiss franc over the loan life. If the Swiss franc does depreciate by 6 percent, the effective financing rate would be 1.52 percent. This implies that there is a 5-percent probability that the U.S. firm will incur a 1.52-percent effective financing rate on its loan. The second row shows that there is a 10-percent probability of a 4-percent depreciation in the Swiss franc over the loan life. If the Swiss franc does depreciate by 4 percent, the effective financing rate would be 3.68 percent. This implies that there is a 10-percent probability that the U.S. firm will incur a 3.68-percent effective financing rate on its loan. For each possible percentage change in the Swiss franc's value, there is a corresponding effective financing rate. We can associate each possible effective financing rate (Column 3) with a probability of that occurring (Column 2). From these two columns we can attain an expected value for the effective financing rate of the Swiss franc. An expected value of the effective financing rate is determined by multiplying each possible effective financing rate by its associated probability. Based on the information in Exhibit 20.3, the expected value of the effective financing rate, referred to as $E(r_f)$, is computed:

$$\begin{aligned} E(r_f) &= 5\%(1.52\%) + 10\%(3.68\%) + 15\%(6.92\%) + 20\%(9.08\%) \\ &\quad + 20\%(12.32\%) + 15\%(14.48\%) \\ &\quad + 10\%(16.64\%) + 5\%(18.80\%) \\ &= .076\% + .368\% + 1.038\% + 1.816\% \\ &\quad + 2.464\% + 2.172\% + 1.664\% + .94\% \\ &= 10.538\% \end{aligned}$$

It has been determined that the expected value of the effective financing rate for borrowing Swiss francs is 10.538 percent. Given this information, should the U.S firm borrow Swiss francs or U.S. dollars? The answer may depend on what the interest rate is for a U.S. dollar loan. Recall that it is assumed to be 15 percent. If you are

Exhibit 20.3
Analysis of Financing with a Foreign Currency

Possible Rate of Change in the Swiss Franc Over the Life of the Loan (e_f)	Probability of Occurrence	Effective Financing Rate If This Rate of Change in the Swiss Franc Does Occur (r_f)
−6%	5%	(1.08)[1 + (−6%)] − 1 = 1.52%
−4	10	(1.08)[1 + (−4%)] − 1 = 3.68
−1	15	(1.08)[1 + (−1%)] − 1 = 6.92
+1	20	(1.08)[1 + (1%)] − 1 = 9.08
+4	20	(1.08)[1 + (4%)] − 1 = 12.32
+6	15	(1.08)[1 + (6%)] − 1 = 14.48
+8	10	(1.08)[1 + (8%)] − 1 = 16.64
+10	5	(1.08)[1 + (10%)] − 1 = 18.80
	100%	

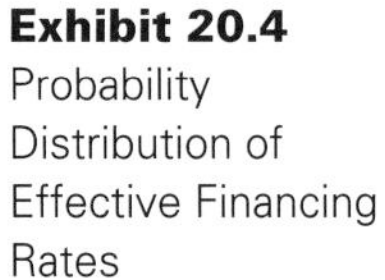
Exhibit 20.4
Probability Distribution of Effective Financing Rates

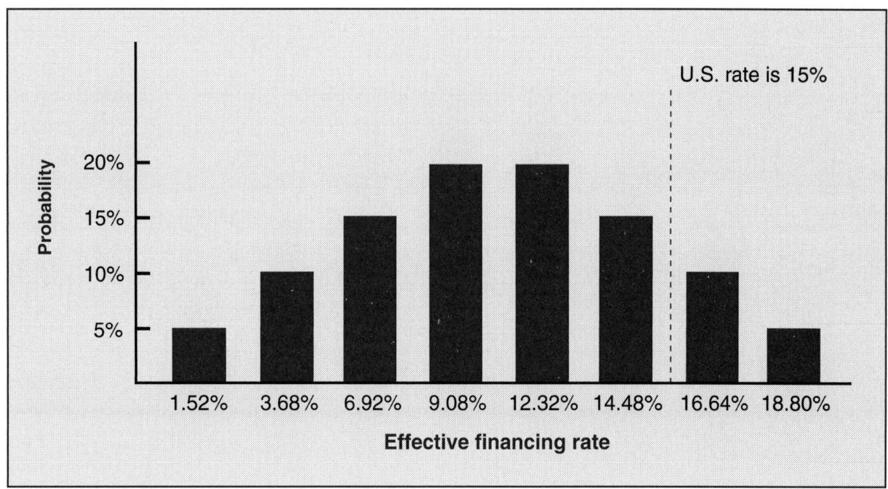

the treasurer of the U.S. firm, are you going to borrow U.S. dollars (and pay 15-percent interest) or borrow Swiss francs (with an expected value of 10.538 percent for the effective financing rate)? You may choose to borrow U.S. dollars since you desire to know with certainty the rate you will pay for your loan. However, you may be willing to borrow Swiss francs if you feel the potential reduction in financing costs from a Swiss franc loan outweighs the risk involved. What is the risk in this case? Using Exhibit 20.3, you can see that the risk reflects the 5-percent chance (probability) that the effective financing rate on Swiss francs will be 18.8 percent and the 10-percent chance that the effective financing rate on Swiss francs will be 16.64 percent. Either of these possibilities represents a greater expense to the U.S. firm than would be incurred if it borrowed U.S. dollars. For this reason, some of the more conservative firms may choose to avoid the uncertainty by simply borrowing U.S. dollars. Other firms may be willing to borrow Swiss francs and tolerate the risk.

To further assess the decision regarding which currency to borrow, the information in Columns 2 and 3 of Exhibit 20.3 is used to develop a probability distribution in Exhibit 20.4. This exhibit illustrates the probability of each possible effective financing rate that may occur if the U.S. firm borrows Swiss francs. Notice that the U.S. interest rate (15 percent) is included in Exhibit 20.4 for comparison purposes. There is no distribution of possible outcomes for the U.S. rate since the rate of 15 percent is known with certainty (no exchange rate risk exists). There is a 15-percent probability that the U.S. rate will be lower than the effective rate on Swiss francs and an 85-percent chance that the U.S. rate will be higher than the effective rate on Swiss francs. This information can assist the firm in its financing decision.

Actual Results from Foreign Financing

The fact that some firms utilize foreign financing suggests that they believe reduced financing costs can be achieved. To assess this issue, the effective financing rates of the Swiss franc and the U.S. dollar are compared in Exhibit 20.5 from the perspective of a U.S. firm. The data are segmented into annual periods.

The borrowing of Swiss francs was most advantageous from 1980 through 1984. During these years, the franc depreciated substantially, so that the effective

Exhibit 20.5
Comparison of Financing with Swiss Francs versus Dollars

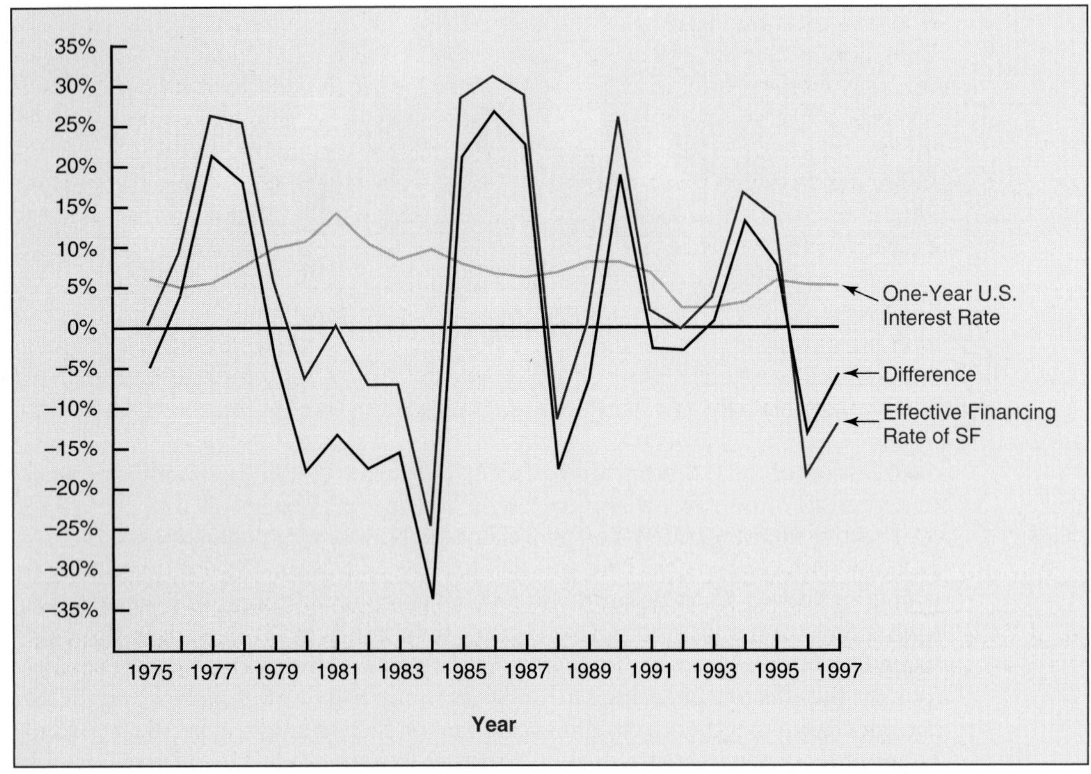

financing rate on francs was usually negative from a U.S. firm's perspective. The difference between Swiss franc and dollar financing rates during these years ranged from 14 percent to 34.5 percent. As an extreme example, the Swiss franc's effective financing rate was –24.9 percent in 1984, versus 9.6 percent for dollars, causing a difference of 34.5 percent. A U.S. firm that borrowed francs rather than dollars to obtain a $1,000,000 loan would therefore have reduced financing costs by $345,000 (34.5% × $1,000,000).

The results of borrowing francs have not always been so favorable. In the mid-1980s, the Swiss franc appreciated, causing its effective financing rate (from a U.S. perspective) to be high. Therefore, U.S. firms that borrowed francs during this time incurred much higher financing costs than they would have if they had borrowed dollars.

http://
The Commerzbank site at www.commerzbank.com offers various charts on exchange rates and interest rate fluctuations as well as a number of economic analyses.

Exhibit 20.5 demonstrates the potential savings in financing costs that can be achieved if the foreign currency depreciates against the firm's home currency. It also demonstrates how the foreign financing could backfire if the firm's expectations are incorrect and the foreign currency appreciates over the financing period.

To illustrate the short-term financing dilemma, consider the situation of Asian subsidiaries of U.S.-based MNCs during the 1997–1998 Asian crisis. These subsidiaries commonly borrow local currencies on a short-term basis to finance some of their operations. The borrowing of local currencies reduces the firms' exposure to exchange rate risk because their cash inflows can be used to repay their financing

Nike Problem

Nike's International Short-Term Financing

Nike has extensive operations in Japan, where interest rates are usually very low. Thus, Nike is able to borrow short-term funds to support its operations in Japan at a very low interest rate and does not expose itself to additional exchange rate risk. The revenue generated by the Japanese subsidiary can be used to pay yen interest payments. Nike could consider using borrowed yen to support its operations in other Asian countries where interest rates are higher, such as in Indonesia and in Hong Kong. However, since repayment would ultimately be in yen, Nike would be subject to exchange rate risk if it borrowed in this manner.

Discussion: Should Nike's parent borrow funds denominated in yen at a low interest rate and convert the funds to dollars to support operations in the United States? Assuming that the Japanese subsidiary periodically remits earnings to the United States, does this strategy increase the exchange rate risk of Nike?

expenses. However, some of the subsidiaries used other currencies (including the U.S. dollar) for financing because the interest rate from borrowing U.S. dollars was between 7 and 9 percent at the time versus more than 15 percent in Indonesia and Thailand. During the crisis, the interest rates reached 20 to 25 percent in Thailand and 50 percent in Indonesia.

The Asian subsidiaries had to decide whether to borrow locally at these high interest rates or attempt to obtain cheaper financing from other countries and be subject to even higher effective financing rates if the Asian currencies continued to weaken substantially. Because Indonesia's currency weakened so much during the crisis, local firms that borrowed funds from other countries to avoid the high interest rate ultimately incurred an effective financing rate of about 90 percent because it took more currency to obtain the currency that was initially borrowed to repay the loan.

FINANCING WITH A PORTFOLIO OF CURRENCIES

While foreign financing can result in significantly lower financing costs, the variance in foreign financing costs over time is higher. MNCs may be able to achieve lower financing costs without excessive risk by financing with a portfolio of foreign currencies, as demonstrated here.

Assume a U.S. firm needs to borrow $100,000 for one year and obtains the following interest rate quotes:

- Interest rate for a one-year loan in U.S. dollars = 15%
- Interest rate for a one-year loan in Swiss francs = 8%
- Interest rate for a one-year loan in Japanese yen = 9%

Due to relatively low quotes for a loan in Swiss francs or Japanese yen, the U.S. firm may desire to borrow in a foreign currency. If the U.S. firm decides to use foreign financing, it has three choices based on the information given: (1) borrow only Swiss francs, (2) borrow only Japanese yen, or (3) borrow a portfolio of Swiss francs and Japanese yen. Assume that the U.S. firm has established possible percentage changes in the spot rate from the time the loan would begin until loan repayment for both the Swiss franc and Japanese yen, as shown in Column 2 of Exhibit 20.6. For each possible percentage change that might occur, a probability of that occurrence is disclosed in the third column.

Based on the assumed interest rate of 8 percent for the Swiss franc, the effective financing rate is computed for each possible percentage change in the Swiss franc's spot rate over the loan life. There is a 30-percent chance that the Swiss franc will appreciate by 1 percent over the loan life. If the Swiss franc appreciates by 1 percent, the effective financing rate will be 9.08 percent. Thus, there is a 30-percent chance that the effective financing rate will be 9.08 percent. Furthermore, there is a 50-percent chance that the effective financing rate will be 11.24 percent and a 20-percent chance that it will be 17.72 percent. Given that the U.S. loan rate is 15 percent, there is only a 20-percent chance that the financing in Swiss francs will result in a higher financing cost than that of domestic financing.

The lower section of Exhibit 20.6 provides information on Japanese yen. For example, the yen has a 35-percent chance of depreciating by 1 percent over the loan life, and so on. Based on the assumed 9-percent interest rate and the exchange rate fluctuation forecasts, there is a 35-percent chance that the effective financing rate will be 7.91 percent, a 40-percent chance that it will be 12.27 percent, and a 25-percent chance that it will be 16.63 percent. Given the 15-percent rate on U.S. dollar financing, there is a 25-percent chance that financing in Japanese yen will be more costly than domestic financing. Before examining the third possible foreign financing strategy (the portfolio approach), determine the expected value of the effective financing rate for each foreign currency by itself. This is accomplished by totaling the products of each possible effective financing rate and its associated probability as follows:

Currency	Computation of Expected Value of Effective Financing Rate
Swiss francs	30%(9.08%) + 50%(11.24%) + 20%(17.72%) = 11.888%
Japanese yen	35%(7.91%) + 40%(12.27%) + 25%(16.63%) = 11.834%

The expected financing costs of the two currencies are almost the same. The individual degree of risk (that the costs of financing will turn out to be higher than domestic financing) is about the same for each currency. If the U.S firm does choose to finance with only one of these foreign currencies, it is difficult to pinpoint (based on our analysis) which currency is more appropriate. Now, consider the third and final foreign financing strategy: the portfolio approach.

Using the information in Exhibit 20.6, there are three possibilities for the Swiss franc's effective financing rate. The same holds true for the Japanese yen. If a U.S. firm borrows half of its needed funds in each of the foreign currencies, then there will be nine possibilities for this portfolio's effective financing rate, as shown in Exhibit 20.7. The first two columns list all possible joint effective financing rates. The third column computes the joint probability of that occurrence assuming that exchange rate movements of the Swiss franc and Japanese yen are independent. The fourth column shows the computation of the portfolio's effective financing rate based on the possible rates disclosed for the individual currencies.

Exhibit 20.6
Development of Possible Effective Financing Rates

Currency	Possible Percentage Change in the Spot Rate Over the Loan Life	Probability of That Percentage Change in the Spot Rate Occurring	Computation of Effective Financing Rate Based on That Percentage Change in the Spot Rate
Swiss franc	1%	30%	(1.08)[1 + (.01)] – 1 = .0908, or 9.08%
Swiss franc	3	50	(1.08)[1 + (.03)] – 1 = .1124, or 11.24%
Swiss franc	9	20	(1.08)[1 + (.09)] – 1 = .1772, or 17.72%
		100%	
Japanese yen	–1%	35%	(1.09)[1 + (–.01)] – 1 = .0791, or 7.91%
Japanese yen	3	40	(1.09)[1 + (.03)] – 1 = .1227, or 12.27%
Japanese yen	7	25	(1.09)[1 + (.07)] –1 = .1663, or 16.63%
		100%	

An examination of the top row will help to clarify the table. This row suggests that one possible outcome of borrowing both Swiss francs and Japanese yen is that they will exhibit effective financing rates of 9.08 percent and 7.91 percent, respectively. The probability of the Swiss franc's effective financing rate occurring is 30 percent, while the probability of the Japanese yen rate occurring is 35 percent. Recall that these percentages were given in Exhibit 20.6. The joint probability that both of these rates will occur simultaneously is (30%)(35%) = 10.5%. Assuming that half (50%) of the funds needed are to be borrowed from each currency, the portfolio's effective financing rate will be .5(9.08%) + .5(7.91%) = 8.495% (if those individual effective financing rates occur for each currency).

Exhibit 20.7
Analysis of Financing with Two Foreign Currencies

(1)	(2)	(3)	(4)
Possible Joint Effective Financing Rates		Computation of Joint Probability	Computation of Effective Financing Rate of Portfolio (50% of Total Funds Borrowed in Each Currency)
Swiss Franc	Japanese Yen		
9.08%	7.91%	(30%)(35%) = 10.5%	.5(9.08%) + .5(7.91%) = 8.495%
9.08	12.27	(30%)(40%) = 12.0	.5(9.08%) + .5(12.27%) = 10.675
9.08	16.63	(30%)(25%) = 7.5	.5(9.08%) + .5(16.63%) = 12.855
11.24	7.91	(50%)(35%) = 17.5	.5(11.24%) + .5(7.91%) = 9.575
11.24	12.27	(50%)(40%) = 20.0	.5(11.24%) + .5(12.27%) = 11.755
11.24	16.63	(50%)(25%) = 12.5	.5(11.24%) + .5(16.63%) = 13.935
17.72	7.91	(20%)(35%) = 7.0	.5(17.72%) + .5(7.91%) = 12.815
17.72	12.27	(20%)(40%) = 8.0	.5(17.72%) + .5(12.27%) = 14.995
17.72	16.63	(20%)(25%) = 5.0	.5(17.72%) + .5(16.63%) = 17.175
		100.0%	

A similar procedure was used to develop the remaining eight rows in Exhibit 20.7. From this table, there is a 10.5-percent chance that the portfolio's effective financing rate will be 8.495 percent, a 12-percent chance that it will be 10.675 percent, and so on.

Exhibit 20.8 displays the probability distribution for the portfolio's effective financing rate that was derived in Exhibit 20.7. This exhibit shows that financing with a portfolio (50 percent financed in Swiss francs with the remaining 50 percent financed in Japanese yen) has only a 5-percent chance of being more costly than domestic financing. These results are more favorable than those of either individual foreign currency, as explained next.

Portfolio Diversification Effects

When both foreign currencies are borrowed, the only way the portfolio will exhibit a higher effective financing rate than the domestic rate is for *both* currencies to experience their maximum possible level of appreciation (which is 9 percent for the Swiss franc and 7 percent for the Japanese yen). If only one does, the severity of its appreciation will be somewhat offset by the other currency's not appreciating to such a large extent. The probability of maximum appreciation is 20 percent for the Swiss franc and 25 percent for the Japanese yen. The joint probability of both of these events occurring simultaneously is (20%)(25%) = 5%. This is an advantage of financing in a portfolio of foreign currencies. The U.S. firm has a 95-percent chance of attaining lower costs with the foreign portfolio than with domestic financing.

The expected value of the effective financing rate for the portfolio can be determined by multiplying the percentage financed in each currency by the expected value of that currency's individual effective financing rate. Recall that the expected value was 11.888 percent for the Swiss franc and 11.834 percent for the Japanese yen. Thus, for a portfolio representing 50 percent of funds borrowed in each currency, the expected value of the effective financing rate is .5(11.888%) + .5(11.834%) = 11.861%. Based on an overall comparison, the expected value of the portfolio's

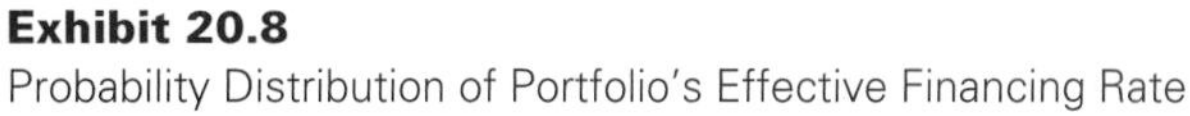
Exhibit 20.8
Probability Distribution of Portfolio's Effective Financing Rate

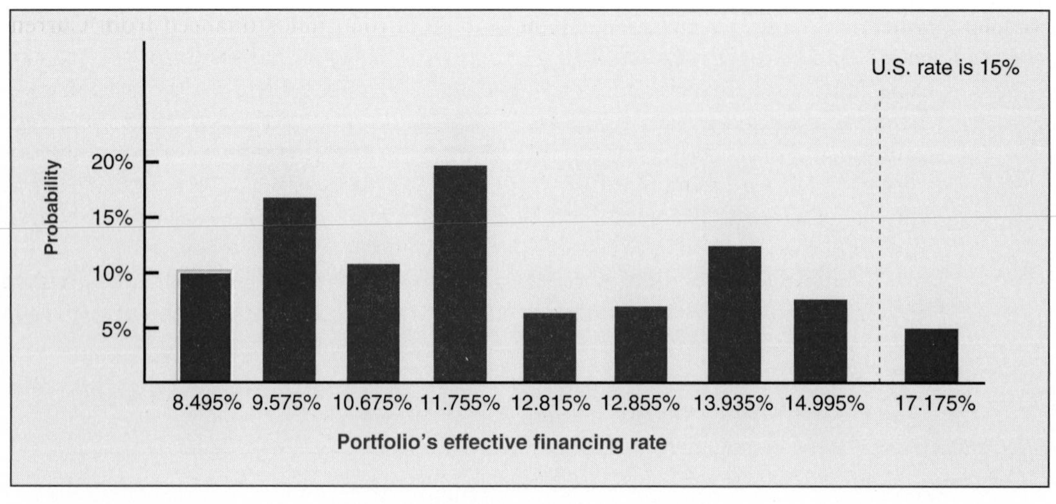

effective financing rate is very similar to that from financing solely in either foreign currency. However, the risk (of incurring a higher effective financing rate than the domestic rate) when financing with the portfolio is substantially less.

In the example, the computation of joint probabilities requires the assumption that the movements in the two currencies are independent. If movements of the two currencies were actually highly positively correlated, then financing in a portfolio of currencies would not be as beneficial as demonstrated, since there is a strong likelihood of both currencies experiencing a high level of appreciation simultaneously. If the two currencies are not highly correlated, they are less likely to simultaneously appreciate to such a degree. Thus, the chances that the portfolio's effective financing rate will exceed the U.S. rate are reduced when the currencies included in the portfolio are not highly positively correlated.

This example includes two currencies in the portfolio. Financing with a more diversified portfolio of additional currencies that exhibit low interest rates may even increase the probability that foreign financing will be less costly than domestic financing, since several currencies are not likely to move in tandem and therefore simultaneously appreciate to offset the advantage of their low interest rates. Again, the degree to which these currencies are correlated with each other is important here. If all currencies are highly positively correlated with each other, financing with such a portfolio would not be very different from financing with a single foreign currency.

Repeated Financing with a Currency Portfolio

A firm that repeatedly finances in a currency portfolio would normally prefer to compose a financing package that exhibits a somewhat predictable effective financing rate on a periodic basis. The more volatile a portfolio's effective financing rate over time, the more uncertainty (risk) there is about the effective financing rate that will exist in any period. The degree of volatility depends on the standard deviations and paired correlations of effective financing rates of the individual currencies within the portfolio.

We can use the portfolio variance as a measurement for degree of volatility. The variance of a two-currency portfolio's effective financing rate $[VAR(r_p)]$ over time is computed as

$$VAR(\mathrm{r}_p) = w^2_A\sigma^2_A + w^2_B\sigma^2_B + 2w_Aw_B\sigma_A\sigma_B\mathrm{CORR}_{AB}$$

where w^2_A and w^2_B represent the percentage of total funds financed from Currencies A and B respectively, σ^2_A and σ^2_B represent the individual variances of each currency's effective financing rate over time, and $CORR_{AB}$ reflects the correlation coefficient of the two currencies' effective financing rates. Since the percentage exchange rate change plays an important role in influencing the effective financing rate, it should not be surprising that $CORR_{AB}$ is strongly affected by the correlation between the exchange rate fluctuations of the two currencies. A low correlation between movements of the two currencies may force $CORR_{AB}$ to be low.

To illustrate how the variance in a portfolio's effective financing rate is related to characteristics of the component currencies, assume the following information based on historical information of several three-month periods:

Mean effective financing rate of Swiss franc for three months = 3%
Mean effective financing rate of Japanese yen for three months = 2%
Standard deviation of Swiss franc's effective financing rate = .04

Standard deviation of Japanese yen's effective financing rate = .09
Correlation coefficient of effective financing rates of these two currencies = .10

Given this information, the mean effective rate on a portfolio (r_p) of funds financed 50 percent by Swiss francs and 50 percent by Japanese yen is determined by totaling the weighted individual effective financing rates:

$$\begin{aligned} r_p &= w_A r_A + w_B r_B \\ &= .5(.03) + .5(.02) \\ &= .015 + .01 \\ &= .025, \text{ or } 2.5\% \end{aligned}$$

The variance of this portfolio's effective financing rate over time is

$$\begin{aligned} VAR(r_p) &= .5^2(.04)^2 + .5^2\,(.09)^2 + 2(.5)(.5)(.04)(.09)(.10) \\ &= .25(.0016) + .25(.0081) + .00018 \\ &= .0004 + .002025 + .00018 \\ &= .002605 \end{aligned}$$

This example suggests how an MNC can use historical data to determine the mean effective financing rate and variance of a two-currency portfolio. Thus, it can compare various financing packages to see which package would be most appropriate. The MNC may be more interested in estimating the mean return and variability for repeated financing in a particular portfolio in the future. There is no guarantee that past data will be indicative of the future. Yet, if the individual variability and paired correlations are somewhat stable over time, the historical variability of the portfolio's effective financing rate should provide a reasonable forecast.

To recognize the benefits from financing with two currencies that are not highly correlated, reconsider how the variance of the portfolio's effective financing rate would have been affected if the correlation between the two currencies was .90 (very high correlation) instead of .10. The variance would be .004045, which is more than 50 percent higher than the variance when the correlation was assumed to be .10.

The assessment of a currency portfolio's effective financing rate and variance is not restricted to just two currencies. The mean effective financing rate for a currency portfolio of any size will be determined by totaling the respective individual effective financing rates weighted by the percentage of funds financed with each currency. Solving the variance of a portfolio's effective financing rate becomes more complex as more currencies are added to the portfolio, but computer software packages are commonly applied to more easily determine the solution.

IMPACT OF SHORT-TERM FINANCING ON THE MNC'S VALUE

Short-term financing can affect the value of an MNC, as shown in Exhibit 20.9. The cost of obtaining short-term funds reflects a financing expense for MNCs. To the extent that the MNC's parent can achieve short-term financing in currencies that will reduce its short-term financing expenses, it can maintain less cash to cover such expenses, which frees up additional cash flow and adds value to the MNC.

Short-term financing decisions by foreign subsidiaries also affect the valuation of MNCs because they can affect the timing and the amounts of the foreign currency cash flows that are ultimately remitted to the U.S. parent. For example, if a foreign

Exhibit 20.9
Impact of Short-Term Financing Decisions on an MNC's Value

Expenses Incurred from Short-Term Financing

$$V = \sum_{t=1}^{n} \left\{ \frac{\sum_{j=1}^{m} \left[E(CF_{j,t}) \times E(ER_{j,t}) \right]}{(1+k)^t} \right\}$$

V = value of the U.S.-based MNC
$E(CF_{j,t})$ = expected cash flows denominated in currency j to be received by the U.S. parent in period t
$E(ER_{j,t})$ = expected exchange rate at which currency j can be converted to dollars at the end of period t
k = the weighted average cost of capital of the U.S. parent company
m = number of currencies
n = number of periods

subsidiary is able to obtain short-term financing at a very low interest rate, this will increase the amount of foreign currency cash flows that will ultimately be received by the U.S. parent and will therefore enhance the value of the MNC.

SUMMARY

- MNCs may use foreign financing to offset anticipated cash inflows in foreign currencies so that exposure to exchange rate risk will be minimized. Alternatively, some MNCs may use foreign financing in an attempt to reduce their financing costs. Foreign financing costs may be lower if the foreign interest rate is relatively low or if the foreign currency borrowed depreciates over the financing period.
- MNCs can determine whether to use foreign financing by estimating the effective financing rate for any foreign currency over the period in which financing will be needed. The expected effective financing rate is dependent on the quoted interest rate of the foreign currency and the forecasted percentage change in the currency's value over the financing period.
- When MNCs borrow a portfolio of currencies that have a low interest rate, they can increase the probability of achieving relatively low financing costs if the currencies' values are not highly correlated.

SELF-TEST FOR CHAPTER 20

(Answers are provided in Appendix A at the back of the text.)

1. Assume that the interest rate in New Zealand is 9 percent. A U.S. firm plans to borrow New Zealand dollars, convert them to U.S. dollars, and repay the loan in one year. What will be the effective financing rate if the New Zealand dollar depreciates by 6 percent? if the New Zealand dollar appreciates by 3 percent?

2. Using the information in question 1 and assuming a 50-percent chance of either scenario occurring, determine the expected value of the effective financing rate.

3. Assume that the Japanese one-year interest rate is 5 percent, while the U.S. one-year interest rate is 8 percent. What percentage change in the Japanese yen would cause a U.S. firm borrowing yen to incur the same effective financing rate as it would if it borrowed dollars?

4. The spot rate of the Australian dollar is $.62. The one-year forward rate of the Australian dollar is $.60. The Australian one-year interest rate is 9 percent. Assume that the forward rate is used to forecast the future spot rate. Determine the expected effective financing rate for a U.S. firm that borrows Australian dollars to finance its U.S. business.

5. A U.S. company plans to repeatedly borrow two currencies with low interest rates whose exchange rate movements are highly correlated to finance its U.S. operations. Will the variance of the two-currency portfolio's effective financing rate be much lower than the variance of either individual currency's effective financing rate? Explain.

QUESTIONS AND APPLICATIONS

1. Explain why an MNC parent would consider financing from its subsidiaries.

2. Discuss the use of specifying a break-even point when financing in a foreign currency.

3. Discuss the development of a probability distribution of effective financing rates when financing in a foreign currency. How is this distribution developed?

4. Once the probability distribution of effective financing rates from financing in a foreign currency is developed, how can it be used in deciding whether to finance in the foreign currency or the home currency?

5. How can a U.S. firm finance in euros and not € necessarily be exposed to exchange rate risk?

6. Explain how a firm's degree of risk aversion enters into its decision on whether to finance in a foreign currency or a local currency. What motivates the firm to even consider financing in a foreign currency?

7. Assume a U.S.-based MNC needs $3 million for a one-year period. Within one year, it will generate enough U.S. dollars to pay off the loan. It is considering three options: (1) borrowing U.S. dollars at an interest rate of 6 percent, (2) borrowing Japanese yen at an interest rate of 3 percent, or (3) borrowing Canadian dollars at an interest rate of 4 percent. The MNC has forecasted that the Japanese yen will appreciate by 1 percent over the next year and that the Canadian dollar will appreciate by 3 percent. What is the expected "effective" financing rate for each of the three options? Which option appears to be most feasible? Why might the MNC not necessarily choose the option reflecting the lowest effective financing rate?

8. How is it possible for a firm to incur a negative effective financing rate?

9. If interest rate parity does not hold, what strat- € egy should a U.S. firm consider when it needs short-term financing? Assume a U.S. firm needs dollars. It borrows euros at a lower interest rate than that for dollars. If interest rate parity exists and if the forward rate of the euro is a reliable predictor of the future spot rate, what does this suggest about the feasibility of such a strategy? If the MNC expects the current spot rate to be a more reliable predictor of the future spot rate, what does this suggest about the feasibility of such a strategy?

10. A U.S. firm needs dollars. Assume that the U.S. € one-year loan rate is 15 percent, while a one-year loan rate in euros is 7 percent. By how much must the euro appreciate to cause the loan in euros to be more costly than a U.S. dollar loan?

11. A U.S.-based MNC decides to borrow Japanese yen for one year. The interest rate on the borrowed yen is 8 percent. The MNC has developed the following probability distribution for the yen's degree of fluctuation against the dollar:

Possible Degree of Fluctuation of Yen Against the Dollar	Percentage Probability
–4%	20%
–1	30
0	10
3	40

Given this information, what is the expected value of the effective financing rate of the Japanese yen from the U.S. corporation's perspective?

12. Assume that interest rate parity exists. If a firm believed that the forward rate was an unbiased predictor of the future spot rate, would it expect to achieve lower financing costs by consistently borrowing a foreign currency with a low interest rate?

13. Assume a U.S firm considers obtaining 40 percent of its one-year financing in Canadian dollars and 60 percent in Japanese yen. The forecasts of appreciation in the Canadian dollar and Japanese yen for the next year are as follows:

Currency	Possible Percentage Change in the Spot Rate Over the Loan Life	Probability of That Percentage Change in the Spot Rate Occurring
Canadian dollar	4%	70%
Canadian dollar	7	30
Japanese yen	6	50
Japanese yen	9	50

The interest rate on the Canadian dollar is 9 percent, and the interest rate on the Japanese yen is 7 percent. Develop the possible effective financing rates of the overall portfolio and the probability of each possibility based on the use of joint probabilities.

14. Why might a corporation attempt to borrow a portfolio of foreign currencies even when it needs to make payments in its local currency?

15. Does borrowing a portfolio of currencies offer any possible advantages over the borrowing of a single foreign currency?

16. If a firm borrows a portfolio of currencies, what characteristics of the currencies will affect the potential variability of the portfolio's effective financing rate? What characteristics would be desirable from a borrowing firm's perspective?

17. Boca Inc. needs $4 million for one year. It currently has no business in Japan but plans to borrow Japanese yen from a Japanese bank because the Japanese interest rate is three percentage points lower than the U.S. rate. Assume that interest rate parity exists; also assume that Boca believes that the one-year forward rate of the Japanese yen will exceed the future spot rate one year from now. Will the expected effective financing rate be higher, lower, or the same as financing with dollars? Explain.

18. Jacksonville Corporation is a U.S.-based firm that needs $600,000. It has no business in Japan but is considering one-year financing with Japanese yen because the annual interest rate would be 5 percent versus 9 percent in the United States.

    a. Can Jacksonville benefit from borrowing Japanese yen and simultaneously purchasing yen one year forward to avoid exchange rate risk? Explain.
    b. Assume that Jacksonville does not cover its exposure and uses the forward rate to forecast the future spot rate. Determine the expected effective financing rate. Should Jacksonville finance with Japanese yen? Explain.
    c. Assume that Jacksonville does not cover its exposure and expects that the Japanese yen will appreciate by either 5 percent, 3 percent, or 2 percent, with an equal probability of each occurrence. Use this information to determine the probability distribution of the effective financing rate. Should Jacksonville finance with Japanese yen? Explain.

19. € Assume that the U.S. interest rate is 7 percent and the euro's interest rate is 4 percent. Assume that the euro's forward rate has a premium of 4 percent. Is the following statement true: "Interest rate parity does not hold; therefore, U.S. firms could lock in a lower financing cost by borrowing euros and purchasing euros forward for one year." Explain your answer.

20. Orlando Inc. is a U.S.-based MNC with a subsidiary in Mexico. Its Mexican subsidiary needs

a one-year loan of 10 million pesos for operating expenses. Since the Mexican interest rate is 70 percent, it is considering borrowing dollars, which it would convert to pesos to cover the operating expenses. By how much would the dollar have to appreciate against the peso to cause such a strategy to backfire? (The one-year U.S. interest rate is 9 percent.)

21. Assume the following information. Raleigh Corporation needs to borrow funds for one year to finance an expenditure in the United States. The following interest rates are available:

	Borrowing Rate
U.S.	10%
Canada	6
Japan	5

The percentage change in the spot rates of the Canadian dollar and Japanese yen over the next year are as follows:

Canadian Dollar		Japanese Yen	
Probability	Percentage Change in Spot Rate	Probability	Percentage Change in Spot Rate
10%	5%	20%	6%
90	2	80	1

If Raleigh Corporation borrows a portfolio, 50 percent of funds from Canadian dollars and 50 percent of funds from yen, determine the probability distribution of the effective financing rate of the portfolio. What is the probability that Raleigh will incur a higher effective financing rate from borrowing this portfolio than from borrowing U.S. dollars?

22. Assume that a U.S. firm has a foreign subsidiary in Asia that commonly obtained short-term financing from local banks prior to the Asian crisis. Explain why the firm may not be able to easily obtain funds from the local banks since the crisis.

Internet Application

23. The Bloomberg Web site provides interest rate data for many different foreign currencies over various maturities. Its address is:

http://www.bloomberg.com

a. Go to the "Markets" section of the Web site and then to "International Yield Curves." Review the different three-month interest rates among countries. Assume that your U.S.-based MNC could borrow funds for 1 percent above the annualized risk-free (government) rates shown at the Bloomberg Web site. Which country has the lowest three-month interest rate? Which country has the highest three-month interest rate?

b. As a cash manager of a U.S.-based MNC that needs dollars to support U.S. operations, where would you borrow funds for the next three months? Explain.

c. If you were working for a foreign subsidiary based in Thailand and needed to borrow to fund local operations, where would you borrow short-term funds? Explain.

Running Your Own MNC

24a. Given that your business has receivables in a foreign currency, you may want to consider financing in that same foreign currency to offset the exposure. Compare the recent interest rate of the foreign currency of concern to the U.S. interest rate: Is the foreign interest rate typically higher or lower than the U.S. interest rate? Would you use financing in that currency to offset receivables? Explain.

b. Explain how you could use foreign financing for your business in a manner that would reduce your exposure to exchange rate risk. Be specific.

Blades, Inc. Case

Use of Foreign Short-Term Financing

Recall that Blades, Inc., has recently decided to establish a subsidiary in Thailand in order to manufacture "Speedos," Blades primary roller blade product. The Thai subsidiary is expected to be operational by early next year, and all baht-denominated net cash flows generated by the subsidiary will be remitted to the U.S. parent. Blades has also decided to finance part of the initial investment of 550 million baht by issuing yen-denominated bonds and has completed its initial negotiations with its Thai customers and suppliers. Also recall that all roller blades manufactured in Thailand will be sold to Thai retailers. As a result of these actions, Ben Holt, Blades' chief financial officer (CFO) is confident that the Thai subsidiary will operate as profitably as expected.

Since construction of the new plant in Thailand is nearly finished, Ben Holt realizes that he must focus his attention on the short-term financing that will be needed to operate the plant successfully. Specifically, his forecasts indicate that Blades will sell 120,000 pairs of Speedos to the retailers he has identified in Thailand. Blades expects to charge a price of 5,000 baht per pair of Speedos in its first year of operating the Thai subsidiary. The materials needed to manufacture these 120,000 pairs will be purchased from Thai suppliers. Blades expects the cost of the components necessary to manufacture one pair of Speedos to be approximately 3,500 baht in its first year of operating the Thai subsidiary.

Because Blades is relatively unknown in Thailand, Blades' suppliers have indicated that they would like to receive payment as early as possible. Conversely, Blades' customers have insisted on open account transactions, which would require payment for the roller blades approximately three months subsequent to the sale of the roller blades. Furthermore, the production cycle necessary to produce Speedos, ranging from purchase of the materials to the eventual sale of the product, is approximately four months. Because of these considerations, Blades expects to collect its revenues approximately six months after payment has been made for the materials, such as rubber and plastic components, needed to manufacture Speedos.

Ben Holt would like to establish a reputation as a good business partner in Thailand, since Blades will be operating its Thai subsidiary for ten years. Consequently, it is important to Mr. Holt that payment be remitted to the Thai suppliers on time. Ben Holt has identified at least two choices for satisfying Blades' working capital needs resulting from its Thai operations. First, Blades could borrow Japanese yen for six months, convert the yen to Thai baht, and use the baht to pay the Thai suppliers. When the accounts receivable in Thailand are collected, Blades would convert the baht received to yen and repay the Japanese yen loan. Second, Blades could borrow Thai baht for six months in order to pay its Thai suppliers. When Blades collects its accounts receivable, it would use these receipts to repay the baht loan. Thus, Blades would use the revenue generated in Thailand in order to repay the loan, whether the money was borrowed in yen or in baht.

Ben Holt's initial research indicates that 180-day interest rates in Japan and in Thailand available to Blades are 4 percent and 6 percent, respectively. Consequently, Ben Holt favors borrowing the Japanese yen, as he believes this loan to be cheaper than the baht-denominated loan. However, he is aware that he should somehow incorporate the future movements of the yen-baht exchange rate in his analysis, but he is unsure how to accomplish this. However, he has identified the following probability distribution of the change in the value of the Japanese yen with respect to the Thai baht and of the change in the value of the Thai baht with respect to the dollar over the six-months period of the loan:

Possible Rate of Change in the Japanese Yen Relative to the Thai Baht Over the Life of the Loan	Possible Rate of Change in the Thai Baht Relative to the Dollar Over the Life of the Loan	Probability of Occurrence
2%	−3%	30%
1	−2	30
0	−1	20
1	0	15
2	1	5

Ben Holt has also informed you that the current spot rate of the yen (in baht) is THB0.347826, while the current spot rate of the baht (in dollars) is $.023.

You, a financial analyst of Blades, Inc., have been asked to answer the following questions for Ben Holt:

1. What is the amount, in baht, Blades needs to borrow in order to cover the payments due to the Thai suppliers? What is the amount, in yen, Blades needs to borrow in order to cover the payments due to the Thai suppliers?
2. Given that Blades will use the receipts from the receivables in Thailand to repay the loan and that Blades plans to remit all baht-denominated cash flows to the U.S. parent whether it borrows in baht or dollars, does the future value of the yen with respect to the baht affect the cost of the loan if Blades borrows in yen? Does the future value of the baht with respect to the dollar affect the cost of the yen loan?
3. Using a spreadsheet, compute the expected amount (in U.S. dollars) that will be remitted to the United States in six months if Blades finances its working capital requirements by borrowing baht versus borrowing yen. Based on your analysis, should Blades obtain a yen- or baht-denominated loan?

Small Business Dilemma

Short-Term Financing by the Sports Exports Company

At the current time, the Sports Exports Company focuses on producing footballs and exporting them to a distributor in the United Kingdom. The exports are denominated in British pounds. Jim Logan, the owner, plans to develop other sporting goods products besides the footballs that he produces. His entire expansion will be focused on the United Kingdom, where he is trying to make a name for his firm. He remains concerned about his firm's exposure to exchange rate risk but does not plan to let that get in the way of his expansion plans because he believes that his firm can continue to penetrate the British sporting goods market. He has just negotiated a joint venture with a British firm that will produce other sporting goods products that are more popular in the United States (such as basketballs) but will be sold in the United Kingdom. Jim will pay the British manufacturer in British pounds. These products will be delivered directly to the British distributor rather than to Jim, and the distributor will pay Jim with British pounds.

Jim's expansion plans will result in the need for additional funding. Jim would prefer to borrow on a short-term basis now. Jim has an excellent credit rating and collateral and therefore should be able to obtain short-term financing. The British interest rate is one-fourth of a percentage point above the U.S. interest rate.

1. Should Jim borrow dollars or pounds to finance his joint venture business? Why?
2. € Jim could also borrow euros at an interest rate that is lower than the U.S. or British rate. The values of the euro and pound tend to move in the same direction against the dollar but not always by the same degree. Would borrowing euros to support the British joint venture result in more exposure to exchange rate risk than borrowing pounds? Would it result in more exposure to exchange rate risk than borrowing dollars?

21 International Cash Management

The term **cash management** can be broadly defined to mean optimization of cash flows and investment of excess cash. From an international perspective, cash management is very complex because of different laws among countries that pertain to cross-border cash transfers. In addition, exchange rate fluctuations can affect the value of cross-border cash transfers.

The specific objectives of this chapter are to

- explain the difference in analyzing cash flows between a subsidiary perspective and a parent perspective,
- explain the various techniques used to optimize cash flows,
- explain common complications in optimizing cash flows, and
- explain the potential benefits and risks from foreign investing.

Cash Flow Analysis: Subsidiary Perspective

The management of working capital (such as inventory, accounts receivable, and cash) has a direct influence on the amount and timing of cash flow. Working capital management and the management of cash flow are integrated. We discuss them here first before focusing on cash management.

Begin with outflow payments by the subsidiary to purchase raw materials or supplies. The subsidiary will normally have a more difficult time forecasting future outflow payments if its purchases are international rather than domestic because of exchange rate fluctuations. In addition, the possibility exists of substantially higher payments due to appreciation of the invoice currency. Consequently, the firm may wish to maintain a large inventory of supplies and raw materials so that it can cut down on purchases if the invoice currency appreciates, and instead draw from its inventory. Still another possibility is that imported goods from another country could be restricted by the host government (through quotas, etc.). In this event, a larger inventory would give a firm more time to search for alternative sources of supplies or raw materials. A subsidiary with domestic supply sources would not experience such a problem and therefore would not need as large an inventory.

Outflow payments for supplies will be influenced by future sales. If the sales volume is substantially influenced by exchange rate fluctuations, its future level becomes more uncertain, which makes outflow payments for supplies more uncertain. Such uncertainty may force the subsidiary to maintain larger cash balances in order to cover any unexpected increase in supply requirements.

Subsidiaries use their raw materials and/or supplies in their production process. If their finished goods are exported overseas, the sales volume may be more volatile than if the goods were only sold domestically. This could be due to the fluctuating exchange rate of the invoice currency. Demand for these finished goods by importers will most likely decrease if the invoice currency appreciates. The sales volume of exports is also susceptible to business cycles of the importing countries. If the goods were sold domestically, the exchange rate fluctuations would not have a direct impact on sales, although they would still have an indirect impact since they would influence prices paid by local customers for imports from foreign competitors.

Sales can often be increased when credit standards are relaxed. However, it is important to focus on cash inflows due to sales rather than on sales themselves. Looser credit standards may cause a slowdown in cash inflows from sales, which could offset the benefits of increased sales. Accounts receivable management is an important part of the subsidiary's working capital management because of its potential impact on cash inflows.

The subsidiary may be expected to periodically send dividend payments and other fees to the parent. These fees could represent royalties or charges for overhead costs incurred by the parent that benefit the subsidiary. An example is research and development costs incurred by the parent, which would improve the quality of goods produced by the subsidiary. Whatever the reason, payments by the subsidiary to the parent are often necessary. When dividend payments and fees are often known in advance and denominated in the subsidiary's currency, forecasting cash flows is easier for the subsidiary. The level of dividends paid by subsidiaries to the parent is dependent on liquidity needs, potential uses of funds at various subsidiary locations, expected movements in the currencies of subsidiaries, and host-country government regulations.

After accounting for all outflow and inflow payments, the subsidiary will find itself with either excess or deficient cash. Thus, it will periodically need to either invest its excess cash or borrow to cover its cash deficiencies. If it anticipates a cash deficiency, short-term financing is necessary, as described in the previous chapter. If it anticipates excess cash, it must determine how the excess cash should be used. Investing in foreign currencies can sometimes be attractive, but exchange rate risk makes the effective yield uncertain. This issue is discussed later in this chapter.

Liquidity management is a crucial component of a subsidiary's working capital management. Subsidiaries commonly have access to numerous lines of credit and overdraft facilities in various currencies. Therefore, they may maintain adequate liquidity without substantial cash balances. While liquidity is important for the overall multinational corporation (MNC), it cannot be properly measured by liquidity ratios. Potential access to funds is more relevant than cash on hand.

Centralized Cash Management

Each subsidiary should manage its working capital by simultaneously considering all of the points discussed thus far. Often, though, each subsidiary is more concerned with its own operations than with the overall operations of the MNC. Thus, a **cen-**

tralized cash management group may need to monitor, and possibly manage, the parent-subsidiary and intersubsidiary cash flows. This role is critical since it can often benefit individual subsidiaries in need of funds or overly exposed to exchange rate risk. Kraft's treasury department, for example, is centralized to manage liquidity, funding, and foreign exchange requirements of its global operations. And Monsanto's centralized system for pooling different currency balances from various subsidiaries in Asia creates an estimated annual savings of hundreds of thousands of dollars per year.

Exhibit 21.1 is a complement to the following discussion of cash flow management. It is a simplified cash flow diagram for an MNC with two subsidiaries in different countries. While each MNC may handle its payments in a different manner, Exhibit 21.1 is based on simplified assumptions that will help illustrate some key concepts of multinational cash management. The exhibit reflects the assumption that the two subsidiaries periodically send loan repayments and dividends to the parent or send excess cash to the parent (where the centralized cash management process is assumed to take place). These cash flows represent the incoming cash to the parent from the subsidiaries. The parent's cash outflows to the subsidiaries can include loans and the return of cash previously invested by the subsidiaries. The subsidiaries also have cash flows between themselves, due to purchasing of supplies from each other.

Exhibit 21.1
Cash Flow of the Overall MNC

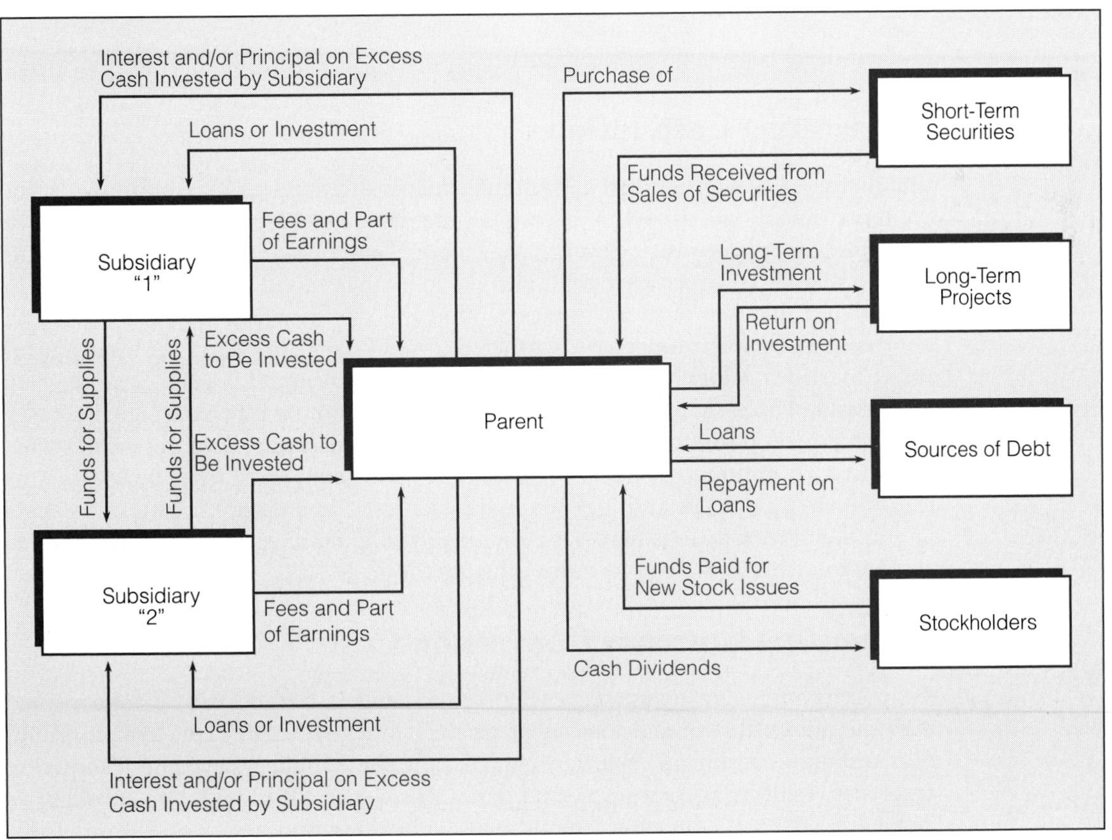

While each subsidiary is managing its working capital, there is a need to monitor and manage the cash flows between the parent and the subsidiaries, as well as between the individual subsidiaries. This task of international cash management should be delegated to a centralized cash management group. International cash management can be segmented into two functions: (1) optimizing cash flow movements and (2) investing excess cash. These two functions are discussed in turn.

The centralized cash management division of an MNC cannot always accurately forecast events that affect parent-subsidiary or intersubsidiary cash flows. It should, however, be ready to react to any event by considering (1) any potential adverse impact on cash flows and (2) how to avoid such an adverse impact. If the cash flow situation between the parent and subsidiaries results in a cash squeeze on the parent, it should have sources of funds (credit lines) available. On the other hand, if it has excess cash after considering all outflow payments, it must consider where to invest funds. This decision is thoroughly examined shortly.

TECHNIQUES TO OPTIMIZE CASH FLOWS

Cash inflows can be optimized by

- accelerating cash inflows
- minimizing currency conversion costs
- managing blocked funds
- managing intersubsidiary cash transfers

Each of these tasks is discussed in turn.

Accelerating Cash Inflows

The first goal in international cash management is to accelerate cash inflows, since the more quickly the inflows are received, the more quickly they can be invested or used for other purposes. Several managerial practices are advocated for this endeavor, some of which may be implemented by the individual subsidiaries. First, a corporation may establish **lockboxes** around the world, which are post office box numbers to which customers are instructed to send payment. When set up in appropriate locations, a lockbox can help reduce mailing time (**mail float**). The processing of incoming checks at a lockbox is usually taken care of by a bank on a daily basis. A second method for accelerating cash inflows is the **preauthorized payment,** which allows a corporation to charge a customer's bank account up to some limit. Both the preauthorized payment and lockboxes are even used in a domestic setting. Because international transactions may have a relatively long mailing time, these methods to accelerate cash inflows can be quite valuable for an MNC.

Minimizing Currency Conversion Costs

Another technique for optimizing cash flow movements, **netting,** can be implemented with the joint effort of subsidiaries or by the centralized cash management group. This technique optimizes cash flow by reducing the administrative and transaction costs that result from currency conversion. Consider an MNC with two subsidiaries located in different countries. Any time one subsidiary purchases goods from a second subsidiary, it may need a foreign currency to make payment. The second subsidiary may do the same when purchasing goods from the first subsidiary. Both subsidiaries could avoid (or at least reduce) the transaction costs of currency conversion if they netted out the payments, accounting for all of their transactions over a given period to determine one net payment.

Over time, the use of netting has become increasingly popular. Its key benefits are as follows. First, it reduces the number of cross-border transactions between subsidiaries, thereby reducing the overall administrative cost of such cash transfers. Second, it reduces the need for foreign exchange conversion since transactions occur less frequently, thereby reducing the transaction costs associated with foreign exchange conversion. Third, the process of netting forces tight control over information on transactions between subsidiaries. Thus, there is a more coordinated effort among all subsidiaries to accurately report and settle their various accounts. Finally, cash flow forecasting is easier since only net cash transfers are made at the end of each period, rather than individual cash transfers throughout the period. Improved cash flow forecasting can enhance financing and investment decisions.

A **bilateral netting system** involves transactions between two units: between the parent and a subsidiary, or between two subsidiaries. A **multilateral netting system** usually involves a more complex interchange among the parent and several subsidiaries. For most large MNCs, a multilateral netting system would be necessary to effectively reduce administrative and currency conversion costs. Such a system is normally centralized so that all necessary information is consolidated. From the consolidated cash flow information, net cash flow positions for each pair of units (subsidiaries, or whatever) is determined, and the actual reconciliation at the end of each period can be dictated. The centralized group may even maintain inventories of various currencies so currency conversion for the end-of-period net payments can be completed without significant transaction costs.

Exhibit 21.2 is an example of an intersubsidiary payments matrix that totals each subsidiary's individual payments against each of the other subsidiaries. For example, the first row implies the Canadian subsidiary owes the French subsidiary the equivalent of $40,000, the Canadian subsidiary owes the Japanese subsidiary the equivalent of $90,000, and so on. During this same period, these subsidiaries have also received goods from the Canadian subsidiary, for which payment is due. In the second column (under Canada), the table suggests that the French subsidiary owes the Canadian subsidiary the equivalent of $60,000, the Japanese subsidiary owes the Canadian subsidiary the equivalent of $100,000, and so on.

Since subsidiaries owe each other, currency conversion costs can be reduced by requiring that only the net payment be extended. Using the intersubsidiary table, the schedule of net payments is determined as shown in Exhibit 21.3. Since the Canadian

Exhibit 21.2
Intersubsidiary Payments Matrix

Payments Owed by Subsidiary Located in:	U.S. Dollar Value (in Thousands) Owed to Subsidiary Located in:				
	Canada	*France*	*Japan*	*Switzerland*	*U.S.*
Canada	—	40	90	20	40
France	60	—	30	60	50
Japan	100	30	—	20	30
Switzerland	10	50	10	—	50
U.S.	10	60	20	20	—

Exhibit 21.3
Netting Schedule

Net Payments to Be Made by Subsidiary Located in:	Net U.S. Dollar Value (in Thousands) Owed to Subsidiary Located in:				
	Canada	*France*	*Japan*	*Switzerland*	*U.S.*
Canada	—	0	0	10	30
France	20	—	0	10	0
Japan	10	0	—	10	10
Switzerland	0	0	0	—	30
U.S.	0	10	0	0	—

subsidiary owes the French subsidiary the equivalent of $40,000 but is owed the equivalent of $60,000 by the French subsidiary, the net payment required is from the French subsidiary to the Canadian subsidiary, amounting to the equivalent of $20,000. Exhibits 21.2 and 21.3 convert all figures to U.S.-dollar equivalents to allow for consolidating payments in both directions so the net payment can be determined.

There can be some limitations to multilateral netting due to foreign exchange controls. Although the major industrialized countries typically do not impose such controls on netting, some other countries do. For a third class of countries, netting is prohibited. Thus, an MNC with subsidiaries around the world may be able to implement the multilateral netting system over only some of its subsidiaries. Obviously, this will limit the degree to which the netting system can reduce administration and transaction costs.

Managing Blocked Funds

Cash flows can also be affected by a host government's blockage of funds, which might occur if the government requires all funds to remain within the country in order to create jobs and reduce unemployment. To deal with funds blockage, the MNC may implement the same strategies used in the case of high host-country government taxation. To make efficient use of these funds, the subsidiary may be instructed by the MNC to set up a research and development division, which incurs costs and possibly generates revenues for other subsidiaries.

Another strategy is to use transfer pricing in a manner that will increase the expenses incurred by the subsidiary. A host country government is likely to be more lenient on funds sent to cover expenses than on earnings remitted to the parent.

When subsidiaries are restricted from transferring funds to the parent, the parent may instruct the subsidiary to obtain financing from a local bank rather than from the parent. By borrowing through a local intermediary, the subsidiary is assured that its earnings can be distributed to pay off previous financing. If the earnings were to be sent to the parent, the host government could enforce a blockage of funds.

As an example of managing blocked funds, subsidiaries of a U.S. MNC based in the Philippines were prevented from exchanging their Philippine pesos into U.S. dollars to send these dollars home. To deal with such restrictions, one general manager reportedly loaded pesos into his luggage and took them to Hong Kong, where he converted them into U.S. dollars. A better way of dealing with such restrictions is to find a use for the currency within the host country. For example, in the case of the Philippine government restriction, one company held its corporate meeting in Manila so it could use the pesos to pay the expenses of the meeting (hotel, food, etc.) in pesos. This approach is somewhat similar to sending the funds to the parent, since it is likely that the parent would have paid the expenses of the corporate meeting had it been held in the parent's country.

Managing Intersubsidiary Cash Transfers

Proper management of cash flows can also be beneficial to a subsidiary in need of funds. Assume that Short Sub needs funds, while Long Sub has excess funds. If Long Sub purchases supplies from Short Sub, it could provide financing by paying for its supplies earlier than necessary. This technique is often called **leading.** Alternatively, if Long Sub sells supplies to Short Sub, it could provide financing by allowing Short Sub to lag its payments. This technique is called **lagging.** The leading or lagging strategy can make efficient use of cash and therefore reduce debt. Some host governments prohibit the practice by requiring that a payment between subsidiaries occur at the time at which goods are transferred. An MNC would need to be aware of any existing laws that restricted use of this strategy.

Complications in Optimizing Cash Flow

Most complications encountered in optimizing cash flow can be classified into three categories:

- company-related characteristics
- government restrictions
- characteristics of banking systems

Each complication is discussed in turn.

Company-Related Characteristics

In some cases, optimizing cash flow can become complicated, due to characteristics of the MNC. For example, if one of the subsidiaries delays payments to other subsidiaries for supplies received, the other subsidiaries may be forced to borrow until the payments arrive. A centralized approach that monitors all intersubsidiary payments should be able to minimize such problems.

Government Restrictions

The existence of government restrictions can disrupt a cash flow optimization policy. For example, some governments prohibit the use of a netting system, as noted earlier. In addition, some countries periodically prevent cash from leaving the country, thereby preventing net payments from being made. These problems can arise even for MNCs that do not experience any company-related problems.

Characteristics of Banking Systems

The abilities of banks to facilitate cash transfers for MNCs will vary among countries. Banks in the United States are advanced in this field, but banks in some other countries do not offer services needed by MNCs. For example, MNCs prefer some form of zero-balance account, where excess funds can be used to make payments but earn interest until they are used. In addition, some MNCs benefit from the use of lockboxes. Such services are not available in some countries. In addition, there may be insufficient updating on the MNC's bank account information, or fees for banking services may not be broken down in a detailed manner. Without full use of banking resources and information, international cash management is limited in its effectiveness. In addition, an MNC with subsidiaries in, say, eight different countries will typically be dealing with eight different banking systems. Much progress has been made in foreign banking systems in recent years. As time passes and a more uniform global banking system emerges, such problems may be alleviated.

INVESTING EXCESS CASH

Along with optimizing cash flow, the other key function of international cash management is investing excess cash. International money markets have grown to accommodate corporate investments of excess cash, one of the key markets being the Eurocurrency market. The dollar volume of deposits has more than doubled since 1980. Eurodollar deposits commonly offer MNCs a slightly higher yield than bank deposits in the United States. Many MNCs utilize the Eurocurrency market as a temporary use of funds. For example, Westinghouse maintains over $400 million in Eurodollar deposits. Many MNCs also establish deposits in nondollar currencies in the Eurocurrency market. While Eurodollar deposits still dominate the market, the relative importance of nondollar currencies has increased over time.

In addition to their use of the Eurocurrency market, MNCs can also purchase foreign Treasury bills and commercial paper. Improved telecommunications systems have increased access to these securities in foreign markets and allow for a greater degree of integration among money markets in various countries.

There are several aspects of short-term investing that deserve consideration by the MNC. First, should the excess cash of all subsidiaries remain separated or be pooled together? Second, how can the MNC determine the effective yield expected from each possible alternative? Third, what does interest rate parity suggest about short-term investing? Fourth, how can the quoted forward rate be used to evaluate the short-term investment decision? Fifth, how can forecasted exchange rates influence the short-term investment decision? Finally, is it worthwhile to diversify investments among currencies? Each of these questions is discussed in turn.

Centralized Cash Management

An MNC's short-term investing policy can either maintain separate investments for all subsidiaries or employ a centralized approach. Recall that the function of optimizing cash flows could be improved by a centralized approach, since all subsidiary cash positions could be monitored simultaneously. With regard to the investing function, centralization allows for more efficient usage of funds and possibly higher returns. The term *centralized* implies that excess cash from each subsidiary is pooled until it is needed by a particular subsidiary. To understand the advantages of such a system, consider that the rates paid on short-term investments such as bank deposits are often higher for larger denominations. Thus, if two subsidiaries have excess cash of $50,000 each for one month, the rates on their individual bank deposits may be lower than the rate they could obtain if they pooled their funds into a single

$100,000 bank deposit. In this manner, the centralized (pooling) approach generates a higher rate of return on excess cash.

The centralized approach can also improve the efficiency of working capital management by reducing the MNC's overall financing costs. To illustrate, suppose that Subsidiary A has excess cash during the next month of $50,000, while Subsidiary B needs to borrow $50,000 for one month. If cash management is not centralized, Subsidiary A may use the $50,000 to purchase a one-month bank certificate earning, say, 10 percent (on an annualized basis). At the same time, Subsidiary B may borrow from a bank for one month at a rate of, say, 12 percent. The bank must charge a higher rate on loans than it offers on deposits. With a centralized approach, Subsidiary B could borrow Subsidiary A's excess funds, thereby reducing its financing costs. This approach is limited since the excess cash of one subsidiary may be denominated in a currency different from that needed by the other subsidiary. While the cash transfer is still possible, the chance of exchange rate fluctuations could discourage it.

The pooling of invested funds and matching of subsidiaries with excess funds may result in excessive transaction costs. For example, consider an MNC whose subsidiaries are transacting in several different currencies. A fully centralized approach would require all excess funds to be pooled and converted to a single currency for investment purposes. In this case, the advantage of pooling may be offset by the transaction costs incurred when converting to a single currency. Centralized cash management could still be valuable, though. The short-term cash available in each currency could be pooled together so that there would be a separate pool for each currency. The excess cash of subsidiaries in a particular currency could still be used to satisfy other subsidiary deficiencies in that currency. In this way, funds could be transferred from one subsidiary to another without incurring transaction costs that banks charge for exchanging currencies. This strategy would be especially feasible if all subsidiary deposits were deposited in branches of a single bank so that funds could easily be transferred among subsidiaries.

Our discussion of using excess cash has emphasized two suggestions: (1) pool together short-term cash denominated in a particular currency whenever possible in order to get the highest return on short-term bank deposits with a given maturity and (2) attempt to accommodate short-term financing needs of subsidiaries with excess funds available at other subsidiaries whenever possible.

When a firm has any cash remaining, it may consider whether to cover any payables positions in foreign currencies. If the firm has future cash outflows in foreign currencies that are expected to appreciate, it may desire to cover such positions by creating short-term deposits in those currencies. The maturity of a deposit would ideally coincide with the date at which the funds are needed.

Any remaining funds can be invested in domestic or foreign short-term securities. In some periods, foreign short-term securities will have higher interest rates than domestic interest rates. The differential can be substantial, as is illustrated in Exhibit 21.4. However, firms must account for the possible exchange rate movements when assessing the potential yield on foreign investments, as explained next.

Determining the Effective Yield

Consider a U.S. firm that invests in a deposit denominated in the currency reflecting the highest interest rate and then converts the funds back to dollars when the deposit matures. This strategy will not necessarily be feasible, since the currency denominat-

Exhibit 21.4
Short-Term Annualized Interest Rates Among Currencies (as of February 3, 1999)

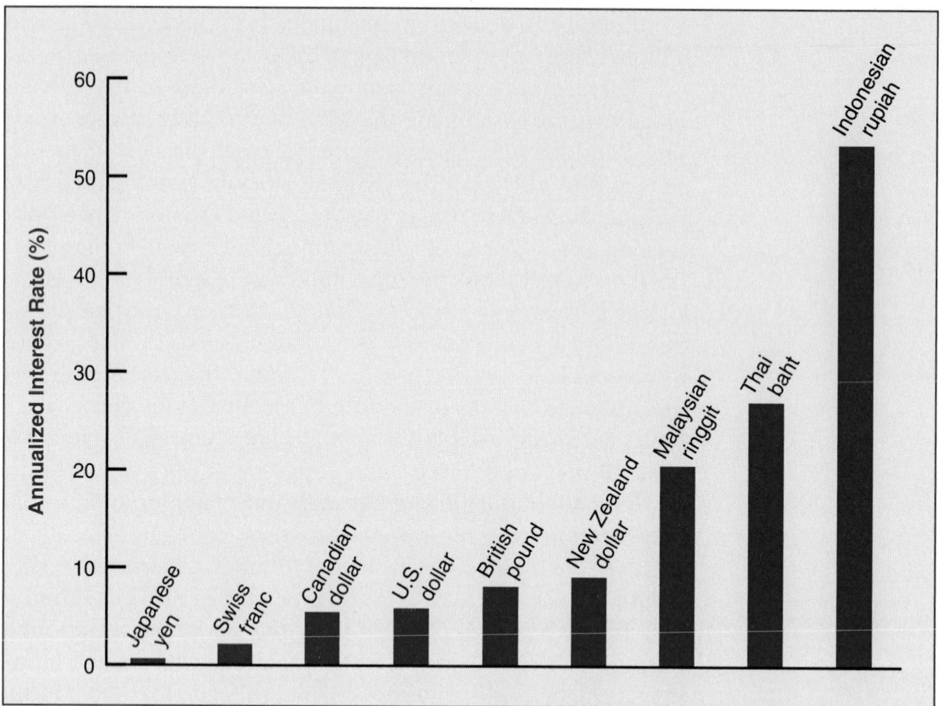

ing the deposit may depreciate over the life of the deposit. If it does, the advantage of a higher interest rate may be more than offset by the degree of depreciation in the currency representing the deposit. It is the deposit's **effective yield,** not its interest rate, that is most important to the cash manager. The effective yield of a bank deposit considers both the interest rate and the rate of appreciation (or depreciation) of the currency denominating the deposit and can therefore be very different from the quoted interest rate on a deposit denominated in a foreign currency. An example follows to illustrate this point.

Assume that Quant Co., a large U.S. corporation with \$1,000,000 in excess cash, could invest in a one-year deposit at 6 percent but is attracted to higher interest rates in Australia. It creates a one-year deposit denominated in Australian dollars (A\$) at 9 percent. The exchange rate of the Australian dollar at the time of the deposit is \$.68. The U.S. dollars are first converted to \$1,470,588 (since \$1,000,000/\$.68 per A\$=\$1,470,588) and then deposited in a bank. One year later, Quant Co. will receive A\$1,602,941, which is equal to the initial deposit plus 9-percent interest on the deposit. At this time, assuming Quant Co. has no use for Australian dollars and will convert them into U.S. dollars. Assume that the exchange rate at this time is \$.72. The funds will convert to \$1,154,118 (computed as A\$1,602,941 × \$.72 per A\$). Thus, the yield on this investment to the U.S. corporation is:

$$\frac{\$1{,}154{,}118-\$1{,}000{,}000}{\$1{,}000{,}000}=.1541, \text{ or } 15.41\%$$

The high yield is attributed to the relatively high interest rate earned on the deposit, plus the appreciation in the currency denominating the deposit over the investment period.

If the currency had depreciated over the investment period, the effective yield to the U.S. corporation would be less than the interest rate on the deposit and could even be lower than the interest rate available on U.S. investments. For example, if the Australian dollar had depreciated from \$.68 at the beginning of the investment period to \$.65 by the end of the investment period, Quant Co. would have received \$1,041,912 (computed as A\$1,602,941 × \$.65 per A\$). In this case, the yield on the investment to the U.S. corporation is:

$$\frac{\$1{,}041{,}912-\$1{,}000{,}000}{\$1{,}000{,}000}=.0419, \text{ or } 4.19\%.$$

The examples provided here illustrate how appreciation of a currency denominating the foreign deposit over the deposit period will force the effective yield to be above the quoted interest rate. Conversely, depreciation will create the opposite effect.

The previous computation of the effective yield on foreign deposits is conducted in a logical manner. A quicker method is shown here:

$$r = (1 + i_f)(1 + e_f) - 1$$

http://

Visit www.bloomberg.com for the latest information from financial markets around the world.

The effective yield on the foreign deposit is represented by r, i_f is the quoted interest rate, and e_f is the percentage change (from the day of deposit to the day of withdrawal) in the value of the currency representing the foreign deposit. The term i_f is used in Chapter 20 to represent the interest rate when borrowing a foreign currency. In this chapter, the interest rate of concern is the deposit rate on the foreign currency. In our example, e_f represents the percentage change in the Australian dollar (against the U.S. dollar) from the date Australian dollars are purchased (and deposited) until the day they are withdrawn (and converted back to U.S. dollars). In our first example, the Australian dollar appreciated from \$.68 to \$.72, or by 5.88 percent over the life of the deposit. Using this information as well as the quoted deposit rate of 9 percent, we find that the effective yield to the U.S. firm on this deposit denominated in Australian dollars is

$$\begin{aligned} r &= (1 + i_f)(1 + e_f) - 1 \\ &= (1 + .09)[1 + (.0588)] - 1 \\ &= .1541, \text{ or } 15.41\% \end{aligned}$$

which is the same rate computed using the first approach.

To test your ability to use the formula for the effective yield, apply it to our revised example, in which the Australian dollar depreciated from \$.68 to \$.65, or by 4.41 percent. Based on the quoted interest rate of 9 percent and the depreciation of 4.41 percent, the effective yield is

$$\begin{aligned} r &= (1 + i_f)(1 + e_f) - 1 \\ &= (1 + .09)[1 + (-.0441)] - 1 \\ &= .0419, \text{ or } 4.19\% \end{aligned}$$

which is the same rate computed earlier for this revised example.

The effective yield could be negative if the currency denominating the deposit depreciated to an extent that more than offset the interest accrued from the deposit. For example, if a U.S. corporation sets up a foreign deposit in euros that has a quoted interest rate of 9 percent and the euro depreciates against the dollar by 12 percent, the effective yield is

$$\begin{aligned} r &= (1 + .09)[1 + (-.12)] - 1 \\ &= -.0408, \text{ or } -4.08\% \end{aligned}$$

The result here suggests that the firm will end up with 4.08 percent less in funds than it initially deposited.

Up to this point, only bank deposits have been considered. There may also be other short-term foreign securities available. Any available securities denominated in a particular currency should have somewhat similar yields. As with bank deposits, the effective yield on all other securities denominated in a foreign currency is influenced by the fluctuation of that foreign currency's exchange rate. Our discussion will continue with a focus on bank deposits for short-term foreign investment. Yet, the implications of our discussion can be applied to other short-term securities as well.

Implications of Interest Rate Parity

Recall that covered interest arbitrage is described as a foreign short-term investment with a simultaneous forward sale of the foreign currency denominating the foreign investment. One might think that a foreign currency with a high interest rate would be an ideal candidate for covered interest arbitrage. However, such a currency will normally exhibit a forward discount that reflects the differential between its interest rate and the investor's home interest rate. This relationship is based on the theory of interest rate parity. Investors cannot lock in a higher return when attempting covered interest arbitrage if interest rate parity exists.

Even if interest rate parity does exist, short-term foreign investing may still be feasible but would have to be conducted on an uncovered basis (without use of the forward market). That is, short-term foreign investing may result in a higher effective yield than domestic investing, but it cannot be guaranteed.

Use of the Forward Rate as a Forecast

If interest rate parity exists, the forward rate can still be a useful indicator to the U.S. firm's investment decision. Consider the following information:

One-year U.S. interest rate = 6%
One-year Australian interest rate = 9%
Spot rate of Australian dollar = $.65
One-year forward rate of Australian dollar = $.6321
Amount of excess funds available at U.S. firm = $400,000

The U.S. firm may first consider using covered interest arbitrage by investing in Australian dollars (A$) and covering the position. This would result in the purchasing of A$615,385 (computed as $400,000/$.65 per A$). At the end of one year, the U.S. firm will receive A$670,770 (computed as A$615,385 × 1.09). It can lock in the number of U.S. dollars received when converting those Australian dollars back to U.S. dollars by selling Australian dollars one year forward. At the forward rate of $.6321, this amounts to $424,000 (A$670,770 × $.6321 per Australian dollar). The effective yield here is

$$\frac{\$424,000 - \$400,000}{\$400,000} = .06, \text{ or } 6\%$$

This is not more lucrative for the U.S. firm than simply investing in the United States.

Now consider a second possibility, in which the U.S. firm does not cover in the forward market. Assume that the actual spot rate of the Australian dollar at the time the deposit matures turns out to be $.6321. This is the same exchange rate that the U.S. firm could have negotiated in the forward market when the deposit was created. We know from the previous example that at this exchange rate the investment will yield about 6 percent, the same as the yield on a U.S. investment.

If the actual spot rate of the Australian dollar after one year turns out to be more than $.6321, the total U.S. dollars received from the investment will be more than $424,000, and the effective yield will be more than 6 percent (and therefore more rewarding than a U.S. investment). If the actual spot rate after one year turns out to be less than $.6321, the total U.S. dollars received will be less than $424,000, and the effective yield will be less than 6 percent (and therefore less rewarding than the U.S. investment). This example demonstrates that if interest rate parity exists, we can use the forward rate as a break-even point to assess the short-term investment decision. When investing in the foreign currency (and not covering the foreign currency position), the effective yield will be more than the domestic yield if the spot rate of the foreign currency after one year is more than the forward rate at the time the investment is undertaken. Conversely, the yield of a foreign investment will be lower than the domestic yield if the spot rate of the foreign currency after one year turns out to be less than the forward rate at the time the investment is undertaken.

http://

Visit ciber.bus.msu.edu for links to numerous valuable sites related to international business.

Relationship with the International Fisher Effect. When interest rate parity exists, MNCs that use the forward rate as a predictor of the future spot rate expect the yield on foreign deposits to equal that on U.S. deposits. While the forward rate is not necessarily an accurate predictor, it can still be a reasonable forecasting tool if it provides unbiased forecasts of the future spot rate. Being unbiased suggests that it underestimates or overestimates the future spot rate with equal frequency. Thus, the effective yield on foreign deposits is equal to the domestic yield, on average. MNCs that consistently invest in foreign short-term securities will earn a yield similar on average to what they could earn on domestic securities.

Our discussion here is closely related to the international Fisher effect (IFE). Recall that the international Fisher effect suggests that the exchange rate of a foreign currency is expected to change by an amount reflecting the differential between its interest rate and the U.S. interest rate. The rationale behind this theory is that a high nominal interest rate reflects an expectation of high inflation, which could weaken the currency (according to purchasing power parity). If interest rate parity exists, the forward premium or discount reflects that interest rate differential and represents the expected percentage change in the currency's value when the forward rate is used as a predictor of the future spot rate. The IFE suggests that firms cannot consistently earn short-term yields on foreign securities which are higher than those on domestic securities, since the exchange rate is expected to adjust to the interest rate differential on average. If interest rate parity holds and the forward rate is an unbiased predictor of the future spot rate, we can expect the IFE to hold.

The IFE may appear to hold for some currencies and not for others. To determine whether IFE holds, the effective yield from investing in a foreign currency can be compared to that of domestic investing. If the effective yields of the two alternative investments in short-term securities are similar over time on average, then the results would support the IFE. This comparison is conducted in Exhibit 21.5 for a firm that has invested its excess cash in British money market securities rather than in U.S. money market securities because of the relatively high British interest rates. The top graph shows that when the British pound appreciated, as in the 1985–1988

Exhibit 21.5
Investing Cash in British Pounds versus Dollars

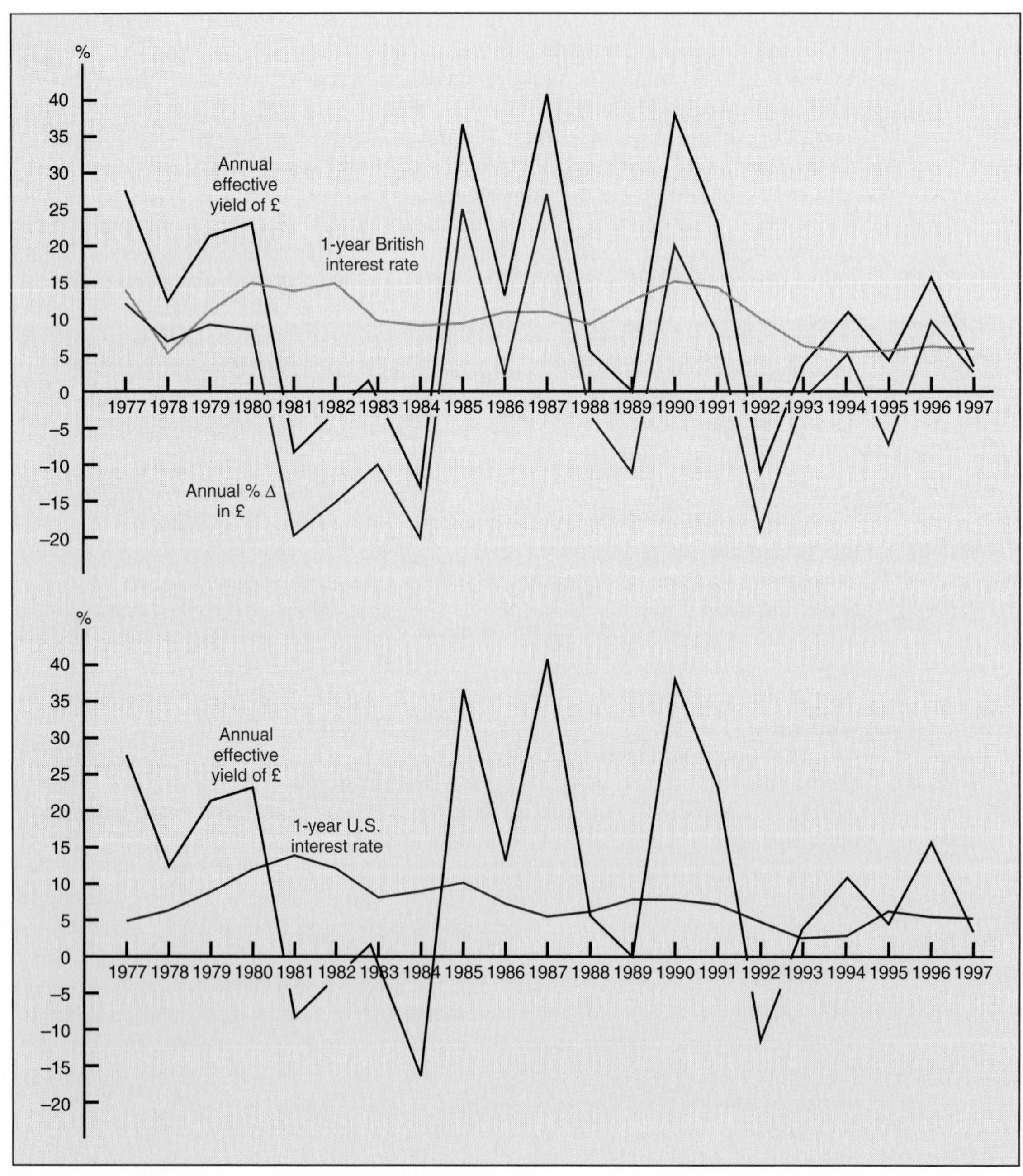

period, the effective yield from the British investment was much higher than the British interest rate. As an extreme example, in 1987 the one-year yield on the British investment exceeded 40 percent.

However, the risk of the British investment is possible depreciation of the pound, which occurred in some periods (such as in the 1981–1984 period and in 1992). In these periods, the effective yield on the British investment was negative. As an extreme example, in 1981 the pound depreciated against the dollar by 20 percent, and the effective yield on the British investment was –8.98 percent. This implies that the firm would have received fewer funds from its money market investment than what it initially invested. Overall, the top graph shows how the effective yield of a foreign investment is dependent on the currency's movement over the investment period.

The lower graph compares the effective yield on the British investment (derived in the top graph) to the U.S. interest rate. This graph illustrates how a foreign investment can generate much higher returns when the foreign currency strengthens, but much lower returns when the foreign currency weakens.

The key implications of interest rate parity and the forward rate as a predictor of future spot rates for foreign investing are summarized in Exhibit 21.6. This exhibit explains the conditions necessary in order for investment in foreign short-term securities to be feasible.

Exhibit 21.6
Considerations When Investing Excess Cash

Scenario	Implications for Investing in Foreign Money Markets
1. Interest rate parity exists.	Covered interest arbitrage is not worthwhile.
2. Interest rate parity exists, and the forward rate is an accurate forecast of the future spot rate.	An uncovered investment in a foreign security is not worthwhile.
3. Interest rate parity exists, and the forward rate is an unbiased forecast of the future spot rate.	An uncovered investment in a foreign security will on average earn an effective yield similar to an investment in a domestic security.
4. Interest rate parity exists, and the forward rate is expected to overestimate the future spot rate.	An uncovered investment in a foreign security is expected to earn a lower effective yield than an investment in a domestic security.
5. Interest rate parity exists, and the forward rate is expected to underestimate the future spot rate.	An uncovered investment in a foreign security is expected to earn a higher effective yield than an investment in a domestic security.
6. Interest rate parity does not exist; the forward premium (discount) exceeds (is less than) the interest rate differential.	Covered interest arbitrage is feasible for investors residing in the home country.
7. Interest rate parity does not exist; the forward premium (discount) is less than (exceeds) the interest rate differential.	Covered interest arbitrage is feasible for foreign investors but not for investors residing in the home country.

Use of Exchange Rate Forecasts

While MNCs do not know how a currency's value will change over the investment horizon, they can use the formula for the effective yield provided earlier in this chapter and plug in their forecast for the percentage change in the foreign currency's exchange rate (e_f). Since the interest rate of the foreign currency deposit (i_f) is known, the effective yield can be forecasted given a forecast of e_f. This projected effective yield on a foreign deposit can then be compared with the yield when investing in the firm's local currency. For example, assume a U.S. firm has funds available for one year. It is aware that the one-year interest rate on a U.S. dollar deposit is 11 percent and the interest rate on an Australian deposit is 14 percent. Assume that the U.S. firm forecasts that the Australian deposit will depreciate from its current rate of \$.1600 to \$.1584, or a 1 percent decrease. The expected value for e_f [$E(e_f)$] will therefore be –1 percent. Thus, the expected effective yield [$E(r)$] on an Australian dollar-denominated deposit is

$$
\begin{aligned}
E(r) &= (1 + i_f)[1 + E(e_f)] - 1 \\
&= (1 + 14\%)[1 + (-1\%)] - 1 \\
&= 12.86\%
\end{aligned}
$$

In this example, investing in an Australian dollar deposit is expected to be more rewarding than investing in a U.S.-dollar deposit. Keep in mind that the value for e_f is forecasted and therefore is not known with certainty. Thus, there is no guarantee that foreign investing will truly be more lucrative.

Deriving the Value of e_f That Equates Foreign and Domestic Yields. In recognition that e_f is uncertain, the U.S. firm may attempt to at least determine what value of e_f would make the effective yield from foreign investing the same as that from investing in a U.S. dollar deposit. To determine this value, begin with the effective yield formula and solve for e_f as follows:

$$
\begin{aligned}
r &= (1+i_f)(1+e_f)-1 \\
(1+r) &= (1+i_f)(1+e_f) \\
\frac{(1+r)}{(1+i_f)} &= (1+e_f) \\
\frac{(1+r)}{(1+i_f)} - 1 &= e_f
\end{aligned}
$$

Since the U.S. deposit rate was 11 percent in our previous example, that is the rate to be plugged in for r. We can also plug in 14 percent for i_f, so the break-even value of e_f would be

$$
\begin{aligned}
e_f &= \frac{(1+r)}{(1+i_f)} - 1 \\
&= \frac{(1+11\%)}{(1+14\%)} - 1 \\
&= -2.63\%
\end{aligned}
$$

This suggests that the Australian dollar must depreciate by about 2.63 percent to make the Australian dollar deposit generate the same effective yield as a deposit in U.S. dollars. Any smaller degree of depreciation would make the Australian dollar deposit more rewarding. The U.S. firm can use this information when determining whether to invest in a U.S. dollar or Australian dollar deposit. If it expects the Australian dollar to depreciate by more than 2.63 percent over the deposit period, it will prefer investing in U.S. dollars. If it expects the Australian dollar to depreciate by less than 2.63 percent, or to appreciate, its decision is more complex. If the potential reward from investing in the foreign currency outweighs the risk involved, then the firm should choose that route. The final decision here will be influenced by the firm's degree of risk aversion.

Use of Probability Distributions. Since even expert forecasts are not always accurate, it is sometimes useful to develop a probability distribution instead of relying on a single prediction. An example of how a probability distribution is applied follows.

Assume a U.S. firm is deciding whether to invest in Australian dollars for one year. It finds that the quoted interest rate for the Australian dollar is 14 percent, and the quoted interest rate for a U.S.-dollar deposit is 11 percent. The firm then develops a probability distribution for the Australian dollar's possible percentage change in value over the life of the deposit. The probability distribution is displayed in Exhibit 21.7. From the first row in the exhibit, we see that there is a 5-percent probability of a 10-percent depreciation in the Australian dollar over the deposit life. If the Australian dollar does depreciate by 10 percent, the effective yield will be 2.60 percent. This implies that there is a 5-percent probability of the U.S. firm's earning a 2.60 percent effective yield on its funds. From the second row in the exhibit, we see that there is a 10-percent probability of an 8-percent depreciation in the Australian dollar over the deposit period. If the Australian dollar does depreciate by 8 percent, the effective yield will be 4.88 percent, which means there is a 10-percent probability of the U.S. firm's generating a 4.88 percent effective yield on this deposit. For each possible percentage change in the Australian dollar's value, there is a corresponding effective yield. Each possible effective yield (Column 3) is associated with a probability of that yield occurring (Column 2). An *expected value* of the effective yield of

Exhibit 21.7
Analysis of Investing in a Foreign Currency

Possible Rate of Change in the Australian Dollar Over the Life of the Investment (e_f)	Probability of Occurrence	Effective Yield if This Rate of Change in the Australian Dollar Does Occur
−10%	5%	(1.14) [1 + (−.10)] − 1 = .0260, or 2.60%
−8	10	(1.14) [1 + (−.08)] − 1 = .0488, or 4.88%
−4	15	(1.14) [1 + (−.04)] − 1 = .0944, or 9.44%
−2	20	(1.14) [1 + (−.02)] − 1 = .1172, or 11.72%
+1	20	(1.14) [1 + (.01)] − 1 = .1514, or 15.14%
+2	15	(1.14) [1 + (.02)] − 1 = .1628, or 16.28%
+3	10	(1.14) [1 + (.03)] − 1 = .1742, or 17.42%
+4	5	(1.14) [1 + (.04)] − 1 = .1856, or 18.56%
	100%	

the Australian dollar is derived by multiplying each possible effective yield by its corresponding probability. Based on the information in Exhibit 21.7, the expected value of the effective yield, referred to as $E(r)$, is computed this way:

$$E(r) = 5\%(2.60\%) + 10\%(4.88\%) + 15\%(9.44\%) + 20\%(11.72\%) + 20\%(15.14\%) + 15\%(16.28\%) + 10\%(17.42\%) + 5\%(18.56\%)$$

$$= .13\% + .488\% + 1.416\% + 2.344\% + 3.028\% + 2.442\% + 1.742\% + .928\%$$

$$= 12.518\%$$

Thus, the expected value of the effective yield when investing in Australian dollars is approximately 12.5 percent.

To further assess the question of which currency to invest in, the information in Columns 2 and 3 from Exhibit 21.7 is used to develop a probability distribution in Exhibit 21.8, which illustrates the probability of each possible effective yield that may occur if the U.S. firm invests in Australian dollars. Notice that the U.S. interest rate (11 percent) is known with certainty and is included in Exhibit 21.8 for comparison purposes. A comparison of the Australian dollar's probability distribution

Exhibit 21.8
Probability Distribution of Effective Yields

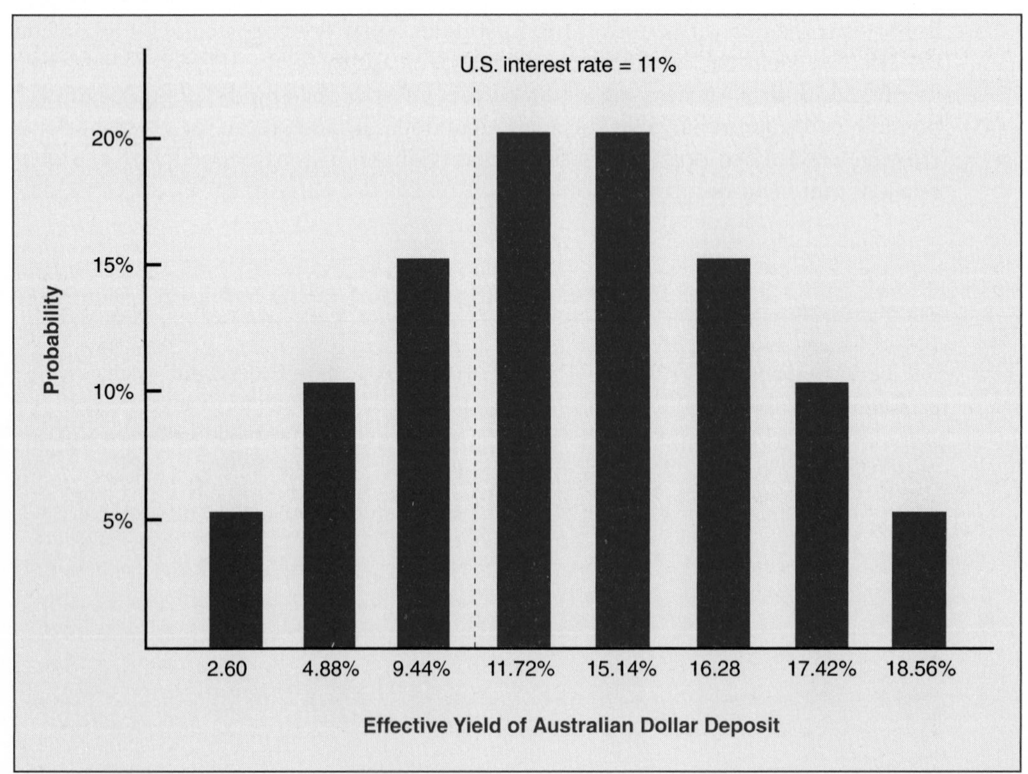

against the U.S. interest rate suggests that there is a 30-percent probability that the U.S. rate will be more than the effective yield from investing in Australian dollars and a 70-percent chance that it will be less.

If you are the treasurer of the U.S. firm, are you going to invest in U.S. dollars (and earn 11 percent with certainty) or invest in Australian dollars (with an expected value of 12.5 percent for the effective yield)? You may choose to invest in a U.S.-dollar deposit since you prefer knowing with certainty the yield you will earn from your investment. Or you may feel the potential reward from investing in Australian dollars outweighs the risk involved. The risk is the 5-percent chance (probability) that the effective yield on the Australian dollar deposit will be 2.60 percent, or the 10-percent chance the effective yield on the Australian dollar deposit will be 4.88 percent, or the 15-percent chance the effective yield on Australian dollars will be 9.44 percent. Each of these possibilities represents a lower return to the U.S. firm than what it would have earned had it invested in a U.S.-dollar deposit. This explains why some of the more conservative firms choose to avoid the uncertainty and invest in U.S. dollars.

Diversifying Cash Across Currencies

Because an MNC is not sure how exchange rates will change over time, it may prefer to diversify cash among securities with different currency denominations. This way it avoids the possibility of incurring substantial losses due to a particular currency's depreciation. Limiting the percentage of excess cash invested in each currency will reduce the MNC's exposure to exchange rate risk. The degree to which a portfolio of investments denominated in various currencies will reduce risk depends on the currency correlations. Ideally, the currencies represented within the portfolio will exhibit low or negative correlations with each other. When currencies are likely to be affected by the same underlying event, their movements tend to be more highly correlated, and diversification among these types of currencies does not substantially

Nike Problem

International Cash Management

At a given point in time, Nike may have at least $400 million in cash balances. Thus, short-term investing decisions can have an important effect on Nike's value. Since Nike has several subsidiaries, it may wish to maintain some cash in the respective local currency of each subsidiary for liquidity. However, it may also want to consider maintaining any cash beyond some limited level in currencies that offer an attractive yield and are not expected to depreciate against whatever currency where the funds will ultimately be used. Furthermore, Nike may consider creating short-term investments in currencies with high interest rates where future cash outflows are anticipated. For example, if Nike anticipates an expansion of facility in the United Kingdom (where interest rates are usually higher than in the United States), it may invest funds there.

Discussion: Should Nike consider investing funds in Latin American countries where it may expand facilities? The interest rates are high and the proceeds from the investment could be used to help support the investment. When would this strategy backfire?

reduce exposure to exchange rate risk. For example, MNCs that invested their cash in Asia in 1997 earned a higher interest rate than what was possible in the United States, but Asian currencies, such as the Indonesian rupiah, the Malaysian ringgit, the South Korean won, and the Thailand baht, depreciated by more than 50 percent against the U.S. dollar in less than one year. Consequently, subsidiaries based outside of Asia that attempted to benefit from the high Asian interest rates earned negative effective yields on their investments, suggesting that they received less than what they initially invested. Diversification of cash among these currencies was not beneficial in this case because all of the currencies weakened in response to the Asian crisis. The potential benefits from investing in a portfolio of currencies is more thoroughly discussed in Appendix 21.

Using Dynamic Hedging to Hedge Investments

Some commercial banks have begun to offer **dynamic hedging** for firms that invest in short-term securities denominated in foreign currencies. Unlike some other hedging techniques, dynamic hedging does not guarantee home currency cash flows to be received at a future point in time. It reflects periodic hedging by the bank, wherein hedges are applied when the currencies held are expected to depreciate and removed when they are expected to appreciate. In essence, the objective is to protect against downside risk while benefiting from the favorable movement of exchange rates.

Consider a manager assigned to perform dynamic hedging for a U.S. firm that has invested in British pounds. If the pound begins to decline and is expected to depreciate further, the manager will sell pounds forward for a future date at which the pound's value is expected to turn upward. If the manager is very confident that the pound will depreciate in the short run, most or all of the position will be hedged. Now assume that the pound begins to appreciate before the forward contract date. Since the contract will preclude the potential benefits from appreciation of the pound, the manager may buy pounds forward to offset the existing forward sale contracts. In this way, the manager has removed the existing hedge. Of course, if the forward rate at the time of the forward purchase exceeds the forward rate that existed at the time of the forward sale, a cost is incurred to remove the hedge.

The manager may decide to remove only part of the hedge, offsetting only some of the existing forward sales with forward purchases. With this approach, the position is still partially protected if the pound depreciates further. Overall, the performance from using dynamic hedging is dependent on the manager's ability to forecast the direction of exchange rate movements.

Impact of International Cash Management on an MNC's Value

An MNC's international cash management can affect its value, as shown in Exhibit 21.9. If an MNC's foreign subsidiary can invest its cash in currencies that offer a higher return than what is available from investing in local securities, it can increase the level of its foreign currency cash flows. Thus, it would have increased the expected dollar cash flows that will ultimately be received from the foreign subsidiaries as the foreign currency cash flows are remitted to the U.S. parent. In addition, the U.S. parent may be able to increase its own cash flows by conducting effective international cash management when managing its excess cash.

Exhibit 21.9
Impact of International Cash Management on an MNC's Value

Returns on International Cash Management

$$V = \sum_{t=1}^{n} \left\{ \frac{\sum_{j=1}^{m} \left[E(CF_{j,t}) \times E(ER_{j,t}) \right]}{(1+k)^t} \right\}$$

V = value of the U.S.-based MNC
$E(CF_{j,t})$ = expected cash flows denominated in currency j to be received by the U.S. parent in period t
$E(ER_{j,t})$ = expected exchange rate at which currency j can be converted to dollars at the end of period t
k = the weighted average cost of capital of the U.S. parent company
m = number of currencies
n = number of periods

SUMMARY

- Each subsidiary of an MNC can assess its cash flows by estimating expected cash inflows and outflows to forecast its balance in each currency. This will indicate whether it will have excess cash to invest or a cash deficiency. The MNC's parent may prefer to use a centralized perspective, in which the cash flow positions of all subsidiaries are consolidated. In this way, funds could be transferred among subsidiaries to accommodate cash deficiencies at particular subsidiaries.
- The common techniques to optimize cash flows are (1) accelerating cash inflows, (2) minimizing currency conversion costs, (3) managing blocked funds, and (4) implementing intersubsidiary cash transfers.
- The efforts by MNCs to optimize cash flows are complicated by (1) company-related characteristics, (2) government restrictions, and (3) characteristics of banking systems.
- MNCs can possibly achieve higher returns when investing excess cash in foreign currencies that either have relatively high interest rates or may appreciate over the investment period. However, if the foreign currency depreciates over the investment period, this may offset any interest rate advantage of that currency.

SELF-TEST FOR CHAPTER 21

(Answers are provided in Appendix A at the back of the text.)

1. Country X typically has a high interest rate, and its currency is expected to strengthen against the dollar over time. Country Y typically has a low interest rate, and its currency is expected to weaken against the dollar over time. Both countries have imposed a "blocked funds" restriction over the next four years on the two subsidiaries owned by a U.S. firm. Which subsidiary will be more adversely affected by the blocked funds, assuming that there are limited opportunities for corporate expansion in both countries?

2. Assume that the Australian one-year interest rate is 14 percent. Also assume that the Australian dollar is expected to appreciate by 8 percent over the next year against the U.S. dollar. What is the expected effective yield on a one-year deposit in Australia by a U.S. firm?

3. Assume that the one-year forward rate is used as the forecast of the future spot rate. The Malaysian ringgit's spot rate is $.20, while its one-year forward rate is $.19. The Malaysian one-year interest rate is 11 percent. What is the expected effective yield on a one-year deposit in Malaysia by a U.S. firm?

4. Assume that the Venezuela one-year interest rate is 90 percent, while the U.S. one-year interest rate is 6 percent. Determine the break-even value for the percentage change in Venezuela's currency (the bolivar) that would cause the effective yield to be the same for a one-year deposit in Venezuela as for a one-year deposit in the United States.

5. Assume interest rate parity exists. Would U.S. firms possibly consider placing deposits in countries with high interest rates? Explain.

QUESTIONS AND APPLICATIONS

1. Discuss the general functions involved in international cash management.

2. What is netting, and how can it improve an MNC's performance?

3. How can an MNC implement leading and lagging techniques to help subsidiaries in need of funds?

4. Explain how the MNC's optimization of cash flow can distort the profits of each subsidiary.

5. How can a centralized cash management system be beneficial to the MNC?

6. Why would a U.S. firm consider investing short-term funds in euros?

7. Assume that a U.S.-based MNC has $2,000,000 in cash available for 90 days. It is considering the use of covered interest arbitrage, since the euro 90-day interest rate is higher than the U.S. interest rate. What will determine whether this strategy is feasible?

8. Assume that a U.S.-based MNC has $1,000,000 in cash available for 30 days. It can earn 1 percent on a 30-day investment in the United States. Alternatively, if it converts the dollars to Mexican pesos, it can earn 1.5 percent on a Mexican deposit. The spot rate of the Mexican peso is $.12. The spot rate 30 days from now is expected to be $.10. Should this firm invest its cash in the United States or in Mexico? Substantiate your answer.

9. Assume that a U.S.-based MNC has $3,000,000 in cash available for 180 days. It can earn 7 percent on a U.S. Treasury bill or 9 percent on a British Treasury bill. The British investment requires conversion of dollars to British pounds. Assume that interest rate parity holds and that the MNC believes the 180-day forward rate is a reliable predictor of the spot rate to be realized 180 days from now. Would the British investment provide an effective yield that is below, above, or equal to the yield on the U.S. investment? Explain your answer.

10. Repeat question 9, but this time assume that the firm expects the 180-day forward rate of the pound to substantially overestimate the spot rate to be realized in 180 days.

11. Repeat question 9, but this time assume that the firm expects the 180-day forward rate of the pound to substantially underestimate the spot rate to be realized in 180 days.

12. Assume that the one-year U.S. interest rate is 10 percent and the one-year Canadian interest rate is 13 percent. If a U.S. firm invests its funds in Canada, what percentage will the Canadian dollar have to depreciate to make its effective yield the same as the U.S. interest rate, from the U.S. firm's perspective?

13. A U.S.-based MNC plans to invest its excess cash in Mexican pesos for one year. The one-year Mexican interest rate is 19 percent. The probability of the peso's percentage change in value during the next year is as follows:

Possible Rate of Change in the Mexican Peso Over the Life of the Investment	Probability of Occurrence
−15%	20%
− 4	50
0	30

What is the expected value of the effective yield based on this information? Given that the U.S. interest rate for one year is 7 percent, what is the probability that a one-year investment in pesos will generate a lower effective yield than could be generated if the U.S. firm simply invested domestically?

14. If a U.S. firm believes that the international Fisher effect holds, what are the implications regarding a strategy of continually attempting to generate high returns by investing in currencies with high interest rates?

15. A U.S. firm considers placing 30 percent of its excess funds in a one-year Singapore dollar deposit and the remaining 70 percent of its funds in a one-year Canadian dollar deposit. The Singapore one-year interest rate is 15 percent, while the Canadian one-year interest rate is 13 percent. The possible percentage changes in the two currencies for the next year are forecasted as follows:

Currency	Possible Percentage Change in the Spot Rate Over the Investment Horizon	Probability of That Percentage Change in the Spot Rate Occurring
Singapore dollar	−2%	20%
Singapore dollar	1	60
Singapore dollar	3	20
Canadian dollar	1	50
Canadian dollar	4	40
Canadian dollar	6	10

Given this information, determine the possible effective yields of the portfolio and the probability associated with each possible portfolio yield. Given a one-year U.S. interest rate of 8 percent, what is the probability that the portfolio's effective yield will be lower than the yield achieved from investing in the United States? (See Appendix 21.)

16. Why would a firm consider investing in a portfolio of foreign currencies instead of just a single foreign currency?

17. Tallahassee Company has $2 million in excess cash that it has invested in Mexico at an annual interest rate of 60 percent. The U.S. interest rate is 9 percent. By how much would the Mexican peso have to depreciate to cause such a strategy to backfire?

18. € Dallas Company has determined that the interest rate on the euro is 16 percent, while the U.S. interest rate is 11 percent for one-year Treasury bills. The one-year forward rate of the euro has a discount of 7 percent. Does interest rate parity exist? Can Dallas Company achieve a higher effective yield by using covered interest arbitrage than by investing in U.S. Treasury bills? Explain.

19. € Consider a U.S. firm with no European business that has cash invested in six European countries, each of which uses the euro as its local currency. Are the MNC's short-term investments well diversified and subject to a low degree of exchange rate risk? Explain.

Internet Application

20. The Bloomberg Web site provides interest rate data for many different foreign currencies over various maturities. Its address is:

    http://www.bloomberg.com

    a. Go to the "Markets" section of the Web site and then to "International Yield Curves." Review the different three-month interest rates among countries. Assume that your U.S.-based MNC could invest funds for 1 percent above the annualized risk-free (government) rates shown in the Bloomberg Web site. Which country has the highest one-year interest rate?
    b. As a cash manager of an MNC based in the United States that has extra dollars that can be invested for one year, where would you invest funds for the next year? Explain.

c. If you were working for a foreign subsidiary based in Japan and could invest Japanese yen for one year until the yen are needed to support local operations, where would you invest the yen? Explain.

Running Your Own MNC

Managing Cash

21. Given that you receive periodic payments in foreign currency for your exports, explain how you could effectively use cash management. That is, explain how you would use the funds as they are received. If you had some existing short-term debt, would you prefer to invest the cash in short-term securities or would you pay off the debt?

Blades, Inc. Case

International Cash Management

As chief financial officer of Blades, Inc., Ben Holt is reasonably satisfied with the performance of Blades' subsidiary in Thailand. The subsidiary recently began production of "Speedos," Blades' primary product, which will be sold to various retailers in Thailand. Preliminary orders from Thai retailers indicate that Blades will be successful in meeting the forecasted demand for "Speedos" during the first year of the Thai subsidiary's operations. Specifically, the orders indicate that 120,000 pairs of "Speedos" will be sold to Thai retailers for an average price of 5,000 Thai baht per pair. This forecast is based on the most recent information.

The Thai subsidiary needed to pay for the rubber and plastic components necessary to produce the 120,000 pairs of "Speedos" approximately six months before accounts receivable resulting from the sales by the Thai subsidiary were collected. Since the average cost per pair of "Speedos" runs at approximately 3,500 Thai baht, Blades has decided to finance the Thai subsidiary's working capital needs by borrowing 420 million baht in Thailand at an interest rate of 6 percent. The subsidiary will collect the accounts receivable resulting from the sale of "Speedos" next month. These accounts receivable will be used to repay the loan's principal and interest.

Ben Holt is currently planning to instruct the Thai subsidiary to remit any remaining baht-denominated cash flows back to the United States. However, he has noticed that Blades would be able to invest funds in Thailand at a relatively high interest rate compared to the United States. Specifically, Blades could invest the remaining baht-denominated funds for one year in Thailand at an interest rate of 15 percent. Ben Holt attributes the high interest rates in Thailand as an indication of the uncertainty resulting from recent events in Thailand.

If the funds are remitted back to the U.S. parent, the excess dollar volume resulting from the conversion of baht is either used to support the U.S. production of "Speedos" if needed or is invested in the United States. Specifically, they would be used to cover cost of goods sold in the U.S. manufacturing plant, located in Omaha, Nebraska. Since Blades used a significant amount of cash to finance the initial investment necessary to build the plant in Thailand and purchase the necessary equipment, Blades' U.S. operations are strapped for cash. Consequently, if the subsidiary earnings are not remitted back to the United States, Blades would have to borrow funds at an interest rate of 10 percent to support its U.S. operations. Any funds remitted by the subsidiary that are not used to support U.S. operations will be invested in the U.S. at an interest rate of 8 percent. Ben Holt estimates that approximately 60 percent of the funds remitted by the subsidiary will be needed to support U.S. operations, while the remaining 40 percent would be invested in the United States.

Ben Holt is consequently faced with two alternative plans. First, he could instruct the Thai subsidiary to repay the baht loan (with interest) and invest any remaining funds in Thailand at an interest rate of 15 percent. Second, he could instruct the

Thai subsidiary to repay the baht loan and remit any remaining funds back to the U.S., where 60 percent of the funds would be used to support U.S. operations and 40 percent of the funds would be invested at an interest rate of 8 percent.

Ben Holt has contacted you, a financial analyst at Blades, Inc., to help him in analyzing the two different options available to Blades. Mr. Holt has informed you that the current spot rate of the Thai baht is $0.0255, and the baht is expected to depreciate by 5 percent over the coming year. He has provided you with the following list of questions he would like you to answer:

1. There is a tradeoff between the higher interest rates in Thailand and the delayed conversion of baht into dollars. Explain what this means.
2. If the net baht received from the Thailand subsidiary are invested in Thailand, how will U.S. operations be affected?
3. Construct a spreadsheet that compares the cash flows resulting from two plans. Under the first plan, net baht-denominated cash flows (received today) will be invested in Thailand at 15 percent for a one-year period, after which the baht will be converted to dollars. Under the second plan, net baht-denominated cash flows are converted to dollars immediately and 60 percent of the funds will be used to support U.S. operations, while 40 percent are invested in the United States for one year at 8 percent. Which plan is superior given the expectation of the baht's value in one year?

Small Business Dilemma

Cash Management at the Sports Exports Company

Ever since Jim Logan began his Sports Exports Company, he has been concerned about his exposure to exchange rate risk. The firm produces footballs and exports them to a distributor in the United Kingdom, with the exports being denominated in British pounds. Jim has just entered into a joint venture in the United Kingdom in which a British firm produces sporting goods for Jim's firm and sells the goods to the British distributor. The distributor pays pounds to Jim's firm for these products. Jim recently borrowed pounds to finance this venture, which created some cash outflows (interest payments) that partially offset his cash inflows in pounds. The interest paid on this loan is equal to the British Treasury bill rate plus 3 percentage points. His original business of exporting has been very successful recently, which has caused him to have revenue (in pounds) that will be retained as excess cash. Jim must decide whether to pay off part of the existing British loan, to invest the cash in the U.S. Treasury bills, or to invest the cash in British Treasury bills.

1. If Jim invests the excess cash in U.S. Treasury bills, would this reduce the firm's exposure to exchange rate risk?
2. Jim decided to use the excess cash to pay off the British loan. However, a friend advised him to invest the cash in British Treasury bills, stating "the loan provides an offset to the pound receivables, so you would be better off investing in British Treasury bills than paying off the loan." Is Jim's friend correct? What should Jim do?

APPENDIX 21

Investing in a Portfolio of Currencies

Large financial corporations may consider investing in portfolios of currencies, as illustrated in the following example. Assume a U.S. firm needs to invest $100,000 for one year and obtains these interest rate quotes:

Interest rate for a one-year deposit in U.S. dollars = 11%
Interest rate for a one-year deposit in Singapore dollars = 14%
Interest rate for a one-year deposit in British pounds = 13%

Due to relatively high quotes for a deposit in Singapore dollars or British pounds, it is understandable that the U.S. firm may desire to invest in a foreign currency. If the U.S. firm decides to use foreign investing, it has three choices based on the information given here:

- invest in only Singapore dollars
- invest in only British pounds
- invest in a mixture (or portfolio) of Singapore dollars and pounds

Assume that the U.S. firm has established possible percentage changes in the spot rate from the time the deposit would begin until maturity for both the Singapore dollar and British pound, as shown in Column 2 of Exhibit 21A.1. We shall first discuss the Singapore dollar. For each possible percentage change that might occur, a probability of that occurrence is disclosed in the third column. Based on the assumed interest

Exhibit 21A.1
Development of Possible Effective Yields

Currency	Possible Percentage Change in the Spot Rate Over the Deposit Life	Probability of That Percentage Change in the Spot Rate Occurring	Computation of Effective Yield Based on That Percentage Change in the Spot Rate
Singapore dollar	–4%	20%	(1.14) [1 + (–4%)] – 1 = 9.44%
Singapore dollar	–1	50	(1.14) [1 + (–1%)] – 1 = 12.86%
Singapore dollar	+2	30	(1.14) [1 + (2%)] – 1 = 16.28%
		100%	
British pound	–3	30	(1.13) [1 + (–3%)] – 1 = 9.61%
British pound	0	30	(1.13) [1 + (0%)] – 1 = 13.00%
British pound	2	40	(1.13) [1 + (2%)] – 1 = 15.26%
		100%	

rate of 14 percent for the Singapore dollar, the effective yield is computed for each possible percentage change in the Singapore dollar's spot rate over the loan life. In Exhibit 21A.1, there is a 20-percent chance the Singapore dollar will depreciate by 4 percent during the deposit period. If it does, the effective yield will be 9.44 percent. Furthermore, there is a 50-percent chance the effective yield will be 12.86 percent and a 30-percent chance it will be 16.28 percent. Given that the U.S. deposit rate is 11 percent, there is a 20-percent chance that investing in Singapore dollars will result in a lower effective yield than investing in a U.S. dollar deposit.

The lower section of Exhibit 21A.1 provides information on the British pound. The pound has a 30-percent chance of depreciating by 3 percent during the deposit period, and so on. Based on the 13-percent interest rate for a British pound deposit, there is a 30-percent chance the effective yield will be 9.61 percent, a 30-percent chance it will be 13 percent, and a 40-percent chance it will be 15.26 percent. Keeping in mind the 11-percent rate on a U.S. dollar deposit, there is a 30-percent chance that investing in British pounds will be less rewarding than investing in a U.S.-dollar deposit.

Before examining the third possible foreign investing strategy (the portfolio approach) available here, determine the expected value of the effective yield for each foreign currency, summing up the products of each possible effective yield and its associated probability as follows:

Currency	Computation of Expected Value of Effective Yield
Singapore dollar	(20%)(9.44%) + 50%(12.86%) + 30%(16.28%) = 13.202%
British pound	(30%)(9.61%) + 30%(13.00%) + 40%(15.26%) = 12.887%

The expected value of the Singapore dollar's yield is slightly higher. In addition, the individual degree of risk (the chance the return on investment will be lower than the return on a U.S. deposit) is higher for the pound. If the U.S. firm does choose to invest in only one of these foreign currencies, it may choose the Singapore dollar since its risk and return characteristics are more favorable. Yet, before making its decision, the firm should consider the possibility of investing in a currency portfolio, as discussed here.

The information in Exhibit 21A.1 shows three possibilities for the Singapore dollar's effective yield. The same holds true for the British pound. If a U.S. firm invests half of its available funds in each of the foreign currencies, then there will be nine possibilities for this portfolio's effective yield. These possibilities are shown in Exhibit 21A.2. The first two columns list all possible joint effective yields. The third column computes the joint probability of each possible occurrence. The fourth column shows the computation of the portfolio's effective yield based on the possible rates disclosed for the individual currencies shown in the first two columns. The top row of the table suggests that one possible outcome of investing in both Singapore dollars and British pounds is an effective yield of 9.44 percent and 9.61 percent, respectively. The probability that the Singapore dollar's effective yield will occur is 20 percent, while the probability that the British pound's effective yield will occur is 30 percent. The joint probability that both of these effective yields will occur simultaneously is (20%)(30%) = 6%. Assuming that half (50%) of the funds available are invested in each currency, the portfolio's effective yields will be .5(9.44%) + .5(9.61%) = 9.525% (if those individual effective yields do occur).

Exhibit 21A.2
Analysis of Investing in Two Foreign Currencies

Possible Joint Effective Yield			
Singapore Dollar	British Pound	Computation of Joint Probability	Computation of Effective Yield of Portfolio (50% of Total Funds Invested in Each Currency)
9.44%	9.61%	(20%)(30%) = 6%	.5 (9.44%) + .5 (9.61%) = 9.525%
9.44	13.00	(20%)(30%) = 6	.5 (9.44%) + .5 (13.00%) = 11.22%
9.44	15.26	(20%)(40%) = 8	.5 (9.44%) + .5 (15.26%) = 12.35%
12.86	9.61	(50%)(30%) = 15	.5 (12.86%) + .5 (9.61%) = 11.235%
12.86	13.00	(50%)(30%) = 15	.5 (12.86%) + .5 (13.00%) = 12.93%
12.86	15.26	(50%)(40%) = 20	.5 (12.86%) + .5 (15.26%) = 14.06%
16.28	9.61	(30%)(30%) = 9	.5 (16.28%) + .5 (9.61%) = 12.945%
16.28	13.00	(30%)(30%) = 9	.5 (16.28%) + .5 (13.00%) = 14.64%
16.28	15.26	(30%)(40%) = 12	.5 (16.28%) + .5 (15.26%) = 15.77%
		100%	

A similar procedure was used to develop the remaining eight rows in Exhibit 21A.2. There is a 6-percent chance the portfolio's effective yield will be 11.22 percent, an 8-percent chance that it will be 12.35 percent, and so on.

Exhibit 21A.2 shows that investing in the portfolio will likely be more rewarding than investing in a U.S.-dollar deposit. While there is a 6-percent chance the portfolio's effective yield will be 9.525 percent, all other possible portfolio yields (see Column 4) are more than the U.S. deposit rate of 11 percent.

Recall that investing solely in Singapore dollars has a 20-percent chance of being less rewarding than investing in the U.S. deposit, while investing solely in British pounds has a 30-percent chance of being less rewarding. The analysis in Exhibit 21A.2 suggests that investing in a portfolio (50 percent invested in Singapore dollars, with the remaining 50 percent invested in British pounds) has only a 6-percent chance of being less rewarding than domestic investing. These results will be explained.

When an investment is made in both currencies, the only time the portfolio will exhibit a lower yield than the U.S. deposit is when *both* currencies experience their maximum possible levels of depreciation (which is 4-percent depreciation for the Singapore dollar and 3-percent depreciation for the British pound). If only one of these events occurs, its severity will be somewhat offset by the other currency not depreciating to such a large extent.

In our example, the computation of joint probabilities requires the assumption that the movements in the two currencies are independent. If movements of the two currencies were actually highly correlated, then investing in a portfolio of currencies would not be as beneficial as demonstrated here because there would be a strong likelihood that both currencies would experience a high level of depreciation simultaneously. If the two currencies are not highly correlated, they will not be expected to simultaneously depreciate to such a degree.

The current example includes two currencies in the portfolio. Investing in a more diversified portfolio of additional currencies that exhibit high interest rates can even increase the probability that foreign investing will be more rewarding than the U.S. deposit. This is due to the low probability that all currencies will move in tandem and therefore simultaneously depreciate to offset their high interest rate advantages. Again, the degree to which these currencies are correlated with each other is important here. If all currencies were highly positively correlated with each other, investing in such a portfolio would not be very different from investing in a single foreign currency.

Repeated Investing in a Currency Portfolio

A firm that repeatedly invests in foreign currencies usually prefers to compose a portfolio package that will exhibit a somewhat predictable effective yield on a periodic basis. The more volatile a portfolio's effective yield over time, the more uncertainty (risk) there is about the yield that portfolio will exhibit in any period. The portfolio's variability depends on the standard deviations and paired correlations of effective yields of the individual currencies within the portfolio.

We can use the portfolio variance as a measurement for degree of volatility. The variance of a two-currency portfolio's effective yield (σ^2_p) over time is computed as

$$\sigma^2_p = w^2_A\sigma^2_A + w^2_B\sigma^2_B + 2w_Aw_B\sigma_A\sigma_B CORR_{AB}$$

where w_A and w_B represent the percentage of total funds invested in Currencies A and B respectively, σ^2_A and σ^2_B represent the individual variances of each currency's effective yield over time, and $CORR_{AB}$ reflects the correlation coefficient of the two currencies' effective yields. Since the percentage exchange rate change plays an important role in influencing the effective yield, it should not be surprising that $CORR_{AB}$ is strongly affected by the correlation between the exchange rate fluctuations of the two currencies. A low correlation between currency fluctuations can force $CORR_{AB}$ to be low.

To illustrate how the variance in a portfolio's effective yield is related to characteristics of the component currencies, consider the following example. The following information is based on several three-month periods:

Mean effective yield of British pound over 3 months = 4%
Mean effective yield of Singapore dollar over 3 months = 5%
Standard deviation of British pound's effective yield = .06
Standard deviation of Singapore dollar's effective yield = .10
Correlation coefficient of effective yields of these two currencies = .20

Given the previous information, the mean effective yield on a portfolio (r_p) of funds invested as 50 percent into British pounds and 50 percent into Singapore dollars is determined by summing up the weighted individual effective yields:

$$\begin{aligned} r_p &= .5(.04) + .5(.05) \\ &= .02 + .025 \\ &= .045, \text{ or } 4.5\% \end{aligned}$$

The variance of this portfolio's effective financing rate over time is

$$\begin{aligned}\sigma^2_p &= .5^2(.06)^2 + .5^2(.10)^2 + 2(.5)(.5)(.06)(.10)(.20)\\ &= .25(.0036) + .25(.01) + .5(.0012)\\ &= .0009 + .0025 + .0006\\ &= .004\end{aligned}$$

There is no guarantee that past data will be indicative of the future. Yet, if the individual variability and paired correlations are somewhat stable over time, the historical variability of the portfolio's effective yield should be a reasonable forecast of the future portfolio variability.

PART V INTEGRATIVE PROBLEM

Short-Term Asset and Liability Management

Kent Co. is a large U.S. firm with no international business. It has two branches within the United States, an eastern branch and a western branch. Each branch currently makes investing or financing decisions independently, as if it were a separate entity. The eastern branch has excess cash of $15 million to invest for the next year. It can invest its funds in Treasury bills denominated in dollars or in any of the three foreign currencies in which it does business. The only restriction enforced by the parent is that a maximum of $5 million be invested or financed in any foreign currency, in order to limit the exposure to any single foreign currency.

The western branch needs to borrow $15 million over one year to support its U.S. operations. It can borrow funds in any currency in which it does business (although any foreign funds borrowed would need to be converted to dollars to finance the U.S. operations). The only restriction enforced by the parent is that a maximum equivalent of $5 million can be borrowed in any single currency. A large bank serving the Eurocurrency market has offered Kent Co. the following terms:

Currency	Annual Interest Rate on Deposits	Annual Interest Rate Charged on Loans
U.S. dollar	6%	9%
Australian dollar	11	14
Canadian dollar	7	10
New Zealand dollar	9	12
Japanese yen	8	11

The parent of Kent Co. has created one-year forecasts of each currency which can be used by the branches in making their investing or financing decisions:

Currency	Today's Spot Exchange Rate	Forecasted Annual Percentage Change in Exchange Rate
Australian dollar	$.70	–4%
Canadian dollar	.80	–2
New Zealand dollar	.60	+3
Japanese yen	.008	0

Questions

1. Determine the investment portfolio composition for Kent's eastern branch that would maximize the expected effective yield while satisfying the restriction imposed by the parent.
2. What is the expected effective yield of the investment portfolio?

3. Based on the expected effective yield for the portfolio and the initial investment amount of $15 million, determine the annual interest to be earned on the portfolio.
4. Determine the financing portfolio composition for Kent's western branch that would minimize the expected effective financing rate while satisfying the restriction imposed by the parent.
5. What is the expected effective financing rate of the total amount borrowed?
6. Based on the expected effective financing rate for the portfolio and the total amount of $15 million borrowed, determine the expected loan repayment amount beyond the principal borrowed.
7. When the expected interest received by the eastern branch and paid by the western branch of Kent Co. are consolidated, what is the net amount of interest received?
8. If the eastern branch and the western branch worked together, the eastern branch could loan its $15 million to the western branch. Yet, one could argue that the branches could not take advantage of interest rate differentials or expected exchange rate effects among currencies. Given the data provided in this example, would you recommend that the two branches make their short-term investment or financing decisions independently, or that the eastern branch lend its excess cash to the western branch? Explain.

APPENDIX A
Answers to Self-Test Questions

ANSWERS TO SELF-TEST QUESTIONS FOR CHAPTER 1

1. MNCs can capitalize on comparative advantages (such as a technology or cost of labor) that they have relative to firms in other countries, which allows them to penetrate those other countries' markets. Given a world of imperfect markets, comparative advantages across countries are not freely transferable. Therefore, MNCs may be able to capitalize on comparative advantages. Many MNCs initially penetrate markets by exporting but ultimately establish a subsidiary in foreign markets and attempt to differentiate their products as other firms enter those markets (product cycle theory).
2. In the late 1980s and early 1990s, West European countries removed many barriers, which allowed more potential for efficient expansion throughout Europe. Consequently, U.S. firms may be able to expand across European countries at a lower cost than before.

   During the same period, Eastern European countries opened their markets to foreign firms and privatized many of the state-owned firms. This allowed U.S. firms to penetrate these countries to offer products that previously had been unavailable.

   In the early 1990s, the United States, Canada, and Mexico agreed to cut trade barriers. Some U.S. firms may benefit by penetrating the Canadian and Mexican markets.
3. First, there is the risk of poor economic conditions in the foreign country. Second, there is country risk, which reflects the risk of changing government or public attitudes toward the MNC. Third, there is exchange rate risk, which can affect the performance of the MNC in the foreign country.

ANSWERS TO SELF-TEST QUESTIONS FOR CHAPTER 2

1. Each of the economic factors is described, holding other factors constant.

   a. *Inflation.* A relatively high U.S. inflation rate relative to other countries can make U.S. goods less attractive to U.S. and non-U.S. consumers, which results in fewer U.S. exports, more U.S. imports, and a lower (or more negative) current account balance. A relatively low U.S. inflation rate would have the opposite effect.
   b. *National Income.* A relatively high increase in the U.S. national income (compared to other countries) tends to cause a large increase in demand for imports and can cause a lower (or more negative) current account balance. A relatively low increase in the U.S. national income would have the opposite effect.

c. *Exchange Rates.* A weaker dollar tends to make U.S. products cheaper to non-U.S. firms and makes non-U.S. products expensive to U.S. firms. Thus, U.S. exports are expected to increase, while U.S. imports are expected to decrease. However, some conditions can prevent these effects from occurring, as explained in the chapter. Normally, a stronger dollar causes U.S. exports to decrease and U.S. imports to increase because it makes U.S. goods more expensive to non-U.S. firms and makes non-U.S. goods less expensive to U.S. firms.

d. *Government Restrictions.* When the U.S. government imposes new barriers on imports, the U.S. imports decline, causing the U.S. balance of trade to increase (or be less negative). When non-U.S. governments impose new barriers on imports from the United States, the U.S. balance of trade may decrease (or be more negative). When governments remove trade barriers, the opposite effects are expected.

2. When the U.S. imposes tariffs on imported goods, foreign countries may retaliate by imposing tariffs on goods exported by the United States. Thus, there is a decline in U.S. exports that may offset any decline in U.S. imports.
3. The Asian crisis caused a decline in Asian income levels and therefore resulted in a reduced demand for U.S. exports. In addition, Asian exporters experienced problems, and some U.S. importers discontinued their relationships with the Asian exporters.

ANSWERS TO SELF-TEST QUESTIONS FOR CHAPTER 3

1. Bid/ask spread = (Ask rate – Bid rate)/Ask rate
   = (\$.80 – \$.784)/\$.80
   = .02, or 2%
2. $\text{FR premium (or discount)} = \frac{\$.188 - \$.190}{\$.190} \times \frac{360}{90} = -.0421, \text{ or } -4.21\%$
3. MNCs use the spot foreign exchange market to exchange currencies for immediate delivery. They use the forward foreign exchange market and the currency futures market to lock in the exchange rate at which currencies will be exchanged at a future point in time. They use the currency options market when they wish to lock in the maximum (minimum) amount to be paid (received) in a future currency transaction but maintain flexibility in the event of favorable exchange rate movements.

   MNCs use the Eurocurrency market to engage in short-term investing or financing or the Eurocredit market to engage in medium-term financing. They can obtain long-term financing by issuing bonds in the Eurobond market or by issuing stock in the international markets.

ANSWERS TO SELF-TEST QUESTIONS FOR CHAPTER 4

1. Economic factors affect the yen's value as follows:

   a. If U.S. inflation is higher than Japanese inflation, the U.S. demand for Japanese goods may increase (to avoid the higher U.S. prices), and the Japanese demand for U.S. goods may decrease (to avoid the higher U.S. prices). Consequently, there is upward pressure on the value of the yen.

b. If U.S. interest rates increase and exceed Japanese interest rates, the U.S. demand for Japanese interest-bearing securities may decline (since U.S. interest-bearing securities are more attractive), while the Japanese demand for U.S. interest-bearing securities may rise. Both forces place downward pressure on the yen's value.
c. If U.S. national income increases more than Japanese national income, the U.S. demand for Japanese goods may increase more than the Japanese demand for U.S. goods. Assuming that the change in national income levels does not affect exchange rates indirectly through effects on relative interest rates, the forces should place upward pressure on the yen's value.
d. If government controls reduce the U.S. demand for Japanese goods, they place downward pressure on the yen's value. If the controls reduce the Japanese demand for U.S. goods, they place upward pressure on the yen's value.

The opposite scenarios of those described here would cause the expected pressure to be in the opposite direction.

2. U.S. capital flows with Country A may be larger than U.S. capital flows with Country B. Therefore, the change in the interest rate differential has a larger effect on the capital flows with Country A, causing the exchange rate to change. If the capital flows with Country B are nonexistent, interest rate changes do not change the capital flows and therefore do not change the demand and supply conditions in the foreign exchange market.
3. Smart Banking Corp. should not pursue the strategy because a loss would result, as shown here.

   a. Borrow $5 million.
   b. Convert $5 million to C$5,263,158 (based on the spot exchange rate of $.95 per C$).
   c. Invest the C$ at 9% annualized, which represents a return of .15% over six days, so the C$ received after six days = C$5,271,053 (computed as C$5,263,158 × [1+.0015]).
   d. Convert the C$ received back to U.S. dollars after six days: C$5,271,053 = $4,954,789 (based on anticipated exchange rate of $.94 per C$ after six days).
   e. The interest rate owed on the U.S.-dollar loan is .10% over the six-day period. Thus, the amount owed as a result of the loan is $5,005,000 (computed as $5,000,000 × [1+.001]).
   f. The strategy is expected to cause a gain of ($4,954,789 – $5,005,000) = –$50,211.

Answers to Self-Test Questions for Chapter 5

1. The net profit to the speculator is –$.01 per unit.
   The net profit to the speculator for one contract is –$500 (computed as –$.01 × 50,000 units).
   The spot rate would need to be $.66 for the speculator to break even.
   The net profit to the seller of the call option is $.01 per unit.
2. The speculator should exercise the option.
   The net profit to the speculator is $.03 per unit.
   The net profit to the seller of the put option is –$.03 per unit.

3. The premium paid is higher for options with longer expiration dates (other things being equal). Firms may prefer not to pay such high premiums.

Answers to Self-Test Questions for Chapter 6

1. Market forces cause the demand and supply of yen in the foreign exchange market to change, which causes a change in the equilibrium exchange rate. The central banks could intervene to affect the demand or supply conditions in the foreign exchange market, but they would not always be able to offset the changing market forces. For example, if there were a large increase in the U.S. demand for yen and no increase in the supply of yen for sale, the central banks would have to increase the supply of yen in the foreign exchange market to offset the increased demand.
2. The Fed could use direct intervention by selling some of its dollar reserves in exchange for pesos in the foreign exchange market. It could also use indirect intervention by attempting to reduce U.S. interest rates through monetary policy. Specifically, it could increase the U.S. money supply, which places downward pressure on U.S. interest rates (assuming that inflationary expectations do not change). The lower U.S. interest rates should discourage foreign investment in the U.S. and encourage increased investment by U.S. investors in foreign securities. Both forces tend to weaken the dollar's value.
3. A weaker dollar tends to increase the demand for U.S. goods because the price paid for a specified amount in dollars by non-U.S. firms is reduced. In addition, the U.S. demand for foreign goods is reduced because it takes more dollars to obtain a specified amount in foreign currency once the dollar weakens. Both forces tend to stimulate the U.S. economy and therefore improve productivity and reduce unemployment in the United States.

Answers to Self-Test Questions for Chapter 7

1. No. The cross exchange rate between the pound and the C$ is appropriate, based on the other exchange rates. There is no discrepancy to capitalize on.
2. No. Covered interest arbitrage involves the exchange of dollars for pounds. Assuming that the investors begin with $1 million (the starting amount will not affect the final conclusion), the dollars would be converted to pounds as shown here:

$$\$1 \text{ million}/\$1.60 \text{ per } £ = £625{,}000$$

The British investment would accumulate interest over the 180-day period, resulting in

$$£625{,}000 \times 1.04 = £650{,}000$$

After 180 days, the pounds would be converted to dollars:

$$£650{,}000 \times \$1.56 \text{ per pound} = \$1{,}014{,}000$$

This amount reflects a return of 1.4 percent above the amount U.S. investors initially started with. The investors could simply invest the funds in the United States at 3 percent. Thus, U.S. investors would earn less using the covered interest arbitrage strategy than investing in the United States.

3. No. The forward rate discount on the pound does not perfectly offset the interest rate differential. In fact, the discount is 2.5 percent, which is larger than the interest rate differential. U.S. investors do worse when attempting covered interest arbitrage than when investing their funds in the United States because the interest rate advantage on the British investment is more than offset by the forward discount.

   Further clarification may be helpful here. While the U.S. investors could not benefit from covered interest arbitrage, British investors could capitalize on covered interest arbitrage. While British investors would earn 1-percent interest less on the U.S. investment, they would be purchasing pounds forward at a discount of 2.5 percent at the end of the investment period. When interest rate parity does not exist, investors from only one of the two countries of concern could benefit from using covered interest arbitrage.
4. If there is a discrepancy in the pricing of a currency, one may capitalize on it by using the various forms of arbitrage described in the chapter. As arbitrage occurs, the exchange rates will be pushed toward their appropriate levels because arbitrageurs will buy an underpriced currency in the foreign exchange market (increase in demand for currency places upward pressure on its value) and will sell an overpriced currency in the foreign exchange market (increase in the supply of currency for sale places downward pressure on its value).
5. The one-year forward discount on pounds would become more pronounced (by about one percentage point more than before) because the spread between the British interest rates and U.S. interest rates would increase.

ANSWERS TO SELF-TEST QUESTIONS FOR CHAPTER 8

1. If the Japanese prices rise because of Japanese inflation, the value of the yen should decline. Thus, even though the importer might need to pay more yen, it would benefit from a weaker yen value (it would pay fewer dollars for a given amount in yen). Thus, there could be an offsetting effect if PPP holds.
2. Purchasing power parity does not necessarily hold. In our example, Japanese inflation could rise (causing the importer to pay more yen), and yet the Japanese yen would not necessarily depreciate by an offsetting amount, or at all. Therefore, the dollar amount to be paid for Japanese supplies could increase over time.
3. High inflation will cause a balance of trade adjustment, whereby the United States will reduce its purchases of goods in these countries, while the demand for U.S. goods by these countries should increase (according to PPP). Consequently, there will be downward pressure on the values of these currencies.
4. $$\begin{aligned} e_f &= I_h - I_f \\ &= 3\% - 4\% \\ &= -.01 \text{ or } -1\% \\ S_{t+1} &= S(1 + e_f) \\ &= \$.85[1 + (-.01)] \\ &= \$.8415 \end{aligned}$$

5. $$e_f = \frac{(1+i_h)}{(1+i_f)} - 1$$
$$= \frac{(1+.06)}{(1+.11)} - 1$$
$$\cong -.045, \text{ or } -4.5\%$$
$$S_{t+1} = S(1+e_f)$$
$$= \$.90[1+(-.045)]$$
$$= \$.8595$$

6. According to the IFE, the increase in interest rates by 5 percentage points reflects an increase in expected inflation by 5 percentage points.

   If the inflation adjustment occurs, the balance of trade should be affected, as Australian demand for U.S. goods rises while the U.S. demand for Australian goods declines. Thus, the Australian dollar should weaken.

   If U.S. investors believed in the IFE, they would not attempt to capitalize on higher Australian interest rates because they would expect the Australian dollar to depreciate over time.

Answers to Self-Test Questions for Chapter 9

1. U.S. four-year interest rate = $(1+.07)^4$ = 131.08% or 1.3108. Mexican four-year interest rate = $(1+.20)^4$ = 207.36% or 2.0736.

$$p = \frac{(1+i_h)}{(1+i_f)} - 1 = \frac{1.3108}{2.0736} - 1$$
$$= -.3679 \text{ or } -36.79\%.$$

2. Canadian dollar $\dfrac{|\$.80 - \$.82|}{\$.82} = 2.44\%$

   Japanese yen $\dfrac{|\$.012 - \$.011|}{\$.011} = 9.09\%$

   The forecast error was larger for the Japanese yen.
3. The forward rate of the peso would have overestimated the future spot rate because the spot rate would have declined by the end of each month.
4. Semistrong-form efficiency would be refuted since the currency values do not adjust immediately to useful public information.
5. The peso would be expected to depreciate because the forward rate of the peso would exhibit a discount (be less than the spot rate). Thus, the forecast derived from the forward rate is less than the spot rate, which implies anticipated depreciation of the peso.
6. As the chapter suggests, forecasts of currencies are subject to a high degree of error. Thus, if a project's success is very sensitive to the future value of the bolivar, there is much uncertainty. This project could easily backfire, because the future value of the bolivar is very uncertain.

Answers to Self-Test Questions for Chapter 10

1. Managers have more information about the firm's exposure to exchange rate risk than do shareholders and may be able to hedge it more easily than shareholders could. Shareholders may prefer that the managers hedge for them. Also, cash flows may be stabilized as a result of hedging, which can reduce the firm's cost of financing.
2. The Canadian supplies would have less exposure to exchange rate risk because the Canadian dollar is less volatile than the Mexican peso.
3. The Mexican source would be preferable because the firm could use peso inflows to make payments for material that is imported.
4. No. If exports are priced in dollars, the dollar cash flows received from exporting will depend on Mexico's demand, which will be influenced by the peso's value. If the peso depreciates, Mexican demand for the exports would likely decrease.
5. The earnings generated by the European subsidiaries will be translated to a smaller amount in dollar earnings if the dollar strengthens. Thus, the consolidated earnings of the U.S.-based MNCs will be reduced.

Answers to Self-Test Questions for Chapter 11

1. Amount of A$ to be invested today = A$3,000,000/(1+.12)
   = A$2,678,571
   Amount of U.S. $ to be borrowed to convert to A$ = A$2,678,571 × $.85
   = $2,276,785
   Amount of U.S. $ needed in one year to pay off loan = $2,276,785 × (1+.07)
   = $2,436,160
2. The forward hedge would be more appropriate. Given a forward rate of $.81, Montclair would need $2,430,000 in one year (computed as A$3,000,000 × $.81) when using a forward hedge.
3. Montclair could purchase currency call options in Australian dollars. The option could hedge against the possible appreciation of the Australian dollar. Yet, if the Australian dollar depreciates, Montclair could let the option expire and purchase the Australian dollars at the spot rate at the time it needs to send payment. A disadvantage of the currency call option is that a premium must be paid for it. Thus, if Montclair expects the Australian dollar to appreciate over the year, the money market hedge would probably be a better choice, since the flexibility provided by the option would not be useful in this case.
4. Even though Sanibel Co. is insulated from the beginning of a month to the end of the month the forward rate will become higher each month, because the forward rate moves with the spot rate. Thus, the firm will pay more dollars each month, even though it is hedged during the month. Sanibel will be adversely affected by the consistent appreciation of the pound.
5. Sanibel Co. could engage in a series of forward contracts today to cover the payments in each successive month. In this way, it locks in the future payments today and does not have to agree to the higher forward rates that may exist in future months.

6. A put option on SF2,000,000 would cost \$60,000. If the spot rate of the SF reached \$.68 as expected, the put option would be exercised, which would yield \$1,380,000 (computed as SF2,000,000 × \$.69). Accounting for the premium costs of \$60,000, the receivables amount would convert to \$1,320,000. If Hopkins remains unhedged, it expects to receive \$1,360,000 (computed as SF2,000,000 × \$.68). Thus, the unhedged strategy is preferable.

Answers to Self-Test Questions for Chapter 12

1. Salem could attempt to purchase its chemicals from Canadian sources. Then, if the C\$ depreciates, the reduction in dollar inflows resulting from its exports to Canada will be partially offset by a reduction in dollar outflows needed to pay for the Canadian imports.

   An alternative possibility for Salem is to finance its business with Canadian dollars, but this would probably be a less efficient solution.
2. A possible disadvantage is that Salem would forego some of the benefits if the C\$ appreciated over time.
3. The consolidated earnings of Coastal Corp. will be adversely affected if the pound depreciates because the British earnings will be translated into euro earnings for the consolidated income statement at a lower exchange rate. Coastal could attempt to hedge its translation exposure by selling pounds forward. If the pound depreciates, it will benefit from its forward position, which could help offset the translation effect.
4. This argument has no perfect solution. It appears that shareholders penalize the firm for poor earnings even when the reason for poor earnings is a weak euro that has adverse translation effects. It is possible that translation effects could be hedged to stabilize earnings, but Arlington may consider informing the shareholders that the major earnings changes have been due to translation effects and not to changes in consumer demand or other factors. Perhaps shareholders would not respond so strongly to earnings changes if they were well aware that the changes were primarily caused by translation effects.
5. Lincolnshire has no translation exposure since it has no foreign subsidiaries. Kalafa has translation exposure resulting from its subsidiary in Spain.

Answers to Self-Test Questions for Chapter 13

1. Possible reasons may include
   - more demand for the product (depending on the product)
   - better technology in Canada
   - fewer restrictions (less political interference)
2. Possible reasons may include
   - more demand for the product (depending on the product)
   - greater probability to earn superior profits (since many goods have not been marketed in Mexico in the past)
   - cheaper factors of production (such as land and labor)
   - possible exploitation of monopolistic advantages
3. U.S. firms prefer to enter a country when the foreign country's currency is weak. U.S. firms normally would prefer that the foreign currency appreciate after they

invest their dollars to develop the subsidiary. The executive's comment suggests that the euro is too strong, so any U.S. investment of dollars into Europe will not convert into enough euros to make the investment worthwhile.

4. It may be easier to engage in a joint venture with a Chinese firm, which is already well established in China, to circumvent barriers.
5. The government may attempt to stimulate the economy in this way.

Answers to Self-Test Questions for Chapter 14

1. In addition to earnings generated in Jamaica, the NPV is based on some factors not controlled by the firm, such as the expected host government tax on profits, the withholding tax imposed by the host government, and the salvage value to be received when the project is terminated. Furthermore, the exchange rate projections will affect the estimates of dollar cash flows received by the parent as earnings are remitted.
2. The most obvious effect is on the cash flows that will be generated by the sales distribution center in Ireland. These cash flow estimates will likely be revised downward (due to lower sales estimates). It is also possible that the estimated salvage value could be reduced. Exchange rate estimates could be revised as a result of revised economic conditions. Estimated tax rates imposed on the center by the Irish government could also be affected by the revised economic conditions.
3. New Orleans Exporting Co. must account for the cash flows that will be forgone as a result of the plant, because some of the cash flows that used to be received by the parent through its exporting operation will be eliminated. The NPV estimate will be reduced after this factor is accounted for.
4. (a) An increase in the risk will cause an increase in the required rate of return on the subsidiary, which results in a lower discounted value of the subsidiary's salvage value.
   (b) If the rupiah depreciates over time, the subsidiary's salvage value will be reduced because the proceeds will convert to fewer dollars.
5. The dollar cash flows of Wilmette Co. would be affected more because the periodic remitted earnings from Thailand to be converted to dollars would be larger. The dollar cash flows of Niles would not be affected so much because interest payments would be made on the Thai loans before earnings could be remitted to the United States. Thus, a smaller amount in earnings would be remitted.
6. The demand for the product in the foreign country may be very uncertain, causing the total revenue to be uncertain. The exchange rates can be very uncertain, creating uncertainty about the dollar cash flows received by the U.S. parent. The salvage value may be very uncertain; this will have a larger effect if the lifetime of the project is short (for projects with a very long life, the discounted value of the salvage value is small anyway).

Answers to Self-Test Questions for Chapter 15

1. Acquisitions have increased in Europe to capitalize on the inception of the euro, which creates a single European currency for many European countries. This not only eliminates the exchange rate risk on transactions between the participating

European countries, but it also enables one to more easily compare valuations among European countries to determine where targets are undervalued.

2. Common restrictions include government regulations, such as antitrust restrictions, environmental restrictions, and red tape.
3. The establishment of a new subsidiary allows an MNC to create the subsidiary it desires without assuming existing facilities or employees. However, the process of building a new subsidiary and hiring employees will normally take longer than the process of acquiring an existing foreign firm.
4. The divestiture is now more feasible because the dollar cash flows to be received by the U.S. parent are reduced as a result of the revised projections of the krona's value.

Answers to Self-Test Questions for Chapter 16

1. First, consumers on the islands could develop a philosophy of purchasing homemade goods. Second, they could discontinue their purchases of exports by Key West Co. as a form of protest against specific U.S. government actions. Third, the host governments could impose severe restrictions on the subsidiary shops owned by Key West Co. (including the blockage of funds to be remitted to the U.S. parent).
2. First, the islands could experience poor economic conditions, which would cause lower income for some residents. Second, residents could be subject to higher inflation or higher interest rates, which would reduce the income that they could allocate toward exports. Depreciation of the local currencies could also raise the local prices to be paid for goods exported from the United States. All factors described here could reduce the demand for goods exported by Key West Co.
3. Financial risk is probably a bigger concern. The political risk factors are unlikely, based on the product produced by Key West Co. and the absence of substitute products available in other countries. The financial risk factors deserve serious consideration.
4. This event heightens the perceived country risk for any firms that have offices in populated areas (especially next to government or military offices). It also heightens the risk for firms whose employees commonly travel to other countries and for firms that provide office services or travel services.
5. Rockford Co. could estimate the net present value (*NPV*) of the project under three scenarios: (1) include a special tax when estimating cash flows back to the parent (probability of scenario = 15%), (2) assume the project ends in 2 years and include a salvage value when estimating the *NPV* (probability of scenario = 15%), and (3) assume no Canadian government intervention (probability = 70%). This results in three estimates of *NPV*, one for each scenario. This method is less arbitrary than the one considered by Rockford's executives.

Answers to Self-Test Questions for Chapter 17

1. Growth may have caused Goshen to require a large amount for financing that could not be completely provided by retained earnings. In addition, the interest rates may have been low in these foreign countries to make debt financing an attractive alternative. Finally, the use of foreign debt can reduce the exchange

rate risk since the amount in periodic remitted earnings is reduced when interest payments are required on foreign debt.

2. If country risk has increased, Lynde can attempt to reduce its exposure to that risk by removing its equity investment from the subsidiary. When the subsidiary is financed with local funds, the local creditors have more to lose than the parent if the host government imposes any severe restrictions on the subsidiary.
3. Not necessarily. German and Japanese firms tend to have more support from other firms or from the government if they experience cash flow problems and can therefore afford to use a higher degree of financial leverage than firms from the same industry in the United States.
4. Local debt financing is favorable because it can reduce the MNC's exposure to country risk and exchange rate risk. However, the high interest rates will make the local debt very expensive. If the parent makes an equity investment in the subsidiary to avoid the high cost of local debt, it will be more exposed to country risk and exchange rate risk.
5. The answer to this question is dependent on whether you believe unsystematic risk is relevant. If the CAPM is used as a framework for measuring the risk of a project, the risk of the foreign project is determined to be low, because the systematic risk is low. That is, the risk is specific to the host country and is not related to U.S. market conditions. However, if the project's unsystematic risk is relevant, the project is considered to have a high degree of risk. The project's cash flows are very uncertain, even though the systematic risk is low.

Answers to Self-Test Questions for Chapter 18

1. A firm may be able to obtain a lower coupon rate by issuing bonds denominated in a different currency. The firm converts the proceeds from issuing the bond to its local currency to finance local operations. Yet, there is exchange rate risk because the firm will need to make coupon payments and the principal payment in the currency denominating the bond. If that currency appreciates against the firm's local currency, the financing costs could become larger than expected.
2. The risk is that the Swiss franc would appreciate against the pound over time since the British subsidiary will periodically convert some of its pound cash flows to francs to make the coupon payments.

   The risk here is less than it would be if the proceeds were used to finance U.S. operations. The Swiss franc's movement against the dollar is much more volatile than the Swiss franc's movement against the pound. The Swiss franc and the pound have historically moved in tandem to some degree against the dollar, which means that there is a somewhat stable exchange rate between the two currencies.
3. If these firms borrow U.S. dollars and convert them to finance local projects, they will need to use their own currencies to obtain dollars and make coupon payments. These firms would be highly exposed to exchange rate risk.
4. Paxson Co. is exposed to exchange rate risk. If the yen appreciates, the number of dollars needed for conversion into yen will increase. To the extent that the yen strengthens, Paxson's cost of financing when financing with yen could be higher than when financing with dollars.
5. The nominal interest rate incorporates expected inflation (according to the so-called Fisher effect). Therefore, the high interest rates reflect high expected inflation. Cash flows can be enhanced by inflation because a given profit margin

converts into larger profits as a result of inflation, even if costs increase at the same rate as revenues.

Answers to Self-Test Questions for Chapter 19

1. The exporter may not trust the importer or may be concerned that the government will impose exchange controls that prevent payment to the exporter. Meanwhile, the importer may not trust that the exporter will ship the goods ordered and therefore may not pay until the goods are received. Commercial banks can help by providing guarantees to the exporter in case the importer does not pay.
2. In accounts receivable financing, the bank provides a loan to the exporter secured by the accounts receivable. If the importer fails to pay the exporter, the exporter is still responsible to repay the bank. Factoring involves the sales of accounts receivable by the exporter to a so-called "factor," so that the exporter is no longer responsible for the importer's payment.
3. The guarantee programs of the Export-Import Bank provide medium-term protection against the risk of nonpayment by the foreign buyer due to political risk.

Answers to Self-Test Questions for Chapter 20

1. $r_f = (1 + i_f)(1 + e_f) - 1$

   If $e_f = -6\%$, $r_f = (1 + .09)[1 + (-.06)] - 1$
   $= .0246$, or 2.46%

   If $e_f = 3\%$, $r_f = (1 + .09)(1 +.03) - 1$
   $= .1227$, or 12.27%

2. $$E(r_f) = 50\%(2.46\%) + 50\%(12.27\%)$$
   $$= 1.23\% + 6.135\%$$
   $$= 7.365\%$$

3. $$e_f = \frac{(1 + r_f)}{(1 + i)} - 1$$
   $$= \frac{(1 + .08)}{(1 + .05)} - 1$$
   $$= .0286, \text{ or } 2.86\%$$

4. $E(e_f)$ = (Forward rate – Spot rate)/Spot rate
   = (\$.60 – \$.62)/\$.62
   = –.0322, or 3.22%

   $E(r_f) = (1 + i_f)[1 + E(e_f)] - 1$
   $= (1 + .09)[1 + (-.0322)] - 1$
   $= .0548$, or 5.48%

5. The two-currency portfolio will not exhibit much lower variance than either individual currency because the currencies tend to move together. Thus, the diversification effect is limited.

Answers to Self-Test Questions for Chapter 21

1. The subsidiary in Country Y should be more adversely affected because the blocked funds will not earn as much interest over time. In addition, the funds will likely be converted to dollars at an unfavorable exchange rate because the currency is expected to weaken over time.
2. $E(r) = (1 + i_f)[1 + E(e_f)] - 1$
   $= (1 + .14)(1 + .08) - 1$
   $= .2312$, or 23.12%
3. $E(e_f) =$ (Forward rate – Spot rate)/Spot rate
   $= (\$.19 - \$.20)/\$.20$
   $= -.05$, or –5%
   $E(r) = (1 + i_f)[1 + E(e_f)] - 1$
   $= (1 + .11)[1 + (-.05)] - 1$
   $= .0545$, or 5.45%
4. $$e_f = \frac{(1+r)}{(1+i_f)} - 1$$
   $$= \frac{(1+.06)}{(1+.90)} - 1$$
   $= -.4421$, or -44.21%

   If the bolivar depreciates by less than 44.21 percent against the dollar over the one-year period, a one-year deposit in Venezuela will generate a higher effective yield than a one-year U.S. deposit.
5. Yes. Interest rate parity would discourage U.S. firms only from covering their investments in foreign deposits by using forward contracts. As long as the firms believe that the currency will not depreciate to offset the interest rate advantage, they may consider investing in countries with high interest rates.

Appendix B
Supplemental Cases

Chapter 1 Ranger Supply Company

Motivation for International Business

Ranger Supply Company is a large manufacturer and distributor of office supplies. It is based in New York but sends supplies to firms throughout the United States. It markets its supplies through periodic mass mailings of catalogues to those firms. Its clients can make orders over the phone, and Ranger ships the supplies upon demand. Ranger has had very high production efficiency in the past. This is attributed partly to low employee turnover and high morale, as employees are guaranteed job security until retirement.

Ranger already holds a large proportion of the market share in distributing office supplies in the U.S. Its main competition in the U.S. comes from one U.S. firm and one Canadian firm. A British firm has a small share of the U.S. market but is at a disadvantage because of its distance. The British firm's marketing and transportation costs in the U.S. market are relatively high.

While Ranger's office supplies are somewhat similar to those of its competitors, it has been able to capture most of the U.S. market because of its low prices charged to retail stores, which is a result of its high efficiency. It expects a decline in the aggregate demand for office supplies in the U.S. in future years. However, it anticipates strong demand for office supplies in Canada and in Eastern Europe over the next several years. Executives of Ranger have begun to consider exporting as a method of offsetting the possible decline in domestic demand for its products.

a. Ranger Supply Company plans to attempt penetrating either the Canadian market or the Eastern European market through exporting. What factors deserve to be considered in deciding which market is more feasible?
b. One financial manager has been responsible for developing a contingency plan in case whichever market was chosen imposed export barriers over time. This manager proposed that Ranger should establish a subsidiary in the country of concern under such conditions. Is this a reasonable strategy? Are there any obvious reasons why this strategy could fail?

Chapter 2 MapleLeaf Paper Company

Assessing the Effects of Changing Trade Barriers

MapleLeaf Paper Company is a Canadian firm that produces a particular type of paper not produced in the United States. It focuses most of its sales in the U.S. In the past year, for example, 180,000 of its 200,000 rolls of paper were sold to the U.S., with the remaining 20,000 rolls sold in Canada. It has a niche in the U.S., but because there are some substitutes, the U.S. demand for the product is sensitive to any changes in price. In fact, it had estimated that the U.S. demand rises (declines) three percent for every one percent decrease (increase) in the price paid by U.S. consumers, other things held constant.

A 12 percent tariff had historically been imposed on the exports to the U.S. Then on January 2, a free trade agreement between the U.S. and Canada was implemented, eliminating the tariff. MapleLeaf was ecstatic about the news, as it had been lobbying for the free trade agreement for several years.

The Canadian dollar was worth $.76. MapleLeaf hired a consulting firm to forecast the value of the Canadian dollar in the future. The firm expected the Canadian dollar to be worth about $.86 by the end of the year and then stabilize after that. The expectations of a stronger Canadian dollar were driven by an anticipation that numerous Canadian firms would capitalize on the free trade agreement more than U.S. firms, which would cause the increase in the U.S. demand for Canadian goods to be much higher than the increase in the Canadian demand for U.S. goods. (However, no other Canadian firms were expected to penetrate the U.S. paper market.) MapleLeaf expected no major changes in the aggregate demand for paper in the U.S. paper industry. It was also confident that its only competition would continue to be two U.S. manufacturers that produce imperfect substitutes of the paper. Its sales in Canada were expected to grow by about 20 percent by the end of the year because of an increase in the overall Canadian demand for paper and then remain level after that. MapleLeaf invoiced its exports in Canadian dollars and planned to maintain its present pricing schedule, since its costs of production were relatively stable. Its U.S. competitors would also continue their pricing schedule. MapleLeaf was confident that the free trade agreement would be permanent. It immediately began to assess its long-run prospects in the U.S.

a. Based on the information provided, develop a forecast of MapleLeaf's annual production (in rolls) needed to accommodate demand in the future. Since orders for this year have already occurred, focus on the years following this year.
b. Explain the underlying reasons for the change in the demand and the implications.
c. Would the general effects on MapleLeaf be similar to the effects on a U.S. paper producer that exports paper to Canada? Explain.

Chapter 3 Gretz Tool Company

Using International Financial Markets

Gretz Tool Company is a large U.S.-based multinational corporation with subsidiaries in eight different countries. The parent of Gretz provided an initial cash infusion to establish each subsidiary. However, each subsidiary has had to finance its own growth since then. The parent and subsidiaries of Gretz typically use Citicorp (the largest bank in the U.S., with branches in numerous countries) when possible to facilitate any flow of funds necessary.

a. Explain the various ways in which Citicorp could facilitate Gretz's flow of funds, and identify the type of financial market where that flow of funds occurs. For each type of financing transaction, specify whether Citicorp would serve as the creditor or just an intermediary.
b. Recently, the British subsidiary called on Citicorp for a medium-term loan and was offered the following alternatives:

Loan Denominated In	Annualized Rate
British pounds	13%
U.S. dollars	11%
Canadian dollars	10%
Japanese yen	8%

What characteristics do you think would help the British subsidiary determine which currency to borrow?

Chapter 4 Bruin Aircraft Inc.

Factors Affecting Exchange Rates

Bruin Aircraft Inc. is a designer and manufacturer of airplane parts. Its production plant is based in California. About one-third of its sales are exports to the United Kingdom. While Bruin invoices its exports in dollars, the demand for its exports is highly sensitive to the value of the British pound. In order to maintain its parts inventory at a proper level, it must forecast the total demand for its parts, which is somewhat dependent on the forecasted value of the pound. The treasurer of Bruin was assigned the task of forecasting the value of the pound (against the dollar) for each of the next five years. He was planning to request from the firm's chief economist forecasts on all the relevant factors that could affect the pound's future exchange rate. He decided to organize his worksheet by separating demand-related factors from supply-related factors, as illustrated by the headings below:

Factors that can affect the value of the pound	Check (✓) here if the factor influences the U.S. demand for pounds	Check (✓) here if the factor influences the supply of pounds for sale

Help the treasurer by identifying the factors in the first column and then checking the second or third (or both) columns. Include any possible government-related factors and be specific (tie your description to the specific case background provided here).

Chapter 5 Capital Crystal Inc.

Using Currency Futures and Options

Capital Crystal Inc. is a major importer of crystal from the U.K. The crystal is sold to prestigious retail stores throughout the U.S. The imports are denominated in British pounds (£). Every quarter, Capital needs £500 million. It is presently attempting to determine whether it should use currency futures or currency options to hedge imports three months from now, if it will hedge at all. The spot rate of the pound is $1.60. A three-month futures contract on the pound is available for $1.59 per unit. A call option on the pound is available with a three-month expiration date and an exercise price of $1.60. The premium to be paid on the call option is $.01 per unit.

Capital is very confident that the value of the pound will rise to at least $1.62 in three months. It has been very accurate in its previous forecasts of the pound's value. The management style of Capital is very risk-averse. Managers receive a bonus at the end of the year if they satisfy minimal performance standards. The bonus is fixed, regardless of how high above the minimum level one's performance is. If performance is below the minimum, there is no bonus, and future advancement within the company is unlikely.

a. As a financial manager of Capital, you have been assigned the task of choosing among three possible strategies: (1) hedge the £ position by purchasing futures, (2) hedge the £ position by purchasing call options, or (3) do not hedge. Offer your recommendation and justify it.
b. Assume the previous information that was provided, except for this difference: Capital has revised its forecast of the pound to be worth $1.57 three months from now. Given this revision, recommend whether Capital should (1) hedge the £ position by purchasing futures, (2) hedge the £ position by purchasing call options, or (3) not hedge. Justify your recommendation. Is your recommendation consistent with maximizing shareholder wealth?

Chapter 6 Hull Importing Company

Effects of Pegging the Pound to the ECU

Hull Importing Company is a U.S.-based firm that imports small gift items and sells them to retail gift shops across the United States. About half of the value of Hull's purchases comes from the United Kingdom, while the remaining purchases are from Mexico. The imported goods are denominated in the currency of the country where they are produced. Hull normally does not hedge its purchases.

In previous years, the Mexican peso and pound fluctuated substantially against the dollar (although not by the same degree). Hull's expenses are directly tied to these currency values because all of its products are imported. It has been successful because the imported gift items are somewhat unique and are attractive to U.S. consumers. However, Hull has been unable to pass on higher costs (due to a weaker dollar) to its consumers, because consumers would then switch to different gift items sold at other stores.

a. Hull expects that Mexico's central bank will increase interest rates, and that Mexico's inflation will not be affected. Offer any insight on how the peso's value may change and how Hull's profits would be affected as a result.
b. Hull used to closely monitor government intervention by the Bank of England (the British central bank) on the value of the pound. Assume that the Bank of England intervenes to strengthen the pound's value with respect to the dollar by 5 percent. Would this have a favorable or unfavorable effect on Hull's business?

Chapter 7 Zuber Inc.

Using Covered Interest Arbitrage

Zuber Inc. is a U.S.-based MNC that has been aggressively pursuing business in Eastern Europe since the Iron Curtain was lifted in 1989. Poland has allowed its currency's value to be market-determined. The spot rate of the Polish zloty is \$.40. Poland also has begun to allow investments by foreign investors, as a method of attracting funds to help build its economy. Its interest rate on one-year securities issued by the federal government is 14 percent, which is substantially higher than the 9 percent rate presently offered on one-year U.S. Treasury securities.

A local bank began to create a forward market for the zloty. This bank was recently privatized and has been trying to make a name for itself in international business. The bank has quoted a one-year forward rate of \$.39 for the zloty. As an employee in Zuber's international money market division, you have been asked to assess the possibility of investing short-term funds in Poland. You are in charge of investing \$10 million over the next year. Your objective is to earn the highest return possible while maintaining safety (since the firm will need the funds next year).

Since the exchange rate has just become market-determined, there is a high probability that the zloty's value will be very volatile for several years as it seeks its true equilibrium value. The expected value of the zloty in one year is \$.40, but there is a high degree of uncertainty about this. The actual value in one year may be as much as 40 percent above or below this expected value.

a. Would you be willing to invest the funds in Poland without covering your position? Explain.
b. Suggest how you could attempt covered interest arbitrage. What is the expected return from using covered interest arbitrage?
c. What risks are involved in using covered interest arbitrage here?
d. If you had to choose between investing your funds in U.S. Treasury bills at 9 percent or using covered interest arbitrage, what would be your choice? Defend your answer.

Chapter 8 Flame Fixtures Inc.

Business Application of Purchasing Power Parity

Flame Fixtures Inc. is a small U.S. business in Arizona that produces and sells lamp fixtures. Its costs and revenues have been very stable over time. Its profits have been adequate, but Flame has been searching for means of increasing profits in the future. It has recently been negotiating with a Mexican firm called Coron´ Company, from which it would purchase some of the necessary parts. Every three months, Coron´ Company would send a specified number of parts with the bill invoiced in Mexican pesos. By having the parts produced by Coron´, the company is expected to save about 20 percent on production costs. Coron´ is only willing to work out a deal if it is assured that it will receive a minimum specified amount of orders every three months over the next ten years, for a minimum specified amount. Flame will be required to use its assets to serve as collateral in case it does not fulfill its obligation.

The price of the parts will change over time in response to the costs of production. Flame recognizes that the cost to Coron´ will increase substantially over time as a result of the very high inflation rate in Mexico. Therefore, the price charged in pesos likely will rise substantially every three months. However, Flame feels that, because of the concept of purchasing power parity (PPP), its dollar payments to Coron´ will be very stable. According to PPP, if Mexican inflation is much higher than U.S. inflation, the peso will weaken against the dollar by that difference. Since Flame does not have much liquidity, it could experience a severe cash shortage if its expenses were much higher than anticipated.

The demand for Flame's product has been very stable and is expected to continue that way. Since the U.S. inflation rate is expected to be very low, Flame likely will continue pricing its lamps at today's prices (in dollars). It believes that by saving 20 percent on production costs it will substantially increase its profits. It is about ready to sign a contract with Coron´ Company.

a. Describe a scenario that could cause Flame to save even more than 20 percent on production costs.
b. Describe a scenario that could cause Flame to actually incur higher production costs than if it simply had the parts produced in the United States.
c. Do you think that Flame will experience stable dollar outflow payments to Coron´ over time? Explain. (Assume that the number of parts ordered is constant over time.)
d. Do you think that Flame's risk changes at all as a result of its new relationship with Coron´ Company? Explain.

Chapter 9 Whaler Publishing Co.

Forecasting Exchange Rates

Whaler Publishing Co. specializes in producing textbooks in the United States and marketing these books in foreign universities where the English language is used. Its sales are invoiced in the currency of the country where the textbooks are sold. The expected revenues from textbooks sold to university bookstores are shown in Exhibit B.1.

Whaler is comfortable with the estimated foreign currency revenues in each country. However, it is very uncertain about the U.S.-dollar revenues to be received from each country. At this time (which is the beginning of Year 16), Whaler is using today's spot rate as its best guess of the exchange rate at which the revenues from each country will be converted into U.S. dollars at the end of this year (which implies a zero percentage change in the value of each currency). Yet, it recognizes the potential error associated with this type of forecast. Therefore, it desires to incorporate the risk surrounding each currency forecast by creating confidence intervals for each currency. First, it must derive the annual percentage change in the exchange rate over each of the last fif-

Exhibit B.1
Expected Revenues from Textbooks Sold to University Bookstores

University Bookstores In	Local Currency	Today's Spot Exchange Rate	Expected Revenues from Bookstores This Year
Australia	Australian Dollars (A$)	$ .7671	A$38,000,000
Canada	Canadian Dollars (C$)	.8625	C$35,000,000
New Zealand	New Zealand Dollars (N$)	.5985	N$33,000,000
United Kingdom	Pounds (£)	1.9382	£34,000,000

teen years for each currency to derive a standard deviation in the percentage change of each foreign currency. By assuming that the percentage changes in exchange rates are normally distributed, it plans to develop two ranges of forecasts for the annual percentage change in each currency: (1) one standard deviation in each direction from its best guess to develop a 68-percent confidence interval, and (2) two standard deviations in each direction from its best guess to develop a 95-percent confidence interval. These confidence intervals can then be applied to today's spot rates to develop confidence intervals for the future spot rate one year from today.

The exchange rates at the beginning of each of the last sixteen years for each currency (with respect to the U.S. dollar) are shown here:

Beginning of Year	Australian $	Canadian $	New Zealand $	British Pound
1	$1.2571	$.9839	$1.0437	£2.0235
2	1.0864	.9908	.9500	1.7024
3	1.1414	.9137	1.0197	1.9060
4	1.1505	.8432	1.0666	2.0345
5	1.1055	.8561	.9862	2.2240
6	1.1807	.8370	.9623	2.3850
7	1.1279	.8432	.8244	1.9080
8	.9806	.8137	.7325	1.6145
9	.9020	.8038	.6546	1.4506
10	.8278	.7570	.4776	1.1565
11	.6809	.7153	.4985	1.4445
12	.6648	.7241	.5235	1.4745
13	.7225	.8130	.6575	1.8715
14	.8555	.8382	.6283	1.8095
15	.7831	.8518	.5876	1.5772
16	.7671	.8625	.5985	1.9382

The confidence intervals for each currency can be applied to the expected book revenues to derive confidence intervals in U.S. dollars to be received from each country. Complete this assignment for Whaler Publishing Co., and also rank the currencies in terms of uncertainty (degree of volatility). Since the exchange rate data provided are real, the analysis will indicate (1) how volatile currencies can be, (2) how much more volatile some currencies are than others, and (3) how estimated revenues can be subject to a high degree of uncertainty as a result of uncertain exchange rates. [If you use a spreadsheet to do this case, you may want to retain it, since the case in the following chapter is an extension of this case.]

Chapter 10 Whaler Publishing Co.

Measuring Exposure to Exchange Rate Risk

Recall the situation of Whaler Publishing Co. from the previous chapter. Whaler needed to develop confidence intervals of four exchange rates in order to derive confidence intervals for U.S.-dollar cash flows to be received from four different countries. Each confidence interval was isolated on a particular country.

Assume that Whaler would like to estimate the range of its aggregate dollar cash flows to be generated from other countries. A computer spreadsheet should be developed to facilitate this exercise. Whaler plans to simulate the conversion of the expected currency cash flows to dollars, using each of the previous years as a possible scenario (recall that exchange rate data are provided in the original case in Chapter 9). Specifically, Whaler will determine the annual percentage change in the spot rate of each currency for a given year. Then, it will apply that percentage to the respective existing spot rates to determine a possible spot rate in one year for each currency. Recall that today's spot rates are assumed to be as follows:

Australian dollar = $ .7671
Canadian dollar = $ .8625
New Zealand dollar = $ .5985
British pound = £1.9382

Once the spot rate is forecasted for one year ahead for each currency, the U.S.-dollar revenues received from each country can be forecasted. For example, from Year 1 to Year 2, the Australian dollar declined by about 13.6 percent. If this percentage change occurs this year, the spot rate of the Australian dollar will decline from today's rate of $.7671 to about $.6629. In this case, the A$38,000,000 to be received would convert to $25,190,200. The same tasks must be done for the other three currencies as well in order to estimate the aggregate dollar cash flows under this scenario.

This process can be repeated, using each of the previous years as a possible future scenario. There will be 15 possible scenarios, or 15 forecasts of the aggregate U.S.-dollar cash flows. Each of these scenarios is expected to have an equal probability of occurring. By assuming that these cash flows are normally distributed, Whaler uses the standard deviation of the possible aggregate cash flows for all 15 scenarios to develop 68-percent and 95-percent confidence intervals surrounding the "expected value" of the aggregate level of U.S.-dollar cash flows to be received in one year.

a. Perform these tasks for Whaler in order to determine these confidence intervals on the aggregate level of U.S.-dollar cash flows to be received. The methodology described here is used by Whaler, rather than the simple combining of results of individual countries (from the previous chapter), since exchange rate movements may be correlated.
b. Review the annual percentage changes in the four exchange rates. Do they appear to be positively correlated? Estimate the correlation coefficient between exchange rate movements with either a calculator or a spreadsheet package. Based on this analysis, you can fill out the following correlation coefficient matrix:

	A$	C$	NZ$	£
A$	1.00			
C$		1.00		
NZ$			1.00	
£				1.00

Would aggregate dollar cash flows to be received by Whaler be more risky than they would if the exchange rate movements were completely independent? Explain.
c. One executive of Whaler suggested that a more efficient way of deriving the confidence intervals would be simply to use the exchange rates instead of the percentage changes as the scenarios and derive U.S.-dollar cash flow estimates directly from them. Do you think this method would be as accurate as the method now used by Whaler? Explain.

Chapter 11 Blackhawk Company

Forecasting Exchange Rates and the Hedging Decision

This case is intended to illustrate how forecasting exchange rates and hedging decisions are related. Blackhawk Company imports goods from New Zealand and plans to purchase NZ$800,000 one quarter from now to pay for imports. As treasurer of Blackhawk, you are responsible for determining whether and how to hedge this payables position. Several tasks will need to be completed for you to make these decisions. The entire analysis can be performed using LOTUS.

- Your first goal is to assess three different models for forecasting the value of NZ$ at the end of the quarter (also called the future spot rate, or FSR):

- Using the forward rate (FR) at the beginning of the quarter. Using the spot rate (SR) at the beginning of the quarter.
- Estimating the historical influence of the inflation differential during each quarter on the percentage change in the NZ$ (which leads to a forecast of the FSR of the NZ$).

The historical data to be used for this analysis are provided in Exhibit B.2.

a. Use regression analysis to determine whether the forward rate is an unbiased estimator of the spot rate at the end of the quarter.
b. Use the simplified approach of assessing the signs of forecast errors over time. Do you detect any bias when using the FR to forecast? Explain.
c. Determine the average absolute forecast error when using the forward rate to forecast.
d. Determine whether the spot rate of the NZ$ at the beginning of the quarter is an unbiased estimator of the spot rate at the end of the quarter using regression analysis.
e. Use the simplified approach of assessing the signs of forecast errors over time. Do you detect any bias when using the SR to forecast? Explain.
f. Determine the average absolute forecast error when using the spot rate to forecast. Is the spot rate or the forward rate a more accurate forecast of the future spot rate (FSR)? Explain.
g. Use the following regression model to determine the relationship between the inflation

Quarter	Spot Rate of NZ$ at Beginning of Quarter	90-Day Forward Rate of NZ$ at Beginning of Quarter	Spot Rate of NZ$ at End of Quarter	Last Quarter's Inflation Differential	Percentage Change in NZ$ Over Quarter
1	$.3177	$.3250	$.3233	–.05%	1.76%
2	.3233	.3272	.3267	–.46	1.05
3	.3267	.3285	.3746	.66	14.66
4	.3746	.3778	.4063	.94	8.46
5	.4063	.4093	.4315	.58	6.20
6	.4315	.4344	.4548	.23	5.40
7	.4548	.4572	.4949	.02	8.82
8	.4949	.4966	.5153	1.26	4.12
9	.5153	.5169	.5540	.86	7.51
10	.5540	.5574	.5465	.54	–1.35
11	.5465	.5510	.5440	1.00	–.46
12	.5440	.5488	.6309	1.09	15.97
13	.6309	.6365	.6027	.78	–4.47
14	.6027	.6081	.5409	.23	–10.25
15	.5491	.5538	.5320	.71	–3.11
16	.5320	.5365	.5617	1.18	5.58
17	.5617	.5667	.5283	.70	–5.95
18	.5283	.5334	.5122	–.31	–3.05
19	.5122	.5149	.5352	.62	4.49
20	.5352	.5372	.5890	.87	10.05
21(Now)	.5890	.5878	(to be forecasted)	.28	(to be forecasted)

Exhibit B.2
Historical Data for Analysis

differential (called *DIFF* and defined as the U.S. inflation minus New Zealand inflation) and the percentage change in the NZ$ (called PNZ$):

$$PNZ\$ = b_0 + b_1\, DIFF$$

Once you have determined the coefficients b_0 and b_1, use them to forecast PNZ$ based on a forecast of 2 percent for DIFF in the upcoming quarter. Then, apply your forecast for PNZ$ to the prevailing spot rate (which is $.589) to derive the expected FSR of the NZ$.

h. Blackhawk plans to develop a probability distribution for the FSR. First, it will assign a 40-percent probability to the forecast of FSR derived from the regression analysis in the previous question. Second, it will assign a 40-percent probability to the forecast of FSR based on either the forward rate or the spot rate (whichever was more accurate according to your earlier analysis). Third, it will assign a 20-percent probability to the forecast of FSR based on either the forward rate or spot rate (whichever was less accurate according to your earlier analysis).

   Fill in the table that follows:

Probability	FSR
40%	
40	
20	

i. Assuming that Blackhawk does not hedge, fill in the following table.

Probability	Forecasted Dollar Amount Needed to Pay for Imports in 90 Days
40%	
40	
20	

j. Based on the probability distribution for the FSR, use the table that follows to determine the probability distribution for the real cost of hedging if a forward contract is used for hedging (recall that the prevailing 90-day forward rate is $.5878).

Probability	Forecasted Dollar Amount Needed If Hedged with a Forward Contract	Forecasted Amount Needed If Unhedged	Forecasted Real Cost of Hedging Payables
40%			
40			
20			

k. If Blackhawk hedges its position, it will use either a 90-day forward rate, a money market hedge, or a call option. The following data are available at the time of its decision.

- Spot rate = $.589
- 90-Day forward rate = $.5878
- 90-Day U.S. borrowing rate = 2.5%
- 90-Day U.S. investing rate = 2.3%
- 90-Day New Zealand borrowing rate = 2.4%
- 90-Day New Zealand investing rate = 2.1%
- Call option on NZ$ has a premium of $.01 per unit.
- Call option on NZ$ has an exercise price of $.60.

   Determine the probability distribution of dollars needed for a call option if used (include the premium paid) by filling out the following table:

Probability	FSR	Dollars Needed to Pay for Payables
40%		
40		
20		

l. Compare the forward hedge to the money market hedge. Which is superior? Why?

m. Compare either the forward hedge or the money market hedge (whichever is better) to the call option hedge. If you hedge, which technique should you use? Why?

n. Compare the hedge you believe is the best to an unhedged strategy. Should you hedge or remain unhedged? Explain.

Chapter 12 Madison Inc.

Assessing Economic Exposure

The situation for Madison Inc. was described in this chapter to illustrate how alternative operational structures could affect economic exposure to exchange rate movements. Ken Moore, the vice president of finance at Madison Inc., was seriously considering a shift to the proposed operational structure described in the text. He was determined to stabilize the earnings before taxes and believed that the proposed approach would achieve this objective. The firm expected that the Canadian dollar would consistently depreciate over the next several years. Over time, it has been very accurate in its forecasts. Moore paid little attention to the forecasts, stating that regardless of how the Canadian dollar changed, future earnings would be more stable under the proposed operational structure. He also was constantly reminded of how the strengthened Canadian dollar in some years had adversely affected the firm's earnings. In fact, he was somewhat concerned that he might even lose his job if the adverse effects from economic exposure continued.

a. Would a revised operational structure at this time be in the best interests of the shareholders? Would it be in the best interests of the vice president?
b. How could a revised operational structure possibly be feasible from the vice president's perspective but not from the shareholders' perspective? Explain how the firm might be able to ensure that the vice president will make decisions related to economic exposure that are in the best interests of the shareholders.

Chapter 13 Blues Corporation

Capitalizing on the Opening of Eastern European Borders

Having done business in the United States for over fifty years, Blues Corporation has an established reputation. Most of Blues' business is in the United States. It has a subsidiary in the western section of Germany, which produces goods and exports them to other European countries. Blues Corporation produces many consumer goods that could possibly be produced or marketed in Eastern European countries. The following issues were raised at a recent executive meeting. Offer your comments about each issue.

a. Blues Corporation is considering shifting its European production facility from western Germany to eastern Germany. There are two key factors motivating this shift. First, the labor cost is lower in eastern Germany. Second, there is an existing facility (currently government owned) in the former East Germany that is for sale. Blues would like to transform the facility and use its technology to increase production efficiency. It estimates that it would need only one-fourth of the workers in that facility. What other factors deserve to be considered before the decision is made?
b. Blues Corporation believes that it could penetrate the Eastern European markets. It would need to invest considerable funds in promoting its consumer goods in Eastern Europe, since its goods are not well known in that area. Yet, it believes that this strategy could pay off in the long run because Blues could underprice the competition. At the current time, the main competition consists of businesses that are perceived to be inefficiently run. The lack of competitive pricing in this market is the primary reason for Blues Corporation to consider marketing its product in Eastern Europe. What other factors deserve to be considered before a decision is made?

c. Blues Corporation is currently experiencing a cash squeeze because of a reduced demand for its goods in the United States (although management expects the demand in the United States to increase soon). It is currently near its debt capacity and prefers not to issue stock at this time. Blues Corporation will purchase a facility in Eastern Europe or enact a heavy promotion program in Eastern Europe only if it can raise funds by divesting a significant amount of its U.S. assets. The market values of its assets are temporarily depressed, but some of the executives think an immediate move is necessary to fully capitalize on the Eastern European market. Would you recommend that Blues Corporation divest some of its U.S. assets? Explain.

Chapter 14 North Star Company

Capital Budgeting

This case is intended to illustrate that the value of an international project is sensitive to various types of input. It also is intended to show how a computer spreadsheet format can facilitate capital budgeting decisions that involve uncertainty.

This case can be performed using an electronic spreadsheet such as EXCEL. The following present value factors may be helpful input for discounting cash flows:

Years from Now	Present Value Interest Factor at 18%
1	.8475
2	.7182
3	.6086
4	.5158
5	.4371
6	.3704

For consistency in discussion of this case, you should develop your computer spreadsheet in a format somewhat similar to that in the Capital Budgeting chapter, with each year representing a column across the top. The use of a computer spreadsheet will significantly reduce the time needed to complete this case.

North Star Company considered establishing a subsidiary to manufacture clothing in Singapore. Its sales would be invoiced in Singapore dollars (S$). It has forecasted net cash flows to the subsidiary as follows:

Year	Net Cash Flows to Subsidiary
1	S$ 8,000,000
2	10,000,000
3	14,000,000
4	16,000,000
5	16,000,000
6	16,000,000

These cash flows do not include financing costs (interest expenses) on any funds borrowed in Singapore. North Star Company also expects to receive S$30 million after taxes as a result of selling the subsidiary at the end of Year 6. Assume that there will not be any withholding taxes imposed on this amount.

The exchange rate of the Singapore dollar is forecasted in Exhibit B.3 based on three possible scenarios of economic conditions.

The probability of each scenario is shown below:

	Somewhat Stable S$	Weak S$	Strong S$
Probability	60%	30%	10%

Fifty percent of the net cash flows to the subsidiary would be remitted to the parent, while the remaining fifty percent would be reinvested to support ongoing operations at the subsidiary. North Star Company anticipates a 10-percent withholding tax on funds remitted to the United States.

Exhibit B.3
Three Scenarios of Economic Conditions

End of Year	Scenario I: Somewhat Stable S$	Scenario II: Weak S$	Scenario III: Strong S$
1	.50	.49	.52
2	.51	.46	.55
3	.48	.45	.59
4	.50	.43	.64
5	.52	.43	.67
6	.48	.41	.71

The initial investment (including investment in working capital) by North Star in the subsidiary would be S$40 million. Any investment in working capital (such as accounts receivable, inventory, etc.) is to be assumed by the buyer in Year 6. The expected salvage value has already accounted for this transfer of working capital to the buyer in Year 6. The initial investment could be financed completely by the parent ($20 million, converted at the present exchange rate of $.50 per Singapore dollar to achieve S$40 million). North Star Company will go forward with its intentions to build the subsidiary only if it expects to achieve a return on its capital of 18 percent or more.

The parent is considering an alternative financing arrangement. With this arrangement, the parent would provide $10 million (S$20 million), which means that the subsidiary would need to borrow S$20 million. Under this scenario, the subsidiary would obtain a 20-year loan and pay interest on the loan each year. The interest payments are S$1.6 million per year. In addition, the forecasted proceeds to be received from selling the subsidiary (after taxes) at the end of 6 years would be S$20 million (the forecast of proceeds is revised downward here because the equity investment of the subsidiary is less; the buyer would be assuming more debt if part of the initial investment in the subsidiary were supported by local bank loans). Assume the parent's required rate of return would still be 18 percent.

a. Which of the two financing arrangements would you recommend for the parent? Assess the forecasted *NPV* for each exchange rate scenario to compare the two financing arrangements and substantiate your recommendation.
b. In the first question, an alternative financing arrangement of partial financing by the subsidiary was considered, with an assumption that the required rate of return by the parent would not be affected. Is there any reason why the parent's required rate of return might increase when using this financing arrangement? Explain. How would you revise the analysis in the previous question under this situation? (This question requires discussion, not analysis.)
c. Would you recommend that North Star Company establish the subsidiary even if the withholding tax is 20 percent?
d. Assume that there is some concern about the economic conditions in Singapore which could cause a reduction in the net cash flows to the subsidiary. Explain how EXCEL could be used to reevaluate the project based on alternative cash flow scenarios. That is, how can this form of country risk be incorporated into the capital budgeting decision? (This question requires discussion, not analysis.)
e. Assume that North Star Company does implement the project, investing $10 million of its own funds with the remainder borrowed by the subsidiary. Two years later, a U.S.-based corporation notifies North Star that it would like to purchase the subsidiary. Assume that the exchange rate forecasts for the somewhat stable scenario are appropriate for Years 3 through 6. Also assume that

the other information already provided on net cash flows, financing costs, the 10-percent withholding tax, the salvage value, and the parent's required rate of return is still appropriate. What would be the minimum dollar price (after taxes) that North Star should receive to divest the subsidiary? Substantiate your opinion.

Chapter 15 Redwing Technology Company

Assessing Subsidiary Performance

Redwing Technology Company is a U.S.-based firm that makes a variety of high-tech components. Five years ago, it established subsidiaries in Canada, South Africa, and Japan. The earnings generated by each subsidiary as translated (at the average annual exchange rate) into U.S. dollars per year are shown in Exhibit B.4.

Each subsidiary had an equivalent amount in resources with which to conduct operations. The wage rates for the labor needed were similar across countries. The inflation rates, economic growth, and degree of competition were somewhat similar across countries. The average exchange rates of the respective currencies over the last five years are disclosed below:

Years Ago	Canadian Dollar	South African Rand	Japanese Yen
5	$.84	$.10	$.0040
4	.83	.12	.0043
3	.81	.16	.0046
2	.81	.20	.0055
1	.79	.24	.0064

The earnings generated by each country were reinvested rather than remitted. There were no plans to remit any future earnings either.

A committee of vice presidents met to determine the performance of each subsidiary in the last five years. The assessment was to be used to determine whether Redwing should be restructured to focus future growth on any particular subsidiary, or to divest any subsidiaries that might experience poor performance. Since exchange rates of the related currencies were affected by so many different factors, the treasurer acknowledged that there was much uncertainty about their future direction. The treasurer did suggest, however, that last year's average exchange rate would probably serve as at least a reasonable guess of exchange rates in future years. He did not anticipate any of the currencies experiencing consistent appreciation or depreciation.

a. Use whatever means you think are appropriate to rank the performance of each subsidiary. That is, which subsidiary did the best job over the five-year period, in your opinion? Justify your opinion.
b. Use whatever means you think are appropriate to determine which subsidiary deserves additional funds from the parent to push for additional growth. (Assume no constraint on potential growth in any country.) Where would you recommend the parent's excess funds be invested, based on the information available? Justify your opinion.

Exhibit B.4
Translated Dollar Value of Annual Earnings in Each Subsidiary (in millions of $)

Years Ago	Canada	South Africa	Japan
5	$20	$21	$30
4	24	24	32
3	28	24	35
2	32	36	41
1	36	42	46

c. Repeat question (b), but assume that all earnings generated from the parent's investment will be remitted to the parent every year. Would your recommendation change? Explain.
d. A final task of the committee was to recommend whether any of the subsidiaries should be divested. One vice president suggested that a review of the earnings translated into dollars shows that the performance of Canadian and South African subsidiaries are very highly correlated. The VP concluded that having both of these subsidiaries did not achieve much in diversification benefits and recommended that either the Canadian or South African subsidiaries could be sold without forgoing any diversification benefits. Do you agree? Explain.

Chapter 16 King Inc.

Country Risk Analysis

King Inc., a U.S. firm, is considering the establishment of a small subsidiary in Bulgaria which would produce food products. All ingredients can be obtained or produced in Bulgaria. The final products to be produced by the subsidiary would be sold in Bulgaria and other Eastern Bloc countries. King Inc. is very interested in this project, since there is little competition in that area. Three high-level managers of King Inc. have been assigned the task of assessing the country risk of Bulgaria. Specifically, the managers were asked to list all characteristics of Bulgaria that could adversely affect the performance of this project. The decision as to whether to undertake this project will only be made once this country risk analysis is completed and accounted for in the capital budgeting analysis. Since King Inc. has focused exclusively on domestic business in the past, it is not accustomed to country risk analysis.

a. What factors related to Bulgaria's government deserve to be considered?
b. What country-related factors can affect the demand for the food products to be produced by King Inc.?
c. What country-related factors can affect the cost of production?

Chapter 17 Sabre Computer Corporation

Cost of Capital

Sabre Computer Corporation is a U.S.-based company that plans to participate in joint ventures in Mexico and in Hungary. Each joint venture involves the development of a small subsidiary that helps produce computers. The main contribution of Sabre is the technology and a few key computer components used in the production process. The joint venture in Mexico specifies joint production of computers with a Mexican company owned by the government. The computers have already been ordered by educational institutions and government agencies throughout Mexico. Sabre has a contract to sell all the computers it produces in Mexico to these institutions and agencies at a price that is tied to inflation. Given the very high and volatile inflation levels in Mexico, Sabre wanted to assure that the contracted price would adjust to cover rising costs over time.

The venture will require a temporary transfer of several managers to Mexico plus the manufacturing of key computer components in a leased Mexican plant. Most of these costs will be incurred in Mexico and will therefore require payment in pesos. Sabre will receive 30 percent of the revenue generated (in pesos) from computer sales. The Mexican partner will receive the remainder.

The joint venture in Hungary specifies joint production of personal computers with a Hungarian computer manufacturer. The computers will then be marketed to consumers throughout the Eastern

Bloc countries in Europe. Similar computers are produced by some competitors, but Sabre believes it can penetrate these markets because its products will be competitively priced. While the economies of the Eastern Bloc countries are expected to be somewhat stagnant, demand for personal computers is reasonably strong. The computers will be priced in Hungary's currency, the forint, and Sabre will receive 30 percent of the revenue generated from sales.

a. Assume that Sabre plans to finance most of its investment in the Mexican subsidiary by borrowing Mexican pesos and to finance most of its investment in the Hungarian subsidiary by borrowing forint. The cost of financing is influenced by the risk-free rates in the respective countries and the risk premiums on funds borrowed. Explain how these factors will affect the relative costs of financing both ventures. Address this question from the perspective of the subsidiary, not from the perspective of Sabre's parent.
b. Will the joint venture experiencing the higher cost of financing (as determined in the previous question) necessarily experience lower returns to the subsidiary? Explain.
c. The Hungarian subsidiary has a high degree of financial leverage. Yet, the parent's capital structure is mostly equity. What will determine whether the creditors of the Hungarian subsidiary charge a high-risk premium on borrowed funds because of the high degree of financial leverage?
d. One executive of Sabre suggested that since the cost of debt financing by highly leveraged Hungarian-owned companies is about 14 percent, its Hungarian subsidiary should be able to borrow at about the same interest rate. Do you agree? Explain. (Assume that the chances of the subsidiary's experiencing financial problems are the same as those for these other Hungarian-owned firms.)
e. There is some concern that the economy in Hungary could become inflated. Assess the relative magnitude of an increase in inflation on (1) the cost of funds, (2) the cost of production, and (3) revenue from selling the computers.

Chapter 18 Devil VCR Corporation

Long-Term Financing

Devil VCR Corporation is a U.S.-based company that produces videocassette recorders. Three years ago, Devil established a production facility in the United Kingdom, since it sells VCRs there. Devil has excess capacity there and will use that facility to produce the VCRs that are to be marketed in Singapore. The VCRs will be sold to distributors in Singapore and invoiced in Singapore dollars (S$). If the exporting program is very successful, Devil Corporation will probably build a facility in Singapore, but it plans to wait at least ten years.

Prior to this exporting program, Devil Corporation decided to develop a hedging strategy to hedge any cash flows to the U.S. parent. Its plan is to issue bonds to finance the entire investment in the exporting program. Virtually all expenses associated with this program are denominated in pounds. Yet, the revenue generated by the program is denominated in Singapore dollars. Any revenue above and beyond expenses is to be remitted to the United States on an annual basis. Aside from the exporting program, the British subsidiary will generate just enough in cash flows to cover expenses and therefore will not be remitting any earnings to the parent. Devil Corporation is considering three different ways to finance the program for ten years:

Issue ten-year, Singapore dollar-denominated bonds at par value; coupon rate = 11%.
Issue ten-year, pound-denominated bonds at par value; coupon rate = 14%.
Issue ten-year, U.S.-dollar-denominated bonds at par value; coupon rate = 11%.

a. Describe the exchange rate risk if Devil finances with Singapore dollars.
b. Describe the exchange rate risk if Devil finances with British pounds.
c. Describe the exchange rate risk if Devil finances with U.S. dollars.

Chapter 19 Ryco Chemical Company

Using Countertrade

Ryco Chemical Company produces a wide variety of chemical products that are sold to manufacturing firms. Some of the chemicals used in its production process are imported from Concellos Chemical Company in Brazil. Concellos uses some chemicals in its production process that are produced by Ryco (although Concellos has historically purchased these chemicals from another U.S. chemical company rather than from Ryco). The Brazilian cruzeiro has been depreciating continuously against the dollar so that Concellos' cost of obtaining chemicals is always rising. Concellos will probably pay twice as much for these chemicals this year because of the weak cruzeiro. It probably will attempt to pass most of its higher costs to its customers in the form of higher prices. However, it may not always be able to pass higher costs from a weak cruzeiro: Its competitors make all their chemicals locally, and their costs are directly tied to Brazil's inflation. Its competitors sell all their goods locally. This year, Concellos planned to charge Ryco a price in cruzeiros that was substantially above last year's price.

Representatives from Ryco are flying to Brazil to discuss its trade problems with Concellos. Specifically, Ryco wants to avoid its exposure to the high inflation rate in Brazil. This adverse effect is somewhat offset by the consistent decline in the value of the cruzeiro, which allows Ryco to obtain more cruzeiros with a given amount of dollars every year. However, the offset is not perfect, and Ryco wants to create a better hedge against Brazilian inflation.

a. Describe a countertrade strategy that could reduce Ryco's exposure to Brazilian inflation.
b. Would Concellos be willing to consider this strategy? Is there any favorable effect on Concellos that may motivate it to accept the strategy?
c. Assume that countertrade is agreed upon by both parties. Why would the cost of obtaining imports still rise over time for Concellos? Would Concellos earn lower profits as a result?

Chapter 20 Flyer Company

Composing the Optimal Currency Portfolio for Financing

As treasurer for Flyer Company, you must develop a strategy for short-term financing. The firm, based in the United States, currently has no transaction exposure to currency movements. Assume the following data as of today:

Currency	Spot Exchange Rate	Annualized Interest Rate
Australian dollar	$.75	13.0%
British pound	1.70	12.5
Canadian dollar	.86	11.0
Japanese yen	.006	8.0
Mexican peso	.17	11.5
New Zealand dollar	.60	7.0
Singapore dollar	.50	6.0
South African rand	.16	9.0
U.S. dollar	1.00	9.0
Venezuelan bolivar	.0008	12.0

Your forecasting department has provided you with the following forecasts of the spot rates one year from now:

	Strong $ Scenario	Stable $ Scenario	Weak $ Scenario
Australian dollar	$ .66	$ .76	$ .85
British pound	1.58	1.73	1.83
Canadian dollar	.85	.85	.91
Japanese yen	.0055	.0062	.0072
Mexican peso	.14	.173	.18
New Zealand dollar	.53	.59	.63
Singapore dollar	.45	.48	.52
South African rand	.15	.155	.17
U.S. dollar	1.00	1.00	1.00
Venezuelan bolivar	.00073	.00079	.00086

The probability of the strong dollar scenario is 30 percent, the probability of the stable dollar scenario is 40 percent, and the probability of the weak dollar scenario is 30 percent. Based on the information provided, prescribe the composition of the portfolio that would achieve the minimum expected effective financing rate based on each of the following risk preferences:

1. *Risk-neutral* — Focus on minimizing the expected value of your effective financing rate, without any constraints.
2. *Balanced* — Borrow no more than 25 percent in any foreign currency.
3. *Conservative* — Borrow at least 60 percent U.S. dollars and no more than 10 percent of the funds from any individual foreign currency.
4. *Ultraconservative* — Do not create any exposure to exchange rate risk.

Fill out the following table:

	Portfolio's Effective Financing Rate Based on:			
Risk Preference	**Strong $ Scenario**	**Stable $ Scenario**	**Weak $ Scenario**	**Expected Value of Effective Financing Rate**
Risk-neutral portfolio				
Balanced portfolio				
Conservative portfolio				
Ultraconservative portfolio				

Which portfolio would you prescribe for your firm? Why?

Chapter 21 Islander Corporation

Composing the Optimal Currency Portfolio for Investing

As treasurer for the Islander Corporation, you must develop a strategy for investing the excess cash that will be available for the next year. The firm, based in the United States, currently has no transaction exposure to foreign currency movements. Assume the following data as of today:

Currency	Spot Exchange Rate	Annualized Interest Rate
Australian dollar	.75	13.00
British pound	1.70	12.5
Canadian dollar	.86	11.0
Japanese yen	.006	8.0
U.S. dollar	1.00	9.0

Your forecasting department has provided you with the following forecasts of the spot rates one year from now:

	Strong $ Scenario	Somewhat Stable $ Scenario	Weak $ Scenario
Australian dollar	$ .66	$ .76	$ .85
British pound	1.58	1.73	1.83
Canadian dollar	.85	.85	.91
Japanese yen	.0055	.0062	.0072
U.S. dollar	1.00	1.00	1.00

The probability of the strong dollar scenario is 30-percent, the probability of the somewhat stable dollar scenario is 40-percent, and the probability of the weak dollar scenario is 30-percent. Based on the information provided, prescribe the composition of the investment portfolio that would maximize the expected value of the effective yield for each of four possible risk preferences:

1. *Risk-neutral* Focus on maximizing the expected value of your effective yield, without any constraints.
2. *Balanced* Invest no more than 25-percent in any foreign currency.
3. *Conservative* Invest at least 50-percent of the funds in the U.S. dollar and no more than 10 percent of the funds in any individual foreign currency.
4. *Ultraconservative* Do not create any exposure to exchange rate risk.

Fill out the following table:

	Forecasted Effective Yield for:			
Risk Preference	Strong $ Scenario	Somewhat Stable $ Scenario	Weak $ Scenario	Expected Value of Effective Yield
Risk-neutral portfolio				
Balanced portfolio				
Conservative portfolio				
Ultraconservative portfolio				

Which portfolio would you prescribe for your firm? Why? (You may find it helpful to draw bar charts that show the probability distribution of effective yields for each of the portfolios, placing one bar chart above another.)

Appendix C
Fundamentals of Regression Analysis

Businesses often use **regression analysis** to measure relationships between variables when establishing policies. For example, a firm may measure the historical relationship between its sales and its accounts receivable. It can then forecast the future level of accounts receivable based on a forecast of sales, using the relationship detected. Alternatively, it may measure the sensitivity of its sales to economic growth and interest rates so that it can assess how susceptible its sales are to future changes in these economic variables. In international financial management, regression analysis can be used to measure the sensitivity of a firm's performance (using sales or earnings or stock price as a proxy) to currency movements or economic growth of various countries.

Regression analysis can be applied to measure the sensitivity of exports to various economic variables. This example will be used to explain the fundamentals of regression analysis. The main steps involved in regression analysis are

1. Specifying the regression model
2. Compiling data
3. Estimating the regression coefficients
4. Interpreting the regression results

Specifying the Regression Model

Assume that your main goal is to determine the relationship between percentage changes in the U.S. exports to Australia (called *CEXP*) and percentage changes in the value of the Australian dollar (called *CAUS*). The percentage change in the exports sent to Australia is the **dependent variable** since it is hypothesized to be influenced by another variable. While you are most concerned with how *CAUS* affects *CEXP*, the regression model should include any other factors (or so-called **independent variables**) that could also affect *CEXP*. Assume that the percentage change in the Australian *GDP* (called *CGDP*) is also hypothesized to influence *CEXP*. This factor should also be included in the regression model. To simplify the example, assume that *CAUS* and *CGDP* are the only factors expected to influence *CEXP*. Also assume that there is a lagged impact of one quarter. In this case, the regression model can be specified as

$$CEXP_t = b_0 + b_1(CAUS_{t-1}) + b_2(CGDP_{t-1}) + u_t$$

where

b_0 = a constant
b_1 = regression coefficient that measures the sensitivity of $CEXP_t$ to $CAUS_{t-1}$
b_2 = regression coefficient that measures the sensitivity of $CEXP_t$ to $CGDP_{t-1}$
u_t = an error term

The t subscript represents the time period. Some models, such as this one, specify a lagged impact of an independent variable on the dependent variable and therefore use a $t-1$ subscript.

Compiling the Data

Now that the model has been specified, data on the variables must be compiled. The data are normally input onto a spreadsheet as follows:

Period (t)	*CEXP*	*CAUS*	*CGDP*
1	.03	−.01	.04
2	−.01	.02	−.01
3	−.04	.03	−.02
4	.00	.02	−.01
5	.01	−.02	.02
.	. . .	. . .	. . .
.	. . .	. . .	. . .
.	. . .	. . .	. . .

The column specifying the period is not necessary to run the regression model but is normally included in the data set for convenience.

The difference between the number of observations (periods) and the regression coefficients (including the constant) represents the degrees of freedom. For our example, assume that the data covered 40 quarterly periods. The degrees of freedom for this example is 40 – 3 = 37. As a general rule, analysts usually try to have at least 30 degrees of freedom when using regression analysis.

Some regression models involve only a single period. For example, if you desired to determine whether there was a relationship between the firm's degree of international sales (as a percentage of total sales) and earnings per share of MNCs, last year's data on these two variables could be gathered for many MNCs, and regression analysis could be applied. This example is referred to as **cross-sectional analysis,** whereas our original example is referred to as a **time-series analysis.**

Estimating the Regression Coefficients

Once the data have been input into a data file, a regression program can be applied to the data to estimate the **regression coefficients.** There are various packages such as EXCEL or LOTUS that contain a regression analysis application.

The actual steps conducted to estimate regression coefficients are somewhat complex. For more details on how regression coefficients are estimated, see any econometrics textbook.

Interpreting the Regression Results

Most regression programs provide estimates of the regression coefficients along with additional statistics. For our example, assume that the following information was provided by the regression program:

	Estimated Regression Coefficient	Standard Error of Regression Coefficient	*t*-statistic
Constant	.002		
$CAUS_{t-1}$	.80	.32	2.50
$CGDP_{t-1}$	.36	.50	.72
Coefficient of determination (R^2) = .33			

The independent variable $CAUS_{t-1}$ has an estimated regression coefficient of .80, which suggests that a 1-percent increase in *CAUS* is associated with a .8-percent increase in the dependent variable *CEXP* in the following period. This implies a positive relationship between $CAUS_{t-1}$ and $CEXP_t$. The independent variable $CGDP_{t-1}$ has an estimated coefficient of .36, which suggests that a 1-percent increase in the Australian *GDP* is associated with a .36-percent increase in *CEXP* one period later.

Many analysts attempt to determine whether a coefficient is statistically different from zero. Regression coefficients may be different from zero simply because of a coincidental relationship between the independent variable of concern and the dependent variable. One can have more confidence that a negative or positive relationship exists by testing the coefficient for significance. A *t*-test is commonly used for this purpose, as follows:

Test to determine whether $CAUS_{t-1}$ affects $CEXP_t$

$$\text{Calculated } t\text{-statistic} = \frac{\text{Estimated regression coefficient for } CAUS_{t-1}}{\text{Standard error of the regression coefficient}} = \frac{.80}{.32} = 2.50$$

Test to determine whether $CGDP_{t-1}$ affects $CEXP_t$

$$\text{Calculated } t\text{-statistic} = \frac{\text{Estimated regression coefficient for } CGDP_{t-1}}{\text{Standard error of the regression coefficient}} = \frac{.36}{.50} = .72$$

The calculated *t*-statistic is sometimes provided within the regression results. It can be compared to the critical *t*-statistic to determine whether the coefficient is significant. The critical *t*-statistic is dependent on the degrees of freedom and confidence level chosen. For our example, assume that there are 37 degrees of freedom and that a 95 confidence level is desired. The critical *t*-statistic would be 2.02, which can be verified by using a *t*-table from any statistics book. Based on the regression results, the coefficient of $CAUS_{t-1}$ is significantly different from zero, while $CGDP_{t-1}$ is not. This implies that one can be confident of a positive relationship between $CAUS_{t-1}$ and $CEXP_t$, but the positive relationship between $CGDP_{t-1}$ and $CEXP_t$ may have occurred simply by chance.

In some particular cases, one may be interested in determining whether the regression coefficient differs significantly from some value other than zero. In these cases, the *t*-statistic reported in the regression results would not be appropriate. See an econometrics text for more information on this subject.

The regression results indicate the **coefficient of determination** (called R^2) of a regression model, which measures the percentage of variation in the dependent variable that can be explained by the regression model. R^2 can range from 0 to 100 percent. It is unusual for regression models to generate an R^2 of close to 100 percent, since the movement in a given dependent variable is partially random and not associated with movements in independent variables. In our example, R^2 is 33 percent, suggesting that one-third of the variation in *CEXP* can be explained by movements in $CAUS_{t-1}$ and $CGDP_{t-1}$.

Some analysts use regression analysis to forecast. For our example, the regression results could be used along with data for *CAUS* and *CGDP* to forecast *CEXP*. Assume that *CAUS* was 5 percent in the most recent period, while *CGDP* was –1 percent in the most recent period. The forecast of *CEXP* in the following period is derived from inserting this information into the regression model as follows:

$$
\begin{aligned}
CEXP_t &= b_0 + b_1(CAUS_{t-1}) + b_2(CGDP_{t-1}) \\
&= .002 + (.80)(.05) + (.36)(-.01) \\
&= .002 + .0400 - .0036 \\
&= .0420 - .0036 \\
&= .0384
\end{aligned}
$$

Thus, the *CEXP* is forecasted to be 3.84 percent in the following period. Some analysts might eliminate $CGDP_{t-1}$ from the model because its regression coefficient was not significantly different from zero. This would alter the forecasted value of *CEXP*.

When there is not a lagged relationship between independent variables and the dependent variable, the independent variables must be forecasted in order to derive a forecast of the dependent variable. In this case, an analyst might derive a poor forecast of the dependent variable even when the regression model is properly specified, if the forecasts of the independent variables are inaccurate.

As with most statistical techniques, there are some limitations that should be recognized when using regression analysis. These limitations are described in most statistics and econometrics textbooks.

USING EXCEL TO CONDUCT REGRESSION ANALYSIS

Various software packages are available to run regression analysis. The following example is run on EXCEL to illustrate the ease with which regression analysis can be run. Assume that a firm wants to assess the influence of changes in the value of the Australian dollar on changes in its exports to Australia based on the following data:

Period	Value (in Thousands of Dollars) of Exports to Australia	Average Exchange Rate of Australian Dollar Over That Period
1	110	$.50
2	125	.54
3	130	.57
4	142	.60
5	129	.55
6	113	.49
7	108	.46
8	103	.42
9	109	.43
10	118	.48
11	125	.49
12	130	.50
13	134	.52
14	138	.50
15	144	.53
16	149	.55
17	156	.58
18	160	.62
19	165	.66
20	170	.67
21	160	.62
22	158	.62
23	155	.61
24	167	.66

Assume that the firm applies the following regression model to the data:

$$CEXP = b_0 + b_1\, CAUS + u$$

where

$CEXP$ = percentage change in the firm's export value from one period to the next

$CAUS$ = percentage change in the average exchange rate from one period to the next

u = error term

The first step is to input the data for the two variables in two columns on a file using EXCEL. Then, the data can be converted into percentage changes. This can be easily performed with a COMPUTE statement in the third column (Column C) to derive *CEXP* and another COMPUTE statement in the fourth column (Column D) to derive *CAUS*. These two columns will have a blank first row, since the percentage change cannot be computed without the previous period's data. Many students already know how to use EXCEL to create a COMPUTE statement and to apply the COMPUTE statement all of the data within a column. If you do not, ask a friend for a few minutes of help.

Once you have derived *CEXP* and *CAUS* from the raw data, you can perform regression analysis as follows. On the main menu, select "Tools." This leads to a new menu, in which you should click on "Data Analysis." Next to the "Input Y Range," identify the range C2 to C24 for the dependent variable as C2:C24. Next to the "Input X Range," identify the range D2 to D24 for the independent variable as D2:D24. The "Output Range" specifies the location on the screen where the output of the regression analysis should be displayed. In our example, F1 would be an appropriate location, representing the upper-left section of the output. Then, click on OK, and within a few seconds, the regression analysis will be complete. For our example, the output is listed below:

SUMMARY OUTPUT

Regression Statistics	
Multiple R	0.8852
R Square	0.7836
Adjusted R Square	0.7733
Standard Error	2.9115
Observations	23.0000

ANOVA

	df	*SS*	*MS*	*F*	*Significance F*
Regression	1.0000	644.6262	644.6262	76.0461	0.0000
Residual	21.0000	178.0125	8.4768		
Total	22.0000	822.6387			

	Coefficients	*Standard Error*	*t Stat*	*P-value*
Intercept	0.7951	0.6229	1.2763	0.2158
X Variable 1	0.8678	0.0995	8.7204	0.0000

	Lower 95%	*Upper 95%*	*Lower 95.0%*	*Upper 95.0%*
Intercept	–0.5004	2.0905	–0.5004	2.0905
X Variable 1	0.6608	1.0747	0.6608	1.0747

The estimate of the so-called slope coefficient is about .8678, which suggests that every 1-percent change in the Australian dollar's exchange rate is associated with a .8678-percent change (in the same direction) in the firm's exports to Australia. The *t*-statistic is also estimated to determine whether the slope coefficient is significantly different than zero. Since the standard error of the slope coefficient is about .0995, the *t*-statistic is (.8678/.0995) = 8.72. This would imply that there is a significant relationship between *CAUS* and *CEXP*. The R-Square statistic suggests that about 78 percent of the variation in *CEXP* is explained by *CAUS*. The correlation between *CEXP* and *CAUS* can also be measured by the correlation coefficient, which is the square root of the R-Square statistic.

If you have more than one independent variable (multiple regression), you should place the independent variables next to each other in the file. Then, for the X-RANGE, identify this block of data. The output for the regression model will display the coefficient, standard error, and *t*-statistic for each of the independent variables. For multiple regression, the R-Square statistic is interpreted as the percentage of variation in the dependent variable explained by the model as a whole.

Using the "COPY" Command

If you need to repeat a particular type of computation for several different cells, you can use the COPY command. You must highlight the particular cells in which the computation is performed and instruct EXCEL (by clicking on "Edit") to copy that computation to whatever range of cells you desire.

Appendix D
Focus on an MNC

One way to fully understand the concepts in this text is to apply the concepts to one particular MNC in which you are interested. For the MNC that you select, use its annual report and other information to answer the following questions. If the question is not directly answered by the annual report, provide the related information that is disclosed in the annual report and use your opinion to answer the question.

Chapter 1 Concepts

a. Describe the main business of the MNC.
b. What is the goal of the MNC according to the annual report?
c. Describe the international business methods used by the MNC (such as exporting, importing, international joint ventures, development of foreign subsidiaries, etc.).
d. Given the specific countries where the MNC does its business, do you think that the MNC experiences significant agency problems?
e. In what countries does the MNC expect to expand in the near future? Why does the MNC see opportunities in those countries? What are the risks of pursuing new business in those countries?

Chapter 2 Concepts

In what countries does the MNC export products? How has the MNC's export business been affected by recent changes in the factors that can affect the degree of international trade (such as national income of foreign countries, inflation of foreign countries, or exchange rate movements)?

Chapter 3 Concepts

a. How is the foreign exchange market used by the MNC?
b. How is the Eurocurrency market used by the MNC?
c. How is the Eurobond market used by the MNC?
d. Does it appear that the MNC issues stock in foreign countries? (Determine if its stock is listed on foreign stock markets.)

Chapter 4 Concepts

What are the currencies that the MNC uses to conduct its international business? How have the values of these currencies changed in the last year? (To answer this question, review a recent foreign exchange table provided by any business newspaper and another table containing quotations from a year ago.) The answers to this question will be used in later chapters to determine how the firm was affected by changes in the values of these currencies.

Chapter 5 Concepts

Does the MNC use currency futures or options for its international business? If so, explain how.

Chapter 6 Concepts

Does the main foreign currency used by the MNC change on a daily basis against the dollar? (To answer this question, review the foreign exchange table for the last two or three issues of any business newspaper.)

Chapter 7 Concepts

Look in the Money Rates section of *The Wall Street Journal* (or in any other business newspaper) or on the Internet and find the interest rate of the main foreign currency used by the MNC. Compare this interest rate to a comparable U.S. interest rate (which is also provided in the Money Rates section). Is the foreign interest rate higher or lower than the comparable U.S. interest rate? Given this information, do you expect that the forward rate of the foreign currency would have a discount or a premium? Determine what the forward rate discount or premium is by reviewing the foreign exchange table in *The Wall Street Journal* or any other business newspaper.

Chapter 8 Concepts

Does it appear that the MNC is concerned about exchange rate movements? Based on this answer, does the MNC appear to believe that purchasing power parity holds (so that any exchange rate effects are offset by inflationary effects)? Explain.

Chapter 9 Concepts

If the MNC used the 90-day forward rate (a market-based forecast) to forecast the spot rate 90 days from now, would it expect its main foreign currency (the one that it uses most frequently) to appreciate or depreciate?

Chapter 10 Concepts

a. In what ways is the MNC exposed to exchange rate risk?
b. How were the MNC's cash flows recently affected by exchange rate movements according to its annual report?
c. How were the MNC's consolidated earnings affected due to translation exposure according to its annual report?

Chapter 11 Concepts

Does the MNC hedge any of its transaction exposure? If so, what techniques does the MNC use to hedge its transaction exposure?

Chapter 12 Concepts

Does the MNC hedge any of its translation exposure? If so, what techniques does it use to hedge its translation exposure?

Chapter 13 Concepts

a. Review the possible benefits from direct foreign investment identified in this chapter. Which of these benefits apply to the MNC's direct foreign investment?
b. Do you think that the economic growth levels of the countries where the MNC does business are highly correlated? Given your answer to the previous question, do you think that the performance levels of the MNC in each country are highly correlated?

Chapter 14 Concepts

a. Does it appear that the MNC has had a large capital budget for foreign projects recently?
b. Identify the countries where the MNC has recently implemented new projects. (This can usually be determined by reviewing the geographical segment data in the annual report and assessing the change in the MNC's assets in each geographic region over the last few years.)

Chapter 15 Concepts

Has the MNC undergone any restructuring (including international acquisitions or divestitures) recently? If so, describe the restructuring. Does this restructuring reflect a change in the focus of the MNC's business?

Chapter 16 Concepts

Given the foreign countries where the MNC does most of its international business, describe the types of country risk to which the MNC is exposed.

Chapter 17 Concepts

a. For the foreign country in which the MNC does most of its business, explain how you would estimate the MNC's cost of capital used to support its business in that country.
b. Given the foreign countries in which the MNC does most of its international business, do you think the MNC uses mostly equity or debt to support its foreign projects? Explain.

Chapter 18 Concepts

Does the MNC borrow foreign currencies on a long-term basis? If so, does it appear that the MNC is borrowing the currencies that it needs to support its existing international business?

Chapter 19 Concepts

a. What types of payment methods do you think the MNC uses to pay for imports?
b. What types of trade finance methods does the MNC use according to its annual report? If these methods are not described in the annual report, what trade finance methods do you think the MNC uses based on its operations?

Chapter 20 Concepts

Does the MNC borrow short-term funds in foreign currencies? If so, does it appear that these funds are borrowed to finance existing business denominated in those foreign currencies?

Chapter 21 Concepts

Does the MNC invest in short-term securities denominated in foreign currencies? Are the funds denominated in the same currencies that the MNC commonly uses to conduct its foreign business operations?

GLOSSARY

Absolute form of purchasing power parity. Also called the "law of one price," this theory suggests that prices of two products of different countries should be equal when measured by a common currency.

Accounts receivable financing. Indirect financing provided by an exporter for an importer by exporting goods and allowing for payment to be made at a later date.

Advising bank. Corresponding bank in the beneficiary's country to which the issuing bank sends the letter of credit.

Agency problem. Conflict of goals between a firm's shareholders and its managers.

Airway bill. Receipt for a shipment by air, which includes freight charges and title to the merchandise.

All-in-rate. Rate used in charging customers for accepting banker's acceptances, consisting of the discount interest rate plus the commission.

American depository receipts (ADRs). Certificates representing ownership of foreign stocks, which are traded on stock exchanges in the United States.

Appreciation. Increase in the value of a currency.

Arbitrage. Action to capitalize on a discrepancy in quoted prices; in many cases, there is no investment of funds tied up for any length of time.

Asian dollar market. Market in Asia in which banks collect deposits and make loans denominated in U.S. dollars.

Ask price. Price at which a trader of foreign exchange (typically a bank) is willing to sell a particular currency.

Assignment of proceeds. Arrangement which allows the original beneficiary of a letter of credit to pledge or assign proceeds to an end supplier.

Balance of payments. Statement of inflow and outflow payments for a particular country.

Balance of trade. Difference between the value of merchandise exports and merchandise imports.

Balance on goods and services. Balance of trade, plus the net amount of payments of interest and dividends to foreign investors and from investment, as well as receipts and payments resulting from international tourism and other transactions.

Bank for International Settlements (BIS). Institution which facilitates cooperation among countries involved in international transactions and provides assistance to countries experiencing international payment problems.

Bank Letter of Credit Policy. Policy that enables banks to confirm letters of credit by foreign banks supporting the purchase of U.S. exports.

Banker's acceptance. Bill of exchange drawn on and accepted by a banking institution; it is commonly used to guarantee exporters that they will receive payment on goods delivered to importers.

Barter. Exchange of goods between two parties without the use of any currency as a medium of exchange.

Basel Accord. Agreement among country representatives in 1988 to establish standardized risk-based capital requirements for banks across countries.

Bid price. Price that a trader of foreign exchange (typically a bank) is willing to pay for a particular currency.

Bid/ask spread. Difference between the price at which a bank is willing to buy a currency and the price at which it will sell that currency.

Bilateral netting system. Netting method used for transactions between two units.

Bill of exchange (draft). Promise drawn by one party (usually an exporter) to pay a specified amount to another party at a specified future date, or upon presentation of the draft.

Bill of lading. Document serving as a receipt for shipment and a summary of freight charges and conveying title to the merchandise.

Bretton Woods Agreement. Conference held in Bretton Woods, New Hampshire, in 1944, resulting in agreement to maintain exchange rates of currencies within very narrow boundaries; this agreement lasted until 1971.

Call. See currency call option.

Call option on real assets. Project that contains an option of pursuing an additional venture.

Capital account. Account reflecting changes in country ownership of long-term and short-term financial assets.

Carryforwards. Tax losses that are applied in a future year to offset income in the future year.

Cash management. Optimization of cash flows and investment of excess cash.

Central exchange rate. Exchange rate established between two European currencies through the European Monetary System arrangement; the exchange rate between the two currencies is allowed to move within bands around that central exchange rate.

Centralized cash flow management. Policy that consolidates cash management decisions for all MNC units, usually at the parent's location.

Coefficient of determination. Measure of the percentage variation in the dependent variable that can be explained by the independent variables when using regression analysis.

Cofinancing agreements. Arrangement in which the World Bank participates along with other agencies or lenders in providing funds to developing countries.

Commercial invoice. Exporter's description of merchandise being sold to the buyer.

Commercial letters of credit. Trade-related letters of credit.

Comparative advantage. Theory suggesting that specialization by countries can increase worldwide production.

Compensation. Arrangement in which the delivery of goods to a party is compensated for by buying back a certain amount of the product from that same party.

Compensatory Financing Facility (CFF). Facility that attempts to reduce the impact of export instability on country economies.

Consignment. Arrangement in which the exporter ships goods to the importer while still retaining title to the merchandise.

Contingency graph. Graph showing the net profit to a speculator in currency options under various exchange rate scenarios.

Counterpurchase. Exchange of goods between two parties under two distinct contracts expressed in monetary terms.

Countertrade. Sale of goods to one country which is linked to the purchase or exchange of goods from that same country.

Country risk. Characteristics of the host country, including political and financial conditions, that can affect the MNC's cash flows.

Covered interest arbitrage. Investment in a foreign money market security with a simultaneous forward sale of the currency denominating that security.

Cross exchange rate. Exchange rate between currency A and currency B, given the values of currencies A and B with respect to a third currency.

Cross-border factoring. Factoring by a network of factors across borders. The exporter's factor can contact correspondent factors in other countries to handle the collections of accounts receivable.

Cross-hedging. Hedging an open position in one currency with a hedge on another currency that is highly correlated with the first currency. This occurs when for some reason the common hedging techniques cannot be applied to the first currency. A cross-hedge is not a perfect hedge, but can substantially reduce the exposure.

Cross-sectional analysis. Analysis of relationships among a cross-section of firms, countries, or some other variable at a given point in time.

Currency Board. System for maintaining the value of the local currency with respect to some other specified currency.

Currency call option. Contract that grants the right to purchase a specific currency at a specific price (exchange rate) within a specific period of time.

Currency cocktail bond. Bond denominated in a mixture (or cocktail) of currencies.

Currency diversification. Process of using more than one currency as an investing or financing strategy. Exposure to a diversified currency portfolio typically results in less exchange rate risk than if all of the exposure was in a single foreign currency.

Currency futures contract. Contract specifying a standard volume of a particular currency to be exchanged on a specific settlement date.

Currency put option. Contract granting the right to sell a particular currency at a specified price (exchange rate) within a specified period of time.

Currency swap. Agreement to exchange one currency for another at a specified exchange rate and date. Banks commonly serve as intermediaries between two parties who wish to engage in a currency swap.

Current account. Broad measure of a country's international trade in goods and services.

Delphi technique. Collection of independent opinions without group discussion by the assessors who provide the opinions; used for various types of assessments (such as country risk assessment).

Dependent variable. Term used in regression analysis to represent the variable that is dependent on one or more other variables.

Depreciation. Decrease in the value of a currency.

Direct foreign investment (DFI). Investment in real assets (such as land, buildings, or even existing plants) in foreign countries.

Direct Loan Program. Program in which Ex-Im Bank offers fixed-rate loans directly to the foreign buyer to purchase U.S. capital equipment and services.

Direct quotations. Exchange rate quotations representing the value measured by number of dollars per unit.

Discount. As related to forward rates, represents the percentage amount by which the forward rate is less than the spot rate.

Documentary collections. Trade transactions handled on a draft basis.

Documents against acceptance. Situation in which the buyer's bank does not release shipping documents to the buyer until the buyer has accepted (signed) the draft.

Documents against payment. Shipping documents that are released to the buyer once the buyer has paid for the draft.

Double-entry bookkeeping. Accounting method in which each transaction is recorded as both a credit and a debit.

Draft (bill of exchange). Unconditional promise drawn by one party (usually the exporter) instructing the buyer to pay the face amount of the draft upon presentation.

Dumping. Selling products overseas at unfairly low prices (a practice perceived to result from subsidies provided to the firm by its government).

Dynamic hedging. Strategy of hedging in those periods when existing currency positions are expected to be adversely affected, and remaining unhedged in other periods when currency positions are expected to be favorably affected.

Economic exposure. Degree to which a firm's present value of future cash flows can be influenced by exchange rate fluctuations.

Economies of scale. Achievement of lower average cost per unit by means of increased production.

Effective yield. Yield or return to an MNC on a short-term investment after adjustment for the change in exchange rates over the period of concern.

Efficient frontier. Set of points reflecting risk-return combinations achieved by particular portfolios (so-called efficient portfolios) of assets.

Equilibrium exchange rate. Exchange rate at which demand for a currency is equal to the supply of the currency for sale.

Equity multiplier. Assets divided by equity.

Eurobanks. Commercial banks that participate as financial intermediaries in the Eurocurrency market.

Eurobonds. Bonds sold in countries other than the country represented by the currency denominating them.

Euro-clear. Telecommunications network that informs all traders about outstanding issues of Eurobonds for sale.

Euro-commercial paper. Debt securities issued by MNCs for short-term financing.

Eurocredit loans. Loans of one year or longer extended by Eurobanks.

Eurocredit market. Collection of banks that accept deposits and provide loans in large denominations and in a variety of currencies. The banks that comprise this market are the same banks that comprise the Eurocurrency market; the difference is that the Eurocredit loans are longer term than so-called Eurocurrency loans.

Eurocurrency market. Collection of banks that accept deposits and provide loans in large denominations and in a variety of currencies.

Eurodollar. Term used to describe U.S. dollar deposits placed in banks located in Europe.

Euronotes. Unsecured debt securities issued by MNCs for short-term financing.

European Central Bank (ECB). Central bank created to conduct the monetary policy for the countries participating in the single European currency, the euro.

European Currency Unit (ECU). Unit of account representing a weighted average of exchange rates of member countries within the European Monetary System.

Exchange Rate Mechanism. Method of linking European currency values with the European Currency Unit (ECU).

Exercise price (strike price). Price (exchange rate) at which the owner of a currency call option is allowed to buy a specified currency; or the price (exchange rate) at which the owner of a currency put option is allowed to sell a specified currency.

Export-Import Bank (Ex-ImBank). Bank that attempts to strengthen the competitiveness of U.S. industries involved in foreign trade.

Factor. Firm specializing in collection on accounts receivable; exporters sometimes sell their accounts receivable to a factor at a discount.

Factoring. Purchase of receivables of an exporter by a factor without recourse to the exporter.

Financial Institution Buyer Credit Policy. Policy that provides insurance coverage for loans by banks to foreign buyers of exports.

Fisher effect. Theory that nominal interest rates are composed of a real interest rate and anticipated inflation.

Fixed exchange rate system. Monetary system in which exchange rates are either held constant or allowed to fluctuate only within very narrow boundaries.

Floating rate notes (FRNs). Provision of some Eurobonds, in which the coupon rate is adjusted over time according to prevailing market rates.

Foreign bond. Bond issued by a borrower foreign to the country where the bond is placed.

Foreign exchange market. Market composed primarily of banks, serving firms and consumers who wish to buy or sell various currencies.

Foreign investment risk matrix (FIRM). Graph that displays financial and political risk by intervals, so that each country can be positioned according to its risk ratings.

Forfaiting. Method of financing international trade of capital goods.

Forward contract. Agreement between a commercial bank and a client about an exchange of two currencies to be made at a future point in time at a specified exchange rate.

Forward discount. Percentage by which the forward rate is less than the spot rate; typically quoted on an annualized basis.

Forward premium. Percentage by which the forward rate exceeds the spot rate; typically quoted on an annualized basis.

Forward rate. Rate at which a bank is willing to exchange one currency for another at some specified date in the future.

Franchising. Agreement by which a firm provides a specialized sales or service strategy, support assistance, and possibly an initial investment in the franchise in exchange for periodic fees.

Freely floating exchange rate system. Monetary system in which exchange rates are allowed to move due to market forces without intervention by country governments.

Full compensation. An arrangement in which the delivery of goods to one party is fully compensated for by buying back more than 100 percent of the value that was originally sold.

Fundamental forecasting. Forecasting based on fundamental relationships between economic variables and exchange rates.

General Agreement on Tariffs and Trade (GATT). Agreement allowing for trade restrictions only in retaliation against illegal trade actions of other countries.

Gold standard. Era in which each currency was convertible into gold at a specified rate, allowing the exchange rate between two currencies to be determined by their relative convertibility rates per ounce of gold.

Hedge. To insulate a firm from exposure to exchange rate fluctuations.

Hostile takeovers. Acquisitions not desired by the target firms.

Imperfect market. The condition where, due to the costs to transfer labor and other resources used for production, firms may attempt to use foreign factors of production when they are less costly than local factors.

Import/export letters of credit. Trade-related letters of credit.

Independent variable. Term used in regression analysis to represent the variable that is expected to influence another (so-called "dependent") variable.

Indirect quotations. Exchange rate quotations representing the value measured by number of units per dollar.

Interbank market. Market that facilitates the exchange of currencies between banks.

Interest Equalization Tax (IET). Tax imposed by the U.S. government in 1963 to discourage U.S. investors from investing in foreign securities.

Interest rate parity. Theory specifying that the forward premium (or discount) is equal to the interest rate differential between the two currencies of concern.

Interest rate parity (IRP) line. Diagonal line depicting all points on a four-quadrant graph that represent a state of interest rate parity.

Interest rate parity theory. Theory suggesting that the forward rate differs from the spot rate by an amount that reflects the interest differential between two currencies.

Interest rate swap. Agreement to swap interest payments, whereby interest payments based on a fixed interest rate are exchanged for interest payments based on a floating interest rate.

International Bank for Reconstruction and Development (IBRD). Bank established in 1944 to enhance economic development by providing loans to countries. Also referred to as the World Bank.

International Development Association (IDA). Association established to stimulate country development; it was especially suited for less prosperous nations, since it provided loans at low interest rates.

International Financial Corporation (IFC). Firm established to promote private enterprise within countries; it can provide loans to and purchase stock of corporations.

International Fisher effect. Theory specifying that a currency's exchange rate will depreciate against another currency when its interest rate (and therefore expected inflation rate) is higher than that of the other currency.

International Fisher Effect (IFE) line. Diagonal line on a graph that reflects points at which the interest rate differential between two countries is equal to the percentage change in the exchange rate between their two respective currencies.

International Monetary Fund (IMF). Agency established in 1944 to promote and facilitate international trade and financing.

International mutual funds (IMFs). Mutual funds containing securities of foreign firms.

Intracompany trade. International trade between subsidiaries that are under the same ownership.

Irrevocable letter of credit. Letter of credit issued by a bank that cannot be cancelled or amended without the beneficiary's approval.

Issuing bank. Bank that issues a letter of credit.

J-curve effect. Effect of a weaker dollar on the U.S. trade balance, in which the trade balance initially deteriorates; it only improves once U.S. and non-U.S. importers respond to the change in purchasing power that is caused by the weaker dollar.

Joint venture. Venture between two or more firms in which responsibilities and earnings are shared.

Lagging. Strategy used by a firm to stall payments, normally in response to exchange rate projections.

Leading. Strategy used by a firm to accelerate payments, normally in response to exchange rate expectations.

Letter of credit (L/C). Agreement by a bank to make payments on behalf of a specified party under specified conditions.

Licensing. Arrangement in which a local firm in the host country produces goods in accordance with another firm's (the licensing firm's) specifications; as the goods are sold, the local firm can retain part of the earnings.

Locational arbitrage. Action to capitalize on a discrepancy in quoted exchange rates between banks.

Lockbox. Post office box number to which customers are instructed to send payment.

London Interbank Offer Rate (LIBOR). Interest rate commonly charged for loans between Eurobanks.

Long-term forward contracts. Contracts that state any exchange rate at which a specified amount of a specified currency can be exchanged at a future date (more than one year from today). Also called long forwards.

Louvre Accord. 1987 agreement between countries to attempt to stabilize the value of the U.S. dollar.

Macroassessment. Overall risk assessment of a country without considering the MNC's business.

Mail float. Mailing time involved in sending payments by mail.

Managed float. Exchange rate system in which currencies have no explicit boundaries, but central banks may intervene to influence exchange rate movements.

Margin requirement. Deposit placed on a contract (such as a currency futures contract) to cover the fluctuations in the value of that contract; this minimizes the risk of the contract to the counterparty.

Market-based forecasting. Use of a market-determined exchange rate (such as the spot rate or forward rate) to forecast the spot rate in the future.

Medium-Term Guarantee Program. Program conducted by Ex-Im Bank in which commercial lenders are encouraged to finance the sale of U.S. capital equipment and services to approved foreign buyers; Ex-Im Bank guarantees the loan's principal and interest on these loans.

Microassessment. The risk assessment of a country as related to the MNC's type of business.

Mixed forecasting. Development of forecasts based on a mixture of forecasting techniques.

Money market hedge. Use of international money markets to match future cash inflows and outflows in a given currency.

Multibuyer policy. Policy administered by Ex-Im Bank that provides credit risk insurance on export sales to many different buyers.

Multilateral Investment Guarantee Agency (MIGA). Agency established by the World Bank that offers various forms of political risk insurance to corporations.

Multilateral netting system. Complex interchange for netting between a parent and several subsidiaries.

Multinational restructuring. Restructuring of the composition of an MNC's assets or liabilities.

Negotiable bill of lading. Contract that grants title of merchandise to the holder, which allows banks to use the merchandise as collateral.

Net operating loss carrybacks. Practice of applying losses to offset earnings in previous years.

Net operating loss carryforwards. Practice of applying losses to offset earnings in future years.

Netting. Combining of future cash receipts and payments to determine the net amount to be owed by one subsidiary to another.

Net transaction exposure. Consideration of inflows and outflows in a given currency to determine the exposure after offsetting inflows against outflows.

Non-deliverable Forward Contracts (NDFs). Like a forward contract, represents an agreement regarding a position in a specified currency, a specified exchange rate, and a specified future settlement date, but does not result in delivery of currencies. Instead, a payment is made by one party in the agreement to the other party based on the exchange rate at the future date.

Nonsterilized intervention. Intervention in the foreign exchange market without adjusting for the change in money supply.

Ocean bill of lading. Receipt for a shipment by boat, which includes freight charges and title to the merchandise.

Open account transaction. Sale in which the exporter ships the merchandise and expects the buyer to remit payment according to agreed-upon terms.

Overhedging. Hedging an amount in a currency larger than the actual transaction amount.

Parallel bonds. Bonds placed in different countries and denominated in the respective currencies of the countries where they are placed.

Parallel loan. Loan involving an exchange of currencies between two parties, with a promise to reexchange the currencies at a specified exchange rate and future date.

Partial compensation. An arrangement in which the delivery of goods to one party is partially compensated for by buying back a certain amount of product from the same party.

Pegged exchange rate. Exchange rate whose value is pegged to another currency's value or to a unit of account.

Perfect forecast line. A 45-degree line on a graph that matches the forecast of an exchange rate with the actual exchange rate.

Petrodollars. Deposits of dollars by countries which receive dollar revenues due to the sale of petroleum to other countries; the term commonly refers to OPEC deposits of dollars in the Eurocurrency market.

Plaza Accord. Agreement among country representatives in 1985 to implement a coordinated program to weaken the dollar.

Political risk. Political actions taken by the host government or the public that affect the MNC's cash flows.

Preauthorized payment. Method of accelerating cash inflows by receiving authorization to charge a customer's bank account.

Premium. As related to forward rates, represents the percentage amount by which the forward rate exceeds the spot rate. As related to currency options, represents the price of a currency option.

Prepayment. Method which exporter uses to receive payment before shipping goods.

Price-elastic. Sensitive to price changes.

Privatization. Conversion of government-owned businesses to ownership by shareholders or individuals.

Product cycle theory. Theory suggesting that a firm initially establish itself locally and expand into foreign markets in response to foreign demand for its product; over time, the MNC will grow in foreign markets; after some point, its foreign business may decline unless it can differentiate its product from competitors.

Project Finance Loan Program. Program that allows banks, Ex-Im Bank, or a combination of both to extend long-term financing for capital equipment and related services for major projects.

Purchasing Power Parity (PPP) line. Diagonal line on a graph that reflects points at which the inflation differential between two countries is equal to the percentage change in the exchange rate between the two respective currencies.

Purchasing Power Parity (PPP) theory. Theory suggesting that exchange rates will adjust over time to reflect the differential in inflation rates in the two countries; in this way, the purchasing power of consumers when purchasing domestic goods will be the same as that when they purchase foreign goods.

Put. See currency put option.

Put option on real assets. Project that contains an option of divesting part or all of the project.

Quota. Maximum limit imposed by the government on goods allowed to be imported into a country.

Real cost of hedging. The additional cost of hedging when compared to not hedging (a negative real cost would imply that hedging was more favorable than not hedging).

Real interest rate. Nominal (or quoted) interest rate minus the inflation rate.

Real options. Implicit options on real assets.

Regression analysis. Statistical technique used to measure the relationship between variables and the sensitivity of a variable to one or more other variables.

Regression coefficient. Term measured by regression analysis to estimate the sensitivity of the dependent variable to a particular independent variable.

Reinvoicing center. Facility that centralizes payments and charges subsidiaries fees for its function; this can effectively shift profits to subsidiaries where tax rates are low.

Relative form of purchasing power parity. Theory stating that the rate of change in the prices of products should be somewhat similar when measured in a common currency, as long as transportation costs and trade barriers are unchanged.

Revocable letter of credit. Letter of credit issued by a bank that can be cancelled at any time without prior notification to the beneficiary.

Semistrong-form efficient. Description of foreign exchange markets, implying that all relevant public information is already reflected in prevailing spot exchange rates.

Sensitivity analysis. Technique for assessing uncertainty whereby various possibilities are input to determine possible outcomes.

Simulation. Technique for assessing the degree of uncertainty. Probability distributions are developed for the input variables; simulation uses this information to generate possible outcomes.

Single-Buyer policy. Policy administered by Ex-Im Bank which allows the exporter to selectively insure certain transactions.

Single European Act. Act intended to remove numerous barriers imposed on trade and capital flows between European countries.

Small Business Policy. Policy providing enhanced coverage to new exporters and small businesses.

Smithsonian Agreement. Conference between nations in 1971 that resulted in a devaluation of the dollar against major currencies and a widening of boundaries (2 percent in either direction) around the newly established exchange rates.

Snake. Arrangement established in 1972, whereby European currencies were tied to each other within specified limits.

Special Drawing Rights (SDRs). Reserves established by the International Monetary Fund; they are used only for intergovernment transactions; the SDR also serves as a unit of account (determined by the values of five major currencies) that is used to denominate some internationally traded goods and services, as well as some foreign bank deposits and loans.

Spot market. Market in which exchange transactions occur for immediate exchange.

Spot rate. Current exchange rate of currency.

Standby letter of credit. Document used to guarantee invoice payments to a supplier; it promises to pay the beneficiary if the buyer fails to pay.

Sterilized intervention. Intervention by the Federal Reserve in the foreign exchange market, with simultaneous intervention in the Treasury securities markets to offset any effects on the dollar money supply; thus, the intervention in the foreign exchange market is achieved without affecting the existing dollar money supply.

Straddle. Combination of a put option and a call option.

Strike price. *See* **Exercise price.**

Strong-form efficient. Description of foreign exchange markets, implying that all relevant public information and private information is already reflected in prevailing spot exchange rates.

Structural Adjustment Loan Facility (SAL). Facility established in 1980 by the World Bank to enhance a country's long-term economic growth through financing projects.

Supplier credit. Credit provided by the supplier to itself to fund its operations.

Syndicate. Group of banks that participate in loans.

Syndicated Eurocredit loans. Loans provided by a group (or syndicate) of banks in the Eurocredit market.

Target zones. Implicit boundaries established by central banks on exchange rates.

Tariff. Tax imposed by a government on imported goods.

Technical forecasting. Development of forecasts using historical prices or trends.

Tenor. Time period of drafts.

Time-series analysis. Analysis of relationships between two or more variables over periods of time.

Time series models. Models that examine series of historical data; sometimes used as a means of technical forecasting, by examining moving averages.

Trade acceptance. Draft that allows the buyer to obtain merchandise prior to paying for it.

Transaction exposure. Degree to which the value of future cash transactions can be affected by exchange rate fluctuations.

Transfer pricing. Policy for pricing goods sent by either the parent or a subsidiary to a subsidiary of an MNC.

Transferable letter of credit. Document that allows the first beneficiary on a standby letter of credit to transfer all or part of the original letter of credit to a third party.

Translation exposure. Degree to which a firm's consolidated financial statements are exposed to fluctuations in exchange rates.

Triangular arbitrage. Action to capitalize on a discrepancy where the quoted cross exchange rate is not equal to the rate that should exist at equilibrium.

Umbrella policy. Policy issued to a bank or trading company to insure exports of an exporter and handle all administrative requirements.

Unilateral transfers. Accounting for government and private gifts and grants.

Weak-form efficient. Description of foreign exchange markets, implying that all historical and current exchange rate information is already reflected in prevailing spot exchange rates.

Working Capital Guarantee Program. Program conducted by ExIm Bank which encourages commercial banks to extend short-term export financing to eligible exporters; Ex-Im Bank provides a guarantee in the loan's principal and interest.

World Bank. Bank established in 1944 to enhance economic development by providing loans to countries.

World Trade Organization. Organization established to provide a forum for multilateral trade negotiations and to settle trade disputes related to the GATT accord.

Writer. Seller of an option.

Yankee stock offerings. Offerings of stock by non-U.S. firms in the U.S. markets.

INDEX